ASHE Reader on
Finance in Higher Education

Second Edition

Edited by

John L. Yeager
University of Pittsburgh

Glenn M. Nelson
University of Pittsburgh

Eugenie A. Potter
University of Michigan

John C. Weidman
University of Pittsburgh

Thomas G. Zullo
University of Pittsburgh

James L. Ratcliff
ASHE Reader Series Editor

ASHE Reader Series

PEARSON
Custom
Publishing

Printed in the United States of America

10 9 8

Please visit our web site at www.pearsoncustom.com

ISBN 0–536–62882–3

BA 993004

PEARSON CUSTOM PUBLISHING
75 Arlington Street, Suite 300, Boston, MA 02116
A Pearson Education Company

Contents

SECTION III.
INSTITUTIONAL RESOURCES   235

SECTION IV.
HIGHER EDUCATION EXPENDITURES

299

General Introduction

In the five years since the publication of the last ASHE Reader on Finance, the landscape in higher education has changed substantially. The media, national commissions, private think tanks, professional organizations, and the economy itself have been significant forces in reshaping the various contexts—theory, public opinion, government policy, and institutional practice—in which higher education financial issues are addressed. In many cases, these forces are not new, but as the twentieth century makes way for the twenty-first, they are reasserting their influence with dramatic results. The first order of business, then, for this latest edition of the Finance Reader is to describe briefly how the national landscape of higher education finance has been altered since 1996, as a prelude to the selected readings that comprise the heart of this collection.

The influence of the media, and media stories on higher education finance, is extremely powerful. To a substantial extent, the media shapes public opinion on many issues. When the issue is as complex and multifaceted as higher education finance, the role of the media becomes even more pronounced. One of the most vivid examples was the *Time* Magazine "Special Investigation" on college tuition in its March 17, 1997, issue. On the cover was a title guaranteed to catch the attention of almost anyone with even a remote interest in higher education finance—student, parent, faculty, administrator, trustee, or state legislator: "How Colleges are Gouging U," with the 'U' in traditional block college letter style. In the article, *Time* reporter Erik Larson set out to discover "Why Colleges Cost Too Much." Amid the growing public rumblings about the escalation in college tuition throughout the 1990s, the article was a clarion call, taking the issue to a whole new level in terms of public consciousness, and political urgency.

Contemporaneous with (and sometimes prompted by) the media stories were reports in the late 1990s by various national commissions, think tanks, and professional organizations that sought to come to terms with several dimensions of the higher education finance puzzle. In an attempt to demonstrate the value of higher education, and perhaps to bolster flagging public confidence in the public higher education enterprise, the National Association of State Universities and Land Grant Colleges produced two reports: *For Every Dollar Invested . . . The Economic Impact of Public Universities* (1996) and *Value Added—The Economic Impact of Public Universities* (1997). According to the 1997 report, "Unfortunately, during the last decade, parents, legislators, and governors often have overlooked these benefits [of higher education] in the face of rising tuition bills and the need to cut state spending. Instead, all too often, the spotlight has focused on the costs of public higher education."

Also in 1997, the Commission on National Investment in Higher Education issued its report, with the dramatic title *Breaking the Social Contract: The Fiscal Crisis in Higher Education*, which explored the costs of higher education and the institutional reforms that had to be made to ensure access and affordability in higher education. A year later, the National Commission on the Cost of Higher Education (appointed by Congress—another indication of this issue's political urgency) released its report, *Straight Talk About College Costs and Prices*, which urged colleges and universities to take the public's concern over rising tuition more seriously. That same year, 1998, the Institute for Higher Education Policy, as part of the New Millennium Project on Higher Education Costs, Pricing, and Productivity, produced *Reaping the Benefits: Defining the Public and Private Value of Going to College*. This report, citing the "growing public scrutiny of higher education, combined with limited or reduced government spending," sought to articulate the benefits of college attendance and make the case for the value of higher education, much as Howard Bowen had done almost thirty years earlier in *Investment in Learning: The Individual and Social Value of American Higher Education.*

Of course, all of higher education—public and private, two-year and four-year—operates against the backdrop of the American economy, which for much of the 1990s has been in the longest period of expansion in American history. Fueled by record low unemployment, a stock market that more than quadrupled its value during the decade, and very stable inflation, the American economy has played an enormous role in higher education finance, from the extraordinary gains in institutional endowments to robbing some institutions of prospective students who instead take their chances in a very favorable job market.

It is surprising that within the context of such a prosperous economy there exists a continuous public emphasis on higher education cost reduction and cost containment. As state financing of higher education stabilizes, there has been an increased shift from government appropriations to tuition, which has directly affected students and their families. Federal and state support to students has also been shifting from grants to loans. This shift in public policy means that the primary burden for payment of tuition costs now rests with students at a time when tuition is rapidly becoming the major, and in some case almost the only, significant source of institutional revenue.

In response to this situation, institutions have aggressively sought to reduce costs through such actions as reduction of tenured faculty positions, an increase in the use of part-time faculty, and better cash management practices. Higher education has also undertaken new revenue generating activities, including facilities rental, expanded continuing education programs, increased efforts to raise private gifts, technology transfer programs, and venture capital endeavors. Many of these efforts have been successful, but most have relatively little impact on overall institutional financial well-being. Tuition is, and will remain, the primary source of institutional revenue.

These changing patterns of financing higher education have been exacerbated by such factors as relentless institutional aspirations, competition, and the pressures of tech-

nology. Colleges and universities continually seek to improve the quality of programs and faculty, expand and upgrade facilities, and provide additional student amenities—many of which are in direct response to student demands. Attracting and retaining quality faculty, students, and programs require major commitments of scarce resources. Institutional competition exists and will continue for the most qualified students as well as the funds to support research and development projects.

In the last decade, sophisticated distance education programming has quickly established itself a major competitor to campus-based programs, along with specialized corporate-based institutions. These changes will have a profound effect on traditional institutions in terms of providing cost effective undergraduate, graduate, and continuing education services. The capacity of traditional institutions to compete will depend upon their ability to offer high quality programs at competitive prices. Another major area of concern is the rapidly escalating costs associated with technology for instruction, research, and management support. In most if not all cases, these costs must be passed on to students in the form of higher tuition or increased student fees. This litany of financial pressures represents a challenge that will require a great deal of skill to navigate, as well as a concerted effort on the part of institutions to define their particular strengths and missions through the development of strategic plans and transformational strategies. Institutional survival is at the very core of these activities.

It seems unlikely that so much could have possibly changed between the publication of the last edition of the ASHE Reader on Finance in Higher Education and this one: a realignment of public and political opinion, driven in large part by stories in the media, and the enormous pressure on higher education to respond; the release of numerous reports—concerned either with making the case in favor of higher education to a skeptical society or with charting a new course for its survival in the face of grave challenges; the explosion of the national economy (and the economies of many states)—and the inevitable question of when the history-making expansion will end. If this is the millennial edition of the ASHE Reader, then the context for this reader is, in keeping with the millennial spirit, appropriately dramatic and tumultuous. It is hoped that the articles in this Reader, and the introductory comments offered by the editors, will prove useful for students and scholars as they seek to understand the important and complicated issues of higher education finance.

PURPOSE OF THE READER

The purpose of this Reader is to serve as an instructional resource reference for students, scholars, and practitioners working in the area of higher education finance as they address many of the issues and challenges described above. This purpose can only be achieved if a wide and diverse set of interrelated perspectives and agendas can be integrated, communicated, and understood.

ORGANIZATION OF THE READER

One of the most difficult questions confronting the editors was the organization of the Reader. We quickly recognized that there were many reasonable alternative organizational structures from which to choose, each having its own specific advantages and drawbacks. Regardless of the structure, we acknowledge that it represents only an artificial delineation between topics since there is a great deal of overlap and interrelatedness between these topics. The organizational structure ultimately selected is reflective of the literature and many of the major topics that we include in our own teaching, writing, and research. Further, while drawing on the wisdom and vision of previous editors and their editions, this Reader has been expanded to include sections on several emerging themes that the editors of this edition believe merit careful consideration.

For example, the rapid globalization of higher education and the resulting increase in cross-fertilization of ideas and approaches to financing and budgeting in higher education represents an exciting new area for analysis. As a result, a new international section has been added that examines higher education finance from a global perspective. Another new section, on strategic planning and resource allocation, has been included in recognition of the growing interest in linking institutional strategic planning with budget practices. A third new section, on ethics, has also been introduced. At first, this may seem like an unusual addition, but it is a deliberate recognition of the increasing importance that ethical standards and practices have on institutional financial activities.

The editors have also developed a brief, new reference section that identifies web sites in the areas of higher education finance and budgeting. We hope these web sites provide the reader with ready access to the most current information in the field and proves to be a useful tool for all audiences. Many of the web sites included in this section were helpful to the section editors as they searched for publications on particular topics. If this section does prove valuable, we suggest that a list of relevant web sites become a part of all future readers, and that the ASHE Executive Committee consider the development of a central web site to collect and keep track of these links to new and important knowledge.

We also departed from previous Readers in that the traditional section featuring "classical" works in higher education finance has been discontinued. Those articles that have become the bedrock of our understanding of financial activities in higher education have been reviewed and are included along with contemporary works in the appropriate section. Section editors focused primarily on identifying articles published after 1990 to offer the most recent examples of pertinent scholarship.

As a result of these modifications, this Reader is divided into eight sections, each addressing a specific set of topics related to higher education finance. A Section Editor was appointed for each of the eight sections, and this section editor was responsible for coordinating the development of each section. These responsibilities included identifying prospective articles, assembling review panels for each section, managing the review process, making the final decisions regarding article selection, and preparing summary introductions. The following is a list of the eight sections and Section Editors for this Reader:

Section I: Economics and Financing of
  Higher Education
John C. Weidman

Section II: Government Financing of Higher Education

Glenn M. Nelson

Section III: Institutional Resources

Thomas O. Zullo

Section IV: Higher Education Expenditures

Glenn M. Nelson

Section V: Strategic Planning and Resource Allocation

John L. Yeager

Section VI: Institutional Financial Management

John L. Yeager

Section VII: Ethics and Higher Education Finance

Eugenie Potter

Section VIII: International Financing of Higher Education

John C. Weidman

As noted, one of the most important tasks of each Section Editor was the selection of a review panel for each section. These review panels performed an essential function in the preparation of the Reader by helping with the identification of prospective articles and the selection of articles to be included. The members of these review panels for each section are listed in the section introductions. Each of the eight review panels consisted of three to six members, resulting in a total of 51 faculty members and practicing professionals who participated in the review and preparation of this collection.

The process of identifying, reviewing, and selecting articles was extensive. A national call for outstanding articles was distributed to major higher education organizations and publications. Section Editors solicited members of each review panel for recommendations regarding prospective articles, and also conducted literature reviews of relevant reference databases. Initial efforts to identify articles resulted in more than 500 prospective articles. These articles were then reviewed, and a

shorter list of articles was compiled. Ultimately, 58 articles were selected for inclusion.

Due to space limitations, obviously not all articles identified and reviewed could be included, though we believe those that are included in this collection are representative of the best available scholarship. The editors' attempt to expand the number of topics covered in this Reader made it more difficult to attain complete coverage. The field of higher education finance is simply too large and complex to permit an exhaustive treatment within a single publication. Further, the ASHE Reader Editorial Board stated that only published articles or book chapters could be included. This meant the exclusion of a number of excellent papers that were presented at professional association meetings in recent years. We anticipate that the best of these articles will be published over the next few years, and that they will eventually appear in future editions of this Reader.

ACKNOWLEDGMENTS

We recognize that this Reader would not have been possible without the input and efforts of several individuals in addition to the Section Editors. The preparation of this Reader was a team effort in which all members played important roles and whose efforts are greatly appreciated by the editors. In each section introduction, the members of the review panels are identified and recognized.

We would like to acknowledge our Assistant Editors, Lisa DeFrank-Cole and John (Jay) Cole. Lisa played a critical role in the overall management of the process, ensuring that editors adhered to deadlines and that appropriate resources were available for the successful development of the Reader. Lisa's organizational skills, encouragement, and enthusiasm kept our team on track. Jay was a valuable addition to the team by assisting the editors with identifying articles for review, conducting the review process, and contributing to the composition of the introductions. Jay's knowledge of the relevant higher education literature proved to be an important asset.

Laurie Cohen, our Research and Reference Analyst, supplied excellent library reference assistance to the Section Editors, and provided important guidance to them in the identification of articles germane to their particular sections.

Mary Jane Alm, our Administrative Assistant, provided critical back-up and support services, and coordinated the distribution of Reader materials and correspondence.

In addition to his contribution as a reviewer for the section on government financing, Ed Hines also helped the editors by sharing his comments, and the comments of his students, regarding the 1996 edition of the ASHE Finance Reader.

Any shortcoming of this Reader is purely the responsibility of the editors. We hope that this collection of articles will serve well the needs of the ASHE membership, other faculty, practicing professionals, and students who are working in the area of higher education finance.

Glenn M. Nelson

Tom Zullo

John C. Weidman

Eugenie Potter

John L. Yeager

SECTION I

ECONOMICS AND FINANCING OF HIGHER EDUCATION

INTRODUCTION

Given the constantly changing landscape in the economics and financing of higher education, one of the most important criteria for selecting articles for this section was timeliness. In an effort to capture the most recent "lay of the land," six of the seven articles in this section were published in the last two years. These articles reveal a modern landscape that is complex and diverse, from tuition dilemmas to definitions of costs and productivity, from the special economic role of community colleges to the privatization of higher education. This section will give readers a basic map for navigating these complicated subjects, and encourage further reading for more detailed understanding.

The first article asks the provocative question, "Financing Higher Education: Who Should Pay?" D. Bruce Johnstone provides a thorough answer by first describing the economic, social, and political context for American higher education, then moving to an accessible discussion of efficiency, productivity, and revenue sources as these concepts relate to higher education, and concluding with predictions (some dire) regarding the future of the higher education enterprise. This article is essential for any reader seeking a sophisticated introduction to the universe of financial issues in higher education.

The second article by Johnstone also asks a very important question—"Patterns of Finance: Revolution, Evolution, or More of the Same?" Johnstone answers this question by describing current patterns of financing higher education in three areas—total resources, costs per unit, and apportionment of costs—and then concluding that in the first decade of the new millennium, American higher education can look forward to "more of the same" when it comes to many long-standing financial concerns.

"Subsidies, Hierarchy, and Peers: The Awkward Economics of Higher Education," by Gordon Winston, addresses a very significant point—the extent to which the "economic analogy" can be applied fairly and effectively to higher education. Many commentators and pundits have argued that higher education is, or at least should be, a business, and a college student is, in fact, a customer. After a careful consideration of the economic circumstances of higher education, including an insightful analysis of the financial hierarchy among institutions, Winston asserts that the "awkward economics" of higher education confounds the use of traditional business analogies in describing the economic behavior and dynamics of colleges and universities. This is one of two articles included from a special issue of the *Journal of Economic Perspectives* (Vol. 13, No. 1, 1999) devoted to the economics of higher education.

Perhaps no single issue has dominated more media attention, or prompted greater public unease, than the issue of tuition. Acknowledging the high-profile and contentious nature of tuition, the Institute for Higher Education Policy prepared a report, "The Tuition Puzzle: Putting the Pieces Together." The report explains how and why tuition has increased in recent years, and goes a step further to offer recommendations to states and institutions on how to prevent tuition from increasing apace.

Given the rising costs of tuition, it is reasonable to ask whether the payoffs to higher education are worth the price. James Monks addresses this question in "The Returns to Individual and College Characteristics." He finds that graduates from highly or most selective colleges and universities earn significantly more than their counterparts who graduated from less selective institutions. These patterns are, however, mediated by race and gender. The findings provide considerable food for thought in the ongoing debates on the returns to individuals for investments in earning degrees from various types of higher education institutions.

Inclusion of the article, "The Community College: Educating Students at the Margin Between College and Work," by Thomas Kane and Cecilia Elena Rouse, is a recognition of the importance and uniqueness of community colleges as an institutional type in America. In their article, Kane and Rouse trace the history of the community college, discuss the effects of community college attendance on educational attainment and wages, illustrate the flaws in modern financing of community colleges, and comment on the role that these institutions will play in a future of increased demand for post-secondary education and a technological sea change in educational delivery. Readers unfamiliar with community colleges—and those already well-acquainted—will both find much of value in Kane and Rouse's analysis.

Echoing the theme of privatization in other countries, explored in the section on International Financing of Higher Education, is the seventh article. "Privatizing Higher Education," by Kevin Sontheimer, seizes the reader's attention with his claim that there are no good arguments in favor of publicly-supported higher education, an incendiary assertion in America, where public support of higher education has become enshrined as a civic principle. Sontheimer proceeds to discuss the privatization process, including a realistic treatment of various problems that would face a privatization effort. Read in conjunction with the articles on privatization in the International section, this article should stimulate interesting discussion both for and against privatization in higher education.

The following reviewers contributed to the selection of the works included in this section:

Laurie Cohen, University of Pittsburgh

Jann E. Freed, Central College

Donald E. Heller, University of Michigan

D. Bruce Johnstone, State University of New York at Buffalo

John C. Weidman, University of Pittsburgh

CHAPTER 1

FINANCING HIGHER EDUCATION

Who Should Pay?

D. BRUCE JOHNSTONE

The funding of higher education is a large and complex topic. It is complex in part because of its multiple sources of revenue and its multiple outputs, or products, which are only loosely connected to these different revenue sources. Furthermore, these revenue and expenditure patterns vary significantly by type of institution (university, four-year college, two-year college), mode of governance (public or private), and state. Within the private sector, expenditure levels as well as patterns of pricing and price discounting vary greatly according to institutional wealth and the depth, demographics, and family affluence of the applicant pool. In the public sector, these patterns also vary according to state funding levels, tuition policies, and enrollment limits set by state governments or public multicampus governing boards.

The topic is large because finance underlies much of the three overarching themes of contemporary higher education policy: *quality*, and the relationship between funding and quality in any of its several dimensions; *access*, or the search for social equity in who benefits from, and who pays for, higher education; and *efficiency*, or the search for a cost-effective relationship between revenues (particularly those that come from students, parents, and taxpayers) and outputs (whether measured in enrollments, graduates, student learning, or the scholarly activity of the faculty).

Within these broad themes lie public and institutional policy questions that are informed, if not answered, by economic and financial perspectives. How, if at all, can costs—especially to the taxpayer and the student—be lowered without damage to academic quality or to principles of access and participation? What are appropriate ratios of students to faculty and to professional and administrative staff at various kinds of institutions? What are reasonable conceptions and expectations of higher educational productivity? How can institutional aid, or price discounting, be used to maximize net tuition revenue in the private sector? Are taxpayer dollars in the public sector best used to hold down tuition, or should they go toward expanding need-based aid, with public tuitions raised closer to the full average costs of undergraduate instruction? Are public aid dollars best used for grants and loan subsidies? What of public aid based on academic promise and performance rather than family need? And what is the appropriate response by institutions and governments to the pervasive condition of austerity in higher education, whether brought on by declining enrollments, declining state assistance, or runaway costs?[1]

Although this chapter concentrates on American higher education, the financial principles and problems are much the same worldwide.[2] Our understanding of the particular financial conditions and problems of American higher education can be sharpened by noting what is peculiar to the

Source: Altbach, Berdahl, and Gumport, Editors. *American Higher Education in the Twenty-First Century: Social, Political, and Economic Challenges*, (The Johns Hopkins University Press: NJ, 1999), ch. 13.

financing of the American university: the sheer size, and consequent accessibility, or what the Europeans call "massification"; the large private sector, which includes the most and the least prestigious institutions; and the great reliance on nongovernmental revenue—mainly tuition but also private gifts and return on endowments.

Who pays and who should pay? Students and parents? Taxpayers? Philanthropists? How much higher education? At what cost or level of efficiency? These questions can be adequately addressed only within the broader context of American society in the late 1990s.

THE ECONOMIC, SOCIAL, AND POLITICAL CONTEXT

Higher education is recognized both as an engine of economic growth and as a gatekeeper to individual positions of high remuneration and status. Advanced education—particularly in high technology, information processing, and sophisticated management and analysis—is thought to be essential to maintaining America's economic position in the increasingly competitive global economy. It follows that most jobs of high remuneration and status will require an advanced degree, probably beyond the baccalaureate, and it further follows that the lack of postsecondary education creates a likelihood of marginal income and status. These propositions, however, do not mean that advanced education necessarily makes individuals more productive or that all recipients of advanced education will find remunerative, high-status employment. Higher education can make individuals more productive; but it can also simply screen, or select, for the kinds of intellectual, social, and personal characteristics required for the high-remuneration, high-status jobs that may be available. In short, higher education is essential for most good jobs, and the absence of education beyond high school will be an increasingly formidable barrier to obtaining them; but the mere possession of an advanced degree will guarantee neither good, nor lasting, employment.

American society is being increasingly polarized by class, race, and ethnicity. More and more children grow up in poverty, both rural and urban. The dilemma presented by

higher education's gatekeeper function is that access to, and especially success in, college and university remains highly correlated with socioeconomic class. This correlation has not significantly diminished in recent years, even though American higher education is more accessible than the higher education systems of other countries. Thus, with the increasing polarization of income in the 1980s and 1990s, and with the increasing relationship of economic success in life to success in college, there is reason to be alarmed at the degree to which our colleges and universities perpetuate, and even accelerate, the intergenerational transmission of wealth and status.

As to the political context, American society, or at least a voting electorate, is becoming increasingly conservative. Key elements of this conservatism include resistance to the notion of a benign government, to social welfare programs, and to transfer payments from the rich to the poor. Insofar as there is to be a public agenda for education, it is to be advanced through private, or at least market-oriented, mechanisms: charter schools and vouchers for education reform and tuition tax credits and portable need-based aid to increase accessibility to higher education. A third element of this resurgent conservatism is increasing concern over crime and moral laxity, coupled with a diminishing inclination to view social deprivation or racism as an acceptable excuse for "deviant" (i.e., non-middle-class) behavior.

These themes are intertwined, of course. For example, the political inclination to seek private solutions to what used to be viewed as public problems is given impetus by declining public revenues—which, in turn, is a function, at least in part, of the globalization of the economy and the increasing propensity of wealthy individuals to flee to low-tax havens and to move their enterprises to low-wage economies. There are also internal inconsistencies among these themes: for example, increasing dissatisfaction with governmental intrusion contradicts not only the demand for more costly and intrusive accountability but also direct political intervention into matters of curriculum and programs. But these economic, social, and political themes, for all their complexity, provide a context for consideration of the three broad issues of higher education finance:

- *The size of the nation's higher educational enterprise.* How much publicly supported higher education does the nation need, or will it choose to afford, measured either in total expenditures or as a percentage of the nation's gross domestic product?

- *The efficiency and productivity of this enterprise.* What should higher education (particularly public) cost per unit, whether the unit is students enrolled, degrees granted, scholarship produced, service rendered, or combinations thereof?

- *The sources of revenue to support this enterprise.* Who pays for the costs of higher education? Students and parents? Government and taxpayers? Philanthropists?

SIZE OF THE ENTERPRISE

The American higher education enterprise is enormous, even when controlling for our great wealth and population. For example:

- Total current-fund expenditures for all institutions of higher education in 1993/94 were $173,350,617,000, of which total education and general expenditures (that is, excluding institutionally provided room and board, other auxiliary enterprises, university hospitals, Pell grants, and certain other expenditures) were $136,024,350,000.[3]

- The total expenditure on higher education, including all institutional current-fund expenditures plus additions to plant value, or about $200 billion, is about 3 percent of the nation's gross national product.[4] Among the seven highly industrialized countries, the United States is second only to Canada in higher education expenditure as a percentage of gross domestic product, spending more than France, Germany, Italy, Japan, or the United Kingdom.[5] (Per student expenditures, however, are less than those of most other affluent nations.)

- A total of 14,305,658 students, full- and part-time, were enrolled in the fall of 1993.[6] These students included 62 percent of all high school graduates from the immediately preceding year. Thirty-one percent of all young people aged twenty-two to twenty-four and 60 percent of all young people aged eighteen to nineteen were in some postsecondary institution in 1994. Finally, 22 percent of all persons over the age of twenty-five claimed in 1994 to have completed at least four years of college.[7]

- These students were enrolled in 3,688 colleges and universities, including 1,641 public and 2,047 private institutions, enrolling 11,184,080 and 3,116,570 students, respectively. In addition, some 1,027,713 students were enrolled in 6,737 noncollegiate postsecondary (mainly short-term vocational) institutions, more than 5,000 of them proprietary.[8]

By these and other measures, it is clear that America has chosen to support a large, accessible (both in cost and in admission standards), and highly diverse system (some would say a "nonsystem") of higher education. These "choices" are made in the form of literally millions of decisions by parents and students to pay the costs of college, thereby giving expression to the value they place on higher education for themselves or for their children, and by even more citizens and elected officials, mainly at the state level, who spend tax funds to maintain public colleges and universities, to provide assistance, mostly via student aid, to private colleges and universities, and finally, to support an academic research enterprise that is far and away the largest and most productive in the world.

As the nation approaches the millennium, four forces will expand this already large enterprise. The first is an expansion of the eighteen-to-twenty-four-year-old age cohort. Between 1996 and the year 2006, this traditional college-going age cohort will increase by about 16 percent. The middle-age cohort will continue to decline as the low birth rates of the 1960s and 1970s work their way through, resulting in a possible decline in nontraditional enrollments. Projections of enrollment growth between 1996 and 2006 by the National Center for Education Statistics range from a high of 27 percent to a low of 4 percent, with a middle estimate of 14 percent, or a projected enrollment growth for the decade of just under 2 million students.[9]

This growth will occur unevenly, concentrated mainly in the high-growth states of the West, Southwest, and South. Probably nowhere is there such anxiety over a state's ability to accommodate a projected explosion of student enrollments as in California, where experts are forecasting "tidal wave II," during which the colleges and universities of California may need to accommodate at least 450,000 additional students over the next decade, at a projected additional cost in 1995/96 dollars of $5.2 billion annually—if California is to maintain its historic accessibility to publicly supported higher education.[10]

A second force for more higher education is an expansion of participation and completion due to a perception of higher private rates of return and the perceived need for at least some higher education for positions of remuneration and status. If efforts to reduce the current high attrition rates in U.S. colleges prove successful, there will be a significant increase in enrollment even without any expansion of first-time participation.

A third force, related to the above, is the accretion of degree level sought by the average student. This phenomenon is probably a function of the increasing amount and complexity of knowledge, the increasing educational demands of the productive economy (whether for actual skills, or simply for higher education's screening function), and the tendency of most professions to enhance their status by requiring ever more education prior to entry and perhaps more continuing education to maintain current licensure.

A fourth force, identified more through conjecture than hard evidence, is the incentive for enhancement that seems to be built into the traditions of the academy. William Massy and Robert Zemsky identify this force as "the ratchet."[11] It manifests in a perpetual dissatisfaction on the part of professors, staff, and administrators with the status quo and in a determination to do more and better: to teach new materials, to advise students more effectively, to perform more sophisticated (and usually more costly) research, and generally to advance in the highly competitive pecking order of individual and institutional scholarly prestige, without regard to whether more and better is either cost-effective or demanded by those who must pay the bills.

THE EFFICIENCY AND PRODUCTIVITY OF THE ENTERPRISE

Another issue within the financing of higher education is the efficiency with which all of these resources are employed in the higher educational enterprise and their productivity. Productivity and efficiency look at both costs, or expenditures, and at benefits, or outputs. These concepts deal with costs *per:* whether per student (which, of course, is not really an output but which has the advantage of being easily and unambiguously measured), or per unit of research, or per unit of learning (however measured), or per learning added by the institution. Because the real outputs of the university (the discovery, transmission, and promulgation of knowledge) are both multiple and difficult to measure, and because revenue, at least for the support of instructional expenditures, follows student enrollment in both the public and the private sectors, the cost per student inevitably and overwhelmingly dominates approaches to questions of productivity and efficiency. But we ought never to forget that enrollment, however measured—and however sensitive to fields of study, levels of education, or methods of instruction—is still merely a proxy for the hard-to-measure real output, which is student learning.

Variation in Unit Costs

In the production of goods, there are usually multiple ways of combining productive inputs —mainly different combinations of labor, capital, materials, and managerial effectiveness—to produce a unit of output. The most efficient combination of inputs is determined by the alternative manufacturing technologies and the relative costs of the inputs. Given a set of input costs and a set of technologies for combining inputs into desired outputs, there is an unambiguous most efficient way: that is, a lowest cost per unit. The efficiency, then, of any alternative producer or production process can be measured by how that producer or that process compares to that most efficient way.

Higher education is not as fortunate as these goods-producing enterprises. The technology of university production (of learning and scholarship) is unclear and highly idiosyncratic to the institution, the department, and the individual professor. We do know that per student costs vary greatly. Thus, higher education is generally assumed to be more costly at research universities than at undergraduate colleges due to the higher salaries, lower teaching loads, and more extensive academic support (e.g., libraries and computer facilities) accorded the faculty of the research university. However, the direct instructional costs (especially at the margin) of at least freshmen and sophomores at a typical public research university can be rather low due to the prevalence of low-cost teaching assistants and very large lecture courses—in contrast to the typical public four-year college, where most instruction is carried out by regular faculty in moderate-sized classes, albeit with heavier average teaching loads. In the end, it is probably appropriate to claim that per student costs at a research university are higher than at a four-year college; but it must not be forgotten that this is so at least partly because of certain assumptions and cost allocations that, while reasonable, are nonetheless judgmental and sometimes questionable.

Among like institutions, most interinstitutional variation in per student costs can be attributed to differences either in the amenities provided to the students (recreational and cultural facilities, for example, or academic and student services support staff) or in the costs of faculty. Differential faculty costs, in turn, reflect differences not only in salary (which are low for part-time faculty, who provide much of the teaching at low-cost colleges, and high for the full-time senior professoriate at prestigious private colleges) but also in that other major faculty expense, time (which translates into light teaching loads at wealthy colleges and heavy teaching loads at low-cost "access" colleges).

Howard Bowen, in his classic 1980 study of higher education costs, found great variation in costs among seemingly similar institutions with seemingly similar outcomes.[12] Among a sample of research and doctoral-granting universities arranged from lowest to highest in per student expenditures, the average university in the third quartile spent twice as much per student as the average in the second quartile, and the highest-spending university in the sample spent almost seven and one-half times as much as the first quartile average. Variation among colleges was less, but the colleges in the third quartile of per student costs still spent about 50 percent more than the colleges in the second quartile. More recent data on current-fund expenditures on instruction shows per student spending of $7,573 at universities, $4,788 at "other four-year," and $2,727 at two-year colleges.[13]

This great spread in unit costs is seen by some as profligacy on the part of the highest-cost institutions. Bowen accounts for such variation with his revenue theory of costs, which states that institutions raise all the money they can (which, in the case of highly endowed institutions with wealthy alumni that continue to attract children of affluent families, is a very large amount indeed), and spend all that they raise, purposefully and honorably, even though the amounts spent do not emerge from any discernible production function, as such, as in the industrial manufacture of goods.[14]

But even if the "cost" we use to calculate the cost per student at Harvard were to mean the same thing as the "cost" in per student costs at, say, neighboring Wheelock College or at UMass, Boston, we still cannot say unambiguously that Wheelock and UMass, Boston, are more efficient or more productive than Harvard. They may be cheaper per student, to be sure, but whether they are more efficient requires a measure of output that we do not have and that we probably could not agree upon. And if Harvard were to contest its possible characterization as "inefficient" or "unproductive," it would point to the extraordinary knowledge and competence of its graduates, or to the lifetime of added benefits that Harvard presumably helped to produce, or the value to the society (uncaptured by private lifetime income streams) that Harvard "created."

In short, without better agreement on the proper outputs of higher education, not to mention how to weigh and how to measure them, we are left with cost per full-time equivalent student, as best as we can measure it, as an index of productivity—and as something that should presumably get lower (or cheaper) in response to the demands of students, parents, and taxpayers that higher education become less costly.

Inflation in Unit Costs

Actually, the problem of unit costs and efficiency (or inefficiency) in higher education is less a function of unit costs, per se, and more a function of the seemingly inexorable increase of such costs and of the resulting tuition increases at rates considerably in excess of the rate of inflation. This is the "cost disease" described by William Baumol as characteristic of the so-called productivity-immune sectors of the economy, which are generally labor-intensive, with few opportunities for substitution of capital or new production technologies for labor (live theater, symphony orchestras, social welfare agencies, and education).[15] Unit costs in such enterprises track their increases in compensation. Because workers in such enterprises (e.g., faculty) typically get the same wage and salary increases as those in the productivity-sensitive, goods-producing sectors of the economy, in which constant infusions of capital and technology produce real productivity gains and allow unit cost increases to be less than compensation increases, the unit costs in productivity-immune sectors will inevitably exceed those in goods-producing sectors. Thus, unit-cost increases in higher education will be "above average." And since the rate of inflation is nothing more than a weighted average of many price increases, it is inevitable that unit costs—and thus tuitions—in higher education will rise in normal years faster than the rate of inflation.

This is the normal, or default, condition in higher education: unit costs increase slightly in excess of the prevailing rate of inflation and tuition increases even more, substantially exceeding the prevailing rate of inflation, resulting in the following:

- State governments shift the cost burden from taxpayers to students and families through very high percentage tuition increases in the public sector.
- Private colleges put more of their marginal tuition dollar back into student aid, thus requiring even larger tuition increases to keep up with rising costs.
- Faculty compensation increases exceed compensation increases generally prevailing in the economy.
- Higher education becomes "input rich" in the form, say, of more technology per student, higher faculty and staff to student ratios, or more costly physical plant per student.

All of these factors have been at work for the past decade or more, resulting in very substantial tuition increases in both the private and the public sectors. From 1975 to 1995, tuitions rose at private universities by 105 percent, at private colleges by 108 percent, at public universities by 1105 percent, and at public two-year colleges by 228 percent (Table 1.1).[16] The very high rates of tuition increase in the priciest private colleges are the result of an enrichment of the amenities, a lowering of faculty/student and staff/student ratios, and the increase in institutionally provided financial aid (i.e., a lowering of the net revenue yield from a dollar of tuition increase). Rising tuitions in the public sector is overwhelmingly caused by the withdrawal of state tax revenue and a shift in relative cost burden from the taxpayer to students and parents.

TABLE 1.1
Annual Tuition, Private and Public Colleges, 1974/75–1994/95 ($)

Year	Private Institutions		Public Institutions	
	University	College	University	Two-Year
1974/75	2,614	1,954	599	277
1979/80	3,811	3,020	840	355
1984/85	6,843	5,135	1,386	584
1989/90	10,348	7,778	2,035	756
1994/195	14,510	10,698	2,982	1,914
% increase 1990–95	40	86	47	153
% increase 1985–95	24	108	115	228

Source: National Center for Education Statistics. *Digest of Education Statistics, 1995* (Washington, D.C.: U.S. Department of Education, 1995), table 306.

Diverging Trajectories of Costs and Revenues

The natural trajectory of unit costs in higher education, as described above, is steeply upward, at rates in excess of prevailing rates of inflation. The corresponding rate of increase of anticipated revenues is substantially flatter, being dampened by the following:

- Price resistance from upper-middle-class parents, apparently less willing to accept tuition increases that are considerably in excess of inflation and that take increasing portions of family income.[17]

- Price resistance from older students and from graduate and advanced professional students facing mounting debt loads.[18]

- Decreasing support from governors and state legislatures faced with other compelling public need, decreasing federal financial assistance, and restive or angry state taxpayers.

- Increasing costs of "big science" without concomitant increases in federal research support.

- Decreasing support for academic health centers, caught between cost-cutting insurers and low-cost alternative providers.

The resulting scenario is frightening, especially for high-cost research universities and for public colleges and universities that face declining state tax revenues and increasing enrollment without the benefit of substantial endowments, wealthy alumni, internationally eminent scientists, or deep and affluent applicant pools. Some institutions have turned their fortunes around through vigorous cost cutting, restructuring, and moving into a narrow market niche, but the late 1990s will be a period of great uncertainty and continuing financial stress for most colleges and universities.[19]

SOURCES OF REVENUE FOR THE ENTERPRISE

The financing of higher education poses the question of how the costs should be apportioned among four parties: parents, students, taxpayers, and philanthropists.[20] Parents would finance their children's education from current income, savings, or future income via increased indebtedness. Students would finance their own education from savings, summer earnings, term-time earnings, and future earnings via loans or graduate tax obligations. Taxpayers at the federal, state, and local levels would finance students' education through taxes on income, sales, property, assets; business or manufacturing taxes (via the higher prices of the goods or services so taxed) or through the indirect "tax" of inflation brought about by public deficit spending. And philanthropists would finance students' education either through endowments or current giving.

The sharing and shifting of the costs among these parties is a zero-sum game, in which a lessening of the burden upon, or revenue from, one party must be compensated either by a reduction of underlying costs or by a shift of the burden to another party. Thus, if state taxpayers' share of higher education costs is to be lessened, that reduced share must either lead to reduced institutional costs or be shifted, probably to students and parents via higher tuition. But if parents cannot pay or have enough political power to limit, by statute or regulation, a higher parental contribution (as happened when voter pressure forced Congress to eliminate home equity from the assets considered in determining "need" for awarding federal Pell grants), the burden would shift to students, principally through higher debt loads. This scenario—lower taxpayer contributions, reduced institutional budgets, higher tuitions, level parental contributions, and much higher debt burdens—is exactly what has happened in the last decade or two.

The policy questions sharpened by the cost-sharing perspective are as follows:

- What is the appropriate amount that should be expected from parents to cover the higher educational costs of their children? Is this share to be a function only of current income, to be met by family belt tightening? Or are parents also expected to have saved from the past or to borrow against the future? Are assets to be figured in the calculation of need? How long should parental financial responsibility continue: through undergraduate years only, or until the age of, say, twenty-four or twenty-five? And what is the expected contribution from a noncustodial parent?

- With regard to student share, are there any limits to the hours of term-time work compatible with full-time study? Are there any limits to the amount of indebtedness that students should be allowed to incur in pursuit of their education? Should this limit be a function of likely completion of studies or of the anticipated earning power of the intended occupation or profession? Would this deferred payment obligation be best handled via a conventional mortgage-type loan, an income-contingent obligation, or a graduate tax obligation (assuming that the present value of the repayment stream under all options would yield the same repayments, at least over a cohort of borrowers)?

- Should public (taxpayer) financial support be linked to governmental ownership and ultimate control, as in the support of public higher education? Or should taxpayers support certain costs divorced from control, such as vouchers (e.g., Pell grants), which support both public and private—and even proprietary—sectors of higher education? Should taxpayer support per student continue to be a function mainly of family income and sector costs (e.g., public research universities as opposed to public community colleges)? Or should the government, through the financial aid system, differentiate among students by their academic potential or attempt to influence their choice of academic field or intended occupation?

There has been a considerable increase in education costs borne by students and parents, mainly through higher tuitions, especially in the 1980s for private institutions and in the 1990s for public institutions (Table 1.1). However, before drawing conclusions about either the relative shares borne by students, parents, and taxpayers or the impact of these increasing costs, we need to adjust for the impact of inflation, for increases in family incomes, and for the effects of financial assistance. Table 1.2 shows the cost of higher education in the percentage it took (after financial aid) of family incomes at selected levels.

Tables 1.3 and 1.4 show how the expenses of private and public institutions, both high cost and low cost, are met through combinations of family contributions, federal and state aid, loans, and institutional (philanthropic) grants for high-, middle-, and low-income families.

Some observations from Tables 1.3 and 1.4:

- The costs of college borne by the student and parent are high but are very high only for relatively affluent families at high-cost private institutions.

- Meeting the high costs at expensive private colleges and universities without substantial parental contributions requires both very high institutional, or philanthropic, support as well as very substantial student indebtedness.

TABLE 1.2
Tuition, Room, and Board as Percentage of Family Income, by Income Percentile,
Public and Private Colleges, 1979–1994 (constant 1975 $)

Year	Public Institutions			Private Institutions		
	25th Percentile	50th Percentile	75th Percentile	25th Percentile	50th Percentile	75th Percentile
1979	15.1	9.1	6.3	34.3	20.7	14.4
1984	20.5	11.7	7.7	49.3	28.1	18.5
1989	21.4	12.0	7.9	57.1	32.1	21.2
1994	26.2	14.2	9.1	71.3	38.7	24.8
% increase 1979–94	74	56	44	108	87	72

Source: National Center for Education Statistics, The Condition of Education, 1996 (Washington, D.C.: US. Office of Education), 1996, 62.

TABLE 1.3
Student Budgets at Private Institutions, Sources of Support, by Family Income ($)

Source of Support	High-Cost Institution			Low-Cost Institution		
	Low-Income Family	Middle-Income Family	High-Income Family	Low-Income Family	Middle-Income Family	High-Income Family
Parental contribution	0	3,000	25,500	0	2,000	16,500
Federal grants	4,000	0	0	4,000	0	0
State grants[a]	3,000	1,500	0	3,000	1,500	0
Institutional grants	13,500	16,000	0	4,000	6,500	0
Student summer savings	1,500	1,500	1,500	1,500	1,500	1,500
Student term-time earnings	2,000	2,000	0	2,500	2,500	0
Student loans	5,000	5,000	2,000	3,000	4,000	0
Total from taxpayer[b]	8,365	2,865	546	7,819	2,592	0
Total from parents[c]	0	3,000	25,500	0	2,000	16,500
Total from student[d]	7,135	7,135	2,954	6,181	6,908	1,500
Total from philanthropists[e]	13,500	16,000	0	4,000	6,500	0

Note: Low income, $12,000; middle income, $38,752; high income, $100,000. Most high-cost private colleges use the College Scholarship Service or a similar system, which yields a higher family contribution. Many systems use the concept *family contribution,* which includes the summer savings assumption.

a. State need-based grant assumes approximately 75% of New York State Tuition Assistance Program (the most generous in the nation).

b. Total from taxpayer is sum of federal and state grants plus the present value of loan subsidies.

c. Total from parents is the expected family contribution minus assumed summer savings from the student.

d. Total from student is the sum of term-time earnings, summer savings, and the present discounted value of expected loan repayments.

e. Total from philanthropists represent all institutional grants.

TABLE 1.4
Student Budgets at Public Institutions, Sources of Support, by Family Income ($)

Source of Support	High-Cost Institution ($12,000)			Low-Cost Institution ($6,000)		
	Low-Income Family	Middle-Income Family	High-Income Family	Low-Income Family	Middle-Income Family	High-Income Family
Parental contribution	0	2,500	8,500	0	2,000	4,000
Federal grants	3,000	0	0	2,340	0	0
State grants	2,000	750	0	1,160	250	0
Institutional grants	0	0	0	0	0	0
Student summer savings	1,500	1,500	750	500	1,500	1,000
Student term-time earnings	2,000	2,500	750	1,000	1,250	1,000
Student loans	3,500	4,750	2,000	1,000	1,000	0
Total from taxpayer	5,955	2,050	545	3,775	525	0
Total from parents	0	2,500	8,500	0	2,000	4,000
Total from student	6,045	7,450	2,955	2,225	3,475	2,000
Total from philanthropists	0	0	0	0	0	0

Note: See table 1.3.

- The key to financial accessibility lies less in level of tuition, or even in expected parental contribution, than in students' willingness to incur substantial indebtedness. Total student debt for four or more years of undergraduate education, plus three or more years of graduate or advanced professional school, can easily reach $50,000 to $100,000 or more, presenting the student with a repayment obligation that can either discourage advanced higher education altogether or distort career and other life choices.

- High-cost public institutions (high tuition plus residency) require substantial indebtedness, considerably diminishing the price advantage over high-cost private institutions.

From time to time, a proposal is made that direct public funding of state colleges and universities, at least for the support of instruction, be drastically reduced or eliminated altogether, with tuitions raised to full or near full cost, eliminating or greatly reducing what the proponents of this view call the "subsidy" to the students and families of students attending public colleges and universities. In place of direct state revenue, which currently supports from 60 to 90 percent of public four-year undergraduate instructional costs, proponents of the high-tuition, high-aid model would substitute a much expanded program of need-based grants, which would diminish as parental or student incomes rose. The grants would phase out entirely for families and students whose income was deemed sufficient to pay the full cost of tuition in addition to other expenses.[21]

The high-tuition, high-aid model is based on claims of efficiency and equity. The efficiency claim begins with the tenet of public finance theory that any public subsidy of a good or a service that consumers are likely to purchase anyway, in the absence or diminution of the subsidy, is an inefficient use of public tax dollars. The tax dollars released, if public sector tuitions were allowed to rise, would supposedly go toward public needs of greater priority: more need-based student aid, health care, public infrastructure, tax cuts, or public deficit reduction. And if the demand for public higher education should decline as a result of lower subsidies and higher prices, this too

might be a move in the direction of a more efficient use of the nation's resources. Subsidies can generate overproduction of a good or service, and a higher priced public higher education might discourage ambivalent, ill-prepared students whom advocates of high tuition and high aid assume are taking up space and wasting precious resources in our public colleges and universities.

A corollary of the efficiency claim is that there exists, at least in some states, underutilized capacity in the private higher education sector that could be filled at relatively low marginal cost. A shift of tax dollars from the direct support of public colleges and universities to need-based student aid, portable to the private sector, would presumably shift enrollments there and enable the socially optimal level of enrollments to be supported more in the private sector but at a lower additional net cost to the taxpayer.

The equity argument in favor of high tuition, high aid is based on two assumptions: first, that public higher education is actually partaken of disproportionately by students from upper-middle-income and affluent families; and second, that the state taxes used to support public higher education tend to be proportionate or even regressive and thus are paid by many lower-middle-income and poor families, who are unlikely to benefit. Thus, the high-tuition, high-aid model of public higher education finance is claimed to be more equitable than across-the-board low tuition because it targets all public subsidy only on the needy and imposes full costs on students or families affluent enough to pay.

The case against the high-tuition, high-aid model rests partly on the oversimplification and political naïveté of the case made on its behalf; summarized above, and partly on the case to be made for the very existence of a public higher education sector. The case against high tuition, high aid may be summarized by four points.

First, a "sticker price" of $15,000 to $18,000 for a full-time year at a public college or university would almost certainly discourage many from aspiring to higher education, even with the prospect of financial aid or a lower tuition for those in need.[22] The total costs to students and parents of a year of full-time study at a public four-year college or university, as shown in table 1.3, make even public higher education today a relatively heavy financial burden for most families and for nearly all independent students. This fact alone does not fully negate the more theoretical arguments of efficiency and equity presented on behalf of full-cost or near-full-cost pricing for public higher education, as summarized above. But even with financial aid, costs at a public college might seem daunting to many students and their parents, especially to students from disadvantaged and nonwhite families.

Second, a high-tuition, high-aid policy would lessen the quality of public colleges and universities. The purpose of high-tuition, high-aid plans is to reduce state tax revenues currently going to public colleges and universities, even though some proponents claim that this revenue loss would be made up by increased revenue from the much higher tuitions paid by the more well-to-do. Private sector proponents of high tuition, high aid, however, make no secret of their aim to shift enrollments and tuition dollars of middle- and upper-middle-income students (or at least the most attractive and able ones) from the public sector to the private sector. With little or no price advantage left in the public sector; with the resource advantage of large endowments, wealthy alumni, and the tradition of philanthropic support in the private sector; with the patina of elitism and selectivity associated with private colleges and universities (especially in the Northeast); and with greater constraints and burdens remaining on the public sector, many of the nation's 1,600 public colleges and universities would become places for students whom the private colleges, now priced the same as public colleges, do not accept. Such an erosion in the relative status and quality of public colleges and universities does not seem to be in the nation's public interest.

Third, high tuition does not guarantee high aid. Governors, legislators, and voters, continually pressed by public needs exceeding available resources, are likely to support that part of the public sector in which they perceive that they or their children have a stake. They are much less likely to maintain the financial aid, or "tuition discount," portion of the public higher educational budget when it is devoted almost exclusively to the poor. The not unlikely consequences of a policy of high tuition, high aid,

rather than the purported enhancements of efficiency and equity, are higher tuition, lower taxes, inadequate aid, diminished access, and deteriorating public colleges and universities.

Fourth and fundamentally, the high-tuition, high-aid model is a denial of the appropriateness of higher education as a public good. The nation's public colleges and universities have been built and supported over the last century and a half not merely to provide a subsidized education to those who might not otherwise have an opportunity for higher education. Rather, voters and elected officials wanted public colleges and universities that would attract and hold the best and brightest students and scholars, serve society, aid the economy, and be a signal of the state's culture. The high-tuition, high-aid model essentially denies most of these public purposes to public higher education and substitutes only a public subsidy for those who are too poor to afford what would become an otherwise unsubsidized, expensive, and essentially privatized product. States need to consider whether these continue to be important reasons for supporting public higher education or whether they mainly want to get needy students into some college, in which case high tuition, high aid is almost certainly, as public finance theory correctly states, less expensive to the taxpayer.

SUMMARY AND CONCLUSIONS

The financial fortunes of American colleges and universities vary greatly by institution. Those relatively few private institutions with large endowments, traditions of generous alumni giving, and deep and affluent student applicant pools will experience continuing cost pressures but will be able to increase revenues commensurably and continue to prosper. Some public institutions similarly situated with deep and affluent applicant pools, with established traditions of philanthropic support, and with research strengths in areas of continuing public investment (e.g., biomedical and applied sciences) will prosper. Some less-well-endowed private institutions will seize a specialized market niche, either vocational (e.g., health-related professions) or cultural/ideological (e.g., conservative Christian) and, with good management and low faculty costs will also prosper. Most private colleges and universities, however, will feel a fierce revenue squeeze, primarily driven by the lack of growth in the number of upper-middle-class parents able or willing to pay the high tuitions and in the number of students willing to take on increasing levels of indebtedness. And most public colleges and universities will continue to experience flat or declining state tax support, forcing even higher tuition, more program closures, and an increasing reliance on part-time and adjunct faculty.

As more and more colleges and universities exhaust the available cost-side measures for increasing productivity, interest is turning to increasing productivity by enhancing higher education's output, or learning.[23] Expressed another way, the major remaining productivity problem in higher education may not lie in excessive costs but in insufficient learning—a function of such features as redundant learning; aimless academic exploration; the unavailability of courses at the right time; excessive nonlearning time in the academic day, week, and year; insufficient use of self-paced learning; and insufficient realization of the potential of collegiate-level learning during the high school years. Enhancing the productivity of learning, then, would reduce vacation time and other time spent in other-than-learning activities; provide better advising and other incentives to lessen aimless curricular exploration; enhance opportunities for self-paced learning, perhaps through the aid of instructional technology; minimize curricular redundancy; and maximize the potential of college-level learning during the high school years.

Technology in the form of personal computers, new instructional software, the internet, and instructional videocassettes, will profoundly affect the way faculty and advanced students conduct research, and it will enrich some teaching. However—aside from some pockets of distance learning and users of a virtual university, generally limited to nontraditional and technologically inclined students—technology will mainly enable more and better, not cheaper, learning.

The shift in burden from parents and taxpayers to students, paid for with more part-time (and even more full-time) work and much more debt, will continue, but there is reason to believe that the long-expected price resistance

is happening. Marketing will become even more frenzied, and so will governmental efforts to "solve the problem" without spending any taxpayer revenue: tuition prepayment, tax-exempt savings plans, non-need-based price discounting, income-contingent repayment plans, and the like.

State higher education budgets will be smaller, but this reduction will be accompanied by greater flexibility and performance criteria, such as premiums to institutions that improve retention and completion rates. Most institutions have been shaping their missions for years to adjust to more low-income, minority, older, part-time, and place-bound students; greater applied and vocational interest among most students; and less revenue and the need to trim or eliminate that which is neither excellent nor popular nor central to the institution. In short, much of the vaunted restructuring that management consultants and many observers and analysts of higher education have been calling for as a solution to the financial dilemma of U.S. colleges and universities is probably not a solution at all, for the simple reason that it has been going on for years. Most of the smaller and comprehensive colleges have reallocated resources and altered their programs and faculty profiles dramatically; many have changed mission altogether. Many of those that have not are either rich or private or both and have no need to change dramatically (at least no need that can be called a public policy issue).

The largest class of institution for which this is not necessarily the case are those universities, largely regional and with minimal or uneven scholarly reputations, that continue to pursue the research university model but that are unlikely to penetrate the top ranks, measured by the scholarly prestige of their faculty or their graduate programs. Here, pressures to control costs are likely to focus on an increasing separation of funding for instruction and research, much as has occurred in the United Kingdom. If these measures are successful, the result could be less indirect public subsidization of faculty scholarship, a widening difference in faculty workloads, and a reduced administration overhead on competitive research grants.

Although American higher education does more than the systems of any other nation to provide postsecondary opportunities to those from low socioeconomic backgrounds, the larger American society is becoming not only more unequal but also more predictable in intergenerational transmission of higher educational attainment. In other words, the children of well-educated, well-off parents generally achieve and persist in college, and those of the very poor, unless they are very bright and very lucky, generally do not. The likely continuation of sharply rising public tuitions, political attacks against remedial courses, elimination of affirmative action considerations in admissions and financial aid, and the conservative assault against curricula acknowledging multicultural values will likely accentuate this pattern.

NOTES

1. The prevailing condition of austerity in higher education is described in David W. Breneman, *Liberal Arts Colleges: Thriving, Surviving, or Endangered?* (Washington, D.C.: Brookings, 1994); Carol S. Hollins, *Containing Costs and Improving Productivity in Higher Education* (San Francisco: Jossey-Bass, 1992); D. Bruce Johnstone, *Working Papers in a Time of Fiscal Crisis* (Albany: State University of New York, 1992); William B. Simpson, *Managing with Scarce Resources* (San Francisco: Jossey-Bass, 1993).

2. D. Bruce Johnstone, "The Costs of Higher Education: Worldwide Issues and Trends for the 1990s," in *The Funding of Higher Education: International Perspectives*, ed. Philip G. Altbach and D. Bruce Johnstone (New York: Garland, 1993). For a perspective on the austerity of higher education in developing countries and the similarity with the United States and Europe in both analyses and policy solutions, see Adrian Ziderman and Douglas Albrecht, *Financing Universities in Developing Countries* (Washington, D.C.: Falmer, 1995).

3. National Center for Education Statistics, *Current Funds Revenues and Expenditures of Institutions of Higher Education: Fiscal Years 1986 through 1994* (Washington, D.C.: U.S. Department of Education, 1996), table 2.

4. National Center for Education Statistics, *Digest of Education Statistics, 1995* (Washington, D.C.: U.S. Department of Education, 1995), table 30.

5. National Center for Education Statistics, *The Condition of Education, 1996* (Washington, D.C.: U.S. Department of Education, 1996), 162.

6. National Center for Education Statistics, *Digest of Education Statistics, 1995*, table 165.

7. National Center for Education Statistics, *Condition of Education, 1996*, indicator 7; National Center for Education Statistics, *Digest of Education Statistics, 1995*, tables 8, 6.

8. National Center for Education Statistics, *Digest of Education Statistics, 1995*, tables 165, 233, 350.

9. National Center for Education Statistics, *Projections of Education Statistics to 2006* (Washington, D.C.: U.S. Department of Education, 1996), chap. 2.

10. *The Challenge of the Century,* (Sacramento: California Postsecondary Education Commission, 1995). The privately financed California Policy Center sets the number at 488,000; see *Shared Responsibility: Strategies to Enhance Quality and Opportunity in California Higher Education* (San Jose: California Higher Education Policy Center, 1996).

11. William F Massy and Robert Zemsky, "The Lattice and the Ratchet," *Policy Perspectives* 2 (1990). See also, Robert Zemsky and William F. Massy, "Toward an Understanding of Our Current Predicaments," *Change,* Nov/Dec. 1995.

12. Howard R. Bowen, *The Costs of Higher Education* (San Francisco: Jossey-Bass, 1980), 116–19.

13. National Center for Education Statistics, *Digest of Education Statistics, 1995,* table 343.

14. Bowen, *Costs of Higher Education,* 19–26.

15. William J. Baumol and William G. Bowen, *Performing Arts: The Economic Dilemma* (New York: Twentieth Century Fund, 1966); William G. Bowen, *The Economics of the Major Private Universities* (Berkeley, Calif.: Carnegie Commission on the Future of Higher Education, 1968).

16. For accounts of recent tuition increases, see Arthur Hauptman, *The College Tuition Spiral* (Washington., D.C.: College Board and American Council on Education, 1990); Carol Francis, *What Factors Affect College Tuition?* (Washington, D.C.: American Association of State Colleges and Universities, 1990); Michael S. McPherson, Morton Owen Shapiro, and Gordon C. Winston, *Paying the Piper: Productivity, Incentives, and Financing in U.S. Higher Education* (Ann Arbor: University of Michigan Press, 1993); Michael Mumper, *Removing College Price Barriers: What Government Has Done and Why It Hasn't Worked* (Albany: State University of New York Press, 1996).

17. "$1000 a Week: The Scary Cost of College," *Newsweek,* Apr. 29,1996.

18. National Center for Education Statistics, *Student Financing of Graduate and First-Professional Education, Contractor Report* (Washington, D.C.: U.S. Department of Education, 1993).

19. David Leslie and E. K. Fretwell, *Wise Moves in Hard Times: Creating and Managing Resilient Colleges and Universities* (San Francisco: Jossey-Bass, 1996). See also David W Breneman, *Higher Education on a Collision Course with New Realities* (Washington, D.C.: Association of Governing Boards, 1994). Reprinted with permission by American Student Assistance.

20. Some consider "business" a possible fifth party to bear a share of higher education

costs. However, grants from business to higher education can be viewed in one of three ways: (1) as the purchase of a service, whether research or specialized training, in which case the grant should cover the costs of the added service but is not expected to bear a share of the core instructional costs of the college or university; (2) as voluntary contributions coming out of owner profits, in which case they would fall under "philanthropy"; or (3) as contributions considered part of the cost of doing business, included in the price of the products and paid for by the general consumer, like a sales or consumption tax, in which case the incidence, or burden, is indistinguishable from that of other taxes and may be considered to be included, at least conceptually, in the "taxpayer" party. See D. Bruce Johnstone, *Sharing the Costs of Education* (New York: College Board, 1986).

21. The case for high tuition, high aid was popularized in W. Lee Hansen and Burton A. Weisbrod, *Benefits, Costs, and Finance of Pub-* *lic Higher Education* (Chicago: Markham, 1969). See also Carnegie Commission on Higher Education, *Higher Education: Who Pays? Who Benefits? Who Should Pay?* (New York: McGraw-Hill, 1973); Frederick J. Fischer, "State Financing of Higher Education: A New Look at an Old Problem," *Change,* Jan./Feb., 1990; and McPherson, Shapiro, and Winston, *Paying the Piper.* The case against draws heavily on D. Bruce Johnstone, *The High-Tuition-High-Aid Model of Public Higher Education Finance: The Case Against* (Albany: State University of New York, for National Association of System Heads, 1993).

22. The figures assume nontuition expenses of $8,000 annually and tuition expenses of $7,000 to $10,000, or approximately 75 percent of undergraduate instructional costs.

23. D. Bruce Johnstone, *Learning Productivity: A New Imperative for American Higher Education* (Albany: State University of New York Press, 1992).

CHAPTER 2

PATTERNS OF FINANCE

Revolution, Evolution, or More of the Same?

D. BRUCE JOHNSTONE

This examination of the prospect of revolutionary change in patterns of financing American higher education in the next decade begins with a consideration of current patterns of financing along three dimensions: total resources, cost per unit, and apportionment of costs (Johnstone, 1993a, forthcoming). I pose several questions for each dimension, describing ways in which current patterns might change and suggesting the likelihood of such changes being revolutionary or evolutionary. My personal conclusion is that the next decade will consist largely of struggling in the same ways with the difficulties all too familiar from the current decade.

CURRENT PATTERNS AND MAJOR ISSUES

The patterns and discernible trajectories of higher education finance in any country may be described along three dimensions:

1. The total resources devoted to higher education and to its traditional products of teaching, research or scholarship, and service. The most important part of this sum is the total of public, or taxpayer-provided, resources.
Currently, measured by the scale of resources, American higher education must be characterized as enormous, even controlling for our great population and great wealth. This observation is true whether "scale" is measured by the proportion of the traditional college-age population matriculating, enrolling, or completing college, or by the percentage of adults currently enrolled or having some tertiary degree, or by the percentage of total gross domestic product or of total public expenditures devoted to higher education (Johnstone, 1991). On the dimension of total financial resources devoted to higher education, or the scale of the aggregate enterprise, speculations about radical changes in the near-term future would include these questions:

- Is higher education likely in the next decade to claim an appreciably greater or lesser amount either of the nation's total resources, or more narrowly, of our public (taxpayer-originated) resources?

- If there is to be some "revolutionary change" in scale, and if that change is to involve that which institutions of higher education mainly do—which is to teach—would such a change

Source: *The Review of Higher Education*, Spring 1988, Volume 21, No. 3, pp. 245–255. Copyright © Association for the Study of Higher Education. All Rights Reserved (ISSN 0162-5748).

entail more or fewer students entering into the system, thereby changing what we have come to describe as participation, or access? Or might it more likely entail more (or less) higher education for the average student enrolled, thus changing persistence or completion or the prevalence of post-baccalaureate education, or perhaps the amount of continuing or lifelong education, but without radically changing the proportion of any age cohort ultimately accessing higher education?

- Or might the change in scale have to do more with the total time and resources that the nation's more than 500,000 full-time and nearly 300,000 part-time faculty presently devote to research and the dissemination of knowledge (and the volume of articles and books published and the number of scholarly conferences) as opposed to teaching? This change might yield considerably more teaching and commensurably less scholarship for little or no change in the total resources devoted to the nation's higher education enterprise.

2. The productivity, or efficiency, or cost per unit of the higher educational enterprise, whether these "units" be numbers of students taught, units of actual learning, or new knowledge generated.

Because teaching (actually, learning) is the main, although by no means the only, product of American higher education, and because we still have no reliable, affordable measure of the learning added by the college or university, the dominant measure of efficiency in higher education is the cost per student credit hour, or cost per full-time equivalent student. This cost, in turn, is a function of: (a) the average faculty and staff costs, which are determined mainly by the level of salaries and whether the faculty and staff are full-time, with benefits, or part-time, with low wages and no benefits; (b) the prevailing faculty/staff-to-student ratio, which, given the traditional teaching paradigm, is mainly a function of class size and teaching loads; and (c) expenditures for items other than teaching, whether technology, facilities, student affairs, marketing and public relations, or general administration. In the near term, speculations of "revolutionary changes" in the productivity or efficiency of American higher education would ask, for example, these questions:

- Are average teaching loads or class sizes likely to be enlarged substantially, and thus more students taught per faculty member, with or without the benefit of new instructional technologies?

- Can and will the cost of faculty and staff be otherwise substantially lowered, most likely through the further hiring of low-paid, part-time faculty instead of moderately paid, full-time faculty and staff and/or through contracting out more of the university's noninstructional activities?

- Can and will the prevailing instructional paradigm of "courses" and "classes" meeting for fixed periods of time (e.g., semesters or terms), each with a number of students and an instructor, change in the direction of more independent study or other modes of self-paced learning? More importantly, can such changes significantly lower the cost per student or per graduate or per some other realistic measure of student learning?

- Can the seemingly irreversible trend toward more administrative and professional (nonteaching) staff be turned around so that more of the resources go directly toward teaching, or at least toward teaching and scholarship?

3. Finally, how the burdens of meeting these costs, whatever they may be, are apportioned among parents (from current income, savings, or debt), students (from part-time earning and debt), taxpayers (directly, through support of institutional expenditures or indirectly, through student grants and loan subsidies), and philanthropists (through endowments and current gifts).

The current pattern of financing American higher education along this dimension is characterized by a substantial and increasing reliance on revenues from sources other than the government or taxpayer—particularly from parents and students through tuition, and from philanthropists or donors. This pattern (less reliance on taxpayers) is seen especially in the public sector and particularly in the more costly (and generally the more selective) public research universities. Speculations about "revolutionary change" along this dimension focus mainly on the degree to which, and the form by which, public tuitions may rise at even greater rates than in the recent past, displacing even more taxpayer resources. Such increases may possibly be accompanied by more need-based grants to preserve accessibility, but the outcome will essentially be the privatizing of the financing of public higher education (Hansen & Weisbrod, 1969; Carnegie Commission, 1973; McPherson & Winston, 1993). Consider these questions:

- Will "high tuition-high aid" become the dominant pattern of public higher education finance, with public-sector tuitions set at, or very near, full cost, accompanied by higher need-based grants from both federal and state government? Such a change would shift enrollment from the public to the private sector, possibly causing either the radical transformation or the closure of some public institutions.

- Will radically new forms of deferred payment plans—very long term loans, income-contingent repayments, or graduate taxes—be implemented to mask, if only cosmetically, the effects of even greater shifts of financial responsibility to students?

- If "high tuition-high aid" is to be a growing pattern, will the "high aid" part of the equation actually materialize as promised by its proponents? Or will the real result (and perhaps, for some, the real agenda) be high tuition, only modest aid, based on merit as well as need, greatly diminished access at the "low end" of the continuum of academic preparedness, and, as suggested above, an increasingly privatized public sector?

- Might "high tuition-high aid" occur only or mainly at the post-baccalaureate level, leaving the mix of enrollments and missions essentially unchanged (as between the current public and private sectors) at the undergraduate level, but

greatly raising tuitions and creating the above-mentioned impacts at the graduate, advanced professional, and continuing education levels?

FINANCE, INSTITUTIONAL MISSIONS, AND PREVAILING TEACHING-LEARNING PARADIGMS

Patterns of finance are inextricably connected with institutional missions and the prevailing teaching-learning paradigms in American higher education. It is difficult to contemplate radical changes in patterns of finance that do not either arise from, or cause, profound changes in the substance of the higher educational enterprise, For example, what if a decision were made to no longer award financial aid mainly on the basis of parental income, as now, but on the basis of academic promise and performance—i.e., to deny financial assistance to lower-achieving students in spite of financial need? Such a decision would almost certainly drive out of higher education hundreds of thousands and possibly millions of students who may be marginally prepared academically and who are often ambivalent about higher education. Many of these students now try for a college education, and sometimes succeed, because they feel that college can lead to a better life as long as the attempt is financially possible without the prospect of unmanageable debt. Debt can be made somewhat more manageable through longer repayment periods and by linking repayments to future earnings. But a debt is still a debt, even if it is dressed up as a "graduate tax" or an "advance on future income"; and a big debt, even in fancy dress, is still daunting, particularly to those who are ambivalent about higher education to begin with.

Greatly increasing the public sector tuition and providing financial aid based largely on merit would have profound financial consequences for the nation's higher educational enterprise, public and private. It would lead to the downsizing and even the closure of many less selective institutions. On the positive size, such a consequence would save significant public resources. On the negative side, it would have a major and almost certainly detrimental impact on the lives of those no longer accommodated. But these are not really so much revolutionary changes in the pattern of financing higher education as a revolutionary change in the peculiarly American *vision* of opportunity and social mobility, in which our colleges and universities, through their present patterns of finance, play such a significant role.

Similarly, a significant number of the nation's "regional" public doctoral-granting universities (as opposed to the nationally or internationally eminent public research universities) could teach students at a lower cost if they were to cease operating as research universities and if their faculty instead were given the high teaching loads characteristic of two- or four-year teaching colleges. But such a change, even if it were to be politically possible (which it almost certainly is not), would not lead to a more productive institution, but rather to a fundamentally different kind of institution: cheaper in per-student costs perhaps (although low-cost graduate teaching assistants would no longer be available), but not necessarily cheaper in per-student learning. Unquestionably it would be less productive in scholarship and probably in service to the community. Again, this change would be not so much a radical shift in a pattern of finance as a radical redefinition of the very missions of these dozens or hundreds of institutions.[1]

In fact, the only way to create revolutionary changes in the patterns of higher educational finance that would not require or cause radical change in the missions of the institutions or in the nature of the prevailing teaching-learning paradigm would require either of two circumstances or assumptions. The first is the assumption already held by many citizens and elected officials that there is substantial waste in colleges and universities that could be eradicated simply with better management, less diversion of resources into expensive nonteaching activities, and a rejuvenated work ethic, all of which, we assume, would lead to significantly lower per-student costs. The problem with this assumption is that it is almost certainly untrue of most or all of the nation's nearly 1,500 community colleges and most of the nearly 1,000 less-selective, regional, baccalaureate and comprehensive colleges, public and private alike.[2] In these institutions, teaching loads are already high, faculty and staff costs almost always low (due to very large numbers of part-time faculty

and low-cost contract staff), and amenities lean. Fund raising and marketing, even at the public campuses, are already aggressive. Inflation-adjusted budgets have been cut for most of the past ten or fifteen years. The low-hanging fruit of productivity gains has long since been picked. In contrast, high-cost colleges and universities with well-paid faculty, low teaching loads, low student-faculty ratios, modern facilities, and other amenities almost certainly have not yet taken all possible efficiencies—or at least cost reductions. But these colleges and universities are expensive, not because the taxpayer is picking up higher costs, but because parents, students, and donors have paid handsomely, and continue to do so, for precisely the kinds of "extras" that such colleges feature. They may also have faculty who are paid near the top of the faculty pay scale and who teach fewer courses than faculty at other institutions. But most of these faculty are both hard-working and astonishingly productive in doing what they were hired (and ultimately promoted) to do: internationally recognized scholarship that brings prestige to their institution, their colleagues, and ultimately to their students (regardless of who actually teaches them). The Harvards, Stanfords, and Williamses may be expensive, at least relative to most other colleges and universities. But it is difficult to call them unproductive, when parents and students are lining up to be given the opportunity to buy what these and other high-cost institutions provide: a great learning ambiance, prestige, and future benefits that come from selectivity and a lifetime of rewarding associations. It would be foolish to predict any significant change—let alone a "revolutionary" change—in the financial patterns of such institutions.

This is not to say that there will not be changes in how colleges and universities are financed, even without dramatic change in the underlying teaching-learning paradigm. State governments can always withdraw even more money, forcing public colleges and universities to raise tuition even more sharply, to further reduce faculty costs (by having fewer and/or more part-time), to cut academic and support programs, to reduce enrollments, and possibly, in the most extreme cases, to close campuses. But however disaffected state politicians and even the electorates may be, at least in certain states, there is as yet no evidence that either the voters or the elected officials want either to limit access dramatically or to downgrade the scholarly missions of their research universities to the point of substantially diminishing their prestige, wherever they currently are in that fiercely competitive institutional pecking order. Although a few private colleges may go out of business, there are actually more private institutions of higher education in the mid-1990s than there were in the mid-1970s. Private colleges have shown themselves incredibly robust: more vulnerable, in the end, to adverse demographics than to finances per se. And if a few go out of business altogether, their demise will strengthen (slightly) those that remain, rather than signal any radically new financial pattern in the sector generally.

OUTSIDE THE BOX: ALTERNATIVE TEACHING-LEARNING PARADIGMS

The analyses and speculations above have all been predicated on a continuation of the predominant teaching-learning paradigm: that is, degrees are awarded through an accumulation of course credits, and most course credits are awarded through traditional didactic instruction, in which an instructor teaches, by lecture, discussion, or combinations thereof, directly to a class of students at a set time of the day/week for a fixed period of weeks. Large classes with relatively inexpensive instructors who also teach several other large classes are very inexpensive. Very small classes with costly professors who teach few of them are relatively expensive. Some radically different paradigms exist, some of which may be less expensive per unit of learning but all of which, to be less expensive, must yield more student learning per dollar spent on faculty, probably with the aid of technology and/or self-paced learning. Many alternative paradigms—for example, teaching that is enriched with live (synchronous) distance learning via high-resolution, interactive fiber optic cable, or individualized self-paced distance instruction via video cassettes and e-mail—hold the prospect of substantially more powerful teaching and learning, and perhaps an extension of participation (already extremely high in the United States). But these technological changes will most likely bring greater, not lesser, per-student costs.

Clearly, new teaching-learning paradigms that feature technology-assisted, asynchronous instruction (e.g., videos and instructional software) and that assume a large volume of learners can be highly cost-effective, virtually by definition. The "virtual university;" made theoretically possible by the Internet, generally proclaimed by proponents of the new Information Age, and endorsed in 1995 by some western governors, is such an example. And surely, some, perhaps many, who are "into the Internet," who are self-motivated, and who are unable or unwilling to partake of traditional higher education may take advantage of such technology-aided, cost-effective learning. The potential for changing the nature and the financing of graduate and other forms of post-baccalaureate education, including continuing professional education as well as strictly recreational and self-improvement learning, is enormous.

However, most traditional-age undergraduate students engage in higher education for purposes other than, or at least in addition to, learning: for the prestige of being admitted to a selective institution, for the fun of college life, or for the social learning that comes of interacting with fellow students, professors, and other adult professionals. Such students will achieve few if any of these life goals from the Internet or from other forms of self-paced learning.

By this reasoning, radical new patterns of higher education finance predicated on conceivable "out of the box" possibilities presented by the new learning technologies are likely to have a major cost-reducing impact more on firm-specific and continuing professional education, or on personal or recreational forms of postsecondary education, but not on mainstream undergraduate education nor on elite graduate higher education, except when such education is enriched—and made more expensive—as additional resources are brought to it.

RADICAL CHANGES IN "WHO PAYS?"

This resistance to change in the first two dimensions leaves the third dimension of higher education finance—the sharing of costs among parents, students, and taxpayers—in which there might be some revolutionary change in financial pattern, with or without fundamental change in institutional mission or in the dominant teaching-learning paradigm. Indeed, the core premise of the "high tuition-high aid," argument is that significant additional costs could be shifted from the taxpayer to the middle- and upper-middle-class parent without altering the accessibility of higher education, the missions of institutions, or the nature of the teaching-learning process.

The argument against high tuition-high aid is more political than economic. Suffice it to say for the purpose of this section that a full-scale adoption of "high tuition-high aid," even if it did not ultimately diminish access and participation, would profoundly alter the relative fortunes of the public and private sectors of higher education, dramatically shifting more academically prepared students to the private sector and relegating to many or even most of the nation's more than 1,600 public colleges and regional universities the task of educating those students that the private sector chooses not to accept.

The next decade is likely to see a continuation of the pressures on state treasuries. Businesses, entire industries, and affluent individuals have become increasingly mobile, seeking tax breaks as well as cheap labor, sunshine, and social amenities. These factors all put great strain on the taxing capacity of states. Furthermore, the federal government is trying to extricate itself from spending obligations on health and human services, which will place additional pressure on already strained state budgets. With the theoretical logic of "high tuition-high aid" and the current (mid-1990s) ambivalence about such once-dominant social goals as "access" and "equal opportunity," the result is likely to be a continued shift of costs from the state taxpayer to the family and particularly to the student.

At the same time, a truly profound further shift in the direction of "high tuition-high aid" is unlikely for two reasons. First, affordable public higher education has broad political appeal. Welfare and other transfer payments as well as many forms of governmental regulation (and the offending public sector bureaucrats) may be vulnerable to the social and economic conservatism that emerged in the mid-1990s. But affordable public higher education is something that conservative middle-class voters get for their taxes, and there is no evidence that either voters or elected officials are ready to eliminate relatively low tuitions at most public sector institutions.

Second, the major shift in the direction of higher public-sector tuition may already have occurred in most states by the mid-1990s. Although stipulating the real costs of undergraduate education is difficult and a bit subjective, it is likely that public-sector tuition in many states is already covering between one-third and one-half of the real costs of undergraduate instruction. Clearly, this fraction could increase still more, particularly in some states of the South and West that continue the tradition of very low public tuition. But there is no evidence to suggest any imminent, profound, national shift toward the elimination of a significantly subsidized public sector tuition.

FINANCING HIGHER EDUCATION IN THE COMING DECADE: MORE OF THE SAME

Predicting future patterns in something so large, complex, and politically robust as higher education finance is simultaneously difficult and simple. It is difficult because the effects of two critical determinants—politics and technology—are, for different reasons, very difficult to predict. At the same time, it is simple because this very vastness—together with the enormous variation already in the system, both in the per-student expenses and in the sharing of these costs, plus the existence of powerful parties with stakes in the status quo—all make revolutionary change unlikely. That there are problems or dissatisfactions with the current patterns of higher education finance, or that radical alternatives are conceivable and technically feasible, does not make them likely. My best prediction is that there will be no revolutionary change in the financial patterns of mainstream American higher education, although there may well be radical changes on the peripheries, such as continuing professional education, or learning for strictly recreational purposes. But the most likely changes in financial patterns in the coming decade are the following:

- *Scale:* Higher education will continue to expand slightly in scale and, therefore, in the percentage it takes of the nation's gross domestic product. The proportion of high school graduates going on to higher education will remain about constant, but the numbers of the traditional college-age cohort will increase slightly. The rates of those achieving completion and post-baccalaureate continuation will also increase slightly.

- *Financial assistance:* Financial assistance will be increasingly "managed" in the form of individualized price discounting for cost-effective enrollment management, or the meeting of net tuition revenue goals. Less aid will be available to the very needy high-risk student.

- *"Access"* in the traditional meaning of the term will actually diminish, with less financial aid available to those least prepared and/or academically ambivalent about college.

- *Productivity:* The resources consumed per student—a rough measure of productivity or efficiency—will continue to decline slightly in real terms in most institutions in response to tightening public (mainly state) revenues and to increasing family resistance to tuition and other cost increases. Well-endowed, selective institutions will be the exception, but they will maintain this selectivity by scholarships, or price discounting, which both their wealth and their market power make possible. Most institutions will control costs mainly as they have for the past decade: by trimming full-time faculty and staff and deferring maintenance. Dramatic changes in financial patterns via "restructuring" or "reengineering" will not be the norm.

- *Technology:* The use of instructional technology will continue to increase, although unevenly among institutions, faculties, and individual professors, and mainly as add-ons or enrichment, rather than as a change in the prevailing undergraduate instructional production function.

- *Learning productivity:* Other forms of learning productivity will increase—particularly college-level learning in high school and greater use of the full academic year—but the proportion of students completing a baccalaureate in less than the traditional four years will

not increase appreciably nor will the underlying per-student instructional costs.

- *Cost-sharing:* The portions of instructional cost borne by the parent in the form of higher public tuition and by the student in the form of term-time or "stop out" earnings or loans will continue to creep upward. Still they will fall considerably short of the full or near-full cost advocated by the proponents of "high tuition-high aid."

- *"Special programs" to obscure the shift of the burden from taxpayer to the student and family:* Government, both federal and state, will continue to propose, and occasionally to implement, programs or devices that cost the taxpayer nothing and do nothing to alter the underlying cost of instruction but which will make rising debt burdens more manageable, at least for some students, or otherwise lower the cost to the middle- and upper-middle income families who are financially able to prepay tuition.

- *Financing on higher education's periphery.* Far more dramatic changes in finance, both in underlying instructional costs and in who pays for these costs will be seen on the periphery of higher education: in firm-specific and other forms of continuing professional education, in the extension of higher education to place-bound students or to the elderly, and to technologically oriented individuals pursuing post-baccalaureate learning for recreation or self-improvement.

In summary, the decade will see continued pain, turbulence, and dissatisfaction with the financing of higher education—in short, more of the same.

NOTE

1. The Carnegie (1994) classification system lists 65 public Doctoral I and II institutions. They award at least ten doctorates annually in three or more disciplines but fall short of the Research II category, which requires 50 doctoral degrees and $40 million or more in federal research support.

2. This number includes the Carnegie (1994) classifications of Comprehensive/Master's I and II and Baccalaureate II.

REFERENCES

Carnegie Commission on Higher Education. (1973). *Higher education: Who pays/who benefits? Who should pay?* New York: McGraw-Hill.

Carnegie Foundation for the Advancement of Teaching. (1994). *A classification of institutions of higher education.* Princeton, NJ: Carnegie Foundation.

Hansen, W. L., & Weisbrod, B. (1969). *Benefits, costs, and finances of public higher education.* Chicago: Markham Publishing.

Johnstone, D. B. (forthcoming). Financial issues in American higher education. In P. G. Altbach, R. O. Berdahl, and P. J. Gumport (Eds.), *American higher education in the twentieth century: Social, political, and economic challenges.* Baltimore: Johns Hopkins University Press.

Johnstone, D. B. (1991). Higher education in the United States in the year 2000. *Prospects, 31*(3), 430–422; reprinted in Z. Morsy & P. Altbach (Eds.), *Higher education in international perspective* (pp. 178–90). New York: Garland Press.

Johnstone, D. B. (1992). *Learning productivity: A new imperative for American higher education.* Albany: State University of New York.

Johnstone, D. B (1993a). The costs of higher education: Worldwide issues and trends for the 1990s. In P. Altbach and D. B. Johnstone (Eds.), *The funding of higher education: International perspectives* (pp. 3–24). New York: Garland Press.

Johnstone, D. B. (1993b). *The high tuition-high aid model of public higher education finance: The case against.* Albany: State University of New York.

Massy, W. F, & Zemsky, R. (1996). Information technology and academic productivity. *EDUCOM Review, 31*, 12–15.

McPherson, M. S., Schapiro, M. O., & Winston, G. C. (1993). *Paying the piper: Productivity, incentives, and financing in U.S. higher education.* Ann Arbor: University of Michigan Press.

Twigg, C. A. (1996). *Academic productivity: The case for instructional software.* Washington, D.C.: EDUCOM.

CHAPTER 3

SUBSIDIES, HIERARCHY AND PEERS

The Awkward Economics of Higher Education

GORDON C. WINSTON

The editors of this journal, Alan Krueger, Brad De Long, and especially Timothy Taylor, did much to improve the paper in style and substance. My thanks, too, to Henry Bruton, Jared Carbone, Jill Constantine, Al Goethals, Doug Gollin, Bill Jaeger, Ethan Lewis, Steve Lewis, Larry Litten, Sarah Turner, Estelle James, Mike McPherson, Mike Rothschild, Morty Schapiro, James Shulman, Paula Stephan, Ivan Yen, Dave Zimmerman, discussions at the Southern Economic meetings, seminars at the Williams economics department, the Williams Project summer conference, the University of Virginia, Macalester, the NBER higher education workshop, and the Stanford Forum in Aspen—all of which forced me to think harder about these matters. Finally, I am especially grateful to Bill Bowen and James Shulman for the continued support of the Andrew W. Mellon Foundation through its support, in turn, of the Williams Project on the Economics of Higher Education.

Higher education is a business: it produces and sells educational services to customers for a price and it buys inputs with which to make that product. Production is subject to technological constraints. Costs and revenues discipline decisions and determine the long-run viability of a college or university. "But higher education is not just a business." While that statement is often meant to imply that higher education is nobler than business—more decent and humane in the purposes it serves—it can also mean that even in economic terms higher education is, in important ways, simply different from a business.

This paper asks how well our extensive experience with commercial businesses—and the microeconomic theory of firms and markets that has evolved to describe them—helps in understanding the economics of higher education. That experience and those insights will be used by trustees, politicians, administrators, lawyers, reporters and the public, as well as by economists, to understand and evaluate the behavior of colleges and universities. So it is useful to ask how safe it is to use "the economic analogy" in the context of higher education, drawing parallels between universities and firms, students and customers, faculty and labor markets, and so on. The discussion here seeks to identify the key economic features of higher education that make it different from familiar for-profit industries and to ask what difference those differences make.

This is a stick that can be picked up from either end. One approach is to start with meticulous economic theory and see how far it can be made to encompass the economic realities of higher education. An excellent recent paper by Rothschild and White (1995) does that. In their matching model, students and colleges meet in complex competitive markets, where students provide simultaneously both monetary payments and quality inputs in the ways they affect other students' learning, and institutions provide both individual financial aid grants and educational services that build human capital. All actors are perfectly informed and both markets clear, which means in this case that gross tuition (the sticker price) and individual financial aid grant awards are all determined by the interactions.

This paper picks up the stick from the other end. I will start with the economic realities of higher education to see how far toward useful theoretical precision they can be pushed. It is inherently the less rigorous end of the stick, but I would argue equally important when the task is to make economic sense of a complicated and unusual industry. It is the most effective route to identifying where our familiar economic formalisms and assumptions may become seriously inappropriate.

THE ECONOMIC CIRCUMSTANCES OF HIGHER EDUCATION

In identifying what appear to be the central economic characteristics of higher education, I will begin with the fundamental fact that few institutions of higher education are for-profit firms. I will draw on the literature in this area to explore how the institutional imperatives of a nonprofit differ from profit-making businesses. I will then add three further elements to the picture: a measure of the student subsidies found in U.S. higher education as revealed in 1995 data; the fact that the production of education depends to some extent on peer effects generated by the student-customers themselves; and that higher education is a sharply hierarchical industry with a range of institutions from richer to poorer, a fact that has surprising relevance for costs, prices, subsidies, and competition.

Higher Education as a Nonprofit Enterprise

In a seminal article, Henry Hansmann (1980) identified the legal and economic rationale for the nonprofit firm as a situation in which, because of asymmetries of information, the buyer is highly vulnerable to sellers' opportunism. In markets where customers are little informed about what they are buying, they can easily be taken advantage of—at the extreme, consumers may not be informed about whether

they have bought anything at all. Did the CARE package get delivered in Somalia? Was the contribution to public radio actually used to support programs? More often, consumers know that they have bought something, but they also know that they are vulnerable to receiving a service of lower cost and quality than they expected and paid for. Given the asymmetries of information, though, it may be impossible to draw up a contract that guarantees that the expected quality in all its dimensions will be provided. As a result, nonprofits are frequently found in the markets for things like nursing homes, day care and education.

Markets like these are sometimes referred to as "trust markets" because of that vulnerability. The nonprofit structure of suppliers encourages the honest if profit-sacrificing behavior that justifies trust. By reducing incentives for the opportunistic behavior, nonprofits become the preferred suppliers in certain settings: they increase the probability—and the confidence of donors or buyers—that they're getting what they are paying for, tending to offset the contract failure inherent in such asymmetric markets.

It can be added that any investment decision, perhaps especially including investments in human capital, proceeds in the face of a considerable degree of ignorance of how it will turn out and whether the hoped-for future gains will indeed materialize. People investing in human capital through a purchase of higher education don't know what they're buying— and won't and can't know what they have bought until it is far too late to do anything about it. Education is a typically one-shot investment expenditure, a unique rather than a repetitive purchase, more like buying a cancer cure than groceries (Litten, 1980; Winston, 1988). Indeed, it is an uncertain investment often made in large part by a parent on behalf of a child, adding yet another layer of murkiness as to how well a rational choice model applies in this context.

The key legal and economic characteristic of nonprofit enterprises is a "non-distribution constraint" (Hansmann, 1980). Nonprofit firms are allowed to make profits, and usually do; the term "nonprofit" does not mean that revenues never exceed expenditures. Instead, it means that there is no outsider to whom the enterprise can legally distribute those profits as the normal firm distributes profits to its owners. Indeed, a nonprofit has no owners—it owns itself. Of course, the behavior of a nonprofit firm must respect the fact that its total costs cannot long exceed its total revenues, so the firm may appear to be profit-motivated in its attempts to raise revenue, when in fact it is only recognizing the reality that it is budget-constrained.

The non-distribution constraint can be fudged, Hansmann noted, by transfer pricing that inflates rewards to suppliers of purchased inputs—as when managers like United Way's William Aramony or the "Praise the Lord" television ministry's Jim and Tammy Bakker compensate themselves or their relatives too generously. Moreover, managers can and do shift profits around within a multiproduct nonprofit firm, using those from activities they don't much like to cross-subsidize those they do (James, 1978; Weisbrod, 1988). Profits made from undergraduate education, for instance, might support administrators' perks, the teaching of graduate students, or high-powered Rose Bowl football teams. Nonprofits may also have the problem that because they cannot be taken over in a capital market, like a publicly owned firm, no indirect disciplinary forces can operate in that guise (Rose-Ackerman, 1996). Further, it is unusual for the management of a nonprofit, operating at least partly outside such market tests, to recognize accurately the economic cost of its capital services in production (Winston, 1993). So the point here is not that the nonprofit form is without its own set of issues or problems, but rather that the non-distribution constraint serves to soften the incentive that a for-profit supplier has to take advantage of the partially informed buyer.

Because of the non-distribution constraint, and the sometimes fuzzy objectives of nonprofits, the managers of nonprofit firms are motivated by a less tidy incentive structure than we attribute to those running for-profit firms. It is a commonplace, of course, that even applied to for-profit firms "profit maximization" is an oversimplification—but it is an oversimplification that usually works. In nonprofits, the non-distribution constraint makes the purpose of profit maximization unclear and no equally simple alternative presents itself. Part of the analytical problem is that nonprofit managers often share the overall objectives of the organization; that is, they work for nonprofit firms because they care strongly about objectives like diversity or equal opportunity through educational access (Bowen and Bok, 1998) or delivering food to children in Somalia or medical care for the homeless. Rose-Ackerman (1996) labels these incentives "ideological" and (a bit harshly, I think) the nonprofit administrator motivated by them an "ideologue."

In higher education, managers appear motivated by what Clotfelter (1996) calls "the pursuit of excellence," a general goal which in practice means maintaining or improving the quality of the educational services they supply and the equity with which they are provided (Bowen and Breneman, 1993). This striving for academic excellence is often defined relative to other institutions. In that sense, the goal has a positional aspect, one that can border on a striving for status and relative rankings. Along similar lines, James (1990) suggests that if colleges and universities have a single-valued objective function, it is something like "prestige maximization."

Hansmann (1980) distinguished two sources of revenue for nonprofit firms. Some, like churches, are supported by charitable donations from people who endorse the firm's ideological purposes. Hansmann called these "donative nonprofits." Others, like day-care centers, are supported more conventionally by the sale of goods or services. They are "commercial nonprofits." Colleges and universities have both of these sources of revenue. They are supported by charitable contributions and by sales revenues, and thus are "donative-commercial nonprofits." Donative revenues result from the various charitable motives of their donors; in the case of education, such motives include a dedication to equal opportunity under the belief that education is a human capital investment, an appreciation of the externalities of an educated citizenry, an alum's sense of obligation to repay past subsidies,[1] a desire to bathe in the reflected glory of an improving alma mater, and so on. Commercial revenues are supported by more conventional personal consumption and investment incentives.

In higher education, of course, sales proceeds in the form of net tuition receipts are the commercial revenues that combine with charitable donations, broadly defined as legislative appropriations, current gifts, and asset earnings from the accumulated past donations embedded in endowment and physical plant. (The prudent management of current operations also adds to asset accumulation.) Long-run survival for the college, like the business firm, requires that total costs not continually exceed total revenues.

But, in sharp contrast to the business firm, donative-commercial nonprofits can and do subsidize their customers, selling them a product at a price that is below the costs of its production.[2] This sustainable excess of production cost over price—the continuing ability of a college to subsidize all of its customers, not just cross-subsidize some at the expense of others or briefly let price fall below cost—is a defining economic characteristic of higher education, both public and private.

From Hansmann (1980), then, I want to take: the emphasis on information asymmetries and a high level of ignorance and faith embedded in the college purchase decision; the central role of the non-distribution constraint; the more complex managerial motivation that values equity and academic quality, implying that the relative position of the institution takes on special importance; and a recognition that the costs of production in colleges and universities are covered by a combination of charitable donations (past and present) and sales revenues. To this list, I want to add two more elements that I have come to believe are defining economic characteristics of the firm in higher education.

Peer Effects: Customer-Input Technology

The technology of producing much of what is sold in higher education is unusual in that colleges can buy important inputs to their production only from the customers who buy their products; that is, higher education uses a customer-input technology. While this relationship may be clearest in a college's production of something like intercollegiate sports entertainment—where only its own students can play on its teams—it is of greater importance in the production process for high quality academic education where, to a significant degree, students educate both themselves and each other, and the quality of the education any student gets from college depends in good measure on the quality of that student's peers.[3] Inputs of faculty and facilities matter, too, of course, but the quality of both individual students and of the student body as a group counts for a great deal in the quality of educational services the institution delivers.

This point has long been recognized in a variety of casual ways, in that average SAT scores or other indicators of student quality are often used as a measure of institutional quality (Turner, 1996). Both admissions offices and the rating organizations like *U.S. News and World Report* put great stake in the fact that student and institutional quality go hand in hand (Klitgaard, 1985; Litten, 1980; Rosovsky, 1990).

I want to suggest a deeper point: that as an argument of the educational production function, peer quality is, technically, an input to a college's production and one that cannot be bought from anyone other than its own customers. Peer quality is an input that costs, an input that may or may not have substitutes, and an input whose use will be adjusted to reflect its costs, available substitutes, and resources. The formal model by Rothschild and White (1995) mentioned earlier built its analysis on the simultaneity of the two transactions implicit in this technical relationship: the student-as-customer pays a price for education while the same student-as-supplier-of-input is paid a wage rate by the school (a financial aid grant if general subsidy is ignored), leaving a net tuition payment as their difference. Later on, I want to suggest that an important feedback operates through this technical relationship.

A school's student-customer population defines and restricts the sources of an input important to its product. Because different customers bring different measures of those inputs—quite apart from their demand for the product, some students will supply high quality inputs while others will not—institutions have strong incentives to care about the identity of those to whom they will sell, and to try to control or influence who their customers will be. Schools are able to do this through excess demand queues that allow them to select those to whom they will sell.[4] In this situation, the familiar models of microeconomic theory in which buyers are anonymous and sellers don't care which buyers they serve are clearly inappropriate.

The Hierarchy of College and Universities

Some schools are rich and some are poor. A hierarchy of institutions results from their donative wealth and the present and past differences among them in raising and accumulating donative resources. These differences in wealth, in turn, strongly influence their current commercial circumstances. Schools that get a lot of donated resources from endowments and legislatures and gifts and their capital stocks can and do sell their educational services, in their commercial role, at a lower price or higher production cost and quality. So Williams sells its $65,000 a year education for an average price net of financial aid grants of about $20,000. The "market" for higher education is very different from commercial markets. Competitive forces will still play out, but they will do so on a strikingly uneven playing field.

Table 3.1 is taken from a recent study of student subsidies at most of the accredited, degree-granting colleges and universities in the United States (Winston and Yen, 1995, updated with 1994–95 data).[5] The data include 2739 institutions, of which 1420 are public and 1319 are private. Student subsidies (column 2) are simply the average cost of a student's education (column 3) less the tuition and fees the student pays for it net of financial aid grants (column 4). The price/cost ratio (column 5) is the proportion of the student's educational costs covered by the student's payment.

A bit more needs to be said about educational costs since these data represent an economist's inclusive description of production costs rather than what is found in either college fund accounting or familiar for-profit accounts. Most important, these costs include a calculated yearly rental rate to recognize that the costs of physical capital services must be added to reported "Educational and General (E&G)" spending, hence the label "E&G&K." Capital costs account, on average, for nearly 25 percent of educational costs (Winston and Lewis, 1997). Furthermore, an effort was made to eliminate non-educational costs from total E&G and capital costs as far as the data allowed. A lot of questions about educational costs remain (Winston and Yen, 1995; Winston, 1998a), especially at complex multi-product universities, but it is reassuring that those more complicated institutions behave the same in our data and analysis as the simpler liberal arts and two-year colleges.

The schools are ranked by decile in Table 3.1 according to the subsidies per student shown in column 2. Part of the subsidy (cost

TABLE 3.1
Costs, Prices, Subsidies, and Hierarchy, 1995

Ranked by Dollar Value of Subsidy	Enrollments	Average Student Subsidy	Costs: Educational "E&G&K"	Price: Net Tuition & Fees	Price/Cost Ratio
	(1)	(2)	(3)	(4)	(5)
	FTE	$	$	$	%
All Institutions	3,500	8,200	12,000	3,800	31.5%
Public	5,100	8,700	9,900	1,200	12.4%
Private	1,700	7,700	14,200	6,500	45.9%
Decile 1	3,300	22,800	28,500	5,700	20.1%
Decile 2	3,800	11,100	14,900	3,800	25.4%
Decile 3	4,300	9,300	12,300	3,000	24.4%
Decile 4	4,500	8,200	11,000	2,800	25.6%
Decile 5	3,700	7,300	9,900	2,600	26.6%
Decile 6	3,900	6,500	9,400	2,900	30.8%
Decile 7	3,500	5,800	8,700	2,900	33.1%
Decile 8	3,500	5,100	8,400	3,300	39.5%
Decile 9	2,900	4,100	8,700	4,600	52.5%
Decile 10	1,600	1,800	7,900	6,100	77.4%

Source: Winston-Yen, 1995 (updated); based on US Department of Education IPEDS data. Includes 2739 institutions, of which 1420 are public and 1319 are private. All dollar amounts are per FTE student averaged over institutions. Col. 3: Educational costs include the share of E&G spending devoted to instruction plus the rental rate for physical capital. Col. 4: Tuition and fees net of grant aid.

less net price), it should be noted, is given as financial aid to some students (sticker price less net price) while the rest is given as a general subsidy to all students (cost less sticker price). The total subsidy reflects the donative or charitable component of the school's per student revenue; the net price is the commercial component. Together, these two sources of revenue cover the costs of a year's education; costs exceed net price in equilibrium, but only by as much as a school's available donative resources will allow. So despite the fact that all firms in the higher education industry must meet the same non-negative profit constraint, that constraint will mean very different things in costs, prices, and subsidies to different schools because of the very different levels of donative resources they command.[6]

It's useful to make all this more concrete. The average student subsidy in U.S. higher education is an impressive $8,200 a year; the student pays $3,800 for $12,000 in education. Moreover, the subsidy is about the same in public and private schools even though average cost and price are very different. Although it is not explicit in Table 3.1, financial aid represents only $2,150, or about 25 percent of the average subsidy, despite getting the lion's share of attention, while the general subsidy given to every student by a sticker price set well below costs takes the lion's share of the money with $6,050.

But the most striking fact in Table 3.1 is the uneven distribution of that average subsidy; that is, the wide range of subsidies that are supported by differences in the donative resources available to different colleges and universities. Even across the crude decile groupings of the table that lump very different schools together—especially in the top and bottom deciles—wealthy institutions have far more donative resources with which to subsidize their students than do poor ones. The average school in the top decile gives each student a subsidy of nearly $22,800 a year from donative resources—to support a $28,500 education—while the average school at the bottom gives each student a $1,800 subsidy to help pay for a $7,900 education. One result is that the student at the bottom actually pays a higher net dollar price than the student at the top! Were we to separate the data from public and private sectors, these differences would be even more striking.

It is a fact of fundamental importance to the economics of higher education, then, that any differences in managerial skill or luck or location or imagination among schools will often be overwhelmed by differences in sheer donative wealth that become differences in price, cost, and subsidy. Moreover, these differences are so very great that it seems fair to believe that they capture a good measure of institutional quality. Quality is a tricky issue, of course; assessing the quality of schools or students is never a simple matter (McPherson and Winston, 1993). But differences across schools and students are very great, so it seems useful if crude to think of student quality in terms of intellectual/academic abilities and of school quality as dependent on expenditures per student and average peers. This will capture important aspects of education, even if it neglects a great deal.

What, tangibly, does a "student subsidy" look like? What's the difference between a school with a big one and a school with a small one? The school with bigger student subsidies has more and better maintained buildings and grounds, more computers, a more distinguished and influential faculty with lighter teaching loads that leave more time for public engagement and research, a richer menu of student services from psychological to career counseling, better food and fewer double or triple dorm rooms, smaller classes, more varied courses and programs, more outside speakers and debates, and extracurricular activities that are better funded. All that at a price that's low relative to the cost of supplying these items. That implies, in turn, better students who have survived a more demanding selection process. While most high-subsidy schools are also high-cost schools, Cooper Union uses its ample subsidy resources to sell a $35,000 a year education at a net tuition that the data behind Table 3.1 show to be slightly negative.

The schools in the top decile of Table 3.1 include all the usual suspects (along with the military academies and a few medical schools with enough undergraduate enrollments to have made the cut): Cal Tech, Johns Hopkins, Harvard, Princeton, Stanford, Yale, Amherst, MIT, Williams, Swarthmore, Berkeley, UCLA, Penn, Carleton, Colgate, the Universities of Washington and Minnesota, SUNY Buffalo, and Chapel Hill, and more. In the bottom decile are, predictably, all the accredited, degree-granting, for-profit colleges and universities—including prominently Phoenix and DeVry—with their negative subsidies, along with nonprofits like the Cincinnati Mortuary College, the Art Institute of Pittsburgh, and Machzikei Hadath Rabbinical College. And so on.

IMPLICATIONS FOR ANALYSIS OF HIGHER EDUCATION

These characteristics of nonprofit organizational form, peer effects with a customer-input technology, and the hierarchy will modify the way firms and markets work. I want to suggest some of the implications of these aspects of higher education.

Colleges as Firms That Rely on Customer-Inputs

It is useful to return to the framework of Rothschild and White (1995) because that paper made a very useful contribution to these issues by modeling an industry's behavior when firms operate with technologies that depend on customer-inputs. Their aim was to show that efficient allocation of product among customers and inputs among firms would emerge from a competitive market, and they used higher education as their case in point.

In their model, two prices are determined in the market for higher education. One is the market-clearing price for the firm's product, which could vary across firms, and the other is the market-clearing price for each customer's input, which could vary among customers to reflect the different quantities of the input each might supply. Over all of its customers (students), total sales revenues for each firm (college) had to equal total costs of production for a zero profit equilibrium. All markets are fully informed and competitive with zero profit equilibria and with no donative revenues. In this market, it turns out that students are indifferent to where they go since they know they will get the same benefit per dollar spent on educational product at Harvard or the University of Oregon or at the poorest of the nation's private two-year colleges-and they pay the same market clearing price for it.[7] Colleges are indifferent among students since they'll pay the going competitive wage for a unit of student quality, whoever it is attached to. Schools and students always know the student's true quality and agree on it. Individual students and schools face infinitely elastic supply and demand and indifferent choices, all at prevailing prices that they can't affect.

The Rothschild and White (1995) model serves nicely to recognize the simultaneous purchase-sale/sale-purchase relationships between firm and customer under a customer-input technology. Strong students pay a lower net tuition than weak ones because they contribute more on the margin to the educational activities of the university and hence get more financial aid. This is true, too, of the good athlete though that person's factor contribution takes a different form, supporting a different one of the university's products, and it is true as well of the effective graduate teaching or research assistant.

But setting their analysis in a fully informed, perfectly competitive, profit maximizing, market-clearing, no-donations industry did much to limit the relevance of the Rothschild and White (1995) model to higher education—and, indeed, they include a "Limitations" section acknowledging as much. The list of the key economic characteristics of higher education in the previous section paints a picture of a real world of higher education in which very different educational quality is produced in very different schools at very different cost and sold at very different prices—gross and net—to students with very different input characteristics who get very different subsidies and are often selected from very long queues of applicants, leaving a lot of unsatisfied demand. All of this exists in a world of massive ignorance about what is being bought and sold. The assumptions in the Rothschild and White (1995) framework appear to go beyond innocent abstractions.

Controlling to Whom They Sell

One factor that is obscured by the assumptions of perfect information is that a firm that depends on its own customers to supply an important input to production will care very much about who those customers are and how well-equipped they are with the input that matters. If it can, the firm will try to control who its customers are.

Colleges exercise control over whom they sell to by generating excess demand and then selecting the students with the characteristics they most desire from the resulting queue (Klitgaard, 1985; Rosovsky, 1990; Litten, 1991; Duffy and Goldberg, 1998; Bowen and Bok, 1998). Indeed, selectivity, as measured by the ratio of applicants to admissions, average test scores, and high school grades is one of the most significant and sought-after descriptions of a college's educational quality—so much so that some colleges have aggressively manipulated the numbers.[8] High quality colleges are selective because that is the way they assure an ample input of student quality.

Excess demand only occurs when student demand is robust at the relevant price relative to supply. So selectivity requires, simultaneously, the generation of demand and the restriction of supply. This is much like an efficiency wage where a "too high" wage rate is paid so that an employer can select individual workers on the basis of their desirable characteristics. Indeed, what's going on here may be readily understood in efficiency wage terms as large subsidies can be seen as large real wages paid for student quality. From this perspective, the question of why we observe this seemingly clumsy subsidize-and-select system instead of simply paying a market-clearing wage for student quality has an efficiency wage answer—the existence of a "too high" wage rate for student quality allows the institution to control what quality is and who they think has it (Akerlof and Yellin, 1988). (Indeed, it's hard to see how a market for student quality could work otherwise—it's simply too hard for a buyer and seller to identify quality and agree on its amount.) A similar efficiency wage mechanism appears to work in hiring faculty at wealthy schools, where long queues of applicants at wages well above market-clearing support a selection process that is completed with the granting of tenure after a long probationary period and searching evaluation (McPherson and Winston, 1983).[9]

Identifying the determinants of student demand for higher education—and more so for an individual school—is not a simple matter but at base, demand must surely be influenced by what a student gets and what that student pays. On one hand, that requires attention not to the sticker price, tuition, but to the net price, after adjustment for any grant aid. But more

important in a world of highly variable student subsidies and college quality, neither of those prices necessarily reflects what the student will actually get. That is described by a school's student subsidy (cost minus net price) or—putting the same thing in relative instead of absolute terms—its price/cost ratio, what the student pays for a dollar's worth of educational spending and quality. These are in columns (2) and (5) in Table 3.1; while subsidies range from $22,800 down to $1,800, a student pays 20 cents for each $1 of educational spending in the wealthiest decile and 78 cents for each $1 of educational spending in the poorest.

But since colleges work with a customer-input technology, an important part of institutional quality is due to the quality of one's peers. So student demand is sensitive, too, to the quality of a school's students. That means that not only do students teach students in the educational production process, but because that fact is known to potential students, demand is affected by a school's existing student quality. Again, this fact is clear to admissions offices and U.S. News and World Report. Increased demand, ceteris paribus, increases excess demand and the opportunity for selectivity, and therefore for future student quality. A feedback is created through which student quality tends to be concentrated in those schools with significant donative resources—which become more attractive because of the quality of their students. We think of high student quality as the result of selectivity; this feedback suggests that selectivity is a result, too, of high student quality.[10] A related feedback appears to amplify differences in faculty quality, too; good students appeal to good faculty and good faculty appeal to each other.

Strategic restrictions of supply imposed by schools play a larger role in this process than it might at first appear. Restrictions on supply are needed, of course, to turn demand into excess demand to allow selectivity. A college that accepted all applicants—that couldn't enforce binding supply restrictions—could not be selective and would not be able to increase student quality through demand expansion.

But enrollment restrictions work to protect excess demand and selectivity in another and potentially more important way, too. Since the donative resources available to a private college or university are effectively fixed in the short run, the level of enrollment determines how broadly those resources will be spread; what the subsidy per student will be. There are fixed resource flows as well as fixed costs. So a private college has two good reasons not to satisfy demand fully: to increase selectivity directly and to increase subsidy per student, hence demand, hence selectivity indirectly. A public college more frequently relies for donative revenues on legislative appropriations that rise with increasing enrollments. Their incentive for restricting supply, then, is more focused on the maintenance of excess demand for selectivity. But though public colleges would appear to be denied the goal of admissions selectivity in the interests of access, it can often be met in the small by creating internal supply restrictions that govern entry into high-subsidy honors college programs or by selective flagship campuses within the larger university system. The University of California at Berkeley, for example, the flagship campus of that state's system, has a disproportionate (and increasing) share of the high-SAT freshmen within the University of California system (Frank and Cook, 1995).[11]

To summarize: a school controls the quality of its customers' input to the production process by using its donative resources to pay student subsidies that attract more students than its restricted supply can accommodate, then selecting from the resulting excess demand queue those students with the most desirable input qualities. Since the quality of existing students is attractive to potential applicants, present student quality feeds back to increase future student quality. Clearly, the greater the donative resources, the greater the school's control over student quality or, putting it the other way around, with meager donative resources, a school will have difficulty being very selective with respect to student quality. Differences in both of these directions appear to be amplified by potentially strong feedback.[12]

Producing Education Using Different Input Proportions

Schools differ markedly in their ability to command student quality inputs through the mechanism of donative wealth leading to excess demand and selectivity. They adapt to their different circumstances by producing education in very different ways, using factor proportions that economize on scarce student quality. Those schools that command most of the student quality input tend to choose an educational production technology that amplifies the effects that those high quality students have on each other. They often feature residential colleges whose living arrangements facilitate student interaction. They are often geographically separated; they have small classes so that students interact, too, in the classroom; they use a non-vocational, "impractical" curriculum; they concentrate on students of compatible "college age" whose interactions can best create peer effects.

Very wealthy schools with high quality students use that peer input as a substitute for other inputs. Thus, Harvard offers large undergraduate classes taught by teaching assistants; Clotfelter (1996) reports that the average class size in social science at Harvard in 1991–92 was 242 students and that just 48 percent of the social science students were taught by regular faculty. This technique would produce an inferior undergraduate product were it not offset by an ample number of excellent fellow-students. If peer quality is as important as I suspect, such schools—so long as they can attract and select superior students—can get by with a lot of corner-cutting in the direct inputs used in their undergraduate education. It's doubtful that a university with weaker peers could get by with impunity in doing the same thing.

Of course, peer effects can be powerful both for better and for worse. With an anti-academic student culture, what is amplified may be hostility to learning and academic values. No one who saw the positive academic effect of the removal of fraternities from the Williams campus in the early 1960s could doubt the powerful influence on the educational process of a reinforcing negative student ethos, and its removal (more generally, see Moffat, 1989).

Schools that have less of the student quality input shift to technologies with less of student interaction—increasing commuter populations, larger classes, wider age and cultural disparities among students, more vocational curricula, and so on. At the extreme are schools producing distance learning with little or no student interaction and little contribution from one student's qualities to another student's education.

Summary: The Firm in the Higher Education Industry

The firms in higher education appear to display the following characteristics: they have donative as well as commercial revenues so that costs can and do exceed sales revenues by a great deal, subsidizing their customers; there are very different levels of donative revenues among different institutions; those donative revenues are fixed in the short run for private schools but typically expand with enrollment in public schools, which has influenced schools' incentives to restrict or expand enrollment; firms use a production technology in which an important input, student quality, can be purchased only from their customers; firms control who they sell to by using their donative resources to generate an excess demand that allows them to select among potential customers for student quality; higher student quality feeds back to increase demand, hence student quality; and schools will adjust the production technology they use for education in response to how they are positioned by their donative revenues.

THE MARKET, HIERARCHY AND COMPETITION

The economic characteristics that describe individual firms in higher education have significant implications for how these firms will interact in a market. If, for instance, colleges relied only on commercial resources—on sales proceeds—they would all compete in the market under the same conditions of success and survival. A similar sort of balanced competition would arise if donative revenues per student were equal at all schools; in this situation, competition might bid price-cost ratios to equality, though less than one, across the market. Or if colleges were always price-takers in the markets for education and for student quality, they would not restrict supply to generate excess demand and select their students on quality. But none of this appears to be the case.

Four particular market characteristics seem most important. All schools in the market sell below cost, subsidizing their customers. Because different schools have very different access to donative resources to support those

subsidies, they fall into a sharply differentiated subsidy hierarchy. Because schools use a customer-input technology with a strong feedback through demand to reinforce student quality, the hierarchy based on donative wealth becomes highly skewed. A school's position, vis-à-vis its competition, both signifies its "excellence" and affects its ability to attract scarce student quality. This section discusses how these characteristics affect the disciplinary pressures of market competition.

Hierarchy and the Positional Nature of Success

The higher education market is strongly hierarchical with firms differentiated initially by their access to donative resources—the subsidy rankings of Table 3.1—and what those resources will buy. The hierarchy that starts with differential access to donative resources is then amplified by the feedback from those resources to institutional quality to student quality to demand to selectivity to greater student quality, along the lines already laid out. At the top of the hierarchy are the schools well-endowed with donative wealth—large endowments and expensive plants in the case of private schools and, additionally, large government subsidies in the case of public schools—that offer expensive and high quality education at highly subsidized prices and that therefore disproportionately attract high quality students, and employ an educational technology to take advantage of those students. Movements down the hierarchy bring less of student quality and more use of methods of educational production that don't so much rely on peer quality. Movement down the hierarchy, too, means less of excess demand until schools encounter increasing problems of selling the product at all—from an excess demand at the top that controls quality, to near market-clearing demand in the middle where quantity and quality trade off, to excess supply and empty classroom seats and dormitory beds at the bottom. Strategies to augment demand—like increased reliance on distance learning or foreign or older students or vocational curricula—become crucial for schools with less donative wealth.

With institutions in highly differentiated circumstances, the positional nature of much academic success and the role of emulation, status, and relative prestige become especially important in motivating institutional behavior. At the top are the schools with the largest donative resources that set standards for emulation across the market. But while that wealth establishes the targets of emulation, it also creates an effective, classic barrier to entry and to upward movement within the hierarchy. Schools accumulate wealth both to overtake those above them in the pecking order and, perhaps more important, to fend off those who would overtake them from below. Since current donative income at private schools can be used either for subsidies to entice current students or for saving to augment their wealth to entice future students, the rich, within this hierarchy, get richer while the positional ranking itself remains remarkably stable (Kerr, 1991). Historically, the process has conferred significant first-mover advantages to those who led the pack (Noll, 1998). The feedback cycle is only compounded by the fact that higher student quality implies higher postgraduate incomes, which induce more generous alumni giving, further augmenting donative wealth and skewing the hierarchy.

Table 3.2 shows the distribution of some of the student quality characteristics that go with the subsidy hierarchy. The deciles in Table 3.2 include institutions ranked again according to subsidy per student. What's reported—selectivity, average SAT scores, National Merit Semifinalists and the proportion of the entering class from the top 10 percent of their high school class—are the familiar measures of student quality that, if subsidy indeed leads to selection on student quality, should be correlated with subsidies. And they are correlated, significantly so.

Table 3.3 reports some suggestive measures of the changing production technology used across the hierarchy. Institutions with larger subsidies, and thus greater selectivity and more of the student quality that gives them an opportunity to exploit peer effects in production, have a large share of undergraduates living together, more undergraduates in a common under-25 age bracket, and fewer programs of vocational training, part-time degrees, and adult education. The U.S. market structure, of course, is not so tidy as a focus on these highly aggregated tables might seem to imply. Cutting across that ranking by student subsidy are important regional, ideological, and curricular dimensions that differentiate among schools on criteria other than donative resources. College

TABLE 3.2
Subsidies and Student Quality

Ranked by Dollar Value of Subsidy	Percent Applicants Accepted	Mean SAT score	Percent in Top 10 Percent of H.S. Class	Percent National Merit Semifinalists
	(1)	(2)	(3)	(4)
All Institutions	83.2%	970	19.7%	0.7%
Public	88.1%	940	14.7%	0.3%
Private	78.0%	990	22.7%	1.0%
Decile 1	67.1%	1090	37.5%	2.7%
Decile 2	78.6%	1000	22.5%	0.9%
Decile 3	81.6%	950	19.2%	0.6%
Decile 4	85.1%	970	18.8%	0.6%
Decile 5	84.9%	950	18.2%	0.6%
Decile 6	87.1%	940	16.5%	0.4%
Decile 7	86.9%	940	16.6%	0.4%
Decile 8	88.6%	930	14.7%	0.2%
Decile 9	87.1 %	940	16.5%	0.4%
Decile 10	84.7%	920	12.3%	0.2%

Sources: Winston and Yen (1995).
Observations: Applicants accepted, 2,525; SAT, 924; HS Class, 1,483; Merit Scholars, 943.
All variables are significantly related to subsidy deciles.

TABLE 3.3
Subsidies Demand Augmentation, and Educational Technologies

Ranked by Dollar Value of Subsidy	Undergraduates in Dorms	Undergraduates over Age 25	Undergraduates in Vocational Programs	Schools with Part-Time Degree Prog.	Schools with Adult Education
	(1)	(2)	(3)	(4)	(5)
All Institutions	46.5%	32.1%	9.6%	88.5%	81.7%
Public	29.2%	39.9%	6.4%	95.1%	92.6%
Private	56.3%	23.6%	13.0%	81.7%	70.2%
Decile 1	60.7%	23.7%	5.4%	67.6%	66.9%
Decile 2	58.0%	26.1%	7.7%	84.5%	73.5%
Decile 3	47.1%	29.7%	9.4%	92.2%	80.5%
Decile 4	47.3%	31.2%	9.2%	93.8%	82.0%
Decile 5	43.7%	34.0%	9.7%	94.7%	86.9%
Decile 6	42.3%	33.5%	10.3%	93.0%	85.8%
Decile 7	40.2%	35.5%	10.2%	95.1%	90.8%
Decile 8	40.1%	36.4%	9.0%	92.9%	92.0%
Decile 9	38.1%	35.0%	12.2%	93.8%	87.4%
Decile 10	34.1%	35.6%	12.6%	77.5%	70.5%

Sources: Winston and Yen (1995).
Observations: Dorms, 1,637; Over 25, 2,283; Vocational, 2,567; Part-time, 2,573; Adult Education, 2,531.
All variables are significantly related to subsidy deciles.

students resist being far from home (Litten, 1991) and programmatic and ideological differences like religious denomination are often important to them (Rose-Ackerman, 1996). Only at the top of the hierarchy is the market truly national and even that is a quite recent development (Hoxby, 1997); it is no accident that the rating agencies like *U.S. News and World Report* separate national and regional rankings. Keeping these qualifications in mind, though, it is useful still to focus on the wealth differences that will have their effects even within national, regional and ideological branches.

Competition and Prices

How might competition function in this kind of hierarchical market and with what effect on prices? Competition among schools appears to be limited to overlapping "bands" or segments of similarly wealthy schools within the hierarchy (with the further separation by geography and ideology). As one observer put it, "A school competes only with the ten schools above them and the ten below, even if there are more than 3,300 in the country." Access to

donative resources is the barrier to entry into competition with schools in the bands above while competitive pressures—like price discounting for certain desirable students—slowly "wick up" the hierarchy from below (Bronner, 1998). Competition at the top and bottom of the hierarchy takes place in markets for two very different things. At the bottom, it's competition in the product market for customers who will buy the output; at the top, it's competition in the input market for scarce student (and faculty) quality that will improve a school's educational quality and position.

Competition at the top is heavily positional. "Excellence" and "prestige" drive colleges, but these goals can be judged only with respect to others. The bottom line for any school is its access to the donative wealth that buys quality and position. Several authors have described the conflict between individual and social rationality and the wasteful dynamics of positional markets (Frank and Cook, 1995; Hirsch, 1977). Essentially, the notion is that the players become trapped in a sort of upward spiral, an arms race, seeking relative position; in the case of education, it may, in the extreme, involve expensive "competitive amenities" that do not produce sufficient benefit to justify their cost directly, but are important to an individual school because others are offering these amenities. Schools at the very top are accorded, what is more, great respect as objects of emulation even when they have little effect on a school's own market band—how many schools style themselves as "The Harvard of _____"?

The behavior of prices in this market will be determined by different factors in different parts of the market. Indeed, the basic question, "Why do tuitions keep rising?" has proven hard to answer mainly because there is no single answer. There appear to be three quite different answers appropriate to three quite different parts of the market.

For public institutions, tuition has gone up because, since the mid-1980s, their donative resources have gone down as a manifestation of a national tax revolt and disenchantment with higher education (Winston et al., 1998). Most public schools have faced the hard choice of either cutting educational spending—and quality—or increasing price. They've typically done some of both. Because the price that students pay for public education has covered so small a part of costs—just 12 percent in 1995—and their subsidies so large a part, even a small percentage reduction in public support has meant a large percentage increase in tuition and large headlines.

For the private institutions that compete to sell their services, sticker prices have risen to allow more price discrimination, in the form of financial aid, among potential buyers. In the four years between 1986–87 and 1990–91, on average, private schools used 42 percent of their sticker price increases to increase financial aid; in the next four years, the share of the increase in announced prices they committed to financial aid increased to 60 percent—with the change concentrated in the hardest-pressed part of the private sector (Winston et al., 1998; Winston, 1998b).[13]

Finally, for the wealthy private institutions that compete to buy scarce student quality, the positional race has created pressure on each school to obtain more donative resources, both to attract students now and to save to be ready to attract students in the future. Any school could opt out of that arms race, unilaterally, only at the risk of being overtaken by hungry schools from below, an institutional sin border-

ing on fiduciary irresponsibility. So we've seen perpetual and ever-larger capital campaigns and real tuition increases despite a bonanza of unprecedented endowment earnings from the stock market boom. In a positional market, there's never too much of a good thing—or even much stomach for asking that question—and in the hierarchy, wealth is quite fundamentally a good thing (Winston, 1997).

The Church and the Car Dealer

This positional competition at the top is especially worrisome when it is embedded in an industry of donative-commercial nonprofits with a customer-input technology that induces competition for customer quality. The donative-commercial firm is essentially part church and part car dealer—devoted partly to charity and partly to commerce, to "ideology" and "rationality." The result is a tension between doing good and doing well. It plagues administrators trying to decide which behaviors— those of the charity or those of the firm—are appropriate to a college or university. It also creates real if often unrecognized ambiguities for society's evaluation of such an industry.

Such conflicts are nowhere clearer than in the Justice Department's antitrust action a few years ago against a group of leading private colleges and universities that used to meet to coordinate their offers of financial aid for those students whose applications overlapped two or more of those schools (Carlton et al., 1995).[14] The schools saw their action as coordinating a charitable mission—that of increasing equality of opportunity by assuring access to an expensive and high quality education by high quality students who couldn't otherwise afford it. Overlap meetings were necessary to focus aid subsidies on low-income students, since without coordination parental haggling and individual school's positional bidding for student quality would divert those resources from low-income students who were willing but unable to pay the full price to high-income students who were able but unwilling to pay it. The Justice Department, in sharp disagreement with the schools, saw overlap meetings as simple commercial (net) price fixing. The conflicting views were charity versus commerce. While most of the Ivy League schools signed a consent decree that barred coordination over a wide range of activities, MIT went to court. The Justice Department won in trial court—colleges and universities are commercial entities—but MIT won on appeal—colleges and universities are, importantly, also charities.

The conflict between the roles of church and car dealer is such that both sides appear to have been right. The Department of Justice, despite its reversal on appeal, effectively stopped the coordination of tuition and financial aid among these schools. As a result, price competition has, indeed, slowly crept to the top of the hierarchy in the market for student quality where these schools jockey for position. The first high-level skirmish was that between Stanford and Harvard in 1995 working through "early decision" policies that shook up admissions practices throughout these schools. But spring of 1998 seems likely to go down as the beginning of real competition at the top end of the student quality market, as major changes in price through financial aid policies were initiated first by Princeton (to the apparent benefit of low-income students), then picked up by Yale (for middle-income students) (Gose, 1998), turned into a merit-packaging-within-need-based-aid policy by Swarthmore, and opened wide by Harvard's invitation to renegotiate any initial aid award (Bronner, 1998) and its late September escalation that increased grant aid by $2,000 across the board (Arenson, 1998; Pertman, 1998).

That competition does not appear to have much tempered sticker price increases, though. Indeed, it may well push them up to cover, among other things, more aid-discounting. As we've seen, the competition has modified aid policies as these schools sensed that they were losing position in the competition for high-quality students. Price discrimination—aid policy—is increasingly tailored to a student's willingness to pay (McPherson and Schapiro, 1998). Ironically, a strong case can be made that without the ban on coordination, these schools would likely have acted jointly against the threat to their mutually recognized ideological values (and their vulnerability to congressional pressure as their continued price increases seem to be creating a major public relations problem). Without coordination, each school, individually, risks a great deal not to go along with the others. But more fundamentally, by not acting together they are risking abandon-

ment of 30 years of the need-blind admission and need-based aid policy that has been one of their primary charitable contributions, increasing equality of opportunity by weakening the connection between income and high quality private education (McPherson and Shapiro, 1998; Bowen and Bok, 1998).

For the public sector, the donative-commercial nature of colleges and universities also underscores an emerging threat. In what Californians call "The Second Tidal Wave," college enrollments are projected to increase nationally by 10–30 percent in the next decade—as many as three million more students (Macunovich, 1997). Since the average student in a public college or university in Table 3.1 pays only one-eighth of the total cost of the education received, those figures suggest that three million new students will bring $3.6 billion in new tuition revenues, but if each of them gets the same kind and quality of public education students are getting now they will cost $29.7 billion. The pressing questions are "Who's going to pay the rest?" or "How is public higher education to be modified to reduce that cost?" (Trow, 1997).[15]

CONCLUSION

This paper suggests that standard economic intuition and analogies, built on an understanding of profit-making firms and the economic theory that supports it, are likely to be a poor guide to understanding higher education and to making predictions and public policy. One who thinks a college is like any other business will look in all the wrong places. Salop and White (1991), for example, presented the justice Department's antitrust case against the overlap schools in this journal as a strong one, drawing standard welfare conclusions keyed to competition and efficiency. But it's not clear what it means to use those familiar welfare criteria when, in long-run equilibria, firms' price-to-cost ratios range from decile averages of 0.067 (top public) to 0.89 (bottom private), reaching 1.0 only for the highly atypical for-profit college. It's also not clear how those welfare criteria apply when quantity rationing is used in complex ways to cut demand (Bowen and Bok, 1998)—to reduce, for instance, Williams's applicant pools of 4,500 down to freshman classes of

500—making a hash of concepts like the role of the preferences of the (nonexistent) "marginal non-aided student." I suspect that if Salop and White had the information in Table 3.1 about the awkward realities of the costs, prices, subsidies, and hierarchy that structure higher education—information that has become available only since they wrote—their careful analysis of the relevance of antitrust laws would have turned out differently. Our economics and intuitions about for-profit business don't just obscure what's happening in colleges and universities, they can also seriously distort understanding and policy.

NOTES

1. Alumni donations are sometimes seen as the repayment of the student's subsidy as an implicit loan from the college in recognition of an imperfect human capital market (Hansmann, 1990, 1996). However, that idea doesn't fare well empirically (Clotfelter, 1998). For an extensive discussion of donor motivation, see Rose-Ackerman (1996).

2. This can usefully be made more precise. The all-purpose equation for the sources and uses of funds in a firm, whether profit or nonprofit, is $p + dr = c + v + d$, where p is commercial revenue, dr is donative revenue, c is costs, v is retained earnings or institutional savings, and d is dividends. Thus, the left-hand side of the equation is sources of revenue, and the right-hand side is uses, what happens to that revenue. In any for-profit firm, donated revenue $dr = 0$. In any nonprofit firm, dividends $d = 0$. In a donative nonprofit, $p = 0$. In a donative-commercial nonprofit like a college, only $d = 0$. So its customers are subsidized in an amount of $s = c - p$ and its donative resources cover subsidies and saving.

3. Though I believe that interaction among good students plays the central role—a belief being investigated empirically with Al Goethals and Dave Zimmerman at the Williams Project—even in a hub-and-spoke view of education, the professor at the hub can cover more ground or go deeper into subjects the more able are the individual students on the spokes, especially if the professor adjusts the pace of the course, as most of us do, to the students' apparent comprehension (Goethals et al., 1998).

4. Though it is often said that only 20–30 percent of all colleges and universities can choose their students (Bowen and Bok, 1998), Table 3.1 and 3.2 below show that even at the bottom of the pecking order, the average school rejects more than 10 percent of its applicants.

The rub comes when the school's chosen level of selectivity leaves it with excess capacity and it must scramble to fill the class (Breneman, 1994).

5. From Department of Education IPEDS (Integrated Postsecondary Data System) data, those schools were eliminated that: a) were not in one of the 50 states and Washington DC; b) reported zero enrollment or current expenditures; c) had fewer than 20 percent undergraduates among their students; or d) were not given a Carnegie classification.

6. Institutional saving will be largely ignored in what follows. It has been shown to be important for wealthy schools (Weber and Winston, 1994), playing a central role in building future wealth to support a future competitive position. Recently, that saving has been pushed to very high levels in wealthy schools by the stock market (Winston, 1997), ambitious capital campaigns and continued real tuition increases. But data are not yet available to assess its importance for the general population of institutions of higher education.

7. There's a bit of a fudge in the Rothschild and White (1995) model as the product of education is called "human capital," allowing them to have the price of human capital driven to equality across schools without, given differences in productivity, requiring that tuitions are equal. I'm not quite sure what it would have meant to the interpretation of their findings to say that their institution's product was "educational services." I suspect it would have made a mess, but maybe it's mostly semantics.

8. See the *Change* piece (Webster, 1992) on the deceptions that *U.S. News* has encountered in trying to get accurate data from colleges and universities for its ratings, especially the gimmicks used to inflate and distort selectivity numbers. See also Stecklow's (1995) *Wall Street Journal* article on colleges' misrepresentation of their students' SATs.

9. Interestingly, White and Rothschild (1993) speculated on why the elite graduate professional schools charged such low prices of their customers—why they capture so little of the rent that their students earn from their education. The answer, it would appear, has much to do with the price (wage) those high-subsidy schools are paying for the exceptional quality of their students. Schools of lower quality may capture a larger proportion of their students' rents because, this approach would suggest, they are buying lower quality students and hence paying less for them.

10. Frank and Cook (1995) documented this concentration of student quality in higher education as a primary illustration of "winner-take-all" markets.

11. It is significant that since 1900, most of the expansion of higher education has taken place in the public sector, as Goldin and Katz explore

in their paper in this symposium, and what expansion there has been in the private sector has come largely from new entrants. The difference in the mechanisms that award donative revenues to schools would appear to be an important part of the explanation for this.

12. There are other explanations for what, beside peer effects, might make schools care so about student quality. Liebowitz and Margolis (1994) discuss network effects; Basu (1989) and Becker (1991) emphasize the appeal of one's association with people and institutions of status and prestige that are surely reinforced by the exclusivity of strict selection. But these are not mutually exclusive, so arguing that one effect is present doesn't argue that another is not. A car, for a familiar example, can provide both transportation and status and the status component will be much influenced by who else owns that kind of car. But your Mercedes isn't any safer, nor will it stop shorter or hold the road better if other Mercedes owners are rich or obnoxious or Grand Prix drivers. Your children's learning, however, will be greater if it happens in the company of other good students (Goethals et al., 1998).

13. In the conventions of college accounting, financial aid is seen as a cost of operation; it is as if the full sticker price were collected from every student and then some was given back to selected students as a financial aid payment. Economists, in contrast (and an increasing number of commentators), see financial aid as a discount from a sticker price, so it is collected in full only from non-aided students. This doesn't matter to the calculation of subsidies (as the difference between cost and price) so long as "cost" and "price" are appropriate to each other: both are measured with or both without financial aid. Note that, ceteris paribus, the only thing the sticker price does is to divide the subsidy into the general subsidy that everyone gets and financial aid. So the result reported in the text simply asked how much of an increase in price went to increased aid and how much to increased costs, net of aid.

14. They were: MIT, Brown, Columbia, Cornell, Dartmouth, Harvard, University of Pennsylvania, Princeton, Yale, Amherst, Barnard, Bowdoin, Bryn Mawr, Colby, Mount Holyoke, Middlebury, Smith, Trinity, Tufts, Vassar, Wesleyan, and Williams (Salop and White, 1991).

15. It's tempting to decide that those grim questions result from a confusion of average and marginal cost. Not only is it the conventional wisdom for colleges and universities but the whole cottage industry of student enrollment management consultants takes as self-evident that the cost of a marginal student is much lower than average cost. Unfortunately, it doesn't work out that way. A couple of years after the low-marginal-cost

argument is used to justify expanding a student body, the Provost and Deans of Students and Faculty tour the campus and declare that there's awful overcrowding of dorms, dining rooms and classes, so expansion is necessary. If it's done, costs will have risen; if it's not done, overcrowding remains and product quality is degraded. What seems at issue is that in thinking (and teaching) about marginal cost, economists make an implicit assumption that the quality of the product remains exactly the same with an incremental unit of output. (It always does implicitly in my micro lectures.) But in a college that is not likely—if additional students are really to be provided with the same quality of educational services, it means more classrooms and dorms and professors and the rest which, unless there's genuine excess capacity or large economies of scale or scope, quickly adds up to something close to average cost. Any excess capacity that does exist in U.S. higher education is unlikely to be located very near the three million additional students. So marginal cost looks a whole lot like average cost in higher education.

REFERENCES

Akerlof, George A., & Janet L. Yellen. (May 1988). Fairness and unemployment. *American economic review.* 78, pp. 44–49.

Arenson, Karen W. (1998). Harvard, joining others, plans rise in financial aid. *The New York times,* p. A20, Sept. 17.

Basu, Kaushik. (1989). A theory of association: Social status, prices and markets. *Oxford economic papers.* October, 41, pp. 653–71.

Becker, Gary S. (1991). A note on restaurant pricing and other examples of social influences on price. *Journal of political economy,* 99, pp. 1109–16.

Behrman, Jere R., et al. (October 1996). The impact of college quality on wages: Are there differences among demographic groups? Discussion Paper Number 38. Williams Project on the Economics of Higher Education.

Breneman, David W. (1994). *Liberal arts colleges: Thriving, surviving, or endangered?* Washington D.C.: The Brookings Institution.

Bronner, Ethan. (June 21, 1998). College efforts to lure the best set others back. *The New York times,* The National Desk.

Bowen, William G. & David Breneman. (1993). Student aid: Price discount or educational investment. *Brookings review.* Winter, 11, pp. 28–31.

Bowen, William G. & Derek Bok. (1998). *The shape of the river: Long-term consequences of considering race in college and university admissions.* Princeton: Princeton University Press.

Carlton, Dennis W., Gustavo E. Bamberger, & Roy J. Epstein. (1995). Antitrust and higher education: was there a conspiracy to restrict financial aid? *RAND journal of economics.* Spring, 26:1, pp. 131–47.

Clotfelter, Charles T. (1996). *Buying the best: Cost escalation in elite higher education.* Princeton: Princeton University Press.

Clotfelter, Charles T. (1998). *Alumni giving to private colleges and universities.* Duke University, April.

Duffy, Elizabeth A., & Idana Goldberg. (1998). *Crafting a class: College admissions and financial aid, 1995–1994.* Princeton: Princeton University Press.

Frank, Robert H. & Philip J. Cook. (1995). *The winner-take-all society.* New York: The Free Press.

Goethals, George R., Gordon C. Winston, & David Zimmerman. (1998). Students educating students: The emerging role of peer effects in higher education. Presented at the Forum for the Future of Higher Education, Aspen, September.

Gose, Ben. (1998). Recent shifts on aid by elite colleges signal new push to help the middle class. *The chronicle of higher education.* Academe Today, March 6.

Hansmann, Henry. (1980). The rationale for exempting nonprofit organizations from corporate Income Taxation. *Yale law journal.* November, 91, pp. 54–100.

Hansmann, Henry. (1990). Why do universities have endowments? *Journal of legal studies.* January, 19, pp. 3–42.

Hansmann, Henry. (1996) *The ownership of enterprise.* Cambridge: The Belknap Press of Harvard University Press.

Hirsch, Fred. (1977). *Social limits to growth. A twentieth century fund study.* Cambridge: Harvard University Press.

Hoxby, Caroline M. (1997). How the changing market structure of U.S. higher education explains college tuition. Harvard University, mimeo. September.

James, Estelle. (1978). Product mix and cost disaggregation: A reinterpretation of the economics of higher education. *Journal of human resources.* Spring, 13, pp. 157–86.

James, Estelle. (1990). Decision processes and priorities in higher education. In Hoenack, Stephen A., & Eileen L. Collins. (Eds.), *The economics of American universities.* Buffalo, NY State University of New York Press.

Kerr, Clark. (1991). The new race to be Harvard or Berkeley or Stanford. *Change.* May/June pp. 8–15.

Klitgaard, Robert E. (1985). *Choosing elites.* New York: Basic Books.

Liebowitz, S. J., & Stephen E. Margolis. (1994). Network externality: An uncommon tragedy. *Journal of economic perspectives.* Spring, 8, pp. 133–50.

Litten, Larry H. (1980.) Marketing higher education. *Journal of higher education.* 51:1, pp. 40–59.

Litten, Larry H. (1991). *Ivy bound: Observations and reflections on how students choose colleges.* College Board.

Macunovich, Diane. (1997). Will there be a boom in the demand for U.S. higher education among 18 to 24 year-olds? *Change.* May/June, 29:3, pp. 34–44.

Masden, Scott E. (1995). Old school ties: Financial coordination and the governance of higher education. *Journal of economic behavior and organization.* September, 28:1, pp. 23–48.

Massy, William F., & Robert Zemsky. (1992). Faculty discretionary time: Departments and the academic ratchet. Discussion Paper No. 4, Stanford Institute of Higher Education Research, May.

McPherson, Michael S., & Gordon C. Winston. (1983). The economics of academic tenure: A relational perspective. *Journal of economic behavior and organization.* December.

McPherson, Michael S., & Gordon C. Winston. (1993). The economics of cost, price, and quality in U.S. Higher Education. In McPherson, Schapiro, & Winston. (Eds.). *Paying the piper productivity, incentives, and financing in U.S. higher education.* Ann Arbor: The University of Michigan Press.

McPherson, Michael S., & Morton Owen Schapiro. (1998). *The student aid game: Meeting need and rewarding talent in American higher education.* Princeton: Princeton University Press.

Moffat, Michael. (1989). *Coming of age in New Jersey.* New Brunswick: Rutgers University Press.

National Commission on the Cost of Higher Education. (1998). *Straight talk about college costs and prices: Report of the national commission on the cost of higher education.* Phoenix: The Oryx Press.

Noll, Roger G. (1998). *Challenges to research universities.* Washington: The Brookings Institution.

Pertman, Adam. (1998). Harvard OK's big boost in student aid. *The Boston globe.* September 17, p. 1 c. 6.

Rose-Ackerman, Susan. (1996). Altruism, nonprofits and economic theory. *Journal of Economic Literature.* June, 34, pp. 701–28.

Rosovsky, Henry. (1990). *The university: An owner's manual.* New York: W. W. Norton & Company.

Rothschild, Michael & Lawrence J. White. (1995). The analytics of pricing in higher education and other services in which customers are inputs. *Journal of economic literature.* June, 103, pp. 573–86.

Salop, Steven C., & Lawrence J. White. (1991). Policy watch: Antitrust goes to college. *Journal of economic perspectives.* Summer, 5:3, 193–202.

Stecklow, Steve. (1995). Cheat sheets: Colleges inflate SATs and graduation rates in popular guidebooks. *Wall Street journal.* April 5, Sec A, p. 1.

Trow, Martin. (1997). The development of information technology in American higher education. *Daedalus.* Fall, 126:4, pp. 293–314.

Turner, Sarah. (1996). A Note on Changes in the returns to college quality. Mimeo, University of Michigan, April 1.

Weber, Valerie and Gordon Winston. (1994). The economic performance of Williams, Amherst, Swarthmore and Wellesley: 1988–9 to 1992–3: A global comparison. Discussion Paper No. 28. The Williams Project on the Economics of Higher Education, September.

Webster, David S. (1992). Rankings of undergraduate education. In *U.S. news and world report* and *Money*: Are they any good? *Change*. March/April, Pp. 19–31.

Weisbrod, Burton A. (1988). *The nonprofit economy*. Cambridge: Harvard University Press.

White, Lawrence J., & Michael Rothschild. (1993). The university in the marketplace: Some insights and some puzzles. In Clotfelter, Charles T., & Michael Rothschild. (Eds.). *Studies of supply and demand in higher education: A national bureau of economic research project report*. Chicago and London: University of Chicago Press.

Winston, Gordon C., & Ethan G. Lewis. (1997). Physical capital and capital service costs in U.S. Colleges and Universities: 1993. *Eastern economic journal*, 23:2, 165–89.

Winston, Gordon & Ivan Yen. (1995). Costs, prices, subsidies, and aid in US higher education. Discussion Paper Number 32, The Williams Project on the Economics of Higher Education, July.

Winston, Gordon C., Jared C. Carbone, & Ethan G. Lewis. (1998). What's been happening to higher education: Facts, trends, and data, 1986–97 to 1994–95. Discussion Paper No. 47, The Williams Project on the Economics of Higher Education. March.

Winston, Gordon, C. (1993). The Capital Costs Conundrum: Why are Capital Costs Ignored and What are the Consequences? *The NACUBO business officer*, June, pp. 22–27.

Winston, Gordon C. (1988). Three problems with the treatment of time in economics: Perspectives, repetitiveness and time units. In Tiechgraber, Richard F. III & Gordon C. Winston. (Eds.). *The boundaries of economics.* Pp. 30–52. Murphy Institute Studies in Political Economy Series. New York: Cambridge University Press.

Winston, Gordon C. (1997). Do elite schools make big profits? Presented at the Forum for the Future of Higher Education, Aspen Institute, September 23.

Winston, Gordon C. (1998a). A Guide to Measuring College Costs. Williams Project on the Economics of Higher Education, Discussion Paper No. 46, January.

Winston, Gordon C. (1998b). For-profit higher education: Godzilla or chicken little? Presented at the University of Virginia Conference on the Economics of Higher Education, October.

CHAPTER 4

THE TUITION PUZZLE

Putting the Pieces Together

THE INSTITUTE FOR HIGHER EDUCATION POLICY

PREFACE

This report is one in a series published under the aegis of The Institute for Higher Education Policy's *New Millennium Project on Higher Education Costs, Pricing, and Productivity*. Sponsored by The Institute for Higher Education Policy The Ford Foundation, and The Education Resources Institute (TERI), the project is a multi-year effort to improve understanding and facilitate reform of the complex system for financing higher education.

The report was drafted by Jane Wellman, with primary analytic support and guidance provided by Katheryn Volle Harrison, Alisa Federico Cunningham, Colleen O'Brien, and Jamie Merisotis. We would like to thank the members of the project Advisory Group who provided excellent feedback and advice on earlier drafts of the report. We also would like to express our appreciation to the many other colleagues who provided comments and ideas for the report, including Robert Atwell, Judith Eaton, T. Edward Hollander, Andrew Malizio, and David Rhodes. Special thanks to our colleagues at The Ford Foundation for their ongoing encouragement and support for our work in this area, especially Jorge Balan, Alison Bernstein, and Steven Zwerling. We heartily acknowledge the contributions of these individuals to this report and recognize that they are not responsible for any errors of omission or interpretation contained herein.

The *New Millennium Project* team is co-directed by Jamie Merisotis, President, and Jane Wellman, Senior Associate, at The Institute for Higher Education Policy. Project staff include: Colleen O'Brien, Managing Director; Diane Gilleland, Senior Associate; Thomas Parker, President of TERI; Katheryn Volle Harrison and Alisa Federico Cunningham, Research Analysts; and Christina Redmond and Mark Harvey, Project Assistants.

The project also is being guided by an Advisory Group of national experts in higher education. Advisory Group members include:

- Vera King Farris, President, Richard Stockton State College;
- Augustine Gallego, President, San Diego Community College District;
- D. Bruce Johnstone, Professor of Higher Education, SUNY Buffalo;
- Gerald Monette, President, Turtle Mountain Community College;
- Barry Munitz, President and CEO, The J. Paul Getty Trust, *Chair*;

Source: *The Tuition Puzzle: Putting the Pieces Together,* Feb. 1999, Institute for Higher Education Policy, Washington, DC.

- Michael A. Olivas, William B. Bates Professor of Law, University of Houston; and

- Carol Stoel, Co-Director, Teacher Education, Council for Basic Education.

EXECUTIVE SUMMARY

The dilemma of rising college prices is one of the most troubling aspects of higher education policy. How and why have prices gone up? Has financial aid kept college affordable despite the rising prices? Is there a "problem" with tuition, and if so, is it mostly a public relations problem, or have rising prices hurt the capacity of higher education to maintain affordable educational access, institutional choice, and quality? Despite stacks of reports on the topic, the different pieces of the tuition puzzle have not been fit together.

This report ties together data and information from numerous sources in order to help identify the pieces of the tuition puzzle in higher education. The goal of the report is to provide new insights into the causes and consequences of rising college prices, and to question whether rising prices are inevitable, or if something can be done about them. The report includes a summary of what has happened with college tuition increases in the last two decades, what has caused the increases, what they have meant for student access and college choice, and how governments and institutions have responded to these increases. It concludes with a synthesis of the consequences of the overall tuition puzzle, recommendations for change in tuition policies—both at the institutional and the state policy level—and suggestions for further research.

The research summarized in the report shows the following:

- Overall, average tuition and fees increased almost fivefold over the last two decades, or nearly doubled after adjusting for inflation. The significant investment in student financial aid has helped to ease, but not erase, the consequences of higher prices.

- One of the most significant causes of higher prices has been the declining role of public revenues, which are partially

offset through higher prices. The revenue problem is compounded by institutional spending habits, particularly increased support for student aid as well as for research and other activities. Competition in the higher education market has contributed to price increases in selective institutions, rather than stabilizing or decreasing prices, as would be expected.

- Access to college, as measured by the proportion of people going to college, is being maintained despite the higher prices, though gaps between low- and high-income students remain a serious concern. When the higher prices are compared to the economic costs of not going to college, clearly the costs of not going outweigh the price of attendance, even at the higher tuition levels. But if earnings alone are the measure of the worth of the additional investment required for a bachelor's degree, the benefit has not increased nearly as much as the price; incomes for baccalaureate degree holders have remained steady.

- There has been an enrollment response to the higher prices, with incremental shifts away from community colleges by middle- and upper-income students and toward research institutions by the richest students. Low-income students—who are more "price responsive"—have largely remained concentrated in public two- and four-year institutions. The enrollment shifts mean that higher education is at risk of becoming more economically stratified by sector at the end of the 1990s than any time in the previous two decades.

- Because of the necessity to find cost savings, spending on instruction in most types of institutions has not kept pace with spending in other categories, notably research and public service. At the same time, institutions are becoming more entrepreneurial in finding new revenue sources, not just from tuitions but from private and philanthropic sources. The combination of cuts and new revenue sources means a more fragmented revenue base, with less institutional activity directly associated with instruction.

- Much of the response to rising prices from both federal and state policymakers has been focused on efforts to increase financial options to help students meet the higher prices, and to improve public information about college prices. Neither of these responses are intended to actually reduce the price of college.

- Despite the higher prices, there has not been a systematic restructuring of tuition price structures as part of the public policy response. The pretense that college tuitions should be kept as low as possible is maintained in policies and political habits that thwart efforts to restructure prices and manage costs.

- State and federal policymakers have been active co-contributors (along with institutional leaders) to the increase in college tuitions, because they believe that higher education can afford to make up cuts in public revenues through increased tuitions and more financial aid. Unless different budget rules are developed, the game of tuition "chicken" that is ritualistically played across the country is likely to continue.

The report concludes that it is not inevitable that tuitions must continue to increase as they have in the past. Pricing and aid structures and budgetary policies can be adopted that moderate the rate of increases and protect access, choice, and quality. Solving the tuition puzzle requires multi-pronged strategies that address both the internal habits of the academy and the external political culture surrounding it.

Recommendations for States

The single pressure point most likely to be helpful in addressing rising prices is changed tuition policies at the state level, which are designed to address both the internal practices of higher education and the state political and budget environment in which tuition decisions are made. Specific suggestions include:

- State budget practices and tuition policies need to be rewritten, to be realistic

and mutually reinforcing. In states where tuitions are increasing rapidly but are still characterized by policymakers as low, this pretense should be scrapped in favor of realistic price structures that permit moderate increases but keep college affordable. Policies should be set so that tuitions increase at rates no greater than per capita personal income annually.

- State policy leaders should examine the match between public subsidies and private resources across all of higher education to ensure that state funds are being spent consistently with public priorities. Evidence about how resources are spent by revenue source and budget category should be developed for all public institutions, and for state-supported student aid at private institutions.

- The role of financial aid in maintaining economic access to higher education should be protected through a reevaluation and (if necessary) a realignment of state aid programs, including policies about funding sources for institutional aid in the public sector.

- State policy leaders should set the goal that higher education's share of general revenues will not continue to decline, unless there is evidence that the continued investment in higher education is no longer a priority.

Recommendations for Institutions

Institutions of higher education, both public and private, must take steps to address rising tuitions and restore public and policymaker confidence. Specific suggestions to accomplish these objectives include:

- The role of tuition revenue in institutional planning and budgeting must be changed. Rather than building the budgets by first developing resource needs for access and quality, and then generating revenue to match, institutions should move away from cost-plus pricing to value-based pricing. Tuition limits should be set first, and then plans for raising revenue from other sources and for institutional needs should follow.

- Price structures should be reviewed and, if necessary, realigned. Greater differentiation among prices by level of instruction and program should be permitted. Higher tuitions at the graduate and professional levels, in particular, should be encouraged, and/or costs for these programs reduced, to protect public support for undergraduate education.

- Instruction should be protected at the same time that costs are cut and productivity increased. Attention to the quality of teaching and learning must be maintained as a priority. Analyses and action plans should be undertaken to ensure that lower rates of growth in spending for instruction relative to other spending categories do not contribute to lower quality or effectiveness. Plans for cost savings in some areas should be accompanied by plans to reinvest in other priorities.

- Academic and program planning must be integrated with long-term resource planning, and not maintained as essentially separate efforts within the institutions. Institutions need to develop realistic projections of long-term enrollments matched to scenarios of what can be accomplished at different revenue levels, and then make difficult decisions about focus, program, and priority. Faculty need to be better informed about the costs of programs, and the consequences of choices about future priorities.

- Institutions must take responsibility for strengthening their capacity to define the terms of public accountability that they are prepared to meet.

I. INTRODUCTION

The dilemma of rising college prices is one of the most troubling aspects of higher education policy. How and why have prices gone up? Has financial aid kept college affordable despite the rising prices? Is there a "problem" with tuition, and if so, is it mostly a public relations problem, or have rising prices hurt the capacity of higher education to maintain affordable educational access, institutional choice, and quality? Despite stacks of reports on the topic, the different pieces of the tuition puzzle have not been fit together.

Part of the difficulty in answering these questions is that they are complicated, since higher education is a complex industry. Some of the public policy debate about college prices is obsessed with quibbling about technical details, in search of analytical precision. Further, the answers to these questions are slightly different for the various sectors of higher education—public, private, two-year, and four-year. Generalizations that might be accurate from a national perspective also can be misleading about particular institutions or particular states. But although generalizations can be misleading, a review of a wide-range of research on the topic shows a remarkably consistent analysis of the issue of rising college prices in higher education.

This report ties together data and information from numerous sources in order to help identify the pieces of the tuition puzzle in higher education. The goal of the report is to provide new insights into the causes and consequences of rising college prices, and to question whether rising prices are inevitable, or if something can be done about them. We've used the analogy of the tuition puzzle to convey an image of a mosaic of facts, explanations, and policy responses concerning rising college prices. Readers are cautioned against searching for symmetry among the different puzzle pieces: some are big pieces, some are small; some are clearly about causes, while others seem to be part cause and part response to the problem. By learning from what we know, rather than what we can't answer, the pieces of the puzzle can be fit together to develop strategies that match solutions to the problems uncovered.

The report includes a summary of what has happened with college tuition increases in the last two decades, what has caused the increases, what they have meant for student access and college choice, and how governments and institutions have responded to these increases. It concludes with a synthesis of the consequences of the overall tuition puzzle, recommendations for change in tuition policies—both at the institutional and state policy level—and suggestions for further research.

Definitions of Terms

The language that is typically used to analyze student tuitions, financial aid, and college finances unfortunately blurs the words "price" and "cost" in such a way as to confuse most readers and analysts. For instance, "cost" can alternatively mean tuition only, or tuition and living expenses, or per-student expenditures by institutions. To avoid some of these confusions, we propose to use the term price to mean the amount charged to or paid by the consumer, and cost to refer to money spent by the institution to provide education, as well as other education-related services. Price, therefore, includes tuition, fees, room and board, books and supplies, and other living expenses, even though some analysts exclude room and board and living expenses from the definition of college prices. We believe this terminology is preferable, because the price is what consumers of higher education have to meet to pay for college. In addition, to keep the discussion as uncluttered as possible, the unit of analysis in this report is usually full-time, full-year undergraduate students. Other terms that are used include:

Total price—Tuition, fees, room and board, books and supplies, and other living expenses (financial aid is not taken into consideration).

Sticker price—Tuition and fees charged by institutions to students (financial aid is not taken into consideration).

Net price (grants)—Total price minus grant aid received by the student.

FTE student—Full-time equivalent (FTE) student is the term used to describe enrollment adjusted by attendance status, which counts all full-time students and a portion of part-time students.

Expenditures—An institution's Education and General expenditures (E&G) include instruction, research, public service, academic support, student services, institutional support, operation and maintenance of plant, scholarships and fellowships, mandatory transfers, and nonmandatory transfers. Total expenditures include E&G expenditures plus auxiliary enterprises, hospitals, and independent operations.

Instructional costs—This includes only those expenditures that are classified as directly attributable to instruction (primarily faculty compensation). The indirect costs of instruction from libraries, departmental research, student services, museums, community service, and administration are excluded from this analysis. The source for instructional costs and most other cost information is the federal IEPDS database.

IPEDS—The Integrated Postsecondary Education Data System (IPEDS) is the major federal data collection tool for both financial and enrollment data in higher education. Prior to 1986, IPEDS was called the Higher Education General Information Survey (HEGIS).

Public institutions—Postsecondary institutions that are chartered by state or local governments, with public governing boards, including those with constitutional autonomy.

Private institutions—Private, not-for-profit postsecondary institutions (unless otherwise noted).

II. THE TUITION PUZZLE

The tuition puzzle is composed of several key pieces: how college prices have increased; the causes of higher prices; consequences for student access and choice; and responses to higher prices.

A. How College Prices Have Increased

The Size of Price Increases
The basic facts about how much prices have increased are largely undisputed:

- Overall, sticker prices (average tuition and fees) increased almost five-fold from 1976–77 to 1996–97, or nearly doubled after adjusting for inflation (NCES, 1997).

- Between the mid-1970s and the early-1980s, tuition[1] increased steadily, but remained at relatively constant levels when adjusted for inflation. Since the early-1980s, however, sticker prices have continued to grow faster than inflation for all institutional types (See Figure 4.1).

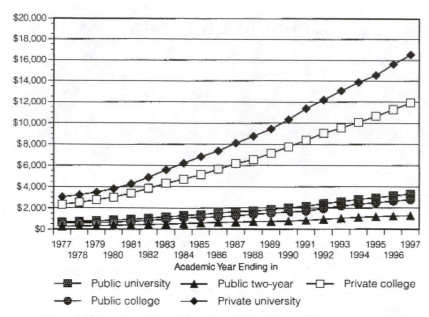

Figure 4.1 Average Tuition and Fees by Type of Institution, Academic Year 1976–77 to 1996–97
In constant 1996–97 dollars

Note: College is equivalent to "other four-year institutions," i.e., not universities. 1996–97 figures are preliminary. Constant dollars are calculated using CPI-U (1982–84 =100). Private includes for-profit institutions. Private two-year institutions were excluded from this analysis.

Source: NCES, 1997.

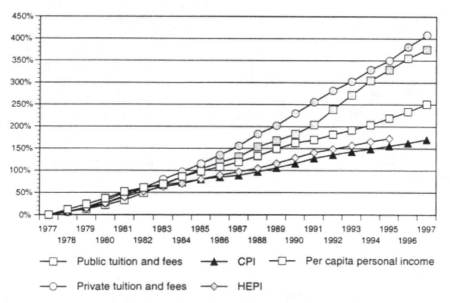

Figure 4.2   Trends in Tuition and Fees, Price Indices, and Personal Income, 1977–1997

Note: The Consumer Price Index (CPI) and the Higher Education Price Index (HEPI) are calculated for the academic year, (ending in the given year), as are tuition and fees. Per capita personal income is for calendar years. Private institutions include both non-profit and for-profit institutions. 1996–97 data for tuition and fees are preliminary.

*Source:*NCES, 1997; U.S. Bureau of the Census, 1997a.

- Tuition has increased in both the private and public sectors of higher education by rates exceeding growth in most major price indices, including students' and families' ability to pay (as measured by per capita personal income). Over the entire period of 1976–77 to 1996–97, tuition increases were greatest in the private sector in terms of both percentage changes and dollar amounts. Since

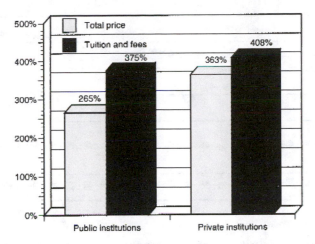

Figure 4.3 Increase in Prices between 1976–77 and 1996–97
In constant 1996–97 dollars

Note: Private Institutions include both non-profit and for-profit. Total price includes tuition, fees, room, and board. 1996–97 data are preliminary.

Source: NCES, 1997.

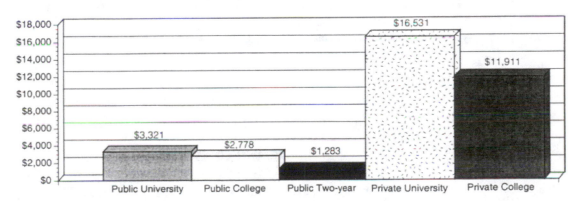

Figure 4.4 Average Tuition and Fees by Type of Institution, 1996–97

Note: College is equivalent to "other four-year institutions," i.e., not universities. Private institutions include both non-profit and for-profit. 1996–97 data are preliminary.

Source: NCES, 1997.

1989–90, however, public sector tuition has risen by a larger percentage, although from a lower base than in the private sector. Annually, prices increased faster in the private sector than in the public sector in the late 1980s, whereas the public sector had higher rates of growth in the early 1990s (See Figure 4.2).

- The biggest increase in total prices was due to tuition increases, and not living expenses, books, or other student expenses. Measures of trends in total prices show a slightly slower increase

than trends in sticker prices alone (See Figure 4.3).

Net Prices[2]
The wide range of prices for higher education reflects the diversity of types of institutions across the country. Despite the high tuition at some institutions, tuition is relatively low at the overwhelming majority of institutions. In 1995–96, only 81 of 3,600 colleges and universities—less than 3 percent—charged $20,000 or more for tuition and fees (ACE, 1998b). More than three-quarters of the students enrolled in

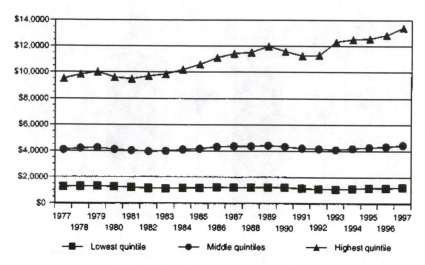

Figure 4.5 Changes in Mean Family Income, 1977–1997
In constant 1997 dollars

Note: Families as of March of the following year. Constant dollars adjusted with CPI-U.
Source: U.S. Bureau of the Census, 1997b.

TABLE 4.1
Average Net Price by Income Level, 1989–90 and 1995–96
In constant 1996 dollars

Average net price, 1989–90

	Private Four-year	Public Four-year	Public Two-year
$0–$9,999	$10,104	$5,884	$4,995
$10,000–$19,999	$10,720	$6,605	$5,599
$20,000–$39,999	$11,630	$7,585	$5,714
$40,000–$59,999	$13,512	$7,934	$5,963
$60,000 and up	$17,691	$9,382	$6,378

Average net price, 1995–96

	Private Four-year	Public Four-year	Public Two-year
$0–$9,999	$11,771	$7,032	$3,942
$10,000–$19,999	$9,478	$6,061	$4,005
$20,000–$39,999	$11,629	$7,950	$5,057
$40,000–$59,999	$13,788	$9,022	$5,633
$60,000 and up	$17,811	$10,441	$5,486

Real change, 1989–90 to 1995–96

	Private Four-year	Public Four-year	Public Two-year
$0–$9,999	17%	20%	−21%
$10,000–$19,999	−12%	−8%	−28%
$20,000–$39,999	0%	5%	−11%
$40,000–$59,999	2%	14%	−6%
$60,000 and up	1 %	11 %	−14%

Note: Net price is total price of attendance (tuition and fees plus living and other expenses) less grant aid only. Analysis includes only full-time, dependent undergraduates, including those who did not receive grant aid. The 1989–90 and 1995–96 data are not completely comparable.
Source: NCES, 1990, 1996.

higher education are in the public sector, where average tuition remains quite low (NCES, 1996, 1997).

Yet looking only at sticker prices does not really explain "affordability"—whether the amount that students and their families actually pay for college is within their reach—as incomes have changed over time. Between 1977 and 1997, average family incomes increased after adjusting for inflation by 41 percent for the highest income quintile, increased at a lower rate for families in the middle quintile, and actually declined slightly for the lowest income group (See Figure 4.5). Financial aid is designed to maintain affordability despite changes in prices and income. To make this possible, campuses would have had to be very diligent in distributing grant aid in such a way as to compensate for rising prices and different trends in average family income.

However, an analysis of changes in average net price—total price less grant aid—by income level in the 1990s reveals this did not occur. After adjusting for inflation, the average net price of attending four-year institutions—both public and private—increased the most for the lowest income families. Only at public two-year institutions did net prices decline across the board, suggesting that affordability was maintained primarily at community colleges (See Table 4.1).

Public Reactions to Higher Tuition Levels

How college prices are perceived is as important as the facts about tuition increases, since perceptions influence the behavior of both students and public policymakers. Several analysts have examined how the general public views higher education prices, as well as how policy leaders look at them. Research commissioned by the American Council on Education (ACE) shows that concern about the price of college is near the top of the list of things parents worry about for their children—greater than their concerns about the quality of public schools, health care for their children, or even the fear that their children will be the victims of crime (ACE, 1998a). The public doesn't understand why prices are going up, although those with an opinion mostly think they are caused by "high-priced" faculty. The public continues to think that the price of college is usually worth it, yet the majority think that the price increases are unfair and that colleges aren't concerned with affordability for the average family.

Analysis commissioned by the California Higher Education Policy Center in 1993—the height of tuition increases in public higher education in California—showed that concern over higher prices led to public pressure to completely overhaul the educational system in that state. Several years later, similar research showed that the call for restructuring abated considerably once the prices stabilized (Immerwahr, 1993, 1998).

Public worry extends to skepticism from policymakers, particularly at the state level, where there is a pervasive belief that higher prices are a reflection of skewed institutional spending priorities. The Education Commission of the States' (ECS) survey of state policymakers reveals that they believe higher education does not spend its money wisely, and that tuition increases could be avoided if colleges realigned their spending with those areas the public most cares about, particularly undergraduate education and job preparation (ECS, 1998). This agenda linking increased evidence of accountability to the possibility of future funding increases echoes the call put forth by others in recent years (see, for example, Wingspread Group, 1993).

B. The Causes of Higher Prices

Declining Role of Public Revenue

The consensus from several different studies is that one of the most significant causes of higher tuitions is the changing role of public revenue (GAO, 1998; Davis, 1997; McPherson and Schapiro, 1998), which declined in relative terms between 1980–81 and 1994–95. The relative decline occurred despite the fact that public revenue dollars have continued to increase—even on an inflation-adjusted, per full-time equivalent (FTE) student basis. Because growth in public funding has not kept pace with overall revenue needs, institutions have turned to other sources to fill the gap—specifically, tuition revenue. Thus, tuition revenue per FTE has grown at a faster rate than both public revenue and total revenue per FTE (See Table 4.2).

As a result, the composition of revenue has shifted, in both the public and the private sectors. In 1980–81, taxpayer revenue from all sources accounted for 63 percent of total rev-

TABLE 4.2
Percentage Change in Revenue per FTE,
1980–81 to 1994–95
In constant 1994–95 dollars

Public Institutions	Revenue per FTE		Percentage Increase from 1980–81 to 1994–95
	1980–81	1994–95	
Tuition and fees	$1,442	$2,814	95%
Federal government	$1,435	$1,695	18%
State government	$5,095	$5,505	8%
Local government	$420	$611	45%
Gifts	$285	$609	114%
Endowment	$56	$89	59%
Other	$2,453	$4,004	63%
Total	$11,185	$15,327	37%

Private Institutions	Revenue per FTE		Percentage Increase from 1980–81 to 1994–95
	1980–81	1994–95	
Tuition and fees	$6,482	$11,545	78%
Federal government	$3,325	$3,921	18%
State government	$340	$581	71%
Local government	$133	$160	20%
Gifts	$1,641	$2,391	46%
Endowment	$909	$1,285	41%
Other	$4,863	$7,347	51%
Total	$17,691	$27,230	54%

Note: Private institutions include both non-profit and for-profit.

Source: NCES, 1997.

TABLE 4.3
Percentage Share of Revenues by Source, Academic Years 1980–81 to 1994–95

Public Institutions	1980–81	1990–91	1994–95
Tuition and fees	13%	16%	18%
Federal government	13%	10%	11%
State government	46%	40%	36%
Local government	4%	4%	4%
Gifts	3%	4%	4%
Endowment	0%	0%	1%
Other	22%	25%	26%
Total	100%	100%	100%

Private Institutions	1980–81	1990–91	1994–95
Tuition and fees	37%	40%	42%
Federal government	19%	15%	14%
State government	2%	2%	2%
Local government	1%	1%	1%
Gifts	9%	9%	9%
Endowment	5%	5%	5%
Other	27%	27%	27%
Total	100%	100%	100%

Note: Because of rounding, details may not add to totals. Private institutions include both non-profit and for-profit.

Source: NCES, 1997.

enue in public institutions and 22 percent in private institutions, while revenue from tuition and fees covered 13 percent and 37 percent, respectively. By 1994–95, the relationship between revenue sources had changed dramatically, with a 12 percentage point decrease in the share of total revenue that came from public tax sources at public institutions and a 5 percentage point decline at private institutions. This was accompanied by a substantial increase in tuition revenue as a share of total

revenue—by 5 percentage points in the both the public and private sector (See Table 4.3).

The decline in the role of public revenues has affected both the public and private sectors, although the specific relationships differ slightly. In the public sector, there is a direct relationship between lower state revenues and higher tuition and fee levels. A recent U.S. General Accounting Office (GAO) study found that for every dollar lost in state tax revenues, there has been a 75 cent increase in tuition in public institutions (GAO, 1998). As state revenue decreased as a percentage of total revenue from 46 percent in 1980–81 to 36 percent in 1994–95, the share of tuition and fees revenue increased from 13 percent in public institutions in 1980–81 to 18 percent in 1994–95. In response, public institutions have tried to diversify their revenue base, in part through increased fundraising from the philanthropic sector. As a result, the share of overall revenues from philanthropic sources (including gifts and endowment) in the public sector increased by 2 percentage points between 1980–81 and 1994–95.

However, a shift toward non-public revenue sources in the public sector has meant less institutional flexibility in allocation decisions. Even though the roles of revenue sources have shifted, and other revenue sources have been found to abate the relative decline in public resources, there are fewer unrestricted resources available for general institutional purposes. For instance, gift revenue is frequently targeted by donors for limited purposes.

For private institutions, the decline in the role of total taxpayer revenue was not as steep as in the public sector, but the relative decline in federal revenue was felt more sharply than in the public sector—the share of revenue from federal resources declined from 19 percent in 1980–81 to 14 percent in 1994–95. The proportion of revenue from philanthropic sources has remained the same. Combined, the share of revenue from federal and philanthropic sources in the private sector declined by 5 percentage points; in comparison, there was a 5 percentage point increase in the share of total revenues paid from tuition. Private institutions received slightly more (less than 1 percentage point) in state revenue as a proportion of total revenue in 1994–95 than in 1980–81.

Another consequence of funding shifts is that competition for revenue between the public and private sectors is increasingly intense. The stable sources of revenue that used to be counted on to pay for the overall purposes of the institution have declined, to be replaced by a more fragmented and competitive revenue base. Public institutions are pursuing philanthropic funds more than in the past, and private institutions are vying for state revenues more than before. Along with increased competition comes greater consumerism, and more fragmentation of institutional attention needed to maintain a diverse funding base.

Increased Institutional Spending on Student Aid
The need for more tuition revenue has been fueled in part by internal spending patterns, and in particular, by increased spending on student aid. Several analysts (see McPherson and Schapiro, 1998, and National Commission on the Cost of Higher Education, 1998) have

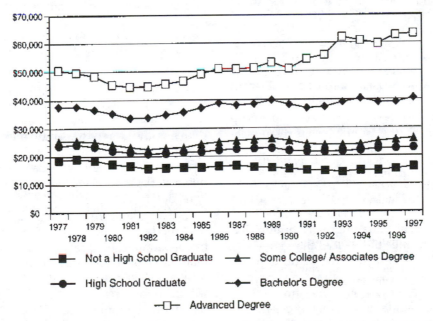

Figure 4.6 Mean Earnings of Workers 18 Years of Age and Older by Educational Attainment, 1977 to 1997 In constant 1997 dollars

Source: U.S. Bureau of the Census, 1998.

TABLE 4.4
Percentage Increases in Top Three E&G Expenditure Categories by Sector, 1986–87 to 1993–94

Research and Doctoral Universities (Carnegie Research I & II, Doctoral I & II)

Public		Private	
Unrestricted scholarships	85%	Unrestricted scholarships	83%
Funded research	30%	Institutional support	27%
Public service	24%	Instruction	27°%

Comprehensive Universities (Carnegie Comprehensive I & II)

Public		Private	
Unrestricted scholarships	51%	Funded research	137%
Public service	35%	Unrestricted scholarships	94%
Restricted scholarships	13%	Restricted scholarships	31

Liberal Arts Colleges (Carnegie Liberal Arts I & 11)

Public		Private	
Funded research	164%	Unrestricted scholarships	91%
Unrestricted scholarships	57%	Funded research	45%
Public service	42%	Library	27%

Community Colleges (Public Carnegie Two-Year Schools)

Funded research	175%
Restricted scholarships	58%
Unrestricted scholarships	54%

Note: All expenditure amounts were adjusted for inflation and presented in 1993–94 current dollars before percentages were calculated. The universe of institutions includes only those for which data were available in 1986–87, 1990–91, and 1993–94. Unrestricted scholarships represent institutional student aid and restricted scholarships represent student aid from other sources.

Source: McPherson and Schapiro, 1998.

concluded that increased spending for institutional aid is another significant "driver" of higher prices. The increased spending occurred in both the public and private sectors, although many analysts have noted that higher spending is a relatively greater cause of rising tuitions in the private sector (Hauptman and Krop, 1998; Davis, 1997; McPherson and Schapiro, 1998).

Underlying the shift to greater tuition discounting—reducing the price charged—is a self-conscious effort by many institutions to use enrollment management strategies to redistribute subsidies and at the same time protect student access. Students who have the means to do so are charged the full sticker price, and a portion of the tuition revenues is redirected to need-based financial aid, which is then pack-

aged to go to poor students or to students with desired characteristics. Such strategies have many variations, ranging from admitting students without regard to financial need and meeting their full need, to deliberately shaping a financial aid strategy that maximizes the quality of incoming students as well as the revenue obtained from them.

At the same time, the "high tuition/high aid" model has been advocated for many years by a number of analysts (see in particular Hansen and Weisbrod, 1969; and Fischer, 1990) as a more efficient and equitable way to distribute public resources, by funding students based on economic need rather than general appropriations to institutions. The model involves lowering direct support to public institutions, raising public tuition and fees to close to full-cost levels, and using public resources for need-based grants or targeted tuition discounts. The theory is that even with tuition increases, access can be protected through increased institutional aid. This strategy is similar to the enrollment management mechanisms used within institutions, but redistributes revenue across higher education sectors.

The ultimate effect of both of these strategies has been to increase institutions' provision of student aid. Analyses conducted by McPherson and Schapiro (1998) and others confirm that institutional aid accounts for one of the largest categories of spending increases per FTE student within higher education. With the exception of private comprehensive universities, public liberal arts colleges, and community colleges, institutional spending for "scholarship" expenditures from unrestricted revenues increased at rates that outpaced any other expenditure category (See Table 4.4).

Spending for "Prestige"

Several higher education analysts believe that another example of competition contributing to rising prices lies in spending to increase prestige, or gaining a competitive market advantage. This theory is presented most clearly in the essay "The Lattice and the Ratchet," by Zemsky and Massy (1990), and reiterated in Massy's testimony before the National Commission on the Cost of Higher Education (Massy, 1997). Their analysis is that the competitive market has increased the value of prestige, and when colleges are faced with the option of cutting, spending, or increasing prestige, they will choose the latter course, since with higher prestige comes greater resources. While harder to quantify empirically than student aid spending, the analysis of expenditure trends and costs done by McPherson and Schapiro (1998) offer some corroborative evidence from research universities to support Zemsky and Massy's theory. Their analysis shows that the two sectors in higher education that have seen the greatest internal spending increases outside of student aid are the public and private research universities. Most of these increases were in public service and research, not in instructional areas.

It's the Economy

To borrow an aphorism from Clinton campaign strategist James Carville, one simple answer to the reason for higher college prices is "it's the economy, stupid." The rising economic necessity of college attendance has increased college enrollment rates. This "wage premium" has allowed demand to continue increasing, despite higher prices, contrary to normal economic logic. Whereas in past generations Americans could make a reasonable living with just a high school education, the changing workplace demands higher skills and places a higher premium on credentials than ever before. Some college attendance or post-high school technical training has become a prerequisite for many entry-level jobs.

The gap in earnings for baccalaureate degree holders and high school graduates has widened. In 1977, workers who had attained a bachelor's degree earned 58 percent more than did workers whose highest level of education was high school; by 1997, this gap had risen to 77 percent. The gap in average earnings between advanced degree holders and high school graduates has widened even further: 112 percent in 1977 and 176 percent in 1997 (U.S. Bureau of the Census, 1998). Average annual earnings of workers 18 years of age and older, adjusted for inflation, show divergent patterns according to educational attainment. The earnings of advanced degree holders have increased considerably since 1977 and the earnings of workers with bachelors degrees have increased slightly, whereas the earnings of high school graduates have declined over this period. When higher prices are compared to future earnings for bachelors degree holders, the economic payoff from going to college has not increased at the same rate that the price of attending college has. Therefore even though the economic value of college has grown, it is because the penalty of not going to college has increased, more than because of the economic payoff from going.

A "Non-Cause": Spending For Instruction

While the data indicate that the preceding factors may have some impact on the rise in tuition, it is important to note what the research says about factors that have *not* contributed to the price increases. Public opinion polling and interviews with policy leaders show a com-

TABLE 4.5
Salary of Full-time Instructional Faculty
In constant 1995–96 dollars

All	1970–71 $49,431	1995–96 $49,309	Percentage Change 0%
Professor	$69,841	$64,540	–8%
Associate professor	$52,751	$47,966	–9%
Assistant professor	$43,466	$39,696	–9%
Instructor	$36,402	$30,344	–17%
Lecturer	$43,544	$34,136	–22%
No Rank	$47,967	$42,996	–10%
Public	$50,379	$48,837	–3%
Public four-year	$51,033	$51,172	0%
Public two-year	$49,176	$43,295	–12%
Private	$45,187	$50,466	12%
Private four-year	$45,987	$50,819	11%
Private two-year	$33,696	$31,915	–5%

Source: NCES, 1997.

TABLE 4.6
Percentage Change in Faculty Composition by Full-time/Part-time Status, 1970–71 to 1993–94

Year	Full-time Number	% Share	Part-time Number	% Share
1970–71	369,000	78%	104,000	22%
1971–72	379,000	77%	113,000	23%
1972–73	380,000	76%	120,000	24%
1973–74	389,000	74%	138,000	26%
1974–75	406,000	72%	161,000	28%
1975–76	440,000	70%	188,000	30%
1976–77	434,000	69%	199,000	31%
1977–78	448,000	66%	230,000	34%
1979–80	445,000	66%	230,000	34%
1980–81	450,000	66%	236,000	34%
1981–82	461,000	65%	244,000	35%
1982–83	462,000	65%	248,000	35%
1983–84	471,000	65%	254,000	35%
1984–85	462,000	64%	255,000	36%
1985–86	459,000	64%	256,000	36%
1986–87	459,000	64%	263,000	36%
1987–88	523,000	66%	270,000	34%
1989–90	524,000	64%	300,000	36%
1991–92	536,000	65%	291,000	35%
1993–94	546,000	60%	370,000	40%

Percent increase in part-time instructional faculty from 1970–71 to 1993–94: 256%

Percent increase in full-time instructional faculty from 1970–71 to 1993–94: 48%

Note: Data unavailable for missing years.

Source: NCES, 1997.

monly held perception that spending for faculty—protected by the tenure system—is one of the major internal cost drivers (ACE, 1998a; ECS, 1998). Yet the national trend data simply don't support that point of view: average faculty salaries in constant dollars have declined since 1970–71 at public institutions, and have risen only slightly at private institutions (See Table 4.5). The number of part-time faculty has increased overall (NCES, 1997).

An analysis of changes in various categories of E&G expenditure by McPherson and Schapiro (1998) includes data on per-student spending for instruction compared with per-student spending on other categories of expenditure for 1986–87 and 1993–94. They show that, in real terms, private institutions have been able to increase per-student spending on instruction over this period (especially private research universities), whereas public institutions generally have not. Spending on instruction per student actually declined in the public comprehensive colleges and liberal arts colleges. At the same time, per-student spending for other categories of spending, such as research and public service, has increased at faster rates than per-student instructional spending. Only in private research universities has instructional spending grown at a more rapid pace than most other categories. As a result, the composition of total E&G spending has shifted slightly away from instruction and toward such categories as research and public service for some types of institutions—in particular, public research universities (See Table 4.7). This shift is probably attributable both to cost cutting efforts and to increased funding opportunities outside of instruction.

The Dilemma of Federal Policy and Price Increases

One of the more debated and unresolved pieces of the tuition puzzle is the role that federal loan increases have had on higher prices. Some analysts contend that federal loan capital has allowed institutions to raise tuitions, and to redirect a portion of the additional revenue to institutional aid (see Hauptman and Krop, 1998). These analysts infer a direct causal relation between loan availability and the tuition discounting phenomenon. Others contend that blaming the federal student loan system for college tuitions is like blaming the egg for the chicken, since colleges had to increase tuitions because of the declining role of public funding, not because of federal aid availability. At the nub of the debate is disagreement about what interventions the federal government might consider to discourage tuition increases without instigating price controls on one hand, or hurting student access on the other.

But while the loan programs so far have not provided the "smoking gun" proof that federal funding practices have caused tuition increases, the federal government may not be able to remain above the fray for long. In 1997, Congress and President Clinton created new tuition tax credits to allow parents and students to help pay for college tuitions.

For eligible students attending public institutions, the Hope Scholarship should represent a substantial discount on sticker prices (Zucker, 1998). In those states where tuitions remain relatively low—such as California, Florida, Texas, and North Carolina—the benefit to the students, the state and the institutions from the federal credit will be less. As a result, tax analysts in these states have begun to note that the states might want to reevaluate their policies of maintaining low tuition in order to recapture the federal tax benefit. Recognizing that states now have the incentive to increase public tuitions to take advantage of federal tax incentives, Secretary of Education Richard Riley has publicly urged Governors and State legislatures against increasing their public tuitions. At the moment, the political mood against tuition increases, along with the strong economy, have kept such shifts from occurring. But the pipe has been laid, and absent a change in federal policy, state tuition increases that will be directly attributable to federal financing policies are likely (Burd, 1998).

TABLE 4.7
Real Change in E&G Expenditure Categories per FTE Student Between 1986–87 and 1993–94

	Instruction and Self-supported	Funded Research	Public Service	Academic Support	Library Expenditures	Student Services	Institutional Support	Operations and Maintenance	Restricted Scholarships	Unrestricted Scholarships	Plant Additions
Public:											
Research and Doctoral	6%	30%	24%	15%	12%	15%	4%	−5%	11%	85%	−2%
Comprehensive	−1%	5%	35%	8%	5%	12%	1%	−14%	13%	51%	−12%
Liberal Arts	−4%	164%	42%	0%	0%	2%	−7%	−20%	19%	57%	−33%
Two-Year	0%	175%	10%	−7%	1%	8%	−5%	−9%	58%	54%	7%
Private:											
Research and Doctoral	27%	15%	23%	−5%	24%	26%	27%	13%	17%	83%	−1%
Comprehensive	11%	137%	6%	3%	28%	25%	3%	−2%	31%	94%	22%
Liberal Arts	14%	45%	11%	18%	27%	22%	8%	−1%	22%	91%	13%

☐ Rate of increase is the same or lower than instruction

▨ Rate of increase is faster than in instruction

Note: All expenditure amounts were adjusted for inflation and presented in 1993–94 constant dollars before percentages were calculated. The universe of institutions includes only those for which data were available in 1986–87, 1990–91, and 1993–94.

Source: McPherson and Schapiro, 1998.

TABLE 4.8
Average Difference in Tuition and Fees Between
Private and Public Institutions
In constant 1996–97 dollars

	Ratio of Private to Public Universities	Difference (in Dollars)	Ratio of Private to Public Colleges	Difference (in Dollars)
1976–77	4.43	$6,394	4.19	$4,867
1996–97	4.98	$13,210	4.29	$9,133

Note: Adjusted for inflation using CPI-U (1982–1984 = 100).
Source: NCES, 1997.

C. Consequences for Student Access and Choice

Student Access

The changing role of financial aid in relation to price and the internal dynamics of the higher education student marketplace have been studied extensively (Heller, 1997; McPherson and Schapiro, 1998; National Commission on the Cost of Higher Education, 1998). Heller concludes from his summary of recent analyses that as prices go up, enrollments go down, even with the provision of aid. According to Heller, the consensus among researchers is that every $100 increase in tuition results in a drop in enrollments of 0.5 to 1.0 percentage points across all types of institutions. Decreases in financial aid also lead to declines in enrollment, with the effect differing depending on the type of aid awarded. In general, enrollments are more sensitive to grant awards than to loans or work-study.

However, access to college, as measured by the proportion of people going to college, has increased consistently over the period from 1977 to 1997. Nationally, 67 percent of recent high school graduates enrolled in college immediately after high school in 1997 (64 percent for men; 70 percent for women), increasing from just 51 percent in 1977. Enrollment has been rising for all income groups throughout most of the 1980s and 1990s. However, the gap between low- and high-income students is still close to 30 percentage points (NCES, 1998). Therefore, it does not appear that overall access has been affected negatively by rising prices, though gaps between low- and high-income students remain a serious concern.

Institutional Choice

While overall access may have been maintained, it is clear that the growing price gap between public and private colleges increasingly has made attendance at some private institutions a financially prohibitive choice for many students. Reducing the size of the price gap between public and private institutions has been a goal for many policy leaders over the last two decades, particularly those who are worried about the potential loss of institutional diversity and quality that might accompany a lessening of opportunity in that sector. In the early 1970s, the Carnegie Commission on Higher Education recommended that a national goal be set to maintain private/public price differentials of roughly 2.5 to one (Carnegie Commission on Higher Education, 1973). The "tuition gap" between private and public institutions has changed over the past two decades, but has not met the Carnegie recommendations. Measured as a ratio, the size of the gap has remained about the same: between 1976–77 and 1996–97, private tuition has remained more than four times higher than public tuition. At the same time, the size of the gap—measured in constant dollar amounts—has increased significantly, to an average of $13,210 in the university sector and $9,133 in the collegiate sector.

But the most important impact on student enrollment choice may not have been isolated to public/private price distinctions; there is a growing body of research showing structural shifts of enrollments by institutional mission as well. As Heller (1997) points out, lower-income students are more sensitive to changes in tuition and aid than are students from middle- and upper-income families. Increased aid, therefore, has not been enough to prevent negative enrollment consequences, particularly among the lowest income students.

One of the most revealing pieces of research about the structural consequences of increased prices on enrollments has been presented by McPherson and Schapiro (1998). They show that the different sectors of higher education are more economically segregated now than in the past. While the percentage of lower-income freshmen attending public two-year institutions has remained steady—having risen slightly from 46 percent in 1980 to 47 per-

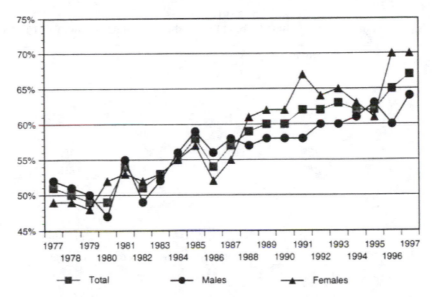

Figure 4-7 College Enrollment Rates of High School Graduates, 1977 to 1997

Note: Enrollment in college as of October of each year for individuals ages 16 to 24 who graduated from high school during the preceding 12 months. Includes GED recipients.

Source: NCES, 1997; U.S. Bureau of Labor Statistics, 1997.

cent in 1994—students from wealthier families have fled from these institutions. The percentage of middle-income students attending public two-year institutions fell from 39 percent to 34 percent, upper middle-income went from 28 percent to 22 percent, upper-income decreased from 17 percent to 14 percent, and the richest students fell from 15 percent to 9 percent. At the same time, a greater percentage of the richest freshmen attended public and private universities in 1994 than in 1980 (See Table 4.9). The bottom line is that higher education risks becoming more economically stratified by sector now than any time in the last two decades, despite the substantial investment in student aid.

D. Responses to Higher Prices

There seem to be five basic responses by institutional, state, and federal policymakers to rising college prices: 1) expansion of programs to make it easier for families to pay for college; 2) improved public information to students and parents about college prices; 3) cost reduction strategies; 4) initiatives to improve productivity; and 5) state-level tuition policy and budget practices. To borrow a medical analogy, the first two strategies can be described as both

symptomatic and therapeutic, designed to increase options and improve awareness, but not intended to get at the root causes of tuition and price increases. The latter three are more systemic.

Expansion of Programs to Make It Easier for Families to Pay for College

Expansion of funding options—through expanded borrowing, prepayment plans, and new tax benefits—has been the area of tuition *budgetary* policy that has received the most public policy attention in the last 10 years. While some of these efforts have focused on increasing need-based student aid, there has been a considerable expansion of efforts to ensure that middle- and upper-income families have more options to help pay for college as well. Prepaid tuition plans, college savings plans, and private loan plans that offer a wide range of repayment options are very common now; they are all ways that the tuition bite can be softened for families who do not qualify for need-based financial aid (see Olivas, 1993, for a fuller discussion of prepaid tuition plans). Some state aid programs, such as Georgia's politically popular Hope Scholarship program, feature funding that is packaged with early outreach programs designed to enhance aca-

TABLE 4.9
Percentage Distribution of Freshmen by Institutional Type and Income Background, Fall 1980 and Fall 1994

1994	Public			Private		
	Two-year	College	University	Two-year	College	University
Total	31%	24%	19%	3%	17%	6%
Lower	47%	23%	11%	3%	13%	3%
Lower-middle	39%	25%	15%	3%	15%	3%
Middle	34%	25%	18%	3%	17%	4%
Upper-middle	22%	26%	25%	2%	18%	7%
Upper	14%	20%	28%	3%	22%	13%
Richest	9%	13%	25%	4%	27%	22%

1980	Public			Private		
	Two-Year	College	University	Two-year	College	University
Total	36%	20%	18%	4%	17%	5%
Lower	46%	23%	10%	6%	13%	2%
Lower-Middle	42%	21%	13%	5%	15%	3%
Middle	39%	20%	17%	4%	16%	4%
Upper-middle	28%	20%	25%	3%	18%	7%
Upper	17%	16%	27%	3%	25%	13%
Richest	15%	12%	20%	3%	32%	20%

Note: College is equivalent to "all other four-year institutions," i.e., not universities. Because of rounding, details may not add to totals.

Source: McPherson and Schapiro, 1998.

demic preparation for college. The most prominent national example of programs targeted at middle and upper-income families is the federal Hope Scholarship tax credit. Furthermore, a number of institutions have contracted with private tuition payment companies to work with families (for a small fee) to allow them to spread college payments over a 10- or 12-month period (McDonald, 1995).

Improved Public Information to Students and Parents about College Prices

Research continues to show that the general public overestimates the price of college, and underestimates the availability of financial aid. This misinformation then contributes to lowered expectations which can affect college enrollment options. As a result, many states and institutions are embarking on public information efforts, designed to improve public understanding about college prices and the different ways to meet them. The most prominent national example of such a campaign is one now being led by the American Council on Education. Their "College is Possible"

campaign is a national coalition of organizations and institutions joined together to improve public information about college prices. To the extent that students are opting away from college or choosing lower-priced institutions out of misperceptions about tuition and financial aid, this strategy may be helpful in the long run to reduce negative enrollment consequences from price increases. However, even if successful in improving consumer decisionmaking, these campaigns cannot be presumed to help directly with stabilizing price increases.

Cost Reduction Strategies

There can be no disputing that higher education as an industry has responded to reduced resources through cost cutting. Information from the National Association of College and University Business Officers (NACUBO), the Learning Productivity Network, the American Council on Education, and the National Commission on the Cost of Higher Education shows considerable evidence of institutional efforts to hold down spending. Unfortunately, there is no accepted way to quantify the effect of these kinds of initiatives on total costs or prices. Cost cutting strategies can be grouped into three categories: cost deferral strategies, strategic cost reductions, and permanent cost restructuring.

- *Cost deferral strategies* are ways that institutions respond to short-term budget shortfalls by avoiding spending. Hiring freezes, purchasing deferrals and reductions in maintenance, grounds, and building repairs are common examples. Cost deferrals are ways to save money without permanently reducing the base expenditures. In fact, in the case of deferred maintenance, cost deferrals can end up driving up long-term costs.

- *Strategic cost reductions* are reductions in expenditures while maintaining most functions. Strategic cost reductions typically occur in administrative and support areas. NACUBO encourages institutional members to identify strategies they have used to cut costs, and now manages a national competition designed to advertise strategies they have used to cut costs, and now manages a national competition designed to advertise strategies and promote best practices. Many of the NACUBO network cost reduction strategies are examples of strategic cost reductions in areas such as utilities savings, cost savings through pooled purchasing, and savings in employee benefits costs through shifts to HMO plans (NACUBO, 1977).

- *Permanent cost restructuring* eliminates some functions, and permanently reduces the costs of others. Examples of permanent cost restructuring are eliminating low-enrollment courses, shutting down programs, and replacing full-time faculty with part-time faculty. The trends noted earlier in hiring patterns of full-time and part-time faculty suggest that this kind of cost restructuring has been a common phenomenon in higher education.

Initiatives to Improve Productivity

Several researchers are beginning to focus attention on finding ways to generate sus-

tained improvements in productivity by joining cost reductions with quality and outcome improvements. The national leader in this arena has been D. Bruce Johnstone, who has put together a "Learning Productivity Network" at the State University of New York at Buffalo. Johnstone argues that the only way that institutions can address the long-term imbalance between resources and needs is through sustained productivity increases. He provides several examples of ways that institutions can permanently reduce costs through greater attention to efficiency improvements, including year-round-operations; reducing redundant course taking through improved counseling and better scheduling; and reducing time-to-degree through more efficient course sequencing, including better use of high school time to generate college credit (Johnstone, 1993; Johnstone and Maloney, 1998).

Massy (1997) is also focusing research to develop alternative measures of institutional quality which focus on sustained outcomes rather than on traditional resource input measures. Different ways of measuring quality have to be found before goals can be set for how much can occur through productivity. In simple terms, productivity can be said to occur when quality is increased and costs are maintained, or when costs are reduced but quality is maintained. The issue of productivity is a remarkably painful one for higher education, in part because faculty assume it is a codeword for higher workload, and because the culture of the academy pretends to reject utilitarian or market-based notions of production and efficiency. As a result, most institutional quality assessments avoid looking at use of resources as one element of quality. It is simply taken as a given that more money means better quality. The assessment movement clearly has not caught up with cost measurement.

State-Level Tuition Policies and Budget Practices

One of the responses that seems not to have occurred is systematic attention to tuition policy, particularly in the public sector, and to the relation between tuition and costs. This area has not been the topic of much research. As a result, a brief discussion of how public tuition policies are designed, and what has happened to them in the current environment, is provided here.

Tuition policy in higher education is set at two levels: by institutions, under the authority of governing boards or trustees; and by states, through laws or budget practices that implement tuition decisions. The federal government does not have tuition policies for higher education, although it can be said to be an intensely interested observer of tuition policy, since one of the goals of federal aid programs is to enable access to higher education. Also, the student aid need analysis formulas take price of attendance into account in determining award amounts.

While state tuition policies are immediately relevant to the public sector, they are germane to the private sector as well, because tuition is a key ingredient in how higher education budget appropriations are put together. Private institutions also are keenly interested in state student aid and in the trade-offs between direct appropriations to public institutions in contrast to student aid funding. Private institutions are politically important, as they participate in the creation of state tuition policies, even though the policies do not apply directly to their institutions.

The general structure for state tuition policies are as follows:

- *Mission-based tuition policies.* Every state has some form of mission-based tuition policy, with the lowest tuitions charged to students in two-year institutions, and charges calibrated upward to the highest amounts in research universities.

- *Policy or philosophic underpinning.* Most states have some policy statements that assert their basic philosophy or policy framework for tuition. A 1992 survey found that the majority of states with a tuition "policy" report that they have a low- or moderate-tuition philosophy, rather than a "high-tuition" or "full-cost" policy (Lenth, 1993). "Low" was defined to mean keeping tuitions as low as possible; "moderate" was a cost-sharing approach; and "high" meant students would bear more of the cost increases than the state. A number of states did not claim to have a tuition policy, but set tuitions based on charges in comparable institutions in other

TABLE 4.10
Variation in Tuition Philosophy and Procedures Among the States, 1992

Philosophy/ Procedure	Number of States		
	Research Universities	State Colleges & Universities	Community Colleges
Low-tuition philosophy	8	6	14
Moderate-tuition philosophy	18	21	19
High-tuition philosophy	5	5	3
"Indexed" to comparable institution	7	6	4
Institution-level decisions only	12	10	8
Total	50	48	48

Source: Lenth, 1993.

states, or on individual institutional circumstances (See Table 4.10).

- *Authority to set tuition.* The authority to set tuition is generally shared among the legislature, governor, governing boards, and sometimes the campuses in multi-campus systems. As such, decisions about tuition charges occur where there is broad-based shared responsibility between government and higher education, rather than authority to act unilaterally, which is clearly held by one side or the other. This means that tuition decisions are political, and that a number of interest groups try to influence the process.

- *Indexing of tuitions.* Most states have policies that focus more on how increases in tuition will be indexed rather than on the base tuition structure. These policies allow tuition to increase according to some measure of inflation or ability to pay, or in comparison to peer groups.

- *Cost-based tuition differentials.* Many states set some prices in high-cost areas at greater levels than others in order to recapture some of the revenues associated with the greater costs. These cost-based price structures are known as differentials. Tuition differentials are typically charged to non-resident students, for instance, where many state laws specify that the out-of-state students shall be charged prices that equal the full cost to the state to provide the education. Tuition differentials also are charged for some graduate and professional programs. In 1998, for example, 32 states charged graduate students in the public universities more than undergraduates, a differential averaging around $500 more per year for graduate students, or roughly 14 percent of average residential tuition of $3,500 for undergraduates (Washington Higher Education Coordinating Board, 1998).

Despite the use of some cost differentials, most tuition structures are not consistently cost-based. The costs of instruction in research universities are typically much higher than in comprehensive or community colleges, yet the student share of costs—as measured by tuition and fees as a percentage of education and general revenues—was lowest in the public research universities, followed by community colleges (See Table 4.11) (Lenth, 1993).

- *Cost-sharing arrangements.* Another variation on cost-based policies are cost-sharing tuition structures. Usually applied to tuition increments or increases rather than the base structure, cost-sharing arrangements assign some portion of the share of new costs to the taxpayers or to students. An example of cost sharing used to index revenues can be found in Minnesota, which has a "shared responsibility" arrangement for splitting new revenues between the state and the student (Minnesota Higher Education Coordinating Board, 1994).

The problem with state tuition policies is that they tend to be swept away by the power of funding decisions. And the structural shifts in budget policies at both the federal and state level mean that higher education funding is being squeezed. At all levels of government,

TABLE 4.11
Tuition and Fee Revenues as a Percentage of Total Institutional Revenue and E&G Expenditures at Public Institutions, 1975–76 to 1990–91

	Tuition and Fees as a Percentage of Total Revenues	Tuition and Fees as a Percentage of Total E&G Expenditures
1975–76		
Public Research	12%	16%
Public Four-Year	18%	22%
Public Two-Year	16%	18%
1980–81		
Public Research	12°/a	15%
Public Four-Year	18%	21%
Public Two-Year	15%	17%
1985–86		
Public Research	13%	17%
Public Four-Year	19%	23%
Public Two-Year	15%	17%
1990–91		
Public Research	15%	18% (25%)*
Public Four-Year	22%	26% (39%)*
Public Two-Year	17%	19% (45%)*

* Figures in parenthesis exclude "restricted" E&G expenditures, which is primarily specialized research expenditures. This exclusion is not available for prior years.

Source: Lenth, 1993.

efforts to reduce taxes and control spending have created budget structures that constrain spending on "discretionary" items.

At the state level, higher education funding is part of a relatively small portion of the state budget that governors and legislatures can control, unencumbered by federal or state entitlement laws that constrain their options. The portion of the budget that is available for discretionary spending is declining, and with it, the general fund revenue base for higher education. General tax appropriations to higher education went from nearly 16 percent of total state spending in Fiscal Year 1987 to 13 percent in 1997, at the same time that spending for Medicaid increased from 8 percent to almost 15 percent, and corrections rose from 5 percent to 7 percent (NASBO, 1998).

State budget decision-makers, faced with hard decisions and unwilling to raise taxes, believe that tuitions can be raised to substitute for lost general funds without fundamental negative consequences on programs or services. This *de facto* tuition policy that has been adopted by state government is one that has been called "passive resistance"—or letting natural forces take their course (Roherty, 1997). In the current political environment, those natural forces mean that general funds will decline, and tuitions will go up.

Along with the structural budget issues is the political process between higher education and state government that accompanies tuition increases. Most states are on record as having policies that college tuitions will be kept as low as possible. Rather than having policies that manage prices, increases are avoided in good times, while charges increase sharply in bad times. What happens as a result is a "boom and bust" phenomenon, with tuition increases ratcheting upwards in double digits in some years, and holding at zero or even being rolled back in other years. If institutional leaders attempt to smooth out increases, they risk approbation from state political leaders, students, and the media. Because tuition increases are a political hot potato, and because responsibility for approving them is shared between the academy and state government (including the governor and the legislature), the result is a form of tuition "chicken," where each waits for the other to take the initiative. It is therefore not surprising that tuition increases often occur at the very end of the state budget process, too late for students and families to make enrollment decisions.[3]

III. PUTTING THE PIECES OF THE PUZZLE TOGETHER

Summary and Conclusions

College prices have increased nearly five-fold over the last two decades, mostly because of public funding reductions at both the federal and state levels. The price spiral has been exacerbated by institutional spending patterns, particularly to increase funding for student aid in order to maintain access and affordability. There is also some evidence that research institutions are increasing spending,

primarily outside of instruction, in order to maintain or enhance their market position. These responses suggest that competition in the higher education market has contributed to price increases in selective institutions, rather than stabilizing or decreasing prices, as would be expected.

Access to college, as measured by the proportion of people going to college, is being maintained despite the higher prices, though gaps between low- and high-income students remain a serious a concern. When the higher prices are compared to the economic costs of not going to college, clearly the costs of not going to college outweigh the price of attendance, even at the higher tuition levels. But if earnings alone are the measure of the worth of the additional investment required for a bachelor's degree, the benefit has not increased nearly as much as the price; earnings for baccalaureate degree holders have remained steady.

Institutions have invested significantly in student aid to help keep college affordable. In fact, institutional expenditures to pay for more grant assistance have been one of the largest cost increases in higher education. Many more funding options are available to ensure that cash is available to pay for college as well, through increased borrowing and repayment options. And families are being encouraged to save money for college, through tuition prepayment, savings plans, and federal tax changes that have increased the attractiveness of those options. Efforts to increase public awareness about ways to pay for college, and about the real facts of college affordability, are underway, designed to address negative and frequently inaccurate public perceptions about college prices.

Because of the necessity to find cost savings, spending on instruction in most types of institutions has not kept pace with spending in other categories, notably research and public service. At the same time, institutions are becoming more entrepreneurial in finding new revenue sources, not just from tuitions but from private and philanthropic sources. The combination means a more fragmented revenue base, with less institutional activity directly associated with instruction.

Much of the response to rising prices from both national and state policymakers has been focused on efforts to increase financial options to help students meet the higher prices, and to improve public information about college prices. Neither of these responses are intended to actually reduce the price of college. At the institutional level, institutions are engaged in widespread cost cutting efforts, including some recent efforts to address both productivity and costs. These cost cutting and productivity efforts hold the most promise to reduce the tuition increases by holding down costs. They also risk further cuts in funding for instruction, simply because it is a core function of most institutions. But most important, because a root cause of the tuition problem is the role of public revenues, the problem can't be solved through cost cutting or even increased productivity alone. These steps have to be part of a comprehensive institutional response to the tuition problem, including attention to the revenue side.

There has not been a systematic restructuring of tuition price structures as part of the public policy response to higher prices. There is also a huge gap in most states between the stated tuition policies and the policies that are enforced through the state budget and funding practices. Most state tuition policies are designed as revenue policies more than as pricing strategies. Price structures have not been recalibrated to reflect the new revenue realities. To the contrary, the stated tuition policy for most public institutions is that tuitions should be kept as low as possible—a pretense that is in sharp contrast to the *de facto* policy that tuitions can increase when state revenues decline. Because the policies are not acknowledged, tuition charges go up and down in a boom and bust phenomenon, without a restructuring of price structures to better reflect costs or student ability to pay. Serious attention is simply not paid to the relation between price and cost, and to where public subsidies are being put both at the institutional level and across all of higher education. Pricing policies are based on spending, rather than on internal costs or expenditure patterns. What that means is that as spending increases, tuition increases. The general inattention to the distribution of public subsidies and program costs also masks important funding patterns across institutions, where the student share of costs is highest in the baccalaureate institutions, and lowest at the research universities.

While inattention to tuition policies and price structures may have contributed to the problem, they clearly have not been the primary cause of it. A more prominent reason is that rising tuition, particularly in the public sector, is the consequence of *de facto* state budget policies that have acknowledged that tuitions can increase, and the path of least resistance for both state decision-makers and institutional leaders has been to let the role of public revenues decline, and the tuitions to rise. The diminishing role of state funding in turn has led to increased competition for private resources between the public and private sector, which then has led to greater spending.

Rising college prices are the biggest single threat to public and political support for higher education. State and federal policymakers have been active co-contributors (along with institutional leaders) to the increase in college tuitions, because they believe that higher education can afford to take cuts in public revenues by making up revenue losses in increased tuitions, and through increases in financial aid. At the same time, the pretense that college tuitions are still "low" is maintained in policies and political habits that thwart efforts to restructure prices and manage costs.

The booming economy of the 1990s has meant that state higher education budgets are once again in a growth mode. As a result, the rate of tuition increases has slowed, and some states have even tried to roll back tuitions. The commitment to maintain tuitions with no more increases has become a popular political slogan among governors across the nation. But the new public funding is unfortunately not due to a changed budgetary position for higher education. Both at the federal and state level, higher education remains caught in the discretionary budget squeeze, with budgets unlikely to grow to accommodate both workload and inflationary increases over the next decade. Because times are good, pressure is on once again to cut taxes; in 1997–98, there were more tax cut initiatives being considered at the state legislative level than any time since the late 1970s. When the economy slows, as it inevitably will, tuition increases once again by default will become the primary backup revenue source. Institutions will then be back in the budget position they were in the late 1980s, with a low tuition base and the declining role of public revenues.

Recommendations for Institutions and States

It is not inevitable that tuitions must continue to increase as they have in the past. Steps can be taken to ensure that college remains affordable, and to stabilize funding to protect access and quality for future generations that is at least equivalent to what it has been in the past. But to do that, steps have to be taken to change the political and policy context within which tuition decisions are made—both within the institutions and at the state policy level. In the final analysis, the tuition puzzle is also a political and policy puzzle, caused by the gradual disinvestment in higher education as a public good, and exaggerated by the culture and spending habits within higher education. Solving the puzzle requires multi-pronged strategies that address both the internal habits of the academy and the external political culture surrounding it. Such efforts will require new kinds of advocacy from higher education, including not just better public relations but evidence that resources that are invested in the academy are used in a manner consistent with public priorities. It will also require attention to the public policies surrounding higher education finance, and the consequences of an increasingly privatized system of finance on educational opportunity and quality for future generations.

Recommendations for States

The single pressure point most likely to be helpful in addressing rising prices is changed tuition policies at the state level, which are designed to address both the internal practices of higher education and the state political and budget environment in which tuition decisions are made. Specific suggestions include:

- State budget practices and tuition policies need to be rewritten, to be realistic and mutually reinforcing. In states where tuitions are increasing rapidly but are still characterized by policymakers as low, this pretense should be scrapped in favor of realistic price structures that permit moderate increases but keep college affordable. Policies should be set so that tuitions increase at rates no greater than per capita personal income annually. State leaders also should support institutional efforts to control prices through state budget policies that encourage such efforts.

- State policy leaders should examine the match between public subsidies and private resources across all of higher education to ensure that state funds are being spent consistently with public priorities. Evidence about how resources are spent by revenue source and budget category should be developed for all public institutions, and for state-supported student aid at private institutions. The basic structure of prices for all three public sectors should be reevaluated using cost and revenue data, and restructured when necessary to ensure that the student share of costs is highest at the graduate and professional levels, and lowest at lower division levels.

- The role of financial aid in maintaining economic access to higher education should be protected through a reevaluation and (if necessary) a realignment of state aid programs, including policies about funding sources for institutional aid in the public sector. The realignment of student aid should also include a fresh look at the relation between public and private sector prices, and goals should be set for the ideal tuition "gap" that should be permitted in order to encourage choice as well as access.

- State policy leaders should set the goal that higher education's share of general revenues will not continue to decline, unless there is evidence that the continued investment in higher education is no longer a priority.

Recommendations for Institutions

Institutions of higher education, both public and private, must take steps to address rising tuitions and restore public and policymaker confidence. Specific suggestions to accomplish these objectives include:

- The role of tuition revenue in institutional planning and budgeting must be changed. Rather than building the budgets by first developing resource needs for access and quality, and then generating revenue to match, institutions should move away from cost-plus pricing to value-based pricing. Tuition limits should be set first, and then plans for raising revenue from other sources and for institutional needs should follow.

- Price structures should be reviewed and, if necessary, realigned. Greater differentiation among prices by level of instruction and program should be permitted. Higher tuitions at the graduate and professional levels, in particular, should be encouraged, and/or costs for these programs reduced, to protect public subsidies for undergraduate education.

- Instruction should be protected at the same time that costs are cut and productivity increased. Attention to the quality of teaching and learning must be maintained as a priority. Analyses and action plans should be undertaken to ensure that lower rates of growth in spending for instruction relative to other spending categories do not contribute to lower quality or effectiveness. Plans for cost savings in some areas should be accompanied by plans to reinvest in other priorities.

- Academic and program planning must be integrated with long-term resource planning, and not maintained as essentially separate efforts within the institutions. Institutions need to develop realistic projections of long-term enrollments matched to scenarios of what can be accomplished at different revenue levels, and then make difficult decisions about focus, program, and priority. Faculty need to be better informed about the costs of programs, and the consequences of choices about future priorities.

- Institutions must take responsibility for strengthening their capacity to define the terms of public accountability that they are prepared to meet.

Suggestions for Future Research

The analyses in this report suggest that there is a complex array of explanations, causes, and consequences of rising tuitions which are unlikely to be changed through existing policy structures or by the market. The consequences of this tuition puzzle are greater economic and sectoral stratification within higher education,

combined with the continued erosion of public and political support for higher education.

While more successful policy models might be found to turn the price spiral around, this is unlikely to happen until greater consensus develops about the size, cause, and long-term consequences of rising college tuition. At the moment, this consensus frankly does not exist. To the contrary, the unspoken acknowledgment seems to be that it is inevitable that tuition will increase, and that higher prices can be accommodated without fundamentally hurting the purposes or quality of higher education. The inferences we have drawn from these analyses suggest that this view is basically incorrect—the problem has long-term consequences that potentially are extremely harmful to the purposes of higher education. However, the connections we have drawn between problem, cause, consequence, and solution clearly need further exploration. Additional attention needs to be paid in particular to the implications of this analysis for future policy interventions, at the national/federal levels as well as by states and institutions. The consequences of these trends on educational quality need more careful study and attention.

The following areas are the highest priorities for more research:

1. **Price elasticity.** Most of the research on student price response is more than 20 years old. The current recruitment environment enables students to get better information about college prices than was generally the case in the late 1970s, and there are more funding options available. New research is needed about how students in the current environment react to prices and aid, by income level and sector.

2. **The role of prepaid tuition and college saving plans.** Prepaid tuition and college saving plans are spreading, but little is known about how they will affect college-going decisions and prices. More and more families are using these plans. As these individuals show up ready to be enrolled, the guarantee provided by states could create a financial liability that they are unable to meet. This could result in higher prices in some cases. Further, because of the enrollment limi-

tations placed on students participating in most plans, student choice about where to go to college also could be affected.

3. **Matching resources with quality.** There has been a good deal of attention to strengthening institutional effectiveness through assessment of student learning outcomes. The accountability agenda now in place in many states emphasizes "outcomes" and student learning. Yet the relationship of resources to quality—not as a substitute measure, but as a legitimate dimension of quality—appears to have evaporated from the assessment agenda. Measurement of costs as one element of institutional assessment has to be put squarely back on the assessment and accountability agenda.

4. **Measurement of costs.** Despite the fact that many states have policies based in part on internal costs, there is relatively little attention to cost measurement, and to public clarity about cost and subsidy patterns within institutions and across sectors. The issue of cost measurement becomes particularly murky when applied to graduate education, where the question of how to account for both direct and indirect research costs is challenging methodologically and politically. For these reasons, national data on the relative cost of graduate education in contrast to undergraduate education is extremely hard to obtain.

   The problem of cost measurement is not primarily a methodological one. Costing methodologies exist that would allow institutions to measure costs while maintaining flexibility in institutional decisions about how to apply the methodology. But the culture of the academy has been to resist cost measurement and to portray public communication about costs as both technically impossible and politically dangerous. Attention needs to be paid to new approaches to cost measurement, not just from the business and finance community, but from the academic side of the institution. As one part of this, analysis of costs and subsidies should be

made part of the assessment agenda within the academy.

5. **The role of colleges in the higher education continuum.** One of the most disturbing conclusions of this research is that the pricing and subsidy patterns may be pushing students toward research institutions on one hand and community colleges on the other. The evidence shows that there has been an incremental shift away from community colleges by middle- and upper-income students and toward research institutions by the richest students. Low-income students—who are more "price responsive"—have largely remained concentrated in public two- and four-year institutions. The enrollment shifts mean that higher education is at risk of becoming more economically stratified by sector at the end of the 1990s than any time in the previous two decades. Without denigrating the quality or capacity of either of these sectors, the erosion of the middle—traditional baccalaureate level education—may have serious negative consequences for higher education. Much more needs to be known about what is happening, and why.

6. **The role of distance learning.** The research that has been conducted to date is overwhelmingly focused on conventional higher education; the emerging role of proprietary institutions, as well as of distance-delivered higher education, have not yet been integrated into the research literature. It is possible that the analysis of the whole puzzle might change slightly if those additional pieces were better understood. The extent to which distance learning can provide access at lower cost and comparable quality is particularly important to understand.

NOTES

1. In this analysis, tuition includes tuition and fees unless otherwise noted.
2. The net price referred to in this analysis is net price (grants).
3. Research conducted by colleges in California has shown that the enrollment losses occur

when tuition spikes, but that the students tend to return in subsequent semesters or future years. (Unpublished research conducted by the Los Rios Community College District, and the Los Angeles Community College District, cited in CPEC, 1990.) This research suggests that if tuition increases are moderate and predictable, then students can plan to meet them and the negative enrollment consequences can be lessened.

REFERENCES

American Council on Education (ACE). (1998a). *Research on public perceptions of college costs and student aid.* Washington, DC: ACE.

_____. (1998b). "College is possible: Myths and realities about paying for college." From the College is Possible website (www.collegeispossible. org).

Burd, Stephen. (1998.) Riley urges colleges not to raise tuition or lower aid in response to tax credits. *Chronicle of higher education.* December 18.

California Postsecondary Education Commission (CPEC). (1990*). Technical background papers.* Prepared for the Higher Education at the Crossroads report. Sacramento, CA: CPEC.

Carnegie Commission on Higher Education. (1973*). Higher education: Who pays? Who benefits? Who should pay?* New York, NY: McGraw Hill.

CPEC. See: California Postsecondary Education Commission.

Davis, Jerry. (1997). *College affordability: A closer look at the crisis.* Washington, DC: Sallie Mae Education Institute.

Education Commission of the States (ECS). (1998). *Survey of perceptions of state leaders.* Denver, CO: ECS.

Fischer, Fred. (1990). State financing of higher education: A new look at an old problem. *Change.* January/February.

GAO. See: U.S. General Accounting Office.

Hansen, W. and B. Weisbrod, (1969). *Benefits, costs, and finance of public higher education.* Chicago: Markham Publishing Company.

Hauptman, Arthur, & Cathy Krop. (1998). Federal student aid and the growth in college costs and tuitions: Examining the relationship. In *National commission on the cost of higher education,* (1998), pp. 70–83.

Heller, Donald E. (1997). Student price response in higher education: An update to Leslie and Brinkman. *The journal of higher education.* Vol. 68, No. 6 (Nov/Dec.), pp. 624–659.

Immerwahr, John. (1993*). The closing gateway: Californians consider their higher education system.* With John Farkas. San Jose, CA: The Public Agenda Foundation and the California Higher Education Policy Center.

_____. (1998). *The price of admission: The growing importance of higher education: A national survey of Americans' views.* San Jose, CA: The National Center for Public Policy and Higher Education, Spring.

Johnstone, D. Bruce. (1993). *Learning productivity: A new imperative for American higher education.* Albany NY: State University of New York (SUNY).

Johnstone, D. Bruce and Patricia Maloney. (1998). Enhancing the productivity of learning: curricular implications. In Groccia & Miller. (Eds.). *Productivity in higher education.* San Francisco, CA: Jossey Bass.

Lenth, Charles S. (1993). *The tuition dilemma: State policies and practices in pricing public higher education.* Denver, CO: The State Higher Education Executive Officers (SHEEO), December.

Massy William F. (1997). Remarks on restructuring higher education. In *National commission on the cost of higher education,* 1998, pp. 84–91.

McDonald, Sheila. (1995). *Tuition payment plans. The dilemma for colleges and universities: Internal vs. external administration.* Newport, RI: Tuition management Systems, Inc.

McPherson, Michael & Morton Schapiro. (1998). *The student aid game.* Princeton, NJ: Princeton University Press.

Minnesota Higher Education Coordinating Board. (1994). *The design for shared responsibility and the result of its implementation.* Minneapolis, MN: Minnesota Higher Education Coordinating Board.

National Association of College and University Business Officers (NACUBO). (1997). *Payment and pricing practices, results of a national survey.* From the NACUBO website (www.nacubo.org).

National Association of State Budget Officers (NASBO). (1998). *1997 state expenditure report: Executive summary.* Washington, DC: NASBO, May.

National Commission on the Cost of Higher Education. (1998). *Straight talk about college costs and prices.* Phoenix, AZ: Oryx Press.

NCES. See: U.S. Department of Education. National Center for Education Statistics.

Olivas, Michael. (1993). *Prepaid college tuition plans: Promises and problems.* New York: The College Board.

Roherty Brian. (1997). The price of passive resistance in financing higher education. In Callan & Finney. (Eds.). *Public and private financing of higher education: Shaping public policy for the future.* Phoenix, AZ: Oryx Press.

U.S. Bureau of the Census. (1997a.) Selected per capita income and product items in current and real (1992) dollars. Table No. 722. *Statistical Abstract of the United States.* From the Census website (www.census.gov/statab/freq/98s0722.txt).

_____. (1997b). Table F-3: Mean income received by each fifth and top five percent of families: 1966 to 1997. *Current population survey data.* From the Census website (www.census.gov/hhes/income/histinc/f03.html).

_____. (1998). Table F-3: Mean earnings of workers 18 years old and over, by educational attainment, by race, Hispanic origin, and gender: 1975 to 1997. *Current population survey* data. From the Census website (www.census.gov).

U.S. Bureau of Labor Statistics (BLS). (1997) College enrollment and work activity of 1997 high school graduates. Supplement to *Current population survey, 1997*. From the BLS website (www.bls.gov).

U.S. Department of Education. National Center for Education Statistics (NCES). (1990). National Postsecondary Student Aid Study, 1990 (NPSAS: 90). Data Analysis System.

_____. (1996). *National postsecondary student aid study, 1996* (NPSAS: 96). Data Analysis System.

_____. (1997). *Digest of education statistics*. Washington, DC: U.S. Government Printing Office.

_____. (1998). *The condition of education*. Washington, DC: U.S. Government Printing Office.

U.S. General Accounting Office (GAO). (1998). *Tuition increases and colleges' efforts to contain costs.* HEHS98–227. Washington, DC: U.S. Government Printing Office.

Washington Higher Education Coordinating Board. (1998). *A national comparison: tuition and required fees.* Olympia, WA: Washington Higher Education Coordinating Board.

Wingspread Group on Higher Education. (1993). *An American imperative: Higher expectations for higher education. An open letter to those concerned about the American future.* Racine, WI: The Wingspread Group.

Zemsky Robert & William Massy. (1990). The lattice and the ratchet. *Policy perspectives*. (A publication of the Pew Higher Education Research Program, Philadelphia, PA). Vol. 2, No. 4 (June).

Zucker, Brian. 1998. The hope tax credit and implications for tuition and financial aid. Unpublished memo prepared for the University of North Carolina General Administration. Chapel Hill, NC.

CHAPTER 5

THE RETURNS TO INDIVIDUAL AND COLLEGE CHARACTERISTICS

Evidence from the National Longitudinal Survey of Youth

JAMES MONKS

There is growing interest in the heterogeneity of earnings among college graduates. This study examines earnings differentials across both individual and institutional characteristics. Using data from the National Longitudinal Survey of Youth, it can be seen that graduates from highly or most selective colleges and universities earn significantly more than graduates from less selective institutions. Additionally, graduates from graduate degree granting and research universities, and private universities earn more than their counterparts from liberal arts colleges and public institutions. There is, however, variation across racial and gender groups in the returns to individual and college characteristics. These findings are important in an educational environment where the (market) value of a liberal arts education is under scrutiny, and where the higher costs of private versus public colleges and universities are being questioned.

1. INTRODUCTION

The vast majority of the economics literature on the returns to a college degree has emphasized the level of education in enhancing earnings ability. The first generation of the literature focused on quantifying the returns to an additional year of school or on the diploma effects of receiving one's degree. More recently, researchers have begun to address the full breadth of college experiences and to explore heterogeneity in the returns to education. In particular, there has been a growing interest in the returns to both individual and institutional characteristics.

The existing literature tends to only control for a limited number of college quality or selectivity measures (Bok & Bowen, 1998; Dowd, 1998; Davies & Guppy, 1997; Behrman, Constantine, Kletzer, McPherson & Schapiro, 1996a; Behrman, Rosenzweig & Taubman, 1996b; Brewer & Ehrenberg, 1996; Brewer, Eide & Ehrenberg, 1996; Daniel, Black & Smith, 1995; Loury & Garman, 1995; Fox, 1993; James & Alsalam, 1993; Litten & Smith, 1993; Rumberger & Thomas, 1993; James, Alsalam, Conaty & To, 1989). To my knowledge no study examines the earnings of liberal arts college graduates relative to graduates from larger research-oriented institutions, conditional on individual and institutional quality and control. This study examines the impact of selectivity, control, and college type on earnings. I limit the analysis to these institutional characteristics because these are the institutional qualities that are most visible to prospective students and employers.

Source: *Economics of Education Review* 19 Issue 3, (June 2000) pp. 279–289.

This study examines the returns to college quality conditional on public versus private control and on the Carnegie classification of the institution. In addition, individual ability measures and labor market experiences, including Armed Forces Qualifications Test (AFQT) score (as a measure of academic ability and preparation), experience, tenure, race, gender, industry and occupation, are also controlled for. By using the National Longitudinal Survey of Youth (NLSY) to match individuals and institutions I am able to estimate the impact of college quality on the log of hourly wages, within institutional type and conditional upon individual characteristics. Conversely, I am able to estimate the returns to other institutional characteristics conditional upon quality. This is especially important in an educational environment where the (market) value of a liberal arts education is under scrutiny, and where the higher costs of private versus public colleges and universities are being questioned (McPherson & Schapiro, 1991).

I find strong evidence of higher earnings among the graduates of more selective institutions. There is also evidence of a premium for attending a larger graduate degree granting university, rather than a liberal arts college, and weak evidence that graduates of private institutions earn more than graduates of public institutions. While this pattern of returns to institutional characteristics holds for most groups, there is heterogeneity in the magnitude of the returns to institutional attributes based on race and gender. For example, it appears that males receive a higher return to attending a graduate degree granting university and a private institution than females; in contrast, there does not appear to be a significant difference in the earnings of non-white college graduates from public versus private institutions, while whites are penalized by the market for attending a public college or university. Additionally, non-whites from a highly or most selective institution earn a much higher premium than their white counterparts.

The remainder of the article is divided into four main topics. The next section outlines the sample chosen and constructed for this study. This is followed by a description of the underlying economic model and econometric methodology used to estimate the earnings across college characteristics. The next section presents the results of the regression analyses, and the final section summarizes these results.

2. DATA

This study utilizes the National Longitudinal Survey of Youth. The NLSY is a survey of individuals from 1979 to 1996.[1] The respondents were aged between 14 and 22 at the beginning of the survey, in 1979, and aged between 28 and 36 in 1993. This data set is particularly useful for this study since it tracks college-aged individuals through their college years and into their early labor market experiences.

This paper exploits the Federal Interagency Committee on Education (FICE) codes reported by NLSY respondents for each spell of college attendance. Beginning in 1984, the NLSY asked each respondent who reported attending a college or university the name of the three most recent colleges attended and the dates they attended each institution. These responses were then recorded using the college or university's FICE code. Additionally, each respondent was asked their highest degree received and the date they received this degree. By matching the date they received their baccalaureate degree to the college spell information I was able, in most cases, to determine the FICE code of the respondent's baccalaureate degree granting institution.

Respondents from the military and disadvantaged white subsample were excluded from the sample used in this study (Table 5.1). Those respondents who had not completed 16 years of schooling by 1993, the survey's end at the time of writing, were also excluded from the sample. In some cases (452 respondents) the date that the respondent received his baccalaureate degree could not be determined either because it was simply not reported or because by the 1988 survey, when the NLSY first asked the respondent's highest degree ever received, the respondent had earned a masters degree or higher so the date of the baccalaureate degree was never reported. For 52 of the respondents, the NLSY staff could not find a FICE code to coincide with the reported college or university. An additional 224 individuals were excluded from the sample because their reported FICE code could not accurately be matched to the data sets discussed below to extract the institutional characteristics.

TABLE 5.1
Sample Construction

	Number of Persons	Number of Person-years
Total NLSY sample	12,686	
Less the military subsample	– 1280	
Less the poor white subsample	– 1643	
Less highest grade completed < 16	– 7945	
Less college graduation date unknown	– 452	
Less college FICE code unknown	– 52	
Less non-matching or two year FICE code	– 224	
Chosen respondents	1087	9348
Less employment status recode not working	– 29	– 1865
Less rate of pay less than $2.93 or more than $500	– 6	– 409
Less unreported industry or occupation	0	– 6
Less highest grade completed > 16 by 1993	– 315	– 2002
Less incomplete work history	– 3	– 89
Sample chosen	734	4977

The reported FICE code of each college graduate from the selected sample from the NLSY was matched to the Computer Aided Science Policy Analysis and Research (CASPAR) database developed by Quantum Research Corporation for the National Science Foundation (NSF). The CASPAR database is a compilation of data from surveys of universities and colleges conducted by the NSF Division of Science and Resources Studies. The control of the institution (public or private) and the Carnegie classification (2-year, liberal arts, masters, doctoral, research or specialized) were identified by matching the NLSY reported FICE code to this database. The measure of college quality used in this study was taken from *Barron's Profiles of American Colleges* (Anon, 1987). Barron's reports a single summary measure of selectivity (non-competitive, less competitive, competitive, very competitive, highly competitive and most competitive) based on the entering class's SAT and ACT scores, class rank, high school grade point average, and the percentage of applicants who were accepted. The 1987 Barron's selectivity ranking is used since it falls roughly into the middle of the survey years, and there is evidence of a high degree of correlation across time in the selectivity ranking of colleges and universities (Kingston & Smart, 1990). There is also evidence to suggest that a categorical measure of college quality is preferable to a linear measure in estimating the returns to education (Kingston &

Smart, 1990). In some of the cases, the reported FICE code could not be matched to the CASPAR database or to the Barron's Profile because the reported college was a single university branch and the NSF or Barron's reporting unit was the entire university system, or vice versa. There were also observations where the reported baccalaureate granting institution was a 2-year college. The observations where these discrepancies occurred were excluded from the sample.

The sample resulting from the above restrictions contained 1087 individuals and 9348 person-year observations. Only those person-year observations following the individual's graduation from college were included in the sample. This sample was limited further to those observations where the primary activity was working; the hourly rate of pay was greater than or equal to $2.93 or less than $500; valid industry and occupation were reported; and a complete work history of experience and tenure were reported.[2] The sample was also restricted to those individuals whose highest grade completed was 16 by 1993. This focuses the investigation on earnings differentials among working college graduates who do not continue their education (by 1993) and does not address possible returns to college characteristics that may arise due to increases in the probability of achieving a graduate degree or to possible increases in employment probabilities. The chosen sample has 734 individuals,

TABLE 5.2
Comparison of NLSY to *Digest of Education Statistics* and
***Barron's Profiles of American Colleges* Summary Statistics**

Individuals: (n = 734)	NLSY	DES
Percent male	48%	49%[a]
Percent white	72%	85%[a,b]
Average age adjusted AFQT score	1.73	NA
Percent attended non or less competitive	27%	NA
Percent attended competitive	45%	NA
Percent attended very competitive	21%	NA
Percent attended highly or most competitive	6%	NA
Percent attended liberal arts colleges	22%	16%[c]
Percent attended masters, doctoral or research universities	77%	83%[c]
Percent attended public institutions	63%	67%[c]

College and universities: (n = 407)	NLSY	Barron's and DES
Percent non or less competitive	27%	33%
Percent competitive	44%	48%
Percent very competitive	20%	12%
Percent highly or most competitive	8%	7%
Percent liberal arts colleges	28%	35%[d]
Percent masters, doctoral and research universities	69%	64%[d]
Percent public institutions	52%	28%[d]

a   Percent of bachelor's degrees awarded by characteristic in the 1984–1985 academic year.
b   Percent of bachelor's degrees awarded to individuals who were white, non-Hispanic.
c   Percent of individuals enrolled in 1985 by type of institution.
d   Percent of institutions by type and control from the DES, for 1985–1986.

407 colleges and universities, and 4977 person-year observations.

The NLSY has a lower rate of college attendance and graduation than the population at large because it oversamples blacks and Hispanics who tend to have lower enrollment rates than whites. These over-represented subsamples were included in this study in order to more efficiently estimate the returns to both individual and institutional characteristics across racial groups. Because of the large number of respondents excluded from the sample, a close examination of the remaining respondents is warranted. Table 5.2 compares summary measures of the respondents and colleges from the sample chosen from the NLSY to the *Digest of Education Statistics* (DES) (US Department of Education, 1984–1986) and Barron's Profiles summary measures.

A strict comparison of the respondents from the NLSY sample to the DES is not possible because the NLSY is a sample of college gradu-

ates currently working and the DES is a survey of either current college graduates or enrollees. However, comparisons of these two groups would likely reveal any gross misrepresentation of the population of college graduates in the NLSY. The amount of males in the NLSY is 48%, in comparison to 49% in the DES.[3] The NLSY does have a much lower percentage of white college graduates, 72%, than the DES, 85%. This is likely to be attributable to the oversampling discussed above and will be addressed in the following empirical tests. Because of the relatively small number of respondents who attended both non-competitive and most competitive institutions these categories were combined with less competitive and highly competitive, respectively. This increases the frequency of each cell count and improves the efficiency of the estimated returns to these categories. There appears to be sufficient variation in the percentage of individuals who attended each category of college selectivity. The sample from the NLSY

TABLE 5.3
Summary Measures

Variable	Mean	Standard Deviation	Minimum	Maximum
Experience (weeks/52)	7.79	3.34	0.38	18.46
Tenure (weeks/52)	3.04	2.82	0.02	16.50
Male	0.51	0.50	0.00	1.00
White	0.80	0.40	0.00	1.00
Armed Forces Qualification Test	1.75	0.59	0.03	3.09
Public institution	0.63	0.48	0.00	1.00
Masters, doctoral or research university	0.76	0.43	0.00	1.00
Specialized institutions	0.01	0.08	0.00	1.00
Non or less competitive	0.27	0.44	0.00	1.00
Competitive	0.45	0.50	0.00	1.00
Very competitive	0.21	0.41	0.00	1.00
Highly or most competitive	0.06	0.24	0.00	1.00
1979 net family income (in $10K)	2.55	1.46	0.00	7.50
1979 net family income missing	0.22	0.42	0.00	1.00
Log hourly wage	2.18	0.47	1.08	6.08
Year	88.48	3.17	79.00	93.00
Number of person-year observations	4977			

seems to have a higher percentage of liberal arts college graduates, 22%, than the DES, 16%. This may be because the NLSY is composed of college graduates and the DES measures college attendees. If liberal arts colleges have higher graduation rates then we ought to expect a higher percentage of college graduates attended liberal arts colleges than are currently enrolled. Sixty-three percent of the NLSY sample attended a public institution and the DES reports a comparable 67% of enrollees at public institutions. In summary, it appears that the sample of individuals from the NLSY is comparable to the population of college students, with the noted exception of race.

A word of caution is necessary in comparing the NLSY sample of colleges to Barron's and the DES. The NLSY is a number of graduates weighted sample of colleges. The probability of observing a college is directly proportional to the number of graduates from that college relative to the population of college graduates. It is therefore to be expected that the sample of institutions from the NLSY will favor large, public, graduate degree granting institutions relative to the cross-section of all colleges and universities. This comparison is made simply to determine whether there is adequate variation in the number of each type of institution in the sample so that I am not inadvertently estimating returns

to individual colleges rather than college characteristics. There appears to be a sufficient number of colleges in each category of selectivity, Carnegie classification and control in order to draw inferences concerning earnings differentials across these characteristics.

In addition to the institutional characteristics, I have controlled for individual attributes which determine wages. In particular, I control for actual work experience since the age of 18 (weeks of work divided by 52), and its square, and tenure (weeks at current employer divided by 52), and its square. This accounts for differences in pre- and post-college work experience and subsequent on-the-job human capital accumulation. A respondent's AFQT score is used to control for differences in individual academic ability. Since the Armed Services Vocational Aptitude Battery (ASVAB) of tests used in the construction of the AFQT score were given at a single point in time, differences in results may arise due to differences in the ages of the sample and not necessarily because of differences in academic ability. This problem is minimized by calculating the ratio of each person's test score to the average test score for his or her age. Finally, the 1979 net family income is used as a control for an individual's ability to pay.[4] Table 5.3 provides means, standard deviations, minimums and maximums for all of the variables for the entire sample.

3. MODEL

This section focuses on the underlying economic model and methodology used to estimate the earnings differentials across institutional characteristics conditional upon individual traits and labor market experiences. Properly controlling for relevant individual attributes and a number of college characteristics enhances the understanding of variation in earnings across specific college characteristics. The process underlying the human capital investment decision to enroll in a particular college is one which relates wages to human capital such as experience, tenure, and individual and institutional characteristics.

Institutional characteristics may influence earnings conditional on individual characteristics for a number of reasons. First, institutions may facilitate the accumulation of human capital at different rates. For example, if there are peer effects, then attending a selective institution where one is surrounded by bright students may increase human capital accumulation. Similarly, if the instructional quality is better at private institutions, then graduates of private colleges and universities may have greater human capital. Classroom dynamics and overall curricular design may also be important in the production function of human capital. If this is true, then graduates of different types of institutions may have accumulated different levels of human capital. A second reason why institutional characteristics may influence earnings separately from individual characteristics is that employers may identify institutional attributes as a signal of ability. This may especially be the case if institutional characteristics are more visible than individual ability measures.

The human capital and signaling explanations for the potential importance of institutional characteristics in determining earnings are not mutually exclusive. It may be that graduates of certain types of institutions earn more because of both human capital and signaling. In either case, individuals attempting to maximize the net present value of lifetime wealth would attempt to enroll in those institutions whose graduates earn a premium.

Further compounding the college choice decision is that (most) institutions are selective to some degree in their admissions processes. So not only do individuals choose institutions based on future earnings and costs, but institutions choose individuals based on individual characteristics, such as academic ability, and in some cases ability to pay. As a result, an individual's academic ability and financial resources are primary determinants in the college matriculation process.

A reduced-form equation relating the log of wages at time t, for individual i, who attended institution j, as a function of individual and institutional characteristics is:

$$\text{In} \quad W_{ijt} = X_{0it}\beta_1 + X_{il}\beta_2 + Q_j\beta_3 + \delta_i + \varepsilon_{ijt} \quad (1)$$

where $\text{In } W_{ijt}$, is the log of hourly wages; X_{0it} are individual time varying labor market experiences; X_{0il} are nontime-varying individual characteristics which influence earnings; Q_j are college characteristics; δ_i is a normally distributed individual specific error component; and ε_{ijt} is a normally distributed random error. Estimation of Eq. (1) will result in biased estimates of the returns to institutional characteristics because it does not account for the selection process by individuals and institutions in the enrollment process.

Individuals are clearly not randomly allocated to different institutions and institutional types. They are both chosen by the institution and choose the institution themselves. Accounting for this selection process is at best difficult and problematic. Attempting to correct for selection using various estimation techniques relies on assumptions which may act to exacerbate the problem. For example, Brewer et al. use multinomial logit to estimate the institutional type chosen. This approach becomes complicated as the number of institutional characteristics are increased, and it also assumes the independence of irrelevant alternatives, which is not likely to be the case in choosing which college to attend. Additionally, the instrumental variable estimation approach followed by Behrman et al. (1996a) works well when there are few variables to instrument, but when the number of college characteristics increases this approach too becomes problematic.

Because I include a number of institutional characteristics among the regressors, I am unable to use either a multinomial logit correction or instrumental variables. As a result, I attempt to control for the college selection process in the least restrictive means possible by including among the regressors individual attributes which influence the enrollment process. Because academic ability and ability to pay are primary determinants in the college selection process, I include among the regressors of Eq. (1) one's AFQT score and 1979 net family income. In as much as AFQT score and family income are controls which may not fully capture the endogeneity of the institutional characteristics, the resulting estimates of the coefficients on the institutional characteristics may be biased. One should not interpret the coefficients on the institutional characteristics as a true return to these characteristics in the sense of what an individual randomly assigned to this institution could expect to receive. Instead these coefficients reflect the average earnings of graduates from institutions of certain types, conditional upon their observable individual characteristics.

The log of hourly wages is first regressed against experience, experience squared, tenure, tenure squared, a male dummy variable and a white dummy variable as a benchmark for the incorporation of individual academic ability measures and college characteristics. This specification is then expanded to include the additional college selectivity, control, classification dummies and AFQT score, and then the respondent's 1979 net family income. All specifications are estimated using generalized least squares to control for heteroskedasticity introduced to the disturbance structure from the individual specific error component.

Additionally, a number of previous analyses have found significant differences across demographic groups in the returns to education (Bok & Bowen, 1998; Cohn & Addison, 1998; Cooper & Cohn, 1997; Behrman et al., 1996a; Loury & Garman, 1995; Card & Krueger, 1992). I allow for varying coefficients across demographic groups by performing separate regression analyses by race and gender. Most other studies of the returns to institutional attributes ignore possible differences across demographic groups in the impact of college characteristics on labor market outcomes. Because labor market and higher education opportunities may differ across these groups, the returns to these opportunities may differ as

well. If the accumulation of human capital varies across certain groups within an institution, perhaps due to peer effects or the classroom dynamics of race and gender, then the earnings of graduates of certain institutional types may vary across these groups. Bok and Bowen (1998) found that black students at selective institutions "under-performed" relative to what would be predicted based on their standardized test scores.[5] Therefore standardized test scores may not accurately control for systematic differences across groups of students in academic performance while in college, and the returns to institutional characteristics may vary across demographic groups as a result. It may also be the case that race and gender may interact with institutional characteristics in forming a signal to employers of ability. Additionally, Kolpin and Singell (1997) show that in the presence of affirmative action, individuals from a preferred group may receive different rates of return to their individual and institutional characteristics.

While a complete test of these hypotheses is beyond the scope of this study, I allow for possible variation in the returns to individual and institutional characteristics by estimating separate regressions for males and females, and whites and non-whites. Chow tests are performed to test for the existence of significant variation in the coefficients across gender and racial groups.

4. RESULTS

I begin by regressing the log of hourly wages against experience, experience squared, tenure, tenure squared, a dummy if the individual is male and a dummy if the individual is white.[6] There are the usual concave increases in log wages over experience and tenure. Males earn significantly higher earnings than females, and there appears to be no significant difference in earnings among white and non-white college graduates. These results are presented in specification 1 of Table 5.4.

Including AFQT scores, institutional characteristics, and industry and occupation dummies (results not shown for industry and occupation) among the regressors, specification 2 of Table 5.4 does not significantly change the quadratic returns to experience

TABLE 5.4
Returns to College Characteristics. Dependent Variable: Log Hourly Wages.

	Specification 1	Specification 2	Specification 3
Intercept	1.533***	1.295***	1.242***
	(0.035)	(0.064)	(0.066)
Experience	0.077***	0.071***	0.071 ***
	(0.006)	(0.006)	(0.006)
Experience squared/10	– 0.019***	– 0.017***	– 0.017***
	(0.004)	(0.004)	(0.004)
Tenure	0.037***	0.035***	0.035***
	(0.005)	(0.005)	(0.005)
Tenure squared/10	– 0.025***	– 0.023***	– 0.023***
	(0.005)	(0.005)	(0.005)
Male	0.155***	0.128***	0.131 ***
	(0.026)	(0.022)	(0.022)
White	0.035	– 0.049*	– 0.069*
	(0.029)	(0.029)	(0.030)
Armed Forces Qualification Test		0.111***	0.107***
		(0.022)	(0.022)
Public institution		– 0,045*	– 0.033
		(0.027)	(0.027)
Masters, doctoral or research		0.137***	0.126***
		(0.031)	(0.032)
Specialized institution		0.189**	0.169*
		(0.089)	(0.089)
Non or less competitive		– 0.047*	– 0.042
		(0.028)	(0.028)
Very competitive		0.081***	0.079***
		(0.030)	(0.030)
Highly or most competitive		0.151***	0.131***
		(0.049)	(0.050)
Net family income			0.030***
			(0.008)
Adjusted R-squared	0.86	0.89	0.89
Number of observations	4977	4977	4977

Notes: (1) Standard errors are in parentheses. (2) Specifications 2 and 3 include dummy variables for industry and occupation, and missing AFQT and net family income, not shown. (3) Significant: *** at the 1% level; ** at the 5% level; * at the 10% level.

and tenure, nor the male premium. The sign of the coefficient on the white dummy variable is now negative, and significantly different from zero. The omitted variable in this specification is non-white, female, competitive, private, liberal arts college graduate. There is a positive and significant return to academic ability, as measured by the age-adjusted AFQT score. Additionally, graduates from publicly controlled institutions earned 4.5% less than graduates from privately con-trolled institutions.[7] On the other hand, graduates from graduate degree granting research institutions earned approximately 14% more than graduates from liberal arts colleges.[8] This result is consistent with the findings of Dowd (1998) and Pascarella and Terenzini (1991), both of whom found significant differences across college versus university graduates. Graduates from specialized institutions earned approximately 19% more than liberal arts college graduates.

There is strong evidence of a positive and significant relationship between wages and college quality, as measured by Barron's selectivity measure. Even after conditioning on AFQT score, gender, race, experience, tenure, control of institution, classification of institution, and industry and occupation, graduates from more selective colleges and universities earn more than graduates from less selective institutions. In particular, graduates from non or less competitive institutions earned approximately 5% less than graduates from competitive institutions; graduates from very competitive institutions earned 8% more; graduates from highly or most competitive colleges and universities earned 15% more than competitive college graduates.

Specification 3 of Table 5.4 includes the respondent's 1979 net family income in order to control for differences in familial resources which may influence the college selection process (Loury & Garman, 1995). While net family income appears to have a positive and significant impact on log wages, its inclusion among the regressors does not significantly alter the coefficients on the other individual or institutional characteristics. Individuals from more competitive institutions and larger research institutions earn significantly more than their counterparts from less selective institutions and liberal arts colleges.

A number of alternative specifications were also tested. The college selectivity dummies were interacted with experience to test for differences in the profile of earnings over time by college quality. No significant pattern emerged. Additionally, the AFQT score and college selectivity were interacted to see if individual academic ability and institutional quality were complements. Again, no significant pattern emerged. Finally, both the public control dummy and Carnegie classification dummies were interacted with quality, but neither proved significant.

Table 5.5 presents the results of separate regression analyses by gender. A Chow test that the relationship between log hourly wages and the regressors is the same for males and females fails to reject the null at even the 10% significant level. While the overall returns to institutional characteristics are qualitatively the same for both males and females, there are some noteworthy differences in the magnitude of the

individual effects. Specifically, female graduates of specialized institutions earn significantly more than their male counterparts. On the other hand, while both men and women graduates from graduate degree granting institutions earn more than liberal arts college graduates, males receive a larger premium for attending graduate degree granting and research institutions than females. Females also have a higher return to AFQT score and a larger non-white premium, although these differences are not significantly different from zero.

The final analysis (Table 5.6) examines differences in the returns to individual and institutional characteristics by race. In this case the Chow test rejects the null, at the 1% significance level, that the relationship between log hourly wages and the regressors is the same for whites and non-whites. While the coefficients on institutional quality are not significantly different from zero for non-whites, the magnitude of these effects is larger. In particular, non-white graduates of highly or most competitive institutions earn a larger premium than whites. This result is consistent with earlier studies that explicitly examine returns to institutional quality across racial groups. For example, Behrman et al. (1996a) find greater returns to college quality among non-whites than whites, and Loury and Garman find a larger return to college selectivity among blacks than whites.

The returns to graduating from a masters, doctoral or research university are not substantially different for whites and non-whites. The returns to public institutions are different across racial groups. White graduates of publicly controlled institutions earn significantly less than white graduates of privately controlled institutions, while the earnings of non-white graduates of publicly controlled institutions are not significantly different from the earnings of non-white graduates of private institutions. Additionally, non-white graduates of specialized institutions earn a premium that is not realized by white students.

Studies that fail to adequately address the sometimes substantial differences in the returns to both individual and institutional characteristics across gender and racial groups are obfuscating the true relationship between these interactions. It may be further interesting to perform separate regression analyses within

TABLE 5.5
Returns to College Characteristics. Dependent Variable: Log Hourly Wages.

	Males	*Males*	*Females*	*Females*
Intercept	1.642***	1.324***	1.581***	1.325***
	(0.047)	(0.085)	(0.046)	(0.124)
Experience	0.095***	0.088***	0.057***	0.055***
	(0.009)	(0.009)	(0.009)	(0.009)
Experience squared/10	− 0.030***	− 0.027***	− 0.007	− 0.007
	(0.005)	(0.005)	(0.005)	(0.005)
Tenure	0.026***	0.025***	0.050***	0.047***
	(0.007)	(0.007)	(0.008)	(0.008)
Tenure squared/10	− 0.017***	− 0.014**	− 0.035***	− 0.034***
	(0.006)	(0.006)	(0.008)	(0.008)
White	0.032	− 0.035	0.040	− 0.096**
	(0.040)	(0.039)	(0.040)	(0.045)
Armed Forces Qualification Test		0.079***		0.132***
		(0.029)		(0.032)
Public institution		− 0.054		− 0.021
		(0.037)		(0.039)
Masters, doctoral or research		0.177***		0.081*
		(0.043)		(0.045)
Specialized institution		0.037		0.427***
		(0.105)		(0.158)
Non or less competitive		− 0.050		− 0.032
		(0.038)		(0.039)
Very competitive		0.078*		0.080*
		(0.040)		(0.043)
Highly or most competitive		0.138**		0.139**
		(0.065)		(0.073)
Net family income		0.032***		0.027**
		(0.010)		(0.013)
Chow statistic (df: 34, 4909)		0.35		
Adjusted *R*-squared	0.87	0.91	0.85	0.88
Number of observations	2514	2514	2463	2463

Notes: (1) Standard errors are in parentheses. (2) The second specifications for both males and females include dummy variables for industry and occupation, and missing AFQT and net family income, not shown. (3) Significant: *** at the 1% level; ** at the 5% level; * at the 10% level.

both racial and gender groups, however there were too few observations for non-white females and non-white males.

While the underlying causes of the varying returns to institutional characteristics across demographic groups is beyond the scope of this paper and the limitations of the data set, these results raise important questions concerning the educational experiences on campus of different groups, labor market treatment of different groups from similar

institutions, and the potential interaction of individual and institutional characteristics in signaling ability.

The higher returns to quality realized by non-white graduates found in this study appear consistent with a model of affirmative action in hiring developed by Kolpin and Singell (1997), where individuals from a preferred group earn a premium not realized by other individuals with comparable institutional affiliations. If this is indeed the case,

TABLE 5.6
Returns to College Characteristics. Dependent Variable: Log Hourly Wages.

	Whites	Whites	Non-whites	Non-whites
Intercept	1.571 ***	1.184***	1.524***	1.117***
	(0.034)	(0.086)	(0.059)	(0.129)
Experience	0.074***	0.067***	0.087***	0.081***
	(0.007)	(0.007)	(0.012)	(0.012)
Experience squared/10	– 0.016***	– 0.014***	– 0.027***	– 0.023***
	(0.004)	(0.004)	(0.007)	(0.007)
Tenure	0.042***	0.040***	0.024***	0.020*
	(0.006)	(0.006)	(0.010)	(0.011)
Tenure squared/10	– 0.029***	– 0.027***	– 0.015	– 0.012
	(0.006)	(0.005)	(0.010)	(0.010)
Male	0.152***	0.141***	0.159***	0.111**
	(0.030)	(0.026)	(0.051)	(0.053)
Armed Forces Qualification Test		0.121***		0.093**
		(0.027)		(0.044)
Public institution		– 0.066**		0.035
		(0.031)		(0.066)
Masters, doctoral or research		0.127***		0.143*
		(0.036)		(0.077)
Specialized institution		0.026		0.411**
		(0.109)		(0.208)
Non or less competitive		– 0.049		– 0.012
		(0.032)		(0.061)
Very competitive		0.070**		0.087
		(0.033)		(0.075)
Highly or most competitive		0.100*		0.176
		(0.057)		(0.116)
Net family income		0.027***		0.049**
		(0.009)		(0.023)
Chow statistic (df: 34, 4909)		2.75		
Adjusted R-squared	0.86	0.90	0.85	0.86
Number of observations	3652	3652	1325	1325

Notes: (1) Standard errors are in parentheses. (2) The second specifications for both whites and non-whites include dummy variables for industry and occupation, and missing AFQT and net family income, not shown. (3) *** significant at the 1% level; ** at the 5% level; * at the 10% level.

then minorities have an added incentive to gain admission to highly selective institutions. Furthermore, recent judicial and policy decisions restricting consideration of an applicant's race in admissions are likely to reduce the number of minority graduates from top institutions, and may further raise the earnings premium for minority graduates from highly selective institutions. Clearly, additional analyses designed to explicitly explore the underlying causes of the differences across demographic groups in the returns to institutional quality found in this and other studies is warranted.

5. CONCLUSION

In the context of an educational environment that is increasingly questioning the market value of a liberal arts education, and the increasing costs of private institutions and more selective colleges and universities, relatively little is known about the labor market returns to these institutional characteristics. This study contributes to the literature on the heterogeneity of returns to college by incorporating a more comprehensive list of institutional attributes and examining the earnings of graduates across these institutional characteristics. Furthermore, this paper investigates the impact of individual and institutional characteristics on earnings across racial and gender groups.

I find significant returns to college quality. Additionally, there appears to be a premium for graduating from a graduate degree granting or research institution relative to graduating from a liberal arts college. There is weak evidence that alumni/ae from private institutions earn more than graduates from publicly controlled institutions. These results, however, vary across race and gender.

These results reveal the importance of controlling for a broader range of institutional attributes in estimating the impact of college characteristics on earnings and in more closely examining heterogeneity in the returns to college experiences across racial and gender groups. The underlying causes of these differences across demographic groups are still unknown. Similarly, there remains much work to be done in uncovering the reasons for the college characteristic premiums discussed above. For example, it is still unknown whether the wage premiums earned by more selective, private, university students are due to greater human capital accumulation, signaling of higher ability, or both.

NOTES

1. At the initial time of this study, the 1994 and 1996 survey responses were not available. As a result, this study only uses the annual NLSY data from 1979 to 1993.
2. All dollar values are constant dollar (CPI-U. 1983/84 = 100). $2.93 represents the 1983/84 real dollar value of the 1993 minimum wage of $4.25.
3. The *Digest of Education Statistics* does not report standard errors in order to test for significance in the difference between the variable means.
4. For those individuals who either did not take the ASVAB battery of tests used in the con-

struction of the AFQT score or had missing 1979 net family income, a dummy variable indicating that the variable was not reported was included among the regressors and the individual was assigned the average value for that variable from the sample used in this study.
5. Bok and Bowen (1998) use the Scholastic Aptitude Test (SAT) as their standardized test.
6. White is defined here as those respondents identified as non-black, non-Hispanic; non-white is defined as those respondents identified as black or Hispanic.
7. I am following convention and a rough approximation by referring to the coefficient on a dummy variable in a natural logarithm regression as the percentage wage effect. A more accurate measure of the percentage change would be $\exp(\beta) - 1$.
8. Separate dummy variables for masters, doctoral and research universities were initially included, but an F-test that their coefficients were equal could not be rejected at the 5% level.

REFERENCES

Anon (1987). Barron's profiles of American colleges. Woodbury, NY: Barron's Educational Series, Inc.

Behrman, J. R., Constantine, J., Kletzer, L., McPherson, M., & Schapiro, M. O. (1996a). Impact of college quality choices on wages: are there differences among demographic groups? Mimeo, Williams Project on the Economics of Higher Education.

Behrman, J. R., Rosenzweig, M. R., & Taubman, P. (1996). College choice and wages: estimates using data on female twins. *Review of Economics and Statistics, 78*(4), 672–685.

Bok, D., & Bowen, W. (1998). *The shape of the river.* Princeton, NJ: Princeton University Press.

Brewer, D. J., & Ehrenberg, R. G. (1996). Does it pay to attend an elite private college? Evidence from the senior high school class of 1980. *Research in Labor Economics, 15,* 239–271.

Brewer, D. J., Eide, E., & Ehrenberg, R. G. (1996). Does it pay to attend an elite private college? Cross cohort evidence on the effects of college quality on earnings. Working Paper No. 5613, Cambridge, MA: National Bureau of Economic Research.

Card, D., & Krueger, A. B. (1992). School quality and black-white relative earnings: a direct assessment. *Quarterly Journal of Economics, 107,* 151–200.

Cohn, E., & Addison, J. T. (1998). The economic returns to lifelong learning in OECD countries. *Education Economics, 6*(3), 253–307.

Cooper, S. T., & Cohn, E. (1997). Internal rates of return to college education in the United States by sex and race. *Journal of Education Finance Summer, 23,* 101–133.

Daniel, K., Black, D., & Smith, J. (1995). College quality and the wages of young men. University of Pennsylvania, mimeo.

Davies, S., & Guppy, N. (1997). Fields of study, college selectivity, and student inequalities in higher education. *Social Forces, 75*(4), 1417–1438.

Dowd, A. C. (1998). Returns to field of study and institutional type among elite college graduates. Cornell University, mimeo.

Fox, M. (1993). Is it a good investment to attend an elite private college? *Economics of Education Review, 12*(2), 137–151.

James, E., & Alsalam, N. (1993). College choice, academic achievement and future earnings. In E. P. Hoffman, *Essays on the economics of education.* Kalamazoo, MI: W. E. Upjohn Institute for Employment Research.

James, E., Alsalam, N., Conaty, J. C., & To, D. (1989). College quality and future earnings: where should you send your child to college? *American Economic Association Papers and Proceedings,* May 1989, 247–252.

Kingston, P., & Smart, J. (1990). The economic payoff to prestigious colleges. In P. Kingston, & L. S. Lewis, *The high status track: Studies of elite private schools and stratification.* Albany, NY: State University of New York Press.

Kolpin, V., & Singell, L. D. (1997). Asymmetric information, strategic behavior and discrimination in the labor market. *Economic Theory, 12,* 175–184.

Litten, L. H., & Smith, C. E. (1993). Variations in short-term incomes among graduates of selective colleges and universities. Consortium on Financing Higher Education, mimeo.

Loury, L. D., & Garman, D. (1995). College selectivity and earnings. *Journal of Labor Economics, 13*(2). 289–308.

McPherson, M. S., & Schapiro, M. O. (1991). *Keeping college affordable.* Washington, DC: Brookings Institution.

Pascarella, E. T., & Terenzini, P. T. (1991). *How college affects students: findings and insights from twenty years of research.* San Francisco: Jossey-Bass Publishers.

Rumberger, R. W., & Thomas, S. L. (1993). The economic returns to college major, quality, and performance: a multilevel analysis of recent graduates. *Economics of education review, 12*(1), 1–19.

US Department of Education (1984–1986). *Digest of education statistics.* Washington, DC: US Department of Education.

CHAPTER 6

THE COMMUNITY COLLEGE

Educating Students at the Margin between College and Work

THOMAS J. KANE AND CECILIA ELENA ROUSE

We thank Lauren Broom for expert research assistance, Mark López for help with some calculations, and Brad De Long, Alan Krueger, John Siegfried, Timothy Taylor, and participants at the JFEP Symposium on Higher Education held at Macalester College on June 26, 1998 for helpful comments. Kane acknowledges the generous support of the Andrew W. Mellon Foundation.

Community colleges have assumed an increasingly central role in the nation's education and training system. Between 1980 and 1994, the proportion of 18 to 24 year-olds enrolled in college grew by more than one-third, from 26 to 36 percent. Nearly half of this increase in enrollment was absorbed at community colleges (U.S. Department of Education, 1997, Tables 178 and 186, p. 188, 196). Yet despite the increasing interest in community colleges among both students and policymakers as a potential source of education for workers seeking to upgrade their skills, relatively little is known about them.

We have four goals in this paper. The first is to provide background on the history and development of community colleges in the United States in the last half century. Second, we survey the available evidence on the impacts of community colleges on educational attainment and earnings. Third, we weigh the evidence on the impact of public subsidies on enrollment at community colleges and explore some weaknesses in the current higher education financing structure. Finally, we reflect on how the students who have been responding to the rise in the payoff to education are to be absorbed by our postsecondary training institutions.

THE HISTORY AND DEVELOPMENT OF COMMUNITY COLLEGES

In the late 19th century, when William Rainey Harper, founding president of the University of Chicago, developed a plan to separate the first two years of college from the second two years, he started a movement that would revolutionize higher education. The plan, modeled after the German "Gymnasium," was to create university-affiliated six-year high schools and two-year colleges, called "junior colleges," that would teach students the lower-division "preparatory" material. Although their evolution differed across the country, junior colleges were generally designed to increase access to higher education without compromising and burdening the existing four-year

Source: *Higher Education : Handbook of Theory and Research*, Volume XIV; J. Smart and W. Tierney (eds.), 1999. Agathon Press.

colleges. These colleges are generally defined as "any institution accredited to award the associate's in arts or science as its highest degree" (Cohen and Brawer, 1982, pp. 5–6). This definition includes comprehensive two-year colleges and many technical institutes (both public and private), but it excludes publicly funded vocational schools, adult education centers, and most proprietary schools. In this article, we use the terms "community college," "junior college," and "two-year college" interchangeably.[1]

The first phase in the expansion of junior colleges began after World War II when millions of former military personnel were given a tuition voucher under the GI Bill to attend college. Between 1944 and 1947, enrollments in junior colleges nearly doubled. The end of the Korean War brought another similar increase in junior college enrollments (Witt et al., 1994). The final phase in the expansion occurred in the 1960s, when the first baby boomers began to reach college age, Vietnam War veterans began to return home, and Americans enrolled in college to avoid the military draft. Over the 1960s, the number of junior colleges more than doubled and enrollments quadrupled (Witt et al., 1994). This immense expansion led Clark Kerr, an architect of the California higher education system, to term the junior college the great innovation in American higher education in the 20th century (Brint and Karabel, 1989, p. v).

Originally, junior colleges focused on what is termed the "transfer function": students would complete two years of a general undergraduate education and earn an associate's degree (AA) at the two-year college, and those who wanted and were capable would transfer to a four-year college to complete a bachelor's degree. Since then, two-year colleges have broadened their mission to include vocational degree programs, continuing adult education programs, and workforce, economic and community development programs. In addition, community colleges have traditionally striven to increase access to higher education through an open admissions policy—often not even requiring a high school diploma—and low, or no, tuition. In 1996–97, full-time students paid, on average, $1,283 for annual tuition and required fees at public two-year colleges compared to $2,986 at public four-year colleges (U.S. Department of Education, 1997).

Although private junior colleges were common at the turn of the century—at that time, only 26 percent of two-year colleges were public—96 percent of the 5.5 million students enrolled in two-year colleges in 1995 were enrolled in public institutions (U.S. Department of Education, 1997). These 5.5 million students represent 38 percent of enrollments in all postsecondary institutions and 48 percent of enrollments in public institutions (U.S. Department of Education, 1997). Figure 6.1 shows the importance of community colleges by graphing the proportion of first-time first-year students enrolled in public two-year colleges from 1955 through 1995. In 1955, only 17 percent of all such students were enrolled in a public two-year college; today, that percentage has grown to 44 percent.

This explosion in enrollment in community colleges was powered primarily by the growth in part-time students. Part-time enrollments in public two-year colleges increased 222 percent between 1970 and 1995, compared to an increase of 63 percent in full-time enrollments.

Figure 6.1 Proportion of First-time First-year Students in Public Two-year Colleges

Source: Digest of Education Statistics (1997).

Today, roughly 65 percent of community college students attend part-time.

Although community colleges exist nationwide, they are not equally represented in all states. In California, which enrolls one-fifth of all students enrolled in public two-year colleges, 47 percent of all college enrollments are in public two-year colleges—compared to Louisiana and Montana which each have less than 7 percent. States with more developed four-year college systems tend to have less developed two-year college systems, and vice versa, suggesting that states choose to invest in one system or the other (Rouse, 1998).

The faculty at two-year colleges also differs from that at four-year colleges. The master's degree is the highest degree of 64 percent of full-time faculty in public community colleges, while 68 percent of four-year comprehensive college faculty have doctorates. Almost two-thirds (60 percent) of the faculty at public two-year colleges teach part-time, compared to one-third of comprehensive four-year college faculty. Only 32 percent of the full-time faculty at public two-year colleges hold a rank of either associate or full professor, compared to over 60 percent at public four-year universities. Instead, community colleges rely more heavily on non-tenure track faculty; 40 percent of community college faculty hold a rank of instructor or lecturer and 11 percent have no rank; for comparison, 11 percent of faculty at comprehensive and 8 percent at public research universities hold the rank of instructor or lecturer, and fewer than 1 percent have no rank (U.S. Department of Education, 1997). Of course, the heavy reliance on part-time and adjunct faculty help maintain community colleges' flexibility to respond to changing educational needs in the community.

Community college faculty also spend far more time on teaching than their four-year college counterparts. Two-year college faculty spend 69 percent of their time teaching and 4 percent of their time conducting research or scholarship (the bulk of the rest of their time is spent on administration, non-teaching service, and professional development), while faculty at comprehensive public four-year colleges spend 60 percent of their time teaching, and faculty at public research universities spend 40 percent of their time teaching. Similarly, 58 percent of faculty at community colleges teach more than 15 hours per week, compared to 18

percent of faculty at comprehensive four-year colleges and 7 percent of faculty at public research universities (U.S. Department of Education, 1997). The focus on teaching both lowers the educational costs and is hailed by many students as an advantage of attending a community college, particularly for those who seek more personal attention in the classroom.

WHO GOES TO COMMUNITY COLLEGE?

About one-third of all high school graduates will attend a community college at some point in their lives (Rouse, 1994). Compared to students who first enroll in a four-year college, community college students are more likely to be the first in their family to attend college and are much less likely to have parents who have graduated from a four-year college. The combined student body of community colleges is 70 percent white, 11 percent black, and 11 percent Hispanic. Almost 36 percent of community college students are at least 30 years old, compared to only 22 percent of public four-year college students. As noted above, most community college students attend part-time.

A community college education appeals to many students because of the lower costs of attendance. The average tuition is less than one-half that at public four-year colleges, and because community colleges are located in most towns and cities, many students can live at home while attending college.[2] Community colleges have also lowered other costs of attendance. Courses are not only offered during the "traditional" daytime hours, but also at night and on weekends. Many community colleges offer courses at work sites, or via audio, video, or computer technologies. As a result, 84 percent of community college students work while also attending college compared to 78 percent of students attending public comprehensive four-year colleges. Although the proportion of students reporting some employment is comparable at two-year and comprehensive four-year colleges, roughly one-half of those attending a community college who are employed report work as their primary activity, compared to only one-quarter of those attending public comprehensive four-year colleges (Horn, Becktold and Malizio, 1998).

Do the attractively low tuition and neighborhood convenience of community colleges divert students from four-year colleges? Or do they provide a place in higher education for those who would not have otherwise attended college? Of course, the social importance of this issue ultimately depends on the extent to which the type of institution one attends affects one's educational attainment, as we discuss below. The few studies that attempt to address such issues tend to find that community colleges draw both types of students, although it appears that slightly more than half of community college students are non-traditional students who probably would not have attended four-year institutions (Grubb, 1989; Rouse, 1995, 1998). This suggests that community colleges have increased overall educational attainment, and that a major role of community colleges is to provide a place in higher education for those not traditionally served by the four-year college system.

THE CHANGING SHAPE OF A COMMUNITY COLLEGE EDUCATION

Originally, students at community colleges completed courses that mimicked the first two years of a university curriculum before transferring to a four-year college. As a result, most students followed an academic curriculum delivered in a traditional manner. Today, however, community college courses have taken a variety of other approaches.

A significant fraction of community college students enroll in terminal (usually vocational) degree programs. Community colleges also serve an important remediating function within our higher education system. In 1995, almost all public two-year colleges provided remedial courses, compared to 81 percent of public four-year institutions (Lewis, Farris and Greene, 1996). About 41 percent of community college students took at least one remedial course compared to only 22 percent of public four-year college students. There seems to be an increased interest in limiting the amount of remediation done at four-year colleges; for example, the trustees of the City University of New York (CUNY) voted in May 1998 to deny admission to students who cannot pass reading, writing, and mathematics proficiency tests

(Arenson, 1998). If educational offerings of four-year colleges are limited in this way, the remediation role of community colleges is likely to increase.

As another example of their flexibility in adapting to labor market conditions, a growing number of community colleges are providing contract training—that is, classes offered to employees of a business, industry, labor union, or public agency—often at a site designated by the contracting agency. As of the late 1980s, 94 percent of community colleges provided at least one course by contract. The most common form of contract training was teaching the job-specific skills needed to perform a job, to improve current performance, or to prepare for advancement on a contract basis with firms; 93 percent of community colleges provided such courses (Lynch, Palmer and Grubb, 1991). Sixty percent of community colleges provided contract courses in basic reading, writing, or math skills. The median ratio of contract enrollment (in 1988–89) to regular credit enrollment was 0.22, indicating that at one-half of colleges there was one or fewer contract students for every five or so regularly enrolled students (Lynch, Palmer and Grubb, 1991). Krueger and Rouse (1998) evaluated one such workplace education program in which a community college provided basic literacy education to employees at a manufacturing company and a service company. They reported positive and significant effects of the training on the wage growth and job progression of employees at the manufacturing company, but no such effects at the service company.

THE NET EFFECT OF COMMUNITY COLLEGES ON EDUCATIONAL ATTAINMENT

One concern among observers of community colleges is that as they provide education services in nontraditional ways, the quality of such services may suffer. Critics point to the fact that community college students typically do not complete many college credits. Figure 6.2 shows the distribution of credits completed at two-year colleges.[3] The credits have been divided by 30 so as to represent years of enrollment on the horizontal axis. The figure shows that a majority of students who ever enroll in a two-year college complete one year or less; 35

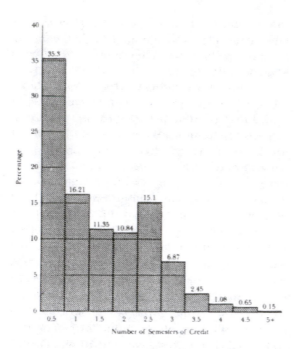

Figure 6.2 Distribution of Two-year College Credits (among those with positive two-year college credits)

Source: Authors' calculations using the *High School and Beyond.*

percent of students complete only one semester or less.

Similarly, Table 6.1 shows degree attainment, 10 years after high school, by whether students first attended a two- or four-year college.[4] Of all students who enroll in a two-year college, over one-half do not complete any degrees. About 15 percent complete a certificate, another 16 percent attain an associate's degree and about 16 percent complete at least a bachelor's degree. In contrast, nearly 60 percent of four-year college entrants complete at least a bachelor's degree. The remaining columns of the table refer to opinions that the students expressed about their own future while seniors in high school. While the percentages of students who complete a degree increases among two-year college students who would either be "disappointed if they do not complete college," or feel they are "'definitely' able to complete college," or for whom "a bachelor's degree is the lowest level of education with which they would be satisfied," degree completion still lags considerably behind that of four-year college students.

The skewed distribution of completed credits and the relatively small proportion of

students who complete degrees raises an important question: Do two-year college students simply maintain modest educational objectives or is there some aspect of two-year colleges that discourages students from completing more courses? Policymakers in certain states, such as California and New York, are considering limiting enrollment at four-year colleges and encouraging students to begin at a two-year college (Trombley, 1991; Kelley, 1998, p. 2). A key question is whether such a policy will affect the educational attainment of those students denied admission to a four-year college. If educational outcomes of students who begin in a community college only differ from those who begin in a four-year college because the two-year college students desire less education, then students who begin at a two-year college with a certain level of desire for schooling should fare as well as those who begin at a four-year college. However, if it appears that some aspect of community college discourages otherwise equally motivated and prepared students from completing more courses, which is one possible interpretation of Table 6.1, policymakers might ask why.

One could argue that two-year college students attain less education than four-year college students because, although two-year and four-year college students have the same aspiration levels while seniors in high school, their desired level of schooling changes over time and this change is unrelated to the type of institution that the individuals attend. Of course, if this is the case, policymakers need not be concerned about differences in educational attainment between the two types of institutions. However, it is also possible that the difference is due to some effect of community colleges. Clark (1960) and Brint and Karabel (1989) argue that the vocational education and terminal degree programs of community colleges are not conducive to completing four years of college, even for those who aspire to a four-year college degree. Their thesis is that two-year colleges are not appropriate institutions for students interested in completing a four-year degree because transferring can be costly and burdensome; conversely, they argue, the four-year college environment helps to keep students focused on the bachelor's degree. Essentially these authors argue that many students lack the necessary information to make an informed decision

TABLE 6.1

Degree Attainment by Type of First College Attended and by Degree Aspirations in the 12th Grade

(among high school seniors in 1982/degree attainment as of 1992)

Highest Degree Attained	All	Disappointed if Do Not Complete College	"Definitely" Able to Complete College	BA+ is Lowest of Level of Education With Which Would be Satisfied
		Two-year College Students		
None	53.7	47.8	60.1	44.9
Certificate	14.6	12.8	12.9	8.5
Associate's Degree	16.1	18.7	14.8	12.8
Bachelor's Degree	14.8	19.5	11.3	31.0
Graduate Degree	0.8	1.1	0.8	2.9
All		68.0	73.4	17.9
		Four-year College Students		
None	29.4	26.7	39.4	22.5
Certificate	5.3	3.8	6.1	2.5
Associate's Degree	6.4	6.1	7.7	2.8
Bachelor's Degree	48.5	52.2	41.8	56.8
Graduate Degree	10.4	11.3	5.0	15.5
All		87.1	83.5	56.0

Note: Authors' calculations using the High School and Beyond sophomore cohort (self-reported postsecondary attendance and degree attainment). The cells represent percentages of the column. All percentages are weighted using the fifth follow-up panel weight. "Two-year Students" are those who started at a two-year college; "Four-year Students" are those who started at a four-year college.

between two- and four-year colleges, and so they do not fully realize in attending a two-year college that they are reducing their chances of completing a four-year degree.

The potential importance of starting at a two-year or four-year college on eventual educational attainment is an empirical issue. But the effect is difficult to estimate, because desired levels of schooling and academic preparation are difficult to measure. Some authors have concluded that students who begin at a two-year college complete less education, on average, than similar students who begin at a four-year college (Alba and Lavin, 1981; Anderson, 1981; Breneman and Nelson, 1981; Dougherty, 1987; Velez, 1985). However, these studies limit their analysis to students who have already started at a college. As a result, they not only miss an important component of the mission of community colleges—to include students who ordinarily would not attend college—but they also bias their estimates of the effect of having been diverted

from a four-year college on educational attainment. Rouse (1995) accounts for all students, not just those who have started college, and also uses college proximity as an instrumental variable that is correlated with the type of college first attended, but hypothetically uncorrelated with educational attainment (conditional on the type of college attended). As with other authors, she finds that students who begin at a two-year college (and who otherwise would have attended a four-year college) complete less schooling—about three-quarters of a year—than those who begin at a four-year college. However, unlike the previous literature, she also finds that starting at a two-year college does not appear to affect the likelihood of attaining a bachelor's degree for those diverted from a four-year college. Therefore, it appears there is some negative effect of starting at a two-year college on years of education completed for an individual who would otherwise have attended a four-year college, perhaps because with so few students living on-campus, peer effects are not as strong as on four-year campuses and because transferring from a two-year to a four-year college can be difficult and burdensome.

LABOR MARKET PAYOFFS TO COMMUNITY COLLEGE

Despite the fact that community colleges enroll a large share of those starting college—and an even larger share of those persuaded by public subsidies to enter college—we know relatively little about the relationship between community college coursework and future earnings. The standard educational attainment question used by the U.S. Bureau of the Census inquires about years of schooling completed (or, more recently, degrees received)—not about the type of institution one attended. The resulting lack of data has been a serious limitation for research on community colleges.

Evidence from Panel Survey Data

The handful of available analyses of the labor market payoffs to community colleges has relied on panel surveys beginning with high school-age youth, which follow respondents through college and beyond, eventually observing sample members' earnings in the years after college. Table 6.2 summarizes the results from six papers estimating the relationship between community college attendance and earnings.[5] Five of the papers attempt to control for prior differences in academic preparation between college entrants by using either a standardized test score or high school class rank (or both) as regressors. The paper by Jacobson, LaLonde and Sullivan (1997) uses information on earnings prior to college entry to "control for" such differences.

One could draw two primary generalizations from the results reported in Table 6.2. First, as reported by Leigh and Gill (1997) and Kane and Rouse (1995), the average community college entrant (who never attended a four-year college), who enrolls but does not complete a degree, earns 9 to 13 percent more than the average high school graduate with similar high school grades and/or test scores between the age of 29 and 38. Second, Kane and Rouse

(1995), Grubb (1995), and Monk-Turner (1994) estimate that each year of credit at a community college is associated with a 5–8 percent increase in annual earnings—which happens to be the same as the estimated value of a year's worth of credit at a four-year college.

Most of the above results are based on the labor market experiences of those who entered community college soon after high school. However, given the recent policy interest in retraining for older workers, the earnings impacts for older adults is of particular interest. The papers by Leigh and Gill (1997) and by Jacobson, LaLonde and Sullivan (1997) provide what evidence we have on this issue. Leigh and Gill test for differences in the educational wage differentials for those entering college at different ages, and do not find evidence that the earnings differentials associated with associate degrees or with community college coursework are any different for the one-third of those who attend community college after age 25. Jacobson, LaLonde and Sullivan's analysis of samples of displaced workers suggests that the earnings differential associated with a year of community college coursework is approximately 2–5 percent. However, the authors estimate substantially larger returns (on the order of 15 percent per year) for courses in more quantitatively or technically-oriented courses such as vocational health, technical/professional, and technical trade courses, and science and math academic courses, but find negligible returns to non-quantitative courses like sales/service, non-technical vocational, social science/humanities, health/physical education/consumer-oriented, and basic education. Despite these gains, the average earnings of displaced workers did not return to pre-displacement levels.

Evidence from Differentials by State and Over Time

An alternative approach to analyzing the labor market effects of community colleges is to use evidence on historical differences in the prevalence of community and four-year colleges between states and over time. We used the micro-data from the 1990 census to estimate the difference in each state in the log of annual earnings between high school graduates (with no postsecondary training) and those with "some college, no degree," for 25–34 year-old

TABLE 6.2
Summarizing Research on Labor Market Effects of Community College Education

Authors:	Data Sources:	Covariates:	Annual Earnings Differential (relative to high school graduates)		
			A.A. Degree Holders:	Some College No Degree:	
Leigh and Gill (1997)	NLSY (1993)	*Ability Measure:* AFQT Score *Other Covariates:* Race, ethnicity age, gender, work exp., region, part-time emp.	.235 (.040) (No sig. diff. over age 25)	2-Yr Coll 4-Yr Coll	.118 (.031) .093 (.035)
Kane and Rouse (1995)	NLSY (1990)	*Ability Measure:* AFQT Score *Other Covariates:* Race, ethnicity, age, gender, work exp., region, part-time emp., parents' education.	.271 (.038)	2-Yr Coll 4-Yr Coll	100 (.030) .125 (.036)
	NLS-72 (1986)	*Ability Measure:* H.S. Class Rank, NLS-72 Test Score *Other Covariates:* Race, ethnicity, gender, work exp., region, part-time employment, parental income.	.159 (.034) (Differential larger for women)	Per Year: 2-Yr Coll 4-Yr Coll	.061 (.016) .061 (.012)
Grubb (1995)	NLS-72 (1986)	*Ability Measure:* NLS-72 Test Scores, H.S. Grades *Other Covariates:* Race, ethnicity, parental income, an index of parental socio-economic status, work experience, tenure on current job, indicators for firm-provided training.	Voc. AA .106 (.033) Acad –.021 AA (.044)	Per Year: Voc 2-Yr Voc. 4-Yr Acad 2-Yr Acad 4-Yr	.046 (.042) .120 (.025) .047 (.025) –.012 (.014)
Jacobson, LaLonde and Sullivan (1997)	Displaced workers in PA and WA.	*Ability Measure:* Person Fixed-Effects *Other Covariates:* Prior industry, age	—	2-Yr. PA 4-Yr, WA	.015 (.004) .052 (.005)
Monk-Turner (1994)	Parnes NLS	*Ability Measure:* IQ Score (on H.S. Transcript) *Other Covariates:* Race, gender, parental educ., region, work exp. marital status, educational plans.		Per Year: 2-Yr Coll 4-Yr Coll	.054 (.02) .079 (.01)
Heineman and Sussna (1977)	HS Graduates (Class of 1964 and 1967)	*Ability Measure:* H.S. Class Rank *Other Covariates:* Race, age, gender, work exp., parental family income, parental education, religion, military service.	.150	—	

Note: In the studies which report impacts by year or by gender, the above estimates represent weighted averages using sample sizes as weights. Standard errors for the pooled estimates were calculated under the assumption of independence. Where impacts were reported in dollars, we divided by the relevant average annual earnings to convert to percentages. Where impacts were reported in units of log earnings, we reported log earnings differentials, which approximate percentage differences.

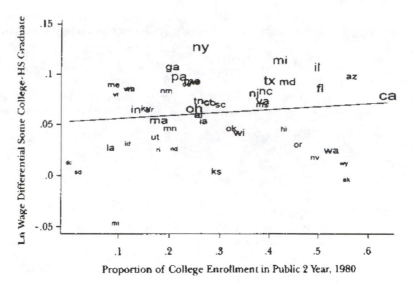

Figure 6.3 The "Some College" Wage Differential and Community College Enrollment by State

Note: Ln wage differentials for 25–34 year-old males estimated by state using the 1990 5% PUMS. The wage differentials were estimated with separate log wage equations for each state, including regressors for age (10 categories), race/ethnicity, and category of educational attainment. The size of the symbol for each state reflects the reciprocal of the standard error on the estimated coefficient.

Source: Bane and Rouse (1995).

males.[6] (In an attempt to categorize the men by the states in which they were trained, the income differentials were measured by the state in which men were living five years earlier.) In Figure 6.3, we then plot these state average earnings differentials by the proportion of enrollment in each state in community colleges. If those attending community colleges were receiving lower earnings differentials from college attendance than those attending four-year colleges, we might expect to see a downward sloping graph. As is apparent from Figure 6.3, there is no strong relationship between the "some college" earnings differential and the proportion of enrollment in community colleges.[7] In fact, the "some college/high school graduate" earnings difference in California—with relatively large community college enrollments—is higher than the national average. Moreover, as we reported in Kane and Rouse (1995), there is no evidence that the "some college" earnings differential has fallen over time as community college enrollments have risen.

Experimental Evidence

The non-experimental evidence summarized to this point suggests substantial effects of community college training on annual earnings.

However, experimental evaluations of training programs have offered a much less optimistic appraisal of the impacts of classroom training for the unemployed and out-of-school youth.[8] For instance, in 1986, the U.S. Department of Labor commissioned an experimental evaluation of training provided to adults and out-of-school youth under the Job Training Partnership Act. Because many of the training providers under the Job Training Partnership Act (JTPA) were community colleges—indeed, over one-half of community colleges receive JTPA funds (Lynch, Palmer and Grubb, 1991)—the results of the JTPA evaluation provide another indirect assessment of the labor market value of a community college education.

The primary difference between the non-experimental results summarized above and the results of the typical randomized controlled experiment lies in the fact that the experiments can only estimate the incremental impact of a new opportunity for training—not the value of the training itself. For instance, many members of the control group in the JTPA experiment received classroom training at the very same institutions where the treatment group members received their training—they just paid for the training themselves or took advantage of other government programs, such as the federal Pell Grant program, to help pay the cost. Thus, the experimental evidence provides no direct evidence on the value of training vs. no training, but rather estimates only the difference between the training opportunities provided to the treatment group and the training opportunities available elsewhere. The more similar JTPA training was to training available elsewhere, the more likely one would find a zero incremental impact of the JTPA program.

Indeed, this may explain the divergence between the results of the JTPA evaluation and the non-experimental estimates cited above. The impacts of the JTPA program on earnings were not statistically distinguishable from zero for several subgroups—leading some observers to conclude that classroom training had little impact. However, the differences in the amount of classroom training received by the treatment and control groups were also quite small.

In fact, if one translates the point estimates of the educational wage differentials arising out of the JTPA experiment into the framework we have been using, the results are quite comparable in magnitude. For example, during the final year of the JTPA evaluation follow-up, the average adult woman assigned to classroom training earned $282 (5.1 percent) more than those in the control group (Orr et al., 1994). They also received 147 hours more training than those in the control group. If there are 420 hours of classroom training in a typical academic year (that is, 14 weeks per semester, 15 classroom hours per week, and two semesters a year), then our point estimate would be that receiving an academic year's worth of training would have been associated with an annual earnings differential per year of 14.6 percent. Similar results hold for the adult male and female youth groups, although the impacts for male youth were smaller than the 5 to 8 percent differential implied by the non-experimental estimates. In other words, even though the JTPA experimental estimates were generally not statistically distinguishable from zero, because alternative training opportunities were so readily available to the control group, the implied estimates of the differential per year of training received were generally on the high end of the non-experimental estimates above. Heckman, Hohmann, Khoo and Smith (1997) have used the JTPA data to generate non-experimental

estimates of the value of classroom training. Their results also suggest substantial private internal rates of return to classroom training, albeit with more ambiguous social returns.

The Payoff to Completing an Associate's Degree

With only about 16 percent of community college entrants completing an associate's degree, the incremental value of degree completion itself has been central to the policy debate over community colleges. While the evidence presented in the last section suggests there are returns to completing community college credits, some argue that the main return to attending a community college comes with completing an associate's degree.

The evidence in Table 6.2 reports the total earnings differential between associate's degree recipients and high school graduates, inclusive of any credits completed. (One exception: the associate's degree effects reported for Grubb (1995) should be interpreted as incremental to the number of credits completed.) Completing an associate's degree appears to be associated with a 15 to 27 percent increase in annual earnings. Since estimates suggest that two years of community college credit is associated with a 10 to 16 percent increase in earnings (that is, the 5 to 8 percent annual gain times two), there appears to be some additional gain to the associate's degree itself. The evidence also suggests that this differential is larger for women, largely reflecting the value of nursing degrees where the earnings gain is especially pronounced (Kane and Rouse, 1995; Grubb, 1995).[9]

Discontinuities in the relationship between average log earnings and years of schooling completed at 14 and 16 years of schooling have traditionally been interpreted as reflecting the value of completing an associate's or bachelor's degree (Hungerford and Solon, 1987).[10] However, before 1992, the standard Census Bureau question on educational attainment did not allow one to distinguish between those who had completed an associate's or bachelor's degree and those who had completed 14 or 16 years of schooling without degrees. To assess whether the return to the associate's degree reflects a "sheepskin effect" or the effect of having completed two years of college, Jaeger and Page (1996) exploit a 1992 change in the Census Bureau educational attainment question; the earlier question focused solely on years of schooling completed, while the new one inquires about degree completion. After matching responses in the March 1991 *Current Population Survey* (including the question regarding years of schooling completed) and March 1992 survey (with data on degree completion), they found that white men with associate's degrees earn 8–19 percent more than men reporting similar years of schooling completed, but no degrees, and white women with associate's degrees earn 24–31 percent more than women reporting similar years of schooling completed, but no degrees. Again, it seems that nursing degrees account for much of the importance of associate's degrees for women (Kane and Rouse, 1995).

However, such estimates likely overstate the direct effect of degree completion for two reasons. First, the estimates are not adjusted for prior differences in family background and ability between degree completers and dropouts—because such information is not available on the Current Population Survey. It appears that those completing degrees not only have higher earnings than others with similar years of schooling, but they also seem to have higher prior test scores and more advantaged family backgrounds as well, and so controlling for these other factors would shrink the effect of degree completion.

Second, the magnitude of sheepskin effects may partially reflect the nature of measurement error in self-reported measures of educational attainment. Kane, Rouse and Staiger (1997) develop a technique for estimating the amount of measurement error in both self-reported and transcript-reported schooling in the NLS-72. Their findings suggest that respondents are more likely to misreport the number of years of college they have completed than they are to misreport degrees completed. While more than 95 percent of those who report a bachelor's degree 7 years after graduating from high school are estimated to be reporting accurately, one-third of those who report 3 years of college credit are estimated to have completed only 0, 1 or 2 years of college. Similarly, among those who report 1 year of college, 30 percent are estimated to actually have 0, 2 or 3 years of college. As a result, estimates based on self-reported schooling are likely to provide an accurate esti-

mate of the earnings of those with a bachelor's degree and underestimate the differences in earnings per year of college for those without a bachelor's degree. Any discontinuity of earnings between those reporting 3 years of college and those reporting a bachelor's degree is likely to be exaggerated. In other words, the "sheepskin" effects reported in the literature may well be due in part to the nature of the reporting error in educational attainment.

Finally, even what remains of the "sheepskin" effect, after controlling for individual heterogeneity and measurement error, overstates the relative value of degrees and understates the anticipated value of postsecondary entry for those who do not complete degrees. There may be an option value to college entry for those uncertain of their prospects for finishing (Manski, 1989; Altonji, 1991; Comay et al., 1973). If the returns to education are uncertain or if youth are uncertain as to whether they are "college material," youth may gain some information in the first few months of college which helps to resolve the uncertainty. The wage differentials only reflect later monetary payoffs to college attendance. However, to the extent that the decision to enroll in college is an experiment for many, the anticipated outcome of that experiment may be sufficient to justify the public and private investments required, even if, after running the experiment, students do not finish the degree. This argument also suggests that we might wish to avoid proposals which seek to limit aid to those who complete degrees, as is occasionally suggested as a policy response to the high non-completion rates at community colleges (for example, Fischer, 1987).

A ROUGH APPROXIMATION OF THE PRIVATE AND SOCIAL RATES OF RETURN

How do the earnings differentials associated with a year at a community college compare to the costs of attendance? Using the average annual earnings of current 25–64 year-old workers (employed full-time, full year) to estimate future earnings and employing a discount rate of 6 percent, the present value of expected lifetime earnings for the average male high school graduate in 1992 would have been $480,500 (in 1997 dollars)[11] The present value of a 5 to 8 percent increase in lifetime earnings for someone with career income of $480,500 would be $24,000 to $38,400 before taxes or $15,600 to $25,000 after taxes (assuming a combined federal and state tax rate of 35 percent).

The full cost to a family of a year at a community college includes both the earnings foregone by students as well as the cost of tuition. (We have left out room and board, since individuals would have to eat even if they were not in school). In 1992, the average income of a male 18–24 year-old high school graduate working full-time, full-year was $19,400 (in 1997 dollars). Foregoing nine months at that salary would imply costs of $14,600 before taxes or $9,500 after taxes. As mentioned above, a minority of students actually seem to forego nine months of full-time earnings, since a majority of both two-year and four-year college students work while they are in school. Nevertheless, such calculations provide a rough approximation of the "unit price" of a year of full-time schooling, even if relatively few students decide to "purchase" a full nine months away from work.

Adding in the private cost of tuition at the average public two-year college, the rise in after-tax lifetime income of $15,600 to $25,000 would be larger, but not dramatically larger, than the estimated private cost of $10,800 ($9,500 in foregone after-tax earnings plus $1,300 per year for tuition).

Calculations along these lines also reveal why it may not be surprising that the earnings differential associated with a year at a community college is similar in magnitude to that associated with a year at a four-year college. Although the tuition charges at community colleges are typically lower ($1,300 per year compared to $3,000 at the average public four-year institution), the vast majority of the private cost of attendance is foregone earnings, not tuition. To the extent that students are choosing on the margin between two-year and four-year colleges, we might expect students to attend each type of college to the point where the payoffs were similar.

Given the size of the public subsidies directed at community colleges, the average tuition families face ($1,300) is considerably less than the actual cost of a year of full-time education. Rouse (1998) estimates that average variable cost of a year in community college is $6,300 (in 1997 dollars).[12] However, this figure does not include capital costs, which Winston and Lewis (1997) estimate to be an additional $1,700 per student (27 percent of expenditures per student). To the extent that the private cost families face is considerably lower than the actual cost of the resources required to produce a year at a community college, we might fear students would over-invest in post-secondary education. However, even if we were to count only the earnings increases associated with community colleges (and ignore any of the other hard-to-measure benefits, such as civic participation or greater social mobility), the estimated 5 to 8 percent earnings differential would imply gains roughly the same as the full cost of the resources used: the combined cost of pre-tax earnings and expenditures per pupil of $22,600 is comparable in magnitude to the $24,000 to $38,400 estimate of the present value of future earnings differentials.

Although these back-of-the-envelope calculations can of course be subjected to criticism on many dimensions, it thus appears possible that a year of community college increases earnings by an amount roughly equal to the value of the resources used to produce that year.

STUDENT FINANCING ISSUES

Community colleges are heavily dependent upon public subsidies for their operations; 62 percent of current-fund revenues are appropriated by state and local governments (U.S. Department of Education, 1997, Table 328, p. 344). Because students must be enrolled at least half-time to qualify for many federal aid programs such as the guaranteed student loan programs, only a quarter of community college students report receiving state or federal grant aid to help cover the cost of tuition and fees (U.S. Department of Education, 1992–93, Table 3–1a, p. 62).

Future demographic trends are likely to strain the ability of states to maintain this commitment in coming years. The size of the traditional college-age population (that is, 15 to 24 year-olds) has declined by 15 percent since 1980, partially relieving the cost pressure produced by rising college enrollment rates. However, this college-age population is now projected to rise by one-fifth over the next 15 years (Campbell, 1994). The rise is projected to be particularly dramatic in California, where the number of 15 to 24 year-olds is projected to increase at roughly twice the national rate. If the labor market wage premiums favoring college entry persist, and college enrollment rates remain high, states are likely to be forced to choose between raising tuition and increasing public expenditures on higher education.

Should states decide to increase tuition, it is likely to have an unusually large impact on community college enrollments. The demand elasticities with respect to upfront costs of college entry are quite high. After reviewing 25 estimates of tuition price responses, Leslie and Brinkman (1988) reported a median estimate of a 4.4 percentage point difference in postsecondary entry for every $1,000 difference in tuition costs (in 1997 dollars).[13] A number of others have found similar results, including Cameron and Heckman (1998b), Rouse (1994), Kane (1995), Kane (1994) and McPherson and Schapiro (1991). Enrollment at two-year colleges appears to be particularly sensitive to tuition changes (Kane, 1995; Rouse, 1994; Manski and Wise, 1983).

In addition, students seem to be more sensitive to tuition changes than to changes in future wage differentials. While the payoff to college was rising dramatically during the 1980s, the proportion of high school graduates entering college within two years of high school rose by only 7 percentage points, from 65 to 72 percent (U.S. Department of Education, *Condition of Education, 1997,* p. 64). Using the estimates of tuition sensitivity described above, a tuition increase of $1500 would have been enough to have wiped out that rise in college entrance rates—even though the present value of the college earnings differential rose by far more than $1500 during the 1980s.

One potential explanation for the sensitivity of students to the tuition costs at community colleges is that they face borrowing constraints in the private capital market. Indirect evidence on this point is provided by Card (forthcoming), who summarizes evidence suggesting higher marginal returns to schooling for disadvantaged groups than for the population as a whole. Such findings may result from the fact that lower-income families have more difficulty arranging financing for college. In a similar vein, most studies find that large differences in

college entry by family income remain, even among those with similar test scores and academic performance in high school.[14]

The most obvious constraints which limit family borrowing for community college are the explicit limits on student borrowing in the federal student loan programs. Since 1992, the most a dependent student could borrow under the Stafford loan program has been $2,625 during the freshman year, $3,500 during the sophomore year and $5,500 per year thereafter. Independent students who are married, have dependents, are veterans or are over age 24 can borrow an additional $4,000 per year during their first two years and an additional $5,000 per year thereafter. However, such amounts may not be sufficient to pay living expenses on top of tuition bills. Some states and institutions have their own loan programs, but in 1992–93, less than 1 percent of undergraduates received either a state loan (0.5 percent) or an institutional loan (0.4 percent); in contrast, 20 percent of undergraduates received federal loans. A third source of borrowing constraints may be the confusing nature of the application process. Several studies cited in Orfield (1992) suggest that low-income families are often unaware of eligibility rules and procedures.

An important challenge will be to create a financing structure that will allow community colleges to expand in the next few years to meet the training needs of the population—and then eventually to contract as the relevant population declines. The current system of "backward-looking" means-testing, which looks back at the parents' income to determine student eligibility for financial aid, is more appropriate for the student of traditional college age and is less well-suited to the population of community college entrants. If community colleges are to remain an engine of innovation in postsecondary education, we will require similarly creative and flexible financing strategies to match. As an alternative to the current form of financing with several advantages would be greater reliance on income-contingent loans—that is, loans where the amount of repayment depends to some extent on future income earned—as discussed in this journal in Krueger and Bowen (1993). The expected subsidy implicit in an income-contingent loan is lower than the cost of a dollar in appropriations to public institutions, which in turn means that families and youth would have a stronger incentive to allocate society's educational resources in a prudent manner. Moreover, the means-test implicit in income-contingent loans does not involve the same difficulty in distinguishing students who are "dependent" on parents' resources from those who are "independent."

CONCLUSION

For the past five decades, the debate over access to higher education and the role of higher education in economic development has implicitly been a debate about community colleges. In any discussion involving marginal incentives, community colleges have been the margin. They have been the gateway for those on the verge of enrolling in college: older students, those who cannot afford to attend full-time, and those who need to develop their basic skills. Ironically, though, we know less about community colleges than about other sectors of higher education. The evidence we do have, as summarized above, suggests that community colleges increase aggregate educational attainment, and are associated with higher wages, even for those not completing degrees.

If current labor market conditions persist, we can expect significant increases in demand for postsecondary training slots in the future, due to the projected growth in college-age cohorts. Historically, community colleges have been the buffer, absorbing much of the increase in enrollment when veterans returned from war or when demand for skilled labor outpaced supply. Enrollment at community colleges also has swelled much more dramatically than at other institutions during economic downturns, when opportunity costs of such investments in training are lowest (Betts and McFarland, 1996).

Recent technological developments in distance learning will likely allow colleges to be even more responsive to changes in demand for higher education and have raised hopes of improving productivity in instruction.[15] Community colleges are participating in this growing trend. In 1995, 58 percent of public two-year colleges were offering distance learning courses serving over 400,000 students (or about 7 percent of their total enrollment).[16] However, community colleges are not the only institu-

tions turning to distance learning: two-thirds of public four-year colleges offered such courses in 1995 and an additional 25 percent were planning to offer such courses by 1998. To the extent that geographic accessibility and flexible scheduling have been a traditional source of community colleges' market niche, the technological revolution may allow other institutions, such as four-year colleges and private for-profit institutions, to compete more effectively in the markets traditionally served by community colleges.[17] The net result of these technological changes—whether they lead to an increasing or decreasing role for community colleges in the future—remains to be seen.

NOTES

1. Although we use the terms interchangeably, we know of no private "community" colleges while "junior" and "two-year" colleges are both public and private.
2. Rouse (1994) shows that college proximity is an important determinant of college attendance. We discuss the literature on the effects of tuition below.
3. Figure 6.2 is based on authors' calculations from the *High School and Beyond Post-secondary Transcript* file, which is for students who were sophomores in 1980 (the "sophomore cohort"). The figure includes only students who had a complete set of (cumulative) transcripts and who had earned any credits at a two-year college as of 1992; the distributions are weighted by the post-secondary transcript weight. If the sample is limited to those who have no four-year credits, the distribution looks quite similar.
4. Proprietary schools were not counted as college for this exercise; therefore, if a student first attended a proprietary school and then attended either a two- or four-year college, we count the two- or four-year college as the "first" school attended.
5. Hollenbeck (1990) and Surette (1997) also report results consistent with those in Table 6.2 using the National Longitudinal Study of the Class of 1972 (NLS-72) and the National Longitudinal Survey of Youth (NLSY) respectively.
6. To match as closely as possible the state where the person was educated, sample members were categorized by their state of residence in 1985, when they would have been 20 to 29. The regressions also adjusted for race/ethnicity and year of age.
7. Weighting by the reciprocal of the standard error of each estimate, the slope coefficient in Figure 6.3 was .038 with a standard error

of .029, meaning that for every 10 percentage point increase in the proportion of students in the state enrolled in community colleges, the estimated wage differential is estimated to rise by a statistically insignificant third of a percentage point.

8. For instance, in a recent summary in this journal, LaLonde (1995) concluded: "Finally, the National JTPA Study found that . . . those men assigned to a strategy that offered classroom training did not appear to benefit from JTPA services."

9. The estimated earnings differential for associate's degree completion for women falls by one-third when one includes a dummy variable for nurses.

10. In contrast, studies of the relationship between log earnings and the number of years of schooling suggest that the percentage increase in earnings between the 13th and 14th years of schooling is similar to that between the 12th and 13th years of schooling; there is no discontinuity (for example, Park, 1994).

11. This may be a conservative estimate since we are implicitly assuming no real wage growth. However, it may also be overly optimistic, since the continuing increases in college enrollment may eventually lead to a decline in earnings differentials.

12. Excluding "fixed costs" such as research, administration, student serves and admissions, her estimate would be $4,200.

13. Leslie and Brinkman's (1988, appendix table 6) actual estimate was that a $100 increase in tuition in 1982–83 dollars was associated with a .7 percentage point decline in enrollment among 18–24 year-olds. We have converted to 1997 dollars in the text.

14. Kane (1998), Manski and Wise (1983) and Hauser and Sweeney (1997) report differences in postsecondary entry by family income, conditioning on both parental education and student test scores. Using the NLSY, Cameron and Heckman (1998a) find differences in college entry by family income to be greatly reduced, but not eliminated, after including controls for AFQT scores.

15. The Department of Education defines distance learning as ". . . education or training courses delivered to remote (off-campus) locations via audio, video, or computer technologies" (Lewis et al., 1997).

16. The most common form of the distance learning is one-way pre-recorded video classes (67 percent), although half of public two-year colleges also offer two-way interactive video.

17. We thank Michael Rothschild for pointing out the potential vulnerability of community colleges as the technology for distance learning improves.

REFERENCES

Alba, Richard D., & David E Lavin. (1981). Community colleges and tracking in higher education. *Sociology of education.* 54, pp. 223–37.

Altonji, Joseph. (1991). The demand for and return to education when education outcomes are uncertain. National Bureau of Economic Research. Working Paper No. 3714, May.

Anderson, Kristine L. (1981). Post-high school experiences and college attrition. *Sociology of education.* 54, pp. 1–15.

Arenson, Karen W. (1998). CUNY to tighten admissions policy at four-year schools. *New York times.* May 27, Section A, Page 1.

Barbett, Samuel F., Roslyn Korb & MacKnight Black. (1988). *State higher education profiles: 1988 Edition.* Washington, D.C.: National Center for Education Statistics.

Betts, Julian & Laurel McFarland. (1996). Safe port in a storm: The impact of labor market conditions on community college enrollments." *Journal of human resources.* 30:4, pp. 742–65.

Bloom, Howard S. et al. (1994). *National JTPA study overview: Impacts, benefits and costs of Title II-A: A Report to the U. S. Department of Labor.* Bethesda: Abt Associates, January.

Breneman, David W., & Susan C. Nelson. (1981). *Financing community colleges: An economic perspective.* Washington, D.C.: The Brookings Institution.

Brint, Steven & Jerome Karabel. (1989). *The diverted dream: Community colleges and the promise of educational opportunity in America, 1900–1985.* New York: Oxford University Press.

Bruno, Rosalind R., &Andrea Curry. (1996). *School enrollment—social and economic characteristics of students: October 1994.* U.S. Bureau of the Census, Current Population Reports, pp. 20–487. Washington, D.C.: U.S. Government Printing Office.

Cameron, Stephen V., & James J. Heckman. (1998a). Life cycle schooling and dynamic selection bias: Models and evidence for five cohorts of American males. *Journal of political economy.* 106:2, pp. 262–333.

Cameron, Stephen V., & James J. Heckman. (1998b). The dynamics of educational attainment for Blacks, Hispanics, and Whites. Working Paper, Columbia University Department of Economics, September.

Campbell, Paul R. (1994). *Population projections for states, by age, race and sex: 1993–2020.* U.S. Bureau of the Census, Current Population Reports, pp. 25–1111. Washington, D.C.: U.S. Government Printing Office.

Card, David E. (Forthcoming). The causal effect of education on earnings. In Orley Ashenfelter & David E. Card. (Eds.). *Handbook of labor economics, Volume 3.* New York, NY: North-Holland.

Clark, Burton R. (1960). The 'cooling-out' function in higher education. *American journal of sociology.* 65, pp. 569–76.

Cohen, Arthur M., & Florence B. Brawer. (1982). *The American community college.* San Francisco: Jossey-Bass Publishers.

Comay, Y., A. Melnick, & M. Pollatschek. 1973. The option value of education and the optimal path for investment in human capital. *International economic review.* 14, pp. 421–35.

Dougherty, Kevin. (1987). The effects of community colleges: Aid or hindrance to socioeconomic attainment? *Sociology of education.* 60, pp. 86–103.

Fischer, Frederick. (1987). Graduation-contingent student aid. *Change.* November/December, pp. 40–47.

Griliches, Zvi. (1977). Estimating the returns to schooling: Some econometric problems. *Econometrica,* 45, pp. 1–22.

Grubb, W. Norton. (1993). The varied economic returns to postsecondary education: New evidence from the class of 1972. *Journal of human resources.* 28:3, pp. 365–82.

Grubb, W. Norton. (1995). Postsecondary education and the sub-baccalaureate labor market: Corrections and extensions. *Economics of education review.* 14:3, pp. 285–99.

Grubb, W. Norton. (1988). Vocationalizing higher education: The causes of enrollment and completion in public two-year colleges, 1970–1980. *Economics of education review,* 7, pp. 301–19.

Grubb, W. Norton. (1989). The effects of differentiation on educational attainment: The case of community colleges. *Review of higher education,* 12, pp. 349–74.

Hauser, Robert M. and Megan Sweeney. (1997). Does poverty in adolescence affect the life chances of high school graduates? In Greg J. Duncan & Jeanne Brooks-Gunn. Eds.), *Consequences of growing up poor.* New York: Russell Sage.

Heckman, James J. et al. (1997). Substitution and drop out bias in social experiments: A study of an influential social experiment. University of Chicago Working Paper, August.

Heineman, Harry N. & Edward Sussna. (1977). The economic benefits of a community college. *Industrial relations.* 16:3, pp. 345–54.

Hollenbeck, Kevin. (1993). Postsecondary education as triage: Returns to academic and technical programs. *Economics of education review.* September, 12:3, pp. 213–32.

Horn, Laura J., Jennifer Berktold, & Andrew G. Malizio. (1998). *Profile of Undergraduates in U.S. Post secondary Education Institutions: 1995–96.* Washington, D.C.: National Center for Education Statistics.

Hungerford, Thomas, & Gary Solon. (1987). Sheepskin effects in the returns to education. *Review of economics and statistics,* 69:1, pp. 175–77.

Jaeger, David A. and Marianne E. Page. (1996). Degrees matter: New evidence on sheepskin effects in the returns to education. *Review of economics and statistics.* 78:4, pp. 733–40.

Jacobson, Louis S., Robert J. LaLonde, & Daniel G. Sullivan. (1997). *The returns from community college schooling for displaced workers.* Federal Reserve Bank of Chicago, WP-97-16, June.

Kane, Thomas J. October (1994). College attendance by blacks since 1970: The role of college cost, family background and the returns to education. *Journal of political economy,* 102:5, pp. 878–911.

Kane, Thomas J. (1995). *Rising public college tuition and college entry: How well do public subsidies promote access to college?* National Bureau of Economic Research Working Paper No. 5164, April.

Kane, Thomas J. (1998). *Are college students credit constrained?* Working Paper, Kennedy School of Government, Harvard University, May.

Kane, Thomas J., & Cecilia Elena Rouse. (1995). Comment on W. Norton Grubb. The varied economic returns to postsecondary education: New evidence from the class of 1972. *Journal of human resources.* Winter, 30:1, pp. 205–21.

Kane, Thomas J., & Cecilia Elena Rouse. (1995). Labor-market returns to two- and four-year college. *American economic review.* June, 85:3, pp. 600–14.

Kane, Thomas J., Cecilia Elena Rouse & Douglas Staiger. (December 1997). Estimating returns to schooling when schooling is misreported. Unpublished paper, Kennedy School of Government, Harvard University.

Kelley, Pam. (1998). Free K-14 could become the standard in North Carolina. *Community college week.* June, 10:22, p. 6.

Krueger, Alan B. & William G. Bowen. (1993) Policy watch: Income contingent loans. *Journal of economic perspectives.* 7:3. pp. 193–201.

Krueger, Alan B., & Cecilia Elena Rouse. (1998). The effect of workplace education on earnings, turnover, and job performance. *Journal of labor economics.* January. 16:1, pp. 61–94.

LaLonde, Robert J. (1995). The promise of public sector-sponsored training programs. *Journal of economic perspectives.* Spring, 9:2. pp. 149–68.

Leigh, Duane E. and Andrew M. Gill. (1997). "Labor market returns to community colleges: Evidence for returning adults." *Journal of human resources.* Spring, 32:2, pp. 334–53.

Leslie, Larry, &Paul Brinkman. (1988). *Economic value of higher education.* New York: Macmillan.

Lewis, Laurie, Elizabeth Farris, & Bernie Greene. (1996). *Remedial education at higher education institutions in fall 1995.* Washington, D.C.: U.S. Department of Education, National Center for Education.

Lewis, Laurie et al. (1997). *Distance learning in higher education institutions.* Washington, D.C.: U.S. Department of Education, National Center for Education.

Lynch, Robert, James C. Palmer, & W. Norton Grubb. (1991). *Community college involvement in contract training and other economic development activities.* Berkeley, CA: National Center for Research in Vocational Education, October.

Manski, Charles F. (1989). Schooling as experimentation: A reappraisal of the postsecondary dropout phenomenon. *Economics of education review.* 4, pp. 305–12.

Manski, Charles F., & David A. Wise. (1993). *College choice in America.* Cambridge, MA: Harvard University Press.

McPherson, Michael S. and Morton Owen Schapiro. (1991). Does student aid affect college enrollment? New evidence on a persistent controversy. *American economic review,* 81, pp. 309–18.

Monk-Turner, Elizabeth. (1994). Economic returns to community and four-year college education. *Journal of socio-economics,* 23:4, pp. 441–47.

Orfield, Gary. (1992). Money, equity and college access. *Harvard educational review.* Fall, 72:3, pp. 337–72.

Orr, Larry L., et al. (1994). *National JTPA study: Impacts, benefits and costs of Title II-A.* Draft report to the U.S. Department of Labor, March.

Orr, Larry L. et al. (1996). *Does training for the disadvantaged work?* Washington, D.C.: Urban Institute.

Park, Jin Heum. (1994). Returns to schooling: A peculiar deviation from linearity. Princeton University Industrial Relations Section Working Paper No. 335, October.

Pincus, Fred L. (1981). The false promises of community colleges: Class conflict and vocational education. *Harvard educational review.* 1980, 50, pp. 332–61.

Rouse, Cecilia Elena. (1994). What to do after high school? The two-year vs. four-year college enrollment decision. In Ronald Ehrenberg. (Ed.), *Contemporary policy issues in education.* Ithaca, NY: ILR Press, pp. 59–88.

Rouse, Cecilia Elena. (1995). Democratization or diversion? The effect of community colleges on educational attainment. *Journal of business economics and statistics.* April, 13:2, pp. 217–24.

Rouse, Cecilia Elena. (1998). Do two-year colleges increase overall educational attainment? evidence from the states. *Journal of policy analysis and management.* Fall, 17:4, pp. 595–620.

Surette, Brian J. (1997). *The effects of two-year College on the labor market and schooling experiences of young men.* Working paper, Finance and Economics Series, Washington, D.C.: Federal Reserve Board, June.

Tinto, Vincent. (1985). College proximity and rates of college attendance. *American educational research journal.* 10, pp. 277–93.

Trombley, William. (1993). College running out of space, money. *Los Angeles times.* October 18, 3A.

U.S. Department of Education. (1997). *Condition of education 1997.* Washington, D.C.: National Center for Education Statistics.

U.S. Department of Education. (1997). *Digest of education statistics 1997.* Washington, D.C.: National Center for Education Statistics.

U.S. Department of Education. *Student financing of undergraduate education, 1992–93.* U.S. Government Printing Office: National Center for Education Statistics.

Velez, William. (1985). Finishing College: The effects of college type. *Sociology of education.* 58, pp. 191–200.

Winston, Gordon C. & Ethan G. Lewis. (1997). Physical capital and capital service costs in U.S. colleges and universities: 1993. *Eastern economic journal.* Spring, 23:2, pp. 165–89.

Witt, Allen A., et al. (1994). *America's community colleges: The first century.* Washington, D.C.: The Community College Press.

CHAPTER 7

PRIVATIZING HIGHER EDUCATION

KEVIN C. SONTHEIMER

This chapter focuses on higher education in the United States, but the issues considered are relevant to almost all countries since in virtually all countries the provision of education at the post-secondary level is dominated by the public sector. The United States is different from most countries in this regard in that the public sector presence in higher education has become dominant only more recently (but having its origin with the Morrill Act of 1862), in fact being a post-World War II phenomenon. The United States is also different in that even at this date there still is a substantial private sector component to higher education, and many of the reputedly best institutions of higher learning in the United States are private. Thus the possibility of privatizing the public sector institutions might seem more feasible in the United States than in other countries.

The richness and extent of the public sector in supporting and providing higher education services in the United States is well exemplified by the arrangement in Pennsylvania. The Pennsylvania situation also exemplifies the potential that remains for private sector provision of higher education services (and research services). The situation in Pennsylvania is given in Table 7.1.[1] The data show that private colleges and universities in Pennsylvania still remain the largest provider of services to full-time (FT) students among the categories distinguished. To provide a clearer picture of the Pennsylvania situation, it should be noted that only one of the four state-related universities (The Pennsylvania State University) receives most of its education funds from the public sector as a direct subsidy. Three of the four state-related universities receive less than half of their education funds as a direct public sector subsidy. Thus the extent of the private portion of higher education in Pennsylvania is larger than the categories of Table 7.1 might indicate.

The fact that private sector provided education is still robust and viable in terms of market share makes it a clear, practical, and reasonable alternative institutional form as a provider of education services. Indeed, the fact that some of the very best providers of higher education in terms of quality are private institutions makes the case for private education even stronger. A typical ranking of universities and four-year colleges according to perceived quality usually has the top twenty positions dominated by private institutions. So empirically, whether assessed in terms of relative quality or financial sustainability, the private sector is a highly viable alternative to public sector provided higher education.

What are the arguments in favor of or against public sector provided higher education? First, there are no strong philosophical or economic arguments for the public sector to be the provider of higher education services. The public good argument for higher education is weak at best. While there are productivity gains from the education received at the post-secondary level, there is no evidence that the productivity improvements are not properly compensated via the market (i.e., there

Source: *Privatizing Education and Educational Choice: Concepts, Plans, and Experiences*, S. Hakim, P. Seidenstat and G. Bowman (eds.), 1994, Praeger Publishers, Inc.

TABLE 7.1
Institutional Categories and Enrollments in PA Higher Education (Fall Term, 1991)

	No.	Enrollments		Percentages	
		FT	PT	FT	PT
State Universities	14	76,670	20,180	20.4	9.9
State-Related Universities	4	103,311	38,627	27.5	18.9
Community Colleges	13	38,196	74,322	10.2	36.4
Private State-Aided Institutions	11	35,294	12,297	9.4	6.0
Private Colleges & Universities	76	112,939	54,774	30.1	26.8
Theological Seminaries	17	1,611	1,389	0.4	0.7
Private Junior Colleges	9	3,873	2,560	1.0	1.3
State School of Technology	1	510	—	0.1	—
Total	145	375,404	204,149	100.0	100.0

are no significant external economies). The public good argument via the political requirements of the democratic process also is strained when it comes to post-secondary education. The affordability or access argument based on distributional considerations (whether argued as another version of a public good case, or simply based on interpersonal, distributional considerations without any reference to externalities or social stability as a public good) also is weak, since private provision of the services with public finance to those individuals meeting subsidization criteria is a feasible option. There are, in fact, no strong philosophical or economic arguments in favor of publicly provided higher education.

The fact that there are no compelling philosophical or economic arguments in favor of public sector provision of higher education services does not make a case against publicly provided higher education.

What are the arguments against publicly provided higher education? First, there are the inefficiencies that derive from tying subsidies to specific providers. If subsidies are provided to individuals there are well known utility gains thereby captured by allowing the individual to assign the subsidy to the provider of choice rather than requiring the individual to have to restrict his/her choice to a particular subset of institutions in order to gain the subsidy.

Second, there is the catalogue of problems typically associated with institutions that are part of the public sector—for example, intertemporally soft budget constraints that

derive from the incremental budget process even if the political unit providing the funding has a balanced budget requirement. In the instances in which there are no balanced budget requirements, then the deficit potential of the public unit translates into a soft budget potential for the subsidiary educational unit even within a budget period. In fact, the existence of a balanced budget requirement for the political unit providing funding does not guarantee that there cannot be a soft budget constraint for a subsidiary unit, such as an educational institution; it only provides some pressure to enforce budget constraints on subsidiary units.

Indeed, the catalogue of problems that applied to state enterprises in the former socialized economies of Central and Eastern Europe apply to public institutions of higher education in the United States (though there is a significant difference of degree due to a competing private sector, a rivalrous political process, and a relatively aggressive and unconstrained press in the United States). Pennsylvania provides a good example of the intertemporal softness of budget constraints that the incremental budget process yields. Using student full-time equivalent (FTE) data as a rough measure of productivity, the data of Table 7.2 demonstrate how the real resource cost of higher education has increased far in excess of the FTE measure of output. The fact that the faculty growth was below the administrative and professional support services, further suggests that the main growth was for wasteful uses of resources.[2]

TABLE 7.2
PA Growth in FTE Students versus Administration and Other Personnel

(Percentage Change from 1980–1981 to 1989–1990)

Characteristics	Percent Growth	
	State Universities	State-Related Universities
No. of FTE Students	22.9%	10.2%
No. of Instructional Faculty	3.5%	3.6%
No. of Executives, Administration and Managerial Personnel	56.6%	42.3%
No. of Other Professional	94.5%	28.9%
No. of Non-professional	10.5%	20.3%

THE PRIVATIZATION EXPERIENCE

The main lesson of all the efforts to execute large scale privatization of industry is that it is not easy. It is not easy even when there is widespread popular support and strong political will behind the privatization effort at its outset.[3] It is definitely not easy when there is ambivalence among the political authorities and/or among the population as Russia now demonstrates.

The second lesson is that unless the transition process is well designed so as to make the costs of transition low, both the popular support and the political will for privatization will weaken as the process proceeds, and the privatization program might not be completed, as was the case in Great Britain. The case of Great Britain is especially instructive of the difficulties of large scale privatization. Despite the advantages of the parliamentary system, a popular government with a substantial majority in Parliament, sophisticated capital markets thoroughly integrated into international markets, a world-class banking system, and so on, approximately only twenty or so firms were privatized over a period of approximately twelve years. Privatizing large scale enterprises is not easy!

The latter lesson includes the subordinate lesson that having a well-defined goal or goals for privatization is not enough to sustain support through a transition process. Goals will be abandoned if the realized costs during the transition are too high or endure too long. A program of privatization must have well-defined goals and the process of transition must not be too traumatic in that the costs associated with dislocations must not be too high, too concentrated, and endure too long. An indefinitely long path of moderate annual costs due to inefficiencies can rationally be chosen by consumers to be superior to a path with an up-front period of high costs followed by a sustained period of low costs. The intertemporal preferences of the public matter.

THE TRANSITION PROCESS: BENEFITS AND COSTS

The benefits of privatizing higher education would be broadly distributed in that the untying of public subsidies from specific institutions will allow large numbers of students to capture the utility gains to be had from larger choice sets. To the extent that the privatization of higher education would break the connection between soft budget constraints and increasing tax burdens, the general population would experience lower tax loads. The latter gains are not inconsiderable since higher education in the United States shares features in common with medical care, and they are that both have been experiencing price increases well above those of other final product and service categories and that both absorb a large portion of public expenditures (though medical costs clearly dominate higher education expenses as a proportion of gross national product).[4] So the benefits of privatization would be widely but not universally shared.

On the other hand the costs of privatization would be distributed much more narrowly. As is typical of privatization efforts, the principle costs are the employment/income losses and relocation costs that would have to be absorbed by employees in inefficient enterprises. A secondary loss is the value of the employment stability that is characteristic of public enterprise that would be sacrificed in converting to a private enterprise without tied public subsidies. Because the losses would be large to the individuals involved, and concentrated geographically (large urban public universities, the colleges of college towns), the lesson of Public Choice Theory is that the political efforts of the potential losers in opposing privatization can readily dominate the efforts of the potential gainers.

Negotiating the transition process of privatization is an exercise in the application of Public Choice Theory. It is necessary to structure the distribution of costs and benefits of privatization intertemporally and across the electorate so as to sustain political support.[5] This fact greatly influences the transition process proposed here for privatizing higher education in the United States. The feasibility of a privatization process hinges at least as much on political as economic considerations.

The specific problems with the privatization of higher education have to do with employment maintenance, regional incomes considerations, the salability of capital assets, and the fact that higher education services are highly subsidized by the private sector as well as the public sector. Since the private sector subsidies provided to public institutions are tied to the institutions via endowment funds and capital assets, all of the subsidies cannot be made portable. Also, the newly privatized institutions would have to compete with heavily subsidized sales by pre-existing private institutions. The primary component of the mechanism proposed for achieving a privatized higher education sector is a phased-in voucher system. A second component of the mechanism is a sale process for capital assets that provides for a preferential Employee Stock Ownership Plan (ESOP) bid. The privatization process is described and the likely transition experience developed in the following sections.

Employment Maintenance

Much of the efficiency gains of privatizing education would be lost if employment guarantees were given to those presently employed in the public universities, colleges, and other postsecondary educational institutions. Providing for the privatization of the institutions and untying the public subsidies to students from the institutions to allow students to vote with their feet, while guaranteeing employment in place for faculty and staff, would impose a heavy cost burden offsetting the utility gains of

the students. Therefore such employment guarantees cannot be a part of a meaningful or serious privatization plan. Thus a problem is: how to put forward a program that is both serious and does not provide the foundation for its own defeat by not forestalling the opposition that a clear and present danger of unemployment would induce?

Regional Income

Resistance to privatization proposals does not just come from those for whom the threat of unemployment might be clear and present, or those in their immediate families. The notion of income and employment multipliers are well known and accepted parts of the common economic and political conceptual frameworks. Any threat of employment or income loss to a well specified subset of a community is seen to be a threat to the community as a whole, and sometimes in a distorted and exaggerated way. The resistance factor that a privatization program would induce has a multiplier associated with it.

The resistance multiplier is larger than the actual income or employment multipliers since the anticipation of who will bear the burden of the multiple employment or income losses is a matter of probability. If the employment multiplier is two, and the anticipated direct employment loss might be 5 percent of the work force so that the full loss would be 10 percent, it is quite possible that 25 percent of the work force could feel significantly threatened, for example. That is, for every additional job to be lost due to the direct effect there could be, for example, as many as five employed persons who feel that there is a reasonable probability that their position could be the one lost via the multiplier effect. A one in five chance of becoming unemployed is likely to raise the political concerns of anyone.

The regional multiplier concerns that might stem from the threat of unemployment and income losses as a result of privatization thus make the importance of dealing with the employment maintenance problem all that much greater. The regional multiplier of resistance is undoubtedly understated in the preceding paragraph since it neglects what might be called the sympathy factor.

Just as the multiplier effects result in the magnification of the resistance to privatization, so too they can magnify the reduction in resistance to privatization as the perceived threats are reduced. There is both a positive side and a negative side to multiplier effects.

Salability of Capital Assets

A second major feature of any privatization scheme is the way it deals with the disposition of the capital assets of the to-be-privatized enterprises. The privatization can allow for the piecemeal disposing of some or all of the assets, or it can keep them intact in a bundle. If some assets can be disposed of piecemeal, then the privatization plan provides for the downsizing or restructuring of enterprises up-front in the privatization process. If the scheme allows for the piecemeal disposing of all the assets, then the scheme is basically treating the enterprise as a bankrupt organization. This is not part of what is normally understood to be the focus of privatization and so will be ruled out here. It will be ruled out not because of any objection in principle, but for the pragmatic reason of trying to minimize the opposition to privatization.

The piecemeal disposing of some of the capital assets of the enterprise up-front in the process tends to raise the insecurity level of the employees and community because of the increased probability of transitional employment dislocations. Thus such a feature of a privatization program is a negative feature to be avoided, *ceteris paribus*. The piecemeal disposing of some capital assets up-front also will reduce the viability of the remnant enterprise after privatization, reinforcing the opposition to privatization. The privatization scheme to be proposed will provide that public institutions of higher learning to be privatized be privatized intact (i.e., all the capital assets kept in one bundle). After privatization, however, *qualified* piecemeal disposition of assets will be provided for.

One of the typical problems of privatization schemes in formerly socialist economies is determining the value of the capital assets of the state enterprises. The book values of the capital assets typically are meaningless, the revenue and cost data of the enterprises are almost meaningless if not meaningless, and the same is true for all capital assets in any specific region within any of the formerly socialist economies. Not only are the specific capital asset values subject to huge uncertainties, but also site values are subject to huge uncertainties.

The problem of capital asset value determination in the formerly socialist economies has a reflection in the public institutions of higher education in the United States. The problem is that most state or community owned institutions do not keep capital accounts. Thus there is more difficulty in accurately assessing the values of the capital assets than is typically the case for commercial assets. However, because the institutions are embedded in functioning market economies and site values therefore are determinable with much greater accuracy, the problem of capital asset valuation is not so severe as in formerly socialist economies. Still the estimated values of the capital assets of institutions of higher learning would have greater standard deviations associated with them than is typical of commercial firms in a well-functioning market economy. This would be especially true for the case of institutions which constitute a significant portion of the economic base of the local community, as, for example, the public college of a college town.

Because of the risk associated with the purchase of the capital assets via the pricing problem, the sale of such assets is somewhat problematic. The risk factor would induce a discounting of the sale value of the assets.

Private Sector Subsidies

Special feature of the market for higher educational services is the ubiquity of subsidies to the buyers of the services. Most private colleges and universities, not just public institutions, sell their services below cost. The subsidies come from the use of endowment income to pay for portions of overhead and operating costs and to further reduce the price imposed on the consumer via scholarships and student aid packages. Other subsidies are effectively provided by donors funding the construction or renovation of capital assets. Higher education is further subsidized by special tax treatment for private institutions.

The existence of subsidization of the sale of educational services by the already private institutions poses a problem for a to-be-privatized public institution. If the buyers of the formerly public institution have to pay the approximate market value of the capital assets, their resulting cost base will put them in a competitively disadvantageous position. The need to pay for all of their capital assets will give the newly private institutions a higher cost structure than their older rival private institutions (on average). Only if the capital assets do not have any good alternative use will capital markets discount the assets sufficiently to put the newly private institutions on a par with the cost structures of their rival and prior private institutions.

For those cases where the capital assets of public institutions have good alternative commercial uses (whether kept intact or decomposed after privatization), the subsidized pricing of rival colleges and universities will help to ensure that the capital assets would move into their alternative uses. That is, in such cases the capital assets would be withdrawn from higher education. This would mean transitional dislocations in employment and income losses up-front in the privatization process.

It might well be that there are excess physical plant and other capital assets in higher education. A process that threatens the abrupt withdrawal of the excess capacity is a process that also threatens quick and severe dislocations in terms of employment and incomes. The dislocations also would be highly concentrated geographically and politically. The process of privatization then should be designed to allow for a smoother withdrawal of excess capital assets (if any).

There is a footnote to be added on the issue of private subsidies to higher education. The vast proportion of subsidies available through public institutions comes from public funds raised via annual tax collections. However, many public institutions now have endowment funds provided by private persons or private sector institutions, and the funds are growing due to significant fundraising efforts by the public institutions. These funds would be non-transferable in the privatization process: they would remain with the institution. (The subsidies yielded by public sector endowments would provide a trivial amelioration of the problem presented by the extensive subsidies available via the extant private institutions.)

THE PRIVATIZATION PROGRAM

A feasible process for privatizing higher education in the United States must first pass the test of political feasibility. Given that higher education in the United States is primarily a state concern and not a national (federal) concern, the political test is a stern one. The test has fifty parts.

The political test means that significant or severe up-front dislocations in employment and income are not acceptable. Other, somewhat less politically potent dislocations to students and prospective students who are attached or hope to become attached to particular institutions that would be threatened by prompt closure or severe downsizing must be accounted for as well. The process must constrain such dislocations in order to be politically feasible.

Employment subsidies to newly privatized institutions would not be an economically or politically appealing mechanism to mitigate significant upfront dislocations. The process should avoid such features. A privatization process that provides a stake for the main interest group that might otherwise oppose the privatization, but that avoids direct employment subsidies, is a more viable process. A mechanism that fits this prescription is well known, and that is to provide for significant employee ownership of the newly privatized institution.

The essential features of the privatization process would be as follows:

1. As a means of coping with the capital asset valuation problem, the privatization program should include a public bid process. The bidding should be for the intact institution, including all assets, any and all bonded or other debt, credits, and contracts of the institution.[6] The bid process should provide for a special ESOP bid to convert the public institution into either a for-profit or non-profit institution of higher learning. The request for bids should provide a certified estimate (as an attempt to provide information of value to all potential buyers) of the worth of capital assets and net worth of the institution. The bidding should require that bids cover at least 40 percent of the estimated net

worth of the institution, except that an ESOP bid need cover only 20 percent of the net worth or 50 percent of the best non-ESOP bid, whichever is greater. If an ESOP bid meets the criteria, then the ESOP bid wins. If only an ESOP bids, the ESOP wins.

2. The revenues obtained from the sale of the institutions of higher learning would be deposited in a tuition fund, the earnings of which would be used to pay for the tuition vouchers to be granted to students.

3. The annual subsidies provided by government funding to the institutions, less the earnings to be obtained from the tuition fund, would be converted into per capita subsidies to students in the form of vouchers usable at any institution of higher teaming within the state. The interstate redeemability of the vouchers would have to be negotiated between the various states.

4. The ESOP would not be allowed to be converted into a public corporation or otherwise sold for at least ten years. Any revenues obtained by the sale of any capital assets during the first ten years would have to be added to the endowment of the institution or invested in other capital assets.

5. Any unfunded pension liabilities would remain the liability of the public sector and would not accrue to the to-be private institutions.

Feature one serves several purposes. First, if no bids would be made for any particular institution that met the stipulated thresholds, it would be a clear demonstration to the general public that the institution in question was producing educational services of dubious value relative to the cost to taxpayers. It would stimulate consideration of closure as a means of promoting a more efficient allocation of resources if there were no buyers as opposed to the likely perpetuation of the institution under the current public funding system. A second purpose is to convert faculty and staff who are stakeholders in the institution by virtue of their employment and possibly emotional attachment into potential shareholders as well as stakeholders. The incomes and employment of the faculty and staff would not be so directly threatened because of the better terms offered to the ESOP, and in fact the faculty and staff would be offered something which they might well value and accept as some compensation for the risk that privatization as an ESOP might entail. This is to promote the feasibility of privatization (alternatively, to reduce the opposition by lowering the perceived costs). Third, by removing the assets of the institutions from the public property lists, the process promotes the possibility that the future costs to the public sector can go down since maintenance and other costs would have been shifted to the private sector. Fourth, the conversion to an ESOP and removing the institutional budget from the state budgeting process also creates an incentive for faculty, staff, and administration to slow the growth of costs and to seek out internal efficiency improvements. Finally, the potential ESOP holds out the prospect of real faculty governance at the privatized institutions. Since faculty governance is often a rallying cry on campuses, this might be another compensation for the risk that the privatization otherwise brings relative to continued public status.

The first feature also deals with the problem of the ubiquity of private subsidies in the private sector of higher education. By reducing the capital cost of the to-be-private institutions, the institutions can compete on a comparable cost basis with the extant private institutions. Thus the survival of the institutions is more a matter of their future cost control and quality of service than their historical development and legacies.

The second feature allows for a reduction in the current tax load carried by taxpayers. This spreads the benefits of privatization to a larger category than just the students who might benefit from the larger choice set of institutions to attend. This benefit is spread thinly, but it is a clear benefit nonetheless.

The third feature allows students to redistribute themselves as dictated by their preferences, rather than as dictated by the tying of subsidies to a particular subset of institutions, and thereby to achieve utility gains without any increased cost to taxpayers. Also, since direct tuition subsidies are not subject to the usual incremental budgeting process as are the budgets of public institutions, some future budgetary savings can be realized. To the extent that the direct subsidy growth can be held below the incremental rate of growth of the public sector institutional and payroll funding, the shifting of the assets reduces the rate of growth of public sector spending and therefore taxes.

The fourth feature is to prevent the faculty and staff, as members of the potential ESOP, from realizing quick capital gains from the transfer of assets. This forestalls public opposition to the privatization that would arise if the faculty and staff could quickly realize gains by immediately selling off the assets transferred from the state. Also, the fourth feature provides the faculty and staff with an incentive to promote the success of the ESOP in addition to the incentive of retaining their employment and salaries. The additional incentive is the prospect of capital gains that might come at the end of ten years if they can make a success of operating their institution in the private sector. The potential for capital gains also holds some potential as a moderating influence on wage and salary growth since the employee-owners can anticipate a trade-off between wage or salary income and capital gains.

Feature five is an important feature to promote the financial viability of the new private institutions. This feature recognizes that the liability at present does not accrue to the (public) institutions, but to the relevant government units (state or local government). It also recognizes that the unfunded liabilities are for benefits based on past service as public employees, and that the liabilities therefore properly should remain with the public sector. Leaving the liability in the public sector does not result in any new liability or future tax burden for the general public.

There is nothing in the five features of the program that prevents the failure of some of the privatized institutions, or their downsizing. To the extent that over time there is a redistribution of students across institutions, those institutions that lose students will have to downsize and/or fail, and those that gain students will grow. Faculty over time will be reallocated as will capital investments. The allocation of inputs over time will become increasingly rational but with a lag relative to the self-allocation of students.

THE TRANSITION

The point of privatizing the public institutions of higher education is not to close them, to eliminate faculty and staff positions, or to cause other and larger regional dislocations. Rather the point is to promote utility gains for present and future students and to reduce the tax burden on taxpayers. Accomplishing the latter will probably entail some employment and income losses, and in some locations failing (closing). In the event that achieving the efficiency gains will entail some significant and localized dislocations, the task then is to not allow the prospect of the dislocations to prevent the realization of any net gains.

The program proposed above is designed to minimize the resistance to changes that will realize the efficiency gains by reducing the up-front costs as much as possible and by giving the prospective losers as great an opportunity as reasonable to protect and advance their situations. Part of this strategy is to avoid rapid and precipitous change. The idea is to allow time for new market positions to be explored and developed.

The use of ESOPs is a critical factor in the transitional strategy. ESOPs are calculated to act more deliberately, if more slowly, in eliminating positions. For this reason a larger role for ESOPs than for non-employee-owned institutions is calculated to reduce the resistance to privatization.

Similarly, the deep discounting of the capital assets of the public institutions is calculated to reduce the opposition to privatization by the employee groups and community support for their opposition. The lump sum subsidy that the discounting represents will be seen as some insurance that the privatized institutions will not fail and maybe not even have to engage in significant downsizing. Indeed, the deep discounting will allow the newly privatized institutions an opportunity to engage in effective competition with the extant private institutions. At the least, it should put off the need for significant downsizing or closing for a substantial period and thereby mitigate the opposition to doing any privatization.[7]

The actual transition from public institutions to a stable arrangement of older private and recently privatized institutions will take some time. Part of the strategy should be to ensure that the transition takes some years as a way of ensuring that the costs of the transition are not bunched up at the beginning of the process. The capital asset subsidies help in that regard. But another step should be taken. The transition should not include a rapid voting-with-the-feet of the current crop of students. A prospect of a rapid and large reallocation of students between institutions should be avoided since it creates a clear prospect of institutional failures. To that end a brake should be placed on the voting-with-their-feet phenomenon.

Feature three of the privatization program provides for the calculation of an annual subsidy per student. Since the total amount available for payment of subsidies will be held constant in the privatization, and the number of eligible students will increase, the average subsidy received will fall. Nonetheless, some students enrolled at the time of privatization will opt to move with the smaller subsidy, and some students will opt to remain where they are and suffer the reduction in subsidy. The latter group would tend to oppose the privatization, so a specifically transitional provision should be added to the program, to wit:

6. Any students enrolled in a public institution at the time of privatization should have the option of remaining at their original but privatized institution with the same effective subsidy they enjoyed before privatization. Any students enrolled at the time of privatization who switch to a different institution must accept the new and lower subsidy. Students enrolled in private institutions at the time of privatization will be eligible for the voucher subsidy wherever they choose to enroll after privatization.

This feature of a privatization program will have two effects. First, it will restrain the voting-with-their-feet by students who are enrolled at the time of privatization, but have no effect on the voting-with-their-feet by future enrollees. It thereby stretches out the period of reallocation of students over a four-year period. Second, it will eliminate the opposition to the privatization program that would be induced by reducing the subsidies received by students who would choose to remain attached to their old institutions after privatization. Both features enhance the feasibility of privatiza-

tion. However, the second effect also entails a higher cost to the taxpayers than an immediate adjustment to the lower average subsidy would entail. This is considered to be an acceptable effect because the higher tax cost would be diffused over a large number of taxpayers, and per taxpayer would be a small and temporary increase, while the benefits associated with the second effect would be concentrated and significant to the affected persons.

Adding feature six to the privatization program would ensure a transition to privatization that would last at least five years and probably more. Features one through six together constitute a program with a transition that keeps the up-front costs low but provides a flow of benefits that begins immediately (though feature six restrains the immediate flow of benefits somewhat). The privatization program also provides an opportunity for those most potentially involved on the cost side to participate and influence their fates via the ESOP arrangement. It also provides them with effective support (the capital asset discounts) for preserving their jobs and incomes within a framework that long-term does not increase the cost of subsidizing higher education and even allows the prospect of reducing the cost.

While the prolonged transition period will delay the failure of some institutions, it will not prevent the failures. Those institutions that cannot compete effectively under the new subsidy arrangement will ultimately fail. The capital asset discount and the initial restraint on voting-with-the-feet only can delay the ultimate rationalization of investments in institutions of higher learning.

CONCLUSION

The present arrangement of tying subsidies to institutions induces efficiency losses by constraining choice. An equally costly program of subsidies that allows individuals to assign the subsidies is possible and achieves utility gains. The program also promises further gains by taking higher education institutions out of the incremental budget processes of the public sector and thereby putting hard budget constraints in the place of soft budget constraints. The privatization program also would reduce current and future tax burdens by moving the maintenance of capital assets off the public budget. Both the number of potential beneficiaries and the potential total benefit are large.

The proposed program stretches out the costs of transition so as to minimize the political opposition to privatization. The program also increases the role and participatory share of the faculty and staff in their institutions, making the transition period less threatening. Clearly some faculty and staff groups will benefit from the self-determined reallocation of students across institutions. The ESOP arrangement allows each faculty and staff group to work out internal arrangements to give them a voice in the management of their institution. It also gives them a greater incentive, along with the hard budget constraints, to restrain cost growth and to eliminate wasteful expenditures.[8] Thus the failures and downsizing of institutions, along with their income and employment losses, are pushed further into the future and the resistance to the privatization is reduced.

The greatest impediment to large scale privatization programs in other countries is the resistance to prospective income and employment losses that come early and strongly in the process. The program proposed here for higher education avoids this problem by stretching out the period of such loss absorption and providing benefits up-front and throughout the transition process.

NOTES

1. The source for the data is *Colleges and Universities: Fall Enrollment 1991* published by the Division of Data Services, Pennsylvania Department of Education.
2. The source for the data is *Selected Output, Input and Efficiency Measures for Major Institutions and Programs of the Pennsylvania Department of Education.*
3. Chile and Great Britain are two cases where there was strong political will and, at least in the case of Great Britain, strong popular support as well. Both Chile and Great Britain had other strong advantages such as well developed capital and other markets (Bogetic and Conte 1992, 2–3).
4. For example, tuition charges for the 1980–1986 period increased by 10.6 percent annually

while the Consumer Price Index increases averaged 4.8 percent (Iosue 1992, 7).

5. It should be noted that even when the burdens and fragility of democratic government do not have to be borne, large-scale privatization proves to be a long and difficult task. The large scale privatization in Chile extended over approximately twenty years and only about 200 enterprises were privatized and another approximately 350 firms were restituted to their prior owners (Bogetic and Conte 1992, 2–3).
6. Estimating the value of the capital and other assets of a firm is not an easy task. The estimates determined in takeover efforts emerge from a process which has been well documented in many cases, and the documentation clearly demonstrates the subjectivity of judgments and approximations of the procedures used. The valuations are well summarized in the following lines: "Whether raider or target, buyer, or seller, the question is, what is the right price? No one knows. . . . Pricing is therefore a matter of conjecture or speculation." (A. Fleischer, Jr., G. C. Hazard, and M. Z. Klipper 1988, 135–136.)
7. The fact that some privatized institutions might grow is ignored because such prospects improve the feasibility of the privatization effort, and the focus here is on how to cope with the potential resistance to privatization.
8. For example, if colleges and universities were ESOP's, it is not at all clear that most of the present large athletic programs would endure.

REFERENCES

Bogetic, Z., & Conte, M. (1992) Privatizing eastern European economies: A critical review and proposal. *Mimeograph,* October.

Fleischer, Jr., A., G. C. Hazard, & M. Z. Klipper. (1988) *Board games: The changing shape of corporate power.* Boston: Little, Brown and Company.

General Assembly of Pennsylvania, Joint State Government Commission. (1992) *Selected output, input and efficiency measures for major institutions and programs of the Pennsylvania Department of Education 1980–81 and 1990–91,* Staff Memorandum. August.

Iosue, R. V. (1992) Higher education: Are we getting our money's worth? In D. E. Eberly. (Ed.). *Leading Pennsylvania into the 21st Century: Policy Strategies for the Future.* Harrisburg: The Commonwealth Foundation.

Pennsylvania Department of Education, Division of Data Services. (1991) *Colleges and universities: Fall enrollments.* Harrisburg: Author.

SECTION II

GOVERNMENT FINANCING OF HIGHER EDUCATION

INTRODUCTION

As two of the largest and most important social institutions in America, government and higher education have a complex relationship that defies easy description and ready understanding. The use of the term "government" implies a monolithic nature, when in fact government consists of public authority at the federal, state, and local levels, each with its own particular powers, procedures, and constituencies. Likewise, higher education is an extremely large tent that covers a bewildering array of institutional types, missions, and governance structures. The complex relationship between government and higher education has many facets but at its core is a single issue: financing. The purpose of this section is to provide an abbreviated but meaningful introduction to the role that government, primarily at the federal and state levels, plays in the financing of America's enormous and diverse system of higher education.

The section begins with a general article on government financing of higher education. The first, "Financing American Higher Education in the 1990s," by Arthur Hauptman, is an excellent primer on the current status of public support for higher education. Hauptman examines the amount of government support for colleges and universities, sources of institutional revenue (including federal, state, and local funding), and the rising importance of student financial aid (particularly loans), before concluding with a useful discussion of financial issues facing higher education in the near future, organized by institutional type.

The second article, "Federal Student Aid and the Growth in College Costs and Tuitions: Examining the Relationship" co-authored by Hauptman and Cathy Krop, focuses on the critical subject of federal student financial aid and its effect on college costs and tuition. After reviewing the impact of federal student financial aid policy over the last quarter-century, the article offers two proposals for reform of federal student aid policy. Given the increase of public concern and political rhetoric over tuition in recent years, this article helps to answer important factual and cause-and-effect questions, while offering compelling options to bring about the fairest and most effective reforms.

To understand current federal financial aid policy, it is very helpful to explore the history of these policies. James Hearn presents a thorough and engaging history in the third article, "The Growing Loan Orientation in Federal Financial Aid Policy: A Historical Perspective." By analyzing the history of the terms and provisions of the Higher Education Act of 1965 and its subsequent reauthorizations, Hearn provides not only a look at the evolution of important financial trends but also a glimpse into the complicated workings of the federal policy domain.

Turning from the federal government to the states, the section continues with an article by David Breneman and Joni Finney, describing "The Changing Landscape: Higher Education Finance in the 1990s." The Breneman and Finney article overlaps slightly with Hauptman in its discussion of revenue sources, but then moves in a very different (and equally effective) direction with a detailed case study analysis of financial contexts in five major states—California, Florida, Michigan, Minnesota, and New York.

Breneman and Finney conclude with an issues and questions list for state policymakers that will serve as very valuable discussion starters.

Drawing an explicit connection between a state's general financial condition and the specific fortunes of higher education, Harold Hovey addresses "The Outlook for State Finances." Hovey's article begins with a general explanation of state budgeting dynamics, continues with a consideration of the prospects for higher education finance in the early 2000s, and closes with an exploration of fiscal impacts on state higher education policy. Hovey skillfully demystifies much of the state level political process, writing with an honesty and clarity that readers should find refreshing and informative.

A third treatment of state government financing of higher education, by Michael Mumper, concentrates on "State Efforts to Keep Public Colleges Affordable in the Face of Fiscal Stress." Citing twenty years of tuition increases, Mumper raises the specter that public higher education is rapidly becoming too expensive for American families of average incomes, and thus a cherished goal of American higher education—access—is jeopardized. In his article, Mumper examines the causes and conditions that precipitated tuition increases across states, describes the range of state policy reactions to such increases, and evaluates the relative effectiveness of these different reactions.

Performance funding is a specific, and controversial, policy mechanism that more and more states are using to hold colleges and universities accountable for the appropriations they receive. In his article, "Linking Performance to Funding Outcomes for Public Institutions of Higher Education: the U.S. Experience," Daniel Layzell gives the reader a critical introduction to the performance funding phenomenon. Wisely, Layzell begins with a discussion of performance indicators—the nuts and bolts of any performance funding scheme—and outlines some of the most significant limitations of the performance indicator systems that have thus far been developed. Only then does Layzell explore the link between performance and funding, and what the future holds for this approach.

James Palmer addresses the special challenges of financing community colleges in "Funding the Multipurpose Community College in an Era of Consolidation." Palmer contends that modern community colleges have three identities, or missions: the flexible institution; the scholastic institution; and the social service agency. He then offers justification for public financing of these institutions based upon each identity. Palmer concludes with the observation that the real challenge in financing community colleges is developing a funding approach that allows a two-year institution to be all three identities, and to fulfill all three missions, simultaneously.

The final article in this section, "Vouchers in American Education: Hard Legal and Policy Lessons from Higher Education," by F. King Alexander, is particularly timely and relevant given the economic and philosophical debates raging over the use of vouchers in public education. But these debates typically occur within the domain of elementary and secondary, not higher, education. Alexander argues that, in fact, federal direct student aid has served as a higher education voucher system during the last twenty-five years, and that the results of the higher education experience holds powerful, cautionary lessons for voucher policies in the K-12 sphere.

The reviewers for this section were:

F. King Alexander, University of Illinois, Urbana-Champaign

Peter H. Garland, Executive Director, Pennsylvania State Board of Education

Edward R. Hines, Illinois State University

Michael Mumper, Ohio University

Sheldon L. Stick, University of Nebraska, Lincoln

Glenn M. Nelson, University of Pittsburgh

CHAPTER 8

FINANCING AMERICAN HIGHER EDUCATION IN THE 1990S

ARTHUR M. HAUPTMAN

In the mid 1990s, American higher education became a $200 billion enterprise. The activities financed by this $200 billion are tremendously diverse, ranging from huge research universities with budgets of several hundred million dollars to small liberal arts colleges with budgets of several million dollars.

This chapter addresses four aspects of how American higher education is financed in the 1990s. First, it examines trends in the overall level of resources devoted to the enterprise. Second, it discusses the current level of dependence on, and trends in, the major revenue sources. Third, it analyzes the changing role of the various financial aid programs in helping students and their families pay for college. Finally; it identifies the critical financial challenges facing different sectors and types of institutions. In each instance, the chapter speculates on future financial trends.

OVERALL LEVEL OF RESOURCES

By most reasonable standards, America has the best-funded system of higher education in the world. Spending by American colleges and universities in the mid 1990s accounted for nearly 3 percent of the Gross Domestic Product (GDP) (U.S. Department of Education, 1996c; U.S. Government, 1995).[1] This is a higher percentage of GDP devoted to higher education than in any other country in the world. It also represents a tripling over the past half century in the proportion of GDP devoted to higher education (see Figure 8.1).

Much of the growth in higher education's share of the American economy comes from the increased proportion of the population enrolled in college. Like the proportion of GDP devoted to higher education, the proportion of the population sixteen years of age and older enrolled at any one time in higher education also has tripled over the past half century (see Figure 8.2).

The increase in the proportion of the economy devoted to higher education, however, reflects more than just increased participation. Spending per student has also grown in real terms over time, doubling over the past half century (see Figure 8.3) and increasing by roughly 25 percent when adjusted for inflation over the past fifteen years.

Overall economic growth will be a key determinant of how fast resources for higher education grow in the future. Based on historical experience and simulations, strong economic growth in the range of 2 to 3 percent real growth per year is likely to produce substantial increases in resource levels for higher education in the future.

Source: *New Directions for Institutional Research*, no. 93, Spring 1997. © Jossey-Bass Publishers.

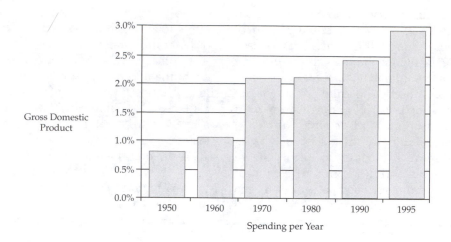

Figure 8.1 Higher Education Spending as a Percentage of Gross Domestic Product

Sources: U.S. Department of Education, 1996c, Table 166, p. 175; U.S. Government, 1995, Table B-1, p. 274.

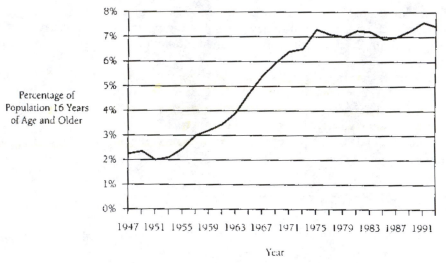

Figure 8.2 Percentage of the Population Enrolled in Higher Education

Sources: U.S. Department of Education, 1996c, p. 176; U.S. Government, 1995, p. 312.

The simulations indicate that this growth in higher education resources will occur even if the proportion of federal and state taxpayer dollars devoted to higher education declines and even if public confidence in higher education in the future is low. (For a discussion of such simulations, see Hauptman, 1992).

On the other hand, low or negative rates of economic growth will most likely result in declining resources per student even if public confidence is high and a larger share of public dollars goes to higher education. In effect, within foreseeable levels of economic growth, the overall size of the economic pie is more important to future resource levels for higher education than is the specific slice of that pie that higher education receives.

REVENUE PATTERNS

This section reviews trends in four major sources of revenues—state and local funding, the federal government, tuitions and fees, and endowment income and private giving. Table 8.1 indicates trends in revenues from each of these sources in the 1980s and 1990s.

Each of the major revenue sources for higher education grew substantially in real terms in the 1980s. This was particularly true in

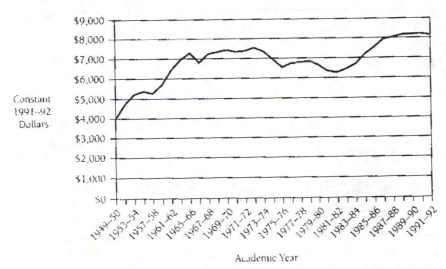

Figure 8.3 Spending per Student in Real Terms Since 1950

Source: U.S. Department of Education, 1996c.

TABLE 8.1
Trends in Major Revenue Sources Since 1980

	Dollars in Billions				Percentage Change		
Revenue Source	1980–81	1985–86	1990–91	(est.) 1995–96	1980–81/ 1985–86	1985–86/ 1990–91	1990–91/ 1995–96
Tuition and fees	13	23	37	55	77	61	49
Federal government	10	13	18	22	30	38	22
State and local government	21	32	43	49	52	34	14
Endowments/gifts	5	8	12	17	60	50	42
Sales and services	14	24	40	50	71	67	25
Other sources	2	3	5	7	50	67	40
Total current fund revenues	65	103	155	200	58	50	29
Inflation rate					31	21	17

the second half of the decade when a growing economy proved to be a boon for higher education. This growth in revenues contributed to a sense of financial well-being, which surrounded higher education for much of the decade. The pattern in the 1990s has been far different, with the rate of growth in resources often less than inflation. In some instances, actual declines in funding in current dollars have replaced previous patterns of growth in constant dollars.

State and Local Financial Commitment

States are the largest source of governmental funding for higher education. In the mid 1990s, they provide roughly $45 billion annually for higher education in general support of public institutions, state student aid programs, and a host of categorical programs.

For most of the past half century, overall state funding of higher education has grown much faster than inflation to support growing enrollments and demands for more services. One notable exception to this trend was the first several years of the 1990s when state spending for higher education stalled and actually fell in current dollars for the first time since these statistics began to be kept in the 1950s.

Since the mid 1970s, however, corrections, health care, welfare, and K-12 education all have eroded higher education's share of state budgets. In the 1980s, a strong economy meant that state support of higher education grew in real terms despite higher education's declining share of state funding. But a weaker economy and continued competition with other functions have made higher education's declining share of state funds a more prominent concern in the 1990s.

Although the state share of institutional budgets has fallen, state funds still represent the primary source of support for public institutions. In the mid 1990s, state funding constitutes roughly 35 percent of current funds revenues for all public institutions, down from 45 percent a decade earlier. As would be expected, state funds are a far less important source of revenue to private institutions, where they have consistently represented 3 percent or less of all institutional revenues.

Local governments contribute roughly $5 billion annually to higher education in the mid 1990s. Almost all of this funding goes to community colleges where local tax dollars typically represent between one-quarter and one-half of current fund revenues. By contrast, local tax dollars represent less than 5 percent of revenues at public four-year institutions, and are an insignificant source of revenue for private institutions.

A growing issue for private institutions is whether they make payments to the community in which they are located in lieu of the taxes they do not pay as a result of their tax-exempt status. This issue of tax exemption and payments-in-lieu-of-tax is a hot one in many communities, particularly in light of several recent court rulings that suggest private colleges should lose their tax-exempt status if they fail to meet certain criteria.

Federal Funding

The federal role in higher education serves three major purposes. First, the federal government sponsors a wide variety of student aid programs, consisting of grants, loans, and work-study, which provide more than two-thirds of all aid available in the mid 1990s. Second, the federal government is the primary funder of university-based research, providing as much as three-fourths of all funding for this purpose. Third, it supports institutions through a wide variety of categorical programs.

For all these functions, the federal government spends about $25 billion annually on higher education in the mid 1990s, excluding any tax breaks that relate in various ways to higher education expenses. Thus, the federal government spends roughly half of what state and local governments spend on higher education. Roughly half of the $25 billion annual federal commitment to higher education is devoted to the various federal student aid programs.

Measuring the federal presence in student aid and the financing of higher education can be confusing, however. One source of confusion is that the face value of federal student loans does not appear on the federal budget; instead, only the subsidies, default payments, and administrative costs associated with these loans are budgetary items.[2] Thus, the more than $10 billion that the federal government annually spends on student aid in the mid 1990s leverages more than $30 billion in financial aid that is provided to students.

It is also difficult to measure precisely the size of federal student aid relative to institutional budgets because most of the aid does not appear in statistical reports as a federal revenue to institutions. Instead, these funds appear as part of the tuition and fees or room and board items that the aid supports.

Student Charges

Tuitions and other student charges in both the public and private sectors have increased at roughly double the rate of inflation for the past fifteen years. Although the annual percentage growth in student charges has slowed in the mid 1990s from previous patterns, it still is roughly double the rate of inflation.

Although the overall percentage growth in tuition and fees has been similar between the two sectors, the patterns and the reasons for this growth have been distinctly different. Tuitions continue to be the principal source of revenue for private institutions. In the mid 1990s, they account for roughly two-fifths of all current funds revenues of private institutions, a proportion that has remained largely the same over the past several decades. Tuitions and other charges at private institutions tend to increase faster during times of economic prosperity, when colleges believe their students and their families can afford the higher rates of increase, and when the costs of various factors of production including faculty, staff, and utilities tend to increase at faster rates than during recessions.

By contrast, tuitions at public institutions tend to increase faster during times of economic recession, as states have more difficulty in maintaining their financial commitment to public institutions because of shortfalls in tax revenues. As state funds become more constrained, tuitions are increased to make up for the shortfalls. As a result, tuitions as a share of all revenues have grown at public institutions. In the mid 1990s, tuition and fees represent about one-fifth of total revenues at public institutions, up from less than one-sixth a decade earlier.

The growth in public sector tuitions is largely a function of state funding patterns. When the economy is strong, and state revenues are growing, the growth in public sector tuitions and fees tends to be relatively moderate. During recessions, when state tax revenues flag, tuitions increase more to make up for the shortfall in state revenues. Thus, public sector tuitions tend to increase the most when students and their families can least afford to pay them.

The growth in tuitions and fees in both the public and private sectors over the past decade and a half mirrors the tremendous growth in the college wage premium—the difference between what college graduates earn and what those without a degree earn. In the 1990s, the college wage premium is at its highest level ever, and many in higher education point to the growth in the college wage premium as a principal argument for the need to send more students to college (U.S. Department of Education, 1996c).[3]

But this emphasis on the private benefits of higher education may undercut arguments for greater public support. It also may be short-lived, as the college wage premium is cyclical depending on a number of economic and demographic trends. For example, if more people graduate from college in the future, the college wage premium could decrease as labor-market shortages shift.

Endowment Income and Private Giving

The size of endowments and the strength of alumni and other private giving are among the most distinctive features of American higher education. This reliance on private giving, in addition to tuitions, represents a primary reason that America devotes such a high proportion of its economy to higher education, as most countries rely much more on public resources to fund their higher education systems.

Private giving has been a particularly important revenue source for independent institutions, where endowment income and private gifts on average represent 10 to 15 percent of total revenues. Contrary to the common perception, however, most private colleges do not have substantial endowments. Roughly one hundred private institutions have endowments with market values in excess of $100 million; endowments of the remaining fifteen hundred private institutions are much smaller.

Nonetheless, for many private colleges, fundraising has long represented the critical ingredient that allows them to be independent of government and to stay in business. Without this source of funds, most private institutions would either have to come under the aegis of state governments or would be forced to charge substantially higher tuitions than they do.

Fundraising is increasingly part of the responsibilities of public sector officials as their institutions seek to replace shortfalls in state funding and reduce the need to raise tuitions. The most notable trend in this regard is the growth of foundations at public colleges and universities, which typically operate separately from the institution itself. But national statistics on public colleges and universities do not accurately reflect this important trend because foundation activities typically are not included in data reported by institutions.

CHANGING ROLE OF STUDENT AID IN PAYING FOR COLLEGE

Over the past three decades, student aid, especially loans, has become increasingly prominent in the financing of American higher education. In 1995–96, roughly $50 billion in student financial aid was provided in all forms from federal, state, institutional, and private sources. (See College Board, 1996, for information on student financial aid presented throughout this chapter.) More than four-fifths of this total aid was provided to students enrolled in higher education institutions; the remainder was for students enrolled in trade schools and other forms of short-term training programs that are not included in the higher education statistics. The $40 billion in federal aid represents roughly two-fifths of the estimated $100 billion in total costs of attendance that college students faced in the 1995–96 academic year.

The growth over time in the overall amount of student aid available consists of mixed trends in the three major forms of student aid—need-based grants, loans, and work-study.

Need-Based Grants

Need-based grants initially were the primary form of student financial assistance. In the past two decades, however, grants have been replaced by loans as the principal source of aid. The federal Pell Grant program is by far the largest government-sponsored grant program, spending about $6 billion annually in the mid 1990s. This level of spending represents more than a doubling in real terms over the level two decades earlier.

Despite this real increase in funding, the buying power of Pell Grants has not increased over this time, for several reasons. First, as already mentioned college tuitions and other charges have increased substantially faster than inflation since 1980, thereby negating the effect of increased federal spending for Pell Grants. Second, the number of Pell Grant recipients has also grown since the mid 1970s, thereby reducing the growth in per-recipient award levels. Third, the mix of aided students has changed over time, with lower-income students representing an increasing proportion of Pell Grant recipients. As a result of these different factors, the maximum Pell Grant award has declined when adjusted for inflation over the same time period that overall funding level for the program has increased in constant dollars.

The other principal federal grant program, Supplemental Educational Opportunity Grants, has not enjoyed as much of an increase as Pell Grants, its younger counterpart. What the program receives in annual appropriations in the mid 1990s is about one-tenth of what the Pell Grants program now receives and is roughly the same in real terms as what it received in the mid 1970s.

Student Loans

Loans over the past two decades have become a major source of financing higher education. In the mid 1990s, they represent more than half of the total amount of financial aid, compared to one-fifth or less two decades ago. Total borrowing for college now reaches $30 billion annually. Loans now finance roughly one-third of total charges for college tuition, fees, room, and board, up from less than one-tenth two decades ago (see Figure 8.4).

This increased reliance on loans has raised a number of worrisome consequences. First,

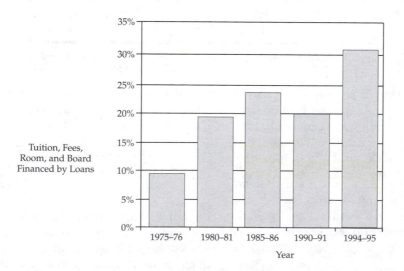

Figure 8.4 Percentage of Tuition, Fees, Room, and Board Financed by Loans

Source: College Board, 1996.

more borrowing by students represents a generational shift in responsibilities from parents to their children. Second, although there are no conclusive data, many fear that the growth in indebtedness may adversely restrict student choices of the colleges they attend and the careers they enter. Third, the huge increase in student indebtedness may serve as a major obstacle to how much many institutions can charge in the future.

For many years, most borrowing was by students enrolled in either independent or proprietary institutions. One of the most marked developments in the past decade however, is that borrowing is much more prevalent among students enrolled in public sector institutions than used to be the case. For example, students at public four-year institutions now borrow roughly one half of all subsidized student loans, up from one-third a decade ago.

Students in public sector institutions also represent a large share of the borrowers in the unsubsidized loan program that was authorized in 1992, partially a function of middle-income students not qualifying for subsidized loans because of the lower costs of attendance in that sector. Similarly, a recent survey indicates that roughly one-half of all baccalaureate recipients borrow, regardless of whether they graduate from a public or private institution.

College Work-Study

The federal College Work-Study program regularly is cited as among the most effective student aid programs, because students have to earn the benefit rather than being given money in the form of grants or borrowing with the possibility of default. Yet, the roughly three quarters of a billion dollars that the federal work-study program receives in appropriations in the mid 1990s is roughly one-quarter less in real terms than what the program received in federal appropriations two decades ago.

ISSUES FACING DIFFERENT SECTORS OR TYPES OF INSTITUTIONS

The preceding discussion does not take into account one of the fundamental facts of higher education in America, namely, that the financial condition of different types of institutions

and the challenges they face in the years ahead vary substantially. This final section identifies some of the major financial issues and challenges faced by public and independent institutions as well as those faced by four major types of institutions—research universities, comprehensive universities, liberal arts colleges, and community colleges.

PRINCIPAL ISSUES FACING PUBLIC AND PRIVATE INSTITUTIONS

Public and private institutions tend to be far more similar in their expenditure patterns than in their revenues (U.S. Department of Education, 1996b;[4] McPherson and Schapiro, 1994). For example, instruction constitutes between one-quarter to one-third of the total budget in both the public and private sectors, research accounts for between 5 and 10 percent of total spending, and public service represents less than 5 percent of total spending in both types of institutions. Operation and maintenance of plant represent about 7 percent of total spending for both public and private institutions, student services represent about 5 percent of the budget in both types of institutions, and academic support activities account for between 6 to 7 percent of total spending in both sectors.

The only spending category in which there is a substantial difference between public and private institutions is scholarships and fellowships (which should not be viewed as a spending category anyway but should be categorized more appropriately as a revenue discount). However they are measured, scholarships and fellowships average more than 10 percent of the budgets of private institutions but constitute less than 5 percent of the budgets of public institutions.

It is on the revenue side where the public and private sectors have their real differences. Tuition and fees constitute one-sixth of the total revenues of public institutions but nearly two-fifths of all private institutional revenues. State funding is the principal source of funds for public colleges and universities, representing on average more than two-fifths of all their revenues. Endowment income and annual gifts provide more than 10 percent of all revenues of private institutions but less than 5 percent of public sector revenues. Because of the differences in their structures and in their principal sources of funds, public and private institutions tend to face distinctly different sets of financial issues.

Changing Patterns of State Support

The principal financial issue facing public colleges and universities in this country is how much support they will receive from state governments in the future and whether the rules and formulas that govern how states allocate funds to institutions will change in light of changing demographic and economic factors.

One concern about public colleges and universities, which is very much related to the more limited funding they now receive from states, is the increased *time-to-degree* for their undergraduates, who on average now take in excess of five years to graduate. This increase in time-to-degree may in part be a function of restricted state funding, which, when it leads to enrollment caps in many states and fewer course offerings at many public institutions, limits the ability of students to enroll in the courses they need to graduate.

The fact that tuitions are rising rapidly at many public colleges at the same time that students are frozen out of classes and taking longer to complete their degrees does not help the public's perception of public higher education. Unlike public institutions, where lengthening in the time-to-degree is a major concern, private colleges' average time-to-degree has not changed materially over time.

Private college officials have a keen interest in how states finance public institutions, although they are less directly affected by this source of support than their public counterparts. Their biggest worry in this regard is that public institutions, by virtue of their state subsidy, are able to charge a much lower price than private institutions, placing them at a competitive disadvantage.

Growing Gap Between Resources and Expectations

All colleges and universities are faced with rising expectations in the form of growing numbers of students and families believing that higher education is the principal ticket to success in our society and worrying that they will not be able to buy that ticket. This growth in expectations is fueled by such demographic factors as the projected increase in the number of high school graduates, which confirm that the demand for higher education will increase rapidly for the foreseeable future.

Public institutions will tend to bear the brunt of these rising expectations, as historical trends indicate that most of the new students who aspire to higher education will enroll in public institutions. In addition, in most of the southern and western states, where the demand for college will be greatest, a relatively large share of college students are enrolled in public institutions.

Private college officials face a slightly different problem in this regard. Unlike their public sector counterparts, they are not expected to educate most of the growing numbers of students for whom higher education previously was an impossible dream. The private college "problem" is mostly one born of the perception of having inadequate resources at the same time that the tuitions they charge are reaching once unimaginable heights. It is this juxtaposition of high prices and nice facilities on the one hand and claims of poverty on the other that poses one of the biggest public relations challenges for private institutions in this country.

Limits of High Tuition-High Aid

The most fundamental financial issue facing the broad range of private colleges and universities in this country is whether they are approaching or have exceeded the limits of the "high tuition-high aid" strategy that served them so well in the 1980s. Most private colleges raised their tuitions much faster than inflation in the 1980s and reinvested an increasing percentage of these tuition dollars in financial aid. The concept underlying this effort was to increase resource levels while at the same time increasing the diversity of their student bodies through the aggressive use of student aid discounts. For most institutions, this strategy worked well in the 1980s.

Whether most private institutions can continue with this high tuition-high aid strategy is a real question. First, there is growing consumer resistance to further steep tuition hikes after more than a decade of rapid increases. Second, as a higher proportion of students are aided, a smaller proportion of each additional tuition dollar is available for purposes other than student aid, unless institutions abandon need-based aid policies.

The dilemma that many private colleges are now facing can be summarized by the following question: Is it possible to increase tuitions, improve diversity, and prevent the exodus of middle-class students, yet still have enough money left over from student aid requirements to pay for program and facility improvements? The answer in the 1980s seemed to be yes for most institutions. With higher charges and more aid recipients in the 1990s, however, the answer now for most private colleges seems to be no.

Interestingly, as many private colleges are questioning the viability of the high tuition-high aid strategy, more and more states and public institutions are debating whether such an approach makes sense for them. Many public institutions now find themselves in a position similar to that which faced private institutions in the early 1980s—they are charging tuitions that are far less than what many of their students would be willing to pay to attend. Not surprisingly, therefore, a number of states and individual public institutions are borrowing from the private college model and using a high tuition-high aid strategy as a means for dealing with shortfalls in state funding for higher education.

ISSUES FACING DIFFERENT TYPES OF INSTITUTIONS

As many differences as there are in the financial challenges facing public and private institutions, the real diversity in the financial issues that colleges and universities face and in their economic situations emerges when different types of institutions are examined. The following discussion focuses on the principal financial issues faced by four types of institutions—research universities, in both the public and private sectors; comprehensive institutions; private liberal arts colleges; and community colleges. Collectively, these four types of institutions account for four-fifths or more of all higher education enrollments in the United States.

Research Universities

Over the past half century, federal support of campus-based research has become a critical component of financing research universities in this country. Federal grants and contracts now account for roughly one-fifth of all revenues for these institutions in both the public and private sectors; the bulk of this support is for campus-based research activities. This degree of dependence on federal funds defines a set of issues that research universities face related to the receipt and use of these funds.

One such issue is the continuing set of controversies related to indirect cost recovery, including what costs are legitimately regarded as being part of research activities. Another issue is the inadequacy of research facilities, which previously were funded separately by the federal government but now are essentially financed out of the indirect cost pool. The pattern of federal research funding over time—for example, the changing mix of defense- and non-defense-related research—is still another issue in this area.

Whereas all institutions must grapple with achieving an appropriate balance between teaching, research, and service, a research university is the type of institution where these tensions are most pronounced. This level of tension means that research universities must periodically address the question of how to ensure that undergraduate education receives the appropriate amount of attention in institutional discussions, policies, and budgets.

In addition, the complexity of research universities has also become a financial issue for these institutions as they have grown in the scope and diversity of activities for which they are responsible. These are big organizations, with annual budgets that often exceed $100 million, and with many constituencies and complex management problems that often include running large health care facilities, big-time athletic programs, and large physical plants that may cover many square miles, not to mention the challenging job of educating thousands of students. The task of running organizations like this should not be minimized in considering the issues facing them.

Comprehensive Institutions

Possibly the single most important issue facing comprehensive institutions is the pressure they face to become research universities. This pressure becomes an issue because typically these institutions lack the resources to make this transition successfully. For every comprehensive that succeeds in becoming a research-oriented institution, many more fail and end up with strained budgets and disgruntled students who worry about what kind of education they are receiving.

A comprehensive also is the type of institution that will feel the greatest pressure to accommodate the growing numbers of students who will be coming out of high school seeking a baccalaureate. To the extent that sufficient funds are not likely to be provided for this purpose, however, these institutions will face a large task.

To the extent that faculty shortages emerge or worsen in certain fields of study in the future, comprehensive institutions are most likely to feel the impact. Research universities and premier liberal arts colleges are now, and are likely to remain, the institutions most successful in attracting new faculty talent. They will also be most able to recruit existing faculty to fill whatever gaps exist in the future mix of their faculties. The result of these flows of new and existing faculty will be that any faculty shortages will have the most impact at the comprehensive institutions.

For several reasons, comprehensive universities also may be most affected by the application of technology and telecommunications to learning processes, particularly through distance learning. First, they are the public institutions that are most likely to have a mismatch between growing demand and inadequate resources and thus may be most interested in exploiting technology. Second, these institutions serve a higher proportion of more nontraditional students than other four-year institutions. These are the students who are more likely to be interested in the possibility of distance learning in the home than students of more traditional college age. Third, comprehensive institutions tend to be more flexible and more attuned to market forces than research universities and liberal arts colleges and therefore may be more willing to experiment with technological applications to learning.

Liberal Arts Colleges

One of the most noticeable trends in American higher education in recent decades has been a growing vocationalism in which students view the value of the education and the degree they receive as directly connected to the jobs they get once they graduate. Liberal arts colleges more than any other type of institution seem to be swimming against this tide of vocationalism by insisting on the intrinsic value of a liberal education (Breneman, 1994).

The critical and distinctive essence of liberal arts colleges is their small size, small classes, heavy interaction between faculty and students, and a streak of independence from political forces. These strengths, however, also may represent the Achilles' heel of these institutions. Many liberal arts colleges lack the critical mass and resource base to withstand external shocks as well as competition for their best students from research universities and public comprehensive institutions. These institutions face the issue of whether they can maintain or add quality to their programs without ruining their ability to compete with less expensive alternatives.

A liberal arts college also is the type of higher education institution that seems most subject to competitive pressures of various kinds. One such pressure is from peer colleges, which often are competing for the same pool of students. This competition for students involves a wide range of institutional policies, including tuition setting; student financial aid; the quality of academic, dormitory, and recreational facilities; and amenities, among others.

Another competitive pressure for liberal arts colleges comes from public institutions, which can offer their programs at a fraction of what private institutions charge because of the large state subsidies they receive. It is this competition from public universities that seems to most engage many private college officials when they are asked about the pressures their institutions face.

These competitive pressures—with other private colleges and with the public sector—relate to the basic financial calculus that most private colleges, but especially liberal arts colleges, must solve. One equation in this calculus is how to maintain or add to the quality of programs and services without reaching beyond the ability of the market to pay for them. A second equation is how to cut costs without affecting quality. These are tough questions that liberal arts college officials regularly must address.

Community Colleges

Most community colleges rely heavily on local property taxes as a primary source of support; these revenues typically pay for one-quarter or more of a community college's budget. Over the past several decades, local property taxes have come under attack for a number of reasons, including charges of regressivity and unfairness in their application. Local taxes have also been the subject of a number of state tax-cutting initiatives, referenda, and legislation. Continued taxpayer resistance to property and other local tax sources could spell big trouble for community colleges, which rely so much on these sources of revenues.

Although community colleges are rightly regarded as one of the great success stories of American higher education, two persistent concerns about them are their low graduation rates and low levels of articulation with four-year colleges. Though many students enroll in community colleges for purposes other than receiving a degree or transferring to a four-year institution, the rate at which community college students either complete their programs or transfer is very low. This lack of success undercuts the credibility of community colleges as academic institutions and therefore could reduce their future levels of public and private financial support.

Because their mission is so fundamentally tied to the goal of providing access, community colleges provide a disproportionate share of the growing amount of remediation that American higher education institutions are being asked to provide to correct inadequate preparation of students in elementary and secondary education. One of the financial issues associated with remediation is that, typically, the institutions that provide it are not adequately compensated for the costs of providing it. Thus, the institution always feels behind to the extent that its revenues do not meet the costs associated with remediation. A related issue is that loans are being used to finance much of remedial education. To the extent that many of the students who take remedial courses will not be able to pay off their loans, we as a society are consigning them to a future of being bad credit risks and a permanent burden to society.

A community colleges is also the type of institution that is most involved with the provision of vocational training for specific job-related skills. This involvement in vocational training raises a number of related financial issues. One such issue is the keen competition that community colleges face from proprietary trade schools, which offer programs that provide many of the same sets of skills as community college training programs.

Competition and cooperation with businesses is another issue raised by the degree to which vocational training is offered by community colleges. Many community colleges have come to rely on the revenues from their programs that provide training for the employees of local businesses on a contract basis. But to the extent that businesses become dissatisfied with the performance of the community college and seek alternative providers or decide to train their own employees, the financial foundation of the community colleges erodes. The considerable overlap that exists between education and training programs at both the federal and state levels is still another issue related to the vocational training that community colleges provide. The confusion that is created by this overlap, and the lack of a systematic approach for financing short-term vocational training, may be contributing to the fact that America lags behind many other industrialized countries in developing specific skills geared to the needs of the workplace.

IMPORTANCE OF INSTITUTIONAL RESEARCH

This chapter has been drawn with a broad brush, aimed at providing the big picture of how higher education is financed in America in the 1990s. Although institutional researchers focus on the financing and the demographics of a particular institution, the trends and issues presented in this chapter provide a context for understanding the issues that individual institutions face.

What states are doing, how the federal role in higher education may be changing, overall trends in giving, and the degree to which financial aid is being provided and in what forms are all considerations within which institutional plans must be realized.

As this chapter has also indicated, these overall trends will have different implications for different institutions. A factor that may be critically important for one type of institution may be largely irrelevant for another. To be successful, the plans of each institution must incorporate consideration of overall trends as well as the issues facing particular types of institutions.

NOTES

1. Spending and revenue figures for higher education in this chapter are from the U.S. Department of Education's *Digest of Education Statistics* (1996c). The data source for national economic activity, population trends, and price indices is the U.S. Government, *Economic Report of the President*, 1995.
2. Further adding to the confusion, with recent changes in federal budget rules, the annual federal costs of student loans are now estimated on a *present value basis;* that is, the flow of costs are estimated over the life of the loan and discounted back to their present value, whereas spending for grants and other forms of aid continues to be shown on an annual basis.
3. Because of data limitations, the college wage premium is typically calculated by comparing the annual earnings of individuals with differing levels of education. The primary data source is U.S. Department of Commerce, Bureau of the Census, *Current Population Reports.* These data are summarized in the U.S. Department of Education's *Condition of Education* (1996a). In the mid 1990s, wage and salary workers twenty-five to thirty-four years old

with four or more years of college had more than twice the earnings of, individuals who did not complete high school. For males, this wage differential was only 50 percent in the 1970s when there was considerable discussion of people being overeducated.
4. Data for different spending categories come from U.S. Department of Education, National Center for Education Statistics, *Current Funds Revenues and Expenditures of Institutions of Higher Education* (1996b).

REFERENCES

Breneman, D. (1994). *Liberal arts colleges: Thriving, surviving, or endangered?* Washington, D.C.: Brookings institution.

College Board. (1996). *Trends in student aid.* Washington, D.C.: College Board.

Hauptman, A. M. (1992). *The economic prospects for American higher education.* Washington, D.C.: Association of Governing Boards of Universities and Colleges and the American Council on Education.

McPherson, M., & Schapiro, M. (Sept. 1994). Expenditures and revenues in American higher education. Williamstown, Mass.: Williams Project on the Economics of Higher Education.

U.S. Department of Education, National Center for Education Statistics. (1996a). *Condition of education.* Washington D.C.: U.S. Government Printing Office.

U.S. Department of Education, National Center for Education Statistics. (1996b). *Current funds, revenues and expenditures of institutions of higher education.* Washington, D.C.: U.S. Government Printing Office.

U.S. Department of Education, National Center for Education Statistics. (1996c). *Digest of education statistics.* Washington D.C.: U.S. Government Printing Office.

U.S. Government, President's Council of Advisers. (1995). *Economic Report of the President.* Washington, D.C.: U.S. Government Printing Office.

CHAPTER 9

FEDERAL STUDENT AID AND THE GROWTH IN COLLEGE COSTS AND TUITIONS

Examining the Relationship

ARTHUR M. HAUPTMAN AND CATHY KROP

SUMMARY OF FINDINGS AND RECOMMENDATIONS

The question of whether federal student aid has fueled the growth in tuitions and other charges has been the subject of heated debate at least since William Bennett raised the issue when he served as Secretary of Education during the mid-1980s. Bennett's argument then was that colleges and universities were chasing their own tail by relying on federal student aid to raise their tuitions and other charges at a rate much greater than the general rate of inflation. An alternative view advanced by most higher education officials has been that critics who accuse them of gouging the consumer and the taxpayer are wrong. They argue that there is no correlation between increases in federal student aid and the rapid growth in tuitions and other charges.

As is often the case in public policy debates, both positions probably have been overstated. The purposes of this paper are: 1) to identify possible ways in which federal student aid policies over time may have affected the growth in college costs and tuitions, and 2) to make recommendations for how the possible inflationary effects of federal student aid policies might be ameliorated.

To assess the possible effects of federal student aid policies on the growth in college tuitions, this paper examines the extent to which the different federal student aid programs covered the total costs of attendance (defined as tuition, fees, and room and board) in 1975, 1985, and 1995.

Federal student aid—grants, loans, and work-study—paid more than two-fifths of the total costs of attendance faced by college students in 1995. Federal aid covered nearly one-half of the total costs of attendance for public college students and nearly two-fifths of the costs for private college students.

The proportion of total costs of attendance met through federal student aid has increased dramatically over the past two decades. Federal student aid in 1975 represented less than one-tenth of the total costs of attendance in the public sector and less than one-fifth in the private sector. In 1985, those proportions had grown to about one-third for the public sector and about one-quarter for the private sector.

Federal loans have become a particularly important source of funding for college students and their families.[1] Federal loans accounted for more than one-third of total costs of attendance in 1995, compared to less than one-tenth in 1975. Given the growing importance of federal loans in paying for college, it is

Source: Prepared for the National Commission on the Cost of Higher Education by the Council for Aid to Education (CAE), An Independent Subsidiary of RAND. December 1997.

increasingly difficult to argue that they have had no effect on tuition-setting at many institutions. This is not to say that college officials stay up nights figuring out how they can set tuition and other charges to maximize the federal aid eligibility of their students. Many other factors probably play a more important role in tuition pricing decisions, including the availability of state funding for public institutions, the demands on all institutions for greater quality in the services they offer, the limited possibilities for offsetting efficiencies and economies of scale, and students' continued willingness to pay higher prices as demonstrated by application patterns at many public and private institutions.

At the very least, however, the tremendous growth in the availability of federal loans has facilitated the ability of both public and private colleges to raise their tuitions at twice the rate of inflation for nearly two decades without experiencing decreases in enrollment or other clear signs of consumer resistance. In particular, it seems evident that private colleges could not have stabilized their share of total enrollments over the past two decades without the tremendous expansion in federal loan availability.

The potential effect of federal loans on college tuition levels is magnified by the fact that, since 1981, student eligibility for the federal in-school interest subsidy has been determined by subtracting family resources and grant aid from the student's total costs of attendance. As a result, eligibility for loans and loan subsidies grows as tuitions and other charges increase, constrained by the amount of annual and cumulative loan limits. Thus, whenever federal loan limits increase, the potential link between tuitions and loans strengthens.

By using total costs of attendance, the federal aid formulas also ignore the growing use of discounting at many institutions. While more and more students and families do not pay the full sticker price for tuitions, fees, and room and board, the current aid system continues to calculate federal aid eligibility as though the stated costs are what people actually pay.

Both public and private institutions have greatly increased the discounts they provide in the form of grant aid from their own resources. The aid private institutions provided from their own resources in 1995 equaled one-fifth of the total costs of attendance—triple what it was in 1975. Compared to private institutions, public institutions provide far less aid from their own resources—one-twentieth of total costs of attendance—but the proportion they do provide grew fivefold from 1975 to 1995. When the discounts provided by institutions are subtracted from the total costs of attendance, federal student aid in 1995 covered more than half of public sector costs of attendance minus institutional aid and nearly half of the "net" private sector costs of attendance. Federal loans financed more than two-fifths of the net costs of attendance at both public and private institutions in 1995.

The 1981 decision to use total costs of attendance in determining eligibility for the in-school interest subsidy has had another important effect: a student's qualification for the subsidy now varies depending on where he or she goes to school. Middle income students who are ineligible for loan subsidies if they attend institutions that charge $10,000 may be eligible at institutions that charge $20,000 or more. That is why federal loan subsidies stretch much further up the income scale than do federal grants or the new tuition tax credits, which address this issue by limiting benefits to families with incomes below $100,000.

Federal grants probably have had less impact on college pricing decisions than loans have. Compared to loans, federal grants cover a much smaller share of total costs of attendance. A smaller proportion of students receive grants than borrow, meaning that federal grants insulate a smaller proportion of students from the effects of higher prices than loans do. Perhaps most important, in the largest grant program—Pell Grants—costs of attendance are effectively no longer a factor in award calculation, thereby reducing the potential link between aid and charges.

This paper suggests that although federal policies have not been the principal factor in the growth of college costs and tuitions, the federal government should consider taking two steps to reduce the potential impact of federal student aid on college costs:

- First, the federal government should no longer recognize total costs of attendance in determining eligibility for federal loan subsidies. Instead, only a portion of tuition (say, 50 percent) over some base level (e.g., $3,000, average public sector tuition) and a standard amount of living expenses should be used in determining eligibility for federal loan subsidies. In addition, there should be an overall limit on the amount of federal aid that a student may receive, including unsubsidized loans, with the limit being lower for undergraduates than for graduate and professional school students.

There are precedents for allowing only a portion of costs to be used in federal aid calculations. Since 1992, a standard amount for living expenses has been used in the Pell Grant program. In addition, the two new tuition tax credits only recognize a portion of tuition costs. Partial cost reimbursement for determining eligibility for loan subsidies could have several distinct benefits over the traditional practice of using full costs of attendance. It could: 1) better target low and middle income students for loan subsidies; 2) reduce the government's role in subsidizing student lifestyle choices; and 3) recognize the growing use of discounting by many colleges in the federal student aid equation.

While some will argue that the proposal for partial cost reimbursement is a form of price control, it is not. Institutions would not have to charge below a specified limit in order for their students to be eligible for federal student aid; nor would the federal government need to monitor what institutions charge. This paper makes it clear that federal price controls and federal monitoring of college charges are inappropriate mechanisms for dealing with the issue of college costs. But this paper also makes it clear that the federal government has a right and a responsibility to the taxpayer to make a policy determination about how much of tuitions and other charges it is willing to subsidize.

One purpose of imposing an overall annual limit on federal aid is to ensure that students can still borrow adequate sums through various federal loan programs while minimizing the potential link between college costs and unsubsidized loans, including in the federal Parent Loans (PLUS) program, in which no annual dollar limit currently exists. Another purpose of an overall federal aid limit, however, is to better target the types of aid that various groups of students receive. With an overall limit on federal aid, students from low income families would receive more of their aid package in the form of grants, while upper income students

would mostly borrow in the unsubsidized loan programs up to some overall limit.

Some will argue that if federal loan policies in the future meet only a portion of charges and the annual amount of federal aid students may receive is limited, institutions will respond as they have in the past to cutbacks in federal student aid—i.e., they will raise their prices still further to generate more discounts for students whose aid has been reduced. But past declines in the real value of federal grants could not have been offset through higher tuitions if more loans had not been available to pick up some of the newly created need. If eligibility for loans and loan subsidies is what is being reduced in this case, institutions would be hard pressed to raise their prices to pay for even more discounting. Moreover, many institutions are reaching or have exceeded the limits of the discounting strategy, because each increase in tuitions and other charges now nets fewer and fewer dollars for non-student-aid purposes.

- Second, the federal government should reduce the regulatory and reporting requirements for institutions that demonstrate they are doing a good job in administering the federal student aid programs through low default rates and other measures of performance in the federal aid programs.

Many college officials argue that the costs of complying with a wide range of federal laws, regulations, and reporting requirements have been an important factor in the overall growth of college costs and tuitions. In the federal student aid programs, the prevailing philosophy in both statute and regulations has been to impose the same rules and reporting requirements on all institutions regardless of how well they administer the federal aid programs. Thus, an institution with a student loan default rate of two percent must comply with the same set of requirements as an institution with a 20 percent default rate.

A system of performance-based deregulation could be designed to make distinctions among institutions as to the types and amounts of regulations and reporting requirements that would be required of them, based on a series of readily available program performance indicators. Such a shift in regulatory philosophy in the federal student aid programs not only would reduce the costs of high performing institutions, it also would allow federal officials to focus their limited resources on institutions that demonstrably are not performing at a minimum level.

THE PARAMETERS OF THE DEBATE

The question of whether federal student aid has fueled tuition growth has been the source of heated debate at least since William Bennett raised the issue when he served as Secretary of Education during the mid-1980s. Bennett's argument then was that colleges and universities were chasing their own tail by relying on federal student aid to raise their tuitions and other charges at a rate much greater than the general rate of inflation. Further assertions by Bennett and others making this argument were that college officials explicitly took federal aid into account in setting their prices and that many students spent the federal aid they received frivolously, buying stereos or taking trips.

An alternative view advanced by most higher education officials has been that critics who accuse them of gouging the consumer and the taxpayer are wrong. They argue that there is no correlation between increases in federal student aid and the rapid growth in tuitions and other charges. They further point to the evidence that *decreases* in federal aid may have led to higher tuitions as institutions attempted to make up for federal aid cutbacks by providing more aid from their own resources, paid for by higher tuitions charged to students judged able to pay the full sticker price. Many college officials also believe that the costs of complying with federal student aid and many other federal as well as state regulations has further contributed to inflated cost structures at many institutions.

As is often the case in public policy debates, both positions in this debate probably have been overstated. By and large, the critics are wrong to argue that colleges and universities are setting their prices largely on the basis of the availability of federal aid. Many other factors probably have contributed more to the rapid growth in college costs and tuitions over the past two decades. Expanding demands on both public and private institutions to provide more and

better services have contributed greatly to the cost spiral. Students and parents have indicated through their actions that they are willing to pay a higher price to have good professors, a wide range of programs, more student services, up-to-date facilities, and pleasant surroundings.

Many officials and analysts also point to the growing gap in lifetime earnings between college graduates and those who do not complete college as being a critical factor in allowing institutions to charge higher prices. Under this view, students and their families have been willing to pay higher tuitions because they recognize that the value of a college education is growing commensurably in terms of labor market differentials.

On the other hand, defenders of the current structure are being unrealistic when they argue that federal aid plays no role at all in tuition pricing decisions. Most observers agree, for example, that many proprietary schools price themselves according to how much federal aid is available. One strong indication of this is that when eligibility for federal unsubsidized student loans was restricted for students attending proprietary schools in the late 1980s, tuitions at many of these schools dropped accordingly. But the potential link between college costs and federal student aid is not limited to the proprietary sector.

Perhaps the most compelling evidence that federal aid has had an impact on tuitions at public and private nonprofit institutions comes from examining the extent to which federal aid now covers total costs of attendance. As shown in Table 9.1, federal aid in 1995 constituted roughly two-fifths of the total costs of attendance—i.e., the total amount that college students pay for tuition, fees, and room and board.[2] Federal loans alone covered more than one-third of the total costs of attendance in 1995. By contrast, in 1975, federal aid paid only one-eighth of the total costs of attendance, and loans paid for less than one-tenth of the total bill.

These figures underscore why it is important to differentiate between grants and loans in assessing the possible significance of federal student aid in the college cost equation. Throughout the twenty year period from 1975 to 1995, federal grants paid for less than one-tenth of the total costs of attendance and were awarded to less than one-third of all students. This relatively stable proportion of funding, combined with the

TABLE 9.1
Federal Aid, Federal Loans, Federal Grants, and Institutional Aid as a Percentage of the Costs of Attendance

				Percentage of costs of attendance			
	Federal Loans	Federal Loans Less Institutional Aid	Federal Grants	Federal Grants Less Institutional Aid	Total Federal Aid	Total federal Aid Less Institutional Aid	Total Institutional Aid
Public Institutions							
1975	3%	3%	6%	6%	9%	9%	1%
1985	25%	25%	9%	10%	34%	35%	3%
1995	41%	44%	7%	7%	48%	51%	6%
Private Institutions							
1975	13 %	14%	4%	4%	17%	18%	6%
1985	22%	25%	6%	6%	27%	31%	11%
1995	34%	42%	3%	4%	38%	46%	19%
Total, Public and Private Institutions							
1975	8%	9%	5%	5%	13%	14 %	3%
1985	23%	25%	7%	8%	31%	33%	7%
1995	38%	43%	5 %	6%	43%	49%	12%

Source: NCES, Digest of Education Statistics, various years; and College Board, Trends in Student Aid, various years.

fact that costs of attendance effectively no longer determine the size of the Pell Grant a student receives, suggests that Pell and other forms of federal grant aid have not played a major role in most colleges' pricing decisions.

The growth in the share of the total bill financed by federal loans, by contrast, suggests that increased reliance on borrowing has played a significant role in allowing the rapid growth of college tuitions and other charges over the past two decades. Federal loans have grown tremendously as a proportion of costs of attendance, from less than one-tenth of total costs of attendance in 1975 to nearly two-fifths in 1995. The potential importance of federal loans is reinforced by the fact that one out of every two college students who are eligible to borrow now do so. With so many students borrowing such a high proportion of costs of attendance, it seems that loans must be providing some degree of insulation to institutions when they raise their prices. In the face of these figures, to argue that student loans are not a factor in college tuition patterns is akin to arguing that the ready availability of mortgages has no impact on the price of housing in this country, or that car manufacturers could maintain their

prices even if loans and leases were not available to finance automobiles.

Another striking trend in the financing of higher education over the past two decades is the rapid growth in the grant aid institutions provide in the form of discounts from their sticker price of tuitions, fees, and room and board. As seen in Table 9.1, institutional aid quadrupled as a proportion of total costs of attendance, from three percent in 1975 to 12 percent in 1995. For a variety of reasons, higher education traditionally has accounted for the student aid institutions provide from their own resources as an expenditure item along with faculty salaries and heating bills. But in recent years, a growing number of higher education officials and analysts have recognized that institutionally funded student aid more properly should be accounted for as a discount from revenues, and that the price students pay minus the financial aid they receive is a more appropriate measure of the costs students face than is the sticker prices published in the college catalogue.

There are a number of important differences in the trends in how students in public and private institutions finance their education, as indicated in Figures 9.1 through 9.5. As

Figure 9.1 shows, federal aid in 1995, for example, financed nearly one-half the costs of attendance for public sector students, compared to about one-third those for private sector students. Both public and private institutions have seen the share of costs of attendance met by federal aid increase rapidly between 1975 and 1995. But, whereas federal aid covered a larger portion of costs of attendance in private institutions than in public institutions in 1975, this was no longer the case by 1985.

Most of this growth in the share of costs of attendance covered by federal aid was due to the growth in federal loans (Figure 9.2). Federal loans accounted for about two-fifths of total costs of attendance in the public sector in 1995, up from less than one-twentieth in 1975. For private sector students, federal loans in 1995 paid for about one-third of costs of attendance, up from one-seventh in 1975 and one-fifth in 1985.

Both public and private institutions have greatly increased the discounts they provide in the form of grant aid from their own resources (Figure 9.3). The use of discounts has traditionally been far more prominent in the private sector. There, discounts repre-

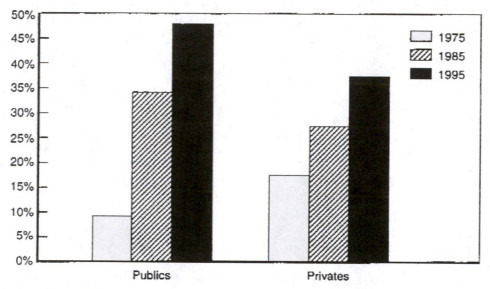

Figure 9.1 Federal Aid as a Percentage of Costs of Attendance

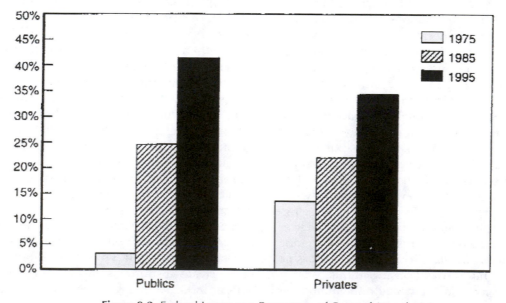

Figure 9.2 Federal Loans as a Percentage of Costs of Attendance

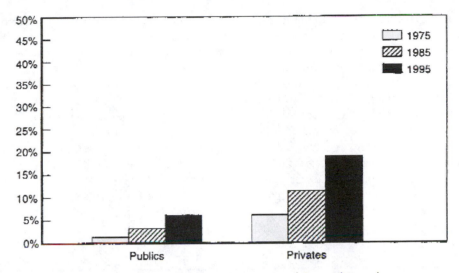

Figure 9.3 Institutional Aid as a Percentage of Costs of Attendance

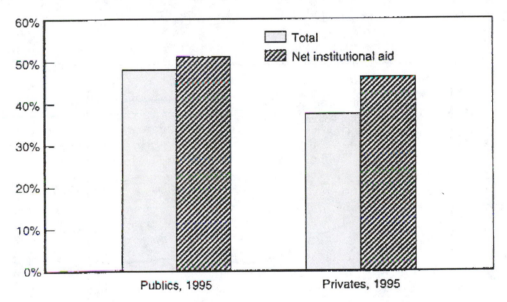

Figure 9.4 Federal Aid as a Percentage of Costs of Attendance

sented nearly one-fifth of the total costs of attendance in 1995, up from one-twentieth in 1975. Discounting is less prominent at public institutions, representing just one-twentieth of costs of attendance in 1995. But the growth in this sector has been rapid—student aid funded by public institutions as a proportion of costs of attendance grew fivefold from 1975 to 1995.

As shown in Figure 9.4, when these discounts are subtracted from the sticker price, federal aid covered just over one-half of the amount students actually paid on a net basis in 1995 in public institutions and almost one-half in private institutions.

In addition, as Figure 9.5 shows, federal loans financed more than two-fifths of the net bill for both public and private sector students in 1995.

Loans have traditionally been a particularly important source of financing for students attending private colleges. In this regard, it is hard to imagine that private colleges could have stabilized their share of college enrollments over the past two decades—which they have, at around 20 to 25 percent of all students—without a healthy growth in student loan availability

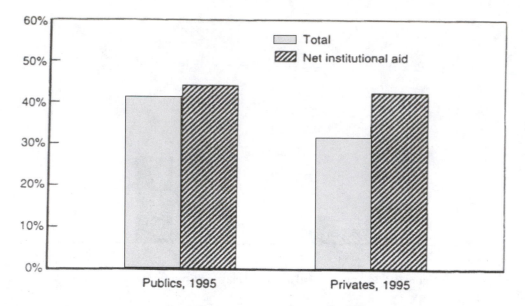

Figure 9.5 Federal Loans as a Percentage of Costs of Attendance

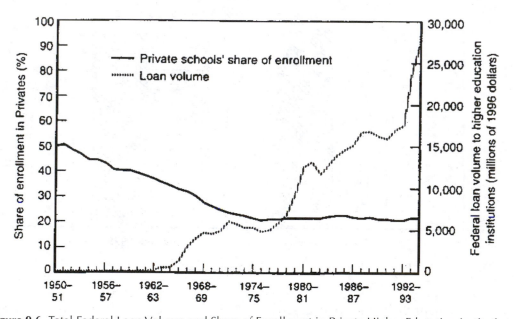

Figure 9.6 Total Federal Loan Volume and Share of Enrollment in Private Higher Education Institutions

(Figure 9.6). This is not to say that federal loan availability has caused private institutions to raise their tuitions or that private college officials spend all their waking hours trying to set tuitions and other charges to maximize the federal aid eligibility of their students. Many other factors can be given greater weight in explaining the growth in tuitions in recent decades, including the pressures to improve programs, facili-ties, and services to compete for the declining numbers of traditional college age students.

But it is also no doubt the case that the growing availability of federal loans has facili-tated the execution of the "high tuition/high aid" strategy that so many private colleges pursued in the 1980s. An integral component of that strategy was to provide financial aid to those students who become "needy" by virtue of the higher prices that are being charged.

And as we have shown, loans represent a large share of the aid that was used to fill this need gap.

Loans traditionally have been far more critical in the financing of private institutions than they have been in the public sector, where tuitions are much lower and the need for loans has been less pressing. And it is clear that loans are not the principal reason public sector tuitions have grown so rapidly in the 1980s and 1990s—that starring role belongs to the slowdown in growth of state support for higher education and the use of tuition to make up for the shortfall in state funding. But the fact that two-fifths of public sector costs of attendance in 1995 were met through loans—up from one-twentieth in 1975—suggests that borrowing must have helped public college students pay the higher tuitions and other charges of the 1980s and 1990s.

RECENT ANALYSES OF THE IMPACT OF LOANS ON COSTS

At least two recent analyses have examined whether a correlation exists between federal loans and the rapid growth in tuitions. Using different methodologies, both studies found no correlation and thus concluded that the growing availability of federal loans has not influenced tuition patterns. Both of these studies, however, present an incomplete picture of the issue, and neither addresses the question of whether a correlation between tuition growth and federal loan availability or the lack thereof is an adequate measure of the possible relationship between tuitions and federal loans.

One of these analyses appears in a memorandum prepared by Jamie Merisotis, of the Institute for Higher Education Policy, for Senator James Jeffords, chairman of the U.S. Senate Committee on Labor and Human Resources. The memorandum to Senator Jeffords presents graphs comparing the annual percentage increases in loan volume and tuitions at public institutions on both a concurrent and lagged basis. The graphs indicate there is no correlation between the annual increases in college tuitions and federal loan volume.

However, studies of year-to-year changes, by their nature, fail to take into account longer term trends and patterns. If the same data in the memorandum to Senator Jeffords are presented on a cumulative basis over time and compared to the growth in the general rate of inflation, there is a much more striking correlation between the growth in loans and tuitions relative to the growth in inflation in both public and private institutions, as Figures 9.7 and 9.8 indicate.

This longer term connection between tuition growth and federal loans seems far more relevant than what happens from year to year. The thrust of our argument in this paper is that college officials set their tuitions each year and then gauge whether students and their families are willing and able to pay the higher prices. In those instances where demand slackens, colleges then either reduce the rate of increase in tuition and other charges in the next year or become even more aggressive with their student aid strategies. In this kind of scenario, growing loan availability over time is a much more important factor in determining students' ability to pay than are annual changes in eligibility rules and limits for federal loan programs.

The other recent analysis of this issue was done by the Coopers and Lybrand consulting group on contract with the American Council on Education. This study used multiple regression techniques to conclude there is no correlation between loan subsidies and the growth in tuitions over the past five years. But for this type of analysis, loan subsidies are an inappropriate measure of the impact of federal loans. The dollar amount that students and their families have borrowed is a much better measure than loan subsidies of the effect of federal loans on college costs, because the amount borrowed represents how much students and their parents do not have to pay out of their own pocket while the students are enrolled. Loan subsidies are also the wrong measure in this case because unsubsidized loans have accounted for most of the increase in federal loan volume since 1992. Unsubsidized loans now represent one-third of all federal loan volume. By looking only at the loan subsidy value, the Coopers and Lybrand study ignored the most significant aspects of recent federal student loan trends.

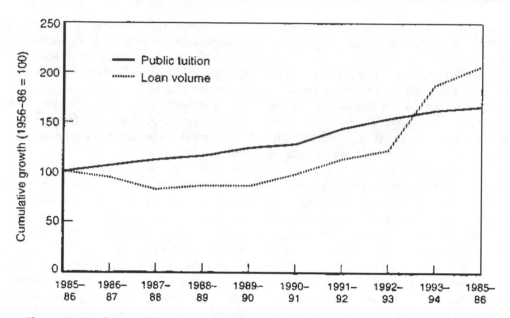

Figure 9.7 Real Growth in Aggregate Tuition and Total Loan Volume at Public Institutions

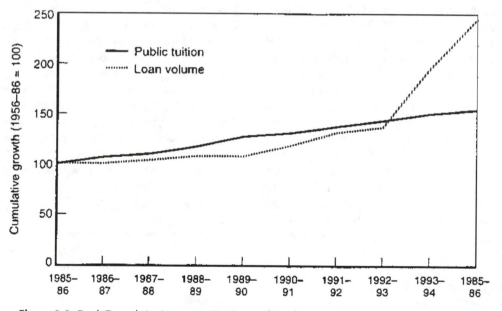

Figure 9.8 Real Growth in Aggregate Tuition and Total Loan Volume at Private Institutions

IS THERE A FEDERAL ROLE IN CONTAINING COLLEGE TUITIONS AND COSTS?

As with assertions about the role of federal aid in the tuition-setting process, proposals about what, if anything, the federal government should do about rising tuitions have been stated in extremes. On the one hand, some would have the federal government limit what institutions can charge or how fast they can increase their tuitions in order to have their students qualify for federal student aid. On the other hand, for those who believe there is no relationship between federal aid policies and tuition inflation, the federal government should play no role in the tuition-setting process.

Both of these extreme responses ignore key historical evidence. Proposals that would allow the federal government to control what institutions can charge seem unwarranted. Past federal efforts at wage and price controls in other industries have been unable to offset much stronger market pressures. But those who advocate no change in the federal student aid programs to address college cost concerns are refusing to recognize the growing role of federal aid, particularly loans, in financing higher education in this country.

The traditional federal policy response to growing college costs and tuitions has been to seek ways to increase aid to keep college affordable. Another way to keep college affordable, however, is to try to keep tuitions and other charges down. The 105th Congress, as evidenced by creation of the National Commission on the Cost of Higher Education, seems prepared to devote considerable time to the question of what, if anything, the federal government might do to encourage institutions to lower the rate of growth in college costs and tuitions.

Some Members of Congress have suggested that the federal government should limit how much institutions can charge in order for their students to remain eligible for federal student aid. Another legislative suggestion has been to limit aid for students attending institutions where tuitions and other charges increase more rapidly than inflation. Both of these approaches, however, would involve the federal government in the process of setting tuitions and other charges, a process in which many would argue it simply does not belong. Either of these approaches also would entail a massive effort on the part of the federal government to monitor how much institutions charge. In the absence of more constructive suggestions for dealing with college costs and tuitions, however, these kinds of federal limits on tuitions and other charges could possibly emerge in the reauthorization process.

The approach of limiting what institutions may charge in order for their students to be eligible for federal aid would be counterproductive, just as past efforts at wage and price controls have failed for other industries. The proposal to limit aid for students attending institutions where tuitions have increased too rapidly would create perverse incentives or lead to accounting tricks. For example, one decision an institution could make to conform its tuition increases to this kind of federal rule would be to cut back on the aid it provides from its own resources. This is certainly not the intention of those who propose such a limit. Another way institutions might react to such a rule would be to restrict tuition growth by shifting to fees or to other charges that would not be subject to the federal limitation. Again, this would not be a particularly desirable or useful result.

TWO PROPOSALS FOR REFORM

This paper proposes that the federal government could address the issue of rising college costs and tuitions in two ways without imposing on institutional autonomy. By making these proposals, we do not mean to imply that federal policies have caused the explosion in college costs and tuitions. As we have already indicated, a number of factors other than federal student aid probably have contributed more to the patterns of tuition inflation in this country. It is worthwhile, nonetheless, to consider whether there are actions the federal government could take to reduce inflationary pressures or incentives that exist in current procedures and rules.

One approach is for the federal government to use only a portion of costs of attendance in determining students' eligibility for loan subsidies and to limit the amount of federal aid students can receive annually, including unsubsidized student and parent loans. The other is to reduce regulatory and reporting requirements for institutions that are judged to be doing a good job in administering the federal student aid programs, thereby reducing their costs of compliance.

PARTIAL COST REIMBURSEMENT AND AN ANNUAL LIMIT ON FEDERAL AID

The federal Guaranteed Student Loan (GSL) program was established in 1965 to ensure that college students would have access to private financed loans that, in the absence of a federal guarantee against default, either would not have been available or would have charged prohibitive interest rates. The program was a federal entitlement in that lenders were insured against default as long as they exhibited "due diligence" in servicing the loan. The federal government was obligated to pay the statutorily set interest rate for borrowers as long as they were in school. In addition, lenders were eligible to receive federal "special allowance" payments to compensate them for the difference between market interest rates and the student interest rate.

To the extent that there may be a policy connection between federal loans and tuition escalation, it can be traced to the decision in 1981 to tie eligibility for federal in-school interest subsidies to a student's need. Prior to passage of the Middle Income Student Assistance Act (MISAA) in 1978, eligibility for the federal in-school interest payment was limited to students with family incomes of $25,000 or less. With the passage of MISAA, which, incidentally, was partially a response to efforts at the time to pass tuition tax credits, the income cap on in-school interest subsidies was removed entirely. In addition, in 1979 the limit on federal special allowance payments was removed so they could float with then volatile market conditions.

These two legislative changes led to the first of several explosions in loan volume in the late 1970s and early 1980s. (Since the mid-1970s, total volume in the federal student loan programs has grown fivefold in real terms.) In response to this boom in student loans, budget reconciliation legislation in 1981 reimposed a cap on which students could receive the federal in-school interest subsidy. But instead of being based solely on family income, the limit imposed in 1981 was based on a student's need—costs of attendance minus expected family contribution and other aid received.

Having a subsidy cap based on need rather than income has changed the dynamics of the federally subsidized student loan programs. With a need-based cap, any increase in student charges potentially translates into greater eligibility for the in-school interest subsidy. The annual and cumulative dollar limits on how much students can borrow become the only thing standing in the way of tuition increases resulting in even more borrowing. As long as loan limits are relatively low, as they were when the need-based cap on the in-school interest subsidy was imposed in 1981 and as they continue to be for certain groups of students, the

connection between loan policy and college charges is tenuous.[3] But when loan limits are increased, the threat of loans spurring further tuition inflation also increases. This is now most obviously the case with the Parent Loans (PLUS) program where there are no dollar limits and a student's costs of attendance are the only limit on how much parents can borrow.

The 1981 policy shift to a need-based subsidy cap also created issues of equity and effectiveness because borrowers' eligibility for the in-school interest subsidy now varies depending on the costs of the institution they attend. A student from a family with $80,000 in family income is now ineligible for federal in-school interest payments if he or she goes to a public institution where the total costs of attendance, including room, board, and other expenses, in addition to tuition and fees, may be $10,000. But if that same student goes to a private institution where the average costs of attendance exceed $20,000, he or she may well be eligible for federal in-school interest payments. At current tuition levels, students with family incomes in excess of $100,000 can qualify for the in-school interest subsidy at the highest-priced institutions. Moreover, eligibility for this interest subsidy continues if the borrower goes to graduate school, thus adding substantially to the long-term federal taxpayer cost.

A need-based subsidy cap can also lead to a situation where the federal government is subsidizing students' lifestyles. For example, if an institution decides to upgrade its dormitories and increases its room fees to pay for the renovations, the federal government could become a partner in this decision by subsidizing loans that reflect the higher cost. Similarly, a student may choose to live in a single dorm room rather than double up, and the government could end up subsidizing this choice. Again, as in the case of higher income students attending higher priced institutions, this subsidy lasts through graduate or professional school and so can be quite expensive to the taxpayer.

Partial Cost Reimbursement

One means for the federal government to address the question of college costs and student aid without intruding on institutional autonomy would be to consider only a portion of a student's total costs of attendance in calculating his or her eligibility for federal loan subsidies. This partial cost reimbursement model would represent a shift from the traditional federal aid practice of recognizing a student's total costs of attendance in determining eligibility for federal student loans. Such a change in policy could have the beneficial effect of decoupling or at least reducing whatever link may now exist between federal aid and tuition setting, since the federal government no longer would match every increase in student charges on a dollar-for-dollar basis.

The federal government could move in the direction of partial cost reimbursement by recognizing a portion of tuition costs (say, 50 percent) above some base level of tuition (say, $3,000, to reflect average tuition and fees at public institutions) and a standard amount of nontuition expenses to determine a student's eligibility for federal loan programs. This proposed change would have no effect on determining eligibility for Pell Grants, which should be allowed to continue to serve as the foundation aid program. In addition, under this proposal, institutions could continue to use the total costs of attendance in determining an individual student's eligibility for the federal campus-based programs.

It also is important to understand that the federal government under the partial cost reimbursement plan described here would not tell institutions how much they could charge. Nor would there be any need to monitor how fast their charges increase. Instead, the federal government would be limiting how much of a student's total costs of attendance can be subsidized through the federal loan programs. In operational terms, what the family is expected to contribute and whatever federal grant aid the student receives would be subtracted from the partial costs of attendance, rather than the current practice of using whatever the institution charges as the upward bound of federal subsidies.

There are precedents for this kind of partial cost reimbursement approach. The Pell Grant program, for example, since 1992 has only recognized a standard living expense in its award formula. And the two newly enacted tuition tax credits—the HOPE and Lifetime Learning tax credits—recognize only a portion of tuitions, precisely to discourage institutions from raising their tuitions in order to capture more federal tax benefits for their students.

Interestingly enough, neither of these precedents was criticized as being an example of federal price controls.

A primary argument against partial cost reimbursement will be that students will no longer be able to go to the school of their choice if they are no longer eligible for subsidized loans. There are at least two counter arguments to this contention. First, students and their parents could still borrow in the unsubsidized loan programs. Second, by not using total costs of attendance as a benchmark, federal policies would finally recognize the growing role of states and institutions in the provision of student aid, unlike the traditional practice where the federal government acts as though it is the only source of funds in the student aid process. Thus, partial cost reimbursement could help to address the growing concern in the Congress that institutions use their sticker price to determine federal aid eligibility for all students, even those who do not pay the full sticker price because of institutional discounts.

Partial cost reimbursement also represents a way to limit how much in the way of family resources students may have and still qualify for the federal in-school interest subsidy. In the current federal student loan structure, the higher the costs of attendance, the higher the income that students can have and still qualify for the in-school interest subsidy. If the federal government were to set limits on how much it would reimburse through subsidized borrowing, the in-school interest subsidy would be better targeted than is currently the case. In addition, if nontuition expenses were limited to a standard amount, the federal government could get out of the business of subsidizing student lifestyle choices.

In effect, partial cost reimbursement is a way to reestablish an income limit on subsidies in the federal student loan programs while improving upon a simple income cap. Unlike a cap on income, subtracting expected family contribution from the partial costs of attendance would have different effects on students whose family incomes are similar but whose other circumstances differ. For example, students from families with two children in college might still be eligible for the subsidy, while another family with similar income but only one child in college would be ineligible. In addition, subtracting a student's family contribution from partial costs to determine eligibility for subsidized loans reduces the "notch effect" that simple income limits can create. With an income cap, students with one dollar less than the limit may participate fully in the program, while those with one dollar more would not be eligible at all, i.e., a notch effect exists at the dollar limit. Under the approach suggested here, one more dollar in family contribution simply would mean the student is eligible for a dollar less in subsidized loans.

Students whose family contribution and other aid are less than their partial costs of attendance would still be eligible for the in-school interest subsidy. Students whose family contribution exceeded the partial cost calculation would be ineligible for subsidized loans, but could still borrow in the federal unsubsidized loan programs. In a time of more limited federal resources, targeting subsidies to those students with lower family incomes regardless of where they go to school and providing unsubsidized loans to meet the cash flow needs of students from families of more substantial means seems far more appropriate than the current policy of providing better-off students with expensive federal subsidies throughout their educational careers.

The important point here is that policymakers ought to decide how far up the income scale they want to provide subsidies, rather than have the limit on who receives the subsidy be a consequence of how much an institution charges, as is currently the case in the federal loan programs. If properly structured, partial cost reimbursement could reduce whatever incentive exists for higher-priced institutions to increase their tuitions, since students with family incomes above the cap would no longer find their eligibility for subsidized loans increase as tuitions rise.

A partial cost approach could lead to lower federal subsidy costs, but that need not be its underlying purpose. Limits on the amount of subsidy that higher income students receive also could be used to increase subsidized loan limits for students from lower income families. If that were the case, the result of adopting a partial cost approach would be a redistribution of subsidies rather than an overall reduction in federal expenditures for student loans.

Some will argue that if federal loan policies in the future meet only a proportion of

tuitions and other charges, many institutions could respond by raising their prices still further to generate more discounts for students whose eligibility to borrow had been reduced. But most institutions in the past could not have offset federal grant decreases through higher discounts if federal loans had not been available to pick up much of the newly created need. If loan eligibility is what is being reduced in this case, institutions would be hard pressed to raise their prices to pay for more aid discounting.

We want to emphasize again that under partial cost reimbursement, institutions could charge whatever they want and there would be no federal role in monitoring their tuitions and other charges. The federal government simply would stop providing subsidized loans to students with family contributions above a certain level.

Imposing an Annual Limit on Federal Aid

The preceding discussion does not address the question of whether students who become ineligible for federal in-school interest subsidies under a partial cost reimbursement approach should be able to participate fully in the federal unsubsidized loan programs, and whether parents should continue to be able to borrow up to the full costs of attendance in the PLUS program.

The dilemma here is as follows: If what students and parents may borrow in the unsubsidized programs is limited to the partial costs of attendance, then many current students and their families will simply not be able to borrow enough through the federal loan programs to attend the institution of their choice. On the other hand, if students can borrow unsubsidized loans up to the total costs of attendance, then nothing will have been done about the issue of college costs and federal loans. Whatever link between college tuitions and federal loans may now exist will simply shift over to the unsubsidized federal loan programs, with lower federal expenditures for student loans but higher borrowing costs for many students.

One solution to this dilemma would be for the federal government to limit how much federal aid students can receive annually, including through the various unsubsidized programs. Each of the federal student aid programs has limits on how much students can receive, but there is no limit on the total amount of federal aid they can receive, either annually or over the course of their education. As a result, rising college tuitions and other charges often are financed through a progression of federal student aid programs. Campus-based aid is added to Pell Grants, subsidized loans are added to the campus-based programs, unsubsidized student loans and PLUS loans are added to the subsidized loan amounts. The total amount of federal aid through the Title IV programs sums up to well in excess of $15,000 for undergraduates and more than $20,000 for students in graduate and professional school fields of study.[4] While few students receive this much in federal aid, adding one federal program on top of another with no sense of an overall limit increases the potential link between college costs and federal aid.

The lack of an overall annual limit on federal aid also contributes to concerns about the fragmentation of the student aid delivery system and an overall lack of coherence in federal policies. If one were to ask how much federal aid a student can receive, few people could answer that question, because an overall figure never appears in the legislation or in federal student aid documentation. Students and their families do not know how much federal aid is available, because the information is never provided. In addition, the absence of an overall limit means no tradeoff exists among federal aid programs. What students receive in grants typically does not affect how much they or their parents can borrow.

Placing a limit on total annual federal aid would build on the proposal for a Student Total Education Package (STEP), the keystone of the 1993 report of the National Commission on Responsibilities for Financing Postsecondary Education. The STEP proposal principally was made to increase awareness about the availability of federal aid and to generate support for more funding of federal aid. But such an approach also could help to reduce the potential link between college tuition costs and federal student aid programs by removing total costs of attendance from of the student aid equation. Imposing an overall limit on how much federal aid students may receive would have another important favorable consequence. It would introduce greater policy coherence into the federal student aid structure by establishing a relationship among the various federal programs.

PERFORMANCE-BASED REGULATORY RELIEF

Colleges and universities, like any other organizations in our society, are obligated to comply with a broad range of federal and state laws and regulations. As issues in our society have become increasingly complex, the breadth of laws and regulations with which higher education institutions must comply has similarly grown.

For colleges and universities, these laws and regulations govern the safety of their workers, the security of their students, and the environmental hazards created in their laboratories. Many higher education officials believe that compliance with federal and state laws and regulations has contributed greatly to increased costs and consequently to the tuitions charged. Some have estimated that as much as ten percent or more of total expenditures at their institutions go toward providing the necessary information to dozens of federal and state agencies.

These concerns are not new, however. The American Council on Education, for example, issued a report in 1976 on the costs of federally mandated social programs at colleges and universities. That report suggested that while the compliance costs to individual institutions were small—less than 5 percent of operating budgets—they were growing much faster than instructional costs or total revenues. Interestingly, the highest cost item identified in the 1976 report was the payment of social security taxes. The belief that federal laws and regulations are adding to the costs of higher education has not abated in the intervening two decades, although environmental regulations are now a more likely target of criticism of excess regulations. Few college officials would now mention social security taxes as a burdensome regulation.

With regard to the federal student aid programs, the prevailing philosophy in both statute and regulation has been to have all institutions comply with the same set of rules and reporting requirements. To participate, all institutions must comply with uniform requirements, including maintaining a default rate in the student loan programs below certain specified levels, meeting certain minimum financial requirements, being accredited by a recognized accrediting agency, and providing annual audits and other information as required by the Higher Education Act and related regulations. In the existing regulatory structure, little or no distinction is made based on how well institutions administer the federal aid programs. Institutions with low default rates and well-run aid offices are subject to the same reporting requirements as institutions with high default rates and understaffed or nonexistent financial aid offices.

The Clinton Administration has proposed moving away from this traditional philosophy. It advocates instead the development of a system in which institutions determined to have done a good job in administering the federal student aid programs would be subject to less intensive regulatory and reporting requirements than those institutions that have not performed as well. The Administration's proposal was prompted in part by comments it had received from a number of college officials who argue that their institutions are doing a good job administering the programs and that they should not be subject to the same rules and regulations as institutions with an inferior track record.

The Administration sponsored a set of discussions in 1995 and 1996 on a preliminary proposal of performance-based deregulation and invited formal written responses from interested parties. While there was considerable interest on the part of many college and university officials in pursuing the notion of performance-based deregulation, the response from much of the higher education community, as represented by their associations, was lukewarm at best. Representatives of at least several of the associations suggested instead that broad-based deregulation was a more appropriate approach to the issue of overregulation in higher education than deregulation based on the performance of institutions. In the heated environment preceding the 1996 presidential campaign and election, the Administration chose to postpone deliberations on its proposal.

The notion of differentiating regulatory and reporting requirements on the basis of how well institutions are administering the federal student aid programs remains a good idea, however, and one worth further exploration and debate. A performance-based deregulation approach would appropriately reward institutions that demonstrate they are doing a good job administering the federal student aid programs. It also would allow federal regulators to target their limited resources for enforcement on those institutions that are not meeting minimal standards in administering the federal student aid programs.

NOTES

1. In this paper, the term *federal loans* refers to the various federally sponsored loan programs, including those financed with federal capital as well as privately financed loans that are either subsidized or guaranteed by the federal government or its agents. The term *subsidized loans* refers to loans for which the federal government pays the interest while the borrower is in school; *unsubsidized loans* are federally guaranteed but provide no federal in-school interest payment. All federal loans are subsidized, however, in that the effective rate of interest, which is set by law, is well below what the private sector charges in the absence of a federal guarantee.

2. Figures for federal student aid provided in this analysis come from College Board, *Trends in Student Aid,* various years. Figures for institutionally funded student aid, costs of attendance, and full-time equivalent student enrollments are as reported in the *Digest of Education Statistics.* Costs of attendance estimates do not include books, supplies, transportation, and other expenses. While the methodology used in this paper differs from one used by Jerry Davis in his recent analysis, *College Affordability,* the results are strikingly similar.

3. Michael McPherson and Morton Schapiro in Chapter 8 of their new book, *The Student Aid Game,* reject the notion that federal loans have contributed to tuition inflation largely on the basis that there are limits on how much students can borrow.

4. These figures do not include veterans' education benefits and other specialized forms of aid, such as scholarships and fellowship programs provided under Title IX of the Higher Education Act. Nor do they include health professional loans and other specialized loan programs not authorized by the Higher Education Act.

CHAPTER 10

THE GROWING LOAN ORIENTATION IN FEDERAL FINANCIAL AID POLICY

A Historical Perspective

JAMES C. HEARN

In the past two decades, the federal government has dramatically changed the ways in which it aids the financing of postsecondary students' attendance. From a roughly equal emphasis on student loans and grants, the government has moved toward an approach dominated by loans. Increasingly, federally supported student aid is loan aid, not grant or work-study aid. Largely as a result of this emerging federal emphasis, loans have grown to well over half of all the student financial aid awarded in this country.

The increased use of loans as the primary instruments of federal student aid policy has created new financial challenges in students' and graduates' lives. The effects of students' rising debt levels, in particular, have been much discussed in the popular press, in the chambers of Congress, and among those closely involved in student aid issues. Often, the language used has been that of crisis. For example, a senator closely associated with the rise of federal student aid grants has worried publicly that rising debt levels might be creating "a new class of indentured servants" (Senator Claiborne Pell, cited in Kosterlitz, 1989, p. 921). In a similar vein, College Board president Donald Stewart said recently that we are facing "a deeply mortgaged future. It may be individuals who pay off the educational debts, but we as a society are co-signing the mortgage—and paying a high social cost as well" (College Board, 1995a, p. 11).

The actual short- and long-term implications of the recent loan explosion have been little studied empirically before now, and the severity of the problem is unclear (Baum, 1996). What *is* clear, however, is that the financial aspects of attending college have changed remarkably since the mid-1970s. To aid understanding of that transition, in this chapter I trace the history of student loans in federal financial aid policy. The emergence of the current federal emphasis on loans is best understood by looking back further than the past two decades and by examining more than the federal loan programs alone. Investigating the programs' development since their inception and in broad political, economic, and social context illuminates why particular paths were taken and how the legacy of taking those paths shapes contemporary policies.

The chapter is organized in three parts. The initial section provides a brief overview of the history of federal loans and other forms of federal student financial aid, focusing particularly on trends in dollar outlays and student participants. The following section profiles in more detail the often colorful policy history of the federal loan programs.[1] In the concluding section, I discuss the

Source: *Condemning Students to Debt: College Loans and Public Policy*, R. Fossey & M. Bateman (eds.), 1998, Teachers College Press, Columbia University, New York, NY.

federal loan programs' evolving role in the financing of higher education.

AN OVERVIEW OF FEDERAL INVOLVEMENT IN STUDENT LOANS

Prior to the passage of the Higher Education Act of 1965, the federal government supplied only one form of aid generally available to all college students: National Defense Student Loans. Originated in 1958, these loans were later renamed National Direct Student Loans, then renamed again, as Perkins Loans. Other federal aid prior to 1965 was specially directed

to particular groups, such as that offered through the Servicemen's Readjustment Act of 1944 (the "GI Bill"). As noted in Table 10.1, all federal student aid totaled a little over one billion dollars in 1963–64 (in 1994 dollars).

Activist national education initiatives in the 1960s expanded the total of direct federal student aid outlays. By providing matching and cost-support funds, the federal government also spurred dramatic growth in other forms of aid in that period. By 1970–71, the total of these two kinds of federally *supported* student aid was $12.5 billion in 1994 dollars.[2] A decade later, the total was nearly twice that amount. Thus, total federally supported aid

TABLE 10.1
Total Aid Awards for Postsecondary Students in the United States
(Selected Years, in Millions of U.S. Constant Dollars)

	1963–1964	1970–1971	1975–1976	1980–1981	1985–1986	1990–1991	Est. 1994–1995
Federally Supported Aid:							
Generally Available Federal Aid:							
Pell Grants (formerly Basic Grants)	0	0	2505	4088	4866	5436	5570
Supplementary Educational Opportunity Grants (SEOG)	0	499	538	630	559	501	546
State Student Incentive Grants (SSIG)	0	0	53	124	103	65	72
College Work Study (CWS)	0	849	789	1131	895	806	749
Loan Programs:							
Perkins Loans	547	898	1231	1188	959	964	958
Income-Contingent Loans	0	0	0	0	0	0	0
Family Education Loans (Non-Direct):							
Subsidized Stafford Loans	0	3791	3389	10,623	11,360	11,075	13,906
Unsubsidized Stafford Loans	0	0	0	0	0	0	7039
Supplemental Loans for Students (SLS)	0	0	0	0	367	1894	32
Parent Loans (PLUS)	0	0	0	0	330	1059	1637
Direct Student Loans (Ford Program):							
Subsidized Stafford Loans	0	0	0	0	0	0	1073
Unsubsidized Stafford Loans	0	0	0	0	0	0	471
Parent Loans (PLUS)	0	0	0	0	0	0	168
Total Generally Available Federal Aid	547	6038	8505	17,784	19,439	21,806	32,221
Specially Directed Federal Aid	565	6508	14,654	6820	2245	1672	2388
Total Federally Supported Aid	1112	12,546	23,159	24,604	21,684	23,479	34,610
State Grant Aid	269	882	1311	1372	1788	2059	2628
Institutional and Other Grant Aid	1297	3125	3126	2782	4040	6379	8929
Total Federal, State, and Institutional Aid	2679	16553	25,857	28,758	27,511	31,917	46,167

Note: These data are adapted from data supplied by the Gillespie and Carlson (1983) and the College Board (1995). See text for details on the data.

grew over 20-fold between 1963–64 and 1980–81. After relative stability in the 1980s, the number began to grow dramatically again, reaching an estimated total of over $34 billion dollars in 1994–95.

Most of the growth in federal student aid has been in programs providing aid generally available to the American public, rather than in aid targeted for special groups such as veterans. As Table 10.1 reveals, the generally available aid programs were over 32 times larger in 1980–81 than in 1963–64. That growth slowed in the mid-1980s but surged again in the later years of the decade. Then, between 1990–91 and 1994–95, generally available aid awards rose a remarkable 48%. At middecade, the programs were 59 times larger than in 1963–64.

The bulk of this recent growth came in the federally supported loan programs, and those programs now compose the great majority of the generally available federal aid. For reinforcement of that point, consider the other generally available federal programs, for grants and work-study support respectively. Federal grant programs include the massive Pell Grants program and the smaller Supplemental Educational Opportunity Grants (SEOG) and State Student Incentive Grants (SSIG) programs. After adjusting for inflation, federal grant aid has grown little for the past decade, totaling $6.2 billion in 1994–95. The other federal non-

loan program, the College Work Study (CWS) program, has actually shrunk since the 1970s, and totaled only $749 million in 1994–95. The combined 1994–95 total of under $7 billion dollars in the Pell, SEOG, SSIG, and CWS programs contrasts dramatically with the over $25 billion committed under the loan programs in that year.

As suggested in the table, the federal government has initiated many loan programs over the years. A brief introduction to those programs will be provided here, with more details to come later in the chapter. Perkins loans, as noted earlier, began in 1958. These are administered by campus aid officials, and funds are supplied directly by the federal government. Income-contingent loans, which allowed students to repay at a set percentage of income, were a separate program for a period in the 1990s, but this program has been discontinued and income-contingent repayment is now provided as an option within other federal loan programs. The Federal Family Education Loan Program (FFELP) includes all the programs based in funds supplied by private lenders, mainly banks and state-licensed or -controlled financing organizations. What is now the subsidized Stafford Loan program under the FFELP was once known as the Guaranteed Student Loan (GSL) program. The unsubsidized Stafford Loan program under

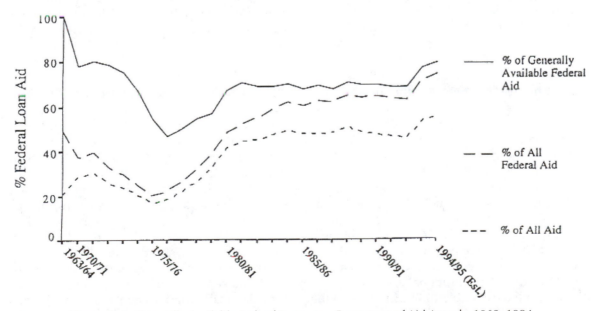

Figure 10.1 Generally Available Federal Loans as a Percentage of Aid Awards, 1963–1994

FFELP is a newer effort to provide loan funds for students not qualifying for federal subsidies on interest while they are in school. A growing share of federal student loans (one third in 1994–95) is now unsubsidized. The Supplemental Loans for Students program was the predecessor of the unsubsidized Stafford Loan program, and has now been phased out of existence. The final FFELP program is the Parent Loans program, known as the PLUS program, which provides unsubsidized loans to the parents of students who do not qualify for sufficient subsidized loan aid to meet educational costs. Recently, three non-FFELP versions of the Stafford and PLUS programs have been funded on a trial basis: Under the new Ford Direct Student Loan Program (FDSLP), funds for loans are provided by the federal government to college aid offices, which in turn directly allocate the loans to students.

These varied loan programs will be discussed in more detail later in this chapter. For now, it is instructive to examine them as a block. Figure 10.1 traces generally available federal loan support as a percentage of aid awards, using the data of Table 10.1. The solid line, for federally supported loans as a percentage of all generally available federal aid, suggests that the federal government's percentage in loans drifted down from a total orientation to NDSL loans in the year immediately preceding the Higher Education Act of 1965 to just under half in 1976–77. Then, the percentage began a quick climb upward to a range between 65 and 70%, where it stayed until 1992–93. In 1993–94, it rose to 76%. In 1994–95, it rose to 78%. The broad-dashed line, for loans as a percentage of all federal aid, tells a similar story. The distance between this line and the solid line above it narrows because of the decline in specially targeted federal aid. Virtually all targeted aid has been in the form of grants, so the gradual disappearance of those forms of aid spelled substantial declines for grant aid as a percentage of all federal aid.

There has also been notable growth in federally supported loans as a percentage of all federal, state, and institutional aid combined, denoted in the figure by the short-dashed line. Over the years since 1980–81, state grant aid has doubled, and institutional and other grant aid has tripled (see Table 10.1). Still, most of the absolute growth in aid totals has come from the

growth of the dollar volume of federal loans. The figure reveals that student financial aid in the United States is increasingly composed of federally supported loan aid. That aid moved from around 20% of all aid in 1963–64 to a low of 17% in 1975–76, then rose to a high of 55% in 1994–95. The fact that federally supported loans are now over half of all aid is especially startling in light of the relatively small role that loans played in overall aid outlays as recently as 20 years ago.

Two elements in the loan data merit further attention: the growth in programs other than the Perkins program, and the increasing use of programs other than the traditional subsidized, nondirect guaranteed student loan program. The increasing dominance of the FFELP and the FDSLP over the Perkins program is clear from the raw data of Table 10.1: Between 1975–76 and 1994–95, the dollar investment in loan programs other than Perkins grew from $3.4 billion to over $24 billion. In the same years, the number of loans other than Perkins loans increased from 922,000 to 7 million (Gillespie & Carlson, 1983; College Board, 1995b). Meanwhile, funding for Perkins loans has grown relatively little in real terms over the years since their inception, and they are not central elements in the recent "loan explosion."

Regarding the second important element in the historical data, policy makers and students have recently made increasing use of programs other than traditional guaranteed student loans. It is instructive to trace the history of the average nondirect subsidized Stafford loan from its inception under the original GSL program to the present. In constant-dollar terms, loans of this kind have actually decreased in size since 1970–71, according to data from the College Board (1995a). Thus, the rising spending for subsidized Stafford Loans has gone largely into additional loans for additional students, not into more generous loans to individual students. The increase in the number of students served by the subsidized Stafford program seems to be related more to increasing college costs and to the increasing number of financially independent (and, therefore, usually more needy) college students rather than to major expansion of program eligibility standards. Indeed, financial eligibility requirements for federal aid programs tightened in real terms over the 1980s, and award sizes stagnated. In response, more students and their families have qualified for modest Stafford loans and also have made more extensive use of other sources of aid, including the growing array of alternative federal loan programs.

Two good cases regarding the latter point are the PLUS program and the unsubsidized Stafford program. Both nondirect and direct PLUS loans averaged over $5,000 in 1994–95, and together those programs served an estimated 351,000 students that year. Similarly, both nondirect and direct unsubsidized Stafford loans averaged over $3,500 that year and together provided an estimated 2.1 million students with loans. In both cases, individual loan amounts were substantially larger than those in the long-standing, nondirect, subsidized Stafford loan program. Together, the number of students served by these alternative programs was far from insignificant. While 4.3 million students received the traditional, nondirect, subsidized Stafford loans in 1994–95, 2.7 million received a nondirect, unsubsidized Stafford loan, a direct, subsidized Stafford loan, a direct, unsubsidized Stafford loan, a nondirect PLUS loan, a direct PLUS loan, or a combination of these (College Board, 1995b).

In sum, federal student aid policy progressed from the relatively small NDSL program of the early 1960s to a substantially greater effort with a roughly equal focus on grants and loans in the 1970s, then in the years since has moved to an even more substantial effort with a renewed emphasis on loans. Although the original NDSL (Perkins) program has grown only modestly over the years since the 1960s, other student loan programs have grown dramatically in dollar terms, in variety, and in coverage of the student population. Behind this striking growth is a colorful political history.

THE POLICY HISTORY OF FEDERAL STUDENT LOANS

Federally supported loans for facilitating postsecondary attendance are a relatively new aspect of the finance of higher education in the United States (Kramer, 1991). Some limited, highly targeted federal loans were made in World War II and, shortly after the war, the Truman Commission, a presidentially appointed panel, argued vigorously for federal student

loans (Presidents Commission, 1947; Woodhall, 1988). Nevertheless, federal financial aid up to the late 1950s consisted almost entirely of specially directed grant aid. At that time, however, federal leaders troubled by the nation's military, technological, and scientific status relative to the Soviet Union came to view investment in education as a productive countermeasure. Overcoming longstanding reservations regarding federal activities in education (see Morse, 1977), they implemented the National Defense Education Act of 1958. The National Defense Student Loan (NDSL) program was a prominent feature of the act. Thus, federal loan programs emerged largely out of noneducational concerns, a typical pattern in federal higher education policy making (see Brademas, 1983; Moynihan, 1975; Schuster 1982).

The NDSL program was the first federal loan program, and indeed the first federal aid program, not targeted toward particular categories of college students. Former NDSL director John Morse (1977) has noted that "it was the national panic (not too strong a word) over Russia's success in launching the first satellite that gave federal aid proponents the opening they needed" to overcome federal leaders' historic reluctance to become involved in higher education (p. 3).

NDSL funds were to be awarded to campuses, which in turn would provide loans to full-time students on the basis of need, as determined by institutions. Preference was to be given to students in the sciences, teaching, mathematics, and modern foreign languages. Forgiveness of loan debts was to be granted to students in certain careers, such as teaching. The loans were to be repaid over long terms at a low interest rate (3%). The government contributed $9 to a school's loan fund for every dollar provided by the institution. All repayments were to be reinvested by institutions in further student loans. In 1958–59, 27,600 students received these new loans, which totaled $9.5 million.

In its first few years, the NDSL program's preferences for students in certain fields were removed. Interestingly, the government consistently underestimated the interest from both students and institutions in participation in these loans, and the roster of institutional and student participants grew substantially. The total NDSL funds requested by institutional applicants regularly exceeded appropriations by a factor of 20 or more in the early years of the program, and the government found itself in the novel and awkward position of judging the relative worthiness of different institutions (Morse, 1977).

The NDSL program was the first federal effort to require testing of students' financial need, and the first to involve a contract between the federal government and institutions (Moore, 1983). For our purposes, however, the historically most notable aspect of the NDSL program is its pioneering of the notion of generally available federally supported loans for college students. Before the late 1950s, loans for college students were largely privately or institutionally originated and based on the income and financial positions of the student's parents (Bosworth, Carron, & Rhyne, 1987; Gillespie & Carlson, 1983). Some states (prominently including New York and Massachusetts) and some across-state associations initiated guaranty funds in the 1950s to support commercial lending to students, but interest on these loans was generally not publicly subsidized (see Barger & Barger, 1981). Although some of these efforts served as models for the development of later federal loan programs (Marmaduke, 1983), there was no significant federal support for commercial, institutional, or state lending to students before the NDSL program.

The development of the NDSL program can be viewed as the initiation of the modern era of federal student aid. The consequences of this program and the federal efforts that followed it were profound for those involved in student-aid work at the campus level. Before the late 1950s, student aid administration was not developed as a professional field and student aid offices were far less complex and systematized than today. Analysis of a student's aid eligibility was rather primitive by current standards, often involving simple income cutoffs. The initiation of the NDSL program brought growing demand for institutions to measure accurately their students' actual financial needs. Seeing that their need analysis efforts could benefit from collective wisdom as well as from economies of scale in formula development and processing expenses, institutions increasingly turned to the College Scholarship Service (CSS), a service organization

begun by the College Board in 1954. Integrating generalized need analysis routines with the unique need and award standards of each institution, the CSS was a harbinger of aggressive modernizing efforts in student aid in the 1960s and beyond.

Despite the stirrings brought on by the NDSL program, however, the student aid arena remained quite small at the federal level for several years. This was all to change remarkably in 1964–65. A new Social Security benefit for recipients with dependents in college and a new aid program for students in health-related fields were initiated at that tithe, but these developments were soon overshadowed by the passage of the watershed U.S. Higher Education Act of 1965.

Emergence of Assertive Federal Policy in Student Aid—1965 to 1972

The bywords of higher education in 1965 were *prosperity* and *growth*. Nationally, unemployment and inflation were low, and productivity was rising. In addition, the many children born in the years after World War II were enrolling in college at high rates. Postsecondary enrollments grew steadily, along with the nations supply of institutions, especially in the community college sector, where new institutions were emerging at the rate of one every week and a half. Dramatic demographic changes in student bodies were in the future, however: Students of this era were more likely than today's students to be full-time, residential, male, and White (Breneman, 1991). Out of this context arose the US. Higher Education Act of 1965.

The act was a product of a wide-ranging educational initiative on the part of Congress and President Lyndon Johnson. All told, the 89th Congress passed more than two dozen acts aimed directly at American schools and colleges. Most of those were closely connected to the Democrats' War on Poverty and Great Society efforts, as well as to the Civil Rights Act of 1964. President Johnson and congressional leaders saw action in education as an effective, politically feasible policy mechanism for achieving their broader goals of eliminating poverty and discrimination in the nation. In the president's view, "The answer for all our national problems, the answer for all the problems of the world, comes down . . . to one single word—education" (cited in Gladieux & Wolanin, 1976, p. 17).

Higher education was to reap especially significant rewards from the president's linkage of educational improvement to emerging national priorities. The Higher Education Act encompassed two approaches to federal support: aid to states and institutions and aid to needy students (Gladieux & Wolanin, 1976; Leslie, 1977; Fenske, 1983). College student aid was covered mainly under Title IV of the act. For student aid, the passage of Title IV represented both a philosophical and a fiscal shift. Philosophically, it expanded the purposes of federal student aid in the equity-oriented direction suggested years earlier by the Truman Commission. Fiscally, the act laid the groundwork for massive growth in the dollars and recipients of federal aid to levels unimagined even in the 1950s.

Under Title IV, the existing NDSL program was renewed, the College Work Study (CWS) program established a year earlier was finalized, and the Guaranteed Student Loan (GSL) and the Educational Opportunity Grants (EOG) programs were inaugurated. The CWS and EOG programs, like the earlier NDSL program, were to be delivered through campus offices (as "campus-based" aid, in the federal terminology). The GSL program was also to be administered out of campus aid offices, although private funds were to be loaned. Thus, the student aid elements of the 1965 act were to be delivered largely through existing institutional aid offices.

The new Guaranteed Student Loan program was a particular interest of President Johnson. Johnson had made his way through college with the help of loans from family friends, a bank, a local newspaper publisher, and his college (Caro, 1983; Hansen, 1987). As a consequence, he strongly supported expanding students' opportunities to borrow. As a senator front Texas in the 1950s, Johnson had introduced loan legislation, which failed to pass (Morse, 1977). The GSL program offered more than simple philosophical appeal for Johnson, however. It was designed in good part as a tactical diversion to head off legislation establishing tax credits for higher education attendance (Morse, 1977; Kramer & Van Dusen, 1986). Thus, the GSL program was not aimed primarily at socioeconomically disadvantaged students. Instead, it was initiated as a small, supplementary program operating at low federal cost and serving those not quite needy enough to qualify for the other new, more need-based aid programs (Kramer & Van Dusen, 1986; Hauptman, 1987). Specifically, the program's main intent was to address middle-income families' liquidity problems by facilitating access to funds from private lenders.

Although it was originally conceived as providing no subsidies at all, the GSL program as legislated provided interest subsidies for students while in school as well as funds to assure that states and private nonprofit agencies would work with the federal government to guarantee student loans made by commercial lenders. The initial federal interest rate subsidy was set at 6% a year while the student was in school and 3% during the repayment period, which began 9 months after graduation. The borrower was to pay the other 3%. Only those with family incomes under $15,000 could receive the subsidy, although unsubsidized GSL's were available to others. Students were given 10 years to repay loans over $2,000, and less time to repay smaller loans.

Banks, savings and loan associations, credit unions, and other financial institutions were invited to participate in the program. The guarantees on loans were to be assured through a federally supported guaranty fund in each state, equal to 10% of the face value of the loans, to protect lenders against loss through default, death, or disability of the borrower. The federal government provided states with deposits to be used to build their own guaranty funds, although most states opted to participate instead in the broader Federally Insured Student Loan (FISL) program.

These initial terms met with some concern from lenders, states, institutions, and students. Money was to be tied up in student loans for many years without payback (causing liquidity problems for lenders), the interest rates set by the government were not sufficiently high for lenders, institutions were frustrated by reporting and regulatory control mechanisms, and states were unenthusiastic about beginning their own guaranty agencies under existing guidelines (Morse, 1977; Breneman, 1991).

Having rejected such alternatives as the development of a national student loan bank (see Panel on Educational Innovation, 1967), the federal government moved to refine the GSL program into a more accepted loan policy vehicle. In 1968, it raised the statutory interest rate to 7% and introduced "reinsurance," which merged existing state guaranty funds with federal insurance support. Nonprofit and state agencies were to provide guarantees, funded by a small administrative allowance, retention of a percentage of collections on defaulted loans, and an insurance premium paid by borrowers. The federal government assured states that it would cover 80% of a state's total losses from student default, death, or disability. This alleviated some of the pressures on state guaranty funds while creating incentives for states to monitor more closely lenders' efforts to collect loan payments.

In 1969, the federal government introduced the "special allowance," which paid all eligible lenders a supplementary amount above the statutory interest rate. The allowance, which was revised every 3 months by a committee of government officials, fluctuated between 1 and 2.5% over the next few years (Moore, 1983). Loan volume grew somewhat as a result, and by 1970, over one million borrowers received just over one billion dollars under the GSL program (Gillespie & Carlson, 1983).

The coming of the early 1970s marked the end of the initial "policy emergence" phase of federal student aid under the Higher Education Act of 1965. Through the combination of new or expanded student aid programs, federal support for spending for generally available student aid grew approximately tenfold between 1963–64 and 1972–73, in constant-dollar terms. Although new grant and work-study programs were a prominent feature of that growth, generally available federal loan programs grew at nearly the same rate.

Years of Policy Refinement and Expansion—1972 to 1978

The academic year 1972–73 marked the beginning of a second phase in the Title IV aid programs history, a phase of policy refinement and expansion. As the 1972 debates on reauthorizing the Higher Education Act approached, policy makers generally agreed that a new, expanded program of aid for college attendance was desirable, but conflict emerged among institutions, policy analysts, interest

groups, and politicians over several issues (Gladieux & Wolanin, 1976; Brademas, 1987). After lengthy, detailed, and exhaustive deliberations, rough consensus was reached over the directions of expansion in the aid programs: toward channeling aid to students rather than to institutions, toward greater emphasis on facilitating student choice among institutions and persistence to the desired degree, toward an expanded pool of eligible applicants for aid, and toward a distinct, foundational role for the federal government in efforts to build equality of opportunity through student aid (Gladieux & Wolanin, 1976).

The newly created Basic Educational Opportunity Grants (BEOG) program was central to each of these directions, in that it allowed needy students to take their aid eligibility to the institutions of their choice, rather than relying on the grant funds available at one institution. Informed choices by students among competing institutions were therefore favored, under the assumption that grant portability would make institutions more sensitive to market forces favoring efficiency and quality. The BEOG program was the federal government's first major, direct, need-based grants program. It was to provide a foundation for students' aid packages, onto which other forms of federal, state, and institutional aid would be added. The 1972 reauthorization also brought expansion of the SEOG program, as well as CWS and NDSL (the latter of which was renamed the National Direct Student Loan program). Also that year, Congress initiated the State Student Incentive Grant (SSIG) program, which provided grant aid jointly with states.

In the context of all these new and expanded commitments, policy makers did not expect major growth in the loan programs (Mumper, 1996). That was to prove an accurate forecast: Federally supported loan volumes remained relatively stable throughout the early and mid-1970s, and loans diminished as a factor in federal aid, accounting during this period for only about one half of all generally available federal student aid, one fourth of all federal student aid, and about one fifth of all student aid (see Figure 10.1).

The primary implication of the 1972 amendments for the loan programs involved their relative priority. Loans were thenceforth to be viewed as supplemental aid for facilitating students' choice and persistence, rather than as a core "access" element in aid packages. Whether someone attended college or not was to be addressed mainly through the BEOG program, with loans and other aid programs providing supplemental support for one's attending a preferred school and attaining one's degree.

A second implication of the 1972 reauthorization for the loan programs was especially portentous. The eligible pool of institutions for federal student aid programs was expanded to include proprietary and vocational institutions. This expansion marked a transformation of the target of federal aid policy from "higher education" into "postsecondary education" (Schuster, 1982). Although the significance of this change was little noted at the time, the newly included proprietary and vocational institutions would come to dominate later reports of fraud and high default rates in loan programs.

Analyses of the 1972 reauthorization sometimes paint the results in glowing terms, but, in truth, the debate was a "debacle" of disunity and frustrated hopes for the interest groups representing higher education institutions (Hansen, 1977, p. 242). Most important, those groups favored maintaining campus officials as the dominant forces in student aid, and therefore strongly opposed the development of the portable, "voucher" concept in the basic grants program. After 1972, however, elements of consensus began to arise among interest groups. A "student aid partnership" emerged, consisting of postsecondary institutions and their associations, state government officials involved in aid policy, federal aid officials in the U.S. Department of Health, Education, and Welfare, and private organizations processing aid applications under contract (Fenske, 1983). In the mid-1970s, the partnership began to voice rather uniform views in keeping with a consensually supported focus on equal opportunity (Hansen, 1977). Policy disputes were rare in those years, and the partnership mainly worked together toward incremental operational and bureaucratic improvements in the programs (Hansen, 1977; Fenske, 1983). Federally supported aid grew 60% in real terms between 1972–73 and 1977–78, largely in the grants programs.

The period may be viewed, therefore, as a time of refinement and expansion of loan pol-

icy. A major example of refinement is the creation in 1972 of the Student Loan Marketing Association (Sallie Mae). A government-sponsored private corporation that was begun to provide liquidity and facilitate the secondary market in the GSL program, Sallie Mae sought to encourage banks' continuing participation in the program by buying loans and allowing pledges of existing student loans as collateral for new loans.

Other 1972 refinements included the introduction of need analysis to the GSL program, to replace the simple income cutoffs used in earlier years. Later in this period, to combat the influences of inflation on GSL program participation, the income level for student eligibility was raised to $25,000. In addition, the government raised overhead payments to state agencies, allowed states to keep up to 30% of their recoveries on defaulted loans to cover administrative costs, and offered 100% federal reinsurance to those states with low default rates. Also, the "special allowance" for lenders was pegged to an adjustable gross yield of 3.5% above the 90-day treasury bill rate.

Partly as a result of these reforms, the number of state loan agencies and participating financial organizations grew in the mid-1970s. Thus, although some other refinements of the time were restrictive on students and institutions, the general tone of the GSL changes in this period was expansive and the program grew notably after years of relative stability.

In the NDSL program, concern over mounting program costs led to the withdrawal of loan forgiveness for students entering military service or teaching careers. This period also brought regular rises in the administrative allowance for reimbursing institutions' NDSL costs. Overall, NDSL funding was rather stable in the mid-1970s.

Despite the seemingly calm surface surrounding the aid programs, however, this was a period of increasing demographic, economic, and political tensions in higher education (Stampen, 1987). In the late 1970s, those tensions erupted. Congress became concerned over the financial needs of middle-class parents of college-bound students, relative to lower and upper-class students (Brademas, 1987), and controversy arose over how to address the perceived problem. Congress debated between expanding the Title IV aid programs to cover more middle-income students and introducing a new program of federal tuition tax credits for college attendance. On this question, the professional and political allies of the aid partnership found themselves uncomfortably split. Longtime direct student aid proponents such as Senators Moynihan and Kennedy joined a coalition of liberal and conservative senators favoring tax credits. President Jimmy Carter and his allies countered that tax credits were wasteful in that they would go to many families who did not need aid to finance attendance, they were hard to control budgetarily, and they came too late in the academic year to influence attendance in the direction of expanded equality of opportunity.

In the end, the congressional proponents of the traditional student aid approach triumphed. The Middle Income Student Assistance Act (MISAA) was passed as the Higher Education Amendments of 1978. As a response to the perceived "middle-income squeeze," MISAA loosened the definition of need to include more middle-income families in the basic grants program and removed the $25,000 income ceiling on eligibility for GSLs. After passage of the act, any student could receive the GSL interest subsidy during enrollment, as well as the program's attractive 7% repayment rate. MISAA thus defined any student facing college expenses as needy enough to warrant federal support (Brademas, 1987).

The Policy Destabilization of 1978 to 1980–81

The passage of the expansive MISAA legislation initiated a period of destabilization of the federal aid policy agenda. Between 1977–78 and 1980–81, total federally supported aid grew a stunning 59% in constant dollars. Growth in the loan programs was especially strong. The removal of the family income ceiling on GSL eligibility in the context of dramatically rising interest rates in the general economy created substantial incentives for middle and upper-income families with discretionary resources to participate in the program.

In 1979, the government acted to assure more aggressive loan marketing to those very families. Responding to complaints by banks and other lenders that general interest rates had risen enough to make unattractive the full GSL interest rate for lenders (i.e., the statutory loan rate plus the special allowance rate), the government implemented a more liberal, variable special allowance. Soon the full interest rate rose as high as 19.5%.

Presented with an opportunity for inflation-proof, government-guaranteed returns, financial institutions quickly intensified their marketing of GSLs to the public. As families increasingly noticed this easily accessible, non-need-based, program, the number of student borrowers in the GSL program grew to 2.9 million in 1980 (College Board, 1993), and yearly program disbursements began regularly exceeding budgeted appropriations by large margins. Underestimates of demand became characteristic of the years immediately following MISAA.

The period was further troubled by growing controversy over the ultimate directions of the loan programs. Although MISAA was traditional in its use of aid awards rather than tax credits, it was a striking departure from the aid coalition's consensus favoring need-based, grants-oriented aid for the disadvantaged students. An "era of good feeling" in federal aid policy had come to an end, replaced by uncontrolled growth and philosophical uncertainty, especially regarding the appropriate clientele for the GSL program. Most participants and analysts attribute the removal of income caps on GSL eligibility to the combination of middle-class pressure for relief from college costs and heavy lobbying efforts by financing-industry officials (e.g., see McPherson, 1989). Stampen (1987) suggests that resistance to the costs of government oversight was also a factor:

> Senator Jacob Javits of New York argued, to a room charged with certainty about the excess of government regulation, that the ceiling on Guaranteed Student Loans should be eliminated so that middle- and upper-income students could become eligible. He reasoned that it was costing the government more to enforce the regulations excluding them than to remove the ceiling. The government's fiscal note, which turned out to be wildly inaccurate, estimated a cost of $9 million. Senator Javits concluded by saying he was not worried that a Rockefeller or two might receive a loan because they would repay many times through higher taxes after graduation. (p. 10)

MISAA's magnanimous terms stimulated a shift to loans in the overall balance of program allocations under Title IV, after several years of increasing emphasis on grants (see Table 10.1 and Figure 10.1). Viewed in retrospect, the middle years of the 1970s may be seen as a grants-oriented anomaly in the history of federal aid policies. The ratio of loans to other generally available federally supported aid in 1980–81 was similar to that of the mid-1960s and to that of the rest of the 1980s (see Figure 10.1). What is more, the ratio actually grew in the 1990s, leaving the grants orientation of the mid-1970s an ever more distant memory.

Of course, the loans emphasis in the late 1970s involved much more money than was present in the 1960s. It also involved much more controversy. The arrival of painful financial pressures on the government at that time led some critics to worry that Congress and the president had promised aid for all needy students while not reserving the funds necessary to achieve those goals (Gladieux, 1980). Although federal officials sought to step up their formal control and oversight of student aid award processes, many analysts argued that the government was not attending closely enough to program efficiency (e.g., appropriate ways to control fraud, abuse, and waste) and fairness (e.g., the acceptability of the use of the GSL program for investment purposes by upper-income families). Some observers decried the blurring of the original purposes of the Title IV programs as aided populations expanded. What is more, the interests of public and private institutions, of higher-cost and lower-cost institutions, of selective and open-admissions institutions, and of proprietary and traditional institutions began to diverge significantly (Gladieux, 1983; Mumper, 1996; Schuster, 1982).

With controversy and fiscal restraint as a backdrop, the 1980 reauthorization of the Higher Education Act focused on redesigning the student aid programs and managing their growth. Congress created the new Parental Loans for Student program (PLUS). This program of loans for parents of dependent undergraduates was similar to the GSL program, but was open to all regardless of need, provided no interest rate subsidy, allowed larger loans, and featured higher interest rates.

That reauthorization also addressed problems with the MISAA legislation and the difficulties posed by continuing high rates of inflation and interest. Official interest rates on NDSL

and GSL loans were raised, but the special allowance for GSL lenders was restricted and the growing GSL-based profits of state lending agencies were curtailed through limiting those agencies' use of tax-exempt bonds to finance student loans.

Although Congress proclaimed as a priority the control of waste, it also imposed ceilings on spending by the Department of Education and thereby reduced the department's audit and program-review capabilities. By the time Ronald Reagan entered office in early 1981, some of the major dislocations of MISAA had been addressed, and the turbulent third phase in the federal aid programs' political history was drawing to an end. The following years would bring a return to some predictability in student aid, but would not bring a return to consensus.

The Policy Drift of 1981 to the Present

The lengthy and ongoing fourth phase in the life of the Higher Education Act may be termed a period of policy drift. The overall size of the federal aid commitment has increased, and loans have continued to grow both in absolute terms and relative to grants. Yet the period has brought no real consensus to the arena regarding growth, loan emphasis, or other policy features.

In the early 1980s, Congress blocked implementation of some aspects of the 1980–81 reauthorization and provided some support for conservatives' efforts to cut federal student aid. College benefits to Social Security survivors were removed and the terms of the new PLUS loan program were toughened. Congress also enacted several measures to slow GSL program growth: Student borrowing was limited by actual need, students with family incomes over $30,000 became subject to need analysis tests for loan eligibility for the first time since 1978, and banks were allowed to charge students a loan origination fee. Loan growth slowed much less than Congress initially expected and hoped, however, and the first year of the Reagan administration was the high-water mark for supporters of retrenching federal student aid.

In the following years, the political rhetoric concerning the aid programs became more heated than ever. In the early 1980s, political conflict over student aid was based not in the details of aid programs themselves, but in the proper funding levels of those programs relative to other social and educational programs. The central parties to the conflict were not so much opposing members of Congress as distinct branches of government. There was an ongoing, almost ritualized battle of wills between the Reagan administration, which favored substantial cutbacks, and the Congress, which tended to oppose such retrenchment. The conflict continued over the years of the Reagan presidency.

Although the relative proportion of total student aid paid by states and institutions, as opposed to the federal government, increased in the 1980s after a long downward trend (see Table 10.1), the overall size of that shift was not nearly so dramatic as one might have expected on the basis of the Reagan administration's rhetoric. It was in this period that Education Secretary William Bennett uttered perhaps the single most famous (or infamous) quotation ever in this arena, arguing for changes in student aid that would require aid-enriched students to pursue "a divestiture of certain sorts: stereo divestiture, automobile divestiture, three-weeks-at-the-beach divestiture" (Fiske, 1985, p. A1).

In the end, the opposing forces reached something of a balance, or an inescapable impasse (Hartle, 1991). The generally available aid programs grew slightly in constant-dollar terms (College Board, 1995b) and by the end of the decade most postsecondary students were receiving at least one kind of federal aid (McPherson & Schapiro, 1991).

Despite the ongoing hostilities between Congress and the Reagan administration, they did share a concern over college students' expanding debt levels, and in this concern they were joined by the popular media (e.g., Fiske, 1986; "The Student Loan Scandal," 1987) and policy analysts (e.g., Hansen, 1987). As participation in loan programs continued to grow in the 1980s, Lawrence Gladieux (1983) of the College Board noted wryly that

> in an age of Visa, MasterCard, massive consumer credit, and "creative financing;" it is perhaps not surprising that loans have been the primary focus of efforts and plans to fill the gap for students and parents. . . . Increasingly, postsecondary education has come to be looked on as another consumer

item to be "financed"—stretched out and paid for from the student's and/or parent's future earnings. (pp. 422–423)

Analysts, policy makers, and media observers also shared a concern over a related problem of the period, the increased incidence of loan defaults in both the GSL and the NDSL programs. Default expenses grew sevenfold in the 1980s in constant-dollar terms (U.S. Department of Education [USDOE], 1992). Although analysts noted that students tend to be young and have few assets, the popular media and congressional critics frequently compared their default rates unfavorably with rates for standard consumer and home loans.

Unfortunately, in both the NDSL, and GSL programs, the incentives and resources for preventing loan defaults were limited in this period. In the NDSL program, institutions were constrained by costs from becoming debt collectors. In the GSL program, lenders were entirely insured against default losses by the provisions of the program, and USDOE oversight was limited by budget constraints and program structure. In addition, critics argued that as participation by educational institutions and students in the proprietary sector increased dramatically in the 1980s, accrediting bodies in that sector may have failed to effectively police their member institutions' aid practices. Finally, there was a willingness of some lenders to lend to students regardless of their institution's default rates and stability, a willingness of guaranty agencies to guarantee such loans, and a willingness of secondary loan markets to provide ongoing financing (Dean, 1994). In the mid-1980s, Congress imposed more stringent "due diligence" requirements on institutions to reduce defaults, limit multiple disbursement of loans to first-year students, and limit interest billings.

In the 1986 reauthorization of the Higher Education Act, NDSLs were renamed Perkins Loans, borrowers were given the option of consolidating their student loans from various federal programs into a single loan under a single, weighted interest rate, and the Supplemental Loans to Students (SLS) program for independent students was initiated. The SLS program was analogous to the PLUS program for dependent students: it provided a way for students to finance the great majority of their college costs through unsubsidized loans.

Although Congress in this reauthorization also toughened need analysis for loan eligibility, placed a limitation on student borrowing to the assessed amount of need, and allowed lenders to charge borrowers a new premium for insurance, GSL program growth continued, no doubt greatly aided by Congress's raising of the allowable loan size and by declines in loan servicing costs, which attracted more and more financial institutions into the program (USDOE, 1992).

Two of the most notable continuing problems of the 1980s in the federal loan programs were problematic loan administration and the ever increasing complexity of the programs. Widely publicized cases of noncompliance in loan servicing lessened public and congressional confidence in the integrity of the loan programs and the quality of their management (Dean, 1994). At the same time, frequent articles catalogued complaints about complexity from policy analysts, aid officers, and students (e.g., see Flint, 1991; "17 Changes in 4 Years," 1990; Wilson, 1988). One of these articles even lampooned in full-page cartoon form the detailed, lengthy process of loan generation and disbursement (Wilson, 1987, p. 25). Kramer and Van Dusen (1986), portrayed the guaranteed student loan program as a Rube Goldberg contraption: "a long series of devices accomplishing by extravagant means something terribly simple, like opening a tin can or putting out the cat" (p. 18). Ironically, the Education Department found that its efforts to meet public demands for greater fiscal integrity in the programs often meant earning the ire of aid officers and others frustrated by program complexity. Sometimes, the department made such sudden regulatory changes that institutions found themselves formally out of compliance without having known of the original, newly instituted regulations (Dean, 1994).

Tuition, fees, and other expenses of college-going rose at unprecedented rates in the 1980s, and the loan programs picked up the majority of the federal contribution to meeting those expenses. Between 1980 and 1990, the number of student borrowers in the GSL program grew from 2.9 million to 3.7 million (College Board, 1993, 1995b). As a result of this rapid, largely unplanned growth in the student loan programs, growth in grant programs was restricted. An increasing share of a limited pool of federal dollars was going to support the expanding volume of the federal loan programs. The federal government's expenses in supporting lenders and guaranteeing loans more than doubled between 1980 and 1985, then grew another 12% between 1985 and 1990 (USDOE, 1992).

Mumper (1996) has termed the late 1980s and early 1990s a period of "continuing deterioration" in the loan programs (p. 100). The U.S. General Accounting Office issued a scathing report in 1992, and congressional attention to loan problems also rose noticeably as the new decade began. Senator Sam Nunn brought his Permanent Senate Subcommittee on Investigations into the loan arena, focusing on abuses among proprietary schools and among private participants in the student loan industry. That committee (Nunn, 1990) found "overwhelming evidence that federal student loan programs and, particularly, those involving trade and proprietary schools, are riddled with fraud, waste, abuse, and pervasive patterns of mismanagement. . . . [W]e did not hear of even a single part of the guaranteed student loan program that is working efficiently and effectively (p. 1)." Senator Nunn concluded that "nothing less than a comprehensive, sustained, and intensive reform effort is needed" (cited in Mumper, 1996, p. 100). Senator Edward Kennedy, noting that "student loan programs may be just one step ahead of disaster" (cited in Mumper, p. 100), endorsed reform as well, and Congress in the early years of the decade enacted legislation aimed at cutting off institutions with especially high student loan defaults.

As the 1992 reauthorization of the Higher Education Act arrived, a number of problems in the loan programs demanded federal attention. Program costs continued to rise, management questions continued to plague program leaders, lower-income students continued to receive more loans and less grant aid than many thought advisable, debt obligations among all kinds of students continued to grow, and rapidly rising college costs convinced many to argue for expanded loan eligibility for middle-income students.

The 1992 presidential campaign figured prominently in debates on these problems. Bill Clinton proposed a national service program to replace existing student loan programs (Clinton, 1992). Clinton linked national service initiatives with student loan reform by stressing that loan programs make repaying the loan a priority, which in turn encourages students to take high-paying jobs offering few returns to society, rather than low-paying jobs that benefit society (Mumper, 1996). After winning a campaign in which this and other student aid issues were frequently discussed, Clinton as president began to pursue formal adoption of his ideas.

His proposals have met with mixed success. Congress passed a scaled-back version of the national service idea, with each award limited to $4,750 a year and the number of participants limited to no more than 100,000 people. Another goal of the administration, alternative GSL repayment periods for students, was implemented. The small federal Income Contingent Loans program was replaced by the offering of income-contingent repayment as an option in other federal loan programs. Congress in 1992–93 also expanded eligibility for the GSL and NDSI, programs, raised the limit on yearly undergraduate borrowing, placed eligibility analysis for all Title IV programs under the rather liberal "Federal Methodology," and reduced Pell eligibility for single independent students and dependent students with earnings. Each of these moves increased the demand for loans further (Zook, 1994). Finally, Guaranteed Student Loans were renamed Stafford Loans, and those loans and the PLUS and SLS loans were folded into the Federal Family Education Loan Program (FFELP).

These last changes were closely connected to the most dramatic policy option considered in the reauthorization of the Clinton years: instituting a "direct lending" program to replace the traditional guaranteed student loan approach. Under this new program proposed by Clinton, institutions would lend federal funds directly to students, without the use of private funds or the involvement of private financial institutions. Direct student loans were broached as an approach to lowering institutions' administrative costs by eliminating the need to deal with multiple private lenders and guaranty agencies participating in the Stafford Loan program. In concert with this change, it was argued, the complexity of the loan programs would be reduced and management in federal student loans improved. Coloring the direct lending debate were proponents' concerns over indications that the student-loan

business was making many people in the financing industry extraordinarily wealthy (see Regional Financial Associates & Jenkins, 1991; Zook, 1993). On the negative side, many institutions expressed concerns over new administrative burdens potentially associated with the direct lending efforts. Their opposition was reinforced by analyses by Sallie Mae and the Congressional Research Service (Dean, 1994).

In the end, Congress, in August 1993, adopted a compromise, trial version of the direct lending program, under which direct lending could be instituted voluntarily at institutions while the traditional nondirect guaranteed loan program would also continue. Volunteer institutions could disburse subsidized Stafford loans, unsubsidized Stafford loans, and PLUS loans directly to students. Both sides expressed confidence that time would tell that theirs was the superior alternative (Zuckman, 1993).

Under the terms of the compromise, the volume of direct loans could grow as a proportion of all lending to as much as 60% of all federal loans by 1998. Private capital is replaced as a source of loan funds by federal treasury funds, secured by the issuance of treasury bonds or the use of tax receipts. Institutions perform the administrative functions formerly performed by private and state lenders. Loan servicing is performed by federally supported contractors. Schools are required to process adjustments in loan amounts, notify servicing contractors of changes in student status, and maintain records of funds receipt and disbursement. The Ford Direct Student Loan Program was adopted as an option by many institutions around the country and began disbursing funds in 1994–95. Intriguingly, Congress left many of the specifics of the program open for interpretation and refinement.

Between the early and mid-1990s, the landscape of student loans changed notably. Contrary to the expectations of many and the hopes of some, growth in the loan programs accelerated rather than slowed. Between 1990–91 and 1994–95, the number of student borrowers in the Stafford program grew from 3.7 million to 6.2 million (College Board, 1995b). Stafford loans came to be provided in traditional and direct form and in subsidized and unsubsidized form. Those with need received the subsidized loan for which the government paid interest during the years in school. Those without measurable need received the new unsubsidized Stafford loan, for which the interest rate was higher, and the student paid the interest accrued during attendance. Unsubsidized Stafford loans grew dramatically after their inception, mainly because of the discontinuation of the unsubsidized SLS program, which served similar purposes and was phased out in 1994–95 (College Board, 1995b).

Interestingly, the 1990s have brought noteworthy decreases in the loan participation rates of students and institutions in the proprietary sector. Stafford loans and other federal loans are now far less tilted to the for-profit sector than they were in the 1980s. Specifically, students in the proprietary sector received only 10% of the subsidized Stafford loans in 1993, down from a high of 35% in the mid-1980s (College Board, 1995b). At the institutional level, most of the more than 500 institutions that dropped out of the federal loan programs between 1992 and 1995 were from the proprietary sector (Zook, 1995). It is in that sector that many of the worst abuses of federal aid programs have occurred, and in that sector that default rates have tended to be highest (Hansen, 1987; Mortenson, 1990). These declines in loans in the for-profit sector suggest indirectly that recent actions to address high default rates in the federal loan programs have been successful on at least some grounds.

CONCLUSION: FEDERAL LOAN EXPANSION IN BROADER CONTEXT

It is impossible to examine the dramatic increase in federal loan support without considering other developments taking place at roughly the same time. While federal loan efforts have been evolving since their great expansion in the late 1970s, total enrollments have risen (rather than falling, as anticipated by many analysts), the demographic characteristics of students have become more diverse, and delayed entry and part-time enrollment have increased (Hearn, 1992). At the institutional level, student aid has increasingly been viewed as an integral element in a wide variety of concerns, including admissions, fund raising, student services, and public relations (Brademas, 1983). At the same time, because of

its close connections to concerns regarding cost patterns, tuition levels, grant support, program duplication, and educational quality, student aid has become a more prominent vehicle for states' initiatives in postsecondary education. Each of these trends is tightly related to the changes in federal loans.

It is especially important to examine simultaneously financing trends at the federal, state, and institutional levels. As Table 10.1 suggests, the federal retreat from grants and movement into loans since the 1970s has been met by some expansion in grant aid for students at the state and institutional levels. States' abilities to respond effectively to changes in federal aid have been hampered, however, by their own economic and political difficulties. Most notably, state efforts have been constrained by uncertainty over the financial feasibility of both the traditional "low-tuition-low-aid" approach to student support and the alternative "high-tuition-high-aid" approach to financing public institutions (Fischer, 1990; Hearn, Griswold, & Marine, 1996). That uncertainty over appropriate tuition and aid levels has also troubled private institutions. Under pressure, some states and some private institutions have been forced to adopt what is in essence the worst of both approaches, a "high-tuition-low aid" approach (Griswold & Marine, 1996). That is, tuitions have been allowed to rise without parallel increases in student aid. A somewhat less regrettable state and institutional response, but still troubling and quite central to the concerns in this chapter, are efforts to use loans rather than grants as the dominant form of student aid in high-tuition-high aid approaches (see St. John, Andrieu, Oescher, & Starkey, 1994).

Clearly, the dramatic rises in public and private institutions' tuition levels since 1980 are closely linked to the parallel expansion of student loans. As colleges' costs for salaries and other items have risen, the burden of meeting those costs has increasingly been placed on students and their families. In some ways, these new demands on them have been immediately felt. For example, need analysis and eligibility analysis formulas for determining students' aid levels have been tightened, bringing more stringent expectations for parental contributions to college expenses, student savings, and summer work earnings, as well as tougher requirements for students wishing to be certified as financially independent of their parents. But much of the increased financial burden on students and their families has been deferred in impact, via demands that students finance more of their college attendance through loans. Postsecondary institutions, financial institutions, and governments are increasingly providing aid to be repaid later, after students are presumably more established in their adult careers. In essence, unable to slow the growth in college costs, unable or unwilling to devote further governmental resources to meet those costs, and unwilling to demand more short-term contributions from students and their families, policy makers have placed much more of the burden of financing attendance on students' future lives. As the imagery and language of "downsizing" and "cost control" have come in the past decade to dominate policy arenas at the local, state, and national levels, many postsecondary leaders are reluctantly accepting students' high debt levels as ongoing facts of life.

It can be argued that appreciably higher student loan levels represent almost as significant a historical development in federal aid policy as the GI Bill or the original Higher Education Act of 1965. Yet, in contrast to those earlier events, the loan explosion has taken place incrementally over a period of years. Some years are more significant than others, of course, but there is no single watershed year in federal loan policy. Mark Twain's old parable of the hot-water frog seems apropos: Dropped in boiling water, a frog will promptly jump out, but dropped in cool water which is being slowly heated to boiling, a frog might well end up being boiled to death. Of course, the consequences of loan expansion are not nearly so dire for students or policy makers. Still, as Twain warns us, intense scrutiny of one's emerging environment is always warranted.

ACKNOWLEDGMENTS

This chapter benefited substantially from the helpful comments of two veteran analysts of federal student loan policy: John Lee, president of JBL Associates of Bethesda, Maryland and Keith Jepson, Director of Financial Aid at New York University. My research assistant, James Eck also deserves thanks, as do Sharon Wilford and Sammy Parker, who assisted me in earlier work on the political history of federal student aid efforts.

NOTES

1. Reference to the work of a number of authors is essential to understanding the policy history of federal student loans. Primary sources for the present work were Gladieux and Wolanin (1976), Morse (1977), Moore (1983), Gillespie and Carlson (1983), Gladieux (1983), Fenske (1983), Hartle (1991), Dean (1994), St. John (1994), College Board (1995b), and Mumper (1996). A political history of all the federal aid programs (including grants and work study as well as loans) is presented in Hearn (1993). Each of these sources may be consulted for further details and perspective on the historical analysis presented here.

2. Several points should be made about the data of Table 10.1 (for details, see College Board, 1995b). First, federally supported aid totals include some funds supplied by institutional, private, and state sources. Importantly, totals for Family Education Loans are for the amounts for the loans themselves, not for the amount supplied by the federal government for subsidies and repayments on those loans. The actual funds supplied by the federal government are substantially smaller than the totals for these loans themselves. Second, the amounts in the table include aid for undergraduate, graduate, and professional students. Third, total loan amounts are underestimated because private loans by individuals, corporations, and schools are not included in figures, and are essentially incalculable (College Board, 1995b). Finally, reported lost values in Table 10.1 are for loan commitments, not the final loan amount, but the two totals are virtually identical.

REFERENCES

Barger, H., & Barger, G. (1981). *College on credit: A history of United student aid funds, 1960–1980*. Indianapolis, IN: Hackett.

Baum, S. (1996, Winter). Is the student loan burden really too heavy? *Educational Record*, 77(1), 30–36.

Bosworth, B., Carron, A., & Rhyne, E. (1987). *The economics of federal credit programs*. Washington, DC: Brookings Institution.

Brademas, J. (1983). Foreword. In R. H. Fenske, R. P. Huff, & Associates (Eds.), *Handbook of student financial aid*, pp. ix-xiii. San Francisco: Jossey-Bass.

Brademas, J. (1987). *The politics of education: Conflict and consensus on capitol hill*. Norman, OK: University of Oklahoma Press.

Breneman, D. W. (1991). Guaranteed student loans: Great success or dismal failure? In D. W. Breneman, L. L. Leslie, & R. E. Anderson (Eds.), *ASHE reader on finance in higher education* (pp. 377–387). Needham Heights, MA: Ginn Press.

Caro, R A. (1983). *The years of Lyndon Johnson: The path to power.* New York: Vintage Books.

Clinton, W. (1992). *Putting people first.* New York: Times Books.

College Board. (1993). *Trends in student aid: 1983 to 1993.* Washington, DC: Author.

College Board. (1995a, December). College costs and student loans up. *College Board News, 24*(2), 1, 11.

College Board. (1995b). *Trends in student aid: 1985 to 1995.* Washington, DC: Author.

Dean, J. (1994). Enactment of the federal Direct Student Loan Program as a reflection of the education policy making process. In J. Jennings (Ed.), *National issues in education: Community service and student loans* (pp. 157–178). Bloomington, IN: Phi Delta Kappa International.

Fenske, R. H. (1983). Student aid past and present. In R. H. Fenske, R. P. Huff, & Associates (Eds.), *Handbook of student financial aid* (pp. 5–26). San Francisco: Jossey-Bass.

Fischer, F. J. (1990). State financing of higher education: A new look at an old problem. *Change, 22*(1), 42–56.

Fiske, E. (1985, February 12). New secretary sees many "ripped off" in higher education. *The New York Times,* pp. A1, B24.

Fiske, E. (1986, August 3). Student debt reshaping. *The New York times,* pp. 34–38, 40–41.

Flint, T. A. (1991). Historical notes on regulation in the federal student assistance programs. *Journal of student financial aid, 21*(1), 33–47.

Gillespie, D. A., & Carlson, N. (1983). *Trends in student aid: 1963 to 1983.* Washington, DC: College Board.

Gladieux, L. E. (1980, October). What has Congress wrought? *Change,* 26–27.

Gladieux, L. E. (1983). Future directions of student aid. In R. H. Fenske, R. P. Huff, & Associates (Eds.), *Handbook of student financial aid* (pp. 399–433). San Francisco: Jossey-Bass.

Gladieux, L. R., & Wolanin, T. R. (1976). *Congress and the colleges: The national politics of higher education.* Lexington, MA: Lexington (Heath).

Griswold, C. P., & Marine, G. M. (1996). Political influences on state policy: Higher-tuition, higher-aid, and the real world. *Review of higher education, 19* (4), 361–389.

Hansen, J. S. (1977). *The politics of federal scholarships: A case study of the development of general grant assistance for undergraduates.* Unpublished doctoral dissertation, The Woodrow Wilson School, Princeton University.

Hansen, J. S. (1987). *Student loans: Are they overburdening a generation?* New York: College Board.

Hartle, T W. (1991). The evolution and prospects of financing alternatives for higher education. In A. M. Hauptman & R. H. Koff (Eds.), *New ways of paying for college* (pp. 33–50). New York: ACE-Macmillan.

Hauptman, A. M. (1987). The national student loan bank: Adapting an old idea for future needs. In L. E. Gladieux (Ed.), *Radical reform or incremental change?: Student loan policy alternatives for the federal government* (pp. 75–89). Washington, DC: College Board.

Hearn, J. C. (1992). Emerging variations in postsecondary attendance patterns: An investigation of part-time, delayed, and non-degree enrollment. *Research in higher education, 33,* 657–687.

Hearn, J. C. (1993). The paradox of growth in federal aid for college students:1965–1990. In J. C. Smart (Ed.), *Higher education: Handbook of theory and research (Vol. 9).* (pp. 94–153). New York: Agathon.

Hearn, J. C., Griswold, C. P., & Marine, G. M. (1996). Region, resources, and reason: A contextual analysis of state tuition and student-aid policies. *Research in higher education, 37* (3), 241–278.

Kosterlitz, J. (1989, April 15). Losers by default. *National journal, 47,* 924–923.

Kramer, M. (1991). Stresses in the student financial aid system. In A. M. Hauptman & R. H. Koff (Eds.), *New ways of paying for college* (pp. 21–32). New York: ACE-Macmillan.

Kramer, M., & Van Dusen, W. D. (1986, May/June). Living on credit. *Change, 18* (3), 10–19.

Leslie, L. L. (1977). *Higher education opportunity: A decade of progress.* (ERIC/AAHE Higher Education Research Report No. 3). Washington, DC: American Association for Higher Education.

Marmaduke, A. S. (1983). State student aid programs. In R. H. Fenske, R. P. Huff, & Associates (Eds.), *Handbook of student financial aid* (pp. 55–76). San Francisco: Jossey-Bass.

McPherson, M. S. (1989). Appearance and reality in the Guaranteed Student Loan Program. In L. E. Gladieux (Ed.). *Radical reform or incremental change?: Student loan policy alternatives for the federal government.* Washington, DC: College Board.

McPherson, M. S., & Schapiro, M. O. (1991). *Keeping college affordable: Government and educational opportunity.* Washington, DC: Brookings Institution.

Moore, J. W. (1983). Student aid past and present. In R. H. Fenske, R. P. Huff, & Associates (Eds.), *Handbook of student financial aid* (pp. 5–26), San Francisco: Jossey-Bass.

Morse, J. (1977). How we got here from there: A personal reminiscence of the early days. In L. Rice (Ed.), *Student loans: Problems and policy alternatives* (pp. 3–15). New York: College Board.

Mortenson, T. G. (1990). *The impact of increased loan utilization among low family income students.* Iowa City, IA: American College Testing Program.

Moynihan, D. P (1975). The politics of higher education. *Daedalus, 104,* 128–147.

Mumper, M. (1996). *Removing college price barriers: What government has done and why it hasn't worked.* Albany, NY: SUNY Press.

Nunn, S. (1990, October 10). Opening statement to the Permanent Subcommittee on Investigations (Hearings on Abuses in Federal Student Aid Programs). Washington, DC: United States Senate.

Panel on Educational Innovation. (1967). *Educational opportunity bank—A Report of the Panel an Educational Innovation to the U.S. Commissioner of Education, the Director of the National Science Foundation, and the Special Assistant to the President for Science and Technology.* Washington, DC: GPO.

President's Commission on Higher Education. (1947*). Higher education for American democracy.* Washington, DC: GPO.

Regional Financial Associates, & Jenkins, S. (1991). *Lender profitability in the student loan program.* Report prepared for the U.S. Department of Education. West Chester, PA: Regional Financial Associates.

St. John, E. P. (1994*). Prices, productivity and investment: Assessing financial strategies in higher education.* (ASHE-ERIC Higher Education Report No. 3). Washington, DC: School of Education and Human Development, George Washington University.

St. John, E. P., Andrieu, S. C., Oescher, J., & Starkey, J. B. (1994). The influence of student aid on within-year persistence by traditional college-age students in four-year colleges. *Research in Higher Education, 35* (4), 455–80.

Schuster, J. H. (1982, May). Out of the frying pan: The politics of education in a new era. *Phi Delta Kappan 63* (9), 583–591.

Seventeen changes in four years: Johns Hopkins grapples with new loan rules. (1990, December 5). *Chronicle of higher education, 37* (14), p. A24.

Stampen, J. O. (1987). Historical perspective on federal and state financial aid. In California Postsecondary Education Commission (Ed.), *Conversations about financial aid.* Sacramento, CA: Author.

Student loan scandal, The. (1987, October 8). *The New York times,* p. 26Y.

US. Department of Education. (1992). *Guaranteed Student Loans Program data book, FY91.* Washington, DC: Author.

US. General Accounting Office. (1992). *Transition series: Education issues* (Report No. GAO/OCG-93–18-TR). Washington, DC: US. General Accounting Office.

Wilson, R. (1987, April 15). Critics Blast Guaranteed Student Loan Program, Charging It Is Too Complex and Is Poorly Policed. *Chronicle of higher education, 33*(31), pp. 1, 24–26.

Wilson, R. (1988, March 16). Student-aid analysts blast loan program, urge big overhaul. *Chronicle of Higher Education, 34*(27), pp. 1, 24.

Woodhall, M. (1988). Designing a student loan program for a developing country: The relevance of international experience. *Economics of education review 7* (1), 153–161.

Zook, J. (1993, June 9). For Sallie Mae's top executives, 1992 was a very good year. *Chronicle of higher education, 37,* p. A23.

Zook, J. (1994, April 27). Record-setting debt: Changes in federal law have brought huge increases in student borrowing. *Chronicle of higher education, 39,* p. A21.

Zook, J. (1995, July 21). Congressional panel warned of growing Pell Grant fraud. *Chronicle of higher education, 41* (4S), p. A26.

Zuckman, J. (1993, August 14). Both sides hope to be No. 1 in dual loan system test. *Congressional Quarterly Weekly Report, 51,* pp. 2230–2231.

CHAPTER 11

THE CHANGING LANDSCAPE

Higher Education Finance in the 1990s

DAVID W. BRENEMAN AND JONI E. FINNEY

In the early 1970s, the Carnegie Commission on Higher Education completed a landmark study that evaluated individual and societal benefits—and responsibilities—regarding higher education. In June 1973, the commission concluded that in relation to higher education, "the proportion of total economic costs borne privately (about two-thirds) as against the proportion of total economic costs now borne publicly (about one-third) is generally reasonable."[1] The commission reached this conclusion based on, among other things, the rationale that about two-thirds of the additional earned income of college graduates is kept by those individuals, and about one-third is taken publicly in the form of taxes. Also influencing its decision was the commission's judgment about the social benefits of higher education at that time.

Current economic circumstances are pressuring public officials and educational leaders to revisit important public policy questions about who pays for, who benefits from, and who *should* pay for higher education. As of yet, however, few of these leaders fully understand or are willing to evaluate the consequences of the fiscal transformations of the 1990s. One of the most significant changes concerns reduced state support for higher education as other spending commitments—especially Medicaid and corrections—have increased dramatically. This reduced state support, coupled with steep increases in tuition and student loan burdens, has resulted in a significant shift from public to private support of higher education. Should these trends continue—and many have argued that they will—governors, legislators, and college and university officials will face even tougher decisions concerning: opportunity (how affordable and available are colleges and universities to the population at large?); costs (to what extent will institutions of higher education need to restructure their services to significantly cut costs?); and quality (what are the core services that specific colleges and universities bring to their states, and how can those services be maintained or improved?).

To more fully understand the challenges and priorities that states will face during the rest of the 1990s and into the next century, this chapter analyzes the most significant shifts in revenue sources for higher education during the recent past, with an emphasis on the economic recession of the early 1990s. In doing so, this chapter draws upon the five case studies that can be found in part II, for they explain in detail how five states financed their systems of higher education during the first half of this decade. The last section of this chapter raises issues that state and institutional leaders should address as they think about the future of higher education in their states.

Source: *Public and Private Financing of Higher Education: Shaping Public Policy for the Future*, J.E. Finney & P.M. Callan (eds.), 1997, Oryx Press.

MAJOR REVENUE SOURCES SUPPORTING HIGHER EDUCATION: EARLY 1990s

Overview

The financial support for higher education in the United States can be described as vast by any measure. Overall, higher education's share of the Gross Domestic Product (GDP) was nearly 3 percent in 1995.[2] Even during the recession of the early 1990s, when overall economic growth slowed from earlier decades, the proportion of the GDP spent on higher education increased. Total revenue from all sources supporting public and private higher education also increased. In 1990, total revenue from all sources supporting colleges and universities was approximately $150 billion (63 percent for public and 37 percent for private institutions). By 1994, total revenue reached approximately $179 billion, with the same percentage distribution between public and private institutions.[3]

As total revenue was increasing, however, a shift occurred in revenue sources: For the first time since the mass expansion of public colleges and universities, tuition overtook state government appropriations to institutions in providing the largest share of revenues for higher education. In 1990–91, tuition and fees for all higher education institutions nationally accounted for $37.4 billion in revenues, whereas revenues from state government appropriations to colleges and universities accounted for $39.5 billion. By 1993–94, tuition and fees had jumped to $48.6 billion while revenues from state governments rose only to $41.9 billion. In terms of share, the switch in funding sources is also apparent: The share of revenues funded by tuition increased from 25 to 27 percent from 1990–91 to 1993–94, while the share of revenues funded by state governments decreased from 27 to 23 percent during the same period.[4]

In relation to public institutions only, the shift from state funding of revenues from tuition is equally dramatic, though the portion of revenues funded by the states is still higher than the portion funded by tuition and fees. As Table 11.1 reveals, however, the gap is narrowing.

If one looks back to 1980–81, specifically focusing on public higher education, the changes in revenue sources are even more dramatic. Figure 11.1 demonstrates a long-term shift from public to private support for education. Although the category "private gifts and contracts" shows the highest percentage change in share and is itself an important indicator of revenue-raising priorities at public institutions, it represented only 4 percent of revenues in 1993–94. The 43 percent increase in share for tuition and fees is far more dramatic in terms of actual dollar amounts, for this category

TABLE 11.1
Percentage of Current Revenue Fund for Higher Education Institutions

	Public Institutions			Private Institutions		
	1990–91	1993–94	Change	1990–91	1993–94	Change
Tuition and Fees	16.3	18.4	12.9	40.4	42.0	4.0
Federal Government*	10.3	11.0	6.8	15.4	14.5	(5.8)
State Government	40.3	35.9	(10.9)	2.3	2.1	(8.7)
Local Government	3.7	4.0	8.1	0.7	0.7	0.0
Private Gifts, Grants, Contracts	3.8	4.0	11.1	8.6	8.6	0.0
Endowment Income	0.5	0.6	20.0	5.2	4.6	(11.5)
Sales and Services	22.7	23.4	3.1	22.9	23.2	1.3
Other Sources	2.6	2.7	3.8	4.5	4.3	(4.4)

* This category includes appropriations, unrestricted grants and contracts, restricted grants and contracts, and revenues associated with major federally funded research and development centers. This same category excludes Pell Grants; federally supported student aid that is provided to students is included under tuition and sales and services.

Source: U.S. Department of Education, National Center for Education Statistics, *Digest of Education Statistics 1996* (Washington, D.C.: 1996), pp. 333–35. Due to the difficulties in compiling data across states, 1993–94 is the most recent year that data on all institutions of higher education are available.

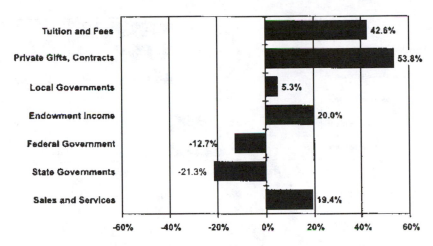

Figure 11.1 Change in Share of Revenues for Public Higher Education, 1980–81 to 1993–94

Source: U.S. Department of Education, *Digest of Education Statistics 1996*, p. 334.

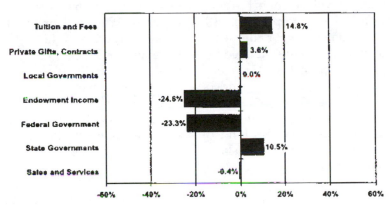

Figure 11.2 Change In Share of Revenues For Private Higher Education, 1980–81 to 1993–94

Source: U.S. Department of Education, *Digest of Education Statistics 1996*, p. 335.

jumped from 13 to 18 percent of total revenues during the period shown. The largest drop, meanwhile, was in state government funding, both in percentage terms and dollar amounts. State government funding as a share of total revenues at public institutions fell from 46 to 36 percent, which represents a decline of 21 percent. Also, the 13 percent drop in share in federal funding is particularly important for research institutions.

Important shifts among revenue sources also occurred at private colleges and universities during the same period, as shown in Figure 11.2. As with public institutions, tuition revenues as a share of total funding increased significantly at the private institutions, from 37 to 42 percent of total revenues. Meanwhile, funding from the federal government as a share of

overall revenues fell from 19 to 15 percent, which represents a 23 percent decline in share during this period. Federal funding is particularly important for private institutions due to their extensive involvement in research. The increase in the share represented by state governments in Figure 11.2 is largely an anomaly, for state governments make up a very small portion of revenues at private institutions. The state government share during the period shown increased only from 1.9 to 2.1 percent of total revenues—an increase that looks significant in terms of percentage change, but is small in terms of overall funding.

If one excludes sales and services (e.g., hospitals, dormitories, restaurants), the shift in revenues from public to private sources is even clearer—and more pronounced (see Figure

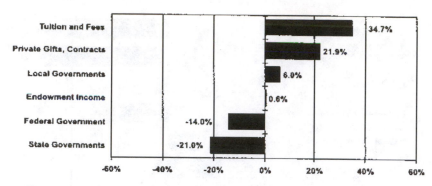

Figure 11.3 Change in Share of Revenues for Higher Education, Excluding
Sales and Services, 1980–81 to 1993–94

Source: U.S. Department of Education, *Digest of Education Statistics 1996,* p. 333.

11.3). Some finance experts view this perspective of change as the most important, arguing that higher education's involvement in hospital services and other auxiliary enterprises masks the most important trends in higher education finance. The share of these revenues funded by tuition and fees increased from 27 to 37 percent (a 35 percent increase), while the share funded by state governments dropped from 40 to 31 percent (a 21 percent decrease). As a result of this shift, the share of these revenues funded by tuition and fees is now larger than the share funded by state governments.

State Revenues

In the early 1990s, the number of observers (for instance, Atwell, Breneman, Hauptman, Johnstone, Schapiro, and Zemsky)[5] began arguing that recent trends in the financing of higher education are not simply another cyclical downturn in state support for higher education, but rather a new era of reduced support likely to be long-lasting. The arguments have been based on the view that most state governments have been experiencing structural deficits brought on by obligations passed down from Washington for social services; growth in medical spending; demographic changes increasing the need for K–12 funding increases, prison spending, and aid to the elderly; and the pressure not just to refrain from tax increases, but to reduce taxes.

From this perspective, higher education has been portrayed as one of a small number of state-supported activities that is discretionary in nature, setting up the potential for legislatures to cut spending there. Additional arguments have focused on states passing up higher education in favor of other state priorities, a result, perhaps, of the years of criticism begun by William Bennett when he was secretary of education. A third view has focused on the ability of colleges and universities—unlike most state activities—to raise funds from non-state sources, including tuition increases, private fund raising, and federal grants.

Whatever the mix of reasons present in each state, we now know from Steven Gold's work that higher education spending did indeed fall as a share of state outlays from 14.0 percent in 1990 to 12.5 percent in 1994—the only area to take such a large decline.[6]

Federal Revenues

A similar pattern is present in federal support for higher education. Grants for students comprise a declining share of total federal student aid. From 1990 to 1996, grant dollars declined from 49 to 42 percent of all federal aid allocated. Loans jumped during the same period from 48 to 57 percent. Campus work-study fell from 3.0 to 1.2 percent.[7] As college costs outpaced inflation during the late 1980s and 1990s, the purchasing power of the Pell Grant, the largest federal grant program, fell sharply. According to The College Board, the maximum Pell Grant now buys less than 30 percent of the average tuition, room and board, and fees at public colleges.

Growth in student borrowing was the most visible change in federal funding during the first half of the 1990s. Stafford Loans—the oldest and largest of the federal education loan programs—jumped by about 43 percent from

1990 to 1994[8] In 1992, the federal government established the unsubsidized Stafford Loan Program, for which all students are eligible—and students have flocked to it. In two years it has grown to provide $7.5 billion to more than two million students, so that it now represents about one-third of federal loan volume and accounts for half the increase in student loan volume since the 1992 reauthorization.[9]

Federal support for research grew from $9 billion in 1990 to $11.8 billion in 1994.[10] Continued growth in federally sponsored research may be problematic as the federal government works to reduce the deficit, balance the budget, and devolve responsibilities to the states. Behind these numbers, a conflict in funding research has been brewing. Due to increased pressure on limited research dollars, federal agencies tend to spread their funds over more proposals, causing gaps in funding that institutions have been trying to close with their own funds.[11] During the 1980s, for instance, institutional support for research was the second fastest growing source of research expenditures, accounting for about 8.5 percent in private universities and 23 percent at public ones by the end of the 1980s.[12] The pressure to reduce federal spending has had an impact on all forms of federal support to colleges and universities.

Tuition Revenues

While sharp tuition increases marked the early years of the 1990s (as shown in Table 11.2),

political resistance to additional tuition increases has increased as low- and middle-income families express fears about college being priced out of reach. As a consequence, the past two years have witnessed only modest increases in public tuition levels in most states. It no longer appears politically feasible to continue double-digit tuition increases, at least for in-state undergraduate students.

The heavy reliance on tuition revenues during the early part of the 1990s and the corresponding high rate of student borrowing represent a generational shift in the responsibilities of paying for higher education from parents to their children. Experts offer a number of opinions about why tuition has increased so rapidly. A recent study completed by the General Accounting Office cites two factors most responsible for the increase in tuition in public institutions: the rise in institutional expenditures and higher education's greater dependency on tuition as a source of revenue.[13] In fact, according to this report, if the shares of funding, by source, had remained constant at 1980 levels, tuition could have been 30 percent lower than it was at the end of 1995.

Sources of Voluntary Support

Colleges and universities have increasingly turned to philanthropy to make up some of the revenue losses, with mixed results. The big change has been the growth of private fund raising by public institutions, but only the most

TABLE 11.2
National Averages in Resident Undergraduate Tuition (in Dollars)

	Universities		State Colleges and Univ.		Community Colleges		Private 4-Year	U.S. CPI*	
	Nat'l Ave.	% Change	Nat'l Ave.	% Change	Nat'l Ave.	% Change	Nat'l Ave.	% Change	
1991	2,156		1,735		947		9,391		4.2
1992	2,410	12	1,940	12	1,052	11	10,017	7	3.0
1993	2,627	9	2,123	9	1,148	9	10,498	5	3.0
1994	2,837	8	2,277	7	1,231	7	11,025	5	2.6
1995	3,032	7	2,402	6	1,314	7	11,709	6	2.8
% Change, 1991–95		41		39		39		25	11.9

* CPI figures are based on calendar rather than fiscal years.

Sources: Washington State Higher Education Coordinating Board, *Tuition and Fee Rates, 1994–95: A National Comparison* (Olympia: 1995), tables 1, 5, 9. Data for the private institutions are from *Chronicle of Higher Education Almanac* 38–42, no. 1 (September 1991 to September 1995 editions). Data for the U.S. Consumer Price Index (CPI) are from the U.S. Department of Labor, Bureau of Labor Statistics, "Consumer Price Index for All Urban Consumers, U.S. City Average," October 1996.

TABLE 11.3
Change In Voluntary Support For Higher Education, 1990–1995 (in Percent)

Alumni	42
Other Individuals	32
Corporations	18
Foundations	28
Religious Organizations	4
Other Organizations	34

Source: Chronicle of Higher Education Almanac 43, no. 1 (September 1996), pp. 17–18.

prestigious universities have realized much from this source. Of the total $12.7 billion given to public and private colleges and universities in 1995, 20 top universities in the country accounted for approximately 23 percent of all giving.[14] Fewer than 1,000 institutions receive 84 percent of all private contributions.[15] Overall, private fund raising by colleges and universities experienced a 30 percent gain from 1990 to 1995. The increases in giving are displayed by source in Table 11.3.

Private Colleges and Universities

Private colleges and universities, faced with an excess supply of spaces at posted prices, have increased their tuition discounts dramatically. In a recent study of 147 private colleges and universities, tuition discounts increased by more than 28 percent from 1990 to 1995.[16] The study showed a wide range of tuition discounts among various types of private institutions. Tuition discounting became so commonplace in small private colleges with relatively low tuition—representing one end of the continuum—that at a third of these institutions, 10 percent (or fewer) of the freshmen paid the published tuition price. Of all the institutions surveyed, fewer than half of the students paid the published tuition price. The practice of tuition discounting raises questions about the role of financial aid in these institutions. Aid dollars are being used more frequently, it appears, to attract the right "mix" of students, rather than to offset the price of college for needy students.

In response to this climate, some colleges have decided to cut tuition since they had so few full-paying students left (for instance, Muskingum College, Bennington College,

and North Carolina Wesleyan College). Haggling over the net price of college became the norm, as more and more families learned that they could bargain with most colleges over the actual price to be paid by the family. Many nonselective private colleges have squeezed about all of the net tuition revenue gains out of their markets, and will find themselves in increasingly difficult financial straits if some form of public policy response is not forthcoming.

STATE POLICY RESPONSES: 1990–1995

Overview

The case studies found in part II provide in-depth examinations of fiscal trends and changes in five states: California, Florida, Michigan, Minnesota, and New York, from 1990 to 1995—as well as state and institutional policy responses to these changes. Case study researchers found a varied range of responses to the changing fiscal climate of the 1990s. No single state can be considered "average" or "normal." It is useful for this reason to look at how these particular states fared and determine to what extent, if any, we can learn more about the common problems states face, as well as learn more about the range of policy responses to these problems.

To better understand the fiscal context of each state, case study researchers collected data from the state and drew upon national comparative data sources as well. The following section summarizes case study findings, and places these findings within a larger national context.[17]

The Context of Change, 1990–1995: Undergraduate Enrollment, Participation, and Growth in Higher Education

In 1994–95, overall undergraduate enrollment in higher education was about 12 million students nationwide[18] The case studies show that during the first half of the 1990s, enrollment increased slowly in Michigan and more rapidly in Florida. During the same period, enrollment at New York's and Minnesota's colleges and universities declined in fairly small numbers. California's enrollment declined more substantially, by

TABLE 11.4
High School Graduates and College Enrollment, Case Study States

	% Change in High School Graduates (1990–95)*	FTE Public Higher Education Students per New High School Graduate[†]	
		1990	1995
California	11.0	4.92	4.51
Florida	8.2	2.92	3.64
Michigan	0.0	3.27	3.71
Minnesota	5.7	3.42	3.32
New York	2.8	2.59	2.81

* The figures in this column are based on projections beginning in 1993.

† A caution is in order here. Because these statistical data are based on students enrolling in public colleges and universities, those states with robust private sectors of education, like New York, look as though fewer of their students attend college compared to the national average.

Source: Figures in the first column are from Western Interstate Commission for Higher Education (WICHE), Teachers Insurance and Annuity Association, and The College Board, High School Graduates: Projections by State, 1992 to 2009 (Denver: 1993), pp. 22–27. Data in the second and third columns are from Kent Halstead, State Profiles: Financing Public Higher Education, 1978–1996 Trend Data (Washington, D.C.: Research Associates of Washington, 1996), pp. 9, 17, 45, 65.

about 200,000 students—mostly at the community college and state university systems.

Enrollment levels alone, however, provide an incomplete picture of change in the states. Enrollment may increase due to increases in the population or because of improved recruiting efforts. A more complete picture of how the changes of the 1990s affected educational opportunity for young people can be seen by also examining the trends in the number of high school graduates from 1990 to 1995, as shown in Table 11.4. This table also shows the full-time-equivalent (FTE) student enrollment in higher education per new high school graduate.[19]

Table 11.4 shows that the number of high school graduates, the primary pool for colleges and universities, increased in every state except Michigan, where it remained constant. The table also shows that the number of public FTE students in higher education (per new high school graduate) dropped in two states: California and Minnesota. This statistic provides the best national comparative measure on college enrollment relative to the size of the high school graduating class. States such as Michigan that experienced no growth in the number of high school graduates, but an increase in the number of public FTE students in higher education (per new high school graduate) either increased the number of high school graduates going to college or increased the enrollment of other full-time students to make up for the decline in high school graduates.

In Florida and New York, the number of high school graduates increased, as did the number of public FTE students in higher education (per new high school graduate). Florida's efforts to increase the number of high school students entering college seems to be working, given steady improvements in enrollment over the past 10 years or so.

In California and Minnesota, on the other hand, the number of FTE students in higher education (per new high school graduate) decreased while the overall pool of high school graduates increased. Of the case study states, California experienced the largest percentage increase in the number of high school graduates, and the largest percentage decrease in FTE students per new high school graduate.

Another important contextual factor to consider in trying to assess a state's record in college participation is the contribution of private colleges and universities. The case study states vary in the size of their private higher education sectors. New York depends most heavily on private colleges and universities to deliver education to its citizens. Minnesota is next in

Figure 11.4 Percentage of Students Enrolled In Private Institutions, 1989 and 1994

Note: Data include both undergraduate and graduate enrollments.
Source: Chronicle of Higher Education Almanac 37 and 42, no. I (September 1990 and 1995).

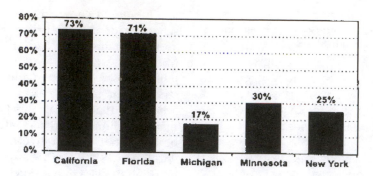

Figure 11.5 Projected Increases in High School Graduates, 1992–2009

Source: WICHE, Teachers Insurance and Annuity Association, and The College Board, *High School Graduates, Projections fry State,* pp. 22–27.

relying on its private colleges and universities. Even in states such as California and Florida, where the total number of students attending private colleges and universities is fairly small, state policies to support private higher education—mostly through financial aid—are important, long-standing commitments made by the state. Figure 11.4 shows the share of students educated in private colleges and universities in each of the case study states.

A final contextual factor that will affect many states over the next decade is the projected growth in the number of high school graduates, with a corresponding projected increase in college enrollments. In the next decade, half the states will see substantial increases in the number of students seeking postsecondary education. Figure 11.5 shows the wide range of growth projected in high school graduates in the case study states. Nationally, high school graduates are projected to increase about 32 percent from 1992 to 2009. In the West, high school graduates are projected to increase 65 percent and in the South and South-Central United States, by 73 percent.[20]

Fiscal Changes in the States from 1990 to 1995

Although some of the changes in how states finance higher education were visible before the 1990s, many of these trends accelerated during the first half of this decade because a large part of the country was in a recession, and because higher education support declined in absolute state dollars during this period. The rapid increase in tuition, combined with growing student indebtedness, became more visible during the 1990s, even though tuition rates had

been moving upward for some time. Changes in state financing of public higher education also affected private colleges and universities.

Case Study Findings

Finding One

For the first time since the mass expansion of higher education, dollars paid by students and their families (tuition) surpassed state appropriations to colleges and universities, which was previously the largest revenue source. Tuition revenue has surpassed state government appropriations to colleges and universities as the largest revenue source for higher education. In terms of actual dollars, tuition and fees for all higher education institutions nationally accounted for $37.4 billion in revenues for 1990–91, whereas appropriations to institutions from state governments accounted for $39.5 billion. In 1993–94, however, tuition and fees jumped to $48.6 billion while revenues from state governments rose only to $41.9 billion.

Finding Two

Higher education's share of state budgets declined nationally and in the case study states. Higher education lost ground in the competition for state resources in the 1990s. As noted by Brian Roherty in chapter 1, beginning in 1990 Medicaid displaced higher education as the second largest state spending category (the first is elementary and secondary education); Medicaid's share of state appropriations rose from 10.2 percent in 1987 to 19.2 percent in 1995. Table 11.5 documents the declining share of state appropriations for higher education in the case study states and nationally.

Finding Three

For the first time in 40 years there was an absolute annual decline in state dollars for higher education. In 1992, states reached a record high of $40 billion in investment in higher education. In 1993, for the first time in 40 years, states provided fewer resources for higher education than they did the previous year—slipping to $39.8 billion. Recovery since 1993 has been steady; states invested $44.4 billion for higher education in 1996.[21]

Table 11.6 shows what happened in the five case study states in terms of appropriations per public FTE student.[22] Only Michigan and Minnesota increased state dollars per public FTE student during the period studied. California, Florida, and New York decreased state appropriations per public student, with the largest decrease—both in absolute and percentage terms—in California. Only Michigan was below the national average in state dollars per student in 1990; by 1995 Michigan moved up to the national average, while California slipped below it.

Finding Four

The student share of the cost of higher education increased in all the case study states and tuition as a share of personal disposable income increased in most states. Tuition as a portion of all higher education revenues (defined as state appropriations plus tuition revenues) grew at a fairly rapid pace in most states across the country, and in all case study states, even those with higher state appropriations per student (see Table 11.7). In 1995, tuition still ranged from a low of 20 percent of all higher education revenues in California, to a high of 45 percent in Michigan. In 1990, California, Florida, and New York were well below the national average in this measure, while Michigan was significantly above it. In 1995, California, Florida, and New York were still well below the national average.

From 1980 to 1995, tuition at four-year public colleges and universities rose nearly three times as much as median household income, making it much more difficult for low- and middle-income families to afford college.[23] With the exception of Florida, tuition followed this same trend in the case study states, as shown in Table 11.8, which portrays tuition relative to personal disposable income.

Data from Tables 11.6, 11.7, and 11.8 reveal the broad range of public policies across the states regarding who pays and who benefits from higher education. Taken together, these

TABLE 11.5
Higher Education Share of State Budget (In Percent)

	1990	1994	Change
California	13.8	11.3	(18.1)
Florida	13.2	11.4	(13.6)
Michigan	14.7	13.7	(6.8)
Minnesota	19.9	17.2	(13.6)
New York	9.8	8.5	(13.3)
U.S.	14.0	12.5	(10.7)

Source: Steven Gold, *State Spending Patterns in the 1990s* (Albany: Center for the Study of the States, SUNY, 1995), pp. 23–30.

TABLE 11.6
State Dollars per Public Student

	State Dollars Per Public FTE Student		Indexed Value*	
	1990	1995	1990	1995
California	4,708	4,416	108	95
Florida	5,583	5,526	128	119
Michigan	4,194	4,648	96	100
Minnesota	4,444	4,939	102	106
New York	5,120	4,918	117	105

* National Index Average = 100.

Source: Halstead, *State Profiles, Trend Data* (1996), pp. 10, 18, 46, 66.

TABLE 11.7
Tuition Revenue Relative to Revenue Supporting Higher Education

	Tuition Revenue Relative to Total Revenue		Indexed Value*	
	1990	1995	1990	1995
California	10.6%	20.0%	41	64
Florida	18.0%	21.4%	69	68
Michigan	39.8%	44.5%	152	142
Minnesota	26.2%	30.1 %	100	96
New York	20.3%	25.7%	78	82

* National Index Average = 100.

Note: Total revenue is defined as state appropriations plus tuition revenue.

Source: Halstead, *State Profiles,* Trend Data (1996), p. 26.

TABLE 11.8
Tuition Relative to Personal Disposable Income
(in Percent)

	1990	1995
California	3.2	5.6
Florida	7.5	7.1
Michigan	17.4	19.3
Minnesota	9.9	11.4
New York	7.1	9.0

Source: Halstead, *State Profiles: Financing Public Higher Education, 1978 to 1995* (Washington, D.C.: Research Associates of Washington, 1995), p. 32.

tables show that state dollars for higher education are declining, students and their families are paying a greater share of the cost of higher education, and, with the exception of one state, tuition is taking a larger bite out of personal income.

Finding Five
During the first half of the 1990s, tuition increased at every type of higher education institution at a rate faster than the Consumer Price Index. In relation to this finding, see Table 11.2 as well as Figure 11.7.

Finding Six
Many states that increased tuition the fastest during the 1990s have frozen or dramatically slowed the growth of tuition. Of the five states (California, Massachusetts, New York, Oregon, and Virginia) that raised tuition by the highest per-

centage from 1990 to 1995 (and also had large enrollments), four have either frozen or slowed the growth of tuition dollars in the last two years—some as the result of public backlash. Only New York continued the high rate of tuition increases into 1994 and 1995.[24] Even New York, however, froze tuition for the 1996–97 school year.

Finding Seven
State student aid programs grew, but increases did not keep pace with the need caused by rising tuition. As Table 11.9 reveals, states made substantial contributions to their student aid programs during the time period studied. Total state dollars for student financial aid increased 41 percent from 1990 to 1995.[25] Of the states studied, however, none claimed that student aid dollars kept up with the double- and triple-digit increases in tuition during this period. New York, where state student aid is structured as an entitlement, was more successful in increasing aid as tuition increased, because those increases are mandated by law.

Although California's overall grant dollars increased during the five-year period, need-based state aid for undergraduates dropped by $23 million from 1991 to 1992. Similarly, while grant aid in Florida over the five-year period rose for Florida's students, state need-based aid declined by about $3 million from 1991 to 1993.

Also, as the five case studies in part II illustrate, states have widely varying priorities for state student aid dollars. For example, in 1994

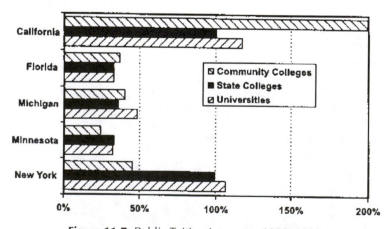

Figure 11.7 Public Tuition Increases, 1990–1995

Note: From 1990 to 1995, the U.S. CPI increased 16.6 percent.
Source: Washington State Higher Education Coordinating Board, *Tuition and Fee Rates,* tables 1, 5, 9.

TABLE 11.9
Increase in State Grant Aid to Students, 1990–1995
(in Percent)

California	33.0
Florida	37.5
Michigan	5.3
Minnesota	20.4
New York	25.4

Note: This table includes aid for both undergraduate and graduate students.

Source: National Association of State Student Grant and Aid Programs, *NASSGAP 26th Annual Survey Report 1994–95 Academic Year* (Albany: New York State Higher Education Services Corporation, 1996), p. 2.

Florida provided its residents with more dollars for non-need-based aid than did all the other states combined. Georgia is now moving along a similar path.

Finding Eight

Students at public institutions in many states are paying for an increasing portion of student aid through tuition increases. More public colleges and universities have, for the first time, used tuition dollars to increase their financial aid programs for students in their institutions. "Tuition discounting," a term used to describe the practice of providing institutional aid to students who cannot pay the full cost of tuition in private colleges and universities, is a practice now found in public institutions. For example, in California from 1990 to 1994, student aid dollars in the public colleges and universities dwarfed total dollars in the state aid program. Minnesota found it necessary for the first time to discount tuition at its flagship institution. In Florida, public policy requires that a percentage of tuition increases is allocated for student aid support at public institutions. Michigan colleges and universities have discretion over tuition dollars and have used these funds to support student aid. Public institutions in New York are seeking the authority to set tuition differentially across institutions, along with more freedom to use these dollars to support financial aid.

This shift in the source of financial aid raises issues of equity. California, Minnesota, and Florida have completed extensive studies about the income distribution of students in the various types of institutions in the state.[26]

All three states found that, on the average, higher income students were attending the large flagship institutions with middle- and low-income students concentrated at the state colleges and universities and community colleges. The private colleges in these states drew, for the most part, students from family backgrounds with incomes higher than those students attending state colleges and universities, but lower than the flagship institutions.

The growth of institutional aid dollars from student tuition revenue raises the policy question of whether institutions or the states are best suited to distribute financial aid dollars. If the current trend of increasing institutional aid from tuition dollars continues, middle-income families will find attending public colleges and universities more expensive.

Finding Nine

Tuition discounting in private colleges and universities increased. While data are not available by state, a national study documented the findings in Table 11.10, which shows that tuition discounting grew at private colleges and universities in the United States.

Finding Ten

Students borrowed more money and more students borrowed to pay for higher education. Even though dollars for need-based grant programs increased during the 1990s, student borrowing across the five states skyrocketed from 1990 to 1995. Changes in eligibility for federal loan programs, as well as rising college prices, account for this growth. From 1990 to 1996, total loan volume in the United States grew from $15.8 billion to $28.5 billion.[27] More detailed information about

TABLE 11.10
Increase in Tuition Discount Rate, 1990–1995
(in Percent)

Small College, Low Tuition	37.5
Small College, High Tuition	28.7
Large College/University	28.0

Source: Lucie Lapovsky, "Tuition Discounting Continues to Climb: NACUBO Study Analyzes Six Years of Data," in *Portfolio* (NACUBO Business Officers, February 1996), p. 21. Data are based on a sample of 147 private colleges and universities.

trends in student borrowing is found in the case studies.

Finding Eleven

Support for state mechanisms to promote student choice to attend private colleges and universities has eroded in some states due to changes in the structure of higher education finance. Significant changes in the support of public policies relative to private colleges and universities have occurred since 1990 in California and in New York, and are also apparent in other states to a lesser degree. Although enrollment increased or held stable in private colleges and universities in the case study states during this period, tuition discounting increased and state support to private colleges decreased. The discounting of tuition and the decreased state support may undermine the investment these institutions will be able to make in their own futures.

Private colleges and universities in California and New York have historically been supported by public policies that have helped make them an integral part of the state system of higher education. Both states provide financial aid to students attending private colleges and universities. The rapid increases in tuition at public institutions have made more students eligible for state aid scholarships, including many students attending public colleges and universities. For the first time since the inception of large state programs for financial aid in both California and New York, students from public institutions are now using a greater share of state financial aid grants than are students from private colleges and universities. These programs were created to provide choice to students who wanted to attend a private college or university.

Other Policy Responses

Other policy responses to changes in the finance of higher education during the 1990s are described in the case studies. However, with the exception of Florida and Michigan, case study researchers found little evidence that the states, in responding to the changes in the 1990s, were guided by either historic or new state policies created for higher education.

Even though Florida was under significant fiscal stress during the 1990s, attempts were made to increase student participation, reduce student time in college, and begin planning to accommodate the projected increases in enrollment expected during the first decade of the next century. While these issues were approached largely in isolation—and none were fully resolved to the satisfaction of educational and political leaders—the state's adjustments to the fiscal pressures of the 1990s appear to have remained consistent with historic public policies in the state, particularly in maintaining access for qualified high school graduates.

Michigan, on the other hand, maintained its commitment to past public policies largely by maintaining the status quo. The state could afford this for two primary reasons. First, although state revenues dipped slightly during fiscal year 1991, revenue growth remained positive during the rest of the recession and higher education stayed a high priority for legislators. As a result, Michigan's system of higher education did not face the cuts that public colleges and universities faced in many other states. Since enrollments were not increasing in Michigan during this period, state funding per student increased significantly. Second, even though tuition increased dramatically in the state as well, students and families paid the higher rates without clamoring for change. With yearly increases in state appropriations to higher education and with a high level of public satisfaction, Michigan's colleges and universities navigated the first half of the 1990s in a fairly stable environment without significant long-term changes.

Neither New York nor California could afford such a strategy. The cuts in state dollars for higher education in New York and California were much more severe than those in Florida. (Michigan's system of higher education enjoyed actual increases each year.) Moreover, the responses to New York's and California's fiscal crises were not only piecemeal and fragmentary, but they also diverged significantly from those states' historic policies. For California, the most drastic result of the early 1990s was that access to higher education decreased during this period, based on several measures described in the case study. As California began to recover from the recession, it has increased state appropriations for public higher education. The state has also begun restoring dollars to the state student aid program to support students attending private colleges and universities. Little planning has been done, however, to address how the state should accommodate the huge increases in enrollment demand expected over the coming decade.

While New York's system of higher education did not see funding cuts as deep as California's public colleges and universities, the fiscal stress on higher education in New York continued well into 1994 and 1995. During these years, tuition increases in the public institutions continued unabated—which marked a significant change in past public policy, for until the 1990s New York had very low or no tuition in its public sector. Although budgets in New York became more stable in 1996, the long-term prospects for increased higher education funding are still dim, as demands for public services increase and the governor continues to pursue his tax-cutting agenda. Unlike California, however, the state of New York has required its institutions of higher education to begin reporting regularly to the legislature on long-term strategies to improve cost effectiveness. Although policy makers and educational leaders are now asking difficult questions regarding accountability, efficiency, and productivity, it remains to be seen whether this discussion will help New York develop new long-term public policies regarding higher education.

During the 1990s in Minnesota, the state's high level of commitment to both public and private higher education eroded somewhat, causing the state's historic policies that generously supported both public and private higher education to come into question. While the state faces a moderate increase in enrollment growth over the next decade, competition for state resources is intensifying. Also increasing is the level of conflict between the public and private institutions of higher education. A proposal to move a significant portion of state funding for public colleges and universities into the state student aid program, available to students at public or private institutions, is under consideration by the governor. With a governor and many legislators also expressing interest in approaches that shift public higher education subsidies away from institutions and toward the "consumer," Minnesota may be

moving toward a more "market-oriented" approach to funding higher education.

ISSUES AND OPTIONS FOR STATE POLICY

As this chapter has described, the state financing of higher education in the 1990s has brought about important structural changes in the financing of higher education in the United States, the most important of these being a dramatic increase in tuition and student borrowing, and a significant decrease in state funding. These changes have resulted in a gradual shift from the state to the individual in paying for higher education. This shift has important consequences, as Brian Roherty has described in chapter 1, concerning the composition of and the demand for higher education in the coming decades. As a result, the fiscal changes of the 1990s bring with them a wide array of public concerns that call into question, as the case studies in part II reveal in greater detail, established state priorities regarding higher education.

Priorities for Higher Education

Unfortunately, many generations find that they have backed into new priorities without having evaluated them—through isolated fiscal or institutional decisions made on an ad hoc basis in response to real and pressing short-term needs. In light of the recent shift in the burden of paying for higher education—at a time when competition for state revenues is expected to intensify and the number of high school graduates is projected to rise in many states—it is especially important that each state revisit its priorities that guide higher education policies. It is toward this aim that the following priorities for higher education, which are not meant to be exhaustive, are listed. These priorities often are in conflict, not only with one another, but also with other state priorities. Several of those listed will no doubt be prominent across many states, while others may be missing entirely from some states. It could be that states facing significant enrollment growth will find themselves adopting similar priorities—or that other factors besides projected enrollment growth are more significant determinants of state priorities.

1. Maintain or improve access to undergraduate programs, including affordability
   a. Maintain low public tuition
   b. Establish or maintain high tuition/high aid policies
2. Enhance the quality of undergraduate education
3. Enhance higher education's role in economic development
4. Ensure accountability for public funds
5. Increase specialization of function among institutions or maintain the system as is by spreading the budgetary pain evenly
6. Help private institutions survive by enhancing their ability to meet state objectives
7. Use financial pressure to force productivity increases within the institutions
   a. Force a reduction in unit costs of education
   b. Force institutions to set priorities among activities (e.g., undergraduate versus graduate programs)
8. Fund technology to enhance productivity
9. Reduce state contributions to higher education to fund other state priorities

Of course it is one thing to establish priorities publicly and another to put them into effect (through annual appropriations, governance policies, institutional decisions, and the like) and it is always the latter that proves to be the acid test. Ironically, however, those states that need to revisit their priorities most are the very ones in which publicly established policies have begun to erode without widespread public debate.

Some have argued that the underlying message of the structural changes in higher education finance during the 1990s is that access has slipped as a priority for many states. In every case study state, for instance, tuition rates and loan volume increased significantly, and in four out of five of the states, tuition was taking a larger portion of disposable income. Yet of the case study states, only in California did enrollments and other factors change so that access was reduced significantly during the first half of the 1990s. During 1994 and

1995, however, the legislature and governor in California agreed to freeze student tuition for a second year, and enrollments have increased again.

Some policy makers appear to be willing to let access slip from their grasp, perhaps on the assumption that we have done all that we can or should do in this area, or perhaps out of a sense that the system simply cannot handle the growth that will occur in some states. (In California, this growth has been referred to as "Tidal Wave II.") Not seeing any way to accommodate this potential growth, these policy makers may prefer simply not to talk about it. Others may believe that we have gone too far in our emphasis on access, and that too many young people are in college who do not deserve to be there. For whatever reason, access as a public priority has not received significant public debate, yet in relation to higher education, it is the issue that arguably affects more families more significantly than any other single issue.

Whereas access appears to have slipped from the lexicon of public debate over higher education, "privatization" has become a buzzword of late, with its meanings not entirely clear. Outsourcing seems to be one meaning, but the more profound one refers to a shift by formerly public universities into a stance of "state-assisted," and ultimately into predominantly private financial status. One dimension of this shift is the growing tendency of public institutions to recycle tuition revenue into student aid, precisely as the private institutions have been doing. Some public university presidents argue that their best policy is, to the extent possible, to behave as if they were leading private institutions. But it is not yet clear what the full impact of this strategy will be on public priorities for higher education.

Issues for Policy Makers

As states go about the task of determining their priorities (either through deliberate or ad hoc means) and as public institutions begin to adopt the revenue-raising strategies of private institutions, it is crucial that policy makers consider the effects of a general shift from state to private support of public higher education. The following issues are presented on the basis of that assumption.

1. We must better understand the effects of the increased reliance of public colleges and universities on tuition and other private revenue, and decreased reliance on state general funds. The increased reliance of tuition dollars in public colleges and universities has also influenced the financing of private institutions. Is more—or less—governmental attention being given to public institutional expenditures of state appropriations? To the amount and distribution of state appropriations for student financial aid?

2. If the changes of recent years toward "privatization" of revenue sources are structural and permanent, we need to better understand the likely effects on public and private higher education institutions and on state and federal public policies for higher education. For example, as the "equity" of state government in the enterprise decreases, how will the traditional relationships of government to the colleges and universities change with respect to accountability and regulation? Is growing deregulation likely, and if so, what form would that take?

3. It is also important to understand how the changing patterns of finance influence expectations that colleges and universities will pursue public policy goals such as access and economic development. What are the implications for public support of particular functions, such as student financial aid and capital expenditures? What are the implications for educational opportunity, affordability, access, and choice?

4. A related issue concerns how states invest their resources. Are there specific changes in state budgetary practices and policies that would encourage institutions to evolve in desired directions (for instance, by placing more emphasis on undergraduate rather than graduate programs)? Can we identify "best practices" in this area?

5. Some assert that evidence is mounting that colleges and universities have become, are becoming, or will become more responsive to market forces than in the past. If colleges and universities are becoming more responsive to markets, should government seek to achieve public purposes through the market, relying more on incentives than on general institutional support through state appropriations? In general, should public support be more focused and targeted than in the past, with less governmental responsibility for the overall well-being of institutions?

6. If colleges and universities are becoming more responsive to markets, then state and federal governments need to determine if there are some functions of higher education that public policies should seek to insulate from market forces. If so, what are these functions? For example, is there a public policy interest in preserving and transmitting knowledge of the classical languages and cultures or in an "academic core" deemed essential for an informed citizenry or in "basic" as opposed to "applied" research?

7. Suppose it were possible for a handful of the most prestigious public universities to be privatized by replacing state institutional support with some mix of tuition, private philanthropy, and contract support. Would this be a desirable public policy? Would there be serious social costs if the most prestigious public institutions were no longer public? (This discussion assumes that privatization is not a realistic possibility for the vast majority of public four-year and two-year colleges and universities.)

8. If public tuition continues to increase, states might debate whether institutions should allocate some percentage of the increased tuition to student aid. Alternatively, states could allocate increased public funds to state-run financial aid programs rather than having each college or university mimic the selective discounting that one finds in the private sector. What is the best way to distribute student aid in public institutions?

9. Many who believe that the changes in state support for higher education of the last five years will not be reversed

have argued that colleges and universities must reduce costs rather than attempt to solve their financial problems solely through increasing revenues. Although many businesses and other institutions in the United States have been following that approach recently, the degree of change has been minimal in higher education. Economist William Baumol has argued, on the other hand, that higher education fundamentally cannot achieve productivity increases, and that we must accept the fact that a steadily growing share of national income will be devoted to higher education (and also to medical care).[26] Which argument is acceptable to the public and state policy makers? Can institutions of higher education improve productivity significantly?

10. There has also been extensive discussion of the potential of the new information technologies to reduce higher education costs (or expand outreach to unserved populations), but the jury is still out on whether new technologies will produce significant reductions in the unit costs of education. Are we likely to see dramatic breakthroughs in costs from this source in the next five to ten years? If so, can public policy help to encourage this trend, or can we assume that incentives are already in place to bring these changes into existence?

11. It is difficult to address new mechanisms of finance when so many of the old ways of funding institutions are tied to how we organize our public colleges and universities. What do new forms and purposes of finance imply for governance systems? Can we identify specific governance patterns that seem best adapted to the circumstances of the next five to ten years? Are system offices (such as the University of California's Office of the President) cost-effective in a time of limited resources? And what of the regulatory powers of certain state governance structures (for instance, Illinois and Virginia)?

CONCLUSION

Clark Kerr, president emeritus of the University of California and former director of the Carnegie Commission on Higher Education, has described the mix of public and private control and financing of colleges and universities in this country as a "halfway house."[29] Changes in the financing of higher education in the 1990s have gradually shifted the burden of paying from the state to the individual. Rapidly increasing costs of operating the "house"—combined with continued intense competition for state resources in most states and projected enrollment jumps in some—threaten to exacerbate those changes. Meanwhile, many public institutions are adopting strategies similar to those of private institutions in raising revenues, yet few are seriously addressing long-term issues concerning productivity. Until state and institutional leaders begin to fully grapple with the effects of the changes in financing during the recession of the 1990s, they are unlikely to fully understand or take responsibility for the changes that are on the horizon.

NOTES

1. Carnegie Commission on Higher Education, *Higher Education: Who Pays? Who Benefits? Who Should Pay?* (New York: McGraw-Hill, 1973), p. 3.
2. U.S. Office of the President, *The Economic Report of the President* (Washington, D.C.: 1995), p. 274.
3. Appropriations, revenue, and other budgetary data are presented in fiscal years, unless otherwise noted.
4. U.S. Department of Education, National Center for Education Statistics, *Digest of Education Statistics 1996* (Washington, D.C.: 1996), p. 333.
5. Robert Atwell, "Higher Education Governance in Despair," in *Journal for Higher Education Management* 11, no. 2 (winter/spring 1996), pp. 13–19; David Breneman, *Higher Education: On A Collision Course with New Realities* (Boston: American Student Assistance, 1993); Arthur Hauptman and Anthony Carnevale, "The Economic, Financial, and Demographic Context of American Higher Education," unpublished paper prepared for the Seminar on Change and the Public Comprehensive University, Aspen Institute Program on Education in a Changing Society, 1996; Bruce Johnstone, "Learning Productiv-

ity: A New Imperative for American Higher Education," in *Higher Education in Crisis: New York in National Perspective*, edited by William Barba (New York: Garland, 1995); Morton Owen Schapiro, Michael McPherson, and Gordon Winston, *Paying the Piper: Productivity, Incentives, and Financing in U.S. Higher Education* (Ann Arbor: UM Press,1993); and William Massy and Robert Zemky, "Cost Containment: Committing to a New Economic Reality," in *Change* 22, no. 6 (November/December 1990), pp. 16–22.

6. Steven Gold, *The Fiscal Crisis of the States: Lessons for the Future* (Washington, D.C.: Georgetown University Press, 1995), p. 68.

7. The College Board, *Trends in Student Aid: 1984 to 1994* (Washington, D.C.: 1994), p. 3; and *Trends in Student Aid: 1986 to 1996* (Washington, D.C.: 1996), p. 3. Numbers for 1995–96 listed as preliminary.

8. The average Stafford Loan per student jumped froth $2,712 in 1990 to $3,061 in 1994, according to The College Board, *Trends in Student Aid: 1984 to 1994*, p. 3.

9. Jacqueline E. King, "Student Aid: Who Benefits Now?" in *Educational Record* 77, no. I (winter 1996), pp. 21–27.

10. These data are based on federal academic research and development obligations according to a survey of 15 federal agencies by the National Science Foundation (1994 numbers are preliminary). Figures cover federal obligations, which are funds set aside for payments. Figures include spending for science and engineering projects only, and exclude spending in such disciplines as the arts, education, and the humanities.

11. Roger Geiger, "Research Universities in a New Era," *in Higher Learning in America: 1980–2000*, edited by Arthur Levine (Baltimore: John Hopkins UP, 1993), pp. 210–42.

12. Ibid.

13. U.S. General Accounting Office, *Tuition Increasing Faster Than Household Income and Public Colleges' Costs* (Washington, D.C.: 1996), p. 20.

14. *Chronicle of Higher Education Almanac* 42, no. 1 (September 1995), p. 25.

15. Ibid., pp. 17–18. Figures are based on a survey of 992 institutions, compiled by the Council for Aid to Education for 1993–94.

16. Lucie Lapovsky, "Tuition Discounting Continues to Climb: NACUBO Study Analyzes Six Years of Data," in *Portfolio* (NACUBO Business Officers, February 1996), p. 21.

17. This section draws upon data from national sources in order to compare the five states studied and to put the case study findings in a national context. Numbers in the case studies may be slightly different, since the case studies relied on a combination of national and state data. Important differences between the sets of data will be noted.

18. *Chronicle of Higher Education Almanac* 39–43, no. 1 (1992–1996 editions).

19. It is possible for a state to show an overall increase in students (head count), while experiencing a decline in the public FTE students per new high school graduate. This can happen due to an increase in the number of part-time students or due to increases in the number of high school graduates.

20. Western Interstate Commission for Higher Education (WICHE), Teachers Insurance and Annuity Association, and The College Board, *High School Graduates, Projections by State 1992 to 2009* (Denver: 1993), pp. 14–15.

21. Edward Hines, *State Higher Education Appropriations 1995–96* (Denver: State Higher Education Executive Officers, 1996). This figure does not include local property taxes appropriated for higher education.

22. It is important to note that the statistics in Tables 11.6 and 11.7 are based on students attending public colleges and universities and, therefore, do not account for support to students attending private colleges and universities in the states. Also, states with large community college systems, such as California, tend to appear low on appropriations per student presented in Table 11.6, due to the lower costs associated with that sector of higher education. Nevertheless, the data provide a picture of changes over time that are useful to note.

23. U.S. General Accounting Office, *Tuition Increasing Faster*, p. 19.

24. Washington State Higher Education Coordinating Board, *Tuition and Fee Rates, 1994–95: A National Comparison* (Olympia: 1995), Tables 1, 5, 9.

25. National Association of State Student Grant and Aid Programs, *NASSGAP 26th Annual Survey Report: 1994–95 Academic Year* (Albany: New York State Higher Education Services Corporation, 1996), p. 2.

26. California Student Aid Commission, *Family Financial Resources of Dependent Undergraduates at California Four Year Institutions* (Sacramento: 1996); Florida Postsecondary Education Planning Commission, *How Floridians Pay for College* (Tallahassee: 1994); and Minnesota Private College Research Foundation, *Ways and Means: How Minnesota Families Pay for College* (St. Paul: 1992).

27. The College Board, *Trends in Student Aid: 1986 to 1996*, p. 4.

28. William J. Baumol and Sue Anne Batey Blackman, "How to Think About Rising College Costs," in *Planning for Higher Education* 23, no. 4 (1995), pp, 1–7.

29. Clark Kerr, *The Great Transformation in Higher Education: 1960–1980* (Albany: SUNY Press, 1991), p. 27.

REFERENCES

Atwell, Robert. (1996). Higher education governance in despair. *Journal for higher education management,* 11, no. 2, winter/spring, pp. 13–19.

Baumol, William & S. A. B. Blackman. (1995) How to think about rising college costs. In *Planning for higher education* 23, summer, pp. 1–7

Breneman, David. (1993). *Higher education: On a collision course with new realities.* Boston: American Student Assistance.

California Student Aid Commission, (1996). *Family financial resources of dependent undergraduates at California four year institutions.* Sacramento.

Carnegie Commission on Higher Education. (1973). *Higher education: Who pays? Who benefits? Who should pay?* New York: McGraw-Hill.

Chronicle of higher education almanac 37–43, no. 1, September 1990-September 1996.

The College Board. (1996). *Trends in student aid: 1986 to 1996.* Washington, D.C.

_____. (1995). *Trends in student aid: 1985 to 1995.* Washington, D.C.

_____. (1994). *Trends in Student Aid: 1984 to 1994.* Washington, D.C.

Florida Postsecondary Education Planning Commission. (1994). *How Floridians pay for college.* Tallahassee.

Gold, Steven. (1995). *The fiscal crisis of the states: Lessons for the future.* Washington, D.C.: Georgetown University Press.

_____. (1995). *Spending Patterns in the 1990s.* Albany: Center for the Study of the States, SUNY.

_____. State support of higher education: A national perspective. In *Planning for Higher Education* 18. no. 3, pp.1989–90.

Halstead, Kent, (1996). Quantitative analysis of the environment, performance, and operation actions of eight state public higher education systems. Unpublished paper. San Jose: The California Higher Education Policy Center.

_____. (1996). *State profiles: Financing public higher education, 1978 to 1996 trend data.* Washington, D.C.: Research Associates of Washington.

_____. (1995). *State profiles: Financing public higher education, 1978 to 1995.* Washington, D.C.: Research Associates of Washington.

Hauptman, Arthur, & Anthony Carnevale. (1996). The economic, financial, and demographic context of American higher education. Unpublished paper prepared for the Seminar on Change and the Public Comprehensive University, Aspen Institute Program on Education in a Changing Society.

Hines, Edward R. (1996). *State higher education appropriations 1995–96.* Denver: State Higher Education Executive Officers.

Johnstone, Bruce. (1995). Learning productivity: A new imperative for American higher education. In William Barba (Ed.), *Higher education in crisis: New York in national perspective.* New York: Garland, 1995, pp. 31–60.

Kerr, Clark. (1991). *Great transformation in higher education, 1960–1990.* Albany: SUNY Press.

King, Jacqueline. (Winter, 1996). Student aid: Who benefits now?" In *Educational Record,* pp. 21–29.

Lapovsky, Lucie. (February 1996). Tuition discounting continues to climb: NACUBO study analyzes six years of data. In *Portfolio.* NACUBO Business Officers, pp. 20–5.

Levine, Arthur (Ed.) (1993). *Higher learning in America, 1980 to 2000,* Baltimore: Johns Hopkins UP.

Massy, William, & Robert Zemsky. (November/December 1990). Cost containment: Committing to a new economic reality. In *Change* 22, no. 6, pp. 16–22.

Minnesota Private College Research Foundation. (1991). *Ways and means: How Minnesota families pay for college.* St. Paul.

Mortenson Research Letter on Public Policy Analysis of Opportunity for Postsecondary Education. (July 1995). *Postsecondary education opportunity,* no. 37, Iowa City, Iowa.

National Association of State Student Grant and Aid Programs. (1996). *NASSGAP 26th annual survey report, 1994–95 academic year,* Albany: New York State Higher Education Services Corporation.

Schapiro, Morton Owen, Michael McPherson, & Gordon Winston. (1993). *Paying the piper: Productivity, incentives, and financing in U.S. higher education.* Ann Arbor, UM Press.

U.S. Department of Education, National Center for Education Statistics, Office of Educational Research and Improvement. (1996). *Digest of education statistics, 1996,* Washington, D.C.

U.S. General Accounting Office. (1996). *Tuition increasing faster than household income and public colleges' costs,* Report B-271081, Washington, D.C.

U.S. Office of the President. (1996). *Economic Report of the President,* Washington, D.C.

Washington State Higher Education Coordinating Board. (1996). *Tuition and fee rates, 1995–96: A national comparison,* Olympia.

_____. (1995). *Tuition and fee rates, 1994–95: A national comparison,* Olympia.

Western Interstate Commission for Higher Education (WICHE), Teachers Insurance and Annuity Association, The College Board. (1993). *High School Graduates, Projections by State 1992–2009,* Denver, WICHE.

CHAPTER 12

STATE FUNDS FOR HIGHER EDUCATION: FISCAL DECISIONS AND POLICY IMPLICATIONS

HAROLD HOVEY

THE OUTLOOK FOR STATE FINANCES

Introduction

Impact of Fiscal Conditions on Higher Education

State funding for higher education has always been heavily influenced by states' fiscal situations. State elected officials have often viewed support of higher education as more discretionary than funding for many other programs. As a result, changes in state fiscal conditions are often multiplied in their impacts on higher education. When finances are tight, higher education budgets are often cut disproportionately. When financial conditions are good, higher education often receives larger increases than most other programs.

These fiscal responses mean that the outlook for state higher education funding depends critically on the outlook for state finances overall. This chapter addresses that outlook.

Baseline Budget Projections

The approach used in this paper is similar to that used by most legislative bodies when developing and enacting budgets and making fiscal projections—typically called *baseline* or *current service* budgeting. The starting point is current spending and revenues. The projections are based on applying current government policies to predicted future changes in the environment in order to measure the fiscal consequences of continuing those policies.

For revenues, that means predicting the revenues from current taxes, given likely changes in the national and state economies. For spending, it means predicting the workloads, such as the number of children in public schools, that drive spending. The underlying assumption is that decision-makers will be tempted to hold constant their spending for units of workload, such as spending per pupil. But to keep activity constant, such as maintaining the same pupil-teacher ratios and quantities of teaching supplies per pupil, spending must reflect inflation as well as growth in workloads.

The result of such an analysis is a current service, or baseline, budget. Such budgets provide the starting point for formulating governors' budgets and considering legislative budget options.

Source: *State Spending for Higher Education in the Next Decade: The Battle to Sustain Current Support*, 1999, The National Center for Public Policy & Higher Education, San Jose, CA.

The time period covered by the forecasts is a fiscal year or biennium, depending on the fiscal practices of individual states.

If the projections indicate that revenues from current taxes likely will exceed the spending needed to maintain current services, the government has fiscal flexibility to expand spending
further or reduce taxes. If there is a projected shortfall, decision-makers must either raise taxes to finance their current programs or curtail their spending patterns.

Some states and the federal government extend their fiscal projections to longer time periods. They use roughly the same approach—basing expected revenues on predicted economic conditions, and basing spending on predicted changes in price levels and workloads for government programs.

The Environment for State Finances

Economic Environment

The condition of the nation's economy is the single most critical factor influencing the fiscal condition of state governments. Economic growth brings large gains for state revenues because of impacts on tax bases. For example, in a rapidly expanding economy, rapid growth in incomes brings rapid growth in income tax revenues and rapid growth in purchases brings rapid growth in revenues from sales taxes. Economic growth also affects spending. Large portions of state expenditures are for means-tested safety net programs, such as cash welfare and Medicaid (health care for low-income households). In strong economic times, more people hold jobs and eligibility for safety net programs is reduced. Conversely, in economic downturns, the caseloads in these programs increase as more people become eligible because of low incomes.

From year to year, the performance of the nation's economy seems quite unpredictable. At any given time, there is constant speculation over whether the nation is on the verge of recession or economic "overheating," that is, rapid but unsustainable growth. Over the long run, economic growth is more predictable. Changes in the nation's real (inflation-adjusted) output are driven by the combination of: (1) the number of workers, and (2) their productivity or output per unit of time. Many factors affect productivity, such as technological innovation, education and training of workers, and capital investment. But over multi-year time periods changes in both productivity and the number of workers have proven to be relatively predictable.

For its projections, this paper relies on the baseline economic assumptions used by the U.S. Congress in its budget deliberations. These assumptions are quite similar to those used by those states that make long-term budget projections, as well as to the assumptions underlying forecasts used in business planning in the private sector.

The projections assume that each year of the forecast period will be characterized by about the same rate of economic growth. This is not because those making the forecasts believe that the nation will be free of periods of slow growth or recession alternating with faster-than-normal growth. It simply means that, without exception, those who make long-term projections of government budgets are not confident of their ability to forecast exactly when these periods will begin and end. They are confident, however, that the variations will average out over the projection period to about the rate of economic growth being assumed.

Demographic Environment

Standard demographic projections from the U.S. Census Bureau underlie both the economic and workload projections used in this report.[1]

Federal Policy

Because federal aid finances about a quarter of all state and local spending, the fiscal outlook of state and local governments is highly sensitive to changes in federal funding. These projections assume that federal aid will continue to finance the same percentage of state and local outlays as in the past. State government costs are also sensitive to federal mandates, which are presumed not to undergo major changes.

Political Environment

There are no assumptions about the relative electoral success of major political parties underlying the projections. This can be viewed as either: (1) an assumption that that success will not change in major ways, or (2) an assumption that such changes are insignificant.[2]

Sensitivity to Assumptions

Long-term fiscal projections are sensitive to the assumptions described above.

Spending Growth Projected to Parallel Personal Income Growth

Total Spending Increases

Detailed projections of state and local spending on a state-by-state basis were developed by State Policy Research, Inc., during 1998. The nationwide projections produced an unsurprising result. To maintain their current services, state and local governments will need to increase their spending by about the same percentage as the increase in total personal income of all Americans. Specifically, over the next eight years, an increase of 39.6% in spending will maintain current services while personal income growth is expected to be about 36.5%. Thus, current service spending can be accommodated with a slight rise in the percentage of incomes spent by state and local governments, from about 16.0% to 16.3%.

Having spending for current services so closely tied to personal income makes sense. First, it is reasonable to expect that voters will support adjusting purchases of public services about as fast as incomes grow. The projections imply improvements in purchasing power, as measured by real per capita income gains. To maintain balance between public and private outlays, citizens are likely to want to devote some of this purchasing power to public goods and services. It makes little sense, for example, to spend more on vehicles while not maintaining roads on which to drive them or on security alarm systems without adequate police responses to the resulting alarms.

Second, many of the factors driving personal income increases are also driving increases in the costs of government. Inflation is the best example. Demography offers other examples. A growth in population not only contributes the workers who produce economic growth, but also produces more citizens to be served by governments. Growth in those segments of the population that create high spending needs, such as children in school, is roughly propor-

tional to the growth in the segments creating economic growth, such as those in the 18 to 65 age group.

Differences Among Functions

Within the growth in total spending for current services, there are differences among major government functions. The somewhat higher-than-average growth of the college-age population and trends in college attendance will likely make higher education costs rise more rapidly than the costs of most other programs. Growth in the population over age 65, and particularly in the population over age 85, will tend to force Medicaid costs—a large portion of which pays for nursing home care—to rise more rapidly than total state and local outlays.

Revenues Grow More Slowly than Personal Income

Problem Widely Recognized

While spending for current services will grow at about the same pace as personal income, state and local revenues from existing taxes will not do so. The result is a shortfall in state and local budgets that is almost entirely attributable to the characteristics of state and local tax systems. This problem with current tax systems is well known. It has been the subject of a series of reports from organizations of state and local officials identifying the problem and proposing reforms in state tax systems to reduce if not eliminate it.[3]

Causes of the Problem

As economists would put it, the problem with state and local tax systems is their low *elasticity*. To provide revenues adequate to finance current service spending without tax increases, these tax systems would have to have *unit elasticity*—that is, growth in revenues would be proportionate to growth in personal income. For example, a 10% increase in personal incomes would result in a 10% increase in tax revenues. Because of its graduated personal income tax rates, the federal income tax would raise much more than 10% additional revenue for every 10% increase in personal income. To offset this tendency, the federal government adjusts the standard deduction and tax bracket break points for inflation every year. But even with the adjustment, federal income tax revenues grow at a better pace than personal income because: (1) personal income growth enters the income tax base, and (2) additional increments of real income (that is, income adjusted for inflation) are taxed at successively higher marginal income tax rates.

State and local tax systems show the reverse. The main culprit is states' high reliance on sales taxes on goods. As individual incomes rise, people spend a successively smaller portion of incremental income on taxed goods and higher proportions on non-taxed outlays for services. Even without increases in personal income, the share of consumer spending associated with goods tends to decline. Because productivity increases are concentrated in manufacturing, prices of manufactured goods tend to decline while those of services, where productivity has less of an impact, tend to rise. As a result, successively larger portions of incomes go to purchase services.

Low elasticity of state and local tax systems is also associated with high reliance on taxes and fees based on units of purchase (e.g., packages of cigarettes, bottles of alcoholic beverages, gallons of gasoline) rather than on prices. For more complex reasons, business taxes also have less-than-unit elasticity, since smaller portions of economic activity are associated with the types of businesses (corporations engaged in manufacturing) for which state and local tax systems were designed.

These characteristics of state and local tax systems mean that every growth of 10% in personal income is associated with growth of about 9.5% in state and local tax revenues.

The Outlook for Funding Current Services

Structural Deficits

With revenues growing more slowly than personal income and outlays growing faster, state and local governments have a *structural deficit* in funding current services. This mismatch between what would be needed to continue current programs and revenues from current taxes is about 0.5% a year. That is, to maintain current services, state and local governments nationwide would have to increase taxes by about 0.5%. Alternatively, they could maintain current tax systems and keep budgets balanced by holding spending growth to about 4.5%

annually rather than the 5% needed to maintain current services.

Problem Not Obvious in Recent Years:

These structural deficits usually appear when states make long-term projections of their fiscal situations. But they are a marked contrast to the widely publicized surpluses that have been appearing in state budgets in recent years. Why the difference?

1. The nation's economy has been growing faster than its long-term sustainable growth rate, swelling state as well as federal tax collections.

2. Unusual percentages of the economic gains from growth have accrued to economic players with higher-than-average tax rates, namely corporations and high-income households.

3. Federal aid, particularly funding associated with welfare reform, has provided windfall revenues for state governments.

4. Several fortuitous circumstances have benefited state finances, including extraordinary returns on pension fund investments (which cut the amounts required for employer contributions), a rapid decline in welfare caseloads, and unusual moderation in cost increases in health care.

5. Gains from these factors have been concentrated at the state level, without corresponding gains in local government finance. Therefore, surpluses reported by states are not indicative of the combined circumstances of state and local governments discussed in this report.

Interdependence of State and Local Finances

The impact of the combination of stronger state and weaker local finances on support of higher education is not obvious at first blush. Because most higher education money comes from states, strong state finances might suggest a favorable environment for higher education spending, regardless of local situations. In practice, however, local fiscal pressures are rapidly translated into state fiscal pressures. Evidence of this appears in discussions of taxes and tax relief. In many states, there is strong sentiment for reducing reliance on property taxes, such as personal property taxes on motor vehicles and residential property taxes. When states seek to reduce burdens of local property taxes, they do so by replacing all or most of the local revenue losses.

Evidence of the interaction of state and local finances also appears in spending. For example, in the state campaigns of 1998, candidates almost universally stressed increasing state aid for local public schools. Besides whatever impact this might have on how well children are educated, one effect is to reduce reliance on local property taxes for funding of schools. This effect can be viewed as using some state revenue growth to enhance local revenue growth, which is not matching the strong growth seen by states.

Problem Likely to be Obvious in Next Few Years

The flip side of the better-than-normal state financial conditions will be, as everyone who looks at the subject concludes, an ensuing period when state finances show worse problems than the normal mild structural deficits. There are two basic reasons for this, one behavioral and one economic.

The *behavioral reason* stems from the tendency to assume that the future will be like the immediate past. This is particularly important in state government, which has institutional factors encouraging a short-term outlook. The old adage that elected officials rarely look beyond the next election has an element of truth. Also important is the turnover of legislators—always rapid, but accelerated by the increasing use of term limits. The office of governor also turns over rapidly, with most governors limited to eight years of continuous service.

These factors mean that the average state legislator and governor in 1999 has never held his or her current office except during the period of unbroken prosperity that has lasted since 1992. In this context, there is a tendency to assume that strong tax collection growth will continue unabated and that actual collections will always exceed those predicted by revenue estimators. Revenue estimators themselves are not immune from adjusting their estimating procedures to deal with their recent errors, which have been underestimates.

So on top of whatever institutional inability state elected officials inherently have to look beyond the next election, all the behavioral factors at work encourage more optimism about future state finances than projections suggest is merited. Historically, this factor alone has led state officials to over-commit their resources by adopting aggressive tax cuts and spending increases.

The *economic reason* to expect a sharp reversal of state fiscal fortunes lies primarily in the likelihood that past economic patterns will be repeated. If they are, the past eight years of rapid growth will be followed by some years of recession or slow growth with resulting negative impacts on state finances.

Problems would arise even if the nation were to revert to its normal long-term growth pattern of increases of about 2.4% in real (inflation-adjusted) Gross Domestic Product rather than the nearly 4% growth in 1998 and 1999. Such a situation would likely reverse some of the five factors listed on page 182 that have contributed to the current strong fiscal positions of the states.

Impacts on Higher Education

The Past

The last five years have been about as good as it gets in state funding of higher education. By all available measures of state government spending, appropriations per full-time equivalent (FTE) student have increased by substantially more than the rate of inflation. Not included in these calculations are the significant developments in state tax policies that have provided special tax treatment for college savings and a variety of tax benefits in some states for outlays for college costs.

This favorable fiscal environment has meant that state elected officials have exerted little pressure for major changes in higher education. With minor exceptions, they have not forced consolidation or closures of institutions, elimination of programs, restrictions on tenure, mandates regarding minimum faculty teaching loads, enrollment caps, and other devices to attempt to force cost reductions. Nor have they squeezed appropriations for public institutions to the point that large tuition increases were required in order for the institutions to match the increases in costs occurring (on a national average basis) at private and public institutions.

In fact, many states have budgeted more favorably for higher education than necessary to match enrollment changes and inflation. Some states have been financing the costs of tuition freezes and a few rollbacks. Many have increased scholarships, particularly in grades 13 and 14. The environment for the establishment of new institutions in rapidly growing states has been favorable, as has the environment for the expansion of offerings at existing institutions.

The Future

The national budget projections suggest that this environment will not continue.

Even if the national economy and state finances return to *normal growth* patterns without a downturn, higher education will find itself in an environment where merely maintaining current services (through appropriations reflecting inflation and enrollment increases) will be difficult. Specifically, if higher education shared the fiscal pain equally with all other functions, spending growth would be slightly below the amounts needed to maintain current services. Without tax increases, appropriations to higher education each year would be about 0.5% short of the total funding needed for maintaining those services. New initiatives in higher education would require offsetting reductions in the current spending base.

In a normal growth environment, higher education would constantly be on the defensive against those seeking deeper cuts in order to finance tax cuts or new initiatives in other fields, such as elementary and secondary education.

If the long-term pattern of normal growth is preceded by *recession* or *slower-than-normal* growth, higher education would experience even more fiscal pressures, recreating the fiscal environment of 1990 to 1993 and 1984 to 1986.

Differences among States

State Situations

Few individual states exhibit the structural deficit of 0.5% a year that is represented by the national average. Both tax systems and spending pressures vary among the states.

Some states rely heavily on personal income taxes with their high elasticity. Others have no personal income tax and rely heavily on sales and excise taxes with quite low elasticity. Some states will see little growth in government workloads, such as those associated with enrollment increases, while others will see faster-than-average growth. Inelastic tax systems and rapid workload growth are frequently found together. Table 12.1 provides the baseline projections (in year eight) of each state's structural surplus (+) or deficit (−) for state and local governments combined.

Reasons for Differences in Outlook

The reasons for the major differences among the states can be divided into three categories: (1) differences in tax systems, (2) differences in spending needs, and (3) differences in economic growth rates.

Most of the states that have surpluses also have *tax systems* that rely heavily on graduated personal income taxes, which take increasing shares of personal income as inflation and economic growth drive those with more income into higher tax brackets. These states do not rely heavily on sales taxes. Of the ten states showing structural surpluses, ten have personal income taxes and nine use graduated rates. Bottom-ranked states typically do not rely significantly on graduated income taxes. The bottom-ranked states typically rely heavily on sales and excise taxes and/or on revenues from royalties, severance taxes, and other revenues associated with natural resources.

Many of the states with surpluses have few demographic pressures on *spending* because of slow population growth and stable or declining school enrollments. This is a characteristic shared by Iowa, Minnesota, Nebraska and several other top-ranked states. Conversely, many of the states showing the largest structural deficits have been showing substantial increases in enrollments, which are expected to continue.

Steady *economic growth* causes both an increase in revenues, because taxes are collected on a stronger economic base, and an increase in spending needs, because of rising population and enrollments. However, these factors do not necessarily produce balanced growth in spending needs and revenues within individual states. The imbalance becomes particularly notable in states where past economic

TABLE 12.1
State and Local Surplus or Shortfall as a Percent of Baseline Revenues in Year Eight of Fiscal Projections

Rank	State	Percent
1	Iowa	2.7%
2	Nebraska	1.5
3	North Dakota	0.9
4	Ohio	0.9
5	Kentucky	0.5
6	Connecticut	0.4
7	Michigan	0.4
8	New York	0.3
9	Maine	0.1
10	Minnesota	0.1
11	Massachusetts	0.0
12	Oregon	–0.1
13	Illinois	–0.4
14	Pennsylvania	–1.3
15	West Virginia	–1.4
16	Wisconsin	–1.5
17	Missouri	–1.8
18	Kansas	–1.9
19	Mississippi	–2.0
20	Oklahoma	–2.1
21	Arkansas	–2.3
22	Louisiana	–2.5
23	California	–2.8
24	Rhode Island	–2.9
25	Delaware	–3.0
26	New Jersey	–3.3
27	North Carolina	–3.7
	United States	**–3.8**
28	Utah	–4.3
29	South Carolina	–4.6
30	Vermont	–4.6
31	Alabama	–4.8
32	South Dakota	–5.0
33	Indiana	–5.7
34	Montana	–5.7
35	Georgia	–6.5
36	Washington	–6.7
37	Virginia	–6.8
38	Colorado	–7.0
39	Maryland	–7.1
40	Texas	–7.8
41	New Hampshire	–8.2
42	Florida	–8.8
43	Tennessee	–9.1
44	Arizona	–10.5
45	Wyoming	–10.6
46	New Mexico	–12.0
47	Idaho	–13.2
48	Hawaii	–15.1
49	Alaska	–16.4
50	Nevada	–18.3

Source: State Policy Research, Inc., 1998.

growth has abruptly slowed. This results in a slowdown in the growth of tax collections without a proportional slowdown in the growth of spending needs (such as when young workers with children are drawn to a state during prosperous times, only to witness an abrupt economic downturn). Hawaii is a good example of this effect.

PROSPECTS FOR FUNDING HIGHER EDUCATION

Introduction and Summary

Understanding the State Perspective

It is understandably difficult for someone oriented to a particular government-financed activity—such as higher education, law enforcement, health care, or public schools—to see beyond the needs for government support of that function. The usual approach from such a perspective is to ignore choices and problems associated with other functions, implicitly assuming that those with overall responsibility can and should make the adjustments—in tax levels and funding of other programs—that are necessary to provide appropriate funding for the activity in question. *In this context, the discussion of baseline structural deficits is easily viewed as a problem that must be tolerated, but somehow should be dealt with by those who are supposed to deal with it, specifically those outside higher education.*

Besides, projections like those presented above are dry as dust when compared with the appealing realities of any government function, such as higher education. Compared with such inviting concepts as broadening access and improving quality in higher education, funding current service budgets for health care or law enforcement sounds like a trade-off that somehow should be made in favor of the more attractive alternative.

A Native American saying asserts that you cannot know a person until you have walked in his moccasins. Most readers of this paper have lifelong careers in higher education, without the experience of having served in major elected offices, with no burning desire to do so, and with limited prospects for doing so even if they choose to do so. They haven't and will not walk in the moccasins of elected officials. For a short time, they must settle for a few written words that attempt to convey the perspective of elected officials.

Higher Education Funding Options

Three appendices, not included, to this report attempt to convey the perspective of elected officials by examining substantive and political arguments about tax increases and, program-by-program, arguments against cutting and for expanding major programs other than higher education. (Readers are presumed to be familiar with those arguments in relation to higher education.)

The gist of the arguments in each appendix and the basic conclusions flowing from them are summarized below. This chapter, in projecting mild structural deficits in most states, indicates that there will be a widespread inability to fund current state and local services with current taxes. If higher education were to share proportionally in adjusting to this problem, it would:

- *not* see expansion of spending patterns for any program except as financed by reductions in another program within total higher education spending by states, and

- share proportionately in spending growth rates that average annually about 0.5% below the levels of total appropriations that are needed to maintain current services.

This conclusion could be avoided by two alternatives, both of which are unlikely. First, state officials might raise taxes, but many reasons make this improbable. Second, state officials might favor higher education spending over other areas of spending by providing disproportionate budget cuts in other programs, but this is unlikely.

State officials might, in fact, make the pain suffered by higher education proportionally greater than that of other programs. This would happen if they opted for the new initiatives in other programs described. Or higher education might suffer more than required to close the structural deficits because state officials insist on additional tax cuts.

The environment described in the appendices, not included, will make it difficult, particularly in some states, to achieve funding of current services for higher education. With a struggle just to maintain current service spending, increases above that level appear unlikely over any decade-long horizon. Specifically, it is likely that the fiscal environment for higher education in most states in the early 2000s will be significantly worse than it was in the late 1990s.

Funding Current Services

Amounts Needed

The baseline projections on which the earlier discussion is based presumes that state governments will continue to provide the same level of support for higher education as they have in the past. Specifically, this is defined as increasing funding enough to cover the expected increases in higher education enrollment with constant real (inflation-adjusted) support for full-time equivalent (FTE) students. To do this, state funding would have to cover per-FTE cost increases associated with general inflation and additional cost increases associated with presumed increases in higher education salaries equivalent to increases being experienced in the private sector.[4] The net effect of these factors is that total state support needs to increase by nearly 6% a year in the baseline projections.

Implications of the Baseline for Higher Education Funding

If 6% increases are, in fact, achieved, state support of higher education would closely resemble the patterns now in existence. This, of course, is the intent of current service or baseline budgets.

Specifically, the total costs of higher education would rise about 4% per FTE student. The share of total costs currently paid by the federal government, state and local governments, and tuition would remain as it is today. Higher education tuition would thus be rising slightly faster than inflation, along with the funding from other sources of support for higher education.

Shifting Spending Priorities Toward Higher Education?

National Situation

Over the past decade, the percentage increases in state support for higher education have been smaller than the percentage increases in total state budgets. The baseline projections imply that this situation will need to be reversed. Specifically, annual increases in state appropriations of about 6% would contrast with annual total budget increases of about 5%. They would exceed annual increases in elementary and secondary budgets of just under 5%. To fund the baseline, state elected officials would be in the position of having to defend an apparent priority for higher education spending—as well as defending the apparent other priority implied by the baseline, Medicaid.

This development implies a significant shift in emphasis from what state officials have been doing over the past decade and from the near-universal statements about spending priorities in the 1998 campaigns. Many candidates talked about a priority for spending on education. For most of them this boiled down to K-12 education.

State Situations

Individual states face dissimilar situations because of expected differences in the budget increases needed to maintain current services. These differences are caused by several factors, including projected increases in higher education enrollments and in the workload factors driving other spending. The differences among states are captured in Table 12.2. The right two columns of the table show the projected increases in total state and local spending needed to maintain current services over eight years, and the spending increases needed for higher education to maintain its current services over the same time frame. The "Annual Average Advantage for Higher Education" is derived by subtracting the growth in all programs from the growth in higher education, and then dividing by eight to give readers a feel for the annual difference.

Based on the national average, spending for higher education would have to increase 1% faster than total state and local spending (the higher education "advantage") if current services are to be maintained for all programs. As Table 12.2 shows, eleven states can cover current services by providing smaller increases to higher education than to their total budgets. These are primarily southern states that saw rapid growth in the 1960s and 1970s, resulting in enrollment bulges for higher education in the 1990s. In the next decade, higher education enrollments will be stable or declining while other portions of the population, particularly those over age 45, expand rapidly.

In a third of the states, current service spending implies providing for annual growth in higher education funding that exceeds by 2% or more the growth rates in total annual spending. This occurs primarily because those states, particularly those in the Southwest, are now feeling the impacts of higher education enrollment of their rapid growth in the late 1970s and 1980s.[5]

Baseline Implies Tax Increases in Most States

The Magnitude of the Fiscal Problem

To provide the level of funding for higher education described above, state officials will need to put themselves, in conjunction with local governments, in a position to fully fund their current service budgets. Nationwide this implies tax increases of about 0.5% a year. A few states would not require tax increases at all, while some others would require tax increases approximating 1% a year.

The baseline projections do not include the impacts of decreases in revenues because of recently legislated tax cuts. Many states have already enacted tax cuts that are being phased in over a period of years. These future cuts will cause budget shortfalls in these states to be larger than the shortfalls presented in the baseline projections. Nor do the baseline projections include the impacts of the many commitments made by individual state elected officials in support of tax cuts that have not yet been enacted.

In combination, these factors suggest that funding the baseline budgets of higher education and other programs implies substantial tax increases. The amounts vary by state. Each state will have somewhat different: (1) baseline budget shortfalls or surpluses, (2) already enacted tax cuts taking effect in future years, and (3) likelihood of enacting additional tax cuts in 1999. Summing these would imply tax increases by state and/or local governments during the early 1990s of as much as 1% a year in many states.

Obviously, state officials are unlikely suddenly to announce that they see a need to start raising taxes just because projections indicate future fiscal problems. Instead, the cyclical patterns that historically have brought about state tax changes reveal that tax increases must appear to be absolutely essential at the time.

TABLE 12.2
Percentage Change in Spending to Maintain Current Services

Rank	State	Annual Average Advantage for Higher Education	Eight-Year Spending Growth Rate	
			All Programs	Higher Education
1	Vermont	5.3%	41.0%	83.3%
2	Nevada	4.9	75.4	114.8
3	Hawaii	4.3	45.3	79.5
4	New Mexico	3.3	52.2	78.9
5	Arizona	3.3	60.6	86.9
6	South Dakota	3.2	40.2	65.7
7	Wisconsin	3.0	36.9	60.8
8	Florida	2.9	46.3	69.6
9	Minnesota	2.8	38.0	60.3
10	Kansas	2.8	37.2	59.2
11	Washington	2.7	44.9	66.4
12	Connecticut	2.4	31.8	51.1
13	Maryland	2.4	40.5	59.6
14	New Hampshire	2.2	44.5	62.0
15	Iowa	2.1	32.0	48.7
16	Oklahoma	2.1	33.7	50.4
17	Alaska	2.1	43.6	60.3
18	Pennsylvania	1.9	32.5	47.4
19	Montana	1.7	43.1	56.7
20	Colorado	1.7	50.8	64.2
21	California	1.7	38.9	52.3
22	Rhode Island	1.6	33.7	46.8
23	North Dakota	1.5	33.2	45.0
24	Oregon	1.4	43.2	54.8
25	Nebraska	1.4	35.9	47.4
26	Missouri	1.3	36.9	47.5
27	Delaware	1.3	43.8	54.3
28	Louisiana	1.3	33.3	43.7
	United States	**1.0**	**39.5**	**47.7**
29	New York	1.0	32.5	40.5
30	Georgia	0.8	50.0	56.4
31	Massachusetts	0.8	36.1	42.3
32	Texas	0.7	45.5	51.5
33	Idaho	0.6	57.8	62.3
34	Virginia	0.5	41.6	45.7
35	Wyoming	0.3	42.4	44.5
36	Utah	0.1	51.0	52.1
37	Michigan	0.1	31.7	32.6
38	Illinois	0.0	33.4	33.8
39	Tennessee	0.0	45.4	45.4
40	Maine	−0.1	31.3	30.4
41	Ohio	−0.2	32.1	30.5
42	Indiana	−0.2	38.7	36.7
43	New Jersey	−0.5	37.1	33.3
44	Arkansas	−0.5	40.2	36.2
45	South Carolina	−0.5	40.0	36.0
46	Alabama	−0.6	38.9	34.3
47	Kentucky	−0.8	35.4	28.6
48	Mississippi	−0.9	37.4	30.5
49	West Virginia	−0.9	29.4	22.0
50	North Carolina	−1.3	45.9	35.3

Source: Calculated from The Outlook for State and Local Finances (Washington, D.C.. National Education Association, 1998), Technical Appendix.

This dynamic is particularly germane because extraordinary economic circumstances can make state fiscal positions look artificially strong in good times, such as those of the late 1990s. In such an environment, state legislatures tend to expand state spending and cut taxes, while still producing balanced budgets—but only so long as the unusually strong economic circumstances continue.

Fiscal Crises

If extraordinarily good times were followed by normal times, it might be possible for states to make fiscal adjustments in less than a crisis environment. However, extraordinarily good times are usually followed by corrections in the private economy called recessions. When these occur, states are usually caught in a situation where their budgets are grossly out of balance. Often state officials are slow to recognize the onset of recession. Because of the timing of legislative sessions and controversy over appropriate solutions, state legislatures are often slow to enact corrective measures once the problem has been recognized. As a result, the magnitude of corrections to maintain balanced budgets is often 5% or more. That is, the corrections imply a combination of spending cuts and tax increases amounting to 5% or more of total spending, often to be continued in effect for several years.

The crisis environment created by unexpected large budget gaps provides the political environment most conducive to state tax increases. Increases are presented as an alternative to such measures as laying off large numbers of state employees, mid-year cuts in school funding that would cause actions like ending extracurricular activities in public schools, mid-year increases in university and community college tuition, and the like.

Even in such a crisis environment, it isn't obvious that state elected officials will act to avoid these results. Their primary objections are likely to be: (1) concern over rising taxes, and (2) concern over the apparent priority being given to higher education over other competitors for funds.

Looking Hard at Higher Education Spending

In the early 2000s, state elected officials will be facing structural deficits yet seeking to fund new initiatives in many programs. They will be confronted with difficulties in raising taxes and cutting current services in other programs. In this context, at an absolute minimum, they and their budget staffs will be subjecting higher education to more scrutiny than in the recent past.

The underlying question about spending will be whether, at the margin, higher education spending is contributing more than spending at the margin in other programs. This question will be raised in a political dimension with the adverse electoral consequences of cuts in higher education compared with cuts affecting public schools, health care providers, and others active in state politics. The question will be raised in a substantive dimension with the values of improvements in higher education compared with the values of improvements in job training, preschool education, preventive health, and other programs.

One underlying question about financing will be whether raising revenues in the form of budgets that encourage university officials to raise tuition (or cut spending) are less painful than raising revenues in the form of tax increases.

Cross-Cutting Approaches

Historically, elected officials have often found comfort in applying a logic equally to all program budgets. Critics can argue that such approaches ignore the relative merits of spending increases and the costs of spending cuts in each program and thus beg the issues elected officials are supposed to decide. A more positive view of the result is to say that elected officials often simply assume that the relative merits of increases and adverse consequences of cuts are about equal across programs, so adjustments associated with changes in state fiscal circumstances should be in roughly equal proportions.

The across-the-board approaches are particularly likely to be employed in situations where the complete state budget process cannot be used to set new priorities based on changed fiscal circumstances. Those situations arise when governors and/or legislative budget committees are charged with adjusting already enacted budgets to deal with unexpected fiscal difficulties.

Historically, the first signs that state budgets are unbalanced usually come during a period for which the current budget has been set, and thus needs to be trimmed in mid-year or in the midst of a biennium. Some of the across-the-board measures adopted in such circumstances have included:

- Uniform holdbacks of appropriations, called pro-ration in some states, by which spending for each function is constrained to 1% to 5% below amounts appropriated;

- Freezes on new hires and promotions;

- Freezes on purchases of new equipment and renovation projects;

- Elimination or curtailment of hiring of seasonal or temporary workers; and

- Restrictions on travel.

As fiscal difficulties persist, the need to formulate new budgets with less total spending than required to maintain current services appears. Across-the-board approaches are often applied in this situation also. Some examples are:

- Freezing spending by holding appropriations in the new budget to the dollar totals provided in the old;

- Adjusting budgets only for changes in workloads (e.g., FTE student counts), thereby requiring state agencies and grantees to absorb costs of employee pay raises and inflation in costs of utilities and purchases; and

- Across-the-board percentage reductions in total spending from a base of either the costs of maintaining current services or the previous year's budget.

While subject to the criticism that these across-the-board efforts are arbitrary, many elected officials are more comfortable with them than with more policy-oriented and less uniform sharing of fiscal pain among program clients and interest groups advocating various forms of spending. Public higher education in most states has seen these across-the-board policies at work in past periods of fiscal adversity and is likely to see them again in the early 2000s.

Singling Out Higher Education for Disparate Spending Cuts

Over the past several decades, state budgets for higher education have reflected two major characteristics. First, the percentage of state spending devoted to higher education has been declining. Second, there have been fluctuations in higher education spending, changes that are linked to state fiscal circumstances.

The Balance Wheel Concept

The fluctuations in higher education spending stem from use of higher education as a "balance wheel in state finance."[6] Typically, when state finances are strong, appropriations for higher education have risen disproportionately to appropriations for other functions. But current service budgets in higher education have been cut disproportionately when state fiscal circumstances are weak.

Selection as a balance wheel results from some perceived characteristics of higher education relative to other objects of state spending. First, higher education institutions have separate budgets with reserves of their own and perceived fiscal flexibility to absorb temporary fiscal adversity, unlike state agencies which do not have these features. Second, higher education is perceived as having more flexibility to translate budget changes into employee pay than state agencies, which are bound by statewide pay scales, and local education agencies, which are subject to collective bargaining and multi-year employee contracts. Third, higher education is seen as having more flexibility to vary spending levels (e.g., through changes in courses offered and class sizes) than most programs, which have spending levels that are more fixed. Fourth, in most states, higher education has the ability to maintain and increase spending levels by shifting larger proportions of costs to users by tuition and fee increases.

Temporary Cuts and Permanent Loss of Budget Share

Use of higher education as a balance wheel has probably been an independent factor leading to the reduction in higher education spending as a share of state budgets. Because the starting point for budgeting is the prior year, disproportionate spending constraints on higher education tend to be perpetuated as state financial circumstances improve.

However, there are other reasons why the higher education share of state spending has been declining. One major reason is totally independent of higher education or of current perceptions of higher education. Through the late 1980s and early 1990s factors unique to Medicaid and corrections were causing rapid annual increases in spending for those programs. Because "shares of the budget" is a zero-sum game, their gains had to come at the expense of shares of other programs. Viewing the same phenomenon another way, the baseline costs of those programs rose rapidly because of changes in federal mandates, workload (e.g., prisoners to be confined, parolees to be supervised, and Medicaid clients, particularly those in nursing homes), and cost factors (e.g., increasing complexity and cost of medical procedures). There were no comparable changes in higher education in most states.

Even with these explanations, it appears that higher education is doing worse in capturing growth in state spending that would be expected based on changes in objective circumstances.[7] In other words, higher education isn't competing successfully with the attractions of other forms of state spending.

The critical question for many readers is undoubtedly whether these factors will continue to impact state support of higher education in the next decade.

The answer to this question cannot be known with certainty. The author's answer is YES. Absent any evidence of change, the author assumes that elected officials' attitudes toward the substantive and political merits of spending on various programs remains as in the past. With attitudes and decision-making procedures unchanged, and with the impacts of strong and weak state fiscal circumstances on higher education spending well known, forecasting state approaches to higher education spending becomes simply a matter of forecasting the state fiscal circumstances likely to prevail in the next decade.

Given the fiscal environment predicted in this paper for the next decade, *the fiscal outlook for state support of higher education is not good* from the perspective of advocates of increased state spending for higher education. Use of higher education as a balance wheel will continue. Higher education will likely share disproportionately in the adverse consequences of the structural deficits likely to become increasingly apparent in most states.

Put another way, the current relatively generous increases in state support of higher education do not reflect changes in patterns and practices in state budgeting. They only reflect the standard response to extraordinarily strong fiscal conditions. They will disappear when those fiscal conditions disappear.[8] Both will disappear soon.

Could These Conclusions be Wrong?

The predictions of widespread structural deficits in state and local government throughout the next decade are the cornerstone of the conclusions in this chapter. Those conclusions are based on many factors, some more predictable than others. Appendix D, not included, discusses the sensitivity of the conclusions to various predictions and assumptions.

FISCAL IMPACTS ON HIGHER EDUCATION POLICY

Central Fiscal Decisions, in Theory

The preceding two chapters deal entirely with purely fiscal decisions of state elected officials. These are decisions from the world of state budget offices and governors, legislative fiscal staffs and legislators, and voters occasionally acting directly on tax and spending measures by initiative and referendum. These decision-makers are treated as though they dealt only with relatively pure fiscal decisions, including:

- The level of taxes and thus spending,
- The allocation of spending among higher education and other major functions, and
- The mechanisms for adjusting spending to unexpected changes in fiscal circumstances.

The major players in these decisions are chairs of appropriating committees, House speakers and Senate presidents, governors, budget directors, legislative fiscal officers, and those interest groups with major effects on overall spending and tax policies. They do not normally have any closer association with higher education than with health care, elementary and secondary education, or other functions.

Of course, fiscal decisions themselves are policy decisions. Furthermore, decisions about budget levels often push detailed policy decisions in particular directions. For example, new programs are more likely to be established in higher education institutions when appropriations exceed costs of maintaining current services. But in the purest view of budgeting, the central fiscal authorities *do not:*

- Determine how the spending totals they set will be allocated within a function, such as by determining divisions between community and institutional mental health, formulas for allocating school aid among school districts, and allocations of higher education funds among levels of instruction, individual institutions, or between scholarships and institutional support.
- Establish policies affecting individual functions except as government-wide policies applicable to all functions, such as civil service pay schedules, contributions to employee retirement plans, and charges levied by central service units such as state computer utilities.

These limited roles of central fiscal authorities are reflected in the normal assignments of responsibilities in executive branches and legislatures. Within the executive branch, state budget offices play the fiscal role, while departments and independent agencies administer functions and are expected to have dominant influence over questions of policy—so long as they operate within fiscal constraints. In the legislatures, appropriating committees have jurisdiction over budgets. But substantive legislation dealing with policies is assigned to other committees such as those dealing with education and health care.

Central Fiscal Decisions, in Reality

As a practical matter, the divisions between central fiscal authorities and those setting policy for individual state functions is never clear and always controversial.

Ambiguity in roles is inherent in the work of elected officials because their responsibilities include both policies within individual governmental functions and central fiscal decisions. They are under no major pressure to separate their roles and often do not do so; therefore, governors frequently use the process for the development of budgets as their primary mechanism for reviewing and making decisions on major policy initiatives. Many legislatures include substantive legislation in their budget bills. It is quite common for legislators and governors to hold many major decisions of a legislative session for final determination as part of grand compromises that include tax policy, the budget, issues with fiscal impacts such as employee pay raises, money issues within functions such as allocation of school aid among school districts, and issues unrelated to money such as those associated with regulatory policy.

Many state budget staffs, both legislative and executive, and legislators serving on appropriating committees see themselves as having more responsibility for policy than the theory summarized above suggests they should have. They feel responsibility for decisions embodied in "their" products, such as their executive budget and their appropriations bills. Some believe that they cannot separate decisions on how much to spend on particular functions from decisions on how it will be spent. For example, they may support additional spending if used for Activity A but not for Activity B. In that situation, to achieve their objectives, they must control sub-allocations of appropriations when Activities A and B are within the same function—as when, for example, both involve higher education spending. Moreover, those in central positions may choose to exercise power simply because they believe they know the right policies and are in a position to use their fiscal power to ensure implementation of the policies they like.

Rightly or wrongly, central fiscal decisionmakers have more impact on policy than theory might suggest they should have. That impact varies from state to state and from year to year based on many different factors, including institutional traditions, statutory frameworks, the impact of dominating personalities, and the preferences of current governors and legislative leaders.

Fiscal Decision-Makers Affecting Higher Education Policy

Random Impacts

Some impacts of fiscal decision-makers on higher education policy are nearly random. For example, a powerful appropriations committee chairperson may use his or her position of power to favor appropriations for a particular higher education institution in his or her district. Or the position of power may lead to larger appropriations for some activity, such as medical education, and lesser ones for others. A powerful budget analyst in an executive or legislative position may influence a variety of policies of interest to him or her, but random events may lead to someone else holding such a position with less or more power to implement policy preferences. This paper has nothing to contribute to the understanding of such situations.

Systematic Perspectives

On some subjects, the impacts of those who draw power from state fiscal processes is not random. It stems from one of two factors, or both:

1. There is a substantial rationale for involvement of central fiscal perspectives in the decision.

2. Central fiscal decision-makers bring a unique perspective to the policy under consideration.

There are many examples where there is a substantial rationale for involvement of central fiscal decision-makers in higher education policy. Each one is controversial, but these are some common ones:

- Policies involving collecting money from the public (e.g., tuition), particularly if state rules allow the collecting agency to supplement spending through using the resulting revenues.

- Policies involving duplication of functions or potential duplication of missions of other agencies, such as providing remedial instruction in higher education.

- Policies with rationales outside of the budgeted function, such as justification of higher education spending based on perceived economic development benefits.

The unique perspectives of those in central fiscal decision-making involve such topics as government-wide approaches to performance measurement and attitudes toward contracting out government functions.

The discussion of individual policies in higher education that constitutes the remainder of this chapter examines the unique policy perspectives commonly found among those dealing primarily with fiscal matters affecting multiple state agencies. The aim is to explain the various perspectives and their impacts on higher education, not to predict the extent to which the perspectives are likely to be implemented.

Tax Expenditures Versus Spending

In economic terms, there is little difference between supporting an activity through direct grants, which count as state spending, and tax concessions, which count as reductions in revenues. This point is so widely understood that the federal government and some states prepare annual reports on *tax expenditures*. Like outlays, tax expenditures involve allocation of scarce state resources. The amounts and purposes can be calculated by treating the revenue reductions as though they were outlays.

Paying some of the costs of attending higher educational institutions provides an example. Suppose, for example, the intent is to employ additional state resources of $600 per full-time pupil in higher education. One approach would be to give the $600 to the institution providing the education. This would count as an outlay, taking the form of an appropriation to the institution. Another approach would be to allow the subsidy to follow the student by awarding $600 to each eligible student in the form of a voucher or its equivalent, a scholarship which could only be used as partial payment of tuition. This would also count as an outlay, but the appropriation would be to a state scholarship commission. Another approach would be to award the student or person paying the tuition a tax credit of $600. This would not be an outlay, but instead would be a reduction in revenue.

Choices between expenditures and tax expenditures are only theoretically unrelated to other policy choices. As a practical matter, whether the decision is made in a tax context or a spending context also influences other important policies. For example, it is relatively easy to defend distributing institutional subsidies only to public institutions. It is much harder to defend confining tuition tax credits only to those attending public institutions.

Central state decision-makers have recently shown a strong bias toward using tax expenditures rather than spending. Many decision-makers wish to make records of reducing taxes. This alone could account for the recent popularity of using tax expenditures in higher education, both at the federal level and in some states.

The impact of both federal and state fiscal conditions on this bias is probably not well understood. When a government is collecting more money than is required to maintain current services, the excess is available for either tax reduction or increased spending. In this situation, but only in this situation, tax expenditures appear to perform double service in public perceptions. On the one hand, they are a reduction in taxes. On the other, they represent added support for the function for which they are provided.

However, when a government is unable or barely able to cover current service spending with current revenues, there are no extra resources available either for added spending or for tax reductions. In such a context, the use of resources for either a tax expenditure or a regular expenditure will require difficult decisions to increase taxes or cut spending in existing programs. No double duty can be performed by a tax expenditure because any tax cut will have to be accompanied by an equal and offsetting tax increase.

In such a context, a different principle of central fiscal authorities applies. Public opinion surveys and the experience of state elected officials suggests that revenue-neutral tax changes are perceived as tax increases. The public clearly sees, and journalists widely publicize, the portion of the revenue-neutral changes that increases revenue. The corresponding reductions are often less clearly perceived and, when perceived, tend to be viewed as promises of politicians to cut taxes that may not be fulfilled.

It follows that the recent emphasis on tax expenditures for higher education may be temporary.

Subsidizing Consumers, Not Providers

Over the past several decades fiscal decision-makers have become increasingly convinced that it is better to provide government support of consumption of any good or service by allocating subsidies to consumers rather than to providers. This approach substitutes decisions by consumers for decisions by government on such topics as which providers prosper and grow, which suffer, and which are eliminated. Adoption of the approach causes massive changes in any field affected by it. Fields most recently affected include the provision of acute medical care (a function most hospitals perform), mental health, and housing.

The impact can most recently be seen in the dramatic changes that have taken place in the operations and ownership of what formerly were public hospitals. There is a potential direct parallel to public higher educational institutions. The response of governments in the United States to people who needed hospital care but could not pay for it was the creation of public hospitals. These hospitals, which included some of the best-known and respected medical facilities in the nation, were typically funded and maintained by local governments, primarily counties.

The major changes in health care are primarily associated with the institution of the Medicaid program, which, in effect, provides open-ended vouchers to those eligible in the form of a Medicaid card which works roughly like a health insurance card. Parallel changes occurred in other government programs such as the provision of health care for veterans and for some members of the armed forces and their dependents. Private (mostly not-for-profit) hospitals were often preferred by these subsidized patients by reason of location, perceived better services, and other reasons. In the many cases where government payments equaled or exceeded costs of treatment, private hospitals aggressively marketed themselves to charity patients. As a result, capacity utilization in public hospitals dropped, costs per patient increased, and for a variety of reasons, the public hospitals were slow to adopt cost-saving measures being adopted in the private sector. Faced with the resulting financial pressures, state and local governments have largely eliminated their public hospitals—closing some, merging others with private institutions, and disposing of others to profit-seeking or not-for-profit corporations.

These results have their critics, but have generally pleased elected officials and their fiscal staffs. Competition is believed to hold costs to below what they would otherwise be. The changes have reduced public employment. Almost by definition, consumers are satisfied as they are experiencing the consequences of their own choices.

Advocates of subsidizing consumers rather than producers are now most publicly apparent in the voucher movement (and pressures for tax credit equivalents of vouchers) in elementary and secondary education. The voucher proposals draw huge controversies, primarily because public education employees perceive the changes as threatening their jobs, a threat those employees have recognized better than their counterparts in public hospitals.

Subsidizing consumers rather than producers in higher education has produced much less visible controversies. However, policy shifts have been substantial, and they can be seen in the details of some programs—such as in shifts of support for teaching in university medical schools. They appear dramatically in the recent adoptions of education saving accounts, tax deductions for tuition, tax credits for tuition, and state-run college savings plans. Most of these programs do not distinguish between private and public institutions as providers of higher education services.

State central decision-makers are moving consistently in many fields toward more support of consumers and less support of providers. The concepts are reflected in the use of tax expenditures rather than outlays for functions such as childcare, care for the elderly, higher education, elementary and secondary education, and job training. They are reflected in changes in financing mental health and daycare services. They are reflected in education plans that seek to increase student choice in attending charter schools or schools outside the district of residence.

To the extent that central decision-makers successfully bring these perspectives to higher education, the results will be a greater emphasis on tax expenditures, a greater emphasis on scholarships, less emphasis on institutional support, and broader participation by private institutions in public support of education of state residents.

How far could such an approach evolve? In higher education, it could evolve to match systems now in existence for other functions, systems in which governments merely buy "slots" that eligible participants use, thereby providing these participants with choice among providers, so long as space is available. Section 8 housing subsidies work this way. Most daycare programs work this way. School voucher plans work this way. Much of job training works this way. So does provision of Medicaid-reimbursed nursing home care.

Public Support of Quality

Government typically provides its services at no cost to the consumer or with charges that are highly subsidized with tax revenues. As a result, there is little limit to potential consumer demand and thus to government costs. Meeting all of the resulting demand is impossible, so governments find ways to limit consumption of what they produce.[9]

A common mechanism for limiting consumption is to declare only a portion of possible consumers as eligible for the service by some test, such as through the low-income tests required for eligibility for government-paid health care, nursing home services, and housing. But long traditions and public policy arguments suggest that many public services must be offered to all. Examples are services of the police, libraries, public parks, museums, public schools, and public higher educational institutions. Although no one likes to talk about the resulting rationing as a matter of policy, public services in these situations normally do not meet the highest standards of quality in their industry. This drives the portion of demand associated with more affluent and/or highly motivated users into private sector providers.

The results are apparent in many fields. Those seeking the highest levels of security services buy alarm systems and hire private guards. Those seeking the best mental health care see private psychiatrists even though supposedly comparable services are available at public expense. Most parents pay private doctors to vaccinate children, even though vaccination is offered as a public health service. Affluent families go to private theme parks while less affluent ones use public parks. Many people seeking their definition of "the best" for their children send them to private schools and universities.

In general, while aspiring to the best, governments provide most services based on views of meeting minimum standards. In this context, widespread support for using tax dollars to bring some state universities to standards of elite private institutions remains an anomaly of public policy that has not escaped the notice of some central decision-makers.

Rationing by User Charges

Many of the staff members populating central fiscal agencies are trained in economic doctrines that place much more value on user charges for public services than the providers and users of the particular services consider appropriate.

In extreme cases—where benefits of government services accrue almost exclusively to the users of the service—this philosophy suggests either that government should not provide the service at all or, if circumstances dictate that it must, the users be charged the full cost of providing services. This approach has much to do with why state governments, despite federal urging, have never participated with their own tax dollars in subsidized housing, why costs of fish and game programs are covered by license fees, why gas taxes and other user fees cover most highway costs, and why heavy fees are charged for applications for state and local permits to conduct various activities.

This orientation to user charges helps explain why there is often more interest in financing portions of higher education outlays with tuition among budget staffs than among students and higher education professionals.

Avoiding Geographic Distinctions

Statewide elected officials, such as governors, are elected by systems in which a vote anywhere counts as much as a vote anywhere else. Legislators are elected in smaller geographic constituencies but must reach decisions by majorities of representatives of such constituencies. Both systems give elected officials strong reasons to never appear to be anything but even-handed in dealing with different geographic areas within a state.

The resulting pressures in allocation of support among public higher educational institutions is well known. These pressures inherently make it difficult to single out particular institutions, and thus particular places, as unique centers of excellence. Instead, all of the pressures lead to one of two policies. One option is access for nearly all high school graduates to excellent state institutions. This policy leads to the conclusion that such institutions should exist in every population center. The other option is concepts of tiers of excellence, with use of the excellent institutions restricted on some basis other than geography such as the stiff admissions requirements used by the University of California.

Budgeting for "Add-Ons" for Missions Not Directly Related to Higher Education

The basic philosophy of budgeting suggests that appropriations should be budgeted to agencies primarily responsible for identifiable missions. This is a bureaucratic version of the concept of subsidizing consumers rather than providers. It is reflected in practices such as budgeting training of employees in the agency with the employees, rather than in appropriations for particular training providers, such as state universities. The philosophy is incompletely implemented even in this simple case and is even less completely implemented in other more fiscally significant cases.

The best current example is the interaction of economic development and higher education objectives. States are pursing economic development competitively and at great expense. Bidding wars have established the going price of luring one new manufacturing job as a one-time outlay (in tax benefits, cash subsidies, free land, provision of public services such as road connections, and more) in the range of $15,000 to as much as $300,000. With this kind of money at stake, state officials concerned with economic development are willing to exert great pressures on higher education administrators to be responsive to real or imagined concerns of business leaders contemplating expansion or new locations. These business leaders are looking for a higher education presence in the fields that interest them and in close proximity to where they are considering locating facilities. Those locations are often not the ones that would be selected on the basis of higher education criteria alone.

Purity in budgeting spending by higher education institutions to achieve economic development objectives will never be achieved. Economic development professionals will always have an interest in minimizing their apparent costs by ensuring that they appear outside their budgets and in such forms as budgets for higher education and reductions in tax collections. Administrators in higher education (and other fields) will always be motivated to claim benefits from their spending in contributing to state objectives outside educating students, of which economic development is an example.

But at least in the theory of budgeting (as imperfectly pursued by central fiscal staffs), those portions of demands on higher education rationalized by state objectives outside of higher education should be budgeted separately.

Conclusions

The likely impacts of the central fiscal perspectives considered in this chapter are much more difficult to forecast than the likely impacts of state fiscal conditions on state spending for higher education. About all that can be said with certainty is that the constant tensions between perspectives of central fiscal decision-makers and managers of state programs, including higher education, seem likely to continue at about the same levels as in the past.

NOTES

1. For more details on assumptions underlying the baseline forecasts, see The Outlook for State and Local Finances (Washington, D.C.: National Education Association, 1998). Some of the workload assumptions are interactive with policies assumed in current policy projections. For example, higher education enrollment is not independent of tuition and access policies. The current service projections presume no change in the percentage of public higher education costs defrayed by tuition payments.

2. A long line of academic studies shows state tax and spending levels, overall and for individual programs, to be insensitive to polit-

ical variables such as party control of governors' offices and legislatures.

3. See for example, Financing State Government in the 1990s (Denver: National Conference of State Legislatures, 1993) and Is the New Global Economy Leaving StateLocal Tax Structures Behind? (Washington, D.C.: National League of Cities, 1998). Both of these studies were endorsed by large numbers of organizations of state and local officials.

4. Because of productivity gains in the economy, private sector wages and salaries rise in real terms. That is, the purchasing power of workers increases, as it historically has. To maintain the alignment of public and private compensation, public sector compensation also must rise somewhat faster than inflation. Specifically, in the projections inflation occurs at about 2.5% and all wages, private and public, rise just over 3.5 % annually, providing a real purchasing power increase of about 1%. The real world implication of this is that simply matching inflation and workload increases is not a tenable long-term policy for governments. Good examples of why this is not good policy can be found in Colorado and Washington, both of which have limits on state spending growth tied to the sum of inflation and population growth. Those limits, approved as a result of voter-initiated measures on state ballots, have forced these states into tight budgets and ultimately to return to voters with requests for waivers of the limits. Such requests were on the November 1998 ballots in both states.

5. These projections obviously depend on the validity of the underlying demo-graphic forecasts, both for higher education enrollment and the other drivers of workloads in government programs. These projections are most reliable for states with large populations and diversified economic bases, and least reliable for states with the reverse, such as Hawaii, Idaho, Vermont, and Wyoming.

6. Higher education is not unique as a balance wheel. Other institutions with similar characteristics, such as state arts agencies and Medicaid providers, also serve this function. In the case of Medicaid providers, the cuts often take the form of shifting billing cycles, for example, creating large one-time savings by moving from payment within 15 days to payment within 60 days.

7. To the author, who works daily with data on the budgets of 50 states, this is an empirically based statement. However, because the adjustments associated with (1) the use of higher education as a balance wheel, (2) federal mandates, (3) workload growth, and (4) uncontrollable cost changes are all difficult to make and controversial, the extent to which higher education's relative unpopularity has been

a factor in declining budget shares cannot be easily demonstrated empirically.

8. This conclusion implies that public K-12 education spending will continue to command strong support among elected officials. This support was strongly in evidence in 1998 in congressional actions on education funding in 1998 and in campaign positions of candidates for state office, despite ample criticism of "throwing money at the problem" aimed at elected officials supporting major spending increases.

9. The default is that queues form which in and of themselves impose a cost in waiting times. National health services in Canada and Europe are illustrations. Free operations are available to all, but waiting periods for non-emergency procedures are months and sometimes years. Another type of queue arises when insufficient quantities of services are provided to meet demand in particular geographic areas. Many state highway programs have this characteristic.

10. One of the likely solutions to financing Social Security will come from mandatory coverage of all state and local workers. In a practice dating from the beginnings of Social Security, some states and local governments are exempt from Social Security coverage. Including them will raise their payroll costs by roughly 15% with sizeable fiscal impacts on the affected states and local governments.

11. The discussion of individual spending categories uses shares of general fund budgets as compiled by the National Association of State Budget Officers in their annual series called State Expenditure Report. In most states, the general fund is the primary component of the state budget and the one usually containing all major outlays for higher education, except capital outlays supported by bond issues. The concept typically excludes from total spending and revenues: (1) trust funds such as those for unemployment compensation; (2) revenues earmarked for particular purposes, such as highways, and the spending of those revenues; and often, (3) large categories of spending not financed by taxes, such as spending financed by university tuition and federal aid.

CHAPTER 13

LINKING PERFORMANCE TO FUNDING OUTCOMES FOR PUBLIC INSTITUTIONS OF HIGHER EDUCATION

The US Experience

DANIEL T. LAYZELL

INTRODUCTION

State-level policy-makers in the US (e.g. legislators, governors) have been monitoring the performance of publicly-funded institutions of higher education since the 1980s via a variety of accountability mechanisms. In the last few years, budgetary constraints, together with policy-makers' ongoing interest in accountability and programmatic outcomes have also brought about a renewed interest in the uses and implications of performance-based budgeting, i.e. allocating resources to institutions according to their achievement of previously established goals, objectives, and outcomes. This is by no means a new concept in public budgeting, either in general or in higher education. The federal Government experimented with this kind of budgeting in the late 1960s and early 1970s and the State of Tennessee has had an ongoing performance-based funding programme for higher education in place since 1978. However, one of the main differences between performance-based funding then and now is the comprehensive nature of some of the initiatives currently under consideration by state policy-makers.

Because the essence of performance-based funding is the system of performance indicators on which the allocation is based, this article will begin with a discussion of performance indicators before moving on to a discussion of performance-based funding systems. Hence, the purpose of this article is to:

- Discuss the different types of mechanisms currently in place for measuring institutional performance.
- Briefly describe recent experiences with performance indicators for institutions of higher education.
- Describe the pitfalls and limitations of performance indicator usage in higher education.
- Discuss the current status of performance-based funding applications at the state level for higher education, including the reported difficulties experienced in their implementation.
- Discuss the future implications of such mechanisms for public higher education in the US.

Source: *European Journal of Education*, Vol. 33, No. 1, 1998.

STATE APPROACHES TO PERFORMANCE INDICATOR SYSTEMS

The development of performance indicators is ultimately based on the desire for accountability. At the state level, accountability is implemented by setting goals and objectives for higher education and periodically assessing progress towards those goals and objectives, using accepted indicators. While setting statewide goals and objectives is an activity that is unique to every State, Ewell & Jones (1994) note four approaches commonly used in measuring progress towards accountability goals and objectives:

- *Inputs, processes, outcomes:* a "production" process model aimed at measuring the value added to departing students, perhaps through pre- and post-assessments.

- *Resource efficiency and effectiveness:* an approach designed to measure the efficient usage of key resources such as faculty, space, and equipment, using ratio analyses or similar techniques.

- *State need and return on investment:* an approach built on the assumption that higher education is a strategic investment for States: it is designed to measure the fit between higher education and state needs (e.g. work force preparation).

- *"Customer" need and return on investment:* an approach built on the notion of "consumerism" that is designed to measure the impact of higher education in meeting individual needs (e.g. retention and graduation rates, employability of graduates).

The four approaches are not independent and the authors note that most States employing performance indicators borrow from one or more of the other areas. Ewell & Jones (1994) further note that:

> the point for policy makers is less to choose among them (the four approaches) as much as it is to ensure that those responsible for developing any planned statewide indicator system recognize the need to be guided by an explicit policy framework . . . (p. 13).

In short, the policy goals and objectives should drive the selection of performance indicators, and not the other way around.

RECENT STATE EXPERIENCES WITH PERFORMANCE INDICATORS

According to a recent survey by the State Higher Education Executive Officers (SHEEO), three-quarters of the States (38) currently report or use performance indicators for higher education in some way (SHEEO, 1997). Their primary uses are for accountability reporting or "consumer information". The survey also found that the most frequent recipients of performance indicator reports were state legislatures and governors. This is not surprising, given that the reporting of performance measures is frequently mandated through state statute.

Gaither (1997) cites several lessons learned from past state experiences with performance indicators:

- The numbers of performance indicators should be kept to a minimum (< 20).

- Performance indicators should not be developed in a top-down manner.

- Both faculty and the state legislature need to be involved in the development of the indicators for lasting success (i.e. gain "buy in").

- One indicator model cannot be applied to all types of institutions effectively without diminishing diverse missions (i.e. one size does not fit all).

- Policy-makers tend to prefer quantitative to qualitative measurement. Indicators should have financial incentives for institutions.

- Performance results must be communicated in a timely and understandable fashion for policy-makers and the public at large.

The relative importance of each of these "lessons" varies. However, it should be noted that each one was probably learned painfully by at least one State during their performance indicator implementation.

LIMITATIONS AND PITFALLS OF CURRENT PERFORMANCE INDICATOR SYSTEMS FOR HIGHER EDUCATION

The use of performance indicators has a number of limitations and pitfalls that need to be at least considered, if not controlled, by those seeking to develop them. These are described in the following sections.

Data Limitations

A significant practical issue that has an impact on the development and implementation of performance indicators is the availability of data. The recent SHEEO survey found this determined the performance indicators used in three-quarters of the 38 States currently using such measures. Four-fifths of the States indicated that they were also engaging in new data collection to support their system of performance indicators.

This practice has both positive and negative attributes. The ability to work with existing data collection systems reduces the start-up time and cost to implement a performance indicator system. It also improves the "comfort level" of those involved and thus the credibility of the process. On the other hand, keeping only to those indicators for which data are currently available may not result in the most useful or appropriate set of performance indicators. The significant number of States that are engaging in new data collection suggests a recognition of this limitation.

More Is Not Necessarily Better: Having too Many Indicators

A common pitfall that many policy-makers fall prey to is the desire to use several performance indicators, thinking that this somehow provides a more complete picture of institutional performance. This is typically a symptom of having no explicit framework to guide the development of performance indicators (see subsection below). It is also often the result of a policy development process where opinions differ as to what is important to measure.

The result of having too many indicators is twofold. First, the more indicators an insti-tution is measured on, the less important any one of those indicators becomes and vice versa. This is due to the fact the process of minimising the number of indicators is a pri-oritisation process that ensures that the resulting performance indicators are viewed as important. Second, as indicators and goals are added, the institution runs the risk of con-flicting goals and results. For example, if pol-icy-makers decide that institutions should show a high level of access and admission for freshmen (i.e. an open-door policy) and high graduation rates, they are likely to find that one is not necessarily compatible with the other.

No Policy Framework for Performance Indicators

A critical pitfall that needs to be avoided is the temptation to rush into developing perfor-mance indicators without an explicit policy framework to guide that development. The first two questions that must be asked are: (1) what does the State view as the most signifi-cant goals to be achieved by higher educa-tion?; (2) how should this be measured? Every policy-maker has his or her own "favourite" indicators that may or may not fit into these broader strategic goals. Without these strategic goals, performance indicators simply become a laundry list odds and ends that result in bothersome data collection and reporting activities to no end.

To Be or Not to Be: Quantitative vs. Qualitative Indicators

In the development phase of every system of performance indicators, there is a constant tension between the desire to keep things numeric and "measurable" and the desire to address the less tangible but equally impor-tant aspects of the institution. Performance indicator systems that focus solely on quanti-tative measures are more comfortable and familiar for policy-makers, but they may pro-vide a one-dimensional view of the organisa-tion. The development of valid qualitative indicators of organisational performance requires a rigour and discipline that are diffi-cult to achieve. A well-balanced system will include both types of measures.

Confusing 'Inputs,' 'Processes' and 'Outcomes'

One common pitfall of performance indicator systems is the blurring of organisational inputs, processes, and outcomes in the development of measures. For example, one popular "performance measure" that is used by many States is the teaching workload of faculty. While this is an important measure of institutional resource use and says something about an institution's internal budget process, it does not say anything about the instructional outcome. But institutional outcomes do not occur in a vacuum: they are directly related to its inputs and processes. In short, a well-rounded set of performance indicators should explicitly incorporate aspects of organisational inputs, processes, and outcomes, but be up front about the differences among the three.

Lack of Broad 'Buy in' Up Front

The quickest way to doom any new policy initiative, the establishment of performance indicators included, is to develop them without sufficient input from the organisation's key stakeholders. While a more consultative process requires more time, discipline and patience, it is also likely to be more successful and sustainable in the long run.

LINKING PERFORMANCE TO FUNDING: THE LOGICAL NEXT STEP

Performance-based funding is the logical extension of a system of performance indicators and it directly ties together accountability, performance, and funding levels. To understand the unique nature of such mechanisms, we first need to consider the two predominant modes of resource allocation for public institutions of higher education currently in use: incremental budgeting and formula budgeting.

Incremental Budgeting is the traditional and dominant form of government budgeting. It starts with an institution's prior year base budget and allocates increases (or decreases) to that base according to a set of established decision rules or budget guidelines. Examples include inflationary increases for supplies and utilities, or cost of living adjustments for employee

salaries. Policy-makers typically focus here on "cost to continue" items (e.g. increases/ decreases due to inflationary increases or workload changes) and, in some instances, new programme initiatives.

Formula budgeting, on the other hand, refers to a mathematical basis for requesting and/or allocating funds to institutions of higher education, using a set of cost and staffing factors (e.g. cost per credit, student/ faculty ratios) in relation to specified inputs (e.g. student credit hours, enrolment levels). Funding formulae for public higher education have been used by States for more than half a century. They were originally envisioned as a means of distributing public funds for higher education in a rational and equitable manner and have evolved over time into relatively complicated mechanisms with multiple purposes and outcomes.

Performance-based budgeting is different from the first two modes of allocating resources to public colleges and universities currently used, since 'resources flow only after the recipient of the funds can demonstrate that a specified outcome has, in fact, been produced' (Jones, 1997). In short, incremental and formula budgeting methods have a "needs based" approach to resource allocation, while performance-based budgeting/funding adopts a more "merit based" approach.

According to Carter (1994), a performance-based budget has the following four characteristics:

- It presents the major purpose for which funds are allocated and sets measurable objectives.

- It reports on past performance and uses common cost classifications that allow programmes to be compared rather than focusing on line comparisons.

- It offers management flexibility to reallocate money as needed and to provide rewards for achievement or penalties for failure.

- It incorporates findings from periodic programme evaluations that are supported by credible information that can be independently audited.

Jones (1997) further notes that, for a performance-based funding initiative to be implemented, the following four elements must be in place:

- The objectives to be attained—either outcomes or demonstration of good practice.

- The 'metrics of success'—specific measures or definitions on which performance is calculated.

- The basis of reward—the benchmarks of success.

- The method for resource allocation.

Performance-based funding initiatives for higher education have had some success, most notably in Tennessee (Folger, 1989). Tennessee's incentive funding programme and the additional funding received by institutions both directly and indirectly as the result of this programme have been held up as the prime example of these benefits. Ashworth (1994) cautions, however, that fully implementing performance-based funding has two fundamental problems. First, 'uniform agreements on the values that would have to be cranked into a formula do not exist, and data are not available within reason or within tolerable costs to feed such a formula system' (1994, p. 11). Secondly, it is conceivable that if all funding were distributed on a performance basis there could be significant redistribution of funds from year to year. This would adversely affect an institution's ability to plan and execute, ultimately defeating the purpose of performance budgeting.

CURRENT STATUS OF PERFORMANCE-BASED FUNDING EFFORTS FOR HIGHER EDUCATION

Despite these potential limitations, the concept of performance-based funding is alive and well in several States. The recent SHEEO (1997) study found that 22 States were using performance indicators as the basis for allocating resources to their institutions of higher education, either directly or indirectly.

One way to assess the impact of a policy initiative is to view it from a longitudinal perspective. Table 13.1 presents a comparison of the status of performance-based funding for higher education at the state level in 1994 and

1997, based on the results of two different studies. The 1994 data are from a study based on a 50-State survey conducted by Layzell & Caruthers (1995), while the 1997 data are from the recent SHEEO survey. While there were some differences between the two surveys, they were minor in a methodological sense, since the SHEEO survey was itself based on the survey form developed by Layzell & Caruthers (1995). Hence, these two studies present two valid points of comparison. Several points illustrated in this table bear discussing. First, the number of States which reported they used performance-based funding grew significantly between 1994 and 1997, from 9 to 22. Of the 22 States which reported using performance indicators for allocating resources in 1997, seven reported that there was a *direct* link between the use of performance measures in resource allocation and 15 indicated that there was an *indirect link*. There is a subtle but significant difference between having a direct or an indirect link in performance-based funding. Having a direct link means that the attainment or lack of attainment of an objective as measured by any performance indicator has a direct impact on the resources provided to the institution. For example, if an institution's funding were partially based on the attainment of a 60% graduation rate for all entering freshman within six years and the institution had only a 45% graduation rate, this would result in a negative impact on the resources provided to the institution. But having an indirect link in place provides for a much more subjective interpretation in applying performance indicators in the resource allocation process. That is, while performance indicators play a role in allocating resources to institutions in such a model, other factors are also considered. Thus, in our previous example of the six-year graduation rate, the institution would not necessarily be assured of a reduction in funding or other negative consequences.

As indicated in Table 13.1, the same number of States indicated their intention to implement performance-based funding in the future (within the next two years) in both 1994 and 1997. Interestingly, five of the States that had indicated their intention to implement such an initiative in 1994 had set up one by the time of the 1997 survey. Also notable is the fact that five States which had indicated no intention to

TABLE 13.1
Status of State Performance-based Funding Programmes for Higher Education: 1994

Performance-based Funding (P-BF) in Place

1994	1997		Plan to Implement P-BF in Future		No Current Plans to Implement P-BF	
	Direct Link	Indirect Link	1994	1997	1994	1997
Arizona	Arkansas	Arizona	Idaho	Indiana	Alabama	California
Arkansas	Colorado	Connecticut	Kentucky	Louisiana	Alaska	New Jersey
Colorado	Florida	Delaware	Mississippi	Maine	Delaware	New Mexico
Connecticut	Kentucky	Hawaii	New Mexico	Maryland	Georgia	Oklahoma
Florida	Missouri	Idaho	N. Dakota	Minnesota	Illinois	W. Virginia
Minnesota	Ohio	Illinois	Ohio	S. Carolina	Indiana	Wisconsin
Missouri	Tennessee	Iowa	Oregon	S. Dakota	Kansas	
Nebraska		Kansas	Pennsylvania	Utah	Louisiana	
Tennessee		Mississippi	S. Carolina	Virginia	Maine	
		Montana	S. Dakota	Wyoming	Maryland	
		N. Carolina			Massachusetts	
		Oregon			Michigan	
		Rhode Island			Nevada	
		Texas			New Jersey	
		Washington			New York	
					N. Carolina	
					Texas	
					Utah	
					Vermont	
					Washington	
					Wisconsin	
					Wyoming	
(n = 9)	(n = 7)	(n = 15)	(n = 10)	(n = 10)	(n = 22)	(n = 6)

Sources: Layzell & Caruthers, 1995; SHEEO, 1997.

Note: There were 9 non-respondents in the 1994 survey and 11 non-respondents in the 1997 survey.

implement performance-based funding for higher education in 1994 indicated in the 1997 survey that they had plans to implement it within two years. More notable is the fact that six States which had indicated no intent to implement performance-based funding in 1994 reported the current, though indirect, use of performance indicators in the resource allocation process in 1997. These changes are indicative of the incremental change in attitudes to performance-based funding for higher education.

The State of South Carolina presents an interesting case study regarding the future of performance-based funding for higher education. In 1996, the South Carolina legislature, prompted by a group of private business leaders in the State, implemented the most significant performance-based funding programme to date. It has been implemented by the State Commission for Higher Education and is based on institutional performance across 37 specific performance indicators which will be phased in by the year 2000. At that point, 100% of state funding for public higher education will be allocated on the basis of institutional performance in these indicators. The significance of this programme becomes quite clear when one considers that other state performance-based funding initiatives allocate between less than 1% and 4% of state funding for higher education (Burke & Serban, 1997).

REPORTED DIFFICULTIES RELATED TO PERFORMANCE-BASED FUNDING IMPLEMENTATION

A recent study by Burke & Serban (1997) explored, amongst other things, the difficulties experienced by States in implementing performance-based funding initiatives. It was based on a survey of various people involved in the implementation process, including governors, legislators, state-level higher education officials, institutional governing boards, institutional administrators, and faculty leaders.

The survey found that the three main factors consistently mentioned by these people as major difficulties in implementing performance-based funding are: (1) the selection of performance indicators; (2) the selection of "success" criteria (benchmarks of success); (3) the small amount of funding allocated for the initiative. Clearly, the first two are key factors to the success of any performance-based funding initiative. The inability of a State to successfully overcome these roadblocks would effectively scuttle the initiative. The third factor reflects the need to provide a meaningful incentive for institutions to take performance funding seriously. If the dollar value is too low, neither institutions nor policy-makers will be likely to find performance-based funding worth the effort.

PROSPECTS FOR THE FUTURE

The rapid growth in the number of States which have been using performance-based funding in recent years for their institutions of higher education and the large number of States planning to adopt this in the near future suggest that this practice will be in place for the foreseeable future. The recent SHEEO survey results suggest that States may choose mechanisms that link performance and funding levels more indirectly (as opposed to directly) as a way to "test out" performance indicators and address technical implementation issues without damaging institutional resources. Clearly, the development and use of performance indicators will continue to be strongly tied to data availability and the related technical capabilities of States. Also, the large number of States

which at present use an "indirect linkage" between institutional performance and funding levels suggests a desire to maintain an element of subjectivity in the state resource allocation process for higher education.

The author would offer four suggestions to those who are considering developing performance-based funding initiatives for higher education institutions:

- *Keep it simple.* This ranges from using a minimum number of performance indicators to the development of the actual resource allocation mechanism. Unnecessary complexity only serves to hinder implementation and communication to key individuals involved in the process.

- *Communicate and clarify often.* Making sure that everyone involved understands the goals and objectives of the development process and that each step is clearly described will greatly facilitate the implementation of performance-based funding.

- *Leave room for error and experimentation.* Given that the development of performance indicators is likely to result in unforeseen difficulties, the process of developing a performance-based funding programme should also leave room for error and experimentation at the beginning.

- *Learn from others' experiences, but develop your own programme.* The process of learning from others' experiences, good and bad, with the development and implementation of performance-based funding is an extremely useful process in the development of one's own programme. However, every State should also ensure that their programme reflects their own particular needs and concerns.

The ultimate question regarding performance-based funding is, of course, whether this will actually serve to improve institutional performance in the long run. It is likely to be at least five years or more before there is any clear evidence regarding the success or failure of these initiatives. However, it should be noted that a large number of those surveyed in the Burke & Serban (1997) study felt that one of the advantages of performance funding was the "potential to improve higher education". This suggests that, at the very least, a positive political environment for the development of performance-based funding models should be in place in the US in the foreseeable future.

REFERENCES

Ashworth, K. W. (1994). Performance based funding in higher education: the Texas case study. *Change,* November/December, pp. 8–15.

Burke, J. C. & Serban, A. M. (1997). *Performance funding and budgeting for public higher education: Current status and future prospects.* Albany, NY: Rockefeller Institute of Government.

Ewell, P. T., & Jones, D. (1994). Pointing the way: indicators as policy tools in higher education. In S. Ruppert. (Ed.) *Charting higher education accountability: A sourcebook on state level performance in-dicators* (Denver, Education Commission of the States).

Folger, J. (1989). *Designing state incentive programs that work.* Paper presented at National Center for Postsecondary Education Governance and Finance Conference on State Fiscal Incentives, Denver, CO, November.

Gaither, G. H. (1997). Performance indicator systems as instruments for accountability and assessment. *Assessment update,* 9, pp. 1–2, 14–15.

Jones, D. (1997). *Perspectives on performing funding: Concepts, practices, and principles* (Unpublished draft).

Layzell, D. T., & Caruthers, J. K. (1995). *Performance funding at the state level: trends and prospects.* Paper presented at the 1995 Association for the Study of Higher Education Annual Meeting, Orlando, FL, November.

State Higher Education Executive Officers (1997). *State Survey on Performance Measures.* Preliminary results.

CHAPTER 14

FUNDING THE MULTIPURPOSE COMMUNITY COLLEGE IN AN ERA OF CONSOLIDATION

JAMES C. PALMER

Today's community college system is a product of the publicly subsidized move to mass higher education during the 25 years following World War II. When the President's Commission on Higher Education (1947) issued its landmark report advocating free schooling through grade 14 for all who could benefit, 315 public junior colleges enrolled 216,325 students (Palmer, 1987). By the time the Carnegie Commission on Higher Education (1970) published *The Open-Door College*, 847 public community colleges enrolled 2,366,028 students (Harper, 1971). Between the publication of these two reports, which anchor both ends of American higher education's greatest growth period, the proportion of individuals between the ages of 18 and 24 who were enrolled in college (two-year or four-year) rose from 12% to 32% (U.S. Bureau of the Census, 1975, p. 383). During the same time period, total government revenues to public institutions of higher education (in current dollars) increased from $453 million annually to $9.2 billion (U.S. Bureau of the Census, 1975, p. 384).

Although enrollments continued to grow after 1970, rising to 5.5 million students in 1992 (Snyder & Hoffman, 1995, p.177), community college claims to increased public subsidies have been more intensely scrutinized. Lombardi (1973) notes that the "golden era of community college financing peaked in the mid-sixties" as the public became more distrustful of social institutions generally and as access to education became a less urgent priority in light of other "local and national concerns . . . crowding education for first demand on public money" (p. 110). The change in fortunes experienced by the community college was characterized by Lombardi as "its most serious crisis since the Great Depression" (p. 111) and was mirrored globally as countries throughout the world found that postwar rates of growth in tertiary education became fiscally unsustainable in the 1970s (Eicher & Chevaillier, 1993). The result for American community colleges is documented in Table 14.1: Between 1977 and 1992, tuition revenues per full-time-equivalent (FTE) student increased by 32%, while state and local appropriations per FTE student decreased by 12% and federal appropriations per FTE student decreased by 58%.

The current era, then, is one of consolidation, marked by an effort to prioritize the purposes of mass higher education and to achieve ever greater operating efficiencies as demand continues to outpace public revenues. The primary fiscal question of the past 25 years has not been "Will the community college survive?" Indeed, the institution remains a well-established part of American higher education and in the 1990s has often enjoyed higher percentage increases in state appropriations than those enjoyed by four-year colleges and universities (Hines, 1994, p. 10). The more

Source: *A Struggle to Survive: Funding Higher Education in the Next Century*, D.S. Honeyman, J.L. Wattenbarger and K.C. Westbrook (eds.), 1996, Corwin Press.

TABLE 14.1
Current Fund Revenues per Full-Time-Equivalent Student (in 1994 constant dollars) at Public Two-Year Colleges, by Type of Revenue Source: Academic Years Ending 1977 through 1992

Academic Year Ending	Total	Tuition and Fees	Federal Appropriations	State and Local Appropriations	Federal Grants and Contracts	State and Local Grants and Contracts	Private Gifts	Endowment	Sales and Services of Educational Activities
1977	$5,727	$962	$114	$4,153	$330	$112	$29	$4	$23
1978	5,744	925	102	4,212	317	132	28	3	24
1979	5,864	928	114	4,262	353	146	27	4	30
1980	5,790	933	78	4,201	365	151	27	5	30
1981	5,516	928	68	3,957	345	154	27	6	31
1982	5,454	980	59	3,911	285	156	29	6	27
1983	5,109	985	41	3,650	221	148	29	7	27
1984	5,243	1,023	45	3,725	229	154	31	8	28
1985	5,719	1,091	43	4,055	265	194	35	8	28
1986	5,981	1,111	37	4,268	268	218	38	8	34
1987	6,059	1,121	45	4,269	251	292	39	9	35
1988	5,905	1,105	43	4,163	240	275	42	5	31
1989	6,052	1,155	40	4,159	254	361	48	6	30
1990	5,904	1,157	39	3,997	249	373	51	6	32
1991	5,891	1,206	41	3,971	246	336	53	6	31
1992	5,743	1,269	48	3,743	260	331	56	5	31

Source: Smith et al. (1995, p. 407).

important question, rather, is "On what basis will public subsidies be made?"

Answers have been made from two standpoints. Scholars with close ties to the community college movement have responded from a policy viewpoint, arguing that state funding plans should be consistent with the tenets of open access, curricular comprehensiveness, local control, low cost to students, and responsiveness to local needs (Martorana & Wattenbarger, 1978; Wattenbarger, 1985). Their goal is to preserve the expanded access to education that emerged in the immediate postwar decades. Economists have applied theoretical constructs. Examples include Breneman and Nelson (1981), who weigh institutional claims for public subsidy against the competing values of market efficiency and social equity, and Garms (1977), who analyzes state funding plans against nine criteria that stress tax equity, access for those unable to attend four-year colleges, minimal duplication of effort between educational sectors, and internal college efficiency.

This chapter takes a different approach, analyzing the question of public subsidy from

the standpoint of educational purpose, for at the heart of today's funding controversies lies the often unrecognized problem of reconciling the conflicting economic imperatives inherent in the community college's multiple educational roles. One role is that of the *flexible institution,* meeting the diverse and idiosyncratic educational needs of local citizens. A second role is that of the *scholastic institution,* leading students to degree completion or to successful entry into higher levels of the graded education system. A third role is that of the *social service agency,* executing government programs that address economic or social ills through education or training. Each offers the public a different picture of the return it can expect (both to individuals and to society at large) on its investment in the community college.

THE FLEXIBLE INSTITUTION

Although community college catalogs describe curricula leading to degrees and certificates, students use the institutions for their own purposes. For example, studies of transfer students reveal wide variations in the ways students use community colleges on the path to the baccalaureate. Some take only one course at the community college either before or after matriculation into the four-year college, whereas others earn well over 100 semester hours of community college credit; the linear sequence of two years at the community college followed by two years at the university applies only to a minority of students (Palmer & Pugh, 1993; Palmer, Stapleton, & Ludwig, 1994). In the vocational arena, students also exhibit diverse patterns of study. Except in allied health and other areas that require licensure, relatively few students complete the associate's degree; student association with the college may range from enrollment in one semester to completion of two or more programs over an extended period of time (Cohen & Brawer, 1989, pp. 215–216).

It can be argued, therefore, that besides maintaining access to degree programs, investment in community colleges (with their relatively loose entry and exit policies) yields the advantage of an institutional flexibility needed for ad hoc, complementary, or even serendipitous learning. Ad hoc learning is undertaken to meet the need for new skills or understandings. An example might be a student who enrolls in a computer science course to cope with new technologies on the job. Complementary learning is undertaken in conjunction with degree programs offered elsewhere. A common example is the university student who concurrently enrolls in a community college course either to remediate skills or to complete a required course that is oversubscribed at the four-year institution. Serendipitous learning involves spontaneous discovery and redirection, as in the case of students who enter a program in one field but discover that they would like to study something else. Adelman (1992) documented these and other patterns of idiosyncratic use in the college-going behavior of respondents in the National Longitudinal Study of the High School Class of 1972 (NLS72), concluding that community colleges are facilitators of "occasional" learning with only a minimal credentialing role. "What the community college does," he maintained, "is to canonize and formalize the many decisions we make as adults to engage in learning for either

limited, highly focused purposes or for general purposes" (p. 22).

Why Invest in the Flexible Institution?

The benefits accrued to individuals through this institutional flexibility are difficult to calculate because the uses and outcomes of the institution are as varied as the students who attend, but at least four types of benefits might be assumed. One is access to education. As Adelman (1992, p. 22) points out, four-year institutions usually have a "culture of credentialism," with an attendant adherence to academic calendars, making it difficult for them to serve occasional learners. Without the community college, these individuals might presumably find few opportunities for structured study.

The second potential benefit, implied in the first, is learning efficiency. The university student who takes a community college course in the summer may decrease the time to degree. Similarly, the employee who takes a computer course to enhance job skills may learn those skills in a more timely and efficient manner with the guidance of an instructor.

The third benefit to individuals entails enhanced earnings. Kane and Rouse (1995a, 1995b) offer evidence of the wage benefits of course taking without earning a credential. Their analysis of the incomes of NLS72 respondents suggests that "both men and women earn more than comparable high school graduates after attending a two-year college whether or not they complete the [associate's] degree" (Kane & Rouse, 1995a, p. 219). Grubb (1995) concurs but argues that much depends on the type of credit earned. His analysis of the same data set suggests that the wage benefits of nondegree holders accrue only to those who earn vocational credits and not academic credits.

Beyond ex post wage differentials, however, Kane and Rouse (1995b) also note the probability of a fourth benefit: an "option value" accrued to those who complete courses without earning a credential. As they explain,

> When one is uncertain about the prospects of completing college before entry, there will be value attached to enrolling in order to discover whether one is "college material." . . . Those who do not exercise the option of completing college and leave

after only a few credits may enjoy only small wage differentials. However, it would be inaccurate to describe college as not having been worthwhile for this group, because the *ex ante* returns may indeed have been large enough to justify the public and private investments. (p. 611)

Presumably, the students' future educational investments will be made on the basis of better-informed judgments.

To the extent that individuals enjoy these benefits, society may also gain through positive externalities. Without flexible community colleges (or institutions like them), individuals would presumably under-invest in the occasional learning (above and beyond employer-provided, on-the-job training) needed to remain employable in a rapidly changing economy. Aggregate consumer investment in post-compulsory education would be less efficient because consumers would not have the insights gained through the opportunity to experiment by taking occasional courses. (It would be as though consumers in the automobile market were asked to make purchasing decisions without test drives.) Society might also lose the net increase in educated citizens that presumably results with the freedom afforded by community colleges to test one's educational intentions and skills in a low-risk atmosphere that facilitates easy entry and exit. Romano (1986b) implies this benefit in his suggestion that discount rates used in the calculation of the return on investment in education at two-year and four-year colleges should include a "risk factor" that recognizes the tendency of the former to attract students for whom traditional baccalaureate-granting institutions are intimidating. As he explains, "If . . . the risk of going to a 4-year college is perceived to be higher . . . than that of going to a 2-year college, then the future stream of earnings for the 4-year choice would have to be discounted at a higher rate" (p. 162).

Funding the Flexible College

Given the presumption of societal benefits, a case can be made for public subsidy of the flexible community college. These subsidies would ideally be made in ways that encourage the maintenance of easy access and exit, rewarding enrollment of any kind regardless of the stu-

dent's length of association with the institution. Because the educational needs of area citizens will presumably vary between localities, funding mechanisms should, in Garms's (1977) words, "enhance, rather than impede, the ability of the community college to respond to the particular needs of the community it serves" (p. 38). Local administrators should be given a high level of autonomy in setting academic policy and administering funds, points that have been emphasized by many community college leaders (Martorana & Wattenbarger, 1978; Wattenbarger, 1985).

Effectiveness in the use of funds would be measured in terms of consumer satisfaction with the college experience. Indicators of the extent to which idiosyncratic student goals have been met might also be emphasized.

Those who would tie funding to the college's role as a flexible institution nonetheless face the challenge of defining priorities among a potentially infinite set of individual training and education agendas that students bring with them. To do otherwise is to suggest that society offer the colleges a blank check, subsidizing the enrollment of all comers. But whose agenda is more worthy of public support? Economic analysis leads to conflicting views. For example, Breneman and Nelson (1981) claim that vocational education yields few positive externalities and should be paid for by students and their employers, who are the presumed beneficiaries of such training. Yet Romano (1986a) cautions that public subsidy of vocational education might be required in the face of employer fears that workers will move or change jobs, thereby making it difficult for businesses to recoup their training costs. These fears might limit employer contributions to training, leading to the possibility "that in the face of no publicly-financed training programs, fewer people would be trained than is economically justified" (p. 12).

Even if priorities were made, the colleges would still face the difficulty of pigeonholing students into priority categories. Which of the students in a photography class, for example, are honing job skills and which are pursuing a personal avocation? Answers to these types of questions remain as elusive as the goals of the students themselves. In the end, flexible responsiveness to idiosyncratic educational agendas becomes an ever more infeasible institutional purpose as the need to prioritize those agendas increases. The natural fallback is to the prescriptive stance of the degree-granting scholastic institution.

THE SCHOLASTIC INSTITUTION

Advocates of a scholastic focus for the community college, notably Cohen and Brawer (1987, 1989) and Eaton (1994), question the supposed benefits and efficiencies of the flexible institution. They emphasize the importance of student placement and guidance through sequenced degree programs, arguing that students may otherwise wander through the curriculum without demonstrable results. Attention to sequenced learning according to prescribed curricula, they maintain, is also necessary to sustain transfer opportunities for baccalaureate-seeking students. From the scholastic viewpoint, the flexible institution offers what Cohen and Brawer (1989) call a "nihilistic curriculum represented by students taking classes at will" (p. 386). All efficiencies are lost: "This is chaos, not college" (p. 386).

The scholastic philosophy figures heavily in policy responses to the fiscal problems of the post-1960s. For example, McCabe (1981) called on community colleges to follow the lead of Miami-Dade Community College: tightening matriculation processes through rigorous entrance testing and placement, insisting that students master basic skills prior to enrollment in college-level courses, providing continual feedback to students as they progress through their programs, and strictly enforcing standards of academic progress with the understanding that public subsidy of a student's education will be discontinued if those standards are not met. In California, the exigencies of a declining state economy were met during the 1980s and 1990s with policies that reflect many of McCabe's precepts. The state instituted a matriculation program emphasizing testing, placement, and the mutual responsibility of college and student to work toward the completion of educational goals (California Community Colleges, 1984). As the gap between enrollment demand and available funding expanded in the 1990s, a task force convened by the board of governors of the California community colleges drafted recom-

mended registration guidelines that give first priority to matriculated students who intend to transfer, earn a credential (associate's degree or certificate), acquire entry-level job skills, or upgrade job skills. Among matriculated students, priority was to be given first to continuing students, followed by recent high school graduates, other new or returning students, and new students who already hold the baccalaureate (Walters, 1994).

Why Invest in the Scholastic Institution?

These measures emphasize individual and societal returns on investment in degree attainment. Some are economic, dealing principally with the earnings advantages that accrue to at least some degree holders. Although Kane and Rouse (1995a, 1995b) show that college dropouts earn higher wages than high school graduates who accumulate no college credits, their analysis of NLS72 respondents also suggests a sheepskin effect for women who earn the associate's degree and for men who earn the baccalaureate. In these cases, those who hold the credential enjoy higher earnings than similar students who earn the equivalent of two or four years' college credits but who do not earn, respectively, the associate's degree or the baccalaureate. Analyzing the same data set, Grubb (1995) comes to a similar conclusion but again cautions that much depends on the student's curriculum. He argues that the sheepskin effect enjoyed by women applies only to those who earn vocational degrees and not to those who earn associate's degrees in academic fields. Obviously, much depends on whether the degree is an entry-level requirement for job seekers. As Kane and Rouse (1995b) note, the sheepskin effect enjoyed by women earning two-year degrees probably reflects "the value of the associate's degree in nursing, since one-quarter of the associate's degrees for women [in the NLS72 study] were awarded in the field of nursing" (p. 605).

A second and potentially more compelling set of considerations, however, lies in the intrinsic value of the bachelor's degree within a society that views the four-year credential—rightly or wrongly—as the principal mark of achievement in undergraduate education. The high visibility of the bachelor's degree, which contrasts sharply with the obscurity of the relatively unknown associate's degree (Adelman, 1992, pp. 25–26), places considerable pressure on the community college to maintain its place in the graded system of education, offering students the maximum opportunity for transfer to baccalaureate-granting institutions. From this standpoint, the scholastic stance offers important advantages. Its emphasis on matriculation, guided progress through a sequenced curriculum, and enforcement of academic standards reinforces the goal of degree attainment, promising efficiency for students who will proceed purposely rather than haphazardly toward the baccalaureate; for individual community colleges, which will minimize the costs associated with continually reregistering students who attend sporadically; and for state higher education systems, which will be characterized by greater linkages between two-year and four-year institutions. Because of the disproportionally large numbers of minority and low-income students at community colleges (as opposed to four-year colleges), it can also be argued that the scholastic stance promotes equity, offering a path to the baccalaureate for those who have been underrepresented in the ranks of bachelor's degree graduates (Palmer & Eaton, 1991, pp. 19–20).

A third set of potential benefits is pedagogical in nature, based on the assumption that adherence to prerequisites and academic standards throughout the curriculum may limit faculty tendencies to cope with wide-ranging student skills by watering down expectations for learning. Richardson and Rhodes (1985) take this stance, arguing that "open access defined as the opportunity to take all but the limited-seat, high-cost technical programs" has diminished instructional quality, thereby limiting educational opportunity (p. 286). They maintain that "qualified students who wish to earn legitimate college and occupational credentials are handicapped by college-level courses that are taught at less-demanding levels in order to accommodate underqualified students" (p. 286). This view has been supported by interviews and ethnographic research that portray the community college faculty as casualties of an acculturation process that leads many new teachers to compromise their commitment to academic standards (London, 1978; Richardson, Fisk, & Okun, 1983; Seidman, 1985; Weis,

1985). Without the corrective measures of the scholastic stance, the result may be a diminished return on societal investment in the community college as an avenue for educational advancement.

Funding the Scholastic Institution

Besides employing registration priorities favoring matriculated, degree-seeking students (as has been recommended in California), funding systems designed to yield the benefits and efficiencies implied in the scholastic framework would have three features that make them radically different from the fiscal structures that support community colleges today. One would be a performance-based approach to funding that ties subsidies (at least partially) to documented evidence of student learning. This performance-based approach would rest heavily on assessments of curriculum effects, demonstrating the extent to which program completers have the knowledge and capacities that are expected of graduates.

A second feature, inherent in the first, would be the diminution of enrollment in the calculation of subsidies. Noting that enrollment-based funding mechanisms were developed to cope with the rapid growth of the 1950s and 1960s, McCabe (1981) suggests that they have become detrimental in the subsequent, less affluent era. He argues that the colleges have "become entrapped by an essential need to sustain enrollment in order to remain economically viable" (p. 8), often to the detriment of the institution's academic viability. "Legislators who demand improved quality and higher standards," he maintains, "must help by freeing the colleges from the bondage of enrollment-driven funding formulas" (p. 10). This stance would be heartily approved by those who feel that faculty efforts to maintain high expectations for students are thwarted by an enrollment-at-all-costs attitude.

Finally, the scholastic stance demands the fiscal and administrative separation of the credit curriculum, which leads to degree completion, from the continuing education curriculum, which accommodates occasional learning. Cohen and Brawer (1989) have argued that the intermingling of these two functions, which have essentially different purposes, diminishes each and confounds education for personal consumption with education for the benefit of society. They maintain that students pursuing occasional learning should be enrolled in a self-supporting college extension division and not in credit classes, which should be offered in a separate subsidized program for degree seekers. Their approach models those employed in universities and in the higher education systems of foreign countries, aligning funding intent with educational purpose:

> Other nations have been more vigorous in steering . . . personal interest students to self-pay activities or government funded programs provided through community education structures and operated through local government agencies. American universities tend to shunt them to their extension divisions. Community colleges function in a shadow world of enrollment-driven, program differentiated funding for students whose aspirations are as mercurial as their use of the institutions is indistinct.
>
> (Cohen, 1993, p. 74)

THE SOCIAL SERVICE AGENCY

Largely unmindful of the philosophical distinctions and fiscal nuances of the flexible and scholastic viewpoints, legislators are nonetheless intent on demonstrating the utility of their appropriations. One approach has been the use of categorical funds that underwrite college efforts in economic development projects or other social programs. In Illinois, for example, formula-derived funding for the community colleges is augmented by economic development grants and other special appropriations that support small business centers, training programs for displaced workers, and other projects that are designed to boost the economy of local communities or enhance the skills of the local workforce (Illinois Community College Board, 1994). Such nonformula components have seen increasing use in state funding plans nationally (McKeown & Layzell, 1994, pp. 321–322). Between 1977 and 1992, the constant-dollar revenues per full-time-equivalent (FTE) student received by community colleges in the form of state or local grants and contracts increased by 196%, the largest increase in any of the eight revenue categories tracked by the United States Department of Education (see Table 14.1).

This trend is wholly in line with Lombardi's (1973) prescient observation that "slowly but surely community colleges are becoming dispensers of social welfare" (p. 114). The acceptance of and active competition for government contracts to carry out economic development and social welfare programs has been accelerated by a perceived need on the part of colleges to diversify their funding base. For example, fiscal uncertainties in California led Newmyer and McIntyre (1992) to recommend, among other policy initiatives, the pursuit of "a greater share of [federal] funds for vocational education, such as the Perkins Act and JTPA" (pp. 24–25). Community college leaders have also used economic development projects, particularly those that are developed in partnership with area businesses, to enhance the institution's image and utility. Zeiss (1989) maintains that linkages with business could be the vehicle that erases the identity problem of community, technical, and junior colleges that has so long endured. . . . By examining their frame of reference, focusing on a target market, and promoting a point of difference, community colleges can easily become recognized as a vital part of their communities, states, and nation. (pp. 3–4)

Why Invest in the College as Social Service Agency?

From the economic perspective, public investments in these projects imply efficiencies in the production of social benefits, such as net increases in employment, reductions in welfare dependence, or reductions in the rate of small business failure. For example, the Illinois Community College Board reports annually on the estimated number of jobs that are saved, retained, or created through investment in economic development grants (see, e.g., Illinois Community College Board, 1996). So long as these jobs represent a net increase in employment and not simply the economic gain of Illinois at the expense of employment in other states (a potential danger pointed out by Grubb, 1989), they presumably reflect a positive return on public investment.

A second, more subtle benefit lies in the potential efficiencies of the funding mechanism itself; because contracts target funds for specific purposes, usually requiring rigorous assessments of results, they avoid the vagaries of general institutional support. Eicher and Chevaillier (1993) note the attractiveness of this direct funding to policy makers worldwide who feel that subsidies for the general operation of institutions (such as those subsidies awarded simply on the basis of enrollment) offer few incentives for increasing productivity or reducing costs. They point out that such doubts are less frequently raised in the case of "specific support given only on a temporary basis and subject to evaluation. . . ." Hence, "funding based on contracts and signed between the government and each institution recently has been advocated at the higher education level" (p. 484).

Finally, community college leaders and commentators have raised the possibility of increased efficiency in government delivery of social services. They argue that the nation's community colleges, with their commitment to vocational training and their ethos of responsiveness to local needs, constitute an established adult education system that can consolidate and coordinate the delivery of diffuse government programs for human resource development. For example, Katsinas and Swender (1992) and Katsinas (1994) suggest that these advantages are not always understood by administrators who oversee government manpower development programs, with the result that funding is inefficiently spread across several community-based organizations (CBOs), sometimes involving community colleges, sometimes not. Hence, "community colleges must actively promote a national strategy of human resource policy development that places them in a primary brokering role, extending and in many cases replacing those functions previously performed by CBOs" (Katsinas & Swender, 1992, p. 22). This picture of the community college is one in which the institution is at the center of government workforce development efforts, coordinating credit programming with "non-FTE-based employment and training, welfare-to-work, and adult literacy systems" (Katsinas, 1994, p. 25). The inefficiencies inherent in the overlapping regional jurisdictions of adult lit-

eracy agencies, regional economic development councils, and other agencies that administer programs funded by the Job Training Partnership Act (JTPA) and the Family Support Act of 1988 (such as the JOBS program) would be eliminated as community college districts become the service regions for all.

Funding the Community College as Social Service Agency

The desired advantages of these funding arrangements may not be realized if hidden costs remain unrecognized in funding mechanisms. These costs are incurred through the paperwork burden of government contracts, the strictures within legislative mandates that impede responsiveness to local needs, and the tendency to involve colleges in noneducative work for which the institution may be ill suited. Each should be avoided.

Paperwork documenting compliance with contract obligations cannot be avoided. But it can lead to inefficiencies when it makes unwarranted demands on staff time (potentially to the detriment of clients) or when the information it generates has only marginal utility. For example, college staff working with public aid recipients may devote a great deal of time to collecting and reporting data that say more about the month-to-month compliance of clients with public aid rules and regulations than about the progress the students make in their educational programs. Clearly, the data collection mandates imposed on the colleges, although required by law, may be of little or no use to the colleges in their attempt to help public aid recipients.

College action can also be restricted by legislative prescriptions that preclude creative responses to local problems. For example, Katsinas (1994) urges community colleges to become local coordinators for the federally funded JOBS programs. But does the JOBS program as developed in the Family Support Act of 1988 offer an optimal welfare-to-work mechanism? Herr, Halpern, and Conrad (1993) say no, pointing to research evidence suggesting that its emphasis on education limits its utility for all but the most able public aid recipients. They maintain that "the welfare-to-work transition is not a single leap from education to employment" (p. 115). For some individuals, it is a long and difficult period of adjustment because "at a more basic level, it is about personal growth and change" (p. 115). Hence, they question the utility of immediately placing welfare recipients in education programs and suggest alternative approaches that may not be fundable under the current law.

If this analysis is correct, community colleges may buy into a flawed mechanism, offering their curricula as the path out of welfare for area citizens who have more immediate, noneducational needs. In the extreme, the ideal of community responsiveness could be turned on its end as colleges develop programs whose starting points are legislative mandates rather than community nuances. Because these mandates change constantly, there is the added danger that college services to local communities will evolve incoherently, thereby thwarting the efficiencies seen by Katsinas (1994) in government use of community colleges as a nexus for social service programs. Eicher and Chevaillier (1993) have noted that "specific grants do not ensure the long-term stability that institutions need, and they can be given more in accordance with passing priorities and fancies of elected bodies than with a thought-out pattern of development" (p. 513).

The recognition that solutions to social problems entail more than formal education also leads to the question of how far community colleges should stray from their traditional educative roles. If the colleges are viewed as the solution to social ills rather than part of the solution, expectations of the colleges may rise exponentially. Welfare-to-work programs that start with an emphasis on education may add on services related to personal counseling, legal advice, or reference and referral to emergency housing shelters. It quickly becomes evident that success of the college program requires careful coordination with other community-based agencies. Otherwise, the college may go beyond its expertise and endanger its reputation as an educational institution. As Vaughan (1991) notes, college leaders should protect the educational core of the community college mission:

> Waiting at the edge of the mission are any number of problems that need solutions. Indeed, the problems are too numerous to be addressed effectively by any single

entity in society Thus, priorities must be established. . . . To try to be all things to all people is both to dissipate the mission beyond recognition and to pull so many resources from the core that the community college no longer functions as an institution of higher learning. Once this happens, the community college has trouble justifying funds from the sources that normally finance higher education. (p. 32)

All of these cautions point to imperatives in contracted funding for college economic development or social welfare programs. First, reporting requirements, although necessary, should yield useful information about program success and not be so burdensome as to reduce client services. Although colleges must remain accountable, there is clearly a point of diminishing returns at which staff investment in paperwork endangers program effectiveness. There is also a point at which legislative strictures diminish college responsiveness to local needs. This responsiveness will be endangered to the extent that funding is tied to specific, centrally prescribed actions rather than to desired outcomes. Piland (1995) notes this danger in California, arguing that if the state's community colleges are to fulfill their potential as catalysts of local economic development they must be freed of regulatory and legislative micromanagement.

Finally, special purpose contracts should not expect more from the community college than the institution can deliver. Gottschalk's (1977) observation that community colleges "provide the educational component of solutions to social problems" (p. 9) is a useful rule of thumb, suggesting that contracted funds will yield the greatest return when targeted to educational services. At the most, community colleges might serve as brokers, funneling funds to community-based organizations for noneducative services. But success in this role presupposes minimal political conflict between CBOs and community colleges. This conflict is rarely discussed by those calling on community colleges to coordinate government social welfare programs.

BALANCING MEANS AND ENDS IN A MULTIPURPOSE COLLEGE

Although each can be discussed separately, the flexible, scholastic, and social service philosophies are thoroughly intertwined in today's community college as it serves the diverse constituency of mass higher education. The flexible institution, evident in and encouraged by enrollment-driven subsidies, benefits occasional learners. The more prescriptive scholastic institution, evident in curriculum structures outlined in college catalogs (and tacitly supported by state policies that allow funding for enrollment in credit programs only), recognizes the needs of degree-bound students. The social service agency, evident in the growing use of special purpose contracts that involve colleges in social and economic development programs, recognizes the needs of displaced workers, public aid recipients, and others who can profit from a coordinated "one stop" approach to the receipt of government subsidized education and training benefits.

But it is hard to see how the three can be combined in ways that allow each to flourish to its full potential (Cohen & Brawer, 1989, pp. 277–278). College funding mechanisms necessarily represent a trade-off (by default or design) between the benefits of the flexible, scholastic, and social service institutions. For example, the benefits derived from citizens' opportunity to engage in occasional learning are diminished to the extent that colleges introduce matriculation policies or other initiatives that stress sequenced learning and degree completion. Similarly, increased use of special purpose contracts that involve community colleges in economic development programs divert at least some administrative attention away from more traditional service areas.

As the public seeks ever greater returns on its investment, it is appropriate to ask how the lost opportunities inherent in these tradeoffs can be minimized. One potential answer lies in the argument that these lost opportunities are (in aggregate) the inevitable cost of a greater good: the presence of a community-based institution that can meet local needs as they change over time. Efficiencies are maximized through administrative judgments that, based on study of these needs, offer the most appropriate mix of the flexible, scholastic, and social service approaches.

Another answer, however, lies in the conviction that the attempt to mix educational functions is inherently wasteful and that the community college must be fundamentally changed.

Eaton's (1994) call for a collegiate emphasis is an example. She would concentrate community college efforts on postsecondary degree programming, leaving remedial education, workforce development, and other noncollegiate functions to other agencies that are more capable of carrying out these ends; the colleges would be funded accordingly with the goal of maximizing the efficiencies and benefits of the scholastic institution. Cohen and Brawer (1989) offer a compromise approach to the same end, maintaining institutional comprehensiveness but insisting on clear fiscal and administrative divisions within the college that separate units with different educational functions. For example, the unit serving degree-seeking students would be separate from the unit serving ad hoc learners; each unit would be funded separately because each takes on an entirely different task for students pursing different ends.

These answers imply a more reasoned, means-ends approach to funding than is usually the case in the public arena. Cohen (1993) has correctly observed that "as always, the nature of college services is driven less by intramural educational philosophy than by the ability to sustain revenues" (p. 74). It remains to be seen whether the contemporary period of consolidation and fiscal parsimony will lead to decisions that are driven more by considered debate about institutional purpose than by fiscal opportunism.

REFERENCES

Adelman, C. (1992). *The way we are: The community college as American thennometer.* Washington, DC: Office of Educational Research and Improvement, U.S. Department of Education.

Breneman, D. W., & Nelson, S. C. (1981). *Financing community colleges: An economic perspective.* Washington, DC: Brookings Institution.

California Community Colleges, Board of Governors. (1984). *Student matriculation: A plan for implementation in the California community colleges.* Sacramento: Author. (ERIC Document Reproduction Service No. ED 261738)

Carnegie Commission on Higher Education. (1970). *The open-door college.* New York: McGraw-Hill.

Cohen, A. M. (1993). Trends and issues in community college finance. *Community College Review, 20*(4), 70–75.

Cohen, A. M., & Brawer, F. B. (1987). *The collegiate function of community colleges.* San Francisco: Jossey-Bass.

Cohen, A. M., & Brawer, F. B. (1989). *The American community college.* San Francisco: Jossey-Bass.

Eaton, J. S. (1994). *Strengthening collegiate education in community colleges.* San Francisco: Jossey-Bass.

Eicher, J.-C., & Chevaillier, T. (1993). Rethinking the finance of post-compulsory education. *International Journal of Educational Research, 19,* 445–519.

Garms, W. I. (1977). *Financing community colleges.* New York: Teachers College Press.

Gottschalk, K. (1977). Can colleges deal with high-risk problems? *Community College Frontiers, 6*(4),4–11.

Grubb, W. N. (1989). *The developing vocational education and training "system": Partnerships and customized training.* Washington, DC: Office of Vocational and Adult Education, U.S. Department of Education. (ERIC Document Reproduction Service No. ED 329 680)

Grubb, W. N. (1995). Response to comment. *Journal of Human Resources, 30,* 222–227.

Harper, W. A. (1971). *Junior college directory.* Washington, DC: American Association of Junior Colleges.

Herr, T., Halpern, R., & Conrad, A. (1993). Changing what counts: Rethinking the journey out of welfare. *Applied Behavioral Science Review, 1,* 113–149.

Hines, E. R. (1994). *State higher education appropriations, 1993–94.* Denver, CO: State Higher Education Executive Officers.

Illinois Community College Board. (1994). *A fiscal profile of the Illinois public community college system: Fiscal years 1966–1994.* Springfield: Author.

Illinois Community College Board. (1996). *Workforce preparation grant report for fiscal year 1994.* Springfield: Author.

Kane, T. J., & Rouse, C. E. (1995a). Comment on W. Norton Grubb, Grubb, "The varied economic returns to postsecondary education: New evidence from the class of 1972." *Journal of Human Resources, 30,* 205–221.

Kane, T. J., & Rouse, C. E. (1995b). Labor-market returns to two- and four-year college. *American Economic Review, 85,* 600–614.

Katsinas, S. G. (1994). Is the open door closing? The democratizing role of the community college in the post-cold war era. *Community College Journal, 64*(5), 22–29.

Katsinas, S. G., & Swender, H. J. (1992). Community colleges and JTPA: Involvement and opportuni-

ty. *Community, Technical, and Junior College Journal, 62*(6), 18–23.

Lombardi, J. (1973). Critical decade for community college financing. In J. Lombardi (Ed.), *New directions for community colleges: Vol. 2. Meeting the financial crisis* (pp. 109–120). San Francisco: Jossey-Bass.

London, H. B. (1978). *The culture of a community college.* New York: Praeger.

Martorana, S. V., & Wattenbarger, J. L. (1978). *Principles, practices, and alternatives in state methods of financing community colleges and an approach to their evaluation, with Pennsylvania as a case study.* Report no. 32. University Park: Center for the Study of Higher Education, University of Pennsylvania.

McCabe, R. H. (1981). Now is the time to reform the American community college. *Community and Junior College Journal, 51*(8), 6–10.

McKeown, M. P., & Layzell, D. T (1994). State funding formulas in higher education: Trends and issues. *Journal of Educational Finance,* 319–346.

Newmyer, J., & McIntyre, C. (1992). *Funding gap study.* Sacramento: California Community Colleges Board of Governors. (ERIC Document Reproduction Service No. 351 066)

Palmer, J. C. (1987). *Community, technical, and junior colleges: A summary of selected national data.* Washington, DC: American Association of Community and Junior Colleges. (ERIC Document Reproduction Service No. ED 292 507)

Palmer, J. C. (1995). *Results of a formative evaluation of the opportunities program.* (Available from the Illinois Community College Board, 509 South 6th Street, Room 400, Springfield, IL 62701)

Palmer, J. C., & Eaton, J. S. (1991). Building the national agenda for transfer: A background paper. In J. S. Eaton (Ed.), *Setting the national agenda: Academic achievement and transfer* (pp. 17–52). Washington, DC: American Council on Education.

Palmer, J. C., & Pugh, M. B. (1993). The community college contribution to the education of bachelor's degree graduates: A case study in Virginia. In J. S. Eaton (Ed.), *Probing the community college transfer function* (pp. 45–70). Washington, DC: American Council on Education.

Palmer, J. C., Stapleton, L., & Ludwig, M. (1994). *At what point do community college students transfer to baccalaureate-granting institutions: Results of a 13-state study.* Washington, DC: American Council on Education.

Piland, B. (1995). Facing the 21st century: California community colleges at the crossroads. *Community College Journal, 65*(3), 24–28.

President's Commission on Higher Education. (1947). *Higher education for American democracy.* Washington, DC: Government Printing Office.

Richardson, R. C., Jr., Fisk, E. C., & Okun, M. A. (1983). *Literacy in the open-access college.* San Francisco: Jossey-Bass.

Richardson, R. C., Jr., & Rhodes, W. R. (1985). Effective strategic planning: Balancing demands for quality and fiscal realities. In W. A. Deegan & D. Tillery (Eds.), *Renewing the American community college* (pp. 284–302). San Francisco: Jossey-Bass.

Romano, R. M. (1986a). An economic perspective on the public financing of the community college. *Community College Review, 14*(2), 8–13.

Romano, R. M. (1986b). What is the economic payoff to a community college degree? *Community/ Junior College Quarterly of Research and Practice, 10,* 153–164.

Seidman, E. (1985). *In the words of the faculty.* San Francisco: Jossey-Bass.

Smith, T. M., Perie, M., Alsalam, N., Mahoney, R.P., Bae, Y., & Young, B. A. (1995). *The condition of education, 1995* (NCES Report No. 95-273). Washington, DC: Office of Educational Research and Improvement, U.S. Department of Education.

Snyder, T. D., & Hoffman, C. M. (1995). *Digest of education statistics, 1995.* Washington, DC: Office of Educational Research and Improvement, U.S. Department of Education.

U.S. Bureau of the Census. (1975). *Historical statistics of the United States: Colonial times to 1970.* Washington, DC: Author.

Vaughan, G. B. (1991). Institutions on the edge: America's community colleges. *Educational Record, 72*(2), 30–33.

Weis, L. (1985). *Between two worlds: Black students in an urban community college.* Boston: Routledge & Kegan Paul.

Walters, J. E. (1994). *Registration priorities: A report.* Sacramento: Chancellor's Office, California Community Colleges. (ERIC Document Reproduction Service No. ED 374 878)

Wattenbarger, J. L. (1985). Dealing with new competition for public funds: Guidelines for financing community colleges. In W. A. Deegan & D. Tillery (Eds.), *Renewing the American community college* (pp. 253–283). San Francisco: Jossey-Bass.

Zeiss, T. (1989). Roles of community, technical, and junior colleges: Positive image opportunity. In T. Zeiss (Ed.), *Economic development: A viewpoint from business* (pp. 3–6). Washington, DC: American Association of Community and Junior Colleges.

Chapter 15

Vouchers in American Education

Hard Legal and Policy Lessons from Higher Education

F. King Alexander

As government and public debate intensifies over the issue of American educational reform, parental choice and the use of educational vouchers for elementary and secondary education has once again emerged as perhaps the most contentious educational and legal theme in legislatures throughout the United States. Voucher proponents claim that public schools maintain a monopoly on grammar and high school educational opportunities and this system shields public schools from marketplace influences and promotes declining, or at best, mediocre academic results. Moreover, they claim that the choice of the consumer and the competition of the marketplace create efficiencies that drive down costs. Opponents declare that vouchers are not only unconstitutional but they would have a detrimental impact on public education by diverting essential resources away from the majority of the nation's children and schools. Further, they argue that vouchers are premised on the assumption of social separation and will thereby ultimately create inequalities in the social structure and denial of education opportunity. What makes this recent debate different from previous voucher disputes is that many current advocates of school voucher policies increasingly cite as favorable precedent the effectiveness of direct student aid programs in higher education. It is maintained that federal and state direct student grant programs constitute a legal voucher and do not violate federal or state law. Voucher advocates also declare that such governmental policies have successfully expanded student choice without detrimentally impacting resources for public higher education.[1]

This study was designed to analyze two and one-half decades of experience with direct student aid grants in order to shed some light on whether a philosophical shift in funding higher education is occurring at the state level. The information presented in this paper provides a brief overview of the legal struggle to adopt direct student aid policies in higher education and the subsequent growth of state direct student grant programs. This paper will also analyze how public and private institutions of higher education benefit from state direct student aid policies. Because direct student grants to higher education is, in fact, a kind of legally protected voucher, the higher education experience may portend the ultimate effects of recent thrusts to provide vouchers for private elementary and secondary education.

Despite claims of the potential impact of educational vouchers in America's school system, very little evidence is available to judge the merits of the claims made by both sides in the voucher debate because public financing for elementary and secondary education in the United States has been pri-

Source: *Journal of Education Finance*, 24 (Fall 1998), 153–178.

marily confined to publicly managed schools. Due to constitutional prohibitions against the use of public funds for religious purposes, school vouchers have been limited to a few state experimental programs. In order to justify the expansion of such programs, governors, policy officials, and business leaders have turned to federal and state direct student aid policies in higher education as desirable precedents of effective governmental voucher initiatives.

During the last fifty years, a vast amount of experimentation has occurred at federal and state levels with direct student aid policies for higher education. At the federal level, direct student aid has been advanced in the form of grants and loans. In 1995–96, over $6 billion in grant program aid and $28 billion in loan program assistance were allocated to students through federal direct student aid programs.[2] Among state governments direct student grant programs have also rapidly grown and constitute anywhere from less than 1 percent of state appropriations in Hawaii to nearly 23 percent of state appropriations in New York.[3] In most states students are free to use direct grants at any institution of their choice including public, non-profit private, and increasingly, for-profit private postsecondary institutions. Voucher supporters insist that these programs have successfully demonstrated that such policies not only increase student choice but also expand educational opportunity. To fully understand the applicability of the voucher concept in higher education and its effect on educational opportunity, it is first necessary to provide an historical overview of the debates encompassing the origins of the American voucher concept and the adaptation of federal and state direct student aid grant programs.

THE ORIGINS OF THE AMERICAN VOUCHER CONCEPT

The recent debate over the potential effects of school vouchers is not new to American education. Voucher proponents frequently seek to lend verisimilitude to their cause by citing advocacy of such historical eminents as Adam Smith, Thomas Paine, and John Stuart Mill.[4] Since these three greats tend to be repeatedly cited by various voucher advocates and appear

to be largely alone as reputable voices on which a philosophical basis for vouchers is premised, a closer look at their views is warranted. With regard to Smith, they observe his free market principles and his aversion to monopolistic control by the state that he contends inhibits the competitive impulses of human beings. The voucher proponents argue that Smith's "invisible hand" of competition will work to improve education as Smith asserted and documented for commerce and industry. Smith thought highly of the economic consequences of selfishness, that man by taking care of his own happiness would invariably and inadvertently attend to the needs of others. But Peter Gay[5] points out that while on the whole, Smith thought that governmental regulation is highly undesirable, in his later writings he concluded that the "free-play of self-interest led to enduring, often harmful conflict," and did not necessarily maximize resources.[6] Smith speaks with great disdain of the "mean rapacity" of the private monopolizing spirit that makes some men servants and others rulers of mankind. Thus, Smith generally concluded that even though economic greed was not necessarily moral or virtuous, it nevertheless was good for business and a fact of life. To argue that Smith intended that there should not be some guiding "visible hand" of expressing the public common good in matters as essential to social conduct as education is to misconstrue his intent. Without some regulation, unbridled license to take advantage of others would result in great miscarriages of justice. Accordingly, "the state should do something to protect ignorant consumers against fraudulent producers and employers . . . common humanity should prevail over *laissez faire*."[7]

Therefore, any reference to the ideas of Adam Smith as representing conclusive philosophical precedent for vouchers in the United States today misappropriates much of what he actually said and believed. To cite Smith as an advocate for vouchers largely ignores the context of his era and the varying circumstances of place and time that delimit the application of his *The Theory of Moral Sentiments* and his *Wealth of Nations*. Remember, Smith published the former in 1759, and the latter in 1776. Smith, as Gay observes, was not a "system-maker," but an observer and an explainer.[8] His comments, in which he proposed that the state give money directly to parents for the education of their children, were premised on his appreciation for education as a necessary protection of the poor and ignorant against avarice of those more fortunate who have the private means to advance their own education. Smith saw that the state must make provisions for education in order to mitigate the ravages and predaciousness of the marketplace. Not being a "system-maker" and predating the conceptualizations of public systems of education of Rush, Jefferson, Madison, Condorcet, Diderot, and others, Smith was deprived of experiences that would have given him knowledge of the value of merits of public common schools that were to only come to fruition generations later. At the time of the American Revolution and the promulgation of the American Constitution in Philadelphia in 1787, even the founding fathers of the Republic "did not deem the subject of public education important enough to warrant consideration in the Convention."[9] Society had not yet reached the level of humane social sophistication and economic understanding to provide for universal public education. And even though Smith strongly advocated universal education,[10] he had no conceptual framework to know what it should look like when finally implemented. In the United States, except for limited examples in New England, education remained a private matter. Too, according to Cubberley, "Everywhere except in Catholic countries, education as an affair of the State had not been thought of."[11] By 1792 France did not have any public schools and only 36,000 pupils were enrolled in Catholic schools, in a nation of 26 million people. In England and Scotland, the land of Smith's experience, education was considered to be no business of the state and public common schools were only beginning to appear a century after Smith's death. It was only in the larger German states that education had been declared a state function, and Adam Smith was not a product of that culture or system and could not have effectively evaluated its efficacy.

Second, it is to greatly minimize Smith's contributions for one to assume that he was so entirely consumed with the reality of the merits of competition that he would exclude all other social considerations. Smith throughout his writings evinces a healthy regard for the equality of the human condition. Any possible

proposal of Smith for vouchers as direct government aid to parents to pay for private schooling would have conjured in Smith's mind an abiding concern for an underlying standard of social equity. As Smith's writings so clearly indicate, he would have undoubtedly recognized that to supplement family wealth with a voucher, paid by state tax funds, would result in a state created disadvantage for those children with little private means. Distribution of state funds to create further advantage for those who already have the means to attend private schools would fly in the face of Smith's concern that "Civil government, so far as instituted for the security of property (money), is in reality instituted of the rich against the poor. . . ."[12] Thus, Smith would have suspected that those in control of government would collaborate in devices, such as vouchers, to enhance the condition of the rich and inhibit the prospects of the poor.

Smith was not a metaphysician, he, as a reader of Hume, Voltaire, Rousseau and Condillac's,[13] was well aware of the importance of the scientific method and its inherent conflict with the teaching of religious dogma in private schools of that era. Smith was a friend and disciple of David Hume, and both Smith and Hume were wary of the limitations that organized religion placed on science and the advancement of knowledge. As intellectuals of the Enlightenment they believed that the affairs of the state should not be entangled with the affairs of the church. Smith was an empiricist and a scientist of political economy who based his conclusions on observation and evidence and not on metaphysics and superstition. He regarded religion as a human need, but he strongly inveighed against it being conjoined with the activities of the state. In short, Smith was an ardent supporter of the Jeffersonian concept of "separation of church and state." To suggest that Smith would be an advocate for vouchers today in America and to provide tax funds in aid of private and parochial schools overlooks a foundational element in Smith's beliefs.[14]

In this light, those who propose vouchers in the name of Adam Smith evidence a lack of diligence in their readings of *Wealth of Nations*. In this great book, Smith devotes an entire chapter to the problems intrinsic in the state's appropriation of public tax funds for aid of the church. Smith noted that with the decline of feudalism and the emergence of industrialization, trading and commerce became more attractive for investments of church monies, and educational and charitable interests of the church decreased. Smith said that in the produce of manufactures and commerce, "the clergy, . . . found something for which they could exchange their rude produce, and thereby discovered the means of spending their whole revenues upon their own persons, without giving any considerable share of them to other people.[15] Here Smith insinuated his basic belief in the nature of capitalism into his interpretation of the economic pursuits of the church. Thus, according to Smith, the marketplace became a lucrative alternative for investment of church resources and the church, inevitably attracted by the "invisible hand," gravitated away from its earlier charitable pursuits. This weakened commitment drove the church to seek state tax funds to maintain its religious schools for which it no longer saw a sufficient economic return.

Moreover, Smith inveighed most fervently against this new found propensity of the church to obtain tax funds to support its formerly charitable activities; he said in *Wealth of Nations* that "it may be laid down as a certain maxim, that, all other things being supposed equal, the richer the church, the poorer must necessarily be, either the sovereign on the one hand, or the people on the other. . . ."[16] Thus, in view of Smith's aversion to mingling of matters of church and state and because church related schools make up well over 80 percent of private elementary and secondary schools in America, and church related colleges and universities constitute a large portion of higher education institutions, it would be extremely difficult to rationally maintain that Smith would be a proponent of a voucher scheme that would increase the relative financial condition of churches, church schools or colleges, to the detriment of the state or people.

In their zeal to add precedential value to their claims, the advocates of vouchers frequently add Thomas Paine to their pantheon of philosophical adherents. As in the case of Adam Smith, such claims are undoubtedly highly speculative when one considers Paine's foundational beliefs and the time, place and historical context in which they were formu-lated. Those who reach out to Paine as a pillar of voucher advocacy presumably buttress their argument with his footnotes to his discussion of "Ways and Means" of government in his *Rights of Man*, wherein he said that "Public schools do not answer the general purpose of the poor."[17] In the absence of public schools, he recommended that a welfare system be established in which poor parents would be given rebates in a type of negative income tax system, "pay as a remission of taxes to every poor family, out of surplus taxes, and in room of poor-rates, four pounds a year for every child under fourteen years of age; enjoining the parents of such children to send them to school. . . ."[18]

Yet, further inspection of Paine's writings indicates considerable doubt in the interpretation of Paine's intent. Most importantly, to conclude that Paine was a voucher-man fails to consider that he wrote the *Rights of Man*, 1791 and 1792, in response to Burke's *Reflections on the Revolution in France*, November 1790, in which he attacked virtually every aspect of Burke's observations. One of the points most basic to Paine's critique was that Burke had advocated the uniting of church and state and Burke had censured the National Assembly of France for not merging the two. Paine, a deist, and later accused of being an atheist, pointed out that "persecution is not an original feature in any religion; but it is always the strongly marked feature of law-religious, religion established by law."[19] In other words, Paine believed that religious persecution would ultimately result when the state assisted churches in promulgating laws to finance and support religion. Paine observed that "The union of church and state has impoverished Spain,"[20] and if the National Assembly of France should follow the counsel of Burke and the "error of Spain," it would itself fall into "folly."' Thus, it would be difficult to imagine that Paine would knowingly suggest a funding scheme for education that would result in a massive flow of public monies from the state taxpayer for the enhancement of a church or church schools. It is unlikely that Paine would not readily see that the funding of church schools and colleges would be tantamount to falling to Burke's scheme of the uniting of church and state.

Further, at the time Paine published his *Rights of Man* he did not have the benefit of observing a public school system in operation.

Paine himself was born and lived his youth and early adulthood in England, before coming to America to join the Revolution in 1774, and publishing *Common Sense* on January 9, 1776. Paine's England had no public common schools and such schools in the American colonies were found only in limited circumstances in towns or cities in New England. No state systems existed. Pennsylvania had only a few pauper schools. Massachusetts had not enacted its first general state law until 1789, two years after Paine had returned to England.[22]

Even the law in France of 1793, known as the Bouquier Law, did not create a "system" of public schooling, but rather created a voucher program that committed the state to pay the tuition of each student to attend primarily Catholic schools. Dissatisfaction with this voucher plan quickly led to its repeal and the enactment of the Lakanal Law, of 27 brumaire year III (November 17, 1794), that created the first system of secular public common schools in France. Public schools had not been proposed in France until Condorcet, the chairman of public instruction, presented his plan for a system of state schools to the revolutionary Legislative Assembly on April 21, 1792. Even then, however, the implementation of the public school was delayed until May 4, 1793 when Condorcet renewed his appeal saying that the state "has a right to bring up its own children; it cannot confide this trust to family pride nor prejudices of individuals. . . . Education should be common and equal to all. . . ."[23] It is instructive to note that Joseph Lakanal, Condorcet, and Mary Wollstonecraft, along with Paine, served on the Committee of Public Instruction during the revolution. It was clear from their deliberations, under the leadership of Condorcet, that the public secular schools of France were conceptualized and enacted with the passage of the Lakanal law.[24] This legislation quickly brought to an end the national voucher system that had been in operation for only one year. On October 28, 1793, the revolutionarily convention ordained that no ecclesiastic could be appointed as a teacher in state schools. This initiated the idea of secular public schools in France.

Thus, when Paine came to France in 1789, he could not have observed a public common school system in operation and his footnote in his proposal on "Ways and Means" in his *Rights of Man* reflected merely his notion of public schools based on limited observations of a few schools in cities in the emerging colonial states of America. The nemesis of all public schools at that time was scarcity of population in rural areas in the United States and France, and Paine's view reflected as much.[25] Paine's footnote goes on to state that "Public schools do not answer the general purpose of the poor. They are chiefly in corporation towns, from which the county town and villages are excluded; or, if admitted, the distance occasions a great loss of time. Education, to be useful to the poor, should be on the spot. . . ."[26] Thus, Paine's indictment of earlier public schools can be taken primarily as a commentary on their scarcity, their lack of development and pervasiveness, and the greater availability of private schools, and not as a philosophical denunciation of the concept. Thus, Paine's experience had not enabled him to gain perspective regarding the benefits of a comprehensive system of public schools, due to the fact that such schools did not exist when he wrote "Ways and Means" in 1792.[27] Little wonder, then, that Paine would propose a tax rebate for parents to pay for education for their children in any school that may have been available at that time. Only his later actions as a member of Condorcet's Committee on Public Instruction provide evidence of Paine's emerging understanding of public education as an important state responsibility.

It would, therefore, appear to stretch credulity to assume that Paine's comments would ipso facto place him in the pro-voucher camp. Without considerations of time and place and context, it would be just as reasonable to assume that all of the great political philosophers, antedating the creation of public common schools in America, England, and France, would have advocated vouchers. They would have certainly known nothing else. Thus it would appear to be a crass overstatement to assume that Paine would have supported a voucher or direct student aid plan. On the contrary, it could probably be reasonable to assume that had he known of the major contributions and benefits that were to ultimately flow from the creation and operation of America's common school system and her elaborate system of great public research universities, public colleges, and public community colleges, Paine would have been most wary of the voucher agenda of today.

As with Adam Smith and Thomas Paine, to assume that John Stuart Mill would have advocated vouchers for either elementary and secondary schools or for higher education in 21st century America requires a considerable leap of logic. To interject Mill's views into today's discussion of the merits of vouchers without consideration of social and historical context suggests considerable improbable conjecture. Mill believed that it was a "self-evident axiom that the State should require and compel the education, up to a certain standard, of every human being who is born its citizen."[28] In short, Mill was a strong advocate of compulsory universal education and he argued that the state was obliged to see that the parent did not fail in the responsibility to educate the child. In fact, he elevated the parent's failure to educate the child to the level of a "moral crime."[29] He even extended such "moral crimes" of parents to having children in excessive numbers when they did not have the economic means to support them.[30]

Even though Mill asserted state authority to compel education, he admonished that the state should not take "upon itself to direct that education."[31] His objection to a state education was founded in his belief that the state would "mould" people in a way that pleases the "predominant power in the government . . . ."[32] "To understand his objection requires one to read further, however. Why did Mill oppose state education? The answer is that he did not oppose state education *per se*, rather, he opposed the forces that control state education. These forces, according to Mill, in the context of his time, were the "monarch," the "priesthood," the "aristocracy,"[33] or other like objectionable majority. At the time that Mill wrote *On Liberty*, England was not yet as free as it is today of monarchial aristocratic control; it was not until much later that the House of Commons could pass a budget bill free from control and influence of the monarch and the hereditary House of Lords. Mill's primary objection to state education was that it tended to be controlled by the church and was not secular. Unlike the United States where separation of church and state prevailed, in England there was, of course, a state church, the Church of England. Both state and church had long and lurid histories of denial of civil liberties and throughout his life Mill, as a learned man, considered much of the historical losses of liberty to be attributable to church control of the state. Mill took great pains to explain how educational examinations should be purged of religious indoctrination.[34] Limited by his own experiences, Mill could not visualize a common secular public school or a secular state university system as exists in the United States today. Yet, Mill repeatedly evidenced his limitations as an English Protestant by his castigation of the Catholic Church. He believed that education should be objective and oriented toward open disputation on all subjects in pursuit of truth,[35] but he darkly observed that Catholic education is so structured as to deny to the laity "mental freedom" and the teachers in parochial schools, representing the clergy, will always advance their particular sectarian cause.[36] According to Mill, "If the teachers of mankind are to be cognizant of all that they ought to know, everything must be free to be written and published without restraint."[37] He observed that religious creeds that are visited upon passive children as "received beliefs," always heard lauded and never discussed "or challenged" violate all the principles on which education should be founded."[38]

The secular education system of the United States, so rigorously defended by the judicial system pursuant to the rights guaranteed by free speech and expression, and religion provisions of the First Amendment, could not have been foretold by Mill when he published *On Liberty* in 1859. The Fourteenth Amendment was not enacted until 1868 and the expansiveness of the First Amendment of the Constitution's free speech, expression and religious protections did not develop as legal interpretations for almost a century thereafter.[39] With regard to liberties and rights, England has always lagged far behind America. Mill died in 1873 and England did not, itself, require compulsory school attendance until 1880 and it was not until 1944 that England enacted what could actually be considered a comprehensive publicly financed and operated state school system. As late as 1943, R.H. Tawney questioned the continued existence of state aid for the aristocratic English "public" and Church of England schools when he said that: "the existence of a group of schools reserved for the children of the comparatively prosperous . . . is or is not, as the world is today, in the best interests of the nation. It cannot be decided by the venerable device of describing privileges as liberties."[40]

Herein Tawney captures the primary problem that Mill would have had with vouchers. Precious little exists in Mill's writings, that taken as a whole and in context, would suggest, with any certitude, that he would not have seen the fatal conflict inherent between vouchers for state aid to church schools and his ideas of liberty. As Tawney so clearly reveals, it is much too easy for advantage and privilege to masquerade as liberty. The essence of Mill's *On Liberty* inveighs against limitations and inhibitions of the human mind regardless of the purpose, intent, and source of the restraint, whether by monarch, church, or aristocracy.

One can only conclude that to capture the posthumous endorsement of these philosophers for the various voucher schemes requires a more comprehensive treatment of philosophic thought than has been given by voucher advocates thus far. Too, the claim that the experience of vouchers in higher education in the form of direct student aid presents an admirable and effective precedent for the adoption of vouchers for elementary and secondary schools is likewise highly problematic.

HIGHER EDUCATION VOUCHER PROGRAMS

The appropriateness of expansion of education beyond homes and churches is incumbent to the American common school concept. The belief that education of all persons is essential to the democratic form of government has ultimately fueled the movement for the creation of state schools for elementary, secondary, and higher education. However, concerns about the viability of private education led many to advocate the educational voucher in the 1940s and 1950s. A defining event occurred when soldiers returned from World War II and Congress enacted the "Serviceman's Readjustment Act" or as it was more commonly known "The G. I. Bill". Prior to that event, the federal government played a minimal role in the financing of American higher education. With the passage of this Act, Congress began to assert a new interest in expanding higher educational opportunities for all Americans.[41] Supported by a strong private college and university lobby, the "G. I. Bill" allowed students to take public funds to colleges of their choice including private and religious institutions. The Act represented the first comprehensive governmental voucher program in American higher education.

Less than one decade later, Milton Friedman popularized the voucher concept by proposing a funding system where the public would finance schools and colleges but not administer them. He selectively used those passages from Smith and Mill that supported his point of view and rejected the idea that government schools were necessary. Friedman's proposal was an unrestricted voucher scheme whereby parents would receive public resources to attend any educational institution of their choice. According to Friedman, this system would grant parents greater freedom of choice, dissolve the education monopoly held by public institutions, and make schools more efficient and effective by introducing more competition.[42]

Today, forty years after Friedman's proposal, only a couple of restricted pilot voucher programs exist in state elementary and secondary educational systems.[43] In higher education, on the other hand, the state voucher concept has progressed quite differently. Encouraged by the popularity of the "G. I. Bill" and stimulated by private institutional concern about public college and university enrollment growth, the 1950s and 1960s witnessed a momentous policy debate over federal programs that changed the course of future funding of higher education. The outcome of this debate would also influence the way that most state governments would view voucher schemes for higher education.

Beginning with President Eisenhower's recommendations that the federal government supply scholarships or "vouchers" to undergraduates to take to the institution of their choice, the issue of directly aiding students rather than institutions dominated federal policy discussions for the next decade. During that period, federal financial assistance to higher education substantially grew to include an array of new projects such as grants to undergraduates, federal direct and guaranteed loans, work-study programs, graduate fellowships, and construction assistance. With the passage of the Economic Opportunity Act of 1964 and the Higher Education Act of 1965, Congress set a course of providing financial aid directly to needy students to use at most colleges or universities of their choice.[44] To understand the significance of the Act, it is important to recognize that all federal need-based student aid prior to 1965 came entirely in the form of National Defense Student Loans (NDSL). Under the Higher Education Act of 1965, NDSL was augmented and a variety of new programs were established including the Guaranteed Student Loans Program and the Educational Opportunity Grants Program, later renamed the Supplemental Educational Opportunity Grants Program.[45]

Seven years later, Congress passed the Higher Education Amendments of 1972 continuing the funding policies advanced in the Higher Education Act of 1965. The Amendments of 1972 established the Basic Educational Opportunity Grants Program (later renamed Pell Grants), the State Student Incentive Grants Program, and increased support for existing direct student aid grant and loan programs. The passage of the 1972 Amendments ushered in an era where full-fledged public support of private and parochial colleges and universities would continue unabated through direct student aid programs. The contentious debate over whether funds should be used for private and religious purposes had come to an end and the federal government had embraced the concept of indirectly aiding these institutions by means of direct student aid. For the federal government, this was a major philosophical shift from a time of little federal funding for higher education to a period of expanded aid to both public and private institutions. By adopting direct student aid polices, the federal government also was implementing a new funding concept that was contrary to the public institutional aid funding approaches used by most states at that time.

For institutional aid advocates, including many of the nation's largest public college and university organizations, the federal decision to advance the direct student aid concept instead of institutional aid concept was devastating. During the long debate, institutional aid advocates expressed grave concerns that direct student aid policies would disproportionately favor tuition reliant private institutions.[46] This would create a policy environment that would lead to continual cost increases in order to acquire greater federal aid allocations. Institutional aid advocates were also concerned that the federal policy shift to direct student aid was more than an issue of expanding educational opportunities to needy students. The federal passage of the 1965 Act and the 1972 Amendments provided private institutions with a way to receive public funding indirectly through student aid, or vouchers, at a time when most states prohibited the distribution of public resources to privately incorporated institutions. For many public education advocates, the adoption of the federal direct student aid concept meant that the federal government was circumventing many state funding laws and no longer recognized distinctions between public colleges and universities.

After nearly three decades of federal direct student aid policies and billions in public resources allocated to college students, many of the institutional aid advocates predictions about direct student aid have materialized.[47] For example, of the over 35 billion dollars supported through federal direct student aid programs in 1995–96, students attending private institutions received over 34 percent of all grant allocations and 62 percent of loan program resources, despite enrolling only 24 percent of the FTE student population.[48] Also, a higher percentage of private college students receive federal aid and larger awards than do public institution students.

By the mid-1970s, it was clear that the federal government had adopted a need-based voucher approach to funding collegiate accessibility for needy student populations. Students could now take limited public resource allocations to public and most private institutions of their choice. Within a decade, direct student aid programs would once again be expanded by Congress to include less needy student populations and accredited for-profit institutions.[49] By the late 1970s, the federal voucher scheme for funding higher education was fully operational.

FEDERAL INFLUENCE ON STATE POLICY AND LAW

Perhaps the most significant development that transpired during the federal policy shift to the voucher idea was the immense influence that these concepts had on state higher education policy. Prior to the Higher Education Act of 1965, only five states had adopted very limited direct student aid policies. Nearly all state constitutions prohibited appropriations of public money to any institution not under state control.[50] With the passage of the 1972 Higher Education Amendments and the creation of the State Student Incentive Grants (SSIG), the federal government sent a message to states that direct student aid programs were necessary at both the federal and state levels.

The primary purpose for the creation of the SSIG Program was to encourage states to fund direct student aid programs by providing federal money to be matched by state funds. This was an important policy directive initiated by the federal government during a period when most states refused to allow public resources to flow directly or indirectly through students to private institutions. For states, this was a twofold issue of public accountability and constitutionality. Unlike the Federal Constitution, state constitutions presented challenging restrictions. At the federal level, the policies adopted by Congress in the 1960s cleared the way for public funds to flow to private institutions in a variety of forms including direct student aid. In many states, however, this was an extremely controversial issue despite favorable United States Supreme Court decisions that watered down the constitutional restrictions against aid to religions and religious institutions.[51] State constitutions have a long history of being more specific and restrictive than the federal constitution in allowing public resources to be used by privately incorporated businesses, schools, and colleges. For those seeking to extend state aid to private higher education, whether to institutions or to their students, state constitutions presented numerous legal obstacles. Many private colleges and universities are religiously affiliated and aiding private institutions indirectly through students was often contested based on state constitutional clauses barring religious institutions from receiving public appropriations. Along with these religious clauses were various other provisions that banned the use of public moneys for private purposes. These state constitutional barriers created difficulties for direct student aid and private college advocates in

designing higher education funding schemes emphasizing widespread student choice, a rationale for aid to private institutions.[52] For example, prior to 1973, Colorado's constitution had been interpreted to bar grants or scholarships to students who attend private institutions, whether or not such aid is also available to students at public institutions.[53] In Nebraska, the state supreme court ruled in 1973 that a law authorizing state grants of up to $500 to students attending private institutions was unconstitutional.[54] In South Carolina, where 36 percent of full-time students attended private colleges and universities, any public aid to students at sectarian institutions was also ruled unconstitutional by the state supreme court.[55] In other states such as Utah, Wyoming, Virginia, Alaska, and Delaware, state constitutional provisions against aiding privately incorporated institutions or enterprises were upheld on several occasions prior to 1970.

However, it was not long before the federal government's policy shift to direct student aid began to influence state court decisions and legislation. Induced by a landmark U.S. Supreme Court decision in *Tilton v. Richardson*, in 1971, upholding the Higher Education Facilities Act of 1963, the idea emerged that there were legal distinctions between higher education and K-12 education. The *Tilton* case set off a wave of federal legislation in the early 1970s where the Supreme Court upheld public aid to private denominational higher education institutions while striking down programs aiding primary and secondary schools.[56]

In conjunction with these federal rulings, states began to change their own interpretations and contesting many restrictive laws that had been in place for decades.[57] After the *Tilton* case, the wall of separation between church and state began to crumble allowing direct and indirect funding of private higher education. Within three years Georgia (1972), Florida (1972), Massachusetts (1972 & 1974), Colorado (1973), and Virginia (1972 & 1974) amended their constitutions to permit direct student aid loan and grant programs.[58]

As political pressure grew from the private sector and states became more interested in acquiring federal State Student Incentive Grant (SSIG) matching funds, states increasingly adopted direct student aid policies making public funds available to private institutions.

Since the establishment of direct student aid voucher programs at the federal level in 1965 and 1972, many states have upheld student-oriented assistance as constitutional.[59] In each of these cases, the rationale used by the courts in determining the constitutionality of the programs rested on three basic assumptions. First, the funds must be granted to students not pursuing degrees in theology or divinity at public and accredited private institutions. Second, the funds must be granted on the basis of student financial need. Third, the funds must be granted directly to the students who must restrict their use for educational purposes.[60] For many state policy-makers, establishing direct student aid programs for needy students was perceived as a political compromise between public postsecondary officials and voucher proponents, like John Silber of Boston University, who proposed that all state higher education outlays be allocated in sizable vouchers to students.[61] Initially, states demonstrated an aversion to adopting such extensive voucher policies because they disregarded the student's ability to pay; however, as direct student aid programs grew in most states, new programs premised on merit and tuition equalization concepts between public and private institutions became more prevalent.

Once the legal barriers were cleared at the state level, legislatures quickly enacted a series of direct student aid policies that met these three basic assumptions. The implementation of these policies meant that states could also benefit from federal SSIG resource aid. By 1976, only four years after the inception of the SSIG program and five years after the *Tilton* case, thirty-nine states had either reversed existing restrictions or increased funding to direct student aid "voucher" programs for the avowed purpose of expanding opportunities while providing state dollars to private higher education. As Table 15.1 shows, once the legal restrictions were removed in many states during the 1970s, the direct student aid concept became nearly universal. Student aid programs quickly emerged as the most widespread means of indirectly channeling state dollars to private colleges and universities.

When analyzing the history of federal direct student aid programming, the impact of the SSIG Program is often underestimated. From the year of its inception in 1974 to 1996,

TABLE 15.1
Number of States Establishing Direct Student Aid Programs

Year	1966	1976	1986	1996
No. of States	6	39	46	50

Source: *Higher Education in the States,* and NASSGAP, Academic Year 1995–96.[62]

SSIG federal resource contributions to states and institutions totaled more than $1.5 billion, reaching their highest annual levels in the late 1980s. For the federal government and private institutions, SSIG proved to be an overwhelming success. Today, state direct student grants are in place in fifty states and constitute nearly $3 billion dollars in financial assistance to students. Even recent congressional discourse over the future of the SSIG program indicated that the overall objectives of the program, to entice states to adopt and expand the direct student aid voucher philosophy, have been achieved.

GROWTH OF STATE HIGHER EDUCATION VOUCHER PROGRAMS

By 1980 the majority of states had adopted the direct student aid concept as one of many strategies being used to expand postsecondary access. With few constitutional limitations, many state legislatures used direct student aid grants as an incentive for students to attend private institutions. Many state officials and private institution leaders justified creating such programs arguing that the overall share of students at private institutions was a viable economic alternative to subsidizing enrollments in public colleges and universities. During the next two decades, state allocations to direct grant programs grew from $645 million in 1976–77 to $2.9 billion in 1995–96, constituting nearly half of the total federal direct student aid grant appropriations in 1996.[63]

The rapid programmatic growth of direct student aid programs at the state level indicates the emergence of two important trends. First, the data show that there has been a gradual shift by states toward funding direct student aid programs, despite claims by private university officials that state legislatures are not interested in expanding the programs. In 1976–77, state direct student aid grant funds accounted for 4.8 percent of all state appropriations. By 1996, nearly two decades later, state allocations to such programs accounted for 6.6 percent of all state appropriations. This increase shows that states continue to follow the federal government's policy incentives to expand student aid programs by emphasizing the student voucher concept in postsecondary education.

In a number of states, spending on direct grant programs, as a percentage of state appropriations, is considerably higher than the national average of 6.6 percent (see Figure 15.1). In New York and Vermont, where states have a long history of providing grants to students attending private institutions, grant program funds constitute over 20 percent of state appropriations. In Illinois and Pennsylvania, states with politically influential private universities, resource allocations to direct student aid programs are double the national averages at 14.2 and 14.1 percent. In Georgia, a state that has rapidly risen among the states with the greatest amount of direct student grants due to an infusion of $160 million generated by the merit-based Georgia HOPE Scholarship Program,[64] grant program resources constitute over 13.6 percent of state appropriations. These numbers illustrate the great variances that exist when direct student aid grant programs are compared among states. Such data show how some states have embraced the voucher con-

cept and steadily allocate increasing resources for that purpose.

The second trend shows a consistent increase in merit-based direct student aid programs as compared to need-based programs. Currently, the vast majority of state grant funds are distributed through need-based programs, however, many states are beginning to expand direct student aid vouchers beyond need-based categories. During the last five years, merit-based aid programs have gained support as enticements for meritorious students to either remain in their home state or to immigrate to the host state for the purposes of pursuing a postsecondary education. The philosophical justification for adopting and expanding merit-based programs is even more problematic in the policy arena than need-based programs. Implementing publicly funded merit-based aid programs to supply middle-class and upper-class families with tuition subsidies to attend private institutions does not comport with the original justifications for most direct student aid policies.

States are now allocating more resources to merit-based programs than in the past. As Table 15.2 shows, for every dollar spent on merit-based student aid in 1980–81, $7.53 was spent on need-based student programs. In 1995–96, the ratio was reduced to $5.66 for need-based programs to every one dollar spent on merit-based programs. During this same period, from 1980–81 to 1995–96, merit-based aid also increased from 10 percent of all state

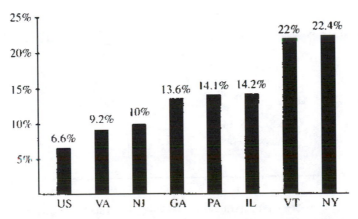

Figure 15.1 State Direct Student Aid Grant Program Resources as a Percentage of State Appropriations for Selected States (1995–96)

Source: NASSGAP (1995–96) & the Grapevine (1997)

TABLE 15.2
State Dollars Spent on Need-Based Student Aid versus Merit-based Aid Programs

Year	1980–81	1985–86	1990–91	1995–96
Amount	$7.53 to 1	$7.63 to 1	$7.25 to 1	$5.66 to 1

Source: Calculated from data in NASSGAP Reports, (1980–81 through 1995–96).

direct student grant expenditures to 15 percent. Though some of this increase is attributable to one state, Georgia, the movement nationwide is nevertheless quite desirable.[65]

Because of state pressure to attract meritorious students and the national publicity and credibility given to Georgia's HOPE grants by President Clinton and the U. S. Congress, other states have begun to join Georgia in creating or substantially expanding non-need-based student aid. Among these states are Kentucky, Maryland, Colorado, Florida, and Ohio.[66] Unfortunately for need-based student aid advocates, the trend toward merit-based vouchers could possibly supersede need-based programs in some states in a few years. This trend is also particularly disconcerting since additional funding for new merit-based student aid programs is often derived from lower-income families through state lottery revenues.

THE IMPACT OF STATE GRANTS ON PUBLIC AND PRIVATE INSTITUTIONS

In earlier debates between direct student aid advocates and institutional aid advocates, many public university officials expressed serious reservations about establishing direct student aid programs at the state and federal levels. Their concerns emanated from the fear that any philosophical shift in policy toward a voucher system in higher education would jeopardize public colleges and universities by creating an environment favoring higher cost institutions. After nearly three decades of state direct student aid policies and over 217 direct student aid grant programs, it is important to show the relative benefits derived by public and private institutions.

One fundamental difference between most state direct student aid programs and traditional institutional funding is that distinctions between public and private institutions are rare, with one important exception; cost variances are almost always factored into direct student aid formulas. In order to expand student choice in a system with dissimilar educational costs, aid formulas regularly grant students attending higher cost institutions a greater share of the available resources. As Figure 15.2 shows, students attending private institutions receive considerably more public taxpayer assistance through state direct student aid programs than do students attending public institutions. Public college and university students receive only

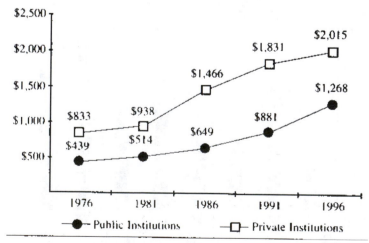

Figure 15.2 Average State Need-based Grant Program Awards to Students in Public & Private Institutions

Source: NASGAP Annual Survey

63 percent of the dollar awards received by students attending private institutions. This disparity has been consistent since the beginning of the student direct aid policies at the state level. In 1976–77, students in private institutions were awarded $394 more per student in state grants than those in public institutions. By 1995–96, private colleges received $747 more per student than did students in public institutions. During the last twenty years, states have done very little to address these disparities. In some cases, a number of states have only exacerbated these differences by creating or expanding grants labeled its "tuition equalization programs." These grant programs therefore tend to reward the highest cost institutions with the largest awards per student.

When comparing aggregate amounts of state direct student grants to public and private institutions during the same period, similar findings emerge. Data indicate that private institutions have traditionally garnered a disproportionate share. In 1995–96, private institutions received 45 percent of all grant dollars expended in state direct student aid programs even though they enrolled only 24 percent of all full-time students. This disparity between public and private student aggregate awards is not a recent development. Since the inception of state direct student grant programs, private college and university students have traditionally received over half of all direct student need-based grant funding. Only during the last five years have aggregate dollar awards for pri-

vate college students fallen from 50 percent to 45 percent of all direct grant dollar awards. Despite this recent decline however, data clearly show why private institutions continue to demand that state governments expand existing voucher programs and the "student choice" concept. Private institutions benefit indirectly through the disproportionate amount of public resources allocated to their students from these state policies.

This inequality and disproportionality is also magnified by the fact that enrollment of lower-income students,[67] as a percentage of freshman class, at private institutions has declined or stayed virtually the same since the inception of state grant programs. In fact, since the late 1975s state expenditures for direct student aid grant programs have increased significantly while lower-income enrollment as a percentage of the entering student population has not increased accordingly. As Figure 15.3 shows, lower-income freshman enrollment at private institutions, as a percentage of all entering freshman, has declined since the inception of the state direct aid programs. In 2-year private institutions, lower-income freshman enrollment, as a percent of all freshman, has declined from 35.2 percent in 1975 to 33.4 percent in 1996. A comparable result is true for private 4-year institutions which enroll virtually the same percentage of lower-income freshman as they did twenty-one years ago. The only modest increase in lower-income enrollment in the private sector was experienced by private universities which

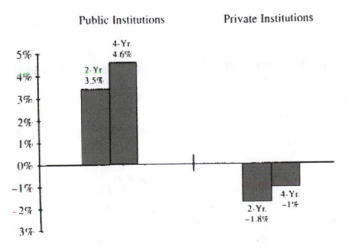

Figure 15.3 Percentage Point Change in Lower-Income Freshman as a Share of All Freshman Population, 1975–1996

Source: Calculated from data in *The American Freshman: National Norms for Fall 1975;* and *1996.*

increased from 10.2 percent in 1975 to 14 percent to 1996. Despite this increase, there was an over-all decline of 1 percent in private 4-year college enrollment of lower-income freshman.

Figure 15.3 also shows that both public 2-year and 4-year institutions experienced mod-erate gains in lower-income freshman atten-dance as a share of all entering freshman stu-dents. In public 2-year institutions, where lower-income enrollment is considerably higher than the 4-year campuses, lower-income enrollment expanded from 28.8 percent in 1975 to 32.3 percent in 1996. This increase is espe-cially significant because of the rapid expansion of enrollments in public 2-year institutions. Public 4-year institutions also made significant advances in the enrollment of lower-income students since the mid-1970s. Lower-income freshman enrollment, as a share of all entering freshman, increased by 4.6 percentage points constituting the largest gains in lower-income freshman participation. These data indicate that despite enrollment increases experienced in all public and private institutional sectors since the mid-1970s, substantive advances in lower-income student enrollment as a percentage of all entering freshman have been experienced only in public 2-year and 4-year colleges and universities.

CONCLUSION

The fate of the current voucher debate will greatly influence the governance and character of American education for decades. The political discussions are intense because the stakes are extremely high. For primary and secondary edu-cators concerned about the legal and fiscal rami-fications of supplying private schools with pub-lic money, the experiences of direct student aid policies in higher education advance a number of important lessons to be considered. After a quarter of a century of federal and state voucher systems in higher education, public colleges and universities find themselves shortchanged in funding. Initially, higher education vouchers, in the form of federal direct student aid, were justi-fied as a means to expand educational opportu-nity and to provide lower-income students with choices to obtain high quality education in pri-vate colleges. It was also justified as a way to indirectly support private colleges with public

resources. Today, growing disparities in expendi-tures per student continue to favor private higher education while lower-income student access to private institutions remains limited. This is occurring despite the fact that greater amounts of federal funds per student are now expended through direct student grants and subsidized loans for students in private colleges than for students in public institutions.

As the results presented in this paper show, state governments have followed federal policy directives in removing many legal barriers to providing aid to private institutions and creat-ing voucher schemes for financing higher edu-cation. In most states, the constitutionality of providing significant amounts of public funds to private and religious institutions through direct student aid is no longer a contested issue. Today, funding for state direct student aid pro-grams constitutes a growing proportion of all state funding for higher education. Even with means test methods designed to concentrate greater assistance on lower-income students, the voucher programs create disparities in favor of private institutions and correspondingly appear to contribute little to expanding educa-tional opportunities or choice. As greater pro-portions of state voucher programs also shift from need-based to merit-based aid, it may be anticipated that lower-income students may have further diminished opportunities.

These findings should not be surprising to many historians or voucher opponents because even Adam Smith foretold with substantial pre-science the expected effects of voucher or direct student aid programs over two hundred years ago by stating, "People of the same trade sel-dom meet together, even for merriment or diversion, but the conversation ends in a con-spiracy against the public, or in some con-trivance to raise prices."[68] The disparity issues that are inherent in the voucher scheme suggest that this form of financing, by its very nature, will generally result in greater inequality between public and private school students. If the experience in higher education is a valid indicator, then one can expect that voucher plans at lower educational levels will produce only marginal increases in choice for lower-income students while greatly increasing inequalities of revenue between public and pri-vate schools: In higher education, private col-lege students garner nearly twice as much direct student grant aid at the state level than public colleges, with little impact on the redistributional effects that choice is supposed to produce. As higher education demonstrates, the negative effects of inequality produced by vouchers will almost certainly outweigh the perceived positive effects of the choices promised by vouchers.

NOTES

1. See comments presented by Minnesota Governor Arnie Carleson and Wisconsin Governor Tommy Thompson at the 1997 National Conference of Republican Governors.
2. The College Board, 1997–98.
3. See the National Association of State Student Grant Aid and Aid Programs (NASSGAP), *27th Annual Survey Report, 1995–96 Academic Year* (Albany: New York State Higher Education Services Corporation, February 1996).
4. See J. J. Hanus, and P. Cookston, Jr. *Choosing Schools: Vouchers and American Higher Education* (Washington, D.C.: American University Press, 1996), 24–25; M. Gronseth, "Educational Vouchers," a report submitted to the Minnesota House of Representatives (Minneapolis: Government Research Department, December 1985): 1–2; J. Areen and C. Jencks, "Educational Vouchers: A Proposal for Diversity and Change," in *Educational Vouchers, Concepts, and Controversies,* ed. G. La Noue (New York: Teachers College Press, 1972), 49; S. Arons, "The Peaceful Uses of Education Vouchers," in *Educational Vouchers, Concepts, and Controversies,* ed. G. La Noue (New York: Teachers College Press, 1972), 71–72.
5. Peter Gay, *The Enlightenment, The Science of Freedom* (New York: W. W. Norton & Company, 1977), 364.
6. Ibid., 365.
7. Gay. *The Enlightenment,* 367.
8. Ibid.
9. Ellwood P Cubberley, *Public Education in the United States* (Boston: Houghton-Mifflin Co., 1934), 84–85.
10. Adam Smith, *Wealth of Nations,* Book V, cI., 1776. (New York: Random House, Inc. Modern Library Edition, 1937).
11. Cubberley, *Public Education in the United States,* 85.
12. Gay, *The Enlightenment,* 366–367.
13. A condillac's *Scientific Method* was published in 1749.
14. Ibid.
15. Smith, *Wealth of Nations,* 755.
16. Ibid., 764–765.
17. Thomas Paine, *Rights of Man,* in "Ways and Means of Improving the Condition of Europe, Interspersed with Miscellaneous Observations," London, February 9, 1972. (New York: Penguin Books, 1984), 245.
18. Paine, *Rights of Man,* 241.
19. Paine, *Rights of Man,* 87.
20. Ibid.
21. Ibid., 88.
22. Ellwood P. Cubberly, *Public Education in the United States* (Boston: Houghton Mifflin Company, 1934), 2; Eric Foner, *Introduction to Rights of Man* (New York: Penguin Books, 1984), 13.
23. Will and Ariel Durant, *The Age of Napoleon* (New York: Simon and Schuster, 1975), 127.
24. Jack Fruchtman, Jr., *Thomas Paine* (New York: Four Walls Eight Windows, 1994), 239.
25. Isser Woloch, *The New Regime, Transformations of the French Civic Order, 1789–1820* (New York: W. W. Norton & Company, 1994), 184.
26. Paine, *Rights of Man,* 245.
27. Incidentally, Paine was a member of the National Convention in France in 1793, when Condorcet's great plan for secular public schools was enacted.
28. John Stuart Mill, "On Liberty in Utilitarianism," in *On Liberty, Essay on Bentham,* ed. Mary Warnock (New York: Meridian Books, 1962), 238.
29. Ibid., 239.
30. Ibid.
31. Ibid.
32. Ibid., 239–240.
33. Ibid.
34. Ibid., 240–241.
35. Ibid., 165.
36. Ibid., 165.
37. Ibid., 166.
38. Ibid., 167–168.
39. *Everson v. Board of Education,* 330 U.S. 671 S. Ct. 504 (1947).
40. R. H. Tawney, "The Problem of the Public Schools," in *The Radical Tradition: Twelve Essays on Politics, Education, and Literature* (London: Allen & Unwin, 1964), 72; Workers' Educational Association, *The Public Schools and the Educational System* (London, 1943), 2, 180. See: John Lawson & Harold Silver, *As Social History of Education in England* (London: Methuen & Co., Ltd., 1973), 420.
41. R. Hofstadter, and W. Smith, *American Higher Education: A Documentary History,* Volume II (Chicago: The University of Chicago Press, 1961), 971.
42. S. K. Alexander and R. G. Salmon, *Public School Finance* (Needham Heights, Mass: Allyn and Bacon, 1995), 222.
43. See J. Witte, *First Year Report: The Milwaukee Parent Choice Program* (Madison: Wisconsin Department of Public Instruction, 1991); and J. Witte, "Who Benefits from the Milwaukee Choice Program," in *Who Chooses? Who Loses? Culture, Institutions, and the Unequal Effects of School Choice,* eds. B. Fuller and R. Elmore (New York: Teachers College Press, 1996).

44. L. E. Gladieux and T. R. Wolanin. *Colleges and the Congress: The National Politics of Higher Education* (Lexington, Mass: Lexington Books, 1976).

45. See J. C. Hearn, *The Paradox of Growth in Federal Aid for College Students, 1965–1990, Handbook of Theory and Research*, Vol. IX (New York: Agathon Press, 1993).

46. M. M. Chambers, *Higher Education: Who Pays? Who Gains?* (Danville, IL.: The Interstate Printers, 1968).

47. See T. Kane, "Lessons from the Largest School Voucher Program," in *Who Chooses? Who Loses? Culture, Institutions and the Unequal Effects of School Choice*, eds. B. Fuller and R. Elmore (New York: Teachers College Press, 1996). 173–186.

48. F. K. Alexander, "Private Institutions and Public Dollars: an Analysis of the Effects of Federal Direct Student Aid on Public and Private Institutions of Higher Education," *Journal of Education Finance* 23 (1998): 390–416.

49. The Middle Income Student Assistance Act (MISAA) expanded student accessibility to federal direct student aid programs.

50. See M. M. Chambers, *Financing Higher Education* (Washington, D.C.: The Center for Applied Research, Inc., 1963).

51. See "Child Benefit Theory," in *Cochran v. Louisiana Board of Education*, 281 U.S. 370 (1930); and Everson v. Board of Education, 330 U.S. 1 (1947): 17–18.

52. A. E. Howard, *State Aid to Private Higher Education* (Charlottesville: the Michie Company, 1977), 14–17.

53. Colorado Constitution, Article IX, 7.

54. *State ex rel. Rogers v. Swanson*, 192 Neb. 125, 219 N. W. 2d 726 (1974).

55. See *Harkness v. Patterson*, 179 S. E. 2d 907 (S.C. 1971).

56. *Hunt v. McNair*, 413 U.S. 734 (1973).

57. Howard, *State Aid to Private Higher Education*, 3–17.

58. Ibid., 16–17.

59. See *Lendall v. Cook*, 432 F. Supp. 971 (E.D. Ark., 1977); *Americans United for the Separation of Church and State v. Rogers*, 538 S. W. 2d 711 (Missouri, 1977); and *Americans United for the Separation of Church and State v. State of Colorado*, 648 P. 2d 1072 (Colorado, 1982).

60. See Tenn. Code Ann. 49–5013–5021.

61. See D. W. Breneman and C. E. Finn, *Public Policy and Private Higher Education* (Washington D. C.: The Brookings Institute, 1978), 50.

62. *Higher Education in the States*, vol. 5, no. 3 (Denver, CO: Education Commission of the States, 1976), 148. Only Utah, Hawaii, Arizona, Idaho, Montana, and Wyoming do not have any state initiated direct student aid programs. SSIG was not included as a state initiated program.

63. *National Association of States Student Grant and Aid Programs* 1980–81; 1985–86; 1990–91; and 1995–96 (Albany, N.Y.: State of New York Higher Education services Corporation).

64. Helping Outstanding Students Educationally (HOPE), Georgia Student Assistance Commission.

65. Since the initiation of Georgia's HOPE Scholarship Program in 1993, merit-based programmatic aid has accounted for 95 percent of all direct grant aid to Georgia.

66. Kentucky's HOPE Scholarship proposes to use lottery funds for student scholarships or grants to attend any accredited institution in the State of Kentucky. If passed, the maximum student award will equal the tuition costs of the most expensive public institution, the University of Kentucky. Maryland's HOPE Scholarship is not a need-based award, however, it does exclude students who come from families earning more than $60,000. The program goes into effect in 1998–99. Florida, Colorado, and Ohio have expanded public funds to existing merit-based programs during the last five years.

67. For the purposes of this study, students from families earning less than $10,000 in 1975 and $30,000 in 1996 were considered lower-income students.

68. See Gay, *The Enlightenment*, 366.

SECTION III

INSTITUTIONAL RESOURCES

INTRODUCTION

The articles relating to Institutional Resources are divided into three broad thematic areas: Tuition, Endowment/Investments, and New Ventures. Tuition is an institutional resource common to all institutions of higher education. While the percentage of an institution's budget may differ between the public and private sectors, tuition charges for both have been increasing at rates greater than that of inflation. At the same time, the percentage of revenue that public institutions receive from state and local governments has been decreasing. A third factor in the equation effecting tuition is the increase in student aid in the form of loans (as opposed to grants) from the federal and state governments. In "Tuition and Student Aid in Public Higher Education: Searching for an Organizing Principle," Stampen and Layzell discuss the approaches to financing higher education from low-tuition, low-aid through the high-tuition, high-aid approach. They argue that higher education must determine what is meant by high-quality education and what is the cost to produce it. On the matter of the relationship between the increasing availability of student loans and tuition rates, Hauptman ("Have Federal Loans Contributed to Higher Tuition?") and Balz ("Show Me the Data") suggest that there is no reliable evidence showing that undergraduate tuition has increased to capture more federal loan money.

The second institutional resource presented in this section is that of Endowment/Investment. The bull market of the 1990s has brought with it a substantial growth in endowment funds. This has resulted in the somewhat pleasant problem of developing and following a spending policy for the realized increase in revenue from this source. Tharp ("Growing the Endowment in a High-Risk Environment") presents the example of the strategies developed by Oberlin College for investment and spending in the current environment. He notes that increasing the endowment requires the management of the three interdependent factors of endowment: spending rates, investment policy, and fund-raising. Morrell ("Success in Investing: Integrating Spending Policy into Asset Allocation Strategy") addresses the issue of asset allocation strategies and notes that institutions should always be aware of the need to make periodic adjustments. Nahm and Zemsky ("The Role of Institutional Planning in Fund-Raising") deal with the always-perplexing issue in fund-raising of need-driven investments versus donor-driven gifts. They point out the importance of trustees becoming planning advocates if an institution is to be successful in fund-raising activities. Yoder ("Investing Planned Gifts: Proper Management Yields Big Dividends") discusses the investment of planned gifts to institutions of higher education. He identifies common administrative problems, factors focusing greater attention on planned gifts, and steps that can be followed for better investment.

With the rising costs of financing higher education, almost every type of institution is searching for "other" sources of income. Major research institutions have become quite active in the areas of technology transfer and the development of "spin-off" companies. Matkin's article ("Organizing University Economic Development: Lessons from Continuing Education and Technology Transfer") discusses technology transfer from the context of non-traditional, non-core functions of the institution, and how the institution is viewed by society. He argues that the more successfully an institution performs non-traditional functions, the more likely it is to retain its institutional identity. All types and sizes of institutions of higher education are also establishing retirement communities, particularly for alumni. The article by Horwitz and Rolett ("Retirement Communities: A Financially Rewarding Educational Approach") addresses the issues that institutions should consider before undertaking the establishment of retirement communities. Of particular note is the idea that, in addition to retirement communities being a direct source of revenue, the residents can also be a source for the development of planned giving. This section concludes with excerpts from a National Association of College and University Business Officers ("Athletics and Their Costs") report on college athletics. Debunking the popular myth that college sports are profitable, the report reveals that, in fact, the vast majority of institutional athletic programs lose money. By taking a much closer look at the financial realities of college athletics, this article also suggests a variety of strategies that institutions can follow to bring the costs of their sports programs under control.

Members of the Institutional Resources review panel were:

Arnold J. Gelfman, Brookdale Community College

Ernest Goeres, West Virginia University

William G. Laird, Carnegie Mellon University

John M. Lyons, University of Alabama at Birmingham

Thomas G. Zullo, University of Pittsburgh

CHAPTER 16

TUITION AND STUDENT AID IN PUBLIC HIGHER EDUCATION

Searching for an Organizing Principle

JACOB O. STAMPEN AND DANIEL T. LAYZELL

State and federal support for public colleges and universities is increasingly uncertain. The single largest funder of public higher education, state governments, accounted for 34 percent of the total current funding revenues of public institutions in fiscal year 1993, down from 43 percent in FY 1984 (U.S. Department of Education, 1996). The result has been increasing reliance on tuition and fee revenue to finance rising institutional costs. From 1980–81 through 1994–95, tuition at public four-year colleges and universities increased 234 percent, compared to an 82 percent increase in median household income, a commonly used indicator of families' ability to pay for college. Moreover, increases in federal grant aid failed to keep pace with increases in tuition. A 1995 annual survey of college freshmen found that 71 percent of the respondents, a thirty-year high, worried that they might not be able to pay for the schooling required for their careers (Astin, Korn, Mahoney, and Sax, 1995).

Still another challenge is the increasing market competition in higher education as new for-profit educational providers move into place alongside traditional public and private colleges and universities (University of Pennsylvania, 1996). Emergence of for-profit institutions and establishment of corporate universities signal a shift in general confidence away from public higher education at a time when rising costs are of paramount concern. These forces lead some observers to suggest that higher education is moving from a "producer-dominated" market to a "consumer-dominated" market where students, not institutions themselves, determine who will survive (Mingle, 1996).

Paradoxically, there are few indications that public higher education is becoming less important. Roughly two of every three four-year college students are enrolled in public institutions. When two-year institutions are added, the public share rises to eight out of ten students in postsecondary education. Those who graduate do well. The earnings advantages of four-year college graduates over nongraduates increased dramatically in recent years. A baccalaureate recipient "in 1980 earned about 43 percent more per hour than a person with a high school diploma. By 1994, this earnings advantage had increased to 73 percent" (U.S. General Accounting Office, 1996, p. 14). At the same time, the individual return on investment in a college degree is at a record high. After slipping to single digits in the 1970s, the college diploma earns an annual return (after accounting for inflation) of 13–14 percent on its cost (Lee and Rosh, 1996). The returns for public college students are even higher because these figures also include the cost of attendance at private institutions. Finally, young four-year college graduates are also three times more likely to be

Source: *New Directions for Institutional Resarch*, no. 95, Fall 1997. © Jossey-Bass Publishers.

employed than high school graduates of the same age (Becker, 1992; Lee and Rosh, 1996). Collectively, these factors would seem to bode well for public higher education. Still, the public is restive.

Why have tuition rates increased beyond the public's perception of what higher education ought to cost? According to one source, "in recent years many states and public institutions appear to have allowed tuition rates to increase in excess of the principles and guidelines written into existing policy, and to jump ahead of public perceptions of what higher education ought to cost. The result not only undermines these policies but puts public support and understanding as well as students' ability and willingness to pay at risk" (Lenth, 1993, p. 1).

Numerous explanations are offered for rising college costs. These include weakened state support for higher education because of such competing priorities as prisons, K-12 education, welfare, and Medicare; increasing involvement in the state funding debates on the part of special interest groups not always supportive of education (Fenske, Besnette, and Jordan, 1996); and more dependence on federal student aid (Fenske, 1997). Hearn, Griswold, and Marine (1996) add that although there has been an overall rise in tuition prices, there are many inconsistencies that can be explained by regional differences, state population size (only for student aid), economic development, public-private higher education mix, and state planning agencies. Whatever the causes, state and public higher education decision makers have increasingly distanced themselves from the traditional low-tuition philosophy. At the same time, they have not adopted the high-tuition, high-aid approach, nor any other.

This chapter explores the interplay between tuition and student aid policies and public higher education during a period that begins immediately before the War on Poverty and ends at the foot of the "bridge to the twenty-first century." Specifically, we are curious about the impacts of these policies on (1) quality and access to public two-year and four-year colleges and funding for instruction, (2) satisfaction with public higher education among policy makers and the public, and (3)

the technical and political feasibility of continuing present arrangements. We begin by briefly sketching the recent history of government efforts to expand access to public higher education. Then we review trend data on enrollment and expenditures for tuition, student aid, and instruction in public two-year and four-year colleges and universities. We conclude with a discussion of alternative paths to greater quality and access in public higher education.

All financial data reported here are expressed in constant 1995 dollars, calculated by multiplying current-year dollars by the 1995 Consumer Price Index and dividing by the current-year CPI. Specifically, Figures 16.1 through 16.3 draw on the *Higher Education Finance Data Bases: 1890–1995*, which is compose of data reported in the federal *Digest of Educational Statistics*, *The Projection of Educational Statistics*, the College Board's *Trends in Student Aid*, and earlier governmental and private databases (Stampen, Hansen, and Luebke, work in progress). Analysts seeking a longitudinal view of higher education developments have often had their hopes frustrated by gaps in collected data, frequent changes in definitions of key variables, and missing information. The *Higher Education Finance Data Bases* is a work in progress that monitors changes in federal definitions of key data elements, extends time series by estimating data for missing years; and uses the results of important government and nongovernment surveys to estimate missing variables. The institutional database begins in 1890 and extends to 1995. A separate student aid database covers the years between 1945 and 1995.[1]

SYSTEMWIDE CHANGE: THE EMERGENCE OF FEDERAL STUDENT AID

Earlier, we traced the expansion of student aid awarded on the basis of demonstrated financial need, thereby setting the stage for exploring national longitudinal data for clues about how to assess policies affecting public higher education. Specifically, we are searching for a set of criteria that institutional researchers can use to evaluate current and future financing alternatives.

Enrollment Growth

Several well-documented factors foreshadowed the growth in enrollment explicated in Linsley's chapter, including the invasion of campuses by members of the baby boom generation, state-funded expansion of instructional capacity in public institutions, rising demand for access among nontraditional consumers (women, minorities, and older adults), the growth in federal need-based grant and loan programs after 1972, growing high school graduating classes (until 1980), and a sharply increasing rate of return on individual investment in higher education. Although it is risky to single out any one of these factors as causal, it is interesting that the rapid growth in the early years and slower growth later roughly parallels changes in policy makers' perceptions of the value of higher education. Previous research is not entirely clear about who benefited from student aid and the other War on Poverty initiatives during this time, but it is evident that overall enrollment increased rapidly at the same time that these initiatives were at their maximum force. A backlash began to build against federal student aid following the 1980 election of Ronald Reagan, whose campaign was sharply critical of the nation's "liberal" education establishment. The *Nation at Risk* report (National Commission on Excellence in Education, 1983) is an example of this criticism. After Reagan's election, one of the first acts of Congress was to vote a ceiling on the growth of student aid (Stampen and Reeves, 1986). At the same time, the new administration, especially its outspoken Secretary of Education William Bennett, exhorted schools and colleges to shift their attention away from student aid and to raise academic standards. As far as the federal government was concerned, higher education needed reform more than new money.

The federal and state governments responded to a weakening economy by becoming more concerned about the quality of the workforce and the nation's competitive position. This in turn made expanded investment in student aid less feasible politically, because it was blamed for eroding academic standards. The continued growth in enrollments in the 1980s appeared mainly to be due to the rising rate of return on individual investments in higher education, not so much because college graduates were more in demand but because there was less work for people without higher education. For example, Murphy and Welch found that between 1979 and 1986 "the rise in the college premium for less-experienced workers was generated by a decline in the real wage for high school graduates of 15.7 percent and a rise in the real wage of college graduates of 8.5 percent" (1992, p. 128).

Students Pay for More Than Instruction

Some data suggest that tuition is rising because the cost of instruction at colleges and universities is rising even faster. For example, a recent GAO study found that "in terms of expenditures per student, school spending for instruction was the largest single factor contributing to the increase in college expenditures from the school year 1980–81 through 1993–94" (U.S. General Accounting Office, 1996, p. 29). Figure 16.1 compares average tuition, room, and board (TRB) expenses with expenditures for instruction per full-time-equivalent (FTE) student and shows that the accuracy of this finding is related to the point in time when it is assessed.

The GAO finding is supported only if we compare expenditures for instruction in 1980 and 1993: real dollar expenditures increased by roughly 30 percent in constant 1995 dollars (from $3,587 to $4,655). However, a different understanding emerges from a longer view. Specifically, expenditures for instruction have fluctuated over the past thirty-five years within a fairly narrow range above $4,000 per FTE. In 1980, the year the GAO began its comparison, expenditures were atypically low because of factors associated with unanticipated inflation. Actually, support for instruction in public higher education has been quite flat for several decades.

Still another impression emerges if we expand the definition of instruction to include other costs related to instruction. There are important differences between instruction expenditures and instruction-related (I-R) expenditures. Instruction is annually reported by the U.S. Department of Education (1996) under the heading of "instruction and departmental research." Specifically, *instruction* refers to faculty pay for activities that are included in the normal workload of most college faculty and a modest amount of time for teaching-related research. Hence, this category essentially includes salaries and fringe benefits for faculty.

The term *instruction-related* requires some explanation. In earlier years, the statistic most often used in place of I-R to represent instruction-related expenditures was educational and general expenses (E&G), which continues to be reported annually by the U.S. Department of Education. However, E&G has been criticized because it includes expenditures for research, scholarships and fellowships, operation of the physical plant, and other factors that are only tangentially related to instruction activities. I-R, on the other hand, combines several subcategories of expenditures that are more closely related to instruction. In addition to expenditures for instruction, I-R includes expenditures for "academic support," including libraries, student services, public service (a form of instruction), institutional support (academic administration), mandatory transfers from scholarships and fellowships (that is, money the institution can allocate to instruction-related activities). Finally, I-R includes inde-

pendent operations, funds used to pay for substitutes for faculty doing research for federally funded research and development centers (Hansen and Stampen, work in progress).

When we compare expenditures for instruction and I-R since 1960, we see the latter rising somewhat faster than the former. Most striking is the decline of instruction as a fraction of I-R expenditures, from 67 percent in 1960 to 56 percent in 1995. By 1995, slightly more than half of every dollar invested in I-R was spent on instruction. Most of the difference is explained by the increasing cost of administration, which some argue is attributable to the existing compliance-driven government accountability system (Bergman, 1991).

Figure 16.1 also enables us to compare the amounts students and their families pay to attend public colleges without considering student aid, and how much society directly pays for instruction. In 1960, expenditures for instruction and average TRB were nearly equal. Since then, however, TRB has increased faster than expenditure for instruction, which suggests that either the instruction has become more efficient or students are simply paying more.

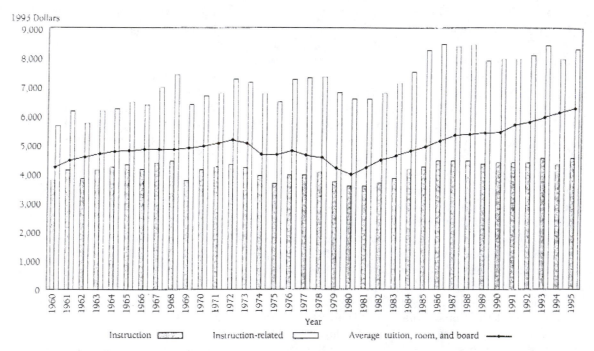

Figure 16.1 Public Higher Education Expenditures for Instruction and Instruction-Related Costs per FTE Student; and Average Tuition, Room, and Board Expenses

Source: Stampen, Hansen, and Leubke, work in progress.

Student Aid Exceeds Tuition Revenue

Perhaps the most surprising news (Figure 16.2) is that investment in student aid exceeds revenue from tuition. In addition to paying for the classrooms, society also appears to provide enough student aid to more than cover the cost of tuition. Tuition is, of course, only one price component of college cost. Need-based grants and loans also are intended to help students who cannot afford the cost of room, board, books, and other educational expenses. When we compare student aid with the latter, we see a widening gap after 1980. However, Figure 16.2 is somewhat misleading because most public college students do not receive student aid. For example, in 1992–93, 46 percent of the students at public universities received some form of financial aid (need-based and not). At public two-year colleges, only 27 percent received any aid (Tuma and Malizio, 1995). Nevertheless, showing the average amount of aid per FTE student gives the reader a sense of the magnitude of investment in student aid to compare with what students pay for tuition and the total cost of attendance.

Figure 16.2 also shows how sensitive tuition and student aid levels are to changes in political priorities. In 1960, federal student aid, which was mainly composed of veterans benefits, equaled roughly one-third the amount of tuition, room, and board and was playing a diminishing role in financing access even though the overall cost of college attendance was gradually rising. President Johnson's War on Poverty began in 1964 at the low ebb when student aid was only one-eighth of TRB. Bipartisan support for eliminating college attendance barriers through federal investment in need-based student aid increased after the beginning of the War on Poverty, through the Nixon-Ford era and into the Carter administration. During this period, public tuition either remained stable or declined. After that, investment in student aid rose to slightly over half of TRB in 1975, and then plateaued until 1980. Since 1980, the ratio of TRB to aid per student has fluctuated around two to one (U.S. Department of Education, 1996).

The downward slope in federal student aid during the 1960s reflects declining veterans benefits after the Korean War, followed by the rapid expansion of need-based aid in the

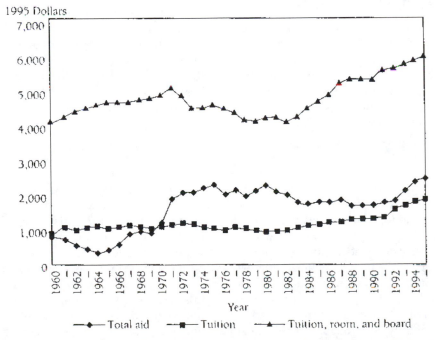

Figure 16.2 Average Tuition; Tuition, Room, and Board; and Student Aid per FTE Student

Source: Stampen, Hansen, and Leubke, work in progress.

late 1960s and early 1970s. Student aid flattened after 1975 due to the phasing out or downsizing of large categorical programs such as a $1 billion decline in post-Vietnam veterans benefits and an even larger reduction from the phasing out of the Social Security Education Benefits program for dependents of injured or deceased workers (Stampen, Hansen, and Luebke, work in progress).

After 1980, politics placed downward pressure on federal need-based student aid and state tuition subsidies. Tuition rose and student aid fell. Reagan's 1980 election campaign argued that the federal government had no authority from the U.S. Constitution to finance higher education. For this reason, the president called for transferring funding for federal student aid programs to the states. Others criticized student aid for not substantially increasing the enrollment of low-income and minority students, while still others attacked the exclusion of middle-income students. But instead of falling, enrollment in public higher education leveled off for several years (around 1975 to 1985) before gradually turning upward again. Since the election of President Clinton in 1992, tuition and student aid have risen together.

The Increasing Importance of Loans

Figure 16.3 shows that the volume of need-based grants (federal and state) was almost negligible until 1967. Grants peaked at about 16 percent of total aid awarded in 1980 and then stayed at a constant level of about 12 percent between 1982 and the present. The space between the bottom lines in the figure shows the volume of need-based loans (that is, the remainder after subtracting grants, loans, and the very small College Work Study program). Loans have exceeded grants since 1980 by a widening margin, particularly in the 1990s. Finally, the space between the top lines shows that the volume of grants and loans awarded without regard to demonstrated need (for example, aid for veterans, Social Security beneficiaries, health care professionals, and so forth) has dramatically decreased since 1980, in part because of the phasing down of categorical programs.

In 1995, roughly 50 percent of available aid per student ($1,321) was in the form of loans, and about 30 percent ($751) in need-based

grants. Fully 20 percent ($519) was nonneed-based grants. Even if both types of grants are combined, the volume of loans still would exceed the volume of grants. Need-based grants account for only a small share of the total aid necessary to compensate low-income students for the recent rise in tuition. Moreover, given the current political mood, it seems unlikely that Congress will substantially increase the proportion of aid in the form of grants. Hence, even though investment in student aid continues to exceed tuition revenue, the percentage of aid in the form of need-based loans continues to increase while the percentage in the form of need-based grants decreases. This is especially disturbing since students from low-income backgrounds may be particularly reluctant to assume substantial debt. It is also noteworthy that investment in need-based grants on a per-FTE-student basis is not much greater than investment in nonneed-based grants.

Growing Concerns About Access and Quality.

The composition of student aid appears to support Mumpher's assessment (1996) of the effects of student aid policy on access over the past three decades: the availability of loans for middle-income and upper-income students assures them of a choice of colleges, but grant aid is insufficient to ensure access for the low-income students for whom student aid was originally intended. The above data also raise questions about quality. What students and their families now pay for in tuition, room, and board exceeds what institutions spend directly on instruction. This means they are paying for increasing percentages of administrative overhead and support services. But even if much more is spent on instruction, how do we know whether it is adequate? To a surprising extent, any means of determining how much it costs to produce a high-quality education has largely been ignored. In part, this is a legacy of the philosophy of student aid, in whose heyday it was widely assumed that all forms of postsecondary education were of more or less equal quality and that the only barrier to access was financial. It is also in part a consequence of the politically driven accountability system that demands compliance with constantly shifting political mandates rather than evidence of long-term effectiveness.

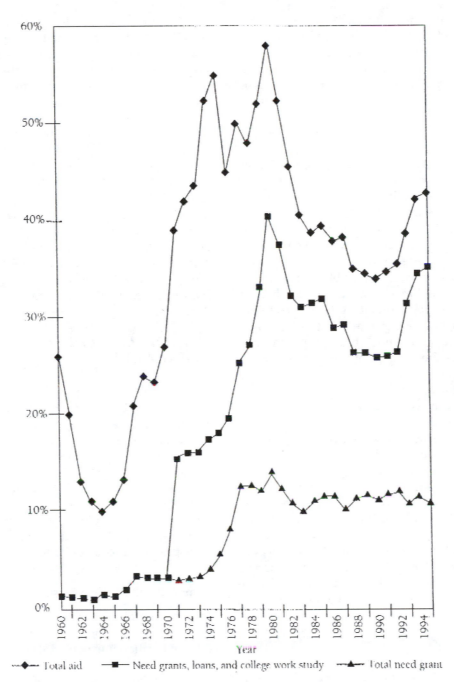

Figure 16.3 Need and Nonneed Grants, Loans, and Work Study per FTE Student as a Percentage of Average Tuition, Room, and Board Charges

WHERE DOES ALL THIS LEAD US?

Experienced observers of higher education finance are well aware of the cyclical nature of funding for colleges and universities. For example, there is some evidence that the most recent downturn in state funding for higher education is stabilizing, if not reversing in many states. However, the difference now is that there are some structural changes taking place both externally and internally to higher education that indicate a return to business-as-usual is not likely. Policy makers and the public are demanding more evidence of student achievement and institutional efficiency before they provide additional resources. The new questions are: Can higher education accomplish more learning with less money? Is access, in and of itself, necessarily a good thing? What do students receive in return for their tuition dollars? What do state and federal governments receive in return for the subsidies they provide?

Increasingly, quality and access are measured not by traditional inputs (for example, high levels of institutional funding versus a broad-based student body) but rather by the return on investment to the individual. In other words, quality and access, which were seen as opposing priorities, now appear to be closely connected. Consequently, public higher education needs an organizing principle that can effectively support financing both quality and access. Such an effort is needed now because neither the old nor the proposed new approaches are capable by themselves of providing the necessary support to ensure the health of the enterprise.

What can we learn from previous experience that helps define a new organizing principle for financing public higher education? We believe that there are three main lessons. First, any policy or set of policies needs to be both technically coherent and politically feasible. That is, policy or policies must be relatively easy to communicate with broad constituencies, must take into account both the multiple sources of funding for public higher education and the cost of providing instruction, and must also set sustainable limits on costs to taxpayers. A $50 billion national loan bank, or for that matter any other new high-cost solution, is not going to win enough support to be implemented.

Second, policy must support both quality *and* access. It makes no sense to view support for institutions and student aid programs separately, because the goals of each are intertwined. The effectiveness of need-based student aid programs depends on the quality of instruction received by all students. This was articulated in the Higher Education Amendments of 1992, where "institutional quality" was introduced as a criterion for institutional eligibility to participate in federal student aid programs.

The third lesson is that there must be some sense of long-term accountability built into policy. Increasing competition from other sectors of government for tax dollars implies that policy makers will increasingly demand some evidence of return on their investment in higher education. In other words, how do we develop methods to identify institutions that are adding high value to their students so that other institutions can emulate their practices? Such methods would ensure that everyone might know what it costs to produce high-quality education. Below, we use three criteria to evaluate alternative policy options for financing public higher education: Is the policy technically coherent and politically feasible? Does it support both quality and access? And is there a built-in accountability mechanism?

THE LOW-TUITION, LOW-AID ALTERNATIVE

This policy approach is based on keeping tuition as low as possible by providing all governmental subsidies to institutions. The need for student aid is dramatically reduced under this alternative because tuition is set well below the cost of instruction. This was the alternative under which the original California master plan and the City University of New York were developed. The University of Wisconsin, for example, established tuition rates at 20 percent of instructional costs until the late 1960s.

Technical and Political Feasibility

In this alternative, society pays for instruction and parents pay for room, board, books, and other educational expenses. The net impact on the taxpayer might not be much different than now since the increased cost of the instructional subsidy would be somewhat offset by reduced need for student aid. However, it is highly unlikely that this alternative would receive wide support, given the amount and increasing proportion of institutional revenues made up by tuition and fees at public institutions ($20.8 billion in FY 1994; *Digest of Educational Statistics,* 1996, Table 319). Also, removing students who vary greatly in their ability to pay as an important source of financial support for instruction would make institutions more dependent on state instructional subsidies that may be inadequate to support high-quality instruction. In addition, moving toward low tuition would very likely be opposed by advocates of private higher education, who would see the move as a threat to their competitive position.

Promoting Quality and Access

Clearly, this policy promotes access by keeping tuition low. However, the value of access depends on whether the subsidies received by the institutions are adequate to meet the costs of providing high-quality instruction and actually are spent on instruction.

Accountability Mechanism

Based on the large investment required by taxpayers to maintain a "low tuition" policy, institutions would have a significant incentive to demonstrate accountability to policy makers and the public, or risk losing funds. However, since policy makers have only a hazy understanding of how high-quality instruction is produced, let alone what it costs, there is little direct incentive for institutions to demonstrate accountability for student learning.

THE HIGH-TUITION, HIGH-AID ALTERNATIVE

This alternative takes the exact opposite approach from the low-tuition model by providing the majority of the governmental subsidy directly to the individual student instead of the institution. As such, tuition rates are significantly higher and much more reflective of the actual cost of providing instruction. Subsidies are provided to students in the form of need-based aid. Under this alternative, institutions then would recycle a proportion of increased revenues to institutional need-based aid. This is a variant of a "voucher" system, wherein all students are provided with a set level of funding and are allowed to apply it to the institution of their choice.

Technical Coherence and Political Feasibility

This model is often viewed by economists as technically superior to the low-aid approach because it adjusts subsidies to the individual student's *ability to pay* the cost of instruction. Students from higher socioeconomic backgrounds receive less subsidy than poorer students because they have more personal resources at their disposal. In short, the subsidy is applied more "efficiently." However, Congress and the state legislatures have been, and are likely to remain, unwilling to fund need-based student aid on a scale large enough to make this model work. State initiatives aimed in this direction have not been successful. For example, public institutions in Vermont recently attempted to apply this approach, but downswings in the state economy and the level of federal student aid undermined its effectiveness (Lenth, 1993). In addition, it seems highly unlikely that state policy makers would warmly embrace a policy that requires both reallocation of existing institutional base budgets to student aid programs *and* raising tuition rates.

Promoting Access and Quality

The extent to which access would be promoted under this model is unclear. Access would advance if the subsidies received by students at different socioeconomic levels to augment personal resources were sufficient to overcome the present financial barriers they face. However, this cannot happen if resources are insufficient (as was the case in Vermont). It is also unclear that quality would advance. Conventional wisdom predicts that competition among public institutions for students and their subsidies also promotes quality. However, private institutions have always operated in this manner, and increasingly public institutions are doing the same. There is little evidence that any changes have produced quality.

Accountability Mechanism

Clearly, under the high-tuition, high-aid alternative institutions become more directly accountable to their students than to society. Sometimes accountability to students and society are synonymous, as when graduates acquire desired knowledge, skills, and wisdom within a reasonable period of time, find jobs, or are able to gain access to additional study. At other times, students may only be exposed to (at best mediocre) courses in more or less exclusive surroundings; students may enjoy it, but society may not be well served. In terms of accountability, the problem with the high-tuition, high-aid approach is essentially the same as that with the low-tuition approach: there is no direct connection between the method of financing and the duality of learning.

THE TAX INCENTIVE ALTERNATIVE

Under this model, state and federal governments allow individuals to deduct a certain amount from their personal income taxes for college expenses. An example of this is President Clinton's Hope Scholarship proposal to allow deductions of $1,400 for tuition and up to $10,000 for educational expenses.

Technical Coherence and Political Feasibility

This approach, while politically attractive, fails on two fronts. First, there is no direct connection to the cost of instruction or other sources of public college and university funding. Second, any new tax deduction means a loss of tax revenue with which to support government programs. This is not an insignificant issue when the competition for tax revenues and public concern over existing tax burdens are both becoming more intense.

Promoting Access and Quality

Targeted deductions are primarily a middle-class issue. Individuals on the low end of the income scale would realize little benefit from this approach. Institutional quality becomes a non-issue as well. Thus, access and quality are neither promoted nor hurt under this scenario.

Accountability Mechanism

Because no direct link leads to overall financing of public higher education, accountability is neither encouraged or disencouraged.

TUITION AND STUDENT AID BASED ON COST OF QUALITY

Under this model, institutions qualify for tuition subsidies and participation in federal student aid programs in part because their students are making good academic progress. Also, faculty and administrators use sound practices to supporting teaching and learning (that is, practices documented by competent research). Through standard accrediting and budgetary processes, state and federal sponsors would consider whether the collective efforts of individual institutions succeed in adding value to students. Institutions with credible evidence of effectiveness would be first in line for support. Other institutions would be lower in the pecking order or under mandate to shore up weak aspects of their operations. The role of institutional research would be to continuously analyze institutional operations and to facilitate adding value to students and other "customers of learning."

Obstacles to adopting the new approach include lack of consensus about the meaning of quality learning and generalized fear of government intrusion. However, we need not resolve all controversies about teaching and learning to develop reasonably good predictors of institutional effectiveness. Improvement efforts can draw on extensive research literatures covering key aspects of institutional quality, including institutional research and analysis (Ewell, 1989), teaching and learning, and student success and persistence (Pascarella and Terenzini, 1991; Cabrera, Castaneda, Nora, and Hengstler, 1992; Tinto, 1995). Moreover, tuition subsidies and eligibility to participate in student aid programs are already contingent on accreditation and budgetary standards. The difference between the new approach and the existing ones is that the latter are input-driven, whereas the former depends on knowing what satisfactory outputs are and how to achieve them.

What we do not yet know is what it costs to provide higher education that produces highly satisfactory outputs. But we may soon find out. Pilot testing is underway for opening the federally sponsored Malcolm Baldrige Award for Quality to educational institutions. Although institutions need not follow any set approach, competitors must display strength in seven categories of activity: institutional leadership, information and analysis, strategic and operational planning, human resource development and management, educational and business process management, institutional performance results, and student focus and student and stakeholder satisfaction. Colleges and universities that have already begun to explore what it takes to score well on "the Baldrige" represent the major institutional categories; examples include public two-year colleges (Delaware County Community College, Maricopa Community College), public four-year institutions (Truman State University, University of Minnesota at Duluth), research universities (Pennsylvania State University), and private nonprofit institutions (Alverno College, Samford University). Seymour and Associates (1996) extensively discuss their experiences in applying these standards and offer a critique of the Baldrige standards themselves.

The operating and instructional costs of the winners of the Baldrige competition offer initial estimates of the cost of quality, which we could improve over time either in connection with the Baldrige or through other arrangements. Whatever quality costs, tuition at public institutions could remain set at 20–30 percent of the cost of instruction as it already is in most states. Need-based student aid could also remain linked to the tuition rate to ensure equitable access. State appropriations could fill the remaining difference between the cost of instruction and tuition. As Lenth (1993) observes, "state policies generally attempt to take the total cost of education into account in setting tuition rates but do this in very inconsistent ways" (p. 11). Knowing what quality costs and what else besides money is required to produce it could add consistency. The key is to have a clear understanding of how to establish combinations of costs and institutional behaviors that produce desired levels of learning.

Technical Coherence and Political Feasibility

This approach is technically coherent in that it recognizes the cost of providing a combination of high-quality instruction and appropriate student aid. It is pragmatic in that it would require only adjustments at the margins of the policies already in place to most states.

Promoting Access and Quality

The cost-of-quality approach would not damage current levels of access to public higher education and would likely improve it by better aligning tuition and student aid with the cost of instruction. Quality is also promoted under this model, assuming that the total dollar amount received by the institution is sufficient to meet its true costs.

Accountability Mechanism

Accountability is present within this model from both efficiency and effectiveness viewpoints. Since tuition and student aid are linked to the cost of instruction, institutions would he expected to demonstrate to both policy makers and students that they are doing what they can to operate efficiently. From the standpoint of demonstrating effectiveness, institutions would be expected to show that societal and individual investments in higher education provide a reasonable return. The success of this policy alternative, of course, depends on identifying effective and reasonably efficient public institutions and using them as models for estimating costs, while facing the political realities of excluding those institutions deemed to be deficient.

IMPLICATIONS FOR INSTITUTIONAL RESEARCH

A real strength of public higher education in the United States is the wide variety and choice it presents. This diversity extends to the issues of tuition and student aid policies. Setting tuition for public higher education among the states ranges from a highly centralized activity (requiring legislative approval) to highly decentralized (institutions having full authority to set tuition). Likewise, programs to set student aid policy vary from relatively large and well integrated to small and insignificant. Also, some states allow (or require) their institutions to set aside a portion of tuition revenue for student aid, while other states do not.

It would be naïve to suggest that there is any simple, all-encompassing solution to the challenges the current array of tuition and student aid issues pose for public higher education. Each institution and state has its own unique set of historical traditions, political factors, and legal parameters within which tuition and student aid policy must be forged. What we try to present, however, are some basic criteria that can be employed in evaluating any pol-

TABLE 16.1
Evaluation of Policy Alternatives

Policy Alternative	Quality	Access	Accountability	Feasibility
Low tuition, low aid	Mixed	Positive	Mixed	Negative
High tuition, high aid	Mixed	Mixed	Negative	Negative
Tax and savings incentives	Mixed	Negative	Negative	Mixed
Cost-of-quality-based tuition and aid	Positive	Positive	Positive	Positive

icy option (Table 16.1). Institutional researchers can play a significant role in both identifying potential policy alternatives and providing objective analyses for decision makers concerning the viability of the alternatives. Current policy discussions on tuition and student aid are flush with anecdotes and poorly reasoned solutions. What is sorely needed is a well-thought-out proposal for reforming financing that meets the long-term needs of individual students and society. Specifically, how do colleges and universities add value to students' learning experiences, and how can we develop standard methods for determining whether an institution is good enough in terms of both quality and access to warrant investment in it?

Institutional research has a critically important role in promoting interinstitutional and intrainstitutional collaboration across a wide range of issues. Individual colleges and universities often find it difficult to describe the quality of the educational services they provide, and governments often cite this as a reason for eroding support. Institutional researchers might respond by identifying what is different about institutions whose students do better than others serving similar clientele. Here, correlations between expenditures and student performance are needed. Exploring interactions among various approaches to the teaching-and-learning equation and instructional costs could be very illuminating.

Public colleges enroll the vast majority of students from low-income backgrounds, and research tells us a great deal about the problems they face. Yet we do not know enough about low-income students who succeed. Analysis of their experiences might assist institutional leaders in doing better. This is particularly needed at a time when many public institutions are beginning to behave like their counterparts in the private sector by recycling tuition income to offer targeted aid. It is important to know the extent of such practices and whether they serve students and public policy.

NOTE

1. Copies of the working versions of the Higher Education Financial Data Bases are available from Jacob Stampen.

REFERENCES

Astin, A. W., Korn, W. S., Mahoney, K. M., & Sax, L. J. (1995). *The American freshman: National norms for fall 1995.* Los Angeles: Cooperative Institutional Research Program, American Council on Education, and University of California.

Becker, W. E. (1992). Why go to college? The value of an investment in Higher Education. In W. E. Becker & D. R. Lewis (eds.), *The economics of American higher education.* Boston: Kluwer.

Bergman, B. R. (1991). Bloated administration, blighted campuses. *Academe, 77* (6), 12–16.

Cabrera, A .F., Castaneda, M. B., Nora, A., & Hengstler, D. (1992). The convergence between two theories of college persistence. *Journal of higher education, 63* (2), 143–164.

Ewell, P. T. (1989). *Enhancing information use in decision making.* New Directions for Institutional Research, no. 64. San Francisco: Jossey-Bass.

Fenske, R. H. (1994). A brief primer on student financial aid. *Report of the commission on student costs and financial assistance.* Phoenix: Arizona Board of Regents.

Fenske, R. H., Besnette, F. H., & Jordan, S. M. (1997). The process of setting tuition in public university systems: A case study of interaction between governing board and campus management. In A. Hoffman (ed.), *Managing colleges and universities: Issues for leadership.* Maryville, Mo.: Prescott.

Hansen, W. L., & Stampen, J. O. (Work in progress). *Balancing quality and access in the financing of higher education.*

Hearn, J., Griswold, C., & Marine, G. (1996). Region, resources, and reason: A contextual analysis of state tuition and student aid policies. *Research in higher education, 37* (3), 241–278.

Lee, S., & Rosh, D. Nov. 18, 1996). Educonomics. *Forbes*, p. 112.

Lenth, C. S. (1993). *The tuition dilemma: State policies and practices in pricing public higher education*. Denver: State Higher Education Executive Officers.

Mingle, J. (Sept. 1996). Remarks made at the University of Wisconsin System Institutional Research Conference, Madison.

Mumpher, M. (1996). *Removing college price barriers: What government has done and why it hasn't worked*. Albany: State University of New York Press.

Murphy, K. M., & Welch, F. (1992). Wages of college graduates. In W. E. Becker & D. R. Lewis (eds.), *Economics of American higher education*. Boston: Kluwer.

National Commission on Excellence in Education. (April, 1983). *A nation at risk: The imperative for educational reform*. Washington, D.C.: U.S. Government Printing Office.

Pascarella, E. T., & Terenzini, P .T. (1991). *How college affects students: Findings and insights from twenty years of research*. San Francisco: Jossey-Bass.

Seymour & Associates. (1996). *High performing colleges: The Malcolm Baldrige national quality award as a framework for improving higher education*. Maryville, Mo.: Prescott.

Stampen, J. O., Hansen, W. E., & Luebke, R. H. (Work in progress). Higher education finance data base: 1890–1995. Machine readable data file. Madison, Wis.: Department of Educational Administration.

CHAPTER 17

HAVE FEDERAL LOANS CONTRIBUTED TO HIGHER TUITION?

ARTHUR M. HAUPTMAN

Congress established the national commission on the Cost of Higher Education in 1997 to investigate the growth in college costs and to suggest what, if anything, the federal government should do about it. Under the auspices of the Council on Aid to Education, I wrote a report to the commission with Cathy Krop, a researcher with the RAND Corporation, that examined the relationship between college costs and federal student aid. We reached two conclusions:

- The ready and growing availability of federally sponsored loans has been a key factor in the rapid growth of college tuition and other charges over the past two decades—a period when tuition has increased at roughly twice the rate of inflation.

- Federal grant aid has played a less substantial role in growth of college tuition than loans, in large part because grants now provide far less financing than loans.

Our report also makes a very controversial recommendation we think might help moderate tuition increases in the long run: In determining a student's eligibility for subsidized loans, the federal government should recognize only a portion of a student's costs of attendance. This would replace its current policy, which subsidizes student borrowers up to the full costs of attendance. In addition, we suggest there should be an overall limit on the amount of federal aid students may receive in any year.

In its final report, the National Commission essentially ignored the relationship between student loans and college tuition, relegating our report to an obscure footnote. Skeptical commission members and other critics make the following two arguments for not addressing this issue. First, they say no empirical evidence exists that proves loans contribute to college cost increases or that college officials are using federal student-aid programs to gouge the public. And second, even if federal loans have contributed to tuition increases, there is nothing short of price controls that the federal government can do to address this issue.

To set the record straight, our report does not argue that federal loans are the principal cause of tuition inflation, nor does it argue for federal price controls of colleges. Quite the contrary. Many other factors are more important in determining tuition levels, and federal price controls are a bad idea and unlikely to work.

Source: *Trusteeship,* Vol. 6, March/April 1998, Association of Governing Boards of Universities and Colleges.

HERE ARE THE NUMBERS

The conclusions in our report were driven by a fairly simple analysis. We examined the share of the total bill for tuition, fees, and room and board that was financed by federal student aid—grants, loans, and work-study—in 1975, 1985, and 1995. We found that federal student aid as a proportion of the costs of attendance has grown dramatically over the past two decades. Federal aid paid for more than 40 percent of all costs of attendance in 1995, up from about 12 percent in 1975. Federally sponsored loans alone paid for more than 30 percent of the total bill in 1995, up from less than 10 percent in 1975.

These facts, which no one on the commission questioned, led us to conclude that federal loan availability has played a key role in financing higher education. Federal loans more than tripled as a proportion of the total costs of attendance over the past two decades, while college tuition and other charges were increasing at twice the rate of inflation. This is powerful evidence of a connection between federal loans and college costs.

Given this growing dependence on loans as a source of financing college costs, saying that loans have had no impact on college tuition patterns is akin to saying that mortgages and changing interest rates have no impact on housing prices. In the case of housing, changing mortgage availability and interest rates certainly influence housing prices. In the case of colleges, when an institution sets its price, the response by potential students and their families certainly is affected by the availability of loans.

Put another way: If federal student loans had been unavailable over the past two decades would tuition be so high today? Certainly not at private colleges and universities. The availability of student loans has played a critical role in the ability of these institutions to stabilize their share of enrollments over the past two decades after a quarter century of declining market share. As for public higher education, loans have become a more prominent factor in financing college tuition and fees only in the last decade. Here, too, it is hard to imagine that the rapid price hikes of the early 1990s could have occurred without the greater availability of loans.

A FINE DISTINCTION

To say that loans have *contributed* to the growth in tuition rates is not the same as saying that tuition rates have increased *because* of the availability of loans. We do not believe college officials are staying up late at night trying to figure out how to maximize the eligibility of students for federal aid. (There is evidence, however, that some proprietary schools set prices according to federal aid availability.) Other factors—such as the availability of state funding for public institutions and the demands on all institutions for greater quality and diversity in the services they offer and the students they serve—are more important in explaining why college tuition rates rose so fast.

The same analysis of aid as a proportion of costs of attendance led us to conclude that federal grants are not contributing as much as loans to higher tuition rates. Federal grants account for less than 10 percent of the total bill students faced in the mid-1990s, the same as in the mid-1970s. In the Pell Grant program—the largest federal grant program—costs of attendance are not really a factor in the award calculation.

In response to this evidence that loans have affected college tuition patterns, our report suggests the federal government no longer use a student's total cost of attendance in calculating eligibility for student loans in which the federal government pays the interest while the borrower remains in school. Instead, what if federally subsidized loan programs were to count only a portion of tuition over a certain base level and recognize a standard amount of living expenses?

The crux of this proposal is that the federal government should establish a policy for determining how much students should be eligible to borrow on a subsidized basis. Currently, that amount is determined by default based on what each individual institution has decided to charge. Students who no longer would be eligible to borrow on a subsidized basis still would be fully eligible to borrow in the unsubsidized loan program.

Critics of this partial-cost reimbursement approach argue it would be a form of federal price controls. It is not. The federal government would not dictate to institutions what to charge, nor would it need to monitor what institutions charge. The federal government should not be in that game.

But the federal government has a responsibility to American taxpayers to determine how much of the costs of attendance it is willing to subsidize. And there is ample precedent for such an approach in existing legislation. Since 1992, the Pell Grant program has only recognized a standard amount for a student's living expenses. In addition, the two new tuition tax credits enacted in 1997 recognize only a portion of tuition costs in their eligibility formulas. Interestingly enough, no one has argued that these provisions represent a form of federal price controls.

For partial-cost reimbursement to work effectively, the federal government also would have to set limits to prevent unreasonable shifts in financing tuition and other charges from subsidized loans to unsubsidized loans, which are more expensive to students. That is why we also suggest limiting the total amount of federal aid students would be eligible to receive in any given year. Because no such annual limit currently exists, programs are stacked one upon another with no governing philosophy. With an overall limit on federal aid, however, lower income students would receive a greater proportion of their federal-aid

package in the form of grants; the federal government would pay the in-school interest on loans to middle-income students; and students from families with higher incomes would borrow mostly from the unsubsidized loan program up to a specified overall limit.

The combination of partial-cost reimbursement and an annual limit on federal aid would have other beneficial effects. Federal loan subsidies would be better targeted to students from lower income families; currently, students from families with incomes exceeding $100,000 are subsidized if they attend high-priced institutions. In addition, the federal government would recognize the growing role of states and institutions in providing aid; by using total costs of attendance as a criterion for eligibility, current policy ignores these aid sources.

That the cost commission was unwilling to address the relationship between college tuition and student loans does not mean a relationship does not exist. The public is still concerned that college costs too much, and many people take the commonsense view that federal student aid has played a major role in the growth of college tuition and other charges. In the long run, the higher education community will be better served if leaders take responsible positions on this issue rather than hope it goes away.

CHAPTER 18

SHOW ME THE DATA

FRANK J. BALZ

Please mull two questions as you read this. First, have you ever participated in a board meeting in which you calculated the change in your institution's undergraduate tuition based on the availability of federal student loans? And second, what legitimate public policy could be served by preventing or restricting students' access to loan programs for their college education?

In fiscal year 1996 alone, 6.1 million individuals borrowed $26.3 billion under various federal student-loan programs. Millions of students from low-income and moderate-income families who might not otherwise have been able to afford a higher education have benefited from these loans. Indeed, for recipients of federally subsidized Stafford loans in 1995–96, the median family income of undergraduates who were financially dependent on their parents was $39,000. For financially independent students, median family income was just $15,000.

Yet in spite of the size and importance of the federal student-loan programs, there is surprisingly little statistical information on some of their basic aspects. For example, no published data reliably identify how much of the total institutional loan volume undergraduates borrowed in the Federal Family Education Loan Program, although this information is available for the direct-loan program. The data gaps are significant barriers to our understanding of how federal student loans work at the institutional level.

Some individuals have tried to compensate for the paucity of good information with assumptions and preconceptions that simply cannot be supported by the available data. To proffer far-reaching conclusions without having important data can dangerously mislead public-policy makers. The purported relationship between the growth of federal student loans and the increase in undergraduate tuition is a good example of this phenomenon.

Comparing trends in overall student loan volume—including subsidized and unsubsidized Stafford Loans, PLUS loans, and loans for both undergraduate and graduate students—with trends in average undergraduate tuition and fees is a meaningless exercise. Patterns of borrowing and statutory loan limits are very different for undergraduate and graduate students. To assume a proportional split between undergraduate and graduate student borrowing and assign it to all institutions over time only compounds the problem.

The basic mechanics of the loan programs are very different. For example, the federal government pays the interest on subsidized loans while students attend college; for unsubsidized loans, students have the option of paying interest while in college or adding the interest to the total to be repaid upon graduation; interest and principal on a PLUS loan begins immediately after the loan is taken out. Different criteria determine eligibility for each of these programs.

Although some progress has been made toward a valid, systematic analysis of the relationship between student loans and undergraduate tuition, the research is far from complete. To date, no reliable evidence shows undergraduate tuition has been increased to capture more federal student loans. In the

Source: *Trusteeship*, Vol. 6, March/April 1998, Association of Governing Boards of Universities and Colleges.

absence of a new data source or analytical technique, it is irresponsible to suggest otherwise.

Even fewer data are available on private loans. No one has documented the extent to which students and their families have used personal loans, home-equity loans, and other private loan sources to finance higher education. Although it may be tempting to assume that the advent of unsubsidized federal loans added to the level of borrowing, these loans may have replaced some portion of existing private borrowing by merely shifting the source of funds. Without the data to study this hypothesis, any assertion is just chatter.

ILLUSORY BENEFITS

Undeterred by the lack of research, some individuals speculate that restricting student access to loans or loan subsidies will appropriately shrink undergraduate tuition. Don't believe it.

Basic economic theory holds that the relative price of a commodity depends on supply and demand. The demand for a college education is increasing partly because it is important for success in an economy that requires advanced skills. The supply is influenced by the importance society places on higher education, as well as by the basic cost structure of institutions. No sector in the American economy is made more economically efficient by arbitrary restrictions on capital—including higher education.

The most likely effects of restricting federal loan eligibility would be to force institutions to make up the shortfall with institutional funds, to force students to choose colleges based more on price than on educational program, or to push students into more expensive private loan alternatives and increase the total price they pay for higher education. Restricting loan eligibility would not reduce tuition.

The average cumulative debt for undergraduate students who borrowed and who completed their senior year in 1995–96 was approximately $13,000. If these students paid 10 percent interest on a private loan, instead of the current 8.25 percent rate for a Stafford Loan, the total cost of the loan over a ten-year repayment period would increase by nearly $1,500.

An important fact has become lost amid the statistics on the growth in student borrowing. The $2,625 maximum loan amount for a first-year undergraduate was unchanged in the 1992 amendments to the Higher Education Act. It has not been changed for ten years. Regardless of how much institutions have raised their tuition, students have been making their decisions to begin college based on the same freshman student-loan maximum for the last decade. Institutions have not gained any additional revenue from these students' federal student loans through increases in tuition.

THE FALLACY OF THE SUBSTITUTE

Some argue that increases in federal student-loan subsidies prevent increases in federal student-grant programs or that decreases in federal loan subsidies will "free up" funds for increases in federal student-grant programs. Both of these statements are wrong.

Federal savings derived from reducing subsidies to loan programs cannot be used to increase federal grants. The federal budget generally is divided into two types of spending: (1) entitlements, which allow anyone who qualifies to receive the benefit, such as student loans and tax-related programs, and (2) appropriated programs, such as Pell Grants, which are limited each year by what the Congress is willing to provide.

Federal budget rules have placed a wall between spending for entitlements and spending for appropriated programs. Savings derived from changes to entitlement programs can be used only for other entitlement programs or tax changes. Savings in an appropriated program can be used only for funding another appropriated program—not for entitlement programs. Under federal budgeting laws, including the recently enacted bipartisan balanced budget agreement, it is impossible to shift spending on loan subsidies to Pell Grants, for example.

In the absence of basic data to carry out an appropriate analysis about the relationship between federal student loans and undergraduate tuition—no less uncovering conclusive evidence—a rush to judgment is foolhardy. Policy makers, the U.S. Department of Education, and the research community must marshal the resources to treat this issue responsibly. Let's aim our efforts in that direction, instead of developing policy recommendations based on unfounded speculations.

CHAPTER 19

GROWING THE ENDOWMENT IN A HIGH-RISK ENVIRONMENT

CHARLES THARP

Charles Tharp is a principal of Charles Tharp Associates in Washington, D.C., consultants on investment policy and structures for endowments and pension funds. A graduate of fYale, he earned an M.A. in international law at England's Oxford University, and has worked as an investment adviser to corporations, as head of the U.S. government's Pension Benefit Guaranty Corporation, and from 1989 to 1995 as treasurer and chief investment officer at Oberlin College, where he reduced expenses while enlarging the endowment measureably. His recent clients include The World Bank, the Kingdom of Jordan, and several foundations.

In his poem, *Dover Beach*, Matthew Arnold, himself an educational reformer, wrote of a "darkling plain . . . where ignorant armies clash by night." He might well have been describing the annual debate on many U.S. campuses in the 1990s over their budgets. Financial discipline has emerged in the 1990s as a pre-eminent concern.

The financial strains have caused numerous colleges and universities—especially private institutions—to look more closely at the way their endowments are performing. Some universities have already made major changes in the management of their endowments; but others are only beginning to understand that wise management of their endowed assets is a strategic way to increase operating income over the long term. Unfortunately, trying to squeeze greater growth from an endowment in the late 1990s requires special thoughtfulness because of the rapidly changing and increasingly high-risk environment.

Endowments are a distinctive feature of American higher education. At least 20 U.S. universities have endowments larger than $1 billion, with Harvard's at $9 billion. Another 200 colleges and universities have endowments of more than $100 million, and perhaps 500 more of the nation's 2,200 four-year institutions hold assets of more than $25 million (*Chronicle* 1997). Managing such large amounts has become a serious business.

Harvard University now has a staff of 150 to do so; and one of its portfolio managers, Jonathan Jacobson, has drawn faculty criticism because he earned $6.1 million last year ($200,000 salary plus performance bonuses), 25 times as much as Harvard's president. Jack Meyer, head of Harvard Management, defends the huge compensation by saying, "Jon has provided over $300 million in value added to the endowment in the past five years." Jacobson's portfolio of stocks has generated a 30 percent annualized return, double that of the Standard and Poor's 500 Index, so Meyer claims, "Jon is the biggest benefactor Harvard has ever had" (Bary 1996).

Source: *Planning for Higher Education*, Vol 25, Summer 1997, p. 1–8. Society for College and University Planning, Washington, D.C

At 1500-student Berea College in Kentucky, vice president for business and finance Leigh Jones was able to contribute more than $16 million to the college's 1996–97 budget from earnings on the college's $485 million endowment. To help him with the endowment he uses the chair of the trustee's investment committee, who is a venture capitalist with Primus Venture Partners in Cleveland, and retains Cambridge Associates, a Boston-based investment consulting firm (Cropper 1996). Berea's endowment includes investments in real estate, venture capital projects, and foreign stocks (19%).

Berea College is far from alone in its purchase of foreign stocks. A survey of college investments revealed that in fiscal 1995–96, an average of 9.5% was invested in foreign securities, up from 2.4% in 1990–91 (Nicklin 1997). And the University of Vermont, in an effort to increase the return on its $101 million endowment, has put $4 million into a risk-arbitrage fund, which invests in companies involved in mergers, spinoffs, and acquisitions.

THE BIG THREE

To grow an endowment a college or university must manage three factors:

- the endowment spending rate
- investment policy for the endowment
- fund raising, to add to the endowment

The three factors are separate but not independent. A high annual spending rate (6% or more) gradually reduces the size of the endowment by lowering the reinvestment rate. Shrewd investments result in endowment growth and better returns for use in meeting operating expenses, as do new monies from fund raising. There are less obvious correlations too. For instance a few studies have indicated that when alumni and other donors perceive that the college has conservative financial policies and/or successful investment returns on its endowment they are likely to donate more money to the college.

I will not discuss fund raising, even though it is very important for endowment growth. But I want to suggest some ways that institutions should approach the endowment spending rate and the handling of their investments.

The endowment spending rate is the most difficult factor to control because it is critical for the institution's annual financial needs and is also central to the long-term stability and growth of endowment assets. (The endowment's payout is the amount of funds transferred each year from the endowment for use in the school's annual budget.) How should a college balance the need for income for annual expenses with the desire to increase the endowment for the future? How should it balance the claims of present faculty and students with those of the cohorts of the future? I think institutions should do some financial modeling as a starting point for understanding the choices.

At Oberlin College we extensively modeled the probable results of different investment scenarios and spending levels, and of different spending formulas. The president and Board of Trustees had determined to avoid the mistakes of their predecessors in withdrawing too much from the endowment each year, and had agreed that a new endowment spending formula was needed. The old rule had been to withdraw up to 5.5% of the endowment's current value for use in the annual budget; but budgetary pressures often caused the endowment spending rate to rise even higher. This practice still goes on at many colleges, with some institutions drawing 7% or more. After study, we developed a new formula to balance the college's operating income needs with protection of its capital and provision for long-term endowment growth.

Our approach was based on that developed at Stanford University (Massy 1990). The idea underlying the Stanford formula is this: the endowment spending rate each year should be based on the previous year's level of endowment payout, plus an annual inflation adjustment. This protects the institution's budget by starting with the actual sum provided the previous year, plus an inflation estimate. But there is also an embedded target payout rate—say 4% or 5%—taken as a percentage of a moving average of the endowment's market value over the past two or three years. This "smoothing" formula moves the payout back toward general levels even if the market results have been volatile. Thus, if the market lifted the value of the college's endowment up 3%

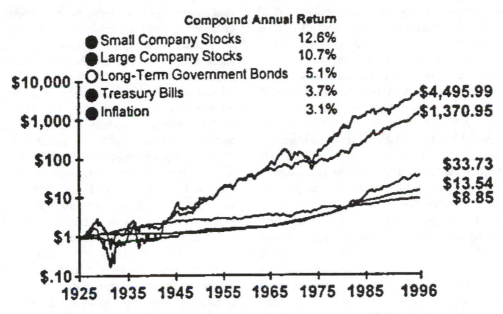

Figure 19.1 Growth of $1.00 invested in various asset classes, 1926–1996.

Source: Ibbotson Associates © 1997.

three years ago, up 8% two years ago, and down 14% in the current year, the college would have its 4% or 5% payout rate based on the average of the past *three* years, not on the current 14% downturn.

The two key questions for Oberlin College were: (1) what target rate to establish, and (2) what balance to strike between the needs of the annual budget and the needs for endowment growth in making annual adjustments.

We knew from experience what damage a 5% or 6% payout rate could do over time. And we observed with keen interest the results of a more conservative 3.5% or 4% payout rate at a competitor such as Swarthmore College, which grew its endowment from half that of Oberlin's 30 years ago to twice that of Oberlin's today. Oberlin's president and board chose an endowment spending target of 4%.

On the second question, they decided to weight the college's budget needs at 60% and the endowment growth needs at 40%, and to smooth market volatility by valuing the endowment over a 36-month moving average of market prices. This combination gave greater security to the annual budget expectations while reserving a healthy weight for long-term savings. Here is the formula we adopted:

$$.6 \ (xg) + .4 \ (yz) = P$$

where x = previous year's payout in dollars

g = expected growth from other sources of revenue, expressed as 1.0 plus the percentage rate of change

y = market spending rate, expressed as a percentage

z = market value of the endowment, defined as the average of the prior 36 months' market values.

P = payout in dollars

Thus, to arrive at a good endowment spending rate two ingredients are essential. One is the smoothing formula to protect the college's or university's annual income from the endowment from the zig-zag swings of the market. (Swarthmore has even placed their venture capital investments in a special fund outside the regular endowment to further insulate the college from a sudden drop in asset values.) The other is a low—and strictly adhered to—spending target of, say, 3.5% or 4% to immunize the endowment from erosion by inflation and to permit endowment growth through reinvestment compounding.

The second ingredient requires a very strict financial discipline to prevent incursions into the endowment corpus. (I recall one college treasurer telling me, when I asked why his spending rate was routinely 9% or 10%, "We have only $30 million, so we might as well spend it.") It is essential to have a conservative spending formula in place before embarking on an aggressive investment program. To do otherwise is to expose the institution to dangerous levels of risk.

HOW TO INVEST FOR THE FUTURE

As colleges and universities seek to manage their endowments more strategically in the late 1990s, the one thing that must be kept in mind is risk. This is the greatest challenge of asset management today. If the decade of the 1960s was the golden age of stockpicking and go-go portfolios, and the 1980s was the heyday of asset allocation, the 1990s is the decade of risk management. Today a college's investment committee does not manage stocks, it manages risk.

In the 1960s numerous colleges and universities improved their endowments considerably by investing in growth stocks and new high-tech companies. But when the stock market collapsed in 1973–74, with a 52% fall in U.S. equity markets in 24 months, followed by double-digit inflation in the late 1970s, the damage to higher education was considerable. The 1980s became the boom time for S&P Index funds and other large, diversified "passive" funds that could offer returns equal to that of the market and reduce a board's exposure to criticism. In the decade between 1980 and 1990, the Salomon Broad Bond Index rose 127%, more than doubling its value, but the S&P Index rose 212.6%, more then tripling. From 1994 to 1997 common stocks have had another surge, again led by "brand-name" stocks and new high-tech firms. (See Figure 19.1.) But a number of older investment hands, including Federal Reserve chairman Alan Greenspan, have grown wary. Risk management is now primary.

How does a college manage risk? I suggest that two sets of actions are necessary. The first set of actions is to get the management of your portfolio in order. The second set pertains to managing your managers.

It is dismaying, but a majority of colleges and universities, including some famous ones, need to improve their strategic management. Oberlin, a remarkable academic institution, was an example. Oberlin in 1950 and 1960 was one of the wealthiest institutions in the nation, measured by endowment per student. By the 1980s this had changed. At one point its endowment returns ranked last among the 33 colleges it considered its peers. The college's holdings of common stocks was 20% below the NACUBO mean. About 30% of its endowment was in cash or cash equivalents. The college's financial condition had slipped to the point where a new president had to recruit new talent for the trustee investment committee and develop a fresh strategic vision.

To move toward superior portfolio management, the first step is an *assessment* of the exact state of the endowment and the college's essential needs. It is imperative to know the true economic value of the endowment's assets and liabilities. There is no need to survey every asset or need of the institution; simply conduct a survey of present resources and commitments. For the inventory of assets, a college needs a conservative accounting approach to valuation, done by a qualified staff or by an outside auditor, or both. This is especially important for assets such as land, real estate, venture capital, and foreign securities.

And *financial reporting* needs to be frequent and accurate. At Oberlin, the trustees believed they had less than 10% of the endowment sidelined in cash. So their quarterly reports asserted. But investigations revealed that the equity managers also held cash instead of common stocks, so actually more than one-third of Oberlin's total endowment was not in the market.

Peer comparisons are helpful too. How well are similar institutions with similar size endowments performing? Is your institution behind, roughly even with them, or ahead? What is their distribution of investments compared to yours? Be sure to include the most outstanding performers among your set of peers so that you have a realistic sense of what can be accomplished. These benchmarks are extremely helpful in evaluating the performance of the managers of parts of your endowment.

With accounting, better reporting systems, and performance measurements an institution is ready to make fundamental changes in the endowment's structure and handling. At Oberlin we closed down loss-making operations, reinvested the cash, let go underperforming managers, and restructured the portfolio. (See Figure 19.2.)

WHICH ASSETS ARE BEST?

Now you are ready to construct an integrated investment model for the institution. The endowment model will have a subpart which includes the flow of funds from new gifts, including the maturation of deferred giving programs, and the payments from the endowment for current use by the college. Most important, you will have to decide on asset allocation (Williamson 1993).

Studies have shown that up to 90% of long-term investment returns depend heavily on asset allocation, or what proportion of funds you put to work in each investment class over time (Ibbotson and Brinson 1993). How you allocate assets is more important than what stocks or bonds you choose, when you buy or sell your investments, or which professional firms you choose to manage your funds. The major classes of investment alternatives, in order of risk, from least to greatest, are:

- cash equivalents
- U.S. investment-grade bonds
- non-U.S. fixed-income securities
- U.S. common stocks
- non-U.S. common stocks
- real estate
- venture capital, or private securities
- special situations

This list is not exhaustive. Some universities invest in commodities, junk bonds, oil wells, or prime farmland like Washington's Whitman College, where 7% of the $167 million endowment is in farms (Mercer 1996).

Constructing the asset allocation model can be done in-house if sufficient skills among the staff, trustees, and professors of finance are available. But most colleges will need to bring in an outside expert to help.

The college or university will need to set some long-term performance goals for (1) the endowment fund as a whole and (2) each asset class in the endowment. These choices will depend on the risk and reward levels of each asset class, how large the endowment is, and how much risk the institution leaders are able to handle.

At Oberlin we inserted benchmarks of achievement in our contracts with the managers of each of our classes, discussing these goals up front and reaching a clear agreement. Sometimes managers would propose weaker bogeys, for obvious reasons. It's important to have benchmarks that are fair and realistic, but sufficiently ambitious. It's also important to monitor the transactions of the investment managers that the university selects through such means as monthly reconciliations, telephone calls, and bringing in the lead managers to report to the trustees regularly on their progress.

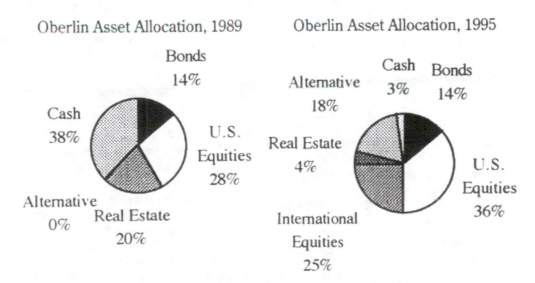

Figure 19.2   Oberlin Asset Allocation, 1989 and 1995

The choice of investment firms to manage the asset classes—bonds, foreign stocks, real estate, venture capital investments, emerging growth stocks, etc.—is the second most important endowment decision after asset allocation. (Colleges with very small endowments may choose to turn over their endowment funds to a single, multi-capability firm.) Be careful, however, of hiring too many outside managers: too many to oversee properly, too many slivers of funds on too many plates.

In selecting investment firms to manage the college's assets, your institution should keep a few things in mind.

1. Be sure to establish a benchmark of expected returns for each asset class, with an explicit understanding of the risk parameters, against which the firm is to manage the allocation.

2. Decide early who will have the authority to hire and fire the asset manager, and who will conduct the search for the best firms to manage each asset. A search consultant may be needed, and the annual *NACUBO Endowment Study* lists the firms used by other colleges (NACUBO 1996). Typically, the institution's financial staff will investigate the firms and recommend the hiring decision to the trustees' investment committee, who will make the final choice.

3. Your issue of a request for proposals from prospective managers should describe the expectations and risk parameters, and should ask for detailed information about such things as the size of the firm in capital and in personnel, assets under management, performance data, some client names to contact for references, the background of the account manager who would handle the college's account, and the firm's investment philosophy and procedures. I suggest that international firms not be overlooked in the searches, especially for investments in foreign securities.

4. In discussing the finalists, hold round-table discussions among the administrators and trustees (and the consultant, if one is used).

5. In negotiating the contract, be certain that the benchmark against which the firm will be judged, termination provisions, fiduciary insurance, and other key items are crystal clear. Every precaution should be taken so that there is no misunderstanding whatsoever. The written agreement should contain all these items to minimize later disagreements (Spitz 1992).

THE NEW, RISKY CLIMATE

What is risk? One definition puts it, "Risk is how likely it is that one morning I may not have enough to pay my bills." For a college, that would translate to not having sufficient endowment returns for next year's operating budget. What if the stock market falls by one third, and the 4% expected from your $90 million endowment, or $3.6 million, was suddenly only 4% of $60 million, or $2.4 million?

Many academics, and most of Wall Street, define risk mainly in terms of price volatility—the likely rises and falls in stock and bond prices. Others define risk as the relative chances of making high returns or none at all. For instance, venture capital deals or investments in possible new oil fields can bring extraordinary returns. But venture capital start-ups can collapse, and oil wells can come up dry. Generally, high-risk investments can yield high returns or big losses, while low-risk investments yield lower returns but little chance of sizable losses.

With the U.S. stock market recently trading at record high levels, with instability in such places as China, the former Soviet Union, and the Middle East, and with foreign currencies shifting frequently, the investing environment has become more risky. At the same time, higher education's voracious needs for more income have become ever more intense. What should university financial planners do? Risk management has become paramount in the late 1990s.

Again going back to Oberlin, we used our endowment model to perform simulations of hundreds of possible scenarios, varying both market conditions and asset allocations. One purpose of the simulations was to test probabilities and risk tolerances. Would the college officers be willing to take a 5% chance of a 20%

increase in endowment if it meant a 10% chance of a 20% loss? The simulations were valuable.

We were able to quantify the tradeoffs, and we learned some things we did not know. For example, the risk-reward frontier was not a continuum. Diversification using some additional asset classes could reduce volatility without reducing expected returns.

Investment in foreign stocks is one example. Recent studies show that returns on U.S. stocks tend to be equal to, or only a half percentage point lower than, returns on foreign stocks if the currency risk is hedged. But if the currencies are not hedged, the low correlations between U.S. and foreign stock returns mean the volatility of a portfolio holding both kinds of assets can be significantly reduced. So Oberlin College decided to increase its international exposure substantially. Oberlin was not alone. In Indiana both Earlham College and the University of Notre Dame now have more than 20% of their endowment dollars invested in overseas stocks and bonds (Nicklin 1997), as do dozens of other colleges and universities. Remember, you are managing risk, not stocks.

Asset diversification—the wise and prudent allocation of assets—has become a key feature for good endowment management in higher education. However, some forms of diversification may carry too high a risk. "Alternative" investments in limited partnerships with limited disclosure is an example. Likewise for the use of derivatives, which can be a valid tool for hedging risk but can be the opposite when hedge fund operators use them to leverage up risk and a client's exposure. A good rule for colleges is: "Don't invest in what you don't understand, and don't approve what your asset manager can't explain."

At Oberlin, our endowment performance went from 33rd among 33 peer institutions in January 1989 to returns that were above the median by June 1995. With an endowment of $203 million in 1989 and $288 million in 1995, we generated $147 million in investment returns, including the money taken by the college for its annual budgets. Strategic endowment management can make a substantial difference for an institution's financial (and academic) health.

Harvard's endowment, for instance, has risen from $1.8 billion in 1977 to $9.1 billion in 1997, helping that university maintain its eminence. Atlanta's Emory University, with an extraordinary 22.5% annualized return over the past five years, has zoomed to a $3 billion endowment, greater than that of M.I.T., Cornell, or Columbia. Yale, with only 22% of its endowment now in U.S. common stocks and increased diversification into venture capital, leveraged buyout funds, real estate, hedge funds, and foreign stocks, had a 25.7% return on its endowment in 1996 and has grown its endowment to $4.9 billion (Bary 1996). Georgetown, Loyola University in Illinois, Grinnell College, Occidental College, and Wake Forest are among those who have increased their endowments *10-fold* over the past 30 years (Wingert 1993).

With colleges and universities facing a more constricted financial future in the coming decade, they will need to devote more expert attention to the management of their endowments. Keep the endowment payout rate as low as possible (3.5% to 4.5%). Allocate your assets wisely. And manage for risk as well as for high returns.

REFERENCES

Bary, A. (1996). Harvard's men. *Barron 's,* December 2.

Chronicle of higher education. (1997). February 14: A35–36.

Cropper, C. (1996). Where the education is built on principal. *New York times,* July 7.

Ibbotson, R. & Brinson, G. (1993*). Global investing: The professional's guide to the world capital markets.* McGraw-Hill.

Massy, W. (1990). *Endowment perspectives, policies, and management.* Association of Governing Boards.

Mercer, J. (1996). Stocks, bonds, and farmland. *Chronicle of higher education.* July 28: A27–28.

NACUBO. (1996). *The 1995 NACUBO endowment study.* National Association of College and University Business Officers (NACUBO).

Nicklin, J. (1997). More colleges look overseas to diversify their endowments. *Chronicle of higher education,* March 21: A41–42.

Spitz, W. (1992). *Selecting and evaluating an investment manager.* National Association of College and University Business Officers (NACUBO).

Williamson, J. P. (1993). *Funds for the future: College endowment management for the 1990s.* The Common Fund Press.

Wingert, D. (1993). *The growth of college endowments, 1960–1990.* The Common Fund Press.

CHAPTER 20

SUCCESS IN INVESTING

Integrating Spending Policy into Asset Allocation Strategy

LOUIS R. MORRELL

There are no secrets to the successful management of investment funds. Sound principles and practices for effective endowment management were established long ago. First, one must clearly define success in terms of objectives. Whether an individual investor, a foundation, or an endowment fund is involved, the concept of success is the same. Investment funds exist to provide an income stream to support the financial needs of the investor—in the present, in the future, or both.

While many people fail to realize the importance of this aspect of investment management, the capital markets are fully aware of it. Fundamental security analysis focuses on the expected future flow of cash. When cash will be received and the probability that it will be received are critical factors in determining the present value (price) of a security. The capital markets are also concerned about the real value of the income stream and the return of principal. The analyst is aware that dollars received in the future must be discounted to reflect the impact of inflation on those dollars. Thus, as a general rule, an investor will demand a return that is increasingly higher as the scheduled time period in which repayment of the investment is extended. The capital markets are also aware of the added investment return that comes from the earlier receipt of income. A dollar today can be invested for incremental return, making it more valuable than a dollar tomorrow.

Another critical factor to be considered is risk. Not only are the capital markets focused on the level of expected investment income; they are also concerned about the probability of receiving such income as well as the future return of principal. A question that is often asked is: "How much will I receive, and what is the probability that I will receive it?" Each factor that adds an element of uncertainty either increases the size of the return that an investor demands or lowers the price that an investor is willing to pay for an investment.

Too many colleges and universities start the investment process by focusing on asset allocation with insufficient regard for their investment return requirements. Other institutions set asset allocations that are more risky than they need to be for a desired outcome. Success in investing requires the establishment of an asset allocation strategy capable of meeting the institution's needs (growth of principal and income distribution) at the lowest possible risk.

CRITICAL ISSUES IN INVESTMENT MANAGEMENT

Achieving success in the investment process centers around three critical issues—asset allocation, spending policy, and risk management.

Source: *NACUBO Business Officer*, Vol. 30, 1997, p. 38–42.

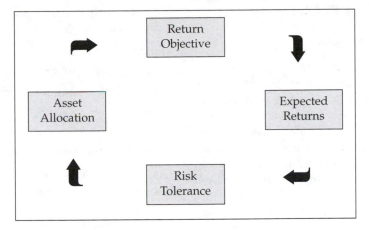

Figure 20.1

Asset Allocation

Studies have clearly demonstrated that asset allocation (asset mix) accounts for more than 90 percent of investment return. The most comprehensive research, conducted by Brinson, Hood, and Beebower in 1986, studied the performance results of a large group of investment funds, with similar asset mixes, over a 10-year period. Researchers observed that funds with similar asset mixes had similar investment results. The use of different investment managers or the practice of shifting assets around within asset classes had a very limited influence on comparative performance results. However, as the variation among asset classes becomes greater, so do the variations in investment returns. For example, funds with higher equity exposures provide higher returns than funds with lower equity exposures. Also, within the asset classes, the mix has an impact on investment return. For instance, in the fixed income category, a higher mix of international, high-yield, and convertible bonds provides greater return than a portfolio consisting solely of U.S. Treasury bonds.

Spending Policy

Spending policy also has an impact on investment success. Spending too much today has a double barrel impact on the future. Excessive withdrawals reduce the balance available for expenditure, while the lower balance in the fund earns less return. At the same time, spending too little deprives the current beneficiaries of endowment income. Funds exist to support programs and activities. Is a dollar earned better invested as part of the continuing portfolio or expended for scholarship aid, a form of human investment?

Risk Management

Dealing with risk is a critical factor in investment management. Risk and reward are directly linked in that they generally move in the same direction. To achieve a higher return one must be willing to accept a higher level of risk.

However, in investing one can get a free lunch. By combining different assets that individually would have high returns at a high risk level, such returns can be maintained while the risk level of the combined assets is reduced. In effect, the risk of one asset neutralizes the risk of another asset. Such a relationship (correlation among assets) is demonstrated in what is called "the efficient frontier." The relationship is displayed on a graph with risk as the horizontal axis and return as the vertical axis. Combinations of asset mixes are plotted to show the reward/risk relationship between each along a line called the efficient frontier. One is thus able to assess the probable outcome of different asset mixes to ascertain the combination that is most acceptable in terms of risk and reward. As a general rule, one should always attempt to minimize risk for any given investment return objective. This can be achieved through the adoption of selective asset mix.

THE INVESTMENT PROCESS

Setting the Return Objective

The initial step in the investment process calls for a college or university to determine the income distribution that it wants to make. To protect the principal of a fund and ensure that income expended is tied to the changing market value of the fund, most endowments spend between 5 percent and 6 percent of the moving market value of the fund. Income distributions can be higher or lower depending upon the financial requirements of the organization. Establishing the distribution rate is the first step in the process. In setting the rate, the institution should consider its total income requirements and other sources of funding. The income demand upon the investment fund must be reasonable and consistent.

As an example, assume that based on an institution's long-range financial plan, the investment fund is expected to provide 5.3 percent of its moving market value to support operating expenses. To protect the economic value of the fund, one must forecast inflation in the period ahead (generally 10 years). One approach would be to average the long-term inflation rate with a rate experienced over a shorter term. For example, if the rate of inflation was 2.8 percent over an extended time period and 3.8 percent for the past 10 years, one could average the two to estimate inflation at a rate of 3.3 percent.

Finally, the college or university must decide whether it wishes to include a factor in its investment return to provide for additions to endowment principal. This decision, in effect, is a matter of balancing present needs against future needs. For example, higher education leaders generally agree that colleges and universities must slow the rate of annual tuition increases in the future. To do so will require a reduction in the rate of annual expense growth and the identification of higher sources of nontuition revenue. One such alternative income source could be the endowment.

Returning to the example, assume that investment return of 2 percent is to be added to the principal of the fund. Therefore, based on the above conclusions and decisions, the total return objective would be as follows:

Return Applied to Operations	5.3%
Return for Inflation Offset	3.3%
Return for Principal Enhancement	2.0%
Total Return	10.6%

Establishing the Asset Allocation

The next step in the process involves setting an asset mix to provide the required return at the lowest level of risk.

The initial decision centers around identifying asset classes that are to be included in the portfolio. Some funds may have restrictions preventing certain types of assets from being included in the asset mix. Investment committee members may strongly oppose particular asset classes. Once the permissible investments are identified, a return rate for each must be projected. One approach could be to weigh long-term and more recent term results, with an adjustment factor to add a margin of safety. An example of such a projection is shown in Table 20.1.

The next step involves establishing correlations among asset classes in terms of performance outcome. Asset classes that move in the same direction are highly correlated, those that move less dramatically in the same direction are lowly correlated, and those that move in opposite directions are negatively correlated. Table 20.2 presents an example of correlations. This step introduces the factor of diversity, allowing an institution to achieve a given return with greatly reduced risk by spreading its funds among different asset classes. This result occurs because different asset classes react differently to the same economic environment or market conditions.

Using the assumptions contained in the above example, a series of models would be run to show asset combinations that are projected to provide the target return of 10.6 percent. This method is referred to as a probability optimizer. Each model allocation should also show the standard deviation for that particular mix of assets. The expected returns, standard deviations, and cross-correlations are combined to build model portfolios.

TABLE 20.1
Asset Returns (Historic and Projected)

Asset Class	Historic Returns	Recent Results	Average	Safety Adjustment	Projected Returns
Large Cap Equities	14.6%	15.3%	14.9%	–3.4%	11.5%
Small Cap Equities	20.3%	14.5%	17.4%	–5.3%	12.1%
U.S. Treasury Bonds	7.2%	7.8%	7.5%	6.0%	
Corporate Bonds	9.6%	8.1 %	8.9%	–2.0%	6.9%
International Equities	18.9%	16.9%	17.9%	–5.9%	12.0%
Real Estate	8.5%	10.5%	9.5%	–1.5%	8.0%
Convertible Bonds	13.8%	9.0%	11.4%	–2.3%	9.1%

Objective: To forecast future rates of return for various asset classes by taking into consideration historic returns and more recent returns and adding a safety margin.

TABLE 20.2
Asset Correlations

Asset Class	Large Cap	Small Cap	U.S. Treasury	Corporate Bonds	International Equities	Real Estate	Convertible Bonds
Large Cap Equities	1.0						
Small Cap Equities	0.78	1.0					
U.S. Treasury Bonds	0.28	0.19	1.00				
Corporate Bonds	0.34	0.22	0.90	1.00			
International Equities	0.47	0.37	0.18	0.22	1.00		
Real Estate	0.61	0.74	0.34	0.34	0.37	1.00	
Convertible Bonds	0.79	0.73	0.35	0.36	0.38	0.57	1.00

Note: The development of correlations is a means of expressing the reward-risk relationship of a blend of different assets. The expected return of two or more assets is the weighted average of the expected return of the asset. The risk is a function of the cross-correlation of returns between the groups. Correlations are not static and do change with phases in the economic cycle.

TABLE 20.3
Projected Returns, Asset Allocations

	Standard	Mix 1	Mix 2	Mix 3	Mix 4	Mix 5	Mix 6
Lg Cap Stks	60.0	9.0	12.0	37.0	41.0	21.0	60.0
Sm Cap Stks	0.0	7.0	9.0	10.0	10.0	20.0	10.0
Intl Eq	0.0	10.0	10.0	10.0	10.0	20.0	10.0
Cvts	0.0	0.0	0.0	0.0	0.0	0.0	0.0
Total Equity	60.0	26.0	31.0	57.0	61.0	61.0	80.0
Dom Bds	38.0	64.0	59.0	43.0	39.0	39.0	20.0
T-bills	2.0	10.0	10.0	0.0	0.0	0.0	0.0
Return	9.2	7.6	7.9	9.7	9.9	10.6	11.0
Risk	10.3	6.4	6.8	9.7	10.2	10.3	12.5

An example of the models is provided in Table 20.3. The Standard column shows a traditional mix of assets found in many portfolios. As noted, in the Mix 5 column, a return of 10.6 percent would be achieved with a standard deviation of 10.3 percent. The same level of risk (standard deviation of 10.3 percent) is found in the traditional mix of assets labeled Standard. However, the traditional mix has a projected annual return rate of only 9.2 percent. This clearly demonstrates how modeling can identify an asset mix with a higher projected return at no increase in risk.

Investment committee members must understand the application of standard deviation to the model portfolios. Standard deviation measures variability (risk) by recording the assets' range of returns over a given time period. One standard deviation is the maximum amount of variability that has occurred 68 percent of the time. As shown in Table 20.3, the standard deviation of the model portfolio is 10.3 percent. This simply means that the returns from the model portfolio fell, most of the time, within 10.3 percent of their annual average returns, or between .3 percent (10.6 percent less 10.3 percent) and 20.9 percent (10.6 percent plus 10.3 percent). If an investment committee is not prepared to accept such a level of volatility, it must reduce its return expectations or the rate of income distribution from the endowment.

Dynamic Nature of Asset Allocation

A college or university should establish a strategic asset allocation that over the long run will provide investment returns that meet the investment goals with an acceptable level of risk. However, periodic adjustments should be made when one or more of the following changes take place:

- Shift in the institution's risk tolerance
- Modification in need for income distribution
- Change in expected returns in the capital markets

CONCLUSION

Success in investing hinges on the integration of spending policy into asset allocation strategy. The formula for success requires colleges and universities to devise an asset allocation strategy capable of meeting the institution's needs for income and growth in principal at the lowest possible risk.

Chapter 21

The Role of Institutional Planning in Fund-Raising

Rick Nahm and Robert M. Zemsky

Rich Nahm is senior vice president for planning and development, and Robert M. Zemsky is professor and director of the Institute for Research on Higher Education at the Univeristy of Pennsylvania. This article is adapted from their chapter in Educational Fund Raising, *edited by Michael J. Worth, © 1993, American Council on Education Series on Higher Education and Oryx Press. The book, sponsored by Council for Advancement and Support of Education, is available from AGB and ACE/Oryx.*

Two disturbing maxims are making the rounds in higher education development offices. The first holds that "Try as one will, fund-raising ends up donor-driven rather than need-driven." In other words, the money that is raised is the money that can be raised because alumni, friends, corporations, and foundations are most prepared to support their own priorities. The more successful the fund-raising—particularly leadership gifts—the more likely that donor interest, rather than academic need, will determine the future shape of the institution.

The second maxim is no less troubling: "Successful fund-raising programs cost more money than they raise because major donors expect more from the institution." This idea maintains that to please today's donors, fund-raising has moved toward "add ons" and "new ventures." The donor wants to leave his or her mark on the institution and so is prepared to supply a lead gift: the first dollar, but not the middle or the last. In return, the institution builds buildings and names them for donors who provide less than half the construction funds and no operating funds. It establishes and fills endowed chairs, though the income from the gift may supply less than half the cost of maintaining a faculty member and none of the "extras" associated with a chair.

The reality that haunts fund-raisers—presidents, chief development officers, and board chairs—is that they can't win for losing. They cannot use a focused fund-raising effort either to shift or sharpen institutional priorities. Instead, such an effort is likely to leave the institution with its mission more blurred, simply because accommodating faculty and student needs with donor interest usually means giving in to all and hoping that enough money will turn up to pay for the promises.

Also, fund-raising cannot become a means of securing the institution's financial future because it adds commitments, often multiplying the cost of doing business. Rising expectations on the part of the entire institution, particularly those areas without ready access to donors, puts added pressure on the budget. The need to keep everyone happy acts as a flywheel, accelerating expenditures throughout the institution.

Source: Trusteeship, Vol. 6, May/June 1995, p. 22–26, Association of Governing Boards of Unversities and Colleges.

Institutional leaders also are learning to their dismay that fund-raising can raise questions about the institution's management by inadvertently highlighting internal divisions. When separate departments independently market their own programs to the same limited pool of major donors, including the same corporations and foundations, donors cannot help but wonder whether anyone is in charge and whether the institution really knows where it is going. Unseemly disputes over priorities among departments or between faculty and administration only add to the sense of drift. This explains why development officers always advise that faculty be brought into the effort, whatever the cost, as a crucial early step in fund-raising planning. The harshest criticism, however, is reserved for those institutions that announce the successful completion of a campaign on Monday and a major budget crisis on Tuesday. The donor and campus communities feel betrayed and are quick to blame an administration that clearly did not know what it was doing.

In this climate, most leaders settle for fund-raising programs that avoid major mistakes. When they reach their announced goal, there is little of the euphoria with which they began their campaigns. Glad their ordeal is over, these leaders publicly welcome the chance to spend more time on campus, while privately wondering if this may be the moment to bring their administration to a successful close.

ALTERNATIVE MODELS

Fund-raising in higher education is at a crossroads. At stake is not only the character and purpose of fund-raising but also the institutional role of development professionals. One response is to separate fund-raising from the general operation of the institution. The development operation would become a quasi-independent foundation serving those parts of the institution that have access to well-defined donor communities and the ability to bear the full cost of intensive fund-raising.

The political and financial independence of such a fund-raising foundation would require that supported projects be fully funded; it also would mean that this fund-raising would be largely independent of institutionally defined goals and priorities. Under this model, the cost of fund-raising itself would be the responsibility of the client program, department, or school. Fund-raising would become "financially responsible," but at the cost of surrendering any claim that the institution as a whole would benefit from the gifts. (Many public universities do conduct their fund-raising through separate foundations, and some of these problems have surfaced.)

The preferred (though more difficult) alternative is to ensure that fund-raising is need-driven rather than donor-driven, capable of providing operating budget relief and integrated with the institution's vision. The challenge is twofold: (1) how to best overcome the unrealistic expectations that fund-raising unleashes across institutions and (2) how to best control the trend toward supporting add-ons and new programs, rather than an institution's mission and programs.

Our solution derives largely from our experience in planning and executing a major fund-raising effort for the University of Pennsylvania. We do not suggest that the problems Penn faced are necessarily similar to institutions of different scale and mission, nor can we say that Penn solved all its problems. We do believe, however, that the basic strategy we put in place has wide applicability for every institution planning a new fund-raising program.

At the core of Penn's strategy was a decision to use the university's academic plan, "Choosing Penn's Future," to structure a major campaign and subsequent fund-raising. Every aspect of the campaign—from its concept and organization to its language and symbols—had its roots in this planning process. Penn's academic priorities for the 1990s and beyond became campaign priorities. From the outset, organizing the fund-raising effort was a joint effort of the development and planning staffs. As the vice president for development and university relations, and the chief planning officer, we served as cochairs of the operations committee that oversaw campaign planning.

THE INSTITUTIONAL PLAN

The most successful planning is simple and straightforward, combining common sense and academic tradition to define institutional priorities. Good planning involves the three following elements:

First, a good plan articulates a *vision* of the institution, supplying language and symbols by which an institution collectively comes to understand what it wants to be. Visions are statements of purpose that relate to current and long-term expectations. The process of developing such a statement of vision, if successful, helps to draw together the institution in common search of unifying themes.

Second, a good plan is an *agenda*; it answers the question, "What do you want to accomplish over the next five years?" In this guise, a good plan is basically a list of proposed actions consistent with the vision on which the plan depends. The items on the agenda should be more about building and establishing educational programs than about administrative or fiscal reform, though the latter are often important preconditions.

Third, good plans convey a sense of *scale and priority*. They propose actions that individually are within the grasp of the institution's capacity for change. The proposed agenda cannot be a laundry list of every pet project of every member of the community. A plan is about choices, about focused investments in a relatively limited number of ventures that best suit the institution's collective sense of its own future. The choices presented in the plan must appear reasonable to those inside and outside the institution, particularly when measured against the institution's financial capacity.

Plans that have these three elements—vision, agenda, and scale—need not be elaborate documents. The shorter the better, perhaps a maximum of 30 double-spaced typed pages. More important than either length or detail is the process by which the plan is developed, vetted, and finally owned by the institution's internal and external constituencies.

To begin with, the institution's leadership is primarily responsible for drafting the plan. The leaders must cull ideas and proposals from a broad base. In that sense, a good planning process is "bottom up." The vision the plan articulates and the specific agenda it proposes must come from the community. Neither, however, is likely to be the work of a committee. The administration in general, and the president in particular, must first listen carefully to the community and then artfully meld those ideas and initiatives into a coherent statement of vision and an agenda. Once drafted, that statement must be discussed, amended, and revised, with the administration and president always bearing first responsibility for the new draft.

The resulting academic plan provides the primary text for all institutional discussions. It takes substantial energy on the part of an administration to draft a plan the entire institution comes to accept as its own. That energy is only possible if the planning discussion itself is at the center of the administration's agenda. The planning process becomes the arbiter of what is and is not important. The result is an academic plan and planning process that knits together an institution. A successful plan gives substance to a common vision by defining symbols as well as actions that collectively promise to make the institution greater than the simple sum of its parts.

BUILDING IN FUND-RAISING

The promise to make an institution greater than the sum of its parts makes possible an integrated fundraising effort. Even the most practical items necessary for a smoothly functioning fundraising program can be derived from a well-formed academic plan shared by an inclusive planning process. In broad sketch, those "practical items" fall into four specific categories, which—when integrated into institutional planning—become keys to success in academic fund-raising.

Developing the Message

The crucial first step is the development of the case, or rationale, for support. This can be as basic as a theme for an annual-giving drive or as complex as a case statement for a major campaign. If the fund-raising message derives from the academic plan, it will give potential donors a clear, consistent, well-developed presentation of the institution's priorities. It will not only answer the question, "why us," but also "why now" and "what for." And it will become an educational tool inside and outside the institution—one that helps move donors toward needs and serves as a scorecard to judge the success of the fund-raising effort.

Setting Priorities

Like the message, the list of priorities should be compelling, direct, and short. For donors, a long list of apparently unconnected needs becomes a disincentive to giving, fueling a perception that the institution functions as a "black hole," continually swallowing money. It is extremely important to develop priority needs into a concise list of gift opportunities that, when funded, will clearly advance the institutional plan. When fund-raising objectives are presented in this context, needs become opportunities, and gifts become investments.

Managing Prospects

An important aspect of a prospect-management system is the extent to which it is need-driven versus donor-driven. This orientation affects the entire fund-raising program. If the institutional plan provides the guiding principle for prospect management, then it will affect every decision—whether it involves a policy issue, such as the role of annual giving in a campaign, or a strategy for cultivation, solicitation, and stewardship for one prospective donor.

The charter of effective prospect management contains many clauses. None is more important than matching identified and cultivated prospects to appropriate needs as defined by the institution's academic plan. Difficult as it is to maintain a need-driven prospect-management program, it is impossible without an academic plan that can tell donors simply and directly, "You are important to our institution because you understand our needs!" The donor's personal good fortune and success thus become the means through which to achieve well-defined institutional goals and priorities. First comes the donor's loyalty and interest, next comes the plan, and only then is the potential gift defined by placing it in the larger context of that plan.

Prospect management essentially is a matching process that helps limit needless competition and mindless gifts. The test used to establish the match is this straightforward question: "Is this prospect best matched with this fund-raising objective or need?" Most issues can be resolved similarly.

Organizing the Program

If the message and priorities for fund-raising and the development of prospect management are based on the institutional plan, then basically the overall fund-raising program should be organized in the same manner. Everything from budget and staffing levels to the fund-raising timetable should be guided by the institutional plan's goals, objectives, and strategies, taking on—in general—its characteristics. The planning and organization of fund-raising should be seen as a logical extension of the institution's overall planning and organization.

Carrying Out the Plan

The ultimate test for success in connecting institutional academic planning with a fund-raising program is the extent to which an institution's governing board embraces the goals and objectives of the plan and actively engages in the fund-raising effort. Need-driven investments in an institution, rather than donor-driven gifts, will become the rule only if board members become eager advocates for the processes of institutional planning and strategic fund-raising.

Before the board can be expected to buy in to the process, an institution's internal constituents must believe in the course that has been set and have confidence in the institution's ability to accomplish its stated goals and objectives.

When everything falls into place, the results can be extraordinary. Uniting an institution's vision with its fund-raising capacity to move the institution to new heights or in new directions is the most satisfying activity in institutional advancement. This characteristic is what separates the great programs from the very good ones.

CHAPTER 22

INVESTING PLANNED GIFTS

Proper Management Yields Big Dividends

JAY A. YODER

Jay A. Yoder is Vassar College's investment analyst. He is a chartered financial analyst.

The last two decades have seen great strides in endowment management. Most colleges and universities have implemented well-reasoned investment policies containing specific asset allocation guidelines.

Table 22.1 illustrates these advances by comparing the composition of endowment funds in 1980 and 1995. Colleges and universities have increased their allocations to better performing asset classes such as equities and alternative investments (including real estate, venture capital, and leveraged buyouts) while reducing their holdings of the poorest performing long-term investment—cash equivalents. Regular measurement and scrutiny of investment results along with comparisons to the performance of other institutions are now the norm. The cumulative result of these actions has been improved investment performance and greater contributions to the budgets of colleges and universities.

This high level of attention and sophistication is present in very few investment programs for planned giving assets. Planned gifts generally refer to all those gifts that provide an income stream to a beneficiary, usually until his or her death, at which time the principal becomes available for the institution's use. Included are charitable gift annuities, pooled income funds, and charitable remainder trusts.

Historically financial officers have often viewed the task of investing these assets as little more than a distraction from greater concerns such as planning, budgeting, accounting, and myriad other responsibilities. The reasons for this attitude include time constraints, the typically small size of planned giving assets in comparison to endowment assets, little knowledge in the finance office about planned gifts, and lack of concern by governing board members, donors, and senior management.

The result is often a simplistic or ad hoc investment approach brought about by the lack of formal investment policies and asset allocation guidelines (how much to invest in stocks versus

	1980	1995
TABLE 22.1 **Composition of Endowment Funds**		
Stocks	51.7%	56.7%
Bonds	28.8%	29.9%
Cash Equivalents	14.7%	6.5%
Alternative Assets/Other	4.8%	6.9%

Source: *NACUBO Business Officer,* Vol. 29, 1996, p. 42–45.

bonds versus U.S. Treasury bills). Investment performance—not surprisingly—is less than optimal. This lack of attention to investment matters can have a negative impact on the ultimate success of an institution's planned giving program. Simply delegating investment responsibility to a bank or money manager without strong direction and knowledgeable oversight does little to mitigate three common problems.

PROBLEM 1: INAPPROPRIATE INVESTMENT STRATEGIES

Planned giving assets should be invested to provide the greatest possible remainder value to the institution after meeting all obligations to donors. This generally means investing a large portion of gifts in common stocks. Yet, many planned giving programs—to their detriment—continue to have a huge percentage of their assets in bonds or, even worse, U.S. Treasury bills.

Cambridge Associates' 1994 Planned Giving survey found that 30 percent of institutions had 25 percent or fewer of their gift annuity assets allocated to equities. Why do so many colleges and universities have so few holdings in the asset class that has historically provided the highest returns? One college officer clearly stated the often-heard argument for this "conservative" policy in his gift annuity program: "Our board only wants to try to make sure that as much of the donors' principal is still there when they die."

Some historical analysis reveals the flaws in this reasoning. Assume that on January 1, 1985, an institution had $3 million of gift annuities or charitable annuity trusts paying out an average of 6 percent. This entire amount was set aside, invested solely in U.S. Treasury bills. Eleven years later, on December 31, 1995, the value of this pool was slightly above $3 million. If the entire amount had been invested in government bonds, the pool would have grown to a significantly greater $5.6 million. However, had these funds been invested entirely in stocks (as represented by the S&P 500 Index), the pool's value would have risen to an astounding $11.4 million. This represents more than three times the value resulting from a T-bills only

policy and double the return from holding government bonds. Multiply this example by a much larger planned giving program over several decades and one can see that institutions can forfeit tens of millions of dollars by following conservative, but clearly inappropriate, strategies.

If one wishes to ensure that "as much of the donors' principal is still there when they die," a diversified portfolio with a heavy emphasis on equities is required.

PROBLEM 2: NO TRACKING OF INVESTMENT PERFORMANCE

Most finance officers have data on the investment performance of their endowment over the most recent quarter or the latest fiscal year. However, few institutions track this information for their gift annuity pool or charitable remainder trusts. Current yield figures for pooled income funds are usually available, but there is often no calculation or tracking of total returns. Publication and dissemination of this information (to governing board members, donors, or planned giving officers) with comparative benchmark data is rarer still. Yet, it is impossible to measure the success of one's investment strategy and the implementation of that strategy (whether by the treasurer's office or outside money manager) without this information. As a result, inappropriate investment strategies and poor performance are not flagged and go uncorrected. The lack of investment performance tracking leads directly to a third problem.

PROBLEM 3: NO PERFORMANCE COMPARISONS

The investment performance of any money manager, pension fund, or endowment can easily be compared to that of its peers. Such averages are widely compiled and publicized. Unfortunately, this is not the case for planned gifts. There is very little information, and none that is publicly available, that would enable an institution to compare the investment results of its pooled income funds or charitable remainder trusts to the performance of other institutions. In 1995, Vassar College's gift annuity pool earned 24 percent, the college's pooled income funds earned from 19 percent to 33 percent, and its managed charitable remainder trusts as a group earned 21 percent. Many might rate these investment returns as excellent, but U.S. stock and bond markets were very strong last year. Other institutions might have achieved even better results. Unfortunately there is no way of knowing. This is an area that is "crying out" for a bank, consultant, or other third-party to step up and fill the void by collecting and publishing this much-needed comparative performance information. The availability of peer comparisons could be the biggest single contributor toward motivating institutions to upgrade their investment approach in the area of planned gifts.

Three major factors are causing institutions to focus greater attention on the investing of planned gifts. Each of these issues alone is a sufficient catalyst, but together they represent a powerful force. The first is a legal requirement that has existed for quite some time, while the latter two are more recent phenomena.

CATALYST 1: FIDUCIARY RESPONSIBILITIES

Colleges and universities serving as trustees for their pooled income funds or charitable remainder trusts are required to meet the fiduciary responsibilities of loyalty and reasonable care (prudence). The "prudent man" rule has been the traditional trust law standard since 1830. It requires a fiduciary to "conduct himself faithfully and exercise sound discretion" based on observations of "how men of prudence, discretion, and intelligence manage their own affairs. . . ." However, the Employment Retirement Income Security Act of 1974 (ERISA) upgraded this standard to what is now known as the "prudent investor" or "prudent expert" rule. It requires that fiduciaries act with the "care, skill, prudence, and diligence under the circumstances then prevailing that a prudent man acting in a like capacity and familiar with such matters would use in the conduct of an enterprise of like character and with like aims." In other words, the fiduciary bar has been raised from a simple prudent (lay)man level to the level of a prudent man with investment knowledge and experience—an expert.

Although ERISA technically applies only to pension plans, it provides the formal framework for what is expected of all fiduciaries. Observers agree that this higher standard would probably be applied to any fiduciary in litigation alleging lack of prudence. Observers also generally concur that a prudent expert must have a well-reasoned and written investment policy statement containing asset allocation guidelines. In addition, he or she must diversify assets, monitor investment performance, and control investment expenses.

A college or university that does not have such policies and procedures for planned giving is exposing itself to potential litigation from disgruntled donors, beneficiaries, heirs, and co-remaindermen.

CATALYST 2: RAPID GROWTH OF PLANNED GIVING PROGRAMS

Vassar has experienced 35 percent growth in the market value of planned gifts under management over the past two years. The number of life-income arrangements at the University of Colorado Foundation has increased 47 percent in the past two and one-half years. Similar growth has been noted at many institutions.

The volume of planned gifts flowing into colleges and universities is forcing greater attention on all program aspects, including investment strategy. Planned gifts are one of the few sources of financial support available to colleges and universities that are likely to grow significantly over the next several years.

CATALYST 3: INTERESTED PARTIES ARE DEMANDING MORE INFORMATION

Development offices report that donors are becoming increasingly sophisticated, asking more astute questions and seeking more information about the investment of their gifts. More planned giving officers are earning certified financial planner or chartered financial consultant designations, thus increasing their awareness of investment matters. They are wisely asking the finance office more questions about investment strategies and requesting detailed data on asset allocation and investment performance. Similar inquiries from governing board members concerned about their fiduciary responsibilities are also increasing.

The challenge now facing many institutions is nothing less than a complete upgrading of their investment approach for planned giving assets. What steps do colleges and universities need to take to begin this process?

STEP 1: IMPROVE COMMUNICATION BETWEEN THE FINANCE AND DEVELOPMENT OFFICES

Financial officers responsible for the investing of planned gifts, or overseeing an outside bank or money manager, need to increase their knowledge about the planned giving vehicles offered by their institutions. To invest these assets appropriately, financial officers must understand the return objectives, acceptable risk tolerances, legal restrictions, and time horizons of the various types of planned gifts offered by their college or university. At the same time, they need to educate planned giving officers, donors, and governing board members about the investment strategies they have implemented to accomplish those return objectives within the above-mentioned constraints.

STEP 2: APPLY THE LESSONS LEARNED AND ADOPT THE SUCCESSFUL STRATEGIES EMPLOYED IN THE MANAGEMENT OF ENDOWMENT ASSETS

Colleges and universities must adopt clear, well-reasoned investment policies and specific asset allocation guidelines. Institutions must also ensure sufficient diversification, regular measurement of investment performance using appropriate benchmarks, and adequate control of expenses. Typically greater allocations to the higher returning asset classes (especially stocks) will be a natural by-product of this process. Not only will fiduciary obligations be fulfilled, but both life income beneficiaries and institutions will benefit from growing income streams and greater remainder values, respectively.

STEP 3: HIRE EXPERTISE

Too many institutions are penny-wise and pound-foolish in this area. Although usually lumped together under the same umbrella, investment expertise is completely independent from and different than accounting or financial expertise. An investment professional with a solid understanding of planned giving vehicles who can create investment policies and asset allocation guidelines, implement a successful strategy, and track and report investment results against proper benchmarks will earn his or her salary many times over. Institutions without existing staff expertise or the capacity to employ such a person can hire a consultant or outsource to a firm knowledgeable in both planned giving and investment management. Well-informed oversight, however, is still a necessity.

Many colleges and universities have experienced significant growth in planned giving assets, a trend that is expected to continue in the foreseeable future. To obtain the maximum benefit from their planned giving efforts, institutions must pay increased attention to investment matters. Colleges and universities that devise and implement appropriate investment strategies for their planned giving programs will earn big dividends in the years ahead.

CHAPTER 23

ORGANIZING UNIVERSITY ECONOMIC DEVELOPMENT

Lessons from Continuing Education and Technology Transfer

GARY W. MATKIN

This chapter describes how American universities have placed continuing education and technology transfer activities either within the university organizational structure or in relation to it. It also describes the dynamics in universities that affect the way these organizational forms are selected and whether or not they are successful. This description and the implications drawn from it should help university administrators position new or expanding economic development initiatives in the organization or select appropriate external organizational forms to carry them out. The description should also help those outside the university, including potential partners, beneficiaries, and government officials, be better informed and better able to influence university decisions about what part the university should play in economic development and how that part should be played.

Organizational issues surface early when expansion of a university's role in economic development is considered—the activity must be housed somewhere, the people carrying out the activity must report to someone, and they must be paid by some entity. Over the years, universities have developed a wide variety of organizational arrangements both within the traditional academic departmental and disciplinary structures and as auxiliary enterprises. Also, as corporations, universities have the legal ability and an increasing propensity to establish or become involved in a variety of external legal entities, including profit and nonprofit corporations, partnerships, real estate investment trusts, and loosely organized consortia. This list of possible organizational forms for university-sponsored economic development activities is thus both long and confusing. The choice of an appropriate form usually is not limited by internal precedent or legal strictures. Instead, it is influenced by many considerations. This chapter discusses some of these considerations and seeks to guide those responsible for university economic development through the many issues that must be addressed.

The following analysis is based on the author's informal study of continuing education organizations over the last twenty years and a more formal study of university technology transfer conducted in 1990 (Matkin, 1990). The chapter begins with some definitions and then describes a number of organizational models for continuing education (CE) and technology transfer, explaining the advantages and disadvantages of each model. Implications from these descriptions are related to some important large-scale trends in university organizational development, concluding with some advice to university administrators and those outside the university who are involved in university economic development efforts.

Source: *New Directions for Higher Education*, no. 97, Spring 1997 © Jossey-Bass Publishers.

DEFINITIONS

The terms *continuing education, technology transfer,* and *economic development* are imprecise and have been used to represent very broad and overlapping areas of activity. Defining these terms therefore requires describing the overlap among them and limiting definitions to a domain that makes the terms useful in discussion.

In the professional field of *continuing education,* this term is used to describe part-time degree programs, noncredit programs, and a variety of other educational experiences that include those involving informal interactions among teachers and students and even technical assistance programs. For our purposes, defining CE is less important than describing how it relates to technology transfer and economic development. Most CE is really knowledge, rather than technology transfer. Only CE directed at the dissemination of research in technical fields meets my definition of technology transfer. The relationship of CE to economic development is harder to limit. Certainly, however, a well-educated and trained workforce is an essential element in economic development. Therefore any CE directly aimed at helping individuals do better in the workplace, as opposed to providing general education or cultural enrichment, would fall into the economic development category.

Technology transfer means the transfer of the results of basic and applied research to the design, development, production, and commercialization of new or improved products, services, or processes. University technology transfer generally refers to the relatively recent activities of technology licensing and other activities directed at creating relations with industry and business development that allow technology licensing and the joint development of a technology to take place. Technical assistance and industrial liaison programs and some aspects of business incubators and research parks can be considered technology transfer activities. Thus, the term *university technology transfer,* in order to preserve any meaning, should not include the traditional university missions of teaching matriculated students and basic research. By this definition, all university technology transfer activity is also economic development.

Of the three terms being discussed, *economic development* encompasses the widest variety of activities. As it relates to universities, economic development means those activities designed to encourage or promote the economic development of a region, state, or country. I agree with other authors in this volume that for the most part university activities are directed at regional economic development. Universities are often called upon to aid state and local government through programs designed to create new business or attract existing businesses to the region, create jobs, provide technical assistance to local industry, or help in training or retraining people for employment.

In addition to these specific activities, it is increasingly recognized that universities can be instrumental in creating an environment supportive of economic growth by improving the quality of life in an area (Rybczynski, 1995) or by "augment[ing] the social structure of innovation" (Feldman, 1994, p. 68), sometimes called the "innovative milieu" (Saxenian, 1994, pp. 41–43, and Castells and Hall, 1994, p. 246). For the purposes of this chapter, *economic development* will refer primarily to specific activities undertaken by universities that go beyond the teaching and research normally considered to be the institution's core activities.

MODELS OF CONTINUING EDUCATION

University-sponsored continuing education has a relatively long history. A convenient date to mark its beginning is 1915, the year of the first conversing of the members of what was to become the National University Extension Association (NUEA). By that time, many large state universities, perhaps led by the University of Wisconsin, had well-established and active extension divisions. Early meetings indicate clearly that the leaders of the extension movement viewed their mission as different from those of their parent institutions but also worthy of full recognition and incorporation into the center of higher education. This different-but-worthy view has been reflected in a number of organizational structures for CE and in a history of debates about the appropriate role of CE in universities. The modern version of these debates has focused on whether university CE should be carried out by a centralized or decentralized unit and assigned to established units of the institution, such as schools, colleges, or departments. A survey of institutions reveals patterns of organization, and a growing body of literature addresses the effectiveness and appropriateness of these patterns. Following is a brief description of four models for organizing CE—the decentralized model, the centralized model, the hybrid model, and the buffer-external model.

The Decentralized Model

In the decentralized model, CE is developed and offered through a number of different units of the university. Professional schools are usually the primary providers of CE in decentralized institutions. Each school determines the nature and extent of its offerings and typically performs many or all of the functions necessary to support such offerings, including marketing, enrollment processing, logistical support, and even record keeping. At the University of Missouri, Columbia, most of the professional schools offer their own CE programs; the School of Business offers executive education, the School of Law offers courses in continuing legal education, and other schools (engineering, library science) also support and staff their own programs. In decentralized institutions, including the University of Missouri, CE in areas not covered by other departments may be offered through an extension or CE office.

The main advantage of the decentralized model is that it keeps the CE function close to the faculty and to departmental interests, thus perhaps encouraging faculty involvement in CE. Faculty and departments can reap the financial rewards of CE and benefit from its many other positive aspects, including closer relationships with professional constituencies and expanded contacts with the community. Decentralized efforts tend to have a greater effect on a narrowly targeted subject area or market niche.

The main disadvantage of the decentralized model is that it tends to serve the needs and desires of the faculty and the department rather than the market. This internal focus often dooms the CE effort to financial failure and to a narrow focus that is fragile and subject to a rapidly changing marketplace. Decentral-

ized functions also tend to be smaller in scale than centralized efforts. Other disadvantages are that the decentralized model is difficult for university administrators to control and coordinate with other efforts; economies of scale in marketing, registration, and other CE functions are difficult to achieve; and the institutional effect of an important educational and service function is diffused. Decentralization usually places CE in the hands of faculty who have many other tasks to do and often lack the skills or dedication necessary to sustain a CE effort. This is particularly a problem when the faculty reward structure does not recognize CE as an important element of faculty roles.

The Centralized Model

In the centralized model, most CE is offered through a unit dedicated to the CE function. Program development, implementation, marketing, and many other operations necessary for carrying out CE, including registration and record keeping, are performed by this single unit. The unit is often called extension or continuing education and is usually controlled by an administrator with the title of director or dean. Even in highly centralized institutions, however, some CE may be carried out by other units, often with the help of the central unit. All but one of the campuses of the University of California system have centralized provisions of CE, although there are small amounts of CE undertaken separately by other units.

The main advantage of the centralized model is that it focuses efforts on CE and makes clear where the responsibility for CE resides. The CE function is more easily controlled and coordinated with other university functions, including alumni relations, development, community relations, and outreach efforts. Economies of scale can be achieved more easily, particularly in marketing, where efforts to market the CE offering can be combined with efforts to promote the institution as a whole. Faculty efforts in CE can be leveraged through the use of CE professionals, who can handle the details of program development, selection, and implementation. A centralized CE unit is usually more market focused and realistic about the market potential of proposed programs. It can more easily create a critical mass of programming, and can often generate from internal sources the venture capital needed to initiate new programs.

The main disadvantage of the centralized model is that it can remove the CE function from the faculty and academic departments, thus discouraging faculty involvement in CE. It often results in arguments over control of resources. The centralized CE unit often wants to retain surplus funds to initiate more CE programs whereas academic units want to use some of those surpluses for faculty and departmental projects. The true cost of operating a successful CE program is revealed in centralized units, which can produce debates about how high CE overhead is or should be.

The Hybrid Model

Completely decentralized or centralized models rarely exist; most universities combine the models to some degree. The sharing of the CE function may be along either program or functional lines. Programmatic sharing occurs when certain kinds of programs or certain subject areas are allocated to a centralized or departmental unit. For instance, a university might have a centralized extension unit that does all continuing education except executive education, which is the responsibility of the business school, or alumni CE, which is handled by the alumni relations office. Functional sharing occurs when a centralized CE unit provides support for the CE efforts of other campus units. For instance, the centralized CE unit might help other units market their programs, enroll their students, or prepare course materials. SUNY at Stony Brook is a hybrid model, with the provision of CE divided both programmatically and functionally between an extension unit and professional schools.

Theoretically, if arrangements are carefully worked out, the hybrid model can capture the advantages and minimize the disadvantages of the other two models. In practice, however, hybrid models can be confusing, and jurisdictional disputes can proliferate as market demands change and as the intellectual landscape is altered by technology and events.

The Buffer-External Model

This model conducts CE through an organizational structure outside the institution, often a not-for-profit entity aligned with the institution through ownership of stock or control of the board of directors. Sometimes the entity is associated with a foundation established for fundraising. This model is usually used only for certain kinds of CE activity, not for the full range of CE offered by a university. An example of such an entity is the nonprofit corporation established by a regional entity to foster economic development. An important part of that program is workforce education in targeted areas. As a nonprofit university organization, the entity could engage any higher education institution it chose to deliver the education and could seek funding and pay faculty without regard to university constraints.

The main advantages of the external model are that it can avoid restrictive policies placed on universities and can be more flexible and responsive to the marketplace than internal organizations. For instance, external organizations can be useful when universities are bound by restrictions on faculty compensation or on the use of CE funds earned through the university. In cases in which the institution does not have an established role in CE or its reputation is tarnished, a separate entity might be able to gain greater credibility and establish stronger ties with the community than the university could. Sometimes the buffer-external model can facilitate the formation of partnerships among entities that would have difficulty cooperating in other organizational forms.

There are many disadvantages to the external model. Employees of external organizations often do not enjoy the same benefits as university employees, the use of the name of the university is sometimes a problem, and the university relinquishes some control of the CE function to the external organization. The issue of academic credit can also be problematic, and public relations and the service image of the university may suffer.

MODELS OF TECHNOLOGY TRANSFER

In contrast to CE, organized university technology transfer is a relatively new phenomenon, dating from the late 1970s. At that time, universities began to be seen as major engines of economic development, particularly in relation to the commercialization of university-produced intellectual property. Central to university technology transfer was the expansion of the technology licensing function, as opposed to the passive patenting function. This function was soon supported by many other technology transfer mechanisms, including research consortia, industrial extension (technical assistance) programs, industrial liaison or affiliates programs, spin-off enterprises, research parks, start-up firm incubators, consultant services, and venture-capital funds.

This proliferation of activity produced a matching proliferation of organizational forms, so many that a categorization scheme is required to describe them. This scheme is pictured in Figure 23.1. The scheme shows the relationship of each organizational form to the central core of the university; which is pictured as the largest circle. Following is a description of each of the organizational forms shown in the figure.

The Integrated Organization

The integrated organization usually is faculty operated, reports to a dean or other academic officer, requires heavy faculty involvement, provides resources to and uses the resources of a department or research unit rather than the university as a whole, and is assigned no or very little separate administrative space. Affiliate programs and research consortia often fall into this category. The industrial liaison program of the College of Engineering of the University of California at Berkeley is a typical example of an integrated organization. It is administered by the dean's office and is housed on campus.

In a very few cases, an integrated organization can be accorded full-fledged status as a university entity. Feller (1994) cites the example of the University of Maryland's Biotechnology Institute, which has coequal status with other UM campuses, its own president, and its own tenure-eligible faculty. The advantages of integrated organizations are that they involve faculty, encourage one-to-one interaction between

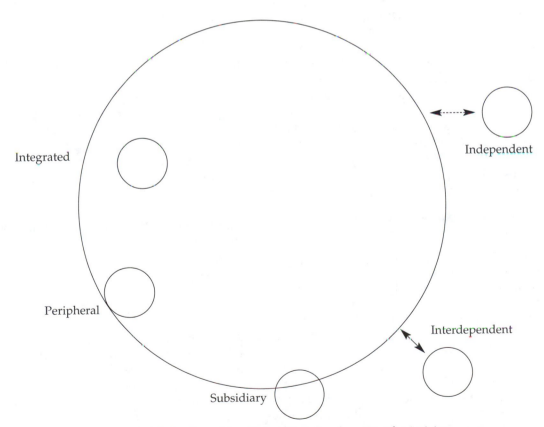

Figure 23.1 Models for Organizing University Technology Transfer Activity

faculty and industry, and help to shape the culture of the university toward favoring technology transfer. The disadvantages are that the activity of such organizations is rarely controlled or coordinated by the central administration, organizational stability and success are dependent on faculty who have many other tasks to perform, and external constituencies may view the organizations as too self-serving.

The Peripheral Organization

The peripheral organization is not usually operated by faculty or within the departmental structure. Instead, it is most often run by non-faculty professionals who report to a member of the administrative cadre of the institution, have an administrative staff, and occupy identifiable space. Many technology licensing offices, continuing education units, technical assistance programs, and special facilities use this model. The Office of Technology Licensing at the University of California, Berkeley, is an example. Housed off campus with a staff of ten, the director of the office reports to the provost for research. The advantages of peripheral organizations are that they employ professionals whose job it is to perform the activity, they have relative organizational stability, they are accountable to and controlled by the central administration, and their activities can be coordinated with other parts of the university more easily than those of integrated organizations can be. The disadvantages are that peripheral organizations tend to have a life of their own, become less aligned with faculty interests, and can exercise a power over the culture of the university and the public's perception.

The Subsidiary Organization

The subsidiary organization has a separate legal form in which the university holds equity (usually a nonprofit corporation) and has a governance structure that is at least nominally separate from the university. It interacts frequently with organizations and individuals outside the university community and usually serves only a few faculty members. Research parks and, again, technology licensing operations often use this model, and it is the preferred model for venture-capital and fund-the-gap activities. The advantages of subsidiary

organizations are that they afford some legal and public relations protection for the university and can escape university policies that stifle technology transfer activity. For instance, they can compensate professionals on incentive schemes rather than using university-based compensation plans. This model also provides for greater accountability and can serve to buffer university activities from commercial activities. The disadvantages of subsidiary organizations are that the relationship between the organization and the university is often not clear, faculty are even less likely to be involved than in the peripheral model, and the university often has even less control over the organization's operations.

The Interdependent Organization

The interdependent organization is a separate legal entity in which the university has little or no equity and over which the university does not exercise total control but is in some ways dependent on the university. Some alumni organizations and university foundations, such as the Wisconsin Alumni Research Foundation (WARF), and some venture capital funds are representative of this category Although WARF's bylaws specify that its efforts are dedicated to the purposes of the university, no university officer sits on its board. The university has agreed to provide WARF with rights to its intellectual property in return for research funding. The advantages of interdependent organizations are that, more completely than the previously described types, they separate incompatible activity from the university and buffer the university from negative public relations and charges of undue influence while still allowing the university to exercise some control. The main disadvantage is that much control is relinquished and therefore the risk of embarrassment or scandal may be increased.

The Independent Organization

The independent organization is usually related to the university through contractual or informal arrangements, with the university exercising no control and usually possessing little or no equity in the organization. An example is Research Corporation Technologies, Inc., which contracts with a number of universities to license university-developed technologies. The main advantage of independent organizations is that they provide real separation of the activity from the university and thus usually offer lower risk of all kinds. The disadvantages are that the university usually gives up considerable value in the transaction and can exercise only limited control over the activities of the organization.

Organizational forms fitting within these models are frequently combined to achieve the desired balance among control, buffering, and autonomy. For instance, a subsidiary foundation—perhaps a nonprofit corporation formed to hold ownership of university-developed intellectual property—may own wholly or in part a for-profit independent corporation formed to exploit a technology based on such intellectual property.

DYNAMICS AND IMPLICATIONS

The organizational models just described do not exist in a static relationship to core university functions, but rather change and evolve. These descriptions, therefore, need to be supplemented with some consideration of the dynamics at play and of the models' implications for the larger university organization.

Again, several patterns emerge. The first might be called the *failed integration pattern.* This pattern is recognized by Feller (1994) as a way in which U.S. universities have historically responded to new missions, "accreting" them and then attempting to integrate them with core missions and existing organizational arrangements such as colleges and departments. When these efforts at integration fail, the missions are retained as separate, self-contained, specialized, and often autonomous organizational entities that exist as long as they can attract funding or serve important political constituencies. Much of the infrastructure that has developed to support technology transfer can be seen as fitting this pattern—it was only weakly related to the educational mission, benefited only a few faculty, and violated academic traditions. But because it gave promise of being self-supporting (or even productive of income) and seemed consistent with values held by society, it was allowed to form and grow (Geiger, 1993). Many small-business

assistance centers also fit this category; they are first placed in schools of business and then often, when the faculty members do not respond, are given to extension to administer.

Another dynamic might be called *spin-off,* or *centrifugal,* pattern. This dynamic is characterized by a tendency for the organizational forms to move outward from the university— from the integrated organization to the peripheral organization, from the peripheral to the subsidiary, and so on. This pattern occurs because of a variety of factors.

First, as the functions occurring within the organizations grow and become more important, they are more likely to require nonfaculty professionals to manage and operate them. This happens partly because there is considerable resistance in institutions and among faculty to devoting large amounts of faculty time and energy to noncore functions. And few faculty-reward systems presently recognize noncore activities. Professionals, in their turn, are usually specialists who demand recognition and autonomy and often feel constrained by university rules and processes. For instance, it is logical to compensate technology licensing officers on some incentive scheme, but most universities find such an approach uncomfortable. Second, as the new functions become more market-oriented, complex, differentiated from core functions, or professionalized, the university begins to lose control of the activities and thus has a greater need for the buffering effect provided by subsidiary, interdependent, and independent organizations.

These dynamics combine to create a more fragmented university, in which it becomes increasingly difficult to reconcile disparate missions and to preserve the traditional definition of the role of the university or to define that role in any coherent way at all. They also result in a less faculty-centered institution. Perhaps most important, these dynamics contribute to the emerging *phenomenon of the periphery,* in which what have been considered noncore university functions are beginning to influence and interact with the core in new and sometimes disturbing ways.

Several recent studies and commentaries on university organizational trends have noted this phenomenon. Burton Clark (1995), in his continuing study of innovative universities in Europe, found that the universities that stand out from the rest have four elements in common: (1) an innovative, self-defining idea, (2) an infrastructure with an integrated administrative core, (3) a discretionary funding base, and (4) an innovative developmental periphery. Clark's examples of the elements of this periphery all fall into our definition of economic development. In Clark's view, development of such a periphery is crucial to the success of innovative universities.

Zemsky and Massey (1995) present a less positive view. They see current universities as consisting of "expanding perimeters" and "melting cores," with considerable tension between the two (p. 41). It is well documented that perimeters of universities have been expanding as the institutions assume new roles and seek more resources. This expansion has occurred at the same time that resources for core functions have declined, relative to the costs of those functions, and core functions have not been able to improve productivity or respond appropriately to calls for increased accountability. For example, between 1990 and 1995 university extension revenue at the University of California statewide increased 21 percent (from $110 million to $133 million), and royalty income from intellectual property almost tripled (from $22.5 million to $63.1 million). Over the same period the state of California reduced its support of the universities by almost one-third, from about $1.8 billion to $1.35 billion. This has resulted in a shift and a tension: those along the perimeter now appear less often as venerable citizens of an ancient academy than as the owners and managers of their own enterprises—more concerned with specific outcomes, with the processes of production, and with the kinds of deliverables the market demands. What now worries these entrepreneurs is the center's need to tax the perimeter in order to sustain its core functions, for which there is no longer sufficient revenue. The more that programs, individual faculty, and staff provide for themselves, the more convinced they become that their hard-won earnings are at risk of being siphoned off by a central administration with little discipline and less purpose (Zemsky and Massey, p. 44).

At the extreme, the essential question for those along the perimeter will become whether continued affiliation with a university is worth the tax. A negative answer is not without precedent; there have been a number of cases in which research institutes (Stanford Research Institute, for example), service bureaus, and consulting groups have left their sponsoring universities to take up an independent existence.

FACTORS TO BE CONSIDERED IN ADOPTING OR ASSESSING AN ORGANIZATIONAL DESIGN

As university administrators face the task of organizing economic development activities, they must match the needs of their situation with the characteristics of the organizational models just described. They will also need to consider the dynamics among then). Some of the factors to be kept in mind should be apparent from the preceding descriptions; others emerge from an assessment of the current organizational capacity and culture of the university. Here is a list of those factors and how they might be applied.

Role of the Faculty

Some assessment needs to be made of the role the faculty is expected to play in the economic development activity and how consistent this role is with established faculty roles. The larger the role the faculty is expected to play and the more consistent their involvement is with established faculty roles, the more logical some form of integrated model is, absent other factors to the contrary. Little or incompatible faculty involvement argues for organizational forms at or beyond the periphery of the university.

Degree of Control

Some university economic activities require a high degree of control by the university, either to assure the success of the activity or to protect the interests of the university. The peripheral organization has the potential for the closest control by the university administration; integrated models usually are controlled by constituent parts of the university rather than its central administration, and subsidiary, interdependent, and independent organizations require by definition some sharing of control with others.

Degree of Buffering

This factor is related to degree of control because, beyond the peripheral model, an inverse relationship usually exists between degree of control and degree of buffering—the more control, the less buffering. The protection or buffering, afforded by subsidiary, interdependent, and independent forms may be of three kinds: protection from market or financial risk, protection from legal liability or potential litigation, and protection from negative public relations.

Interaction with Partners and Degree of Community Involvement

Many forms of economic development involve individuals and organizations outside the university organizational structure, and the degree and nature of their involvement has a significant bearing on the form of organization to be chosen. In some cases, even with anticipated heavy involvement of the community, a university organization of the peripheral or subsidiary kind is appropriate because the university can serve as a neutral convener of groups not used to interacting with each other. In other cases, it is useful to deemphasize university involvement in order to give community groups a sense of ownership and empowerment. For the most part, interdependent or independent organizations are most appropriate for activities requiring significant involvement by outside agencies or groups.

Internal Factors

Many other factors, both internal and external to the university, must be taken into account when deciding how to organize university economic development efforts. Because external situations are so varied, it is difficult even to generalize about external factors. Many of the internal factors are also difficult to specify; but they fall into describable categories. *Organizational capacity* is an important general issue. Does the university have the internal capacity to perform the function, or should the function be handled outside the university by some other entity? Can *existing units* within the university administer the activity or will some *new entity* and accompanying infrastructure have to

be developed? Is the new activity consistent with the *organizational culture* of the university, or will dissonance with that culture cause it to encounter sabotage, resistance, neglect, or reluctant and condescending support? Does the university have a *history* supportive of and consistent with the new activity, or has some scandal or past difficulty permanently colored institutional perception of that kind of activity? Do any special *financial, management,* or *risk issues* need to be addressed? For instance, does the university accounting system have the capacity to handle the transaction volume or reporting requirements of the new activity? Will the university subject itself to risks not covered by current institutional insurance programs? Finally, and most important, does the new activity or program have the *commitment of leadership* essential to its success? Few economic development programs will have smooth sailing right from the start. They will encounter problems that only committed leaders can overcome.

Knowledge of Regional Development

There is a more critical determination university administrators must make, one that can influence the choice of organizational form profoundly but one that also is more important than organizational form. That determination is: How best can economic development be brought to a target region by a university? Too often a university is pressed into economic development activities that cannot succeed because other critical elements of economic development are lacking. For instance, the University of California, by virtue of its contract for managing the Los Alamos National Laboratory, recently has been asked to promote high-technology industry in northern New Mexico, a sparsely populated area. In the author's view, these efforts are unlikely to succeed.

What is often lacking on the part of both universities and the communities they serve is an understanding of the very complex process of regional economic development. Required is the identification of an appropriate starting point. For instance, the University of California, San Diego CONNECT program, was created because the business infrastructure in San Diego was not sufficiently developed or sophisticated to support high-technology entrepreneurialism. Once the community had been organized through the CONNECT program, the university had a much more receptive market for its intellectual property and the university research community developed new linkages to the industrial community.

These two examples also illustrate the relationship between technology transfer and economic development. Effective university technology transfer, that is, technology that results in economic development, is only one of several important components of economic development. For instance, as has been the case in northern New Mexico, technology transfer has been effective in creating new, start-up, high-technology businesses, which move away to more urban areas when they become successful. Universities need to learn a great deal about the dynamics of regional development so that they can educate their local communities, adjust expectations to what reasonably can be accomplished, and structure university involvement appropriately; thus avoiding a no-win situation.

IMPLICATIONS FOR EXTERNAL GROUPS AND ORGANIZATIONS

Perhaps the most important lesson of this discussion for external groups and organizations is that there is no such entity as *the university*. Universities are composed of many organizational units that open have different and even conflicting agendas. An understanding of the relationships among the parts of the university and the dynamics of these relationships can help external groups influence university activities. External groups can help their university partners gain power and avoid internal conflict, they can shoulder their share of the responsibility for activities, and they can avoid pressing universities beyond their capacities and competencies.

As external groups and agencies enter into partnerships and other kinds of arrangements with universities, they need to do their own careful assessment not only of the university as a whole but also of the organizational unit(s) within the university to which they will relate and on which they may depend. Using the guidelines in the preceding section, they need to assess the correctness of the organizational

fit of the university entity charged with responsibility for the activity, asking their own questions about the commitment of leadership, the stability and staying power of the organizational unit, and the relationship of the activity to the core activities of the university. Increased knowledge and sophistication on the part of university constituencies about university organization and dynamics can make a significant contribution to the success of regional economic development.

Recent organizational changes in the University of California's technology licensing function illustrate many of these factors and implications. The regents of the University of California established a centralized patent office in the 1960s to control the university's patentable intellectual property. The main functions of the office were to inventory and then protect with patents, when appropriate, inventions and discoveries made by university researchers. As the number of inventions rose and as pressures from the faculty and the public to license and place intellectual property into commercialization mounted, the capability of the staff to handle the work was well exceeded. The regents delegated authority over the office of the office of the president of the university, and the staff of the office was expanded. The emphasis was placed on licensing rather than protecting intellectual property.

In 1989, a new director was hired, and along with a senior vice president, proposed that a nonprofit foundation be formed to handle regents' intellectual property and a for-profit corporation be formed to handle venture capital accumulation and investment. These ideas were dropped after a lengthy controversy prompted primarily by faculty concerns and played out in the press. However, faculty on the nine campuses continued to complain bitterly about the lack of service, even from the expanded office, and the business community complained about the difficulty in doing business with the university. Berkeley and UCLA asked for and were granted permission to start their own campus technology licensing offices. These two were followed by UC San Diego, and UC San Francisco and UC Davis are now in the process of establishing their own offices.

This story, briefly told, is a realistic example of several aspects described throughout this chapter. First, it is clear that the regents' primary concern in the early years was control. Control is most effectively exercised by a centralized unit. As the control function grew, it became a barrier to development, which upset key constituencies. When professionals were hired to serve these constituencies better, they quickly sought release from controls by trying to move from a peripheral organizational form to a subsidiary organizational form, illustrating the centrifugal force postulated earlier. However, the subsidiary form was dropped when it threatened to move the function too far from faculty control. Now the university is trying to locate the function closer to the faculty of each campus. This scenario illustrates the importance of faculty and the conditions under which a decentralized model might be more appropriate.

CONCLUSION

There can be no doubt that regional economic development activities have become a permanent part of the agenda for American higher education. Those activities are likely to expand in the next few years and become more important in the lives of both universities and the communities they serve. The way in which universities organize such activities will both determine and reflect some fundamental shifts in university organizational structure and a radical redefinition of the role of the university in society. University economic development activities, including continuing education and technology transfer, are now part of the innovative, entrepreneurial, expanding perimeter of higher education, which has a fluid and uneasy relationship with the core and tradition of higher education.

The more successful universities are in performing noncore, nontraditional functions, the more likely they will be able to retain coherent institutional identity in our society—yet the more different that identity will be from the traditional one that has survived since the Middle Ages. Of course, failure at these activities may well precipitate another kind of crisis. In spite of this double bind, those of us on the perimeter are optimistic, confident, and excited about our role in the university community, which we expect to continue far into the future.

REFERENCES

Castells, M., & Hall, P. (1994). *Technopoles of the world.* London: Routledge.

Clark, B. (1995). Case studies of innovative universities: A progress report. Paper prepared for the 17th annual forum of the European Association for Institutional Research, Zurich. Aug. 17–30.

Feldman, M. P. (1994). The university and economic development: The case of Johns Hopkins University and Baltimore. *Economic development quarterly, 8*(1), 67–76.

Feller, I. (1994). The university as an instrument of state and regional economic development: The rhetoric and reality of the U.S. experience. Paper presented at the Center for Economic Policy Research Conference, Stanford University, Mar. 18–20.

Geiger, R. L. (1993). *Research and relevant knowledge.* New York: Oxford University Press.

Matkin, G. W. (1990). *Technology transfer and the university.* New York: Macmillan.

Rybczynski, W. (1995). The rise of the college city. *New York times magazine,* Sept. 17, p. 58.

Saxenian, A. (1994). *Regional advantage.* Cambridge, Mass.: Harvard University Press.

Zemsky, R., & Massy, W. F. (1995). Expanding perimeters, melting cores, and sticky functions: Toward an understanding of our current predicaments. *Change, 27*(6), 40–49.

CHAPTER 24

RETIREMENT COMMUNITIES

A Financially Rewarding Educational Approach

MICHAEL D. HORWITZ AND RODERIC L. ROLETT

Michael D. Horwitz is a consultant for Tenenbaum & Associates in Boston. Roderic L. Rolett is vice president of Herbert J. Sims & C., Inc.

In the face of declining student enrollment, escalating costs, and tightening funding sources, higher education administrators are recognizing the need to maximize revenues, efficiently use resources, and minimize costs while maintaining—or improving—the academic excellence of their institutions.

Many institutions are targeting real estate assets as a source of additional revenue. A fresh look at real estate reveals an often underutilized asset—excess land. In many cases, disposition of underutilized assets can result in development that is compatible with or supportive of the institution's purpose, as well as financially rewarding.

Retirement communities are becoming a popular use for undeveloped land owned by colleges and universities. The University of Virginia and Wellesley, Oberlin, Skidmore, and Springfield colleges have all considered providing retirement housing for faculty, staff, and alumni. A retirement community offers an institution the opportunity to pursue its mission of providing public service to the community, expanding knowledge, training professionals, and teaching humanitarian values. On-site retirement housing furnishes additional educational opportunities, allowing faculty members and students to conduct field studies and participate in internships in such areas as gerontological studies, physical therapy, therapeutic recreational services, and rehabilitation services. The provision of alumni retirement housing can enhance an institution's ties to its alumni, which in turn boosts the recruitment of new students and fund raising.

Retirement communities are culturally and environmentally compatible with colleges and universities. Retirees seek a stable and supportive environment in which they can achieve their potential to continue learning, contribute to the community, and meet new friends. When their community exists in conjunction with an educational institution, senior citizens may take advantage of opportunities to remain physically and intellectually active by auditing courses, enrolling in continuing education programs, joining exercise classes, and attending cultural events and programs. The unique affiliation with a retirement community reduces senior citizens' apprehensions about committing to a major lifestyle and financial change.

Why the sudden interest in retirement housing? A study of national demographic trends shows that the number of elderly in the United States is growing twice as fast as the rate of the overall population. The share of the population age 65 and over grew from 5 percent in 1920 to 12

Source: *NACUBO Business Officer*, Vol. 24, January 1991, p. 33–35.

percent in 1987. The 65-and-over population is projected to more than double in the next 50 years, from 30 million to 68 million.

TYPES OF RETIREMENT HOUSING

When most people think of housing for the elderly, they think of nursing homes. However, only about 5 percent of the elderly population are in nursing homes at a given time. With more and more women in the work force, the traditional care giver is no longer available to care for elderly parents; retirement communities have risen as a substitute. Communities that cater to the healthy elderly as well as the infirm elderly are needed. To meet the growing demand for such communities, a spectrum of housing types has emerged, from facilities that only provide shelter, such as apartments and single family subdivisions, to nursing facilities that offer maximum care and service. The forms of ownership also vary—including cooperative, condominium, entrance fee, and rental.

Congregate Housing

Several forms of housing cater to those elderly who require assistance in home maintenance, cooking, and social activities, as well as the security of on-site health care. A popular form of housing that is gaining acceptance throughout the country is referred to as "congregate housing." Congregate housing appeals to the senior citizen who is less active than he or she once was and has begun to view household upkeep as a burden. The average resident is in his or her late 70s.

Congregate housing provides amenities for independent senior citizens without substantially impinging on a person's sense of independence or offering contractual medical care or daily living assistance. Services provided include meal service, although residents generally have their own private kitchens; housekeeping; linen service; recreational and social activities; transportation; security; and emergency call buttons. Additional services available on a fee-for-service basis include home health care, assistance with the activities of daily living, and wellness programs.

Continuing Care Retirement Communities

A number of facilities provide a continuum of care to their residents. Continuing care retirement communities provide health care (nursing or assisted care) on a fee-for-services basis at an on-site nursing home or through a contract with a nearby nursing home. The provision of services that cater to independent as well as frail elderly allows couples to stay together in a community if one spouse becomes temporarily ill and requires supervised medical care. The trend toward "aging in place" has created a great demand for continuing care retirement communities.

Life Care Communities

The most complete form of elderly housing is a life care community. Skyrocketing health care costs have led to a demand for programs that place a ceiling on living and health care costs. A life care community offers the same range of programs and services provided by continuing care retirement communities, plus full nursing home care at no additional fee.

FEASIBILITY STUDIES

Colleges and universities often need external real estate and financing expertise to create the strategic framework that is required to reap benefits from untapped, illiquid real estate assets.

Especially where a specific type of development such as elderly housing is desired, an institution can benefit from the services of an objective real estate professional who understands both the proposed development and marketing process and the institution's needs and preferences.

The external consultant must consider the institutional objectives in setting up a retirement community—the policies of the educational institution and financial, space, and facility needs. In some cases, a full evaluation of the institution's facility and real estate assets is required as a basis for jointly determining needs and strategies for institutional space usage and availability and disposition of excess assets.

Market Research

Before actually developing a retirement community, the institution must confirm market support for such housing. A market research study should be prepared to identify the appropriate segment of the senior citizen spectrum to address. A study of demographic, income, net worth, and home ownership patterns should be combined with a survey of existing, proposed, and rumored competitive projects to determine the level of unsatisfied demand for elderly housing. This study should be followed by focus group or telephone surveys to examine the issues of site selection, product type, ownership model, and pricing.

Financial Feasibility

A financial feasibility analysis provides the detailed financial information necessary to confirm that the project can be built according to plans. A financial feasibility study should include projected income, balance sheets, and cash flow statements. Health care and actuarial risks are often part of this analysis, with input from insurance professionals. A key component of a feasibility study is the determination of the optimal financing method available, which often includes tax-exempt bond financing.

An institution's ability to finance specialized projects can be enhanced with the aid of a staff member or adviser who understands the lender's credit criteria and structuring requirements. Knowledge of the capital and elderly housing markets is essential to determine the optimal financing method for the development of a retirement community. This information can be incorporated into the formula used to determine the value of the land dedicated to the project and the cash flows required to support the project's debt service payments.

DEVELOPING THE PROJECT

After the marketability and feasibility of the project are confirmed, a qualified developer—preferably with experience in marketing and operating an elderly housing facility—must be chosen.

The institution should assemble a team of architects, engineers, attorneys, and other professionals, and draw upon institutional in-house resources to meet the challenges posed by the complex real estate opportunities.

Successful development of the retirement community requires a unique blend of resources (e.g., land and seed money) and skills. Skills such as familiarity with local land use practice, knowledge of design features for the elderly, service management and operations expertise, marketing, construction, and regulations are prerequisites for developing a quality retirement community. Institutions that want to directly develop a retirement community usually follow one of two general models:

- They set up a not-for-profit or for-profit company to conduct a joint venture with an experienced developer. The institution could contribute the land or other resources (e.g., seed money and alumni contacts) and retain significant control over the development. In these cases, the college or university needs to identify national and local development teams that specialize in retirement housing. Other local institutions, such as hospitals, often are interested in participating.
- They independently develop the retirement community. Where necessary and appropriate, the institution should hire professionals to facilitate the development.

Administrators should prepare a report that describes the proposed site, market, financial findings, and intended structure. Qualified developers should be solicited to make formal presentations to the institution. Then a competitive bid process should be conducted. Though many real estate developers dislike the competitive bid process, it provides the landowner with the opportunity to realize a high return.

Unless the institution wants to sell the land outright, the retirement community usually will be structured as a participating ground lease, whereby the educational land owner receives prepaid ground rent, annual rent, contingent rent, and transaction rent from the retirement community. The retirement community is often established as a not-for-profit

501(c)(3) corporation. The total value of the rental income will depend upon the economics of the retirement community and the ability of the community to support a particular series of rental payments. Leases are generally structured for 75 years. When the lease expires, it can be extended or the institution can take possession of the community and turn it into dormitories or continue to operate it as a retirement community.

The zoning and regulatory processes involved in developing a retirement community can extend beyond two years. Generally, financing is not available until the community has presold (refundable deposits) 50 to 70 percent of the units. The initial feasibility study, developer selection, zoning, regulatory approval, and pre-marketing period can run from two to three years. Construction can take one to two years, bringing the period from conceptualization to move-in to at least five years.

Despite the investment of time, retirement communities can provide a compatible and profitable use of underdeveloped land. Retirement communities that operate in conjunction with colleges and universities enhance alumni relations, stimulate research and professional training, and contribute to the institution's operating budget or endowment through a sale or ground lease.

CHAPTER 25

ATHLETICS AND THEIR COSTS

Excerpts from a Revealing New Report

NACUBO

The National Association of College and University Business Officers has recently published "The Financial Management of Intercollegiate Athletics Programs." Here we present excerpts from several of its crucial sections. Copies of the entire report can be obtained by calling the NACUBO publications desk at (202) 861-2560. The cost is $30 for NACUBO members, and $40 for non-members. Please refer to source code NU1055 when ordering.

Athletics has become an accepted part of the higher education experience. Colleges and universities have made intercollegiate athletics an important co-curricular activity for both participants and alumni, and many feature athletics programs in their marketing materials. Colleges and universities have become a major source of athletic events for American sports fans, many of whom have come to prefer watching their favorite collegiate team over the local professional team. The NCAA "Final Four" comes as professional basketball teams are fighting for spots in the NBA playoffs; yet newspaper and television coverage of the collegiate tournament regularly preempts news about its professional counterpart.

The market forces described have created the public misperception that intercollegiate athletics programs are profit-making enterprises for most colleges and universities. This perception is based on extensive media attention to a very small program segment (football and basketball) of higher education institutions. According to the Knight Commission, 70 percent of Division I athletics programs now lose money.[1] The most recent NCAA survey of revenues and expenses revealed that in 1989 the average profit of Division I-A intercollegiate athletics programs was $39,000, and all other divisions averaged deficits ranging from $145,000 to $782,000.[2]

While a large number of higher education administrators recognize that their institutions may never realize profits from intercollegiate athletics, many choose to build up their programs or selected teams for the visibility they believe major athletics programs will provide. Many colleges and universities believe that even if their athletics programs lose money, the exposure they receive from a television appearance or occasional bowl game will increase public recognition and interest in their institutions. Underlying this idea is the belief that such recognition will translate into increased applications, enhanced fundraising opportunities, and a more receptive ear from legislators and the local community.

Other institutions see their entry into large-scale intercollegiate athletics as a form of public service, with the college or university becoming a source of local or regional pride. This view is

Source: *Academe*, November–December 1993.

reflected in the NCAA's Division I and Division II philosophy statements, which describe intercollegiate athletics programs as having a "dual objective" of serving "the general public (community, area, state [and nation, in the case of Division I members])" as well as the campus community.

Regardless of whether an institution builds up its athletics program to generate revenues or to enhance its publicity, the institution must recognize the potential for financial abuses and rapid cost increases in athletics programs. The college or university must therefore build in mechanisms that will ensure sufficient institutional oversight and control of the intercolle-

giate athletics program. Opinions about the appropriate role for athletics in institutions of higher education are numerous and diverse. Whatever one's views, the financial and public relations risks of intercollegiate athletics programs cannot be disputed. These risks and ways to minimize them are the subject of this briefing paper.

Intercollegiate athletics programs typically have several sources of operating revenues as well as access to funding for capital needs. Table 25.1 describes the average magnitude of each revenue source and its proportion of total athletics program revenues.

TABLE 25.1
Principal Revenue Sources Fiscal Year 1989
(Dollar Amounts in Thousands)

Average Amount in 1989 and Percentage of Total Revenues	Division I			Division II		Division III	
	I-A	I-AA	I-AAA	With FB*	W/O FB**	With FB	W/O FB
Total ticket sales not reduced by contract settlements	$3,399	$438	$238	$93	$44	$16	$3
Percentage of total	35%	18%	20%	13%	9%	13%	2%
Student activity fees for athletics admissions	$890	$900	$697	$234	$170	$152	$142
Percentage of total	4%	18%	24%	12%	13%	11%	25%
Student assessment unrelated to admissions	$950	$1,259	$811	$360	$326	$237	$229
Percentage of total	3%	14%	17%	20%	13%	27%	35%
Guarantees and options received	$792	$145	$39	$25	$10	$2	$2
Percentage of total	8%	6%	3%	2%	2%	1%	31 %
Contributions from alumni and others	$1,546	$299	$151	$102	$54	$32	$12
Percentage of total	15%	11%	10%	11%	10%	12%	6%
Bowl games, tournaments, and television revenues	$1,470	$100	$151	$15	$33	$2	$2
Percentage of total	14%	3%	9%	1%	1%	0%	0%
Direct state or other government support	$1,363	$1,045	$423	$495	$518	$355	$112
Percentage of total	5%	18%	4%	25%	40%	20%	15%
All other revenues	$1,558	$301	$181	$158	$73	$50	$35
Percentage of total	16%	12%	13%	16%	12%	16%	16%

*With football

**Without football

Source: Revenues and Expenses of Intercollegiate Athletics Programs by Mitchell H. Raiborn.

National Collegiate Athletic Association (Overland Park, Kansas: 1990).

- *Ticket sales* in football and basketball have historically been the major source of revenue for large college sports programs, though in recent years ticket income has become a decreasing proportion of the entire revenue picture.

- *"Student activity fees "*and *"student assessments"* are often used interchangeably. The NCAA, however, accounts for the two separately in analyzing sources of athletics program revenue. In the NCAA's terminology, activity fees are charged exclusively for admissions to athletic events, while assessments are fees collected from students that are not directly related to admissions. In either case, these fees are charged to students above and beyond their tuitions.

- *Television broadcast fee revenues* represent a significant portion of total revenues only for Division I-A institutions.

- *Booster club and alumni donations ("contributions from alumni and others")* have been one of the fastest growing revenue sources. When the NCAA began its financial studies in 1965, such donations accounted for five percent of total revenue at major football schools. By 1989, this figure had increased to 15 percent among Division I-A institutions.

- *Direct state or other government support* revenue data combine figures for both public and private institutions. As a result, these data do not provide a fully accurate picture for either group. In comparing public and private institutions in each division, the proportion of total revenues that direct government support represents is comparable only in Division I-A (5 percent for public and 3 percent for private institutions). Among the other divisions, public institutions receive between 20 and 46 percent of total revenues from direct government support (except in Division I-AAA, where public institutions receive only 8 percent), while private institutions receive between zero and 3 percent of total revenues from direct government support.

- *Guarantees and options* are the share of ticket receipts contractually assured to an institution when it is the visiting team. These income sources are not a significant revenue source for institutions outside of Division I-A and perhaps I-AA. According to literature on intercollegiate athletics finances, guarantee revenues and expenses are often not reported because (1) they are not included in the NCAA guidelines for accounting and auditing as revenue objects and (2) they vary greatly from year to year.[3]

- *Corporate sponsorship revenues* comprise direct payments from sponsors for logo use, the naming of bowl games, as well as shoes and uniforms donated for use by collegiate teams. Unfortunately, the NCAA does not collect data on revenues from these sources. Moreover, it appears that no one does. Former Education Secretary Lamar Alexander's 1992 report to Congress identified twenty-four revenue elements commonly compiled in studies of intercollegiate athletic finances. Only one item that could be considered a form of corporate sponsorship was even on the list, and the most recent data were collected in 1970. What remains are anecdotal data. For example, some sense of the magnitude of these dollars among major athletics programs can be gathered from reports that a Division I-A institution lost several hundred thousand dollars in corporate sponsorships after being placed on probation.[4]

- *All other revenues* is a noteworthy category not simply because it is included in the NCAA's survey but because it represents a significant proportion—12 to 16 percent—of total revenues among all NCAA divisions. Beyond that, there is little analysis available to shed light on what is included in this category. One would assume it includes any funding provided an athletics program out of central university funds, among other things.

Most intercollegiate athletics programs have access to funding for capital needs through two sources: debt service and restricted giving. The relatively small proportion of institutions that reported debt service costs in the most recent

NCAA survey of revenues and expenses may indicate that few athletics programs issue debt on their own. The proportion of survey respondents reporting information on debt service ranged from 55 percent in Division I-A to 7 percent in the Division III "with football" segment. Debt is not generally issued by an athletics department itself because "special purpose" debt is not as easily obtained as debt issued by the institution as a whole. Many of these institutions therefore consider debt service an institutional budget item and guarantee athletic facility construction bonds with projected tuition and fee revenues.

Basic equity considerations arise regarding the use of tuition and fee monies generated from all students for debt service on capital projects that benefit only a small subset of students. Where an athletics facility is intended for the use of all students—for intramurals, physical education courses, and leisure-time athletic pursuits—debt service might legitimately be funded from general university revenues. For capital projects that are for the exclusive use of athletes—such as team locker rooms, academic support facilities, and the like—debt service might be more appropriately paid out of the athletics program's budget.

Restricted giving is another source of funds for athletics department capital needs. Naming opportunities such as those associated with athletic facilities are often appealing to alumni and boosters. It is not uncommon to find athletic facilities named for one donor and batting cages, long-jump pits, and weight rooms named for others.

Capital campaigns may include specific athletics capital needs and seek high-level giving for these needs. In pursuing such interests, an institution should consider the impression it makes regarding institutional priorities if a large proportion of a capital campaign appears to be oriented toward meeting athletics needs.

In addition, an institution's development office should consider the effect that designating a proportion of anticipated giving for athletics needs has on total "donor capacity." For example, when a goal of $100 million is set for a capital campaign, this figure represents the institution's best estimate of its total donor capacity from all sources during the campaign period. If a portion of this capacity is anticipated to be $25 million in restricted giving for athletics, that $25 million is not available to support other needs of the institution (which rely on the remaining $75 million donor capacity).

Unrestricted gifts also can be used for athletics program capital needs. In the late 1980s, for example, a large university announced the construction of a $6 million indoor football practice field and weight training facility, for which $3 million of funding came from unrestricted gift funds.[5] While a university always retains the privilege of using unrestricted gifts for the purposes it chooses, presidents and institutional advancement vice presidents should consider whether funding a high proportion of facilities used primarily by athletes from unrestricted monies runs contrary to the wishes of many donors.

Between 1985 and 1989, revenue sources related to athletics events (e.g., ticket sales, conference distributions, etc.) decreased as a combined percentage of total revenues. Unearned or passive revenue sources, such as alumni contributions and government support, have increased as a combined percentage of total revenues.[6]

This pattern indicates that intercollegiate athletics has become more dependent on sources of revenue external to athletics themselves—a conclusion that has strong implications for the institutional control of athletics programs. If the pattern continues, institutional leaders concerned about maintaining control of their athletics programs must ask themselves about the conditions that may be attached to unearned or passive revenues. Some unearned revenues, such as alumni and booster donations, represent opportunities for groups entirely outside of the institution to exercise financial leverage over athletics, perhaps reducing institutional control.

In considering potential revenues from television contracts, from adding games to a sports season and from booster clubs and corporate sponsors, the institution should take care to avoid undue influence of university decision-making by parties external to the institution or those not accountable for the results of their decisions.

As the Knight Commission recommended, presidents should critically review contractual relationships with television networks. Allowing the networks to dictate the terms and conditions for televising college sports reduces institutional control over what are often educational as well as athletic decisions. This is particularly the case where the terms of a television contract intrude into areas that are central to the university's educational mission. (For example, the effect on student athletes of playing in away games scheduled for 9:00 p.m. or later on weekday nights and attending classes early the next morning.)

The potential volume of dollars that booster organizations can bring to an athletics department often gives these clubs significant influence over athletics directors (ADs) and athletics administrators. Rarely is the impact of booster decisions on the institution as a whole taken into consideration. One notable example is booster endowments for coach positions. Such endowments may pay the entire salary of a coaching position or provide a supplement to compensation set by the university (often through set bonuses). Where booster clubs establish such endowments independently, they may hinder efforts of the university to maintain an overall institutional compensation scheme.

Among institutions with major athletics programs, the market for coaches has led to salaries that are well above those paid to professors and senior administrators. This situation is comparable to what occurs at institutions with professional schools, where top salaries are paid to doctors or lawyers on the faculty in order to compete with the salaries these professionals might make in private practice. Booster monies may allow the university to pay a more competitive salary to coaches or to free up monies it had committed to compensation for other purposes. In order to maintain institutional oversight, however, it is important that the university be a part of decisions to establish such endowments.

Several revenue sources, if not managed properly, bring with them threats to the university's public image, especially its perceived academic reputation and institutional priorities.

When student fee increases raise the overall cost of a college education, they affect the amount of financial aid for which a student is eligible. If a large portion of these fee increases is intended to support the athletics department budget, then increasing amounts of state and federal financial aid are in effect providing support for athletics. Presidents and trustees should assess the potential resistance of taxpayers to using state and federal financial aid to support services and activities unrelated to the educational mission of colleges and universities. The institution also should consider the effect on its public image when using taxpayer dollars in this way.[7]

Several states have passed laws prohibiting the direct use of taxpayer dollars for athletics program support. However, because of the diverse financial relationships between athletics programs and their institutions, tax dollars that go for general support of the institution are frequently used to support the athletics program. Presidents need to be cognizant of the extent to which government monies are provided directly. But, more importantly, they need to understand how they are using tax monies as an indirect subsidy of athletics in order to make informed decisions about the legitimacy of this practice.

Taxpayers who are aware of this use of their tax dollars may resent it. In 1988, an Arkansas survey found that "almost 75 percent of Arkansans favor limiting state spending on college athletics . . . 71 percent favor requiring college athletics programs to be self-supporting.[8]

State prohibitions against using taxpayer dollars for athletics purposes may reflect the public's belief that athletics is not a central purpose of higher education. These prohibitions also reflect the misconception that athletics can be a self-supporting activity.

However, by refusing to spend tax dollars on athletics, states are implicitly indicating that athletics are not legitimate programs of colleges and universities worthy of public support. Such an attitude widens the gulf between athletics and academics.

Overassociation with commercial sponsors also may project an image for an institution that it does not want. In accepting contracts with corporate sponsors, an institution must guard against tarnishing its reputation as a predominantly academic institution in the eyes of the public (or in the eyes of legislators responsible for appropriating tax dollars).

Some revenues from corporate sponsors challenge the ability of an institution to account adequately for and capture all revenues that flow to its athletics program. Shoe companies generally contract directly with a coach in making merchandise contributions. As a result, contract revenues and the merchandise itself flow directly to the coach and are not under the university's direct financial control (or oversight). There is some legitimacy to coaches' claims that shoe companies seek their endorsement when the companies make such contracts. However, it is equally legitimate to claim that shoe companies also seek association of their products with the university's name and the reputation of its athletics program. Institutions should consider establishing agreements with coaches that govern revenues obtained from shoe contracts, much as institutions presently have royalty agreements with faculty who develop marketable products while employed by the university.

Unanticipated tax pressure on an institution may also result from some corporate sponsorship revenues. Increasingly, the IRS is questioning the legitimacy of tax exemptions that institutions claim on revenues obtained from corporate sponsors when these revenues can be construed nor as charitable donations but, in effect, fees for advertising. This is particularly the case in regard to advertising on stadium scoreboards and in game programs.

Growth of operating expenses, in the aggregate, has outpaced both inflation and athletics revenue growth.[9] Between 1985 and 1989, the annual growth rate of athletics program expenses increased in all divisions except I-AAA, and the "no football" segment of Division III. More important, in all divisions except the segment of Division III without football, expenditure growth increased more rapidly than did revenue growth over the period.

Despite public belief to the contrary, the large majority of college and university athletics program expenditures have always exceeded revenues. As former Education Secretary Alexander's report to Congress notes, "While most collegiate athletics programs have been operating in the red for decades, the recent publicity given to billion-dollar television contracts has led to an intensity of questioning as to how deficits can still exist."[10] The report goes on to note that these deficits have continued as "revenues and costs in intercollegiate athletics have risen along with revenues and costs of everything else." However, more recent observations "point out that the number of institutions losing money in intercollegiate activities has risen, principally because of the disparity between the rate of increase in revenues and the rate of increase for expenditures."

The NCAA Special Committee to Review Financial Conditions in Intercollegiate Athletics, established in 1992, was charged in part with seeking ways to reduce athletics program costs. Some of the issues dealt with by the committee and frequently discussed in the literature on intercollegiate athletics costs deserve special emphasis.

Salaries of ADs and coaches in many major athletics programs are in many instances much higher than salaries for most academic personnel. A study of the salaries of ADs and football and basketball coaches done by *USA Today* in 1986 determined that most ADs at major sports colleges and universities received over $75,000 a year plus perks and benefits. By comparison, faculty salaries averaged $45,360 in 1991–92 ($51,080 among doctoral institutions, a category into which many institutions with major athletics programs fall).[11] Moreover, while this discrepancy between salaries of athletics personnel and those of faculty is significant, one can assume that it would be far greater were the data compared for the same year.

Presidents can expect that non-athletics faculty will continue to question why their salaries are so much lower than those of athletics department personnel. Moreover, public awareness of this discrepancy will increase as media reports about both intercollegiate athletics programs and overall college and university financial matters continue. The institutional priorities implied by athletics salaries that are high relative to academic personnel salaries will make it increasingly difficult for universities to define their mission as primarily academic. Presidents and trustees should consider how this will affect institutional image and the public's confidence and support in the long term.

Presidents also need to consider how they can begin to reduce personnel in athletics programs as a cost containment measure. Data on overall growth in university administrative personnel and in athletics departments generally supports the view that athletics programs are often overstaffed. College and university leaders must be prepared to evaluate athletics department staffing levels in terms of the institution's overall mission rather than the need to produce winning teams.

Athletic scholarship expenses grew enormously during the 1980s, primarily as a result of the rapid growth of tuitions during that period, but now need to be brought into line with other expenses. Universities can consider several approaches to containing athletic scholarship expenses:

- *Reduce the number of scholarships allowed by the NCAA.*

- *Restrict financial assistance to athletes to need-based scholarships only.*

- *Reduce team and recruitment travel costs.*

  The NCAA Special Committee has made several specific recommendations for reducing team travel and recruitment travel costs, including limits on the form of team transportation and further restrictions on off-campus recruiting contacts.

  An important consideration for university leaders in regard to athletic recruitment costs is the return on this investment to the institution's academic reputation. If the institution views its academic reputation as central to its mission, it must ask whether it makes sense to spend vastly more money recruiting athletes than academically talented students or students with other talents and characteristics desired by the university. In the long term, will the institution's reputation benefit more from producing professional athletes or producing future scientists, doctors, teachers, and civic leaders? [12]

- *Control equipment expenditures.* Because collegiate athletic equipment is expensive, making options for cost reduction in this area is limited. While equipment expenditures are less than 10 percent of total expenses in almost all divisions, they still represent sizable dollar amounts. In 1989 the total cost of equipping a Division I-A football team was estimated at $1,200 per player, plus costs for practice equipment and coaches' equipment. Ice hockey equipment costs were estimated at $1,000 per player, and the cost of equipping a facility for gymnastics began at $50,000. [13]

Reasoned cost reduction efforts demand a full understanding of the sources of various expenses. Full reporting on expenses by individual sports is rarely available. The common practice of grouping numerous operating expenses into a category called "Expenses Not Related to Specific Sports" makes it difficult to obtain a full picture of the sources of athletic costs. Where cost reduction efforts consider eliminating or scaling back some teams, accurate expense information by sport is particularly important. In addressing the gender equity of an entire athletics program, it is necessary to know the true costs of each sport in order to ensure that resources are expended fairly.

The most recent NCAA survey of revenues and expenses shows that athletics departments report from 24 to 37 percent of their total expenses as Expenses Not Related to Specific Sports. A recent NACUBO *Business Officer* article noted that most expenses in this category could be allocated to specific sports based on criteria such as number of athletes in each sport, ratio of direct expenditures or ticket sales of each sport, or use of facilities by each sport. [14]

Many efforts at cost containment can only be accomplished by reducing pressure to spend ever-increasing amounts of money on various aspects of intercollegiate athletics programs. The extreme competitiveness of intercollegiate athletics frequently poses a challenge to such efforts, regardless of the expenditure area. Attempts to reduce salaries, staffing levels, athletic scholarships, travel, or equipment can always be criticized as moves that will reduce the competitiveness of athletic teams.

To make informed choices regarding the financial management of intercollegiate athletics programs and to achieve and maintain financial stability, institutions will require accurate and uniform methods of accounting for and reporting athletics department revenues and expenditures. Before an institution can determine the best method by which to operate its athletics program, it must have a clear picture of the financial status of its program. Developing uniform methods for all institutions to report the true revenues and expenses of their athletics programs will also make it possible to compare athletics programs meaningfully and to develop benchmarks of fiscal stability. Such comparisons may also create a healthy peer pressure, in which athletics programs strive to operate more efficiently than their opponents.

NOTES

1. *A New Beginning for a New Century,* Final Report of the Knight Foundation Commission on Intercollegiate Athletics, (Knight Foundation: Miami, 1993): 7.

2. *Revenues and Expenses of Intercollegiate Athletics Programs,* Mitchell H. Raiborn. (National Collegiate Athletic Association: Overland Park, Kans., 1990).

3. Alexander, Secretary of Education, 1992 Report to Congress.

4. *College Sports, Inc.* by Murray Sperber, (Henry Holt and Co.: New York, 1990): 64.

5. Sperber, p. 131.

6. Raiborn, p. 21

7. *The Old College Try: Balancing Athletics and Education,* John R. Thelin and Lawrence I. Wiseman. Report No. 4. (School of Education and Development, The George Washington University: Washington, D.C.: 1989): p. 54.

8. Sperber, p. 91.

9. Raiborn, p. 34. Also a comparison of Tables 2.1 and 3.1 in that source.

10. Alexander, p. v.

11. *The Chronicle of Higher Education Almanac,* August 26, 1992.

12. A similar view is expressed in Sperber, p. 114.

13. Sperber, p. 116.

14. *Time to Tell the Whole Story: Uncovering the True Cost of University Athletics,* Peter Hughes. (NACUBO *Business Officer,* May 1992).

SECTION IV

HIGHER EDUCATION EXPENDITURES

INTRODUCTION

How much colleges and universities spend, and how and why they spend it, are among the chief practical concerns in higher education finance. However, campus financial administrators seldom have the time, or the inclination, to reflect on their strategies and procedures in the form of published scholarship. For many of them, and for the institutions they work for, the bottom lines are achieving institutional prosperity, productivity, and efficiency, not explaining how they achieve these things. By the same token, relatively few higher education scholars have chosen to tackle the issue of institutional expenditures as an area for research and investigation. Fortunately, there are a handful of administrators and scholars who have reflected on the issue of expenditures, and they have enriched the scholarship on the finance of higher education with their analyses. This section includes eight of these analyses, designed to make readers more aware not only of the importance of expenditures as a financial issue, but also of the complexity of the subject.

While a decade old, John Waggaman's monograph on "Strategies and Consequences: Managing the Costs in Higher Education" remains a vital survey of the various costs incurred by colleges and universities. Waggaman examines the spectrum of cost pressures in higher education, from unmet needs and administrative costs, to faculty costs and research-related expenses. Although the environment has changed somewhat, Waggaman's enumeration of the major forces continues as a useful guide for students.

Writing as the trickle of public criticism of higher education became a flood in the late 1980s and early 1990s, William Massy discusses what inhibits productivity in administrative and support areas, explains how to identify these inhibitors, and offers a plan for making institutions more productive. His words of caution, and his suggestions for improvement, have even greater urgency today as demands grow louder for higher education to be more accountable and effective. Massy's understanding of organizational behavior, and his ability to analyze it in straightforward terms (combined with his strategic use of effective anecdotes from industry and academe), makes this article both robust and accessible for general readers.

Larry Leslie and Gary Rhoades search for explanations in their article, "Rising Administrative Costs." Citing the skyrocketing costs of administration, particularly in comparison to the costs of instruction and research, they offer a series of hypotheses to account for these cost increases, then assess the reasonableness of each hypothesis through findings in the scholarly literature and observations of current trends and conditions in higher education. This approach should prompt substantial discussion as readers compare their own impressions and observations with those of Leslie and Rhoades.

Without question, one of the most significant expenditures in higher education today is technology. In "Forecasting Financial Priorities for Technology," Martin Ringle, a technology administrator, argues that given the rapid pace of technological change, institutional strategies for the financing of new technologies need to be extremely responsive. Drawing on the technology finance models of twenty-five liberal arts colleges, Ringle describes the issues these institutions have faced, from staffing and equipment, to maintenance and organizational change. Ringle's discussion of the liberal arts college experience with financing technology is readily generalizable to other institutional types. John Oberlin, also a technology administrator, outlines the foundation for a new financial strategy for managing information technology in his article, "The Financial Mythology of Information Technology: Developing a Game Plan." Oberlin debunks seven myths of information technology on his way toward advocating for a new approach to financing this always volatile and often misperceived aspect of contemporary higher education.

A more tangible example of an institution's expenditures is its physical plant. Encouraging administrators to reconsider the management of campus facilities, William Daigneau asks,

"The Physical Plant: Asset or Liability?" Daigneau articulates four dimensions of the facilities challenge: obsolescence, efficiency, technology, and economics, and considers whether most colleges and universities are prepared to address these issues. He suggests that by applying techniques from for-profit management, institutional leaders can develop strategic plans for facilities management that will help to avert a physical plant crisis.

The final two articles in this section turn from a focus on the inanimate (technology, facilities) to the animate-specifically, faculty. James Hearn offers an insightful analysis of "Pay and Performance in the University: An Examination of Faculty Salaries." Acknowledging that faculty salaries are generally the single largest item in academic budgets, Hearn takes a look at the history of faculty salaries and data on current faculty salary conditions, then explores the relationship between salaries and faculty productivity—an increasingly contentious issue, both socially and politically. He concludes with an appraisal of institutional policy options related to faculty salaries. Supplementing Hearn's discussion on salaries is Jay Chronister's article on "Benefit and Retirement Issues in Higher Education." Chronister inspects a series of important issues, including the aging of the faculty, the increased cost of fringe benefits, and the absence of a mandatory retirement age, and closes with the implications of these trends and developments for institutional expenditures.

The reviewers for this section were:

Paul Brinkman, University of Utah

Walter A. Brown, George Washington University

James C. Hearn, University of Minnesota

Michael T. Miller, San Jose State University

Glenn M. Nelson, University of Pittsburgh

CHAPTER 26

STRATEGIES AND CONSEQUENCES

Managing the Costs in Higher Education

JOHN WAGGAMAN

COSTS AND COST PRESSURES

Many factors are involved in generating costs and cost pressures. Constituent demands for more services and institutional demands for more resources stimulate cost pressures. The passage of time also increases costs as faculty, buildings, and equipment age and require increased resources to provide a minimum quality of services (Balderston 1974). Changing external conditions over which an institution has little control—economic, demographic, governmental, and postsecondary competitive factors—also stimulate costs. Inflation, recession, reduced birth rates and male college attendance rates, new government regulations, and other external variables demand expenditures unrelated to the educational functions of colleges and universities (Hauptman 1990).

Another source of cost pressures arise from an institution's quest for prestige and quality. Expanded aspirations unchecked by an understanding of costs and revenue sources are especially demanding. Expanded aspirations exist when an institution creates new programs, expands old ones, "stockpiles" faculty for these programs before enrollment growth, and takes other action to increase academic prestige and status. One might call this "risky planning," since the source of revenues to support this growth might not materialize. After expansion comes stabilization, which brings only modest increases of enrollments and revenues accompanied by rising expenditures (Baldridge 1974).

Adjusting to little growth, no growth, or recessionary cutbacks might only dampen cost pressures, not reestablish a new balance between revenues and expenditures. Reduced revenues might pressure a stable institution to restrict enrollment; that action might be followed by two-year institutions wishing to become colleges that offer bachelor's degrees. In states in which enrollment demand is increasing and public institutions are beginning to restrict enrollment, new private institutions might begin to emerge or branch campuses of out-of-state institutions appear to serve the surplus student demand.

Institutions that need students (and revenues) will take a variety of steps. The decisions to increase financial aid to students and expand the number being funded by allocating a greater share of general revenue for this purpose to aid recruitment might represent what Balderston calls a "conscientious overcommitment." Similarly, public institutions that enroll students beyond the number the state will subsidize might be fulfilling an important part of their mission but will create a demand for more funds across the board. One should note that accepting students without public subsidy will reduce instructional costs per full-time equivalent student and also probably reduce the quality of teaching and learning if the policy is continued for any period of time. Increasing revenues and costs of instruction might be appropriate if other institutional resources are being used efficiently and quality needs to be improved.

These and other factors stimulate cost pressures; they will be examined in this section. In the next section, the management and control of costs will be considered.

Cost Pressures from Unmet Needs

A universe of cost pressures arise from the unmet needs of various groups in and outside of higher education. These pressures include current and potential clientele groups, mandates from external sources, the demands (internal and external) for new programs or for enhancement of existing programs, and the suggestions of funding sources. When the pressures stimulate action, they increase expenditures and without more revenues raise the costs of higher education. Cost pressures—some persisting for many years—make strong demands on current institutional budgets and future budget requests.

External sources like governments, foundations, industry, alumni, benefactors, parents, and clients of programs provided by colleges and universities make demands for services and frequently offer resources in exchange. If the services demanded cost more than the resources provided, then some way must be found to bring them into balance. In response, the services demanded could be cut back, the payment or subsidy offered might be increased, existing resources could be reallocated from ongoing programs, or revenues might be increased from another source. The alternatives available are given such weight as the politics and self-interest of the institution seem to justify. For example, a public institution might elect to continue to admit students, even though they would not be funded under a state budget formula which limits the enrollment to be subsidized.

In some instances, external sources mandate programs or services and fail to adequately, fully, or even partially fund the mandates. State and federal government demands based on new social policy oftentimes fall in this category—such as affirmative action programs and implementation of new health and safety standards. Another demand, often a contract requirement, comes from some foundations and government funding sources who will not pay all or most

overhead costs for projects they want completed. In other cases, they restrict the amount of overhead to exclude such elements as computer services or purchasing reference books. In these instances, the offer of resources for some services is made on a "take it or leave it" basis and, if accepted, the institution must fund part of the cost of the project from revenues designated for instruction or other purposes.

Inflation is a key factor in increasing costs. It is especially difficult to "fund" when the economy is stagnant and state revenues are declining or not growing. When revenues cannot keep up with inflation, attempts usually are made to raise tuition and fees; unfortunately, this action can reduce or flatten enrollment in some institutions, further reducing revenues and increasing the unit cost of instruction. Responding in these circumstances to the demands for new programs to fulfill unmet needs is especially difficult or nearly impossible.

"Mandated" Cost Increases

Mandated increases in costs arise from changing economic conditions, threats to financial solvency or profitability, and changes in governmental social policy. Stagnating or declining economic conditions reduce tax collections and funds for both private and public higher education. Worsening economic conditions reduce the discretionary income that students and their families need to pay tuition. In such conditions, both public and private institutions often attempt to raise tuition to make up for the expected decline in revenues. The alternative to the preceding chain of events is for institutions to postpone salary increases and/or cut programs every time the economy or enrollments dip. Strategic planning is a means to anticipate and manage the dips in the economic and demographic cycles (Morrison, Renfro, and Boucher 1984; Cope 1987). However, more than good intentions are needed to make planning work properly and usefully, as one anonymous reviewer reported.

Mandated increases affecting faculty and staff costs are many and substantial: social security charges, retirement programs, health insurance, workers compensation premiums, and salary increases resulting from minimum wage laws or collective bargaining. Institutional administrators who find they do not have enough funds to pay competitive salaries to hire staff and faculty at the skill levels needed find the market is demanding that they raise salaries. Colleges and universities in metropolitan areas face stiff wage competition from the federal government, the public school systems, and the private sector. In a state like Florida, many of the growing community colleges find that they cannot pay high-enough starting salaries for faculty with master's degrees to compete with the salaries paid beginning public school teachers with bachelor's degrees.

A biennial survey of 1989 retirement and insurance benefits by TIAA-CREF indicates that fringe benefits make up 21.1 percent of the payroll for the average college and university employer (*Business Officer* 1991, p. 12). Both larger and comprehensive institutions had higher rates, as did those in the Mid-Atlantic region. Rising health insurance costs are a significant example of a competitive or mandated cost pressure.

Institutions have found little relief for a wide variety of other cost increases; they don't have the ability to substitute other less costly goods or services, for example. Postage increases, travel charges, property insurance, and utilities have all increased in cost due to changes in technology, work load, and the availability of raw materials such as oil and gasoline. Although such cost increases are not clearly "mandates," they are virtually unavoidable. In the short run, most colleges and universities have little opportunity to change technologies or services to improve their costs.

Another set of costs which appear to be unavoidable are those resulting from natural disasters and their equivalent. The former include earthquakes, tornadoes, ice and snowstorms, and floods. The second category of disasters is illustrated by such tragic events as accidents, suicides, and the murder of students on or near campus. The result of the latter is that counseling and security programs of all kinds must be enhanced, lighting improved on campus, emergency telephones installed, and additional staff hired to prevent reoccurrence of such terrible events. Other critical events are fires, power outages (which damage sensitive equipment), student riots, and single-minded destruction of art work and library books. Insurance, which itself is becoming more costly, can cover some—but not all—of the losses from these events.

Another mandate-like expenditure is the payment that public and private institutions make to local governments and public service organizations. The need and justification for these payments is that nonprofit institutions pay no taxes but do generate a demand for services from police and fire departments, water and sanitation facilities, hospitals, and emergency medical services. The classic example is a city's need to buy an aerial-ladder fire truck after a university builds a nine-story residence hall, social science building, or bell tower. A Midwestern university in this situation donated land and funds for the construction of the fire house and the purchase of the ladder truck; the city then paid the salaries and benefits of the employees who staffed the facility 24 hours a day.

Similarly, a large college or university in a small town might stimulate a need for a nearby hospital to operate fully staffed prenatal, maternity, and pediatrics units, plus treatment facilities for terminal illnesses like cancer and AIDS. The university might have to help solicit gifts to enlarge a hospital and then annually conduct voluntary giving drives to raise funds to support facility operation.

Payments in lieu of taxes to municipalities are rising as local governments try to find more revenues. In 1990, Harvard is reported to have added $100,000 to its already $1 million annual contribution to the city of Cambridge, Mass. (*Business Officer* 1991). The same report indicated that Yale earlier had agreed to pay New Haven, Conn., "more than $2 million over the next five years for fire services and street improvements" (p. 15). Such other cities as Evanston, Ill., and Pittsburgh have attempted or are considering a levy of taxes on university students or research grants and some properties, because the higher education institutions in their cities do not pay taxes for the services they receive. In an even more unusual situation in 1991, the federal government's Environmental Protection Agency asked 13 colleges and universities in South Carolina to join with 100 companies and governmental units to pay the $10 million cost of cleaning up a hazardous waste site.

Another special cost situation with few alternatives involves universities that have medical schools. Medical schools that operate their own teaching hospitals provide a variety of medical services to various groups. Various pressures exist to maintain minimum patient charges in order to obtain patients on whom medical students can learn their profession. Many medical services are very costly and require the hospital to seek as much reimbursement as possible from the patients, insurance firms, or government agencies (which pay for indigent patients).

When government does not offer a minimal reimbursement for indigent patients, the university medical school and its hospital can't do much except to raise the charges to those who can pay, which eventually means everyone with health insurance! University hospitals that provide this public service—needing patients, rarely can restrict the choice of patients to treat. Incidentally, university medical centers established to provide services for students now are finding that students without health insurance are leaving their schools with unpaid medical debts. Either the university and the doctors must be willing to absorb these debts, or they must require students to enroll with health insurance (Collison 1989).

Administrative Costs

Administrative costs have been rising as the number of administrative and academic support personnel has increased (Grassmuck 1990). Administrators might have increased as much as 60 percent between 1975 and 1985, a period in which faculty increased by 6 percent. This same trend can be found in the research sector of universities as reported below.

One analysis of this growth suggests that three sets of conditions explains it: regulation and micromanagement; consensus management; and expansion of administrative entrepreneurism ("The Lattice and the Ratchet" 1990). The first category focuses on the requirements of those external to the colleges and universities who audit and inspect and who demand reports of activities and plans. Administrative staff are necessary to respond specifically to the external regulators. As greater statewide coordination, regulation, and governance has emerged since 1960, public institutions have found it necessary to increase the staff who work with state and system officials. In many institutions, it was found necessary to create an equal or greater number of staff positions to match the state staff and the work load it generated.

The second category focuses on the need to spend greater amounts of time and staff on consultation among administrators in order to ensure that all appropriate "interests"—internal and external—are represented in the decision-making process of colleges and universities. Consensus management requires a lot of time, energy, and input from many sources. Consultation has expanded as more faculty committees have been created to help govern institutions; democracy also has its costs.

The third category suggests that staff costs continue to rise as the better-qualified staff delivers better services, develops expertise, and corners the market (like faculty) in their specialty area. These conditions lead to competition among the experts, hiring of more staff, expanded services, additional higher salaries—in other words, the ratchet effect. The analysis suggests that as faculty have increasingly lessened their ties to the institution for which they work, the role of the support staff has grown in importance. (The presumption that faculty at one time were much more involved in university governance and administration ought to be tested, just as these explanations deserve verification studies.)

Administrative salaries are a small share of current institutional costs, but it has risen. According to a national survey of administrative compensation published in the March 1991 issue of *Business Officer*, salaries rose by 5.4 percent, somewhat ahead of 4.7 percent inflation in 1990; this might have been a compensatory increase from the effects of inflation in 1989. The previous year, inflation was 5.1 percent and salary increases were 4.5 percent. Public institutions had larger administrative salary increases in 1990 than private institutions. The median salaries of chief business officers varied by the degree level of the institution and its budget size.

The ability of higher education institutions to pay a median salary that keeps up with inflation is an important achievement; whether that rate of increase extends throughout the administrative hierarchy was not reported. Attempts to keep salary increases at least equal to inflation is a cost pressure, even if meritorious in its intent.

The increase in the minimum wage set by federal law reveals the difficulties resulting from a well-intentioned public policy. In 1990, the minimum hourly wage moved from $3.35 to $3.80; on April 1, 1991, it increased to $4.25. The 1989 law that set these rates also created a lower training wage for teenagers; in 1991, it increased from $3.35 to $3.62.

Colleges and universities hire semi-skilled adult workers at hourly rates or what rates the market requires for service jobs; it also pays students hourly wages for shelving books in libraries. However, if the budgets of institutions do not increase to cover the additional cost of the higher minimum wages, then fewer students are hired by the library. That's what happened at many colleges and universities in 1990; the number of students employed in the library at Florida State University decreased by 25 percent that year for these reasons. Similarly, some students working at fast-food restaurants and other service businesses faced the prospect of unemployment after 1991. The 1991 increase also might stimulate a ratchet effect in which higher paid hourly workers demand a proportionate increase in their hourly wages. The ripple effect of these mandated wage increases has a number of undesirable consequences even when we agree that the minimum wage is not a living wage and should be increased.

Faculty Costs and Characteristics

Faculty Salary Costs

The faculty salary costs of an institution vary according to the degree qualifications, academic rank, and seniority of its faculty. An institution with a large number of faculty who hold doctoral degrees and are full professors with 20–25 years of service will be expensive. According to the March/April 1991 issue of *Academe*, the primary source for national faculty salary data, the all-ranks average faculty compensation for 1990–91 was between $35,480 and $49,320. The all-institution average was $43,720, which rose 5.4 percent over 1989–90, although the increase fell below the rate of inflation for the first time in many years.

Salaries at four-year public institutions increased at a lesser rate than those at private or church-related institutions. The expectations for 1991–92 and later are grim because many states have had to cut back funds for higher education and many other services during the recession. The pressures to find salary funds had escalated in both public and private insti-

tutions when inflation recently was above 5 percent and insurance and other costs, which continue to rise, absorb a larger share of salaries.

Many cost pressures are related to faculty salaries: inflation, competitiveness with the salaries of other professions, faculty shortages, higher salaries for new faculty, demands for reduced work loads, increased cost of fringe benefits, and others, such as the employment of a spouse. Obvious pressures exist to raise salaries to attract faculty and to keep those already employed. Because faculty salaries are such a large portion of the current operating expenditures of institutions, these cost pressures have significant effects on current and future budgets and instructional costs.

Inflation. The impact of inflation in the 1970s, when faculty salaries were left behind, often is used to explain the increase in salaries, institutional budgets, and tuition in the 1980s. "Despite recent actions to narrow the gap, faculty salaries today on average are still about 9 percent lower than in 1971–72" (Hexter 1990, p. 1; Hauptman 1990). The onset of the 1990–1992 national recession will further restrict the ability of institutions to close the 1970s inflation gap; its growth will create more cost/revenue pressures. What happens when the recession ends and state tax collections and private giving rise is dependent on the robustness of the recovery, inflationary pressures, and the public's willingness to provide greater funds.

Some have had an earlier experience with this problem. A 1960s salary policy at Indiana University, a large multi-campus research institution, was labeled "catch up and keep up." The need to regain the purchasing power of faculty and staff salaries lost during the recessions of the early 1960s led to a variety of stratagems to increase appropriations. At this particular institution, the catch-up salary policy was designed to increase the salary ranking of the institution among its peers in the Big Ten. However, when all institutions in the league attempted to increase their salaries at the same time (because revenues were increasing at the end of the recession), the rankings did not change, even though everybody became better off!

The state legislature wanted to see the ranking improve, because members were told that would be the consequence of a large catch-up appropriation; obviously, some legislators were unhappy. Cost pressures did lead to risk-taking so that the university could remain competitive. Stanford is a university that strives to keep salaries at one or two percentage points above inflation to remain top ranked and competitive nationally and worldwide.

Are faculty overpaid? The president of York College of Pennsylvania, Robert V. Isoue, asserts that faculty are underworked, not overpaid (*Higher Education Costs* 1988, p. 234). He draws a comparison between underpaid high school teachers with multiple responsibilities (Russell 1931, p. 23) and the large majority of faculty members who are better paid, but do not conduct any research and teach only nine hours. Increasingly, the level of faculty workload is seen as a cost pressure; it is discussed later in this text.

Retirement. One of the prime factors that might affect instructional costs in the near future is faculty retirement. In the next 25 years, as many as 40 percent of faculty (and administrators) in most two- and four-year institutions could retire; some say the exit will be at a steady pace (Bowen and Sousa 1989). However, many academic administrators are expecting a surge of retirements by 1994. The state university system of California estimates that it will need 8,000 to 9,500 replacement faculty and an additional 6,000 to cover enrollment increases by 2002 (Jewett 1989).

Another uncertainty about faculty retirement trends is the question of what will happen when the age cap requiring retirement is removed for faculty in 1994. In that year—unless Congress acts to the contrary—there will no longer be a mandatory retirement age for faculty. Currently, the average retirement age is a fraction over 65. If faculty retire later, the salary costs should increase; administrators wonder whether they need to create better incentives for early retirement. Unfortunately, such action might accelerate the anticipated increase in retirements among the faculty who began teaching in the 1960s—creating unwanted shortages of experienced faculty. An added complication to this complex situation: Will one of the side effects of the 1990–1992 recession be that 65-year-old faculty members postpone retirement until economic conditions

and current salaries begin to rise across the board again? Remember that some retirement programs take the last five years of salary to compute the monthly retirement benefit.

Retirements mean that the fundamental cost structure of faculty could change significantly by the year 2010. Faculty costs could fall as more faculty are hired at the assistant rank; or, salary costs could increase as institutions bid for a relatively small pool of graduates to replace the retirees. By 1997, about four candidates will be available for every five openings in the arts and sciences (Bowen and Sosa). One of the primary factors that could be holding down faculty costs now is the increasing use of part-time faculty. The 1970s saw part-timers grow from 22 percent to about 34 percent of total faculty (Frances 1990); that trend might have reached 38 percent or higher by 1990 (Leslie 1991). It is much higher in community/junior colleges.

Salary Fairness and Equity Issues

Two faculty salary fairness issues that generate budget requests and therefore pressure the costs of instruction are salary compression and salary inversion. The latter occurs when a department must pay a higher salary to a new faculty member than it pays the experienced faculty already employed. This occurrence lowers morale and leads to demands for better salaries and more equitable workloads. Salary inversion occurs because recruiting new faculty responds to the pressures of competitive market/salary conditions, the availability of alternative employment opportunities, increases in productivity or expertise, inflation, or special local factors such as geographic area cost of living. Institutions might adopt a "catch up and keep up" budget and fund-raising strategy to cope with this condition. They can pressure their state legislatures and private benefactors to increase institutional revenues to cope with this problem just to keep their best teachers and researchers.

Another kind of salary issue is the compression of rates that result when faculty and staff receive similar salaries or when salary varies little by rank among faculty or staff. Similarly, salary levels between administrators and faculty can become closer when pay for the former is held steady and pay for the faculty is increased. Steady-state funding or actual reductions in funding over several years are often the root cause of these conditions; whether they constitute a problem depends on faculty and staff perception. In a capitalistic society in which money talks, undifferentiated salaries by skill level and seniority can fail to perform as incentives for achievement or a continuation of high-quality work. The interim president of the University of South Carolina stated in March 1991 that his institution annually set aside as much as $200,000 to adjust salaries found to be caught in the conversion-inversion tangle.

One of the potential cost items regarding fair faculty salaries is what might be called "the price of salary sex equity." The potential consequences can be estimated from a simple calculation. Multiplying the 1982 estimate that a $1,000–3,000 salary discrepancy per female faculty member exists (Koch 1982) by the U.S. Department of Education's 1985 estimate of 128,063 full-time female instructional faculty produces an estimate of a very large potential future funding obligation: $128,063,000 to $384,189,000.

The size of the salary disparity for women in higher education seems to be growing. In 1972–73, the average salary of female full-time faculty was 83 percent of the average male faculty salary. By 1990, females were averaging 75 percent (National Center for Education Statistics 1990; Hexter 1990). In addition to the back pay for the salary differences, institutions could face large legal fees and fines if discrimination is proved. One difficult aspect of this issue is that few legislatures separately fund sex equity. In the public institutions, the funds for equity salary adjustments often must come from the total funds appropriated by the state for faculty salaries or salary increases. The demand for salary equity funding is a definite cost pressure; it has been around for more than 20 years.

Another development that might turn into a faculty salary cost pressure is the growing differences of average salaries by discipline (Hexter 1990). Salaries already vary by degree level of institution, rank of faculty, gender, race and ethnicity, region, and control (public, private, and church). Hexter reported that salary increases have been greater by roughly one percentage point for engineering and computer science faculty than other fields and about two points over education faculty (p. 5).

The pressure to equalize salaries across disciplines does not seem to have an active voice in 1991. Faculty labor unions often demand equal pay for equal work; they want the external market forces muted inside the institutions when they see higher salaries set for certain disciplines such as business finance or computer science.

Salary Costs from Benefit Programs

Some fringe benefits generate costs even when they have no direct cost. An example is the personnel policy that permits new parents to take unpaid leave for three to six months after the birth or adoption of a child. The cost arises from the search and support for a teaching replacement when faculty colleagues can't absorb the increased instructional load. Finding an appropriate and qualified temporary instructor for a short period is not easy in many cities and towns. Qualified people in the high-cost disciplines such as physics, chemistry, computer science, engineering, and accounting just might not be available. It might be necessary to bring qualified faculty out of retirement or even to employ lesser qualified individuals. In the high-cost programs, even the temporary instructors might be more costly than the faculty who are taking leave.

Another side to this situation: The vacant position often is filled with part-time faculty who are paid at rates less than those of full-time instructors. If qualified part-timers are available, this arrangement actually might reduce the cost of instruction; what it does for the quality of instruction and adherence to the basic curriculum is another matter. Clearly, these are important trade-offs that arise from a benefit program that many find desirable.

A further development of this policy that can generate instructional costs has emerged; it involves a college permitting a faculty member to reduce his or her teaching load while still being paid a full-time wage. Carol Kleiman, a national newspaper columnist who focuses on labor matters, wrote that Albright, Baldwin-Wallace, Beloit, Hood, Knox, and Macalester colleges had implemented either paid or unpaid family leaves; fathers, as well as mother employees, were included at many of these institutions (1991). A college would need added resources to cover the increased instructional costs from the reduced teaching loads if other faculty couldn't cover the added work load and temporary teachers had to be found.

It should be noted that these very humane family-leave policies benefit the colleges by encouraging faculty to stay on rather than taking leave or resigning. The policy might help reduce the turnover of faculty and also help women to build a tenure-earning career at their colleges. The policies do have costs and do generate cost pressures among institutions that compete for faculty; however, their long-range benefits might outweigh the initial costs. The plan bears watching.

Fringe Benefits

According to a 1990 TIAA-CREF fringe-benefits survey of 634 institutions, retirement and insurance plans cost 21.1 percent of college and university payrolls. The average amount per employee was $6,206; the median $4,635. The average percentages varied by type of institution (the highest was public comprehensive universities at 24.5); by region (Mid-Atlantic was highest, the Southwest and South were lowest); by size (larger institutions spent more); and by control (public institutions spent more than private).

No two-year colleges were included in the TIAA-CREF survey. These percentages cover an entire institutional payroll and would be substantially different for separate groups like faculty, technical, and clerical employees. The percentages of benefit deductions vary by groups within an institution, especially when an important part of the benefits are in flat dollar amounts for all employees. Then the lower paid employees could have a larger percentage of their paychecks devoted to fixed-dollar benefit charges, for example. A large public university with such a system (set by the state) could have 28 percent insurance costs for faculty and 34 percent for clerical and service employees for the same kinds of coverage.

The TIAA-CREF survey reported that legally mandated benefit expenditures averaged 6.6 percent of payroll. Social security taxes were the largest mandatory charge and accounted for 5.9 percent of total payroll. Administrators were most likely to pay the maximum charge for social security: 7.6 percent. Workers' compensation programs averaged 0.7 percent and unemployment compen-

sation costs were 0.1 percent. Fringe benefits are the cost category with the highest rate of growth (Frances 1990, p. 13). However, it is the social security taxes, Frances says, that drive the cost increases. It should be noted that not all higher education institutions participate in the social security system.

Pension-retirement plans averaged 8.0 percent of payroll; they could be 15–18 percent of the faculty payroll. Insurance benefit expenditures averaged 6.5 percent of payroll, with 6.1 percentage points designated for health insurance. Long-term disability income insurance averaged 0.3 percent of payroll; travel accident insurance was 0.1 percent. Many different kinds of plans exist—some with coverage defined narrowly (for full-time, low-risk employees, for example) or more inclusively, and with several different kinds of coverage. Collective bargaining contracts may determine the kinds and costs of many benefit packages.

The rising cost of health insurance is placing a strain on fringe benefit budgets. These costs are rising so consistently that the 28 public community colleges of Florida had asked again in 1991–1992 for separate appropriations exclusively for health insurance. In the profit sector, businesses are reporting annual increases of 20 percent in their health insurance costs (Kramon 1991). An insurance consulting firm reports that the health costs per employee have escalated from $1,942 in 1987 to $2,646 in 1989, a 36 percent increase (Roush 1991). Driving up costs are the billions of health care bills remaining unpaid to doctors and hospitals that subsequently are shifted to taxpayers and people with health insurance.

In Florida, the unpaid bills are estimated to total $1.6 billion; 18 percent (2.2 million people) of the population is without health insurance (Troxler 1991). The Florida Legislature is attempting to pass measures to control this situation. A large number of changes in health insurance are being adopted nationally, including charging more for those at risk (smokers and overweight people, for example); rates also are being differentiated according to the extensiveness of the coverage desired. These and many other approaches are being tried in the attempt to hold down health care insurance costs, which are not yet contained!

In states in which the salary and benefits of public colleges and universities are controlled by government, individual institutions might have little say about the rising cost of health insurance. If handicapped by poor state management and stable appropriations, the rising costs of health insurance and retirement are likely to become a drain on the funds allocated for salaries or salary increases, when the latter exist.

Work Load and Productivity

A former president of two public universities (one on the East Coast, the other in the upper Midwest) suggests that the reduction of teaching load per faculty member is one of the most serious causes of rising costs in higher education. A current president of a large public university in the South says there is little evidence that productivity of faculty increases as the teaching load is reduced. In a related vein, faculty are working less as the academic year has shortened—a reduction of one month since the 1960s (Cheney 1990). The consequence of reducing the teaching work load is the pressure to hire more faculty or use an increasing number of part-time/adjunct faculty or graduate teaching assistants.

Several surveys of faculty about their work load have been conducted over the years. One of the latest is the 1988 National Survey of Postsecondary Faculty sponsored by the National Center for Education Statistics. In 1990, Fairweather, Hendrickson, and Russell prepared a special report for NCES describing the activities and work load of faculty reported in the 1988 survey. The data reported here are taken from their paper.

Using the data from both two-year and four-year institutions, the survey revealed that the average faculty work week in 1988 was 53 hours. Forty-six hours (87 percent) occurred at the home institution, four hours (7 percent) were in other paid activities, and three hours (6 percent) were in unpaid service activities. Faculty in research and public doctoral institutions reported above-average work weeks; faculty in private comprehensive institutions and in public two-year colleges showed work weeks below the all-institution average (pp. 2–4). However, the survey revealed that community college faculty spent more time teaching and teaching more students than any other group. Generally, faculty at the research and doctoral-granting institutions spent less time teaching

than the comprehensive and liberal arts groups. The differences reflect the missions of these institutions.

Faculty in the senior ranks or those who were tenured worked more than the all-institutional average work week (pp. 2–5). Teaching activities took above-average time for faculty in business, education, the humanities, and natural sciences. Other significant disciplinary differences included:

> Faculty in education, the fine arts, and the humanities spent a less than average percentage of their time on research activities. Faculty in education were the only members who spent a higher than average percentage of their time on administration and on service (pp. 2–5).

These self reported sample data depict a faculty that works much more than a 40-hour week. Such data present a significantly different picture than one shown in the rousing book *ProfScam* by Charles Sykes (1988).

The matter of faculty work load is one of the most troubling in all of higher education. Institutional and national data exist in fragments, and no reliable standard definitions are used. Great differences exist between programs and disciplines within and between institutions; to protect the autonomy and independence of the academic units that make decisions about the most effective use of their human resources, there is little enthusiasm for collecting work-load data. The latter is true even though a number of states have work-load laws of one kind or another that demand institutions to make good-faith efforts to compile such data.

Within academe a clear feeling exists that spending time and money to perfect a data collection system will only consume resources that could be better used for the primary purposes of teaching, research, and public service. Also, it is believed that the data collected from such a system will not improve the efficiency or effectiveness of institutional operations. However, parents, taxpayers, and legislators increasingly are clamoring for institutions to carefully examine their work-load policies and to confront the issue of who should teach undergraduates and how much time the average faculty member should spend on teaching. These complaints seem lodged more about teaching in large public institutions that tend to have larger classes than in private colleges and universities, although none are immune to these complaints. It should be realized that smaller classes increase the cost of instruction.

State work-load laws or administrative rules specify, on average, the number of hours faculty should devote to instruction. Florida has a 12-hour law for university faculty, but the law permits administrators to make exceptions for professional activities that are judged equivalent to regular classroom instruction (Florida Statutes 240.243). The equivalencies include directed individual study, thesis and dissertation supervision, supervision of interns, and other special kinds of instructional arrangements. Teaching large classes and preparation time for new courses also can be designated equivalents. The larger and more research-oriented universities require more and different exceptions to the 12-hour law. Additional equivalents have been approved for research and service, some administration, and student advising. Faculty in the law and medical schools are exempted from the requirements of the Florida statute.

A proposal in the Florida Senate to remove almost all of the exemptions was considered and defeated in spring 1991. The stimulus for the proposal was that more than one-third of the faculty at the two primary research universities were teaching only six hours, while some of the other universities had only 10 to 15 percent of their faculty teaching a similarly reduced work load; here also the differences were based on institutional missions. The legislative analysis of this proposal, which would also raise the minimum contact hours to 15, indicated that these "under-loaded" research faculty would have to increase their instructional activities by 150 percent.

In committee debate, the Senate sponsor asserted that 500 fewer positions were being used by the universities for instruction than had been fueled by the legislature; he estimated that some $60 million appropriated for instruction was not being used for that purpose. The chancellor of the university system responded by pointing out that more than 1,200 research positions were still being funded that had been authorized back in the 1960s. The ostensible purpose of the legislative proposal was to "increase student access to courses required for graduation and enable students to graduate sooner, thus reducing their educational expenses." Although this proposal had little chance of passing the 1991 legislative session (and didn't), it dealt with issues that have been raised in many states over the past five years. No one expects these issues to go away; a lingering recession only can stimulate interest in proposals to increase faculty work load and thereby reduce the cost of instruction.

The central point to be pondered from the preceding data and information is whether instructional costs are being pushed up by faculty who have reduced teaching loads; unfortunately, there is no good answer. There are isolated reports that some institutions are hiring replacement faculty before they are needed and not requiring these individuals to teach at all. The latter is said to be one of many ways administrators are coping with the shortage of new faculty expected in the late 1990s. During an economic recession, the pressures are even greater to hire part-time faculty—and where available, teaching assistants—to hold down costs. In public institutions, administrators are pressured not to fill authorized faculty positions, but to take the funds and hire adjunct faculty and graduate students. This strategy also allows more and smaller teaching sections in undergraduate courses. Whether this practice is beneficial to students remains to be documented; however, it is believed to help control salary and instructional costs.

Instructional Costs

The largest component of instructional costs is faculty salaries and benefits, considered previously. Other instructional costs include libraries, computers, television and media equipment, laboratories and scientific instruments, and such specialized facilities as theaters, music halls, art studios, and gymnasiums. However, it is the push for additional programs (majors), new graduate degree subjects, new technical specialities, and new courses to accompany the new programs which drives up instructional costs. Some of the pressures for new programs arise from the possibility of serving a new market, of faculty gaining greater independence, of pioneering the development of new fields, and of adding to an institution's prestige. During the 1990–92 recession, larger classes might have become the norm and instructional costs decreased; the educational consequences of this change might not be known.

Instructional Systems

One of the newer terms describing television teaching is distance learning. Through the use of telephone transmission lines, cable television, and satellite relays, it now is possible to schedule educational programming 24 hours a day. Many states are building these instructional systems for kindergarten through high school students. Some states, like Indiana, used everything but satellites in 1967 to provide professional continuing education for lawyers, nurses returning to practice, and other professionals. Instruction for engineering students in Florida is being offered using the methods of distance learning.

The use of two-way audio with video communication permits interaction between an instructor and students. The technology permits one instructor to teach two or three classes simultaneously. If a camera is available at each learning site, the instructor can rotate weekly among the sites to physically (rather than electronically) interact with different classes. Elaborate course planning, preparing attractive visual aids, and avoiding "talking heads" are required to present electronic instruction. Great care must be taken if a quality video production is to be made for subsequent broadcast. Even with these electronic wonders, some kind of staff assistance is required at the additional learning sites; if they are faculty or higher paid teaching assistants, then the cost of instruction per student credit hour might not decline at all.

The distance-learning technology requires substantial capital investment to cover the cost of constructing satellite receivers and sending equipment, for example. Usually a network must be established, costs determined for operating the system, and backup arrangements made for the times when the power goes off, equipment malfunctions, or other interruptions occur to the scheduled transmission. Both administrators and coordinators as well as instructors and technical staff are needed for a basic distance-learning system. All of these systems and their costs often become supplementary to the traditional systems of instruction.

At some point, evaluations will have to be made to determine if this form of instruction generates the same (or a greater) level of learning as the traditional in-class model and whether it is worth the added cost of the telecommunications technology and the additional support staff. Presently, colleges and universities are being pressured to adopt electronic instructional systems to expand access to place-bound students. In the past, it was hoped that the emerging electronic teaching technology could replace faculty; instead, it was found that the technology was used to supplement the faculty members' efforts and thus raised the costs of instruction. Whether learning was enhanced from these technological augmentations has not been demonstrated to the satisfaction of most faculty.

Libraries. The electronic revolution has taken libraries by storm in the last five years. First came large national computerized data base utilities for bibliographic research, then placement of the same data on compact disks. Next came the national and state system data bases of college library books, then the addition of the journal indexes onto the book systems. The next information retrieval development will be to permit computer retrieval of the text of journal articles from either CD-ROM system or regional/national article data bases, when the copyright problems can be solved. The text of books would be likely to follow if their copyright problems could be worked out. Some text retrieval of journal articles already is available on CD-ROM. This portends the power to search an enormous number and variety of texts. The widespread use of electronic bibliographic files appears to have increased the use of inter-library loans to obtain copies of journal articles unavailable in some college libraries.

These developments are an example of using technology to stimulate greater use of library materials; but in some cases, this has added duplicate costs. (For example, both the hard copy of the journal indexes must be subscribed to because the electronic data bases on compact disks are only leased, not purchased so they can be updated quarterly.) In addition to the rising costs of new technology, the costs of serial publications such as scientific journals have increased enormously—some as much as 600 percent over the last three years.

Many major universities (Berkeley, Texas, North Carolina, SUNY Albany) have been reviewing and cutting their journal subscriptions not only to balance their budgets, but also to try to restore some of the funds taken from the book budget that were required to pay the journal price increases. In all, the relatively low salaries paid to librarians has helped hold down library costs. Libraries often take about 6 percent of an institution's budget; older and larger institutions would spend more. New or additional library space probably will be needed by the year 2000 as well as a larger investment in electronic data bases and computer terminals to access the new journals that will exist only in computer data bases. All of the preceding are growing cost pressures.

Complex Enrollment Issues

A minimum enrollment often is specified before a new public institution, campus, center, or program can be created. The presumption is that a specific minimum enrollment justifies the higher administrative costs, because the small enrollments aren't economically efficient. The idea that size determines an efficient operation is an old one in economics and business; it also seems to apply to higher education. A minimum size of 500 to 1,200 full-time equivalent students often is suggested in state master plans. However, much research remains to be completed before generalizable criteria exist to create new institutions and programs.

Declining enrollment on a campus leads to concern for the survival of an institution. It is the pressure of increasing costs due to declining revenues that begins the concern for all manner of cost control strategies, discussed in the next section. Decreases in enrollment initially increase costs per unit of instruction. Generally, an increase in enrollment will reduce overall unit costs. However, educational costs might not decline if expenditures rise significantly to obtain the new enrollment, as for marketing and recruiting, financial aid, counseling and advising, records and registration, retention programs, and student services. One of the consequences of decreasing enrollment is that fewer students remain among whom to spread the fixed costs such as the cost of operating buildings, libraries, and administration. If no other sources cover these costs,

then tuition must be increased for this purpose. That's usually what is done by state universities (Hauptman 1990).

Concerns about the costs related directly to services provided to students leads to some very complex issues. Questions have been raised during research about the causes of increases in tuition. One of these issues is whether declining revenues and rising costs (for instruction, for example) drove up tuition or whether tuition was increased to permit greater expenditures—maybe for computers or more financial aid for students. The first assumption is that the prices for goods and services purchased for higher education have increased faster than inflation. The second idea asserts that institutions have been spending money on new types of products and services, or purchasing more of them.

Kirshstein and others summarize the preceding and other explanations (1990). They then report their research results using national aggregate data and their own simulation model to test the workings of these two explanations (pp. 81–84). The research indicated that both sets of factors were operating on both public and private institutions in the period 1980–1985; however, rising tuition revenues did not significantly stimulate additional expenditures in the period 1975–1980. The 1980–1985 period saw expanded and expensive efforts to recruit a declining pool of high school graduates, especially by the private institutions which primarily depend upon tuition revenues.

Research Expenses

The results from a survey of university department heads in 1985 revealed that 72 percent believed a lack of equipment was preventing critical experiments. The need to establish a research infrastructure to attract scientists, graduate students, technical support staff, and funders (revenue providers) generates cost pressures on universities. For those who have the resources, keeping up with the rising costs and holding together research teams while funding agencies make decisions about continuing project support add to research costs. Institutions without reserves to cover these gaps in external funding risk the loss of valuable support staff.

Research and Support Staff

The need for talented researchers, research apprentices (graduate students), support staff, and others connected with research activities continues to grow. Scientists, mathematicians, and engineers in universities require competitive salaries and benefits to remain in their home institutions; their highly technical skills enable them to readily find high-quality employment in government laboratories, research and development firms, and for-profit corporations with a need for scientific analysis. Similarly, the need for large stipends to attract and hold graduate students in science is very important.

In recent years, fewer Americans have been attracted to doctoral programs in science; the remaining need for research apprentices has been filled with foreign students to the point at which these individuals constitute one-third to one-half (or more) of graduate science enrollment. The decline of federal research fellowships and the forecasted oversupply of scientists in the 1970s are offered as reasons for the current enrollment situation. The future need for more scientists is leading universities now to "stockpile" scientific faculty: College enrollments nationwide are expected to increase after 1995, and the faculty hired in the 1960s are expected to retire in the 1990s. Clearly, stockpiling is expensive and workable, but only available to those with the funds.

Support staff. A key component in the cost of research is the support staff, referred to as research support personnel by Hensley in his 1985 testimony before a task force of the U.S. House Committee on Science and Technology (*University Research Infrastructure* 1986). Although the exact size of this group is not known, Hensley estimated it to exceed 500,000 people. Included in this large group are 12 functional classes: grant and contract officers, program development officers, business managers, clerical personnel, academic officers, research center staff, animal caretakers, laboratory personnel, shop personnel, medical personnel, agricultural extension and experimental station staff, and others. The first half dozen classes have a strong administrative focus but are necessary to keep the research enterprise going. People in these classes are involved in research activities at various times: some during the pre-award stage, some during the conduct of the research, and others throughout the entire process of sponsored research. People who hold these positions are part of the research infrastructure.

Not included are the student assistants or research investigators who carry out the essential research activity. Hensley reports that 75 percent of all those working in research are support staff; faculty researchers constitute the remaining 25 percent. It should be noted that many—if not most—of these staff people are employed only as long as contracts and grants are received to pay their salaries. However, research directors do everything possible to keep together a research team; the pressure sometimes leads to bad financial practices.

Research Equipment and Facilities

The need for better research equipment and better funding for such equipment was reported in detail in a 1985 report by the American Association of Universities, *Financing and Managing University Research Equipment* (reprinted in *University Research Infrastructure* 1986). The report summarized the need with these conclusions from an earlier survey:

1. Of the university department heads surveyed, 72 percent reported that lack of equipment was preventing critical experiments.

2. Universities' inventories of scientific equipment showed that 20 percent was obsolete and no longer used in research.

3. Of all instrument systems in use in research, 22 percent were more than 10 years old.

4. Only 52 percent of instruments in use were reported to be in excellent working condition.

5. 49 percent rated the quality of instrument-support services (machine shop, electronics shop, etc.) as insufficient or nonexistent (p. 462).

A key cost pressure has been reducing federal funds for leasing or purchasing equipment; a 78 percent decline (in constant dollars) occurred during 1966–1983. (However, the federal government was still the largest funder of equipment—54 percent—in use in universities during 1982–1983.) Federal funding has been an important source to cover the rising cost of the sophisticated tools and facilities for scientific research in American higher education. Of the $20 billion spent on civilian research and development, about $6 billion is invested in university research (*University Research Infrastructure* 1986, p. 6).

Cost Reimbursement

The overhead cost-reimbursement rates authorized by the federal government for research grants and contracts vary to the extent an institution can justify the costs permitted to be recovered. A survey of 30 universities with large research expenditures showed different rates between public and private institutions: "The average indirect recovery rate of private universities was 63.6 percent in 1986, as against an average of 42.8 percent for the public university campuses" (Balderston 1990, p. 48). The private universities believe it would be disastrous for them if they didn't recover a maximum amount of indirect costs.

For the public institutions, the recovery rates might be low because state government provides so much of the basic funding. Often the state governments demand that portions of the reimbursed overhead funds are returned to them because of their support for the public institutions. As a result, public university research administrators often believe they are denied the funds to which they are entitled. The belief is widespread among all university research administrators that the federal government does not pay a full share of an institution's indirect costs.

Faculty researchers often complain that their grant proposals are handicapped by high cost-recovery rates because they increase the total cost of the grant project, They request that their institutions absorb more of the indirect costs, which would have the effect of shifting such costs to non-research units. Faculty in private universities with the highest indirect cost rates feel they are losing out in the competition for research projects, because their total project budget is too high.

During the past decade, the cost-reimbursement standards of the federal government have changed; to researchers and administrators, this has led to the systematic underestimation of university needs. In 1985, one of President Reagan's science advisers, Dr. Bernadine Healy, testified before a Congressional committee that facilities-use allowance reimbursements "are

based on an average useful life of 50 years for a university laboratory. The actual average useful life of a laboratory is probably about 20–25 years, as it is for industrial laboratories.

As for research equipment, in addition to having unrealistically long amortization periods—fifteen years, in contrast to the actual six to eight—the government also micromanages the purchase of new equipment" (*University Research Infrastructure* 1986, p. 13).

Cost Studies

Cost pressures can be anticipated by carefully analyzing the factors in the environment most likely to impact an institution. Reports of inflation, economic stagnation and decline, new federal laws, the possibility of postal increases, desegregation court decisions about Southern university systems, and many other developments will demand an assessment of their potential impact on higher education. One way that college and university administrators could respond to these reports is that each one could assume responsibility for surveying the external environment for future changes. However, a strategic planning analysis would require a coordination of these efforts just to identify cost pressures that would require institutional planning and management. Enrollment changes also must be monitored along with the emergence of competing institutions to determine if the student market has altered due to external or internal conditions.

Tracking enrollment and cost changes within an institution is another strategy. It requires a great attention to detail and systematic study; organizations like NACUBO and NCHEMS can provide guidance in such activities. Unfortunately, one of the first services to be discontinued when revenues decline is the analysis of the use of resources within an institution. These times are the ones most in need of good cost analysis, especially if little planning or forecasting has been done to anticipate a possible decline in revenues. When coupled with a focus on managing and controlling costs, these studies of both external and internal factors help an institution shape its future.

REFERENCES

Balderston, F. E. 1974. *Managing Today's University.* San Francisco: Jossey-Bass.

_____. 1990. "Organization, Funding, Incentives, and Initiatives for University Research: A University Management Perspective." In *The Economics of American Universities,* edited by S. A. Hoenack and E. L. Collins. Albany, N.Y.: State University of New York Press.

Bowen, W. G., and J. A. Sousa. 1989. *Prospects for Faculty in the Arts and Sciences.* Lawrenceville, N.J.: Princeton University Press.

Business Officer. May 1991. Monthly publication of NACUBO.

Cheney, L.V. 1990. *Tyrannical Machines: A Report on Educational Practices Gone Wrong and Our Best Hopes for Setting Them Right.* Washington, D.C. : National Endowment for the Humanities.

Collison, N-K. June 7, 1989. "Officials Warn of a Crisis in Student Health Insurance as Medical Costs Soar and Companies Revise Policies." *Chronicle of Higher Education:* A31-2.

Cope, R. G. 1987. *Opportunity from Strength: Strategic Planning Clarified with Case Examples.* ASHE-ERIC Higher Education Reports No. 87–8. Washington, D.C.: ERIC Clearinghouse on Higher Education. ED 296 694. 149 pp. MF-01; PC-06.

Fairweather, J. S., R. M. Hendrickson, and S. H. Russell. 1990. "A Portrait of the Full-Time Faculty Position: Activities and Workload." Revised draft of special issue report no. 2. Washington, D.C.: National Center for Education Statistics.

Financing Managing University Research Equipment. 1985. In *University Research Infrastructure.* 1986. Appendix 3.

Frances, C. 1990. *What Factors Affect College Tuition? A Guide to the Facts and Issues.* Washington, D.C.: American Association of State Colleges and Universities. E 317 149. 71 pp. MF-01; PC-03.

Grassmuck, K. March 28, 1990. "Big Increases in Academic-Support Staffs Prompt Growing Concerns on Campuses." *Chronicle of Higher Education:* Al.

Hexter, H. 1990. "Faculty Salaries in Perspective." *Research Briefs* [ACE] 1: 1–7.

Higher Education Costs. 1988. Hearing before the Subcommittee on Postsecondary Education of the Committee on Education and Labor, U.S. House of Representatives, 1987. No. 100-47. Washington, D.C.: U.S. Government Printing Office.

Kirshstein, R. J., and D. R. Sherman, V. K. Tikoff, C. Masten, and J. Fairweather. 1990. *The Escalating Costs of Higher Education.* Washington, D.C.: Office of Planning, Budget, and Evaluation, U.S. Department of Education. ED 328 114. 161 pp. MF- 01; PC- 07.

Kleiman, C. January 2, 1991. "College Lures Parental-Minded Professors With Paid-Leave Policy." *Tallahassee Democrat:* 3D.

Koch, J. V. October 1982. "Salary Equity Issues in Higher Education: Where Do We Stand? *AAHE Bulletin:* 7–14. ED 222 162. 9 pp. MF-01; PC-01.

Kramon, G. March 24, 1991. "Medical Insurers Vary Fees to Aid Healthier People." *New York Times.* 1+.

"The Lattice and the Ratchet." June 1990. *Policy Perspectives* 2: 1–8 [Pew Higher Education Research Program].

Leslie, D. L. May 10, 1991. Personal communication.

Morrison, J. L., W. L. Renfro, and W.I. Boucher. 1984. *Futures Research and the Strategic Planning Process.* ASHE-ERIC Higher Education Reports, No. 84-9. Washington, D.C.: ERIC Clearinghouse on Higher Education. ED 259 692. 141 pp. MF-01; PC-06.

National Center for Education Statistics. 1990. *Faculty in Higher Education Institutions, 1988.* NCES 90–365. Washington, D.C.: U.S. Government Printing Office. ED 321 628. 209 pp. MF-01; PC-09.

Roush, C. March 24, 1991. "Small Employers Ill Over Health Benefits." *Tampa Tribune.* B1+.

Sykes, C. J. 1988. *ProfScam: Professors and the Demise of Higher Education.* Milwaukee, Wis.: Reardon & Walsh.

TIAA-CREF 1990. *College and University Employee Retirement and Insurance Benefits Cost Survey.* New York: Teachers Insurance and Annuity Association.

Troxler, H. March 26, 1991. "Gorilla's Claws May Be Cut By Lawmakers." *Tampa Tribune.* F1.

The University Research Infrastructure and the Federal Government. 1986. Hearings before the Task Force on Science Policy of the Committee on Science and Technology, House of Representatives. 99th Congress, Vol. 6, No. 101. Washington, D.C.: U.S. Government Printing Office.

CHAPTER 27

IMPROVEMENT STRATEGIES FOR ADMINISTRATION AND SUPPORT SERVICES

WILLIAM F. MASSY

William F. Massy is Director at the Stanford Institute for Higher Education Research at Stanford University. This work was sponsored by the National Center for Postsecondary Governance and Finance at the University of Maryland College Park.

In a report on the problem of increased research overhead published in the late 1980s, the Association of American Universities brought attention to the need to hold the line on administrative and support costs. Picking up where the AAU left off, William Massy acknowledges the necessity for administrators to improve their own area before they can address the question of productivity in academic departments. In this chapter, Dr. Massy responds to the problem by discussing factors that reduce productivity in administrative and support areas, presenting a step-by-step process for diagnosing such problems and laying out the elements of an effective productivity improvement strategy.

We are all familiar with the history of cost escalation in colleges and universities and the negative impression this has made on the general public. For example, an article entitled "The Untouchables" in the November 30, 1987, issue of *Forbes* asked the question: "Are colleges picking our pockets?" According to this piece, "Efficiency and cost cutting are demanded of unions and industry. Even government is under pressure to deliver value for the dollar. Why then does higher education get away with delivering a deteriorating product at ever increasing prices?" As Chester E. Finn Jr. has stated in "Judgment Time for Higher Education: In the Court of Public Opinion," the court of public opinion is concluding that institutions of higher education are not as efficient or productive as they should be.

Parents are becoming more and more concerned about whether they will be able to afford college, and, indeed, many are asking themselves whether the financial sacrifice associated with sending a child to a high-priced private college is warranted. Cost increases at public institutions often trigger sharp political debates, and students everywhere demonstrate against tuition hikes at their schools. Higher education officials argue that the money is needed to maintain or increase quality, but they are challenged by those who demand to know if the quality gained is worth the price.

There are two general explanations of why education costs keep rising. They are higher education's "cost disease" and its "growth force."

Cost disease accounts for expenses escalating faster than the rate of inflation. Most operating costs in education are wage driven, and competition in the labor market links a school's salary increases to

Source: Anderson, Richard E., & Meyerson, Joel W. (1992). *Productivity and Higher Education: Improving the Effectiveness of Facilities, and Financial Resources.* Peterson's Guides, pp. 49–83.

the rate of productivity improvement in the national economy. The theory is borne out by the behavior of the higher education price index (HEPI) in relation to the consumer price index (CPI). The former rose at an annual rate of 6.4 percent for the period 1961–86, while in the same period the latter rose by 5.3 percent—a difference of 1.1 percent. (The differential was 1.0 percent for the decade of the 1960s; 1.0 percent for the 1970s when, in an effort to cope with the oil crisis, higher education allowed salaries to lag; and 2.3 percent for the 1980s, when salaries caught up.) The cost-disease explanation points out that as long as a school's student-faculty ratio remains constant, its unit costs will tend to grow in real terms. Steady erosion of student-faculty ratios will have adverse effects on quality.

Growth force applies to the phenomenon of budgets growing faster than can be accounted for by mere cost increases. It is usually due to the addition of new academic programs and the reluctance of administrators to dismantle old programs and reallocate funds to the new ones. The need for new academic programs springs from the dynamism of knowledge development and the creativity of college and university faculty and students. An institution that fails to innovate will soon fall behind—an outcome that university officers rightly seek to avoid. Add-ons are also the rule in administration and support services. The cost of meeting a new government regulation, for instance, or supplying a newly demanded service is usually layered on top of existing costs.

More specific reasons why college and university costs are continually increasing include the constant need for new technology, rising utility costs, and, of course, the accretion of organizational slack. Whatever the causes, current fund expenditures per full-time equivalent (FTE) student in all higher education institutions grew at an annual rate of 1.4 percent over the HEPI between 1975–76 and 1985–86. (The figures for public and private institution were 1.2 percent and 1.6 percent, respectively.) Much ingenuity, energy, management skill, and motivation are needed to innovate and meet new requirements with constant or declining resources, and it appears to critics of higher education that these have not been forthcoming.

Why, they ask, are new programs, functions, and services usually add-ons to budgets instead of replacements for existing activities?

Why don't investments in new facilities and equipment reduce costs rather than add to them? Why don't institutional leaders put more emphasis on productivity? Why is there so much pressure to increase quality and so little to improve cost effectiveness? Why do support-service departments seem to suffer the same productivity malaise as the academic departments with seemingly less justification?

I have chosen to focus on this last question and offer some suggestions for improving administrative and support service productivity.

GROWTH OF ADMINISTRATION AND SUPPORT COSTS

Administration and support costs amount to some 30 percent of education and general (E&G) expenditures at public institutions and over 40 percent at private institutions, according to Arthur M. Hauptman's report, "Why Are College Charges Increasing? Looking into the Various Explanations." As shown in Table 27.1, most indirect costs (other than for libraries) are growing faster than direct costs. Administration and student services are the growth-rate leaders in both public and private institutions, and their effect on budgets is compounded by the fact that between them they account for 25 percent of E&G expenses. Most institutions would do well to focus on these service areas when looking at costs. Although all the cate-

TABLE 27.1
Growth Rates of Key Expense Categories for Public and Private Higher Education 1975/1976 to 1985/1986

	Public	Private
Indirect		
Administration	5.0%	7.6%
Student Services	4.9%	8.3%
Libraries	0.4%	1.6%
Operations and maintenance	3.4%	5.0%
Direct		
Instruction	2.7%	4.5%
Research	5.1%	3.5%
Public service	3.6%	7.0%

Computed from "Why Are College Charges Increasing? Looking into the Various Explanations;" Table 4, by Arthur M. Hauptman.

gories in the table are important to consider, demonstrable progress in containing administration and support costs is a necessary precursor to addressing the question of productivity in academic departments.

Growth-Rate Analysis

The first step in getting a grip on administrative and support costs is to systematically observe the pattern of cost increases during the preceding three to five years. (A variation on this procedure is to calculate increases in FTE employees by organizational unit, based on payroll records for a fixed date in each benchmark year.) The analysis can proceed as follows: (1) from the pattern of cost increases, develop a chart outlining the administration and support services organization; (2) extract data for two or more benchmark years according to this chart; (3) calculate the annualized growth for each organizational unit in the tree; and (4) focus attention on the high-growth units. If no assignable cause for high growth can be found, the unit is a prime candidate for cost reduction. It is hard to determine in advance what organizational level to look at, so it is best to start at a fairly minor level in the organization and then look at more levels until you can reach conclusions about what is meaningful growth.

The Cambridge, Massachusetts-based MAC Group of management consultants performed such an analysis for a midwestern research university a few years ago. The operating units were ranked according to growth rate in expenditures, and attention was focused on those that fell outside the norm for the organization—the outliers. Special study was made of the outliers that showed higher-than-average expenses. On closer investigation, it turned out that some of the extremes were due to readily assignable causes such as reorganization or a high-level management decision to add to service levels. In other cases, the growth seemed to be due to steady accretion.

Marginal Cost

Sometimes indirect costs are driven by changes in the scale of direct activities like instruction and research. The slope of this relation is, of course, the marginal or incremental cost of the indirect activity with respect to the direct one.

Everyone who has taken an economics course knows about marginal costs, but there seem to be few applications for the concept in colleges and universities. There are, however, three ways in which one can examine higher education's marginal costs: the regression method, the fixed- and variable-cost method, and the incremental-cost method. Briefly, the first is a statistical procedure usually based on time-series data. The second assigns each element of expense into a fixed or variable (i.e., marginal) component based on a detailed understanding of the process involved. The third attempts to identify and quantify the components of cost that vary with a given external variable.

Information about marginal costs helps interpret the growth-rate analysis results described earlier. It may be possible, for instance, to normalize some of the growth rates for changes in the cost-driving activities. As an example, when looking at growth rates in an accounting office, one might observe that transactions (T) are growing at x percent per year, that costs (C) are growing at y percent over the university's index of cost rise for continuing activities, and that marginal costs (MC) are about z percent of total cost. The following formula can be used to calculate the change in cost expected in that accounting office on the basis of the changed transaction volume.

$$\Delta T = xT$$
$$\Delta C = yC$$
$$MC = z\, C/T$$
$$\Rightarrow \text{normalized } y = (1+y) \,/\, (1+xz)$$

Suppose x = 3 percent, y = 1.5 percent, and z = 30 percent. Substituting these numbers in the above formula yields normalized y = 1.015/(1 + 0.03 × 0.30) = 1.006, a growth rate of only 0.6 percent. The difference between 1.5 percent net expansion and 0.6 percent net expansion adjusted for volume growth would make a big difference in one's thinking about what has been happening in that office.

This example assumes that there is only one cost-driving variable. Of course there may be multiple variables, in which case, to separate their individual effects the regression method may be required. It is best, however, to begin with a single cost-driver variable for each organizational unit. (It may be necessary to disaggregate another level or two to find a unit with one main driver.) There is, of course, no harm in having different cost drivers for different organizational units—it is required if the analysis is to be comprehensive. The preliminary specifications for an institution-wide cost study at Stanford, for instance, include the following cost drivers.

- Employee head count—used in the controller's office for payroll and in personnel services.

- Accounting transactions—used in the controller's office for general accounting.

- Number of separate funds—used for fund accounting and in the treasurer's office.

- Building square footage—used in operations and maintenance, security, and health and safety.

Remember, these are not the only cost drivers. The important thing is to start somewhere and build an internally consistent set of measures that can normalize observed and requested expense growth rates. The model can be refined according to individual needs, but even rough marginal cost measures are useful.

How can conclusions be reached about growth-rate outliers that cannot be explained by cost drivers? First, identify some other assignable cause that is acceptable from the standpoint of productivity—for example, new regulations. It is important not to accept rationalizations. Much of what is explained away as increased complexity turns out to be bureaucratic accretion, the nemesis of productivity. The rule should be to take a hard look at all the outliers and some units that are not outliers but, because of known external forces that might have been expected to reduce their work load, should have been. The second step is to examine the units for productivity-degrading factors.

FACTORS THAT DEGRADE PRODUCTIVITY

Left to themselves, most organizations are not only sluggish in adopting productivity-enhancing innovations but actually tend to self-destruct in regard to productivity. This self-destruction can be compared to the thermodynamic concept of entropy. In the state of lowest potential, any closed system will "run down" in the sense that its energy will eventually distribute itself evenly. The only way to counter this tendency is to introduce new energy from the outside to keep the system efficient. Before discussing ways that leaders in higher education can introduce energy and information to their organizations and avoid running down productivity, however, I'd like to first examine the three main destructive forces.

Organizational Slack

Organizational slack can stem from simple inattention to efficiency—in which case "fat" is an apt descriptor. Slack can also arise when employees are prevented from performing effectively or when their personal goals are inappropriately substituted for those of the organization. The latter situation, known as resource diversion, gives rise to the view that people will pursue their own interests at the expense of the organization's at every opportunity. Substitution of personal for organizational goals can take the form of loafing, appropriating the organization's resources for personal use, or, perhaps, becoming obsessed with one's own rights and privileges.

Slack is not always bad. Too strong an emphasis on efficiency can demotivate employees and possibly stunt innovation. The beneficial aspects of slack are even more important in higher education than in industry, and they are most important in research universities where innovation must be a way of life. This is why faculty sometimes question the overzealous pursuit of efficiency in academic departments. (Their concerns are reinforced by the fact that what may seem like slack to an outsider is actually the contemplation necessary to produce new discoveries.)

On the administrative and support side of colleges and universities though, the value of slack is about the same as it is for business and government—some slack is a good investment for the future but too much is an unacceptable drag on current operations. James March, in his article "Emerging Developments in the Study of Organizations," put it well when he wrote:

> Under good conditions, slack search generates ideas, many of them too risky for immediate adoption. When conditions

change, such ideas are available as potential solutions to new problems. An organization is able to meet brief periods of decline by drawing on discoveries generated, but overlooked, during better times. A prolonged period of adversity or of exceptional efficiency in avoiding slack depletes the reservoir and leaves the organization vulnerable.

Slack tends to build up in good times and be squeezed out when times turn bad. J. Paul Austin, chairman of the United States Steel Corporation during the 1950s, once told me that U.S. Steel was "like a big bear—building up fat during economic booms and then hibernating, maintaining itself by shedding fat, during recessions." The cyclical process seems inevitable, but if it is not controlled, the slack may build to dysfunctional levels during good times and the eventual squeezing out may be incomplete. An organization should restructure itself to improve during the course of each cycle rather than simply allow history to repeat itself over and over again.

Accretion of Unnecessary Tasks

Everyone can be busy performing his or her assigned duties with energy and intelligence, and yet the organization as a whole may lack productivity. The key is in deciding what tasks are to be performed or, more precisely, in determining whether the tasks, taken separately and as an ensemble, contribute optimally to the long-range purpose of the whole organization.

Productivity is a measure of effectiveness. It reflects an assessment of the usefulness of what is being done, as well as the ratio of outputs to inputs, per se. Effectiveness, however, is not the same as efficiency, which is based on the narrower measure of the resources required to accomplish a particular task without regard to the task's ultimate value.

There are many reasons for the accretion of tasks. Workers or managers may lack competence and thus create unnecessary work for others—when a personnel department must clean up an employee relations mess left by an overbearing supervisor, for instance. A work unit might create unnecessary tasks by suboptimizing their resources, which can result in a redundancy of effort—as when two depart-

ments teach the same subject, each to half the optimal number of students. If not corrected decisively, certain types of incompetence and suboptimization can become the organizational norm.

Escalating spirals of administrative interactions are another prime cause of task accretion. A good person is hired to perform a certain task. That task results in the discovery of new problems, creating the need to perform additional tasks. Others in the organization are drawn in since they must respond to the new initiatives. Coordinating everyone's efforts means that time is being spent in meetings. Soon, additional people must be hired to keep up with the increased work load. They, in turn, find new problems and create work for others—thus perpetuating the spiral. As Jane Hannaway phrased it in her study *Supply Creates Demands: An Organizational Process View of Administrative Expansion*, "The supply of administrators creates its own demand." This problem can be seen not only in education but in all sectors of business and government. For example, government bureaucracies grow inevitably and inexorably as they respond to new sets of problems. These problems beget new organizations or increase the number of layers in existing organizations. This is one reason why heavily regulated industries have many layers of management.

Instituting procedures to correct problems without periodically examining how the procedures can be refined is a common cause of task accretion. Another cause can be two procedures developed for different purposes that cover much of the same ground. Whatever the situation, it is certain that continual layering of new procedures to address new problems will in time degrade productivity. Conscious decisions and much energy are required to reverse the trend and strip away the layers or their cumulative effect will stifle organizational effectiveness at an ever-increasing rate.

Function Lust

Controllers think that their job is important and tend to want to do more of it. The same is true for auditors, planners, builders, landscape architects, lawyers, and even minute-takers in the myriad meetings that characterize colleges and universities. Student-service professionals, librarians, and computer experts are not exempt either. All can make a perfectly plausible case for how the institution could benefit by more being produced from their specialty. While the phrase "function lust" is perjorative, the motives of those who perpetuate the notion are, at least in their own eyes, pure. All these functions are important; otherwise the institution would not have created job openings for them in the first place. The problem is that specialists are not necessarily in the best position to gauge their own importance in relation to other institutional needs. They can do a good job of assessing absolute importance but are less successful in determining relative priorities and in negotiating trade-offs with other functions.

An outgrowth of function lust is the incentive to increase one's job responsibilities and get promoted, which also contributes to administrative task accretion. Job classification systems that offer advancement on the basis of budget size or the number of people supervised are particularly prone to this malady. Organizations whose managers permit "turf wars" invite accretion because the incentives are to staff up in order to beat competing departments instead of trying to cooperate with them. A certain amount of competition can be healthy, but too much is wasteful.

DIAGNOSING PROBLEMS

While information about expenditure or staff growth rates for organizational units can point toward areas where productivity is suspect, these quantitative measures cannot provide information on why. Informal managerial evaluation is the method of choice for diagnosing problems. There is no substitute for "management by walking around," especially in areas where there is reason to suspect subtly hidden difficulties. Unfortunately, though, even the most perceptive managers may well miss systemic issues—i.e., those that involve more than one function or unit—if they rely solely on intuitive processes. More formal approaches can be of greater effectiveness, especially if the organization is embarking on a major productivity enhancement effort.

The Process-by-Function Matrix

Certain key administration and support operations are common to all colleges or universities of a given size and type, regardless of how they are organized. These operations can be displayed in a process-by-function matrix where function refers to activities generally associated with an organizational unit. A hypothetical example of such a matrix is presented in Table 27.2.

The important processes of hiring and paying people are depicted in the first two columns of the matrix. Each process is initiated by an operating department. (The initiating department may be either academic or nonacademic.) The action must then be approved by the appropriate dean or, in the case of nonacademic units, the vice president or his or her delegate. Actions on high-level positions must be approved by the president or by the provost's office. In many cases, the Affirmative Action officer must approve the new hire as well. The personnel department will review and render an opinion sometime during the process. Though personnel may not have the last word, its view is taken into account by the aforementioned decision makers. The payment screening section of the controller's office may be asked to verify that funds are available and that the hiring or salary is consistent with the project budget and with other contractual requirements if this is a sponsored agreement. Of course, the payroll department and the general accounting department get involved in processing the transaction when it finally comes to pass.

Often the process will loop back to involve a given function more than once. Consider the process of purchasing, for example. This is done many thousands of times annually and, while it would seem to be a simple task, it actually is very complicated. The transaction usually originates in an academic or operating department. The typical pattern is for a purchase order to be checked for fund availability by the payment screening group and then be sent to procurement for vendor selection and, if applicable, negotiation of price and terms. Procurement writes a purchase order and notifies the vendor, the originating department, and accounts payable. The order is shipped directly to the originating department, which is responsible for matching the purchase order to the packing

TABLE 27.2
A Hypothetical Process-by-Function Matrix

Function	Human Resources		Purchasing (general)	Purchasing (equipment)		Submitting Research Proposals	Procurement Contracts	
	Hiring People	Paying People		Gov't. Projects	Univ. Funds		Gov't. Projects	Univ. Funds
Academic or operating department	✔	✔	✔	✔	✔	✔	✔	✔
School dean or vice president	✔	✔	✔	✔	✔	✔	✔	✔
President or provost	✔	✔			✔			✔
Dean of research				✔		✔	✔	
Affirmative Action office	✔	✔						
Personnel office Employment	✔							
Compensation		✔						
Employee relations		✔						
Controller's office Payment screening	✔		✔	✔	✔		✔	✔
Accounts payable			✔	✔	✔		✔	✔
Payroll	✔	✔						
General accounting	✔	✔	✔	✔	✔	✔	✔	✔
Sponsored projects office						✔		
Legal office							✔	✔
Facilities office							✔	✔
Procurement department			✔	✔	✔			

Computed from "Why Are College Charges Increasing? Looking into the Various Explanations," by Arthur M. Hauptman.

slip and notifying procurement and accounts payable that the desired goods have been received and are satisfactory. In the meantime, the vendor sends a bill to accounts payable, which matches it to the appropriate receiving notice. The bill is paid (perhaps after a lag to optimize the financial float) and the transaction is entered into the general ledger. It then appears on the originating department's budget and expenditure statement. Is it any wonder that faculty complain about slow turnaround and departmental administrators are driven to their wits' end trying to keep track of outstanding expenditure commitments?

Similar descriptions could be given for the other processes in the matrix. Though this is only a hypothetical example, most people who know colleges and universities will recognize it as a familiar pattern.

Process Flowcharts

The next step is to develop flowcharts for the processes shown in the matrix. Flowcharts help to organize information about the order in which activities are typically or necessarily performed. Useful insights can be added by showing the range of delay times and perhaps the number of man-hours required to transact each step. The approach should be pragmatic; use a level of detail that illuminates the process, not one that obfuscates it into a maze of unimportant detail. Remember, these are *management displays,* not engineering or computer program specifications. Their purpose is strategic. They are not meant to provide detailed instructions for workers or first-line supervisors. In short, the process flowchart provides essential information about the order in which the gross tasks that make up a process are (or should be) performed, not about how each task should be performed. Each flowchart should take up no more than a single letter-sized page, so that it will fit into a ring binder.

Importance, Reliability, and Redundancy

With the flowchart created, I am ready to turn to diagnosis, which begins with the analysis of importance, reliability, and redundancy. (I have decided to call this IRR, partly because it does provide an "internal rate of return.") The IRR tests are applied to each element of the flowchart.

Because it was included in the process-by-function matrix, the process as a whole has already passed a general test determining its importance. But this is not necessarily the case for its individual elements. The first stage is to scrutinize each step of the process. Tasks that have accreted into the system will not automatically pass if the test is performed rigorously.

One of the main impediments to purging tasks is the argument that deleting a step will degrade the quality of the process. Quality is a loaded word at colleges and universities, and one should not allow that assertion to trump the question of importance—even if the assertion is demonstrably true. The answer lies in recognizing that there are two kinds of quality.

- *Design quality* is the quality designed into the product or service. A BMW has greater design quality than, say, a Ford, and it is more expensive. For some purposes and purses, the BMW represents the best price-quality trade-off; for others, the Ford wins out. It is possible even to construct examples where the Ford is better in absolute terms—regardless of price. Driving in high crime areas or where parts and specially trained mechanics are hard to find are two cases in point. The key idea is that more design quality is *not* always better; it needs to be calibrated to the task or situation at hand.

- *Implementation quality* deals with how well the product or service meets its specifications. If the product is to be a Ford, let it be a well-built Ford. It should be the same whether assembled Monday morning or Wednesday afternoon—no lemons allowed. American industry has learned the hard way that implementation quality should always be maximized. "Do it right the first time" is an important principle both for customer satisfaction and for productivity. Everyone can take pride in producing the best possible implementation quality, but not everyone need aspire to build BMWs.

Taking advantage of higher education's reverence for quality in order to enhance implementation quality is a good thing. Allowing this reverence to mandate unneeded levels of design quality in administration and support services is not. Therefore, one should go through each process flowchart and ask whether the tasks are specified at the minimum acceptable level of design quality. High implementation quality should be insisted on, but academic program needs should rule out unnecessarily expensive work specifications in the administrative and support areas. Implementation quality rarely increases costs significantly. Indeed, an institution probably is paying for this kind of quality anyway, and the only question is whether it is getting its money's worth. Implementation quality is obtained by hiring good people, training them well, and providing good leadership and supervision.

Although reliability is related to design quality and implementation quality, it is worthy of separate consideration for two reasons. First, certain designs will be unreliable even with perfect implementation—these should be avoided if the penalty for failure is even remotely high. Second, issues of reliability tend to be systemic rather than oriented toward the individual process elements.

The assessment of total quality cost (TQC) is being used by many companies as a way to consider the reliability question. The objective is to understand what is being spent on maintaining reliability (that is, preventing failures) and correcting failures. Only by looking carefully at both sides of the equation can a reasonable judgment be made about the optimal reliability. In one case, some 80 percent of cost was due to failure, suggesting that the best trade-off might be to spend more on prevention. The trade-off can go the other way, too. An occasional accounting error that can be corrected later is not as consequential as having a part not work as designed or, worse yet, fail in use. Health and safety, systemic financial control weaknesses, and personnel-policy problems are probably the most worrisome risks—the first for obvious reasons, the second because disallowances and defalcations can be very costly, and the last because of the possibility of class-action lawsuits. The total cost of quality should be assessed for each of the processes included in the matrix.

Redundancy is a clear waste of resources unless it is needed for reliability. Redundancy tends to build up as a by-product of administrative task accretion, and it takes conscious effort and energy to identify and eliminate it. This is basically a common-sense matter: go through the process flowchart and simply ask whether each task is also done somewhere else. If the answer is yes, then question whether the redundancy is needed to contain risk (i.e., for reliability) and how much the risk would be increased if it were eliminated. Often the same risks are mitigated several times in complex systems. One can be more vigorous in rooting out redundancies in processes where the risks of failure are in terms of individual transactions rather than systemic operations.

It is also important to determine whether each process should be centralized or decentralized. Some processes are so critical in terms of the need for precise procedures and quality control that they must be centralized in order to achieve the best performance or to contain risks. Others are better left to the creativity and initiative of those closest to them. More situations probably fall into the latter category than one might think, but each instance requires careful analysis. Generally, one dictum is applicable: decide whether a process must be centralized or whether it can be decentralized and then insist that things be done that way. Do not allow a decentralized process to drift toward centralization because of task accretion by staff groups or second-guessing by upper-level line managers. Such behavior can produce a heavy drag on productivity.

Technology

Once it is clear that only essential tasks are being performed, the next question is whether they can be performed more efficiently. Given a fixed set of tasks, substituting capital for labor is the classic approach for improving productivity, and the second industrial revolution (a phrase coined by Herbert A. Simon in the article "The Steam Engine and the Computer: What Makes Technology Revolutionary") represented by information technology provides unusual opportunities. Volumes have been written about the advantages and pitfalls of office automation, so I will limit myself to only a few points.

- Don't try to automate work processes exactly as they are being done by conventional means. The result will nearly always be a more expensive and less satisfactory product than can be obtained by changing work flows to fit the new opportunities. (This is true especially if packaged software is available to do some or all of the job.)

- Strive to input data once only, as close to their original source as possible. Also, minimize paper flow and the need for multiple files. This not only increases the original cost of the job, but adds additional costs if conflicting information requires reconciliation.

- Don't try to get the process exactly right the first time. Modern software development tools permit systems to evolve as people gain experience with them. Often it is best to build a working prototype that will evolve during the project. This avoids endless arguments about once-and-for-all decisions that are so familiar in traditional development environments.

In the long run, automation ran cure the cost disease by substituting a resource whose unit cost is declining in real terms for one whose unit cost is constantly increasing. Sometimes the up-front investment is hard to justify, and it certainly is necessary to be discriminating in terms of proposals. Still, the college or university that is not investing in information technology is likely to be left behind in terms of productivity.

Optimizing Staff Allocations

As with law, accounting, and consulting firms, colleges and universities rely on the services of highly trained professionals—in their support staff as well as their faculty. Productivity improvement in professional-service firms is obtained mainly by substituting less expert and hence less costly people for those with higher levels of expertise. Senior partners leverage their time with that of partners, associates, and research assistants. The cardinal rule is "Always use the least-expert resource that can do the job." Many colleges and universities spend substantial sums on support staff who directly leverage faculty time. Additional sums are spent for lower-level staff who support higher-level people all through administrative and support areas.

Time leveraging in colleges and universities is a double-edged sword. The advantages are the same as in the case of professional firms. However, more leverage is not desirable unless it leads to savings elsewhere. Under what circumstances do such substitutions increase productivity? The answer is easy when talking about for-profit enterprises such as law or consulting firms; the substitution is productive if and only if it increases the partners' income. For colleges and universities the problem is much more difficult because there is no profit measure and, of course, most administrative and support-service outputs are intangible. Individuals often want additional support in order to ease their burdens or to enrich their jobs by unloading repetitive tasks they feel they have fully mastered. The potential for task accretion furthers this phenomenon by offering a ready menu of interesting additional things to do.

THE NEED FOR MANAGEMENT INTERVENTION

Insights into how to diagnose the factors that inhibit productivity in administrative and support services lead to the question "What can be done about them?" What are needed are managerial interventions that afford the possibility of mitigating or reversing the inhibiting factors and that unleash the forces that will enhance productivity and allow more resources to flow to academic operations.

Many of the diagnostic steps discussed in the previous section contain, within themselves, a blueprint for management intervention. The solutions for certain problems are obvious once their existence is understood. Unfortunately, however, a straightforward problem-by-problem attack on productivity often fails to achieve the expected result. The complex interactions among the productivity-inhibiting factors and the people problems associated with change require a carefully thought-out and integrated management intervention strategy.

The growth of medical costs could not be contained until the cost-plus rules of Medicare and Medicaid were amended to establish limits on how much the government would pay for a given procedure or hospital stay. Airline, railroad, and phone companies could not strip away unneeded layers of management and other impediments to productivity until deregulation converted cost-plus into competitive pricing. U.S. industry as a whole could not streamline itself until foreign competition made it a virtual necessity. Similarly, the add-on spiral in higher education must be broken if costs are to be contained. The continued layering of program on program, cost on cost, will sooner or later cause critics of higher education to shift from rhetoric to action. It is better for correction to be accomplished within the academy than imposed from outside. The experience of the medical profession, which a decade ago was seen as singularly unresponsive to the issue of cost containment, supports this thesis.

To arrest the cost-plus spiral higher education must:

- end cost-plus pricing and place strict limits on spending growth, which, in effect, will simulate the discipline of the marketplace; and

- establish planning and resource-allocation processes and incentives to enhance innovation and stimulate resource reallocation from areas with low productivity to those with greater potential.

In other words, the message is "say no, but don't *just* say no." Higher education must simultaneously enforce spending constraints and make sure that its governance and management processes can generate productivity improvement to fund needed innovation.

College and university managers must provide the transitional leadership needed to give productivity high priority—high enough to offset inevitable bureaucratic forces. This requires vision and team building as well as the more traditional applications of legitimate power, tangible incentives, and analytical problem solving. It amounts to answering the question "What must be done in addition to saying no for the institution to change positively?"

The lesson from industry is that while resource constraints are a necessary condition for unleashing productivity improvement and innovation, they are not sufficient. Financial pressure by itself can crush initiative or create conflict over shares of a fixed or shrinking pie. The challenge is to mitigate these effects and turn the financial pressure into a driving force instead of a crushing burden.

Presentation of a coherent and integrated management intervention strategy is beyond the scope of this chapter, but I will describe some of the elements that have to be included in such a strategy. I hope that this will provide practical advice to higher education executives who are charged with productivity enhancement in the administrative and support service areas.

ELEMENTS OF A PRODUCTIVITY—ENHANCING STRATEGY

The sidebar on the following page provides a paradigm for gaining productivity improvement. It sets forth the interactions among four elements: resource constraints; strategic thinking (visions, plans, measures); incentives,

recognition, and rewards; and individual and group empowerment.

Resource Constraints

Approaching the illustration in the sidebar on the following page from the nine-o'clock position immediately reveals the problem—in this context, it might better be described as the "opportunity"—of resource constraints. Meeting these constraints must become a major organizational objective, in effect the enactment of environmental limits by the organization.

Strategic Vision

Organizations, especially complex ones, need a common sense of direction, a way for the organization to manage what Stanley M. Davis in *Future Perfect* has called its "beforemath." A good strategic vision can provide this, exerting a pull to the future that permits people to move with sufficient common purpose to accomplish complex goals over a long period of time. Likewise, a shared paradigm about the organization's technological, market, and financial settings and its internal dynamics and management processes allows individuals to work toward a common goal with more independence than would be possible if they operated on different theories.

One of the most important advantages of a shared strategic vision is that it makes large-scale organizational change possible over a much longer period of time than would otherwise be possible. Such changes are more likely to require cultural adaptation than simpler changes that deal with individual operations or specific skills and routines. Cultural adaptation requires more time to accomplish. Sometimes the time scale is measured in years, during which memories fade and management turns over. A good strategic vision, well articulated and fully internalized as part of the organization's sense of subjective reality, provides the compass to keep the change process on course.

Strategic vision can be externally oriented or internally oriented, and, according to James L. Heskett's "Lessons from the Private Sector," most organizations need both. The former is usually concerned with what is to be accomplished vis-a-vis the outside environment—i.e.,

Gaining Productivity

It is not easy for colleges and universities to increase productivity. The incentives in an academic culture point toward improving quality; there are few obvious incentives for focusing on efficiency and cost effectiveness. It is possible, however, for institutions to contain costs. Under the right conditions, cost containment can trigger increased productivity, thereby helping to achieve improvement in quality.

I believe that there are four conditions necessary for improving productivity.

Strategic Thinking
(visions, plans, measures)

Constraints on available resources

Incentives, recognition and rewards

Individual and group empowerment

Resource Constraints

Resource constraints can be the driving force behind an institution's decision to increase efficiency and productivity. Most educational leaders press hard to enhance quality, but without the effect of resource constraints there is no incentive to consider cost effectiveness in relation to quality. It is no accident that institutions that regard themselves as relatively well-off financially find it hard to increase productivity, even though they have some of the best human and technological resources for tackling the problem.

Individual and Group Empowerment

Productivity improvement depends on the initiatives and skills of faculty and staff on both the individual and the group levels. They are the ones who are most familiar with the work process and who will implement any day-to-day changes. Faculty and staff must be empowered to lead the institution through its difficult choices. Empowerment means believing that one *can* and *should* make a difference and possessing or having access to the skills and resources needed to do the job.

Incentives, Recognition, and Rewards

Incentives and rewards can be offered in the context of tight resource constraints. In fact, they do not need to be monetary or even tangible. They should, however, be devised to encourage workers to think positively about productivity. It is very important to avoid inadvertently creating incentives that undermine productivity. Personnel reductions that are directly attributable to productivity improvement often decrease the potential for additional gains. Recognizing and celebrating a good result or a good effort is also essential. For example, school administrations should recognize faculty efforts to develop new and more productive teaching methods when setting salaries and making promotion and tenure decisions.

Strategic Thinking

The institution's leaders must engage in strategic thinking about productivity improvement. They must define what they mean by gaining productivity and make clear that it is an important part of their vision for the institution. They must develop plans and programs for embedding the vision in the organizational culture at the working level. They must also provide the concepts and support necessary for empowering people to develop and implement productivity-enhancing initiatives. They must arrange for the right incentives, recognition, and rewards and make sure there is follow-through across the organization.

All four conditions are necessary. Without incentives there will be few faculty and staff initiatives. Without strong conceptual leadership, those initiatives will lack focus, coherence, and staying power. Without faculty and staff initiatives, central visions and plans will stagnate because they lack connection to the actual work process and saliency for the people who would have to implement change. Finally, without a clear and binding resource constraint, the drive for quality and the incentives, recognitions, and rewards associated with quality dominate the objective of gaining productivity.

Adapted from the author's contribution to the article "Double Trouble," which was published in the September 1989 issue of *Policy Perspectives.*

clients, competitors, or suppliers of capital. The latter concerns itself more with how the work will be accomplished and the organization's planning and management processes. Some examples of external and internal vision elements based on the service industry are presented in Table 27.3. Service-industry experience has much relevance for college and university administration and support services, which

TABLE 27.3
Sample Vision Elements from the Service Industry

Externally-oriented Elements

- How does the service concept propose to meet customer needs?
- What is good service? Does the proposed concept provide it?
- What efforts are required to bring client service expectations and capabilities into alignment?
- What are the important features of the delivery system?
- How can the actual and perceived differences between the value and cost of services be maximized?
- Where will investments be made and efforts concentrated?

Internally-oriented Elements

- What are common characteristics of employee groups?
- How important are each of these groups to the delivery of service?
- What needs does each group have?
- How does the service concept propose to meet employee needs?
- To what extent are the concept and the delivery system for serving important employee groups internally consistent?
- To what extent have employees been involved in the design of the concept and the delivery system?

Adapted from Exhibits I and II in James L. Heskett's "Lessons from the Private Sector."

TABLE 27.4
Results of the Stanford Finance Service Training Sessions

Good service reinforced as a priority

- Support from top management was made visible in the sessions.
- Importance of good service to clients was recognized.

Clients identified and client relations enhanced through client interviews.

Services clarified and defined

- Unnecessary services were eliminated.
- Valued services were acknowledged.
- Service strengths and issues were identified.

Service skills reviewed

- Characteristics of good and bad service were discussed (accessibility, follow-through, courtesy).
- Effects of Stanford culture on service was examined.

Team building among group members was significantly enhanced (this was the first exposure to team building for some groups).

Self-image of work groups was improved through understanding their contribution to Stanford.

Communications examined

- Work group members in the sessions improved their communications.
- Departmental communications were improved by means of interviews.
- Managers attended sessions and were interviewed.
- Ongoing direct client feedback was initiated.

Many specific service improvements were put in place.

Improvement suggestions identified

- Service improvement plans were developed by every group.
- Management team committed to following up on issues presented by the work groups.

are dedicated to serving clients both inside and outside the academy.

Vision is created and promulgated through analysis and communication and by acting out the vision. For mid-level managers and rank-and-file employees, the latter can be furthered through carefully designed training sessions. On the next page, Table 27.4 presents the results of service training in the Stanford finance division as reported to me by my staff. The benefits of the session included empowerment through confidence building and skill development as well as the creation of a more powerful shared vision of the what, why, and how of providing good service. Extensive feedback from the participants and from their clients confirmed management's assessment that the program was highly successful.

Empowerment

While strategic vision provides a shared sense of what should be done, empowerment provides a powerful force for making things happen—thus providing a new way to think about productivity and change. A recent retreat for my senior finance staff began with a discussion entitled "Empowering Ourselves: What Can I Do to Create a Stanford of the Future to Which I Am Committed?" The investigation began with the meaning of work.

Participants learned that most people work in order to meet some combination of the following objectives.

- To make a living
- To express deepest values
- To create an organization of one's own choosing
- To fulfill potential
- To discover identity

Only the first entry on the list regards work as a means to an end. The others regard it as tapping intrinsic needs. Surprising gains in productivity are possible when these needs are aligned with those of the organization.

The empowered organization contrasts sharply with the traditional, patriarchal organization. Work in the latter tends to be directed toward gaining the approval of one's superiors (the patriarchs), which leads to undue concern about promotion, avoidance of risk, and control of one's work environment. Attention is directed upward (What does the boss think?) and risk is diversified by name-dropping and diffusing responsibility. Management style is often manipulative and calculating. In the empowered organization, however, work means contributing to impor-

tant shared goals, mastering important skills, finding meaning in thought and action, acting out one's sense of integrity, and having a positive impact on people.

Figure 27.1 depicts what is generally expected from an organization. Responsiveness to mission and adaptability to environmental change is at the top of the triangle. Productivity is at the four o'clock position—how well the mission is accomplished will determine the organization's long-run health. The pressure to do more with less is nearly always present. Quality of work life is at eight o'clock—doing the job well over the long haul depends on employee commitment and morale.

How are these things accomplished? The traditional answer has been found within the patriarchal strategy. The best answer, however, is *empowerment*.

The patriarchal strategy concentrates responsibility and leadership at the top and stresses belief in consistency, control, and predictability. The organization tells the employee "Do as I say and I will take care of you." The implicit patriarchal contract is to submit to authority, to deny self-expression, and to sacrifice now for often unstated promises—all in return for being "taken care of." Employees are instruments, tools to be controlled and prevented from diverting resources. The limits of the patriarchal strategy are that it alienates the doing of work from the managing of work, values internal stability for its own sake, encour-

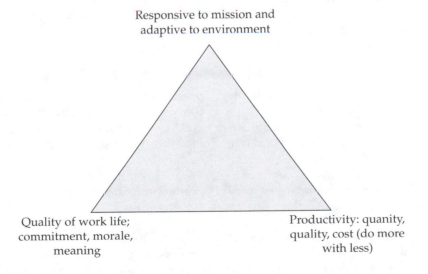

Figure 27.1 What Is Expected of an Organization?

ages narrow functional thinking, limits ownership of plans and ideas, and breeds caution and resistance to change. Over time, employees feel betrayed if rewards are not forthcoming at the level they have grown to expect. The patriarchal strategy tends to produce victims who become envious of victors to the detriment of teamwork and productivity. The balance of forces tends to favor the status quo and to actively inhibit behavior that deviates from it—even if that behavior stands a good chance of furthering the vision.

The empowerment strategy, on the other hand, strives for commitment and leadership at every level and stresses diversity, innovation, and personal responsibility. The organization tells the employee, "We will support autonomy and choice." The empowerment contract is to accept your own authority and accountability, encourage straight communication, and make commitments based on their meaning—not how they may look to the boss. Setbacks are taken at face value rather than as an excuse for feeling like a victim. The value of empowerment is that people will think of the whole organization rather than think in narrow functional or personal terms. The empowered organization values change, so things don't have to be "broke" before they can be improved. (Remember, though, that the improvements should be in implementation quality and not necessarily design quality.) Empowerment allows unique responses as situations demand, with no need to wait for multiple levels of approval or instructions from higher authority. Finally, empowerment integrates the doing of work and the management of work with substantial dividends for productivity.

Employees must empower themselves, though the organization plays a critical role in removing barriers and providing encouragement. In the final analysis, the empowered employee will be strong enough and free enough to decide whether to accept a setback with continued commitment or decline to participate further. The decision to exit may take the form of changing employment or simply hunkering down and riding out the storm—in effect returning to the patriarchal model. This option is always present, and it provides leaders with the continuing challenge of keeping the environment for empowerment green.

Empowerment is not designed solely or even mainly to make people happy. The empowered organization is not "easy," but it does tend to have good morale. The tasks may be demanding, and meaning may be achieved only with great difficulty. Integrity means sailing under your own colors and having the strength to say no (not maybe) when you mean no. This can test relations with others, but contrast it with supervision by intimidation. Browbeating employees and ignoring their wants and needs may give the supervisor a sense of personal power, but that style alienates people and destroys productivity. A friend who is CEO of a major corporation says that while trying to have a positive impact on people is intrinsically gratifying and good, a sufficient reason for acting that way is that it works—it furthers the objectives of the organization. To paraphrase a quote attributed to noted author and former Secretary of the U.S. Department of Health, Education, and Welfare John Gardner, morale is not necessarily happy people and smiling faces. Rather, it is people believing that the organization and its leaders are going in the right direction and doing the right things. For higher education in these times, an important and visible component of the right thing must be to maximize the productivity of administration and support services.

THE ACTION PLAN

Imagine that the diagnoses have been completed and that the necessary preconditions for a successful productivity improvement program have been put in place. The momentum of cost-plus pricing has been arrested, and firm resource constraints have been installed. What specific action steps should be undertaken to channel these positive forces toward administration and support-service productivity improvement?

Communications

The first step is to develop a communications strategy. Wide understanding of the reasons why productivity should be high on the institution's agenda is essential for mounting an effective program. Change itself can be painful, and increased productivity requires firm limits on resource outlays in the face of demands for improved performance. Active participation requires that people understand why they are being asked to endure what may well seem like sacrifices.

But communication should be a two-way street. Creating a shared strategic vision requires listening carefully to what people at all levels of the organization are saying even though in the end the vision is heavily conditioned by the outside environment and determined by the leadership. Changes in the outside environment may best be interpreted by people on the firing line, and the overall vision must relate meaningfully to their goals and sense of reality. Genuine two-way communication is much easier in the empowered organization where one does not have to resort to patriarchal games and the adjudication of claims of victimhood. It is possible for a leader to listen carefully and in good faith to employees without abdicating the responsibility to set the organization's agenda. However, a true leader must be willing to explain a final decision but must not feel compelled to *prove* that it will be the right decision. (Such a burden is impossible. Leaders must be empowered to act on their own judgment, provided they are prepared to be held accountable.)

The communication process can take many forms. Management retreats are popular and they can be very effective. "Town meetings" where leaders meet with middle managers and rank-and-file employees can serve the dual purpose of generating a dialogue between top management and these other groups and facilitating communication among them. Management by walking around is another effective way of communicating.

While every situation is different, it is often a good idea to decide on the broad outlines of the vision in a small group setting before taking it on the road. The small group must include senior management, who must ultimately be responsible for vision content, though others who have taken the time to become expert in the issues can also play an important role. The vision is then refined by give-and-take exposure to broader groups. Finally, the basic content of the message is finalized and promulgated as widely as possible.

Video and other technical aids can be helpful in putting out a coherent and consistent message, since the time and energy of the most senior people—who have the greatest source credibility—is limited. However, there is no substitute for personal involvement. One useful format is for the CEO to videotape a message that is then played before a group in his or her presence, after which there is a discussion and questions session. This conserves the CEO's energy, guarantees the consistency of the message from session to session, and makes it possible for the CEO to think about the group during presentation of the core material.

Management Process

The productivity improvement program will not succeed without a well-thought-out management process for maintaining its place on the organization's agenda and keeping it on track. Experience suggests that the best method is to charge a high-level management group (a steering committee) with this task and then support it with a small staff that will be responsible for planning and follow-through. Keeping the program on the senior people's agenda despite inevitable distractions is a key responsibility for the staff. So is setting reasonably sized specific tasks, making appropriate delegations (with the support of the program's principals), and tracking the delegations to ensure performance. Since facilitating empowerment is a major goal, the staff must avoid the temptation to perform most of the tasks themselves. That would disempower line managers and ultimately undermine the program. One way to make sure this doesn't happen is for the senior people to keep the support staff very small, which would require it to go out into the organization to get things done. This also helps hold the line on task accretion by the staff group.

The usual way to go out into the organization is to delegate particular tasks to individuals or small groups, usually representative managers or staff with specifically relevant expertise. However, one of the lessons of the quality, service, and productivity (QSP) program my colleagues and I developed for Stanford's business and finance division was that an analog to quality circles can be very effective both in solving particular problems and facilitating empowerment. The variant we used was the quality team (we called them QSP teams), a format developed by the Hewlett-Packard Corporation. The team roster was constructed as a diagonal section through the organization, from top to bottom and from side to side. (The traditional quality circle is made up of bottom-level people—e.g., those on the factory floor.) The advantage is breadth of experience plus the ability of the few expert and higher-level participants to get information, assess the implementation possibilities of the group's ideas, and help get things done when the time comes. It is important, however, that these higher-level people consider themselves more as facilitators than as managers, lest the insight and energy of the others be stifled through disempowerment.

The steering committee's role in all this is to help conceptualize the process, set priorities for what tasks need to be attended to, and oversee the work of the staff. Another very important role is to provide an audience to which the work product of the task groups will ultimately be presented. In addition to its obvious value, such a role provides the task groups with a focal point for organizing themselves and a sense of recognition or even reward when they have accomplished their charge. Constructively critical questions from senior managers are in fact a powerful kind of recognition—one of the most powerful a motivated professional can achieve. Furthermore, the presentation sessions provide members of the steering committee with an opportunity to interact with employees from levels they would not usually have contact with and to do so in relation to a problem of mutual importance. We found that the QSP teams facilitate two-way communication and provide opportunities for senior managers to send signals about style and what they think is important.

Analysis and Planning

There is, of course, no substitute for having well-conceptualized and well-thought-out strategies and plans. They deal with the what and how of change, and they must be rooted in the objectively real world as well as in peoples'

sense of subjective reality. For instance, computer systems that cannot work as envisioned because of technological limitations or because they require too much time or money to develop will not be helpful no matter how well they fit in with the vision and people's beliefs about what is important. Engineering, financial, market, contractual, legal, and regulatory factors have to be analyzed in depth in order to see possibilities and avoid mistakes. This kind of fact finding and analysis is part of the content of the delegations and charges to teams referred to in the previous section.

For example, an early action in Stanford's QSP program was to charge a team with trying to understand the elements of good service—what it means, how to get it, how to keep it. The team began the task by doing a systematic literature survey and then decided to talk with a number of companies identified as exemplary service providers. Out of this came some general principles: service must be a major organizational commitment (part of the vision, such as productivity must be); people must be trained in how to provide it, empowered to do so, and then held accountable for following through; and client feedback must be collected, as it is essential to understanding how things are going and to making midcourse corrections. Eventually, what was learned by this team was embodied in the service training program discussed in connection with Table 27.4.

The QSP team on work simplification provides another example. It started by developing a definition and understanding of what is meant by work simplification. This led to the creation of two subteams for doing pilot studies of how Stanford hires and pays people and how Stanford buys things (that is, employment/payroll and procurement/accounts payable). One of their first tasks was to learn about work process flowcharting and then apply it in their own departments. Some of these people discovered they could actually change the way the work was being done. The most spectacular result was in accounts payable, where a change in work flow and procedures reduced the backlog and the use of overtime to virtually nothing while coping with increased transaction volume and maintaining a constant staff—something the finance division had been trying to do for years without success. The final lesson was

TABLE 27.6
Criteria and Suggestions for Individual and Team Rewards

Criteria (typical examples of an employee's willingness to go the extra mile)

- Suggested/developed a system or process that improved the quality, service, and/or productivity of work.
- Suggested/developed a system or process for work-simplification.
- Developed a creative solution to meet the needs of a client or department.
- Assumed additional responsibilities during a period of staff shortage.
- Increased job knowledge by voluntarily participating in cross training.
- Exhibited tact and diplomacy in dealing with faculty, staff, or the outside community on a sensitive issue beyond the normal scope of job.
- Made a difficult decision by using sound judgment and reasoning and carefully weighing alternatives.
- Consistently promoting teamwork by help and cooperation outside of requirements.

Rewards (to be used as a menu of rewards and as a catalyst for new ideas)

- Recognition party or dinner.
- Lunch at Stanford Faculty Club.
- Permission to attend seminars, workshops, and classes outside of university staff development classes.
- Tickets for two to Stanford events such as Lively Arts performances and athletics events.
- Attendance at special lectures, presentations, or other university events.
- Behind-the-scenes tour (perhaps with family) of Stanford facilities such as the linear accelerator, the biological preserve, the marine station, or the hospital.
- A gift from the Stanford bookstore, track house, or art gallery shop.
- Personalized office supplies (pen, etc.).
- A handwritten thank-you note.

From the *Rewards, Recognition, and Incentives Handbook* produced by the Stanford University controller's office.

that much could be accomplished when the people with an intimate knowledge of the process were motivated and empowered to change it and given the tools to do so.

Rewards, Recognition, and Incentives

The "Welcome" section of the Stanford controller's office *RR&I Handbook* begins: "Tom Peters, author of *A Passion for Excellence,* has said that employees come to work equipped with motivation. The manager's job, therefore, is not to motivate, but to capitalize on the resource that is already there by removing minor barriers and constantly recognizing small achievements." The handbook goes on to state: "To be most effective, such recognition must be spontaneous and ongoing. By taking individual responsibility for recognizing our colleagues' daily efforts, we can achieve a culture where recognition is second nature and the incentive to excel accompanies each new task." The *Handbook* presents "simple, straight-forward guidelines for recognizing and rewarding day-to-day efforts," some of which are reproduced in Table 27.6, which appears above. What is particularly impressive is that the guidelines were developed by the line managers themselves rather than by human resource professionals—a tangible example of empowerment.

The more traditional processes of performance evaluations and merit pay should not be overlooked in designing RR&I systems. Written performance evaluations are tremendously important and well worth spending time on. Many organizations, including Stanford, have well-developed processes, including packaged materials and training programs on how to use them. I have found it helpful to ask for a sample of six to twelve of the evaluations written by people who report to me or by those a level lower, who report to them. I do this a month or two after the official performance evaluation season has ended, partly to look at the performance of the evaluated, partly to see whether the evaluator is doing the job conscientiously, and partly to send a signal that I care about the process. With regard to merit pay, the biggest problem is how to increase the range of variation from a point or two from the guideline to as much as two times it. There is no sure way to do this within traditional merit pay systems, though a process wherein senior managers reject packages with unusually small ranges would certainly be a step in the right direction.

Finally, one might consider a nontraditional program of providing merit salary increments not in the base. The idea is that the half or two-thirds of employees who are doing the best job are given salary increments averaging several percent, but these increments would not be added to the person's base salary for compounding in future years. The increment would keep coming as long as performance held up, but it would not be guaranteed. It would be awarded in addition to the normal compounding increments received by everyone, which in the experiment become simple market adjustments. The program is intended to stretch the range of annual merit variations while avoiding the problem of consistently good or bad performance compounding to greater-than-tolerable disparities. The system would be calibrated so that people who don't get the nonbase increment would be slightly below market while those who got the best increments would be above market.

Measurement

The idea of measurement has permeated much of what I have said about productivity improvement. There are a number of reasons for this. First, no system can function effectively without feedback. The ability to assess the gap between performance and expectations is fundamental to midcourse correction, and no one is smart enough or well-informed enough to create a plan that can work without such corrections. Second, rewards, recognition, and incentives require that someone, somehow, makes an assessment of whether work is good, bad, or indifferent. It works the other way too, of course: accountability requires that an assessment be made of results.

I have already discussed one aspect of measurement in connection with communication. Two-way communication is a form of measurement: What's on your mind and how are we, the management, doing? A friend suggested that the way to approach this kind of measurement is to ask, "If I could sit on a bar stool with everyone in the organization for an hour, what would I suggest we talk about?" One way to do that (other than logging many hours on bar stools) is to hold town meetings and insist on candor in the ensuing discussions. Another is to use impromptu written surveys during town meetings, management retreats, and similar functions. The questionnaire does not need to be elaborate, though a degree of consistency will permit comparisons to be made across groups and over time. Sometimes the answers can be tabulated and feedback provided to the group at the same meeting. This usually guarantees that the question-and-answer period will be candid and lively.

Constantly taking the pulse of the organization is one of the keys of effective management. The same is true of client feedback. One of the things the QSP team learned about successful service organizations was that they all go out of their way to obtain systematic feedback from clients and then act on it promptly. The process of acquiring and paying attention to feedback is built into the organization's culture. It is part of its vision and part of its performance evaluation criteria. Experience shows that acting on feedback improves results. Measurement of how productivity improvement is being achieved has to be an integral part of any program.

What feedback is likely to be important in a productivity program? First, there needs to be a systematic attempt to chronicle the specific actions being taken to support the program: what decisions, initiatives, investments, resource reallocations, and work simplification projects are being attempted and what their results are. Sometimes self-assessment is the best or most practical method of evaluation; sometimes it should be done by superiors and sometimes by staff groups, outside consultants, or visiting committees. Whatever the method, the important thing is that there be a description of the action, an a priori statement of the expected outcomes, and an explicit evaluation. The objective is both to learn by doing and to keep score for purposes of RR&I and accountability—the latter being based on the willingness to intelligently act as well as on the efficacy of the final outcome.

The other kind of measure is to keep score on the aggregate performance of operating units with respect to productivity measures. Where the inputs and outputs can be reasonably quantified, the score keeping should be straightforward. Transactions processed per FTE employee is a natural measure in the general accounting department, for instance. Lacking quantification of this sort, it may still be possible to track the number of employees that perform various qualitatively described tasks. It often is possible to measure performance on the basis of budget reallocation that the unit undertakes. Most organizations operate in a dynamic environment, and a long period of organizational stability may well signal a failure to adapt to new requirements or challenges and a stagnation of productivity improvement.

The bottom line is that the organization will tend to pay attention to the things that are posted on the scoreboard—provided, of course, that management makes clear that it is looking at the scoreboard too. The design of a productivity program must include output measures to assess how the program is going. Those measures need to be assessed at the operating unit level where people are close enough to the action to make a difference.

A POSTSCRIPT ON MANAGEMENT STYLE

There is no magic potion for productivity improvement in colleges and universities. Even when dealing with administrative and support services, the obstacles are large and the gains hard won. No large-scale purchase of capital equipment will make the difference. Even when information technology supplants manual processes, the gains are achieved little by little. Small wins by people newly empowered and eager to make a difference are what add up to the final result. The challenge of leadership is to see that the battles are fought on the right ground and for the right objectives; to recognize, reward, and hold people accountable so that the process continues and gains momentum; and to enable people to achieve these wins.

It is a truism that top managers must wholeheartedly support the program, making

it a sine qua non for the organization, if there is to be real success. Their attitude must be positive, and they must be willing to shoulder risks both for the organization and 'for themselves. There should be a bias toward action, an approach that says "try it, fix it" rather than "study it until we're sure it'll work" or "discuss it until we have consensus."

The members of the management team must learn to work together and, above all, must trust one another. Each must carry the others' proxy—to get things done for the good of the organization, they must recognize transgressions and fix them when they occur rather than play "one up." The management team must "zig and zag together," in the words of William F. Miller, former provost of Stanford University and president of SRI International, a nonprofit research institute based in Menlo Park, California. Each member of the team must anticipate what the other will do and make maximum use of that knowledge to get the job done. Not only is this a necessary condition for performing the senior group's tasks effectively but it sets an important example for the rest of the organization. And it applies across the boundary between academic and administrative units as well as within the culture of each.

Finally, it may be useful to initially present the productivity-improvement task as removing impediments rather than as instituting an ideal system all at once. All organizations abound with impediments, and this is especially true of many colleges and universities. Creating the right vision and getting back to neutral on productivity by eliminating redundancy; controlling the cost of quality; or progressing toward work simplification, empowerment, and RR&I represent good initial goals. After a few years, the goal should be to make the whole greater than the sum of the parts through better coordination of functions and global optimization of capital and human resource investments. This is an exciting process. When higher education has mastered it, it shall no longer have to be on the defensive with respect to productivity—the public and the political system will recognize higher education's productivity when they see it.

BIBLIOGRAPHY

Association of American Universities Ad Hoc Committee on Indirect Costs. (1998). *Indirect costs associated with federal support of research on university campuses: Some suggestions for change.* Washington: Association of American Universities.

Allen, Richard, & Paul Brinkman. (1983). *Marginal costing techniques for higher education.* Boulder: National Center for Higher Education Management Systems (NCHEMS).

Barney, Jay B., & William G. Ouchi. (1986). *Organizational economics.* San Francisco: Jossey-Bass Publishers.

Baumol, William J., & Sue Anne Batey Blackman. Electronics, the cost disease, and the operation of libraries. *Journal of the American society for information sciences,* vol. 34 (3): 181–91.

Block, Peter. (1988). *The empowered manager.* San Francisco: Jossey-Bass Publishers.

Bowen, William. (1968). *The economics of the major private universities.* New York: Carnegie Commission on Higher Education.

Davis, Stanley M. (1987). *Future perfect.* Reading, Mass.: Addison-Wesley Publishing Company.

Finn, Chester E., Jr. Judgment time for higher education: In the court of public opinion. *Change,* vol. 20:34–39.

Hannaway, Jane. Supply creates demands: An organizational process view of administrative expansion. *Journal of policy analysis and management,* vol. 7:118–34.

Hauptman, Arthur M. (1988). Why are college charges increasing? Looking into the various explanations. Working draft of a report to the College Board and the American Council of Education, September.

Heskett, James L. (1987). Lessons from the service sector. *Harvard business review,* (March-April): 118–26.

Hoenack, Stephen A. (1983). *Economic behavior within organizations.* New York: Cambridge University Press.

Maister, David H. (1984). Professional service firm management. Memo no. 20. Boston: Harvard Business School (June).

March, James G. (1982) Emerging developments in the study of organizations. *Review of higher education,* vol. 6: 1–18.

Massy, William F. (1984). Productivity and cost increase at Stanford. Discussion paper no. 2. Stanford University Board of Trustees Budget Committee (7 May).

———. (1984). Financing higher education. Tenth annual conference on financing higher education. National Center for Higher Education Management Systems (NCHEMS) (28 November).

———. (1989). "Strategies for productivity improvement in college and university academic departments." Presented at the Forum for Postsecondary Governance, 30 October, Santa Fe, New Mexico.

Meyer, Marshall W. (1985). *Limits to bureaucratic growth.* Berlin: Walter de Gruyter.

Pfeffer, Jeffrey, and Gerald R. Salancik. (1978). *The external control of organizations: A recourse dependence perspective.* New York: Harper & Row, Publishers.

The Higher Education Research Program (Sponsored by the Pew Charitable Trusts). (1989). Double trouble. *Policy perspectives,* vol. 2, no. I (September).

Simon, Herbert A. (1987). The steam engine and the computer: What makes technology revolutionary. *EDUCOM Bulletin,* vol. 22, no. I (Spring): 2–5.

Sullivan, Charles Parker. (1987). The social construction of change in administrative behavior in higher education. Ph.D. diss., Stanford University.

Weber, Max. (1978). Types of legitimate domination. *Economy and society,* vol. I. Guenther Roth and Claus Wittick, (Eds.), 212–301. Berkeley: University of California Press.

Weick, Karl E. (1985). Small wins: Redefining the scale of social problems. *American psychologist,* vol. 39, no. 1: 40–49.

CHAPTER 28

RISING ADMINISTRATIVE COSTS

Seeking Explanations

LARRY L. LESLIE AND GARY RHOADES

The authors wish to acknowledge the insightful comments of Pual Brinkman, Carol Floyd, George Keller, Tony Morgan, and Tom Wickenden, who will recognize how much our article has drawn on and benefited from their thought-provoking suggestions.

Larry L. Leslie is professor of higher education and Gary Rhoades is associate professor of higher education at the Center for the Study of Higher Education, University of Arizona.

By essentially any measure, administrative costs in colleges and universities have risen dramatically during the past two decades, disproportionately more than the costs of instruction and research. Accelerating a four-decade pattern, expenditures for presidents, deans, and their assistants grew 26 percent faster than instructional budgets in the 1980s [3]. The increase for administrative costs per full-time equivalent student in the 1980s, nationwide, was 46 percent, exclusive of monies spent on the administration of libraries, student services, research, and physical plant. Between 1973 and 1974 and 1985 and 1986, the *share* of "education expenditures" spent on administration (institutional support, student services, and academic support minus libraries) increased 2.7 percentage points for all public universities, while the instruction share declined 2.0 percentage points—changes that measure in the billions of dollars, nationally [24]. According to HEGIS/IPEDS data for 1975–86, administrative costs increased faster than academic costs in all higher education sectors [35, 39]. In private colleges, the median rate of increase for administrative and support expenditures was 4 percent per year, in real terms, versus less than 3 percent per year for academic expenditures.

Regarding changes in the number and salaries of administrators, Equal Employment Opportunity Commission data for 1975–85 showed a 6 percent growth in full-time faculty; an 18 percent growth in "executive, administrative, and managerial employees"; and a 61 percent growth in "other professionals," who are degree-holding employees often accounted for in administrative categories.[1] For 1985–90, the increases were 9 percent, 14 percent and 28 percent, respectively [21, 22]. Secretarial and clerical staff grew at a faster rate than faculty. The only group to show a decline was service and maintenance personnel. At some large universities, the numbers were even more dramatic. At UCLA the number of faculty members declined 6.8 percent from 1977 to 1987, at the same time that executive, administrative, and managerial employees increased 35.8 percent. At MIT, faculty members increased by 7.6 percent from 1981 to 1989, whereas administrative personnel increased by 37 percent. Even when faculty numbers increased substantially, as at Ohio State University, where they increased by 29.2 percent between 1979 and 1989, the increase in executive,

Source: *Journal of Higher Education*, Vol. 66, No. 2 (March/April 1995) ©1995 by the Ohio State University Press.

administrative, and managerial personnel well outpaced that growth, being 71.2 percent, while other professionals increased by 139 percent.[2] If we consider salaries, the declines were somewhat less for administrators: between 1971 and 1972 and 1984 and 1985, the average real salaries of faculty and administrators declined by 16 and 13.1 percent, respectively. When those figures are disaggregated for administrators, the data reveal increased salary dispersion among administrators, as well as among faculty [26, 33].

Concerns are widespread. Three-quarters of the member institutions of the Association of American Universities report having recently attempted to reduce administrative costs [23]. State legislators and institutional trustees specifically have targeted administrative costs; in two states legislatures recently have mandated 10 percent reductions in administrative expenditures. When Arizona's Joint Legislative Budget Committee launched a study of administrative costs in higher education in 1992, Arizona became only the most recent of several states to express concern over the increasing allocation of higher education's resources away from instruction to institutional administration. In chairing the subcommittee responsible for the Arizona study, it has become clear to the senior author of this article that the Arizona study, like similar efforts in many other states, merely will estimate and compare growth in administrative costs to comparable costs in peer institutions, over time. By contrast, in this article we hope to focus future studies of costs in ways that will sharpen the understanding of why administrative costs rise and will inform decision making and practice.

Knowing where administrative costs have increased is crucial to understanding causes. Unfortunately, such data tell us little about the nature of or the explanations for spiraling administrative costs. The data are aggregated at too high a level to permit identification of causes. Our aim is to conceptualize the probable causes of increased administrative costs in hypotheses that can be examined empirically. We develop, herein, propositions that account for escalating costs in different branches and levels of higher education administration. We focus on prevailing economic assumptions and predominant explanatory frameworks as found in the literature. We also develop our own

explanations, focusing on the analytical value of two sets of constructs: the "internal position" (that is, organizational distance among) and budgetary authority of administrators, and the relationship between internal administrative stratification and external structures of power.

WHAT ARE ADMINISTRATIVE COSTS?

Whatever expenditure categories are used to measure and explain administrative costs, there will be some dispute about definitions. A good example is "academic support." Some will argue that only a modest portion of academic support costs are administrative in nature, for that category encompasses all costs associated with libraries, museums, academic computing, and other support activities, whereas others may hold that any support activities should be viewed as "administrative." Although open to disagreement, among finance professionals administrative costs generally are taken to be either institutional support or the combination of institutional support, academic support (minus libraries), and student services, as these categories are defined in *College and University Business Administration* [36].

WHAT DO THE INCREASES TELL US?

Most faculty, like the authors of this article, probably would uncritically accept the assumptions that faculty are the primary "production workers" in colleges and universities and that resource shifts away from production activities such as teaching and research are undesirable. Many administrators take issue with the first assumption, arguing that nonfaculty personnel also produce higher education outputs and, more important, are superior to faculty at enhancing revenues, thereby calling into question the assumption that resource shifts away from faculty-centered activities are problematic.[3] How, then, should we judge the empirically documented resource shift?

One issue is whether increased administrative costs have contributed to improved administrative services. Administrative cost increases may signal improved services to clients. Unfortunately, most institutions do not evaluate administrative services through the kinds of client assessments used to evaluate faculty teaching. A survey of AAU member institutions revealed that virtually none of the universities regularly review their nonacademic units [9].

Ultimately, of course, the issue is not whether administrative cost increases reflect improved administrative services; the issue is whether expended resources might have served the institution better if the expenditure had been for instruction, research, or service. In this broader calculus, administrative expenditures are conceptualized as opportunity costs, that is, revenues forgone by production activities. In the end, evaluating expenditure trends is a matter of priorities, of what one values, and of the power to enact those value preferences. We address such matters only incidentally.

Our primary purpose is to provide readers with a conceptual apparatus for exploring the causes of administrative cost increases. By identifying some of the forces and processes operative within institutions, we hope not only to enhance understandings of the cost-increase phenomenon, but also to facilitate the assessment and control of administrative costs within institutions.

WHY HAVE ADMINISTRATIVE COSTS INCREASED?

In discussing why administrative costs have increased, we start with economic assumptions about nonprofit organizations and actors regarding revenue maximization, assumptions made by economists and finance scholars who have dominated the discourse about costs. We then address what is perhaps the most commonly identified source of administrative cost increases, government regulation, by linking it to resource dependency and institutional theory, two prevalent bodies of organization theory that often have been utilized in analyzing institutional resource allocation patterns. Subsequently, we consider explanations grounded in current criticisms of universities regarding the increased emphasis on research and of community colleges regarding the alleged failure to focus on institutional missions. We relate these criticisms to classic organization theory regarding size, complexity, and administrative structure.

One of the shortcomings of commonly cited explanations of administrative cost increases is that they do not specify mechanisms that account for how the increases in administrative costs are realized: the patterns are explained at a structural level, but no attention is paid to the way structural effects are translated into action. Therefore, we turn to a range of published accounts of managerial practices, starting with probably the most widely read contributors to the literature on administrative cost and productivity in higher education, William Massy and Robert Zemsky. We then examine institutional theory, currently one of the most prominent organization theories, in order to identify mechanisms that drive administrators' actions. Finally, we develop two accounts of our own to account for managerial actions: the first focuses on the relative internal position and budgetary authority of administrators; the second focuses on the relationship between internal administrative stratification and external structures of power.

In sum, we review the most common, prominent, and important explanations and theories regarding administrative costs, and we generate propositions that connect them to specific patterns of administrative expenditures. Our conceptual analysis, then, seeks to set out in quite specific and measurable terms what patterns of administrative cost increases would be found if a particular explanation of such costs were accurate. Some of the propositions can be seen as contradictory, as we will note; others can be seen as complementary and additive, perhaps accounting for cost increases in different parts of administration. Still others may interact with each other, with one theory defining and specifying the conditions under which and the mechanisms by which another theory is operative. A precedent for examining such interactive effects in the field of organizations was established by Tolbert [50], who focused on institutional and resource dependency theories.

Specifying the relationships among the explanations and theories is beyond our purpose here. There is, for example, no rank order to our propositions. Further, given that individual social science theories tend to account for limited amounts of variance, there is likely to be utility in several of the propositions. However, the propositions do operate at different levels of generality in accounting for costs and thus vary in how fine-grained a level of explanation they can offer. Some of the propositions refer to a level of generality that cannot distinguish variations in costs within administrative subcategories such as institutional support. Others refer to the growth of specific kinds of offices and do not account for increases and costs in other administrative units. Some of the propositions are more geared to administrative costs at the central level of administration; others address variations between cost increases at the central and college levels; and still others speak to variations within and across various administrative levels. Although we ourselves differ as to how much weight should be given to each mechanism driving the increases in administrative costs, we share the belief that how such increases are achieved in the resource allocation processes within higher education institutions must be addressed. This means taking into account administrators' budgetary authority and their perceptions of various units' needs, productivity, and value, which are subjective perceptions shaped by more than objective reality.

CHARACTERISTICS OF PROFIT AND NONPROFIT FIRMS

In the profit sector economists normally begin with the assumption that firms are profit maximizers. A corollary is that they are cost minimizers; that is, the more costs are controlled, the more profits may rise. Management's resource allocations to functions such as administration are connected to the profit motive. Although there are many known limitations to this assumption, it is generally considered to be basic in microeconomic theory and empiricism [42].

In the nonprofit sector the parallel assumption is that nonprofit organizations are *revenue* maximizers [27, 52]. They exist to serve clients. The more revenues one has, the more clients can be served. A related point is the assumption that "professionals" are motivated largely by altruism to clients, rather than by extrinsic rewards.[4]

In the special nonprofit case of higher education, economists and non-economists alike hold that the ultimate aim of revenue maximization is prestige [for example, 5]. In pursuit

of more prestige, institutions spend all the revenue that they can obtain; in essence costs equal revenues. Seen perhaps most clearly in the case of research universities and elite liberal arts colleges, organizational managers and members direct their energies and institutional resources primarily toward activities that will enhance institutional status, particularly in professional circles. The implicit presumption is that resources will be allocated principally to the production activities of instruction and, especially in the case of universities, of research.

Efforts to maintain or improve one's competitive position increase costs, because higher education suffers from "the cost disease" [2]. Higher education is highly labor intensive; productivity improvements are difficult to achieve through new technologies. It is instructive that some higher education services appear not to suffer from this disease, in that their shares of institutional budgets in fact have decreased. Libraries and operations and maintenance functions are examples.

DIVERSIFYING REVENUE SOURCES.

In the 1980s, as shares of revenues from state appropriations declined, institutions of higher education increased their search for additional funds in a manner quite consistent with historic patterns that are characteristic of the private, for-profit sector. Searching for "new sources of supply of factors of production" is how Schumpeter characterized one of the ways by which firms typically seek to regain homeostasis during periods of fiscal stress [46]. Whether it is in generating private funds through voluntary support and tuition increases, in patenting and licensing new technologies and products, or in pursuing arrangements with business, colleges and universities of the 1980s and 1990s accelerated their search for "new money" [19, 32, 44]. The search contributed to a shift in the distribution of organizational expenditures from instruction to research and service and to administration. The more secure funding *base* was state government, whose priority was instruction, whereas marginal revenues came from industry and the federal government, whose priorities leaned more toward service and research. These new realities not only diverted resources away from instruction toward service and research but raised administrative costs, as new offices and administrative assignments were added to lead, encourage, and support such revenue sources.[5]

> Proposition 1: The more an institution emphasizes the generation of alternative revenues, the greater the proportion of resources that are directed to administrative units perceived as (potentially) generating such revenues.

In recent years, for example, development (a euphemism for fund raising) and technology transfer offices in some institutions have come to be seen as vital to generating additional revenues. The focus on perception, that is, potential payoff, is critical because budgetary decisions can be driven as much by perceptions as by realized income. If the proposition is accurate, those nonacademic units perceived by budgetary decision makers as potential revenue enhancers will receive disproportionately large expenditure increases. To test the proposition empirically, one might categorize administrative units as revenue seekers versus service providers, a priori, and then compare expenditure changes for the categories over time. Degree of institutional emphasis on generating alternative revenues could be determined through various documentary records, for example, presidential public statements and board minutes. Relative emphasis on revenue enhancement should be associated positively with proportional change in expenditure for administration.

STATE REGULATION AND ORGANIZATIONAL DEPENDENCY

During the past two decades, governments have increased their regulatory demands on the academy, and the increased regulatory burden often has been identified as the major reason for administrative cost increases. Regulation and ever-expanding requests for information by state and institutional governing boards result in the addition of administrative staff and expenditures.

> Proposition 2: Increased state and federal regulatory pressure on higher education is associated with the growth of administrative staff and expenditure.

Two related, sometimes competing, organization theories—institutional theory [18] and resource dependency theory [41]—bear on this proposition. In the former, organizational structures (and expenditure patterns) are shaped by organizations' efforts to sustain external legitimacy by conforming to the "institutional" environment, a set of normative understandings for a field of organizations— for example, the institution of higher education. Such norms are defined by government, professional associations, and by other successful organizations. By contrast, resource dependency links organizational structures (and expenditure patterns) to the organization's economic dependency on external organizations. Organizations develop structures that are complementary to the structures of the organization's resource providers.

The increasing state regulation of recent years could be interpreted as a clearer and more authoritative definition of what is normative and as having direct economic implications for organizations that are not in compliance. Institutional theory [18] points to three mechanisms through which normative influences of the environment are translated: one of these is the "coercive" mechanism of the state, which leads organizations to develop structures to address various legal and technical requirements of the state and, in the process, increasingly to mirror the state itself. For example, Newton Cattell [11], then federal relations director for the Association of American Universities, developed an "administrative clone theory," in which he argued that whenever legislation bearing on higher education was passed by the (federal) government, a new office was established in government to administer the law, and subsequently a "clone" of that office appeared on most major university campuses in America. Resource dependency theory would also point to organizations' increasing administrative expenditures to ensure compliance with state regulations and avoid economic penalties. At the same time, colleges and universities are increasing revenues from sources other than the state, which could have led many institutions to create still other structures complementary to external organizations other than the state. The driving force is economic dependency on an external organization, not normative conformity to the institutional environment. State regulations will be a factor only if there are some significant economic sanctions or consequences attached to noncompliance, whereas for institutional theory such regulations will affect organizational structure even if they are not enforced.

By tracking increases in the number of new regulations and requirements or of increased enforcement, researchers could follow the paper trail left by government regulators. Such measurements could then be associated directly with increases in the staff and/or expenditures of the affected units. The University of Michigan has made precisely these connections in a documented effort to respond to state criticism of administrative cost increases [49].

ORGANIZATIONAL COMPLEXITY AND ADMINISTRATIVE COST

A related argument in the literature is that increased administrative costs are due to changing external demands and internal developments that have led colleges and universities to become increasingly complex in terms of their nonacademic responsibilities and their academic structures. The theoretical grounding for the complexity view is contingency theory [31], which holds that there is a positive relationship between an organization's technology and its formal structure. The more complex the technology or the technological demands internally, the more complex the organizational and administrative structures of the organization. A limitation of the theory is that it does not enable one to specify where nor how administrative costs will rise. Brinkman and Leslie [8], in reviewing sixty years of research on economies of scale in higher education, found that both institutional size and complexity were positively related to essentially all expenditure patterns, *especially* to administrative costs.[6] Blau [4] reported a relationship between differentiation and numbers of administrators, a finding that mitigates against administrative economies of scale through greater size alone.

In the literature, complexity is generally operationalized in terms of mission, with teaching institutions being regarded as less complex than public research universities.[7] Increased complexity may stem from an increased emphasis on research or service or from an increasing complexity within mission components, such as within the teaching function. This phenomenon was witnessed in the transition of many junior colleges to comprehensive community colleges over the past several decades.

Normative data suggest that public service and especially research are relatively costly to administer [5, 20]. It follows that because research and service recently have expanded faster than instruction, administrative costs also have grown disproportionately. Quite aside from administrative cost increases, for universities the decline in the *share* of budgets devoted to instruction can easily be seen as an artifact of growth in research and service: if budget shares increase in two of three mission areas, the share for the third (instruction) must decline, all else equal. The foregoing suggests proposition 3.

> *Proposition 3:* The more complex an institution becomes, the greater the share of its expenditures that will be devoted to administration.

Testing this proposition should be fairly straightforward. One would need first to classify institutions by complexity changes over time and then, via regression analysis, compare institutional changes in administrative costs. The necessary data could be obtained from HEGIS/IPEDS. (Such data for 1975–86 do *not* appear to support the proposition [35].) For example, one could compare administrative cost changes for major research universities to those for selective liberal arts and community colleges. Within a sector, one could compare institutional types that have increased in complexity to those that have been more stable, for example, comprehensive community colleges to junior colleges.[8] Regression analysis or adjustments would be necessary to control for important confounding variables, such as the changing amount of research and public service activity in universities. Problems of circularity between cause and effect would have to be addressed, and a more (statistically) sensitive method for classifying institutions by complexity might be required. For example, one might utilize number of degree programs per institution as the independent variable rather than the more abstract notion of mission complexity. Moreover, it would be necessary to determine whether the administrative cost increases were realized in administrative units that oversee the more complex functions and activities.

ACCOUNTS OF MANAGERIAL ACTIONS: THE ADMINISTRATIVE LATTICE

A major shortcoming of the explanations considered thus far is that they may account for shifts in the budget shares of instruction and administration at a structural level without specifying the mechanisms that contribute to such shifts. In other words these explanations largely imply that associated administrative cost increases are inevitable outcomes of recent structural changes in higher education: There is no discretion in increasing administrative expenditures; decisions are determined technologically, not discretionarily [42]. Under the "deterministic" model, evidence is normative; appropriate data sets reveal how money is in fact being spent within institutions, and little more. By examining the *mechanisms* for expenditure changes, however, one may be able to separate the increases conceptually into determined and discretionary components. To put the matter simply, an institution may need to respond to some change in the environment; it may not need to appoint a new vice president to do so.

One of the most prominent accounts of managerial actions driving the escalation of administrative costs is Massy and Zemsky's conception of the "administrative lattice" [38]. Although they emphasize the interaction effects between "external drivers" of administrative cost increases, such as regulation and the internal forces associated with the lattice, Zemsky and Massy [54] point to three internal processes that contribute to proliferating administrative staff and costs, each of which we translate into a proposition.

> *Proposition 4:* Increases in administrative costs are a function of administrators taking on functions formerly performed by faculty.

> *Proposition 5:* Increases in administrative costs are a function of the growth of consensus management in administration.

> *Proposition 6:* Increases in administrative costs are a function of the self-perpetuating growth of administration.

Proposition 4 is consistent with the argument commonly found in discussions of academic productivity: that faculty have increasingly turned their attention away from instruction and advising to research. The corollary is that administrators (or professional staff) have taken on some of the foregone tasks. The case of advising is most easily tested: if this shift has occurred, we would expect to find disproportionate increases in particular student services components of administrative costs and in the number of positions providing direct academic services to students (academic advising, but not, for example, student health). A thorough test of proposition 4 would also have to demonstrate a substantial reduction in faculty time spent on advising. For example, one could compare over time faculty self-reports of their activity. Even though such self-reports may be suspect, there is little reason to believe that faculty have become more or less truthful, temporally. Ideally, one would examine time series data for a panel of institutions; second choice would be time series data for different institutions.

The concept of consensus management, in proposition 5, refers to managers' efforts to promote participative management and ensure extensive involvement in decision making *in central administration matters*. (Consensus management is *not* the same as shared governance, which involves faculty and administrators at all levels.) In some cases, consensus management can involve the risk aversion that is believed to be more typical of managers in nonprofit organizations than in for-profit enterprises. Consensus management is expensive: democratic processes create more work, for more people and therefore lead to the addition of staff. If proposition 5 is correct, we would expect to observe larger increases in the number of administrative positions than in either nonpersonnel expenditures or average personnel salaries. Moreover, we would expect to find proportionally more of the new administrative positions in central administration than in subordinate administrative units.

Proposition 6 refers to the tendency for administrators to generate the need for more administration, implying pejorative intent. In part this proposition may be valid due to the principle that "supply creates its own demand" [25]: because administrators not only process work but create work for others. The growth may also be due to administrators' efforts to provide the best services possible; the appropriate test of the spending then is whether the quality gain is cost effective. If proposition 6 is accurate, again we would expect to find that increased costs stem primarily from the addition of administrative personnel.[9] Because this proposition could be seen as a corollary of other propositions, a robust test of the proposition necessarily would attend to the cause of the increased administrative costs—that is, determining how administrators justified the addition of new personnel, and whether those additional personnel affected the quality of service.

ACCOUNTS OF MANAGERIAL ACTIONS: THE NON-COERCIVE MECHANISMS OF INSTITUTIONAL THEORY

One of the most prominent organization theories, currently, offers alternative explanations of the mechanisms that drive managerial actions, including actions related to increases in administrative costs. Noting the increased homogeneity of organizational forms and practices within a set of connected and similarly positioned organizations, institutional theorists such as DiMaggio and Powell [18] have identified three mechanisms that lead organizations to become increasingly similar or "isomorphic." We have already discussed the "coercive" mechanism of the state, in relation to proposition 2. A second mechanism consists of modeling ("mimetic") processes. According to DiMaggio and Powell, in periods of uncertainty, when the technologies for achieving success are unclear, organizations copy the practices of successful organizations. A third mechanism consists of "normative" processes associated with professionalization. As management becomes more professionalized and more involved in professional associations, the organizations in which managers work come to develop similar forms and practices. Such mechanisms could contribute importantly to increased administrative costs.

Proposition 7: Faced with increased environmental uncertainty and with unclear technologies for achieving organizational ends, managers will increasingly adopt the administrative structures developed by successful organizations.

Proposition 8: The more that administrators become involved in professional associations, the more they and their institutions will tend to adopt normative administrative structures and practices.

Proposition 7 might be paraphrased, "If Harvard is doing it, it must be a good idea." An excellent example is the rush to develop administrative offices of technology transfer in the hopes of replicating the revenue-enhancing successes such as those experienced by Stanford, MIT, and Wisconsin. (Note the co-relationship to proposition 1.) Although comprehensive cost-benefit analyses are lacking, the growing conviction in the literature is that for many if not most institutions, so far, costs have exceeded revenues. The test of proposition 7 lies in the timing and justification of new administrative offices and activities. From where did the idea for the new office originate? Is there a pattern of justifying the establishment of new offices by reference to what elites are doing?

The implication of proposition 8 is that once administrative structures are defined as normative in the relevant profession (for example, student affairs), they come to be adopted throughout the networks of higher education administrators. The mechanism is professionals (for example, business officers) keeping up with the "state of the art" in their field, by employing specialists to perform particular tasks or by purchasing new equipment and software systems. Profession-generated definitions of what is state-of-the-art drive decisions about administrative staffing and infrastructures, with their accompanying administrative expenditures. The test of proposition 8 lies directly in the justifications administrators provide for new administrative structures and staff and indirectly in the patterns of (innovation) implementation, by institution, in connection to respective levels of involvement by institutional administrators in professional associations.

The work of Tolbert [50] suggests the value of the institutional (and isomorphic) perspective in explaining administrative cost increases. From a sample of 167 public and 114 private institutions of higher education, Tolbert identified three administrative officers who represented responses to new or developing revenue sources in each of the two sectors, but which already were fully institutionalized in the other sector. For the public sector, she selected the chief development officer, the director of admissions, and the director of alumni relations; for the private sector her selections were chief planning officer, director of information, and director of institutional research. In the former case, these officers had existed in the private institutions for some time because of private institution resource dependency on tuition and voluntary support; in the latter case, the officers had been common in the public sector because of resource dependency upon state government. The officers had been added in each sector in order to open or expand bases of financial support; the publics had sought to increase revenues from voluntary support and from tuition, and the privates had sought to gain resources from state governments. Both cases represent the development of isomorphism between the two sectors of higher education, isomorphism that involved considerable administrative costs. Moreover, one of Tolbert's key points is that when an office has been fully institutionalized (for example, the development functions in the privates), the size of the office is *not* correlated with the amount of funds raised or with the dependency of the institution on such funds. Administrative costs are shaped more by what is defined as normative than by what is in fact necessary or by the amount of work being done.

ACCOUNTS OF MANAGERIAL ACTIONS: THE DISCRETION AND PREFERENCES OF ADMINISTRATORS AS PROFESSIONALS

For many scholars, the professionalism referred to by institutional theorists translates into a drive to excel. Professional administrators are concerned about quality and quantity of service to their clienteles: students, faculty, staff, and laypersons. Thus, better student counseling and more community service activities are sought, as are higher quality

institutional research information and more effective planning. In contrast, many other scholars see professionals as being largely concerned with status attainment and control over their work (and clients). In order to gain and maintain status, professionals compete to "keep up with the Joneses." In the case of administrators, as James [29] suggests, the most highly regarded managers are those who are the "builders;" the revenue maximizers for their own units, not those who cut their own budgets. The beliefs and cognitive frames that define the administration profession encourage administrative growth.

Whatever view we take of professionals, the concept enables us to recognize that members of the occupation enjoy a measure of discretion and to distinguish between allegiance to the profession versus the (employing) organization. This is as true for administrators as it is for academics. As long ago as 1969, Louis Pondy [42] made precisely this point in testing the hypothesis that professional managers can make "discretionary" as opposed to "technologically determined" decisions in allocating resources to administration. Dividing a sample of forty-five manufacturing industries into owner-managed and nonowner-managed firms, he found that "administrative intensity" (number of administrative personnel divided by the number of production personnel) was partially dependent upon whether the manager personally received the profits generated. Pondy concluded that whereas owner-managers were motivated more by profit, nonowner-managers demonstrated an "expense preference," a concept that has become basic to economic theory. His findings are consistent with later work on CEO pay [51].

Economists hold that those who control firms attempt to maximize their personal utilities through their expense preferences. Managers may claim that administrative costs are "determined" by external factors.[10] However, Williamson [53, p. 1047] found empirically, "Not only are the signs [of the coefficients] as predicted, . . . the magnitudes are sufficiently large to render somewhat doubtful the contention that discretionary effects are unimportant." He went on to conclude, "The notion of expense preference constitutes a critical part of the argument" (p. 1054). In the case of higher education managers, Bassett [1] put it more sharply:

In colleges and universities, "the administration" would be unusual if it did not have similar expenditure preferences. So might the faculty, the librarians, and the OMP staff if they were similarly situated. Lip service is paid to the concept of administrators serving the students and faculty, but the comparative expenditure trends are empirical evidence that self-aggrandizing appurtenances of power preferences are in the aggregate being exercised by "the administration."

As Bassett notes, administrators are not alone in their "expense preferences." Much of recent discussion surrounding higher education has focused on the expensive and unproductive faculty preferences that run counter to the interests of the institution and its clients. Perhaps this is all the more reason to note the difference between the expense preferences of professional administrators and the externally determined needs of the organization.

ACCOUNTS OF MANAGERIAL ACTIONS: ORGANIZATIONAL POSITION AND DISTANCE

If both faculty and administrators, indeed all institutional players, have expense preferences, why is it that it is the costs of administration that have increased disproportionately? We believe that much of the answer lies in the locus of budgetary authority and in the concept of organizational distance. As to the former, the expense preferences of faculty can be mitigated by administrators, who possess the formal and most of the effective authority for financial decisions. For example, departmental faculty may wish to add another professor in a particular specialty, but their ability to act on that preference will be subject to their dean and perhaps the provost authorizing a search. In times of economic hardship, it is not uncommon for institutions to "sweep" vacant faculty lines to the central level, forcing academic units to compete for new positions. If the budgetary situation is judged by central administrators to be sufficiently serious, faculty hiring may be frozen or academic programs may be reorganized by central administrators in ways that retrench faculty positions in some parts of the institution. Of course, administrators face the same constraints as faculty in regard to exter-

nal funding; however, it is administrators who possess the authority for internal allocation decisions, and in times of decline authority becomes more centralized.

Why have managers exercised their budgetary authority in ways that have contributed to disproportionate increases in administrative costs? Bassett [1], among others, might suggest that when individuals possess authority, they act in self-aggrandizing ways. If true, expenditure increases simply would be greatest for those administrators and units with the greatest budgetary authority. Without dismissing the possibility, we offer an explanation that focuses on a relationship between organizational structure and managerial perception.

The notion of organizational distance is embedded in political theories, whose importance in resource allocation have been clearly shown [10, 15]. Distance can refer to the physical separation of administrators from academics. Such separation into distinct floors and buildings was identified by Lunsford [34] as a major contributor to the development of separate identities among academics and administrators and to a corresponding sense of "us" and "them." The physical separation among administrators and academics limits their interaction, thus adding psychological distance. Distance also can be operationalized as the number of vertical layers between academics and those central administrators who possess primary formal budget authority.

Those administrators possessing the authority to make allocation decisions are forever faced with the opposing realities of scarce resources and insatiable resource demands. Their eternal dilemma is how to evaluate requests for resources and whose requests to honor, given constraints of time and disparate knowledge about the needs, work, and productivity of various units. As organizational distance between those with budgetary authority and production workers (for example, academics) increases, the needs of the latter come to be less personally and directly known, more abstract and less immediate. The resource allocator will possess more personal and accurate knowledge of the work responsibilities of those who are closer in distance. In the case of heads of reporting administrative units, presidents and provosts often deal more routinely with their vice-presidential colleagues than with subordinates such as college deans. Sometimes they have hired the vice presidents and are responsible for their performance appraisals. Moreover, the resource allocators know directly the increasing demands being placed on these administrative offices, because many of these demands will have come directly from the president or the provost. Further, these needs usually will be perceived in more concrete and dramatic terms than academic needs will be. Cuts in legal staff, accounts receivables, and affirmative action personnel may be seen to have more serious and immediate adverse affects than academic cuts that require faculty to teach more or that increase class size. By contrast, the resource requests of academic deans are characterized by none of these conditions. Although the deans report directly to the provost, the deans are not quite "members of the same club." There is more organizational distance, both physical and psychological. The deans are more subordinates to than they are colleagues of the provost. Perhaps more importantly, the increased demands that have been placed on the deans will be less likely to be known personally and directly to the provost than those placed on the vice presidents; most pressures will have originated at subordinate levels, for example, instructional needs of teaching departments. Further, given the current media and legislative attention being given to faculty teaching loads, the provost and president may be less likely to view resource requests from teaching units as legitimate. As Riggs [45] has argued, administrators are "detach[ed]" from production activities and they demonstrate a tendency to attach first priority to their own needs; and as Niskanen [37] has observed, administrators "conveniently perceive" their own priorities as coinciding with the priorities of their constituencies.

> *Proposition 9:* The greater the organizational distance between the unit and the budgetary decision maker, the smaller will be the proportional increase in the resource allocation to that unit.

In short, it is postulated that budgetary decision makers first take care of their own needs and the needs of those they know well. The closer a unit is in organizational distance to the budgetary decision maker, the larger will be the increase in budgetary allocation, for the decision maker will be more personally aware

of the unit's needs and more likely to hold that those needs are valid. A corollary is that as one moves down through the organizational structure, the smaller will be the discretionary (in accounting parlance, nondesignated and unrestricted) funds allocated to the unit.[11] If proposition 9 is accurate, then we would expect to find that the largest increases in administrative costs will be in central administrative units, with such costs decreasing as one proceeds down through the administrative system to the academic units. Moreover, the growth in administrative costs across academic units of the same administrative level will be relatively equal; that is, differences among units at the same level will be less than differences among units at different organizational levels.[12] Finally, the differences in the ways in which administrators regard budget requests will be explained primarily by organizational distance. The hypothesized relationships, however, may be temporized by specific events, such as periodic legislative criticisms of and mandates to curb administrative costs.

ACCOUNTS OF MANAGERIAL ACTIONS: INTERNAL ADMINISTRATIVE STRATIFICATION AND EXTERNAL STRUCTURES OF POWER

If the explanatory focus of the concept of organizational distance is on internal stratification by vertical layers in the organizational structure, how are we to explain differential allocations to administrative units at the same relative organizational level? Some of the previous propositions provide some possible answers. For example, proposition 1 would point to a unit's perceived potential for generating alternative revenues. Proposition 2 would point to the extent to which particular administrative areas were affected by state and federal regulations. Proposition 8 would point to the unit's level of professionalization. If we were dealing with academic units, functionalist explanations of internal stratification would point to the unit's merit or productivity. Unfortunately, we lack the data and indices for measuring such variables in administration.[13]

We believe that a significant part of the answer lies in the connection of administrative units to external structures of power and privilege. One explanation is that internal stratification among administrative units is a function of the unit's perceived closeness to particular markets. We draw here on a sociology of the professions that speaks to the question of who is being served to explain professional power and stratification [30, 47]. In the past decade in particular, colleges and universities have sought to position themselves close to the high-technology marketplace, in the knowledge and technologies they generate and teach, and in the services they provide. Let us consider just one example. Such positioning has involved lobbying to change state statutes regarding technology transfer [48]: targeting fields with greater potential for increased revenue and setting up offices to facilitate technology transfer to and interaction with private enterprise. We believe that administrative units at the central and at the academic unit levels benefit disproportionately from being perceived as being connected to the high-technology marketplace in particular and to the corporate marketplace in general.

> *Proposition 10:* Increases in administrative costs will be proportionate to the unit's perceived closeness to the high technology and corporate marketplaces.

Of course, one could modify this proposition to emphasize unit connections to other types of markets that are being emphasized by the campus administration. Proposition 10 could be either complementary or contradictory to proposition 9. Its principal explanatory power may be in explaining horizontal differentiation, with such variations coexisting with larger variations among vertical levels in the institution; on the other hand, differences in administrative cost increases may be explained less by the level of the unit than by its perceived closeness to the high-technology and corporate marketplaces. Another test of proposition 10 lies in the ways administrators regard budget requests and justify allocations: Are their views and rationales grounded more in perceptions of the unit's relationship to the market or in their organizational distance from the unit? What do choices made in strategic planning decisions suggest? Who is cut and who is protected?

A second explanation that addresses the relationship between internal administrative stratification and external structures of power is that the former is a function of the ethnicity, gender, and social-class background of the work force and of its clientele. Sociological studies of wage structures now routinely factor in gender and ethnicity and have found that these impact faculty and administrative salaries [12, 40]. Moreover, sociological work on professions points to the importance of client characteristics in stratification among and within professions [14, 28].

> *Proposition 11:* The ascribed characteristics of administrators and their clients (ethnicity, gender, and social-class background) will have an effect on increases in administrative costs among central administrative units and among academic units.

Data on the ascribed characteristics of the work force are available for gender and ethnicity but not for social-class background. It would be possible in matched comparisons of administrative units (for example, general student affairs offices versus offices of minority student affairs) to obtain data on their clients' gender, ethnicity, and for some proxy measures, of social class.

The proposition does not identify the direction of the effect of ethnicity, gender, and social class background. Findings about salaries would suggest a negative effect. Arguments about the costs of compliance with regulations related to women and minorities and about the emphasis on affirmative action and diversity, would suggest a positive effect. In either case proposition 11 does not hold that these characteristics are the principal basis of resource allocation; proposition 11 can be viewed as being complementary to many of the previous propositions.

In posing these last two hypotheses we move away from a disembodied view that treats administrators and their clients generically, or purely in terms of their work-place characteristics (for example, by their function). Instead, we point to the importance of considering the ascribed characteristics of administrators and of the groups and interests they serve.

What Can Be Done about Administrative Costs?

The answer to this question depends on where administrative costs are increasing and why.

The question has yet to be explored empirically in any broad way. In our view, asking focused questions marks a critical step, not only in advancing our understanding of administrative cost increases, but in spurring more effective management of those costs. To this end, we have offered eleven propositions that we hope will help move studies of administrative costs beyond a "norming" approach by which costs are compared among peer institutions. This is a critical contribution because the norming approach merely draws attention to atypically large changes in administrative costs; it ignores the *structural* causes of increases within the entire system or systems.

Developing a fuller understanding of the causes of increased administrative expenditures would substantially strengthen the public image of higher education institutions and the claims these institutions make on public resources. Increasingly, higher education is losing out relative to other state and federal priorities; its share of governmental resources is declining. The most serious allegations have to do with its reduced attention to undergraduate education, its increasing costs particularly as reflected in tuition prices; and its inefficiency in the use of public resources. The disproportionate increase of administrative expenditures relative to instructional ones is directly implicated in these criticisms.

Cost-increase explanations that are grounded in data might better enable presidents and boards to challenge these recurrent criticisms effectively, as well as the perception of institutions as "fat," despite years of cost containment efforts. Such explanations might also constitute a first step toward containing administrative cost increases.

We would expect to find multifactor explanations of administrative cost increases. Moreover, there is no reason to believe that the increases will be the same by institution and by system of higher education. Many of the propositions above can be seen as complementary; each may contribute to the explanations. We cannot hope to provide *the* answer to the disproportionate rise of administrative costs. No matter what the explanations are for the cost increases, there is still the need to determine and to change *how* choices are made, that is, to specify the *mechanisms* by which budgetary choices are made and administrative

costs are increased and to introduce measures that will mitigate against the unchecked operation of these mechanisms. We would argue that this requires a focus on the budgetary authority structure. Pointing to external regulations as a cause for higher costs does nothing to explain how budgetary choices are made: how new offices are created, staff are added, and/or salaries and nonpersonnel expenditures are increased. Similarly, pointing to changes in internal processes, such as the growth of consensus management or the takeover of functions formerly performed by faculty, does little to detract from the fact that it is administrators who possess the formal authority to make decisions about how any marginal revenues will be spent. This power of the purse perhaps is illustrated best by contrasting administrative and faculty authority.

Administrators may be constrained by faculty viewpoints in increasing administrative expenditures, but there is little question as to who wields final authority. For example, particularly in times of fiscal stress, provosts and deans can effectively sweep vacant faculty lines and freeze faculty hiring, often with little consultation with faculty. They can award administrative salary increases, add new administrative positions, and increase administrative operating budgets. The importance of this budgetary authority is evidenced not just by the disproportionate increases of administrative costs but by the fact that the productivity of administrators and the retrenchment of executive, administrative, and managerial employees are not nearly as prominent on current budget cutting agendas as are faculty productivity and retrenchment. Indeed, the former are often not found at all.

It will not be surprising that as faculty members we now suggest that part of the solution to the problem of disproportionate administrative cost increases is increased sharing of budgetary authority with faculty. Nevertheless, this is an important point, for as financial pressures mount in higher education, authority becomes more centralized in an effort to improve accountability. The chain of command lengthens. There appears to be a clear tendency for governing boards to favor ever stronger financial control by higher administrators [43]. We would argue that such centralization is a major part of the reallocation of resources away from instruction to administration. In trying to deal effectively with difficult financial times, institutions are moving in a direction that gives more discretion to administrators, with little promise of containing, let alone reversing, the trend of the last twenty years to shift resources from instruction to administration.

In closing, however, we want to emphasize that sharing budgetary authority with faculty is insufficient to the task of reversing the reallocation patterns in higher education. There are already many mechanisms and processes of "shared authority" between faculty and administrators that have not proven particularly effective. Part of the problem lies in faculty having merely an advisory role in such processes. More than that, faculty have their own expense preferences, and we have little reason to believe that given the authority, faculty will significantly increase the proportion of resources allocated to instruction. Therefore, we might consider somehow giving a more prominent role in budgetary matters to those who have the most direct interest in instruction, students.

Our suggestion should not be considered as support for the current fashion of "total quality management" or of "quality management" [17]. In the application of these management tools in higher education it is far from clear either that students, as opposed to businesses, are the major customers of higher education, or that student input comes in any other form than customer needs surveys. Our suggestion is that we need broader oversight of allocation decisions and broader involvement in making those decisions, not just in advising those who make the decisions. If such oversight and budgetary authority is to be meaningful, sophisticated, and effective, then it must include an understanding of the sources and causes of mounting administrative costs.

NOTES

1. Due to inconsistencies in reporting, EEOC data often are considered suspect by institutions.
2. The disaggregation found in these data is a step in the right direction, but the categories still amalgamate quite different positions. For example, "other professionals" includes li-

brarians, accountants, counselors, athletic coaches, and lawyers, among others.
3. The question of who is an administrator and who is a "production worker" probably is moot The policy question of interest to resource providers (for example, legislators) concerns how much is being spent on instruction and how the instructional share is changing. The growing share committed to "support" is largely what is at issue.
4. The qualification is important, as we shall see later. Many sociologists, including some sociologists of higher education, work out of variations of professionalization theory that emphasize the self-interested and political nature of professional activities [14, 30, 42].
5. In much of the post-World War II era, externally funded research could be seen as contributing both to prestige and revenues.
6. One recent study [13] suggests that there are economies of scope for instruction and research, that producing them together is cheaper than producing them separately. However, as Brinkman [7, p. 123] notes, "Very little research has been done on the question of whether the multiproduct nature of higher education leads to production economies," and "there is much that we do not understand, mostly because we cannot arrive at definitive interpretations of available data" [13, 16].
7. There may be other dimensions of complexity that do not follow the standard institutional hierarchy in higher education, dimensions along which community colleges are more complex than research universities. With a different operationalization of complexity, the findings about the relationship between complexity and administrative cost might be different.
8. This is a suggestion made by Arthur Hauptman.
9. This proposition need not explain the disproportionate increase in administrative costs. Administrators may create their own demand, but so do academics, through the "academic ratchet" [39]. It may be that the rate of growth generated by the administrative lattice is greater than that generated by the ratchet, but there is no explanation of why this should be so.
10. One of our students is seeking to test the Pondy/Williamson dichotomy of discretionary versus determined administrative expenditures [6]. Part of his research has involved comparing the opinions of administrators who have made expenditure decisions with those of other administrators or others situated a level below the decision maker. Nearly every decision was viewed as determined by the decision maker, whereas subordinates saw most decisions as discretionary, identifying valid alternative expen-

diture needs that they considered more important.

11. Departmental "operations" budgets contain most of an academic unit's discretionary funds and thus serve as a good indicator as to how the resource allocation system has functioned. A good test of the corollary to proposition 9 would be to track operations budgets over time to determine to what extent these allocations have increased over the past two decades.

12. Such a pattern could be consistent with most of the previous propositions. For example, proposition 1 would suggest that development offices would realize increased budgetary shares. Such increases could be realized at both the central level and in the various academic colleges, which might add development officers. However, the differences among administrative costs across the academic colleges might still be less than the differences between administrative costs at the central and the collegiate levels.

13. In a recent study, Pfeffer and Davis-Blake [37] seek to examine the wage structures of different administrators according to their functional importance.

REFERENCES

Bassett, W. B. (1983). Cost control in higher education. In J. Froomkin (Ed.), *The crisis in higher education.* New York: Academy of Political Science.

Baumol, W., & S. A, B. Blackman. (1983). Electronics, the cost disease, and the operation of libraries. *Journal of the American society for information sciences,* 34, 181–91.

Bergmann, B. R. (1991). Bloated administration: Blighted campuses. *Academe,* 77 (November/December), 12–16.

Blau, P. M. (1973). *The organization of academic work.* New York: Wiley.

Bowen, H. R. (1980). What determines the costs of higher education. In H. R. Bowen (Ed.), *The cost of higher education,* pp. 1–26. Washington, D.C.: Carnegie Foundation for the Advancement of Teaching.

Bresciani, D. (In progress). Explanation of administrative costs: A case study. Ph.D. dissertation, University of Arizona.

Brinkman, P. (1990). Higher education cost functions. In S. A. Hoenack & E. L. Collins (Eds.), *Economics of American universities: Management, operations, and fiscal environment,* pp. 107–28. Albany: State University of New York Press.

Brinkman, P., & L. L. Leslie. (1986). Economies of scale in higher education: Sixty years of research. *Review of higher education,* 10 (Fall), 1–28.

Brown, M. K. (1989). Developing and implementing a process for the review of nonacademic units. *Research in higher education,* 30, 89–112.

Caruthers, J. K., & M. Orwig. (1979). *Budgeting in higher education.* AAHE-ERIC Higher Education Report no.3. Washington, D.C.; American Association for Higher Education.

Catell, N. O. (1985). The character of the university and the increasing threat of state government intrusion. In L. L. Leslie & H. L. Otto (Eds.), *Financing and budgeting postsecondary education in the 1980s,* pp. 73–78. Tucson, Ariz: Center for the Study of Higher Education.

Chapman, D. W., & A. P. Wagner. (1986). Gender and salaries: The case of admissions officers. *Review of higher education,* 10 (Fall), 85–104.

Cohn, E., S. L. W. Rhine, & M. C. Santos. (1989). Institutions of higher education as multi-product firms: Economies of scale and scope. *Review of economics and statistics,* 71 (May), 284–90.

Collins, R. (1979). *The credential society.* New York: Academic Press.

Covaleski, M. A., & M. W. Dirsmith. (1988). An institutional perspective on the rise, social transformation, and fall of a university budget category. *Administrative science quarterly,* 33 (December), 562–87.

De Groot, H., W. W. McMahon, & J. F. Volkwein. (1991). The cost structure of American research universities. *Review of economies and statistics,* 73, 424–31.

Dill, D. D. (1992). Quality by design: Toward a framework for academic quality management. In J. C. Smart (Ed.), *Higher education: Handbook of theory and research,* vol. 8, pp. 37–83. New York: Agathon Press.

DiMaggio, P., & W. Powell. (1983). The iron cage revisited: Institutional isomorphism and collective rationality in organizational fields" *American sociological review,* 48, 147–60.

Fairweather, J. (1988). *Entrepreneurship and the university: The future of industry-university liaisons.* ASHE-ERIC Higher Education Report no. 6, Washington, D.C.: Association for the Study of Higher Education.

Galambos, E. C. (1987). Higher education administrative costs and staffing. In *Higher education administrative costs: Continuing the study.* Office of Educational Research and Improvement, pp. 27–74. Washington, D.C.: U.S. Department of Education.

Grassmuck, K. (1990). Big increases in academic support staff prompt growing concerns on campuses. *Chronicle of higher education,* (28 March), pp. 1, 32–33.

_____. (1991). Throughout the 80s, colleges hired more non-teaching staff than other employees. *Chronicle of higher education.* 14 August, p. 22.

Halfond, J. A. (1991). How to control administrative cost. *Academe,* 77 (November/December), 17–19.

Halstead, K. (1991). *Higher education revenues and expenditures.* Washington, D.C.; Research Associates of Washington.

Hannaway, J. (1987). Supply creates demands: An organizational process view of administrative expansion. *Journal of policy analysis and management,* 7, 118–34.

Hansen, W. L., & T. F. Guidugli. (1990). Comparing faculty and employment gains for higher education administrators and faculty members. *Journal of higher education,* 61 (March/April), 142–59.

Hanushek, E. A. (1987). Educational production functions." In G. Psacharopoulos (Ed.), *Economics of education: Research and studies,* pp. 33–41. Oxford: Pergamon Press, 1987.

Heinz, J. P., & E. O. Laumann. (1982*). Chicago lawyers: The social structure of the bar.* New York and Chicago: Russell Sage Foundation and American Bar Foundation.

James, E. (1990). Decision processes and priorities in higher education. In S. A. Hoenack & E. L. Collins (Eds.), *The economics of American universities: Management, operations, and fiscal environment,* pp. 77–106. Albany: State University of New York Press.

Larson, M. S. (1977). *The rise of professionalism.* Berkeley: University of California Press.

Lawrence, P., & J. Lorsch. (1967). Differentiation and integration in complex organizations. *Administrative science quarterly,* 12, 1–47.

Leslie, L. L. & D. Breneman. (1993). Introduction. In D. Breneman, R. E. Anderson, & L. L. Leslie (Eds.), *ASHE reader on finance in higher education,* 2nd ed. Lexington, Mass: Ginn.

Levy, L. (1990). Long run trends in administrative salaries. *CUPA journal,* 41 (Summer), 11–20.

Lunsford, T. (1970). Authority and ideology in the administered university In C. Kruytbosch and S. Messinger (Eds.), *The state of the university: Authority and change,* pp. 87–107. Beverly Hills, Calif.: Sage Publications.

Massy, W. F., & T. R. Warner. (1991). Causes and cures of cost escalation in college and university administrative and support services. Stanford Institute for Higher Education Research, discussion paper, January.

National Association of College and University Business Officers. (1992*). College and university business administration.* 5th ed. Washington, D.C.: National Association of College and University Business Officers.

Niskanen, W. (1971). *Bureaucracy and representative government.* Chicago: Aldine.

Pew Higher Education Research Program, The University of Pennsylvania. (1990). The lattice and the ratchet. *Policy perspectives,* 2 (June).

_____. (1991). Profiles *Policy perspectives,* 3 (March).

Pfeffer, J., & A. Davis-Blake. (1987). Understanding organizational wage structures: A resource dependence approach. *Academy of management journal,* 30, 437–55.

Pfeffer, J., & G. Salancik. (1978). *The external control of organizations: A resource dependence perspective.* New York: Harper and Row.

Pondy, L. R. (1969). Effects of size, complexity, and ownership on administrative intensity. *Administrative science quarterly,* 14 (March), 47–60.

Rhoades, G., & S. Slaughter. (1991). The public interest and professional labor: Research universities. In W. G. Tierney (Ed.), *Culture and ideology in higher education: Advancing a critical agenda,* pp. 187–212. New York: Praeger.

_____. (1991). Professors, administrators, and patents: The negotiation of technology transfer. *Sociology of education,* 64 (April), 65–77.

Riggs, F. W. (1960). Prismatic society and financial administration. *Administrative science quarterly,* 5 (June), 1–46.

Schumpeter, J. (1934). *The theory of economic development.* Cambridge, Mass: Harvard University Press.

Silva, E., & S. Slaughter. (1984). *Serving power: The making of the social science expert, 1865–1911.* Westport, Conn.: Greenwood Press.

Slaughter, S., & G. Rhoades. (1993). Changing intellectual property statutes and policies: Revising the terms of professional labor in a public university. *Higher education,* 26, 287–312.

Task Force on Costs in Higher Education. (1990). Enhancing quality in an era of resource constraints. Report of the Task Force on Costs in Higher Education, The University of Michigan, School of Business Administration, 2 March.

Tolbert, P. S. (1985). Institutional environments and resource dependence: Sources of administrative structure in institutions of higher education. *Administrative science quarterly,* 30, 1–13.

Tosi, H. L., & L. R. Gomez-Mejia. (1989). The decoupling of CEO pay and performance: An agency theory perspective. *Administrative science quarterly,* 34, 169–89.

Verry, D. W. (1987). University internal efficiency. In G. Psacharopoulos (Ed.), *Economics of education research and studies,* pp. 65–69. Oxford: Pergamon Press.

Williamson, O. E. (1963). Managerial discretion and business behavior. *American economic review,* 53 (December), 1032–57.

Zemsky, R., & W. F. Massy. (1990). Cost containment: Committing to a new economic reality. *Change,* 22 (November/December), 16–22.

CHAPTER 29

FORECASTING FINANCIAL PRIORITIES FOR TECHNOLOGY

MARTIN D. RINGLE

At the end of the 1980s many colleges and universities developed financial models for technology based on then-current assumptions about student ownership of microcomputers, hardware life-cycles, maintenance contracts, and other factors. Many of these assumptions are no longer valid. With technology costs and revenue opportunities changing so rapidly, it is clear that future financial strategies will need to be more agile and adaptable than ever before. This article presents financial models drawn from more than 20 independent colleges and universities and discusses how they have been used to define a technology financial strategy at Reed College.

Martin D. Ringle is Director of Computing and Information Services at Reed College in Portland, Oregon.

I am grateful to current and past technology officers of the following colleges for thier generous assistance: Amherst, Bowdoin, Bryn Mawr, Bucknell, Carleton, Connecticut, Davidson, Denison, Grinnell, Hamilton, Haverford, Holy Cross, Hope, Kenyon, Lafayette, Middlebury, Oberlin, Ohio Wesleyan, St. Olaf, Smith, Swarthmore, University of the South, Vassar, and Washington College (MD). I would like to thank David Todd and Dave Smallen for the many insights they have provided on these issues over the years; and Marianne Colgrove and Kerri Creager of Reed's office of Computing & Information Services, for their invaluable assistance and feedback.

In 1943, Thomas Watson, chairman of IBM, said, "I think there is a world market for maybe five computers." Nearly 40 years later, Bill Gates, founder of Microsoft, said, "640K ought to be enough for anybody." Remarks such as these underscore a vital point: predicting the future of technology is a risky business, even for the most successful people in the history of computing. Unfortunately, this is the business for which chief technology officers are hired. As the pace of technology accelerates, our ability to deal with an uncertain future—whether through intuition or the process of strategic planning—becomes ever more critical to our institutions.

At the center of every long-range technology strategy—beneath all the policy and procedural statements on standards, equipment, software, networking, and staffing—lies the key to success or failure: the financial model. For many institutions, however, a financial model is barely visible in their technology planning efforts. All too often, neither technology officers nor financial officers have a complete picture of how much the institution is *really* spending on technology nor how such dollars are being spent. Under these conditions, prioritization of funding items for technology is difficult, if not impossible.

Sources: *Cause/Effect,* Fall 1997.

This article examines financial models for technology and the priorities they need to address. The primary data on which the discussion is based are drawn from trends among a reference group of 25 private, liberal arts colleges from 1986 through 1996. In some respects, this is an update of the 1992 paper, *The Cost of Computing: Shining a Light into the Black Hole*, by David Todd and myself.[1]

It should be noted that while many aspects of funding, budgeting, and expense control differ substantially between private undergraduate colleges and other types of institutions, many of the observations in this paper can be applied to almost any college or university.

"SIMPLICITY, SIMPLICITY, SIMPLICITY!"

—Walden, Henry David Thoreau, 1854

Discussions of financial models for technology are often quite complex, especially when they focus on the maze of accounting practices that can be used to manage funding and expense control. The foundation of a good financial model for technology, however, can be understood in relatively simple terms. It must:

- be consistent with an institution's overall priorities;

- accommodate an institution's financial limitations;

- address technology needs as *endorsed by users;*

- and be sufficiently flexible to adapt to changes in funding, technology, staffing, management, and other factors.

Institutional Priorities

A common weakness of many financial models for technology is that they *assume* rather than *explain* the relationship between technology and the institution's other priorities. Technology, officers, immersed in the challenge of keeping up with skyrocketing user demand, frequently overlook the fact that senior officers are juggling funds for technology with other pressing items such as deferred maintenance, faculty and staff salaries, and financial aid. Technology officers must be able to articulate a clear understanding of how technology fits into the overall institutional strategy and what this implies for the total funding picture.

Financial Limitation

An axiom of organizational funding is that there is *never* going to be enough to meet everyone's needs. To be successful, a financial model for technology must be designed with sensitivity to what is possible and practicable, given an institution's financial constraints. Models that focus exclusively on technical or user demands may fail to provide senior officers with realistic options and may not, therefore, be of much value in building a workable funding strategy. It may be necessary, however painful, to acknowledge that an institution simply *cannot afford* to provide certain technology services unless it is willing (and able) to sacrifice funding in some other area of the budget.

User Endorsement

Technology financial planning is all too often a back-room exercise conducted by the chief technology officer, alone or with a small group of trusted colleagues. Such planning does absolutely nothing to moderate user demand nor to promote understanding of the limitations faced by the information technology organization. The more awareness that users have of information technology financial constraints, the better. It is important that a financial strategy reflect, to as great a degree as possible, technology needs as perceived by users. A user endorsement of the financial plan for technology, based on an understanding of fiscal limitations, may help to garner new institutional resources while it helps—at least temporarily—to moderate user demand.

Flexibility

With changes coming so quickly and from so many different directions, it is imperative that the priorities embedded in a financial model be as flexible as possible. Winning strategies are those that make it relatively easy to modify funding sources, allocation priorities, and technology decisions, as circumstances require. In lieu of a single comprehensive, long-range technology strategy, institutions may be better off defining a set of agile and adaptive short-range strategies that fit together to form an overall plan.

THE TOP OF THE LIST: STAFFING

The first thing that usually comes to mind when considering spending priorities for technology is equipment. Increasingly, however, budgetary emphasis for technology in higher education is being directed toward people rather than equipment. In part, this is the result of the growing realization that user satisfaction seems to correlate far more consistently with staff support than it does with hardware availability.

The increasing priority given to staffing is evidenced by the growth in the percentage of the information technology budget devoted to personnel. Within the reference group of liberal arts colleges, for example, expenditures for staff salaries increased from 41 percent in academic year 1989 to nearly 58 percent in 1995 (Figure 29.1). During the same period, median staff size in the reference group grew from 13.9 to 19.3 FTE (Figure 29.2). The two areas of staffing that experienced the greatest growth were user support and network services. Most recently, new staffing has been concentrated in the areas of Web materials development and Web server management.

Despite the growth in staff size, more than 90 percent of the chief technology officers surveyed indicated that the demands for expanded user support and more sophisticated technical services have risen more quickly than increases in staff size. To make matters worse, nearly half of the schools are seeing a reduction in staff longevity[2] and all but a few are feeling intense pressure from salary competition with the private sector. Smaller colleges, especially those located in rural or remote areas, have been very hard pressed to hire and retain qualified staff in numbers that are sufficient to meet the demand.

By all indications, recruiting and retaining high-quality staff is going to become the single biggest financial challenge for information technology organizations in the years ahead, despite the fact that there are more qualified people in the technology job market than ever before. What can be done to address the problem (other than simply increasing the overall information technology budget)?

Allocate More Funds for Personnel

If the percentage of the information technology budget for staffing is relatively low, then one should consider reallocating funds from line items such as maintenance contracts (see below). Schools that are already spending close to (or above) 70 percent of their information technology budgets on personnel, however, should be very wary of increasing staffing dollars further, since this could trigger serious problems with funding for operations, equipment replacement, and so forth.

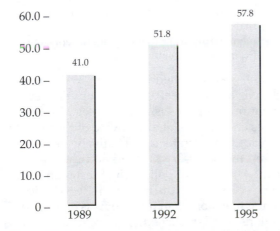

Figure 29.1 Percentage of Budget for Staff Salaries

Percentage of information technology budget allocated for staff salaries

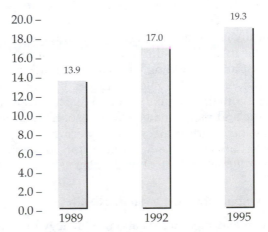

Figure 29.2 Median Staff Size (fte)

Median information technology staff size

Help Your Staff Improve Themselves

Although salary budgets have increased substantially, funds for staff development—workshops, seminars, conferences, and training—have generally remained flat or have decreased during the past five years. Providing opportunities for staff to acquire new skills and take a break from daily routines can be an extremely cost-effective way to improve retention and make staff more valuable to the institution. A reasonable target for staff development funding is 3–4 percent of the total information technology budget. Currently, most schools in the reference group spend between 1 and 2 percent.

Provide Unpaid Leaves

Colleges that allow information technology staff to take periodic unpaid leaves often find that it helps to reduce the cost of recruiting and training new staff. Given the "burnout" conditions of so many information technology jobs, a few months away every few years can be enormously rejuvenating for the staff member and cost-effective for the college.

Outsource

In the past, private institutions, especially smaller ones, had few choices with respect to information technology outsourcing; it was generally an "all-or-nothing" proposition. The lower cost of "doing it yourself" generally won out. Today, there is a growing menu of task-specific outsourcing opportunities that range from piecework Web development to comprehensive network support. While there are drawbacks to outsourcing—for example, staff loyalty is to the third-party provider rather than to the institution—the benefits are increasing. In a fast and forbidding job market, a third-party provider may be able to deliver high-quality staff with little or no disruption due to turnover. More and more small colleges, especially those outside of urban areas, are exploring task-specific outsourcing as a strategy for addressing recruitment and retention problems.

Distribute the Cost of Support Staff

More and more information technology organizations, even the highly centralized ones common at small colleges, are recognizing that support staff in client departments may be easier for an institution to fund than staff in the central organization. Such staff can help to ease the burden on central staff in a variety of ways. Rather than being concerned with "control," information technology organizations should focus attention on the best way to hire and deploy staff.

Restrict Services

Perhaps the least attractive option for making ends meet is to reduce or eliminate existing technology services. In the long run, however, it is wiser to do a few things well than to do everything poorly. Unfortunately, many information technology officers and organizations are myopic when it comes to making this choice. If financial resources are treated as a zero-sum game, then technology services must be viewed likewise. (Feel free to send photocopies of this paragraph to your computing committees, your staff, and your boss.)

EQUIPMENT ACQUISITION, UPGRADE, AND REPLACEMENT

In 1989, Gary Augustson, executive director of Computing and Information Systems at Penn State University, offered a perspective on financial priorities for technology that included the following statement:

> Probably most easily overlooked is the need to plan for replacement of equipment when it becomes obsolete. With today's technology, the useful lifespan of equipment is . . . but a few years. Universities that are struggling to . . . fund . . . equipment hardly want to worry about replacing [it] in the foreseeable future.[3]

These were prophetic words in 1989. As predicted, a great deal of the computing equipment on campuses is now obsolete. While colleges and universities are aware of the need for replacement strategies, relatively few have taken the necessary steps to address the problem. An informal poll of chief technology officers[4] conducted during 1995–1996 indicated that while more than three-fourths of their institutions had established, or were in the process of establishing, policies for the regular replacement of computing equipment, fewer than a quarter of those institutions had identified or allocated sufficient funds with which to carry out those policies.[5] Like deferred building maintenance, this is a problem that promises to get worse as time goes on. What can we do?

Don't Depend on the Kindness of Strangers

Grants, gifts, capital allocations, and end-of-year excess funds are *not* the way to finance equipment replacement. The only effective way to deal with this problem is to do an inventory, price out the total replacement cost, divide by the preferred number of years in the replacement cycle, and then put the resulting figure—underlined and in red—in front of everyone: bosses, committees, trustees, staff, and constituents. The first step in getting a realistic line item in the operating budget for equipment replacement is to do the arithmetic and publish the results.

Take a Careful Look at Unit Cost

It used to be a truism that while the capacity of hardware continually increased, the unit price stayed fairly constant, somewhere between $1,600 and $2,000 for a typical desktop configuration. For strategic budgeting purposes, schools in the reference group used a median figure of $2,000 per desktop for more than six years. During the past year, however, the median figure has jumped to nearly $2,400, driven by the appetites of more sophisticated users who want high-resolution monitors, removable media back-up devices, high-speed network and mobile connections, and other niceties. Can we really afford to provide such platforms? Not likely. We have to restrict the baseline unit cost and somehow limit its growth to the level of inflation.

Increase the Life-cycle

A majority of schools that have equipment replacement policies for desktop computers endorse a life cycle of five years, though about 20 percent have longer cycles (between six and 10 years). A number of colleges and universities, such as Wake Forest, are attempting to support cycles of four years or less. In the private sector, replacement policies of less than three years are not uncommon.

The problem with many of these "endorsed" life cycles is that schools are not fully funding them and, in many cases, simply aren't in a position to do so, now or in the foreseeable future. Funding a four-year replacement policy at the "50 percent level" (as several schools indicate they are doing) is just a politician's way of describing an eight-year life cycle. Schools with a fully funded eight-year cycle, however, may be better off than schools with paper policies that lack realistic institutional support. Facing up to fiscal limitations means deciding how many years (on average) a machine can be useful for faculty, students, and staff-and funding replacements at that level. If an institution can only afford a seven-year replacement cycle, then it needs to acknowledge that fact, budget accordingly, and get on with the rest of its planning activities. If it determines that it simply cannot live with such a cycle, then it needs to provide sufficient cash in the operating budget to shorten the cycle. Period.

Tighten the Perimeter

During the late '80s, many schools discovered that they could get more "bang for the buck" by reallocating used equipment. For example, Brian Hawkins of Brown University and his colleagues correctly pointed out that:

> The half-life of a piece of equipment in an engineering department may be only two years, whereas the half-life of that same piece of equipment in another department may be four years. Reallocation of equipment is essential for the effective utilization of technology over its life cycle.[6]

Nearly every school has exploited this strategy in one form or another. After a decade of reallocation, however, many schools are now finding that their installed base has grown enormously and they are financially unable to include all machines within a regular replacement pool. The only practical solution is to define a sub-set of the installed base—a smaller perimeter—that will be eligible for regular replacement. (Unfortunately, maintaining, rather than replacing, machines can prove to be just as costly in the long run.)

Promote Student Ownership

Each year it becomes a little more practical and a lot more desirable for students to own their own computers. Networked residence halls, falling prices, and more "consumer" availability are helping to accelerate student ownership, currently averaging more than 60 percent. Institutional incentives, such as loan programs, bundled software, one-stop shopping, and convenient user support, can be applied to further increase student ownership.

To Lease or Not to Lease

During the '80s, computer leasing became less and less attractive to colleges as desktop computing grew, the unit cost of microcomputers declined, and interest rates rose. As John Oberlin has insightfully observed, however:

> Leasing has several advantages: 1) it sets a clear expectation that technology will be replaced on a regular life-cycle basis; 2) it shifts the burden of recycling to the vendor, who becomes responsible for disposition of the computers at the end of the lease; and 3) it offers the opportunity . . . for the institution to recapture the salvage value of old technology before it goes to zero.[7]

Schools that simply don't have sufficient cash on hand to establish an appropriate equipment replacement protocol, should look seriously at desktop computer leasing as a way of addressing the replacement problem.

Will NC Save the Day?

With everyone in higher education (and the private and public sectors as well) facing similar problems with regard to equipment replacement, the prospect of a "silver bullet" is extremely tantalizing. Will the *network computer* (NC) envisioned by Larry Ellison of Oracle— and now heralded by Microsoft, Intel, and many others—provide a solution that will radically alter the financial picture? Current wisdom within higher education is that it will not. As many of us recall, 10 years ago it seemed as if microcomputers would have a dramatic financial advantage over mainframe technology, thanks to lower "per seat" costs. When we look at the total cost of ownership, i.e., networking, servers, software, and staffing, it is apparent that we are spending more per seat, not less. Even if the price of an NC or "thin client" falls to $500 (or less) the total cost per seat is going to involve

additional network bandwidth and more server capacity than are required in the distributed environments currently used. Savings to institutions may be far less than expected and, if the experiences of the past 15 years are at all relevant, they may be nil. The NC may be a winner for functional reasons but it isn't likely to help colleges and universities lower their information technology budgets.

MAINTENANCE CONTRACTS

In the '80s, maintenance contracts for centralized hardware (and system software) often consumed 25–35 percent of information technology operating budgets at small colleges. Today, the amount has dropped below 10 percent in most cases and is continuing to decline. A significant factor in this trend has been the movement away from proprietary platforms to more competitively priced open platforms. Schools that haven't made (or completed) this evolution, and who are still spending substantial amounts on maintenance contracts, should move more quickly in this direction.

Take Advantage of Longer Warranties

One of the better ideas to emerge from vendors is the three-year warranty for host and server hardware.[8] Unlike desktop equipment, there is little to be gained by pushing centralized equipment much beyond a three-year lifecycle. This option allows institutions to immediately shift maintenance funds into equipment acquisition and replacement without paying the additional premium embedded in a lease or other credit arrangement.

Do It Yourself

There is a perennial tug-of-war between those who favor maintenance contracts for desktop (and small server) equipment and those who provide in-house maintenance operations. Variables such as proximity to an urban retail environment and the local price of labor make a universal cost-benefit analysis impossible. It is true, however, that many schools are finding that the growing revenue from the maintenance and repair of student (and other) privately-owned equipment is sufficient to subsidize the maintenance costs for college-owned equipment. The speed, reliability, and convenience of in-house maintenance are bonuses on top of the potential financial benefit.

SOFTWARE

While the unit cost of software has been shrinking, the gross cost of software has been steadily rising, because colleges and universities are using more packages from more sources than ever before. Much of the cost of software, however, has become hidden in departmental "supplies" budgets or other nooks and crannies of the institutional operating budget. Rather than seeking to draw these funds back into the central information technology budget, it is wiser simply to endorse this trend and allow software to realize its destiny as a "consumable." (The problems of standards and support can be addressed regardless of how software is purchased.)

INFORMATION TECHNOLOGY AS AN INSTITUTIONAL PRIORITY

There are numerous way to assess an institution's overall priorities. One of the easiest is to look at the percentage of the general operating budget devoted to each item. In the case of information technology, the priority appears to have increased significantly in the past six years. In 1989–90, the median among the reference group was 2.22 percent. By 1995–96 it rose to 3.51 percent, as illustrated in Figure 29.3. Technology leaders within the group are now spending as much as 4 percent to 6 percent.

Another measure that can be used for comparison purposes is the number of information technology dollars in the institutional operating budget being spent per student (i.e., undergraduate FTEs). As shown in Figure 29.4, median expenditures per student among the reference group have almost doubled during the past six years.

While these numbers indicate a trend toward greater institutional emphasis on technology, they shed no light on where additional funds have come from. When asked, many technology officers confess ignorance or reply to the question by saying "the general fund." As those who deal with the finances of colleges and universities are keenly aware, line items do not increase unless other line items decrease or new money is found. So where is the money *really* coming from?

Tuition and Technology Fees

A number of institutions appear to be directing larger portions of tuition increases into technology funding. In a few cases, private colleges and universities indicate that they have added identifiable "technology fees" to their room, board, and other fees. For the most part, though, private liberal arts institutions have been very hesitant about creating "required" fees outside of the tuition structure since this can be interpreted by a wary clientele as a maneuver to hide the real cost of attending college.

Cost-recovery (Usage) Fees

Six years ago, most colleges in the reference group indicated that usage fees played little or no role in their technology funding strategies. (This, of course, is one of the major differences between public and private institutions.) The situation seems to be changing. In addition to the accepted practice of charging for (laser) printing,

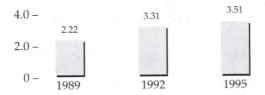

Figure 29.3 Percentage of E&G Budget for Information Technology

Percentage of Education & General (E&G) budget spent on information technology

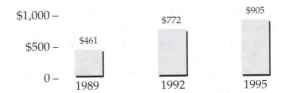

Figure 29.4 Dollars per Student

Information technology dollars spent per student

schools are now levying charges for dormitory network access, PPP dial-in access, and specialized services such as scanning and color printing. Perhaps the most substantial area of usage fees has been telecommunications, where revenues from long-distance services, voice mail, and so forth have been used to underwrite networking and other operating costs.

The area with the greatest untapped potential is usage-based Internet access. Currently, most colleges charge flat fees for residence hall network connections. As institutional costs rise, however, colleges may begin to treat Internet access the same way they treat long-distance telephone services, with connect-time charges rather than flat fees.

One-time Sources

A surprisingly large number of institutions still rely heavily on one-time funding sources, including capital allocations, discretionary funds, gifts, and grants, to subsidize operational increases in technology support. Though the strategy is frequently described as an "interim" approach, data collected during the past 10 years suggest that some institutions have made little or no progress in the direction of moving key operational costs for technology to stable operational funding sources.

The most problematic one-time funding sources are equipment grants. Unless long-term funding (or a long-term funding strategy) is built into the original grant, the equipment quickly becomes an albatross around the neck of the information technology operating budget. Private foundations and public funding agencies have begun to acknowledge this fact, and many are eliminating grants for equipment altogether or requiring that detailed long-term financial commitments be delineated as part of a grant proposal.

Organizational Changes

Another major factor in funding source modification, especially during the past four years, has been increased integration among various technology and information resource organizations. More and more colleges are bringing telecommunications, instructional media, and other services together with computing, networking, and distance education. Most recently, integration of the library with these other services has also increased. For example, in 1989 none of the schools in the reference group had an organization that embraced both technology groups and libraries; nearly 12 percent of the schools have now moved to this type of organization. Whether this becomes a trend—and whether it ultimately helps to improve the funding picture—remains to be seen.

Other Line Items

This is perhaps the most common source of technology funding increases. For obvious (political) reasons, few colleges have been willing to discuss strategies for technology funding that involve reductions of ocher budget line items. (One school, for example, insisted that it doesn't transfer funds from one line to another; it simply *reduces* allocations in one line, *moves* the residual to the general fund, and then *increases* funding in a different line.

THE BOTTOM LINE

While it may be impossible to predict the next wave of technological innovation or the precise curve for the growth of user demand, institutions must develop financial strategies for technology that define flexible priorities and that fit into their overall mission and financial structure. As Gary Augustson correctly pointed out, "There is no simple prescription for success, and what works at one institution may not work at another. Nothing, however, can beat enlightened leadership."[9] It is incumbent on chief technology officers, working closely with senior officers, advisory committees, and other members of the college community, to develop a comprehensive understanding of what the institution is trying to accomplish with technology, how priorities for services and infrastructure relate to one another, where funding will be found, and, of greatest importance, how much technology the institution can actually afford without harming other critical funding priorities.

NOTES

1. This paper appeared in *Computing Strategies in Liberal Arts Colleges,* Martin Ringle, ed., Mass, Addison-Wesley, Inc., 1992, 69–103. David Todd is currently chief information officer at Montana State University, *hdtodd@montana. edu.*

2. Information technology staff longevity at private liberal arts colleges has traditionally been higher than that of many other types of institutions, both in education and the private sector. The median for the reference group, slightly less than five years, continues to be comparatively high though the gap is narrowing especially in very high demand positions, such as database management, networking, etc.

3. J. Gary Augustson, "Strategies for Financial Planning," in Brian Hawkins, ed., *Organizing and Managing Information Resources on Campus,* Educom Strategy Series on Information Technology, 1989, 263–280.

4. The poll was initiated by the author during the Educom95 Post-Conference Workshop and pursued by email in spring 1996. There were 72 responses, mostly (but not exclusively) from liberal arts colleges.

5. Within the reference group of liberal arts colleges, more than 65 percent have developed or are developing policies, while only 20 percent are fully funded.

6. Brian Hawkins, Ron Weissman, and Don Wolfe, "Prescriptions for Managing Information Resources on Campus," in Brian Hawkins, ed., *Organizing and Managing Information Resources on Campus,* Educom Strategy Series on Information Technology, 1989, 229–259.

7. John Oberlin, "The Financial Mythology of Information Technology: Developing a New Game Plan," *CAUSE/EFFECT,* Vol. 19, No. 2, Summer 1996, 10–17.

8. Digital Equipment Corporation and Hewlett-Packard provide three-year warranties on many, though not all, of their host/server lines. IBM provides them on PC but not on UNIX platforms.

9. Gary Augustson, op. cit., 278.

CHAPTER 30

THE FINANCIAL MYTHOLOGY OF INFORMATION TECHNOLOGY

Developing a New Game Plan

JOHN L. OBERLIN

John L. Oberlin (john oberlin@unc.edu) is Interim Director for the Office of Information Technology (OIT) at the University of North Carolina at Chapel Hill. As such, he is responsible for the academic computing center, user services, and communications organizations, as well as for implementing a broad-based financial planning effort for information technology. Formerly, he was Director for Finance and Planning for OIT, as well as Project Director for the Institute of Academic Technology in Research Triangle Park, North Carolina.

New economics are driving campuses to reassess their financial strategies for managing information technology investments. Many institutions will be faced with the prospect of developing an entirely new game plan. This new plan will require collaboration among academic, financial, and technical leaders; a rejuvenation of the collective conventional wisdom on campus; a shift to life-cycle budgeting; an emphasis on technology replacement; explicit plans to recycle old technology off campus; and, most of all, a willingness to recognize and accept the significant financial challenge that evolving information technologies will bring.

The fundamental economic factors underlying information technology are unlike those of more traditional assets. Technologists are finding the new economics to be a slippery slope from which to develop new financial strategies. The rate of technical advancement is accelerating, standards and architectures are changing daily, and prices are falling. Nevertheless, the legacy-based management practices and financial strategies of both technologists and financial officers have changed little in the face of these new realities. The jargon of the technical community is rich with sound bites of financial understanding, yet void of any holistic financial plan to deal with the fundamental economics of information technology. Developing rational and viable financial strategies to accommodate technological change is an institutional imperative for effective information technology management.

THE NEW ECONOMICS OF INFORMATION TECHNOLOGY

The fundamental forces driving the economics of information technology are: (1) the value of information technology is steadily increasing; (2) the demand for technology by institutions, faculty, and students is growing dramatically; (3) the acquisition price per unit of computing power

Source: *Cause/Effect* Volume 19, Number 2, Summer 1996, pp. 10–17, © 1996 Cause.

is rapidly declining; and (4) the total cost of owning and maintaining technology is constantly increasing. At the same time, there is a constant, if not accelerating, rate of change in the underlying technology that makes the economic life cycle of many technologies surprisingly short. These forces change the fundamental economic equations that determine the wisdom of investing in and managing these technology systems. The new economics are briefly summarized below; a more detailed discussion can be found in an article published in the Spring 1996 issue of *CAUSE/EFFECT*.[1]

Lifecycles

Recognizing the economic life cycles of information technology is at the core of understanding the new economics. Each new technology generation has an economic life cycle that is independent of its functional life cycle. Computers rarely wear out. Instead, they become economically obsolete and are replaced. The record of academic institutions is littered with examples of technology at every level—desktop PCs, departmental servers, campus networks, and shared regional supercomputers—that have become functionally obsolete long before their hardware stopped working.

Asset Management

The principles of asset management that apply to buying a computer are fundamentally unlike those of buying a truck. If the physical plant purchased a half-ton pickup truck for $25,000, with an expected life of five years, it would have a capital cost of $5,000 per year. At the end of five years, the truck could be replaced with another truck that would cost more, but still be more or less functionally identical. Computers, on the other hand, are quite different. If the physics department purchased a $25,000 computer and amortized the expense over five years, it would also cost $5,000 per year. However, the physics department will be able to spend significantly less on the replacement and still receive a new computer that is superior to the one it is replacing. In cases where this is true, the rule of thumb for making computer purchases is to adopt a life-cycle model, where

you buy as little as possible and keep it for as short a time as possible.

Financial Pressures

As long as institutions can expect a continual improvement in their return on investments in information technology, they will be compelled to spend an increased percentage of their budget on it. It is a simple economic reality. Any organization in a competitive environment will be forced over time to invest more of its money where the return is greatest. In the case of information technology, where it pays to invest today, it will pay even greater dividends to invest even more tomorrow. This does not imply that technology budgets will expand to 100 percent of the institutional budget. It does, however, mean that we are in an era where technology budgets should be expected to grow steadily over a relatively long period of time.

The Business Case

Traditional wisdom governing technology investment decisions views the investment decision primarily as an expense issue. In reality, it is a cost/benefit issue, where the investment is in the goals of the institution as well as the individuals charged with advancing them. No dean or department head would fill a faculty vacancy based solely on the fact that one applicant might be less expensive than another. It should be equally ridiculous to make investment decisions for technology based solely on cost.

Competitive Economics

The biggest institutional downside of new information technologies is their potential impact on inter-institution competition. For example, if distance learning enabled by technology becomes viable, it could drastically change the competitive landscape. One result would be to break down the regional barriers to competition. If there is new competition, the one thing we can predict with certainty is that there will be winners and losers.

What can institutions do to effectively manage their technology investments in light of these economic forces? What are the fundamental tenets of a new financial game plan for managing those investments?

REEXAMINE THE CONVENTIONAL WISDOM

The first tenet of a financial game plan is to reform the conventional wisdom. Campus constituents need to embrace the evolutionary nature of technology and the subsequent need for institutional change, reengineering, and change management. The need for change should not be seen primarily as a threat; instead, it should be embraced as an opportunity for advancing the institution and empowering individuals. The conventional wisdom needs to accept the tremendous promise of information technology without underestimating the total cost or overstating what it can currently deliver.

Plan for Change

The paradox of planning for information technology is dealing with the rate of change. In times of rapid architectural and technical change, when the need for a viable plan is greatest, the tendency is to abandon planning because of the belief that the changing environment makes planning impossible.

While planning in this environment is difficult, it is not impossible. If the one thing known with certainty is that technology will change, then the one thing that must be planned for is change. Any financial strategy that impedes change is likely to suboptimize or even undermine the investments that rely on it. Moreover, in a competitive environment where information technology can be key, staying ahead of the technology curve may actually be a critical success factor for institutions.

Adapt Strategies to the Rate of Change

The rate of change inherent in information technology systems and the computing industry shows no signs of slowing; if anything, it will continue to accelerate for the foreseeable future. The scholarly record is teeming with false predictions that technological evolution is coming to an inevitable end.[2] Instead, it is becoming increasingly clear that we are not at the end of technology history. Financial strategies will need to support technological evolution so that technologists can optimize campus investments over time. Business models that require long amortization periods, ad hoc purchasing decisions, or monolithic architectures, will almost certainly drive poor purchasing decisions.

Create Financial, Political, and Social Infrastructure

Part of the mythology dominating information technology management is that it is all about technical issues. It can be argued instead that it's actually all about managing change—technical, social, pedagogical, political, and financial. From this perspective, the notion of building technology infrastructure is inconsistent with the notion of constant and rapid change and should be approached with caution. A foundation to build on is one thing; long-term hardware and system investments that are inflexible or static are another. If the phrase "technology infrastructure" means stable hardware, software, or wires in the walls, it borders on being classified as an oxymoron. If it means "long-term" hardware or software, it is definitely an oxymoron.

This doesn't mean there isn't a need for technology infrastructure. However, it does imply that hardware and software may not be the most important aspect of technology infrastructure. The changing nature of technology suggests that standards, architectures, and resource allocation systems that allow us to manage changing hardware effectively may be the real infrastructure needed. More exactly, it's not actually the standards or architectures that are needed. The real infrastructure imperative is to create the underlying processes that can produce the standards, architectures, and governance mechanisms to manage the changing technology.

In other words, the infrastructure most needed to support the information era is financial, social, and political, not technical. Financial infrastructure is the institutional commitment to understand the economics, develop appropriate financial strategies, and fund technology adequately. Social infrastructure is the critical mass of faculty, staff, and students who are willing to accept and work for change. Political infrastructure is the collective resolution of senior administrators, trustees, and legislators to support information technology as a strategic imperative for the campus.

Tell the whole truth

Information technology promises to deliver big benefits down the road, but there will also be big expenses. The cost issue is likely the most misunderstood and misrepresented aspect about the future of information technology. The reluctance of chief information officers (CIOs) and technology leaders at all levels to identify the total costs may amount to "the big lie" for information technology. Their reluctance to document these costs is often justified in the short run, as campus executives, presidents, and trustees cringe at the thought of such large numbers and threaten to shoot the messengers. However, CIOs and other technology leaders may be jeopardizing their long-term credibility and casting technology in a negative light by implying that many of the increased costs are unexpected.

If the biggest financial lie has to do with cost, the second has to do with the benefits of information technology. This is typically born from honest yet excessive enthusiasm. The case for technology is very compelling, but it is not a solution to all things, nor are all the promises deliverable yet. Overselling the benefits may help obtain support or funding in the short term, but will almost certainly jeopardize long-term credibility. Financial planners and CIOs need to be careful to ensure that their business cases don't inadvertently sow the seeds of skepticism as a result of overreaching.

ABANDON LEGACY-BASED THINKING

Considering the relatively short history of information technology, it is rich with legacies—legacy systems, legacy architectures, and legacy assumptions about the economics. Given the rapid change that is inherent in technology, planners need to be careful to constantly reexamine the assumptions on which financial strategies are based. Seven assumptions that bear on the financial case for information technology are briefly reviewed below. They include both legacy assumptions that are clearly no longer valid, and emerging assumptions that seem to be based more on wishful thinking than careful analysis.

Some Economic Myths about Information Technology

- **Myth 1:** Falling computer prices and commodity markets will reduce the total cost of campus expenditures on IT.
- **Myth 2:** Cheap PCs with the power of mainframes are making distributed computing cheaper than central computing.
- **Myth 3:** The marginal cost of supporting another software package, hardware platform, or standard is small.
- **Myth 4:** Information technology investments can be effectively managed through an ad hoc funding process.
- **Myth 5:** Personal computers and distributed computing environments mean an end to central computing authority and enterprise-wide standards.
- **Myth 6:** Emerging technologies and technology-based services will be cash cows for higher education institutions.
- **Myth 7:** Higher education is leading the information technology industry in setting standards and functional requirements.

Myth 1: Falling computer prices and commodity markets will reduce the total cost of campus technology expenditures. Like many of the myths, this is a seductive notion that is easy to buy into. The truth, however, is that falling acquisition prices do little to lower the total cost, and in truth may contribute to increases. As the acquisition price falls, more users buy more technology. The growth in demand for more powerful computers and support is growing faster than prices are falling.

Myth 2: Cheap PCs with the power of mainframes are making distributed computing cheaper than central computing. Similar to the assumption above, this myth overlooks the increase in demand for computing power. More importantly, it fails to take into account the additional support costs associated with maintaining distributed computing systems. There are numerous studies by the Gartner Group that demonstrate the growing total cost of distributed computing.[3]

Myth 3: The marginal cost of supporting another software package, hardware platform, or standard is small. Much of the increased cost of distributed computing systems can be attributed to the decentralized and heterogeneous nature of the environment. The result is a highly complex web of computers and networks that is very difficult and expensive to support. Adding another brand of computer, software version, network protocol, or operating system causes the complexity to grow exponentially. The result is often a more heterogeneous environment and much higher total costs.

Myth 4: Information technology investments can be effectively managed through an ad hoc funding process. One problem with ad hoc funding is that it spawns ad hoc decision-making. This is fundamentally inconsistent with the need for information technology organizations to proactively manage change to ensure maximum effectiveness. A second problem is that individuals and organizations often have no faith that ad hoc funding will be there to replace their three-year-old computers. Therefore, they have strong incentives to purchase today the most expensive computer they can, a practice that leads to excessive spending as well as a loss of future benefits as a result of more timely upgrades.

Myth 5: Personal computers and distributed computing environments mean an end to central computing authority and enterprise-wide standards. PCs are highly valued because of the freedom of choice they give to individuals. Faculty, staff, and students can customize their computing systems to meet their personal preferences. The advent of PCs has clearly reduced the campus hegemony of central computing organizations. But this may be about to change. As stated previously, these environments are becoming increasingly complex and expensive to support, and campuses are under pressure to ensure that it all works together. Similarly, the need on many campuses for enterprise-wide solutions to networking, e-mail, and data storage problems is highlighting the necessity for a stronger central computing authority.

Myth 6: Emerging technologies and technology-based services will be cash cows for higher education institutions. There is a growing consensus that information technolo-gies, and distance learning technologies in particular, will markedly contribute to the financial well-being of many institutions. This belief appears to have its roots in the notion that these new systems will truly disintermediate students from campus and faculty, thus allowing cost savings from reductions in faculty as well as bricks and mortar. There are problems with this assumption. First, the scenario implies that education would be transformed into a highly profitable enterprise. If true, it would spawn a whole new set of profit-motivated competitors that would either drive down prices (and thus profits) or force campuses as we know them today to change radically. In either case, there would clearly be very high costs. Second, even in the best-case scenario, the cost of acquiring and developing the new system will likely make the financial crisis worse before it makes it better.

Myth 7: Higher education is leading the information technology industry in setting standards and functional requirements. Higher education has an important leadership role to play to ensure that emerging technologies deliver on the educational promise. However, the higher education community needs to be mindful that the educational marketplace is only 6 percent of the total technology marketplace, and that the large size of industry and household markets will continue to drive many of the important development decisions and directions.[4]

DO THE RIGHT FINANCIAL ANALYSIS

A frequent charge leveled at higher education is that it is falling behind the curve of what society is demanding of it. Investments in information technology are an opportunity to help close this gap. However, the decision to invest in educational technologies is often restrained by using either conventional methods of capital investment analysis, or no analysis at all, where the conventional wisdom tends toward ignoring hard-to-measure benefits. When a formal analysis is done, the value of technology is almost always underestimated because of a hesitancy to include anything but the most directly obvious benefits.

Adopt Principles of Strategic Cost Analysis

Technology leaders need to expand their level of sophistication when analyzing these decision points and begin adopting the principles of "strategic cost analysis" so their respective institutions can better understand the financial impact of these investments.[5] Shank and Govidarajan argue that traditional methods of financial analysis of information technology investments need to be extended to a more holistic assessment that includes three strategic considerations: value chain analysis, cost driver analysis, and competitive advantage analysis.[6] By doing so, organizations will be better prepared to judge the value of technology. Following the strategic cost management paradigm, institutions will be better prepared to: (1) identify technology's impact on value-creating activities within the organization, (2) understand the cost structure that supports their strategic choices, and (3) realize the implications of how technology allows them to compete more effectively.

Understand Cost/Benefit and Return on Investment

The deciding criterion for investing in technology is not cost, it is cost/benefit. The financial game plan would be incomplete without an understanding of the appropriate scope for cost/benefit assessments. Analyzing investments in either central systems or distributed environments without considering the impact on the other, or on the larger institutional environment, will almost certainly produce poor results. As the demand for information technology grows, individual campus constituent groups will pressure administrators to place their respective technology needs ahead of others.

A challenge for central computing administrators in this environment will be to understand each of these perspectives and function as mediator in the funding equation to ensure that the sum of the parts continues to be greater than the individual pieces—a difficult prospect in a decentralized environment. The challenge will be to balance the demands of individual departments against the needs of the institution as a whole. Solving sub-problems does not solve the larger problem. It would not be unusual for a research university with 25,000 students to own 18,000 computers (not counting student-owned machines) with an asset value of $90 million dollars. Maximizing the return on these investments, department by department, may be much different from optimizing their return for the institution as a whole.

Take a Life-Cycle Approach to Budgeting

There is a great need to understand life cycles and to budget accordingly. Without this approach, colleges and universities will continue to make purchases that suboptimize their investments in information technology. If faculty, departments, and technologists continue to face an ad hoc funding equation when they plan for replacing their current technology, they will continue to make the worst possible investment decisions. Life-cycle budgeting can build confidence, promote coordination, and educate faculty, departments, and campus administrators. It shifts the emphasis away from the acquisition of technology and focuses the financial question on its replacement. The initial acquisition of information technology takes place only once; its life-cycle replacement should be considered a financial perpetuity.

Many skeptics of budgeting and planning for information technology view long-term planning for technology as an oxymoron. Although they may be right in some ways, life-cycle budgeting offers the best chance to prove them wrong. Learning this technique and using it is a critical first step toward overcoming the legacy-based planning biases of the past. Life-cycle planning can be used to: (1) avoid unplanned "expectation inflation," where both planners and users continually underestimate the demand for future information systems; (2) combat unrealistic "life-cycle optimism," where planners are coerced by their own false optimism or pressure from superiors to adopt an overly optimistic estimation of the true life-cycle of technology investments; and (3) clarify the forces driving widespread, but largely uncoordinated, "investment creep," where institutions, schools, and departments continue to marginally expand their technology budgets in an ad hoc fashion despite their best efforts to hold them flat and deny the need.

DEVELOP NEW FINANCIAL STRATEGIES

The dominant financial strategies of the past decade include: (1) positioning information technology as a vehicle for cost savings, typically through simple automation applications; (2) supporting distributed computing at any cost, with the belief that personal computers would lower the total cost of computing; (3) treating the funding gap as a problem to be solved by the technologists; and (4) posing acquisition decisions as ad hoc funding considerations that are truly onetime by nature. These strategies are inconsistent with the new economics of information technology, and if technologists continue to support them, they will be their own worst enemies when dealing with the economics. The strategic importance of information technology demands a reassessment of the financial strategies assembled to support it, as well as the assumptions underpinning them.

Tenets of a New Game Plan

Reform the conventional wisdom

- Plan for change
- Adapt strategies to the rate of change
- Create financial, political, and social infrastructure
- Tell the whole truth

Abandon the Myths of Legacy-Based Thinking

Do the right financial analysis

- Adopt principles of strategic cost analysis
- Understand cost/benefit and return on investment
- Take a life-cycle approach to budgeting

Develop new financial strategies

- Plan on spending more
- Articulate the business case
- Position the funding problem
- Fund information technology as a perpetuity
- Recycle old technology

Plan on Spending More

Institutions must plan to spend more money on information technology if they expect to realize the benefits. According to the Department of Commerce, 1990 was the first year capital spending on the information economy (that is, on computers and telecommunications equipment) exceeded capital spending on all other parts of the nation's industrial infrastructure.[7] The message for higher education is clear: the only credible financial strategy is to spend more or let the technology wave pass by. Superior strategies will focus on architectures and implementations that support the enterprise, build synergy, and eliminate redundancy. These strategies will offer opportunities for cost avoidance, but not cost reduction.

Articulate the Business Case

The case for information technology is that it is a long-term investment in the competitive standing and productivity of the institution. Information technology expenditures do not directly compete with personnel and are actually a necessary investment in human potential. They should be considered an implicit part of the college or university benefit package. It is not unusual for a Research-I university with a student body of 25,000 to spend $40 million a year on information technology. Given the increasing demand and the improving cost/benefit equation, pressure will mount to spend even more, perhaps significantly more. In this environment it will be critically important for senior officials and chief information officers (CIOs) to have a good grasp of the numbers and strong financial controls. Developing and maintaining the business cases will rely on getting the numbers right. New money will be hard to find without a fundamental trust in the system that analyzes and manages these investments.

Position the Funding Problem

Departments, schools, and central computing administrators will need to collaborate to make the case for information technology, but only financial officers, vice presidents, vice chancellors, presidents, trustees, or even legislators will actually be able to solve the financial problems. The funding problem needs to be positioned within the bureaucracy at the appropriate level to have it resolved. Telling a director of academic or administrative computing that a million-dollar funding gap is his or her problem to solve is entirely unacceptable. Similarly, department chairs and deans with funding gaps will have to pass some portion of them forward, as they also can't be solved solely in the academic departments. However, the case of deans and department heads is unique when compared to central computing organizations. Part of the funding gap must be resolved internally in these departments as technology becomes a larger part of their respective budgets. CIOs need to play the lead role in bringing these individuals together and outlining the cases to be made. Many institutions will be looking at expenses of millions of dollars a year (while larger universities will be facing tens of millions of dollars) and will need support and understanding at senior levels before they can proceed.

Fund Information Technology as a Perpetuity

The financial environment for evaluating and managing information technology investments is very complex. These investment decisions are rich with technical, architectural, and management considerations. Moreover, they often involve questions of equity in how resources are allocated, who benefits most, and how much support will be available. These issues, combined with the sheer number of decisions—across central and decentralized units; among faculty, staff, and students; and over academic and administrative units—perpetuate the belief that it is impossible to make rational holistic decisions about these investments. The natural tendency is thus to manage them as a series of ad hoc decisions.

There is, however, hope. The key is to separate the myriad of short-term technical considerations from the longer-term funding decisions. Consider faculty desktop computers. Life-cycle budgeting offers the opportunity to convert this chain of apparent one-time funding decisions into an annual expense. The basic life-cycle equation (number of units × price/unit divided by life-cycle years = annual cost) converts the hardware expense of faculty desktops into a reasonably stable long-term perpetuity.[8] The financial strategy is to identify the perpetuity and manage it over time. There will be many techni-

cal decisions that will vary over the years (what to buy, what standards, what architectures, what operating systems, and so forth), but the financial equation will be more permanent.

Even though the financial perpetuity is more stable than the technology, it will still vary and will need to be managed. The assumptions about quantity, price, and life cycle require continual review and updates. The financial management question is to determine whether the perpetuity is expected to decline, remain flat, or increase over time. The emphasis needs to be on the continuing cost over time, not the arbitrary cost of any particular year.

When this example of faculty computers is combined with other enterprise-wide technology service areas (e.g., networking, data storage, e-mail), a collection of perpetuities can be developed. The financial strategy thus expands to the notion of managing these expenses as a portfolio of perpetuities, where services will come and go, some will grow, and others will decline. The strategic imperative for the institution is to maximize the return on the portfolio.

Recycle Old Technology

Developing strategies to manage technology life cycles is a fundamental requirement of any new financial game plan. Technology rarely wears out, but it does become obsolete remarkably fast. The result is a clear need to recycle old technology on campus as well as off. Recycling old technology on campus has limited potential because it rests on two problematic options—one is to hand down computers from one department to another, the other is to hand down computers from faculty to staff. There are several problems with both of these cases, including: (1) the cost of physically redeploying the technology is high, (2) there are potential problems with equity between departments, (3) it assumes that the computers will be recycled before the end of their life, and (4) it assumes that there are campuswide network standards in place that will allow them to function at all. The greatest downside of recycling computers is the possibility of redeploying obsolete technology that would make the campus support problems worse, not better.

The challenge is thus to develop financial strategies that recycle old technology off campus. The best strategy to accomplish this may be leasing. Leasing has several advantages: (1) it sets a clear expectation that technology will be replaced on a regular life-cycle basis; (2) it shifts the burden of recycling to the vendor, who becomes responsible for disposition of the computers at the end of the lease; and (3) it offers the opportunity, depending on how the lease is structured, for the institution to recapture the salvage value of old technology before it goes to zero.

A leasing strategy that clearly commits an institution to a policy of life-cycling technology has tremendous potential. It represents an institutional commitment to managing change and is an example of the new type of infrastructure needed to manage technology evolution. It highlights the need to not just set campus standards, but to manage them over time. It also creates new urgency and opportunities to partner with vendors. In this scenario, lead vendors would be asked to play a greater support role, manage the transition from one generation of computer to the next, and participate in developing longer-term campus technology architectures.

CONCLUSIONS

The new economics of information technology demand new financial strategies to manage them. The tenets of a new financial game plan must include: (1) a commitment to change the conventional wisdom to recognize the new economic realities, (2) a clear resolution to abandon legacy-based technical and economic assumptions, (3) a shift toward better economic analysis of the investment decisions being made, and (4) an institutional resolution to develop new financial strategies that are consistent with the economic realities of the information era. Two of the most challenging strategies will be the commitment to spend a greater portion of the institutional pie on technology, and the need to manage technology life cycles proactively by focusing on replacement strategies and recycling.

While chief information officers, financial officers, and academic leaders will have to come together to develop and implement these strategies, it is the role of CIOs that is likely to change the most. When viewing information technology systems in aggregate, the CIO's ability to bring information technology to bear on the organizational imperatives of his or her institution might be the single most important factor in determining how technology is valued.

It is not surprising that chief information officers have a difficult job when it comes to delivering a set of services whose value is difficult to quantify and hard to measure directly. To make the information technology function a valuable asset to their respective institutions, CIOs should view their job as adding value to critical areas.[9] They need to know the critical success factors inherent in their institution's plans and be able to link information technology to these plans to create value chains where they are most needed.

As strategists, CIOs need to provide more than just the technology infrastructure. They need to be actively involved in developing the business plans and financial strategies that close the gap between today's realities and tomorrow's promises. It may prove to be more important to have a chief information technology strategist than it is to have a chief technologist.

NOTES

1. John L. Oberlin, "The Financial Mythology of Information Technology: The New Economics," *CAUSE/EFFECT,* Spring 1996, 21–29.
2. Dan G. Hutcheson and Jerry D. Hutcheson, "Technology and Economics in the Semiconductor Industry," *Scientific American,* January 1996, 54–61.
3. Gartner Group, "Total Cost of Ownership," *Management Strategies: PC Cost/Benefit and Payback Analysis,* 1993, 36.
4. "PC Unit Shipments by Key I.S. Market Locations," *IDC's 30th Annual Computer Industry Briefing Session,* 1994. (Track 5-Services/Consumer. Report #5).
5. John K. Shank and Vijay Govindarajan, *Strategic Cost Management: The New Tool for Competitive Advantage* (New York: New York Free Press, 1993).
6. John K. Shank and Vijay Govindarajan, "Strategic Cost Analysis of Technological Investment," *Sloan Management Review* 34 (1992): 39–51.
7. Shoshana Zuboff, "The Emperor's New Workplace: Information Technology Evolves More Quickly than Human Behavior," *Scientific American,* September 1995, 202–203.
8. John L. Oberlin, "Departmental Budgeting for Information Technology: A Life-Cycle Approach" *CAUSE/EFFECT,* Summer 1994, pp. 22–31.
9. Michael J. Earl and David F. Feeney, "Is Your CIO Adding Value?" *Sloan Management Review* 35 (1994): 11–20.

CHAPTER 31

THE PHYSICAL PLANT:
ASSET OR LIABILITY?

Rethinking the Management of Facilities

WILLIAM A. DAIGNEAU

William A. Daigneau is director for university facilities at the University of Rochester.

Higher education has entered a dramatically changed fiscal, social, and technological era. The compounding effect of shortfalls in enrollment, government allocations, research funding, and tuition is forcing a fundamental re-examination of many of the basic tenets of higher education: its role, its goals, and its management. One of the problems, which has risen steadily on the list of issues of highest concern, is the question of what to do with higher education's aging physical plant and the increasing debt burden that many institutions face as they attempt to rebuild, remodel, or restore their facilities.

Particularly perplexing is the failure of traditional solutions to financial difficulties, developed over the past two decades, to provide satisfactory results. In many cases, higher education leaders have found that these solutions are no longer valid approaches because the original assumptions on which they were based have changed so dramatically. For example, administrators often deferred routine expenditures to repair and renew an institution's physical plant knowing they could "catch up" once better days returned. Only new are college and university officials starting to grapple with the possibility that better days may not return soon. Thus, there are few strategies, especially in facilities management, to deal with a possible future featuring low economic and population growth, continued technological change, increased sensitivity to environmental protection, and fundamental shifts in society's demand and expectation for higher education.

The reality of this facilities dilemma recently began surfacing in discussions both within APPA: the Association of Higher Education Facilities Officers and NACUBO. In 1991, NACUBO's Facilities Administration Committee began searching for information that could help guide institutions in considering facilities issues in the context of strategic planning. The committee members found that while much has been written about defining facilities needs, little information has been developed on how to meet those needs without raising more money. Little new information exists concerning potential strategies where total resources are holding steady or decreasing, and the amount available for facilities is shrinking. Higher education leaders have always considered the physical plant as an asset, but may have very little understanding of its dimensions as a liability.

Source: *Business Officer*, Vol. 27, No. 9. National Association of College and University Business Officers.

A PROBLEM WITH FACILITIES?

Higher education is generally recognized as a highly labor-intensive industry. Often, salaries and related benefits costs represent 70 to 80 percent of an institution's annual operating expenses. However, few people understand that higher education is also highly capital intensive. Colleges and universities in the United States own or operate approximately 3 billion square feet of building space. With an estimated replacement value of more than $300 billion, higher education's investment in plant is the single largest asset on its balance sheet, eclipsing many times the value of the more liquid, and hence more visible, financial endowments. On average, each of the 3,300 colleges and universities in the United States owns or operates property valued at almost $100 million. The true expense of this capital invested in an institution's facilities matches that spent annually for labor. In a recent article in *Business Officer*, Gordon C. Winston observed that "Leaving . . . capital costs out of calculation of the educational cost . . . has the same effect, almost to the dollar, as would leaving out all personnel costs, including fringe benefits." (See June 1993 *Business Officer*, page 22.)

Traditionally, higher education has not thought of its sizable investment in plant as a financial asset but as an entitlement. This is reflected not only in attitudes, but also in the tools and methods used to account for and manage these assets. For example, how often does a business officer or treasurer stand in front of the institution's governing board and report on the performance of the physical endowment, as he or she routinely is expected to do for the financial endowment? In a recent review of capital budgeting processes used by some of the largest public and independent universities, David A. Techam did not find one instance where the use of capital or its costs was a factor in establishing project priority or feasibility. Until recently, administrators even ignored the reality that the investment in plant is depreciated.

The benign neglect of such a major component in the delivery of modern education is possible as long as resources are constantly expanding and hard decisions on resource allocation priorities are not necessary. Only after an entitlement or "free good" is recognized as a

liability, or an expense on the financial statements, does the need to manage facilities emerge. Beginning in the 1980s, that is exactly what has happened. The lack of funds to replace or renew an aging physical plant, as well as the reality that revenues are not increasing as fast as expenditures, has left many institutions in a quandary. Some experts believe that economic pressure on higher education will only increase in the next several decades. In a recent publication of the Association of Governing Boards of Universities and Colleges, titled *Trustees and Troubled Times*, the authors stated: "We write as friends of higher education to convey our sense of urgency that great changes are afoot in the United States and the world, and our colleges and universities are not prepared to cope with them. We write as optimists, confident that higher education's leaders, effectively engaged, will do what is best for their institutions and the nation. But we write also as realists: the difficulties ahead for our institutions are real. They are sobering. They cannot be wished away."

LESSONS FROM INDUSTRY

Will the physical plants of universities and colleges, which for so long have been considered significant assets, evolve into serious liabilities? Experiences of other industries in the United States that were also capital intensive provide some sobering lessons. Two of these are the U.S. steel and automaking industries.

Emerging from World War II, the U.S. steel industry seemed invincible. With much of Europe and the Far East in ruin, the United States was blessed with fully operational and up-to-date steelmaking equipment, plentiful raw materials, low energy costs, and well-trained labor. But, within a single generation, U.S. steelmaking would be largely a defunct enterprise. What happened? While many complex factors led to the demise of the U.S. steel industry, one major contributor was the failure of the industry to reinvest continually in and modernize its production facilities, a problem described by Michael E. Porter in his 1985 book *Competitive Advantage*. When severe competition from more efficient, lower cost overseas producers developed, the U.S. steelmakers no longer possessed the financial resources to make sizable reinvestments to replace outmoded technology and worn-out equipment.

An examination of the U.S. auto industry, another capital intensive business, reveals similar patterns to those of the steel industry. The rush by Chrysler, Ford, and now General Motors to close inefficient, outmoded plants and reinvest in new, more productive technology and processes may have saved this industry from a similar fate. But it could be too late. Chrysler, for example, carries a significant debt burden that was acquired to revitalize the company. The limitations that this enormous debt burden impose on Chrysler's ability to react to and take advantage of changes in the marketplace, or to recover from a miscalculation, may ultimately determine the automakers' future, Porter postulated. Chrysler's situation is a somber example to those colleges and universities that are already saddled with considerable debt. As the need increases to replace or renew the large number of facilities constructed in the 1960s and 1970s, will institutions be able to handle the higher debt service requirements?

DIMENSIONS OF THE PROBLEM

The experience of the U.S. steelmaking and auto industries demonstrate one possible outcome when essential reinvestment in plant is ignored or not possible. Does higher education face a similar dilemma? Specifically, how well is higher education prepared to deal with the following issues?

Obsolescence: Are the types of facilities and their condition, constraining factors in higher education's ability to react to changing demographics and societal expectations?

Efficiency: Are universities and colleges overbuilt, not necessarily based on traditional concepts of space utilization, but on the basis of what institutions can afford?

Technology: If the pace of scientific advances continues to accelerate, will the need to modify and re-equip college and university physical plants likewise increase?

Economics: Will the resources be available to retain, let alone repair, the 60 percent of existing space that is now at least 25 years old and will constitute 80 percent of the space by the year 2000?

The degree to which these issues have an impact on higher education over the next several decades no only has significant financial dimensions but also affects the quality and availability of education and research. The central questions for higher education leaders are how to gauge the impact of such issues on their institutions and how to define solutions to deal with them. The answers to these questions represent the essence of strategic planning—the process of establishing the goals and mission of the institution, forecasting the most likely range of possible futures, and then devising strategies that the institution may use to adapt or respond to these possible futures.

Unfortunately, higher education leaders are not well practiced at thinking strategically nor at developing and then implementing business-type strategic plans. A 1979 review of strategic management concepts in not-for-profit organizations by Max S. Wortman, Jr., identified several barriers to effective strategy development: "lack of credibility (of the institution's management both within and outside of the institution), being actionless, constraints of tradition, overly ambitious timetables, and frequent failure in setting prioritites." If asked, many higher education managers would not only concur with Wortman but might add a few more hurdles: unrealistic expectations for revenue, lack of vision or authority (and as a consequence, indecisiveness), and the tendency to ignore or disguise true costs for political reasons. In addition, higher education's governing boards have done little to promote strategic management, not for lack of knowledge of such techniques, but due to the composition and nature of such boards, Israel Unterman and Richard Hart Davis wrote in an article titled., "The Strategy of Not-for-Profits," published in the May-June 1982 *Harvard Business Review.*

Some higher education leaders reading this article will argue that they do plan and will point proudly to the institution's campus master plan on their shelves or to their recently developed "strategic" financial plan that spells out which departments will be cut and by how much. Actually those so-called "plans" are examples of objective setting because they focus on the ends, not the means. Many institutional master or financial plans start from a set of assumptions about the university's mission and a rosy picture of a hoped-for future, regardless of foreseeable trends. Facility master plans, for example, show the optimal configuration of buildings and infrastructure for a given piece of land, often based on an underlying assumption of forever expanding enrollments and programs. These plans show the optimal result or final objective for campus development. Therefore, one often hears when discussing facilities that a certain action is justified because it is "consistent with" or "called for" in the master plan. But if planning is the process of establishing goals, forecasting the future, and deciding the series of actions or steps required to meet those goals, how can the "plan" itself serve as the justification for taking any particular action? A more accurate statement would be that officials are taking an action because it is "consistent with their objectives."

Many in higher education do not understand that the process of master planning is a much different exercise than that of strategic planning. Most existing facility master plans, for example, have an underlying assumption of growth. The question answered by most master plans is "How can an institution best use its land and buildings to meet its future program needs?" Rarely do these plans deal with issues such as the sources of capital required to implement the plans. Nor do such plans address the need for regeneration of existing facilities, environmental protection and enhancement, or new technology that may require less space. No one yet has developed a master plan on how to "shrink" or change a campus in response to obsolescence, efficiency, technology, and economics.

Higher education leaders appear to be doing little, if anything, to plan for a future that does not envision a return to the expansion era of the baby boom once the baby bust ends, sometime in 1996. Under such a scenario, it will be necessary only to dust off these previously prepared "master plans," update them, and give them a new life.

Until this happens, or if it ever does, higher education leaders must continue to confront some rather unattractive realities. In the face of declining resources, students still need to be served, payrolls met, and facilities heated, lit,

and cleaned. The most ominous trend is the growing tendency of the benefactors of higher education (taxpayers, philanthropists, parents, alumni) to balk at feeding institutions' enormous appetites for resources for operations and capital.

In this environment, higher education now shares something with business: the need to compete. College and university leaders must somehow demonstrate that their needs are at least as worthy as society's other needs, such as personal safety, a clean environment, or good transportation. In addition, higher education administrators must increasingly prove to their institutions' traditional benefactors that the resources they currently receive are efficiently and prudently used. While some might argue that higher education is not a business and should not be run like one, it faces some strikingly similar conditions and challenges to those of business. Colleges and universities can benefit from the application of modern management tools and techniques, particularly in the area of strategic management and planning.

STRATEGIC MANAGEMENT OF FACILITIES

Higher education's stock response to the growing dilemma of how to deal with decaying facilities has been to explore various alternatives directed toward one common goal—to increase the amount of funding available to build or remodel facilities. But what strategies have been developed if this effort fails? How will colleges and universities attempt to extend the life of available facilities? How will institutions decide where to spend scarce dollars to bolster current program strengths? How will institutions continue to make and keep facilities safe and accessible? What, if anything, should colleges and universities be doing to seek alternative solutions to managing their facilities during an era of economic austerity? Seeking answers to such questions is germane to the strategic planning process.

There are alternatives. While not widely discussed or considered, institutions might consider options other than the ubiquitous solution of spending more money. Some of these alternatives are similar to those being attempted by industry.

Selective Deferral

Selective deferral differs from the deferred maintenance practiced by higher education for the past 20 years because it is a conscious decision, carrying with it a full understanding of its implications and a plan for recovery. The essence of selective deferral is deciding which facilities are strategically important to the survival or well-being of the institution and which are not. Once determined, resources can be directed toward maintaining, protecting, and modernizing the critically important facilities. Only minimal resources are allocated to nonstrategic buildings. Once the "Value" of the building is fully consumed, the institution either disposes of the facility or pledges a major reinvestment for the building's reconstruction.

A facility might be targeted as nonstrategic for a number of reasons. It might be located at a site that is better suited for an alternative use; the programs housed in the building may be phased out; or eventual modernization of the facility may be economically impractical. Selective deferral includes the establishment of the buildings to be preserved as well as a plan for the nonstrategic buildings once they are no longer usable.

Consolidation and Conversion

A facility may be converted from one use to another for a variety of reasons. Downsizing may reduce the aggregate need for space. Consolidation of the remaining programs frees space for uses that may be strategically important to the institution's mission or that may be treated as surplus space.

A conversion may be the most cost effective alternative for meeting program requirements. For example, it may be less expensive to build or lease new laboratory space rather than renovate a science building constructed 30 or 40 years ago when energy was cheap and building codes were much less restrictive. An older science building might best be converted to meet other needs such as office or classroom uses.

Space may be converted or programs consolidated based on common characteristics of the programs and their compatibility with available space. For example, the computer student lab might be relocated to the library, which normally operates on an extended day, rather than keep the computer science building open and serviced.

Space might be converted to uses unrelated to the mission of the institution to offload operating expenses or generate income. Such uses include research incubators, commercial offices, medical office buildings, health clubs, movie theaters, and retail stores.

Disposal

The demolition of "Old Main," which in the hearts of many alumni and community members may represent the "university," might seem unthinkable. But where is it written that a college or university must keep every structure ever built in perpetuity? Buildings that are no longer owned by an institution do not have to be heated, cleaned, staffed, or maintained. While the renovation of a campus' older buildings may represent an economically attractive alternative to new construction, this is not true for many buildings constructed in the 1960s and 1970s. This period of construction was often marked by the use of materials, energy systems, and designs that may prove more economical to demolish than to keep. While demolition may be the most permanent disposal of a property, other options include sale, sale/leaseback, sale/ground lease, or long-term lease. Divestment is as viable a strategy as is investment.

Although the above alternatives are valid choices, some of these strategies may not be right for a given situation. College X, a small institution that has already instituted extensive sharing of facilities, may find that further consolidation and conversion are not feasible. College Y, a public institution, may be statutorily barred from selling or leasing "public" property. While the two colleges may find that one or more strategies may not be viable, both will probably discover some combination of these or other strategies that will allow them to reshape their facilities mixes in support of both their mission and their revenue streams over the long term. The questions are which strategies are right for a particular institution and how does one go about determining them.

Strategic planning requires increased sophistication in data collection, managerial analysis, risk management, decision-making, and visioning. These management skills are not the most notable attributes of today's higher education management. Given the desire, the higher education leader who genuinely wishes to consider alternatives and to think strategically will not only have to develop these management skills, but will also confront a serious lack of analytical and decision-making tools essential for strategic planning. These needed tools include an accurate and up-to-date inventory of existing space, a realistic appraisal of the value of the institution's buildings, and a complete evaluation of the condition of facilities and their costs to repair or renew. For the cash-strapped college or university, spending money to collect such data will not be viewed as the most prudent use of funds. Even if higher education executives have these needed tools, they will face an even more formidable problem—a poorly defined strategic planning process. A review of the literature turned up few institutional strategic plans, and those that were found often are so general that they could apply to any institution encountering any set of circumstances. Higher education might not have reached the "strategic management stage of development" because leaders have not had to, and perhaps they do not understand how to do it. The problem may be that strategic planning requires a process which is neither well developed nor understood in higher education. A unique planning process that incorporates executive leadership, a new role for an institution's governing board, and the means for an institution to identify and overcome the barriers to effective strategic planning may be required.

THE SOLUTION

The purpose of this article was to focus attention on a significant problem facing colleges

---

Questions About Strategic Facilities Management

Is your institution prepared to make strategic decisions regarding facilities over the next decade? Take this self-test to find out how well you are able to address some critical facility issues.

1. What are your institution's likely requirements for capital funding in the next year? Five years? Ten years?
2. Do the funding agencies (legislatures, foundations, grant makers) believe their capital dollars are spent wisely and most effectively?
3. How will facilities be affected by changes in the methods of program delivery and of technology? How much is this likely to cost?
4. What changes or additions to facilities will be required by fluctuation in the demand for various educational programs? How much will this cost?
5. Which facilities are critical to the institution's long-term viability and success?
6. In a situation of capital rationing, how best should limited capital dollars be spent?
7. What will compliance with present and pending environmental regulations or building codes cost? What is the best strategy for compliance?
8. What is the most cost-effective way to comply with the Americans with Disabilities Act?
9. With limited dollars for capital renewal and for catch-up maintenance, where are these dollars most effectively spent?
10. Which existing space is underutilized and can be reclaimed for more productive uses?
11. Are current space allocation decisions aligned with the institutional vision and program priorities?
12. Will renovation of facilities cost more than new construction?
13. How much and what type of space is needed 10 years from now?
14. To reduce operating expenses, what space or buildings can be disposed of or reused for revenue-producing activities?
15. Which properties adjacent to the campus should be acquired to provide future expansion opportunities or to prevent their use by incompatible activities?
16. Is there a systematic, logical, and financially based methodology to prioritize capital projects? Does it make sense to the governing board, students, faculty, and alumni?
17. What is the most cost-effective way to solve existing facility-related problems? Are there less capital intensive solutions?

The extent to which you have definitive answers to the above questions defines your ability to manage your facilities strategically.

and universities—their leadership's inability to understand, measure, and manage the full financial dimension of higher education's deteriorating infrastructure, and the lack of a process to devise strategies that will help institutions deal with their facilities problem. There are unfortunately very few prescriptions for success to recommend. At the same time, waiting for a "big payday" may not only prove disappointing, but down-right deadly. Higher education leaders can and should develop the tools and processes needed to manage this problem. In this regard, higher education management associations can provide assistance.

APPA and NACUBO's Facilities Administration Committee have concluded that this is a critical issue and believe that the ability of institutions to survive in the 1990s will be in part dependent on how well they manage their physical capital assets. To help institutions in this important area, four distinct subjects require substantive investigation and development. First, the higher education community must understand the extent to which the physical plant may present a potential liability to higher education's long-range stability. Using data that have been collected for the previous deferred maintenance studies, econometric models of higher education finances should be prepared to quantify the financial burden likely to develop over the next two decades as higher education's aging physical plant requires replacement or major repair.

Second, an understanding is needed of what the current state of practice is in the strategic management of facility assets. A review of various institutions' levels of success with strategic management principles, and the degree to which they have led to the development of facilities management strategies, is both necessary and helpful.

Third, higher education management associations need to continue to help institutions develop the tools that are prerequisite to strategy development. Information, provided through publications and seminars, is essential to help institutions develop the following tools: facilities condition audits, space inventory, space utilization, facilities master planning, financial criteria for capital budget decisions, and quality processes such as visioning, mission development, and strategy making.

Fourth, the associations can help lead the effort to integrate the tools and information mentioned above into a process of strategy making for managing facilities. This last step might take the form of a model strategic planning process that institutions could follow.

While the development of a strategic planning process to help colleges and universities make effective decisions about their facilities is not the sole answer to preserving the vitality of the higher education system, it will likely be an essential ingredient to improve overall management. Readers who are interested in participating in any of the aforementioned areas or who have information regarding their institutions' experiences with strategic planning and management should contact the author, or Howard Bell, chair of NACUBO's Facilities Administration Committee and vice president for administrative services at the University of Cincinnati.

CHAPTER 32

PAY AND PERFORMANCE IN THE UNIVERSITY

An Examination of Faculty Salaries

JAMES C. HEARN

James C. Hearn is Professor and Chair, Department of Educational Policy and Administration of the University of Minnesota. His research focuses on organization, policy, and finance in higher education. This paper is a revision of an essay prepared by invitation for the Center of Higher Education Policy Analysis, School of Education, University of Southern California. The author appreciates the research assistance of James Eck and the hlepful comments of Susan Frost, Bill Tierney, and Parker Young.

Faculty salaries are a prominent feature of the reward systems under which academic work is done. Not surprisingly, therefore, they are also becoming a rather prominent element in the recent attention paid to college and university productivity. Among those examining salaries in recent years have been legislators curious over how $100,000 a year professors spend their time, journalists worried about rises in tuition rates, attorneys investigating charges of discrimination in hiring and promotions, and faculty concerned about salary imbalances within and across academic departments. Also increasingly interested in salary structures have been central administrators aiming to manage rising costs. Because faculty salaries are usually the largest single item in academic budgets, they are unquestionably central to the productivity of the enterprise.

The growing internal and external attention to salaries has brought to light the need to develop both conceptualizations and policies in this arena. Too much of the recent attention to the topic has been based on anecdotal and incomplete information. This article, aimed toward providing a more expansive and more balanced perspective, focuses on research universities, the setting in which many of the current controversies over salaries have arisen.

After examining historical patterns and recent salary data, the article explores the tenuous relationship between salaries and performance on campus and approaches to improving postsecondary salary systems. The essay closes with some thoughts on the significance of salaries for leaders seeking more effective academic reward systems.[1] The ultimate goal of the analysis is to help leaders craft salary policies that improve productivity in their institutions.

HISTORICAL PATTERNS IN FACULTY SALARIES IN RESEARCH UNIVERSITIES

For many years, salary issues were relatively invisible in research universities. Analysts rarely studied them, and faculty only rarely complained loudly or mobilized collectively around them

Source: *The Review of Higher Education,* (Summer 1999), Volume. 22, No. 4, pp. 391–410. Copyright © 1999 Association for the Study of Higher Education. All Rights Reserved (ISSN 0162-5748).

(Hansen, 1988b). Even in the context of declines in the 1970s in real and comparative faculty pay (AAUP, 1996b), salaries tended not to be prominent. Faculty labor unions were formed on many other campuses in the 1960s, 1970s, and 1980s but were successfully organized at only a handful of research universities, and university faculties' attitudes toward unionization often depended more on working conditions and job security than on financial concerns (Becker, 1985).

Thus, prior to the 1990s, research universities reflected a distinctive normative legacy concerning faculty salaries. Simply put, that legacy suggested to all concerned that the main rewards of academic life lay beyond mere finances and that, relatedly, faculty salaries were not problematic enough to merit extended policy debate or aggressive mobilization. Citing national survey data, Burton Clark (1987, p. 222) translated this normative legacy into a syllogism which, he argued, represents "the sustaining myth" of academic careers in this country. Paraphrased, Clark's argument is that education is critical to the hopes of humanity and, therefore, the limited material rewards provided by a faculty career are overshadowed by the richness of other kinds of rewards. Support for Clark's inferences comes from a finding that a majority of U.S. research-university faculty in the late 1980s labeled themselves "satisfied" or "very satisfied" with their salaries (U.S. Department of Education, 1990).

Whatever one's views regarding the historical authenticity of Clark's sustaining myth, there are signs that it could be losing some of its hold on faculty and others. While tenured faculty have certainly viewed security and autonomy as valued components of their jobs offsetting any deficits in their compensation (Tierney, 1997), their comfort with existing salary levels and salary policies may decline to the extent that their job security is threatened and their working environment becomes less attractive. For those faculty with nonacademic opportunities, significant improvement in salaries may be needed for retention. Yet dramatic salary gains may be unlikely. It can give faculty no comfort that their salaries are the largest single item on university budgets in a time of growing public scrutiny of those budgets. Policy makers have begun to question traditional assumptions about the performance and pay of faculty, and a variety of observers and analysts have begun to explore alternatives to the ways salaries are currently awarded (Moore & Amey, 1993). The legacy of secrecy, diffidence, and silence may be giving way.

FACULTY SALARIES IN RESEARCH UNIVERSITIES: WHAT CONTEMPORARY DATA SHOW

The 1940 Statement of Principles of the American Association of University Professors [AAUP] noted that tenure is a means not only to academic freedom but also to "a sufficient degree of economic security to make the profession attractive to men and women of ability" (qtd. in AAUP, 1996a). In other words, academic careers on the traditional tenure track should provide sufficient financial rewards to maintain commitment and loyalty. Recent data on twelve characteristics of salary patterns in research universities show mixed success in meeting that goal in the 1990s.

Salaries Relative to Inflation

In the 1990s, the salaries of university faculty are no longer regularly losing ground relative to inflation, as indexed by the Consumer Price Index (CPI). Average salaries are currently at a level roughly equal to that of the early 1970s (AAUP, 1998). In 1997–1998, salary gains of 3.4% doubled the rate of inflation (AAUP, 1998). Recent concerns that the CPI overstates inflation have led some to suggest examining salary trends using a reduced inflation index. When examined using the CPI minus one point, faculty salaries may actually be as much as 15% above their levels in 1972–1973 (AAUP, 1996b). Although overall data of this kind do not illuminate salary variations among individuals, fields, and institutions, there is clearly no sign of a pervasive crisis developing in faculty salaries.

Salaries Relative to Total Income

Faculty's base nine-month academic salaries are not their only sources of potential income. Bowen and Schuster (1986) suggest that faculty earnings fall into four categories: base contract pay for nine months, extra contract pay for 11 or 12 months, extra pay ad hoc for special services such as summer work, and outside earnings from consulting and other services. Among full-time university faculty who have at least some involvement with undergraduate teaching, well under one-half report spending any time at all on consulting or free-lance work, and fewer than one-tenth spend more than four hours a week on such activities (Sax et al., 1996). Base salaries are, therefore, by far the dominant source of income for most faculty.

Salaries Relative to Other Professional Fields

In the last two decades, long-standing salary differences have grown between academics and those in the health professions, law, engineering, and nonacademic science (AAUP, 1998). This deficit in salaries led Linda Bell, lead analyst for the 1997 AAUP report on salaries, to comment that "the large bulk of us do not earn what some of the most poorly paid professionals [in other fields] earn" (qtd. in Magner, 1997, 8).

Differences by Institutional Control

Public and private universities differ in average faculty salaries. Some of these differences are due to distinctive patterns of program offerings, but two patterns are noteworthy. First, salaries are appreciably higher in each faculty rank in the private institutions. Notably, full professors in public doctoral institutions in 1997–1998 earned on average $75,154, while full professors in private doctoral institutions earned on average $95,023 (AAUP, 1998). Second, average faculty salaries have grown more rapidly recently in private institutions. Specifically, salaries grew 66% in the private doctoral sector between 1985–1986 and 1995–1996, while increasing only 52% in the public doctoral sector (AAUP, 1996b).

Field Differences

Two patterns stand Out in recent data on field differences in salary. First, those differences are substantial. Full professors of engineering earned on average about $20,000 more than full professors in education at four-year institutions in 1994–1995 (College and University Personnel Association, 1995). Differences between law or medicine faculty and faculty in the lib-

eral arts are even more striking (Hamermesh, 1988). Second, inequality in salaries among fields seems to lave been growing for decades (Hamermesh, 1988). Over the period 1985–1986 to 1995–1996, the salaries of management faculty in public institutions showed a gain of over 2% a year beyond inflation, while salaries among faculty in foreign languages and literatures barely managed to keep pace with inflation (Tarrant, 1996).

Gender Differences

Women faculty in higher education earn appreciably less than men, regardless of age or the number of hours worked, and there is no indication of any substantive trend since the late 1970s in the relationship of female to male earnings (AAUP, 1996b).[2] The proportions of women faculty have increased overall, and the new entrants have tended to be in the junior ranks, but women's lack of seniority does not seem to play a primary role in their continuing deficit in earnings. The deficit is primarily associated instead with the fact that women are disproportionately located in lower-paying fields without substantial demand outside universities (AAUP, 1997). The relatively few women faculty in business, computer science, and engineering departments tend to be paid far more generously than those in such fields as social work and languages. Nevertheless, within ranks in given fields, there is evidence of gender differences not explainable by other factors (Bellas, 1997).

Racial/Ethnic Differences

There is a striking lack of evidence concerning the relative earnings of different racial/ethnic groups in higher education. Federal and institutional commitments to increasing minority representation on faculties have undoubtedly raised the demand for minority scholars and perhaps put upward pressures on their salaries as well. On the other hand, the number of minority faculty members remains shockingly small (U.S. Department of Education, 1996), and recent evidence suggests that they may still be at some salary disadvantage: Minority faculty salaries in research universities in 1988 averaged over $1,000 less than the average for nonminorities (Fairweather, 1996,

p. 229). Minority faculty may tend to be more junior overall than other faculty and may tend to cluster in lower-paying fields as well; those differences might account for some of the salary deficit.[3] For now, however, it is impossible to draw firm conclusions about relative salaries for similarly situated minorities and nonminorities.

Salary Compression

A significant challenge for academic reward systems is salary compression: the shrinking of inter-rank salary distances due to market conditions. A typical example of compression is the hiring of a junior professor at a salary equal to or above that of a veteran full professor in the same department. In the 1980s salary compression became a significant problem in management, engineering, and some other fields with labor shortages (Tarrant, 1996). Overall, however, the ratio of assistant and associate professors' salaries to full professors' salaries in doctoral institutions remained remarkably steady over the years 1980–1981 to 1996–1997 (AAUP, 1997).

Intersections of Salary Structures with Seniority Distributions

Different fields, institutions, and systems face different seniority structures. In general, a more senior faculty implies higher average salaries and therefore more costs. Changing labor markets and other factors can confound forecasting based on seniority structures. Still, the nation's faculty work force will quite likely grow somewhat younger on average over the next two decades, and average salary outlays per faculty member after inflation are also likely to decline over that period. Faculty hired in the 1960s and 1970s will be retiring in increasing numbers in the coming decade (Hearn & Anderson, 1998). Their departure from the scene will bring changes in the nature of faculty salary distributions. The shape of age-salary profiles is an important factor in budgeting and planning. Just as the aging of the faculty workforce brought higher salaries and higher budgets in the 1980s, the reverse of that trend in the early years of the 21st century may bring some financial savings to institutions, not only through replacement hires at the junior level and the canceling of lines in certain units, but also because part-time, clinical, and non-tenure-track faculty will not receive full salaries and benefit packages.

Intersections of Salary Structures with Faculty Career Stages and Perceived Well-Beings

A national Survey of college faculty found that 75% of the faculty under 35 years old said that personal finances were "somewhat" or "extensively" stressful but that only 46% of those 55–64 and 36% of those over 65 agreed (Sax et al., 1996). Thus, older college faculty view themselves as reasonably secure financially, while younger faculty apparently perceive their financial status as tenuous. It is unclear whether marginally improved salaries alone would significantly ameliorate this perception. The stress may well stem more from the unknowns of the struggle for tenure and promotion than from the inadequacies of current salaries. Still, there is little question that financial matters, whether writ large (long-term financial prospects) or small (current salaries and assets), are quite salient in the personal lives of young faculty.

What Determines Salaries?

Fairweather (1996) found in a 1988 national faculty sample that four nonbehavioral factors positively affected faculty salaries in research universities: rank, being in a private institution, being male, and being in a high-paying field. Fairweather also found several behavioral factors influential, including classroom hours, teaching only graduate students, and publications output. These findings generally match those of earlier studies in research universities (see, for example, Fox, 1985).

Of course, the academic labor market is highly differentiated, largely on the basis of academic disciplines. Fairweather (1996), for example, found that publications played a notably larger role in salaries in the health sciences and business fields than in the humanities. Earlier, Smart and McLaughlin (1978) concluded that fields varied so substantially in the factors critical to their individual faculty's salaries that attempts to identify singular "institutional reward structures" were seriously misguided.

What Do Salaries Determine?

Salaries are a major budget item, so they certainly affect research institutions' financial health, but there is no evidence that salaries strongly affect the attitudes and performance of faculty at those institutions. Beyond a certain minimal standard, salaries as elements in the professional lives of faculty seem to be secondary to rank, tenure, recognition by peers, publications, and working conditions (McKeachie, 1979).

Yet salaries are not trivial to faculty. For one thing, they are tangible. Unlike tenure or promotions, salary changes are an annual event, and dealing with a paycheck is a monthly or biweekly event. More importantly, salary gains may be emphasized on a symbolic level by faculty as legitimation and recognition of their worth to their home institution (Tuckman, 1976). In that vein, *relative* salary and raises can affect a faculty member's attitudes and performance (McKeachie, 1979). The importance of relative pay is heightened by its endurance: Salary differences tend to persist because salary adjustments in the U.S. university tend to be small and incremental (Hansen, 1988a).

The evidence on the importance of salaries to faculty and to institutions clearly merits more consideration. The heart of the question, both conceptually and from a policy perspective, is the connection between salaries and productivity. Do salaries reflect performance? How? In the following section, these questions are explored in more detail.

SALARY STRUCTURES AND FACULTY PERFORMANCE: A TENUOUS RELATIONSHIP

In a number of ways, the salary structures of research universities confound the core tenets of both normative equity theory and neoclassical labor-market theory. I explore some of these contradictions in this section in the context of two theories, introduced with special attention to their connections to performance and productivity issues.[4]

Equity theory is a value-based, prescriptive perspective. In its most familiar form, it is descended from the classic Aristotelian view that equity in organizations or social groups is achieved through proportionality, or at least ordinal consistency. This view translates, in part, into the tenet that organizations should pursue both "horizontal" and "vertical" equity in the ways they treat their employees. Horizontal equity is exhibited by rewarding those of equal worth to an organization equally. Vertical equity is exhibited by rewarding people of greater worth to an organization more generously than those of less worth to the organization. In both domains, organizational worth is the sole criterion for rewards. Factors irrelevant to organizational performance should be irrelevant to organizational rewards.

In contrast to equity theory, neoclassical labor-market theory is descriptive rather than prescriptive. In its usual form, it suggests that in competitive environments, salaries will be tightly connected to the marginal productivity of labor. That is, workers will be paid an amount approximating their contribution to the firm's output: The stronger the worker's performance, the more he or she is to be rewarded financially (Freeman, 1979; Beaumont, 1985). An underpaid worker will move to another competitive organization. Traditional versions of neoclassical labor-market theory would add that those performing a particular set of tasks within an organization (e.g., in a university, teaching, researching, and performing service) would face a rather homogenous external labor market determining the going price of their labor (i.e., salaries). Less traditional versions of the theory recognize more variation in external and internal labor markets.

Common to both equity theory and neoclassical labor-market theory is the notion that salary and performance in an organization should be tightly connected. No one would suggest that these theories' ideal-type notions of the salary/performance relationship fully fit any one actual organization or any set of actual organizations, and few would agree with every one of the theories' implications for university policy. Still, the theories do have philosophical appeal and do seem to be violated by higher education's salary structures. Exploring those violations may contribute to productive dialogue and policy development. Seven areas of disjunction in salaries and performance may deserve particular attention.

Organizational Ambiguities in the Enterprise

Academic organizations—especially research universities—differ from the profit-seeking firms depicted in classical labor-market theories in a number of ways. For one, organizational goals tend to be contested, multiple, and ambiguous. Units in the organization may dissent on what the institution is "all about," and these disagreements are resolved through the acceptance of diverse, often vaguely phrased goals. The differences surrounding goals can also extend to the individual level. To a greater extent than classical theories would predict, faculty may be motivated by nonpecuniary factors only loosely connected to the interests of their home institutions. Relatedly, the technology for achieving goals tends to be unclear in universities. Modes of instruction are extremely varied; and admissions standards, grading standards, curricular design, graduation requirements, and the like are hotly debated. Finally, decision-making authority tends to be diffuse. Notably, who is really in charge of a given domain on campus is not always predictable from an organizational chart, and seemingly parallel or linked units and individuals; may in fact rarely be in contact. These notions are central to organization theorists' focus on "loose coupling" and "anarchic" qualities in higher education (Birnbaum, 1988). In such a setting, those theorists assert, there are multiple individual and organizational definitions of "success," as well as multiple perceptions of how success might be measured. Obviously, these ambiguities will affect locally operational definitions of marginal productivity.

Of particular importance is the existence of multiple products of faculty labor. Beaumont (1985) and others have questioned the relevance of labor-market theories to higher education on the grounds that, in a multiproduct service arena like higher education, labor input and output cannot be precisely quantified. Without such quantification, markets cannot rely on clear-cut assessments of productivity and therefore cannot sort the supply and demand of labor efficiently.

For our purposes, these conclusions by economists and organizational analysts boil down to a convincing litany of doubts about the likelihood of ever determining appropriate levels of compensation in higher education, either from the perspective of equity theory (in determining what is fair, how does one weigh contributions to different kinds of goals?) or from the perspective of labor-market theory (what is marginal productivity in a context of shifting, debatable institutional priorities?).

Within-Unit Salary Dislocations Based on Time of Hire

In some university units, faculty hired more recently receive salaries starkly different from comparable faculty hired in earlier years because of the rising or falling demand for their services in other institutions or organizations. The phenomenon of widely differing salaries for faculty of similar productivity within academic units clearly involves a violation of horizontal equity, i.e., the notion that those doing similar things similarly well should be paid similarly. In general, when rank and other confounding factors are controlled, recent hires are paid more (Webster, 1995), but the opposite pattern has arisen recently in medical schools (Mangan, 1996). While this pattern is no doubt partially caused by real merit differences, the pattern surely also reflects conditions unrelated to performance.

Across-Unit Salary Dislocations Based in Differences in Fields' Internal and External Markets

Like the preceding phenomenon, the phenomenon of widely differing salaries for faculty of similar rank and productivity across academic units involves a violation of horizontal equity. Here, however, the tenet being violated is that those doing similar things similarly well in various parts of the campus should be paid similarly. External markets, and some internal dynamics, have produced salary profiles varying notably by academic units. Differential performance does not seem to explain these variations. Faculty in some areas are simply paid more than similarly performing faculty elsewhere on campus. If one adopts the restrictions of traditional neoclassical theory, defining productivity uniformly across units, the higher salaries of some professors relative to other professionally comparable professors makes no sense. Clearly, there is no single internal or external marketplace for university professors. Instead, fields differ not only in the ways they evaluate productivity but also in the external labor markets they face.

Distinctively Different Salaries for Women

The fact that men and women of comparable abilities, performance, and other characteristics are sometimes rewarded differentially is an archetypal example of horizontal inequity. In an official policy statement based on a research review, the American Association of University Professors (1992) combines equity theory and labor-market theory to suggest that some differences in salaries between men and women are legitimate but that others may very well not be. The association argues further that, within departments, the assignment of tasks tends to be gender-based and tends to disadvantage women in salary contests. Such subtleties often are ignored in analyses of gender inequities. If gender is irrelevant to faculty members' productive capacity, then our focal theories would suggest it should also be irrelevant in the determination of their salaries. Such seems not to be the case.

Moderately Flat Salary Structures Across Fields

Although there are, as noted above, clear differences in salary levels across fields, these differences are not so great as those in the nonacademic world, according to a number of economists (e.g., see Freeman, 1979). If academic salaries fully reflected external markets, the range would be far greater than it really is. In actuality, the potential salary differences are apparently muted by academe's internal values and norms (Freeman, 1979; Bowen & Schuster, 1986). This middling level of by-field variation constitutes a violation of not only the strict labor-market theory assumption that faculty operate in one labor market with consistent definitions of productivity and value but also the more relaxed assumption of other versions of the theory that, if differential salaries by field exist, differences in salaries will *fully* reflect differential market valuations by field. In other words, the existence of a moderate level of salary dispersion across fields may be what is least expected by labor-market theory, but that is precisely what we find in higher education.

As usual, realities are somewhat more complex than ideal-type theories suggest.

Uniform Salary Increments

In many institutions and academic units, salary increments are awarded "across-the-board," i.e., all faculty receive essentially the same percentage raises (Hansen, 1988a). Bowen and Schuster (1986) defend the use of the across-the-board approach on the basis of its low costs (largely avoiding individualized assessments) and its benefits in preserving collegiality and the special nature of higher education. Whether one likes across-the-board raises or not, they clearly involve some significant deviations from equity and labor-market theories. From those perspectives, choosing to adopt the across-the-board approach means choosing to ignore individual and unit differences in performance and thus differences in worth to the institution. Inequities and inefficiencies emerge; and simply put, the connection between salary and productivity is compromised (Becker & Lewis, 1979).

The "Annuity Feature" of Salaries

Regardless of whether a salary system awards raises across-the-board or is more merit-centered, annual salary adjustments in universities are usually awarded on the basis of percentages rather than raw dollar amounts, awards are usually made independently of the base dollar salary, and large individual salary changes from year to year are discouraged (Hansen, 1988a). Effectively, these norms have meant limiting salary raises for most faculty to a small percentage range (usually 2 to 6%). These policies tend to prevent higher-performing, lower-paid faculty from gaining much on lower-performing, higher-paid faculty.

For example, there is rarely any formal consideration of the fact that a 3% raise for a faculty member earning $75,000 is $2,250, while for a faculty member earning $30,000 the same raise is only $900. Even under a strongly merit-centered system, a 3% merit raise for the higher-earning faculty member of the example would provide a greater raise in dollar terms than a 7% merit raise for the lower-earning faculty member. Ultimately, the nation's progressive income-tax system will even this score somewhat in take-home pay, but the fact remains that the poorly performing but higher-paid faculty member would lose little if any economic ground to the high-performing but poorly paid faculty member. Under the normal ranges of faculty salary increments, it would take many years for the latter to catch up with the former, if indeed she ever did.

This phenomenon is an aspect of what is sometimes called the "annuity feature" of faculty salaries: Early salary advantages tend to dissipate very slowly if at all, even in the face of superior performance by others. Under the annuity feature, initial salaries are crucial for future salaries, so dramatic salary advancement for faculty at any rank often depends upon a willingness to leave after obtaining a high initial salary offer elsewhere or at least upon the willingness of an employing institution to match a higher salary offer obtained elsewhere. The great majority of faculty have no outside offers; so for them, initial salaries continue to exert their ancestral holds on later salaries throughout the course of employment at an institution.

If initial salary differences are based in inequities (e.g., gender-based discrimination in salaries), the implications of the annuity feature are even more troubling. Lower initial salaries propel lower savings as well as lower contributions to pension funds. Year after year, the funds lost through unjustified salary deficits could have been compounding in a disadvantaged employee's investment account. Unjustly absent institutional matching funds for pensions could have been compounding as well. Therefore, simply equalizing annual pay for a disadvantaged group at some career midpoint falls far short of truly evening the score. What is more, if unfairly low salaries are allowed to persist unameliorated throughout a working career, their effects do not end with the end of employment: they also can eventually lead to lower retirement benefits.

The annuity feature of academic pay contradicts the theoretical notions that salary changes should be tied closely to merit in both percentage and dollar terms and that existing salaries should reflect current rather than past worth to the organization. Academic compensation systems that add merit pay to base salaries in small percentage increments allow inequities to persist and sometimes grow. Faculty who have long ceased being top perform-

ers tend to have few outside offers, so they remain on campus where they continue to reap the financial advantages of their earlier successes. In contrast, unless special institutional funds are available for making strong counter-offers to faculty being wooed to go elsewhere, high performers who arrived early in their careers may be recruited away by those who can pay salaries better approximating their current worth on the marketplace. Institutional effectiveness and efficiency thereby suffer.

Unfortunately, these fundamental problems are not easily solved. Alternatives to the annuity feature tend to be unattractive and tend themselves to be inconsistent with equity and labor-market theories. For example, awarding lower merit raises (in dollar or percentage terms) to those with higher salaries in a unit, simply on the *a priori* basis of their initial salaries, seems contrary to the spirit of matching salary and current performance. Given the legal and cultural constraints on university salary policies, fully satisfying solutions to the problems generated by the annuity feature may not exist.

IMPROVING SALARY STRUCTURES IN RESEARCH UNIVERSITIES

Salary structures in research universities frustrate simple explanations and simple solutions. Those interested in more closely linking salaries and performance face daunting challenges. Institutions must develop both overarching principles on which their salary structures may be evaluated and specific salary policies based in those principles.

Evaluating Faculty Salary Structures

Institutions need to consider broad criteria on which any salary system, whether current or planned, should be judged. Eight such criteria may be suggested here. First, is the system efficient? That is, does it devote an appropriate level of time and other resources to training, communication, and oversight? Second, are the procedures for salary determination equitable? Do affected parties have a role in the process, for example? Third, are the outcomes equitable for those in different fields, for those suffering from the effects of salary compression, for women, and for racial/ethnic minorities?

Fourth, is the system well understood on campus and, as necessary, beyond the campus? Fifth, does the system allow adequate flexibility for responding to crises and special cases? Sixth, does the system fit with the strategic initiatives, management approach, and organizational culture of the campus? Seventh, does the system make sense from an internal political perspective? That is, does it balance the interests of various parties on campus and reflect current political realities there? Eighth, is the system assessed and evaluated regularly?[5]

Of course, these eight criteria must necessarily be weighted and adapted in particular ways at any given institution. Doing so is not always easy. Judging how well a salary structure deals with questions of salary equity for women faculty can be especially complex and may expose conflicts among the criteria.[6] For example, the route to equitable salaries for women may not be entirely compatible with participatory decision making in certain units, if gender equity is not valued in those units. Relatedly, the costs of achieving salary equity may be greater than some are willing to accept from an efficiency perspective. One of the most difficult salary-related challenges for leaders in academic settings is operationally defining outcome equity, procedural equity, and efficiency and then determining appropriate trade-off's among these three desired outcomes.[7] In the end, the question of judging salary systems becomes thickly intertwined with institutional culture and individual values.

Policy Choices

Specific policy recommendations are rarely appropriate for every institution and, not surprisingly, there are no discernible "silver bullets" for those interested in salary policy. Effective policy development can take place only after detailed review of relevant data and literature, and only after tailoring the results of that review to particular campus circumstances. Still, it may be useful to highlight a few of the more prominent policy choices facing contemporary leaders.[8]

Choice 1: Deemphasizing the External Marketplace
A fundamental aspect of salary policy is the choice of an underlying strategic stance regarding the role of the external marketplace in faculty salary structures. A number of the issues we have discussed in this essay (including salary compression within fields, salary dispersion across fields, gender differences in salaries, and the willingness to make sizable retention counter-offers to current faculty being recruited by other institutions) involve dislocations driven by external markets. Some institutions may choose to deemphasize the influences of the external marketplace. The argument for deemphasizing the market holds that institutions cannot and should not respond aggressively to changes in the marketplace, maintaining instead a more locally determined and presumably more egalitarian approach to salaries. Other institutions may be willing to allow external markets to more directly shape their salary structures. With that choice comes a willingness to accept sizable differences in salaries for individuals in different academic fields (and, in concert, the probability of substantial gender differences in salaries on campus).

Choice 2: Adopting the "Core-Salary" Approach.
In response to growing financial pressures, some institutional leaders have proposed a radically new approach: breaking up the traditional base salary into a stable "core" component and a second component that is "flexible" or "at risk" (see Mangan, 1996). That is, a professor's current and future salaries are unbundled into a foundational component guaranteed year to year and a supplemental component based in research or clinical revenues generated in the current year. Institutions have historically not been allowed to reduce the salaries of individual tenured faculty members without the due process guaranteed by tenure. Operationally, this has meant that even clearly justified efforts at salary reductions have required lengthy hearings and appeals and have often been abandoned. The core-salary approach, if upheld by the courts, would mark the end of this traditional form of financial security for faculty. Individual salaries could be reduced far more easily, facilitating institutional flexibility but perhaps also threatening professors' sense of community and well-being.

Choice 3: Tying Annual Salary Changes More Directly to Annual Performance
In classic economic theory, efficient salary systems allow downward as well as upward movement in individual salaries, in proportion-

ate response to variations in employee performance (i.e., worth to the organization). As noted above, however, universities rarely pursue salary reductions, even when the marketplace suggests them. Beyond the legal challenges lie potentially unpalatable results: Any system tightly aligning pay with performance can create wide salary advantages for those performing well. Such differentiation goes against traditional preferences for rather flat salary profiles. In short, efficiency in salary systems can means dispersion in salary levels, and institutions have to decide whether, for them, that dispersion means unacceptable discomfort.

Choice 4: Standardizing Salaries in Association with Career Ladders

Most faculty work under the contract salary system, in which each faculty member negotiates a salary individually with a representative of the employing institution, usually the head of the home academic unit. A contrasting system is used in the military, government, K-12 education, and a few state systems of higher education: the standardized salary schedule (Beaumont, 1985). Such systems, when used in higher education, offer a single, officially specified salary for each academic rank and, usually, a standard time-in-step salary increase. This approach imposes highly elaborated procedures and a regulated chain of command on salary determinations. The appearance of rigor may help protect such systems against internal disputes and legal challenges. Also, because standardized systems employ straightforward formulaic procedures for salary adjustments, they are often viewed as relatively inexpensive. Such systems can decouple salaries and performance, however, and thus are arguably inefficient as strategic human-resource management tools (Becker & Lewis, 1979).

Choice 5: Decoupling Merit Evaluation for Salary Increases and Faculty Development Efforts

Administrators often seek to reward productive faculty with merit-based salary raises and to improve faculty productivity through individually tailored development efforts. Both of these activities can involve peer observation, self-reporting, and the compilation of documentary evidence on faculty performance. Unfortunately, faculty's incentive to do well in salary evaluations can come into conflict with their incentive to improve their teaching, research, or service. That is, while the most desirable attitude toward faculty-development efforts is a willingness to expose one's own weaknesses for evaluation by others in the interest of improvement, the understandable attitude toward salary determinations is to present oneself in the best possible light in the interest of higher pay. In terms of evaluation research, one process (salary determination) is summative, while the other (faculty development) is formative. When units confound the two processes, the potential for true faculty improvement may suffer. Decoupling the two processes makes sense but seems easier said than done.

Choice 6: Pursuing Internal Consistency in the Determination of Salaries

Many analysts (e.g., Clark, 1987) have observed that flexibility and decentralization contribute to institutional effectiveness. Nevertheless, salary determination may well be an issue requiring aggressive central attention. When there is substantial across-unit and across-time variation in criteria and processes for salary advancement, women, minorities, and others may be disadvantaged (Lee, 1989). Still, some flexibility in reward systems is necessary. Disciplines differ in their markers of scholarly success, and institutions should be wary of forcing one model unbendingly onto all fields. Importantly, administrators should allow enough variation in departments' specific criteria for raises to ensure that distinctive, strategically defensible departmental goals need not be abandoned in order to follow centralized institutional guidelines.

Choice 7: Welcoming Faculty Participation in Determination of Merit-Based Salary Increases

There are benefits to a relatively democratic approach to awarding merit salary increases. When unit faculty are represented in the determination of salary changes, decisions can be consensually legitimated, decision quality may be improved, and administrators may be better protected from charges of favoritism. An elected departmental salary-advisory committee, for example, might buffer a merit-based system from charges of discrimination and lessen legal vulnerability. On the other hand, elected committees may not always reflect the core values of central or unit administrators.

They may produce decisions which are more politically driven or more protective of certain interests or people than would be organizationally desirable from a purely strategic or purely economic perspective. What is more, privacy concerns can arise in some circumstances. In the end, the use of faculty participation in salary determination seems an approach best used contingently and cautiously.

Choice 8: Facilitating Public Scrutiny of Salaries

The public visibility and accessibility of salary information varies appreciably by unit and by institution. Often, leaders are concerned that information about relative salary levels can lead to dissatisfaction (see AAUP, 1992). It is somewhat uncomfortable to argue, however, in a setting driven by democratic and scientific ideals, that professionals benefit from being deprived of information, especially information about something so fundamental. Institutions may at least wish to consider making salary data more available to interested internal and external observers.

Choice 9: Elevating Teaching and Public Service as Criteria for Salary Adjustments

Recent years have brought some reconsideration of the primacy of research in university life (Rice, 1996). Beyond the philosophical rationale for such a move lies some pragmatic reasoning. Societal and political pressures on higher education are trending toward more attention to teaching and service (Rice, 1996). Also, retention-minded administrators may have some practical interest in elevating teaching, which allows faculty less bargaining power in external academic labor markets. Nevertheless, it is unclear how well internal and external authorities will be able to succeed in elevating teaching and service through salary reforms. The research-oriented organizational culture may be highly resistant to change.

CONCLUSIONS

Salaries are only one piece in a mosaic of elements comprising the environment for faculty productivity. More fundamental than the adoption of any of the specific policies and evaluation criteria introduced above is the thoughtful consideration of broader institutional values and strategy. What are the most important equity, effectiveness, and efficiency issues on this campus? What kinds of financial and nonfinancial solutions are most acceptable? What should be the driving principles behind an institution's faculty reward systems, as they relate not only to salary but also to tenure, promotion, and other rewards? How should the institution's mission and core culture shape reward systems?

Only in this wider context is the recent increase in public, legislative, and administrative attention to salaries justifiable, and only in this context can effective salary policy be developed. Alone, salaries are neither the most important motivators for faculty in research universities nor the most uplifting of topics for those who view academe through a transformative lens. A single-minded focus on reforming salary policy alone, without consideration of its place in larger institutional concerns, makes little sense.

Yet a single-minded focus on reforming faculty reward systems without close attention to salaries makes equally poor sense. To ignore salaries is to ignore not only a critical factor in institutional budgets and a central element in public critiques of higher education but also a noteworthy element in professors' feelings of satisfaction and productivity. Indeed, from an administrative perspective, salaries have the advantage of relative concreteness compared to the other factors in the motivational context surrounding professors. An academic leader may find it virtually impossible to learn about, much less influence, the scholarly work schedule or interests of a tenured professor, but he or she *can* change, with relative ease, the ways in which that professor is financially rewarded. Here, at least *marginal* administrative influence on senior faculty performance seems possible. Salaries may be secondary to other factors in the reward context affecting senior professors, but they tend to be notably more measurable and manipulable than those other factors.

The problems in faculty salaries are significant. The opportunities for developing more effective salary policies are real. Salaries' potential as a lever for changing faculty behavior is perhaps more significant than many observers realize. Institutions' futures are highly dependent on their salary structures. In those four simple observations lies ample reason for academic leaders to focus energetically on the topic.

NOTES

1. Because of space limitations, the paper does not consider at any length elements of faculty compensation beyond the standard academic contract, questions relating to faculty unions and collective bargaining, or the salaries of part-time faculty, graduate-student instructors, clinical faculty, and adjunct faculty.

2. The absence of change in overall female/male earnings ratios does not necessarily imply that there have been no improvements in the equity of hiring or remuneration processes in individual cases.

3. Some tentative evidence is available. In a multivariate study using national data, Fairweather (1996) found that minority status was unrelated to salaries in research and doctoral institutions.

4. Obviously, only caricatures of those theories can be presented here. I encourage readers to follow the citations to analysts who have studied the issues in more depth.

5. See Becker and Lewis (1979) and Moore and Amey (1993) for useful examinations of some of these issues.

6. Noting these difficulties, the Commission on Women of the American Council on Education suggests that the criteria for salary decisions, the process for making decisions, and actual salaries should be matters of public record, that all new employees should be informed about how salaries are determined, that institutions should conduct and act aggressively upon salary-equity reviews, and that campuses should establish mechanisms to ensure that the principle of equal pay is incorporated in each round of salary decisions (Moses, 1996).

7. The difficulty of determining amounts for gender equity salary increments is a prominent example.

8. Others have also explored these choices productively. For especially useful discussions, see Becker and Lewis (1979); Fox (1985); Bowen and Schuster (1986); Hansen (1988a, 1988b); and Moore and Amey (1993).

REFERENCES

AAUP. American Association of University Professors. (1992, July–August). Salary-setting practices that unfairly disadvantage women faculty. *Academe, 78*(4), 32–35.

American Association of University Professors. (1996a, January-February). Tenure in the medical school. *Academe, 82*(1), 40–45.

American Association of University Professors. (1996b, March–April). Not so bad. *Academe, 82*(2), 14–22.

American Association of University Professors. (1997, March–April). Not so good. *Academe, 83*(2), 12–88.

American Association of University Professors. (1998, March–April). *Doing better*. Washington, DC: AAUP.

Beaumont, M. S. (1985). *Salary systems in public higher education: A microeconomic analysis*. New York: Praeger.

Becker, W. E. (1985). Maintaining faculty vitality through collective bargaining. In S. M. Clark & D. R. Lewis. (Eds.), *Faculty vitality and institutional productivity: Critical perspectives for higher education* (pp. 198–223). New York City: Teachers College Press.

Becker, W. E., & Lewis, D. R. (1979). Adaptability to change and academic productivity. In D.R. Lewis & W. E. Becker, *Academic rewards in higher education* (pp. 299–312). Cambridge, MA: Ballinger.

Bellas, M. L. (1997). Disciplinary differences in faculty salaries: Does gender bias play a role? *Journal of higher education, 68*(3), 299–321.

Birnbaum, R. (1988). *How colleges work*. San Francisco: Jossey-Bass.

Bowen, H. R, & Schuster, J. (1986). *American professors: A national resource imperiled*. New York: Oxford University Press.

Clark, Burton R. (1987). *The academic life: Small worlds, different worlds*. Princeton: Carnegie Foundation for the Advancement of Teaching.

College and University Personnel Association. (1995). *National faculty salary survey by discipline and rank in public colleges and universities*. Washington, DC: College and University Personnel Association.

Fairweather, J. S. (1996). *Faculty work and public trust: Restoring the value of teaching and public service in American academic life*. Needham Heights, MA: Allyn and Bacon.

Fox, M. F. (1985). Publication, performance, and reward in science and scholarship. In J. C. Smart (Ed.), *Higher education: Handbook of theory and research, Vol. 1* (pp. 255–282). New York: Agathon.

Freeman, Richard B. (1979). The job market for college faculty. In D. R. Lewis and W. E. Becker (Eds.), *Academic rewards in higher education* (pp. 63–103). Cambridge, MA: Ballinger.

Hamermesh, D. S. (1988). Salaries: Disciplinary differences and rank injustices. *Academe, 74*(3), 20–24.

Hansen, L. (1988a). Merit pay in structured and unstructured salary systems. *Academe, 74*(6), 10–13.

Hansen, L. (1988b). Merit pay in higher education. In D. W. Breneman and T. I. K. Youn (Eds.), *Academic labor markets and careers* (pp. 114–137). New York: Taylor and Francis.

Hearn, J. C., & Anderson, M. S. (1998). Faculty demography: Exploring the effects of seniority distributions in universities. In J. C. Smart (Ed.), *Higher education: Handbook of theory and research, Vol. 13* (pp. 235–273). New York: Agathon.

Lee, B. A. (1989). Academic personnel policies and practices: Managing the process. In G. G. Lozier & M. J. Dooris (Eds.), *New directions for institutional research.* No. 63: Managing Faculty Resources, pp. 3–18.

Magner, D. K. (1997, July 3). Increases in faculty salaries fail to keep pace with inflation. *Chronicle of higher education,* p. A8.

Mangan, K. S. (1996, July 26). Medical schools are reining in the salaries of faculty members. *Chronicle of higher education,* pp. A16, 18.

McKeachie, W. J. (1979). Perspectives from psychology: Financial incentives are ineffective for faculty. In D. R. Lewis and W. E. Becker (Eds.), *Academic rewards in higher education* (pp. 3–20). Cambridge, MA: Ballinger.

Moore, K. M., & Amey, M. J. (1993). *Making sense of the dollars: The costs and uses of faculty compensation.* ASHE-ERIC Higher Education Report No. 5. Washington, DC: George Washington University.

Moses, Y. (1996, December 12). Salaries in academe: The gender gap persists. *Chronicle of higher education,* p. A60.

Rice, R. E. (1996). *Making a place for the new American scholar.* Inquiry #1 of the Working Paper Series of "New Pathways: Faculty Careers and Employment for the 21st Century," a project of the American Association for Higher Education.

Sax, L., Astin, A., Arredondo, M., & Korn, W. (1996, September*). The American college teacher: National norms for the 1995–96 HERI faculty survey,* Los Angeles: Higher Education Research Institute, UCLA.

Smart, J. C., & McLaughlin, G. W. (1978). Reward structures in academic disciplines. *Research in higher education, 8,* 39–55.

Tarrant, L. L. (1996, October). *Ten-year trends for average faculty salaries.* Paper presented at the annual meeting of the Southern Association of Institutional Research and the Society for College and University planning, Mobile, AL.

Tierney, W. (1997). Tenure and community in academe. *Educational researcher, 26*(8), 17–23.

Tuckman, H. P. (1976). *Publication, teaching, and the academic reward structure.* Lexington, MA: Lexington Books.

CHAPTER 33

BENEFIT AND RETIREMENT ISSUES IN HIGHER EDUCATION

JAY L. CHRONISTER

The 1990s have been, and will continue to be, a decade of change for higher education. Among the volatile issues that institutions have been forced to address are age and cost factors directly related to faculty and staff. This chapter addresses major retirement and benefit trends and issues that colleges and universities are currently facing. Also, many of the same problems are applicable to other professional staff and nonprofessional staff of the institutions. However, before discussing these issues, it is important to place them in a historical context.

In the 1960s, higher education grew at a significant rate to accommodate the post World War II baby boom. The burgeoning college age population and a social policy that placed emphasis on providing access to postsecondary education led to major increases in the number and size of colleges and universities. According to the National Center for Education Statistics (NCES; 1994a), between 1960 and 1970, enrollments increased from 3.6 million to 8.6 million students (p. 174), and the number of institutions increased from 2,004 to 2,556 (p. 242). One result of this growth in the number of students and institutions was that the number of full-time faculty increased from about 154,000 in 1960 to approximately 369,000 in 1970 (NCES, 1979, p. 104). By 1992–1993, there were 885,796 faculty in higher education, of whom 593,941 were full-time (NCES, 1994c, pp. 9–10).

AGING OF THE FACULTY

The faculty hired during the growth years of the 1960s were a significant portion of the faculty with which higher education entered the decade of the 1990s. In 1977–1978, nearly 17% of the professoriate was age 55 or older, with 2% age 65 or older (National Education Association, 1979, p. 7). By 1987–1988, the percentage of full-time faculty age 55 and older had increased to 25%, with 4% age 65 or older (NCES, 1990, p. 9). Data from the 1993 National Study of Postsecondary Faculty indicate that 26% of the faculty was age 55 or older that year, with 4% age 65 or older, including about 1% age 70 or older (NCES, 1993).

Table 3.1 provides a comparison of the distribution of the ages of full-time faculty and staff between 1987–1988 and 1992–1993. The data in this table reflect the aging trend that has gained increased attention from higher education policy makers. Key points in the table are the decline of faculty under age 35 and between ages 35 and 44 and the increases in the percentage of those over age 45.

Source: *A Struggle to Survive: Funding Higher Education in the Next Century*, 1995, D.S. Honeyman, J.L. Wattenberger & K.C. Westbrook (eds.), Corwin Press.

TABLE 33.1
Age Distribution of Full-Time Instructional Faculty and Staff: Fall 1987 and Fall 1992 (in percentages)

Age	Fall 1987	Fall 1992
Under 35	10.2	7.9
35–44	31.6	28.8
45–54	34.1	37.1
55–59	11.7	13.1
60–64	8.6	8.7
65–69	3.3	3.4
70 and older	0.5	1.0

Source: U.S. Department of Education, National Center for Education Statistics, "1988 National Study of Postsecondary Faculty" and "1993 National Study of Postsecondary Faculty."

The combination of the aging professoriate, constrained financial resources, and the passage of the 1986 amendments to the Age Discrimination in Employment Act (ADEA), which abolished mandatory retirement by reason of age, raised several questions for higher education. Although there was an exemption in the legislation that permitted institutions to retain a mandatory retirement age for tenured faculty until January 1, 1994, there was a concern that without a mandatory retirement age, many faculty would remain with institutions well beyond their productive years and create both academic and financial problems. A 1991 report from the National Research Council concluded that at most institutions few tenured faculty would work beyond age 70, while the possible exception of research universities that had a large proportion of faculty working up to the mandatory retirement age prior to passage of the 1986 amendments to the ADEA (Hammond & Morgan, 1991, p. 2).

Recent reports appear to confirm the conclusions reached by the National Research Council study. *Campus Trends,* 1995 (El-Khawas, 1995, p. 47) reports that between 1993–1994 and 1994–1995, 19% of all institutions reported a net gain in faculty age 65 and over, 65% reported no change, and 16% cited a net loss. When queried as to changes in faculty age 70 and over, 11% cited net gains, 80% indicated no change, and 9% stated they had a net loss. It is the disaggregation of data by type and control of institution where important distinctions arise. Whereas 7% of public institutions reported a net gain in faculty over 70, 18% of all independent institutions

reported a net gain. Distinctions are also evident by type of institution in that 41% of independent research/doctoral universities cited a net gain in faculty age 70 or older, whereas only 16% of the public research/doctoral institutions reported such a gain.

Emphasis on the total number of faculty and the age distribution of those faculty should not obscure the fact that many of the issues for institutions that relate to faculty age, retirement actions, and benefit costs may also be attributable to other professional staff and nonprofessional personnel. Faculty account for about 50% of the professional staff on college and university campuses and about 33% of the total staff. For example, colleges and universities employed approximately 2.6 million individuals in the fall 1991, of whom 1.6 million (62.7%) were professional staff and 950,000 (37.3%) were nonprofessional. Full-time and part-time faculty made up 826,000 (51.6%) of the professional staff (NCES, 1994a, p. 228).

Aging of the professoriate has important implications for higher education for a variety of reasons. An aging faculty is an expensive faculty in terms of salary and total compensation. Using academic rank as a general proxy for age, data from 1993–1994 provide insight into the implications of age/rank for salaries. In 1993–1994, the average salaries for full-time faculty on 9-month appointments were as follows: professors, $60,649; associate professors, $45,278; assistant professors, $37,630; instructors, $28,828; and lecturers, $32,729 (NCES, 1994b). Data derived from the 1993 National Study of Postsecondary Faculty indicate that full-time faculty were distributed across ranks as follows: professors, 30.6%; associate professors, 23.5%; assistant professors, 23.4%; instructors, 13.9%; lecturers, 2.2%; and other, 6.4%. Of all full-time faculty, 26% were age 55 and older, including 48% of the professors and 21% of the associate professors, and nearly 80% of those age 55 and older were tenured (NCES, 1993). It is evident from these data that senior faculty, in terms of age, rank, and tenure status, account for a sizable portion of faculty compensation expenditures and reduce the financial flexibility of institutions as increasing proportions of the faculty reach the higher age classification.

FRINGE BENEFITS

Fringe benefits are an important part of institutional budgets and a significant part of the compensation package for faculty and staff. Most benefit packages provide financial protection for faculty and staff during employment years and address financial concerns of the retirement years. For example, health insurance plans substitute known and regular payments to cover unknown and potentially significant expenses that may arise from medical problems, whereas life insurance and disability insurance provide financial security during employment years. Social Security, pension plans, and, at some institutions, subsidized health insurance coverage provide financial security during the retirement years. Benefit plans provided to faculty and staff vary considerably by type and control of institution and by employee status within institutions (Chronister, 1995).

There are three general classifications of benefits: statutory, voluntary, and support. Statutory benefits are required by law and include Worker's Compensation, Unemployment Compensation, and Social Security. Voluntary benefits are those the institution chooses to offer, or that may be specified in a collective bargaining contract, and include such items as pension plans, health insurance, life insurance, and disability insurance. Support benefits may include such items as housing, parking, tuition repayment programs, and free or reduced costs for cultural and athletic events (Chronister & Kepple, 1987). Table 33.2 provides information on the types of benefits provided to full-time faculty in 1987–1988 and the percentage of institutions offering the benefit.

Approximately 98% of institutions of postsecondary education offered some type of pension plan to full-time faculty and staff in 1987–1988, with 100% of two-year public and four-year public and private institutions providing this benefit. Nearly 100% of all institutions also offered medical insurance coverage for full-time employees. As discussed and analyzed later, pension plans and health insurance programs are two of the most expensive benefits for institutions of higher education to provide, with health insurance costs being the most volatile in recent years.

The institutions vary significantly in terms of the other benefits offered. Life insurance is the third most prevalent benefit, followed by disability insurance, with private institutions more likely than their public sector counterparts to provide the latter. Tuition benefits are more likely to be available for children and spouses at private institutions than at public institutions; however, the public institutions are more likely to provide dental insurance.

Costs of Benefits

The cost of benefits can be viewed from a number of perspectives. First, they can be analyzed on a per-full-time-employee basis, with these

TABLE 33.2
Colleges and Universities Providing Benefits to Full-Time Faculty, Fall 1987 (in percentages)

Type and Control if Institution	Pension	Medical Insurance or Care	Life Insurance	Disability Insurance	Tuition Benefit: Children	Tuition Benefit: Spouse	Dental Insurance or Care	Paid Maternity Leave	Wellness Program	Housing	Meals	Paid Paternity Leave	Child Care
All institutions[a]	98	99	88	79	65	63	59	49	31	11	11	10	4
Four-year public	100	98	90	76	47	53	62	54	40	5	1	14	7
Four-year private	100	99	88	94	99	94	44	60	39	25	16	5	2
Two-year public	100	97	85	70	41	46	73	44	31	0	0	17	4
Other	92	100	89	75	69	55	55	40	15	24	23	4	7

Source: National Center for Education Statistics, 1990, p. 44.

a. All accredited, nonproprietary US. postsecondary institutions that grant a two-year (A.A.) or higher degree and whose accreditation is recognized by the US. Department of Education.

TABLE 33.3
Average Salary, Average Benefit Costs, and Benefit Costs as a Percentage of Average Salary for Faculty on 9 to 10-Month Contracts, by Type of Institution: 1989–1990 to 1993–1994

Type of Institution	1989– 1990	1990– 1991	1991– 1992	1992– 1993	1993– 1994	% Change 1989–1990 to 1993–1994
Associate of Arts						
Salary	33,171	34,717	35,798	36,713	38,412	15.8
Benefits	8,376	9,077	9,630	10,236	10,236	25.1
Benefits % of salary	25.3	26.1	26.9	27.9	27.3	2.0
Bachelor of Arts						
Salary	33,580	35,861	37,446	38,635	39,783	18.5
Benefits	7,862	8,867	9,384	9,762	10,485	33.4
Benefits % of salary	23.4	24.7	25.1	25.3	26.4	3.2
Bachelor of Arts						
Salary	37,147	38,592	40,410	41,515	43,222	16.4
Benefits	9,032	9,767	10,247	10,843	11,352	25.7
Benefits % of salary	24.3	25.1	25.4	26.1	26.3	2.0
Doctoral						
Salary	45,386	47,954	49,415	50,766	52,199	15.0
Benefits	10,144	10,853	11,550	12,023	12,608	24.3
Benefits % of salary	22.4	22.6	23.4	23.7	24.2	1.8
Average						
Salary	39,809	41,947	43,361	44,606	46,186	16.0
Benefits	9,303	10,040	10,649	11,162	11,721	26.0
Benefits % of salary	23.4	23.9	24.6	25.0	25.4	2.0

Note: Based on 1,508 institutions reporting data in all years.

Source: National Center for Education Statistics, *IPEDS Salary Survey,* 1989–90 through 1993–94.

figures traced over time to ascertain the magnitude of change from year to year. A second type of assessment is the analysis of benefit costs as a percentage of salary on an annual basis and over a period of time.

The data in Table 33.3 show the average costs of providing benefits on a per-full-time-faculty basis for the years 1989–1990 through 1993–1994 and highlight several factors with which institutions have had to grapple over the past half decade. First, average benefit costs per faculty member have increased at a rate faster than the rate of average salary increases. Between 1989–1990 and 1993–1994, the average salary increased by 16%, and benefits increased 26%. Benefit costs as a percentage of salary increased from 23.4% to 25.4% over the same period. Important differences in these averages occur when analyzed by type of institution. It was among bachelor's-degree-type institutions that both the largest percentage increases in

average salary and average benefit cost took place; doctoral institutions experienced the lowest increases. Average benefit costs as a percentage of salary were highest among two-year institutions each year, with doctoral institutions, on average, the lowest on that particular ratio.

It is assumed that increased dollars committed to fringe benefits are dollars that might have gone into faculty salaries if the benefit costs had not grown so significantly. Studies have shown that many institutions paid increased benefit costs during years when institutional revenues were reduced or did not grow at a rate commensurate with inflation (El-Khawas, 1991, p. 1).

The three components that serve as the major fringe benefit cost centers for institutions of higher education are retirement contributions, medical/dental plan costs, and Social Security expenditures, regardless of type and control of institution. Among public institutions, these three categories accounted for over 90% of costs in 1993–1994; at private institutions, they accounted for over 80% of expenditures.

Retirement contributions account for between 37.1% and 41.8% of average benefit costs at public institutions and between 24.4% and 34.9% at private institutions (Chronister, 1996). Nearly 100% of institutions provide either a defined benefit or defined contribution pension plan for full-time faculty and staff, although some institutions provide employees with a choice between the two (NCES, 1993).

Defined benefit plans provide the participant with a specific annuity at the time of retirement, usually determined by a formula that consists of a final year average salary (or X years of average highest salary), multiplied by years of service, times a percentage factor, such as 1.5% or 2%. The employer must accumulate the funds needed to pay the annuity, even though the employee may be required to contribute to the fund. The employer's cost in such plans will vary based on investment returns, personnel turnover, and mortality factors (TIAA-CREF, 1995b, p. 1). State pension plans are generally defined benefit plans and in 1987–1988 were made available by 89% of public four-year institutions and 95% of public two-year colleges (NCES, 1990, p. 39). In recent years, there has been increasing concern that many defined benefit plans may be underfunded due to weak state economies that have restricted maintaining adequate contribution levels to fund accounts, "borrowing" from the retirement fund to meet other state needs, or poor investment decisions.

Defined contribution plans are characterized by the specified level of contribution that will be made into participants' individual pension accounts, as opposed to guaranteeing a specific formula-driven annuity at retirement. In these plans, the participant assumes the risk for the adequacy of the retirement annuity because the amount of the annuity is based on the contributions to the fund, the investment earnings on the contributions, and one's age at retirement. The risk for the participant is heavily affected by the financial performance of the investment vehicles in which funds are invested.

The Teachers Insurance Annuity Association and College Retirement Equities Fund (TIAA-CREF) is the most widely offered defined contribution pension plan in higher education. Nearly 60% of institutions offered TIAA-CREF, including 77% of public four-year and 84% of independent four-year institutions, but only 39% of public two-year institutions made it available. About 41% of institutions provide another 403b or 401k plan (NCES, 1990, p. 42). The 1993 National Study of Postsecondary Faculty indicated that 63%, of institutions provide multiple pension plans from which personnel may choose the option in which they wish to participate (NCES, 1993).

Social Security, as an institutional expense, is driven by federal policy in terms of the maximum salary subject to tax and the rate of FICA tax and the Medicare tax that has no salary ceiling. This is a benefit item for which the institution must comply with federal requirements and tax rates, both in terms of the institutional contribution and the employee withholding. With the much publicized concern about the long-term viability of Social Security, both the FICA tax rate and the salary ceiling up to which the rate is applied have been increasing and will undoubtedly continue to increase in the near future. To encourage individuals to work longer and to relieve some of the pressure on the Social Security "trust" fund, the Social Security Amendments of 1983 (P.L. 98–21) revised the normal retirement age beginning in the year 2000. In that year, the normal retirement age will gradually increase to 66 for those reaching age 62 in 2005 and to 67 for those reaching age 62 in 2022 (TIAA-CREF, 1989, p. 3).

As the third major cost center, health benefits have received considerable attention in recent years. The average institutional costs for health coverage for 9- to 10-month faculty in 1993–1994 ranged from 26.0% to 33.4% of total benefit expenditures, depending on the type of public institution, compared with 21.4% to 25.2% at the private institutions, depending on type (Chronister, 1996). Health insurance benefits have been one of the fastest growing cost centers in benefit plans. Between 1977 and 1989, average health care benefits costs for institutions increased from 2.2% to 6.1% of payroll (TIAA-CREF, 1991a).

Health insurance costs have been the focus of a significant number of institutional efforts to control costs. In an attempt to control the increases in the costs of indemnity insurance plans, an increasing number of colleges and universities have been turning to managed health care plans provided by health maintenance organizations or by preferred provider organizations (Hewitt Associates, 1992, p. 7). In attempting to control these costs, it is also common for institutions of higher education to adopt health benefit plans that require faculty and staff to assume a larger share of costs of health care through higher premiums, higher copayments, and larger deductibles.

It is evident from the above that benefit costs have grown faster than faculty (and staff) salaries over the past decade. The problem has been exacerbated by the fact that with constrained financial resources the increases in benefit costs have been achieved at the expense of salary growth and support for other desirable institutional programs. As an example, in 1990–1991, 45% of surveyed institutions reported mid-year budget cuts, and 79% were required to increase spending for health insurance for the year (El-Khawas, 1991, p. 1).

Rising costs of benefits in relation to anticipated financial constraint during the remainder of the current decade will remain a serious fiscal challenge for colleges and universities. Uncertainty at the federal level about how best to address national health care issues and how to resolve the problem of adequate funding for the Social Security system adds to institutional uncertainty for the long term. Many of the cost issues are directly related to the retirement issues addressed in the next section.

RETIREMENT TRENDS AND ISSUES

A discussion of retirement trends and issues must take into account past retirement patterns and changing social, economic, health, and professional variables that affect the retirement decision. It must also be recognized that there are at least two dimensions to the discussion, one being the individual perspective and the other the institutional.

Recent years have been witness to a number of competing and at times diametrically opposed factors affecting retirement decision making on the part of individuals. Among the factors analyzed in this section are increased

longevity for individuals, the economic variables that affect the retirement decision, the nature of incentive retirement plans offered by institutions to encourage retirement, and differences between faculty and staff in terms of retirement.

Longevity

At the midpoint of the decade of the 1990s, higher education faces a longevity challenge similar to that of the rest of society. Longevity is highlighted by the fact that the life expectancy of 65-year-old men and women in America has increased by about two years since 1970 (TIAA-CREF, 1995a, p. 3). The implications of increased longevity are several-fold. Improved health in later years brought about by better health care and advances in medical science provides individuals the opportunity for a longer professional career or a greater number of years of retirement.

Age of Retirement

What are faculty and staff likely to do with this freedom of choice about retirement in the face of increased longevity, better health, and the absence of a mandatory retirement age? Will the choice or decision differ to any degree between faculty and staff or by variables such as discipline, gender, and race/ethnicity? As a basis for attempting to determine whether different cohorts of employees within institutions of higher education differ on the age at which they may retire, some insights can be gained from the results of a study undertaken in spring 1990. Data on the retirement ages of several occupational groups from among 19,126 faculty and staff from a cross section of 130 institutions shows different retirement age patterns by group (Table 33.4). Faculty tend to retire at later ages than do members of the other occupational classifications. Whereas from 52% to 58% of the support staff and professional and management personnel had retired prior to age 65, only 43% of the faculty had retired by that age. Conversely, a much larger proportion of the faculty (28%) had retired after age 65 and into their 70s than had the other occupational groups (13% to 17%) (TIAA-CREF, 1991b).

Two important questions arise from the data in Table 33.4. First, in the absence of a

TABLE 33.4
Distribution of Respondents, by Retirement Age and Former Occupation (in percentages)

Age at Retirement	Total Respondent	Faculty	Administration or Mangement	Professional or Technical Staff	Administration Support Staff	Maintenance Support Staff
Under 65	49	43	57	56	58	52
6524	24	24	21	23	22	26
66 to 69	15	20	13	13	13	10
70 and over	5	8	4	3	3	3
No response	6	4	5	5	4	9
All ages combined[a]	100	100	100	100	100	100

Source: "The NACUBO/TIAA-CREF Survey of College and University Retirees," *Research Dialogues,* No. 31, October 1991, p. 2. Some percentages may not add to 100 because of rounding.

mandatory retirement age, can it be expected that this occupationally differentiated distribution of retirement ages will continue in the future? Second, will retirements continue to cluster at or below age 65? Analysis of actual retirement ages of faculty, other professionals, and nonprofessional staff over the next several years will be necessary to answer the first question. Limited data available from institutions that had abolished mandatory retirement for tenured faculty prior to the January 1, 1994 effective date mandated in the federal legislation indicated that although a few faculty members remained employed there was no great proportion staying on beyond age 70 (Hammond & Morgan, 1991, pp. 27–28). Comparable data are not available on the recent retiree behavior of nonfaculty personnel on college and university campuses.

An interesting perspective on factors that may affect the decision about when to retire or the likelihood of continued employment is presented in "Longevity's Gift: A Second Middle Age" (TIAA-CREF, 1995c), where it is suggested that increased and healthy longevity has created a second middle age between the ages of 50 and 75 that provides individuals the opportunity for a long career. Besides the studies, there is growing evidence that college faculty are using this longer career potential in current retirement planning. Data from the 1993 National Study of Postsecondary Faculty indicate that 17.2% of full-time faculty expect to work to age 70, and an additional 8.6% anticipate working beyond that age. Although 75% of the full-time faculty

who were age 70 in fall 1992 expected to retire in the next three years, only 33% of those over 70 expected to retire in three years (Chronister & Baldwin, in press). These faculty members may indeed be in their "second middle age" in terms of career fulfillment.

Factors Affecting the Retirement Decision

The variables that contribute to the decision to remain employed or to retire may be generally classified as either personal or professional or a combination of the two. Studies have shown that among the most influential factors affecting the decision about whether or not to retire are the availability of a satisfactory retirement income, the health of the individual or the health of a significant other, and the level of satisfaction with one's career and with one's job and place of employment (Gray, n.d.). The majority of factors beyond finances and health that affect the retirement decision of individuals can generally be classified as either push variables (job-related stresses that make the current employment situation unattractive), pull variables (expected postretirement activities that make retirement attractive), and status quo variables (factors that make the continuing employment attractive) (Daniels & Daniels, 1990, p. 70).

Among the variables that may differentiate between faculty and nonfaculty personnel in choosing when they will retire are such work environment variables as the socialization that faculty have received during their graduate study preparation, the latitude they have in how they fulfill their role on campus, and the opportunity for role fulfillment away from campus. This role identity and work context for faculty is significantly different from non-professional staff and some other campus professionals who have limited flexibility in role definition and fulfillment, limited resources for professional development, and limited institutional rewards and recognition. Where faculty may have numerous institutional "status quo" variables affecting their decision about retirement, nonfaculty may be directly affected by work environment and personal variables that serve to "pull" or "push" them toward retirement. The recognition of the variables that affect faculty retirement decisions is critical to institutions that are seeking ways to create faculty and staff turnover through incentive retirement plans or are attempting to discourage faculty and staff from working into their 70s and to take "regular" retirement.

For the "push" or "pull" variables to trigger the actual retirement decision, the need for adequate postretirement income must be satisfied. Concern for adequate income does not center only on immediate postretirement income but on the adequacy of income to offset the long term effects of inflation in the face of longevity. This inflation issue is highlighted in a recent TIAA-CREF publication (Biggs, 1995) about the implications of longevity for a retired couple: "Using our current mortality table, there is a two-thirds chance that one of the two 65-year olds will still be relying on the (retirement) income twenty-five years later at age 90" (p. 2).

Pension Issues

The adequacy of retirement income creates one of the challenges for which the landscape has changed for institutions and faculty in recent years. Over the past decade, colleges and universities have provided faculty and staff with increased numbers of retirement plan choices and increased investment opportunities within the majority of those plans. Placing this higher education change in a national context, a recent report states that between 1975 and 1987 the proportion of workers participating in defined contribution plans for their primary pension coverage increased from 13% to 32%, whereas

the proportion of workers with primary coverage under defined benefit plans dropped from 87% to 68% (TIAA-CREF, 1995b).

With the increase in investment options to employees, institutions have a responsibility to provide educational experiences for employees that assist them in understanding the nature of the differences in investment opportunities so that educated investment decisions can be facilitated (VALIC, 1994). This responsibility does not assume that institutions will give investment advice, but it does assume the need to provide faculty and staff with educational programs that highlight they may need investment advice from a professional financial adviser. The fact that defined contribution retirement plans place the risk of attaining adequate retirement income on the investment decisions of the employee rather than on the institution heightens the need for investment education programs, especially in an environment that provides multiple investment options. The provision of such programs has not become widespread across campuses as yet and is a challenge that faces a growing number of institutions.

The joint responsibility of institutions and employees for effective planning for the achievement of adequate retirement income is highlighted in the following statement:

> The substantial growth of defined contribution plans since passage of ERISA in 1974 underscores an important point about them—individual participants are responsible for their own asset allocation decisions as they direct plan contributions to individual annuity accounts. Clear plan communication and financial educational materials are critical to the success of such participant-directed accounts. Participants also require good financial planning skills for building the personal savings they need to supplement pension and Social Security benefits for an adequate retirement income. (TIAA-CREF, 1995b, p. 1)

Medical Coverage Issues

Integral to retiree financial considerations are concerns about health insurance protection and the cost of such protection. As stated earlier, during employment, institutional health insurance plans provide a known and regular cost to the employee to cover unknown and potentially significant medical expenses. This concern with known and "affordable" health care coverage gains increased significance during the retirement years when medical needs are expected to be greater than during an individual's younger years. Retirees tend to be in a higher "health risk" group for coverage and therefore, if they do not continue in their institution's group plan or another group-based plan, individual expenses for health care coverage can become highly significant for persons on retirement income. Studies indicate that the availability of health insurance for retirees through an institution's group plan at institution, shared, or retiree cost is important in the decision about when to retire.

In an attempt to address concerns about the availability and cost of health insurance, some colleges and universities provide for retirees to continue participation in the institution's group plan at institutional expense. For example, the University of Michigan (1991) provides for retirees and eligible dependents to continue health and dental care coverage with the institution's contribution to the cost of the premium being no more than the university's contribution toward the cost of Blue Cross/Blue Shield (p. 3). This retirement benefit continues until death and is therefore a continuing financial obligation of the institution. That obligation for the University of Michigan currently amounts to about $8 million per year for about 4,000 retirees (Blackburn & Lawrence, 1995, pp. 340–341).

Other institutions address the health care cost concerns of potential retirees by including health benefits as incentives in early retirement plans. The University of Virginia (1995) has provided health benefits for phased retirement plan participants for the period of time the faculty member is phasing into retirement at institutional cost (as though the faculty member were fully employed). Plans such as that of the University of Virginia provide control of institutional costs by specifying the length of time of phased retirement, which is currently five years. Retirees may then continue in the institutional group plan but at their own expense.

With institutional attempts to control health care costs it can be expected that more institutions will use managed care plans and there will be a reduction in the use of indemnity plans. It is very likely that changes in the type of health care coverage provided for employees will also affect retirees in terms of higher-cost premiums and larger deductibles and copayments.

In the absence of the provision of subsidized or otherwise affordable medical coverage, employees may continue employment solely for the purpose of maintaining such coverage. An added concern that has gained increased interest for retirement planning in recent years in relation to health care involves the high cost of long-term care.

FRINGE BENEFIT OPPORTUNITIES FOR PART-TIME FACULTY

Part-time faculty in American higher education have generally had no access, or minimum access, to fringe benefits on college and university campuses. With an expected increased reliance on part-time faculty in the near future, institutions can expect increased requests for benefits for these faculty members. The growth in the use of part-time faculty is highlighted in *Campus Trends*, 1995, which reported that 47% of institutions responding to a national survey have increased the number of part-time faculty, but only 27% have experienced decreases in recent years. These increases have been reported by both public and private institutions (El-Khawas, 1995).

A 1988 survey of colleges and universities found that only about 55% of institutions provided some benefits to regular part-time faculty. Whereas institutions expend the equivalent of about 25% of salary on benefits for full-time faculty, benefits for part-time faculty amounted to about 14% of salary (NCES, 1990, p. 41). About 43% of the institutions provided a pension plan for part-time faculty, and 31% of them subsidized the plan (NCES, 1990, p. 43). Although 31%f institutions offered subsidized pension plans for part-time faculty, only about 20% of all part-timers receive such a benefit (Gappa & Leslie, 1993, p. 162).

Health insurance benefits for part-time faculty members is a topic of intense interest on many college and university campuses, especially where a large proportion of the faculty consists of part-timers. A report based on the 1988 National Survey of Postsecondary Faculty stated that only 16.6% of part-time faculty received subsidized health/medical insurance (NCES, 1990). Gappa and Leslie (1993) found that subsidized medical insurance benefits for part-time faculty were most likely the result of collective bargaining and that there was often a minimum contracted work effort and minimum length of service requirement to establish eligibility.

With the national uncertainty surrounding the availability of adequate and affordable health insurance and health care, the provision of health insurance for part-time faculty who have no other access to subsidized coverage will continue to be an issue placed before institutional policy makers. The issue gains increased significance in that many institutions pay part-time faculty minimum salaries for teaching on a limited basis. Unless a part-time faculty member has another source of income to meet basic expenses and that source also provides health care coverage, the low salary exacerbates the financial condition for this large proportion of the professoriate.

CONCLUSION

Over the past decade, colleges and universities have been faced with the twin challenges of an aging faculty and significant increases in the costs of providing fringe benefits for its workforce. During this same period, constrained financial resources and a variety of external forces have combined to make these challenges more complex, and these factors will continue to affect institutions in the foreseeable future.

The abolition of the mandatory retirement age makes the decision about the age at which personnel will retire an entirely and highly personal decision. Indications are that for the next 10 to 15 years institutions will be required to adjust to a workforce that is older and may have different personal and professional needs and aspirations than does a faculty and staff that is, on average, younger. Affecting the decisions of faculty and staff about when they will retire are concerns about the adequacy of retirement income, the availability of affordable medical insurance or medical coverage of some kind, and opportunities to participate in post-retirement activities that are fulfilling and meaningful. The expectation of a longer retirement period in one's life increases the impor-

tance of retirement planning, including special emphasis on retirement income. Research has shown that personnel who participate in meaningful retirement planning activities are more likely to be satisfied with retirement and to have more adequately planned for the transition in lifestyle that retirement creates. A significant part of that planning process begins early in the career and involves the financial planning related to pension plan choice and investment decisions geared to differing career stages. Retirement planning programs are a resource that the majority of institutions do not provide employees.

Control of the costs of providing fringe benefits will continue to be a challenge to colleges and universities in the foreseeable future. Not only will institutions need to control the cost of such items as health coverage for employees currently covered but they will need to address the needs of a growing number of part-time faculty, the majority of whom do not now have access to subsidized benefits as do their full-time colleagues. This accommodation will need to take place in an environment of constrained financial resources and competition for scarce resources from other institutional functions.

Finally, it is possible that, in view of an aging faculty, colleges and universities will need to develop and implement programs that assist faculty and staff in adapting to changing institutional needs and work role demands.

REFERENCES

Biggs, J. (1995, August). Take a second look at the graded payment. *The participant*, p. 2.

Blackburn, R., & Lawrence, J. (1995). *Faculty at work: Motivation, expectation, satisfaction*. Baltimore: Johns Hopkins University Press.

Chronister, J. L. (1995). Benefits and retirement, 1992–93. *NEA 1995 Almanac of higher education*, pp. 97–108.

Chronister, J. L. (1996). Fringe benefits and retirement: A changing environment. *NEA 1996 Almanac of higher education*, pp. 97–106.

Chronister, J. L., & Baldwin, R. G. (in press). *Faculty retirement and other separation plans*. Washington, DC: National Center for Education Statistics, U.S. Department of Education.

Chronister, J. L., & Kepple, T. R., Jr. (1987). *Incentive early retirement programs for faculty: Innovative responses to a changing environment* (ASHE-ERIC

Higher Education Report No. 1). Washington, DC: Association for the Study of Higher Education.

Daniels, C. E., & Daniels, J. D. (1990). Voluntary retirement incentive options in higher education. *Benefits Quarterly, 6*(2), 68–78.

El-Khawas, E. (1991). *Campus trends, 1991.* Washington, DC: American Council on Education.

El-Khawas, E. (1995). *Campus trends, 1995.* Washington, DC: American Council on Education.

Gappa, J. M., & Leslie, D. W. (1993). *The invisible faculty.* San Francisco: Jossey-Bass.

Gray, K. (n.d.). *Retirement plans and expectations of TIAA-CREF policyholders.* New York: Teachers Insurance and Annuity Association-College Retirement Equity Funds.

Hammond, P B., & Morgan, H. P. (1991). *Ending mandatory retirement for faculty: The consequences for higher education.* Washington, DC: National Academy Press.

Hewitt Associates. (1992). *College and university experience in managed care.* Lincolnshire, IL: Author.

National Center for Education Statistics (NCES). (1979). *Digest of education statistics, 1979.* Washington, DC: U.S. Department of Education.

National Center for Education Statistics (NCES). (1990, January). *Institutional policies and practices regarding faculty in higher education.* (NSOPP-88). Washington, DC: U.S. Department of Education.

National Center for Education Statistics (NCES). (1993). *1993 national study of postsecondary faculty data base.* Washington, DC: U.S. Department of Education.

National Center for Education, Statistics (NCES). (1994a). *Digest of education statistics, 1994.* Washington, DC: U.S. Department of Education.

National Center for Education Statistics (NCES). (1994b). *Salaries, tenure, and fringe benefits. 1993–94.*Washington, DC: U.S. Department of Education.

National Center for Education Statistics (NCES). (1994c). *Faculty and instructional staff: Who are they and what do they do?* Washington, DC: U.S. Department of Education.

National Education Association. (1979). *Higher education faculty: Characteristics and opinions.* Washington, DC: Author.

Teachers Insurance and Annuity Association-College Retirement Equities Fund(TIAA–CREF). (1989). Social Security to increase delayed retirement credit. *The Participant.* New York: Author.

TIAA-CREF (1991a). Trends in payments for employee benefits. *Research Dialogues,* No. 29.

TIAA-CREF (1991b). The NACUBO/TIAA-CREF survey of college and university retirees. *Research Dialogues,* No. 31.

TIAA-CREF (1995a). The retirement security of the baby boom generation. *Research Dialogues,* No. 43.

TIAA-CREF. (1995b). Planning for retirement—the age of individual responsibility. *Research Dialogues,* No. 44.

TIAA-CRIB: (1995c). Longevity's gift: A second middle age. *Research Dialogues,* No. 45.

University of Michigan. (1991). Retirement. In *Standard practice guide.* Ann Arbor: Author.

University of Virginia. (1995). *Phased incentive retirement plan for faculty.* Charlottesville: Author.

VALIC. (1994). The employers education responsibility under 404(c). *Educated Choices,* 3(1).

SECTION V

STRATEGIC PLANNING AND RESOURCE ALLOCATION

INTRODUCTION

Conceptually, a strong symbiotic relationship exists between strategic planning and an institution's resource allocation process. Therefore, it is important that a Reader on higher education finance devote some attention to this relationship. A strategic plan is of little value if resources are not allocated as specified by the plan. Similarly, if the resource allocation process is not guided by the institution's strategic plan, it will be impossible to successfully implement the plan and scarce institutional resources will be wasted. While linking these two components is very important to institutional management, it is a difficult task and there is no easy solution to mapping the strategic plan to resource allocation decisions.

The seven articles included in this section cover a range of topics dealing with the relationship between institutional plans and resource allocation practices. Chaffee's 1981 monograph, "The Link Between Planning and Budgeting," is one of the classic treatments of this issue. Chaffee's article, though twenty years old, remains a valuable and insightful contribution to contemporary discussions of the subject. For those readers unfamiliar with microeconomic theory, Chaffee presents a very clear and concise explication of the microeconomics involved in planning and budgeting, and in so doing, demystifies concepts such as indifference curves and equilibrium points.

Turning to a discussion of the difficulties encountered in linking plans and resources, the section continues with "Why Linking Budgets to Plans Has Proven Difficult in Higher Education." As Schmidtlein notes in the introduction to his article, "Like the Search for the Holy Grail, the theorists and practitioners for many years have maintained a quest for the secret to a successful linkage. Most observers of practice, however, find little evidence that this quest has been successful." Written in 1990, the article does not necessarily reflect the more dynamic strategic planning milieu that has evolved over the last decade, but it does clearly identify the issues associated with attempting to develop the planning-budgeting linkage, and provides a useful extension of many articles that stress the need to develop these linkages. The Brinkman and Morgan article, "Changing Fiscal Strategies for Planning," examines the issues of public trust, multiple revenue sources, revenue maximization, and the need to reallocate resources, and how these issues relate to performance budgeting and responsibility center budgeting. Published in 1997, this article is a valuable complement to the Schmidtlein piece, offering an updated appraisal of the planning and budgeting environment in the mid 1990s.

Shulock and Harrison provide a very concrete example of linking plans and budgets in their article, "Integrating Planning, Assessment, and Resource Allocation." By describing the process followed at California State University, Sacramento, this article presents a good case study and serves as a useful model for those working in public institutions. More important, the case study includes the use of assessment process as part of the larger integrated process, thereby closing the loop between implementation and evaluation. In addition to the detailed description of the process, the authors also pose a number of questions that will serve as an excellent basis for further discussion.

The final article, by Massy, advances a good historical overview of resource allocation practices that also raises a number of important issues. Massy combines a solid, theoretical approach with a strong, practical orientation toward the redesign of budgeting systems. The article outlines many points that could serve to stimulate debate about differing assumptions of decision-making for institutional plans and budgets.

As is evident from the literature, there is no straightforward and easily implemented mechanism that permits plans and budgets to be integrated. The continuously changing internal and external environments require a long-term perspective for this linking process. What is desirable is not always realistic because of resource constraints, personnel, legal regulations, and external pressures, while existing practices are often difficult to change in the short term. The highly political nature of this process strongly influences the outcomes. All of these tensions must be understood and resolved each year when creating a new budget plan. Without an adequate understanding of this process and the accompanying tensions, it is impossible to fully implement a strategic management decision-making model. The articles included in this section provide insight and understanding of important issues that should prompt additional discussion among students and practitioners.

Members of the review panel for this section were:

Glenna G. Brown, University of Alabama at Birmingham

Jack E. Freeman, University of Pittsburgh

Andrea Lex, University of Washington Education Outreach

Elliott L. Mininberg, California State University, Northridge

Rodney Rose, The JCM Group

Frank A. Schmidtlein, University of Maryland, College Park

John L. Yeager, University of Pittsburgh

CHAPTER 34

THE LINK BETWEEN PLANNING AND BUDGETING

ELLEN EARLE CHAFFEE

Administrators in higher education feel mounting pressure to link planning and budgeting as their resources become more scarce and their environments more uncertain. Too often, they turn to theoretically prescribed planning/budgeting systems as solutions.

Microeconomics provides a means of thinking about individual consumption that helps shed light on the nature of the institution's financial problem. It illustrates the complexity of the problem and the inadequacies of prescriptive systems. It also suggests four characteristics of an optimal system that links planning and budgeting. An optimal system (1) estimates changes in income and prices, reducing uncertainty in these areas as much as possible, (2) allows for disproportionate budget shifts, (3) monitors and reflects changes in preferences, and (4) manages conflicting political pressures.

If the decision-making process for linking plans with budgets is to be successfully implemented, it must have the following three features. It must (1) encourage frequent communication between planners and decision-makers, (2) ensure that similar or related decisions are made simultaneously rather than sequentially, and (3) monitor important changes that relate to income, cost, and preference, as well as call attention to these changes so that they receive special notice.

This monograph concludes with a case study that incorporates the four characteristics of an optional system that links planning and budgeting.

INTRODUCTION

The vice-president sat back to think about the budget situation. For the past 10 years, library costs had been skyrocketing, and Greenfield University had allowed the library budget to coast. The librarian's budget request for a 15 percent increase plus a one-time cost of $75,000 was backed by impressive statistics about increases in postage rates and publishing prices. Estimates were high for book and periodical costs for the new interdisciplinary humanities program—a top priority for the school.

The dean of the law school had been insisting on a 19 percent hike for faculty salaries. This year, Greenfield had already lost three top professors to private practice. This was not surprising, considering that their average salary after leaving was nearly double what Greenfield had paid them. The average salary for first-year graduates of the school was more than the salary of assistant professors on the law faculty. Additionally, four more faculty members were being courted by the private sector and other law schools. At this rate, the law faculty would soon be decimated.

Source: *The Link Between Planning and Budgeting*, 1981, National Center for Higher Education Management Systems, Boulder, CO.

As if that were not enough, energy costs were up another 20 percent last year despite a vigorous conservation program, and they were projected to rise another 20 percent next year. The director of the physical plant had been urging a $175,000 capital investment to convert to cheaper fuels.

The dean of Engineering had reported losing at least 100 potential students every year to the competition because Greenfield does not offer electronic and biomedical engineering programs. The projections showed that eventually the tuition and research revenues of these programs would greatly exceed the costs involved, but would first require an expenditure of $50,000 for equipment and other start-up costs.

The vice-president was getting a headache. Her thoughts turned to the long-range plan recently completed by a blue-ribbon committee at Greenfield. Perhaps the plan could offer some guidance for dealing with budget decisions. It called for a return to the liberal arts base upon which Greenfield was founded and had established its reputation. It emphasized energy efficiency, stressed the need to maintain and even improve the quality of the faculty, and warned sternly against allowing any further erosion of the library. The vice-president sketched out solutions based on the long-range plan: (1) fund the library to get enough to cover only cost increases and the costs incurred in supporting the humanities program, (2) deny the special increase for the law faculty above the increase for liberal arts faculty, (3) spend the $175,000 for energy conversion, and (4) deny the engineering request.

It did not feel very good. Maybe she could do more. What were the financial projections? The five-year forecast showed a gap between income and expenses that was equal to 10 percent of the current budget. Last year's budget balanced, but it had been difficult to achieve. No help there. Those projections had not even included the energy conversion project.

THE PLANNING AND BUDGETING PROBLEM

Why is it so tough for vice-presidents at Greenfield (and most other colleges and universities) to link planning and budgeting? It is not enough to blame inflation, demographics, and federal policies, even though these are, indeed, real and serious problems. It should be possible to grasp the nature of the problem and decide upon the most effective way of dealing with it. Decrementalism—making across-the-board cuts —and the serendipity of attrition seem to have accomplished all that they could (but not without creating problems of their own). The fact that administrators were attempting to link plans and budgets indicates a felt need to assert some control over the chaos. It is also an indication of the hope that, in making this linkage the integrity of the institution could be maintained.

To the extent that the interest in linking planning to budgeting leads the administrator to turn to zero-based budgeting or hire strategic-planning consultants, it can divert the administrator from solving the real problem. Useful solutions can be identified only if the nature of the problem is understood.

USING A MICROECONOMIC MODEL

With respect to planning and budgeting, institutions act like consumers. They have needs, desires, and an income that determines the limits of their budget. While there is an unlimited variety of goods available for them to consume, their priorities and pocketbooks reduce the number of choices. But most activities are not considered by them to be consumer activities. If Greenfield could view itself as an individual, economic area of activity and its conflicting needs as choices, a useful planning/budgeting system would be one that helps determine the relative values and priorities of different choices.

Microeconomics provides a means of thinking about individual consumption that sheds light on the nature of the university's problem. Select any two goods that the vice-president is considering and let them comprise one of the trade-offs that faces her. For example, put library restoration on one axis and salary increases for the law faculty on another. In theory, an indifference curve—a curve of marginal utility—could be constructed which represents the relative values of library restoration and law salaries, as shown in Figure 34.1.

The curve's shape is determined by plotting the points that represent purchase combi-

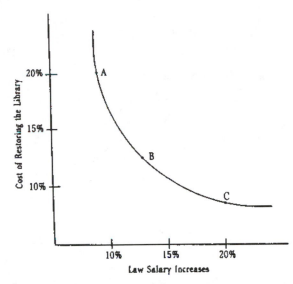

Figure 34.1 Indifference Curve

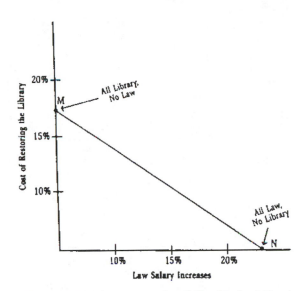

Figure 34.2 Consumption Possibility (Budget) Line

nations about which the consumer is potentially equally pleased or indifferent. According to the curve in Figure 34.1, the consumer would be equally pleased to have any of the three following combinations: (1) about a 20 percent improvement in the library, together with a 10 percent increase in law salaries (point A); (2) a 12 percent improvement in each of these two goods (point B); or (3) an 8 percent improvement in the library and a 20 percent increase in law salaries (point C). These pairs of goods and all other points on the indifference curve represent combinations that the consumer believes to be of equivalent value.

Microeconomics offers suggestions about how to plot an indifference curve. Plotting an indifference curve is so complex, however, that a convincing argument can be made that the task is impossible. The purpose of presenting this analogy is therefore purely conceptual. It is a way to think about the planning/budgeting problem and not a method of acting on the problem. Practical implications are noted later in the monograph.

In theory, the indifference curve is convex to the origin. This is because the law of diminishing marginal returns states that, beyond some point, the more a consumer has of one good, the less value he or she places on having more of the same good. The indifference curve can also be more (or less) curved and tilted toward one of the axes. The form of the single curve is representative of an infinite number of curves that radiate from the origin outwards. A curve which is close to the origin is less desirable than one which is farther out. If the institution's relative preference between library restoration and law salaries changes, so does the shape and tilt of the curve. The curve is a stylized and highly simplified graphic representation of two wants or needs of the institution and their relative values. In fact, the diagram is not just two-dimensional; rather, it extends to as many dimensions as the institution has wants or needs. The curve is therefore extraordinarily difficult to plot. This is a problem addressed later.

Microeconomists add a line to this diagram to represent the individual's "consumption possibility," that is, how much of the two goods the individual's budget can purchase. This is also called the budget line. The total budget for the two goods can buy a certain amount of one good and none of the other. These two points can be identified on the axes. The first is all library restoration and no law salaries (point M in Figure 34.2), and the second is all law salaries and no library restoration (point N). The line drawn from one point to the other includes all the combinations of the two goods that the institution can afford to buy. If the budget goes up, the line moves outward from the origin. The converse is true if the budget goes down. If the price of one good changes, a new point must be identified on the axis to represent the total amount that can be

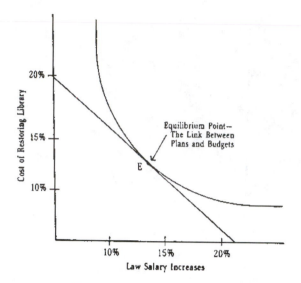

Figure 34.3 Equilibrium Point

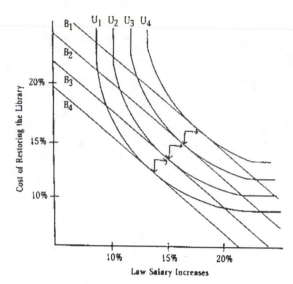

Figure 34.4   Changes in Income as Budget Drift

Incremental or Decremental

afforded. The new budget line would then have a different slope than the old one.

When the indifference curve and the budget line are used together in the diagram, they meet at a single point that represents the optimal amount of each item that a rational consumer purchases. At this point, the consumer gets the most of each good given a certain budget. This is called the equilibrium point (point E in Figure 34.3).

In theory, this point is both what the consumer should *and* does buy. If the indifference curve is thought of as a symbol of Greenfield's plans and the budget line as its budget, then in theory the equilibrium point is the optimal link between its plans and budget. This merits a closer look before the gaps between theory and practice are noted.

In this conceptual model, incrementalism and decrementalism are shifts in the budget line. Consumption steps up to higher, that is, better, indifference curves (from B4 to B1 in Figure 34.4), or it steps down to lower ones (from B1 to B4). This is called budget drift. It works fine if individual preferences—the relative values placed on each item—never change over time. When thus conceptualized, it is clear why budget drift is not satisfactory in the long run. Preferences change as new goods become available, old goods wear out, and new demands are placed on the consumer. Budget drift cannot track them.

What happens when prices change? Depending on the shape of the indifference curve, changing the price of one item affects the amount that can be purchased of both items, as shown in Figure 34.5. This happens because relative preferences of the two items stay the same and the price change acts like a change in the budget. According to this preference ratio, the consumption of both items is adjusted (for example, a move from K to L). If the price of beef goes up while the price of celery stays the same, some celery may be given up in order to eke out a little more beef than seems possible given the price change. This is, however, still less than was purchased before.

Additionally, microeconomists theorize that, at some point when the price of beef is increasing, a similar, less expensive, item can be substituted for some of the beef that would have been bought had there not been a price increase. The vice-president's energy conversion illustrates the point. If the price of oil rises beyond a limit that seems reasonable, only a certain amount of the increased price can be absorbed by decreased consumption, that is, by conservation. The remainder must be absorbed by reduced consumption of other goods. At some point, the physical plant director can start thinking about substituting some other fuel. What makes it especially difficult in the Greenfield

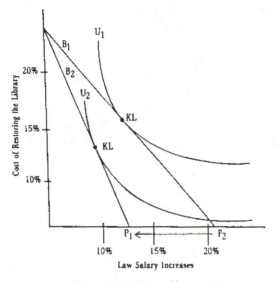

Figure 34.5 Price Change

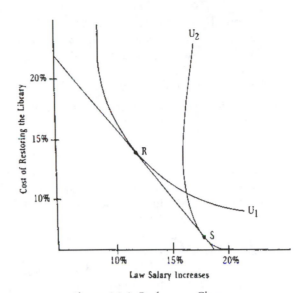

Figure 34.6 Preference Change

case is that the preparation to make the substitution itself carries a cost.

What happens when preferences change? The relative amounts of the two items that are purchased change. It is possible that such a shift means that what is purchased is mostly one item and little of the other (point S in Figure 34.6). Put all these changes together, multiply by the number of dimensions in which the real planning and budgeting problem exists, multiply again by the number of uncertainties that must be anticipated by a one-year budget or by an administrator who thinks about the long term; multiply still again by the number of constituents who claim a role in determining what the indifference curve should look like, factor in the painful cuts and internal dissension caused by scarce resources, and there is little wonder that vice-presidents get headaches and analysts are exhausted! The value of the microeconomic analogy is that it helps to identify the fundamental reasons why achieving an optimal link between plans and budgets is so difficult. Furthermore, it illustrates the problem with incrementalism or decrementalism.

As valuable as across-the-board change is for achieving a sense of stability and for placating some of the internal dissension and claims of unfair treatment, it is simply inadequate for dealing with the complexities of the problems most institutions are trying to resolve. Once any slack in the organization has been removed by

incremental or decremental change, there are only two special circumstances that warrant continued use of the budget-drift approach. The first occurs when the organization achieves a stable equilibrium among all the goods it purchases and the prices of the goods change proportionally. This is, however, an exceptional case. The other use for budget drift occurs when the organization's complexities are virtually impossible to grasp and track. Then there is as much justification for across-the-board change as for any other type of change. Indeed, there is more justification because it conserves energies for solving problems that are solvable.

EVALUATING LINKAGE SYSTEMS

The discussion so far suggests some ideas about the optimal characteristics of a system that links planning and budgeting. The following points suggest what a planning/budgeting system should do:

1. Estimate changes in income and prices, reducing uncertainties in these areas as much as possible.

2. Allow for disproportionate budget shifts, instead of requiring budget drift. As prices and preferences change, optimal budget decisions are likely to require that consumption of one item be changed

more than that of another. In most situations, a budget system that requires, or even encourages, budget drift is not sufficiently flexible to allow the institution to seek an optimal solution.

3. Monitor and reflect changes in preferences. This implies a need to determine whose preferences are to be accommodated and the relative weight that will be assigned to each set of preferences. This is made easier to the extent that the institution is able to identify which of its preferences are constant. The minimum tolerable levels of consumption for as many items as possible must also be identified. These items include academic programs, salary levels by category of employee, library acquisition rates, and items defined in some other terms that are susceptible to this kind of decision.

4. Manage conflicting political pressures. Conflict is generated by at least two factors. One factor is the need to attend to more than one person when identifying the shape of the indifference curve. It is difficult enough for any one person to state a complete preference list. This is compounded enormously when the preference list involves different individuals whose personal well-being lies in protecting their own priorities. The second factor that generates conflict is a scarcity of resources. Contenders for resources attempt to exert influence over the decision about how to allocate resources. The management of conflicting pressures allows the contenders to make themselves known and understood. This process permits nonpowerful but valuable interests to be represented in the final decision.

An Optimal P/B Linking System

1. Estimates changes in income and prices
2. Allows for disproportionate budget shifts
3. Monitors and reflects changes in preferences
4. Manages conflicting political pressures

Figure 34.7 Linking Planning and Budgeting

APPROACHES TO LINKING PLANNING AND BUDGETING

It is useful and instructive to examine existing approaches to linking planning with budgeting from the perspective of the above-mentioned characteristics in order to determine how well they perform. The first, budget drift, neither deals with changes in preferences nor allows for disproportionate budget shifts. Its practitioners estimate changes in income and prices so that they know at what overall level to target the increase or decrease. The system seeks to minimize, but does not manage, conflicting pressures. In effect, it ratifies the existing power distribution in the institution.

Budgeting by "The King's Decree"—autocracy—varies, depending entirely on the characteristics of the king. In many cases, the autocrat cannot invest heavily in monitoring and reflecting changes in preferences among constituents. This holds true particularly when the purpose of autocratic decision-making is to grant primary weight to his or her own preferences. Furthermore, this method is not congruent with one of the significant values of most institutions of higher education, namely, collegiality.

The method identified most often with Harvard—"Each Tub to its Own Bottom"—involves shifting the level of analysis from the institution to the school or to another sub-unit. Since each sub-unit is largely on its own financially, it can link plans and budgets in different ways from other sub-units. There is no inherent reason why the approach should not allow disproportionate budget shifts; and, indeed, if one sub-unit is compared to another, the shifts might turn out to be quite large. The greatest weakness of this method for most institutions is this potential for imbalance between the sub-units. From the point of view of the institution, it is exceedingly difficult to monitor and reflect changes of preference.

The third approach is often referred to as "The Squeaky Wheel Gets the Grease." It is essentially a political model in which the loudest and strongest get the highest proportion of resources. This method allows for disproportionate budget shift. Conflicting internal pressures are not managed, however; they are ratified. It is therefore hard to incorporate institution-wide preferences, and estimates of income and price changes are used only to establish the stakes available in the contest.

The fourth approach, called the "Planning-Programming-Budgeting System" (PPBS), is an old standby that conforms well in theory to the four characteristics of Figure 34.7. This should come as no surprise, since both the microeconomic model of individual choice and PPBS are heavily influenced by the rational model of decision-making. Using PPBS, changes in income and price are estimated, changes in preferences are monitored and reflected, disproportionate shifts are allowed, and conflict is managed. In the translation of theory to reality, however, there are at least three problems with PPBS. First, institutions tend to express preferences and dole out funds in connection with organized departments, while PPBS deals with programs. PPBS is concerned with programs, even if the programs cross departmental boundaries or are subsumed as small parts of organized departments. Second, the management of conflict is achieved through the expectation that rational explanations mitigate disagreements. Third, PPBS has been tried in higher education, but extensive research has not uncovered even one report of an enduring and theoretically true application of the technique in a college or university. For whatever reasons, PPBS does not seem to have survived, much less flourished, in higher education. If this is due to factors other than the reliance of PPBS on the rational model of decision-making (and it is possible that its brief life resulted from the way it was implemented, rather than conceptualized), then faulting PPBS does not necessarily condemn the principles for linking planning and budgeting that are proposed here.

The fifth approach, called "Zero-Base Budgeting" (ZBB), very clearly meets the first three characteristics—estimating changes in prices and income, monitoring and reflecting changes in preference, and allowing disproportionate budget shifts. However, like PPBS, ZBB relies on the persuasion of rational argument. It highlights and exacerbates political conflicts. To the extent that it acknowledges the powerful effects of self-interest, it does so only because of the astuteness of the individual who is orchestrating the process. Furthermore, academic values are difficult to accommodate in the preference functions of ZBB.

A final approach to linking planning and budgeting is strategic planning. Its definitions and forms vary so widely from one proponent of higher education to another that it is difficult to generalize about it. Most clearly, one can say that it is an attempt to monitor and reflect changes in preference, using a particular set of lenses for viewing those preferences—lenses that focus on high-level policy decisions, the environment, and the futurity of present decisions. Most models of strategic planning stop short of dealing with budget details such as estimating changes in income and prices or making disproportionate budget shifts, and they do not manage conflicting budgetary pressures.

IMPLICATIONS OF THE OPTIMIZING CHARACTERISTICS

With the exception of budget drift, none of the above-mentioned systems for linking planning and budgeting has gained wide acceptance and use in higher education. This is not too surprising. The Carnegie book, *Three Thousand Futures*, conveys an appropriate sense of the diversity among colleges and universities and the ways in which they are likely to evolve. Since it is through planning and budgeting activities that these futures will be created, either deliberately or inadvertently, one might expect 3,000 varieties of planning and budgeting activities. Each one would be based on the institution's structure, history, mission, and context, as well as its current situation and the people it employs and teaches. In order to find generalizations that work across institutions, one must operate at the level of principles, not activities.

Such principles are not readily forthcoming, however, because very little empirical or theoretical work focuses on the management of higher education relative to the complexity and scope of the issues which it faces. It is important to communicate at the level of principles, that is, to propose them, debate them, revise them, apply them, throw some of them out, and start over. It is in this spirit that the four characteristics of an optimal system that links planning and budgeting are proposed. The problem is not finding the right system; rather, it is creating one which is unique to the institution and embodies the four characteristics. The discussion which follows suggests the implications of the characteristics for the behavior of planners, analysts, and executive decision-makers.

The most important implication is that an institution that analyzes its current planning/budgeting system from the perspective of a set of principles can find that it is generally doing very well but has limited deficiencies in one or two areas. Once the areas are identified, tinkering at the margin with the present system can solve the problem. This is a solution that is preferable to hiring armies of consultants or starting all over with a new system that is foreign to the school.

The four characteristics can be further analyzed to suggest some activities that should occur in the institution. Planners and analysts should work with decision-makers to identify the internal and external factors that are most critical for determining income, costs, and preferences. The relative importance of the factors varies from one institution to another. The planner needs to analyze the components of these factors, measure their effects, and estimate the ways in which they are likely to change in the future. In this process, the planner deals with both the activities and resources of the institution. The characteristics suggest only two factors that might not be explicit for some planners. These are creativity and iteration.

Creativity is necessary to avoid becoming fixed in old habits and visions, and it is most important in connection with reading and interpreting changes in the preference list. For example, if an institution is in the habit of surveying student opinion about different aspects of institutional functioning, and if the institution decides to start offering classes in the evenings and on the weekends, planners need to recognize that the new classes are attracting new kinds of students whose opinions should also be sampled.

Iteration refers to the need for planners to be in touch with executive decision-makers. Planners must check underlying assumptions and encourage appropriate changes in assumptions. Assumptions are critical to the work of the planner. Assumptions must be made explicit, and they must be congruent with those that executive decision-makers are willing to make. The planner is in an excellent position to detect that the assumptions are proving inadequate to the task, and he or she has the responsibility to bring this to the attention of the decision-makers for joint resolution.

Executive decision-makers have challenges of a different sort. It is up to them to identify and articulate institutional constants—those aspects of values, purposes, structure, and minimum acceptability that change only in the long run, if at all. They must also develop concrete visions of future possibilities that are congruent with the preferences of the institution. Both of these activities are summed up by a political philosopher who stated that the function of leadership is "to find the words that will enable the group to speak as a single voice" (Diesing 1962, p. 200).

Leadership is more an art than a science; it calls for intuitive—not analytical—capabilities. Therefore, analytical tools, like the Institutional Goals Inventory, are of little help. And, on a less abstract level, it is the decisionmaker's responsibility to develop sufficient flexibility in the system to allow disproportionate budget shifts. State schools in Colorado, for example, recently won significant increases in autonomy from legislative control over line-item expenditures.

Finally, the decision-making process for linking plans with budgets must have three features if it is to be able to implement the characteristics suggested earlier. First, it must allow and encourage frequent communication between planners and decision-makers so that assumptions can be checked and revised, and preferences incorporated. Second, in order to make the kinds of tradeoffs envisioned by the microeconomic analogy, similar or related decisions must be made simultaneously rather than sequentially. Third, the process must monitor important changes that relate to income, cost, or preference and call attention to these changes so that they will receive special attention.

A CASE STUDY OF AN OPTIMAL PLANNING/BUDGETING SYSTEM

Each spring, the planners at a university identify the areas about which they had insufficient information the preceding year. These become the subjects of special studies during the summer. Early in the fall, planners from both the academic and business sides of the university begin seven months of weekly meetings that culminate in the presentation of the proposed budget to the Board of Trustees. At these meetings, the planners discuss the kinds of budget requests that they expect to receive, their estimates of income and costs, and the issues about which they need executive guidance. By the second month of meetings, they have produced the first version of what are called "parameters papers"—rough estimates of income and expenses for the next year. Each is divided into about 10 major categories. The first version helps them identify how problematical the budget is likely to be, that is, how large the gap between income and expense projections is likely to be. As more precise information becomes available during the remaining months of meetings, the parameters papers are then reiterated, refined, and reduced to six or seven versions of the papers. In the meantime, recalculations for the parameters papers help identify where major problems are likely to surface. Concurrently, but using different and broader data sources, the group generates successively refined versions of a five-year financial forecast.

Another series of meetings also takes place during this period. The same planners meet every two weeks with the vice-presidents and the president to brief them on current estimates, point out potential problems, and obtain guidance in solving these problems. These meetings help the executives determine their position regarding budget requests. The academic vice-president, for example, writes a protocol letter to the deans describing constraints and priorities as he or she sees them for the coming budget year. In that letter, the vice-president solicits from each dean a budget letter itemizing requests. Each request is supported by analytic rationales and documentation. Before the dean writes the protocol letter, however, the vice-president and the academic planners meet with each dean. These meetings provide for both sides informal assessments of what is needed and what is feasible.

When the budget letters come in from the deans, the academic planners use them to develop a complete list of all requests. Although the vice-president reads all the letters and might discuss questions with the deans, he makes his funding decisions by reviewing the list of all requests. Since neither the vice-president nor his expressed preferences have changed for several years, the deans are likely to have made their requests and written their justifications so as to appeal to these prefer-

ences. Fortunately for all concerned, the vice-president developed his preferences through astute judgments about what was most important to him and the faculty. This feature of the deans' requests makes the vice-president's simultaneous decisions about all requests both easier and more difficult. They are more difficult because they all tend to appeal to his preferences; they are easier because he can hardly lose. Whatever he decides to fund will help the institution achieve what he wants it to achieve.

While the deans' letters are arriving and the list of all requests is taking shape, the weekly and biweekly joint meetings continue. The planners are dealing with financial constraints, and their deliberations both inform and are informed by the planning discussions among the executive decision-makers at several levels. Overall the process is similar to what has been termed "convergent budgeting" (Bacchetti 1978). Plans and budgets are gradually knitted together through an iterative process involving both analysts and decision-makers.

As for developing flexibilities in the system, this university is fortunate in being privately controlled and reasonably secure financially. The challenge is surely greater for public and financially troubled institutions. A flexibility-inducing system in this case is the conditional budget to which are assigned important budget requests that are not critical and are potentially deferrable. The conditional budget items are rank-ordered. Possible sources of funding are identified, including tuition income and indirect cost income that exceeds projections. If and when that income materializes, conditional budget items are authorized in the order that they appear on the list. Another system that promotes flexibility is one-time funding. When a budget request

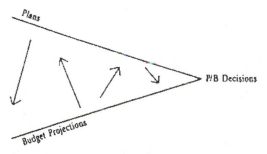

Figure 34.8 Convergent Budgeting

involves an experimental venture, or perhaps a cost that cannot be avoided but is unlikely to be authorized over the long term (for example, the salary of a retiring dean who is returning to the faculty for a short time and will not be replaced when he or she leaves), the request can be authorized. The temporary nature of the authorization is made very clear at the outset, and it is flagged in such a way that it will not slip unnoticed into the permanent budget.

To summarize, many different planning/budgeting systems are required to meet the needs of diverse institutions. It is not necessary to abandon the possibility of finding rationally optimal solutions. The basic principles underlying how the search might be conducted can be identified. In fact, the four characteristics in this monograph are principles that underlie a successful search for the optimal solution.

REFERENCES

Bacchetti, Raymond F. Stanford University, Stanford California. Seminar, 16 October 1978.

Diesing, Paul. (1962). *Reason in Society: Five Types of Decisions and Their Social Conditions.* Urbana, Ill.: University of Illinois Press, 1962.

CHAPTER 35

WHY LINKING BUDGETS TO PLANS HAS PROVEN DIFFICULT IN HIGHER EDUCATION

FRANK A. SCHMIDTLEIN

INTRODUCTION

Within the field of public administration, the belief that budgets should be derived from well-conceived plans appears to be an unquestioned article of faith. Like the search for the Holy Grail, theorists and practitioners for many years have maintained a quest for the secret to a successful linkage. Most observers of practice, however, find little evidence that this quest has been successful. If the secret has been found, its discoverer has shared this knowledge with few practitioners. Some theorists have claimed success, but, like claims for cold hydrogen fusion, the results of their formulations have been inconclusive and controversial. The most notable formulations devised for non-profit organizations have been Program, Planning and Budgeting Systems (PPBS) and Zero-based Budgeting (ZBB), both of which rapidly faded from the scene. Few examples of reportedly successful linkages appear to persist for long. Some, observing these circumstances, suggest that the knowledge and process benefits derived from the search justify continuing the quest even though effective connections remain elusive.

This paper examines some impediments to linking planning and budgeting successfully in higher education institutions. First, it describes various types of planning processes and analyzes the potential they have for producing information needed to guide campus budget processes. In addition, problems affecting the use of formal planning processes in colleges and universities are discussed. The next section describes different concepts of budgeting and explores their characteristics that may limit effective linkages to planning processes and outcomes. Finally, based on these descriptions and analyses, this paper presents some implications and conclusions that may help institutions design more realistic planning and budgeting processes.

The observations contained here are primarily based on an analysis of planning and budgeting literature and on findings and conclusions from two studies in which the author participated: a three-year, nationwide study of higher education institutional planning (Schmidtlein and Milton, 1989) and an earlier study of state higher education budgeting (Glenny and Schmidtlein, 1977).

TYPES OF PLANNING AND THEIR RELATIONSHIPS TO BUDGETING

Institutions can engage in several types of planning processes. In practice, however, they typically employ various mixes of more than one type of planning. Thus, when examining links between plan-

Source: *The Link Between Planning and Budgeting,* 1981, Frank A. Shmidtlein, National Center for Higher Education Management Systems, Boulder, CO.

ning and budgeting, one must be clear about which type of planning, or combination of types, is contemplated. Each type has different implications for achieving such a linkage. Principal types of planning identified in the literature (under various labels) include the following:

Strategic planning. Determining the nature of the environment in which an institution operates (and in which it will be operating), assessing its internal strengths and weaknesses, and developing a "vision" of its future character given these assumptions about its emerging situation.

Program planning. Determining the nature of the programs needed to implement the institution's vision and the types of structures and processes required to support these programs. The term "program," as used here, includes administrative, student service, and public service, as well as academic programs.

Facility planning. Determining the character of the physical facilities needed to implement effectively an institution's programs.

Operational planning. Establishing short-range objectives (typically for a coming budget year or biennium), determining their relative priorities, and deciding the kinds and levels of resources to be devoted to each objective. Sometimes this type of planning is termed "tactical planning."

Budget planning. Determining the goods and services needed to implement desired programs, estimating their costs, determining potential sources of revenues, and reconciling competing claims for resources, given assumptions about revenue limitations.

Issue-specific planning. Determining the policies and actions required to resolve issues affecting a specific campus function or limited set of functions (e.g., computer planning, affirmative action planning, student retention planning, or faculty development planning).

These definitions of the major types of planning are somewhat simplistic; other writers may use different language to describe such concepts, and some would define them differ-

ently. For example, some authors (Keller, 1983) argue that strategic planning encompasses and links many levels of planning. They might suggest that the term "mission planning" would be more appropriate for what is described above as strategic planning. In practice, planning frequently includes several levels and can vary from comprehensive (covering a full range of institutional concerns) to issue specific (dealing only with one or a narrow range of institutional concerns). Whatever definitions one uses, it is important to recognize that there are different levels of planning and that each has different implications for budgeting.

The definitions described were used to emphasize the complex range of activities encompassed by the term "planning" and to illustrate why its generic use can lead to confusion and frustration in practice. They also highlight distinctions that are helpful for analytical purposes. In the following paragraphs, these definitions are used as a basis for examining characteristics of different types of planning that may limit linking them effectively to budgeting.

STRATEGIC PLANNING'S LINKS TO BUDGETING

Ideally, strategic planning, as defined here, leads to agreement on an institution's mission and provides a broad vision of its future directions. It obviously does not provide operational guidance for decisions on specific priorities or on the goods and services an institution should request in a budget document. Indeed, it does not even provide unambiguous guidance for defining and selecting particular programs. Such a vision defines a market niche and an institutional mission appropriate for exploiting that niche. Levels and types of programs can then be specified that will be compatible with that mission, but there is room for debate over the most desirable, specific programs. Consensus on a mission creates a set of shared, often implicit, assumptions that create a context for budget decisions, but this context rarely provides explicit guidance for budget decisions. For example, no one interviewed during the planning and budgeting studies cited earlier reported that they examined a campus mission statement for guidance during budget negotiations.

PROGRAM PLANNING'S LINKS TO BUDGETING

Program plans provide somewhat more specific guidance for budgeting than do strategic plans, but agreement on the character of an institution's programs only partially clarifies what items and amounts should be included in budgets. The size and relative priority of programs fluctuate as their circumstance change. Student choice, political support, faculty recruitment success and many other factors alter priorities among programs from year to year. While operational agreement on programs provides a greater degree of guidance for budget decisions than does consensus on only a strategic vision, there remains a large area for discretionary decisions. Many different flowers can bloom when faculty or administrators begin to determine the specifics and implement a program.

Facility Plannning's Links to Budgeting

In a logical world, one would suppose that facilities plans would be derived from program plans and that, in turn, capital-budget plans would be derived from facility plans. However, these linkages usually are not this explicit and orderly. Often facility plans are developed with only modest guidance from program plans if, in fact, program plans even explicitly exist. Facility plans typically are developed for a full range of campus infrastructure needs for a five- to twenty-year period, priorities are established for meeting these needs, and estimates are made of the costs of these plans. However, immediately preceding or during a budget cycle, assumptions are made about financial costs and feasibility and, for public campuses, the political attractiveness of particular facility projects. Also, in the public sector several different sources of funds may be used to finance a project. Consequently, project timing may depend on when funds from various sources become available. Therefore, priorities frequently shift to align budget requests with these financial constraints and political imperatives. As a result, facility projects that are budgeted for a particular future year typically are not funded in that year.

Facility costs usually are presented in capital budgets that are prepared and reviewed through different processes from those employed in formulating and presenting operating budgets. As a consequence, decisions must be made on the effects the facility budget will have on operating budgets. What will be the impact on utility, maintenance, and similar operating costs? These separate tracks sometimes create difficulties in coordinating the two requests. For example, provisions may not be included in the operating budget for costs associated with a building that, late in the review process, is moved up in the capital-budget-priority rankings.

OPERATIONAL PLANNING'S LINKS TO BUDGETING

The primary function of operational planning is to develop consensus on specific items to be included in a budget, or at least the new items, since most of the items in a budget represent continuing commitments. Operational planning, in theory, should take place before decisions are made on the contents of budget requests. Thus, agreement will be reached and decisions on relative priorities made in a more orderly manner prior to the intense period of effort, with tight deadlines, typical during budget formulation. This concept rests on the hope that through an early planning cycle, analysis can take place and political struggles settled, avoiding their interfering with technical work involved in costing out elements in the budget, identifying fund sources or accounts, and preparing budget justifications. However, in practice, operational planning often takes place as budgetary decisions are being formulated, for reasons discussed later.

BUDGET PLANNING

Budget planning involves making decisions on specific amounts of resources to be devoted to specific purposes for each program. The fine distinction between budget planning and operational planning is based on a recognition that plans seldom can provide sufficiently detailed and complete blueprints for determining the specific items and amounts to be included in requests. Also, the most recent estimates of revenue availability and emerging cost estimates typically result in modifying prior plans. These are among the many reasons why operational planning does not provide complete recipes for budgeters to follow as they perform their technical tasks.

ISSUE SPECIFIC PLANNING LINKS TO BUDGETING

Planning to deal with specific issues typically is generated by external or internal pressures to modify or correct an undesirable situation. The situation is reviewed and analyzed and recommendations made for improvements, perhaps the most common kind of institutional planning. However, if it is the only planning going on, it is often criticized for lacking context and failing to provide a strategic sense of where the institution is headed. Furthermore, since it is not comprehensive, it may not recognize complex relationships among various facets of a campus.

Issue-specific plans may or may not include detailed descriptions of the actions needed to correct the situation or of the budget amounts needed to implement recommendations. Ideally, the budgetary implications of such plans would be made explicit. However, these plans run into the same political circumstances described later and, consequently, may not necessarily be closely linked to budgets.

IMPLICATIONS OF THE DIFFERENT TYPES OF PLANNING

These brief and somewhat simplistic descriptions of different types of planning clearly illustrate the fallacy of discussing generically the linkages between planning and budgeting. Strategic planning and program planning generally provide common assumptions and a general context for formulating budgets, but rarely provide substantial operational guidance for particular budgetary decisions. Operational planning, in theory, should provide more specific guidance for budgeting; however, plans frequently are altered in response to cost and revenue considerations which come into focus as budgets are calculated. In addition, these descriptions of different types of planning are based primarily on what, in theory, should take place. No claims have been made

so far as to whether, in practice, these types of planning actually function as set forth. The next section addresses that issue.

Efficacy of Planning Practices

The belief that budgets can be linked to plans rests on an assumption that it is feasible and cost effective to create reasonably comprehensive plans which can be—and will be—used to guide institutional decisions. The literature and recent research on planning suggest that this assumption is subject to a number of qualifications (Schmidtlein and Milton, 1989; van Vught, 1988). Some factors that hamper applying textbook approaches to institutional planning will be described.

LIMITED POWERS OF PREDICTION

Human beings, undoubtedly well before the use of the oracle at Delphi, have sought to reduce their uncertainty regarding future conditions. Planning is one means toward this end. Planning attempts to gain information and insights into the character of future conditions in order to guide current decisions on courses of action. Persons interviewed regarding planning at their campuses, during the study mentioned earlier, nearly always stressed its importance in preparing their campus to meet emerging conditions. However, in commenting further, they noted the great difficulties of predicting future conditions affecting their institutions and the dangers of over reliance on plans. As one commented, "What comes up is as important as what is planned. That's life."

As a consequence of the uncertain nature of assumptions about future conditions contained in institutional plans, campus staff stressed the importance of maintaining flexibility to react promptly to emerging opportunities and problems. They sought to avoid expending significant amounts of resources to develop plans that in time would be found unwise or impractical. Most emphasized the importance of the process in contrast to the production of a document that rapidly becomes outdated. In addition, they were concerned about planning cycles and plans becoming too rigid, impeding efforts undertake new initiatives promptly and causing them to expend excessive time and resources justifying sensible departures from printed plans.

The uncertainty of predictions contained in plans—and the strategies employed to deal with these circumstances—lead institutional staff to delay decisions when feasible in order to take advantage of the most recent assessments of conditions. Emerging conditions and new information typically resulted in changes in plans right up to the deadlines for budget decisions. Some observers of budget behavior have commented that only externally imposed deadlines and printer's schedules force participants to make controversial budget decisions! These circumstances weaken the feasibility of linking budgets closely to earlier plans and suggest limitations on the feasibility of overly formalized planning practices.

THE POLITICAL CHARACTER OF PLANNING AND BUDGETING

Decisions on plans and budgets are made through institutional political processes. Their contents reflect the outcome of negotiations and the exercise of influence by a wide variety of actors having varying degrees of power and diverse sets of values and preferences. When there are changes in locations and degrees of influence and in values and preferences, earlier plans and budgets are also likely to change. The consensus represented by any plan or budget does not imply a moratorium on the political activities of participants who sought different visions of the future and different decisions. Consequently, issues that were "decided" in plans are frequently reopened with greater fervor during budget negotiations where resources are at stake, not just potential courses of action. The gap in time between completing a plan and formulating a budget permits the emergence of shifts in influence and new perceptions of values and self-interests that can alter earlier plans.

Organizational units nearly always view planning as a means to enlarge their budgets, while central staff frequently seek reallocations and reductions. As a result, unit plans frequently contain "laundry lists" of new items for which they seek resources. One faculty member, commenting on a new planning process at his campus, said the president wanted plans to mesh with the budget. However, people on (planning) committees get "wild eyed" and embarrass the president with demands. The politics of reconciling financially unrealistic unit requests with institution-wide priorities complicates the development of explicit plans.

Often it is not politic to make public the priority ratings attached to units or the elements of their plans. To do so could create a self-fulfilling prophecy. Those with low ratings might lose their most competent and thus most mobile staff, their recruitment opportunities, and their morale. As a consequence, "real" priorities are frequently not revealed in plans. They can be inferred from budgets, but even in these documents, they may not be made explicit. And there are other reasons for not revealing priorities. At one campus, an administrator observed that an earlier president, after discussions of the plan's effects on the budget, lost interest in planning. He didn't want to discuss cost figures in public. The stadium would not have been built as the result of a planning process. "The costs have made us mad. That was where our salary money went." Another campus received a $4.7 million grant to construct a building and employ two additional faculty members, bypassing the normal channels of academic review. The person most closely involved said that the school could not have received the grant if it had been announced in advance and its merits debated on campus. The grant "raised some hackles" among faculty because "any addition changes the balance of power."

The politics of institutional budgeting create many versions of the "Washington Monument Ploy," which gets its name from a story, probably apocryphal, told in Washington budget circles. According to the story, the Department of Interior, when asked to set its priorities for potential budget cuts, listed opening the Washington Monument on weekends as its lowest priority activity in order to appear responsive while recognizing that Congress would never consent to such an action, thus protecting more risky items from budget scrutiny.

Plans are often not an inadequate guide for budget decisions because units typically are reluctant to document their significant problems. They fear—probably correctly—that the press, politicians, and the public will gain inflated impressions of a problem's significance. Their critics and competitors may be able to use such negative information against them in budgetary competitions. As a consequence, plans appear to be better guides for new initiatives than they are for reductions or reallocations. When financial problems become too severe, units can defer planning. At two campuses visited during the planning study, budget crises had resulted in formal long-range planning efforts to be placed on hold. Even in the best of times, organizations tend to view their budget base as a "given" and seek to confine discussions to requests for increases. Cutting budgets usually is a politically difficult task.

EFFECT OF PLANNING PROCESS CONSTRAINTS ON BUDGETING

The observations presented list a few of the constraints on successful institutional planning. Planning seeks to reveal the character of a highly uncertain future and is conducted in a political environment. Consequently, the more specific a plan becomes and, therefore, the more useful it is for providing budget guidance, the more quickly it becomes outdated. Similarly, the more specific a plan becomes, the more likely it will generate political conflict. These circumstances reveal some of the reasons why attempts to link planning to budgeting have had limited success. Consequently, the plans that budget staff might rely on either do not exist or do not provide substantial guidance.

TYPES OF BUDGET PROCESSES AND THEIR RELIANCE ON PLANNING

Budget concepts may be prescribed either by state governments, multi-campus system offices, or campuses. Often a state may employ one budget concept and an institution another, or different agencies within a state may employ different budget concepts in their analyses of institutional budgets. These circumstances increase both the complexity of the budget process and the attempts to derive them from plans.

A number of budget concepts have been described in the literature on the subject. Each of these approaches focuses attention on different organizational concerns. Some focus on the contents of budget increases, others on programs and outcomes, and still others on technical measures of workload or performance. These areas of focus have implications for linking budget processes to planning. Principal budget concepts that have been recommended or utilized in higher education include the following:

Incremental budgeting. Involves establishing a budget "base" for a particular year or biennium and then determining additions to or deletions from that base. However, particular issues affecting the budget base may be examined during budget review when reviewers perceive an issue. Occasionally, more extensive studies of areas in the budget base may be conducted during the budget "off season." Budgets most commonly are presented by "line item," or major objects of expenditure, for each organizational unit.

Formula budgeting. Involves designing and employing a mathematical model or models, typically based on costs and workload or performance factors, to calculate some portion of an institution's budget. Budgets calculated by this method usually contain amounts for each area covered by the formula, such as instruction or libraries, and amounts for functions not included in the formula. When formula budget requests exceed available revenues, reductions commonly are made by reducing the amounts generated by each formula.

Program budgeting. Involves grouping institutional activities that have similar goals into "programs" and, through systems analysis and cost/benefit studies, estimating the resources required to produce the outputs sought from each program. Program categories frequently cut across organizational lines. Budget presentations focus on the results of programs rather than on items to be purchased.

Zero-Based Budgeting. Involves developing budget "decision packages" at the lowest levels of the organization, rank ordering the priority of these decision packages and reviewing and making further decisions on priorities at successive organizational levels. In theory, an assumption is made that every program, or decision package, will be reviewed each year, weeding low priorities from the "budget base."

Performance budgeting. Involves developing indicators of institutional performance and estimating the resources required to maintain selected levels of performance.

In practice, budgets frequently contain features of more than one of these concepts. Higher education institutions generally use incremental or formula concepts to develop their budgets.

The characteristics of planning described earlier show that budgeting generally involves much more than merely costing out pre-existing formal organizational plans. Budget practices, however, also pose problems for planning. Budgets that were agreed upon for the current year are not necessarily followed during the year as new circumstances arise and new understandings develop. Thus, the current budget does not always provide a fully satisfactory reference point for planning. Even more frustrating for planners, particularly in public institutions, decisions on budgets often are delayed or changed after the deadlines for making planning decisions. Thus, planners often do not have a stable set of budget assumptions to serve as a basis for their plans.

PLANNING AND INCREMENTAL BUDGETING

Incremental budgeting focuses on increases in objects-of-expenditure lines, organizational or program categories, and new initiatives. Consequently, it directs planning attention toward the new activities and items sought by an institution. Wildavsky (1964) presented the classic description of this form of budgeting. Incremental approaches to budgeting provide fewer incentives to examine the comparative priorities of items in the budget base. However, a virtue of incremental budgeting is its reducing to manageable proportions the scope of budget considerations. In a sense, it lessens dependence on *a priori* planning since decisions on increases can take place during budget formulation through budget analyses and political negotiations, without necessarily referring to formal plans.

However, time constraints and the stresses of these political debates during the budget process lead people to propose operational planning as a means to settle conflicts over priorities in a more deliberate and thoughtful way prior to the budget formulation cycle. Operational plans to provide guidance for incremental budgeting can range from central staff holding general discussions with units regarding their priorities while, at the same time, providing units with some feedback on overall institutional priorities, to preparing detailed written plans containing lists of specific goods and services sought. As noted earlier, detailed requests for unit budget increases frequently are not constrained by realistic assumptions about available funds. Consequently, units end up frustrated because their detailed planning does not appear to have had a visible effect on budgetary decisions. Campus officials face a difficult dilemma when trying at the same time to encourage unit creativity and initiative and to avoid unrealistic expectations and disillusionment.

Discussion and communication of priorities to campus units in advance of institutional budget negotiations are important. But highly detailed operational plans are time consuming, often reflect unrealistic expectations, and rapidly become dated. Therefore, in many cases, their usefulness may be offset by their costs. Strategic and program planning tends to provide a context for incremental planning and, when successful, provides sets of common assumptions. These forms of planning do not, however, have direct links to decisions on specific priorities, items, and amounts to be included in budgets. Incremental budgets can be derived from plans, but do not depend upon their presence.

PLANNING AND FORMULA BUDGETING

Formula budgeting focuses planning attention on the appropriateness and accuracy of variables included in the formulas and on costs not adequately recognized by formulas. Attention also is directed toward the costs of functions not covered by formulas. This approach to budgeting has been described by Meisinger (1976). State formulas have the virtue of generating a zero-based budget for an institution rather than adding and subtracting from a past year's base. They provide a means to establish equity among campuses and generally direct state attention to technical issues rather than to substantive program issues. But campuses usually do not use state budget formulas to allocate funds internally. Formulas typically generate total amounts for campuses, with inequities from inadequate funding in one area tending to be cancelled out by surpluses generated in another. In some cases, though, different formulas may be used to fund different campus functions and, if transfers among functions are restricted, can set institutional priorities.

Campuses generally value the programmatic autonomy and flexibility a formula budget provides. Internally, if formulas are too rigidly adhered to, they can create distortions and inequities in fund allocations. Institutional units normally seek budgets that are more carefully tailored to their circumstances than would be possible through using all but the most complex and cumbersome formulas. In some cases, however, campuses use simple formulas for internal fund allocation in areas such as faculty travel or instructional materials.

Since formulas reflect what already exists at a campus, or is projected to exist (e.g., project credit hours), they do not necessarily provide incentives for planning, but represent levels of funding that may or may not have been determined through formal planning processes. Although formulas can be designed to give priority to various campus functions, this tends to make them complex and can create unintended negative incentives. Institutions usually are given considerable flexibility to allocate formula-generated funds as they see fit, within the limits of their perceptions of political realities. A campus may engage in planning to determine its substantive directions, and the formula will reflect changes that result from such decisions. A campus also may use planning to determine internal fund allocations, but these decisions will only affect budget requests to the extent that they alter variables used in computing formula amounts. Planning, however, can affect the values used to inflate formulas from year to year. When comparative studies show that formula-generated amounts result in an institution's being at a competitive disadvantage in relation to peer campuses, then adjustments are often made in the formula.

PLANNING AND PROGRAM BUDGETING

Program budgeting focuses attention on the objectives and contents of institutions' academic and administrative programs. The literature on Program-Planning-Budgeting Systems (PPBS) (Hartley, 1968) best describes this budget concept. Examining and seeking justifications for the substance of an institution's programs has considerable intuitive appeal. The analysis of programs during budget review obviously is aided by plans that describe the logic and character of current institutional activities. The review of programs in budgets is also facilitated if prior consensus can be established about their objectives and the outputs required to achieve these objectives. However, problems in defining and measuring outputs was a major factor that frustrated the adoption of PPBS by colleges and universities. Program budgeting—despite its theoretical appeal—has thus proven in practice to be difficult to implement. This difficulty results, in part, from the processes through which program decisions are made in colleges and universities.

As their core staff, higher education institutions have faculty who operate according to principles governing professions. Like other professionals who possess considerable autonomy to make decisions in their highly specialized fields, faculty are given a great deal of autonomy to design, implement, and assess academic programs. New ideas for academic programs and program modifications typically emerge from the interests and expertise of a faculty member or a small group of faculty rather than from planning committees or administrators. Only when initiatives cut across established disciplines, or involve areas of expertise not present in a faculty, are they likely to be generated by campus administrators. Department faculty often believe they have little in common with other departments and frequently consider time spent on joint efforts wasted.

Faculty jealously protect their academic freedom and professional autonomy. As a consequence, they do not welcome the "uninformed" interventions of budget staff and lay policy makers into the substance of their fields. As a consequence, program budgeting, which focuses outsiders' attention on substantive academic matters, often is viewed as inconsistent with the nature and values of the academic enterprise. Budget processes which focus on means and on the equity of resource distributions are less threatening to academic independence. Academics tend to view accountability as resulting from subjecting their performance to the scrutiny of peers in their fields, not through substantive reviews of their work by lay administrators and policy makers. The test of a desirable program, from this perspective, is quality ratings by peers and the program's power in the academic marketplace to attract students, not administrators' judgments during budget reviews. Obviously, there is a legitimate public interest in the substance of academic programs. Academics, however, would argue that there are ways of recognizing this interest that are less intrusive than detailed administrative scrutiny of substantive matters during budget reviews.

PLANNING AND ZERO-BASED BUDGETING

Zero-Based Budgeting (ZBB) (Phyrr, 1973), like program budgeting, focuses budgetary attention on the substance of programs. It assumes that the activities required to achieve institutional objectives can be grouped together into decision packages and ranked according to judgments on their relative priorities. As decision packages are reviewed at successively higher organizational levels, choices among them are made on relative priorities. The development of decision packages requires analysis and planning, and, presumably, decisions on priorities would be based on some coherent vision of the direction in which the institution should proceed. In theory, development of the decision packages should result from a comprehensive review of an institution's activities, and those reviewing the various decision packages would require considerable detailed knowledge of their contents and interrelationships to make proper choices. In practice, both of these assumptions appear questionable in colleges and universities.

Many aspects of budgets are based on long-standing agreements that have political significance. Thus, opening up too broad an array of issues has a potential for creating more political problems than can be dealt with in the time available. In addition, a comprehensive review does not recognize that various issues have differing priorities and that attempting to deal with all of them can impose an unmanageable workload on an organization. Energy required for performing primary instructional, research, and public service functions can be diverted to analyzing and reporting on the importance of the functions. One observer has likened this to a farmer pulling up his cabbage plants every week or so to determine if their roots are growing properly. Furthermore, successive levels of review of decision packages require considerable time and expertise that may not be available. Provosts who are history professors have limited credentials for substantively reviewing alternative directions the physics department might be proposing and vice versa.

The difficulties of relating ZZB to planning are much the same as those already described regarding program budgeting. ZZB assumes a process for defining goals or outputs to serve as a basis for determining priorities that ignores the political nature of setting institutional priorities and the distribution of institutional decision-making authority. This technique requires a formal, structured, and elaborate process that may be more expensive and time consuming than it is worth. Consequently, like program budgeting, ZZB rarely is employed by institutions.

PLANNING AND PERFORMANCE BUDGETING

Performance budgeting assumes an ability to define and agree on the performance measures to be employed in budgets and the ability to attach costs to each of these measures. Elements of this approach do not appear to be used in a comprehensive way as a distinct method of institutional budgeting. Performance budgeting, like formula budgeting, is a rather technical approach to developing budget requests. An attempt is made to define measures of performance and to determine legitimate costs for each. Issues such as the comparative priority of programs and the quality of programs are only indirectly considered through selection of, and changes in, performance measures. As in the case of formula budgets, plans can specify changes that will affect factors used to calculate a performance budget. Plans can establish or imply new performance measures or establish new methods for making cost estimates.

The primary problems in linking planning to performance budgets concern getting consensus on the appropriate indicators of performance, finding ways to measure various types of performance and determining accurately and equitably the costs of achieving a given level of performance. Planning may help with these problems, but, as noted earlier, the political constraints on planning and the character of academic decision making cause difficulties in achieving such a linking.

CONCLUSIONS

Planning takes many forms, which vary in different institutional settings. As a consequence, the relationship between planning and budgeting is complex and often indirect. In addition, there are a number of limitations on the effectiveness of institutional planning: the uncertain nature of future conditions and difficulties in predicting opportunities and threats, the politics of institutional decision making, the distribution of power in institutions, the potential rigidities of formal planning processes, and the time and costs required for comprehensive planning.

Budgeting also takes many different forms and reflects different timetables. Each approach focuses decision making on different institutional concerns. Some forms of budgeting conceptually are more closely linked to planning than others (e.g., program budgeting). However, the approaches to budgeting that have been most explicitly linked to planning—PPBS and ZBB—generally have not been successfully implemented by colleges and universities. Academics value their professional autonomy and academic freedom and resist lay "interference" into substantive academic matters. Consequently, institutions usually do not want budget-office staff members who lack academic credentials to take a leading role in analyzing

alternative approaches to academic programs in the pursuit of resource allocation "efficiencies."

Institutions clearly need to consider their future circumstances and directions and the programs and resources required to move in desired directions. However, the processes and structures they employ in doing so are highly complex and situational. As a consequence, there is considerable evidence that the processes commonly prescribed in the literature on formal planning and on relating planning and budgeting are not proving effective in practice. Perhaps intensive research on the processes being employed to make decisions in institutions will shed some light on what works in practice and will help us revise our theories of planning and budgeting to make them more useful guides to practice.

REFERENCES

Glenny, Lyman & Schmitlein, Frank. (1977). *State budgeting for higher education: The political economy of the process.* Center for Research and Development in Higher Education, University of California, Berkeley.

Hartley, Harry. (1968). *Educational planning-programming-budgeting: A systems approach.* Englewood Cliffs, NJ: Prentice-Hall, Inc.

Keller, George. (1983). *Academic strategy: The management revolution in American higher education.* Baltimore: The Johns Hopkins University Press.

Meisinger, Richard. (1976). *State budgeting for higher education: The uses of formulas.* Center for Research and Development in Higher Education, University of California, Berkeley.

Phyrr, Peter. (1973). *Zero-based budgeting: A practical management tool for evaluating expenses.* New York: John Wiley and Sons, Inc.

Schmidtlein, Frank & Milton, Toby. (1989). College and university planning: Perspectives from a nation-wide study. *Planning for higher education, 17* (3), 1–19.

van Vught, Franz. (1988). Flexibility production and pattern management: Two basic instruments of strategic planning for higher education institutions. The Netherlands: Centre for Higher Education Policy Studies, University of Twente.

Wildavsky, Aaron. (1979). *The politics of the budgetary process,* 3rd ed. Boston: Little, Brown and Company.

CHAPTER 36

CHANGING FISCAL STRATEGIES FOR PLANNING

PAUL T. BRINKMAN AND ANTHONY W. MORGAN

"Long ago, when people wished to discern the shape of things to come, they looked to the stars; today they look at the budget" (Caiden, 1988, p. 42). Today, most analysts of planning and budgeting, at least in the nonprofit sector, assume or advocate a comprehensive, sequential, and rational linking between these two managerial activities. Plans, be they strategic or otherwise, are developed and budgets become the mechanisms for their implementation. In this chapter, we examine this traditional and sometimes normative view, particularly in light of the theme and assumptions of this book.

Most discussions of budgeting focus almost exclusively on the expenditure side of the equation: how expenditure authorizations are allocated to institutions or to units within institutions. Historically, private colleges and universities have been more dependent and therefore more acutely aware of what might be called "revenue markets," including the sensitivities associated with higher tuition levels and donor satisfaction and the connections between those sensitivities or constraints and expenditures. Diversification of revenue sources and increasing competition for revenues in the public sector, however, have made the links between revenue sources and allocation of resources more critical for everyone in higher education. We have therefore paid more attention in what follows to the revenue side of budgeting and the dynamics of planning and budgeting for resources secured in different revenue markets.

Finally, we examine two methods of allocating resources, known as performance budgeting and responsibility center budgeting, against the framework of higher education's need to maintain public trust, its reliance on multiple revenue sources, and its financial future. In the latter context, we also weigh the possibility that colleges and universities might eventually behave more like for-profit than not-for-profit organizations. Our focus is planning and budgeting at the institutional level. We deal with the perspectives of both the central administration within an institution and those of academic and administrative units.

CONTEXT

We believe the following developments are likely to occur and have significant impact on planning and budgeting.

Source: Peterson, M., Dill, D., Mets, L., & Associates (1997), *Planning and Management for a Changing Environment*, Jossey-Bass, pp. 288–306.

Assumptions

1. Many institutions will face a decline in real resources per student (Brinkman and Morgan, 1995).

2. Technology will become ever more pervasive in virtually all higher education endeavors, introduce new levels of competition both from within higher education and from new educational providers, and complicate costing and pricing.

3. The production, control, and management of information will become increasingly important in most organizations.

4. New and expanding markets, such as distance education, will provide opportunities and forces for change.

5. The push for accountability will increase rather than abate.

In short, we envision a fast-moving environment of shifting competition and changing opportunities. Combined with a relatively difficult resource situation, tolerance for error is diminished. Conditions favor the fast and surefooted.

Budgetary Context

Facing that environment is a higher education enterprise whose budgetary practices and characteristics are in some ways less than ideal, given what needs to be done. The salient features are these:

1. The default fiscal strategy for most higher education institutions and their operating units is to increase revenues rather than reduce costs.

2. Most higher education institutions are in multiple "businesses" with different financial objectives and operating within different markets.

3. Most higher education institutions have multiple revenue sources; these sources differ with respect to acquisition and spending rules.

4. Institutions differ significantly from one another in the share of revenue coming from particular sources, as do their individual operating units.

5. Particularly in the academic area, budgetary structures do not always match up well with planning structures. The chemistry department or the office of undergraduate education, for example, may both be planning nodes, but typically the latter is not a budget center. Plans and budgets can also be out of step in a temporal sense.

6. Higher education budgets have multiple purposes. Short-run goals often collide with long-term goals.

7. Higher education budgets tend to be an inertial force; the typical budgeting process is such that anything more than incremental change is likely to meet resistance.

ELEMENTS OF A FISCAL STRATEGY

In what follows, we specify in a normative fashion the elements of a fiscal strategy that need to be present no matter how planning and budgeting are organized and developed.

Resource Acquisition

A fiscal strategy includes responses, explicit or implicit, to certain questions. Is the institution committed to revenue maximization? In balancing the budget, will revenue enhancement normally be the first option, or will it be a second option after expenditure reduction? Will revenue be pursued wherever there are possibilities, or only selectively according to a plan or set of principles?

However these questions are answered, most institutions and their business units would probably agree with the following goals for revenue acquisition: (1) ensure marginal revenue growth, (2) ensure predictable and stable revenue, and (3) find revenues that are flexible in how they can be deployed. Organizations need to develop new revenue sources and expand existing ones in order to meet legitimate organizational needs and keep key constituents happy. The absence of reasonable predictability (as evidenced by planning and budgeting in poor countries) causes enormous problems for both planning and budgeting. Unrestricted revenues are highly prized because they can be used to address a range of needs.

Resource Allocation

A fiscal strategy contains the objectives and the rules for allocating resources. The strategy indicates, first and foremost, the basis upon which allocations are to be made. (Often, this is equivalent to how "need" is to be determined.) Second, budget centers need to be established, as do rules governing how their debts and surpluses are handled. Finally, a procedure for allocation, such as zero-based budgeting, must be specified. Whatever the procedure, the fiscal strategy must include provision for how various short-term and long-term allocation goals are addressed.

Without resource allocation, essentially nothing can happen. Making something happen involves two short-term objectives: (1) meet immediate production and support costs, and (2) impose efficiency. From a longer-term perspective, other objectives must also be addressed: (1) preserve organizational assets, (2) invest in the future, and (3) deploy resources strategically.

Arguably, all of these things that the acquisition and allocation processes ought to do in conjunction with various plans should be incorporated in any institution's overall fiscal strategy. Ideally, all of these objectives would be addressed openly and in an integrated way.

Other Dimensions

Assumptions of declining real resources and emerging competitive forces give impetus to several other important dimensions of planning and budgeting as they generate a fiscal strategy: reallocation, incentives, the links between planning and budgeting, and maintaining political support. Strictly speaking, reallocation of resources is just a type of allocation, but experienced practitioners know the difference between distributive and redistributive politics (Morgan, 1992). Conditions of fiscal stringency combined with rapid change increase the need to bring reallocation strategies front and center. Any fiscal strategy, and especially any serious reallocation effort, must be formulated with explicit incentives as part of the design (Berg, 1985) unless an institution

is prepared to operate in a highly centralized, top-down manner. A fiscal strategy flows out of the intersection of plans and budgets. Explicit attention to that fact should be included within the fiscal strategy itself: how the intersection is managed, who has responsibility for its occurrence, check points, and so on. Finally, fiscal strategies that ignore political realities are likely to be short-lived, especially in difficult times.

With these additional dimensions, it is obvious to us that a fiscal strategy is and should be woven deeply into the fabric of institutional management. Simplistic approaches, such as "we want to do X; can we afford it?" won't do. This becomes even more evident as we examine the issues and strategy options below.

ELEMENTS AND STRATEGIES

We focus on three tasks: maintaining trust in a trust market, managing in the context of multiple revenue sources, and dealing with financial stringency and reallocation. While concerned about a range of planning and budgeting issues, we pay special attention to the extent to which performance budgeting (PB) and responsibility center budgeting (RCB) are likely to be helpful platforms for handling these tasks. In the former approach to budgeting, resource allocations to operating units are linked in some manner to specific levels of performance by those units, such as test scores on a licensure examination (for details, see Ashworth, 1994). In the RCB approach, budget responsibility is highly decentralized, as some or all large operating units, such as a college within a university, are given responsibility for managing all of their own finances. They are assigned revenue, including that from tuition, and must use that revenue to cover their full costs (for details, see Zemsky, Porter, and Odel, 1978; Whalen, 1991).

Maintaining Trust in a Trust Market

Operating in a trust market is a critical ingredient of the environment for higher education institutions. A trust market is characterized by asymmetry of information: the seller knows more about the product or service being sold than does the buyer. For example, few buyers of higher education services truly understand the economics of the enterprise or the qualitative nuances within an academic discipline or an undergraduate education.

In a trust market, business depends on the trust the buyers have in the integrity of the sellers. If the level of trust deteriorates, buyers may at some point refuse to make transactions. It deteriorates if buyers feel they are being taken advantage of, or if they feel that the sellers are not behaving appropriately.

For some time, as Winston (1992) has argued, higher education has been drawing down on what once was a large reservoir of trust. The drawdown has been due to many specific developments and episodes: the rash of criticism of the academy (some of it coming from inside), concerns about workload, salaries that seem high when compared to those of high-profile public figures, occasional but highly publicized instances of scientific fraud committed by university researchers, the overdone aspects of college athletics, the indirect-cost recovery debacle, student loan defaults, the breakdown of consensus on accreditation, and so on. Many of these problems are rooted in higher education's revenue-maximizing behavior, which has intensified since Bowen (1980), among others, called attention to it more than a decade ago. Other problems are rooted in choices about resource utilization, choices that often reflect the private interests of faculty and administrators (James, 1990) or lust for prestige (Garvin, 1980) rather than the interests of constituents.

One such constituent, the federal government, has been showing signs of diminishing trust. The hearings on indirect-cost recovery rates were an example. The message implicit in student right-to-know legislation is quite clear. State governments have also been growing uneasy, as the accountability movement demonstrates. States are interested in reducing the asymmetry of information; they would not be if trust levels remained high. Students have been less vocal, perhaps, but they have been voting with their feet—or at least that is one way of interpreting the increased market share enjoyed by community colleges.

Higher education institutions are facing a dilemma. They are thoroughly accustomed to revenue maximization and setting their own priorities as first principles of fiscal strategy. Yet both behaviors threaten the trust various constituents place in our enterprise. At some point, loss of trust engendered by revenue maximizing results in a net loss in revenue—a classic bind. Similarly, efforts to dictate product and service mix may eventually result in a decline in the demand for those products and services.

There is an obvious need, then, to address these problems. Institutions must learn to focus less on revenue acquisition and more on cost containment. They must better understand their own operations and both the primary and secondary effects of their choices. They must be more forthcoming about their activities and align their priorities with those of their constituents.

A deteriorating trust market and the actions required to reverse the situation indicate a need to strengthen the linkage between planning and budgeting. Planning structures should provide the appropriate venue for consideration of possible second- and third-order effects of alternative fiscal strategies. The loss of trust is just such an effect. No one set out to accomplish that deliberately. Similarly, planning activities should as a matter of course orchestrate the analysis of priorities for both internal consistency and agreement with constituent needs and interests.

From the latter perspective, it would seem that either PB or RCB is likely to be preferable to incremental budgeting. Implementation details are important, of course, but PB in particular has some clear advantages in a trust market.

First, performance budgeting cannot be implemented without serious consideration being given to the range of performances that will be rewarded or supported and to the powerful incentives created by those decisions. Those considerations can and should lead backwards, as it were, to how the institution and its programs are supported, which in turn can and should lead to a discussion about constituents and their interests. Second, if the agreed-upon performance indicators happen to include those favored by constituents, the institution has an obvious basis on which to build and maintain trust. If valued performance goes in some other direction, the institution at least has an evident, visible problem with which to contend. Higher education got into some of its trust problems gradually and in an unplanned way. There is value in bringing priorities and consequences into sharper focus.

We think these advantages of PB could be achieved even if the institution did not quantify the relationship between specific measures of performance and the allocation of resources. Indeed, our preference would be to include performance as an important basis for allocation decisions but not, as a rule, to quantify the relationship because of the imperfect nature of most measures and the difficulty of integrating multiple measures in any mechanical way. Ashworth (1994) and Lasher and Greene (1993) provide helpful assessments of the strengths and weaknesses of PB, albeit in the context of funding institutions and not internal allocation.

Managing Multiple Revenue Sources

From a comparative financing perspective, American colleges and universities are the envy of the world. Historically, higher education institutions in most other nations have received an overwhelming share of their support from a national government and are in turn subject directly and singly to its political and economic vicissitudes. These nations have looked at the diversity of sources of funding available to American colleges and universities as providing some measure of financial stability and alternative avenues for revenue growth. When government funding growth is nonexistent or slow, tuition and private funds might provide a counter-balancing effect. Even the existence of two or three different governments (federal, state, and local) contributing to the support of public institutions is viewed as a stabilizing force, both politically and economically. Not surprisingly, more nations, including several in Europe, are moving away from single-source funding of higher education.

The reality of living with multiple sources of revenue reveals, however, the two edges of this mighty sword. The existence of these multiple streams of revenue substantially undermines simplistic models of planning and budgeting. Most discussions and models of planning and budgeting simplify either by assuming a single revenue source (in the form of an overall bottom line) or focusing on projected differential growth rates as a basis for scenario planning. Yet each revenue source operates in its own "revenue market" that imposes criteria and constraints for acquisition and use of funds. All revenues are not, therefore, interchangeable; nor can they be deployed at will for priorities derived through careful, institutional academic planning. Capital campaigns, for example, are often disillusioning to faculty when they finally confront the reality of a donor-driven philanthropic revenue market. In addition to the constraints and conditions imposed by these various revenue markets, the very existence of multiple streams complicates integrating plans and budgets, particularly at the level of the central administration.

Responsibility Center Budgeting

The existence and growth of multiple sources of revenue, some of which goes directly to units or even individuals within institutions, combined with the complexity of managing from the central administrative level often provide the impetus for RCB, or at least substantial budgetary independence. Substantial independence of subsidiary budgetary units, whether in a formal RCB system or not, poses new challenges to administrators accustomed to traditional paradigms of central planning and budgeting. Institutions operating primarily on a single source of revenue, such as tuition, can of course adopt RCB, but the existence of other significant sources and the experience of attracting and controlling those resources at the unit level whets the appetite of units for more and greater autonomy over both revenues and expenditures. As a rule, then, diversity of revenue sources pushes planning and budgeting responsibilities out from the center, although the extent of this depends on the mix and significance of multiple revenue sources.

RCB is a system whereby all or part of the tuition reflected in enrollments, along with sponsored research and other revenues, is returned to units in proportion to what the unit "earns." In theory, the unit controls its own pricing policy and is responsible for all, or nearly all, of its costs (Berg, 1985). Surpluses and deficits are the responsibility of the unit. Additionally, in most RCB systems, the central administration of an institution oversees a taxing or subvention system where some activities such as libraries, judged to be valued but outside of proper market forces, are subsidized.

Other central services, such as computing or printing, often operate on a charge-back system and must compete with outside vendors.

Just as there is a strong case to be made for PB in a trust market, there are persuasive arguments in favor of RCB in the context of multiple revenue markets and rapidly changing market conditions. The incentive structure created under RCB, for example, is designed with defined responsibility centers as the units of analysis and is intended to force decisions about efficiency and effectiveness of programs to that unit level—close to the action where managers' knowledge of market supply and demand forces is greatest. Although cost consciousness is something academics are not renowned for, it is therefore thrust upon academic and support units, who must operate within what their respective revenue markets produce. Priority setting, regarded by some as the heart of planning, should become very explicit and be debated within the unit.

RCB has been in operation for many years at such well-known private universities as Harvard, Pennsylvania, and Southern California. A newly adopted RCB in a portion of Indiana's public sector (Whalen, 1991) was recently evaluated by Robbins and Rooney (1995). They cite as RCB strengths operational-level flexibility, multi-year planning, information-rich discussions, more explicit and operative incentives, and greater understanding of planning and budgeting.

Any system also has its weaknesses, or at least tendencies that may not well serve certain organizational goals. RCB engenders entrepreneurism—a virtue and a potential vice. The search for revenue can be intense and may lure units far afield from a focused academic mission. Revenue maximization may also overpower concerns for educational quality. Additionally, there are an interrelated set of organizational issues that arise out of RCB with its centrifugal forces. Reimbursement and subvention rates are examples of the administrative pricing complexities with which administrators must deal. Complex subventions involving multifactor taxing and/or subsidization formulas are not only difficult to develop but often contain unintended incentives to which operating units respond. Competing courses may proliferate as a means of securing tuition funds, and professional schools may provide a larger proportion of general education classes than desirable because of favorable course reimbursement rates.

The need for more information and management at the unit level also raises a question of total administrative costs. As units add more development staff, accountants, and managers, and as faculty spend more time on administrative activities, what happens to total institutional administrative costs?

The Role of the Center

RCB, or even just significant levels of revenue flowing directly to units within an institution, raises questions about the role of the central administration, or center, in planning and budgeting for these flows and their uses. For example, if a public medical school derives 10–15 percent of its revenues from the state and competes successfully in revenue markets for research and clinical income, what is the role of the center?

Since much of higher education's legacy for planning and budgeting devolves from the corporate business world (Chaffee, 1985), it is instructive to learn from the debates over the role of the corporate center and its various business units. Large, diversified corporations must operate with two levels of strategy: (1) corporate, to determine which businesses the corporation should be in and how the corporate center should manage those businesses; and (2) business unit, which concentrates on how to operate competitively within the particular market of that business (Porter, 1987). Porter's premise is that diversified companies do not compete, but their constituent business units do. Successful corporate strategy must therefore grow out of and reinforce business-unit competitive strategy. Business-unit strategy or planning, commensurate with RCB strategy in a higher education context, is where the action is and where information about markets and decisions about investments should be made.

How comparable are colleges and universities to diversified corporations and corporate/business-unit strategies? Certainly there is substantial variation by institution, but some do fit this model. Many large universities, four-year colleges, and community colleges run highly diverse "businesses" that operate in very competitive markets. Clark Kerr's term "the multiversity" captures the reality of multiple and diverse activities all sharing a common heating plant. But there are also some significant differences between the collegiate and corporate worlds. One of the most striking is the undergraduate core. A university chemistry department competes nationally for research revenues that flow directly to the department; it also competes in its own graduate student market, complete with competitive stipends. But chemistry departments are an integral part of many undergraduate majors and also contribute to general education programs. No one business unit captures this market for general education or for undergraduate education as a whole.

Another important conceptual issue for linking planning and budgeting in colleges and universities is determining the best level or organizational unit of analysis. Porter's theory defines "strategic business units" as those businesses within a diversified corporation that operate within a defined competitive market of their own. In matters of research and graduate studies, as well as the major itself, the discipline rather than the college is probably the most common parallel to a strategic business unit in the private sector. The exception is professional schools or colleges, where there may not be sufficiently well-defined disciplinary divisions. In other functional areas such as contract instruction, for example, the most appropriate unit may well depend on the size and configuration of the particular institution.

The most suitable level or unit of analysis on which to build a financial strategy therefore varies by type of institution, function, and even institutional context or culture. Thinking through this unit-of-analysis issue raises questions as to the role of the college level, within a university, as well as the central administration in planning and budgeting. If, as Porter's theory implicitly suggests, the department is the fundamental strategic business unit for colleges and universities, what value does the dean or vice-presidential level add?

Fueled by increasingly diverse and independent revenue sources, the natural centrifugal forces within institutions are posing major challenges to traditional models of planning and budgeting, which have focused on the primary role of the central administration while the role of constituent units is appropriate par-

ticipation in central decision processes. What we are seeing is a redefinition of roles and questions being raised as to continuity of leadership and level of management expertise at the strategic business unit or disciplinary level.

Unintended Consequences

Having access to multiple revenue sources can provide stability. During the 1980s and early 1990s, for example, increases in public-sector tuition made up for some of the decreases or slow growth in state support. But stability thus achieved can be costly. Those same increases in tuition contributed to the loss of trust in higher education.

Paradoxically, dependence on multiple sources of revenue can also reduce stability and the institution's control over its own destiny. For example, growth in clinical-practice income allowed medical schools to expand their activities at relatively little direct cost to state government or students. Now, changes in health care threaten that revenue source and pose a very serious problem for medical schools. Institutions that tenure or promote faculty on the basis of extramural funding (Lederman and Mooney, 1995) may be climbing out on a similar limb.

Revenue maximization in conjunction with multiple revenue sources means that institutions are at risk of drifting from their moorings by any number of revenue-related developments. A change in direction that may accompany a change in revenue shares is not necessarily bad, but it might well be if the change in direction is a second-order, unplanned effect rather than an intended outcome—as is usually the case.

Dealing with Financial Stringency and Reallocation

In an environment of declining real resources, productivity gains are critical if institutions are to avoid stagnation and decline. Such gains can be realized either through changes in production functions or through reallocation of resources to higher-value programs and services (growth by substitution).

A prolonged period of financial stringency affects planning and budgeting and underlying fiscal strategies. For example, Massy (1994) hypothesizes that as financial stress increases, nonprofit institutions are likely to behave more like for-profit institutions.

What might that hypothetical response mean in the mid-1990s? We can get a good idea of the implications of such a change from the following strategies, delineated in a recent annual report to investors by a for-profit firm:

- Evaluate each business based on best-practice standards of quality, cost, revenue growth, and profitability

- Invest in high-growth businesses

- Streamline day-to-day processes

- Invest in technology

- Leverage economies of scale

- Improve responsiveness to clients

- Segment markets in new ways

- Allocate resources in a focused way

- Hold expenses at current levels or cut them if planned revenues don't materialize

- Expand high-growth businesses

- Divest businesses that are not producing adequate returns or are no longer central to the more focused strategic direction (Shipley, 1995, pp. 2–3

Are not-for-profit colleges and universities willing and able to conduct themselves in this manner? Most critical in this regard are the prospects for marginal analysis, which is fundamental to the strategies listed above, and for reallocation, which is often an important way of responding to the results of marginal analysis and indispensable in the absence of significant revenue growth.

Both are problematic for higher education. Making them key elements of a fiscal strategy requires a transformation in planning and budgeting. Marginal analysis entails a complex calculus of marginal revenues, costs, and values. Done in the manner of a for-profit firm, it requires agreement on a surrogate for "profitability" and on appropriate ways of determining whether "returns" are "adequate." Better ways of assessing quality and marginal cost would have to be found, too. How many institutions currently have the knowledge to support these calculations? In short, it is difficult to be sanguine about the prospects for the agreements and the addi-

tional knowledge required to support marginal analysis. However, it is conceivable that institutions could benefit by thinking in marginal terms and applying the principles of marginal analysis as best they can even in the face of inadequate information. For example, an academic department can profitably address alternative uses of faculty time, fundamentally a marginal analysis, without measuring precisely either costs or benefits.

Significant reallocation is infrequent, if not rare, in most higher education institutions. The long dependency on increased revenues has created a psychological disposition against reallocation. It is hard to imagine a program that does not have a constituency (either within or outside of the institution) who will resist reallocation when it threatens their interests. Reallocation is further complicated by the diversity of revenues at most institutions. Legal constraints embedded in some revenues can be an impediment to reallocation.

It is apparent, then, that marginal analysis and reallocation, so appropriate in theory, are tough sells in practice. They are tough sells, both cognitively and politically. But times are hard, and therefore what model should be pursued? Should institutions design for, and get tough with, more definitive central planning? Should they conclude that central planning and budgeting will not work and decentralize to something like RCB? Or should they develop a strategy of mixed models? We offer some suggestions in the next section, "Linking Planning and Budgeting."

Some form of PB could be helpful in promoting reallocation, assuming it were possible to reach agreement on the types of performance to be included and the ways in which they are measured. Once in place, these agreements constitute at least one basis for comparing programs at the margin. In addition, if the strategy includes, for example, a tax on all units to create an allocation pool, differential performance over time brings about reallocation "naturally"; the larger the magnitude of the tax rate and the differentials, the more extensive the reallocation. If performance measures are driven by planning goals or planning strategies derive from an analysis of critical issues, this approach to budgeting can support both reallocation and better links between planning and budgeting.

The capability to reallocate resources is, of course, a virtual necessity. The fast-moving higher education environment requires that resources be at least somewhat mobile. Changes in political priorities, technology, competitors, and so on damage and can overwhelm institutions that are locked into spending patterns from another era.

Subventions, while they sometimes entail nothing more than moving resources from the strong to the weak, may also be a shift of resources to areas such as a liberal arts core or a program in theology that are central to the mission of an institution, if not its *raison d'etre*. Like reallocation, then, the capability to undertake subventions in an acceptable manner is a critical component of a good budget system.

Paradoxically, as financial stringency deepens the need for marginal analysis and for reallocation increases, so does the political difficulty of implementing a substantial reallocation tax. Any approach of this type almost certainly establishes powerful incentives that have to be thought out in advance, lest they do serious harm.

In the responsibility center approach to budgeting, it seems that the implicit if not explicit message to the business units is to behave in a for-profit mode. The units are pushed toward marginal analysis, or at least toward comparing the relative value of their various programs and activities in some manner (for example, see Jacquin, 1994). Financial stringency makes this comparative analysis all the more urgent. Conceivably, units could make allocation decisions that would be detrimental to institutional goals or institution-wide responsibilities. For example, various departments could participate too heavily or too little in general education, thus unbalancing it with respect to disciplinary representation.

The central administration can tax business units to create a reallocation pool or use its subventions to bring about reallocation. The reallocation itself can be based on an institutional-level strategic plan. With respect to avoiding the payment of economic rents to business units or otherwise getting effective and efficient use of allocated resources, the center faces an asymmetry of information not unlike that faced by funders outside the institution in a trust market.

LINKING PLANNING AND BUDGETING

We have attempted to show how the ground rules have been evolving for higher education planning and budgeting. If the loss of trust in higher education is to be stemmed and even reversed, if institutions are to come to grips with their complex revenue structures, and if they are to cope with long-term financial stringency, then new links between planning and budgeting need to be formed. It isn't that the general goals of planning and budgeting have changed, but the road maps are undergoing some important revisions. Old solutions are not as appropriate as they once were. In particular, strategists must probe a little deeper to get at second- and third-order effects. When they do so, the linkage between planning and budgeting becomes a little easier to bring about.

Nonetheless, the linkage between planning and budgeting has proven difficult to achieve (Schmidtlein, 1989–90). Planners need to take the initiative if the track record is to improve. We suggest the following strategies to increase the odds of successfully linking planning and budgeting.

Our most basic strategy might be described as selective and opportunistic rather than comprehensive. While some observers would recommend the latter approach, we think it runs the risk of collapsing under its own weight and of requiring busy people to engage in activities that may not always be meaningful. We think a more modest and explicitly opportunistic approach has a greater chance of success at most institutions. Some suggestions follow for finding situations and issues in which the links between planning and budgeting should be most easily forged. Schmidtlein (1989–90) provides a systematic analysis of the prospects for those links in relation to classical approaches to resources allocation such as formula budgeting.

Perhaps the most obvious way to start the search for opportunities is to look for issues where resource allocation can scarcely be done at all without fairly explicit planning. A good example is an effort to develop a long-term strategy for library funding within the framework of the future shape of the library. The information required to support such an effort greatly exceeds what is readily available to budget analysts and line officers. Planners are, or should be, adept at developing information, especially from sources outside the institution. They can bring that to the table along with the perspective that fundamental, long-term questions about the library can only be addressed within the broader framework of institutional mission and programmatic direction.

A similar strategy is to look for emerging issues where the terrain is unfamiliar, or where comparative analysis is helpful (for example, see Middaugh, 1995–96), or where much of the impact is in the future. For example, technology-based distance education seems to be an especially appropriate issue for forging links between planning and budgeting. This is an area where planners can use their environmental scanning skills and whatever skills they might have in bringing together a wide range of ideas and people. It is also an area where revenues options are likely to be quite complex, in terms both of sources and shifts from one-time to base and back again. Immediate and long-term costs for investment and development are important issues, as are long-term maintenance and replacement costs. In short, numerous fiscal and strategic issues arise that are appropriately addressed in a planning mode. An externally imposed need for a major reallocation of resources can be a good opportunity to link plans and budgets. Planning in one form or another, but particularly strategic planning, may generate interest in reallocation, or reallocation needs and opportunities may surface for other reasons. In any case, a thoughtful approach to reallocation requires knowledge that exceeds what is required to budget for day-to-day operations.

Planners need to find or develop tools and techniques that can be useful to the budget process. For example, given the revenue complexities and the allocation challenges discussed above, long-run scenarios make sense; they have been used successfully in the private sector (Shoemaker, 1995). They can increase the chances of realizing the long-run goals of maintaining assets, investing wisely, and offering the right products and services. They can also focus discussions on these goals and, if used in conjunction with a simulation model, provide a quantitative perspective on relationships among long- and short-term goals. Sce-

narios can serve as a platform for discussing higher education's production technologies. Production technologies and production preferences are at stake when an institution attempts to better align itself with constituent interests. Those technologies and preferences and the effects of changing them (or their mix) are part of what is typically addressed in simulation models. (The classic treatment of this type of modeling is in Hopkins and Massy, 1981; a straightforward application can be found in Lovrinic, DeHayes, and Althoff, 1993; and Kundey and Taylor, 1994, provide evidence that budget officers are unlikely to use these tools on their own.)

Finally, linkages between planning and budgeting can sometimes be enhanced by altering what is expected of ongoing planning and evaluation activities. The goal is to force into the open questions that invite the linkage, or in other words, to shape the agenda such that planning and budgeting questions of comparable gravity rise in close proximity to one another. Consider, for example, the typical program review. What if the review has to include a recommendation that the program should grow (however defined), stay the same, or shrink (command fewer resources)? This shifts the ground from what tends to be mostly a tactical discussion ("Are we doing things right?") to a strategic discussion of the extent to which the institution should be engaged in this effort. The appropriate fiscal issues are also likely to arise if substantial resources are going to be needed or are made available for other purposes.

SPECULATIONS

The experience of many institutions in dealing with continuing economic pressures gives them an experiential base for dealing with future conditions. Whether that base includes fundamental changes in planning and budgeting patterns is critical to the institutional cultural changes that lie ahead.

While economic pressures affect institutions quite differently, a second development probably has an even broader impact. The long-promised and anticipated technology revolution looms, but will it ever come? Futurists of the fifties predicted educational technology changes that never happened. The core processes of higher education instruction have remained basically the same for centuries, with some allowance for larger class sizes and modest doses of electronic mediation. Current and projected information technology has the potential for far more fundamental change in those production processes. How seriously should this potential be taken? Should sizeable institutional investments in new technologies and people, far beyond what has been made to date, be made in an effort to get ahead of the curve in anticipation of whole new levels of reconfiguration and competition? Or should institutional leaders, remembering the past, wait and see? It seems to us that for most institutions the risks of an overly cautious approach run much higher than before and therefore compel institutions to engage in new levels of planning for change. Will an institutional culture of caution allow such change in the absence of immediate and compelling external pressures?

A third line of speculation, closely related to this discussion of change, concerns organizations of the future. Charles Handy (1994), a leading management and organizational writer, argues that federalist organizations are best suited to deal with change. The line operating units of organizations, or the federal components that are close to markets and customers, must be given sufficient latitude to operate while the organizational center must focus and limit its efforts to (1) overall system planning, (2) central banking, and (3) designing and monitoring decision processes. If the traditional tendency of the organizational center to overcontrol is allowed, adaptation to changing markets may be hampered.

Organizations, including colleges and universities, must also ask tough questions about their traditional structures. Which administrative offices add value to the organization? Does the dean level of administration add value if the strategic business unit is really the discipline complimented by interdisciplinary programs such as general education? Will the forces of change in the future, reflected primarily through constituents and economic markets, be met by our traditional organizational structures? Or would a movement toward RCB at the departmental level only reinforce disciplinary myopia and power?

While these questions may appear to have more to do with academic governance than planning and budgeting, they are hardly independent. We have discussed two ideal types of planning and budgeting: a more centralized, plan-based model exemplified in performance budgeting and a more decentralized, market model in responsibility center budgeting. While some institutions advocate one or the other, we do not expect to see radical moves to either extreme, but rather mixed models dependent upon both the institutional type and the function within institutions. Massy (1994) argues for a mixed, or hybrid, approach in his concept of "value responsibility budgeting," which combines key elements of incremental, performance, and responsibility center budgeting. While we like the concept, we are less sanguine than he is about the universal applicability of the full hybrid approach across institutions and functions. It makes sense to us, for example, to develop the core of the undergraduate experience, general education, using primarily a plan-based model. Other functions, ranging from research and graduate programs to delivery of contractual instruction, seem suitable candidates for more market-based models. A mix-and-match design of planning and budgeting systems is perhaps the greatest challenge facing those entrusted with developing fiscal strategies for the decades ahead. It is certainly one of the core functions of the organizational center and one that has profound long-term impact.

FURTHER READING

Readers interested in the themes in this chapter might want to examine Meisinger and Dubeck (1994) on the fundamentals of budgeting and financial reporting; Lasher and Greene (1993) on the strengths and weaknesses of various approaches to budgeting; Morgan (1984) on the conceptual roots of various budgeting strategies; Berg (1985) on budget incentives; Massy (1994) on performance, responsibility center, and value responsibility budgeting; Ashworth (1994) on performance budgeting (at the state level); Whalen (1991) on responsibility center budgeting; and Hyatt (1993) on strategic restructuring in the context of linking planning and budgeting.

REFERENCES

Ashworth, K. H. (Nov.-Dec. 1994). Performance-based funding in higher education. *Change*, pp. 8–15.

Berg, D. J. (1985). Getting individual and organizational goals to match. In D. J. Berg and G. M. Skogley (Eds.), *Making the budget process work.* New Directions for Higher Education, no. 52. San Francisco: Jossey-Bass.

Bowen, H. R. (1980). *The Costs of higher education.* San Francisco: Jossey-Bass.

Brinkman, P. T., and Morgan, A. W. (1995). The future of higher education finance." In T. Sanford (Ed.), *Institutional Research in the next century.* New directions for institutional research, no. 85. San Francisco: Jossey-Bass.

Caiden, N. (1988). Shaping things to come: Super budgeters as heroes (and heroines) in the late-twentieth century. In I. S. Rubin (Ed*.), New directions in budget theory.* Albany: State University of New York Press.

Chaffee, E. E. (1985). The concept of strategy: From business to higher education. In J. C. Smart (Ed*.), Higher Education: Handbook of Theory and Research,* Vol. 1. New York: Agathon Press.

Garvin, D. (1980). *The economics of university behavior.* New York: Academic Press.

Handy, C. (1994). *The age of paradox.* Boston: Harvard Business School Press.

Hopkins, D. S. P., & Massy, W. F. (1981*). Planning models for colleges and universities.* Stanford, Calif.: Stanford University Press.

Hyatt, J. A. (1993). Strategic restructuring: A case study. In W. E. Vandament and D. P. Jones (Eds.), *Financial management: Progress and challenges.* New Directions for Higher Education, no. 83. San Francisco: Jossey-Bass.

Jacquin, J. C. (1994). Revenue and expense analysis: An alternative method for analyzing university operations. *NACUBO business officer, 28*(3), 41–47.

James, E. (1990). Decision processes and priorities in higher education. In S. A. Hoenack and E. L. Collins (Eds.), *The economics of American universities.* Albany: State University of New York Press.

Kundey, G. E. & Taylor, E. P. (1994).The financial officer's toolbox: Do financial officers use available methods and tools? *NACUBO Business Officer,* 27(11), 29–32.

Lasher, W. F., & Greene, D. L. (1993). College and university budgeting: What do we know? What do we need to know?" In J. C. Smart (Ed.), *Higher*

education: Handbook of theory and research, Vol. 9. New York: Agathon Press.

Lederman, D., & Mooney, C. J. (Apr. 14, 1995). Lifting the cloak of secrecy from tenure. *Chronicle of higher education,* pp. A16–A18.

Lovrinic, J. G., DeHayes, D. W., & Althoff, E. J. (1993). Developing an economic model: How one midwestern university is approaching cost control." *NACUBO business officer, 27*(1), 34–38.

Massy, W. F. (1994). *Resource allocation reform in higher education.* Washington, D.C.: National Association of College and University Business Officers.

Meisinger, R. J., and Dubeck, L. W. (1994). *College and university budgeting* (2nd ed.) Washington, D.C.: National Association of College and University Business Officers.

Middaugh, M. (1995–96). Closing in on faculty productivity measures. *Planning for higher education,* 24(2), 1–12.

Morgan, A. W. (1984). The new strategies: Roots, context, and overview. In L. L. Leslie (Ed.), *Responding to new realities in funding.* New Directions for Institutional Research, no. 43. San Francisco: Jossey-Bass.

Morgan, A. W. (1992). The politics and policies of selective funding. *Review of higher education, 15*(3), 289–306.

Porter, M. E. (1987). From competitive advantage to corporate strategy. *Harvard business review, 63,* 43–59.

Robbins, D. L., Sr., & Rooney, P. M. (1995). Responsibility center management: An assessment of RCM at IUPUI. *NACUBO business officer, 28*(9), 44–48.

Schmidtlein, F. A. (1989–90). Why linking budgets to plans has proven difficult in higher education. *Planning for higher education, 18*(2), 9–23.

Shipley, W. V. (1995). Chairman's letter. In *1994 annual report.* New York: Chemical Bank, 1995.

Shoemaker, P. J. H. (Winter 1995). Scenario planning: A tool for strategic thinking." *Sloan management review, 36,* 25–40.

Whalen, E. L. (1991). *Responsibility center budgeting.* Bloomington and Indianapolis: Indiana University Press.

Winston, G. C. (1992). Hostility, maximization, and the public trust." *Change, 24*(4), 20–27.

Zemsky, R., Porter, R., & Odel, L. P. (1978). Decentralized planning responsibility. *Educational record, 1978, 59,* 229–253.

Chapter 37

Integrating Planning, Assessment, and Resource Allocation

Nancy Shulock and Mernoy E. Harrison

Nancy Shulock is associate vice president for academic affairs at California State University, Sacramento. She is a graduate of Princeton University and holds a master's in public policy from the University of California-Berkeley and a Ph.D. in political science from the University of California-Davis. Her responsibilities at CSU, Sacramento, include institutional planning and academic resources.

Mernoy E. Harrison is the vice provost for administrative services and campus administrative services officer for the Arizona State University Main Campus. He received his bachelor's in general engineering and his master's in business administration from Stanford University and his Ph.D. in business administration from the University of North Carolina at Chapel Hill. He has served as president of the Western Association of College and University Business Officers and chair of the National Association of College and University Business Officers.

Underestimating uncertainty can lead to strategies that neither defend against the threats nor take advantage of the opportunities that higher levels of uncertainty may provide.
—COURTNEY, H., J. KIRKLAND, AND P. VIGUERIE. 1997. STRATEGY UNDER UNCERTAINTY. *HARVARD BUSINESS REVIEW* 75(6): 68.

The only thing worse than not doing anything to improve your Value Proposition is to move in a direction that takes value away.
—TUCKER, R. B. 1997. ADDING VALUE PROFITABILITY. COLLEGE SERVICES ADMINISTRATION 20(6): 8.

Strategic planning, with its emphasis on defining a university's unique character and identity, was anathema to California State University-Sacramento when it came onto the higher education horizon in the early 1980s. At CSUS planning has evolved from a nonstrategic infancy to an adolescence that has achieved significant linkages among planning, assessment, and resource allocation. It is uncertain when, or even if, the age of maturity will occur. The principal lesson learned in this evolution is that planning is always in a state of development. There is no one best planning process, even for a single institution. The planning process continues to evolve as we learn from experience how best to build the linkages among planning, assessment, and resource allocation. However, the critical value of building these linkages is evident in the experience of CSUS over the past 15 years.

Source: *Planning for Higher Education*, Spring 1998.

THE EARLY YEARS

CSUS is a regional, comprehensive university located in the capital city of the nation's largest state. It is part of the 23-campus California State University system and is relatively young, celebrating its 50th anniversary in 1997. The historic organizational culture of the system was that of a very large state agency, complete with formulas for all aspects of budget and rules for every management circumstance. Individual campuses were viewed almost as bureaus within the agency, with little differentiation in mission. The planning process at CSUS began its modern era in 1984 with the creation of the University Resources and Planning Council (renamed the Council for University Planning four years later). This step marked an attempt by the then-new president to bring all of the activities of the university together to establish a unified set of priorities. Until that point, any planning that occurred was at the unit level, and no large-scale efforts were made to match university resources with planning priorities. The budget was divided largely according to system-wide formulas, and there was little coordination of budgets and plans among the three major divisions—Academic Affairs, Student Affairs, and Business Affairs.

Membership of the new council included faculty, administrators, staff, an alumnus, a community representative, and students. Its charge was to advise the president on the overall direction of the university and, specifically, to make recommendations on the university budget and on other items for which the system administration required campus-wide consultation, for example, capital outlay plans. The reconstitution to the Council for University Planning in 1988 was done in response to a recommendation from the regional accrediting agency to focus the council's activities on long-range planning. The council's revised charge included the development and maintenance of a five-year university plan. This plan was intended to derive from planning carried out at the unit level, where the university was organized into program centers.

Unit plans were required for the next two years, and a university plan was developed from the unit plans in 1991. However, lacking any strategic planning, or other mechanism for setting priorities among unit ambitions, the university plan was a lengthy compendium of objectives submitted by the 18 program centers. There was no guarantee that the large number of objectives were internally consistent across the plan. Indeed, the plan tried to be all things to all people.

LINKING PLANNING AND BUDGETING—RESOURCE PRIORITIES

As the unit plans were being developed and the university plan compiled, a mechanism was adopted to attempt to link planning with budgeting—always a principal goal of any planning process. The council developed a document titled "Resource Priorities" each year to recommend to the president priorities for the following year's budget. Once the president approved it, the vice president for administration was accountable to the council for explaining how his proposed budget reflected the resource priorities.

The effectiveness of this mechanism was limited by the nonstrategic basis to university planning. Lacking any strategic plan, the resource priorities document was merely a reflection of the biases and knowledge bases of

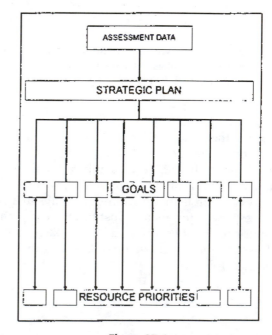

Figure 37.1

the members of the council. It tended to contain overly general items, such as "enhance undergraduate education" and "support student services."

In the past three years, however, two developments have appreciably strengthened the linkage between planning and budgeting provided by the resource priorities. First, the enactment of the university strategic plan provided a framework for the priorities. Beginning with the planning for the 1995–96 budget, the resource priorities were drawn from the various themes of the strategic plan. This guaranteed that there was a broad consensus behind the priorities and that the various priorities would be part of a consistent package that would address the university's vision and goals. Second, the university began to make assessment data available to the council so that priorities could be based on some evidence of the university's condition, not merely on the opinions of council members.

STRATEGIC PLAN

In September 1991, the president directed the council to develop the university's first strategic plan. The council, led in this effort by its Planning Committee, prepared a strategic plan that the president approved in August 1994. The process of completing the plan took three years because of extensive consultation across the university community. The first year was largely devoted to drafting a vision statement and determining the structure of the plan and the various themes. The second year was devoted to consulting with the campus community on the vision statement and drafting the text of the themes. The council drafted six theme papers, and the Academic Senate drafted two.[1] The third year involved extensive consultation on the draft theme papers. No outside consultants were employed in this process because the administration judged that the organizational culture would have resisted, or suspected, a major planning effort guided by outsiders.

The most significant feature of the strategic plan, in terms of how it now drives assessment and resource allocation at CSUS, is its organization into eight themes. There is one goal statement for each theme. Collectively, the eight goals describe the direction in which the university intends to head over the next several years. Implementation of the university's first strategic plan is well under way and is centered around the eight themes. The plan provides a guide for major planning and decision-making efforts and for the allocation of resources: program centers must relate budget requests, hiring plans, and curricular initiatives to the strategic plan; other university plans (for example, telecommunications or facilities) fit their goals within those of the strategic plan; and other university allocation processes (such as lottery funds and the Pedagogy Enhancement Awards Program) require applicants to explain their proposals in the context of the strategic plan.

Most importantly, the strategic plan themes now provide the structure for the resource priorities, which continue to be the principal mechanism for linking planning to budgeting. Beginning with the 1995–96 fiscal year, resource priorities have been identified in relation to the themes of the strategic plan. This has been a major step toward improving the planning process. Whereas past efforts to develop resource priorities to guide the preparation of the subsequent year's budget began with basically a blank slate, current efforts begin within a framework. This framework is no more likely to bring additional resources to the campus than the earlier approach and still offers quite a broad range from which to choose priorities. However, it does ensure that available resources will be directed to areas that have been broadly endorsed as university priorities.

THE ASSESSMENT ERA—PROVIDING THE MISSING LINK IN THE PLANNING PROCESS

Even with the improvement brought about by the adoption of a strategic plan, a piece was still missing in the planning process—there was no objective evidence on which to choose one set of priorities over another, and no mechanisms were in place for determining whether the initiatives that were being implemented were having the intended result. Without evaluation, or assessment, CSUS could continue to direct resources toward a variety of strategic plan initiatives, but it would not know if it had chosen those most in need of attention. And it would not know when it had made progress toward achieving its goals.

Inspired by the opportunity to model a new, evidence-based accreditation process in its 10-year institutional accreditation, CSUS has now immeasurably improved the planning process with the addition of the missing link—assessment. In the 1995–96 academic year, the council began to review theme assessment papers—one for each theme of the strategic plan. These papers have been updated annually as new data become available. The papers prepared by the Office of Institutional Studies, are structured based upon a careful reading of the text of the strategic plan for each theme. Based on what the plan says is important for the achievement of each goal, each theme assessment paper reports on all relevant data from the variety of assessment instruments the university now uses as well as other available institutional data.[2] The result is a rich and complex portrait of how the university appears to be performing in each area. This approach is very different from one that relies on a few key performance indicators. These papers report findings from several standardized surveys, each of which contain numerous questions that may be of relevance to a particular theme.

The adoption of a "culture of evidence," as required by the accreditation review, has dramatically changed the role of the council. The council now spends each fall semester reviewing theme assessment papers for a subset of the themes of the strategic plan—those deemed most important to next year's budget. Small groups of council members review each paper in depth and report their analyses to the full council.[3] They report on the strengths and weaknesses of the university as revealed in the assessment data and suggest any critical issues that seem to require further attention or action. From this review, the council establishes priorities for the subsequent year's budget and develops a list of critical issues to be referred to university governance bodies, deans, and other program center managers for their attention.

Assessment also supports planning activity that occurs at the level of the academic department. Whereas the council reviews assessment data at the aggregate level, program and department data are made available to departments participating in the academic program review process. Departments are now required to develop assessment plans and report on student outcomes, pursuant to those plans, in their self-studies. There are no plans to bring this aspect of university planning to the council's agenda. The council is viewed as best equipped to focus on planning and assessment at the institutional level, with a focus on the attainment of the eight university goals.

Results of the integrated planning efforts at CSUS are already apparent. The following sections describe how assessment has been used to guide resource allocation and influence implementation of the strategic plan. The examples are from the two themes that have received the most attention, in view of their priority within the university—teaching and learning, and campus life.

TEACHING AND LEARNING

Selected Assessment Findings

Assessment information indicated significant student concerns with the scheduling and availability of classes. We teamed from a follow-up survey question that the majority of the respondents preferred to schedule all of their classes on two days a week. The data also showed a pattern of students who face a teaching and learning environment that does not always accord with knowledge of best practices. Students generally study alone, have little contact with faculty outside the classroom, and do not participate widely in faculty research and scholarship. Particular dissatisfaction was reported with academic and career advising. Graduating students and alumni reported that their course work at CSUS did not provide them as well as they would have liked with the technological and communication skills they need. Faculty voiced the concern that innovative teaching is not rewarded as it should be. In addition, only 36 percent of faculty responding to a survey indicated that they were skilled in "using information technology to enhance instruction."

Selected Resource Priorities

As a result of their review of the assessment papers, council members adopted resource priorities for the following year's budget that included a focus on the concerns raised by students and faculty. Some of these priorities are listed as follows:

1. Investigate and encourage the adoption of alternative models of class scheduling and appropriate support services that facilitate students' timely progress through their academic programs.

2. Expand learning in and beyond the classroom to include
   - educating "the whole person" (for example, providing service learning, leadership training, other cocurricular learning experiences, and extracurricular activities that represent bona fide educational experiences for students),
   - involving students in research and creative activity,
   - increasing interaction between faculty/staff and students,
   - involving faculty and students in serving the community in accordance with the "metropolitan university" mission (for example, applied research, internships, and volunteer service),
   - facilitating interaction among students to enhance learning, and
   - encouraging faculty to use pedagogies in the classroom that facilitate "whole person" student development.

3. Use information technology to enhance program quality and improve access to programs and services.

4. Increase faculty ability to use information technology to enhance student learning.

Selected Initiatives

In response to concerns about the class schedule, a new scheduling pattern was implemented to replace the traditional MWF-TTh schedule. In addition, the university adopted an extended semester option. This option allows departments to offer courses, funded by general fund dollars, during the months of January, June, July, and August and include them as part of their fall and spring semester offerings. In response to concerns about the learning environment, the university initiated the Learning Communities program on a pilot

basis for first semester freshmen. In the program 25 to 30 students enroll in two or three General Education classes as a group; the courses complement each other and are linked by a common theme. Faculty are encouraged to integrate the courses, promote group interaction, and provide academic study sessions. In addition to providing some structure to the General Education program, these communities provide students with a sense of belonging to an academic community, addressing a concern noted by students in the survey data. In addition, a new Office of Community Collaboration was established to expand opportunities for students to engage in service learning in the community and to identify opportunities for student/faculty collaboration in community-oriented projects. In response to concerns about the teaching and learning of technology, the university vastly increased the number of computer workstations, lab hours, lab assistants, and computer training opportunities for students. More discipline-specific computer labs have been created so that students can better relate technology to their educational goals. The university library expanded its library instruction program by constructing a new lab for individual student and class use. The library has also increased its staff hours to help students with on-line and traditional research methods. Reference librarians have designed a series of classes to meet student needs for information literacy. The university allotted funds to faculty and departments, on a competitive basis, to encourage integration of information technology into the curriculum, and training opportunities for faculty in information technology have been greatly expanded.

CAMPUS LIFE THEME

Selected Assessment Findings

Data from student and alumni surveys indicated two broad areas of concern. One was the low level of participation by students in what might be called "traditional campus life" activities. Students reported spending little out-of-class time on campus other than to study. They tended to study alone, primarily at home. They did not attend formal campus events with any frequency. They did not report a high level of identification with the university as a whole. Some students cited safety concerns. Initiatives in response to these findings have been aimed at the positive evidence from these surveys: students reported a much higher sense of belonging at the level of the discipline; they indicated high levels of interest in participating in department clubs; 39 percent expressed an interest in living on campus if apartment-style housing were available; they reported considerable interaction with students of various backgrounds in their classes; they reported very high levels of satisfaction with the quality of their academic program and faculty. The second broad area of concern focused on student services. Significant percentages of students reported dissatisfaction with some service offices, with student financial aid at the top of the list. More than half indicated they do not feel well-informed about campus events.

Selected Resource Priorities

In response to these findings the council established the following resource priorities to promote a student-centered environment:

- Improve information provided to the campus community and the region about campus events, activities, and services.
- Improve and expand student services (that is, accessible and high quality services) to facilitate more student time on campus.
- Promote and improve campus safety.
- Investigate the feasibility of providing apartment-style housing on campus.

Selected Initiatives

The campus life theme of the strategic plan was revised to align the university's goals more closely with student needs and concerns. It calls for increased attention to establishing a stimulating set of campus life activities, making the campus welcoming to all students, streamlining the provision of student services, and providing more opportunities for students to participate in activities at the level of the academic discipline. To address the concern that students did not have a sense of belonging to the campus, a larger student life component

was added to the university's outreach, orientation, and new student programs. A new Student Access Center was opened to provide information and support to students about the full range of opportunities and services that are available to them at CSUS. In a major initiative to change the character of student life at CSUS, a housing plan has been approved for one- and two-bedroom apartment-style units with private baths. Academic Affairs made "student centeredness" its highest priority during the 1995–96 academic year. The academic deans and other administrators developed new activities or expanded existing ones that put the needs of students at the center of their plans for the year. These activities included service manuals for students, special events to recognize student achievements, e-mail advising, customer satisfaction surveys, expanded opportunities for experiential learning placements, peer advising, deans' open office hours, and social activities designed to increase student/faculty contact outside the classroom. A number of new initiatives are under way and are aimed at improving information about campus events, including expanded coverage of campus events in the student newspaper, university publications, the CSUS home page, and electronic kiosks. The university has taken a proactive approach to safety on the campus, instituting police bicycle patrols, performing a complete lighting assessment of the campus each month, and reinstituting a night shuttle service. Several improvements have been instituted in student financial aid services.

INSTITUTIONALIZING PLANNING, ASSESSMENT, AND RESOURCE ALLOCATION LINKAGES

The goal of the planning process at CSUS is to integrate planning, assessment, and resource allocation. The university has made great strides in the last three years with the introduction, first, of the strategic plan and, second, of assessment designed to create a culture of evidence. However, assessment at CSUS is inchoate, and strategic planning is only slightly more advanced. Allocating resources, and particularly *reallocating* resources, to accomplish planning goals is a continuing challenge. Each experience with the process yields valuable lessons and new ideas for improvement. Much work and discussion are needed to determine how to improve planning and how to best use assessment data in the planning process. The following section discusses some of these issues.

LESSONS LEARNED

1. *There is no one best planning process.* One of our guiding principles of planning is that there is no one best planning process. Our efforts have never followed any textbook prescriptions. Rather, we have learned from the planning literature but have modified approaches to fit the campus culture. More importantly, we have learned from our own efforts each step of the way and have conditioned members of the council and the university to expect changes. As long as people can see that the evolution is forward, they will accept a dynamic planning process as a positive facet of campus activity.

2. *The assessment that informs planning must be context based.* There is an unlimited amount of data and information that could be provided. The challenge is, therefore, to avoid getting lost in the trees and not seeing the forest. For CSUS, the forest is the eight goals of the strategic plan. Therefore, the assessment information that is presented to the council is the information that has relevance to the themes of the strategic plan that they are reviewing.

3. *The more information provided, the more information requested.* Responsible council members have an insatiable demand for information. Information can always be refined, subtotaled by subgroups, and presented in graphs and tables; that is what members request. The challenge to those guiding the planning effort is to direct the members' focus to the critical issues. Toward that end, we have decided to produce complete theme assessment papers only once every three years. In the intervening years, the assessment papers will follow up on the critical issues that were identified in the

previous complete review. They will track the actions that the various governance groups and administrative units have taken in response to the referrals from the council and track only a few key performance indicators for each theme. The complete results of the surveys we administer regularly will continue to be available for those who wish to pursue other issues in more depth.

4. *The strategic plan and assessment data have the power to move the university, even when resources are not explicitly reallocated.* One of the major reasons for moving into strategic planning at CSUS was the need to accommodate budget reductions. Despite a shortage of new resources and an inability to radically reallocate resources, the existence of the strategic plan themes helped focus campus energy on key issues and changed the topics being actively pursued by campus faculty.

CONTINUING CHALLENGES

1. *How good are the data?* For some of the themes of the strategic plan, data are readily available from institutional sources and student surveys to assemble meaningful indicators of progress. In other areas, however, useful data are scarce. Assessment of the Public Life theme, for example, will require the collection of data from the Sacramento region to enable us to assess how our student and faculty efforts at volunteerism, cultural offerings, technical assistance, applied scholarship, and other collaborations are contributing to the development of the region. As another example, even if agreement is reached on how to define and inventory "faculty scholarship," it is a far more complicated matter to assess its outcomes for the teaching and learning process. We recognize that effort and resources need to be devoted to improving the usefulness of assessment information in a variety of areas

if the planning process is to have useful results.

2. *What does the data mean?* The issue of standards for interpreting the meaning of assessment data is a difficult one. Is it good, for example, that 88 percent of graduating students completing a survey reported that their thesis enhanced their knowledge of their subject? Given that we have hundreds of items of data like that one, it is not practical to develop standards or goals for each item. For many of the items contained in the standardized surveys we administer, national norms are available. But even then, one can question the applicability of those standards. While we have not advanced too far on the issue of standards and data interpretation, it is likely that we will develop goals or standards in some key areas and rely on general reactions and consensus of the council for the interpretation of other areas. The most useful standard will, however, be our past performance, since we will always be able to compare current responses with prior ones. Thus we can readily track progress over time.

3. *How do we ensure that assessment information is central to the resource allocation decisions made at the unit level?* The council operates at a high level, assessing institutional progress and guiding the allocation of resources to its principal operating units. The allocation decisions made in the schools and departments have a substantial impact on the degree to which the strategic plan goals are realized. These decisions need to be informed by assessment information as well.

4. *How durable is the strategic plan itself?* The approach to planning taken at CSUS has proven invaluable in assessing not only the progress we are making toward stated goals, but also the value and currency of the plan itself. Already we have added a new theme and revised two others as a result of discussions in council meetings and elsewhere throughout the university. The council's engagement with assessment data has begun to provide valuable guidance regarding the future direction of the university's strategic plan. The relationship between the themes and assessment is a dynamic interaction in which the themes shape the assessment activities, and the assessment reports reshape the themes. The evolution of the strategic plan itself is perhaps the most profound evidence that the integrated planning process used at CSUS can contribute to institutional advancement.

NOTES

1. The themes were: Teaching and Learning, Academic Programs, Scholarship, Pluralism, Enrollment Planning, Campus Life, Public Life, and Capital Campus.
2. Standardized surveys of entering, continuing, and graduating students, and alumni are administered on a regularly scheduled basis. In addition, an automated registration system requires each student to answer two (of a pool of twenty) questions each semester, providing an ongoing source of valuable survey data. Various other surveys prepared for specific purposes are available, along with standard institutional data.
3. Assessment papers are nonjudgmental presentations of all survey and institutional data judged relevant to the theme at hand. They range from 10 to 20 pages in length, plus supporting tables reporting survey results.

CHAPTER 38

REENGINEERING RESOURCE ALLOCATION SYSTEMS

WILLIAM F. MASSY

The golden age for American universities and colleges began after World War II, when research and graduate education were established as major sources of institutional funding, visibility, and prestige. The postwar period also produced major gains in access, with participation rates climbing from single digits to 20 or 30 percent in many countries.[1] This was a time of great faith in higher education, a time of growth and prosperity for institutions and their faculties. The best institutions set their own agendas—in terms of intellectual rather than market values—and these agendas guided most other institutions as they searched for excellence. Universities and colleges reaffirmed their right to autonomy, the ability to define and control their own standards of behavior, even as the proportion of public funding increased dramatically. For fifty years, the public and their legislators bought into the idea that academic quality is proportional to funding—and hence that higher levels of expenditure per student (more quality) are better than lower ones. This proposition, however, is now being challenged in the United States, Great Britain, and many other countries.

Rising educational demand and the incentives to expand research and scholarship have collided with financial constraints—limitations caused by competing social requirements that outstrip resources even in the fastest-growing economies. Moreover, criticisms about higher education's quality, relevance, and costliness have become commonplace. The result has been a profound shift in how the public views universities and colleges, a shift that was summed up this way by the California Higher Education Policy Center:

> Institutional quality should not be judged solely on the grounds of conventional ideas such as prestige and high levels of expenditure per student, but also on real-world concepts of productivity, student learning, and efficiency in delivering educational services.[2]

WHAT IS DIFFERENT?

In the fall of 1991, a group of twenty-four university citizens from twelve countries, ranging from St. Petersburg University in the east to Stanford in the west, met to think through the new concerns. The group consisted of rectors and presidents, higher education scholars, and leaders of organizations concerned with protecting and preserving scholarly institutions. We met three times during 1991 and 1992, and over the course of our conversations we came to this conclusion:

> *Proposition:* The changes most important to the university are external to it. What is new is the use of societal demand—in the American context, market forces—to reshape the university.

Source: *Resource Allocation in Higher Education,* 1996, W.F. Massy (ed.), Peterson's Guides.

Principal Corollary: The failure to understand these changes puts the university at risk. The danger is that the university has become less relevant to society precisely because it has not fully understood the new demands being placed on it.[3]

The growing demand for higher education stems from peoples' desires to improve their employment prospects and a conviction that obtaining more education will bring dividends in that regard. Governments' and institutions' efforts to improve access have led to what the Europeans call "massification," an increased participation in higher education by students of all backgrounds, including nontraditional students, most of whom simultaneously work in the labor market. In the United States, 60 percent of currently graduating high school seniors can be expected to enroll in college in the fall, while the total number of students enrolling in some form of secondary education throughout the year has reached about twenty million, or 8 percent of the U.S. population, an all-time high.[4] Massification also has spawned a heightened sense of vocationalism, not in the narrow sense of blue-collar training but, rather, in terms of acquiring skills in problem solving, communication, teamwork, and information technology that will prove useful in the world of employment.

Massification and vocationalism focus concern on value for money, the degree to which universities and colleges produce relevant learning in effective and efficient ways. Higher education's critics believe that students are paying more and getting less, that educational productivity has declined. Some critics also point out with increasing stridency that schools do not take full advantage of information technology—that while today's applications demonstrate IT's potential, institutional conservatism stifles truly significant innovation.[5]

Data from the Roper Center of the University of Connecticut's Institute for Social Inquiry document the public's concern about college costs (see Table 38.1). For example, 91 percent of respondents in a 1990 survey felt that most people could not afford college without financial aid. In a 1991 survey, only 25 percent of respondents felt that college was affordable, whereas 87 percent felt that "college costs are rising at a rate which will put college out of the reach of most people." Most worrisome,

though, is the 77 percent of 1991 *Money* magazine readers who, when asked whether "tuitions are fairly priced or overpriced," responded that they are overpriced. This well-off group, who also indicated that college cost did not pose a major problem for them, were questioning higher education's value for money and also, perhaps, our integrity.

The resulting sense of entrapment—being convinced of the need for a college education but worrying about its affordability—threatens to reach dangerous proportions:

> The real anger at higher education comes principally from the makers and shapers of public policy—governors, legislators, regulators, heads of public agencies, and surprisingly, an increasing number from the world of philanthropy. Certainly not all, but clearly too many, of those responsible for higher education's funding believe that colleges and universities have become too isolated from the economic pressures that are forcing most other enterprises to rethink their purpose and mission.[6]

Governmental actions reflect these concerns as well as the underlying changes in the environmental context for higher education. Institutions are responding, as we shall see. First, though, let us examine the drivers of change in somewhat more detail.

Vocationalism

Nontraditional students now represent the new majority in American higher education. They are defined as: "(1) all currently enrolled undergraduates aged 25 or older; (2) all undergraduates under 25 years old who did not proceed directly from high school to college, who attend part-time, or who have 'stopped out' for more than one year.[7] According to the U.S. Census Bureau's *Current Population Survey*, the figure for new-majority students as a share of all undergraduate enrollments grew from about 43 percent in 1978 to about 49 percent in 1987.[8] If current trends continue, these students will represent some 60 percent of enrollment by the end of the decade. Upward trends also have been observed in the U.K., Australia, and continental Europe.[9]

New-majority students focus especially on vocational objectives, but the fear of not finding a job after college is redefining the college

TABLE 38.1
Attitudes about College Costs

	Yes: Can Go without Financial Aid	No: Must Have Financial Aid	Don't Know
Do you think most people can afford to go to college today without financial aid, not?[a]	7%	91%	2%
	Agree	Disagree	Don't know
College costs in general are such that most people can afford to pay for a college education.	25%	73%	2%
I would be able to get a college education at this lime only with low interest loans or grants.[b]	74%	20%	6%
	Agree	Disagree	Don't know
College costs are rising at a rate which will put college out of the reach of most people.[c]	87%	10%	3%
	Overpriced	Fairly Priced	
Do you think tuitions are fairly priced or overpriced?[d]	77%	21%	

Source: Roper Center of the University of Connecticut's Institute for Social Inquiry.

a. Gallup National Poll, adults: June 1990

b. Gallup National Poll, adults: June 1991

c. Gallup National Poll, adults: June 1991

d. Willard and Shullman: National household financial decision makers who worry about money very/fairly often: Autumn 1991

years even for "rite-of-passage" students who proceed directly from high school to college. Even in the most selective residential institutions, vocationalism now affects everything from the choice of major to the demand for job placement student services. While traditional academic programs may contribute to the employment goal, this can no longer be asserted as a matter of principle. In other words, universities are coming to be valued for what they can *do*, not for what they *are*. As we state in "A Transatlantic Dialogue," "The more general consequence of massification is the public's sense that the university ought to be an engine of economic growth and social equilibrium."[10]

The employment motive's impact on U.S. students cannot be overstated. As recently as 1981, nearly 9 percent of the nation's top-paying (upper quartile) jobs were held by blue-collar manufacturing employees with only a high school education. A decade later that figure was 6 percent, which represents an absolute decline of nearly half a million jobs in a labor force that grew by almost twelve million.

America's shift toward a service economy raised the relative earning power of baccalaureate degree holders by some 20 percentage points during the past decade. Even those achieving "some college" are enjoying a significant earnings impact, as employers show increasing reliance on the associates degrees and technical certificates to screen prospective job applicants.[11] A 1993 survey of Californians found that "three out of four . . . agree that even in today's tough economic climate, a young person who goes to college has better economic prospects than one who takes a job right out of high school."[12]

Value for Money

Parents' financial worries and rising levels of educational debt are fueling concerns about value for money. The value being rewarded by the marketplace shows little tolerance for inefficient or indifferent service, and the market pays little heed to traditional scholarly pursuits. According to a recent Pew Higher Education Program *Policy Perspectives:*

The most dramatic change is in what the consuming public has come to expect from higher education—and the increasingly pragmatic, even cynical, terms in which the public evaluates particular colleges and universities. "Rite-of-passage" students, paying parents, and the growing number of adult learners who constitute higher education's "new majority"—all seek a reasonable limit to what institutions charge, access to programs that will result in meaningful jobs, a reduction to bureaucratic impediments to a degree, and, above all, real assurances that shifting financial and political fortunes will not place a higher education beyond their grasp.[13]

The same pragmatism is reflected in governmental efforts to buy educational services as cost-effectively as possible. Competing demands on the public purse, coupled with a growing cynicism about whether institutions can control their costs, provide impetus for new resource allocation and performance assessment strategies.

The concerns about cost and price are not unfounded. Between 1985 and 1990, the period of peak cost escalation in U.S. universities, median inflation-adjusted educational and general expenditures per full-time equivalent (FTE) student grew by 4.9 percent per year at private institutions, 2.6 percent per year in public institutions, and 3.8 percent overall.[14] The figures were even larger for those universities offering major research programs: 5.5 percent per year

TABLE 38.2
Inflation Adjusted Tuition Growth, 1987–93

Year	Private	Public
1987–88	3%	1%
1988–89	4	0
1989–90	4	2
1991–91	3	9
1991–92	4	7
1992–93	3	7

Source: Data from *Chronicle of Higher Education* annual summary of tuition changes deflated by the Consumer Price Index.

for the private research universities, 4.0 percent per year for their public counterparts, and 4.7 percent overall (Figure 38.1). The impact of these growth rates, simply stated, is that in the space of five years, the cost per FTE student in private research universities grew by almost one-third. Given the charges about diminishing educational quality during the same period, complaints about productivity loss in higher education have not surprisingly proliferated.

While unit cost increases can inflame public officials and the media, their impact on the general public is multiplied significantly when they drive up tuition (Table 38.2). Private institutions raised tuition at an inflation-adjusted rate of between 3 and 4 percent during the late 1980s, relying on the perceived linkage between cost and quality to immunize them from public reaction. The increases, however, triggered a

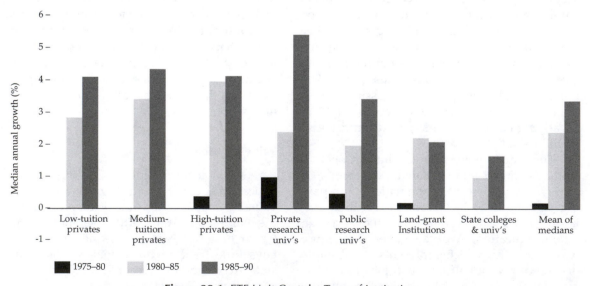

Figure 38.1 FTE Unit Costs by Type of Institution

substantial market and political backlash—indeed, some well-known schools were characterized as "greedy." Private-sector tuition growth has slowed substantially when viewed in nominal rather than inflation-adjusted terms. It declined from 9 percent in 1988–89 to only 6 percent in 1993–94 while remaining essentially constant in real terms—apparently lower inflation has masked the continued increases, but it is doubtful whether such real rates can be maintained when inflation rises again.

Ironically, just as the private-sector pricing pressure seemed to abate, public institutions started raising tuitions at an even faster rate. Beginning in 1991, states tried to mitigate the effects of appropriations cuts on institutional budgets by granting tacit or explicit approval for tuition hikes.[15] In 1990–91, public-sector tuition rose by a startling 9 percent, inflation adjusted, and the next two years brought 7 percent increases. State-funded financial aid rose as well, at an average rate of 8.2 percent from 1991–92 to 1992–93, although the gain matched the increases in cost-of-attendance in only ten of the fifty states.[16] As Arthur Hauptman points out, decreases in state appropriations are often the result of slowdowns in the economy, so that tuition increases tend to occur "when students and their families can least afford it, during tough economic times."[17] The market and political backlash has now reached the public sector, and the rate of tuition increases has abated. Nevertheless, America's public universities and colleges now rely significantly less on direct state support than they did even five years ago.

In 1991, my colleagues on the Pew Higher Education Roundtable and I called for institutions to go on a "revenue diet," and curb the appetite for additional real expenditures by reallocating funds from lower to higher priority work instead of asking for additional funds to finance new programs.[18] We feared that continued cost-rise and attendant tuition increases would erode public confidence in higher education. Justified or not, government edict and market action have now imposed the revenue diet.

The resulting cost-price squeeze means that institutions will have to become more efficient. While efficiency has become something of a bad word in academic circles, both theory and empirical evidence demonstrate powerfully that the more efficient an institution can become, the more it will be able to spend on its chosen high-value activities. Many U.S. institutions are pursuing efficiency gains. Bruce Johnstone, then chancellor of the sixty-campus State University of New York, explained the efficiency objective this way:

> Colleges and universities must become more productive: that is, produce more learning, research, and service at lower unit costs—more efficiently. Market and political forces alike are demanding more productivity from all colleges and universities; public and private, undergraduate and graduate, two- and four-year, selective and less selective.
>
> The challenge is to become genuinely more productive—not just cheaper and shabbier, or less scholarly, or otherwise merely less costly.[19]

To improve efficiency, institutions will have to improve their planning and management systems, tightly focus their activities, and then concentrate on quality—recognizing that they can't afford to do everything while insisting on excellent performance in their chosen areas. Institutions will have to explore continuous improvement and process reengineering methods, which can reduce cost as well as improve quality. Most important, higher education must embrace information technology's potential to transform radically the nature of both academic and administrative work.

Information Technology

Information technology (IT) already represents a significant force in academic life. The Internet, for example, is transforming libraries and scholarly communication. The number of Internet connections has been growing exponentially at 2.9 percent per month, and in early 1993 stood at some 1.8 million sites in 127 countries.[20] Estimating the number of users at 10 per host, this implies 18 million Internet users—and that was in 1993. Vint Cerf, president of the Internet Society since 1991, estimates that the Internet will have 300 million users by the end of the decade.[21]

Internet access provides for information sharing on a worldwide scale. In the past, libraries tried to collect as much material as possible. But now they can share resources in "real time" (defined according to user needs). By developing sophisticated systems for locating and obtaining user-requested materials, libraries can hold down expenditure growth without eroding service quality by adopting a "just in time," as opposed to a "just in case," acquisitions strategy. Similar economics can be obtained in travel by eliminating the need to employ local experts in arcane subject matter. Via the Internet, the expert in Iceland can be accessed as easily as the one on the other side of the campus. Quality teaching and research can come to depend as much on network connections—of both the electronic and human kind—as on the size of the library and the number of experts on staff.

Distance learning offers another example of how IT can transform education. Multimedia concepts now being developed will improve the quality of distance learning enormously while further reducing its cost. Indeed, the distinction between on-campus and distance education will blur to the point where the term *distance learning* no longer has meaning— the technology will deliver the same services whether the distance is across the campus or across the world. IT will leverage facility time and dramatically improve teaching and learning. IT also will alter the economics of education and introduce new competition.

Taking full advantage of information technology will require substantial restructuring. Experience from process reengineering tells us that technology enables significant productivity gains but does not guarantee them.[22] So far institutions have made gains in libraries, electronic mail, administration, and distance learning, but the restructuring of core teaching and learning processes is encountering considerable resistance.

But the day will come. In the 1970s, the Carnegie Council on Higher Education celebrated the university's remarkable stability and permanence with the following observation:

> Taking, as a starting point, 1530, when the Lutheran Church was founded, some 66 institutions that then existed in the Western World still exist today in recognizable forms: The Catholic Church, the Lutheran Church, the Parliaments of Iceland and the Isle of Man, and 62 universities. . . .[23]

No wonder change comes slowly to the academy. But now, in the 1990s, we can add the observation that the fundamental technology of information generation, transformation, storage, transmission, and dissemination—the technology of the university—remained substantially the same from the invention of moveable type until the development of ubiquitous, cheap, and powerful information technology a relatively few years ago. It took decades for the electric motor to transform the factory, but the changes were fundamental. The changes in teaching and learning will be just as fundamental.

INSTITUTIONAL RESPONSES

Recent research shows that institutions follow a predictable pattern when confronted with the changing environment and associated financial difficulties.[24] Almost invariably, the first step is to look for new ways that enhance revenue. Tuition may be raised, sponsored research sought, and gifts solicited, for instance.[25] If the financial gap cannot be bridged with new revenue, institutions cut budgets across the board so the pain can be shared as equally as possible. Often such cuts are accompanied by hiring freezes, travel restrictions, and reductions in capital expenditures. Certain exceptions to this "squeezing strategy" do occur, however. Administrators may harbor secret lists of programs that have outlived their usefulness, but which would be politically difficult to close in normal circumstances. A budget-cutting climate offers the opportunity to move against these "targets of opportunity," usually in the context of speeches about "making hard choices."

What if these tried-and-true responses are not sufficient to restore an institution's financial health? Two kinds of strategies present themselves: *top-down* and *broad-based*. Top-down strategies start by refocusing administrative and support functions and, if necessary, academic programs. By *refocusing* I mean eliminating or downsizing—ending worthwhile services, popular benefits, or even whole academic departments. Downsizing usually means cutting jobs—making the university less an engine of employment. Hopefully this can be accomplished through attrition, but increasingly, U.S. institutions are resorting to outright layoffs. Such actions are painful to all concerned, which leads one to the next response stage: reengineering resource allocation so that future downsizings can be avoided. By improving planning methods as well as associated management information and decision support systems, institutions can improve their elasticity, their ability to adapt to external events without wrenching dislocations.

Broad-based strategies embrace the principles of *continuous quality improvement* (CQI) and *business process reengineering* (BPR). CQI and BPR decentralize quality and efficiency improvement to the individual-worker level. Broadening the base of participation takes longer and requires a different kind of leadership than top-down strategies, but such decentralization is necessary if the university is to become truly efficient and elastic. Employee teams, given the necessary tools and training, are empowered to respond to external events and act on productivity-enhancing opportunities. Performance feedback brings team rewards or, on occasion, a resolve to do better. CQI and BPR now are widely used in business, and universities and colleges are adopting them with increasing frequency.[26] (They are even being used by the Church of England in its efforts to serve members more effectively while making financial ends meet).[27] The vast majority of higher-education applications are in the administrative and support areas, but initiatives aimed at restructuring academic work are beginning to appear.

This book addresses the lower left-hand box of Figure 38.2, "reengineering resource allocation." The remainder of this chapter will describe the problems with traditional budgeting systems and begin to discuss how institu-

tions and governmental units are decentralizing budget decisions to achieve greater effectiveness, accountability, and responsiveness to the preferences of students and other college and university customers. We shall conclude this chapter by asking how academic values can be balanced with market forces in the new decentralized environment, a question that is central to both the theoretical models and practical applications of this book.

Problems with Incremental Line-Item Budgeting

The traditional university controls resources tightly from the center, using what is called line-item budgeting. The line items usually are considered on an incremental basis: that is, items proposed as additions (or deletions, in the case of downsizing) are the only ones to be scrutinized. Limits of time and attention prevent the central authorities from continuously reviewing the ongoing budget base. A variant on centralized budgeting uses formulas to determine the level of each expenditure type (e.g., numbers of faculty, expenditures on staff and supplies) according to student enrollments. This ties the ongoing budget base to activity levels, but such formula-based funding also introduces rigidities into the system.

Centralized budgeting generally prohibits operating units from shifting funds among budget categories. For example, eliminating an approved line item might lead to withdrawal of funds on the grounds that the need had vanished. In other examples, moving money from travel to salaries or vice versa might be discouraged and the use of operating money for equipment purchases expressly prohibited. By controlling everything, administrators believe they can ensure that resources will be used effectively.

Nothing could be further from the truth. Centralized resource allocation systems now are generally recognized to be less effective than ones in which goals are shared, operating units empowered to decide how best to attain the goals, and performance feedback maintained through after-the-fact accountability. We shall illustrate the problems with centralized line-item budgeting by the following account based on the traditional system used at Stanford when, as the newly appointed vice provost for research, I joined the Budget Group in the autumn of 1971.

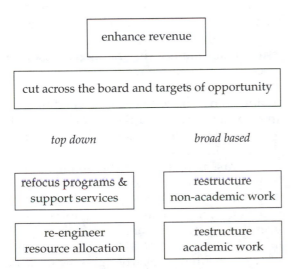

Figure 38.2 Institutional Responses

The year's budget process began with the projection of operating-budget revenue, expected inflation and cost-rise on the existing budget, an inventory of "unfunded liabilities," and a call to operating units for their estimates of "new needs." The latter always produced a large compendium of "requirements," items that the deans and support-service managers believed would be needed to maintain or improve quality and to implement desirable new programs. The lists aggregated to hundreds of items, each specified in detail—for example, a new assistant professor or a new secretary, more teaching assistants, new equipment—and each justified by paragraphs or pages documenting "ineluctable need."

The so-called "maintenance budget," the current-year base escalated by inflation and cost-rise, provided a starting point unless we were in a time of budget adjustments. In other words, operating units owned the purchasing power of their existing budget bases unless specific reductions had previously been negotiated. Stanford did adjust its budgets during the late 1960s and early 1970s, eliminating about seventeen percent of the operating base over an eight-year period.[28] Dollar targets were set, faculty committees consulted, and agreements reached to remove particular line-items. This did not negate the principle that a unit owned the purchasing power of its budget base, since items could be removed only after extensive consultation and negotiation.

The annual budget exercise consisted of "closing the gap," because the sum of requirements invariably exceeded the projected available funding by a wide margin. Gap-closing was accomplished with the aid of a device we called a "migration analysis." New requests and unfunded liabilities were "induced to migrate" across a spreadsheet, stopping in one or another column—the last column representing the jackpot: "funded in the operating budget." Stops along the way included "not funded" and, importantly, "funded outside the operating budget base." The latter meant that funding was on a "one-time basis"—that is, the expenditure was authorized for one year, but ownership of the funds was not passed to the unit. Once authorized, however, these items would often acquire a life of their own and come back to haunt us as unfunded liabilities the following year. The word "no" became very difficult to articu-

late, and efforts to bypass the "not funded" column could reach heroic proportions.

Another heroic struggle involved the estimation of income. Pressures on the tuition, overhead recovery, and gift projections seemed to grow in proportion to the budget gap. Arguments in favor of higher tuition were marshaled, pencils were sharpened on the overhead calculations, and fund-raising strategies were honed. We extended high praise to members of staff who could find new income sources: one year we described our associate controller as "jumping out of the cake" at the eleventh hour with an unexpected new income projection—and for the next few years we eagerly awaited, and implicitly counted on, his repeat performances.

These efforts were not Machievellian. They did not lack integrity. But they did reflect and reinforce a mind-set that focused on the short run and pushed every income source as hard as possible within that context. We did close the gap, and we did balance the budget. At the end of the day, however, it was hard to see what we had accomplished—other than coping with the year's pressures and maintaining peace among the deans and faculty as best we could. The lists of line items approved, not approved, and funded "one-time" did not add up to a coherent strategy. Worse, we were reinforcing a cycle of growing expectations, thus placing ever-stronger pressures on general-funds revenue sources. Yet it all seemed so rational at the time.

Hindsight illuminates many specific shortcomings of the traditional process. Instead of enumerating these shortcomings in detail, however, let us step back and examine the assumptions implicit in traditional resource allocation. While these assumptions are rarely acknowledged explicitly, their influence on resource allocation within colleges and universities remains powerful. So powerful, in fact, that we will sometimes refer to them as principles rather than assumptions.

The first assumption can be summed up by the phrase, "property rights."[29] Once an operating unit has obtained approval for a program, that program has a right to continue unless circumstances change dramatically. Not unlike a tenured professor—as some have pointed out—these property rights are difficult to withdraw absent financial exigency or some even more dramatic event. Program budgets with tenured faculty lines do involve contractual property rights. Faculty and students are viewed as deserving academic freedom: their programs should not be subject to what might turn out to be capricious or malevolent judgments. The property-rights principle means that the purchasing power of the existing budget base should be protected as a first priority and that reductions can be imposed only after due process.

The second assumption holds that academic units are too fragile and their work too important to be disrupted by the hurly-burly of the marketplace. Academic time constants—meaning the gestation of academic work and the duration of faculty employment contracts—are simply too long to accommodate short-term financial fluctuations. The central authorities should shield schools and departments from financial fluctuations to the greatest extent possible. Revenue shortfalls should be covered from central reserves, or budget deficits if necessary, until the need for reductions is irrefutable and academic units have been given time to adapt with minimum disruption. The oft-quoted wisdom that "a great department takes a generation to build, but precipitous action can destroy it in a year" reinforces the arguments for caution to hold academic units harmless from market fluctuations.

The third assumption is closely related to the second. It holds that the central administration should *take responsibility* for the financial health of the academic units. Not to maintain adequate funding for a school or department is perceived as an institutional failure—a perception that can be mitigated but not eradicated by blaming external forces. Funding reductions, which administrators want to avoid if at all possible, are perceived as reducing quality. The idea that funding reductions might trigger improved productivity is foreign to the academy. The predominant view is that less funding means "doing less with less." Searching for ways to be more productive, of doing more with less, is not part of the faculty's job description.[30] The institution is responsible for delivering the funding needed to maintain quality using traditional pedagogical methods.

Deeply embedded in the academic culture, the responsibility principle is also reaffirmed in the faculty marketplace. An institution that fails to provide what its faculty feel they need may well find itself on the short end of competitive raiding activities. This concern for faculty morale and the prospect of losing one's best faculty makes "no" difficult to articulate. The result is a vicious circle: administrations believe their job is to protect academic units and faculty from financial vicissitudes, which reinforces the faculty's belief that this is in fact the institution's responsibility, which lowers the tolerance for budget reductions among deans, department chairs, and faculty.

The three assumptions transform resource allocation from an exercise in investment, where scarce resources are put to the best possible uses, to an exercise in coping and conflict management.[31] Such behavior produces a strategy of minimizing the worst breaches of what is seen as administrative responsibility and resulting losses in morale. Since an unadulterated "no" risks serious disruption, this is avoided where possible—unless, of course, the case for funding can be shown to be flawed in some communicable way. Most requests do represent worthwhile endeavors, however, so budget authorities feel besieged. They feel that they have lost control of the process and that the way to reestablish control is to find new sources of income.

Decentralizing Resource Allocation

Decentralization provides an antidote to the negative consequences associated with line-item budgeting. Performance responsibility budgeting (PRB) and revenue responsibility budgeting (RRB) represent successive steps on the decentralization path, and value responsibility budgeting (VRB), introduced in chapter 12, adopts the best aspects of block and revenue responsibility budgeting while mitigating their most serious difficulties.

Figures 38.3–38.6 provide process flow diagrams for line-item budgeting and for the aforementioned three varieties of decentralized budgeting. The diagrams provide an overview of where funds are allocated and expended, including how the central authorities, operating units, and support units are connected in terms of authority for initiating transactions. The definitions of these three entities depend on the level of budgeting being discussed. For example, in intra-institutional budgeting the

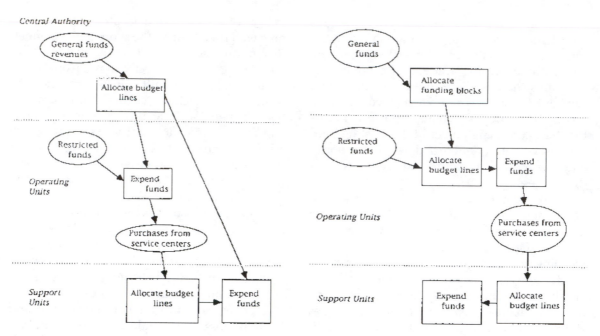

Figure 38.3 Line-Item Budgeting Process Flow Diagram

Figure 38.4 Performance Responsibility Process Flow Diagram

central authority might be a president or provost, the operating entities would be school deans (and possibly department chairs) and support units (other than service centers and auxiliaries). For a state, the central authority would be the system head or perhaps the state budget office, while the operating entities would be campuses or institutions.

In line-item budgeting, which we show to provide a baseline for comparison, the central administration allocates an institution's general funds as indicated at the top of Figure 38.3. In addition, most academic units receive restricted funds in the form of research grants and contracts, gifts, and restricted endowment payouts. Operating units expend funds for personal services (compensation), goods and services from outside, and outputs from service centers and auxiliaries. Service center and auxiliary spending is determined by the units' ability to sell goods and services to other institutional entities (and to outsiders in the case of auxiliaries): purchasing decisions by customers, based on price and quality, provide for resource rationing. Line-item restrictions usually do not govern these support units; rather, they are free to deploy their available funds in ways they believe to be most effective.

Figure 38.4 presents the process flow diagram for performance responsibility budget-

ing. The central authority allocates funding to the operating units in blocks, which can be used as the unit head sees fit. The unit head must allocate resources to lower-level units, which eventually determine individual budget lines against which expenditures can be controlled. The rest of the system works the same as in line-item budgeting, the critical difference being that in performance responsibility budgeting, those closest to the production process—that is, those who possess the best information about the effects of alternative expenditure patterns—make the eventual line-item allocation decisions. Stanford adopted performance responsibility budgeting in the 1980s, when the shortcomings of line-item budgeting became apparent.[32]

In PRB, the central authority determines the size of the block grant by first applying a costing formula and then modifying the block according to judgments based on the unit's performance and plans for the future. The costing formula may simply adjust last year's allocation for inflation, or it may take student numbers and other cost drivers into account. Sometimes the number of tenured faculty appointments is controlled outside the budget process to avoid imprudent long-term commitments, but the number of such regulatory limits tends to be circumscribed. Good performance and plans that advance institutional goals yield added funding—money that can be viewed as a reward for past service or an investment in future prospects. Plans should include information on the unit's revenue enhancement efforts, and less-than-adequate efforts should bring less, not more, funding from the central administration.

In RRB, the central authority allocates revenue lines instead of expenditure lines. Each operating unit is responsible for both its revenues and expenditures. Most revenues are allocated, with only a few truly unattributable lines, such as unrestricted endowment income, placed in the "general revenue" category. General revenues are used to fund central overheads and subventions; alternatively, the general revenues may be allocated by some arbitrary rule (in proportion to assigned revenues, for instance, and then recalled in the form of taxes). As an example of assigned revenues, the tuition "earned" by teaching a certain number of credit-hour enrollment units might be assigned to a school or department, thus comprising "revenue" that the operating unit is free to expend according to its best judgment. The system extends the sensitivity to market forces down through the institution, since operating unit budgets depend on their ability to generate revenue. For example, enrollment shortfalls produce budget consequences, immediately and decisively, the only appeal route being through the difficult subvention route.

The operating units are not generally allowed to expend all their assigned revenue, as demonstrated in Figure 38.5. First, taxes are levied as a percent of revenues, said taxes flowing back to the central authority for redistribution in the form of subventions. The subventions permit the institution to compensate for any market-based revenue shortfalls in relation to cost by applying an "equity judgment." (The equity judgment will reflect the institution's intrinsic values.) For example, a music school that generates little market-based revenue might receive a large subvention, while an affluent business school might pay more in taxes than it gets back in subventions. The taxes also may be used to finance the central authority's own activities, and the activities of support units (other than service centers and

auxiliaries) that do not generate their own revenue. These "income taxes" may be supplemented by "expenditure taxes," overhead payments that also help to fund administrative and support activities.

Revenue responsibility budgeting maximizes entrepreneurship and responsiveness to market forces, but it may prevent the institution from reaching its strategic goals. What the economist calls "externalities" may distort resource allocations, as when one operating unit's decisions adversely affect other units to a powerful extent but the offending unit is immunized from the negative effects by the rules of the budgeting process. An engineering school, for example, might decide to teach its own calculus classes in order to garner the extra income, causing the math department to lose the critical mass of students necessary to fill its classes. Basing the subventions on equity instead of performance limits accountability and fragments planning. Even when externalities are not important, revenue responsibility budgeting may elevate market effects at the expense of institutional values. Institutions try to deal with this problem through subventions, but heavy use of subventions undermines the

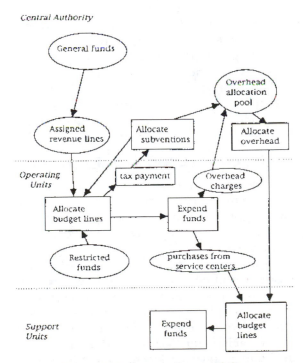

Figure 38.5 Revenue Responsibility Budgeting Process Flow Diagram

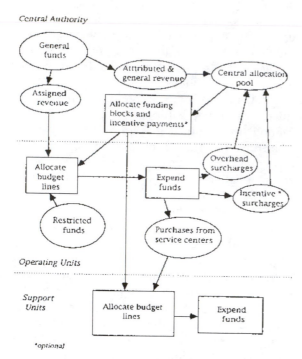

Central Authority

Operating Units

Support Units

optional

Figure 38.6 Value Responsibility Budgeting Process Flow Diagram

sense of revenue "ownership" that forms the core of the responsibility center system. Schools tend to resent revenue taxation, and heavy taxation undermines accountability.

At the other end of the spectrum, performance responsibility budgeting significantly dilutes the effect of market force. The central budgeting authority usually can help smooth over revenue fluctuations, so that the operating units become insensitive to the effects of price and quality on demand. Performance responsibility budgeting also tends to smooth other differences among academic units, including differences stemming from the kinds of performance variations the system is designed to mitigate. Central authorities may defer to the aforementioned property rights principle and forgive performance problems rather than penalize faculty, employees, or students by withdrawing funds.

These considerations have led me to propose a hybrid system, *value responsibility budgeting,* which adopts responsibility center concepts for portions of an institution's revenue base and block allocation concepts for the remainder.[33] As shown in Figure 38.6, the system divides an institution's revenue streams into three categories instead of the two used in revenue

responsibility budgeting. Assigned revenue lines would be those where: (a) the allocation principles are unambiguous and (b) externalities are unimportant. For example, tuition from professional masters enrollments or a specialized course in the major might be assigned, whereas general education enrollments might be withheld and placed in the "attributed revenue" category. Assigned revenues are owned by the operating units as in revenue responsibility budgeting, whereas attributed and general revenues are allocated in blocks as in performance responsibility budgeting. Overhead charges may be assessed, and a new form of transfer, "incentive surcharges," may be invoked to further specific purposes as defined by the central authority.

GOVERNMENTAL RESPONSES

Now that we have examined budgeting issues from within the institution, let us turn to similar issues at the level of state and government funding of higher education institutions. Governmental responses to higher education's changed circumstances can be summarized simply: improve accountability. Officials are coming to believe that traditional resource allocation and regulation systems fail to influence significantly, let alone control, the strategic directions of universities and colleges. Without accountability, the argument goes, institutions have tilted too far toward research and scholarship, failed to adapt to student aspirations and needs, and paid too little attention to efficiency.

To improve institutional accountability, governments are moving away from the common incremental budgeting approach and relaxing line-item control if it is being imposed. They are following the decentralization advice given in 1986 by the University of Oregon's L. R. Jones, Columbia University's Fred Thompson, and the University of Washington's William Zumeta:

> it appears that legislators and executive decision makers in government ought to resist the monopoly biases of budgeteers and lend their support to experiments with competitive service supply and per-unit subsidy arrangements in higher education and elsewhere.[34]

The preferred approaches fall into two broad categories: privatization and performance-based funding, both of which strengthen accountability without unduly meddling in institutions' internal affairs. Privatization has much in common with revenue responsibility budgeting as used within institutions. Performance-based funding is somewhat like performance responsibility budgeting but goes further in holding operating units accountable.

Accountability Killers

In incremental budgeting, the government begins by allocating each university and college a certain sum based on past experience and then discusses how much of an increase (or decrease) will be provided in the coming year. Unfortunately, focusing on strategic issues or on performance in the context of year-to-year increments is very difficult. Institutions assert property rights to use their current base for existing (or at least their own) purposes, arguing that new state initiatives should be funded as add-ons. The system also has disastrous implications for efficiency, as Derek Bok, Robert Zemsky, and I told the Hungarian government after reviewing their options for higher-education reform:

> [The incremental budgeting] method contains mostly negative incentives. University officials have no reason to save money since doing so is likely to lead to reductions in state appropriations in the following year. Instead, officials will be inclined to spend all the money they receive, whether they need it or not, and to exaggerate their problems and needs in order to receive more money in the future. In addition, the system contains no incentive to consolidate or shut down inefficient programs.[35]

The problems with incremental budgeting are similar to those of line-item budgeting, discussed earlier in the context of institutions' internal resource allocation. Often line-item control is combined with incremental budgeting, which compounds the negative effects of both.

Line-item systems were much more common among U.S. state governments a decade ago than they are at present. For example, in studying one large multi-campus university during the 1970s, I found state budget officials

had to approve most significant financial decisions. Today that same university operates under a block grant, which gives its officers the freedom *and* the responsibility to expend funds at times and in ways most likely to achieve state and institutional goals. The change was negotiated in the context of severe appropriations cuts: in effect, the chancellor told the governor that he could not be responsible for making the university more efficient without the power to allocate and reallocate resources internally. The state was committed to the cuts, but realized it had to make a choice: continue line-item control and accept deteriorating quality—a "cheaper and shabbier" university—or delegate authority and hold the institution accountable for offsetting the cuts with improved efficiency. The same rule applies when budget cuts are not imminent: accountability and micromanagement don't mix.[36]

Privatization

In the traditional view of higher education, governments shielded universities and colleges from the pressures of market and political forces. Public policy concerned itself with the health of institutions, on the grounds that universities and colleges are public resources and that education is a public good. The traditional view was founded on the following principles:

- government is the principle provider of public policies relating to universities;
- universities provide education to a limited segment of society as a public good;
- society influences universities by exerting pressure on the government to change its public policy; and
- university traditions of autonomy are designed principally to limit government's capacity to intrude.[37]

Unfortunately, as I noted earlier, government policy and oversight have been unable to assure quality and efficiency to the satisfaction of public officials and their constituents. And if that weren't enough, the same officials are beginning to view the private benefits of a college education (as captured by lifetime salary differentials, for instance) as being more and more important relative to the public benefits of an educated citizenry.

The result has been an increasing "privatization" of higher education by placing greater reliance on tuition and market forces as a substitute for public appropriation. Governments are embracing market principles in hopes that competition will discipline prices, quality, and relevance in ways that bureaucracies cannot, and governments are behaving more like procurers of educational and research services than supporters of institutions. Privatization embraces these principles:

the role of public policy diminishes as public policy becomes less important for defining universities;

universities, often in competition with other segments of higher education, are expected to provide education and educational services to an ever-expanding segment of society;

society influences universities directly through constituency pressures and direct purchases; and

traditional autonomy provides universities less protection from external demands; institutional entrepreneurism rises in response to emerging market opportunities; and the university is less able to integrate demands of external and internal constituencies.[38]

In many parts of America, the public is coming to accept the notion that market mechanisms represent the most practical way to distribute resources, even to the point of determining the relative value of institutional missions according to the enrollments or revenues they garner. Societal demand is being exerted directly on institutions instead of through government mediators.

Privatization need not bring diminished access for disadvantaged students: several mechanisms have been suggested to counteract this trend. Although these mechanisms remain somewhat controversial, most of the controversy stems from a basic disagreement with privatization itself, not the particular mechanism. In at least one state, for example, "serious consideration has been given to ending direct appropriations altogether, replacing them with a voucher system that would make public institutions compete head-on with private institutions for public funds."[39] Even in conventional funding systems, simultaneous increases in

financial aid can help offset the effect of tuition hikes on access. "High tuition-high aid" policies target public funds according to financial need, leaving affluent students to pay the full cost of their education.[40] Adopting such policies would end the concern that:

> Appropriations for public higher education, particularly at flagship institutions, amount to a public tax for the benefit of the economically advantaged whose children neither need nor deserve such subsidy for their college education.[41]

Performance-Based Funding

Where direct competition isn't practical or desired, governments can simulate market actions by making funding contingent on assessed institutional performance. In other words, government exercises the market function by adjusting its purchase-contract prices and quantities in response to changes in absolute or relative institutional performance.

Performance-based resource allocation has its roots in the so-called assessment movement, which became popular in the United States during the 1980s, but the two are not identical. Assessment now focuses on developing feedback for intra-institutional use as much as on producing externally mandated public "report cards." External assessment represents a necessary but not sufficient condition for simulating market action: a mechanism must be present to translate assessment results into meaningful changes in prices or quantities. Assessment can add value even in the absence of such mechanisms by improving information flow into the real market, but this falls under the heading of privatization. Governments that rely on assessment alone, without privatization or performance-based resource allocation, are likely to be disappointed.

America's assessment movement grew in response to concerns about the quality of higher education. At the beginning of the 1990s, at least fifteen states "used some form of student outcome measure as a basis for evaluation by a state agency." Two states, Tennessee and Colorado, "directly linked budgets to an assessment of university outcome measures," and three other states reported pending recommendations for similar policies. More than a dozen additional states were considering assessment, and all six regional accreditation agencies required "some kind of student outcomes assessment in their review process."[42] The U.S. Department of Education has contracted the development of a battery of comprehensive tests for evaluating college learning outcomes, which may (or may not) prove useful for resource allocation. Despite all the activity, however, one must look abroad for the most comprehensive efforts to implement performance-based funding.

The British government has demonstrated its commitment to performance-based funding by separating the allocations for teaching and institutionally funded research, and by basing each allocation on department-level quality assessments.[43] Funds are provided in block grants, with allocations between teaching and research and among departments being a matter for institutional decision. A similar system has been implemented in Hong Kong,[44] and Australia has introduced a program through which institutions that demonstrate extraordinary teaching quality will be rewarded with additional funds.[45]

The separation of teaching and research contrasts markedly with U.S. practice, where self-funded research usually is comingled with educational funding. Sponsored research, which is kept separate in both systems, accounts for a larger fraction of total research expenditures in America than in Britain because Britain funds academic salaries, laboratory infrastructure, and overhead through block grants rather than projects. The U.S. government's budget pressures, however, have transferred more of the burden to institutions in recent years, so the amount of self-funded research now is substantial. Sponsored research proposals are filtered through a powerful market mechanism, peer review, but self-funded research rarely receives such scrutiny. Self-funded research expenditures manifest themselves mostly in more favorable teaching assignments—for example, reduced loads, fewer preparations, smaller classes, and more teaching-assistant support. Such improvements quickly get built into departmental budget bases and may be regarded as property rights by affected faculty, whether or not they actually do meaningful research.

The antidote to such property rights is a system of performance-based assessments, linked to resource allocation. This is not easy, but experiences in Britain and Hong Kong, and in some U.S. universities, indicate that the job can be done.

Evaluating teaching and learning is much harder than evaluating research. The U.K. system remains controversial, for example, even though two different groups (the Funding Council and the Committee of Vice-Chancellors and Principals) currently are actively engaged in evaluation. The task of developing performance measure is not beyond our reach, however. Whereas outsiders have difficulty assessing the delivered quality of teaching and learning, they can fairly easily determine the presence or absence of departmental quality assurance and improvement processes.[46] Evaluators should look for evidence that faculty systematically assess their own work and that of their peers, and then formulate and act upon improvement strategies. Such processes must operate continuously in order to be effective, so the search for evidence is not difficult. (Alas, few departments can muster evidence of continuous teaching quality improvement.[47]) Institution-level reviews are important because they elicit and discipline department-level processes, but the focus should be on the departments themselves, where the ability to assess and improve educational quality truly resides (Figure 38.7).

Quality-process audits should not be confused with the evaluation of inputs (for example, expenditure per student or faculty reputation), which have a deservedly bad name in assessment circles. Performance-based measures should never be based on inputs, since that would be circular. Absent good methods for comprehensively measuring student outcomes, the focus should be on how resources are used—that is, on departmental assessments. Such audits can rely on written submissions supplemented with site visits. The approach is rooted in the principles—eminently reasonable in my opinion—that poor teaching is more

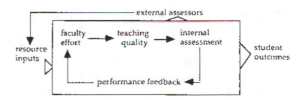

Figure 38.7 Departmental Process Audits

likely to be caused by inattention and failure to focus on student needs than by incompetence, and that quality will improve if faculty work together to continuously improve their performance. Departmental assessments can ascertain what faculty do and how they do it in addition to capacity and competence.

VALUES AND MARKET FORCES

We have seen how market forces are reshaping the university, making it more responsive, more efficient, and more entrepreneurial. The new focus on societal demand is not merely an attribute of our times but the inevitable consequence of massification and democracy. For institutions to ignore the shift would be fruitless and dangerous. Yet how will market forces affect that most fundamental objective of the classic university—to nurture the community of scholars that since ancient times has conserved and advanced mankind's intellectual and cultural heritage? Under what conditions will academic institutions be able to defend intellectual autonomy in the face of privatization and performance-based funding?

Economic theory can shed some light on this question, and the view is not encouraging. According to the theory, nonprofit enterprises like universities and colleges choose their activities (that is, their outputs and the associated processes) to maximize the amount of utility produced, where *utility* is defined subjectively by the institution according to its own value system.[48] This contrasts with the for-profit world, where value is defined in monetary terms by stockholders or other private claimants. Nonprofit enterprises also must take account of productivity factors and market forces (production and demand functions in economic parlance), just like their for-profit cousins, and nonprofits must insure that revenues cover expenditures.

For now, let us simply note that universities cross-subsidize activities with high academic value but low market value by using either fixed revenue—that is, funds that do not depend on current institutional performance—or the proceeds from activities that fetch high prices in relation to their costs. This "discretionary revenue" and the cross-subsidies that flow from it distinguish non-profit enterprises

from businesses, where surpluses may be distributed to owners rather than being plowed back into the entity's own activities.

The traditional university received most of its funding in the form of fixed revenue from historically based government appropriations, endowments, gifts, and the like. (Selective private institutions also have been able to charge high tuition without materially eroding student demand.) Thus, they did not have to worry much about market forces. Decisions were dominated by self-defined values, derived (at least in principle) from scholarly deliberations and defended in the name of intellectual autonomy. We have come to equate this kind of independence with the very essence of a university, but that is an oversimplification. The conditions for value autonomy require a high proportion of discretionary revenue as well as high-minded goals and a nonprofit structure.

Privatization and performance-based funding reduce discretionary revenue, thus altering the relative effects of values and market forces in institutional decision making. Both methods do this by design—indeed, making universities and colleges pay more attention to market forces is their primary goal. These forces—transmitted through the price-quantity reactions of real markets or simulated by performance-based funding mechanisms—trigger institutional adaptive behavior. So far so good. But what happens if the process is allowed to go too far?

The aforementioned economic theory predicts what will happen if discretionary revenues vanish and competition drives prices down to rock-bottom levels: *the university will behave like a business*. The loss of discretionary revenue will eliminate cross-subsidies, and with them will go institutions' ability to pursue values not fully shared by the marketplace. One can prove mathematically that, as budget constraints become tighter and tighter, the nonprofit institution's decision rules converge to the form used by for-profit enterprises. That this is not simply a theoretical proposition can be seen from recent developments in higher education in the Peoples Republic of China—where government funding cuts of 50 percent and more have turned some academic departments into essentially for-profit enterprises.[49] In other words, altruistic-oriented not-for-profit entities become slaves to market forces as their viability comes under threat.

Governmental and institutional policy-makers must find ways to give effective voice to societal demand while avoiding the limiting case where market forces become completely dominant. Universities must commit to reform, to becoming more efficient and to meeting the rising and more varied demands for postsecondary education *before* being forced to do so by extreme market pressure. Governments must find ways to transmit market signals to institutions without placing them at the mercy of sometimes ill-informed and shortsighted shifts in educational demand.

We need a new social compact, both within colleges and universities and between public institutions and the state funding agencies. The new systems should be designed to give market-derived revenue a significant role in university decision making but still retain enough discretionary revenue to maintain autonomy. The universities, for their part, must demonstrate effective stewardship by taking the external society's priorities into account when exercising their autonomy. In the words of "A Transatlantic Dialogue":

> In return for the university's commitment to internal reform, to participating as full partners in the alliance necessary to meet the rising demand for higher education, and to making the provision of social and economic services an integral, indeed equal, part of their missions, public agencies must provide base financial and political support for the university's scholarly functions—which includes protecting and supporting their intellectual and political autonomy.[50]

The compact should extend within universities, to cover schools, departments, and other academic units.

Forging the new social compact will reorient negotiations between governments and universities, and within universities, on a worldwide scale. To quote again from "A Transatlantic Dialogue," the negotiation will take place in the triangular space defined by:

> the rising demand for higher education that has placed a premium on useful knowledge and vocational training;

> the university's own demands that its intellectual autonomy and right to define as well as control its own standards and behavior be respected; and

the demands that the university become both more efficient and more accountable, in order to limit its draw on public resources.[51]

Institutions that can demonstrate relevance, efficiency, and responsiveness to societal demand will enter these negotiations in a stronger position than their more traditional counterparts. They are more likely to be successful in defending their autonomy. Ironically, by becoming more adaptive, universities and colleges will best be able to defend their intellectual values.

NOTES

1. See, for example, participation rates cited in the U.S. Department of Education, *Digest of Education Statistics*, NCES 93–292.
2. The California Higher Education Policy Center, *Time for Decision: California's Legacy and the Future of Higher Education* (San Jose, CA: Discussion Draft, March 1994), 17.
3. "A Transatlantic Dialogue," *Policy Perspectives* 5, no. 1 (1993): 1.
4. Arthur Hauptman, "Higher Education Finance Issues in the Early 1990s," working paper, Center for Research in Education Finance, University of Southern California, June 1992.
5. See for example, Lewis J. Perelman, *School's Out* (New York: Avon Books, 1992).
6. "To Dance with Change," *Policy Perspectives* 5, no. 3 (1994): 6A.
7. "Breaking the Mold," *Policy Perspectives* 2, no. 2 (1990). The calculations are based on data through 1987 and have not been updated, but information from individual institutions suggests that the trend is continuing.
8. Ibid., extrapolation front figure 4 in "Profiles" section, 3.
9. "Innovations in Australian Tertiary Education" (paper presented at the OECD Conference on Current Issues in Mass Higher Education: Financing and Innovation, Chiba City, Japan, 8–11 March 1994); "A Transatlantic Dialogue."
10. "A Transatlantic Dialogue," 3A.
11. "To Dance with Change," 3.
12. John Immerwahr and Steve Farkas, "The Closing Gateway: Californians Consider Their Higher Education System" (Public Agenda

Foundation for the California Higher Education Policy Center, Sept. 1993), iv.

13. "To Dance with Change," 5A.

14. Data source: "A Call to Meeting." *Policy Perspectives* 4, no. 4 (1993): 23B. Community and proprietary colleges are excluded. Educational and general expenditures exclude direct expenditures on sponsored research as well as dormitories and food service, intercollegiate athletics, and similar activities. Research universities are defined as those institutions that belong to the Association of American Universities (AAU); these institutions account for the bulk of the U.S. academic sponsored research. The "overall" figures are the means of medians for all institutional types.

15. State support for higher education declined by 1 percent overall between 1990–91 and 1992–93, according to a recent survey by the Center for Higher Education at Illinois State University. Public appropriations in seventeen states declined between 1 percent and 13 percent, and in an additional twenty states appropriations remained constant or failed to increase enough to keep up with inflation.

16. Kit Lively, "State Spending on Student Aid Rebounds Sharply," *Chronicle of Higher Education.* April 9, 1993, A24.

17. Hauptman, "Finance Issues," 8.

18. "The Other Side of the Mountain," *Policy Perspectives* 5, no. 1 (1991): 2A.

19. Bruce Johnstone, "Enhancing the Productivity of Learning," *American Association of Higher Education Bulletin* (December, 1993).

20. Mark Lottor, Network Wizards, SRI International, Menlo Park, California.

21. *Wired* 12, no. 12 (December 1994): 154.

22. Michael Hammer and James Champy, *Reengineering the Corporation: A Manifesto for Business Revolution* (New York: Harper Business, 1993).

23. Carnegie Council, *Three Thousand Futures: The Next Twenty Years in Higher Education* (San Francisco: Jossey-Bass, 1980).

24. Adapted from "A Call to Meeting," 9B.

25. For examples of revenue-enhancement approaches see D. Bruce Johnstone, "The Costs of Higher Education: Worldwide Issues and Trends for the 1990s" in *The Funding of Higher Education: International Perspectives,* ed. Philip G. Altbach and D. Bruce Johnstone (New York: Garland Publishing), 25–44 ; and William F. Massy, "Building a More Entrepreneurial University" (paper presented at the University Operation and Financial Management Conference, Chinese Taipei, March 25, 1994).

26. Ted Marchese, "TQM Reaches the Academy," *AAHE Bulletin* 44, no. 3 (November 1991), 3–9; and "TQM: A Time for Ideas," *Change* 25, no. 3 (1993): 10-13; Dean L. Hubbard, ed., *Continuous Quality Improvement: Making the Transition to Education* (Maryville, MO: Prescott

Publishing, 1993). The subject also has been the focus of a recent report to England's Committee of Vice-Chancellors and Principals (CVCP).

27. "Nave gazing." *The Economist* 330, no. 7854 (March 12, 1994): 62.

28. For a description of one of these programs see David S. P. Hopkins and William F. Massy, "Budget Equilibrium Program," in *Planning Models for Colleges and Universities* (Stanford, CA: Stanford University Press, 1981).

29. Henry Levin, "Raising Productivity in Higher Education," working paper, PEW Higher Education Research Program, 1989.

30. William F. Massy and Andrea K. Wilger, "Improving Productivity," *Change* 27, no. 4 (July/August 1995): 10–20.

31. Hans DeGroot and Jordan Van der Sluis, "Bureaucracy Response to Budget Cuts: An Economic Model," *Kyklos* 40 (1987): 103–9.

32. William F. Massy, "Budget Decentralization in Higher Education," *Planning for Higher Education* 18, no. 2 (1990): 39–55.

33. William F. Massy, "Resource Allocation Reform in Higher Education," (paper presented at the Conference on Resource Allocation and University Management by the Finance Center of the Consortium for Policy Research in Education; University of Southern California, November 19–20, 1992); Value Responsibility Budgeting seems to have elements in common with the system used by De Montfort University (U.K.), described in Michael A. Brown and David M. Wolf, "Allocating Budgets Using Performance Criteria" in P. G. Altbach and D. B. Johnstone, *The Funding of Higher Education* (New York: Garland Publications, 1993): 173–88.

34. L. R. Jones, Fred Thompson, and William Zumeta, "Reform of Budget Control in Higher Education," *Economics of Education Review* 5, no. 2 (1986): 147–58; see also Mary P. McKeown, "Issues in Higher Education Budgeting Policy," *Economics of Education Review* 5, no. 2 (1986): 159–63 for a discussion of governmental practices and effectiveness circa 1986.

35. Derek Bok, "Universities in Hungary" (Budapest: Citizens Democracy Corps, October 1992), 10; Derek Bok is president emeritus of Harvard University and Robert Zemsky is professor of higher education at the University of Pennsylvania.

36. William F. Massy. "Measuring Performance: How Colleges and Universities Can Set Meaningful Goals and Be Accountable" in *Measuring Institutional Performance in Higher Education,* ed. William F. Massy and Joel W. Meyerson (Princeton, NJ: Peterson's, 1994), 29–54.

37. "A Transatlantic Dialogue." 4A.

38. Ibid., 5A.

39. "To Dance with Change," 5.

40. See Michael S. McPherson and Morton Owen Shapiro, *Keeping College Affordable* (Washington, DC: The Brookings Institution, 1991) for a detailed discussion of high tuition-high aid policies.

41. "To Dance with Change," 6.

42. Serbrenia J. Sims, *Student Outcomes Assessment* (New York: Greenwood Press, 1992), 56–57.

43. Tertiary Education in the United Kingdom" (paper presented at the OECD Conference on Current Issues in Mass Higher Education: Financing and Innovation, Chiba City, Japan, 8–11 March 1994); Graeme John Davies, "Successful Revitalization" (paper presented at the Stanford Forum for Higher Education Future Symposium on "Revitalizing Our Institutions," Pacific Grove, CA, October 7-8, 1993); and various circulars published by the higher education funding councils of England and Scotland.

44. The author, as a member of the Hong Kong University and Polytechnic Grants Committee, is an architect of the new system. For a preliminary description, see Nijel J. French, "Higher Education in Hong Kong: Recent Development and Current Issues" (paper presented at the OECD Conference on Current Issues in Mass Higher Education: Financing and Innovation, Chiba City, Japan, 8–11 March 1994).

45. "Financing Mass Higher Education in Australia" (paper presented at the OECD Conference on Current Issues in Mass Higher Education: Financing and Innovation, Chiba City, Japan, 8–11 March 1994).

46. William F. Massy and Andrea Wilger. "Hollowed Collegiality: Implications for Teaching Quality," *Change* 26, no. 4 (July/August 1944): 10–20.

47. Massy and Wilger, "Improving Productivity," 10–20.

48. See David S. P. Hopkins and William F. Massy. *Planning Models for Colleges and Universities* (Stanford, CA: Stanford University Press, 1981), chapter 3.

49. Personal visits to Beijing; also Yin Qiping and Gordon White, "The 'Marketization' of Chinese Higher Education: A Critical Assessment" (discussion paper 335, Institute of Development Studies, the University of Sussex, 1993).

50. "A Transatlantic Dialogue," 9A.

51. Ibid.

CHAPTER 39

STRATEGIC BUDGETING

DENNIS P. JONES

The most commonly held perspective on budgeting in American higher education is likely that expressed by Caruthers and Orwig (1979, p. 1): "The budget is an instrument that enables the allocation of resources from one organizational unit to another, whether it be from a department to a faculty member, from a college to a department, from a university to a college, or from a funder to the university." This definition brings the distributional function of the budget to the forefront; it describes budgeting as a process unfettered by linkages to plans and priorities. Jones (1984, p. 13), however, emphasized this linkage, noting that "a budget's primary function is to span the distance between intention and action. It is the device by which [an organization] carries out its plans and by which it signals its priorities."

A synthesis of these two, and other, generally similar, definitions yields the conclusion that budgeting is a process of *making decisions that distribute resources to enable action.* Disassembling this composite definition and inspecting the components more closely can be instructive. First, the definition calls attention to the obvious but often overlooked fact that a budget represents a collection of decisions. As such, various approaches to budgeting are best understood by focusing on the kinds of decisions required in the process rather than, on the various processes by which those decisions are achieved. Second, the definition serves to reinforce the notion that the purpose of the budget is to implement the institution's plans; the budget is a major (but not the only) tool for ensuring that institutional goals are pursued and, in the end, achieved.

On a conceptual level, there is seldom serious disagreement with these two points, once articulated and considered. Further, the simple phrase that the budget distributes resources is likely unquestioned as an expression of the essence of what budgeting is about. The overriding concern of most participants in the budgeting process is "Who gets how much?"—a question that reveals a fixation on distribution of financial resources as the centerpiece of budgetary decision making. The central thesis of this chapter is that this focus is entirely too narrow if the intent of the budget is to implement an institution's *strategic* plan. The development of an accompanying strategic budget requires a mechanism that places a series of decisions about the productive assets of the enterprise at the heart of the process.

IMPORTANCE OF STRATEGIC BUDGETING

Experience reveals that the budgeting exercise at many institutions starts and stops with the acquisition and allocation of financial resources. The budget process revolves around the tasks of estimating revenue changes and allocating increases (and, in some case, decreases) among the operat-

Source: *New Directions for Higher Education,* no. 83, Fall 1993. © Jossey-Bass Publishers.

ing units of the institution. To the extent that budget guidelines are prepared centrally, they tend to include estimates of enrollment and revenue changes and to establish limits on price increases that will be allowed in major areas. The size of the salary increases for faculty tends to capture the greatest attention in such guidelines, but it is very common for the guidelines also to establish limits on allowable budgetary increases in such areas as travel, supplies, and equipment. The initial determination of salary increases frequently reflects consideration of salary levels at comparable institutions; targeted levels in other areas typically reflect inflationary changes in the prices of goods and services.

The guidelines may also establish overall limits for the various functional units of the institution: academic affairs, business affairs, student services, and so on. Within the guidelines, departments are asked to submit budget requests. Most such processes also allow special requests for additions to the departments' base budgets—the addition of faculty, for example—or for one-time expenditures for equipment or other items. Such requests are usually dealt with at the midmanagement or vice presidential level, with the basis of judgment most frequently being changes in workload (student demand for courses, larger physical plant to clean, and so on). In almost all cases, the initiative for identifying needs must come from unit heads; institution-level administrators enter the decision-making process when it becomes necessary to choose among competing requests.

This very common approach to budgeting has two noteworthy characteristics. First, it serves to constrain the domain of decisions made within the budget formulation process. The focus of decision making is on the prices that the institution is willing (or required) to pay to maintain the status quo. Fundamental questions about the quantity, quality, mix, and utilization of assets are addressed only when it becomes clear that inaction is no longer an option. Absent that kind of pressure, such questions are answered by assuming that "no change" best serves the needs of the institution.

Second, the approach is fundamentally unit-centered rather than institution-centered, a reflection of the fact that institution-wide administrators are basically reactive rather than proactive participants in the process. As a consequence, some of the core obligations of institutional administrators—to maintain, enhance, and shape the assets and the capacity of the institution as a whole—become subordinated to the sum of the decisions made at the unit level. This delegation of decision authority is unlikely to result in adequate investments in those assets that are everybody's and yet nobody's, such as buildings, certain equipment, and library books. This delegation of authority is also unlikely to result in necessary redistribution of assets, for example, eliminating some administrators and replacing them with faculty or other categories of personnel. When such trade-offs do occur, it is usually because competing alternatives are brought to senior administrators sitting as a court of last resort. But by the time institution-level administrators are confronted with these choices, it is likely that decision makers at lower levels have foreclosed options that would have better served institutional purposes (or that the options that would have better served the institution were never considered).

This approach also ensures that the budgetary levers that institutional leaders can use to change the institution are very short. They consist largely of marginal (incentive or categorical) funds set aside for this express purpose. The possibilities of change are enhanced when assumptions about the asset base of the institution are challenged and changes are made as opportunities allow.

These characteristics make approaches that embody them poor mechanisms for carrying out an institution's strategic plan. When planning is conducted at the strategic (institutional) level and budgeting is centered at the operational (unit) level, the linkages necessary to move an institution in the directions identified in the plan become fragile at best. There is a need for strategic budgeting as well as strategic planning, for an approach to budgeting that reflects an institution-wide perspective on resource allocation, that focuses on the basic asset structure of the institution rather than on the prices of those assets, and that puts central administrators in a proactive rather than a reactive role in this process.

The purpose of this chapter is to propose an approach to strategic budgeting that places decisions about the acquisition, maintenance, and utilization of institutional assets at the center of the budget process. The characteristics of assets that represent decision points in the budget process are examined, and the trade-offs among these decisions are discussed. In addition, the implications of this approach for the procedures of the budget process and for the roles of institutional administrators in the process are presented.

BASIC CONCEPTS OF STRATEGIC BUDGETING

True consumables—payments for insurance, utilities, travel, and expendable office and laboratory supplies—represent a relatively small portion of an institution's budget. At most institutions, the proportion is less than a quarter. Payments for purchased services, particularly the services of part-time faculty, may drive this proportion higher. At the extreme, however, such payments seldom represent more than 30 to 40 percent. The rest of the budget comprises payments made to create or maintain the institution's assets, those tangible things and intangible rights that constitute the valued resources of the enterprise.

Although most of an institution's budget reflects the costs associated with creating and maintaining various kinds of assets (faculty and staff, equipment, physical plant, library and numerous collections, curricula, and such intangible assets as reputation or image), a relatively small portion of the energy that goes into budgeting is directed to decisions about the assets. Instead, attention centers on the financial resources that the institution chooses to invest in these assets on an annual basis. Thus, attention is focused on planned expenditures for faculty salaries rather than on the size and nature of the faculty desired by the institution, on expenditures for library collections rather than on the size and nature of the collection appropriate for the institution, and on the amount of money that can be squeezed out for curriculum development rather than on the philosophy of the institution regarding curriculum review and renewal. By emphasizing the financial resource equivalents of the asset structure in the budget decision-making process, institutional administrators essentially abdicate their responsibility to maintain and

enhance the institution's asset base. In accounting terms, they become fixated on the revenue and expenditure statement to the detriment of a concern with the institution's balance sheet, which focuses on its assets and its net worth.

A very subtle consequence of a budgetary process that puts a premium on decisions about the distribution of financial resources is the delegation of many of an institutions strategic decisions to a managerial group that has neither an institution-wide perspective nor an incentive to act in the best interests of the institution as a whole. Deans, directors, and department chairs can and should be expected to pursue the best interests of their respective units. Unit managers have little cause to concern themselves on an ongoing basis with the level of deferred maintenance on the physical plant, with the annual investments made in equipment or library books, or with the ways in which the institution's funds are invested in the recruitment of a particular type of student body. This is especially true when these priorities conflict with investments in faculty and other personnel. It is the responsibility of executive-level administrators to ensure that the assets of the institution are protected and enhanced as necessary. When they fail to explicitly consider the size and characteristics of the institution's asset structure, the centerpiece of the strategic budget process, they voluntarily cede use of one of the most powerful tools of institutional change to those in no position to use it.

In the accounting sense, assets are defined as "probably future economic benefits obtained or controlled by a particular entity as a result of past transactions or events" (Wainright, 1992, p. 214). In the context of decisions encompassed by the strategic budgeting process, it is useful to consider the following as assets that must be created, maintained, and, over time, shaped to meet the emerging needs of the institution:

Faculty and Staff

Human resources are not considered assets in accounting parlance. However, there are very few college administrators who will not admit, even passionately argue, that its people are a college's or university's most important resource. Further, when institutions of higher education hire regular employees of any type, these are investment decisions. Colleges and universities make social, if not legal, contracts with their regular employees and, in most cases, anticipate indefinite periods of appointment. In many institutions, the commitment often extends beyond the individual employee and attaches to the position filled by that individual.

There are groups of employees—those with temporary or adjunct appointments—to whom institutions do not make such long-term commitments. The budget decisions that surround expenditures for such personnel are more akin to decisions regarding purchase of personal services than to decisions regarding hiring of new employees. Decisions to hire employees on regular appointments are essentially investment decisions, whereas decisions to employ temporary staff or adjunct faculty are essentially decisions to conserve services at a particular level. This distinction between *investment* (in human assets) and *consumption* is maintained throughout this chapter.

Facilities

The physical plant owned by an institution is an asset in the classic accounting sense of the term. The decision to construct or to purchase facilities is an investment decision. Rental of facilities obligates an institution to a series of consumption expenditures.

Equipment

Like the physical plant, owned equipment is an institutional asset. The possibility of renting or leasing equipment rather than buying it again presents institutions with fundamental choices between investment and consumption.

Library Collections

Library books, too, are institutional assets in at least the narrowest sense of the term. The rapidly escalating costs of books and periodical subscriptions, coupled with the advent of new technologies that allow access to information as an alternative to ownership of documents, will increase the necessity of looking seriously at the consumption versus investment decision.

Student Body

Except in rhetorical terms, an institution's student body is seldom considered an asset. However, decisions concerning the clientele to be served are key strategic decisions for an institution, and considerable institutional energy is devoted to enrollment of a student body of a particular size and composition. Further, at many institutions, the investments made in acquiring a student body are exceeded in size only by the investments made in acquiring and retaining the faculty and staff of the institution. The great extent to which budgeting decisions in this area are left to the operational level and are disconnected from planning decisions regarding clientele made at the strategic level is a particularly curious phenomenon in a period of tightly constrained resources.

Endowments and Reserves

Decisions regarding the size of surpluses to be built into the general fund budget, the extent to which resources are to be drawn down to balance the budget, and the size of the contingency reserve to be included as protection against unexpected events are truly strategic budgeting decisions. Decisions about these financial assets represent one of the few areas where institutional administrators have been engaged consistently at the strategic level.

Curricula

Curricula are another area in which institutions make sizable investments without recognizing the results as assets. Investments are not made directly in curricula; rather, they are made in faculty whose time is allocated to the creation of curricula. Failure to recognize curricula as assets has the unfortunate side effect of avoiding recognition that programs, like other assets, deteriorate over time. In the absence of continual attention to renewal, curricula can become institutional liabilities rather than assets.

Image and Reputation

These two factors must be included on the list to draw attention to the fact that assets come in intangible, as well as tangible, forms. Further, these intangible assets are increasingly important to an institution. At a time when competition for students is increasing, any action or condition that sullies an institution's reputation or mars its image can be a serious problem. Investments in image and reputation run the gamut from public relations activities to much less visible efforts to ensure institutional actions consistent with role, mission, and educational philosophy.

The above-listed assets represent institutional capacity; the ways in which they are utilized determine educational outcomes and productivity. Institution-level managers must be held responsible for ensuring that capacity appropriate to the institution's mission is created and sustained. In the final analysis, unit managers are responsible for ensuring that these assets are utilized in ways that efficiently and effectively achieve the academic outcomes established as priorities for the institution.

In taking responsibility for the asset structure of an institution, institutional administrators must focus on requirements at two levels: the acquisition or creation of new assets and the maintenance of existing assets. In higher education, it is common practice to devote considerable time and energy to the creation of new assets and pitifully little to the maintenance of old assets. This is in spite of the fact that all assets depreciate and, without conscious attention, gradually lose their value to the institution. Buildings fall into disrepair, equipment and library books become outdated, and curricula are not revised to incorporate and integrate new knowledge. Personnel, too, can gradually lose their ability to be fully contributing members of the institutional community. Thus, wise administrators are concerned with staff development activities and the need for faculty to have time to recharge their intellectual batteries through sabbaticals, scholarly activities, or other mechanisms.

While the concept of asset depreciation is acknowledged by most campus-level administrators, the allocation of resources to counteract the consequences of the passage of time often are assigned low priority. Even in the best of budgetary times, funds for personnel and program development, replacement of equipment, and renovation of the physical plant are seldom allocated in adequate amounts. Neither funders nor institutional administrators receive acclaim for the unglamorous acts of maintain-

ing the value of the old; recognition attaches to those who create the new.

The decisions associated with creating (or shaping) an institution's assets are more numerous than are typically recognized in any formal sense. In the process of strategic budgeting, the following issues must be addressed:

Quantity of the Asset

This is one of the decision areas in which administrators are most practiced. They are comfortable with decisions that focus on full-time equivalent (FTE) faculty, square feet of building, numbers of students, and size of the endowment. They are less likely to be engaged in determining quantities of equipment or of library collections except as those quantities are reflected in their financial equivalents.

Type of Asset

Within most of the major categories of assets (financial resources being the obvious exception), there are subcategories representing distinctions that cannot be ignored. It is meaningless to deal with FTEs of personnel without distinguishing faculty from clerical staff or to determine physical plant needs without recognizing differences between laboratories and administrative offices. The ways in which personnel assets are shaped are a particularly important reflection of institutional philosophy and represent key strategic decisions. For example, institutions have the choice of delivering learning assistance services through academic departments (utilizing faculty) or through student services units (utilizing non-faculty professionals). The choice that is made can affect not only the budget but also the way in which the institution is perceived by students and the image that is created in the external environment.

Quality of the Asset

Issues of quantity represent commonplace considerations in the budget process; issues of asset quality are dealt with more by default than by advertence. The default condition tends to be the "highest quality" (as in faculty or student) or "state of the art" (in regard to equipment). Alternatives suggesting that assets be of a quality that is "appropriate" or "the minimum required to effectively serve the purpose" are seldom established as standards in higher education. As distasteful as it may be to accept quality standards expressed in this way, the choice is viable, and perhaps even necessary, for many institutions.

Levels of Utilization of the Asset

Expectations regarding levels of utilization of some of the primary assets (personnel and physical facilities, for example) are determinations that are central to the strategic budgeting process. When institutional policy regarding faculty teaching loads is established, a major budgetary decision is also made; the policy has a direct bearing on the number of faculty required to meet student demand.

Price of the Asset

For many institutional assets, considerations of price are not within the decision domain of the institution. Prices of books, for example, are established by the publisher rather than the purchaser. With regard to some assets, however, institutions can establish price, at least within certain limits. Faculty salaries are dictated by the market only to a certain extent; institutions can choose how competitive they want to be within the range established by market mechanisms.

Method of Acquiring the Asset

Finally, strategic budget decision making encompasses a set of decisions about whether capacity is to be owned or rented. Capacity can be acquired through investment in an asset. It can also be acquired through purchase of a service (as when services of adjunct faculty are acquired to replace the services of full-time faculty or when access to information services is acquired as a substitute for the purchase of library resources) or through leasing buildings and equipment. It should also be noted that assets can be acquired through the process of conversion from one type of asset to another. Conversions occur frequently; faculty members become administrators, and classrooms are converted to microcomputer laboratories, for example.

This delineation of a set of institutional assets and of the basic dimensions of this set

establishes a decision-making framework for strategic budgeting that is roughly summarized in Table 39.1. This figure indicates several features of budget decision making at the strategic level. First, it recognizes the basic equation of budgeting: Revenues must equal expenditures. On the revenue side of the equation, it should be noted that budget making involves making decisions as well as making estimates. Decisions such as those that lead to intended changes in the revenue profile or to stabilizing the amount of revenue to be received from a particular source constitute a necessary ingredient of budgeting at the strategic level. Likewise, decisions to utilize resources to offset revenue shortfalls—essentially, to use reserves as sources of revenue—are strategic decisions.

On the expenditure side of the equation, the decisions revolve around not only the mix of assets and consumption items and their characteristics (quantity, quality, price, and so on) but also the trade-offs among these various elements. The price of faculty (their salaries) can be increased if their utilization (work load) can be increased and the quantity thereby reduced. Similarly, the price of faculty may have to be suppressed if it is determined that the number of adjuncts must be reduced so that more freshman courses can be taught by full-time faculty. A layer of complication is added by interactions across types of assets. For example, it may be possible to reduce the overall long-term investment in faculty by increasing the short-term investment in curricula. By investing in restructuring of the general education core curriculum of the college, it may be possible to alter faculty work loads or the number of faculty required to meet student demand. Similarly, a strategic decision to change the undergraduate curriculum so that lower-division students are confronted with fewer large classes has repercussions not only for the faculty asset but potentially for facilities and library collection assets as well.

IMPLICATIONS OF STRATEGIC BUDGETING

Adoption of the basic concept of strategic budgeting has significant implications for both the decision makers and the analysts involved in

TABLE 39.1
Decision-Making Framework for Strategic Budgeting

Assets	Expenditures					Revenues
	Quantity	Quality	Utilization	Price	Total Cost	
Faculty and staff						Tuition and fees
Faculty						Government appropriation
Administrators						
Support						Government grants and contracts
Facilities						
Equipment						Private gifts, grants, and contracts
Collections						
Student body						
Endowments and reserves						
Curricula						Endowment income
Image						Sales and services
Consumption						
Faculty and staff						Other
Faculty						
Administrators						Transfer in (from reserves and so on)
Support						
Facilities						
Equipment						
Collections						
Curricula						
Supplies						
Utilities						
Other services						

the budget-building process. The implications are perhaps greatest for those administrators with institution-wide responsibilities. Their role in the budget process becomes proactive, their basic decisions come early in the budget process, and they will be faced with decisions that cannot help but be unpopular in some instances.

The scope of the early decisions can be seen by referring again to Table 39.1 and recognizing that it outlines the basic contents of the guidelines to be distributed to, and utilized by, unit managers as they build their budgets. This process requires institutional managers to go well beyond their typical steps of reporting revenue estimates and establishing the levels of price increases that will be tolerated in the requests forwarded by the unit heads. Adher-

ence to the concept of strategic budgeting requires institutional administrators, as the individuals responsible for preserving the institution's assets, to declare the level of funding to be set aside for this purpose. In essence, the process is initiated by determining the amounts that will "come off the top" for such purposes as the purchase of equipment and library books and for the renewal and renovation of the physical plant. These allocations, therefore, are less likely to be treated as the sum of whatever remains after unit priorities are established. In addition, the process proscribes the degree of freedom allowed unit managers in making unit-level decisions that have institution-wide implications. The most critical of institution-level decisions involve the leeway allowed unit managers in making decisions about faculty: to unilaterally establish work load policies and, a more commonly encountered practice, to freely determine the substitution of part-time for full-time faculty. It should be noted that these guidelines do not serve as determinants for individual units; however, they do serve to constrain (or, in some cases, expand) the pool of resources for which units compete.

If logically extended, adoption of the concept of strategic budgeting serves to open the gates for discussion of topics that often are avoided, either knowingly or unknowingly, and to reclaim for institutional administrators a role in decisions that are frequently assumed to lie exclusively in the domain of unit administrators. Perhaps the best example of the point is found, again, in the role of institutional administrators in shaping the faculty asset. It is not uncommon to find situations in which the responsibilities of institutional administrators are deemed to end when positions are allocated and prices established. Decisions about the quality or qualities of the individuals hired to fill those positions are frequently left to the unit heads. In the absence of clear understandings between institutional and unit administrators as to sought-after characteristics, this bifurcation of decision-making authority can very easily lead to conditions in which qualities of the faculty employed serve to impede rather than promote achievement of the institutional mission. The classic example is the hiring by teaching institutions of faculty who have research activities as their primary professional interests. There are many other such examples in which the nature of institutional assets is inconsistent with institutional mission and culture.

Implementation of strategic budgeting affects unit heads as well as institutional heads. For deans, directors, and department heads, however, the nature of the effects can be quite varied. On the one hand, when institutional administrators assume explicit responsibility for the maintenance of assets, it is likely that the pool of resources set aside for purchasing books and equipment will be larger than would otherwise be the case. Unit managers typically prefer to relegate such purchases to a lower priority rather than confront strictures in other areas. The down side is that presentation of a more complete set of budget guidelines removes

some decision-making latitude from the domain of unit managers. As noted previously, strategic budgeting does not determine allocation of resources to individual units. That decision is ultimately made through processes that originate at the unit level and work their way up. However, strategic budgeting goes further than is typically the case in specifying the size of the various resource pools for which unit heads eventually compete. In many ways, it could make the job of the unit managers more difficult. In some instances, standard responses to budget balancing—forgoing equipment and purchases and substituting part-time faculty for full-time faculty—could be precluded. More emphasis would likely be placed on issues of faculty quality and work load and of curriculum changes, all topics that most deans and department chairs would just as soon avoid.

Finally, the type of approach to budgeting described in this chapter can have a significant impact on the kinds of analyses done in support of the budget process. Relatively less attention is devoted to compiling information on asset prices, and relatively more energy is devoted to analyses of asset quality and utilization. In addition, the range of assets explicitly considered during the budget process is expanded. As a consequence, analyses that support decisions on the investments required to create or maintain assets such as collections, the student body, and curricula are required on a regular, though not necessarily annual, basis.

SUMMARY

In this chapter, I have suggested the necessity of developing an approach to budgeting that encompasses a set of strategic as well as operational decisions. I have argued that strategic decisions focus on the creation, and maintenance of institutional capacity, whereas operational decisions focus on the utilization of that capacity in ways designed to accomplish specified purposes. As a consequence, strategic budgeting must emphasize institutional assets and the steps that can be taken to move toward an asset profile appropriate to the institution.

Such an approach to budgeting places greater responsibilities on institutional-level administrators and forces them to be proactive rather than reactive in the resource allocation process. These steps lead to an altered distribution of decision-making authority, requiring changes in behavior by all engaged in the resource allocation. Such steps are necessary if linkages between budgeting and strategic planning are to be forged.

REFERENCES

Caruthers, J. K., and Orwig, M. (1979). *Budgeting in higher education*. AAHE-ERIC/Higher Education Research Report, no. 3. Washington. D.C.: American Association for Higher Education.

Jones, D. P. (1984). *Higher education budgeting at the state level: Concepts and principles*. Boulder, Colo.: National Center for Higher Education Management Systems.

Wainright, A. (1992). Overview of financial accounting and reporting. In D. M. Green (ed.), *College and university business administration*. (5th ed.) Washington, D.C.: National Association of College and University Business Officers.

SECTION VI

INSTITUTIONAL FINANCIAL MANAGEMENT

INTRODUCTION

This section addresses the topic of financial management and accounting, moving from a general overview of the institutional budgeting process to a range of more specific and significant issues in institutional financing management. The section begins with an introduction to college and university budgeting by Lasher and Greene, "College and University Budgeting: What Do We Know? What Do We Need to Know?". This article should prove particularly useful to students of higher education who are relatively unfamiliar with the nature of the budgeting process and are seeking a sophisticated primer on the topic. Beginning with a definition of a "budget," Lasher and Greene lead their discussion through a survey of budget types, budget processes, and internal and external factors that influence an institution's budget, followed by a careful consideration of the advantages and disadvantages of different budgeting approaches.

Meisinger and Dubeck ("Fund Accounting") also write with an educated lay audience in mind; their explanation of fund accounting, long recognized as one of the best articles on this subject, provides students with a thorough understanding of the practice and its terminology. Disagreeing with Meisinger and Dubeck about the utility and advantages of fund accounting, Winston ("The Necessary Revolution in Fund Accounting") offers an alternative, "global accounting," which he argues can provide better and more complete information to institutional administrators, and thus result in better management practices. The juxtaposition of these two articles—one explaining and defending the traditional fund accounting method, and the other criticizing that method and offering another option—provides students not only with solid explications from leading experts, but also with the opportunity to compare and contrast the methods and think critically about one of the most fundamental questions in higher education finance: how to organize and report financial information.

Useful to students and practitioners alike, the Taylor, Hewins, and Massy article ("Integrating Strategic Finance and Endowment Management") features some of the best thinking on an integrated approach to institutional financial management. Given the necessity of sound financial management for the continued good health and growth of colleges and universities, this article describes both the processes for, and the importance of, integrated strategic financial planning and investment management.

Attempting to inform the national conversation swirling around the highly publicized increases in the cost of higher education, Rooney, Borden, and Thomas ("How Much Does Instruction and Research Really Cost?") undertook an activity-based costing study of their home institution in an effort to determine the real costs of essential activities: teaching, research, and service. They write about the results of their study, which presents a new and improved cost model that can enhance institutional planning and budgeting efforts. This article also provides diverse audiences, including students, parents, and legislators, with a better understanding of how institutions calculate and represent their costs.

Derived in part from activity-based costing, the concept of responsibility center management, or RCM, has become one of the most notable trends in higher education finance in recent years. Acknowledging the significance of this approach, this section offers two articles on the principles of RCM. The one by RCM trailblazers Strauss, Curry, and Whalen ("Revenue Responsibility Budgeting"), is really three articles in one: Strauss explaining how some of the concepts of RCM can be adapted for use by institutions that do not have a decentralized budgeting system; Curry describing the implementation of RCM at the University of Southern California; and Whalen making the argument for the use of RCM at public colleges and universities. This article provides first-hand accounts from administrators who were on the frontlines and cutting edge of the RCM phenomenon. The second RCM article, by Lang ("A Primer on Responsibility Centre Budgeting and Responsibility Centre Management"), combines a strong theoretical perspective with a discussion of practical application, and serves as a balanced assessment of RCM and its advantages and drawbacks.

From a review of the fundamentals of institutional budgeting to extended examinations of one of the most important budgeting strategies currently employed by colleges and universities, this section seeks to provide a better sense of the intricacies of financial management and accounting. By discussing how institutions organize and report their financial information, and how and why institutions are increasingly held accountable for the quality of their financial reports, this section points to the need for good information. By including recommendations for managing debt in changing financial markets, integrating strategic finance and endowment management, and developing an activity-based cost model for all essential activities, this section suggests how good information can be used by institutions. Finally, by detailing the conceptualization and implementation of responsibility center management as an institutional budgeting strategy, this section demonstrates the application of good information to meet institutional needs. Higher education financial management is, in the end, about information and how it is used.

Members of the review panel for this section were:

Scott C. Kelley, West Virginia University

William Lasher, University of Texas

Arthur Ramicone, University of Pittsburgh

Alan T. Seagren, University of Nebraska, Lincoln

L. Carole Wharton, The Smithsonian Institution

John L. Yeager, University of Pittsburgh

Chapter 40

College and University Budgeting:

What Do We Know? What Do We Need to Know?

William F. Lasher and Deborah L. Greene

INTRODUCTION/OVERVIEW

This chapter reviews what we know and what we don't know about budgeting in American institutions of higher education, and where budgeting is going. We shall revisit the various types of institutional budgets and the institutional budget process. Next, economic, political, and other factors that affect institutional budgets will be explored. Seven approaches to institutional budgeting will then be described, and their strengths and weaknesses highlighted. Since American colleges and universities are not exempt from financial stress—as is all too apparent on so many campuses these days—we shall also examine the issues influencing resource retrenchment and reallocation. Finally, some thoughts will be offered on areas for future research on institutional budgeting.

Webster's New Collegiate Dictionary (1981) defines a budget as "a statement of the financial position of an administration for a definite period of time based on estimates of expenditures during the period and proposals for financing them; a plan for the coordination of resources and expenditures; the amount of money that is available for, required for, or assigned to a particular purpose." Wildavsky (1988, p. 2) defines a budget as a "link between financial resources and human behavior in order to accomplish policy objectives." Simply put, a budget is a spending plan for a given period of time.

Developing a budget is both an art and a science. Since there are never enough resources to satisfy every institutional need, a budget helps to set and communicate institutional priorities (Meisinger and Dubeck, 1984) within the limited resources available. It serves both as an institutional action or operating plan for a given period of time and as a contract. Founders expect specified activities to be accomplished with their funds. For example, students purchase classes with their tuition, legislators purchase a public good, donors purchase a sense of well-being and, perhaps, immortality. A budget doubles as an accountability and control device, against which expenditures can be monitored for compliance. A budget is the result of many political battles, replete with offer and counter-offer, negotiation, and compromise. A budget "lives" over multiple fiscal periods: as last year's actual expenditures, as this year's estimates, and as next year's projections.

The budget process actually consists of multiple budget cycles, overlapping and intersecting each other. While one budget is being developed, another budget is being executed. Still another is being evaluated and audited. The single most critical determinant of the budget for a given fiscal period is the budget from the previous cycle (Meisinger and Dubeck, 1984). Budgets "tend to be altered incrementally to reflect marginal changes" (p. 5), rather than be modified through wholesale changes. Regardless of the latest policy fad or changes in terminology, this year's budget at a

Source: *Higher Education Handbook of Theory and Research*, 1993, Vol. 9; J. Smart (ed.), Agathon Press.

college or university will look remarkably similar to last year's.

It has often been argued that there should be strong ties between an institution's planning function and its budget process. William G. Bowen (1986) has argued this need by enumerating five specific measures that budget officers can take to foster success in reaching hard decisions during the budget process. First, the budget process should be organized so that all elements likely to compete for institutional resources can be considered at the same time. It is critical that resource commitments be made simultaneously, not separately, so that all elements have an equal opportunity of being considered. Second, financial data should "be organized according to the logic of decision making as well as the logic of control" (pg. 16). Bowen advocates program budgeting in the sense that all resources that support a broad objective should be identified with that objective. Additional groupings of resources or expenditures may be necessary, but not for the purpose of assuring that there are sufficient resources budgeted to meet a specific programmatic objective. Third, program data such as the number of students enrolled should be provided along with financial data for each program. Fourth, in addition to the budget year, financial and program data should be provided for several years into the future. Bowen supports long-term planning and using the budget process as one of several planning tools. The picture derived from multi-year budgets helps to highlight areas of institutional commitment and may provide sufficient time to identify the source of necessary resources. Fifth and last, the budget process should be closely coordinated and integrated with institutional planning and control processes.

However, this crucial relationship between planning and budgeting is often confounded by the very nature of planning. Planning is conducted to reduce uncertainty. But the ability of planning to provide a durable, accurate, precise, program of action is constrained by a number of conditions that may be beyond its control. Among these conditions are "the uncertain nature of future conditions and difficulties in predicting opportunities and threats, the politics of institutional decision making, the distribution of power within the institutions, the potential rigidness of formal planning processes, and the time and cost for comprehensive planning" (Schmidtlein, 1989). Planning and budgeting operate on different horizons; a planning cycle may run one to five years while a budgeting cycle generally is limited to one to two years (Meisinger, 1989).

The impact of these intangible, but existing, conditions causes an incongruity between planning and budgeting that is more apparent when looking at the relationship between specific types of planning and the budget process. For example, strategic plans seldom provide specific guidance for budget decisions and program plans. While they delineate which programs and activities should be included in the budget, they do not include the exact amount of funding necessary to operate them. Separate capital budgets usually deal with facilities plans, but there is substantial spillover into the operating budget for utilities, maintenance, and related expenditures. Operational planning may parallel, then converge with, budget planning, but it too may lack the specificity in cost and revenue estimates that is required by budgeting. Issue-specific plans may include more details regarding financing, but lack the comprehensiveness that budgeting requires to encompass all campus programs and activities.

Although the link between planning and budgeting is described and encouraged in the literature, planning rarely provides the detailed operational direction for particular budget decisions. Planning is fixed in the theory side of an institution's program and activities, while budgeting exists more on the application or practice side.

TYPES OF BUDGETS

Meisinger and Dubeck (1984, p. 7-9) have identified six types of budget components: (1) operating budgets, (2) capital budgets, (3) restricted budgets, (4) auxiliary enterprise budgets, (5) hospital operations budgets, and (6) service center budgets. An operating budget generally includes all of the unrestricted funds, and those restricted funds (from endowments and sponsored programs) specified for instruction and departmental support. It is generally viewed as the institution's core budget, and it is the most sensitive to changes in academic program priorities.

A capital budget generally consists of expenditures for major facilities construction, repair, and renovation. The link between the capital budget and the operating budget, though often neglected, is critical to completeness and accuracy in budget development. New facilities burden the operating budget with additional expenditures for utilities and maintenance, while renovated facilities usually lessen the burden.

Expenditures supported by federal and other sponsored research grants and contracts, non-government grants, specified endowment and gift income, and externally-provided student aid generally comprise the restricted budget. This budget affects the operating budget through its support of graduate research assistantships and graduate training grants. The revenue in this budget is generally referred to as "soft money," due to the temporary nature of the projects supported. The level of this budget is the most volatile of the various components, reflecting the uncertainty of project continuation and the potential for the initiation of new projects.

Auxiliary enterprise budgets generally include those institutional support activities that enjoy a dedicated income stream, usually from student user fees and charges to the public for admission to institutional events, activities, or facilities. Auxiliary enterprise units (e.g., dormitories, book stores, intercollegiate athletic programs) are expected to "pay their own way" without receiving support from the tuition or appropriation revenues that support the core operating budget.

A special type of auxiliary enterprise is the institutionally affiliated teaching hospital. The hospital's operating budget includes expenditures for noninstructional hospital services and activities. Its revenues are derived from collected fees that are charged to patients and other users of hospital services. Also, direct legislative appropriations or contracts with state agencies may provide additional income to support the delivery of health care services to indigent patients.

Service centers are support units (e.g., printing shops, telephone systems) that operate within an institution. Revenues for these units typically originate as transfers from other departments or offices within the institution as payment for services rendered. Generally, these budgets are not reflected in the institution's total budget, since the funds have already been counted in the original budgets of transferring departments.

BUDGET PROCESS

Traditionally, budgets have been constructed in successive steps that start with the current year's approved budget (Whalen, 1991). This current approved budget is then adjusted to reflect necessary changes in activities during the fiscal year. (Examples include new appointments, faculty promotions, new programs or activities initiated during the year, reorganizations, and permanent cuts.) This base budget for the next year is then adjusted further to reflect budget policies and planned changes in activities for the upcoming fiscal year.

The budget cycles for public and private colleges and universities are quite similar with the exception that the cycle for public institutions takes more time to allow for state-level, and perhaps system-level, involvement (Meisinger and Dubeck, 1984). Both sectors have phases during which the highest authority (i.e., a state agency or a governing board) establishes the overall procedures that will guide the development of budget requests. The cycle of a public institution generally coincides with state or local government budget cycles (Caruthers and Orwig, 1979). States usually issue technical instructions or guidelines for submitting appropriation requests as many as 9 to 18 months prior to final adoption of the state budget, and 12 to 21 months prior to the beginning of the institution's fiscal year. Some states require a preliminary request and a final request document. At this stage, university activities compete with each other and with other state services such as public education, criminal justice, and mental health

In public institutions, the state's budget instructions are used as the basis for the development of a set of institution-specific instructions, guidelines, or policies. At private institutions, these instructions are developed to reflect the economic and policy environment and the plans of the institution. In either sector, these guidelines indicate that budget *development* is generally a "top-down" activity, initiated from the central administration and imposed on the departments and units lower in the hierarchy. Budget *preparation,* on the other hand, is then begun at the budgetary units and rises to the central administration in a "bottom-up" fashion. This communication can be characterized as information transference within the university's hierarchy. There is, however, an imbalance in the directional flow of information—more information tends to flow upward to central administration than returns to subordinate levels (Meisinger and Dubeck, 1984). Central administration usually requires more information from subordinate levels than is actually necessary for decision making, but rarely provides sufficient feedback to the initiating unit. (At least that is typically the view from the units lower in the hierarchy.)

Expenditure estimates for new and proposed activities are developed. These estimates are affected by the policies outlined in the request guidelines, the effects of inflation, changes in enrollment, new or renovated buildings scheduled to come on-line, and other major developments, as well as the requirements for continuing activities. The resulting request documents are reviewed, possibly modified, prioritized, and summarized at each level as they are transmitted up the institution's hierarchy. In the public sector, the requests are reviewed by campus-level, perhaps system-level administrators, and the institution's governing board before they are submitted to a state-level postsecondary education agency, the legislature, and the governor for their evaluation and review. After submission of the request documents, budget hearings are held to provide additional information about intended activities and related expenditures and to respond to any other inquiries the funders may decide to include. State funding is determined through the normal legislative process and is provided to the institutions through an enacted appropriations bill. At private institutions, the requests are reviewed at the campus level and then submitted to the institutional governing board.

Once the state has determined the level of higher education funding, the funds may be allocated to the state's postsecondary agency for subsequent allocation to institutions; they may be appropriated directly to institutions in a lump sum; or they may be appropriated by line item to specific institutional functions, units, or activities. In any case, the institution revises its operating budget to reflect the differences between the requested amount and the appropriated amount. Since an institution rarely receives 100 percent of the amount it requested, it must recast its budget and may allocate funds to instructional, administrative, and support units differently than originally requested.

At this point in the process, both public institutions and private institutions consider final revenue estimates from all sources, including: tuition and fees, governmental appropriations, investment income, sponsored programs, auxiliary enterprises, and others. Available fund balances from prior year activities are also included as appropriate. Expenditure requests are evaluated against these revenue estimates and tentative budget amounts are allocated to all units. These allocations often set maximum budget levels for each unit. The units then develop more detailed budgets that will be used for the day-to-day operation of the institution. These budgets are reviewed up the institutional hierarchy, summarized by budget staff members, and finally presented to the governing board by the institution's president. Upon receiving board approval, the budget is disseminated to all units.

The budget, once adopted and disseminated, is implemented and monitored. Since the annual operating budget is closely linked to the institution's day-to-day activities, it serves as a control device to keep a rein on expenditures. Expenditure forecasts are typically required throughout the fiscal year (perhaps as often as monthly, but usually no less than quarterly). In public institutions, there are normally reporting requirements to inform state treasury officials about actual expenditures. There may also be reporting requirements before appropriated funds are transferred from the state treasury to institutional current accounts so they can be spent. Transfers among line item appropriations may require approval from the executive and/or legislative branches. In the event of a mid-year adjustment, caused by underrealized income or additional unanticipated expenditures, budget staff members may have to develop information on possible alternative adjustments.

After the close of the fiscal year, the institution will be required to develop an annual financial report concerning its revenue and expenditure activities during the year. This report will then be audited by state, federal, or other officials depending on the institution's governance system and the degree to which it is involved in sponsored activities. These audits will verify the accuracy of the financial reports to assure compliance with various state and federal regulations, as well as generally accepted accounting procedures, and the adequacy of institutional controls and performance.

As has been stated previously, these audit and evaluation activities actually overlap with budget cycles for other years. While last year's budget is being evaluated and audited, this year's budget is being executed and administered, and next year's budget is being planned and developed. Unfortunately, the activity that typically gets short-changed in all of this activity is budget evaluation. Most institutions do not spend sufficient time evaluating the prior year budget to determine whether the objectives of the institution's short-range plans were achieved.

FACTORS THAT INFLUENCE BUDGETS

There are both external and internal factors that affect higher education budgets. External factors include economic, political, and demographic factors, plus the regulatory environment; while internal factors include institutional history, mission, and other characteristics.

Economic Environment

The state of the economy is directly relevant to the fiscal health of higher education. High inflation means that: a static budget will purchase fewer goods and services over time; the real value of faculty salaries will be reduced; and the value of income generated by endowments will be eroded (Layzell and Lyddon, 1990). The strength of the economy also directly affects the level of private contributions to institutions of higher education. In good economic times, monies flow relatively easily to university operating and capital funds. In hard times, not only is charitable giving reduced, but there is more competition among nonprofit sectors for the philanthropic dollar.

During times of rising unemployment, higher education faces a triple threat from more competition for scarcer resources. First, high unemployment signals the demand for additional services, which increases the competition for resources among state services, including higher education. Second, in an economic recession, consumers purchase fewer goods, which leads to fewer tax dollars being collected to pay for federal and state services. In addition, enrollment tends to rise during periods of high unemployment and recession as people take the opportunity to increase their skills in hopes of attaining higher employment levels after the economy starts growing again.

Institutions are directly affected by recession-related problems in federal student aid. Students use the funds from these aid programs to pay the cost of tuition and mandatory fees. As more people enroll in college because they cannot find work and more students become eligible for aid, there is an increase in demand on Pell Grants and College Work-Study Programs. Since the level of federal appropriation has not increased to keep up with demand (there was a $1.4 billion shortfall for the 1991–92 federal fiscal year), the increase in eligible students results in smaller grants for individual students. In some cases, colleges and universities are using institutional funds to make up the shortfall in students' aid packages so they can continue their studies. Also, the rise in student loan defaults, approaching $3.4 billion nationally, has been attributed to the 1992 recession. An institution with a high default rate could be denied future eligibility for federal aid programs for its students, which could harm its tuition and fee revenues (Chronicle of Higher Education, 1992a).

In some states, local economics play a key role for public junior and community colleges, providing one-third to one-half of their operating funds and 100 percent of their capital funds. During an economic downturn, operating budgets at these institutions may be affected simultaneously by decreased state appropriations and static or decreased local support. Taxes linked to local property values generally cannot be raised to equal the entire shortfall from state cutbacks.

Political Environment

The national, state, and local levels of government also affect higher education indirectly through the development of public policy and the imposition of regulations, and directly through special interest appropriations.

National

In July 1992, the Congress reauthorized the Higher Education Act. This will have a wide impact on policy and funding levels providing aid for federal student financial assistance programs, libraries, building construction, renovation, and repair, historically black colleges, and special-purpose institutions. Institutional budgets are also affected by federal research and training grant programs. In addition to the direct costs of these grants, indirect costs are also recovered through institutionally negotiated indirect cost recovery rates. Public and private institutions that receive any kind of federal funds also have to ensure that all programs on campus that benefit from federal funds comply with federal legislation pertaining to civil rights and employment, age, disability, and gender discrimination.

State

A state's legislature, the governor, and the structure of its higher education system all have a tremendous influence on budgeting for public and private higher education (Layzell and Lyddon, 1990). Legislatures are becoming increasingly active in determining higher education policy. As issues become more localized, they try to balance what is good for the state as a whole with what best serves their constituents. While for many states, much of the budget is restricted by federal or state law, (and increasingly by court order), higher education budgets have recently become viewed as a discretionary item (Zusman, 1986). This makes higher education a likely target for legislative scrutiny during difficult economic times. For example, 54 percent of the 1992-93 budget cuts in Ohio came from higher education, while postsecondary spending represents only 12 percent of that state's budget (Chronicle of Higher Education, 1992b). The notion of higher education as a discretionary budget item has also been discussed in the states of California, Illinois, and Texas. This idea is a relatively recent phenomenon, within the last four to six years (Chronicle of Higher Education, 1992c).

Many state legislatures also retain the authority of setting tuition rates. This has a serious effect on the level of tuition revenue institutions can generate. Most states consider tuition as a user fee that supports higher education activities only. They do not view it as a

general tax that can be used to support other items in the state budget, such as highways, health care, or the criminal justice system.

Governors also play an important role in influencing the development of higher education policy. In addition to the authority to approve or veto legislation (including appropriations) that is directly related to higher education, the governor's influence is fully exercised through both his or her leadership on particular issues and through the appointments that he or she makes to cabinet-level positions and to the governing boards of public institutions and systems. The focused attention of the governor on higher education issues may serve as a beacon for other elected officials and the public to take up these issues.

Regulatory Environment

All public and private higher education institutions must comply with various governmental regulations and programs. These requirements represent imposed costs that must be borne by the institution. Bowen (1980) refers to these costs as part of "an educational institution's total cost of doing business." He identified several areas of compliance common to all organizations (personal security, work standards, personal opportunity, participation and due process, public information, and environmental protection) and a few that are critical to the higher education enterprise (emancipation of youth, federal grants and contracts, teaching hospitals, and tax reform). Most recently, disability has been added to this list. Each requirement has a direct and an indirect cost: an actual cost for the program or activity and a compliance cost for maintaining records and reporting on the program or activity. Further, some compliance costs are incurred only one time, while others are recurring. Regardless of whether these costs are direct or indirect, one time or recurring, they must be considered as real costs to be offset either through a corresponding increase in revenue or a corresponding reduction in expenditures in some other area of the budget.

Demographic Characteristics

Several demographic conditions exist that can affect higher education budgets. A state's overall population and its composition has a direct impact on its higher education institutions.

Nationally, the traditional 18-to-24 age cohort is contracting. There will be fewer individuals from this cohort to enroll in postsecondary educational institutions in the near term. However, not all states will be affected equally; the traditional college-going populations of the Sunbelt States are growing, while those in the Midwest have experienced little or no growth (Layzell and Lyddon, 1990). Enrollment declines have both visible and invisible effects on institutional budgets. The loss of tuition is most easily identified. Although the impact of this loss may be partially alleviated by increasing tuition rates, at a certain point the institution will begin to lose enrollment if the increased cost of attendance becomes unaffordable for some students.

The ethnic composition of a state's population can also directly affect institutions of higher education because of variance in persistence to high school graduation. For whatever reasons, minority students tend to drop out of high school at higher rates than majority students. This situation is improving in some states, but it is worsening in others. Fewer high school graduates implies fewer students interested in and eligible for admission to colleges and universities.

Changes in state funding practices may also have an impact on institutions of higher education. Public institutions may experience reductions in state appropriations that result when lower enrollments are factored into the state's formula funding system. For example, Indiana experienced a loss of enrollment in the late 1970s. As a result, the Indiana Commission for Higher Education developed marginal cost factors in its budget process for enrollment changes. Marginal cost factors tend to minimize the funding losses caused by enrollment declines and thereby provide greater funding stability for institutions than do average cost factors. The Indiana Commission also used an actual full-time student equivalent adjustment, rather than estimated annual head count enrollment figures, to make appropriations more accurate in their sensitivity to enrollment (Seitz, 1981).

A less conspicuous but nonetheless real effect of changes in a state's demographic composition is the institution's response. Changes in priorities and internal resources usually accompany an institution's perceived need to approach new markets. An institution may find it necessary to add more resources to recruitment and retention activities to attract and keep more students. To reverse potential declines in traditional cohorts, many institutions look to new markets to attract students. These include part-time students, older students returning to complete a degree or take specific courses, and foreign students (Caruthers and Orwig, 1979).

Institutional Factors

An institution's mission, age, tradition, legal history, and special character shape its budget. The institution's mission, established early in its history by constitution, statute, or governing board, guides much of its instructional, research, and service activity. The mission dictates the scope and breadth of its degree programs and its curriculum, and thus, influences its instructional budget. Different missions require curricula that vary in terms of program mix, level of instruction, method of instruction (e.g., laboratory, clinical, or lecture), and class size. Curriculum requirements also dictate minimum resources for equipment and library holdings. The curriculum also prescribes the level of faculty training. For example, the accrediting body for baccalaureate nursing programs requires that nursing faculty minimally be master's-prepared, while master's level nursing program faculty must be doctorally-prepared. Taken together, these requirements impose a minimum level of resources necessary to provide nursing instruction.

The character of the student body is partially prescribed by an institution's mission through its admission standards. Whether an institution is extremely selective or open to all who apply results in different mixes of students and different levels of academic preparedness. The less prepared a student body is for college-level work, the more remediation will need to be provided by the institution.

Instructional level, the mix of academic disciplines, the nature of the student body, and institutional policies regarding student/faculty ratio determine the size of the faculty, and thus, the cost of faculty compensation (salary and benefits). Most colleges and universities try to keep faculty salaries competitive with like academic institutions while keeping pace with the cost of living (Bowen, 1980). Personnel costs account for a significant portion of higher education costs. Faculty and staff compensation together represent approximately 80 percent of educational and general costs (Halstead, 1991). Faculty compensation alone is estimated to account for at least 64 percent of educational and general expenditures. (Educational and general expenditures include operating expenditures for such core institutional functions as instruction, research, public service, academic support, student services, institutional support, operation and maintenance of physical plant, scholarships, and fellowships.)

Public and private institutions operate under governing boards that are selected under different conditions. A private institution operates with a self-perpetuating board of trustees whose membership is generally nominated and elected by the existing board or by the alumni, whereas the governing boards of public institutions are either elected by the state's voters or appointed by the governor. The governing boards of private institutions usually have significant fund-raising responsibilities in addition to their policy-making duties.

Institutional tradition is related to institutional mission. Nevertheless, different types of institutions have different budget characteristics. For example, historically black colleges and universities, which emerged in reaction to the segregated American society of the 19th century, receive some federal support that is unavailable to other institutions. Similarly, land grant institutions collect noncompetitive federal funds for certain research and service activities. Many private institutions have been adopted wholly or partially by their states and have special funding relationships. A few institutions, such as the service academies and other special purpose institutions, are supported entirely by the federal government.

Numerous, separate public institutions have been reconfigured as multi-campus systems operating under single governing boards. All these examples demonstrate traditional conditions that affect the preparation and implementation of institutional budgets.

An institution's budget is also affected by its overall financial condition, including its level of debt. A limited repertoire of revenue sources affects an institution's ability to support its budget. Public institutions, once completely reliant on state appropriations, now have expanded their funding base to include higher tuition levels, significant fund-raising

efforts, and increased indirect cost revenues from government and private grants and contracts. These increased development activities at public sector institutions are in direct competition for philanthropic funds with those of private institutions. While public institutions increasingly look to private contributions to support their activities, private institutions seek additional support from states to support instructional activities for resident students, research, and some construction projects. These trends are evidence that institutions of higher education will seek revenues from whatever sources seem available. This concept will be discussed further later.

Institutional age is also a significant factor. Older institutions are more likely than younger institutions to have greater physical resources, more degree programs, and more alumni to support them. The age of the physical plant of the campus as well as its size and location also influences the budget. Older buildings require proportionately more funds for maintenance and utilities; larger and urban campuses tend to require additional funds for increased security measures.

Capital renewal and replacement is a topic of growing concern. Postsecondary institutions have tended to balance their budgets during difficult fiscal times by deferring building maintenance, and thereby reducing the physical plant portion of their budgets (Jenny, 1981). The accumulation of deferred maintenance has been identified as a threat to the stability of higher education funding because of the generally poor understanding of capital budgeting, especially maintenance of capital assets (Allen, 1981). In a national survey, Halpern (1987) found that 50 percent of college and university structures will require significant renovation within the next 20–25 years due to age. The cost of backlogged renovation and repairs nationwide was estimated at $60–70 billion, of which one-third was considered "critical" (Rush and Johnson, 1988). The growth of deferred maintenance nationally has been linked to reductions in the level of capital investment in existing facilities and in the level of funding for operations and maintenance (Kraal, 1992). To avoid continued growth in the level of deferred maintenance, the Association of Physical Plant Administrators, the National Association of College and University Business Officers, and the Society for College and University Planning have developed and adopted capital renewal and replacement standards that recommend annual expenditures of 1.5 to 3 percent of the "existing investment in plant and equipment" for postsecondary institutions (Dunn, 1989). Obviously, the deferred maintenance problem will significantly affect institutional budgets in the future if appropriate measures are not taken.

Other Contextual Factors

Howard Bowen, in his far-reaching research on the economics of higher education, formulated the revenue theory of costs and several associated "laws" to help explain higher education financial matters and why institutions budget the way they do. In his 1980 book, *The Costs of Higher Education*, Bowen stated that, "The basic concept underlying the revenue theory of cost is that an institution's educational cost per student unit is determined by the revenues available for educational purposes" (pg. 17). In public institutions, this revenue comes primarily from tuition and state appropriations. In private institutions, it is derived mainly from tuition. In other words, at any given time, the unit cost of education at a particular college or university is determined by the amount of revenue that institution has available to it relative to enrollment.

From this theoretical base, Bowen developed a set of "laws" of higher education costs that describe the motivations and activities of higher education institutions from year to year. These "natural laws" of higher education costs are as follows (Bowen, 1980, pp. 19–20):

1. *The dominant goals of institutions are educational excellence, prestige and influence.* Attainment of these goals is measured by student/faculty ratios, faculty salaries, qualifications of students, the number of library holdings, the quality of facilities, and the amount of equipment available. These things are all resource inputs, not educational outcomes.

2. *In the quest for excellence, prestige, and influence, there is virtually no limit to the amount of money an institution could spend for seemingly fruitful educational ends.* No matter how much an institution has, there is always something else that it needs to meets its mission, improve its programs, or enhance its quality.

3. *Each institution raises all the money it can.* No institution of higher education ever admits to having enough money.

4. *Each institution spends all it raises.* An exception to this is the endowments that are raised where the endowment principal is not spent, but the annual income is. However, these arrangements are designed for the long-term enhancement of the institution, and in that sense are also part of the institution's quest for excellence, prestige, and influence.

5. *The cumulative effect of the preceding four laws is toward ever increasing expenditures.* Questions concerning what higher education ought to cost, or whether higher education could operate more efficiently, are usually raised from outside the institution rather than inside. As a result, there is a basic assumption that institutional budgets must ever increase.

Bowen also noted that these laws were also applicable to other nonprofit organizations such as schools, hospitals, and churches, as well as government agencies.

These laws help explain why private institutions have increased their tuitions so dramatically in recent years. They also indicate why public institutions will naturally turn to students to fund an increasing share of their budgets as state legislatures reduce state appropriations. Bowen would argue that if higher education budgets are to be controlled, the external revenue-providers for higher education—that is, state legislators, the federal government, local governments, students and their families, and donors—must be the source of that control. There are simply too few incentives within colleges and universities to operate with great efficiency or to cut costs.

Three other reasons for the continuation of rapidly increased costs in higher education have been identified by Massy (1989) as cost disease, growth force, and organizational slack. First, due to its high labor intensity, higher education has not been able to accrue great savings nor increase productivity from technological improvements in the workplace. Thus, higher education suffers from a cost disease: its inability to increase productivity means costs will continue to increase. Hopefully, recent advances in the use and sophistication of telecommunications for instruction may provide one remedy to this situation. Second, given its reluctance to eliminate old programs and activities before adding new ones, postsecondary institutions are always moving toward a net increase in programs and activities. This growth force also leads to ever-increasing costs. Finally, the waste and inefficiency common to all organizations, organizational slack, is no kinder to higher education than to other organizations. Additional costs often result from handling the problems that arise from these inefficiencies.

These three reasons and the "natural laws" combine to explain the widespread perception in higher education that budgets must always increase—next year's budget must be higher than this year's—and that the solution to all problems in higher education is more money. Obviously, in the financial environment of the 1990s, the reality at many institutions is that the budget is not going to increase. The additional resources necessary to make that happen are simply not available.

TOOLS FOR INSTITUTIONAL BUDGETING

Caruthers and Orwig (1979) have identified three distinct eras it the evolution of budgeting: (1) the era of executive budgeting, which emphasized control and responded to the perception of waste and inefficiency in organizations; (2) the era of performance-based budgeting, which emphasized management using work measures and cost accounting and responded to a demand for precision in cost attribution and outcome assessment; and (3) the era of programming, planning, and budgeting systems, which emphasized planning and its link to budgeting and responded to the perception of linking dollars to objectives. We may now be in a fourth era, one of budget reform, in response to increasing demands for accountability and reduced public revenues. Many of the reform measures are characterized by aspects of performance budgeting and a strong relationship (at least from a rhetorical standpoint) with strategic planning. Rubin (1988)

also suggests that environmental factors will have an impact on the budget process, that this process will affect outcomes, and that budgets will mirror policy. As in the past, the current drive to overhaul the budget process will no doubt require that institutions continually add on, not substitute, new budgeting requirements.

Over the years, various techniques, methodologies, and approaches have been used by colleges and universities to prepare budgets. In this section, we shall describe several of the better-known approaches, and list some of their strengths and weaknesses.

Incremental Budgeting ("The Science of Muddling Through")

The oldest and most common approach to budgeting is incremental budgeting, which is defined as a "budgeting method that uses essentially the same budget from one year to the next, allowing only minor changes in revenue levels and resource distribution" (Vandement, 1989). Increments or decrements from the base budget are either positive or negative dollar amounts or percentages. Each budget line or group of budget lines is considered separately from others (Caruthers and Orwig, 1979). This approach generally assumes that the basic objectives of the institution, the department, or the program have not changed markedly from the current year, and that they will continue into the next year. New initiatives can be started, and reflected in the budget, but most of the units and programs will see budget changes that reflect only minor changes in existing salary and operating expense levels. Lindblom (1959) referred to this process of determining realistic, successive, budget alternatives that differ only marginally from existing conditions as "the science of muddling through."

The strengths of incremental (decremental) budgeting include the following (Vandement, 1989; Welzenbach, 1982):

- It is relatively simple and easy to understand;
- Budget alternatives are limited to a reasonable set;
- It increases the ability to predict the consequences of budget alternatives with accuracy and confidence;

- It conserves time and energy;
- Its pragmatic approach provides an alternative to other more theoretical approaches;
- It generates limited conflict among resource competitors; every budget item is treated the same;
- It complements long-term organizational commitments during times of fiscal stability;
- It is generally accepted by governing boards and legislators.

The weaknesses of this approach include (Hossler, Kuh, and Bateman, 1989; Vandement, 1989; Welzenbach, 1982):

- It is a nonaggressive approach to management and budget decision making;
- There is a general assumption that the base budget is the absolute minimum, below which the institution cannot function;
- It may easily be affected by internal institutional politics ("the squeaky wheel gets the grease") or by the administration's preferences (budgeting by "king's degree");
- Little incentive is provided to justify continuing programs, to assess their quality, or to cut unproductive programs;
- It is based on inputs, rather than outputs;
- It minimizes conflict rather than selecting the best policy.

Nevertheless, for all of its flaws and "warts," incremental budgeting has been the most widely used approach in institutions of higher education. To paraphrase Winston Churchill, "Incremental budgeting is the worst budgeting approach, except for all the others."

Formula Budgeting

As the name implies, formula budgeting is the application of one or more formulas in the budgeting process (Caruthers and Orwig, 1979). Each formula manipulates certain institutional data based off mathematical relationships between program demand and costs to derive an estimated dollar amount to support future program operation. Formulas are based on his-

torical data, projected trends, and negotiated parameters to provide desired levels of funding. Put another way, formula budgeting is a method that calculates the amount of funding a program requires by applying selected measures of unit costs to selected output measures (Vandement, 1989). As such, formula budgeting is "a combination of technical judgments and political agreements." (Meisinger and Dubeck, 1984, p. 186). This form of budgeting is used mostly at the state level as a method for public institutions to develop their appropriations requests. It is seldom used at the institutional level, although, as discussed later in this section, this may change if cost center budgeting becomes more widely used.

The strengths of formula budgeting include the following (Brinkman, 1984; Meisinger and Dubeck, 1984; Morgan, 1984; Welzenbach, 1982; Caruthers and Orwig, 1979):

- It provides an equitable distribution of funds among institutions;
- It enhances uniformity and ease of budget preparation;
- It provides a useful framework through which colleges and universities communicate with the state legislature;
- It depoliticizes the budgeting process by relying on technical decision making rather than power and influence associated with the traditional political process;
- The quantitative nature of formula budgeting makes decision making appear to be more objective and more routine.

The weaknesses of formula budgeting include (Hossler, Kuh, and Bateman, 1989; Brinkman, 1984; Welzenbach, 1982; Caruthers and Orwig, 1979):

- Although the process may appear to be less political, formula budgeting just shifts the level of political judgments from a traditional program and issues orientation to the level of technical judgments concerning the nature of the mathematical relationships involved in the formula(s);
- Formula approaches are typically enrollment-driven, which may become problematic during periods of enrollment downturns;

- The quantitative nature of formula approaches makes it difficult to include qualitative issues;

- Mechanisms to fund new or innovative programs are typically lacking in formula approaches;

- Formulas perpetuate the status quo because they are based on historical relationships involving existing programs;

- The approach encourages institutions to develop high-cost programs such as engineering or doctoral programs, because the formula generates more funds from such programs;

- Merit-based decisions are typically excluded;

- Many formula approaches do not recognize differences in institutional mission or program;

- Formula approaches tend to have a leveling effect on institutions;

- Formula approaches tend to focus on what can be measured and modeled quantitatively;

- Formulas tend to be overly simplistic and rigid;

- Unintended incentives and disincentives are built-in (such as always rewarding higher enrollment);

- Formulas generally do not recognize economics of scale;

- Such approaches can unintentionally serve as devices of institutional budget control.

This last point deserves additional comment. In those states where formula budgeting approaches are used, institutions insist that the use of appropriated funds not be tied to the unit that generated the funds through the formula. That is, they want the formula used as a revenue generation mechanism, but not as an internal budgeting technique. For the most part, the institutions have been successful in this argument, leaving administrators great discretion in allocating appropriated funds among budgetary units. Of course, the basic amount of support appropriated, and the fact that legislatures rarely appropriate 100 percent of the amount generated by the formula, limits

internal allocation to a large extent. Nevertheless, this decoupling of state appropriation and institutional allocation continues to be a source of distrust between higher education and some public officials in states that utilize formula funding approaches.

Program Budgeting

Many budgeting approaches have been designed in response to the weaknesses found in incremental budgeting. Program budgeting was one of the first attempts to develop a more output-oriented approach. It is defined as a budgeting method "in which budgets are created for specific programs or activities, rather than departments, and each program's budget is apportioned among the several departments that contribute to the program's activities" (Vandement, 1989, p. 129). It is based on allocating funds to related activities that have been grouped together based on their common goals and objectives (Green, 1971).

The primary components of this approach are the program plan, the program budget, and cost-benefit analysis. The process includes developing program goals and objectives, developing alternative activities to meet these objectives, costing each alternative, identifying benefits to each alternative, and selecting the best alternative. These alternatives are forwarded to the next higher administrative unit for review.

A well-known example of program budgeting is Planning, Programming, and Budgeting Systems (PPBS). PPBS strives to match and allocate the appropriate resources that lead to institutionally-desired outputs (Robins, 1986). The concepts of PPBS include (1) a systematic long-range planning process (5–15 years), (2) a selection process for examining mid-range alternatives and objectives (1–5 years), (3) a short-term translation of selected objectives into budgetary data (0–1 year), and (4) a recognition of the costs and benefits of alternatives and objectives over time (Balderston and Weathersby, 1972).

PPBS was used in the early 1960s in the U.S. Department of Defense. By 1965, PPBS was required for budget preparation in most federal agencies (Bowen, 1975). However, the system was not fully integrated into the federal bureaucracy, and shortly died. At the state level, PPBS was thought to provide governors and the legislators with the opportunity to achieve specified goals through the reallocation of state resources. However, in 1966, the American Council on Education rejected PPBS as not being conceptually suited to higher education (Robins, 1986). While PPBS was employed at one time by institutions such as the University of California, Princeton University, and the University of Utah, it is no longer used in higher education. However, because of its theoretical attractiveness, program budgeting still has its proponents. The strengths of program budgeting are (Morgan, 1984; Caruthers and Orwig, 1979):

- It focuses on ends rather than means;
- It relates means to desired ends;
- It provides a sense of institutional direction;
- It does contain qualitative dimensions;
- It creates a better understanding of institutional data bases.

The weaknesses of program budgeting include the following (Hossler, Kuh, and Bateman, 1989; Vandement, 1989; Meisinger and Dubeck, 1984; Morgan, 1984; Welzenbach, 1982):

- It is often difficult in higher education to define what constitutes a program;
- There is often little agreement on specific goals and objectives;
- It is often difficult to identify and measure specific outcomes (many of higher education's outcomes are joint products);
- While it may make sense conceptually to aggregate activities into programs, most organizations are not structured that way;
- Program budgeting is considered an irrelevant operating tool for institutional managers who are responsible for implementing policies and programs;
- The approach focuses on what should be done, rather than how to do it;
- It is unwieldy when used regularly for annual budgeting;
- It fails to take into account institutional missions;

- It falsely assumes that the program cost and other data necessary to make decisions already exist;
- Since programs normally involve several units, it is difficult for institutions to control resources when they are allocated by program;
- It is easier to budget resources to organizational units on the basis of functional need, and to control the resources by unit.

Zero-Based Budgeting

Zero-based budgeting (ZBB) was originally developed by Peter A. Pyhrr, used by Texas Instruments in Dallas in the late 1960s, and exported to Georgia in 1971 for developing the state's FY 1973 budget (Green, 1971). The basic premise behind ZBB is that every activity and program is significant and must be rejustified each year through a series of "decision packages" (Caruthers and Orwig, 1979). It is a microeconomic approach to budgeting (i.e., program and activity objectives are directly translated into elements of the operating plan), whereas program budgeting has a macroeconomic focus (i.e., broad policies are transformed into operating plan elements through a centralized, vertical decision-making process). Under ZBB, each budget unit evaluates its goals and objectives, justifies the need for various activities and their costs and benefits, and develops decision packages for each activity at each level of output. A priority rank is established for each decision package at each hierarchical level. ZBB is a useful approach for developing preliminary budgets for new programs and "start-up" activities. However, it has not been used widely in higher education.

The strengths of zero-base budgeting include:

- It is focused on results and outcomes;
- It is a highly rational, objective approach to budgeting;
- Preparing the decision packages provides an excellent understanding of activities, programs, and organizational units.

The weaknesses of zero-base budgeting include (Morgan, 1984):

- The fact that no budget history is assumed does not recognize continuing commitments, such as faculty tenure, that cannot be changed quickly;
- The process is highly time-consuming and generates a great deal of paperwork;
- The judgments used during the preparation of the decision packages tend to be *ad hoc* in nature;
- The validity and reliability of the criteria and measures used to rank the decision packages may be questionable.

Performance Budgeting

As indicated previously, performance budgeting emerged historically as the second stage in the evolution of budgeting. It is a budgeting approach based on funding desired outcomes or accomplishments (Green, 1971). Although implemented by few states (Banta, 1988; Ewell, 1988, 1985), performance funding developed originally as a cost reimbursement model for resource allocations (Morgan, 1984). It addresses activities rather than objectives, and relies on activity classifications, performance measures, and performance evaluations. It is clearly an approach where institutional funding depends on performing in certain ways and meeting certain expectations.

Performance budgeting was largely unused for many years, but is currently experiencing a renaissance as a state-level budgeting practice that relates resources to activities and outcomes (Banta, 1986; Banta and Fisher, 1984; Bogue and Brown, 1982). Recently, several state legislatures have demonstrated renewed interest in performance funding to ensure accountability by postsecondary institutions.

Some barriers to implementation exist, however. There is disagreement regarding definition and measurement of performance measures. It is often difficult to identify appropriate, measurable criteria on which to judge performance (Caruthers and Orwig, 1979). There is not always a proven relationship between the cause and effect of the criteria and the measures used as proxies for the desired accomplishments. Political reality may prohibit its full implementation, since performance budgeting tends to have little

"pork barrel appeal." That is, since objective measures are used to appropriate funds to institutions, legislators feel they no longer have the ability to provide appropriations to specific institutions, particular those in the area they represent. Another problem is the potential for establishing easily achievable criteria that require little advancement for some institutions. For example, colleges and universities could easily increase the percent of students that graduate by relaxing their grading standards.

Other critical questions in recent cases where performance budgeting has been used include: how much of an institution's appropriation should depend on performance funding, and secondly, should performance budgeting be applied to base funding or incremental funds. If performance criteria are applied to base funds, institutions will not know from year to year (or biennium to biennium) what level of funding to expect. The resulting uncertainty makes it difficult for academic and operational planning to take place. On the other hand, if performance funding is supplemental—that is, provided in addition to base funding—it serves as an incentive to institutions to accomplish the objectives for which the performance funding is provided.

Although some states (e.g. Colorado, Florida, Kentucky, Missouri, South Carolina, Virginia, and West Virginia) have moved toward developing performance measures for their institutions of higher education (Lenth, 1992; Ewell, 1988), only Tennessee has implemented performance budgeting (Lenth, 1992; Banta, 1988). Texas is an example of a state that is moving toward performance budgeting at the present time. The Texas Legislative Budget Board plans to develop an appropriations bill for the 1994–1995 biennium that is based, to some degree, on agency performance for all state agencies and all institutions of higher education. As a result, Texas is in the planning stages of developing performance funding methods for health-related institutions, universities, and community and technical colleges. In 1991, the Texas Legislature instructed the Texas Higher Education Coordinating Board (THECB) to develop a method for distributing state funds to health-related institutions using an outcome-based performance approach. The THECB (1992a) adopted an advisory committee recommendation that would establish core performance measures based on common institutional missions and goals for admission, graduation, licensure, certain postgraduate training, continuing education, research, model training and education projects, and professional, hospital, and clinical services that are defined as unsponsored charity care. Additional measures were provided for enhancements beyond institutional missions and goals that contributed to broader state goals, such as minority participation and training in geographic areas and in particular disciplines where shortages exist within the state. No recommendations were made regarding the percentage of institutional appropriations that should be funded based on these performance measures, nor on whether these funds should be considered part of an institution's base funding or as a supplement.

Although not required to develop a performance funding approach for senior academic institutions, the THECB also recommended that supplemental funds be added to base funding to reward performance in senior universities. The Board proposed that these funds be distributed based on institutional achievement of state goals for instruction, research, and public service as represented by thirteen measures: degrees awarded, course completion, student remediation, minority student enrollment and graduation, community college transfers and graduates, critical skills, graduate/professional study, lower division tenure track teaching, externally funded research, intellectual property income, and faculty service. It is recommended that the Legislature establish thirteen pools of funds from which performance funding can be drawn. Institutions would share proportionately in these pools based on their performance during a given period. The THECB recommended that the total performance funding amount not exceed two percent of base funding for the 1994 fiscal year, five percent of base funding for fiscal 1995, and ten percent in future years.

The THECB also accepted a recommendation from the Texas Public Community/Junior Colleges Association regarding performance funding for those institutions. The Association recommended that 50 percent of performance funding be based on course completion, and 50 percent be based on credentials (certificates and degrees) awarded, transfers to senior institutions, employed course completers, licensure, successful remediation, minority participation, and economic development contribution (i.e., total earnings of all community college students over a base period). While the Association's report made no recommendation regarding the overall percentage of institutional budgets that should be based on these performance measures, it did recommend that these funds be supplemental to community college base funding, which is currently formula-based.

The strengths of performance budgeting include (Morgan, 1984, Caruthers and Orwig, 1979):

- The approach focuses on accomplishments and results rather than on inputs and processes;
- Once defined, it is a relatively simple approach;
- It promotes an equitable allocation of resources to those institutions that meet performance criteria.

The weaknesses of performance budgeting include (THECB, 1992b; Hossler, Kuh, and Bateman, 1989):

- It is difficult to define performance criteria and performance measures;
- There is a tendency to measure that which is measurable and perhaps not deal adequately with important issues (for example, using multiple-choice tests as the only measure of learning);
- Legislators are less able to influence decisions concerning institutions in the areas they represent;
- The time gap between an accomplishment, the measurement of it, and the receipt of the funds may be considerable;
- It is difficult to measure long-term outcomes;
- The approach does not take into account the diversity of various institutional missions in setting universal performance criteria;
- The budgeting and reporting documentation is complex and voluminous.

Incentive Budgeting

Incentive budgeting, like performance budgeting, continues higher education's pursuit of output-oriented budgeting, especially at the state level. Some states are using their budgets to provide incentives to their institutions of higher education for achieving state goals for educational quality. Typically, they set aside a pool of funds earmarked for the achievement of these goals, and once they are met, institutions share proportionately in these funds. Other states operate initiative programs, which provide the funds in advance of goal achievement, based on proposals submitted by institutions. A state's priorities may include specific outcomes, efficient and effective management, decentralized decision making, formula funding (Allen, 1984), remediation, and/or scholarships. Incentive programs give institutions the opportunity to move in the direction of state goals through increased motivation (i.e., additional funding), rather than through coercion (i.e., the threat of funding reductions) and regulation. Colleges and universities are relatively free to participate in those programs where they have the highest likelihood of achieving the objectives.

It may be argued that every budget contains incentives for certain activities and disincentives for others (Folger, 1989). Incentive funding is a mechanism more states are using to encourage institutions of higher education to conduct activities that meet state goals by either adding value to inputs, assuring that certain activities occur, or rewarding specific results. Although terminology varies from state to state, the major types of incentive funding include those programs that reward results after performance has occurred, and those programs that provide prospective funding for new programs and activities that promise the desired results (Berdahl and Holland, 1989). Funding that is awarded based on results is usually referred to as primary incentive funding whereas funding that is allocated prior to achieving the results is referred to as secondary incentive funding. A Texas committee has defined programs that fund results as "incentive funding" and those that fund prospective results as "initiative funding" (THECB, 1990).

Most existing incentive programs concentrate on funding inputs (e.g., centers of excellence, recruitment of eminent faculty, equipment funds), activities and processes (e.g., assessment programs, minority student recruitment/retention, business partnerships), and outputs (e.g. learning outcomes, improved graduation rates). A 1989 survey of fiscal incentive practices by the National Center for Postsecondary Governance and Finance, found that the purpose most often served by incentive programs was economic growth, including technology transfer and applied research to solve state problems. Recruitment of minority students, faculty, and staff was the second most popular category, followed by eminent scholars programs, improvement in undergraduate education, equipment support, and support of basic research. Thirty-two states reported having established some type of incentive funding program. Florida and New Jersey have established the largest number of individual programs, but other states such as Ohio and Tennessee have also been very active in this area (Berdahl and Holland, 1989).

As in the case of performance budgeting, the question of whether the funds for incentive programs will be taken from higher education's base funding or will be added as supplemental funding is critical to institutions. If the incentive programs are supported from funds taken from the base, institutions will be uncertain as to what their basic level of support is. They will be forced to compete for funds that they had previously received. Incentive programs that are supported by funding that is supplemental to basic appropriations truly provide incentives for institutions to achieve the state's specific goals.

The strengths of incentive budgeting include (Holland and Berdahl, 1990; Berdahl and Holland, 1989; Folger, 1984):

- It is a method whereby states can encourage institutions to achieve specific state goals;

- It is an approach that focuses on results and outputs;

- Qualitative issues, such as the quality of educational programs, can be addressed rather than only quantitative issues, such as enrollment levels.

- Incentive programs are most effective when faculty members (i.e., "those closest to the action") are directly involved;

- Incentive programs that use matching funds to leverage private fund raising are especially effective.

The weaknesses of incentive budgeting include (Berdahl and Holland, 1989):

- Measurement of outputs or outcomes in higher education is difficult;

- The tendency is to measure that which is measurable, i.e., that which is quantifiable;

- Since many higher education objectives are difficult to measure directly, proxies (such as test scores) are used; in many cases these proxies become the objective;

- Incentive budgeting is much more effective when supported by funding that is additional to higher education base appropriations, rather than taken from that base;

- Incentive programs tend not to be very useful as accountability measures;

- Incentive programs are not very effective unless a state has developed a comprehensive strategy for higher education improvement; incentive programs should be one part of such a strategy;

- Fiscal incentives tend to emphasize short-term goals rather than long-term planning.

Cost Center Budgeting

Cost center budgeting originated with Harvard's president James Conant who stated that "Every tub stands on its own bottom, each dean balances his own budget" (Caruthers and Orwig, 1979). Under this budgeting approach, academic departments and support units are considered cost centers for fiscal purposes, and are expected to be self-supporting. That is, in each cost center, projected expenditures must be supported by sufficient revenues raised by that center. In an academic department or college, for example, this means that the unit's faculty and staff salaries, its operating expenses, and a share of physical plant costs and other overhead expenditures must be covered by the unit's income from tuition and fees, endowments, gifts, and grants. Some support units are allowed to charge for their services. Never-

theless, under this budgeting approach, any revenue shortfalls in a particular unit must be accompanied by a scaling back of expenditures in order that unit operations can fall within available income.

Currently, some institutions are using an approach called Responsibility Center Budgeting (RCB). This approach is essentially cost center budgeting by another name. Until recently, RCB had only been implemented at private institutions, such as Cornell University, Harvard University, Johns Hopkins University, University of Miami, University of Southern California (where it is known as Responsibility Center Management), University of Pennsylvania, Vanderbilt University, and Washington University. When Thomas Ehrlich became president of Indiana University in 1989, the former provost of the University of Pennsylvania and former dean of the Stanford University Law School brought this innovation to a public institution. The University of Vermont and the University of Alabama-Birmingham have also implemented some form of RCB, but to date, Indiana is the only major research university (as per the Carnegie classification) to do so.

The key concept in responsibility center budgeting is the financial autonomy provided to each budgetary unit (Leslie, 1984). According to Ehrlich, three principles serve as the basis for RCB: "(1) all cost and income attributable to each school and other academic unit should be assigned to that unit; (2) appropriate incentives should exist for each academic unit to increase income and reduce costs to further a clear set of academic priorities; and (3) all costs of other units, such as the library or student counseling, should be allocated to academic units" (Whalen, 1991).

In responsibility center budgeting, tuition and fee income is attributed to the academic unit that generates it, while charges to academic units provide income to support units (Whalen, 1991). Each academic unit is assessed a formula-derived tax for university-wide support services such as libraries, academic computing, academic affairs, student services, physical facilities, and central administration. After all academic and support unit income is estimated for the year, the central administration allocates state appropriated funds among the academic units to offset remaining expenditures.

Among the incentives that make it possible for Indiana University to implement RCB without external interference is the fact that it retains its fund balances at the end of the fiscal year; that is, unspent general revenue funds (i.e., state tax dollars) do not revert back to the state treasury. In addition, Indiana University has legislative authority to use student tuition and fees as well as local funds to supplement state appropriations; that is, these funds are not considered part of the university's appropriation. Finally, the legislature authorized the university to manage its own funds, thus demonstrating a healthy level of trust between the university and the state.

The strengths of cost center budgeting or responsibility center budgeting are as follows (Whalen, 1991; Leslie, 1984; Morgan, 1984; Porter, and Oedel, 1978; Hoenack, 1977):

- It provides a rational approach to budgeting;

- It provides a method for distributing resources that demonstrates an institution's objectives;

- It facilitates accountability (it is easy to track the use of appropriated state funds as they relate to specific state funding decisions);

- There is closer proximity between budget responsibility and control and the institution's operating units;

- Decisions regarding academic changes are made closer to the instructional level;

- Resources can be moved within the institution in direct relation to enrollment patterns;

- The approach is responsive to both public policy and institutional needs;

- It increases competition among "players" (which is good for the consumer);

- It increases the effective use of resources;

- It enhances cooperation among campus units;

- Students have more influence across campus because they can "vote with their feet."

The weaknesses of cost center budgeting include (Whalen, 1991; Hossler, Kuh, and Bate-man, 1989; Leslie, 1984; Meisinger and Dubeck, 1984):

- It is difficult to apply in many institutions because many academic units have considerable service components (e.g. liberal arts departments);

- It may be difficult to classify units as responsibility centers;

- It requires tedious and complex calculations for the allocation of support unit costs to academic units;

- Institutional politics may affect the determination of which unit receives credit for some course offerings or services, or the algorithms that allocate indirect costs;

- Academic programs may become budget-driven;

- Academic units may vie to offer inappropriate service courses just to generate income;

- Central controls may be lacking;

- New fees may be developed to provide dedicated revenue streams for support units;

- It is sometimes difficult to develop equitable cost algorithms for taxing academic units.

Summary

In examining these seven institutional budgeting approaches, it should be remembered that they are not mutually exclusive. Some aspects of one approach may overlap with those of another. The terminology used at a particular institution or in a particular state may contain elements of each approach. This is partly because higher education seems to be constantly trying to move away from incremental budgeting—at least conceptually. Nevertheless, budgeting systems exist that contain decision packages (from zero-base budgeting) within program areas, each with its own formula, and supported by performance measures, with separate incentive funding programs. In the final analysis, however, most institutional administrators are interested in maintaining the funds they were budgeted for this year, and then arguing for the additional funds they need for next year. They frame their requests within the specific budget approach or combination of approaches they are required to use, but their goal is the same, nevertheless.

RETRENCHMENT AND REALLOCATION

Financial stress and uncertainty represent special conditions for budgeters—no more "business as usual." Regardless of whether the stress confronting the institution occurs suddenly or gradually, regardless of whether it is caused by unstable or declining enrollments, reductions in financial support (i.e., tuition, appropriations, fund raising, or endowment income) or other factors, difficult fiscal decisions lay ahead. The basic goal of institutional efforts during these times is to minimize the negative impact on instruction and academic program quality. Institutions respond by using both adaptive and resistive practices to control where reductions take place.

Of course, different types of institutions are affected by financial stress in different ways. Public colleges and universities, for example, feel the greatest impact from declining state and local tax revenues. However, many private institutions that receive direct or indirect public support are also affected. Enrollment declines are most keenly felt at the undergraduate level, largely affecting public state colleges and universities and private, nonselective liberal arts colleges that depend primarily on tuition revenues to support the bulk of their budget revenue. At the graduate level, enrollment declines create difficulties for major research universities that need a critical mass of students to maintain high quality graduate programs (Breneman, 1981). However, at community colleges, open admissions policies and the responsiveness of vocational programs to local community needs help to maintain enrollment levels.

Institutions whose students rely heavily on financial aid are most affected by declines in federal financial assistance programs. Curtailment of federally-supported research centers and programs affects major research universities. All postsecondary institutions are affected by inflation, especially as it boosts the cost of those goods and services that are especially relevant to higher education, such as salaries, fringe benefits, scientific equipment, scholarly books and journals, and utilities.

An institution's ability to respond to financial crises as well as financial opportunities depends on several elements. Among those critical abilities are the institution's financial flexibility, including prior development of reserve funds to meet contingencies, a regular review of the costs and benefits of instructional programs, a regular review of institutional priorities, the diversity of revenue sources, and enhanced communications with faculty, staff, students, and such interest groups as alumni and industry representatives (Vandement, 1989). These elements allow an institution to respond more positively to enrollment fluctuations and financial emergencies and to take advantage of unforeseen opportunities.

Volkwein's (1988) review of state regulatory practices over public postsecondary educational institutions also revealed that there is a relationship between state deregulation and financial flexibility. He found that public universities generally operate more efficiently when subjected to fewer regulations. This underscores the need for flexibility when times are less than ideal. Public universities rely less on state appropriations when they are given incentives for good management. Relief from state control through lump-sum appropriations, campus retention and control of tuition and non-tuition revenues, campus retention of year-end balances, flexibility to shift funds among budget categories, authority to finance capital construction, and biennial budgeting lead to increased flexibility at public research universities. High levels of state control directly and negatively affect institutional efficiency and adaptability, as well as educational effectiveness (Volkwein, 1986).

Under ideal conditions, a postsecondary institution would have the ability to respond to a crisis (Brinkerhoff, 1981). This ability would include having both adequate time to react and the financial flexibility to reallocate funds and make changes in operations without irreparably harming instructional programs. However, the fact that a large proportion of the annual budgets of most colleges and universities are relatively fixed, makes it difficult to make quickly the fiscal changes necessary to shift resources from lower priority to higher priority programs and activities. Unfortunately, the conditions associated with the fiscal crises facing many institutions are rarely ideal.

When confronted with a fiscal crisis, colleges and universities generally try to either resist or adapt depending on their assessment of the severity and the duration of the crisis. Like budgeters in other settings, higher education officials have three basic methods of responding—increasing revenues, reducing expenditures, or some combination of the two. Increasing revenue is a resistive option that allows institutions to maintain current programs and activities. However, campuses may shift energies that should be focused on expenditure savings, retrenchment, and reallocation to increasing revenue as a defense mechanism to avoid difficult decisions. Increasing revenue is not a feasible option for all institutions in all conditions of financial duress. Another related resistive option used to lessen the impact of loss of income from a single source is diversification of funding sources. A broadened base of funds spreads the risk of revenue shortfalls among many revenue sources, rather than relying on only a few.

How colleges and universities allocate resources among units is closely related to each unit's centrality (i.e., the match between the unit's purpose and the institution's mission), its relational power among units within the institution and outside the institution, and the repertoire of resource negotiation strategies it uses (Hackman, 1985). Campus administrators usually review peripheral units first during times of fiscal distress, since it is perceived that their reduction or elimination can occur without harming the integrity of the institution's academic mission.

Bowen and Glenny (1981) have categorized short-term, adaptive responses to fiscal crisis as being either selective or across-the-board reductions of expenditures. Five examples of these techniques include:

- Operational responses that are temporary and have limited impact on instructional programs (e.g. reductions in vacant staff positions, building maintenance, travel, etc.);

- Academic program responses that have little impact on faculty (e.g., reductions in vacant faculty positions, travel to professional meetings, equipment funds, etc.);

- Facility adjustments that rely mainly on attrition;

- Faculty adjustments that rely mainly on academic program considerations (e.g. shifting faculty to service courses as a way of responding to declining majors);

- Procedural responses within the organization (e.g. increased centralization of decision making).

Bowen and Glenny also discuss the fact that several of these reactions erode an institution's budget flexibility over time and limit its options for responding to the problem on a long-term basis. Ordinarily, institutions maintain a certain degree of flexibility through budget and salary savings, the use of part-time and temporary faculty, and the difference between the average costs by which academic programs are typically funded and the marginal costs of additional students. During periods of financial crisis, vacant positions and contingency reserves are usually the first things cut, followed by reductions in support units, supplies, and equipment. Over the short term, these adjustments may allow an institution to withstand brief financial turmoil, but they do not provide long-term solutions. As these types of cuts are made, the institution's budget flexibility is reduced. If the fiscal crisis is short-term, the institution will, over a few years, rebuild a measure of this flexibility. However, if the crisis is long-term, the flexibility will soon be used up, and the institution will be forced to consider more drastic measures.

It is also true that during the early stages of a fiscal dilemma, institutions may choose to make budget cuts across-the-board, with the budgets of all affected campus units being reduced by the same amount or percent. Before long, however, and especially if it becomes clear that the duration of the crisis will be longer term, a realization develops that deeper, more selective reductions are necessary to avoid a slow erosion in the overall quality of institutional programs.

When colleges and universities are confronted with significant reductions in revenues and/or when the duration of the financial crisis appears to be long-term, they must consider more substantive and fundamental changes, such as retrenchment and reallocation. These approaches usually involve reductions in course-offerings, program review, and ultimately the release of faculty and staff in order to achieve financial equilibrium. Obviously, this last option is a painful process for any institution, and one that is entertained only after other alternatives have been exhausted. Nevertheless, this is the situation in which many institutions find themselves in the decade of the 1990s.

Retrenchment, defined as "the dismissal or layoff of tenured faculty, or nontenured faculty in mid-contract" (Mortimer and Taylor, 1984, p. 70), is an adaptive response to long-term fiscal crisis. Since higher education is a labor-intensive enterprise, it stands to reason that any significant reductions in expenditures will ultimately involve reducing personnel. Random faculty attrition is unlikely to provide the necessary budgetary flexibility during a long-term financial dilemma. Rather, reductions in the number of faculty positions in selected programs will probably be required. In her review of institutional experiences in program reduction, Dolan-Green, (1981) found that retrenchment occurs as a result of three broad categories of decisions: program elimination, reallocation of positions, and financial exigency [which the American Association of University Professors has defined as "an imminent financial crisis which threatens the survival of the institution as a whole and which cannot be alleviated by less drastic means (AAUP, 1976)].

One adaptive retrenchment tool that helps institutions identify in which program cutbacks should occur is the review of doctoral programs. In the early 1980s, the Board of Regents of the State University of New York reviewed doctoral programs in both public and private universities in that state. More recently, the Texas Higher Education Coordinating Board completed a statutorily mandated sunset review of more than 600 doctoral programs at the state's public institutions. This resulted in institutions (voluntarily) eliminating 112 low priority programs. Many other institutions have used this technique in recent years to meet fiscal crises. However, it is difficult to complete this process quickly. When a fiscal crisis is imminent, launching a systematic review of doctoral programs will probably not be sufficient to meet the budget challenges associated with the crisis. It can, however, be a useful long-term solution.

Another adaptive aid for institutions experiencing retrenchment is strategic planning, in which the institution identifies its academic niche by reviewing its mission, role and scope, strengths and weaknesses, and eliminating those weak programs that fall outside the mission. An institution may also adopt a resistant approach by redefining its mission so that it is more in line with market demands and by tailoring new programs and recruitment activities to match. Like program review, initiating a strategic planning process is a longer-term solution to dealing with financial crisis.

Reallocation, another long-term, adaptive response to fiscal distress, is a "process whereby resources are distributed according to a plan" (Hyatt and Santiago, 1986, pg. 91). A review of estimated revenues and expenditures suggests alternatives for the reallocation of institutional resources through a series of trade-offs. Additional resources may be provided to some units for selective enhancement and improvement while resources may be reduced for those units identified as "revenue bloated." Other units that have adequate resources that match current activities may have their resource levels maintained. Institutional decisions are made based on academic program quality, unit efficiencies and enrollment fluctuations, revenue options, identification of fixed and variable costs, the spillover effect on other programs, the degree to which programs are in line with the institution's overall mission, and institutional goals and ambitions.

A key issue when an institution is faced with a fiscal crisis and is considering major budget changes is who participates in the decision process and assists in the identification of policy alternatives. During stable economic times, college and university administrators, with advice from the faculty, make decisions regarding the development and maintenance of academic and support programs and activities (Zammuto, 1986). Given the deep cuts that confront many institutions during periods of fiscal crisis, however, many administrators do more than seek advice from the faculty by adopting a decision-making process and style that both informs the college community and invites participation in decision making from various constituencies. The process and the degree to which various campus constituencies are involved in decision making is critical

(Hardy et al, 1983). In many cases, how retrenchment and reallocation decisions are made is as important as what decisions are made (Dill and Helm, 1988).

During difficult financial periods, administrators generally communicate with and seek advice from members of various constituencies from all areas of the institution concerning the nature of the crisis, potential solutions, and the process by which decisions will be made (Hardy et al, 1983; Powers and Powers, 1983; Mortimer and McConnell, 1978). At certain times, institution-wide newsletters or memoranda may be sufficient to provide this information. At others, face-to-face meetings are necessary. The administration may use existing institution-wide committees or establish ad hoc committees for strategic discussions concerning retrenchment or reallocation strategies. These process decisions depend in large measure on the campus situation itself—including governance tradition, financial history, and general institutional character. Consultation and advise usually are obtained from all campus groups that have a stake in the outcome of the decisions, including administrators (especially deans and department chairpersons), faculty, staff, and students. Many institutions also maintain effective communication with other constituencies such as alumni, key donors, and community leaders, and the media. Of course, members of the governing board must give final approval to any major retrenchment or reallocation plans, but it is important that they be kept informed as these plans are developed. Implementation of a decision is at risk of failure if appropriate and adequate communication and participation have been denied to stakeholders (Vroom, 1984).

Bowen and Glenny (1981) suggest that the difficulty in preparing an institutional plan in times of "pervasive uncertainty" and the fact that many educational leaders refuse to acknowledge economic problems both contribute to the institutional paralysis that often occurs in response to a fiscal crisis. They suggest, instead, that by developing a series of alternative resource scenarios in the midst of uncertainty and incomplete information, institutions are better prepared to function under various funding levels. The state of readiness of an institution in anticipation of funding cuts directly affects its ability to respond. Preparation of multiple budget options minimizes the potential disruption of academic and support programs and activities, if anticipated revenues are not realized. Despite the fear that preparation of several budget options will result in lower funding, the existence of multiple funding strategies does not necessarily invite a self-fulfilling prophecy of financial doom. Contingency plans provide immediate options in both hard and good economic times. Such plans strengthen an institution's state of preparedness and its ability to respond to whatever level of financial austerity occurs.

Identifying those academic and support programs and activities that are to be reduced or eliminated is almost always painful and controversial. It is a step that usually occurs only after all other policy alternatives have been examined. When such cuts cannot be avoided, however, institutions are better served when they anticipate carefully how such reassignments, lay offs, or dismissals will be made. As established committees prepare prioritized lists of nonessential academic and support programs and activities that are deemed to be weak and/or peripheral to the institution's mission, many administrators simultaneously develop criteria to determine how faculty and staff from these areas will be selected for reassignment or termination. These criteria usually include such items as tenure status, program need, performance, academic custom and usage, affirmative action, and age.

Tenured and nontenured faculty who are dismissed from their positions have certain rights. In situations involving financial exigency, program reductions, or program discontinuation, these rights include reassignment, retraining, appeal, and reinstatement. Colleges and universities forced to take these actions generally strive to ensure that adequate personnel policies are in place and are followed to guarantee appropriate due process.

Human nature being what it is, and institutions of higher education being the kind of organizations they are, it is only natural that when a college or university is confronted with a fiscal crisis, its leadership will choose to make easy cuts first. As indicated previously, this usually involves such things as reducing travel expenditures, equipment purchases, library acquisitions, funds for long-distance telephone calls, contingency funds; deferring building maintenance; reducing course offerings; not filling faculty and staff positions that become vacant; and increasing revenues, especially tuition and student fees. Normally, cuts in support areas such as physical plant, student services, and administrative areas are emphasized before core academic units are touched. During such periods, it is not unusual for many examples of innovative cost-cutting strategies to be found on the campus.

Nevertheless, as the crisis worsens, more severe actions may be necessary. In the tradition of shared governance, and in an effort to "share the blame/pain," the president or chancellor may choose to request recommendations from vice presidents, deans, faculty members, students, and representatives from other campus stakeholders. Budget priority committees—usually consisting of administrators, faculty members, and student leaders—may be formed (if they do not already exist) to provide recommendations about specific cuts, reorganizations, or programs to be considered for elimination. Normally, however, the last cuts considered will be to tenured faculty members. A "siege mentality" may develop as faculty are forced to consider whether a colleague's program should be reduced or cut all together. The institution may also experience a "brain drain" as faculty members with established reputations receive offers from other institutions to leave and move to financially greener pastures. Unfortunately, this scene is being repeated over and over again as institutions are confronted with expenditure increases and revenue reductions of magnitudes rarely witnessed in higher education in the past.

IMPLICATIONS FOR FURTHER RESEARCH

As colleges and universities learn to function in this new era of financial restraint, and as they are confronted with new levels of distrust on the part of the American public, there are questions concerning whether the budgeting models and approaches that have been used in the past will continue to be appropriate. In general, the question is: Where is higher education budgeting going in these times of persistent uncertainty? More specific questions relate to how higher education budgeting will change as institutions cope with an environment of increasing costs and severe revenue shortfalls. How will they deal with the renewed interest in performance funding? Will more institutions turn to cost center budgeting (or responsibility center budgeting)? How will capital budgeting be changed so that institutions can deal more effectively with the notion of capital renewal and solve the problem of deferred maintenance? Each of these questions provide avenues of future research for scholars interested in higher education finance and governance.

Probably the question that will affect most institutions of higher education in the 1990s is what budget and governance processes will they use to respond to the fiscal crises which will confront them. Although earlier research (such as Hyatt, Schulman, and Santiago, 1984; Leslie, 1984; and Mingle, 1981) offers some insights into how institutions have behaved in the past during such periods, the methods used in those situations may no longer be appropriate because current funding cuts are larger and of longer duration. Budget reductions in the early 1980s were in the range of 2–3 percent. Current reductions are ranging more in the 10–20 percent area. Not only are overall expenditures being trimmed, but entire degree programs and whole colleges are being eliminated. In this new environment, one wonders whether institutions will continue to "take the easy cuts first." Will they continue to make across-the-board cuts first? Will they continue to cut nonacademic support areas and nonpersonnel related costs before they turn to core academic areas? Or will the size or degree of the revenue shortfalls cause them to consider eliminating academic programs that are no longer deemed as being central to the completion of the institution's mission earlier in the process? Case analyses should be completed and the results compared to the earlier literature to answer these questions.

As mentioned previously, institutions have also responded to fiscal crisis in recent years by attempting to increase revenue from other sources to make up for short-falls. Will these attempts continue? For example, students are being asked to carry a significantly larger share of the burden of financing higher education. In the private sector, this trend has been in existence for many years—to a point where many wonder whether the costs are now so high that students cannot afford to attend. The trend is more recent in the public sector. Yet, in response to reductions in appropriations, many states have either raised tuition levels or allowed institutions to raise them. These tuition increases, coupled with reductions in course offerings, have led many students to argue that they are being forced to pay more for less service, especially if they must extend their college careers because they cannot get the necessary coursework to complete their degrees.

Institutions of higher education, both public and private, both four-year and two-year, are increasing the amount of development and fund-raising activities in which they participate. Billion dollar capital campaigns are announced at an increasing rate. Can this continue? Bristol has reported that corporations, foundations and religious organizations, non-alumni individuals, and alumni have each contributed one quarter of all gifts to higher education since 1950 (Bristol, 1991). He also forecast that the average gift from an alumnus would increase from $94.93 in 1990 to $116.52 in 2010. Alumni gifts totaled $2.8 billion in 1990 and are estimated to increase to $11.2 billion by 2010. Bristol identifies five factors that will affect the reliability and likelihood of this prediction: 1) the rate of inflation between now and 2010, 2) the graduation rate for baccalaureate degrees, 3) the average age of alumni in the base (i.e., the number of years that have passed since graduation), 4) history (i.e., the hidden variables cause change in attitudes over time), and 5) the mix of alumni from public and private institutions (since alumni from private institutions tend to support their institutions more generously than alumni from public institutions). Nevertheless, questions remain: Are there sufficient philanthropic dollars available to meet all the perceived needs? Will the competition from other sectors of society, including public elementary and secondary education, reduce the amount of these funds on which colleges and universities can rely?

For public colleges and universities, especially, the proportions of financial support which come from various sectors are changing. At some major research universities, for exam-

ple, state tax dollars provide around one-third of total operating budgets, down from the 50–65 percent levels of years ago. The proportions paid from tuition, outside research support (mostly federal), and gift income have increased greatly. These institutions are becoming "state-assisted" institutions instead of state institutions. What types of governance changes will result from such changes? What impact will those changes have on institutional budgeting processes and approaches?

The history of higher education budgeting is filled with attempts to move from the orientation of incremental budgeting on inputs (e.g. the cost of faculty members, staff, supplies, equipment, travel, etc.) to an orientation on outcomes (e.g. goals, objectives, performance measures). Program budgeting, zero base budgeting, performance budgeting, and incentive budgeting are all more focused on outcomes than is the much-maligned technique of incremental budgeting. Generally, these methods have been used for a time by a few institutions or states and subsequently discarded. However, will institutions continue to try new approaches, only to return to incremental budgeting (perhaps in the current environment it should be called decremental budgeting)? Will those states that have tried incentive budgeting be able to continue their programs if revenues decline? Will the current popularity of performance budgeting continue as a reflection of the accountability movement?

A related question is, how much government oversight is necessary to ensure the quality of higher education? Given the growing distrust of all institutions (including colleges and universities), given the general mood concerning the inadequacy of the public K–12 educational system, and given recent scandals concerning the misuses of public funds (e.g. Stanford University) or exorbitant compensation packages for top officials (e.g. University of California), it is only natural that the quality of institutions of higher education would be called into question. When this is combined with the perception that higher education costs only increase, the fact that benefits are not fully understood, and the realization that fewer funds are available to fund government services in general, it stands to reason that states, especially, will want to have more control over how their appropriations will be spent by public colleges and universities and what they will produce—i.e., they will turn to performance funding systems. If the institutions want this money (and Bowen's revenue theory of cost would lead us to predict that they will always want it), they will have to continue to develop their information systems to collect and report the necessary performance indicators and measures to show their compliance or progress. Implementation of these requirements may be counterproductive in that they shift institutional resources away from core academic activities to peripheral compliance activities.

Perhaps responsibility center budgeting will lead the way to the development of the next generation of budget approaches that simultaneously address the need for stability in a highly volatile environment and the externally-driven demand for increased accountability. While this technique may lead to "the rich getting richer," it may also provide a new mechanism for making difficult reallocation decisions. Many private institutions of higher education have used cost center budgeting for years—with varying degrees of success. Public colleges and universities may want to keep a watchful eye on the progress of Indiana University, and any other institutions that may decide to try this technique, as it implements this budgeting approach.

For the most part in this section, we have focused on the implications for further analysis and research on financial, governance, and procedural aspects of budgeting approaches as they relate to institutional operating budgets. There are, of course, equally important issues related to capital budgeting. While there may be little new building on campuses that are facing funding shortages, there are nevertheless matters of renovation, meeting building maintenance needs that have been too long deferred, and renewing physical plants that are reaching the end of their useful lives. Institutional operating budgets are directly affected by additions of space for classrooms, offices, instructional and research laboratories, recreation, and maybe even parking. Changes in institutional infrastructure automatically impact the operating budget, Since this relationship is often neglected or ignored, new procedures may be necessary to guarantee that operating requirements embedded in capital budget decisions receive consideration during the budget process that is equal to other items. As mentioned, deferred maintenance and capital renewal and replacement should occupy a more prominent place among budget needs. Additional analyses should be carried out to examine such questions as: 1) Will building maintenance and custodial services continue to be deferred as institutions adapt to fiscal constraints? 2) Will the work that has already been done in the area of capital renewal and replacement (Dunn, 1989) provide a useful standard?, and 3) Will new financing methods for capital budgeting and asset management be explored?

In the final analysis, however, we return to the general financial outlook for the 1990s, and what that means for budgeting in institutions of higher education. This environment will require that every college and university reevaluate its mission and—using that mission as a framework—examine the academic programs it offers, the management and care of its capital assets, its policies regarding student admissions and financial aid, its practices with regard to faculty tenure, promotion, and workload, and the allocation of its financial, human, and capital resources. To the extent that their leaders can get outside the bounds of psychological constraints (such as the "business as usual" commitment to traditional ways), and contextual constraints (including the organizational characteristics and cultural boundaries of higher education institutions), more creative budgeting solutions will be identified.

Unfortunately, it seems that many of the decisions being made these days are providing new answers to the age-old questions of, "Who pays for higher education?" and its companion, "Who gains from higher education?" However, these new answers are not being offered as a result of a public policy debate on higher education finance. Rather, they are the corollary results of decisions designed to solve serious economic and political problems. That students and others should shoulder more of the costs of higher education may indeed be a reasonable solution to these problems. However, one would hope that those individuals who make higher education budget decisions would understand that these solutions can change long-standing public policies in addition to meeting current economic needs.

REFERENCES

Allen, R. (1981). Capital budgeting overview. In L. Leslie and J. Hyatt (eds.), *Higher Education Financing Policies: State/Institutions and Their Interactions.* Tucson, AZ: Center for the Study of Higher Education, University of Arizona.

Allen, R. (1984). New approaches to incentive funding. In L. Leslie (ed.), *Responding to New Realities in Funding.* San Francisco: Jossey-Bass.

American Association of University Professors. (1976). Recommended institutional regulations on academic freedom and tenure. 62 AAUP Bulletin 186: 184–191.

Balderston, F., and Weathersby, G. (1972). PPBS in higher education planning and management: part II, the University of California experience. *Higher Education* 1(3): 299–319.

Banta, T. (ed.). (1988). *Implementing Outcomes Assessment: Promises and Perils.* (New Directions in Institutional Research, No. 59.) San Francisco: Jossey-Bass.

Banta, T. (1986). *Performance Funding in Higher Education: A Critical Analysis of Tennessee's Experience.* Boulder, CO; National Center for Higher Education Management Systems.

Banta, T., and Fisher, H. (1984). Performance funding: Tennessee's experiment. In J. Folger (ed.), *Financial Incentives for Academic Quality.* (New Directions for Higher Education, No. 48.) San Francisco: Jossey-Bass.

Berdahl, R., and Holland, B. (eds.). (1989). *Developing State Fiscal Incentives to Improve Higher Education.* Proceedings from a national invitational conference. College Park, MD: National Center for Postsecondary Governance and Finance, University of Maryland.

Bogue, G., and Brown, W. (1982). Performance incentives for state colleges. *Harvard Business Review,* Nov./Dec.: 123–128.

Bowen, F. (1975). Making decisions in a time of fiscal stringency: the long-term implications. Paper presented at a seminar for state leaders in postsecondary education, Denver, CO. ED 202 282.

Bowen, F. (1980). *The Costs of Higher Education: How Much Do Colleges and Universities Spend per Student and How Much Should They Spend?* San Francisco: Jossey-Bass.

Bowen, W. (1986). The role of the business officer in managing educational resources. In L. Leslie and R. Anderson (eds.), *ASHE Reader on Finance in Higher Education.* Lexington, MA: Ginn Press.

Bowen, F., and Glenny, L. (1981). The California study. In L. Leslie and J. Hyatt (eds.), *Higher Education Financing Policies: State/Institutions and Their Interactions.* Tucson, AZ: Center for the Study of Higher Education, University of Arizona.

Breneman, D. (1981). In J. Mingle (ed.), *Challenges of Retrenchment: Strategies for Consolidating Programs, Cutting Costs, and Reallocating Resources.* San Francisco: Jossey-Bass.

Brinkerhoff, J. (1981). The chief institutional officer perspective. In L. Leslie and J. Hyatt (eds.), *Higher Education Financing Policies: State/Institutions and Their Interactions.* Tucson, AZ: Center for the Study of Higher Education, University of Arizona.

Brinkman, P. (1984). Formula budgeting: the fourth decade. In L. Leslie (ed.), *Responding to New Realities in Funding.* New Directions in Institutional Research, No. 43. San Francisco: Jossey-Bass.

Bristol, R. Jr. (1991). How much will alumni give in the future? *Planning for Higher Education* 20, Winter 1991–92: 1–12.

Caruthers, J. K., and Orwig, M. (1979). *Budgeting in Higher Education.* (AAHE/ERIC Higher Education Research Report No. 3. ED 167 857.) Washington, DC: American Association for Higher Education.

Chronicle of Higher Education. (1992a, June 10). Recession takes toll on U.S. aid. 38(40): Al, 20–21.

Chronicle of Higher Education. (1992b, September 9). Drop in state support leaves Ohio colleges wondering how much farther they can fall. 39(3): A23–24.

Chronicle of Higher Education. (1992c, October 7). Budget outlook prompts some college leaders to speak out for higher state taxes. 39(7): A22.

Dill, D., and Helm, K. (1988). Faculty participation in strategic policy making. In J. C. Smart (ed.), *Higher Education: Handbook of Theory and Research.* Vol. IV. New York: Agathon Press.

Dolan-Green, C. (1981). What if the faculty member to be laid off is the governor's brother? In S. Hample (ed.), *Coping with Faculty Reduction.* (New Directions for Institutional Research. No. 30.) San Francisco: Jossey-Bass.

Daugherty, E. (1981). Should you starve all programs or eliminate a few? In S. Hample (ed.), *Coping with Faculty Reduction.* (New Directions for Institutional Research, No. 30.) San Francisco: Jossey-Bass.

Dunn, J. (1989). *Financial Planning Guidelines for Facility Renewal and Adaptation.* (A joint project of The Society for College and University Planning, The National Association for College and University Business Officers, The Association of Physical Plant Administrators of Colleges and Universities, and Coopers and Lybrand.) Ann Arbor, MI: Society for College and University Planning.

Ewell, P. (1988). Outcomes, assessment, and academic improvement: in search of usable knowledge. In J. C. Smart (ed.), *Higher Education: Handbook of Theory and Research,* Vol. IV. New York: Agathon Press.

Ewell, P. (ed.). (1985). *Assessing Educational Outcomes.* (New Directions for Institutional Research, No. 47.) San Francisco: Jossey-Bass.

Folger, J. (1989). Designing state incentive programs that work. In R. Berdahl and B. Holland (eds.), *Developing State Fiscal Incentives to Improve Higher Education.* (Proceedings from a national invitational conference.) College Park, MD: National Center for Postsecondary Governance and Finance, University of Maryland.

Folger, J. (ed.). (1984). *Financial Incentives for Academic Quality.* (New Directions for Higher Education, No. 48.) San Francisco: Jossey-Bass.

Green, J. L., Jr. (1971). *Budgeting in Higher Education.* Athens, GA: University of Georgia Business and Finance Office.

Hackman, J. (1985). Power and centrality in the allocation of resources in colleges and universities. *Administrative Science Quarterly* 30: 61–77.

Halpern, D. (1987). *The State of College and University Facilities.* Ann Arbor, MI: Society for College and University Planning.

Halstead, D. K. (1991). *Higher Education Revenues and Expenditures: A Study of Institutional Cost.* Washington, D.C.: Research Associates of Washington.

Hample, S. (ed.), (1981). *Coping with Faculty Reduction.* (New Directions for Institutional Research, No. 30.) San Francisco: Jossey-Bass.

Hardy, C., Langley, A., Mintzberg, H., and Rose, J. (1983). Strategy formation in the university setting. *Review of Higher Education* 6: 407–433.

Hoenack, S. (1984). Direct and incentive planning within a university. *Socio-Economic Planning Sciences* 11(4): 191–204.

Holland, B., and Berdahl, R. (1990). Green carrots: a survey of state use of fiscal incentives for academic quality. A paper presented at the annual meeting of the Association for the Study of Higher Education. Nov. 1–4. Portland, OR.

Hopkins, D., and Massy, W. (1981). *Planning Models for Colleges and Universities.* Stanford, CA: Stanford University Press.

Hossler, D., Kuh, G., and Bateman, J. M. (1989). An investigation of the anticipated effects of responsibility center budgeting at a public research university: the first year. Paper presented at the annual meeting of the American Educational Research Association, March 27–31. San Francisco.

Hyatt, J., and Santiago, A. (1986). *Financial Management of Colleges and Universities.* Washington, D.C.: National Association of College and University Business Officers.

Hyatt, J., Schulman, C., and Santiago, A. (1984). *Relocation: Strategies for Effective Resource Management.* Washington, D.C.: National Association of College and University Business Officers.

Jenny, H. (1981). The capital margin. In L. Leslie and J. Hyatt (eds.), *Higher Education Financing Policies: State/Institutions and Their Interactions.* Tucson, AZ: Center for the Study of Higher Education, University of Arizona.

Kaludis, G. (ed.) (1973). *Strategies for Budgeting.* (New Directions in Higher Education, No. 2.) San Francisco: Jossey-Bass.

Kraal, S. (1992). A comparative analysis of funding models used to estimate the renovation and renewal costs of existing higher education facilities. Ph.D. dissertation. The University of Texas at Austin.

Layzell, D., and Lyddon, J. (1990). *Budgeting for Higher Education at the State Level: Enigma, Paradox, and Ritual.* (ASHE-ERIC Higher Education Report No. 4.) Washington, D.C.: The George Washington University, School of Education and Human Development.

Lenth, C. (1992). Telephone conversation with D. Greene. October 30.

Leslie, L., and Anderson, R. (eds.) (1986). *ASHE Reader on Finance in Higher Education.* Lexington, MA: Ginn Press.

Leslie, L. (ed.), (1984). *Responding to New Realities in Funding.* (New Directions in Institutional Research, No. 43.) San Francisco: Jossey-Bass.

Leslie, L., and Hyatt, J. (eds.). (1981). *Higher Education Financing Policies: State Institutions and Their Interactions.* Tucson, AZ: Center for the Study of Higher Education, University of Arizona.

Lindblom, C. (1959). The science of "muddling through." *Public Administration Review* 19: 79–88.

Massy, W. (1989). Budget decentralization at Stanford University. *Planning for Higher Education* 18(2): 39–55.

Meisinger, R., and Dubeck, L. (1984). *College and University Budgeting: An Introduction for Faculty and Academic Administrators.* Washington, D.C.: National Association of College and University Business Officers.

Mingle, J., and Associates. (1981). *Challenges of Retrenchment: Strategies for Consolidating Programs, Cutting Costs, and Reallocating Resources.* San Francisco: Jossey-Bass.

Morgan, A, (1992). The politics and policies of selective funding: the case of state-level quality incentives. *The Review of Higher Education* 15(3): 289–306.

Morgan, A. (1984). The new strategies: roots, context, and overview. In L. Leslie (ed.), *Responding to New Realities in Funding.* (New Directions in Institutional Research, No. 43.) San Francisco: Jossey-Bass.

Mortimer, K., and McConnell, T. (1978). *Sharing Authority Effectively.* San Francisco: Jossey-Bass.

Mortimer, K., and Taylor, B. (1984). Budgeting strategies under conditions of decline. In L. Leslie (ed.), *Responding to New Realities in Funding.* (New Directions in Institutional Research, No. 43.) San Francisco: Jossey-Bass.

Powers, D and Powers, M. (1983). *Making Participatory Management Work.* San Francisco: Jossey-Bass.

Robins, G. (1986). From Understanding the college budget. In L. Leslie and R. Anderson (eds.), *ASHE Reader on Finance in Higher Education.* Lexington, MA: Ginn Press.

Rubin, I. (ed.), (1988). *New Directions in Budget Theory.* Albany, N.Y.: State University of New York Press.

Rush, S., and Johnson, S. (1988). *The Decaying American Campus: A Ticking Time Bomb.* (A joint report of the Association of Physical Plant Administrators of Universities and Colleges and the National Association of College and University Business Officers in cooperation with Coopers and Lybrand).

Schmidtlein, F. (1989). Why linking budgets to plans has proven difficult in higher education. *Planning for Higher Education* 18(2): 9–23.

Seitz, C. (1981). The Indiana experience. In L. Leslie and J. Hyatt (eds.), *Higher Education Financing Policies: State/Institutions and Their Interactions.* Tucson, AZ: Center for the Study of Higher Education, University of Arizona.

Texas Higher Education Coordinating Board. (1990). Report of the Initiative and Incentive Subcommittee, March. Austin, TX.

Texas Higher Education Coordinating Board. (1992a). Board agenda item IV-A, Minutes from July Board Meeting. Austin, TX.

Texas Higher Education Coordinating Board. (1992b). Report from Committee on Performance Based Funding for the Health-Related Institutions, July. Austin, TX.

Vandement, W. (1989). *Managing Money in Higher Education: A Guide to the Financial Process and Effective Participation Within It.* San Francisco: Jossey-Bass.

Volkwein, J. (1988). State regulation and campus autonomy. In J. C. Smart (ed.), *Higher Education: Handbook of Theory and Research,* Vol. IV. New York: Agathon Press.

Volkwein, J. (1986). State financial control of public universities and its relationship to campus administrative elaborateness and cost: results of a national study. *The Review of Higher Education* 9(3): 267–286.

Vroom, V. (1984). Leaders and leadership in academe. In J. L. Bess (ed.), *College and University Organization: Insights from the Behavioral Sciences.* New York: New York University Press.

Webster's New Collegiate Dictionary. (1981). Springfield, MA: G. & C. Merriam.

Welzenbach, L. (1982). *College and University Business Administration.* Washington, D.C.: National Association of College and University Business Officers.

Whalen, E. (1991). *Responsibility Center Budgeting: An Approach to Decentralized Management for Institutions of Higher Education.* Bloomington, IN: Indiana University Press.

Wildavsky, A. (1988). *The New Politics of the Budgetary Process.* Glenview. IL: Scott, Foresman and Company.

Zammuto, R. (1986). Managing decline in American higher education. In J. C. Smart (ed.) *Higher Education: Handbook of Theory and Research,* Vol. IV. New York: Agathon Press.

Zemsky, R., Porter, R., and Oedel, L. (1978). Decentralized planning: to share responsibility. *Educational Record* 59: 229–253.

Zusman, A. (1986). Legislature and university conflict: the case of California. *The Review of Higher Education* 9(4): 397–418.

CHAPTER 41

FUND ACCOUNTING (1984)

RICHARD J. MEISINGER, JR. AND LEROY W. DUBECK

Designing an accounting system is an art form. The system can hide information or it can disclose various aspects of an institution's financial situation. Some accounting systems can do both simultaneously.

Most college and university accounting systems are designed in accordance with generally accepted accounting principles, especially those summarized in *College & University Business Administration,* 4th ed. (Washington, DC: National Association of College and University Business Officers, 1982), and *Audits of Colleges and Universities* (New York: American Institute of Certified Public Accountants, 1975). However, in accounting, as in most disciplines, there is disagreement over how to address certain situations. In those instances the accounting methodologies will differ from one campus to another. The design of the accounting system can also be determined in part by the nature of the institution (e.g., public versus independent, research-oriented versus instruction oriented) and the institution's history.

An accounting system does not necessarily reflect all financial transactions that may influence the institution's financial status. Frequently these transactions are described in notes to the institution's financial statement. They might include such items as significant additions to plant and pledges of gifts. Items that do not appear in a financial statement might include a planned bequest by an alumnus to be made at an unnamed future date or the donation of rare books or works of art. The latter items increase the value of the institution's assets but would not be included in the financial statement. One must realize, therefore, that the institution's accounting system may not provide a complete financial picture.

What follows is a layman's guide to fund accounting, the basic framework for most college and university accounting systems. This is a brief overview of the most common types of accounts and funds and summarizes selected accounting principles. Attention is given to basic financial statements. The sample institution referred to throughout this chapter is examined in Tables 41.1 through 41.5.

TYPES OF ACCOUNTS

The Accounting Equation

The accounting equation involves the balanced relationship among three kinds of economic representations: assets, liabilities, and net worth. Assets are economic values that are owned by or are under the control of the institution. They are of two kinds. The first is cash and that which can be converted into cash, such as investments and accounts receivable. The other type of asset is represented by costs incurred at an earlier date that have not yet been attributed to a given fiscal period. Examples

Source: Breneman, Leslie, & Anderson (1993). *ASHE Reader on Finance in High. Ed.* Ginn Press, pp. 465–491.

TABLE 41.1
Sample Educational Institution Balance Sheet June 30,19__ with Comparative Figures at June 30,19__

Assets			Liabilities and Fund Balances		
Current Funds	Current Year	Prior Year	Current Funds	Current Year	Prior Year
Unrestricted			**Unrestricted**		
Cash	$210,000	$110,000	Accounts payable	$125,000	$100,000
Investments	450,000	360,000	Accrued liabilities	20,000	15,000
Accounts receivable, less			Students' deposits	30,000	35,000
allowance of $18,000			Due to other kinds	158,000	120,000
both years	228,000	175,000	Deferred credits	30,000	20,000
Inventories, at lower of cost			Fund Balance	643,000	455,000
(first in, first out basis)			Total unrestricted	1,006,000	745,000
or market	90,000	80,000			
Prepaid expenses and					
deferred charges	28,000	20,000			
Total unrestricted	1,006,000	745,000			
Restricted			**Restricted**		
Cash	145,000	101,000	Accounts payable	14,000	5,000
Investments	175,000	165,000	Fund balances	446,000	421,000
Accounts receivable, less			Total restricted	460,000	426,000
allowance of $8,000			Total current funds	1,466,000	1,171,000
both years	68,000	160,000			
Unbilled charges	72,000	—			
Total restricted	460,000	426,000			
Total current funds	1,466,000	1,171,000			
Loan Funds			**Loan Funds**		
Cash	30,000	20,000	Fund balances		
Investments	100,000	100,000	U.S. government grants		
Loans to students, faculty, and			refundable	50,000	33,000
staff, less allowance of $10,000			University funds		
current year and $9,000			Restricted	483,000	369,000
prior year	550,000	382,000	Unrestricted	150,000	100,000
Due from unrestricted funds	3,000	—	Total loan funds	683,000	502,000
Total loan funds	683,000	502,000			
Endowment and Similar Funds			**Endowment and Similar Funds**		
Cash	100,000	101,000	Fund balances		
Investments	13,900,000	11,800,000	Endowment	7,800,000	6,740,000
			Term endowment	3,840,000	3,420,000
			Quasi-endowment—		
Total endowment and			unrestricted	1,000,000	800,000
similar funds	14,000,000	11,901,000	Quasi-endowment—		
			restricted	1,360,000	941,000
			Total endowment and		
			similar funds	14,000,000	11,901,000
Annuity and Life Income Funds			**Annuity and Life Income Funds**		
Annuity funds			Annuity Funds		
Cash	$ 55,000	$45,000	Annuities payable	$2,150,000	$2,300,000
Investments	3,260,000	3,010,000	Fund balances	1,165,000	755,000
Total annuity funds	3,315,000	3,055,000	Total annuity funds	3,315,000	3,055,000
Life income funds			Life income funds		
Cash	15,000	15,000	Income payable	5,000	5,000
Investments	2,045,000	1,740,000	Fund balances	2,055,000	1,750,000
Total life income funds	2,060,000	1,755,000	Total life income funds	2,060,000	1,755,000
Total annuity and life			Total annuity and life		
income funds	5,375,000	4,810,000	income funds	5,375,000	4,810,000
Plant Funds			**Plant Funds**		
Unexpended			Unexpended		
Cash	275,000	410,000	Accounts payable	10,000	—
Investments	1,285,000	1,590,000	Notes payable	100,000	—
Due from unrestricted			Bonds payable	400,000	—
current funds	150,000	120,000	Fund balances		
Total unexpended	1,710,000	2,120,000	Restricted	1,000,000	1,860,000
			Unrestricted	200,000	260,000
			Total unexpended	1,710,000	2,120,000

TABLE 41.1
(continued)

Assets			Liabilities and Fund Balances		
Current Funds	Current Year	Prior Year	Current Funds	Current Year	Prior Year
Renewals and Replacements			**Renewals and Replacements**		
Cash	5,000	4,000	Fund balances		
Investments	150,000	286,000	Restricted	25,000	180,000
Deposits with trustees	100,000	90,000	Unrestricted	235,000	200,000
Due from unrestricted			Total renewals and		
current funds	5,000	—	replacements	260,000	380,000
Total renewals and					
replacements	260,000	380,000			
Retirement of Indebtedness			**Retirement of Indebtedness**		
Cash	50,000	40,000	Fund balances		
Deposits with trustees	250,000	253,000	Restricted	185,000	125,000
Total retirement of indebtedness	300,000	293,000	Unrestricted	115,000	168,000
			Total retirement of		
			indebtedness	300,000	293,000
Investment in Plant			**Investment in Plant**		
Land	500,000	500,000	Notes payable	790,000	810,000
Land improvements	1,000,000	1,110,000	Bonds payable	2,200,000	2,400,000
Buildings	25,000,000	24,060,000	Mortgages payable	400,000	200,000
Equipment	15,000,000	14,200,000	Net investment in plant	38,210,000	36,540,000
Library books	100,000	80,000	Total investment in plant	41,600,000	39,950,000
Total investment in plant	41,600,000	39,950,000	Total plant funds	43,870,000	42,743,000
Total plant funds	43,870,000	42,743,000			
Agency Funds			**Agency Funds**		
Cash	50,000	70,000	Deposits held in custody		
Investments	60,000	20,000	for others	110,000	90,000
Total agency funds	110,000	90,000	Total agency funds	110,000	90,000

Source: *College & University Business Administration,* 4th ed. (Washington, DC: National Association of College and University Business Officers, 1982), pp. 456–457.

of this second type of asset are capital costs, depreciable equipment, buildings, inventories, prepaid expenses, and deferred charges.

There are also two kinds of liability accounts. The first represents amounts that are owed to organizations or individuals who are outside the institution itself. (An exception to this definition will be discussed later.) In general, liabilities represent amounts owed to others, including creditors, for a variety of reasons. Some liabilities may be amounts that are owed and must be paid in the near term or immediately. Other liabilities may be paid out over a period of many years. The second type of liability account is used to record deferred credits or deferred revenues. These liabilities represent amounts that have been collected in cash or whose collection is anticipated but for which an earnings process has not yet occurred. Until such a process begins, the institution carries these items as a liability.

The relationship between assets and liabilities or the difference between them produces the third kind of account, generally referred to as net worth, equity, or proprietorship. Net worth is also net assets, which represent the net difference between assets and related liabilities. In fund accounting the fund balance equals assets minus liabilities.

The accounting equation is the relationship among these three kinds of accounts and is expressed by the statement that assets minus liabilities equals net worth or by an algebraic transposition of that equation (i.e., assets equal liabilities plus net worth). Another way of interpreting the accounting equation is to state that equities are claims by an owner or creditor against assets.

Real and Nominal Accounts

The accounts used in the accounting system to record asset values, liability values, and net worth or fund balance values are referred to as real accounts. These balances carry forward from the beginning of the organization until its end or until the particular type of asset, liability, or net worth no longer exists. Nominal accounts, on the other hand, expire at the end of a given fiscal period (e.g., the fiscal year) and are created anew at the beginning of the next period. Such accounts—called income and expenses—classify the increases and decreases in net worth and provide more detailed information about the sources and uses of net worth throughout the year. For example, increases in net worth may result from sales, gifts, endowment income, or contributions to capital; decreases may reflect expenses or losses in investments, among other possibilities.

In most cases financial statements deal exclusively with either real accounts or nominal accounts (special types of reports may deal with elements of both at the same time). In examining financial statements it is helpful to remember that net worth or fund balances are changed by increases or decreases in assets or liabilities (i.e., by income and expenses).

The concept of double-entry bookkeeping is built on the accounting equation. Thus, for each economic event that is recorded there is a balanced set of entries to record the event (i.e., a debit and a credit). At all times the system must balance so that debits equal credits. The total of assets must likewise equal the total of liabilities and net worth in the system.

The accounting equation and the principles of real and nominal accounts underlie all accounting and apply to fund accounting as well as to other forms of accounting. The next section examines fund accounting and explains why that methodology is used in college and university accounting systems.

TYPES OF FUNDS

Restricted and Unrestricted Funds

Nonprofit organizations as a group often differ from profit-making enterprises in that they are the recipients of gifts, grants, contributions, and appropriations, which are restricted at the direction of the sources for particular purposes, functions, or activities. A donor, for example, may specify that a gift is to be used only for scholarships. This restriction is legally binding on the institution, which has no authority to use that money for any other purpose. That the institution may already have a scholarship program and that the gift would simply help to finance it

are irrelevant. Another example of a restriction is a donor's specification that only the income from investing the donation may be used.

Restrictions imposed by a donor differ in two important respects from self-imposed limitations established by the governing board or from other kinds of conditions that characterize the relationship between the donor and the grantee (but which are not restrictions). First, the restriction must be set forth in writing or must be related to a representation made in writing. Second, the language used in the written instrument must be restrictive. Restrictive language is characterized by words that indicate a command or a demand or that establish an absolute limitation. The law distinguishes between restrictive language and precatory language, which represents only a wish, a desire, or an entreaty (but which is not restrictive).

If conditions are documented in writing and if the language is appropriately restrictive, the restrictions cannot be changed by the institution acting alone. In some jurisdictions even the institution and the donor together may not change the restriction once the gift has been accepted with the restrictions imposed. The removal of a restriction or the redirection of the resources into a related activity can be accomplished only through a formal or an informal application of the doctrine of *cy pres*. (This procedure requires formal court proceedings and involves the state attorney general.)

Occasionally, ambiguous language is used in the instruments conveying the donation, and sometimes the original documentation is missing. Legal review is almost always required in such situations. Institutions seeking relief through the courts would, if successful, receive a declaratory judgment.

In summary, it is important to distinguish between those resources that are truly restricted and those that are not. *Cy pres* relates only to externally restricted funds and not to internally designated funds (such as those designated in the budget process). The maintenance of the distinction between these two categories is a paramount responsibility of the fund accounting system.

Resources received by institutions are labeled in several ways to indicate the nature of any pertinent restrictions.

Ownership vs. agency relationship. When an institution receives new monies, the first question is whether the resources actually belong to the institution. Funds that do not belong to the institution are called agency funds and represent assets held by the institution on behalf of others. Alternatively, agency funds represent liabilities for amounts due to outside organizations, students, or faculty that will be paid out on their instructions for purposes other than normal operations. Institutions have on occasion used the agency fund classification inappropriately for funds that officials would like to use outside the constraints of the budget process.

Restricted vs. unrestricted. If the monies received by the institution are indeed owned by the institution, the next question is whether the monies are restricted or unrestricted. As noted earlier, the specific nature of the restrictions must be clearly stated.

Expendable vs. nonexpendable. If the monies received by the institution are restricted, it must be determined whether the monies are expendable or nonexpendable. If the monies are expendable (i.e., can be spent), one must ask for what specific purpose, function, activity, or object. If the purpose or character of the expenditure is such that it is a part of normal operations, it is classified in a category that relates it to current operations. If, on the other hand, the restriction is such that the monies must be spent to acquire land, buildings, equipment, or other types of capital assets, the expenditure is classified as a part of plant funds.

Nonexpendable funds can be distinguished by several types of restrictions. For example, endowment funds cannot be spent. Rather, they must be invested, and only the income can be used. It should be noted that income from the endowment represents a new source of funds, and the nature of this money must be determined by the same series of questions outlined above. It is possible for a donor to restrict both the principal (i.e., the endowment monies) and the investment income.

Certain other funds cannot be spent but must be loaned to students or faculty. Under this arrangement the monies will be loaned, the borrowers will repay the loans, and the same resources will be reloaned to other borrowers.

A third nonexpendable fund is the annuity fund or life income fund. Here, the donor provides money to the institution with instructions to pay to an outside party for a period of time either a certain amount of money (in the case of an annuity fund) or the investment income (in the case of a life income fund).

All funds not restricted by the donor are by definition unrestricted. Generally, all unrestricted funds are to be used first as revenue for current operating purposes. A governing board may also designate unrestricted funds for long-term investments to produce income (in the manner of endowment funds), or for plant acquisition purposes (for which restricted funds are normally used).

Thus, certain unrestricted funds are intended for the same purpose as certain restricted funds. In the reporting of college and university financial matters, as evidenced in financial statements, funds that are either restricted or designated for similar types of activities are classified in a group that has a name indicating the purpose. However, within each one of these groups it is necessary to distinguish between those amounts that are in the group by reason of restrictions imposed by donors and those amounts that are in the group by reason of designation by a governing board.

SELECTED ACCOUNTING PRINCIPLES

Accounting principles are the standards that define how economic transactions are to be classified and reported. Recognition of proper accounting principles is important in establishing a college or university accounting system. Most institutions adhere to the accounting principles set forth by the American Institute of Certified Public Accountants (AICPA). These principles should be reflected in an institution's financial statement. When studying a financial statement that has been audited, one should see in the auditor's report a statement as to whether the financial statement has been prepared in accordance with generally accepted accounting principles. If the auditor notes an exception or denies that proper accounting principles have been followed, it will be difficult to evaluate the financial statement in a meaningful fashion.

Funds and Fund Groups

A fund is an accounting entity with a self-balancing set of accounts consisting of assets, liabilities, and a fund balance account, in addition to nominal accounts that measure increases and decreases in the fund balance. Separate funds are established to account for financial activity related to a particular restricted donation, source of restricted funds, or designated amount established by the governing board. These accounting entries are set up to insure the observance of restrictions imposed by donors and of limitations on the use of unrestricted funds that have been established by the governing board. In many cases, however, funds of similar designation and restriction are grouped together for reporting purposes and for purposes of efficient management. Often the assets of like kinds of funds are placed in one set of asset accounts. Similarly, liability accounts related to those assets may be merged. Nevertheless, there would still be a series of individual fund balances for which a separate accounting would have to be performed. The total of all such assets would equal the total of all such liabilities and the total of the fund balances to which they relate. This grouping together for accounting and reporting purposes yields what is termed a fund group. It is important to note that within each fund group it is necessary to continue to distinguish between the balance of funds that are unrestricted and those that are externally restricted. Within the restricted subgroup it is necessary to account for each separate restricted fund balance.

Accrual Basis of Accounting

Accrual-basis accounting is often defined in comparison to cash-basis accounting. In the latter the only transactions recorded are those in which cash comes into the organization or goes out. Thus, an asset or an increase in the fund balance would be recognized only when cash is collected. Similarly, the assets and fund balance would be reduced only when a cash payment is made. Almost nothing else would be accounted for, making the cash-basis of accounting rather unsatisfactory for most reporting and management purposes. Accrual-basis accounting was developed in response to this shortcoming in the cash-basis method. The accrual-basis recognizes fund balance increments (i.e., revenue) when the amount is earned. Expenses and other types of deductions are recognized when the goods or services have been used up. An asset is recognized as an amount that has been received and has continuing value (i.e., unexpired costs), although a payment may not have been made for this amount. The measurement of revenues and expenses is called the accrual basis of accounting because accruals are used to convert cash receipts into revenue and cash disbursements into expenses.

The objective of accrual-basis accounting is to provide a more satisfactory matching of revenues and other fund balance additions with expenses and other fund balance deductions in the accounting period to which the financial statements relate. In other words, the accrual basis attempts to determine the real economic impact of what has occurred during a given period of time rather than simply determining how much cash was received or disbursed.

Interfund Accounting

The concept of interfund accounting relates to maintaining the integrity and self-balancing characteristics of the individual funds. Problems arise, for example, when cash used for the benefit of one fund actually belongs to another fund. To illustrate, assume that an institution has a scholarship fund of $10,000 and has $10,000 in the bank for that fund. Also assume that in the institution's unrestricted current fund is another $10,000 that is available for any purpose. Assume that the institution makes a payment of $1,000 to a scholarship recipient out of the unrestricted current fund bank account, whereas the intent was to use the restricted scholarship fund. If the fund balance of the scholarship fund is reduced along with the amount of cash belonging to the unrestricted current fund, both funds would be unbalanced. That is, their assets (when examined separately) would not be equal to their liabilities and fund balances. In the fund that has made the disbursement (i.e., that has given up the cash), an asset account would be established representing the amount due from the fund that is ultimately to finance the activity. This arrangement puts the unrestricted current fund back in balance. In the restricted fund that is to be used for scholarships, a liability account would be established for the $1,000 paid on behalf of the restricted fund, and the fund balance would be charged the same amount. Again, the restricted fund would now be in balance and there would exist an inter-fund receivable and payable. The asset and liability would at some point be extinguished by a transfer of cash between the funds.

CHART OF ACCOUNTS

The chart of accounts in an accounting system is used to classify each transaction accounted for in the system, facilitating easy and accurate retrieval. It is based on (1) the accounting principles for proper classification of economic phenomena and (2) the reporting needs of management and external parties, calling for segregation of different kinds of transactions so that those transactions may later be aggregated and reported by type. . . .

Accounting systems in higher education usually involve both an alphabetical designation of the account name, which can be read, and a numerical or alpha-numeric designation of the account, which can be used for encoding purposes. This arrangement allows the system to work with a numerical or shortened reference rather than a long rational name.

It is important to remember that the purpose of the chart of accounts is to assist in the locating of discrete kinds of transactions. The only rules are those that make sense in terms of how much information and what kinds of categories should be reported. The information needs of many colleges and universities are the same in certain areas, particularly with regard to the production of basic financial statements.

TYPES OF FINANCIAL STATEMENTS

A college or university's financial statement is generally composed of four segments: (1) balance sheet; (2) statement of changes in fund balances; (3) statement of current fund revenues, expenditures, and other changes; and (4) footnotes to the above segments.

The balance sheet reflects the financial resources of the institution at a given time. The balance sheet contains the assets of the institution, the liabilities, and the fund balances. Thus, the status of the institution is generally expressed in terms of its real accounts. The assets can be viewed as the forms of the institution's financial resources, whereas the liabilities and fund balance are the sources.

The statement of changes in fund balances summarizes the activity within each group of funds during a specific fiscal period. This statement is comparable to the income statement and statement of changes in the stockholders' equity in the for-profit sector. For nonprofit organizations, however, the statement of changes in fund balances covers each set of funds.

The statement of current funds revenues, expenditures, and other changes is a detailed accounting of changes in the current funds column that are included in the statement of changes in fund balances. Sometimes this statement is referred to as the statement of changes in financial position. In fund accounting most useful information is already contained in the balance sheet and the statement of changes in fund balances, often making redundant the information contained in the statement of current funds revenues, expenditures, and other changes. On the other hand, there may be some activity that should be reported and has not been disclosed in any of the statements; this can often be taken care of by enhancing the statements with another presentation summarizing the changes in financial position or by adding footnotes to the financial statements. Footnotes summarize the significant accounting principles used to prepare the statements and provide other information essential to a full understanding of the institution's particular financial environment. No examination of an institution's financial statement is complete without a thorough perusal of the footnotes.

FINANCIAL STATEMENTS: A DETAILED EXAMINATION

Interrelationships of the Three Basic Statements

The balance sheet—a report as of a particular time—states all the financial resources for which the institution's governing board is responsible. In Table 41.2 the balance sheet has

TABLE 41.2

Sample Educational Institution Statement of Changes in Fund Balances Year Ended June 30, 19___

	Current Funds		Loan Funds	Endowment and Similar Funds	Annuity and Life Income Funds	Plant Foods			
	Unrestricted	Restricted				Unexpended	Renewals and Replacements	Retirement of Indebtedness	Investment in Plant
Revenues and other additions									
Unrestricted current fund revenues	7,540,000								
Expired term endowment—restricted						50,000			
State appropriations—restricted						50,000			
Federal grants and contracts—restricted		500,000							
Private gifts, grants, and contracts—restricted		370,000	100,000	1,500,000	800,000	115,000		65,000	15,000
Investment Income—restricted		224,000	12,000	10,000		5,000	5,000	5,000	
Realized gains on investments—unrestricted				109,000					
Realized gains on investments—restricted			4,000	50,000		10,000	5,000	5,000	
Interest on loans receivable			7,000						
U.S. government advances			18,000						
Expended for plant facilities (including $100,000 charged to current funds expenditures)									1,550,000
Retirement of indebtedness									220,000
Accrued Interest on sale of bonds								3,000	
Matured annuity and life income restricted to endowment				10,000					
Total revenues and other additions	7,540,000	1,094,000	141,000	1,679,000	800,000	230,000	10,000	78,000	1,785,000
Expenditures and other deductions									
Educational and general expenditures	4,400,000	1,014,000							
Auxiliary enterprises expenditures	1,830,000								
Indirect costs recovered		35,000							
Refunded to grantors		20,000							
Loan cancellations and write-offs			10,000						
Administrative and collection costs			1,000						
Adjustment of actuarial liability for annuities payable					75,000				
Expended for plant facilities (including noncapitalized expenditures of $50,000)						1,200,000	300,000		
Retirement of indebtedness								220,000	
Interest on indebtedness								190,000	
Disposal of plant facilities									115,000
Expired term endowments ($40,000 unrestricted, $50,000 restricted to plant)				90,000					
Matured annuity and life income funds restricted to endowment					10,000				
Total expenditures and other deductions	6,230,000	1,069,000	12,000	90,000	85,000	1,200,000	300,000	411,000	115,000
Transfers among funds—additions/(deductions)									
Mandatory:									
Principal and Interest	(340,000)							340,000	
Renewals and replacements	(170,000)						170,000		
Loan fund matching grant	(2,000)		2,000						
Unrestricted gifts allocated	(650,000)		50,000	550,000		50,000			
Portion of unrestricted quasi-endowment funds Investment gains appropriated	40,000			(40,000)					
Total transfers	(1,122,000)		52,000	510,000		50,000	170,000	340,000	
Net increase (decrease) for the year	188,000	25,000	181,000	2,099,000	715,000	(920,000)	(120,000)	7,000	1,670,000
Fund balance at beginning of year	455,000	421,000	502,000	11,901,000	2,505,000	2,120,000	380,000	293,000	36,540,000
Fund balance at end of year	643,000	446,000	683,000	14,000,000	3,220,000	1,200,000	260,000	300,000	38,210,000

Source: College & University Business Administration, 4th ed. (Washington, DC: National Association of College and University Business Officers, 1982), pp. 458–459.

columns for two dates (i.e., current year and prior year). The prior-year column is a point of reference and can be used as a standard to evaluate the current year's financial information. Note that for each category of funds, assets equal liabilities and fund balances for both the current year and the prior year.

The statement of changes in fund balances (Table 41.2) has a separate column for each fund group. The purpose of this statement is to show the gross additions to and gross deductions from each of the fund groups, to account for any amounts that may have been transferred from one fund group to another, to report the net change in fund balances for the year for each of the fund groups, and to show beginning balances (in order to account for ending balances).

It is worth examining the beginning and ending balances of the statement of changes in fund balances to trace their origins to the balance sheet. For example, at the bottom of the first column of Table 41.2, the beginning and ending fund balances of unrestricted current funds total $455,000 and $643,000, respectively. In the balance sheet (Table 41.1) these amounts appear on the liability side opposite the term "fund balance" under the heading "current unrestricted funds." The beginning balance on the statement of changes is the prior year's figure of $455,000. The ending figure is the current year's balance sheet figure of $643,000.

The balance sheet shows amounts for each of the fund balances for each of the fund groups. The statement of changes in fund balances reports all activity that resulted in changes in those fund balances during the year. For each different type of addition or deduction there is a separate line caption. Thus, within the accounting system there are separate classifications so that transactions may be reported separately in the statement. The statement of changes in fund balances addresses only the fund balances, not the assets or liabilities.

The statement of current funds, revenues, expenditures, and other changes covers the activity from the beginning to the end of the fiscal year and essentially expands on the information presented in summary fashion in the statement of changes in fund balances. It relates to current funds only and to transactions that have affected the fund balances of the current funds and has no relationship to assets or liabilities or to changes in funds other than current funds. In Table 41.3 the final numbers in each of the first two columns are the same as the net changes for the years that appear in the first two columns of the statement of changes, namely, $188,000 and $25,000, respectively.

The accrual-basis of accounting can lead to confusion when one examines the statement of current funds, revenues, expenditures, and other changes. As mentioned earlier, certain kinds of funds are provided to the institution with earmarks categorizing them as current operating activity. Accordingly, these funds are classified in the group called current restricted funds. When the amounts are received, they are accounted for as additions to those funds, and such additions are reported in the statement of changes in fund balances. The difference between those two kinds of transactions and any transfers produce the net change in fund balance for the year.

An examination of the statement of current funds, revenues, expenditures, and other changes reveals something a bit unusual in terms of revenues. This statement attempts to match pure revenues with expenditures and other transactions in order to derive a more meaningful report that applies the accrual-basis concept to operations for the year. However, in the accrual-basis of accounting one has not "earned" a current restricted fund until that fund has been expended for the purpose for which it was restricted (i.e., a revenue from current restricted funds does not exist until those funds have been expended). This is not unlike the deferred-credit concept in the for-profit sector, whereby a business may receive money from a customer in advance of having rendered the service. The receipt of such monies is treated as a deferred credit. As the services are rendered and the expenses incurred, these amounts are taken into revenue. This reporting convention gives the statement preparer a better basis for matching revenues and expenses, which is one of the objectives of the accrual basis of accounting. The potential confusion here, of course, is that these resources are treated as fund balances rather than as liabilities, as the for-profit sector would treat them. Thus, the two financial statements (Tables 41.2 and 41.3) seem to conflict.

The differences are reconciled by an adjustment made to the statement of current funds, revenues, expenditures, and other changes. The adjustment represents the difference between the additions to current restricted funds for the current year and the amounts earned and therefore reflected in revenue. In the figures under consideration, the adjustment for the current year is the difference between $1,094,000 of additions (Table 41.2) and $1,014,000 recognized as revenue (Table 41.3), or $80,000. However, the adjustment is

TABLE 41.3
Sample Educational Institution Statement of Current Funds Revenues,
Expenditures, and Other Changes Year Ended June 30, 19__

	Current Year			Prior-Year Total
	Unrestricted	Restricted	Total	
Revenues				
Tuition and fees	$2,600,000		$2,600,000	$2,300,000
Federal appropriations	500,000		500,000	500,000
State appropriations	700,000		700,000	700,000
Local appropriations	100,000		100,000	100,000
Federal grants and contracts	20,000	$375,000	395,000	350,000
State grants and contracts	10,000	25,000	35,000	200,000
Local grants and contracts	5,000	25,000	30,000	45,000
Private gifts, grants, and contracts	850,000	380,000	1,230,000	1,190,000
Endowment income	325,000	209,000	534,000	500,000
Sales and services of educational activities	190,000		190,000	195,000
Sales and services of auxiliary enterprises	2,200,000		2,200,000	2,100,000
Expired term endowment	40,000		40,000	
Other sources (if any)				
Total current revenues	7,540,000	1,014,000	8,554,000	8,180,000
Expenditures and mandatory transfers				
Education and general				
Instruction	2,960,000	489,000	3,449,000	3,300,000
Research 100,000	400,000	500,000	650,000	
Public service 130,000	25,000	155,000	175,000	
Academic support	250,000		250,000	225,000
Student services 200,000		200,000	195,000	
Institutional support	450,000		450,000	445,000
Operation and maintenance of plant	220,000		220,000	200,000
Scholarships and fellowships	90,000	100,000	190,000	180,000
Educational and general expenditures	4,400,000	1,014,000	5,414,000	5,370,000
Mandatory transfers for:				
Principal and interest	90,000		90,000	50,000
Renewals and replacements	100,000		100,000	80,000
Loan fund matching grant	2,000		2,000	
Total educational and general	4,592,000	1,014,000	5,606,000	5,500,000
Auxiliary enterprises				
Expenditures	1,830,000		1,830,000	1,730,000
Mandatory transfers for:				
Principal and interest	250,000		250,000	250,000
Renewals and replacements	70,000		70,000	70,000
Total auxiliary enterprises	2,150,000		2,150,000	2,050,000
Total expenditures and mandatory transfers	6,742,000	1,014,000	7,756,000	7,550,000
Other transfers and additions/(deductions)				
Excess of restricted receipts over transfers to revenues		45,000	45,000	40,000
Refunded to grantors		(20,000)	(20,000)	
Unrestricted gifts allocated to other funds	(650,000)		(650,000)	(510,000)
Portions of quasi-endowment gains appropriated	40,000		40,000	
Net increase in fund balances	188,000	25,000	213,000	160,000

Source: College & University Business Administration, 4th ed. (Washington, DC: National Association of College and University Business Officers, 1982), pp. 460–461.

affected by another transaction (indirect costs recovered), which reduces current restricted fund balances but is not reported as a current restricted fund expenditure because it is an application of such funds to current unrestricted fund revenues. The amount for indirect costs is shown in Table 41.2 as $35,000. The difference between $80,000 and $35,000 accounts for the $45,000 adjustment, reported in Table 41.3 as excess of restricted receipts over transfers to revenues. As a result, Table 41.3 does reconcile with the same changes in fund balance amounts shown in Table 41.2 for current restricted funds.

The real purpose of the statement of current funds, revenues, expenditures, and other changes, then, is to provide greater detail about the sources of current revenues and the functions for which current funds are expended. One of the basic accounting principles involved in this statement is that at this level of aggregation revenues are to be reported by source and expenditures by function. This statement also enables the reader to identify the total financial activity for current funds during the year. The totaling function is accomplished through the columnar presentation, whereby current unrestricted funds and current restricted funds, revenues, expenditures, and other changes are combined in a column labeled "total." For comparison a total for the preceding year is provided.

It is interesting to note that the statement of current funds, revenues, expenditures, and other changes can be considered in an entirely different manner. If, for example, it is remembered that the purpose of the statement is to disclose certain types of information, the format of the statement is less mysterious than it might be otherwise. Thus, if details as to the sources of revenue are reported on separate lines in the statement of changes in fund balances (instead of being reported as a single amount as in Table 41.2), it would be possible to eliminate the section on revenues in Table 41.3, which in turn could be used to provide only the required itemization of expenditures by function for the unrestricted, restricted, and total current funds. Then it would be necessary to tell the reader only how the current restricted fund expenditures were financed. That information could be shown either as a tabulation at the bottom of Table 41.3 or in the notes to the financial statements. The discussion above is intended to highlight the importance of the information content rather than the specific format.

The Balance Sheet—Current Funds

The balance sheet in Table 41.1 contains all of the assets, liabilities, and fund balances. They are arranged side-by-side in a horizontal fashion for each fund group throughout the statement. This format enables the reader to examine the assets and liabilities and fund balances of each fund group separately, and to see in juxtaposition with the current year's amounts the amounts that pertain to the previous year.

The first major fund group on the balance sheet is current funds. Within the current fund group a distinction is made between unrestricted current funds and restricted current funds. The current funds represent the results of operating inflows and outflows, or the "working capital" position of the institution. Assets and liabilities are the same as for a business if the account "due to other funds" is read as "due to other subsidiaries" and fund balances are understood as the working capital portion of the institution's total net worth, or equity. Assets represent the liquid resources or unexpired costs that pertain to day-to-day operations, and include such items as cash and investments.

The most frequently used basis for carrying assets is historical cost or, in the absence of cost, the fair value of the asset at date of donation. If the institution chooses, it may follow the market value method of accounting, whereby the carrying values for investments are changed from reporting date to reflect changes in current market values. If this procedure is followed, all investments of all funds must be accounted for in that fashion.

Another asset listed is accounts receivable. Principles of accounting hold that such assets should be stated at their realizable amounts. Statements often show total accounts receivable less an allowance for doubtful accounts, with the net amount reflecting the difference.

Inventories are unexpired costs representing economic values that will have utility in the succeeding year. Inventories of consumable supplies and supplies for resale are included in this category. Some inventories are carried at the lower of cost or market value.

Cost must be determined on some generally acceptable basis (e.g., first-in-first-out, average cost, or last-in-first-out).

Prepaid expenses and deferred charges include items such as prepaid insurance. Here, a policy premium covering more than one year has been paid in advance, with the premium portion that has expired during the year written off as an expense and the unexpired portion carried as the prepaid expense.

The liabilities of current funds are relatively straightforward. The accounts payable and accrued liabilities represent amounts that have to be paid to vendors and others who have provided goods and services to the institution and for which the institution has not yet made a cash disbursement. Student deposits represent amounts that may be applied against tuition at a later date or refunded, depending on the circumstances. Deferred credits represent amounts that have been received in advance by students during registration. After registration and the beginning of classes the credits would be treated as revenue, becoming an addition to the current unrestricted fund balance in that year. (This is another example of the accrual-basis of accounting at work.)

The fund balance is shown separately on the statement (in Table 41.1 it appears as a single amount). If the governing board designates portions of unrestricted current funds for particular current operating purposes, it may be desirable or necessary to subdivide the fund balance between the designated and undesignated portions. It should be kept in mind that a designation is not a restriction.

The assets and liabilities of the current restricted fund group are similar in nature to the assets and liabilities of unrestricted current funds. The same rules and practices apply to the valuation of investments and to accounts receivable. Unbilled charges are usually related to contracts and grants and are amounts that become accounts receivable when billed. A difference between current restricted and current unrestricted funds is that the plural term "fund balances" is used in the restricted current fund, whereas the singular term "fund balance" is used in the unrestricted current fund. Fund balances are grouped in current restricted funds, but because each fund requires separate accountability, the accounts of the institution must maintain a fund balance account for each

source and restriction. In the unrestricted current fund there is need for only one fund balance. Any others would simply be disaggregations of the larger fund balance. Such disaggregations reflect designations by the governing board.

The current fund balances, both unrestricted and restricted, are key reflections of the financial viability of the institutions. In addition to acting as working capital, the current unrestricted fund balance ($643,000 in Table 41.1) represents an accumulated reserve from operations, or retained receipts comparable to retained earnings in a business. This most flexible reserve provides both a cushion against future operating deficits and a source of seed money for desirable new programs of instruction, research, and public service.

The current restricted fund balance ($446,000 in Table 41.1) can be thought of as representing a backlog of future business already committed. The extent of management control over the timing and use of these restricted funds determines the flexibility and importance of the funds in long-range planning. Just as the adequacy of and trends in the amount of working capital and operating reserves in a business must be continually evaluated in terms of sales volume, market risks, inflation, and possible future product needs, so should current fund balances be measured in an educational institution.

The quantity and quality of current fund assets should be routinely reviewed and the offsetting liabilities should be subject to governing board policies and oversight. Excess cash should be temporarily invested in accordance with sound cash management principles. As competition for students intensifies, colleges and universities—particularly the more expensive independent institutions—are under increasing pressure to provide more student assistance. Receivables, which should be compared with operating volumes and with the receivables of peer institutions, are growing. Designing sound collection policies is becoming one of management's more pressing responsibilities.

Inventories ordinarily do not represent very large commitments in service institutions; however, any investment in inventories is not available for other purposes and therefore should be justified by relevant economic considerations. The timing of payments should be in accordance with sound disbursement policies and procedures to avoid either uneconomic prepayments or reputation-damaging late payments. Current fund borrowings should be monitored closely. Techniques for managing and protecting current operating assets and working capital funds include appropriate cash-flow forecasts, reports on the aging of receivables, and reviews of significant changes in inventory levels.

Sometimes an institution's governing board or administration will transfer what might be considered excessive operating reserves, or accumulated current fund balances, to the long-term capital fund groups, with due consideration for any applicable external restrictions. Such transfers would convert the affected operating reserves to invested reserves, possibly increasing investment income but reducing operating flexibility. Likewise, the governing board or administration may "retransfer" any fund balances previously transferred to the long-term capital fund groups back to the current fund balances for needed current expenditures or to make up deficiencies, again with due consideration for any applicable external restrictions. Any retransfer would convert invested reserves to operating reserves, possibly decreasing investment income but increasing operating resources.

Examples of such transfers are shown in the statement of changes in fund balances (Table 41.2) and are discussed in more detail below. While the mandatory transfers are required by debt instruments or third-party providers, the category "unrestricted gifts allocated" ($650,000) represents management transfers of operating funds to loan, endowment, and plant funds, and the "portion of unrestricted quasi-endowment funds investment gains appropriated" ($40,000) represents a management decision to transfer or retransfer invested funds back to operating funds. Both these transfers should be done in fulfillment of current budgeting and long-range financial plans.

Finally, agency funds represent amounts that are received by the institution but that do not belong to it. Generally, the assets would be cash and investments (see illustration in Table 41.1). The accountability for these funds is to outside parties; thus the balance sheet shows a liability for the amounts held for others by the institution. This is the only fund group that does not have a fund balance. In this case, assets equal liabilities and there are no net assets that belong to the institution. For this reason the statement of changes in fund balances has no column for the agency fund. Clearly, the institution must account to the various parties for whom it is holding funds by showing receipts and disbursements, but such information is not required in these highly aggregated, general financial statements.

Statement of Changes in Fund Balances

Long-term capital is required to finance assets that will not be recovered or converted to cash within the normal operating cycle. These assets include land, buildings, and equipment; student loans; and investments that provide an earnings base independent of current supporters. Long-term capital is provided directly by gifts and government appropriations, or indirectly through current operating funds.

Current operating funds may be expended for equipment and minor plant renovations directly from current accounts. Or, they may be transferred to the plant funds group, to be expended for debt service, major plant additions, and renewals and replacements, or to loan funds, or to endowment and similar funds, either as required by external agreements or benefactors (mandatory transfers) or as determined by the administration.

The statement of changes in fund balances (Table 41.2) shows these flows of long-term capital. Under "revenues and other additions," supporters with "private gifts, grants, and contract—restricted" directly provided $100,000 to loan funds, $1,500,000 to endowment and similar funds, $800,000 to annuity and life income funds, $115,000 to funds for spending on plant, $65,000 for retirement of indebtedness, and $15,000 of "in kind" plant or equipment. An expired term endowment provided $50,000 directly for plant, and state appropriations provided another $50,000 for plant expenditures. Investment income (restricted), realized gains on investments, and accrued interest provided a total of $16,000 to loan funds, $169,000 to endowment and similar funds, and $38,000 to the various plant funds.

Transfers among funds include the long-term capital provided through current operations. Mandatory amounts of $340,000 for debt service (principal and interest) and $170,000 for renewals and replacements were transferred to plant funds as required, while $2,000 was transferred to loan funds for a matching grant. In addition, nonmandatory transfers of unrestricted gifts, which might be considered current operating surpluses, were made by the administration in the amount of $650,000, of which $50,000 was designated for loan funds, $550,000 for quasi-endowment (i.e., amounts set aside by the governing board from expendable funds), and $50,000 for plant. Off-setting this was $40,000 as the "portion of unre-stricted quasi-endowment funds investment gains appropriated," or transferred from long-term invested funds to current use.

Loan Funds

The loan funds balance sheet reports the assets, liabilities, and fund balances of the institution's lending subsidiary, maintained principally to help students finance their education. This cap-ital in recent years has been provided increas-ingly by the federal government and accounted for variously as refundable advances (liabili-ties) or restricted grants (fund balances). Loan funds specifically provided by interested pri-vate benefactors become restricted fund bal-ances. The institution must often add matching funds, which then become restricted, or it may transfer unrestricted current funds to increase unrestricted loan resources. These inflows and certain outflows of loan funds, by refunds or write-offs, are illustrated in the statement of changes in fund balances.

Currently, the largest part of the loan fund group is represented by the National Defense Student Loan Program. The amount that has been received since inception, which has not been extinguished through the various kinds of write-off procedures available, must be shown as a separate amount owed to the federal gov-ernment. This amount is ultimately a liability, but it is accounted for as a fund balance to pro-vide an accounting of the increases and decreases in the amounts owed to the govern-ment that otherwise would not appear in the statement of changes in fund balances. It should be noted that when a loan is made, the asset classification changes but the fund bal-ance is not affected.

In Table 41.1 the cash in the loan fund group is to be loaned to students in the future. The investments represent unloaned resources that will be liquidated when needed for loan purposes. The largest asset category is "loans to students, faculty, and staff, less allowance . . ." Because these loans are not always repaid, they should be reported at their net realizable value as of the reporting date. The high default rate has led most colleges and universities to make an allowance in their financial statements for doubtful loans receivable.

The fund balance, as illustrated, is divided between refundable federal government grants ($50,000) and university funds (of which $483,000 is restricted and $150,000 is unre-stricted).

The statement of changes in fund balances shows the kinds of transactions that affect loan fund balances. Government monies are one source of change, as are private gifts and grants restricted to loan purposes. Investments of these funds yield income and gains that also produce changes in the fund balance. In the illustration (Table 41.2), there are no entries for the granting of loans or the repayment of loans because these result only in a change from one asset category to another (i.e., from cash to loans receivable). When the loans are collected, the repayments are deducted from loans receivable and are added back to cash.

Deductions from the loan funds on the statement of changes in fund balances include loan cancellations and write-offs, refunds to grantors, and charges for administrative and collection costs. Fund balances are also reduced by losses on investments of unloaned cash.

Endowment and Similar Funds

The assets of endowment and similar funds are mostly long-term investments. Other assets are uninvested cash, some receivables, and instruments that are convertible to cash. The investments of this fund group are so important that extensive comments concern-ing them generally appear in the notes to the financial statements.

To understand fully the nature of the invest-ments, two kinds of information must be in either the financial statements or the notes to the financial statements: (1) the basis of accounting (e.g., cost or current market value), and (2) the composition of the investment portfolio (e.g., stocks, bonds, mortgages). If accounting is done on a cost basis, information concerning the current market is required, as is information on the performance of the portfolio (e.g., income, gains, and losses in relation to cost and the market). In the example presented, note 1 to the financial statements illustrates the latter type of disclosure (Table 41.5).

1. Pooling of investments. The concept of investment pooling poses a special accounting problem with respect to investments of endowments and similar funds (and occasionally other fund groups). Though the ability to identify the assets belonging to each fund balance is important, as a practical matter totals are often recorded only for groups of funds. For example, in the current restricted fund group no attempt is normally made to keep separate cash balances for each current restricted fund. Instead, there is an amount that represents total cash for all current restricted funds. This total together with other assets equals the total amount of all fund balances in that group.

In a similar manner, the assets of the endowment and similar funds may be pooled to purchase investments for the benefit of all participating funds. This calls for a particular kind of accounting that treats the individual funds in the pool equitably in terms of the distribution of the income earned by the investments and the gains and losses from trading in investments.

The pooling concept involves the use of market values as the basis for calculating the distribution of participation units to each fund as it enters the pool. The procedure can be summarized as follows: the market value of all assets at the beginning of the pool is determined; units are given an arbitrary value and are then assigned to each fund depending on how much each has contributed to the pool. From that point on, the number of units held by each participating fund is used as a basis for distributing the income earned by the pooled assets and the gains and losses arising from the sale or exchange of investments held by the pool. When a new fund enters the pool, the current market value of the assets in the pool is recalculated, a new unit value (which may be higher or lower than the original value) is determined, and units are assigned to participants in the pool. This is also done when a fund is to be withdrawn from the pool. Note that the assignment of units to funds does not mean that the assets themselves are carried at market value. In fact, the assets may be carried at either market value or cost, depending on the accounting procedure adopted.

2. Types of funds. The fund balances in the endowment and similar funds group may represent several different conditions—for example, truly restricted funds such as endowment, or monies set aside by the governing board with the direction that they are not to be expended now (but may be in the future) and that only the income is to be used. Truly restricted funds are restricted in perpetuity, requiring the investment of the money contributed, and are referred to simply as endowment funds. The restriction on the second type of funds above has a terminal date or ends when a particular event takes place. This type of fund is known as term endowment. As of the balance sheet date, by law neither of these types of funds can be expended, and the governing board on its own cannot override that restriction.

By contrast, amounts set aside by the governing board from expendable funds can be expended and are therefore termed "quasi-endowment funds." Sometimes these funds are called "funds functioning as endowments." Both expressions are intended to indicate that the amounts so carried can be withdrawn from this category, restored to the current funds group from which they came, and expended for the purposes for which they were either restricted or designated. The fund group is labeled "endowment and similar funds" in recognition of the nature of quasi-endowment funds. If there are only endowment and term endowment monies, the fund group could be labeled "endowment funds."

3. Principal vs. income. An important consideration in accounting for endowments and similar funds is the need to

distinguish between principal and income. Endowment funds are peculiar in that legally they are not trust funds but are viewed as such for certain purposes. However, accounting conventions that have been established for endowment funds are patterned after trust fund concepts, which distinguish between principal and income. These conventions dictate that the principal be preserved for the benefit of the remainderment of the trust whereas the income is available for the life tenant or the income beneficiary. An institution with an endowment fund, however, is both the remainderment and the life tenant or income beneficiary. One might ask why this concept is important in this situation. One reason for the need to define income is that the donor has stated that the institution can use only the income. Second, there is another party at issue (i.e., the future generation of students who will benefit from the income). Thus, the governing board has the obligation to balance its investment policies so as not to stress either current income or growth to the advantage of a particular generation of students.

The distinction between principal and income determines what monies are accounted for in the endowment and similar funds group. Principal includes the original contribution (or any additional contributions in the case of endowment or term endowment) or, in the case of quasi-endowment, the original transfers (or any subsequent transfers) made by the governing board. Additions to principal would be realized gains or, in accounting for investments at market, the increases in the carrying value of the investments. Deductions would be losses on investments of the endowment fund.

Income gets its definition from tax law, and includes items such as dividends, interest, rents, and royalties. In the case of real estate, income is the rental income less the expenses of operation and depreciation. The income arising from the investment of endowment and similar funds is accounted for in unrestricted current funds if the income is unrestricted, or in the appropriate restricted fund if the income is restricted. A donor occasionally specifies that the restricted income is to be added to the principal. It is important to note that the addition of income to principal by direction of the governing board does not create a true (new) principal in endowment funds.

Some clarification of terms is in order. Restricted endowment funds are actually endowment funds, the income of which is restricted. Quasi-endowment funds are usually classified as unrestricted and only at times as restricted. Unrestricted quasi-endowment funds are amounts that have been transferred from unrestricted current funds. Restricted quasi-endowment funds are established from restricted current funds set aside for investment (only the income is to be used). The accounting for gains, losses, and income of quasi-endowments follows the same rules as the accounting for true endowments; that is, gains and losses are accounted for as part of the principal of the quasi-endowment fund while the income is accounted for in unrestricted current funds (if the quasi-endowment is restricted).

4. Total-return concept. The total-return concept—a relatively new development—eases restrictions on distinguishing between ordinary income and gains. Its intent is to encourage institutions to invest in growth stocks.

Many states have recently enacted laws patterned after a model law that prescribes how investments of institutions should be managed. Under this law it is legally permissible to use a portion of the gains of true endowment funds for the same purposes as ordinary income is used. (It was always possible for the gains of quasi-endowment funds to be so used.) In most states a portion of the gains may now be transferred from the endowment fund. Normally, there are requirements that such transfers can be made only in the face of gains (i.e., it is not possible to make a transfer that would reduce the fund balance below its historical contributed value).

The total-return concept is the means of determining how much of these gains will be used. First, the total earnings potential of the portfolio is estimated (total return is equal to the ordinary income or yield, plus net gains). A spending rate is then calculated that is sufficiently lower than the total-return earnings rate to ensure that the endowment portfolio is supplemented enough to allow for growth (or, at minimum, to compensate for the ravages of inflation). The spending rate is financed first from ordinary income. If the ordinary income is not sufficient to achieve the spending rate, the difference is financed by means of a transfer from gains. In Table 41.2 the transfer of $40,000, shown as "portion of unrestricted quasi-endowment funds investment gains appropriated," represents the amount necessary to cover the spending rate.

Annuity and Life Income Funds

Annuity and life income funds, which are trust funds, are a special group of invested funds temporarily committed to supporting donor-designated beneficiaries (i.e., for the lifetime of the beneficiaries, or until specific time periods have expired, after which the remaining funds become institutional capital, operating or long-term, unrestricted or restricted, depending on the agreements with the donors).

This fund group is subdivided into annuity funds and life income funds. If the amounts of such funds are relatively insignificant, they may be reported as a subgroup within the endowment and similar funds group. The assets are cash and investments in other assets convertible to cash. The objective of these assets is to produce income.

The distinction between the two kinds of funds is as follows: in an annuity fund a fixed amount is established by the donor and must be paid out even if the ordinary income from investment of the fund is not adequate for the purpose. For this reason, in the payment of an annuity an institution may incur a liability greater than the amount of the income. In this case some of the original principal may have to be paid back. Thus, annuity funds are accounted for through a liability account that expresses the current value of all future payments that must be made, taking into consideration as well the future earnings. Any excess of the asset value over this liability is the fund balance. Periodically, the liability is reevaluated with regard to the estimated remaining life of the annuitant. The liability is then adjusted, with a corresponding adjustment made in the fund balance.

For a life income fund there is an obligation either to pay only the income earned by the specific investments of the fund or to pay a rate of return earned by a group of funds. Because only the income that has been earned is paid out, the obligation is limited and no liability exists as with the annuity fund.

Of the $2,505,000 shown as annuity and life income fund balances at the beginning of the year in the statement of changes in fund balances, only $10,000 matured and, as a restricted amount, moved to endowment for institutional use. A total of $800,000 was received under new agreements, and an additional obligation of $75,000 in actuarial liability was recorded, resulting in ending fund balances of $3,220,000.

The subject of annuity life income funds involves a number of rather complex tax, accounting, and legal issues. In many states annuity funds are regulated as forms of insurance and are subject to jurisdiction of the state insurance regulatory body (e.g., reserve deposits may be required).

Plant Funds

Colleges and universities, as distinct from for-profit enterprises and some nonprofit-oriented ones such as hospitals, have traditionally segregated their plant funds accounting and have generally ignored depreciation. The reason is that most plant funds are originally given or appropriated as restricted or, if not, have been so irrevocably committed to fixed assets that they will never be available for any other purpose. If the resulting plant has been donated, the institution cannot very easily justify charging for depreciation or expecting customers to pay for something that was given in the first place to help those customers.

On the other hand, as shown earlier, some colleges and universities not only make capital expenditures out of current operating accounts but also transfer operating funds to plant for debt repayments and plant renewals and replacements, which could be considered a flow of depreciation-like expenses. The flow of funds into and out of plant accounts and the resulting plant assets and fund balances, or equity, are important in the management and protection of that part of the institution's long-term capital.

Direct external contributions to plant funds and amounts of current operating funds transferred to plant during the fiscal year are shown in the statement of changes in fund balances.

At the top section of that statement (Table 41.2), $230,000 in new funds was added directly to unexpended plant funds from various sources. Under the transfers section at the bottom, $50,000 in unrestricted gifts was allocated by administrative decision from current to plant funds. Out of these receipts and the prior unexpended balance of $2,120,000, a total of $1,200,000 was expended for plant facilities (under "expenditures and other deductions" in the middle section of the statement), leaving an unexpended balance at the end of the year of $1,200,000 for future plant needs.

Similarly, $10,000 in new funds was received directly for renewals and replacements and $170,000 was transferred from current funds under third-party requirements (mandatory). Out of these receipts and the beginning fund balance of $380,000, a total of $300,000 was expended for plant facilities, leaving an ending balance of $260,000 for future renewals and replacements. Retirement of indebtedness received $78,000 in new funds from external sources and $340,000 in mandatory transfers from current operations for principal and interest. Out of those inflows and the $293,000 beginning balance, the institution's debt service obligations on its plant were fulfilled (under "expenditures and other deductions" in the middle of the statement), and $300,000 in debt service funds remained for the future.

The last column shows the changes in the institution's net investment, or equity, in its physical facilities (i.e., in its accumulated historical plant cost less associated liabilities). Of the year's additions to net investment in plant, $15,000 was from gifts in kind, $1,550,000 from expenditures by the other plant fund groups and from current funds, and $220,000 from retirement of indebtedness. During the period, $115,000 of plant facilities was disposed of, for a new addition of $1,670,000 and an ending balance of $38,210,000.

Beginning plant fund balances totaled $39,333,000. With all the above additions and deductions, the ending plant fund balances, or the equity in all plant funds, increased only $637,000, to a new total of $39,970,000. It should be noted that only $1,460,000 of the most flexible unexpended and renewal and replacement funds remained; there had been $2,500,000 at the beginning of the period. The

difference was committed irrevocably to "bricks and mortar," or equipment.

Many donors, faculty members, students, and trustees do not realize that depreciation, or the cost of wear and tear on physical facilities, is not usually accounted for in tuition and fee charges or in the expenditures of colleges and universities.

In the statement of changes in fund balances (Table 41.2), the total of current operating funds made available for plant capital includes, under "revenues and other additions," $100,000 (as stated in the parenthetical note) and $220,000 for "retirement of indebtedness" (not interest), and, under "transfers among funds," $170,000 for renewals and replacements and $50,000 "allocated" to plant. Amounts funded from current operations, but really expended for plant, could be considered capital expenditures in lieu of depreciation. In the year illustrated, this would represent only 1.35 percent of the total investment in buildings and equipment, based on the balance sheet amount of $41,600,000 in Table 41.1.

The sample institution obviously depends heavily on funds from external sources for plant maintenance as well as plant additions. Unfortunately, externally restricted funds are more likely to be given for additions than for preservation of current physical facilities. Over time, this can result in buildings and equipment deterioration that is not recognized in operating statements or balance sheet valuations.

Several comments can be made about the four subgroups of the plant fund group.

1. Unexpended. Unexpended plant funds arise from restricted grants, gifts, and appropriations that can be used only for the acquisition of plant. In the sample institution's statement of changes in fund balances (Table 41.2), unrestricted gifts were allocated by the governing board for this purpose. This $50,000 nonmandatory transfer will be accounted for in the unrestricted portion of the balances of unexpended plant funds.

When an expenditure of these funds is made, there is (1) a reduction in the fund balance and in cash, and (2) an equal increase in the plant funds subgroup labeled "investment in plant," where the cost of the asset acquired

Sample Educational Institution Summary of Significant Accounting Policies June 30, 19__

The significant accounting policies followed by Sample Educational Institution are described below to enhance the usefulness of the financial statements to the reader.

Accrual Basis

The financial statements of Sample Educational Institution have been prepared on the accrual basis except for depreciation accounting as explained in notes 1 and 2 to the financial statements. The statement of current funds revenues, expenditures, and other changes is a statement of financial activities of current funds related to the current reporting period. It does not purport to present the results of operations or the net income or loss for the period as would a statement of income or a statement of revenues and expenses.

To the extent that current funds are used to finance plant assets, the amounts so provided are accounted for as (1) expenditures, in the case of normal replacement of movable equipment and library books; (2) mandatory transfers, in the case of required provisions for debt amortization and interest and equipment renewal and replacement; and (3) transfers of a non-mandatory nature for all other cases.

Fund Accounting

In order to ensure observance of limitations and restrictions placed on the use of the resources available to the Institution, the accounts of the Institution are maintained in accordance with the principles of "fund accounting." This is the procedure by which resources for various purposes are classified for accounting and reporting purposes into funds that are in accordance with activities or objectives specified. Separate accounts are maintained for each fund; however, in the accompanying financial statements, funds that have similar characteristics have been combined into fund groups. Accordingly, all financial transactions have been recorded and reported by fund group.

Within each fund group, fund balances restricted by outside sources are so indicated and are distinguished from unrestricted funds allocated to specific purposes by action of the governing board. Externally restricted funds may only be utilized in accordance with the purposes established by the source of such funds and are in contrast with unrestricted funds over which the governing board retains full control to use in achieving any of its institutional purposes.

Endowment funds are subject to the restrictions of gift instruments requiring a perpetuity that the principal be invested and the income only be utilized. Term endowment funds are similar to endowment funds except that upon the passage of a stated period of time or the occurrence of a particular event, all or part of the principal may be expended. While quasi-endowment funds have been established by the governing board for the same purposes as endowment funds, any portion of quasi-endowment funds may be expended.

All gains and losses arising from the sale, collection, or other disposition of investments and other noncash assets are accounted for in the fund which owned such assets. Ordinary income derived from investments, receivables, and the like is accounted for in the fund owning such assets, except for income derived from investments of endowment and similar funds, which income is accounted for in the fund to which it is restricted or, if unrestricted, as revenues in unrestricted current funds.

All other unrestricted revenue is accounted for in the unrestricted current fund. Restricted gifts, grants, appropriations, endowment income, and other restricted resources are accounted for in the appropriate restricted funds. Restricted current funds are reported as revenues and expenditures when expended for current operating purposes.

Other Significant Accounting Policies

Other significant accounting policies are set forth in the financial statements and the notes thereto.

Source: *College & University Business Administration*, 4th ed. (Washington, DC: National Association of College and University Business Officers, 1982), pp. 462–463.

and the increase in net investment in plant are recorded.

Borrowings are an important source of funding for capital outlay. Monies borrowed for acquisition of new plant and equipment are accounted for in this unexpended plant funds subgroup. When the borrowed money is spent, the charge is against the liability account rather than the fund balance. In the investment in plant subgroup the credit is not to net investment in plant but to the reestablishment of a liability.

Construction in progress may be accounted for in unexpended plant funds until the project is complete. Accountability is then established in the investment in plant subgroup. The procedure most commonly followed is to remove the accountability for construction in progress from the unexpended subgroup as quickly as expenditures are made and to carry the construction in progress in the investment in plant subgroup.

2. Renewals and replacements. This subgroup represents monies set aside to renew or replace plant assets presently in use. Here, too, the fund balances (Table 41.2) are subdivided between restricted and unrestricted. One of the sources of renewal and replacement funds is a portion of the mandatory transfer ($170,000 in Table 41.2); when mandatory transfers are received, they are classified as restricted funds. The assets (Table 41.1) consist of cash, investments, and amounts of money that have been turned over to a trustee in accordance with an indenture. These assets ($100,000) are classified as deposits with trustees. Expenditure of these monies results in the reduction of assets and fund balances in this subgroup. Simultaneously, an equal amount is recorded as an increase in net investment in plant and in the investment in plant subgroup. These expenditures often do not result in the acquisition of a capitalizable asset. The amount of such expenditures not capitalized should be disclosed, as illustrated in the parenthetical note on the caption "expended for plant facilities" in the statement of changes in fund balances. (The note states "including noncapitalized expenditures of $50,000.")

3. Retirement of indebtedness. Funds for this subgroup may come from contributions or grants that are made for this explicit purpose and are restricted. (This is the case in the sample institution.) Most frequently, the monies for this subgroup come from a mandatory transfer (note the $340,000 shown in the transfer section of the statement of changes in fund balances). Amounts so received are classified as restricted fund balances. If the governing board sets aside excess funds for the retirement of indebtedness, such amounts in excess of what is required would be nonmandatory transfers and would be classified as unrestricted. Funds for retirement of indebtedness are used to meet two kinds of obligations: (1) interest expense, which should be shown separately (see the $190,000 deduction), and (2) amortization of the debt (see the $220,000 deduction). Amortization of the debt results in another set of entries in the investment in plant subgroup. In Table 41.1 there would be a reduction of the liability for bonds payable equal to the debt amortization payment made in the retirement of the indebtedness funds, and there would be a corresponding credit for increase to the net investment in plant of $220,000. Thus, as debt is reduced the equity in net assets is increased.

4. Investment in plant. The assets of this subgroup consist of the carrying values of land improvements, buildings, equipment, library books, museum collections, and other similar capital holdings with a long-term life. Some of these are depreciable.

These assets are to be carried at their historical cost until disposed of. In earlier years some institutions carried such assets at some other amount (e.g., periodic appraisal value), either out of preference or because the original cost records had been lost or destroyed. When historical cost information is not available, it is permissible for an institution to obtain a professional estimate of the historical costs and to use the estimate as the basis for reporting.

Rules must be established by the institution to determine when a particular expenditure results in the acquisition of a capital asset. For example, items of movable equipment should be capitalized, provided they have a significant value and that they have a useful life that extends beyond at least a year. (Otherwise the items do not have capital value.) The value thresholds vary widely from institution to institution. The Cost Accounting

Standards Board established costing rules for all contractors employing federal funds and set certain limits beyond which an expenditure is classified as a capital addition. Another rule must be made to determine when a renovation becomes a capital asset. For example, a minor renovation probably has little value associated with it and would not be considered a capitalizable asset. On the other hand, a renovation that extended the life of the asset or permitted an entirely new use of an existing facility will probably be capitalized. Finally, new assets are added to the carrying values of the asset section of this subgroup, and assets that have been sold, destroyed, stolen, lost, or otherwise eliminated from the possession of the institution should be removed from the records (i.e., their carrying values should be removed).

If debt is incurred by the institution to finance working capital, it should not be carried in the plant fund but rather as a liability of current funds. This rule holds even though plant assets may be pledged as collateral against the loan. The reader of financial statements needs to know a great deal about the liabilities of plant funds and other liabilities of a long-term nature that may appear in other fund groups. Some disclosure requirements in this regard are therefore illustrated in the notes to the financial statements (see Table 41.5).

The fund balance of the investment in plant subgroup is referred to as net investment in plant. It is not classified as restricted or unrestricted because it is simply the accountability for the net asset values carried in this section. No further future use is intended. Thus, any restrictions that may have been imposed on the funds used to finance these assets generally have been met. There are, however, some instances of gifts that carry restrictions of a second-generation nature. For example, the initial restrictions may require that the funds be used for the acquisition of a building. An additional restriction might require that, in the event the building is later sold, the proceeds of the sale be used for a replacement building. This situation is rare, however.

In the statement of changes in fund balances (Table 41.2), increases in the net investment in plant arise from the expenditure of unexpended plant funds and renewal and replacement funds. Increases also arise from debt reductions (reflected in the decrease in funds for the retirement of indebtedness) and from contributions-in-kind such as a building, land, or equipment.

Decreases in the net investment in plant represent the elimination from the capital assets inventory of those assets that are retired, sold, disposed of, or destroyed. When such assets are eliminated, the total carrying value of the asset is deducted from the asset category and from the net investment in plant. Any cash proceeds received as a result of this retirement are taken in the unexpended plant fund, and, in the absence of any of the secondary types of restrictions mentioned earlier, are classified as an addition to the unrestricted portion of unexpended plant funds. Thus, the net gain or loss from the sale or disposal of the capital asset does not appear separately. Another major deduction would be the depreciation of capital assets (if such a practice is followed).

Net investment in plant can increase for a reason linked to the peculiar operations of colleges and universities. Many institutions include in the operating budgets of the various departments a provision for minor items of equipment. In some cases there is a policy of equipment replacement with respect to certain types of assets. For example, typewriters may be replaced on a scheduled basis. The amount that will be expended annually for this purpose is budgeted in that department. Therefore, the expenditure of current funds for this purpose becomes part of the functional expenditures set forth in the statement of current funds revenues, expenditures, and other changes and in the statement of changes in fund balances for unrestricted or restricted current funds. Another kind of capital outlay that might be financed in a similar manner from current funds expenditures is library books. These expenditures of current funds for the replacement of capital assets are reported first as expenditures of current funds, and are then picked up as assets and as additions to the fund balance of the investment in plant subgroup. In the sample institution $100,000 charged to current fund expenditures is also added to net investment in plant.

TABLE 41.5
Sample Educational Institution Notes to Financial Statements June 30, 19__

1. Investments exclusive of physical plant are recorded at cost; investments received by gift are carried at market value at the date of acquisition. Quoted market values of investments (all marketable securities) of the funds indicated were as follows:

	Current Year	Prior Year
Unrestricted current funds	$510,000	$390,000
Restricted current funds	180,000	165,000
Loan funds	105,000	105,000
Unexpended plant funds	1,287,000	1,600,000
Renewal and replacement funds	145,000	285,000
Agency funds	60,000	20,000

Investments of endowment and similar funds and annuity and life income funds are composed of the following:

	Carrying Value	
	Current Year	Prior Year
Endowment and similar funds:		
Corporate stocks and bonds (approximate market, current year $15,000,000 prior year $10,900,000)	$13,000,000	$10,901,000
Rental properties—less accumulated depreciation, current year $500,000 prior year $400,000	900,000	899,000
	13,900,000	11,800,000
Annuity funds:		
U.S. bonds (approximate market, current year $200,000, prior year $100,000)	200,000	110,000
Corporate stocks and bonds (approximate market, current year $3,070,000, prior year $2,905,000)	3,060,000	2,900,000
	3,260,000	3,010,000
Life income funds:		
Municipal bonds (approximate market, current year $1,400,000, prior year $1,340,000)	1,500,000	1,300,000
Corporate stocks and bonds (approximate market, current year $650,000, prior year $400,000)	545,000	440,000
	2,045,000	1,740,000

Assets of endowment funds, except nonmarketable investments of term endowment having a book value of $200,000 and quasi-endowment having a book value of $800,000, are pooled on a market value basis, with each individual fund subscribing to or disposing of units on the basis of the value per unit at market value at the beginning of the calendar quarter within which the transaction takes place. Of the total units each having a market value of $15.00, 600,000 units were owned by endowment, 280,000 units by term endowment, and 120,000 units by quasi-endowment at June 30, 19__.

The following tabulation summarizes changes in relationships between cost and market values of the pooled assets:

	Pooled Assets		Net Gains (Losses)	Market Value per Unit
	Market	Cost		
End of year	$15,000,000	$13,000,000	$2,000,000	$15.00
Beginning of year	10,900,000	10,901,000	(1,000)	12.70
Unrealized net gains for year			2,001,000	
Realized net gains for year			159,000	
Total net gains for year			$2,160,000	$2.30

The average annual earnings per unit, exclusive of net gains, were $.56 for the year.

TABLE 41.5
(continued)

2. Physical plant and equipment are stated at cost at date of acquisition or fair value at date of donation in the case of gifts, except land acquired prior to 1940, which is valued at appraisal value in 1940 at $300,000. Depreciation on physical plant and equipment is not recorded.

3. Long-term debt includes: bonds payable due in annual installments varying from $45,000 to $55,000 with interest at 5–7/8%, the final installment being due in 19__, collateralized by trust indenture covering land, buildings, and equipment known as Smith dormitory carried in the accounts at $2,500,000, and pledged net revenue from the operations of said dormitory; and mortgages payable due in varying amounts to 19__ with interest at 6%, collateralized by property carried in the accounts at $800,000 and pledged revenue of the Student Union amounting to approximately $65,000 per year.

4. The Institution has certain contributory pension plans for academic and nonacademic personnel. Total pension expense for the year was $350,000, which includes amortization of prior service cost over a period of 20 years. The Institution's policy is to fund pension costs accrued, including periodic funding of prior years' accruals not previously funded. The actuarially computed value of vested benefits as of June 30, 19__ exceeded net assets of the pension fund by approximately $300,000.

5. Contracts have been let for the construction of additional classroom buildings in the amount of $3,000,000. Construction and equipment are estimated to total $5,000,000, which will be financed by available resources and an issue of bonds payable over a period of 40 years amounting to $4,000,000.

6. All interfund borrowings have been made from unrestricted funds. The amounts due to plant funds from current unrestricted funds are payable within one year without interest. The amount due to loan funds from current unrestricted funds is payable currently.

7. Pledges totaling $260,000, restricted to plant fund uses, are due to be collected over the next three fiscal years in the amounts of $120,000, $80,000, and $60,000 respectively. It is not practicable to estimate the net realizable value of such pledges.

Source: College & University Business Administration, 4th ed. (Washington, DC: National Association of College and University Business Officers, 1982), pp. 463–466.

Statement of Current Funds Revenues, Expenditures, and Other Changes

Revenues

The sources of revenue include tuition and fee income; appropriations received from federal, state, and local government sources; grants and contracts from these same sources; private gifts, grants, and contracts; endowment income (i.e., income generated by the investments of endowment and similar funds); and sales and services of educational departments as well as sales and services of auxiliary enterprises (see Table 41.3). The sales and services of a hospital associated with the institution would be shown separately. There may be certain other institutional activities rendering unique services that would be separately accounted for, or accounted for as a separate source.

All unrestricted resources that are earned by the institution or come into the institution for the first time are accounted for initially as unrestricted current fund revenues. By contrast, all restricted amounts are accounted for initially in another fund group depending on the nature of the restriction.

Expenditures

Expenditures are categorized according to the major functions of the institution (e.g., instruction, research, public service). Auxiliary enterprises and hospital expenditures are shown separately.

Mandatory transfers are shown on the statement of current funds, revenues, expenditures, and other changes, together with, but separate from, the current fund expenditures. The transfers are divided according to their relation to the educational and general programs of the institution, to auxiliary enterprises, or to a hospital. On the statement of changes in fund balances, mandatory transfers are shown in the transfers section.

Mandatory Transfers

In the example (Table 41.3) a mandatory transfer represents an amount of cash to be transferred from the unrestricted current fund. It will go to that restricted fund for which the transfer is made. In most cases the transfer is mandated by a debt instrument (e.g., a bond indenture, which requires the periodic setting aside of funds to cover principal repayment), by interest expenses, and by the need to accumulate certain reserves for renewal and replacement. These required amounts are transferred to, accounted for in, and expended from the plant fund group. Through the transfer the amounts are deducted from current funds. In this example the amounts deducted are unrestricted, but when they are accounted for in the plant fund they are classified as restricted amounts because they are placed there by reason of the legally binding instrument.

Another mandatory transfer illustrated in the example is the matching requirement of the National Defense Student Loan program. The loan fund matching requirement in this example is being financed from the unrestricted current fund, and the mandatory transfer is to the loan fund group, where the amount transferred would have to be classified as a restricted balance.

Nonmandatory Transfers

These transfers are discretionary in nature and are carried out by the governing board. Generally, they are amounts that are unrestricted and are shifted from one major fund group to another to reflect designations by the board. When unrestricted current funds are transferred on a nonmandatory basis to another fund group, it is imperative that the label "unrestricted" be carried along so that when it appears in the other group the reader knows that the amount transferred can be reversed. (Mandatory transfers, once made in accordance with the bond indenture, can never be reversed because they must be used exclusively to serve the debt.)

Other Changes

One such change is the accounting for indirect cost recovery from funding sources. The primary source of this kind of cost recovery is fed-

eral funds that are used to finance various sponsored research, training, and other activities. The source of recovery becomes the revenue source used to account for the amount of indirect cost recovery. This accounting is difficult in that indirect costs are part of the total grant received by an institution. This total grant is first accounted for as an addition to a restricted current fund. The indirect cost recovery, however, is not viewed as an expenditure of a restricted fund but rather as an allocation of that amount into unrestricted current fund revenue for the purpose of reimbursing the institution. Two actions must be taken: (1) the amount must be deducted from the fund balance in restricted current funds (this can be seen as a separate line on the statement of changes), and (2) the amount must be recorded as revenue in unrestricted current funds. Although this amount is not separately labeled, it can be traced. In the federal, state, and local grants and contracts amounts in the unrestricted column of the revenue statement (Table 41.3), these three figures total $35,000, which is equal to the amount of indirect cost recovery deducted from the current restricted fund balances under expenditures and other deductions in Table 41.2. Another kind of deduction that is shown separately in both statements (in the amount of $20,000) is the refunding to a grantor of an unspent amount of a current restricted fund.

All revenues, additions, expenditures, and mandatory and nonmandatory transfers collectively yield the net change in fund balances for the year. These amounts must be shown at the bottom of the statement of current funds revenues, expenditures, and other changes, and also near the bottom of the statement of changes of fund balances (just before the fund balances themselves).

Encumbrances

An encumbrance is a commitment to pay for goods or services when such are received. The encumbrance is accounted for as a reduction of available funds (i.e., as a commitment), but must at all times be distinguished from true liabilities. True liability exists once goods or services have been received. In many cases that liability may result in the incurrence of an expense (i.e., when a value is carried forward as unexpired costs, it becomes an asset). Therefore, neither encumbrances that are not true liabilities as of the reporting date nor outstanding unliquidated encumbrances are included in the statement. If the latter are reported at all, they are shown either as a segregation of the fund balance to which they relate or as amounts disclosed in the notes to the financial statements.

Notes to Financial Statements

The purpose of these notes (see Table 41.5) is to provide further disclosure of key information that is considered necessary according to generally accepted accounting principles for colleges and universities. For example, some notes for the sample institution relate to such matters as the composition, market value, and performance of investments; outstanding commitments in the area of major items of construction; obligations under pension plans; and details concerning liabilities for short and long-term debt.

The nature and the means of repayment of any significant interfund receivables must be disclosed in the notes to the financial statements. If the interfund receivable cannot be collected from the owing fund, consideration must be given to making a permanent transfer (thereby eliminating the interfund receivable and payable).

In their financial statements many nonprofit organizations, including a number of colleges and universities, record pledges receivable as assets and as accountabilities. However, many institutions document pledges or have relationships with potential donors such that it is not possible to determine the net realizable value of outstanding pledges. In those circumstances uncollected pledges are not included in the basic financial statements, though all significant pledges must be disclosed in the notes, as illustrated in the case of the sample institution.

FOR FURTHER READING

Easy-to-understand pamphlets on the interpretation of financial statements are distributed by a number of stockbrokerages. One of the best is offered by Merrill Lynch. Although these documents address the for-profit sector, many of the principles of accounting are relevant to the nonprofit sector as well.

A good introduction to fund accounting is provided by Robert N. Anthony and Regina E. Herzlinger, *Management Control in Nonprofit Organizations*, rev. ed. (Homewood, IL: Richard D. Irwin, Inc., 1980). For those readers willing to tackle a technical discussion of accounting, a thorough text is Ray M. Powell, *Accounting Procedures for Institutions* (Notre Dame, IN: University of Notre Dame Press, 1978). A good overview of the technical aspects of institutional accounting is provided by *College & University Business Administration*, 4th ed. (Washington, DC: National Association of College and University Business Officers, 1982).

This chapter is a revision of material contained in *Financial Responsibilities of Governing Boards of Colleges and Universities* (Washington, DC: Association of Governing Boards of Universities and Colleges and National Association of College and University Business Officers, 1979), and *Conference for Women Administrators: Financial Management of Colleges and Universities* (Washington, DC: National Association of College and University Business Officers and Committee for the Concerns of Women in New England Colleges and Universities, n.d.). Permission to use this material has been granted.

CHAPTER 42

THE NECESSARY REVOLUTION IN FINANCIAL ACCOUNTING (1992)

GORDON C. WINSTON

The financial accounts of a college or university do not report economic information for the institution as a whole. Instead, the institution is divided into separate activities and a separate set of financial accounts—income statement and balance sheet—is reported for each of those activities. In effect, each activity at a college is treated as if it were a separate firm (Garner 1991). Often-complex loans and transfers between these "firms" are recorded in each set of accounts. Typically eight or nine separate fund accounts and their interwoven transfers make up the annual financial statement for even a small college. This peculiar system is called fund accounting.

Fund accounting has been a source of complaints among college and university trustees for decades, and among others who seek to determine the true financial condition of a college or university. Like the old saw about the weather, everyone complains but no one does anything about it.[1] I think a better way should and can be developed, especially since much of higher education is experiencing increasing difficulty in financing its operations. This article is an attempt to point the way.

My alternative to fund accounting is the result of a six-year effort to organize the vital economic information about a college's performance in a different and more useful way. I call the alternative *global* accounting because it presents an encompassing—all inclusive and integrated—view of a college's economic activities and its financial status. It is the kind of information that is essential to the management and governance of a college, the kind needed by the Board of Trustees, a faculty oversight committee, and top administrators. It describes the economic effects of each year's activities, and specifically the effects on the college's real wealth.[2]

The structure of global accounting is the antithesis of fund accounting. Instead of dividing the institution into a set of self-contained and balkanized accounting entities, global accounting brings economic information together about the whole college. The aim is to provide an annual picture of the financial condition of a college that is accurate, clear, and accessible.

THE TROUBLE WITH FUND ACCOUNTS

Fund accounting has an honorable history of service to government and nonprofit institutions; and there are still important questions that only fund accounts, or something like them, can answer. What is at issue is the inadequacy of fund accounts to provide the *sole* or *primary* way to frame economic information for colleges and universities. Here are some of the inadequacies:

Source: *Planning for Higher Education*, Vol. 20, No. 4, Summer 1992. pp. 1–16. Society for College and University Business Officers, Washington, D.C.

1. Fund accounts obscure an overall, global understanding of an institution's economic performance.

2. Fund accounts are very hard to read and understand. That is, they are inaccessible without a significant investment of time to grasp their mass of detailed information repeated for each fund and their often complex transfers and interactions among funds.

3. They cause people to focus attention on understandable information that may be partial, misleading, or just marginally relevant. For example, people tend to focus on such items as the size of the operating budget, the budget surplus or deficit, or the market value of the endowment. But the operating budget leaves out a third or more of all current economic activity; budget surpluses or deficits are easily manipulated; and the endowment is only a fraction of the total wealth in even the best endowed universities (Winston 1988).

4. There is an inherent temptation to present misleading information. Separate funds are potential shells that invite shell games. For instance, Williams College, in moving $5 million of current spending off the operating budget in the 1980s, markedly reduced the apparent (but not the actual) growth of its operating expenditures. Swarthmore boasted of 40 years of exactly balanced operating budgets (Swarthmore 1987, 17), a feat which was apparently achieved by transferring to the operating budget fund from other funds (after the fact) whatever dollars were needed to cover operating expenses. Harvard and MIT followed the same convention in the 1970s (Bierman and Hofstedt 1973).

5. Fund accounting reduces higher education's ability to make economic comparisons among colleges and even to understand economic performance over time at a single school.

The rationale for fund accounts in colleges has been that the separate accounts make it easier to monitor performance in specific areas supported by outside agents, donors, and government agencies who give funds to the college for restricted purposes and need to know if those purposes are well served and managed (Harried, et al 1985, 722). That stewardship role remains. But it doesn't justify the use of fund accounts as the primary way of organizing economic information.

Some have tried to make fund accounting serve purposes of both stewardship and governance, for instance, by using ratio analysis (Chabotar 1989). Both these efforts have been only partially successful since they retain the shortcomings of fund accounting. On the other hand, global accounts that define the context and inform the governance and management of a college will always need to be complemented by sub-accounts fitted within the global reporting so that restrictions on the use of funds and other detailed information can be handled.

WHAT IS GLOBAL ACCOUNTING?

The basic structure of global accounting is simple. For each year's economic activity, three elemental facts are reported:

1. How much the college took in from all sources;

2. What it did with that money; and

3. The effect of these on the institution's real wealth.

That is the essential framework. (It is also the framework, often honored in the breach, of the familiar Income Statement and Balance Sheet.) What is centrally important is that the global accounts encompass the institution's complete activities. No flow or claim between the college and some outside agent—of income or expenditure or saving or liabilities—should be left out. And no financial flows or claims between funds should be included.

When we began constructing our system of global accounts, we intended only to reorganize the economic information already repeated in the fund accounts. Our global accounts were derived from the audited, published information, largely by combining fund activities and eliminating double counting among them (Winston 1988). And that worked, at first.

Indeed, a major question was whether the approach that generated global accounts from

Williams College's fund accounts would work too for other colleges. We answered that question when Duncan Mann and I were able to create global accounts for Wellesley, Carleton, Swarthmore, and, for contrast, the 65-institution system of the State University of New York (Winston and Mann). The result was an accounting of the year's total income, total current spending, and total real financial saving or change in the institution's financial wealth.

But not all wealth. It has become increasingly clear that global accounts that merely reorganize existing information create a useful set of global *financial* records which monitor real financial wealth, but they share the shortcoming of fund accounts in being inadequate to the incorporation of *physical capital wealth*. Neither system could account for all of an institution's wealth. At Williams College, for example, they ignore more than half of the college's $645 million of net worth.

So the set of genuinely global accounts presented here, while still heavily dependent on a reorganization of published information, augments those data with a more realistic treatment of land, plant, and equipment, a treatment very much in the spirit of the current literature on capital planning in colleges (Dunn 1989; Probasco 1991). For some potential users, these full global accounts may go too far; not everyone is ready to monitor all of his or her institution's wealth. These users can retreat to the halfway house of global financial accounts, a system that is no worse than conventional accounting in its neglect of capital wealth and is a whole lot better in dealing with the other problems of fund accounting I have noted. So considerable improvement lies in using the global financial accounts, even if they are importantly incomplete. (Table 42.1 is repeated in the appendix as Table 42.1-A to show the same college in the abbreviated form of global *financial* accounts. But the rest of the text will deal with the fully global accounts that include all institutional wealth.)

In a significant and encouraging recent development, Harvard's new *Financial Report*, published in March of 1992, treats the physical capital stock much as described below, even though the increased realism raised Harvard's reported operating expenses by $77 million and gave the university a $42 million budget deficit (Harvard 1992). Harvard's decision not

only reduces the risk to other schools of adopting these innovations in reporting economic information, but it indicates another way for an institution to move toward fully global accounts without embracing them all at once.

A caveat, before I describe the global accounts in detail. Their application is more immediately appropriate to private than to public institutions. The reason, of course, is the often-Byzantine arrangements of responsibility, ownership, and governance that have grown up between public colleges and state and local agencies, arrangements that can affect, *inter alia*, ownership of the school's capital stock, responsibility for tuition levels, and for salaries and fringe benefits, and even control over the use of any endowment wealth. So at public campuses the scope of responsibility and control may sometimes be different from that implied by these accounts. It remains, however, that global accounts, or something like them, are essential to public institutions if anyone is to know the real costs of public education and the effects of a state's policies on each institution's educational wealth.

How elements of global accounts work to form a coherent system of information will be clearer if they are embedded in a concrete example. Two years' data are presented in Table 42.1.[3] Consider the components in turn.

College Income

The income elements in Table 42.1 are fairly straightforward at a small school, but a few comments are useful nonetheless. The set of income sources is exhaustive: all income flowing into the college in the year is included, whether it comes from students,[4] donors, government, borrowers of the college's wealth, or purchasers of services from the college. Gift and Grant Income in Table 42.1 is separated according to the donor's wishes to recognize the fact that part of the gift income is intended to expand the college's wealth and that that part is potentially different from gifts that donors intend should be used at the discretion of the college. Asset earnings include interest, dividends, and capital gains or losses (whether realized or not). Auxiliary income, in a small liberal arts college, consists largely of student charges for room and board. For a university, that line would be both larger and more com-

TABLE 42.1
Global Accounts

	1989–90 $	1990–91 $
1. College Income		
Tuition and Fees	29,262,691	32,543,540
Gifts and Grants:		
To Endowment	7,066,669	8,744,806
To Plant	1,016,397	713,124
All Other	12,664,824	13,951,045
Asset Income:		
Interest and Dividends	17,039,521	15,859,257
Appreciation	18,582,670	6,873,486
Sales, Services and Other	1,950,970	2,724,059
Auxiliary Income	11,599,559	11,862,813
Total College Income	99,183,301	93,272,130
2. Current Expenditures		
Operating Budget Expenditures	62,425,303	66,924,329
Other Current Expenditures	6,304,914	5,634,728
less Current Acct Maintenance	703,276	642,167
Total Current Expenditures	68,026,941	71,916,890
3. Additions to Capital Stock		
Investment in New Plant	9,334,326	2,310,285
less Deferred Maintenance		
Real Depreciation	7,500,000	8,097,195
less Maintenance Spending:		
In Current Account	703,276	642,167
In Plant Fund	3,477,560	4,639,692
Total Deferred Maintenance	3,319,164	2,815,336
Total Additions to Capital	6,015,162	(505,051)
4. Operating Costs		
Current Expenditures	68,026,941	71,916,890
Real Depreciation	7,500,000	8,097,195
Total Operating Costs	75,526,941	80,014,085
5. Wealth (EOY)		
Financial Wealth		
Assets	346,203,972	358,726,081
less Liabilities	50,596,648	49,355,661
Net Financial Wealth	295,607,324	309,370,420
[Endowment Value]	[333,553,551]	[341,572,081]
Physical Capital Wealth:		
Replacement Value	323,887,799	341,438,861
less Accumulated		
Deferred Maintenance	3,319,164	6,290,686
Net Physical Wealth	320,568,635	335,148,175
Net Worth	616,175,959	644,518,595

plicated as would be "Sales, services and other," the catchall income line here.

Current Expenditures

Current expenditures in the global accounts is both a more and a less inclusive category than "spending from the current fund" in fund accounting. It includes all current expenditures and it excludes maintenance spending. Current expenditures are included whether they appear within the operating budget, elsewhere in the current fund, the capital budget, the endowment fund, or somewhere else in the fund accounts. So in global accounting, there is no opportunity to reduce the apparent level or growth of current expenditures by shifting some of them from a closely monitored area like the operating budget to a less scrutinized part of the accounts, like off-budget current fund or endowment fund spending. Spending on maintenance of the plant and equipment is excluded because it is not a current expenditure; it is spending that buys a durable good, the restoration—"renovation and adaption"[5]—of the physical plant.[6]

Additions to the Capital Stock

Predictably, the greatest departure from conventional reporting comes in the global accounts' treatment of the physical capital stock since that aspect of college management and college wealth is so effectively neglected in fund accounting. The purpose of global accounting of the capital stock is to report its real value and record the effects of the year's activities on that value. It serves, too, to inform a more accurate measure of the college's operating costs that recognizes both current spending and real depreciation of the college's physical wealth.

Additions to the capital stock are simply the year's gross investment in new plant less any value lost through deterioration of the capital stock—the year's "deferred maintenance." Investment in new plant is uncomplicated. It includes all additions, acquisitions of new land, plant, and equipment that will augment the capital stock. Deferred maintenance describes how much of the year's real depreciation of the capital stock was not repaired or renovated, how much the physical plant was allowed to deteriorate over the year.[7] Given

depreciation, repairs and renovation reduce deferred maintenance. Deferred maintenance is not a money expenditure, *per se*, of course, but it is an expenditure of part of the capital stock—consequent on time and its use in production—and therefore a very real *cost* of the year's operations. Recognition of deferred maintenance is essential if the full effect of the year's activities on the value of the college's wealth are to be reported.

Real depreciation is an estimate of the potential amount of capital stock worn out or used up in the course of the year's operations, the amount it would have depreciated had there been no repairs, renovation, or adaption. The emphasis on "real" depreciation is intended to distinguish this estimate of *actual* decline in the value of a capital stock over the course of the year, due to time and its uses, from the more familiar but quite different matter of income tax liability in a for-profit firm. (For many, that's what "depreciation" has come to mean, both in accounting and the public mind.) In the global accounts it is pure economic depreciation.

Finally, maintenance spending, as noted above, is much the same as investment in new plant; it increases the value of durable capital through renovation and adaption. So it is treated the same in the global accounts. To the small amount of such spending found in the current account is added that portion of a conventional "investment in plant" entry that in fact pays for renovation and adaption.

In Table 42.1, real depreciation is estimated as 2.5% of the $324 million capital stock with which 1990–91 started, or $8.1 million.[8] But since that was offset in 1990-91 by an estimated $4.6 million of maintenance spending from the capital budget and another $64 million from the operating budget, deferred maintenance for the year is estimated, with rounding, at $2.8 million.[9] If current spending on maintenance had been $8.1 million for the year, deferred maintenance, of course, would have been zero.

Additions to the capital stock are the net result of all this: investment in new plant is augmented by maintenance spending and reduced by depreciation. Additions to the capital stock will be positive when new plant and maintenance, together, are larger than real depreciation, and negative when they are overwhelmed by the year's depreciation.

Operating Costs

In the global accounts, the year's total real operating costs are reported directly. To total current expenditures is added the year's depreciation of physical plant. So both forms of current spending are recognized as operating costs: current expenditures of the usual sort (less maintenance spending) and current spending of the capital stock through depreciation. Together, these describe the costs of the year's operations.[10]

Wealth: Assets and Liabilities

Assets and liabilities together describe the state of a college's wealth at the end of each fiscal year. They are the college's stock variables. Two aspects of the reporting of assets in global accounts should be noted. One is de-emphasis of the college's *endowment*. It shows up in Table 42.1 as a parenthetical notation sandwiched into the list of assets and liabilities that make up the college's wealth. The reason for this dismissive treatment is, simply, that the endowment has come erroneously to be seen as synonymous with "total financial wealth." While that was nearly true when colleges had very few non-endowment financial assets and, importantly, very little debt aside from some stray accounts payable, it is not true for many colleges now.

Again, Williams' numbers are instructive. In 1989, its endowment had a market value of some $307 million. But the college had another $22 million in non-endowment assets[11] for total financial assets of $329 million (Williams 1991). But those assets were encumbered by some $51 million in debt. So the global accounts report net financial wealth of $278 million—total financial assets less total liabilities—as the appropriate measure of the college's financial wealth. In 1990, the endowment was up to $334 million, but net financial wealth only to $296 million.

The other important differences in global accounts' wealth reporting are that physical capital assets—land, plant and equipment—are (a) accounted for in current replacement values rather than "book values" that the college originally paid for them, and (b) adjusted for accumulated deferred maintenance. At Williams, which is an old college, one major instructional building with seven large classrooms and

13,000 square feet has a book value of less than $50,000, and one faculty residence, not large but pleasant, is valued at only $850 (Williams 1991). Most other campuses would offer similar examples of the distortions inherent in using book values. So while the estimates of replacement values inevitably involve some guesswork, they are clearly a whole lot closer to the truth than are historical values. Accumulated deferred maintenance is treated as an offset against the replacement value of the physical assets, leaving net physical wealth as the measure of value of the capital stock. Table 42.1 assumes that there was no deferred maintenance before 1989–90, so there is little immediate difference between capital assets and net physical wealth. But Table 42.4 shows that over a long period, deferred maintenance will significantly reduce the college's net physical wealth. An example is Yale's current pressing problem (*New York Times*, February 3, 1992), with more than $1 billion of deferred maintenance.

Because financial and physical assets and liabilities are measured in the same current value terms, they can be added together to report the college's total wealth, its total net worth. We are adding apples and apples. For many purposes, it is essential to distinguish between these two forms of wealth (and saving); but for others it is useful to recognize total wealth, regardless of its form. In Table 42.1, reporting a total 1991 wealth of $645 million tells a very different and more complete story than either reporting an endowment of $342 million or financial wealth of $309 million.

Saving and Wealth: Flow-stock Relationships

The usual tautological accounting relationship between economic flows and stocks apply to global accounts. Saving is the difference between income and spending over the period. Any change in wealth between two dates equals and must be due to saving over that period; net worth (wealth) at the beginning of a period plus income minus spending has to equal net worth at the end of the period. Of course, real depreciation must be added to current expenditures to account fully for the year's total spending. This done, the stock-flow identity holds for total saving and wealth (net worth) as well as for financial and physical saving and wealth, separately. It is just as relevant to global accounts as it is to one's checking account.[12]

Operating and Capital Budgets

Operating and capital budgets are embedded in the global accounts, serving their managerial and planning functions, but firmly in the context of the college's overall activities. So total operating expenditures—the bottom line in an operating budget like that of Table 42.2— appears in the global accounts as a component of current spending (the largest). The effect, then, of operating budget performance on the college's wealth is incorporated immediately and directly. Though it is not made explicit here, the same is true for a capital budget which is mapped directly into the global accounts in the form of either new investment or as current spending, on renovation and adaption.

Note that while operating *expenditures* are reported in a line in the global accounts, operating revenues do not appear. The reason is that a college's decision on how much of its total income to allocate to an operating budget as "revenue" is an internal and essentially arbitrary one. That decision may be influenced by some accumulated tradition: tuition and fees, for instance, may all go to the operating budget while only some gifts and a formulaic portion

of asset income do. But a college can, by assignment and transfer of its income to and from the budget, make a budget deficit or surplus virtually anything it wants it to be, including, as Swarthmore and others have shown, always exactly zero.[13] Clarity is served, then, by focusing the global accounts on *spending* in the operating budget—or more broadly, on all current spending—as it encompasses an important set of activities in the college's educational enterprise. Attention to the arbitrary assignment of operating budget revenues—the result of shifting money between pockets—and the consequent budget "deficits" or "surpluses" can be replaced by attention to real current spending and to actual performance relative to an approved spending plan.[14]

USING GLOBAL ACCOUNTS

The global accounts structure was first used to organize an historical review of Williams' economic behavior in order to provide a descriptive context for evaluating present and future performance (Winston 1988). It was done at the height of public criticism of cost growth in higher education when it was deemed wise to know how present performance compared with the past. We were able to generate long

TABLE 42.2
Global Accounts: Current Expenditure Component

	1989–90 $	*1990–91* $
Operating Budget		
Salary Pools:		
Faculty	10,194,014	11,415,331
Administrative/Prof	6,029,465	6,315,789
Weekly	11,568,273	12,101,430
Total Salary Pools	27,791,752	29,832,550
Fringe Benefits	7,258,226	7,816,225
Financial Aid	6,517,892	7,719,186
Other Restricted Spending	2,720,321	3,505,429
Manager's Budgets	18,137,112	18,050,939
Total Operating Budget Expenses	62,425,303	66,924,329
Other Current Expenditures	6,304,914	5,634,728
less Maint. Spending in Current Account	703,276	642,167
Total Current Expenditures	68,026,941	71,916,890

data series[15] on income levels and changes in its composition; on spending, its composition and real rates of growth; and on real saving and its distribution between financial and physical capital wealth. The result provided a foundation for economic policies.

But the broader significance of global accounts appears to lie in their ability to describe, monitor, and evaluate a college's current economic performance and in the structure they give to economic planning. First, let's look to how they can help monitor and evaluate economic performance.

The global accounts don't force any specific criteria of performance evaluation on a college except implicitly in describing the totality of the school's economic activity. But they do make it especially easy to monitor the effects on its real wealth of the college's behavior and the economic circumstances it operates in: the difference between income and current spending is saving (or dissaving) and that, dollar for dollar, increases (or decreases) wealth. And global accounts make it easy to break that down to monitor, separately, the

effects of college behavior on financial wealth and on physical capital wealth. There are many good reasons why a governing board might consider a dollar saved in a liquid financial asset to be very different from a dollar saved in constructing or renovating a building. Both are saving, but their different forms carry quite different implications for future flexibility, costs, returns, and performance. Even at the level of total saving, a board may think it wise to maintain real wealth or to increase it or to spend some of it down.[16] Or it may prefer only to monitor real wealth or income or spending or their components, rather than to define explicit policies in those respects. These are all decisions on which the structure of the global accounts is agnostic.

Using the data from Table 42.1, Table 42.3 illustrates one sort of evaluative summary that global accounts can produce to describe, in the broadest terms, a college's performance for a year.[17] Other summary data could be generated, but these I have listed are especially useful in informing broad questions of strategy and governance.

TABLE 42.3
Global Accounts: Summary

	1989–90 $	1990–91 $
1. Saving-Gain (Loss) of Total Real Wealth:	10,171,785	(651,974)
Gain (Loss) of Real Financial Wealth	4,156,623	(146,923)
Gain (Loss) of Real Physical Wealth	6,015,162	(505,051)
Gifts to Increase Real Wealth	8,083,066	9,457,930
Savings to Increase Real Wealth	2,088,719	(10,109,904)
2. Income	99,183,301	93,272,130
Real Growth Rate	–3.26%	–10.19%
3. Spending		
Operating Costs	75,526,941	80,014,085
Deferred Maintenance	3,319,164	2,815,336
Investment in New Plant	9,334,326	2,310,285
Real Growth Rates		
Operating Costs	4.51%	1.18%
Deferred Maintenance	36.27%	–18.99%
Investment in New Plant	4.35%	–76.36%
4. Saving: Gain (Loss) of Total Real Wealth		
Using Smoothed Asset Income	7,276,151	8,600,747

The first line of Table 42.3—saving, or the gain or loss of real wealth—is, in a sense, "the bottom line" of the global accounts. It describes the change in total real wealth that results from the college's activities for the year, recognizing all its sources of income, all its expenditures on current account and new capital and maintenance, all the depreciation of its physical capital stock, and the contrary effects of inflation in eroding the real value of its financial wealth while increasing the nominal value of its physical wealth. In this fundamental measure, the fortunes of the college illustrated in Table 42.3 declined by some $11 million between 1989–90 and 1990–91, from real saving of $10.2 million to real dissaving of $.7 million.

The next four lines in Table 42.3 address two of the many questions that might be asked about the year's total real saving. The first two lines describe the distribution of total real savings between financial and physical wealth. Physical wealth fared better than did financial wealth in 1989–90 but had a slightly larger decline in 1990–91. The next two lines ask what would have happened to saving without the gifts that were targeted to increase wealth. Some of the increase in wealth on line 1 was the result of the explicit intentions of donors who gave the college money for the purpose of increasing its wealth, so that component might well be separated out from any change in wealth, or saving, that was due, instead to the college's decisions and external circumstances during the year. Without the gifts to wealth (to endowment and plant) of $8 and $9 million in the two years, the college would have saved in other ways some $2.1 million in the good year and lost a bit more than $10 million in the bad one. Again, governing boards would differ in their evaluation of these facts. Had the school's performance led to neither saving nor dissaving in those years, that might be considered good work by the board interested in real wealth maintenance, while it would be considered poor performance by a board that wanted, say, to catch up to Amherst or Swarthmore in wealth per student. So again, the global accounts are agnostic on policy aims.

College income is reported next in Table 42.3 in current dollars while its growth is reported in real terms, adjusted for inflation. Together they monitor the flow of total resources into the school over the year.

Direct monitoring of costs and spending levels and their real growth, as presented in the third section of Table 42.3, is a response to the criticisms of higher education in the 1980s and a conviction that real spending growth should be watched closely, both in detailed categories and broadly. Operating costs include both current expenditures and real depreciation as reported in Table 42.1. The year's deferred maintenance is reported as a separate line because of its usual neglect and its potential for causing serious long-term mischief. A board might adopt the policy that deferred maintenance should always be zero (giving top priority to protection of the physical plant, whatever the costs in other objectives). Or it might feel that deferred maintenance is simply one important aspect of performance that needs to be monitored attentively; that is, a board might conclude that deferring maintenance, like any other reduction in saving, can provide money to do other, more important, things. Again, global accounts inform policy by defining required maintenance spending and showing the cost of not doing it. Investment in new plant describes only spending for new physical capital.

The last section in Table 42.3 addresses an evaluation problem for well-endowed schools that report their financial assets at market values and thereby incur potentially large variations in reported income through capital gains and losses caused by market fluctuations. (Year-to-year comparisons of global performance will be hard to interpret if major changes in asset market value have dominated the numbers.) So in this last section of the table, the effect of the year's activities on the college's wealth are re-examined using a five-year moving average of asset income instead of actual asset income for each year. That smoothes out the volatile element while still reflecting its underlying changes in a subdued form.

These data for 1989-90 and 1990-91 illustrate the effect nicely. Between the two years, the college's capital gains income fell by almost $12 million, so much of the striking difference in the effects of performance on real wealth between the two years was due to that sharp (and uncontrollable) decline in income and not, as it might first appear, to the way the college was run in the latter year. Indeed, the effect of operations on real wealth was, with smoothed income, better in the second year. Without that

TABLE 42.4
Global Economic Plan
(Current Dollars—Inflation Rate 5%)

	1989–90 $	1990–91 $	Plan Parameters $	Planned 1991–92 $	Planned 1992–93 $	Planned 1993–94 $	... Projected 2001–02 $
1. College Income							
Tuition and Fees	29,262,691	32,543,540	6.0%	34,500,000	36,600,000	38,800,000	... 61,800,000
Gifts and Grants:							
To Endowment	7,066,669	8,744,806	$9 m	9,000,000	9,000,000	9,000,000	... 9,000,000
To Plant	1,016,397	713,124	$1 m	1,000,000	1,000,000	1,000,000	... 1,000,000
All Other	12,664,824	13,951,045	$14 m	14,000,000	14,000,000	14,000,000	... 14,000,000
Asset Income:							
Interest & Dividends	17,039,521	15,859,257	6.0%	16,800,000	17,800,000	18,900,000	... 30,100,000
Appreciation	18,582,670	6,873,486	6.0%	7,300,000	7,700,000	8,200,000	... 13,000,000
Sales, Services and Other	1,950,970	2,724,059	6.0%	2,900,000	3,100,000	3,200,000	... 5,200,000
Auxiliary Income	11,599,559	11,862,813	6.0%	12,600,000	13,300,000	14,100,000	... 22,500,000
Total College Income	99,183,301	93,272,130		98,100,000	102,500,000	107,200,000	... 156,600,000
2. Current Expenditures							
Operating Budget Expenditures	62,425,303	66,924,329	On Table 42.5	70,900,000	75,200,000	79,700,000	... 127,000,000
Other Current Expenditures	6,304,914	5,634,728	On Table 42.5	6,000,000	6,300,000	6,700,000	... 10,700,000
less Current Acct Maintenance	703,276	642,167	$650,000	650,000	650,000	650,000	... 650,000
Total Current Expenditures	68,026,941	71,916,890		76,300,000	80,900,000	85,800,000	... 137,100,000
3. Additions to Capital Stock							
Investment in New Plant	9,334,326	2,310,285	$7m constant	2,100,000	2,100,000	2,200,000	... 2,600,000
less Deferred Maintenance							
Real Depreciation	7,500,000	8,097,195	2.5% K-stock	8,500,000	9,000,000	9,500,000	... 14,600,000
less Maintenance Spending							
In Current Account	703,276	642,167	$650,000	650,000	650,000	650,000	... 650,000
In Plant Fund	3,477,560	4,649,692	6.0%	4,900,000	5,200,000	5,500,000	... 8,800,000
Total Deferred Maintenance	3,319,164	2,815,336		3,000,000	3,200,000	3,300,000	... 5,200,000
Total Additions to Capital	6,015,162	(505,051)		(900,000)	(1,200,000)	(1,200,000)	... (2,600,000)
4. Operating Costs							
Current Expenditures	68,026,941	71,916,890	As Above	76,300,000	80,900,000	85,800,000	... 137,100,000
Real Depreciation	7,500,000	8,097,195	As Above	8,500,000	9,000,000	9,500,000	... 14,600,000
Total Operating Costs	75,526,941	80,014,085		84,800,000	89,900,000	95,300,000	... 151,700,000
5. Wealth (EOY)							
Financial Wealth							
Assets	346,203,972	358,726,081		373,500,000	387,100,000	400,200,000	... 481,100,000
less Liabilities	50,596,648	49,355,661	$50 m	50,000,000	50,000,000	50,000,000	... 50,000,000
Net Financial Wealth	295,607,324	309,370,420		323,500,000	337,100,000	350,200,000	... 431,100,000
[Endowment Value]	[333,553,551]	[341,572,081]	$350 m	[350,000,000]	[350,000,000]	[350,000,000]	... [350,000,000]
Physical Capital Wealth							
Replacement Value	323,887,799	341,438,861		360,600,000	380,800,000	402,000,000	... 617,000,000
less Accumulated							
Deferred Maintenance	3,319,164	6,290,686		9,600,000	13,200,000	17,200,000	... 66,200,000
Net Physical Wealth	320,568,635	335,148,175		351,000,000	367,600,000	384,800,000	... 550,800,000
Net Worth	616,175,959	644,518,595		674,500,000	704,700,000	735,000,000	... 981,900,000

abrupt decline in asset income, reductions in deferred maintenance and the growth of current spending would have increased saving by $1.3 million, in 1990–91.

Now lets look at global accounting's ability to assist with economic planning.

Global accounts provide the framework for an economic planning model that has the scope and ability to integrate detailed management sub-plans while showing the global economic implications of the school's intended behavior and anticipated circumstances. Tables 42.4 to

TABLE 42.5
Global Economic Plan: Current Expenditure Component

	1989–90 $	1990–91 $	Plan Parameters $	Planned 1991–92 $	Planned 1993–94 $	Planned 1992–93 $	...	Projected 2001–02 $
Operating Budget								
Salary Pools:								
Faculty	10,194,014	11,415,331	6.0%	12,100,000	12,800,000	13,600,000	...	21,700,000
Administrative/Prof	6,029,465	6,315,789	6.0%	6,700,000	7,100,000	7,500,000	...	12,000,000
Weekly	11,568,273	12,101,430	6.0%	12,800,000	13,600,000	14,400,000	...	23,000,000
Total Salary Pools	27,791,752	29,832,550		31,600,000	33,500,000	35,500,000	...	56,600,000
Fringe Benefits	7,258,226	7,816,225	6.0%	8,300,000	8,800,000	9,300,000	...	14,800,000
Financial Aid	6,517,892	7,719,186	6.0%	8,200,000	8,700,000	9,200,000	...	14,700,000
Other Restricted Spending	2,720,321	3,505,429	6.0%	3,700,000	3,900,000	4,200,000	...	6,700,000
Manager's Budgets	18,137,112	18,050,939	6.0%	19,100,000	120,300,000	21,500,000	...	34,300,000
Total Operating Budget Exp.	62,425,303	66,924,329		70,900,000	75,200,000	79,700,000	...	127,000,000
Other Current Expenditures	6,304,914	5,634,728	6.0%	6,000,000	6,300,000	6,700,000	...	10,700,000
less Maintenance Spending in Current Account	703,276	642,167	$650,000	650,000	650,000	650,000	...	650,000
Total Current Expenditures	68,026,941	71,916,890		76,300,000	80,900,000	85,800,000	...	137,100,000

42.6 illustrate such a model. Table 42.4 is a basic global economic plan; Table 42.5 is a sub-account giving more detail on planned current spending, "the operating budget;" and Table 42.6 gives the sort of evaluative summary data just described, here extended to include anticipated future performance over the period of the plan. All values are in current dollars with an assumed 5 percent inflation rate, and past accumulation of deferred maintenance is arbitrarily set at zero at the beginning of 1989–90. All planned and projected values are rounded.

Two years of historical performance data—1989–90 and 1990–91—are the starting point for projections of both anticipated circumstances (inflation, asset market conditions, etc.) and planned college behavior (staffing, salaries, tuition, resource allocation, etc.). The heart of a planning process is, of course, the thoughtful specification of these "planning parameters"—projections of future intentions, plans and expectations. But in terms of the plan structure that is at issue here, after the college has decided on those planning parameters—how it wants and expects the components of the accounts to change in the future—a global economic plan will show the effects of that behavior on the college's real wealth over the period of the plan.

It is, then, a "consistency-and-implications" model. The pieces have to fit together over any year and they have to fit together from one period to the next, satisfying the truism that

wealth at the beginning of the period plus income less spending has to equal wealth at the end of the period. Each period's performance is anchored in the past year's, and the projections are anchored in the most recent history.

The result is neither an optimization model nor an equilibrium model. It can be made into a "long-run financial equilibrium model" if a constant rate of growth of wealth is imposed; but that remains an option and not a characteristic. It is hoped that its more modest logical structure may well be of greater practical value than the more abstract alternatives in actual planning, administration, and governance. The global plan takes the concrete form of a Lotus spreadsheet that is easy to use to ask, repeatedly, the question, "What will be the economic implications of the following behavior, now and in the future?"

The data in Tables 42.4 through 42.6 are based on Tables 42.1 through 42.3. But it is important that they carry no implication about future plans or projections for any actual school. They are illustrative only of the structure of the economic plan. To make very clear, planning parameter values in these tables have been entered as caricatures—most either as the constant rate of growth of the 6 percent (nominal) or as a constant nominal quantity[18] with the hope that a high level of artificiality will make it starkly clear that these tables deal only with a model structure and that no privileged information is conveyed.

TABLE 42.6
Global Economic Plan: Summary
(Current Dollars—Inflation Rate 5%)

	1989–90 $	1990–91 $	Plan Parameters $	Planned 1991–92 $	Planned 1993–94 $	Planned 1992–93 $	... Projected 2001–02 $
1. Saving—Gain (Loss)							
of Total Real Wealth:	10,171,785	(651,974)	Details	(2,200,000)	(3,600,000)	(4,900,000)	...(16,300,000)
Gain (Loss) of Real Financial Wealth	4,156,623	(146,923)	on Tables	(1,300,000)	(2,600,000)	(3,800,000)	...(13,700,000)
Gain (Loss) of Real Physical Wealth	6,015,162	(505,051)	4 and 5	(900,000)	(1,000,000)	(1,200,000)	... (2,600,000)
Gifts to Increase Real Wealth	8,083,066	9,457,930		10,000,000	10,000,00	10,000,000	... 10,000,000
Savings to Increase Real Wealth	2,088,719	(10,109,904)		(12,200,000)	(13,600,000)	(14,900,000)	...(26,300,000)
2. Income	99,183,301	93,272,130		98,100,000	102,500,000	107,200,000	...156,600,000
Real Growth Rate	–3.26%	–10.19%		0.12%	–0.45%	–0.39%	... 0.03%
3. Spending:							
Operating Costs	75,526,941	80,014,085		84,800,000	89,900,000	95,300,000	...151,700,000
Deferred Maintenance	3,319,164	2,815,336		3,000,000	3,200,000	3,300,000	... 5,200,000
Investment in New Plant	9,334,326	2,310,285		2,100,000	2,100,000	2,200,000	... 2,600,000
Real Growth Rates:							
Operating Costs	4.51%	1.18%		0.93%	0.96%	0.95%	... 0.93%
Deferred Maintenance	36.27%	–18.99%		0.40%	1.13%	1.02%	... 0.26%
Investment in New Plant	4.35%	–76.36%		–14.18%	–2.25%	–2.32%	... –3.10%
4. Savings: Gain (Loss)							
of Total Real Wealth	7,276,151	8,600,747		2,600,000	4,000,000	(2,000,000)	...(17,100,000)
Using Smoothed Asset Income							
5. Accumulated Deferred							
Maintenance	3,319,164	6,290,686		9,600,000	13,200,000	17,200,000	... 66,200,000

A cost of artificiality, though, is that the numbers in these tables are less revealing of an actual planning exercise than they would be with more realistic parameter values. Nonetheless, they show that if a college, starting with the historical performance described in the first two columns, were to plan its spending and anticipate income as described by these rates and levels, it would wind up as described in the last four columns. It would see increasing yearly dissaving, loss of more real financial wealth than physical wealth, real income growth hovering around zero with real operating costs that are increasing modestly, declining real new investment and declining but still positive real deferred maintenance.

If that pattern of behavior (and circumstances) continued until the academic year 2001–2, the college would find itself dissaving at an annual rate of $16 million, despite $10 million a year in gifts intended to increase wealth. Most of the dissaving would take the form of drawing down financial assets, but there would still be an accumulated deferred maintenance of some $66 million or a bit less than 10 percent of its equal capital stock (all in 2002 dollars). A governing board, looking at these results, would have to conclude that the projected behavior under the projected circumstances isn't sustainable. Elimination of asset income volatility makes a significant difference in the evaluation of short-run performance. But predictably, it has a declining effect on the evaluation of smoothly projected future performance. So the plan reveals that something more fundamental than asset income volatility is producing unsustainable results.

Given the artificiality of these numbers, the results of these plan projections probably don't deserve much more discussion. They should serve, however, to give a sense of the kind of strategic information that is generated by the global plan. It is, most generally, a description of the future resource implications of the behavior and circumstances envisioned by the college.

PREMISE AND PROMISES

The premise of the global accounts has been that a college's administration or governing board wants to have meaningful and accessible economic information about the college's performance. But that may be naïve. The fact that the operating budget can be a political document is often acknowledged and usually described as regrettable, but it is also of considerable value in avoiding questions and discussions that might be time-consuming, tedious, and challenging to administrative decisions.

That fund accounts can selectively hide or reveal transactions is often convenient. So is the emphasis on endowment wealth, as though there were no other kinds of financial assets and no offsetting debt. And so on. But the difficulty with the manipulation of economic information, or selective optimism in its reporting, is the old one that plagues any departure from scrupulous efforts to report the economic facts: the first victim of distorted economic information is often the author of those distortions.

It is hard to manage a place if you don't know what's going on. This is a lesson learned and relearned in the contexts ranging from the Soviet planned economy to the current gyrations of state and city budgets in New York and California. Unfortunately, as the government parallel suggests, governors and mayors change and so do college administrations, increasing the temptation those transients face to keep their economic numbers looking good and to let the sober facts show up later, "but not on my watch."

More positively, and more importantly, global accounts appear to represent a marked improvement over fund accounting both in informing the long-run policy issues that confront colleges and universities, and in monitoring their economic performance. The information these global accounts present has proven to be the sort that induces and encourages the discussion of strategic fundamentals, of issues that are basic to the governance of the institution, issues that take the form "If we keep on doing what we're doing, or what we're planning to do next year, what will happen to our economic wealth?" Such elemental questions are not readily induced or addressed by the kind of economic information now available with fund accounts to colleges and universities.

Global accounts describe the effect of a year's activities, actual or planned, on all of the college's real wealth, on the distribution of that wealth between financial and physical assets, on deferred maintenance, on levels and real growth of income from its various sources, and of spending on it various objectives. This it does, in an environment of inflation with its opposing effects on the values of financial and physical wealth. Global accounts describe the whole of an institution. Their data are designed to avoid omissions and partial truths, to be clear and accessible, and to direct attention to the most basic economic implications of a college's behavior.

NOTES

1. Actually, 20 years ago Cornell professors Harold Bierman, Jr. and Thomas Hofstedt showed how misleading conventional budget deficits can be, using analysis similar in some ways to this article (1973). Their effort got them an Andy Rooney segment on CBS, a front-page *Wall Street Journal* article; and strenuous objections from campus controllers and presidents, but no changes.

2. The structure of global accounts was developed in 1986–88, given a shot of practicality during my stint as Williams' provost in 1988–90, and refined in 1991. I enjoyed support from the Andrew W. Mellon Foundation through its assistance for the Williams Project on the Economics of Higher Education. William Bowen, Shawn Buckler, Keith Finan, George Goethals, David Healy, Robinson Hollister, George Keller, Duncan Mann, Charles M. Mott, Saeed Mughal, Will Reed, Joseph Rice, Morton Schapiro, David Schultz, and Winthrop Wassener gave me valuable insights and helped improve the analysis. I am especially indebted to Harold Bierman, Roger Bolton, David Booth, Anne MacEachern, and Michael McPherson.

3. These are similar to historical data from Williams' published sources, so no legal issues are raised by their use here. In the description of an economic plan below, I present transparently unrealistic and uninformative planning parameters to illustrate only the structure of the plan and nothing of Williams' expectations or intentions.

4. Tuition and fee income in these accounts is gross. An alternative would leave institutional student aid out of both income and expenditures and report as income only net tuition and fees.

5. "Adaption" refers to action to offset depreciation due to obsolescence, in the trilogy de-

scribed long ago by Terborg. The other sources are depreciation due to use and depreciation due to the elements; these would be addressed by "renovation" spending as used here.

6. Under present practice some of the renovation and adaption is embedded in current spending but the largest part of renovation and adaption spending typically appears as capital spending (labeled "investment in plant"). So usually only a relatively small adjustment to reported current spending is needed to purge total current expenditures of what is more accurately capital spending. At Williams, the maintenance part of current expenditures was only $703,000 in 1989–1990 and $642,000 in 1990–91.

7. "Deferred maintenance" is often used to describe the accumulated result of past failures to spend enough on maintenance to offset real depreciation. It reduces the value of a stock variable. Here we used the phrase, too, to describe a flow—the extent to which this year's maintenance spending failed to offset this year's depreciation. As usual, this year's flow is an increment to the previously accumulated stock. Note that there is nothing necessarily pejorative about "deferred maintenance." Often it will be advisable to let physical capital depreciate.

8. The 2.5% is a conservative estimate. Economists (Schultz 1960; O'Neill 1971) have put it at 2% of the replacement value of plant and equipment per year. But estimates more carefully done by university capital planners get 1.5–2.5% for renovation and another .5–1.5% for adaption (Dunn 1989). So the 2.5% used in the text and tables appears to be a conservative estimate of the total depreciation and therefore of the spending needed to eliminate all deferred maintenance.

9. An important departure from the facilities planning literature lies in the fact that the global accounts identify the year's deferred maintenance without implying that it must therefore be prevented. Recognition of the cost of real depreciation is not the same thing as funding it. (See Dunn 1989, or Probasco 1991).

10. An issue lurks under the surface here. It is the classic neglect of the opportunity cost of capital as a real cost of production in colleges and universities (and nonprofits in general). So it is inaccurate to call "total current costs" total when they leave out, in the case of Williams, roughly $30 million a year of real costs of production, half again as much as is typically reported (Winston 1991). Two facts might recommend that we continue to leave them out, however: (a) the global accounts are concerned with the total flows of income and spending by the institution from and to outside agents, so it may be permissible to neglect a real cost of production that is paid, by virtue of the college's ownership of its capital stock, back to itself as imputed income, even though the resulting accounts seriously distort the costs of production; and (b) strategically, it may be unwise to try to persuade people of the good sense of both the global accounts and an accounting of capital costs at the same time, though a courageous effort would take on both at once.

11. Though they may differ from endowment assets in other ways, the defining characteristic of these financial assets is that they are "owned" within the college, by a fund other than the endowment fund.

12. There is one awkwardness caused by the use of current market or replacement values for physical capital wealth in an inflationary environment. It lies in the need for an inflation adjustment to the value of the physical capital stock from year to year that doesn't appear here (as would be strictly appropriate) as nominal income. Strict adherence to the tautology would have to report the gain in physical asset value due to inflation as income (a physical capital gain) and then assign all of that income saving, thereby justifying the increase in the nominal value of the capital stock. But since that portion of "income" is always "saved" and serves only to keep the replacement value if the capital stock in current dollars, the better choice seems to be to introduce an apparent violation of the stock-flow tautology rather than insert a large piece of funny money income explicitly into the body of the accounts. So the replacement value of physical capital reflects inflation within each year as well as showing the effect of net investment. As presented in Table 42.1, then, the tautology applies directly to financial saving and wealth but not to physical capital or total saving and wealth, unless inflation-induced "physical capital gains income" is included. (For the reader who'd like to confirm this relationship: the replacement value of the capital stock was $300,000,000 in 1989 while the inflation rate was (rounded) 4.85% over 1989–90 and 4.71% over 1990–91, so the inflation adjustments in replacement value are $14,553,473 and $15,240,777 in 1989-90 and 1990–91, respectively. With these, net physical wealth and net worth at the beginning of each period, plus saving and inflation adjustment will equal net physical wealth and net worth at the end of the period.)

13. In addition to Bierman and Hofstedt's brief fame for showing that budgets are often highly misleading—when MIT reported a $5 million deficit, they actually saved $100 million; Princeton's reported $1.5 million deficit went with $151 million in saving; and Harvard's $1.4 million deficit coincided with $314 in saving, *inter alia*—a number of others have tried to sound the same warning. William Nord-

haus, economist and provost at Yale from 1986 to 1988, for instance, recently cautioned against relying on operating budget deficits and surpluses because "actions are generally taken to produce a balanced budget" (Nordhaus 1989, p. 10).

14. Operating revenues are structurally a lot like a child's allowance, the part of the family income the parents assign for her to spend. Whether or not she can get by on, or even save from, her allowance is not an uninteresting question or one always viewed with dispassion. But it would be a mistake of some significance if the parents (or their creditors) were to represent the child's deficit or surplus on her allowance as a measure of the family's economic fortunes for the week. So in the context of higher education, a number of Princeton faculty members were unimpressed with the university's recent and much publicized operating budget deficits, convinced that there had to be more going on there than met the eye (Lyall 1989). Global accounts make it clear that there was.

15. Initially for the 30 years since Williams was a small, all-male college.

16. The four alternative objectives that Dunn described for endowment wealth are relevant in this broader context of total wealth: (1) protect its nominal value; (2) protect its purchasing power, its real value; (3) have wealth grow as fast as operating expenses; or (4) increase wealth per student as fast as that of competing or peer institutions (Dunn 1991, pp. 34–5).

17. The details of getting from Table 42.1 to Table 42.3 are included in an appendix table.

18. In practice, three kinds of parameter values might be used to describe plans and projections: (a) rates of growth (constant or changing from one year to the next), (b) levels (constant on real of nominal terms or changing over time), and (c) functionally dependent parameters reflecting things like the way institutional need-based financial aid expenses depend on tuition decisions.

REFERENCES

Bierman, Jr., H. and T. Hofstedt. 1973. University Accounting (Alternative Measures of Ivy League Deficits). *Non-Profit Report* (May): 14–23.

Chabotar, 1989. Financial Ratio Analysis Comes to Nonprofits. *Journal of Higher Education*, 60 (no. 2): 188–208.

Dunn, Jr., J. 1989. *Financial Planning Guidelines for Facilities Renewal and Adaption.* The Society for College and University Planning.

Dunn, Jr., J. 1991. How Colleges Should Handle Their Endowment. *Planning for Higher Education*, 19 (no. 3): 32–37.

Garner, C. 1991. The Role of Funds. In *Accounting and Budgeting in Public and Nonprofit Organizations.* Jossey-Bass.

Harried A., L. Imdieke and R. Smith. 1985. *Advanced Accounting.* 3rd ed. John Wiley and Sons.

Harvard University. 1992. *Financial Report to the Board of Overseers of Harvard College.* Harvard University.

Lyall, S. 1989. Strife Over Style and Substance Tests Princeton's Leaders. *New York Times*, 4 December (B1).

Nordhaus, W. 1989. *Evaluating the Risk for Specific Institutions.* Yale University.

O'Neill, J. 1971. *Resource Use in Higher Education: Trends in Outputs and Inputs, 1930 to 1967.* The Carnegie Commission on Higher Education.

Probasco, J. 1991. Crumbling Campuses: What Are the Real Costs? *Business Officer*, 25 (no. 5): 48–51.

Schultz, T. 1960. Capital Formation by Education. *Journal of Political Economy* 68: 6.

Swarthmore College. 1987. The Treasurer's Report. In *The President's Report, 1986–87.* Swarthmore College.

Williams College. 1991. *The Treasurer's Report, 1990–91.* Williams College.

Winston, G. and D. Mann. *Global Accounts: Reorganizing Economic Information for Colleges and Universities.* Forthcoming.

Winston, G. 1988. *Total College Income: An Economic Overview of Williams College, 1956–57 to 1986–87.* Williams College.

Winston, G. 1991. Why Are Capital Costs Ignored By Colleges and Universities and What Are The Prospects For Change? *Williams Project on the Economics of Higher Education, Discussion Paper No. 14.* Williams College.

APPENDIX A

TABLE 42.1-A
Global Financial Accounts

	1989–90 $	1990–91 $
1. College Income:		
Tuition and Fees	29,262,691	32,543,540
Gifts and Grants:		
To Endowment	7,066,669	8,744,806
To Plant	1,016,397	713,124
All Other	12,664,824	13,951,045
Asset Income:		
Interest & Dividends	17,039,521	15,859,257
Appreciation	18,582,670	6,873,486
Sales, Services and Other	1,950,970	2,724,059
Auxiliary Income	11,599,559	11,862,813
Total College Income	99,183,301	93,272,130
2. Current Expenditures:		
Operating Budget Expenditures	62,425,303	66,924,329
Other Current Expenditures	6,304,914	5,634,728
less Current Acct Maintenance	703,276	642,167
Total Current Expenditures	68,026,941	71,916,890
3. Capital Expenditures:		
Investment in New Plant	9,334,326	2,310,285
Maintenance in Current Account	703,276	642,167
Maintenance in Plant Fund	3,477,560	4,639,692
Total Additions to Capital	13,515,162	7,592,144
4. Financial Wealth (EOY)		
Assets	346,203,972	358,726,081
[Endowment Value]	[333,553,551]	[341,572,081]
less Liabilities	50,596,648	49,355,661
Net Financial Wealth	295,607,324	309,370,420
5. Financial Saving:		
Total Financial Saving	17,641,198	13,763,096
Breakeven Saving (Inflation Offset)	13,484,575	13,910,019
Real Financial Saving	4,156,623	(146,923)
Real Net of Gifts to Endowment	(2,910,046)	(8,891,729)

APPENDIX B

Performance Calculations

		1989–90 $	1990–91 $
Saving—Gain (Loss) of Real Wealth:		10,171,785	(651,974)
Total Real Saving:	Y-X[hK*(t-1)-(mc+mk)]+iK*(t-1)	38,209,833	28,498,822
Breakeven Saving:	iNFW(t-1)+iK*(t-1)	28,038,048	29,150,796
Gain (Loss) of Real Financial Wealth: Real Saving		4,156,623	(146,923)
Total Financial Saving:	Y-X-K	17,641,198	13,763,096
Breakeven Saving (Inflation Offset):	i(NFW)(t-1)	13,484,575	13,910,019
Gain (Loss) of Physical Wealth: Real Saving		6,015,162	(505,051)
Total Physical Capital Saving	K-[hK*(t-1)-(mc+mk)]+iK*(t-1)	20,568,635	14,735,726
Breakeven Saving (Inflation Offset):	iK*(t-1)	14,553,473	15,240,777
Composition of Saving:			
Financial Saving		41%	23%
Physical Saving		59%	77%
With Smoothed Asset Income			
Saving—Gain (Loss) of Total Real Wealth: Smoothed		7,276,151	8,600,747
Total Saving		35,314,199	37,751,543
Gain (Loss) of Real Financial Wealth		1,260,989	9,105,798
Total Financial Saving: Smoothed		14,745,564	23,015,817
Spending:			
Deferred Maintenance:	hK*(t-1)-(mc+mk)	3,319,164	2,815,336
Real Yearly Growth		36.27%	−18.99%
Current Expenditures:	X-(mc+mk)	68,026,941	71,916,890
Real Yearly Growth		4.72%	0.97%
Operating Costs:	X-(mc+mk)+hK*(t-1)	75,526,941	80,014,085
Real Yearly Growth		4.51%	1.18%
Investment in New Plant		9,334,326	2,310,285
Real Yearly Growth		4.35%	−76.36%

K = new investment; K* = replacement value of capital stock; h = depreciation rate; mc and mk = maintenance spending in Current and Capital-Budget, respectively (both included in X); i = inflation rate; Y = income; X = (current expenditures + mc + mk).

(t-1)=end of previous period.

Chapter 43

Integrating Strategic Finance and Endowment Management

Philip R. Taylor, Roger C. Hewins III, and William F. Massy

Philip R. Taylor is chair, president and founder of P.R. Taylor Associates. Since earning his J.D. from the University of Virginia and a mechanical engineering degree from Northwestern University, he has held positions at Tandem Computers, Hewlett-Packard, Ashland Oil, and Inland Steel.

Roger C. Hewins III is senior vice president of P.R. Taylor Associates and has been active in financial and investment management for more than 12 years. Mr. Hewins holds an M.B.A. from Harvard University and a bachelor's in psychology from Fordham University.

William F. Massy is senior vice president of P.R. Taylor Associates. He has served as Stanford Univeristy's vice president for business and finance, as chief financial officer, and as a professor in the Graduate School of Business. He founded the Stanford Institute for Higher Education Research in the School of Education and currently directs the project on educational quality for the National Center for Postsecondary Improvement. Dr. Massy did his graduate work at the Massachusetts Institute of Technology and holds a baccalaureate from Yale University.

Over the last 25 years, many of the best-managed U.S. colleges and universities have gained control over their financial destinies by adopting a new approach to financial management. This management paradigm integrates sophisticated revenue and expense forecasting and capital planning techniques with the best tools of modern portfolio theory—and it came just in time to rescue these institutions from an extraordinary set of fiscal challenges.

Traditionally, universities tended to take an income-oriented approach to endowment management that was not coordinated in any meaningful way with their management of the rest of the institution. However, the need for an integrated approach became apparent during the fiscal crises of the early 1970s. These were years of financial frustration caused by a halt to a century of expansion for higher education, with ever-increasing pressure on tuition, governmental funding, and program development challenging universities to balance institutional priorities with shrinking budgets.

To make matters worse, the stock market crashed, and with it the endowments of many institutions that honored the holy grail of "investment total return" without fully understanding its implications. No longer would financial management consist primarily of the "prudent allocation of the excess of revenues over expenses."[1] In the future, institutions would need to make optimal use of institutional resources by employing sophisticated long-term planning and investment tools in a comprehensive way.

Source: *Planning for Higher Education*, vol. 26, Winter 1997–1998, pp. 1–11. Society for College and University Planning.

In this demanding environment these large institutions were able to define and make a transition to budgets that supported current programs and sustainable long-term growth. Along the way they refined their decision-making processes and modeling tools, enabling them to anticipate and survive additional financial challenges in the 1980s and 1990s.

THE GOAL: STABLE, PREDICTABLE FINANCIAL ENVIRONMENTS

Colleges and universities with endowment assets less than $400 million face the same challenges as their larger brethren but often lack the resources and experience required to address them as effectively. As a result, when faced with tough budgetary problems, small and midsized institutions too often reach temporary, stopgap solutions. While they seek the same "stable and predictable financial environments in which the academic process can flourish,"[2] they are far less likely to achieve that balance without access to sophisticated decision processes and financial models.

To compound the problem, smaller endowments on average earn far less and yet spend more than larger endowments, actually depleting their assets year by year instead of achieving financial equilibrium.[3] With unbalanced portfolios not at all tuned to specific needs or risk tolerance, a few years (or quarters) of good absolute investment returns are often confused with stability. And fund administrators are surprised when the asset classes they have favored fall precipitously. As a result, universities and colleges with smaller endowments typically do not receive consistent endowment support for their operating expenses and capital costs. With little long-term guidance, the budgeting process frequently becomes a frustrating annual exercise neither integrated with the results of the previous year's decisions nor likely to accomplish the goals of the institution.

It is important to understand how to manage the entire set of responsibilities inherent in the financial officer's commission. These responsibilities are interrelated in crucial ways and cannot be addressed effectively in piecemeal fashion. Only an objective, comprehensive approach to the large task of financial planning and management can be expected to result in long-run financial equilibrium, strong investment performance, and success in achieving the institution's objectives.

This approach should be organized around the following broad themes:

- *Strategic financial management:* Managing the financial planning and cash flow associated with the business of the institution, from overall endowment spending policy to tuition and financial aid, special program expense, salaries, capital budgets, and plant and equipment maintenance.

- *Investment management:* The task of investing the assets of the endowment portfolio, from the setting of objectives and asset allocation to manager selection, monitoring, and evaluation.

We will focus on the key issues in each area. The unifying theme will be the integration of all financial decisions into a coherent, sustainable financial plan. We will also explore the prudent investment process as developed and practiced by the largest and best institutional investors over the last three decades.

STRATEGIC FINANCIAL MANAGEMENT

The unifying objective of an integrated approach to strategic financial management is achievement of long-run financial equilibrium, a set of conditions under which the budget is likely to stay balanced, or approximately balanced, over a number of years (see the discussion of financial step F3, below). For institutions with substantial endowment assets, this means balancing the institution's budget while ensuring that the real (i.e., after inflation) value of the endowment is stable or increasing over time. Smaller institutions typically fail to achieve this balance (see note 1) and as a result deplete their endowments until a crisis forces drastic measures. Larger endowments, through better investment policies, better planning, and larger initial endowments, have done better at achieving financial equilibrium. Much can be learned from their example.

To illustrate how one can put these concepts into practical use, it is helpful to review

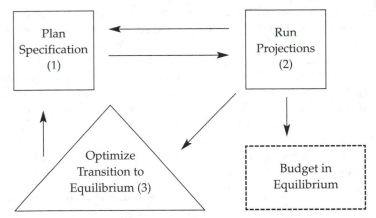

Figure 43.1 The CHOICE-OP™ strategic financial management model is one model for managing the decision-making process. Its tool set simplifies the tasks of projecting an institution's financial position and planning for a smooth transition to budgetary equilibrium. This model was designed to operate iteratively, allowing users to understand and compare the economic impact of several policy scenarios quickly. The user (1) specifies institutional data and growth plans, (2) runs projections, and (3) reviews results. With the benefit of new information, he or she returns to the data specification stage to refine primary planning variable (PPV) inputs. Each cycle complements one's knowledge of the effects of policy changes on the economic outcome. Through its Choice of Opportunities feature the model enables the user to make value judgments between PPVs, and through its Choice Optimization feature it enables the user to optimize the path transitioning from the base case to the equilibrium target.

the methodology of CHOICE-OP™ (see Figure 43.1), a planning and optimization model developed by P.R. Taylor Associates to analyze an institution's entire set of choices and resultant policies—choices and policies that cover investment as well as other strategic financial management decisions.

DECISION-MAKING PROCESS

Running the business of a college or university is a complex task, no matter what size the institution. In addition to the normal constraints, academic financial decisions involve a more subjective value function (that will differ from institution to institution) than exists in the typical business setting. And today, the choice of academic priorities and the supporting financial decisions must reflect market forces as well as institutional preferences. Doing more with less has become the order of the day.

The fundamental questions are, "What resources are (could be) available for programs (operations and capital)?" and "What programs need funding the most?" To induce more efficient and effective operations than in the past,[4] savvy administrators must search for ways in which the educational components can

be rearranged (i.e., "growth by substitution") as well as improved and ensure that the funding sources are available for each. Thoughtful decisions require knowledge of academic disciplines and of institutional strengths and weaknesses. Common sense is also a prerequisite. Even when mixed with a healthy dose of budgetary restraint, these criteria are not sufficient for effective resource allocation. *Process* is the key for successful financial operations management as well as for fiduciary investment management. "While resource allocation does boil down to knowledgeable people making informed decisions, the record shows that *process—the way decisions are made and communicated—powerfully affects outcomes.*"[5]

Several decades of work by the most advanced institutions in terms of planning have revealed just what constitutes good process and what can be expected of it. As anyone who has tried to tackle these problems can attest, there are innumerable planning variables (and financial dependencies) to value and balance. Good process assures that each factor is given its proper consideration and weighting, is analyzed in the context of the whole, and is consistently dealt with as different forecasts and plans are developed. The process described in this article lays the necessary foundation to arrive at optimal solutions. Integrated financial planning thus forms the cornerstone of good process.

The goal is to design and implement operating financial and investment policies that result in long-run financial equilibrium[6] consistent with each institution's academic values. This coordinated approach requires an in-depth understanding of the critical links between investment management and strategic finance. It also requires sophisticated analytic tools to optimize choices from a viable selection of alternatives. The links described below highlight fundamental techniques, software tools, and modern investment principles that can be successfully applied to the financial challenges of any institution.

INTEGRATED STRATEGIC FINANCIAL PLANNING PROCESS

Figure 43.2 illustrates the integrated, strategic financial planning process by emphasizing the building blocks of the institution's financial model.

The financial equilibrium spending rate is the key link between the investment management policies of the endowment (investment steps I1–I5) and the other financial policies gov-

erning the institution's capital structure and funding of operations (financial steps F1–F5). The spending rate should be set with an understanding of the nonuniform nature of expected compounded annual investment returns. The most comprehensive analyses utilize Monte Carlo or equivalent return simulation techniques and payout smoothing functions appropriate to the task. The steps of the strategic financial process are explained below.

Understanding Institutional Needs and Resources

In step F1 of the integrated financial planning process, the institution's so-called primary planning variables (PPVs)[7] and financial resources must be identified and assigned appropriate values. Structural interrelationships that exist among many of the variables of the operating budget are also defined. In general, an analysis of PPVs should (1) separate the associated physical variable from its unit price and (2) incorporate the full incremental cost and revenue associated with each PPV. The decision process will consider whether the unit costs are determined or strongly influenced by an outside market, whether they depend on institutional goals and philosophy, or both.

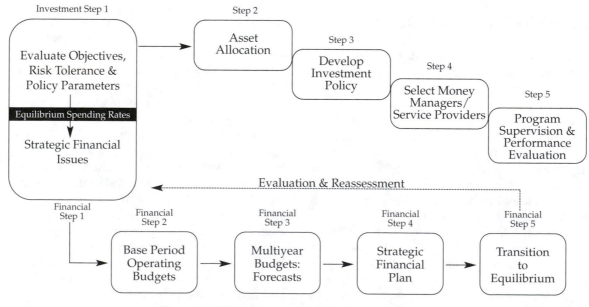

Figure 43.2 Strategic Financial Management Process

This step is inextricably linked to overall investment policy by the financial equilibrium spending rate developed in steps I1 and I2 of the prudent investment process below.

Base Period Operating Budget

Step F2 yields an in-depth understanding of the components that make up the base period (current) operating budget and the institution's goals for future program development. Often, explicit financial submodels are constructed to develop a detailed formulation of the cost, revenue, and demand functions, showing the important linkages that are known to exist between components of the budget. Examples of such submodels include personnel fringe benefits, tuition income, student financial aid, student demand, state public appropriations as a function of institutional factors and state resources, indirect cost recovery on research grants and contracts, and endowment total return and payout. Of course, each of these categories may be further subdivided, depending on the materiality of the item and the complexity of the interrelationships. The determination of which of these budget areas needs to be modeled in depth will vary by institution, as will the relative priorities for the development of the appropriate submodels.

Value measures also play a prominent role in financial decision making. While it is difficult to quantify an institution's values, there is no getting away from the practical necessity of assessing the trade-offs among the key planning variables themselves. This can be done intuitively, possibly with the aid of specialized software tools.[8] However, research has shown how mathematical value functions that sufficiently reflect educational attitudes and judgments can be developed. Such models are essential in devising optimal base period budgets and in choosing preferred long-run strategic plans, as we shall discuss in step F4.

The successful value optimization model will do the following:

- Specify the relevant set of PPVs (i.e., those that are both relevant and to some extent controllable).

- Identify the form and parameters of the constraints (i.e., how the PPVs affect cost and revenue, what the proper demand-and-supply functions are, and whether these functions are to be handled explicitly or subsumed in the value function).

- Present a valid representation of the key administrators' preferences among outcomes of the PPVs.

The latter may be elicited by direct query, through pencil-and-paper questionnaires, or with the aid of an interactive model that varies the inquiries based on the planner's input, and vice versa.

Multiyear Budgets: Forecasts

Building on the process described above, in step F3 we take the next logical step to build dynamic models that deal with more than one period, typically a planning period of three to five years. At its root level, this is a task of estimating the growth rates, year by year, of the PPVs in the budget model. Initially, this is where the pioneer institutions concentrated their modeling efforts and where midsized institutions must begin: cash flow and balance sheet forecasting requirements. Starting with the base period operating budget, various results are forecast using the estimated growth rates for the PPVs. Material outside factors likely to influence the outcomes are also taken into consideration. Happily, you need not start from square one in this exercise; early development efforts by these pioneering institutions yielded sophisticated models of financial and operational performance that are the mainstay of today's more comprehensive approaches.

The overall goal of step F3 is not merely to extrapolate the decisions of the initial base budgeting period to later years, but to define one or more feasible "equilibrium budgets" that can be realistically achieved in the budget year following the planning period, or sooner. By "feasible," we mean consistency with an institution's resources and objectives, including its subjective values as well as financial constraints. By "equilibrium budgets," we mean those likely to result in long-run financial equilibrium (LRFE), the stability concept for financial and physical capital developed by William F. Massy at Stanford University in the early 1970s and now widely recognized as providing the key planning discipline for endowed institutions. Indeed, it is the LRFE concept that enables the planner to satisfy the fundamental challenge of dynamic (multi-period) modeling—to quantify the trade-offs between present and future values of a university's tangible planning variables.

Long-run Financial Equilibrium

- Balance the budget and the long-run growth rates of revenue and expense.
- Develop sustainable tuition, financial aid, and total compensation policies.
- Manage the growth of financial and physical capital.

The essential notion of LRFE is that, in addition to balancing the current budget, managers must ensure that by the end of the planning period the structural growth rates for revenue and expense are approximately equal. This requires managers to link endowment investment strategy and spending policy with budget policy and planning parameters like tuition, financial aid and total compensation growth, physical capital investment and renewal, new program development, and expenditure allocation. Otherwise, regardless of how the base period budget is balanced, there is no certainty that later years' budgets will be balanced or that such budgetary planning will sustain an institution's programs.

In the near term, financial managers of endowed institutions must balance immediate spending imperatives with the need to maintain the purchasing power of financial capital. They must also maintain the right balance between financial capital and physical capital (plant and equipment).

Financial and Physical Capital

- Endowment spending policies: total return and payout targets, smoothing rules.
- Debt discipline: managing liabilities.
- Gross and net endowment support ratios.
- Plant and equipment: investment rates, depreciation, and deferred maintenance.

While everyone appreciates the options and choices made possible by an endowment, this very flexibility places heavy demands on financial managers—demands that require special conceptual tools and models usually not available to small and medium-sized institutions. As one example, many institutions spend too large a fraction of their total investment return and reinvest too little to maintain the endowment's purchasing power. So-called "conservative" (i.e., fixed-income-oriented) investment and payout policies, sometimes instituted to achieve interest and dividend yields sufficient to meet spending needs, can compound the problem. In contrast, strategic financial managers invest for higher total return, determine the spending rate (the link to investment policy) based on long-term equilibrium considerations rather than the happenstance of yield versus capital appreciation, and mitigate volatility through investment diversification and payout smoothing policies.

Similarly, debt by itself can be a powerful leveraging force, but it adds risk to an institution's strategic financial equation and must be considered in the integrated context of endowment total return, payout, and volatility. This consideration produces a policy discipline that is more attuned to an institution's needs than ratings by external agencies; indeed, the existence of such a discipline may actually improve an institution's credit ratings.

In developing payout and debt policies, strategic financial managers should focus on the ratio of endowment spending to total education and general expenditures (the "endowment support ratio"), both gross and net of debt service, as a measure of long-term financial health. A comprehensive strategic financial model must also take account of physical capital renewal. To maintain genuine financial equilibrium, one must avoid the creation of hidden liabilities: investment rates should be commensurate with replacement cost; depreciation and O&M budgets should be scrutinized to avoid deferred maintenance surprises.

In this step a number of feasible forecasts (and combinations of institutional policies) should be evaluated. Prudence could not suggest otherwise, given the sheer complexity of the component interrelationships[9] and the imperfect nature of the inputs. Of course, a single forecast would represent only one of many possible policies for an institution, to the extent that the interrelationships between the PPVs (i.e., internal pricing decisions) or the PPV growth rates themselves fall under institutional control. Moreover, the discipline of the LRFE now makes the analysis manageable; it provides the essential methodology for reducing the overwhelming dimensions of evaluating the trade-offs between present and future values of the many planning variables and their potential combinations.

Thus, planners in the largest institutions experiment with many different forecast scenarios to develop a thorough understanding not just of the numbers but of the inherent trade-offs between alternative institutional value judgments. Rather than proceeding purely by trial and error, many now use computer models to embed the projection and trade-off assumptions, ensuring consistency among the scenarios and exploring a wider range of solutions. When they are satisfied that they have identified at least a few feasible alternatives that might achieve their organizational goals, they move to finalize a strategic plan.

Strategic Financial Plan

In step F4 the professional planner chooses his or her preferred equilibrium scenario from among those feasible scenarios identified in step F3. Feasibility is only a necessary condition for a good plan, not a sufficient one. The forecast model by itself is usually insufficient for planning purposes—while it can project future expected budget surpluses or deficits, it cannot by itself identify strategies for dealing with them.[10] That is the job of the professional planner—to choose the scenario that best suits the institution's objectives.

Here, as in step F2, research shows that the most sophisticated institutions can utilize specialized value optimization models to assist in making this decision. We know from experience that the problems posed by the planner's desire to optimize his or her institution's preferred financial position (and the path to get there) are beyond the functionality of common spreadsheets. In any case, the analyses performed in steps F1 through F3 bolster the planner's overall understanding of the trade-offs affecting his or her decision and facilitate his or her ability to make a reasoned choice.

After planners choose the preferred strategic financial plan, they still must decide how the budget should be adjusted during the planning period as the institution moves to equilibrium. That task is made all the more difficult when the future budget deficits revealed by the step F3 models are very large. Often, a different sort of model will be needed, a "transition-to-equilibrium model" as described in step F5.

TRANSITION TO FINANCIAL EQUILIBRIUM

Step F5 selects the optimal path (e.g., speed, type of budget adjustments) during the planning period to make a transition (year by year) from the base period budget to the chosen financial equilibrium budget. With even a medium-term planning horizon and 15 to 20 primary planning variables, the generalized dynamic optimization problem quickly becomes intractable. The solution lies in partitioning the problem into medium (three- to five-year transition period) and long-range (equilibrium-period) components.

The transition period financial forecast is developed from the bottom up and is highly detailed. Beyond the transition period, the equilibrium-period model is greatly simplified. The set of PPVs is reduced by aggregation: one variable may be used for total expenditures, and in any case constant growth rates are assumed to apply to the period.

The transition path is optimized around (1) a constraint requiring a balanced budget at the end of the transition period, (2) a decision rule for moving the endowment payout rate from its initial value in the base year to the chosen equilibrium value, and (3) weighted preference ranges of select PPVs.

Historically, the sophisticated modeling tools necessary to analyze and optimize the complex relationships described above were only available to institutions committing significant resources to the effort. New, integrated computer models now make those capabilities available to the smallest endowed institutions.

THE STRATEGIC FINANCIAL AND INVESTMENT MODEL

- Projects financial outcomes based on planning and policy parameters.

- Links endowment investment policy and investment return to strategic finance decisions.
- Identifies feasible equilibrium financial positions and assists in the choice of an optimal equilibrium target.
- Calculates policy and budget adjustments needed to make the transition smoothly to financial equilibrium.

Keep in mind that no model by itself can be expected to create an appropriate strategic financial plan. The planner's role in the decision-making process is key. Development of a comprehensive strategic financial and investment plan requires knowledge of an institution's values and an in-depth understanding of its current and projected resources, revenues, operating expenses, and capital needs. It also requires a sophisticated approach to investment management and the links between endowment risk and return and endowment spending.

With common spreadsheet tools, financial planners are able to build base case financial models to analyze and plan institutional budgets, projecting fiscal effects of planned expenditures and exogenous influences. However, most spreadsheet models fall short of needs, because they do not typically incorporate the endowment return and spending parameters that should be developed using modern portfolio models. Nor do they provide any structure or guidance for optimizing an institution's equilibrium position or the path to get there. Clearly, consideration of the linkages between spending and saving requires a more comprehensive approach than afforded by the typical spreadsheet models for projecting revenue and expense.

In short, all four steps above are important for the development of a good plan. Iterative use of these models provides insights that complement the planner's understanding of the consequences of various planning trade-offs and facilitate the planner's choice of optimal equilibrium solutions from among the feasible equilibrium alternatives identified with the projection models.

Once a preferred equilibrium result is chosen, the next logical step is to identify the best transition from the base budget position to the equilibrium target. Only the most sophisticated models provide the software tools needed to implement this step. These more robust integrated models help investment committees assess both the expected long-term effects of alternative spending-saving policies and the risks associated with them. By focusing attention on the key policy questions related to long-term financial equilibrium, committees gain an understanding of the real strategic financial prospects for their institutions.

INVESTMENT MANAGEMENT

Fiduciaries, trustees, and investment committees often fail to prioritize well when allocating their time to their various responsibilities. Specifically, they spend far too much time on the details of various investment strategies, securities, asset classes, and managers, leaving too little time for the paramount issues relating to the overall objectives of their institution, their individual and collective attitudes toward risk in all its forms, and their overall asset allocation and its fit with their objectives and risk tolerance.

This section focuses on overall priorities and the concept of effective delegation. We address the workings of an effective investment committee and introduce the five-step prudent process of investment management, developed and practiced by the largest and best institutional investors over the last three decades.

THE FIVE-STEP PRUDENT PROCESS OF INVESTMENT MANAGEMENT

We start the process (see Figure 43.3) by ensuring effective integration of the strategic financial plan with the investment strategy, then move through strategic asset allocation and the investment policy statement to manager selection issues. In selecting money managers, we focus not on searching for the hottest or most persuasive money managers, but rather on the most effective implementation of the asset allocation and investment policy. Finally, we review a process and specific techniques employed in monitoring and supervising the hired money managers and, more importantly, the portfolio as a whole.

Step I1: Determine objectives, risk tolerance, and policy parameters

Step I1: is the most important—and perhaps most frequently overlooked—step for

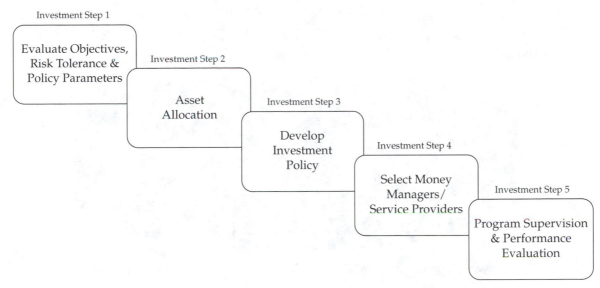

Figure 43.3 The Five-Step Prudent Process of Investment Management

defining one's goals, setting the process in motion, and quantifying what we mean by success. Specific techniques should be used to define institutional objectives in light of the needs identified in the strategic financial planning process, including scenario planning, statistical forecasting, and Monte Carlo simulation, taking account of combinations of investment results and spending policies over various periods of time. No single method is likely to yield a comprehensive view, and this process of exploring in detail alternative scenarios is essential to educate the committee and prepare it to respond to future events and changes.

Specifically, the investment committee needs to know the likely results of its combined policies and decisions for the following two reasons:

- *The committee can only hope to make intelligent decisions in these areas if it understands the long-term impacts of various decisions.* Good trade-offs between risk and reward, program growth and stability, for example, can only be made with this kind of long-range outlook and understanding of the possibilities.

- *A long-term program only works if the committee is able to stay with it.* For example, adopting too aggressive an investment policy could lead to panic by board members or various constituencies in a

down-turn and result in serious program cutbacks.

The committee also cannot simply avoid risk altogether if it hopes to maintain or increase the value of the assets—and the level of supported activities. Specific quantitative projections and qualitative discussions of scenarios and their impacts serve to increase the level of comfort and commitment to the investment policy and ensure continuity in turbulent markets.

The tools of modern portfolio theory enable the well-advised committee to evaluate "minimum-risk" portfolios, which are those portfolios that take the minimum expected risk of fluctuation in value for a given level of expected return. We will look at these tools in step I2, but it is important to anticipate the essential information required to construct an appropriate asset allocation because it is here, in step I1, that the in-depth understanding of return needs and risk tolerance are developed.

Step I2: Asset Allocation

The well-made asset allocation decision flows through the rest of the program, providing the structure and the rationale for the remainder of the tasks and decisions (see Figure 43.4). It defines a set of reasonable expectations for the portfolio and the program as a whole. It determines the specific money management tasks to

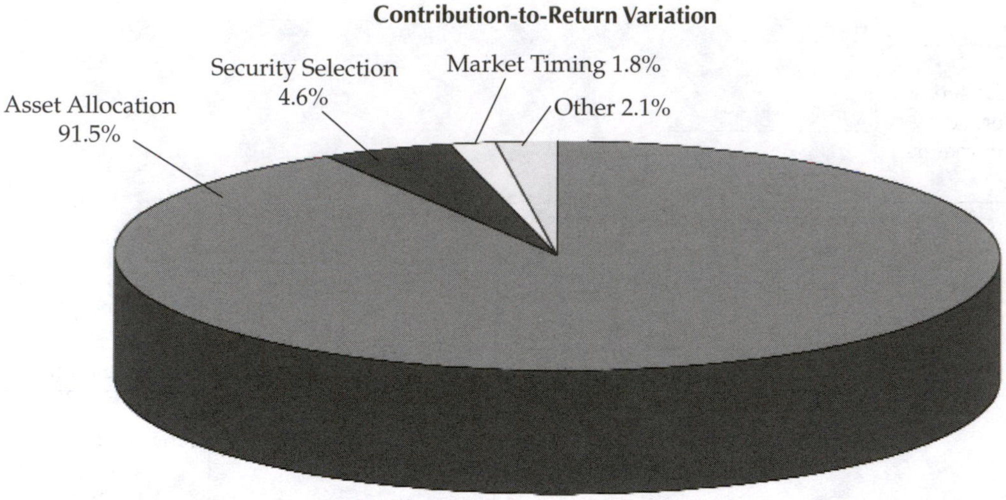

Contribution-to-Return Variation

Figure 43.4 The Importance of Asset Allocation in Explaining Total Portfolio Returns

Source: Brinson, Singer, and Beebowee (1991).

be delegated and the standards for evaluating the performance of selected managers.

Keep in mind throughout the process that this is more about risk control than about maximizing returns. Asset allocation gives the committee a set of reasonable expectations about risk, i.e., how much might be lost. Returns are hard to predict, especially in the short term, but risk can be understood and controlled.

Step I3: Develop Investment Policy

A good investment policy statement (IPS) serves as an effective communication tool among all parties (see Figure 43.5). In step I3, the outstanding investment process followed so far is now documented and communicated to all concerned, from alumni to custodians; from deans to money managers; from future committee members to, if necessary, courts assessing the quality of the fiduciary work of the committee.

The IPS is a living, working document, revised as required, that lays out the investment program and serves as a reference and guide for all parties. It should spell out the results of the first two steps, including the quantitative measures of expected risk and return, the chosen allocation to each asset class and subclass, and portfolio rebalancing parameters. It should assign specific responsibilities for rebalancing, cash investment and reinvest-

ment, and performance reporting. When money managers are chosen, they are added to the IPS. Each of the investment styles is described, including general portfolio holdings and credit guidelines by asset class. The managers need to be identified specifically by style and to know their guidelines.

Over and over the committee and the staff will find that the IPS answers questions and resolves disputes. Producing a good IPS and ensuring that all parties have their copy will solve a lot of problems in advance and will make those that do arise much simpler to handle.

The IPS is the business plan for the endowment—do not invest without one.

Step I4: Select Money Managers/ Service Providers

Now that a program has been established and an asset allocation selected, the committee is ready to select managers. They know just what they want (e.g., $12 million to large cap growth equity) and are ready to look for good, consistent style managers to implement the asset allocation.

The essence of the manager selection process is investment style. The first thing a decision maker needs to know about a group of managers is that they follow consistent styles. Help is needed to do this analysis—it is a major undertaking. The manager databases and analytical capacity to do this work are readily available

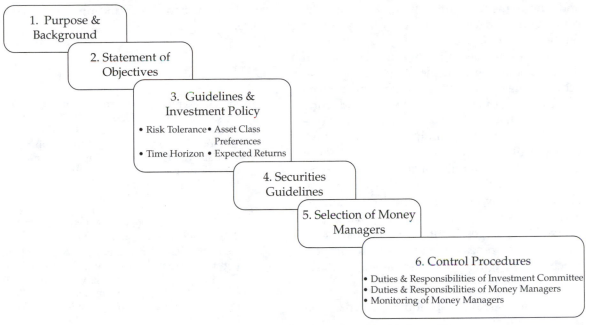

Figure 43.5 The Investment Policy Statement: The Business Plan

Copyright F.R. Taylor Associates, Inc. 1996.

from consultants, although the quality of these resources varies greatly and should be closely scrutinized. Without these resources, the committee lacks essential information and cannot make a good choice of investment managers.

Remember, the committee is implementing an asset allocation to achieve risk control and expected long-term returns. Once a portfolio is constructed thoughtfully with consistent style managers, any out-performance that is achieved is icing on the cake. Managers must be evaluated first on their adherence to specific investment styles, on the stability of their organizations, and on respectable long-term performance in their style.

Step 15: Program Supervision and Performance Evaluation

The asset allocation dictates the portfolio bench mark—created from the appropriately weighted indices. A portfolio universe of similar institutions is also very useful to track over time how the portfolio ranks compared with portfolios of other colleges. Pension plans, for example, can be compared. Over a period of several years a well-implemented portfolio should track its benchmark pretty closely and fare well among its peers. Substantial deviation—in either direction—is cause for concern and examination.

Money managers should be evaluated on an ongoing basis in the same way they were evaluated when they were selected: consistent style management in their peer group and compared to appropriate benchmarks. It is generally advisable, absent specific negative events calling for immediate action (e.g., the resignation of the star portfolio manager or a substantial style deviation), to evaluate the performance of a money manager over a market cycle of several years.

SUMMARY

In this article we have described an integrated approach to financial management for university and college administrators. This approach, made possible by marrying the best of strategic financial management and modern investment management processes, provides administrators with the tools necessary to manage a comprehensive process. Within this process they are able to make a myriad of difficult decisions regarding plant and equipment investment, current spending, investment management, and endowment accumulation, knowing the context for the decisions and their likely impact on the institution as a whole.

The best-managed institutions have shown the way, adopting strategic financial plans that achieve long-run financial equilibrium. In some instances, out of chaotic year-to-year budgeting processes they have created stable and predictable financial environments—they have clearly demonstrated that the results are worth the effort. Moreover, the analytical tools necessary to support an integrated decision-making process are now available to midsized colleges and universities, making this approach, pioneered by the largest institutions, feasible for all.

We have repeatedly stressed the importance of engaging in a disciplined strategic financial process:

- Understand institutional needs and resources.

- Develop a base period operating budget.

- Forecast multi-year budgets.

- Develop a strategic financial plan.

- Choose the optimal path for transition to financial equilibrium.

We should also emphasize that planning models help provide conditions for academic excellence, but of course they can't guarantee it. One key thing they can do is help you consider carefully the various intangibles that need to be built into the decision-making processes, lest these processes be dominated by the tangibles.

As we have discussed, endowment managers need software tools to consider all the factors in a comprehensive fashion, and while the tools should be simple to use they must be complete, stable, and adaptable to your circumstances. Such software tools add considerable value for policing the projection process and evaluating the trade-offs for making the transition to equilibrium.

Similarly, the five-step investment management process provides important discipline for application of modern portfolio tools to endowment management. The long-term differentials between investment returns for large and small endowments provide an excellent example of the benefits of an improved investment process.

NOTES

1. John G. Kemeny, forward in *Planning Models for Colleges and Universities,* by David S. P. Hopkins and William F. Massy (Stanford: Stanford University Press, 1981), p. xix.
2. William F. Massy. "Planning for Stanford's Long-Range Financial Stability: A Time for Hard Choices" in *Stanford University Annual Financial Report* (1974), p. 6.
3. National Association of College and University Business Officers, 1994 NACUBO *Endowment Study* (Washington, D.C.: NACUBO, 1997), pp. 56–5 7, exhibit 8, p. 118, exhibit 15. Figures compare endowments with less than $25 million (small) to those with more than $400 million (large); intermediate sizes show the same trends. Earnings reflect five-year total return.
4. William F. Massy, "Productivity Issues in Higher Education" in *Resource Allocation in Higher Education* (Ann Arbor: University of Michigan Press, 1996), p. 49.
5. William F. Massey, *Resource Allocation in Higher Education* (Ann Arbor: University of Michigan Press, 1996), p. 3.
6. The phrase was coined by William F. Massy in 1973 and is the accepted shorthand way of describing a set of conditions under which a university's budget will stay balanced, or almost balanced, over a period of years.
7. Quantities that have a substantial impact on a university's operating budget and, at least in the short run, are subject to some central university control may be either a base level (e.g., faculty FTEs) or growth rate (e.g., that of faculty salaries).
8. The Educom Financial Planning Model (EFPM), based on the work of David S. P. Hopkins and William F. Massy (see note 1) and located on Cornell University's mainframe computer, provided a rudimentary set of software aids for assessing trade-offs. At its peak of popularity in the early 1980s, EFPM was used by more than 100 institutions located around the world.
9. Our experience has demonstrated that the options and even the values of one period are often hard to reconcile with those of another.
10. David S. P. Hopkins and William F. Massy (a), *Planning Models for Colleges and Universities* (Stanford: Stanford University Press, 1981), p. 133.

Chapter 44

How Much Does Instruction and Research Really Cost?

Patrick M. Rooney, Victor M. H. Borden, and Timothy J. Thomas

Patrick M. Rooney is special assistant to the vice president for long-range planning and an associate professor of economics at Indiana University–Purdue University Indianapolis. He has a bachelor's, master's and Ph.D. in economics from the University of Notre Dame.

Victor M. H. Borden is Director of Information Management and Institutional Research and assistant professor of psychology at Indiana University–Purdue University Indianapolis. He holds a bachelor's in psychology and sociology from the University of Rochester and a master's and a Ph.D. in psychology from the University of Massachusetts.

Timothy J. Thomas is a research analyst with Information Management and Institutional Research at Indiana University–Purdue University Indianapolis. He has a bachelor's in economics from the University of Michigan and is a master's degree candidate in history at IUPUI.

The cost of attending a college or university has risen dramatically over the last 30 years when compared with other public and private expenditures. A recent study by the National Commission on the Cost of Higher Education (1997, 1998) places these increases in the comparative context of other economic indicators. Between 1981 and 1995, tuition at public four-year colleges increased at a rate two to three times higher than the Consumer Price Index, the traditional measure of price inflation. College tuition has also increased faster than commonly accepted measures of income. From 1987 to 1996, disposable per capita income rose 52 percent. The price of public higher education during the same period rose from 95 percent for four-year institutions to 169 percent for two-year institutions.

Rising costs at public universities have been attributed to a broad array of economic, political, and social forces. These include the decline in state appropriations; ever-advancing information and research technologies and their supporting infrastructural requirements; the necessity for expenditures on new and redesigned facilities prompted by enrollment growth and the special needs of newly served student populations; high levels of deferred maintenance; and increasing expenditures on financial aid to attract and retain students.

More generally, Massy and Zemsky (1994) identify two phenomena contributing to increased costs to institutions. They coined the term "academic ratchet" to refer to the increasing focus of faculty roles on specialized research and scholarship rather than on the broader goals of the institution. The second phenomenon, dubbed "administrative lattice," describes how professional

Source: *Planning for Higher Education*, Vol. 27, Spring 1999, pp. 42–54. Society for College and University Planning, Washington, D.C.

administrative structures continually grow more complex to support student life, faculty work, athletic enterprises, and public accountability requirements.

These developments have evoked demands for greater accountability and cost control from many state legislatures and governance boards. Additionally, increasing competition from entrepreneurial institutions, such as the University of Phoenix, has encouraged senior college administrators to support the development of more sophisticated tools to help assess and adjust the alignment of expenses and revenues to the institution's missions, goals, and values.

Higher education institutions have struggled with issues of representing costs for many years. The National Center for Higher Education Management System Resource Requirements Prediction Model (RRPM) of the late 1960s and early 1970s made the use of cost-per-student credit hour as a pivotal planning metric popular among higher education institutions and systems. The popularity of RRPM and several other computer-based planning models for resource allocation declined due to the difficulty in recasting existing data systems and the prioritization of operational functions, such as payroll and registration, ahead of planning needs. Simpson and Sperber (1984) described the kinds of cost information that a department-level administrator would find useful, based largely on distribution of faculty effort over mission-critical activities. Because these and other efforts focused on department-level budgets, they missed the very significant central administrative overhead costs.

Middaugh (1996, 1997) developed a model and collected data nationally to represent instructional costs across a variety of disciplines. The several iterations of the National Study of Instructional Costs and Productivity by Academic Discipline provide useful indicators of instructional effort among full- and part-time faculty and graduate assistants, but the usefulness of its cost information is limited. Like the studies already mentioned, the Middaugh model does not include campus, school, and departmental overheads, thus missing the attribution of central administrative costs. Also, the model attributes all education and general expenses to the instruction function, thereby obscuring the degree to which faculty engage in research and service not specifically funded by sponsored contracts and grants.

This paper describes an institution-wide activity-based costing study conducted at a large, Midwestern, public university located in an urban setting. This program cost study, as it is referred to, provides campus-, school-, and, most importantly, department-level cost information for the full range of mission-critical activities: teaching, research, and service. The study also includes the allocation of all levels of overhead—department, school, and central administration—to the mission-critical activities within each academic unit. Direct and overhead costs are made explicit in this cost model so they can be evaluated separately or together in formulating plans and budgets. The information generated by this model is used with indicators of program quality and accessibility as an integral part of the campus planning and budget processes.

CONCEPTUAL BACKGROUND: ACTIVITY-BASED COSTING

Activity-based costing methods have become a centerpiece in the private sector's efforts to better ascertain costs and revenues associated with the mission-critical activities and product lines of an enterprise. More recently, several colleges and universities have applied activity-based costing methods to the analysis of costs and revenues in higher education. Based on the fundamental principles of activity-based costing, a number of colleges and universities seeking to better manage the costs of higher education have adopted and adapted responsibility-centered management (RCM) (Whalen 1991; Stocum and Rooney 1997; Robbins and Rooney 1995). While activity-based costing and RCM can be used together, each can be used quite independently. Activity-based costing is used to better understand the costs of an activity or set of activities, including overhead. RCM is a broader concept that is a decentralized approach to financial management designed to enhance both academic planning and fiscal efficiency. In an RCM environment each academic and administrative unit is treated as an operating unit called a responsibility center (RC). Each RC assumes primary responsibility for its own fiscal management, including keeping all instructional and other revenues and paying all of the costs of its operation. In this system, the campus administration funds support activities and infrastructure through taxes on the RCs.

Activity-based costing methods and RCM budgeting employs cost drivers to allocate the overhead costs of an enterprise to the primary productive units and their respective activities and products. These methods have been cited as an effective way to assess the costs and contributions of the various activities necessary to the attainment of critical enterprise goals.

As a learning organization, a college or university faces special challenges for engaging in activity-based costing. In the first place, the bottom line relates more directly to the creation, dissemination, and application of knowledge rather than to monetary considerations, although fiscal concerns directly influence an institution's ability to pursue its primary missions. Second, a large component of the cost of higher education is related to how the mission-critical workforce, the faculty, spend their time. Not only does faculty compensation represent a significant portion of a college's or university's costs, but the way faculty use their collective time in pursuing research, teaching, and service activities determines the support costs required in each of those areas.

ORGANIZATIONAL CONTEXT

This study was conducted at Indiana University-Purdue University Indianapolis, an urban public university with more than 27,000 students, 1,500 full-time faculty, 3,500 full-time staff, and a budget of approximately $660 million, including $125 million of externally funded research. The university has 18 academic schools with more than 180 degree programs, ranging from the associate through doctoral levels as well as several of the country's largest first-professional programs in medicine, dentistry, and law. Its internal complexity is compounded by the fact that its academic programs are tied directly to both of the state's large research universities (Indiana University and Purdue University), although it is administratively affiliated with only one of them (Indiana University). As at many public universities, the state appropriation represents a declining portion of the total funding. Tuition and fees, research funds, and other private sources of support represent an increasing proportion.

METHOD

The sophistication and success of an activity-based costing study rests largely on the validity, reliability, and availability of the cost drivers used to allocate overhead expenses to the "product line" of an organization. Like the University of Rhode Island cost study,[1] the current analysis starts with a relatively simple articulation of the mission-critical activities of the university and proceeds to the more complex task of attributing expenditures and revenues to these activities. While the URI study relied almost entirely on student credit hours to attribute revenues and expenses to academic programs and activities, the present study uses a more sophisticated system for allocating costs based on extensions to the existing RCM budgeting and faculty-activity accountability systems.

Defining Mission-Critical Activities

The final target of all revenues and expenditures is the full array of degree programs and department-based service instruction, research, and outreach/public service. More specifically, these mission-critical activities are defined as follows:

- *Undergraduate service instruction.* Instruction and curriculum development associated with courses intended for students not enrolled in the school's or the department's undergraduate degree programs. This includes all credit hour enrollments by nondepartment major students in undergraduate courses.

- *Undergraduate majors.* Instruction, advising, and curriculum development related to maintaining undergraduate degree programs and supporting the students who enroll in them.

- *Graduate majors.* Instruction, program management, and student/curriculum development associated with graduate degree programs, graduate courses, and the students who enroll in them, whether they are enrolled in the school's or department's graduate program or not. No graduate service category was maintained, as the vast majority of these courses would not be offered if there were no graduate degree program.

- *Research and scholarly activity.* Research and scholarship among the faculty in general and among staff specifically hired to support such activity through sponsored grants, contracts, and other restricted sources of funds.

- *Outreach and public service.* Outreach and public service activities among the faculty in general and among staff specifically hired to support such activity via sponsored grants, contracts, and other restricted sources of funds.

The present analysis diverges from the URI study with regard to activity specifications in three notable ways:

- Degree programs are identified only to the department and degree level. That is, the analysis distinguishes between undergraduate, graduate, and professional degrees but does not further distinguish among multiple degree programs at each level (e.g., more than one baccalaureate degree program or master's versus doctoral programs). This organizational level of analysis was chosen to expedite the current study with the expectation that individual program costs could be the focus of a later effort.

- Expenditures are first distributed to administrative activities in the same fashion as they are distributed to the mission-critical activities, as described below. The expenditures associated with administrative activity were then redistributed over the mission-critical activities and thereby treated as an element of overhead (e.g., department and school overhead). See Figure 44.4.

- Fee income from undergraduate courses was allocated between "major" and "service" based on the major of each student enrolled in the section. This allowed differentiation between two students taking the same course for different purposes (majors versus service instruction). Fee income from graduate

courses was allocated solely to the "graduate majors" activity.

Attributing Expenditures and Revenues.

The campus's RCM model is based on the designation of both academic or administrative budgetary centers, the RCs. The academic schools, each headed by a dean, comprise the academic RCs. Administrative RCs consist of the major administrative divisions that are headed by a vice chancellor as well as several other large administrative and academic support units. The campus's RCM model uses a set of cost drivers (e.g., student credit hours, faculty and staff full-time equivalency (FTE), and square footage) to allocate to each academic RC those revenues received centrally (state appropriation) and the costs of central administration and support activities (assessments).[2] In addition, the RCM model and supporting accounting systems allow some revenues (e.g., tuition and fee income) to be attributed directly to academic RCs. Finally, for sponsored grants and contracts and certain other restricted accounts, both revenues and expenditures can be attributed directly to a specific activity (teaching, research, or service) within a school or department using a "higher education function code" that indicates whether the account involved supports research, service, or instructional activities.

Two additional sets of cost drivers were developed for the program cost study. *Organizational cost drivers* attribute to departments (where necessary) those revenues and expenditures that originate or are initially attributed to school and administrative unit accounts. *Activity cost drivers* attribute to the mission-critical activities within schools and departments the nonrestricted funds, which comprise the majority of the annual revenues and expenditures. Figure 44.1 summarizes the revenue and expenditure allocation process.

Starting at the left side of Figure 44.1, most institutional revenues are attributed through the accounting system to the appropriate academic RC. Some revenue sources, such as sponsored grants and contracts, are attributed directly to department and sometimes directly to specific activities within those departments. The top section of the middle column of Figure 44.1 represents the RCM assessments charged

Revenues   **Organizational Structure**   **Activities**

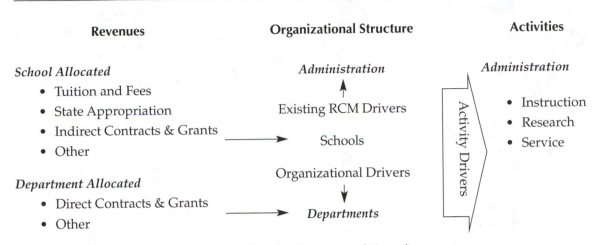

Figure 44.1 Allocating Revenues and Expenditures

to academic RCs to fund administrative RCs. The bottom of the middle column illustrates the use of organizational cost drivers to devolve revenues to the departments. Finally, all revenues are associated with expenditures using the newly developed activity cost drives, which supplement the known restricted expenditures.

Organizational Cost Drivers

Many expenditures, such as all RC assessments for campus administration expenses and revenues, including tuition and fees, originate at the campus level and are then attributed to the academic RC level. For RCs that organize degree programs using a department structure (five of the 14 RCs included in the study), it was necessary to drive these expenditures and revenues down to the department level. The drivers used in this analysis depend on the category of revenue or expenditure. Several possible cost drivers were modeled before settling on those producing the most consistent results across RCs.

The most common drivers are student credit hours (e.g., for tuition and fee revenues and assessments for undergraduate support services) and the proportion of unit full-time academic salaries paid from "Education and General" accounts. For example, the state appropriation is distributed according to the academic salaries driver. Each department receives credit for a portion of the appropriation equivalent to the proportion of total RC full-time academic salaries within that department. That is, if department A accounts for 17

percent of total RC academic salaries, it receives credit for 17 percent of the state appropriation within that school. Similarly, department A would receive a "debit" for 17 percent of the RC assessments, which are also driven by the full-time academic salaries driver. Figure 44.2 illustrates the use of organizational cost drivers to allocate the two largest sources of revenues (tuition and fees and state appropriation) and the overhead expenses (assessments) used to fund central administrative units.

The full-time academic salaries driver was chosen over various modeled combinations of student credit hours, faculty FTE, and staff FTE. The academic salaries driver produced the most stable and consistent empirical results. It is also intuitively appealing in that the academic payroll is the primary "fiscal fuel" for engaging in the mission-critical activities of teaching, research, and service. In addition, state appropriation, faculty salaries, and campus assessments tend to be fairly stable; hence, they are all "quasi-fixed."

Activity Cost Drivers

Once all financial information has been driven to the appropriate unit level, the next step is to move these amounts across the mission-critical activities using the activity cost drivers. As mentioned earlier, certain expenditures and revenues, such as those associated with sponsored grants and contracts, can be attributed directly to activities. In addition to its organizational driver function of attributing tuition and

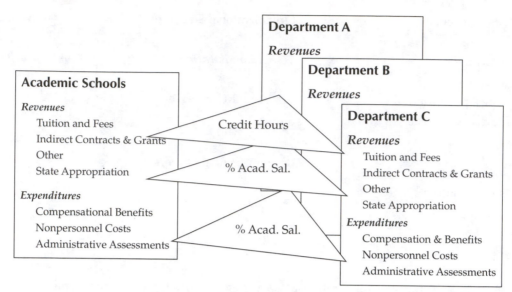

Figure 44.2 Organizational Costs Drivers

fee revenues to departments, student credit hours were used as the activity cost driver to distribute tuition and fee revenues to the three components of instructional activity (undergraduate service, undergraduate majors, and graduate majors).

For expenditures and revenues that cannot be distributed to activities on the basis of either account attributes (the higher education function code) or student credit hours, this analysis employs faculty workload drivers as derived from the Instructional Effort Report (IER)/ Capacity Model.

IER/Capacity Model-Based Drivers

The mission-critical activities to which this analysis targets all expenditures and revenues are directly related to the efforts of full-time faculty. Therefore, the distribution of full-time faculty workload over these activities was chosen as the primary cost driver to distribute a large portion of the annual revenues and expenditures. All academic RCs except the School of Medicine contributed to the IER/ Capacity Model data collection. The School of Medicine had its own even longer-standing system for collecting annual faculty effort distribution data that was entirely compatible for the purposes of this study.

The IER/Capacity Model system has evolved over the last several years from a sim-

ple description of faculty teaching assignment to a more well-rounded but still fairly simplistic description of faculty effort across the mission-critical activities considered in this study (IER/Capacity Model). The most recent iteration of this model was undertaken specifically to generate the activity-based drivers for this analysis. School deans and, in some cases, department chairs were asked to review the instructional workload data for the 1995–96 fiscal year and to supplement it in two specific ways:

- Supplement the scheduled instruction workload information by indicating how each faculty member's remaining workload was distributed across the mission-critical activities plus administration (i.e., service to the university).

- Devise a set of rules to generate workload parameters for scheduled instruction that would replace the existing self-report method.

Because of the relative immaturity of the rule-based system, the self-reports as reviewed by the dean or chair, for both scheduled instruction and other activities, were used in the current analysis. Using the self-reports, each full-time faculty represents 1.00 FTE, regardless of his or her relative workload or productivity.

In reviewing and revising the IERs, deans and chairs were instructed to consider "research and scholarly activity" as a default category for all otherwise nonassigned effort. The data collection forms that were distributed and on which faculty effort was reported showed all noninstructional effort in this default category. Those filling out the forms then noted specific instructional, outreach/service, and administrative roles, with the still-remaining FTE left in the research and scholarship category. This category was further described in the accompanying instruction as being related to such activities as "unfunded" research, "keeping up with one's discipline," and participating in the routine management activities of the academic unit (e.g., completing annual review forms). The nongrant-specific FTE reported in this category was later distributed (by the authors) 40 percent-40 percent-20 percent among the final research, instruction, and administration/management categories, respectively. This convention was chosen to represent common rules of thumb used throughout university departments when defining faculty activity.

Figure 44.3 illustrates the use of activity cost drivers for the major expenditure and revenue categories. Student credit hours were used to allocate tuition and fee revenues to their target activity. The faculty effort data from the IER/Capacity Model data was used to calculate unit-wide distribution drivers. That is, the proportion of effort devoted to the activities, as defined above, was determined across all full-time faculty in a particular unit. These proportions were used to allocate state appropriation across the total instruction, research, services, and administration activities. Student credit hours were then used to backfill appropriations from total instruction into the three categories of instructional activity considered here: undergraduate service, undergraduate majors, and graduate majors. Contract and grant revenues were allocated across activities based on the higher education function code assigned to the specific

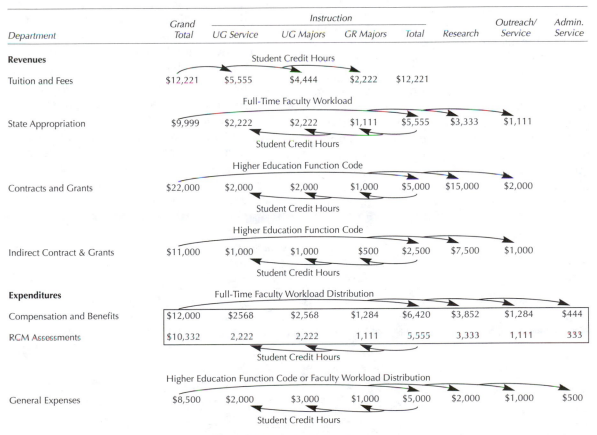

Figure 44.3 Activity Cost Drivers

accounts receiving the income. Indirect contract and grant revenue followed the contract and grant attribution proportionately. Expenditures for compensation and benefits, as well as the RC assessments, were allocated using the same faculty effort/student credit hour drivers used to allocate state appropriation. Finally, general expenses (e.g., supplies, travel, and equipment) were allocated according to either the higher education function code (for restricted accounts) or the faculty workload/student credit hour combination (for unrestricted accounts).

Converting Administrative Activities to Overhead

As discussed above, the model initially included administrative overhead as an activity, but it was then reallocated across the other activities because it is not considered mission-critical. As shown in Figure 44.3, administrative service activities were included as a target of expenditures, although not of revenues. That is, the effort attributed through the IER/Capacity Model to these activities was removed from both the numerator and denominator in determining the faculty workload drivers for revenue distributions but was included for expenditure distributions. It was reasoned that the campus does not receive revenues for the express purpose of administrative management but that management is an overhead cost that should be recognized as consuming resources. Figure 44.4 illustrates the subsequent process by which administrative service-related expenditures were then reallocated to the mission-critical activities using the faculty

workload/student credit hour drivers. These costs thus end up appearing as an overhead expense attributed proportionately to the mission-critical activities.

Generating Measures and Indicators

Having all the drivers necessary to distribute revenues and expenditures to the mission-critical activities, we constructed a set of reports and indicators to communicate the results of the analysis. The primary report consisted of two sections. The first section displayed the revenues and expenditures at the activity level within the unit (school and department, where applicable). The second section outlined a series of measures and indicators derived from the basic table.[3]

The measures and indicators included in the second section of the primary report were chosen to represent several dimensions of program costs in both absolute and relative terms. Specifically, the indicators included:

- *Direct and net contribution.* Revenues minus expenditures for each activity, first for directly attributable revenues and expenditures and then with department-, school-, and campus-level overhead considered.

- *Revenues and expenditures per degree conferred.* A separate accounting of the revenues and expenditures associated with undergraduate and graduate degree programs (combined). This measure was standardized using a three-year average of annual degrees conferred to dampen the annual volatility in the

| Department | Grand Total | Instruction | | | | Research | Outreach/ Service | Admin Service |
		UG Service	UG Majors	GR Majors	Total			
Expenditures								
Compensation and Benefits	$13,920	$1,567	$1,542	$1,014	$4,123	$5,476	$4,321	$6,666
Nonpersonnel	4,978	485	435	734	1,654	2,411	913	1,111
RCM Assessments	5,166	797	323	867	1,987	1,534	1,645	2,222
Total	24,064	2,849	2,300	2,615	7,764	9,421	6,879	9,999
		Full-Time Faculty Workload Distribution						
School Overhead	$9,999	$1,134	$956	$1,139	$3,229	$3,915	$2,855	
			Student Credit Hours					

Figure 44.4 Reallocation of Administrative Service Activities As an Overhead Cost

TABLE 44.1
Distribution of Revenues Across Mission-Critical Activities

| | Target of Revenue | | | |
Source of Revenue	Instruction	Research	Service	Total
Tuition and Fees	100%	0%	0%	100%
Contracts and Grants	5%	73%	22%	100%
Other Income	30%	9%	61%	100%
State Appropriation	84%	14%	2%	100%
Total Revenues	73%	18%	9%	100%

- number of degrees granted in some departments and schools.[4]

- *Revenues and expenditures per major.* Instructional costs standardized according to number of majors in degree program.

- *Revenues and expenditures per student credit hour.* Instructional costs standardized according to total credit hours taught.[5]

TABLE 44.2
Net Contribution of Mission-Critical Activities

Activity	Net Contribution
Undergraduate Service	$4,143,988
Undergraduate Degree Programs	$1,367,533
Graduate/Professional Degree Programs	$3,228,748
Research and Scholarship	$171,406
Outreach/Public Service	$1,087,026

RESULTS

In addition to preparing unit-level reports, the authors prepared a series of summative tables and charts that were disseminated in the broader context of presenting the study for use in the campus-planning and evaluation processes. Given the special nature and large budget associated with the School of Medicine, this unit was excluded from the campus-wide summary tables. Although the use and potential usefulness of the cost study is greatest within the academic units, the overall summary tables are helpful in setting an overall context against which unit summaries can be compared.

Table 44.1 illustrates the overall distribution of revenues, by source, across the mission-critical activities of the campus. As restricted by the model, all tuition and fee revenues are allocated to instructional activities. Three-quarters of the sponsored grant and contract revenue support research activities on the campus, with most other remaining one-quarter used in support of outreach and service activities and only a minor portion of the grant funding going toward instructional activities. The majority of "other income" supports outreach and service activities. This is not surprising for a campus having large health-related programs such as dentistry, which offers fee-based clinical services to the public. Most significantly, the state appropriation was used primarily for instructional activities (84 percent) and in only very modest proportions to support the research and public service activities of faculty.

Table 44.2 displays the net contribution (total revenues minus total expenditures) of the mission-critical activities. The results support what most academics have always believed: undergraduate service courses are the most profitable. What may be somewhat surprising is the fact that in our model, graduate and first professional degree programs (law and dentistry but not medicine) also yielded a modest net contribution. It should be noted that the campus as a whole (excluding medicine) produced nearly a $10 million surplus for this particular academic year.

DISCUSSION

The authors conducted this systematic program cost study to improve both campus planning efforts and accountability to our heterogeneous constituents. This study replicated the URI model in its approach but has made significant refinements in the methodology and the quality of its results. Specifically, this model goes beyond previous efforts by including all levels of overhead—department, school, and central administration—and by using more sophisticated models for determining organizational and activity cost drivers.

As with all cost studies, this model has notable limitations. For example, the timeliness of available data remains a problem. The first iteration of the study was completed in the fall 1997 using information from the 1995–96 fiscal and academic year. While noting the usefulness of the results, deans and department administrators also indicated a need for more recent information to better serve their planning efforts. Efforts are under way to improve the timeliness of data. An Internet-based data entry and retrieval application, which allows for school and department administrators to input faculty effort data directly into a centralized database, will soon be available. This application will provide instant feedback for administrators' specific planning needs as well as the raw data for analyses of this type.

Other limitations in this first iteration relate to the compromises made to ensure that the project would be completed in a reasonable time frame. As mentioned earlier, the current analysis brought all revenues and expenditures down to the unit and degree level (undergraduate versus graduate) but did not distinguish costs among multiple programs at the same degree level within a unit (e.g., two or more baccalaureate programs). We made another compromise due to the level of reliability within the faculty effort data. Specifically, the faculty effort drivers were used to allocate costs broadly to instruction, research, and service, but we did not feel the data were reliable enough to distinguish among the undergraduate major, undergraduate service, and graduate major aspects of instruction. Both these areas of limitations will be addressed in the next iteration of the study. Moreover, future iterations will provide multiple years of results, which will provide a better context for judging the reliability and consistency of the results as well as for judging unit fiscal performance.

Despite these limitations, the study's results have already led to a number of voluntary internal changes. For example, one school had been considering forming stand-alone departments. The conclusion of the dean and his senior staff following this study was that proceeding with this change would reduce the overhead associated with their current program administration structure. Another school is now contemplating raising its tuition for its master's degree program. This study demonstrated that program costs far outpace the tuition revenues for this program, whose graduates can readily realize a large salary upon graduation.

Several deans created or requested more specialized reports and analysis from the study's data to support their annual planning and budget processes. One dean analyzed and compared her school's overhead costs with those of other schools in response to prevailing myths that there were unduly large overhead costs associated with her school's operations. She found her school had only modest overhead costs relative to other schools on campus.

The program cost study results were immediately incorporated into a university-wide planning and evaluation context. For the annual planning and budget process, school deans were provided with a variety of performance measures that relate to the quantities and qualities of students, academic programs, and goal-related activities. The data from the cost study were woven into this process as another source of planning and evaluation information. Taken together, these information sources provide a rich context for evaluating the important issues of program access, quality, and cost.

We expect the uses and applications of the study's results and its later improvements to increase over time and for the results themselves to better reflect the reality of the campus financial environment. The authors have already noted an improvement in the quality of data reported on the faculty effort side, as schools and departments realize how those data are employed and the value of a cost study analysis of this kind.

It is expected that these results will continue to be useful to deans and campus administrators in making decisions to increase or decrease investments in existing programs or whether to initiate new academic programs, and in other administrative decisions informed by financial information. While these decisions should not be based solely on an economic cost-benefit analysis, the economic data should help improve the quality of decisions, especially when augmented with qualitative analysis from program reviews performed by internal and external peers and constituents.

NOTES

1. The URI study may have been the first publicized study that attempted to analyze the full costs and revenues for each degree program, both undergraduate and graduate. It gained notoriety in the press when it was first released, because it showed that its undergraduate programs were generally subsidizing its graduate programs. See Swonger and Mead (1996) and Roush (1996) for more details.
2. For further details on these allocations, the reader can consult Whalen (1991), Robbins and Rooney (1995), and Stocum and Rooney (1997).
3. Upon request, the authors will provide a more complete listing of the organizational and activity cost drivers used to allocate all revenues and expenditures as well as a copy of a sample school or department report.
4. The cost-per-degree indicator in this study is a cross-sectional cost, not a cumulative or longitudinal measure of the cost to confer a degree. That is, the per-degree rate is used to compare annual major instruction costs across departments of varying size and not to determine how much it costs to confer a degree over the length of a student career.
5. In assessing the cost per credit hour, our model was not able to differentiate between undergraduate and graduate credit hours. This is a feature we expect to incorporate in future years as we improve upon the IER/Capacity Model.

REFERENCES

Gilbert, S. W. 1996. Making the Most of a Slow Revolution. *Change* 28(2): 10–23.

Massy, W., and R. Zemsky. 1994. Faculty Discretionary Time: Departments and the "Academic Ratchet." *Journal of Higher Education* 65(1): 1–22.

Middaugh, M. 1996. Instructional Costs and Productivity, by Academic Discipline: A National Study Revisited. Paper presented at the 36th annual Association for Institutional Research Forum, 7 May, in Albuquerque.

_____. 1997. National Study of Instructional Costs and Productivity: Using the Data in Institutional Policy Decisions. Paper presented at the 37th annual Association for Institutional Research Forum, 19 May, in Orlando.

National Commission on the Cost of Higher Education. 1997. *College Tuition Going Up . . . and Up . . . and Up.* 11 February 1998 <http://www.geocities.com/Heartland/Ranch/4851/hi-edcst.html>.

_____. 1998. W. E. Troutt, chair. Straight Talk About College Costs and Prices. Washington, D.C.

Robbins, D., and P. Rooney. 1995. Responsibility Center Management: An Assessment of RCM at IUPUI. *NACUBO Business Officer* 28(9): 44–48.

Roush, W. 1996. URI Tries Downsizing by Formula. *Science* 272: 342–44.

Simpson, W. A., and W. E. Sperber. 1984. A New Type of Cost Analysis for Planners in Academic Departments. *Planning for Higher Education* 12(3): 13–17.

Stocum, D., and P. Rooney. 1997. Responding to Resource Constraints: A Departmentally Based System of Responsibility Center Management. *Change* 29(5): 51–57.

Swonger, A. K., and A. C. Mead. 1996. Program-Level Contribution Analysis—A Tool for Guiding Management at a University. Unpublished report, University of Rhode Island, Rhode Island.

Whalen, E. L. 1991. *Responsibility Center Budgeting: An Approach to Decentralized Management for Institutions of Higher Education.* Bloomington, IN: Indiana University Press.

CHAPTER 45

A PRIMER ON RESPONSIBILITY CENTRE BUDGETING AND RESPONSIBILITY CENTRE MANAGEMENT*

DANIEL W. LANG

Daniel W. Lang, Department of Theory and Policies Studies, OISE/UT, Division of Economics and Management, Scarborough College, University of Toronto

INTRODUCTION

Within the last decade several major universities in the United States and Canada have adopted Responsibility Centre Budgeting (RCB) and Responsibility Centre Management (RCM). As early as the 1970s some universities, before an RCB/RCM taxonomy was developed and elucidated by Edward Whalen at Indiana University (Whalen, 1991), had implemented certain aspects of what is now understood to be encompassed by RCB/RCM.

Responsibility Centre Budgeting and Responsibility Centre Management (RCB/RCM) are now generic terms. At the University of Michigan, RCB/RCM is called Value Centered Management. At Indiana University, the term Responsibility Center Budgeting is no longer used; only Responsibility Center Management is used, as is also the case at UCLA. The comparable term at Ohio State University is Incentive Based Budgeting. At the University of Illinois, Urbana-Champaign, the phrase Mission Focussed Budgeting and Planning is used. The University of Southern California refers to Revenue Centre Management. RCB/RCM, expressed at the school level, is sometimes called School-Based Budgeting, and has close connections to the charter school movement in Alberta and elsewhere (Barlosky & Lawton, 1995).

BASIC ELEMENTS OF RCB/RCM

The first and most important element of RCB/RCM methodology is the calculation of all revenue generated by an academic unit. This includes, obviously, revenue from tuition fees and endowments earmarked for the unit. But, perhaps less obviously, it may also include a share of undesignated endowment and gifts, a share of undifferentiated operating grants, a share of proceeds from the sale or development of university assets, and a share of net revenue generated by university ancillary or auxiliary operations. The revenue thus calculated represents the resource base avail-

---

*A more extensive and theoretical discussion of RCB/RCM based on this research will appear in *Higher Education Management*.

Source: CSSHE (Canadian Society for the Study of Higher Education) *Professional File #17, Winter 1999, Number 17.*

able to the unit. The amount is recalibrated annually to reflect changes in levels of activity that generate revenue, and changes in government funding. Periodic recalibration is important for two reasons: first, it ensures the credibility of incentives and, second, it ensures the reliability of information about costs.

The next and equally important step is the assignment of centrally budgeted indirect costs and overheads to the academic unit. Cost centres are identified. They typically include:

- institutional administration, governance, and management
- development and alumni relations
- financial management
- human resources management
- internal audit
- academic support services (for example, libraries and academic computing)
- student services
- academic administration (for example, research administration)
- occupancy costs
- debt service
- taxes, fees, and levies

These cost centres are broken down and attributed to academic divisions on the basis of an allocative mechanism appropriate to the individual cost centre. For example, financial management costs are assumed on the basis of gross expense budgets, student services on the basis of student population, and human resources on the basis of faculty and staff population.

The revenue base less the indirect and overhead cost allocation then constitutes the net available resource base that the academic unit can apply to its array of academic programs and support activities. However, and very significantly, because the allocation of indirect and overhead costs is transparent and systematic, academic units can make changes in their operations in order to reduce those costs.

In summary, RCB/RCM rests on a few basic operating principles:

- All costs and income generated by each college, faculty, or department are attributed to that unit, appear in its budget, and are under its control.

- Incentives are created and monopolistic barriers removed to allow each academic unit to increase income and reduce costs according to its own academic plans and priorities.

- All costs of administrative and service units are "grossed up" and attributed to academic units. No costs are left unattributed, and the attributed costs themselves include overheads and indirect costs. (For example, the attributed costs of the human resource department include its occupancy costs).

- Decisions about prices (tuition fees) and volume (enrollment) are devolved to the academic units.

- Decisions about optimal balances between costs and revenue are made by the academic units. They set priorities. They link plans and budgets.

- Restrictions on line-by-line budgets are relaxed or eliminated. Each academic unit allocates the global revenue base available to it.

THE LESSONS OF TRIAL AND ERROR

The basic principles on which RCB/RCM have been known and understood for some time, even if the specific RCB/RCM terminology is a more recent development. The theory of RCB/RCM has been described quite well. (Brinkman, 1993; Whalen, 1991). The evolution of RCB/RCM as a formal concept is quite varied. In some cases, like Indiana University, RCB/RCM arose from a fully developed plan that was devised before RCB/RCM was introduced. In other cases, like the University of Toronto, the development was more evolutionary as RCB/RCM was applied to only some major faculties instead of to all faculties. In other universities, like the University of Michigan, RCB/RCM applies fully to expense but only partially to revenue.

This primer takes a practical perspective. It is a "how to do it manual" that asks how RCB/RCM works in practice, and what problems are encountered in the actual implementation of RCB/RCM at the following institutions, all of which have implemented RCB/RCM to some degree: Indiana University, the University of Toronto, the University of Michigan, the University of Illinois at Urbana-Champaign, the University of Minnesota, the University of Pennsylvania, the University of California—Los Angeles, the Ohio State University, Cornell University, the University of Southern California, Clemson University, Worcester Polytechnic University, and Washington University.

The universities that have put RCB/RCM in place have discovered that it offers a number of advantages and disadvantages, some of which were anticipated and some of which became evident only after a period of trial and error.

ADVANTAGES OF RCB/RCM

RCB/RCM emphasizes and exposes costs that are often known but not recognized, or are deliberately not known because of their strategic implications.
While RCB/RCM demands accuracy and a sound methodology for attributing indirect and overhead costs, its ultimate purpose is not to account for costs. There are other reasons for an institution's wanting to know about its cost and income structures. The most obvious of these reasons are to account fully for the costs of research and to ensure that auxiliary or ancillary services that are supposed to be self-funding really are. Less obvious but perhaps ultimately more important is to understand better the dynamics of marginal costs and marginal revenues. In the United States the National Commission on the Cost of Higher Education emphasized the importance of better understanding costs so that they can be better controlled (National Commission, 1998). Because of the way in which research is funded in the United States, American universities that have experimented with RCB/RCM had a prior interest in planning and budgeting schemes that measured and exposed the full costs—direct, indirect, and overhead—of research.

Although a full accounting of cost and revenue is the first and essential step in the RCB/RCM process, it is not the ultimate step. First, RCB/RCM exposes all costs, even for programs and services that are unquestionably necessary and valuable, and for those very reasons are often unexamined, especially in Canadian universities in which there is a conceptual understanding that the costs of research and

instruction can be quite different but in which there are few practical separations of those costs. If one considers that the basic political economy of any university is to optimize the intersection of quality and cost for every program, recognizing the cost structures of high quality programs is just as important as recognizing those of marginal programs. It is equally important to recognize the different cost structures of instruction and research.

Second, RCB/RCM, by assigning responsibility for all costs to the program level, is a key means of translating between budgets and plans. Perhaps more than any other management device, RCB/RCM forges strong and realistic links between planning and budgeting. Thus the idiom by which RCB/RCM exposes and expresses costs is important in and of itself. While linking planning and budgeting is a chronic problem for all colleges and universities, it is a particular problem for many Canadian institutions because of the severe cutbacks in public funding that many of them have suffered in the last decade.

Third, because RCB/RCM has a "bottom line" that forces the reconciliation of all costs and revenue by program or service, it is not possible to mask certain costs or shortfalls in revenue. In several universities that have put RCB/RCM in place this characteristic has made a particular difference for research institutes and centres, ancillary services, and other programs that were presumed to be self-funding. In terms of budget planning, RCB/RCM has a "nowhere to hide" effect which can be as unpopular as it is revealing.

RCB/RCM motivates entrepreneurial behaviour and the generation of revenue.
In most other institutional planning and budget regimes, the generation of revenue is regarded mainly as the responsibility of the university's administration. This is particularly true of Canadian universities. Admissions offices recruit students to ensure that targets for revenue from tuition fees are met. Presidents lobby governments for operating grants. Vice-presidents and development officers organize fund-raising campaigns, cultivate philanthropic foundations, and secure research support. Deans participate in these activities now and then, but the expectation remains that securing revenue is mainly the administration's job. While various

forms of performance budgeting or benchmarking may come into play in setting college, faculty, and departmental budgets (Garner, 1991), those budgets are predominantly expense budgets, and are planned and controlled as such. Revenue is collected centrally and allocated in the form of expense budgets, usually with no direct correlation to sources of revenue. To academic divisions, most services—for examples, libraries, media centres, or campus security—are free goods.

Because income as well as cost is attributed to colleges, faculties. or departments under RCB/RCM. the effect on principals, deans, or chairs is virtually immediate: the generation of revenue counts. Mistaken decisions or even wishful thinking about costs versus benefits makes real differences close to home. Surpluses may be carried forward under RCB/RCM, but so are deficits, which otherwise might be written-off as academic bad luck.

The effect, however, is as subtle as it is immediate. The simple algorithm that more students means more revenue becomes complex as, for example, when marginal instructional costs or, for another example, space costs come into play.

RCB/RCM locates decisions about the allocation of resources where there is the most knowledge to make them intelligently

For the past several decades managers and planners have debated the merits of "top down" planning versus "bottom up" planning as if the choice between them was mutually exclusive (Kail, 1988). In many cases it indeed was. Moreover, the cases in favour of one or the other were often political, aimed in the first instance at securing acceptance of a plan or budget through various levels of participation, or at ensuring compliance through authority. These debates of course begged a question about the quality and soundness of plans in favour of the feasibility of their implementation.

"Sapience" is a term that today is used infrequently, and even then seems abstruse. But it is particularly apt in describing the effect of RCB/RCM on decision-making in universities. Some descriptions of RCB/RCM use the term "proximity" instead of sapience (Whalen, 1991). James March refers to the "limited rationality" of large organizations (March, 1994).

Instead of construing "top down" versus "bottom up" as an either-or choice, RCB/RCM treats them as the outer limits of a continuum in between which the quality of decision-making, especially about plans and budgets, may be optimally located at many different points.

In large, complex institutions—like the typical Canadian research-intensive university—the president and his or her administration usually have the authority to make specific decisions about the allocation of resources to colleges and faculties, and to various services, but may not have the requisite sapience to do so as crucial decisions about plans and budgets are divorced from the reality of scholarship and program delivery. These allocations involve more than finance. They may also involve space, library acquisitions, or computer access.

RCB/RCM, especially RCM, presumes that in terms of sapience the university is not a hierarchical pyramid. Instead, RCB/RCM presumes that the capability to make some decisions is greater lower in the organizational structure, and that those are often decisions about the allocation of resources and about the trade-offs between income and expense.

Unfortunately and perhaps ironically, this advantage of RCB/RCM becomes more salient as the wealth of the institution declines. Deferred maintenance is an especially revealing example in Canadian universities. Physical plant administrators and auditors typically use a variety of formulas to measure the extent to which the value of capital assets have declined due to inadequate maintenance, which is due in turn to reduced budgets for building maintenance and upkeep. There are differences of opinion about the appropriate formula for measuring deferred maintenance (Rush, 1991), but virtually every one of them produces liabilities that are far beyond the capacities of normal operating or capital budgets to resolve. Setting safety and other code compliance aside, most university administrations (as well as provincial governments) have great difficulty setting plans and budgets for reducing deferred maintenance backlogs when available funding constitutes only a small fraction of the overall amount required.

RCB/RCM, in practical effect, puts the question of priorities to the principals and deans who occupy the buildings and facilities in question, and who both presumably and reasonably know best how the condition of the buildings affects the operation of their programs and services. This, of course, cannot reduce the costs of deferred maintenance. It does, however, better allocate whatever scarce funding is available to correct the problem.

RCB/RCM encourages a "buy in" to planning and the acceptance of the need to plan

It has become nearly axiomatic that the first problem in planning, particularly planning that involves reallocation of resources, is convincing academic managers and faculty that there needs to be a plan, and that once there is a plan that it should be taken seriously (Bryson, 1988; Keller, 1983; Lang, 1988).

Typical reactions to the heralds of the need to plan are that:

- There is no real problem.
- The problem is external; the administration should do a better job raising funds.
- The problem is an artifact of the way the university organizes its financial statements (Gordon & Charles, 1997; Winston, 1992).
- If there is a problem, it is that the costs of administration and other institution-wide services are too high. Therefore no reductions need to be made in academic budgets.
- Plans and budgets aren't sufficiently linked to allow individual academic units to depend on them. Decisions about resources will still be made one year at a time, and therefore plans need not be taken seriously.

Because of the form and detail of university budgets under RCB/RCM, the institution's financial condition, including the conditions of its various parts, is obvious and largely undebatable. Thus while there may be and usually is considerable debate about the appropriate planning and budgeting solutions, there is under RCB/RCM broad understanding of the problem and acceptance of the need to solve it.

RCB/RCM reduces the scale of planning and decision-making in large, complex institutions

RCB/RCM is to large scale institutional master planning as distributed computing is to main-frame computing. RCB/RCM redistributes responsibility for planning and budgeting. In this context "redistribute" does not simply mean "relocate" the planning process intact. The central process is disassembled and redistributed. Some of it remains central or "top down" but other parts are moved to new and varied points on the "top down/bottom up" continuum.

The result is a series of plans and budgets which, when taken together like an anthology, form an institutional plan which is of value to governors and government. But each college or faculty need understand only its own plan and budget. Moreover, unlike other budget plans that are developed "bottom up," the RCB/RCM plan does not make any given local plan contingent on other local plans, which is often the case in large-scale planning exercises, and which often is an obstacle to the successful linking of plans and budgets (Griffin & Day, 1997; Schmidtlein, 1989).

For some institutional services—for example, physical plant—the institutional plan can be silent as the demand for service is defined by colleges, faculties, or departments as purchasers of the service. Another way of thinking about this is to understand that most academic and administrative services under conventional forms of budgeting and management operate in centrally controlled supply-side institutional economies. RCB/RCM creates demand-driven buyers markets.

RCB/RCM encourages the creation of markets as well as stimulating responses to markets

Educational planning often revolves around scale and capacity. Demographic change will in time elicit educational change. Whether these changes occur rapidly or slowly, they are essentially reactions, which RCB/RCM may accelerate. But RCB/RCM also stimulates an interest in finding new markets even in the absence of demographic change.

Privatization and marketization are controversial concepts in the public sector, especially in the public educational sector, ranging from vouchers, to charter schools, to radical revision of degree-granting legislation for higher education (Clark, 1998; Marginson, 1997). These, of course, are concepts that operate at the system or jurisdictional level. RCB/RCM is, in practical effect, the institutional version of marketization.

Whatever the arguments for or against privatization and marketization—and there are many (Slaughter & Leslie, 1997)—RCB/RCM can produce very similar effects in terms of the institutional behaviours that lead to improving the fit between social need and economic demand on one hand, and educational diversity and supply on the other hand. This happens because, to the extent that improving the supply/demand fit produces additional revenue, the benefit accrues principally to the college or faculty that offers new or better programs, or expands capacity.

A word of caution about RCB/RCM's capability to encourage market behaviour: the experience of some institutions indicates that market potential is not uniformly or universally distributed among academic programs. For some programs and services the potential for marketization is so minor that it mutes the positive effects of RCB/RCM. This is somewhat more a problem in Canadian universities than in American universities. The combination of large geographic scale and a relatively small dispersed population has meant that many Canadian institutions have not been able to realize as many economies of scale as their American counterparts. A practical consequence is a larger number of excellent or essential programs that are so small as to require subsidies.

RCB/RCM encourages interest in the identification and cost of "backrooms"

Universities, colleges, and schools have a variety of administrative and operational services which under conventional approaches to planning and budgeting are assumed to be distinctive, if not to the individual institution at least to the particular educational sector. Moreover, with a few exceptions, these services are regarded by those who use them as free goods. While their costs are known in the aggregate, their costs to any given faculty or department are not known. Those costs, whether broadly known or not, do not usually include indirect costs and overhead costs. So, their costs, like those of their academic counterparts, are understated.

While these services are often scrutinized carefully under various planning and budgeting regimes— most notably zero-based budgeting—that scrutiny is usually in the form of comparisons or benchmarking which involve the same services at other institutions (Rush,

1994). So university libraries are compared to university libraries and university physical plant departments are compared to university physical plant departments, even if their respective institutions are not really peers.

RCB/RCM, when deployed to its full extent, can break the local intra-institutional monopolies that these services enjoy. Markets are created, sometimes within the institution and sometimes outside the institution. An intra-institutional market, for example, is the acquisition and cataloguing of books which one library might do for another library for a fee. But that same example could apply outside the institution if the arrangement were between, for example, a university library and a metropolitan reference library. Those Canadian provinces that have experimented with various forms of amalgamation in the public sector, particularly Ontario and Nova Scotia, seem attracted to this sort of marketization.

Other services under RCB/RCM might be purchased from the local market. For example, faculties or departments might hire local contractors to do minor building alterations instead of having these services provided by the university's physical plant department. This effect of RCB/RCM can transform the physical plant department, at least partially, from the role of "in house" contractor to the role of building code inspector.

The point here is not to enumerate services that might be offered differently under RCB/RCM. Instead, the point is to illustrate the effect of RCB/RCM on the way in which services are viewed. Once the costs of services are fully known and attributed, and once faculties and departments are enabled to purchase services wherever they choose, the perspective towards the services becomes much more generic.

Since the origins of these services, particularly automated services, are often not visible to users, the services are said to operate in "backrooms." An example from Ontario is an automated student financial needs assessment service which one university operates for a community college for an annual fee. The service is an adaptation of the university's service for its own students. As far as the students at the college know, it is their own service without connection to any other institution.

These "backroom" generic arrangements could of course operate without RCB/RCM. But RCB/RCM creates a much stronger disposition towards thinking in terms of acquiring services from a wider variety of sources, and of benchmarking in terms of "best in class" whereby a university's purchasing department might be compared to that of a manufacturer or a hospital instead of to that of another university (Rush, 1994).

Problems and Disadvantages of RCB/RCM

RCB/RCM may assume more knowledge of costs than an institution might actually have

If the implementation of RCB/RCM at the several universities that have deployed it were to reveal only one thing it would be that the accurate determination and attribution of indirect costs and overhead is absolutely essential and very demanding. The problem has several dimensions.

First, there must be a standard methodology for determining overhead costs. By "standard" one should understand the methodology to apply to all programs and services. This does not mean that the overhead rates would necessarily be uniform, but it does mean that every rate should be determined in the same way.

The following series of tables from the University of Toronto outline the basic steps that a methodology for identifying overhead expenses comprises. Although indirect costs and overhead costs are not exactly the same, in this example and in the application of RCB/RCM generally, they are dealt with as if they were the same. The differences are mainly in terms of how the costs are attributed.

There are two important reasons for using a standard methodology. Deans of faculties and heads of services, at least initially, will almost always question the rates as being too high. These administrators must be confident that the rates are determined consistently across the university. The other reason is that the fiduciary interest in RCB/RCM depends on there being a reconciliation of all costs and incomes across the institution. The deployment of different methodologies could make such a reconciliation impossible.

Methodologies for allocating costs and revenue under RCB/RCM often are not readily available "off the shelf." Most universities that

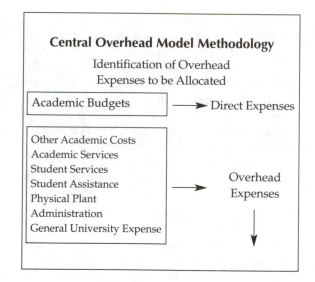

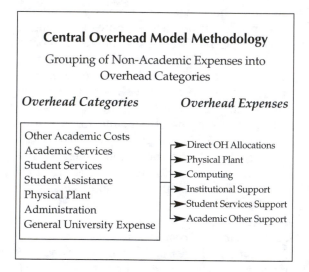

Central Overhead Model Methodology

Direct Overhead Allocations

This category identifies central budgets which can be directly linked to an academic or administrative unit. These costs are stepped down directly to the respective units.

The current model directly allocates

Rent	Tutor Pay Equity
Bridging Fund	Faculty Renewal
COPC Contingency	Administrators on Leave
Enrollment Contingency	Provost's Contingency
Transitional Fund (Old)	Central Equipment Fund

Undergraduate Student Assistance

U of T Grad Opens and Simcoe Specials

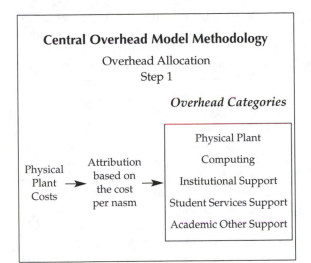

Central Overhead Model Methodology

Overhead Allocation
Step 1

Overhead Categories

Physical Plant Costs → Attribution based on the cost per nasm →

Physical Plant
Computing
Institutional Support
Student Services Support
Academic Other Support

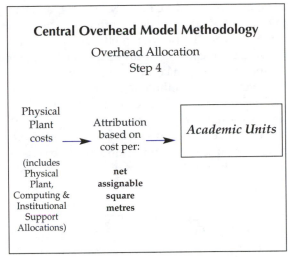

Central Overhead Model Methodology

Overhead Allocation
Step 4

Physical Plant costs

(includes Physical Plant, Computing & Institutional Support Allocations)

→ Attribution based on cost per: →

net assignable square metres

Academic Units

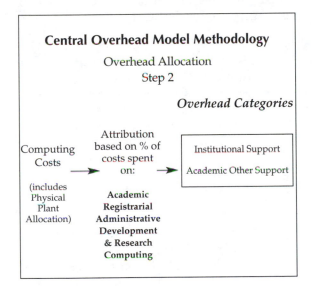

Central Overhead Model Methodology

Overhead Allocation
Step 2

Overhead Categories

Computing Costs

(includes Physical Plant Allocation)

→ Attribution based on % of costs spent on:

Academic Registrarial Administrative Development & Research Computing

→

Institutional Support
Academic Other Support

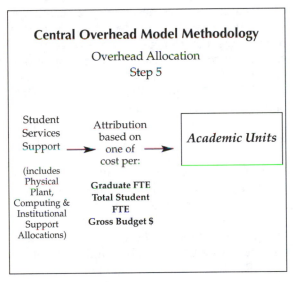

Central Overhead Model Methodology

Overhead Allocation
Step 5

Student Services Support

(includes Physical Plant, Computing & Institutional Support Allocations)

→ Attribution based on one of cost per: →

**Graduate FTE
Total Student FTE
Gross Budget $**

Academic Units

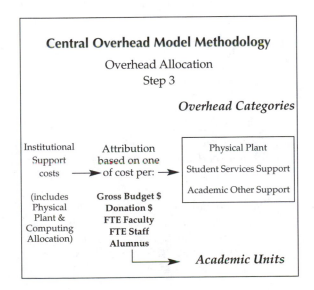

Central Overhead Model Methodology

Overhead Allocation
Step 3

Overhead Categories

Institutional Support costs

(includes Physical Plant & Computing Allocation)

→ Attribution based on one of cost per:

**Gross Budget $
Donation $
FTE Faculty
FTE Staff
Alumnus**

→

Physical Plant
Student Services Support
Academic Other Support

→ *Academic Units*

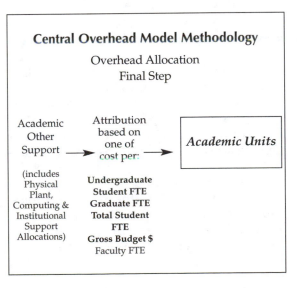

Central Overhead Model Methodology

Overhead Allocation
Final Step

Academic Other Support

(includes Physical Plant, Computing & Institutional Support Allocations)

→ Attribution based on one of cost per:

**Undergraduate Student FTE
Graduate FTE
Total Student FTE
Gross Budget $**
Faculty FTE

→ *Academic Units*

have implemented RCB/RCM report that it can take as many as 18 to 24 months to devise and apply overhead allocation methodologies. For a university facing an immediate and urgent financial crisis, that could be too long to wait.

Second, the methodology must be accurate and inclusive as well as comprehensible—characteristics that often work against one another. But it is nevertheless necessary that the methodology be sufficiently understandable to be credible and to be predictable. Predictability, although apparently a mundane technicality, is essential. A fundamental hope of RCB/RCM is that once cost structures are known, income and expense attributed, and authority delegated, the heads of academic programs and administrative services will seek to minimize those costs and maximize the revenue. So, for example, a dean needs to understand the overhead methodology well enough to know how the overhead rate of his or her faculty might change if it were to occupy less space, reduce its academic complement, or add students. If the methodology cannot pass these tests, RCB/RCM will be little more than an elaborate and expensive accounting exercise.

In terms of comprehensibility and comprehensiveness, it is important to understand that budgets determined under RCB/RCM actually look different from those set under traditional planning and budgeting regimes. Sometimes the differences are large and surprising.

The following table displays the budget of the business school at the University of Michigan before and after the introduction of RCB/RCM, which at the University of Michigan is called "Value Centred Management." The first panel in the table comprises the sources of revenue available to the business school. Note particularly that under RCB/RCM the school receives no allocation from the university's general fund but it does receive all of the tuition and fee revenue that it generates.

The second panel displays the uses or spending of the revenue that is attributed to the business school. Here again the "before and after" contrast is in certain cases very significant. For example, the school's budget under RCB/RCM includes over $2.1 million for the costs of the space that the school occupies. Prior to the introduction of RCB/ RCM use of the school's facilities was a free good to the faculty. The costs were invisible.

Overall, the revenue and expense of the school of business at the University of Michigan under RCB/RCM were approximately 17 per cent higher than previously, and both included items that had never before been part of the school's budget or had even been apparent to the school (see Table 45.1).

Third. the methodology must be replicable. If managers do indeed try to reduce overhead and indirect costs by various means, the RCB/RCM methodology must be sufficiently reliable and robust to allow manipulation and periodic recalculation.

Some methodologies take the form of formal protocols that encompass literally every aspect of institutional revenue and expense from all funds. Here are some examples from actual protocols at various universities that have introduced RCB/RCM:

- Student Services Administration

  Distribute [costs] based on weighted student headcount: Undergraduates = 1.0; Graduates = 0.5; Graduate-Professional = 0.25. The weightings represent our [The University of Michigan] belief that the services provided by these offices are predominantly for undergraduate students but that graduate and professional students also benefit from some subset of the full range of services.

- Library

  The proposed algorithm does not break down the library. Instead it distributes the total budget as a whole. The model is based on the premise that faculty and students at the university [of Pennsylvania] are the primary users of the library. Therefore . . . 50% of the total library budget is distributed based on the number of paid faculty . . . and the remaining 50% based on the number of course units taught.

- Physical Plant

  The physical plant costs associated with the institutional mission [of the University of Minnesota] are allocated to the collegiate units based upon a . . . calculation using the assigned square footage. This basis is derived from a [data] file . . . which provides a listing of instructional activity by building, room number, collegiate unit, course and contact hours per week. This file is linked to other

TABLE 45.1
University of Michigan Business School
Sources and Uses of Funds
Traditional Budgeting, 1995–96
VCM Budgeting, 1995–96, 1996–97 and 1997–98

The Business School Sources	ACTUAL Traditional 1995–96	% of Total Sources	SIMULATED VCM 1995–96	% of Total Sources	PROJECTED VCM 1996–97	% of Total Sources	PROJECTED VCM 1997–98	% of Total Sources
General Fund	29,784,540	36.2	29,784,540		31,401,797			
Provost's Allocation			6,187,785	6.6	5,129,273	5.6	5,129,273	5.4
Tuition and fees			36,160,430	38.7	37,629,433	41.4	38,344,775	40.3
General fund transfers	(44,798)	(0.1)	(44,798)	(0.0)	0	0.0	0	0.0
VPAA GF Transters	1,837,446	2.2	33,291	0.0	900,000	1.0	(40,000)	(0.0)
OVPR GF transfers	3,600	0.0	3,600	0.0	50,000	0.1	5,000	0.0
Federal grants/contracts (Direct)	1,481,307	1.8	1,481,307	1.6	2,000,000	2.2	1,500,000	1.6
Federal grants/contracts (Indirect)	384,667	0.5	384,667	0.4	500,000	0.5	300,000	0.3
Non-federal grants/contracts (Direct)	2,218,153		2,218,153	2.4	1,000,000	1.1	1,000,000	1.1
Non-federal grants/contracts (Indirect)		0.0	0	0.0	0	0.0	100,000	0.1
Cost-sharing transfers	28,625	0.0	28,625	0.0	50,000	0.1	(10,000)	(0.0)
Gifts	9,355,266	11.4	9,355,266	10.0	11,000,000	12.1	11,000,000	11.6
Endowment income	2,494,159	3.0	2,494,159	2.7	2,500,000	2.7	2,850,000	3.0
Investment income	2,401,302	2.9	2,401,302	2.6	2,700,000	3.0	2,530,000	2.7
# External department revenue	28,358,669	34.5	28,358,669	30.3	25,000,000	27.5	28,000,000	29.4
Internal departmental rebillings	3,956,137		3,956,137	4.2	2,000,000	2.2	4,000,000	4.2
VCM revenue to support student svcs.			0	0.0	0	0.0	0	0.0
VCM revenue to support research admin.			0	0.0	0	0.0	0	0.0
VCM revenue to support general admin.			0	0.0	0	0.0	0	0.0
VCM interest to be paid on balances			444,963	0.5	466,766	0.5	471,717	0.5
Total sources	82,259,074	100.0	93,463,557	100.0	90,924,472	100.0	95,180,766	100.0

The Business School Uses	ACTUAL Traditional 1995–96	% of Total Uses	SIMULATED VCM 1995–96	% of Total Uses	PROJECTED VCM 1996–97	% of Total Uses	PROJECTED VCM 1997–98	% of Total Uses
Faculty salaries	19,582,640	27.1	19,582,640	27.3	21,000,000	28.0	23,000,000	28.7
Research scientist salaries	65,302	0.1	65,302	0.1	0	0.0	45,000	0.1
GSA salaries	629,579	0.9	629,579	0.9	650,000	0.9	670,000	0.8
Staff salaries	10,873,353	15.1	10,873,353	15.2	12,400,000	16.5	12,500,000	15.6
Fringe benefits	6,059,932	8.4	6,059,932	8.5	6,600,000	8.8	6,750,000	8.4
# Tuition grants	1,054,343	1.5	1,054,343	1.5	1,100,000	1.5	1,150,000	1.4
# Unit financial aid	6,459,928	9.0	6,459,928	9.0	6,600,000	8.8	6,500,000	8.1
Supplies	8,017,677	11.1	8,017,677	11.2	6,000,000	8.0	7,500,000	9.4
Travel	2,762,501	3.8	2,762,501	3.9	2,600,000	3.5	2,600,000	3.2
Internal rebilled services	2,345,137	3.3	2,345,137	3.3	2,800,000	3.7	2,600,000	3.2
External contracted services	6,701,231	9.3	6,701,231	9.4	6,000,000	8.0	7,500,000	9.4
Miscellaneous expenses	5,452,816	7.6	5,352,716	7.5	6,000,000	8.0	5,300,000	6.6
Inventory acquisitions	0	0.0	0	0.0	0	0.0	0	0.0
# Equipment	849,553	1.2	849,553	1.2	1,500,000	2.0	1,500,000	1.9
# Indirect cost recovered	384,667							
# Transfers to construction	418,795	0.6	418,795	0.6	1,500,000	2.0	1,000,000	1.2
# Net Transters	497,401	0.7	497,401	0.7	250,000	0.3	1,500,000	1.9
TOTAL UNIT OPERATIONS	72,154,856	99.5	71,670,088	100.0	75,000,000	100.0	80,115,000	100.0
OFA/Rackham financial aid			1,220,172	1.7	1,318,607	1.8	1,419,917	1.8
VCM costs for student services			1,793,011	2.5	1,995,043	2.7	1,974,725	2.5
VCM costs for research administration			67,011	0.1	60,671	0.1	80,423	0.1
VCM costs for general administration			5,420,578	7.6	5,564,686	7.4	5,628,431	7.0
VCM costs for facilities			1,981,298	2.8	2,100,657	2.8	2,100,657	2.6
University Participation			1,207,180	1.7	1,283,013	1.7	1,331,313	1.7
Total uses	72,154,856	100.0	83,359,339	116.3	87,322,676	116.4	92,650,467	115.6
Fund Balance Net Change	10,104,218		10,104,219		3,601,797		2,530,299	
Total new VCM attributed costs			11,689,250	16.3	12,322,676	16.4	12,535,467	15.6

data bases to obtain a basis consisting of the cost of the classroom space used by the unit plus the cost of the space that the unit "owns."

- Student Information Systems

The SIS budget will be subdivided into the following three expense categories: student-related; course-related; and divisional production requests. The student-related expenses will be attributed to academic divisions [of the University of Toronto] on the basis of student headcounts. Course-related expenses will be attributed to academic divisions on the basis of the number of courses. Divisional production requests will be allocated to each academic division on a cost per production request.

When one considers the scale and diversity of university budgets, especially those of large research-intensive institutions, the importance and the complexity of RCB/RCM protocols like these become simultaneously apparent. RCB/RCM cannot work successfully without them, but they represent, in terms of time if not money, a very large up-front investment in the RCB/RCM process.

RCB/RCM protocols also involve what might be described as a taxonomy of institutional programs and services. It is not facetious to observe that under RCB/RCM not every program or service can be a responsibility centre. In some respects this observation is a matter of pragmatic common sense. Many programs and services do not and cannot generate revenue. Others do not really deliver a final complete product; they exist only to support other programs that do. In terms of management and organization, the mission and purpose of programs and services—and, in turn, of the institution—could be seriously distorted if every unit behaved as if it were a responsibility centre, in which case the tail would often wag the dog and the RCB/RCM would amount to little more than an elaborate budgetary tautology.

So, another part of the RCB/RCM methodology is a process by which the status of each unit—academic and administrative—in the institution is classified. The following table (Table 45.2) from the University of California at Los Angeles (UCLA) illustrates an RCB/RCM taxonomy. In the UCLA methodology, "RC"

means Responsibility Centre; "AC" means Auxiliary Centre; and "SC" means Service Centre. Responsibility Centres are in virtually all cases academic divisions. In the UCLA example, environmental health and safety ("EH & S") radiation safety services are a Service Centre. An Auxiliary Service (which in Canadian universities might often be called an "ancillary service") is one which is operated on an actual or nominal self-funded basis. A bookstore, student residence, or soil testing service is a good example.

Under RCB/RCM, the direct, indirect, and overhead costs of Service Centres and Auxiliary Centres are allocated to Responsibility Centres as the indirect and overhead costs of those centres, and the net budgets of the Service and Auxiliary Centres become zero.

RCB/RCM requires high level supporting financial information systems

The capability to allow manipulation and recalculation of RCB/RCM overhead and indirect costs rates depends as much on the availability of reliable and accurate data as on the methodology. While most new financial information systems available from a number of vendors—SAP, SCT/Banner, PeopleSoft—are capable of supporting RCB/RCM, some older systems are not. The new systems are expensive. Despite the advantages of RCB/RCM, they might not be sufficient on their own to justify such large scale investments.

Although RCB/RCM inherently involves extensive delegation of authority, and that delegation is essential to the full realization of the advantages of RCB/RCM, it does not relieve the senior administration and the board of governors of their fiduciary responsibilities. Nor should it. Financial liabilities cannot be delegated. Debt is in the end the institution's responsibility. As well, good faculty managers must be protected from incompetent ones, or, more exactly, from the financial consequences of their incompetence.

The implication of all of this is that the institution's financial information system must have a strong and reliable audit capability to give early warnings of poor management at the faculty level. RCB/RCM inherently increases business risk. In this sense RCB/RCM introduces a new demand on financial information systems.

TABLE 45.2
Allocated Expense Changes

	Original Allocation Basis (v. 3.0)	Current Allocation Basis (v. 4.0)	Proposed Changes to Allocation Basis	Notes	RC's	AC's	SC's
Ground Rent	Assignable square feet	Assignable square feet		On-campus space where land was purchased with the property is not assessed ground rent	Yes	Yes	Yes
Operating Cost for Space							
Police/ Community Safety	Assignable square feet	Assignable square feet		Currently allocates 100% of net costs (total expenses less total revenues). Need to define core level of service to be allocated.	Yes	Yes	Yes
EH&S/Radiation Safety	Assignable square feet	1/3 on ASF plus 2/3 on Contracts & Grants Revenue		Includes EH&S (3401) & Radiation Safety (3402). Need to refine.	Yes	Yes	Yes
Other Space Operating Cost	Assignable square feet	Assignable square feet (placeholder for State-funded ASF— block AC's until resolved).	State-funded assignable square feet	Includes all Facilities Mgmt. departments. Need to define core level of service to be allocated.	Yes	No-3	Yes
Replacement Reserve	10 Categories of Space x insurable value	10 Categories of Space x insurable value			Yes	No-1	Yes

No - 1. Already have self-funded replacement reserves

No - 2. Do not receive service from this org.

No - 3. Fees for this org. are already charged directly and are included in direct expenses

No - 4. Organization should not receive allocated expenses but may have some charges—future refinements to the model will correct

RCB/RCM may demand more local managerial skills and appetites than may actually exist

RCB/RCM is as much a managerial system as it is a planning and budgeting system. This is why the architecture and methodology of RCB/RCM must be comprehensible and robust. The tradition of leadership in university faculties and departments depends primarily on scholarly reputation and only coincidentally on administrative skill (Keller, 1983).

Conventional budget planning and management systems are largely centralized and supported by professional financial managers. While the demands that those systems make on the heads of faculties and colleges are not frivolous, neither are they unusual, onerous, or difficult to comprehend. But RCB/RCM in practical effect invests college principals and faculty deans with the responsibilities of CEOs,

which for many academic administrators is a new concept. Most of them are not prepared for such responsibilities. Many do not want to assume them. Virtually none of them was selected and appointed on the assumption that he or she would have to carry out such responsibilities (Blau, 1994).

In other cases the role of the college principal or faculty dean has not changed in order to meet the demands of managing under RCB/RCM but the support staff at the college or faculty level has. In at least three universities that have installed RCB/RCM, senior financial staff from central administrative offices have relocated to divisional offices in order to support RCB/RCM. The overall result is often an unfortunate mismatch between the capabilities of RCB/RCM on one hand and on the other hand the skills and dispositions of those who would use it.

The solution does not lie in reforming or modifying RCB/RCM. The problem is generational. The successful implementation of RCB/RCM may require considerable patience, enough patience to wait for a new generation of academic leadership. Successful implementation may also require additional salary expense for those leaders as they are asked to assume responsibilities and have skills that their predecessors did not.

For publicly-funded institutions there may be an asymmetry between government funding formulas and actual institutional cost structures

In the United States and Canada many if not most schools, colleges, and universities are funded under allocative formulas. There are different types of formulas, each with its own strengths and weaknesses. Some formulas are used in conjunction with other allocative schemes like, for example, performance budgeting. But despite these differences, funding formulas have one thing in common: in one way or another they all make assumptions about institutional cost structures. Some also make algorithmic assumptions about certain forms of income, most notably tuition fees.

The validity of those assumptions is often debated, but valid or not they are inherent to funding formulas and can have a complicating effect on the successful deployment of RCB/RCM. Under RCB/RCM all revenue and all costs are attributed to each faculty or college. Each unit must then adjust its spending patterns to coincide with its revenue patterns. That is the basic idea of "each tub on its own bottom."

The idea is simple enough until one considers the possibility, if not the probability, that large components of revenue may be based on assumptions about costs which are either erroneous to begin with or so generalized that they cannot be validly applied to specific programs in specific institutions. Funding formulas have a powerful homogenizing effect; they are based on averages that treat all programs within certain categories as the same. Therefore for any given program in any given institution under RCB/RCM, the attribution of income may be accurate but may also be unrealistic. It may also assume that the correlation between enrollment and cost is linear when in practical fact it may proceed according to a complex series of step functions unique to each institution. Some universities that have introduced RCB/RCM correct for this by not attributing all income to colleges and faculties. Some is held back and allocated by other means, often and ironically by the same means that preceded the introduction of RCB/RCM. Others correct for the artificial effects of funding formulas by inserting a local formula between the system formula and the RCB/RCM attribution process.

A similar asymmetry may exist within institutions as well if the institutions use internal formulas for making budget allocations (Otten & Savenije, 1990). It is not uncommon for large universities to make allocations according to a series of ratios, for example the number of academic staff to students. The ratios thus constructed are essentially averages that may be appropriate to some faculties but not to others. Thus it might be more accurate to observe that RCB/RCM does not mix well with allocative formulas at any level.

This, of course, is a problem that is in the end part of the case for RCB/RCM. If the linear nature of allocative formulas and the averages that they create are too highly aggregated to reflect local cost structures accurately, as too highly centralized administrative structures do not have enough sapience to know those structures, a move to RCB/RCM removes all assumptions, to continue the example, about staff: student ratios and allows each faculty or department to set its own ratio.

Service teaching and RCB/RCM are not always compatible

From the earliest days of universities one of their roles has been to play a mercantile role among academic disciplines (Haskins, 1923). So today in the multiversity, for example, mathematics departments teach courses for physics departments which in turn teach courses for engineering programs. Curricular regulations make express provisions for elective courses. The variety of permutations and combinations among programs and courses is regarded as a strength of the modern university. Through curricular regulation universities encourage specialization and in a practical sense guarantee markets. Institutional planning and budgeting processes recognize these arrangements by allocating resources to protect high quality programs that otherwise might not be able to support themselves (Kissler, 1997; Vandament, 1989).

RCB/RCM can work against this tradition as individual programs and departments compete with other programs and departments for students, mainly because they do not want to share the revenue which the enrollments generate. But it may also be the case that cost structures—for example, age/salary profiles—may vary among programs and departments, thus causing some programs and departments to "repatriate" courses and offer them themselves. In terms of cost reduction, this consequence might be desirable. In terms of educational quality, the results might be unfortunate, as might have been the case in one university where the faculty of forestry decided to offer its own courses in "English for Foresters."

Another of the effects of RCB/RCM on service teaching, although complicating, reveals and elucidates some of the basic logic of RCB/RCM. The question is about the proper attribution of the income and expense that service teaching generates. The conventional approach—which might be taken even if RCB/RCM were not deployed—is to assign the costs of service teaching to the faculty that provides it. That makes sense from an accounting point of view, which indeed is the point of view of RCB when viewed apart from RCM. It then follows that income ought to be as closely aligned with expense as possible. So the revenue that enrollments in service courses generates is attributed to the faculty that provides the service teaching.

But an ultimate objective of RCB cum RCM is to generate revenue, encourage market-like behaviour, and improve the fit between educational supply and demand. Seen from this perspective, the attribution of revenue ought to be to the faculty that decides on critical balances between enrollment, programs, and resources, and then recruits and registers students, even though some of those students might take some courses in other faculties. The cost of service teaching then would appear as a charge by the faculty that provides the service teaching against the expense budget of the faculty that registers the students and is credited fully for the revenue that they generate.

RCB/RCM also creates markets internal to the institution. In the case of service teaching it is important to consider what is supply and what is demand. The faculties that recruit and register create a demand for service teaching. Provided there is sufficient academic justification, those faculties have a real choice between either offering an entire program themselves or by offering it partially through service teaching provided by other faculties. The reverse is not practicable: providers of service teaching cannot require that their courses be included in other faculties' programs, in other words the supplier cannot have the upper hand. Instead, and also within the basic logic of the RCM side of the RCB/RCM equation, demand in the internal market creates an incentive for faculties that supply service teaching to reduce and control costs, and not simply pass any costs along to other faculties.

Summer sessions in some cases occupy a position comparable to that of service teaching under RCB/RCM. In institutions where the summer session is not a trimester in an integrated twelve month academic calendar, the summer session is an add-on to academic programs much as service teaching is. The summer session has a separate budget and administration. The expense budget is used in practical effect to make internal purchases of instructional time from faculties and departments. Conventional budget and planning regimes attribute income and expense to the summer session instead of to the faculties and departments that provide the instruction and, frequently, the classrooms and instructional laboratories that the summer session physically occupies.

Under RCB/RCM the centre of budgetary planning and management shifts to faculties and departments and away from the summer session administration. The reasoning behind the shift is logical: ultimately, once the cost of organizing and promoting the summer session is set aside, virtually all of the resources that support the session are in the faculties that provide the instruction. While the organizers of summer sessions might find this threatening, it might also improve institutional performance and decision-making as faculties and departments determine the best calendar locations for various courses and gain a better understanding of average costs *versus* marginal costs.

While RCB/RCM can relocate decision-making to levels most capable of making certain decisions, it does not ensure that those decisions will be made at those levels

One of the attractions of RCB/RCM is that it offers the possibility of improving the making of difficult, highly complex decisions. Regardless of the quality of those decisions, they are often very unpopular. Because those decisions are unpopular, senior managers, whether at the institutional, divisional, or departmental level, are inclined to avoid making them. Under conventional planning and budgeting schemes, responsibilities for making certain decisions are organizationally assigned. The responsibilities are difficult to avoid.

But RCB/RCM has an inherent capacity for decision-making "cascades." Just as a university may attribute costs and income to the faculty level, a faculty may assign them to the departmental level, and so on to centres and programs within departments. RCB/RCM by its very nature forces decisions; there couldn't be budgets without them. Thus decisions will ultimately be made at one organizational level or another, and the budgetary consequences of those decisions will be clear.

What might be less clear, however, is the quality or "sapience" of those decisions if the downward cascade does not stop at the level at which the greatest competence and knowledge to make them resides. In other words, the positive correlation between the expansion of RCB/RCM and the quality of decision-making is not infinite. There can be a point at which the expansion of RCB/RCM to lower organizational levels leads to a decline in the quality of decision-making.

RCB/RCM requires new regulatory arrangements

While the description of universities as "organized anarchies" (Cohen &, March, 1974) may be an overstatement, it is true that faculties and departments enjoy considerable degrees of autonomy, especially in terms of who teaches what to whom, appointment of faculty, selection of students, and determination of curriculum. RCB/RCM can expand that autonomy, and in so doing engender greater internal competition among colleges and faculties. When that happens, RCB/RCM needs some sort of forum for local dispute resolution.

Just as nation states have means of curbing the potential excesses of capitalism, universities that deploy RCB/RCM look to similar public regulatory arrangements. One such arrangement is the academic counterpart of a "fair trade commission" which would regulate, for example, the repatriation of service courses and the intra-institutional competition for students. The commission would also ensure that admissions standards would not be compromised to meet unrealistic enrollment and income targets, or that programs inconsistent with institutional missions would not be introduced.

Another regulatory arrangement is similar to a "public utilities commission" which regulates prices and common services. While one first thinks of revenue generation under RCB/RCM as being aimed at enrollment, tuition fees, research grants, consulting income—all essentially external to the institution—RCB/RCM also results in a wide array of internal charges and cost attributions. Some of those charges can be virtually monopolistic, just as a hydro service, or telephone service, or cable television service might be. While RCB/RCM can identify costs with precision, and ensure their attribution, it cannot control or validate those costs. The institutional public utilities commission can, and in turn prevent what otherwise might be described as price gouging.

An institutional public utilities commission can play another role that is also found in the broader economy. As costs are identified and attributed, some academic programs and administrative services may wish to withdraw services that they provide to other parts of the institution, as airlines often wish to do in regard to locations in underpopulated areas. Universities that use RCB/RCM may have to introduce means of regulating the provision of basic services.

While the metaphor of public commissions is apt in describing the roles that they play in deploying RCB/RCM, the role does not necessarily require formal organizational structures. In a number of cases, this is a role played by the chief academic officer.

INSTALLING RCB/RCM COSTS AND PRICES UNDER RCB/RCM

Market driven pricing requires a long-term commitment to RCB/RCM and in turn a long term comprehension of markets and programs costs

RCB/RCM has the effect of stimulating, if not practically requiring, market behaviour at levels within university organization at which such behaviour often is rare. Faculties and colleges have little experience in making decisions about setting prices for their programs and services, and in ensuring that those prices bear a realistic relationship to costs.

For academic degree programs there is a natural tendency to set prices—that is, tuition fees—at whatever levels the market will bear. Although the basic idea is simple to perceive, its implementation is subtle, complex, and slow to evolve. Haste is an enemy of market driven pricing under RCB/RCM. For example, lower tuition fees might support an increase in enrollment, which in turn will produce additional revenue. But increases in enrollment might also produce additional costs. The relationship between enrollment, costs, and prices, however, is not always linear. Thus market-driven pricing might be successful in the short-term but unsuccessful in the long-term, or vice versa.

In the private sector, firms often devise careful strategies for developing, introducing, and pricing new products. Those strategies—for example, Dupont's plan for introducing its miracle fabrics—are sometimes aimed at dominating a market for a long time, in which case initial prices are not necessarily set at the highest possible levels. Instead, the break-even point of income over expense might be as long as three years into the future, with the expectation that the new products will demand large market shares for as long as a decade. The alternative strategy is to recoup development costs by setting prices as high as possible, as soon as possible, which was the case in the introduction of computer technologies. The latter strategy is usually not available to universities because most degree programs, when construed as products, have very long gestation periods.

The point of these examples is not to suggest that there are strong analogies between higher education and the development of new products in the private sector. The point is that as universities introduce RCB/RCM (or other regimes that are highly market driven) they must take as much care as private firms do in determining price strategies and, especially, their time frames. A short horizon is likely to produce deceptive illusions and plant the seeds of future financial distress. RCB/RCM is not a real solution to short term budget problems, their severity notwithstanding. It is a long-term strategy aimed more at the quality of decision-making about the allocation and generation of resources than at the speed with which resources can be reallocated or generated.

Cost driven pricing requires detailed and complete understanding of costs, and of the tolerance of markets to bear those costs. The relationships between costs and time are acute That prices should in some way reflect costs is common sense. It is not, however, widespread common sense in higher education. This is not without reason.

First, some tuition fees are so low as a proportion of cost that they do not really function as prices in an economic sense. Second, degrees have prices in the form of tuition fees, but few colleges or universities are organized exclusively around degree programs in terms of their costs structures. Instead, faculties and departments have several roles: instruction—frequently comprising more than one degree program—research, continuing education and professional development, consulting, and other forms of public service. More significantly, despite a wide range of roles, faculties and departments are supported by single budgets and pools of resources. Attempts to institute PPBS (Planning, Programming, and Budgeting Systems) in higher education have usually met with failure (Balderston & Weatherly, 1972). A private firm's understanding of what constitutes a "cost centre" can be quite different from the comparable understanding in educational institutions in the public and not-for-profit sectors.

One of RCB/RCM's great strengths is that it demands a clear and complete appreciation of costs and the structures that drive them. But, as in the case of market driven pricing, time can make a major difference to an understanding of prices as costs. When new degree programs are introduced or existing programs significantly expanded, they do not reach their steady states for several years. The relationship between income and cost will change each year as the program progresses to its new steady state. In any given year, prices can exceed or fall short of annual costs while matching the average costs that obtain in the steady state.

Most colleges and universities operate on the principle that prices for self-funded programs must at least cover costs, whether or not markets will bear those costs. Costs thus determine the lowest allowable price. This is often regarded as a sound "tough love" practice through which management lessons learned in the private sector are applied in the public sector. But for some programs that approach may be unrealistic from the start, especially for highly specialized programs with low enrollments and for programs with anomalous costs structures (for example, faculties of dentistry that must operate their own clinics without third-party subvention). New programs hardly ever are able cover their costs in the first two or three years of operation because start-up costs and incomplete enrollments—25 per cent in the first year, 50 per cent in the second, and so on—are inherently asymmetrical.

There are ways in which these innate problems can be addressed under RCB/RCM. One is to impose a tax—although that term is not often used formally—on all programs and services in order to fund what amounts to subsidies to certain programs that for one acceptable reason or another cannot cover their full costs. Another is to retain certain income centrally and not attribute it to faculties and programs. This approach is attractive in jurisdictions in which public funding formulas or other allocative schemes do not lend themselves reliably to attribution below the institutional level, as is the case with "infrastructure" grants made by research councils.

Another approach for viewing costs in a broader time frame and thus allowing stronger links between planning and budgeting under RCB/RCM is to make express provisions for internal debt. This approach makes particular sense for the introduction of new programs, sometimes for the closure or radical restructuring on existing programs, and for major capital investments, for example, in laboratories. In those early years in which costs exceed income or savings, the institution can make internal loans to faculties. The loans are real in the sense that the repayments include interest charges as well as principal, and the repayment schedules are built into faculty budgets as any other expense would be, whether or not the institution itself actually incurs an external debt to a lending institution. In cases in which no external debt is incurred—for example, when the institution uses quasi-endowed funds or cash

floats—the internal interest rate is set as an opportunity cost.

Finally, a too rigid or too literal application of the "prices as costs" approach under RCB/RCM runs the risk of driving wedges between activities that should not be organizationally separated. While there are many legitimate debates about whether or not research and instruction should be funded separately and differently from one another, there is a consensus that they complement one another. In most universities faculty are expected to do both, and many facilities and services—libraries, for example—are expected to serve both. RCB/RCM does not require or force the compartmentalization of instruction and research but it does have momentum in that direction against which the institution at large must guard.

At what level should RCB/RCM set prices: by institution, by faculty, or by program?

In the first instance this is an important technical question because it defines the nexus between income and expense. Under RCB/RCM it is a question that must be answered one way or another; it cannot be evaded or deferred. But the question also has much to do with institutional mission, academic organization, and overall financial viability.

Most universities are in fact in several markets: the market for undergraduate degrees in engineering, for example, is not the same as the market for MBA degrees, and so on, even when offered by the same university. This, of course, explains why most (but not all) institutions have schedules of tuition fees with different fees for different programs. But there are other explanations which RCB/RCM tends to expose and emphasize, especially in publicly funded institutions.

First, tuition fees and some other institutional charges and fees have internal as well as external reference points. A comparison of public institutions with high average fees and those with low average fees shows that the ratios among fees are quite similar (University of Toronto, 1996). So, for example, the fee for an MBA program is usually about two times higher than the fee for a BA program within the same institution, regardless of the absolute values of the particular fees in question. This phenomenon may be due as much to government regulation as to institutional policy but the main point in regard to RCB/RCM is that individual faculties and programs may not be able to set their tuition fees entirely independently of other faculties and programs. This suggests that revenue strategies under RCB/RCM may be based more on volume than on prices.

Second, in publicly funded systems of higher education diversity among institutions and programs is often highly sought after but difficult to realize. Institutions often create and support diversity by deliberately deploying "cash cows" and "loss leaders." These are, of course, crass terms that few institutions would openly avow and which no government funding formula recognizes, but the practice exists de facto nevertheless. Programs of very high quality or programs of central importance to a university's mission or reputation are subsidized by programs that may be of lower quality but are more profitable, either because of demand that allows higher fees or because of lower costs. Many governments, especially in Canada, tacitly recognize this by providing funding through block grants.

But RCB/RCM has a tendency towards discouraging diversification that is engendered in this way. This is another reason why some institutions that have deployed RCB/RCM have at the same time introduced various means of internal taxation and cross-subsidization. One must ask, however, whether or not the efficacy of this practice is infinite. In some institutions, the dampening of the connection between the revenue generated by a college or faculty and the actual resource base available to it has become so great that incentives generated by RCB/RCM are weak, which in turn discourages local interest in RCB/RCM.

RCB/RCM AND INSTITUTIONAL PLANS AND MISSION STATEMENTS

The proponents of RCB/RCM correctly point to its capacity to encourage planning, especially strategic planning, down to the grass roots levels of educational institutions. The proponents of mission statements usually categorize them as a form of strategic planning (Bryson, 1988; Schmidtlein, 1989). Some would go on to say that mission statements—both as process and device—are key elements in suc-

cessful strategic planning (Kotler & Murphy, 1981). This juxtaposition suggests that the introduction of RCB/RCM as a planning and budgeting process should have an effect on mission statements. This does not necessarily mean that an institution that installs RCB/RCM will have to change its mission, but it may mean that the form of the mission statement will have to change, as might the means by which the institution determines its mission.

As ubiquitous as the term "mission statement" is in educational planning, it is not always understood with precision. There are in fact several different kinds of mission statements which have been used in higher education (Lang & Lopers-Sweetman, 1991). A brief taxonomy would include the following:

- mission statements as the clarification of goals
- mission statements as smoke screens for opportunism
- mission statements as descriptions of things as they are
- mission statements as aspirations
- historical and philosophical justifications of the status quo
- plans for action
- interrogations which set an agenda for planning
- expressions of scale and capacity
- messianic presidential tablets
- anthologies of missions

For some of these forms of mission statements, the institution's processes for linking plans and budgets—which is what RCB/RCM does—are not fundamentally relevant. The two can co-exist whether or not they actually interact. For other forms, the relationship is symbiotic. And for other forms the two are incompatible to the point of dysfunction.

RCB/RCM to a large degree rules out the *messianic tablet* type of mission statement. This type of mission statement is usually closely identified with the institution's president or chief academic officer, and is expressed in personal terms. It has a philosophical bent and typically describes a plan for institutional reformation or reorganization. The messianic tablet mission statement is the epitome of "top down" planning. This type of mission statement is incompatible with RCB/RCM because its centralized, top down character does not mesh with the high degree of delegation that RCB/RCM entails. RCB/RCM inherently invests less control in central administrations.

Whether determined top down by presidents or as *action plans,* mission statements that require fundamental institutional redirection in short periods of time in response to external factors are also not suited well to RCB/RCM. While RCB/RCM might result in quick action by faculties and departments, it does not force or require such action. Indeed, those faculties and departments that find themselves able to balance income and expense will have relatively little incentive to consider any change at all.

Mission statements that are *anthologies of missions* fit RCB/RCM well because of all the types of mission statements they are the ones that are formed most by broad participation from the bottom up. The anthologies are compilations of plans of various units of the institution, and thus mirror the degree of delegation engendered by RCB/RCM. RCB/RCM brings to those plans a large measure of realism in university management about what is possible and what is not.

Although mission statements are usually associated with individual institutions, there are some mission statements that operate at the system level. RCB/RCM can have a relationship to them too. The relationship depends to some extent on the means that systems used to allocate resources to individual institutions; some of those means—for example, cost based funding formulas—are more suited to RCB/RCM than others. The relationship also can depend on the fiduciary controls that systems use. For example, line-by-line budgeting so predetermines patterns of spending that RCB/RCM would be of little value at the institutional level.

RCB/RCM advances system-wide mission statements that emphasize accessibility and those that call for the reduction of costs in order to close or prevent budget deficits. By attributing revenue to individual faculties and departments, RCB/RCM creates strong incentives to increase capacity and expand accessibility. By identifying all costs and attributing them—along with revenue—to individual faculties and departments, RCB/RCM demonstrates the urgency of the need to balance budgets and forces the balancing.

CONCLUSION: SOME RCB/RCM DOS AND DON'TS

Do not expect RCB/RCM to be useful and effective in all circumstances. Its application should be specific instead of broad.

Its application should be specific instead of broad. RCB/RCM appears to be a creature of circumstance. It has so far been an effective means of addressing a number of specific contemporary problems and issues that confront some universities, and perhaps other large educational institutions as well. As funding shrinks, RCB/RCM can help improve the quality of decisions—as noxious and unfortunate as they may be—about the optimal allocations of resources and balances between income and expense.

Do deploy RCB/RCM to provide incentives towards entrepreneurial behaviour and the generation of revenue

It engenders a broad interest in planning and successfully linking plans and budgets. It provides governors and senior managers with better information about institutional performance.

Do not regard RCB/RCM as an exclusively institutional concept; it should be of more than passing interest to governments and system coordinating agencies

The capability of RCB/RCM to promote better fits between educational supply and demand advances a public policy objective that systems otherwise can realize only by heavy-handed and often ineffective intervention. If boards of governors are better informed, they can relieve some of government's concerns about accountability, and about vexing "How much is enough?" questions. Setting concerns about accountability aside, some provinces might find that, in times of severe financial constraint, it makes better public policy to allow greater institutional autonomy by encouraging marketization which in turn will increase institutional efficiency and effectiveness, not only in controlling costs but also in attracting other sources of revenue (Berdahl, 1993). In such cases, to the extent that system administrations can have an influence on firms of institutional budgeting and planning, they should encourage RCB/RCM as an alternative to regulation.

Do not expect RCB/RCM to be a "quick fix" or inexpensive solution

It takes time and effort to install. Sometimes it requires expensive investments in management infrastructure. It is a long-term commitment to a different management style, the benefits of which may not appear immediately and in fact might not appear until a new generation of academic managers emerges.

Do not expect RCB/RCM to be equally useful and effective in all institutions. It is best suited to large, complex, research-intensive universities and in multi-campus institutions

In his prize-winning essay on corporate power and federalism, Charles Handy acutely describes a paradox of size that afflicts large organizations that must be large and small at the same time (Handy, 1992). While Handy is speaking about private firms, the paradox applies to large universities as well. As institutions they must centrally provide direction, set and enforce standards of quality, ensure cohesion, and create economies of scale. All of which are characteristics of being large. Accountability to governments and boards of governors is also a central responsibility. At the same time they must encourage innovation and efficiency, recognize the differences between accountability and control, and organizationally align competence with decision-making—all of which are characteristics of being small. This does not necessarily mean that RCB/RCM cannot work in smaller institutions. It does, however, mean that for smaller institutions the return on the investment in RCB/RCM might not be large enough to justify its deployment.

Do take into account the ways in which public funding is allocated to universities in implementing RCB/RCM. The success or failure of RCB/RCM can depend on the form that the allocation public takes

Some funding formulas can so distort the connection between revenue and cost that RCB/RCM is difficult to implement without adding an extra layer of complexity between sources of funding and their ultimate allocation.

Do introduce RCB/RCM in order to improve decision-making, but do not expect it to improve all decisions

The beneficial results of RCB/RCM are not automatic. In institutions with several levels of organizational structure, RCB/RCM could be an invitation to "pass the buck" as difficult and unpopular problems about the allocation of resources and the generation of revenue are passed from level to level without stopping at the level where they can be best made.

Do recognize that RCB/RCM, like laissez-faire capitalism, can be prone to excess, and therefore sometimes need regulation

In *The University in Ruins,* Bill Readings takes pains to draw an acute distinction between accountability and accounting, and argues that universities are in danger from regarding accounting as accountability. (Readings, 1996). RCB/RCM looks a lot like accounting with relatively little accountability for anything except the "bottom line." It is indeed true that RCB/RCM has a strong element of accounting, in fact more accounting than would normally be found in other planning and budgeting schemes. Readings and others (Wagner, 1989) go on to say that over-zealous accounting and other applications of the principles of business management to the university undermine the fundamental cultural and moral roles of the university. RCB/RCM does run this risk, but it runs it in both directions.

First, if one assumes that large, complex institutions, like some universities, are too large to be managed well from the top, and for that reason tend towards heavy-handed accounting and accountability, and formulistic allocative schemes, RCB/RCM can be regarded as a means of relocating decision-making to those levels at which fundamental roles are understood and more likely to be protected. But, second and in the other direction of risk, RCB/RCM may ensure only that income and expense are balanced without due regard to those fundamental roles. Universities that deploy RCB/RCM guard against this by creating what we have called here "fair trade commissions" and "public utilities commissions," and by holding back some revenue for allocation on the basis of quality and institutional priority.

Do not assume that RCB/RCM will necessarily or automatically emphasize quality and academic values

In some universities that have adopted RCB/RCM there is a surprising and sometimes ironic concern about quality. The irony is that conventional wisdom presumes that the centre of gravity for concern about quality resides in colleges and faculties. Indeed, a strong reason for moving to RCB/RCM is the presumption that central administrations cannot—whether they admit it or not—make sound and fully informed decisions about the quality of individual academic programs. The surprise is that some universities that have introduced RCB/RCM or have otherwise become highly entrepreneurial report a lack of sufficient emphasis on quality as colleges and faculties seek to maximize revenue (Clark, 1998).

Do not generalize the effects that RCB/RCM may have on collegiality and cooperation. It may be beneficial in some cases and detrimental in others

On the one hand, RCB/RCM promotes collegiality by radically expanding the degree of participation in making crucial decisions about plans and budgets which otherwise would be made centrally at the peak of the organizational pyramid. By exposing and attributing all costs and revenue, RCB/RCM allows a far more extensive understanding within the university community of the institution's overall financial condition.

On the other hand, RCB/RCM in some circumstances engenders intense internal competition among colleges and faculties which discourages collegiality and cooperation. In the spatial terms of an organization chart, then, one might characterize RCB/RCM as promoting vertical collegiality while discouraging horizontal collegiality. As vertical collegiality grows, central administrations necessarily lose some control, particularly if they previously relied on patronage in resource allocation as a means of exerting control. It may also be that as RCB/RCM promotes vertical collegiality the idiom of that collegiality changes. In other planning and budgeting regimes, regardless of the volume of discussion between central administrations and faculties,

the discussion often revolves around resources. As RCB/RCM shifts the centre of gravity of decision-making towards colleges and faculties, the idiom of collegial discourse between, for example, deans and chief academic officers, also shifts, usually in the direction academic plans, standards, and performance measures.

THE FUTURE OF RCB/RCM

Finally, one must ask whether RCB/RCM is a large scale but ephemeral creation of bad financial times or of expanding institutional scale and complexity. RCB/RCM seems to be effective in improving (although not perfecting) the quality of decisions about resource allocation and generation. To the extent that those are difficult and unpopular decisions, universities are attracted to RCB/RCM because it improves decision-making and broadens participation in it. In better financial times that attraction might diminish.

Another attribute of RCB/RCM, however, is its capability to break decision-making log-jams in institutions that are becoming increasingly complex and often larger, regardless of their financial circumstances. In this case the attractions of RCB/RCM are likely to remain compelling and worthy of serious consideration.

There is perhaps an emerging third reason that explains the interest in RCB/RCM. Although much has been said for and against the entrepreneurial university (Clark, 1998; Marginson, 1997; Slaughter & Leslie, 1997) the interest in various forms of marketization and privatization is serious and legitimate. While usually associated with public policy and systems of higher education, marketization, privatization, and entrepreneurial behaviour—in various combinations—may help individual institutions respond successfully to what Burton Clark calls "demand overload" and the asymmetry between the rates at which knowledge is created and the resources made available to sustain it (Clark, 1998). At its inception, RCB/RCM was not closely identified with entrepreneurship, but it is now clear that, intentionally or not, RCB/RCM encourages entrepreneurial or market behaviour and provides a workable organizational structure in which it can be harnessed and productively directed. This, too, suggests that interest in

RCB/RCM will continue even if the financial condition of universities improves.

Since RCB/RCM has the capacity to stimulate and manage market behaviour, it can be an effective institutional response to government and other public demands for a better fit between education and economic and social need. Typically, governments and system coordinating agencies that have these concerns turn to increased regulation and prescriptive funding schemes in order to force the results that they want at the expense of institutional autonomy. RCB/RCM can be a means of producing the desired results without compromising autonomy or inviting heavy-handed government interference.

REFERENCES

Books and Articles

Balderston, F. E. & Weatherly, G. B., (1972). *PPBS in higher educational planning and management: From PPBS to policy analysis*. Office of the Vice President—Planning, University of California.

Barlosky, M., & Lawton. S. (1995). *School-based budgeting*. Toronto, ON: The Quality Schools Project.

Berdahl, R. (1993). *The quasi-privatization of a public honors college: A case study of St. Mary's College in Maryland*. Unpublished paper, University of Maryland—College Park.

Blau, P. M. (1994) *The organization of academic work*, 2nd edition. New Brunswick, NJ: Transaction.

Brinkman, P. (1993). Responsibility Center Budgeting: An approach to decentralized management for institutions of higher education. *Planning for Higher Education*, 21, 49–51.

Bryson, J. M. (1988). *Strategic planning for public and non-profit organizations*. San Francisco, CA: Jossey-Bass.

Clark, B. R. (1998). *Creating entrepreneurial universities*. Oxford, UK: Pergamon.

Cohen, M., & March, J. (1974). *Leadership and ambiguity: The American college president*. New York, NY: McGraw-Hill.

Fielden, J. (1996). *University of X: Delegated management and budgets*. London, UK: Commonwealth Higher Education Service.

Garner, C. W. (1991). *Accounting and budgeting in public and nonprofit organizations*. San Francisco, CA: Jossey-Bass.

Gordon, G., & Charles, M. (1997). Unraveling higher education's costs. *Planning for Higher Education*, 26, 24–26.

Griffin, S., & Day, S. (1997). Progress made on a plan to integrate planning, budgeting, assessment and quality principles to achieve institutional improvement. *AIR Professional File, No. 66*.

Handy, C. (1992). Balancing corporate power: A new federalist paper, *Harvard Business Review*, November-December, 159–182.

Haskins, C. H. (1923). *The rise of universities*. Ithaca: Cornell University Press.

Kail, L. J. (1988). *Financial devolution—Departmental cost centres and incentives*. University of Surrey: Office of the secretary.

Keller, G. (1983). *Academic strategy*. Baltimore, MD: Johns Hopkins University Press.

Kissler, G. R. (1997). Who decides which budgets to cut? *The Journal of Higher Education*. 68(4), 427–459.

Kotler, P. & Murphy, P. (1981). Strategic planning for higher education. *Journal of Higher Education*, 52(5). 470–489.

Lang, D. W. (1988). Planning and decision-making in universities. *Canadian Society for the Study of Higher Education, Professional File, No. 4*.

Lang, D. W., & Lopers-Sweetman, R. (1991). The role of statements of institutional purpose. *Research in Higher Education*, 32(6), 599–624.

March. J. G. (1994). *A primer on decision making*. New York, NY: The Free Press.

Marginson, S. (1997). *Markets in education*. St. Leonards. NSW: Allen & Unwin.

Massy, W. F. (1994). Measuring performance: How colleges and universities can set meaningful goals. In W. F. Massy & J. W. Meyerson, eds., *Measuring Institutional performance in higher education*, (pp. 29–54). Princeton, NJ: Peterson's.

National Commission on the Cost of Higher Education (1998). *Straight talk about college costs & prices*. The Report of the National Commission on the Cost of Higher Education. Phoenix, AZ: Oryx.

Otten, C. & Savenije, B. (1990). The rise and fall of an allocation model: An evaluation of its role as an instrument for policy decisions. *Research in Higher Education*, 31(1), 1–15.

Readings, B. (1996). *The university in ruins*. Cambridge, MA: Harvard.

Rush, S. C. (1994). Benchmarking—How good is good? In W. F. Massy & J. W. Meyerson, eds., *Measuring institutional Performance in higher education*, (pp. 83–98). Princeton, NJ: Peterson's.

Rush, S. C. (1991). *Managing the facilities portfolio*. Washington, DC: NACUBO.

Schmidtlein, F. A. (1989). Center findings reveal planning problems. *News From SCUP*, 19 (4).

Slaughter, S. & Leslie, L. (1997). *Academic capitalism*. Baltimore, MD: Johns Hopkins University Press.

University of Toronto (1996). *Final brief to the advisory panel on future directions for postsecondary education, Appendix VII*. Toronto, ON: Office of the Vice-Provost and Assistant Vice-President, Planning and Budget, University of Toronto.

Vandament, W. E. (1989). Managing money in higher education. San Francisco, CA: Jossey-Bass.

Wagner, R. B. (1989). *Accountability in education.* New York, NY: Routledge.

Whalen, E. L. (1991). *Responsibility Center Budgeting.* Bloomington, IN: Indiana University Press.

Whitaker, G. R. (1995). Value centered management: The Michigan approach to Responsibility Center Management. *The University Record,* January 9.

Winston, G. (1992). The necessary revolution in financial accounting. *Planning for Higher Education,* 20, 1–15.

Institutional Reports

Budgeting policy for the University of Illinois. (1995).

Critical performance measures and benchmarks/performance goals: A guide to their selection and application [at the University of Minnesota.] (1994).

Comments related to the proposal to revise our budgeting strategy, [at the University of Michigan]. (1994).

Cornell University Responsibility Center analysis. (1995).

Cost accounting: A Cornell perspective. (1994).

Incentive based budgeting [at Ohio Stare University]. (1995).

Instructional cost study [at the University of Minnesota]. (1993).

RCM allocation model [at UCLA]. (1995).

Report of the outsourcing advisory group, University of Minnesota. (1996).

Report to the Clemson Board of Trustees, Budget/Funding Task Force. (1994).

Responsibility Center Analysis [at Cornell University]. (1994).

Responsibility Center Budgeting/Responsibility Centre Management at Scarborough College [University of Toronto]. (1996).

Responsibility Centered Management at Indiana University Bloomington—1990–1996. (1996).

Responsibility Center Management at UCLA. (1995).

Responsibility Center Management [at the University of Minnesota]. (1995).

Responsibility Center Management: Issues for discussion [at the University of Pennsylvania]. (1994).

Rethinking administration and Responsibility Centre Budgeting [at the University of Toronto]. (1993).

Revised methodology for distributing allocated cost [at the University of Pennsylvania]. (1994).

Securing the future at UCLA: Improved academic planning and financial management tools. (1995).

Thoughts on the need for a revised approach to accounting and budgeting at Michigan. (1994).

Understanding the revenue and expenditure patterns of the college and its divisions [at the University of Toronto]. (1994).

Value Centered Management at the University of' Michigan. (1995).

Washington University's Budget Structure. (1993).

Chapter 46

Revenue Responsibility Budgeting

Jon Strauss, John Curry, and Edward Whalen

Written by pioneers in the field, the three short pieces in this chapter provide firsthand insights on revenue responsibility budgeting. As we noted earlier, systems of revenue responsibility budgeting are sometimes called responsibility center budgeting or responsibility center management. Jon Strauss discusses some of the principles of responsibility center budgeting and gives examples of how decentralized data can be used even at institutions that do not practice decentralized budgeting. John Curry narrates the actual process of adopting a university-wide responsibility center management system at the University of Southern California in the early 1980s. Finally, Edward Whalen considers the case for adopting responsibility center budgeting at public institutions.

THE WPI EXPERIENCE

Along with Edward Whalen and Robert Zemsky, Jon Strauss was one of the originators of revenue responsibility budgeting and has written extensively on the subject. Strauss helped implement responsibility center budgeting first at the University of Pennsylvania in the 1970s as a budget and finance officer, and then at the University of Southern California in the mid-1980s as senior vice president for administration. While he was president of Worcester Polytechnic Institute (WPI), Jon Strauss encountered resistance to implementing responsibility center budgeting but nevertheless believed that the principles of decentralized management are applicable to a small college environment. In the segment that follows, he presents a brief review of the underlying principles followed by an example of a prototype decentralized management model at WPI. Subsequent sections describe budgeting under decentralized management, potential benefits and pitfalls, and guidelines. He then describes the kind of decentralized management data being used at WPI, to show that even institutions that do not practice responsibility center budgeting management can learn from data constructed around decentralized principles. Jon Strauss is currently vice president and financial officer of the Howard Hughes Medical Institute.—Ed.

Underlying Principles

Experience at the University of Pennsylvania demonstrated that three management principles guide the application and effectiveness of decentralized management in higher education: openness, localness, and merit.

Openness. One of the fundamental tenets of academic freedom that forms the foundation of the entire collegiate experience is free and open exchange of ideas and information. Tradition-

Source: *Resource Allocation in Higher Education*, 1996, W.F. Massy (ed.), University of Michigan Press.

ally, tenure and academic custom have allowed faculty to be largely self-determining: they generate their own support, set their own schedules, recruit their colleagues, and govern their institutions. As a rule, institutions that are dedicated to a management structure that builds upon this foundation are best able to recruit and retain productive and satisfied faculty members—professors who contribute enthusiastically to the attainment of plans they have helped formulate and for which, as a result, they take ownership. Openness is thus a requirement for faculty involvement in the planning and management of the institution.

Localness. If decentralized management can work in the for-profit environment where hierarchical control enjoys a much deeper tradition of respect, then local governance should be a natural in the academic community. In the most radical view, local collegiate governance suggests giving departmental faculties responsibility for their entire academic operations—planning, developing opportunities, generating resources, and achieving excellence, all in addition to their prescribed obligations for instruction, research, and service. Contingent upon the acceptance of these responsibilities, of course, are the authority and the rewards that accompany such a system.

An important benefit of local governance is its simplicity. Because decisions are made by individuals who are in a position to understand best the issues involved (who, incidentally, are often not on the top rungs of the hierarchical ladder), problems can be viewed without complicated models or explanations. The decision makers know at the outset of responding to a challenge that they will be involved in implementing solutions and will be held accountable for outcomes. As a result, decisions tend to emerge more quickly and prudently, and the faculty can adapt their solutions to ever-changing conditions both on campus and off.

Merit. Decisions of the greatest merit are made and implemented openly and at the most local level of the organization. On merit alone are grades awarded, papers published, research support won, salaries earned, promotions made, and tenure granted; moreover, faculty are not only comfortable with, but generally insist upon, using merit to determine alternate courses of action. Merit also provides the principle to weigh several possible local alternatives. Even in the most effective decentralized organizations, overall resources must be allocated in accord with institutional priorities and the performance-risk assessments of "competing" local plans. In the final analysis, academia can no more ignore the principles of financial costs and benefits than the most aggressive Fortune 500 corporations. Moreover, for resource allocation to be effective in an environment of open information and local planning, relative merit must guide every decision.

These three basic management principles framed the set of organizational principles for the implementation of the University of Southern California's Revenue Center Management System.

The closer the decision maker is to the relevant information the better the decision is likely to be.

Stable environments facilitate good planning.

Responsibility should be commensurate with authority and vice versa.

A clear set of rewards and sanctions is required to make operational the distribution of responsibility and authority, as well as to effect their coupling.

While fiscal performance criteria are seductively easy to quantify, achievement of academic excellence requires that academic performance criteria be quantified as well.

The degree of decentralization of an organization should be proportional to its size and complexity.

Successful decentralization requires a centrally maintained management information system providing local and central managers with timely and accurate performance reports.

The central administration should retain sufficient academic and fiscal leverage to facilitate the achievement of institutional goals.

A Specific Example of Decentralized Management Data at the Departmental Level

To give a sense of the major features of policies, procedures, and funds flow in a typical decentralized management system, consider the actual 1991–92 financial results in Table 46.1 for a WPI department under a prototype decentralized management model.

Under this system, the department sees its full revenue and expense activity, restricted as well as unrestricted. Both revenue and expense are further classified as direct and indirect, with direct being under the direct control of the department and indirect being set from outside. The basic logic is that revenue-producing centers will be budgeted and managed with expenses balanced to revenues, and that the financial activity of the revenue centers will sum to the financial activity of the institution.

Individual categories of revenues and expenses are distributed according to the following rules: Tuition revenue is distributed 75 percent to the teaching department and 25 percent to the enrolling department. Restricted scholarship revenue, a distribution of the restricted revenue from all sources of financial aid, is matched to the restricted expenses for financial aid distributed proportionally to tuition. Reimbursed salaries accounts for coverage of committed salaries budgeted as unrestricted from restricted funds.

Financial aid is shown as an indirect expense but more correctly should show as a discount on revenue. The financial aid costs, both unrestricted and restricted, are distributed proportionally to tuition. Some will argue that financial aid should be assigned with the individual student, but this averaging approach reflects the notion that the student is a member of the university and not just the department.

Departmental administration ICR represents that portion of the indirect cost recoveries from restricted activities that are justified based on unrestricted departmental costs, as discussed below. Research incentives, set at 25 percent of the total ICR, are monies the department is allowed to spend based on a historical incentive at WPI. Indirect expenses incurred in the administrative service centers, listed as academic support (library, academic computing) through public service and information, are charged back to the departments based on

TABLE 46.1
Total Resource Management, Revenue and Expense Summary, 1991–92 Fiscal Year

Description	Unrestricted	Restricted
Tuition and fees (undergraduate)	2,399,643	
Tuition and fees (graduate)	733,240	
Endowment revenue		340,134
Scholarship revenue		5,496
Gifts and grants		233,152
Sponsored research		
Other income		
Auxiliary income		
Participation	(783,221)	
Subvention	642,834	
Total revenue	2,992,496	578,782
Faculty salaries	712,629	25,540
Staff salaries	150,405	1,800
Benefits	212,306	6,726
Reimbursed salaries		
Graduate stipends	89,100	60,324
Student help	18,235	5,163
Total compensation	1,182,675	99,553
Graduate assistant tuition	90,620	48,320
Materials and supplies	59,895	21,300
Equipment, expensed	57,947	4,794
Travel	13,667	5,970
Telephone	6,088	
Departmental administration (ICR)	(2,179)	
Research Incentives	17,320	
Total other direct expenses	243,358	80,384
Total direct expenses	1,426,033	179,937
Academic support	219,928	
General administrative	169,296	
Debt service	40,812	
General institutional	36,497	
Depreciation	60,669	
Building repair and maintenance	32,550	
Plant operations and maintenance	145,517	
Departmental utilities	37,433	
General utilities	19,632	
Student services	210,889	
Public services and information	86,362	
Financial aid	563,410	340,134
Cost sharing of research	3,552	(3,552)
Indirect cost recovery	(60,084)	62,263
Total indirect expenses	1,566,463	398,845
Total direct and indirect expenses	2,992,496	578,782

their use (e.g., metered utilities), or potential use (e.g., proportional share of the president's office), of the services. Restricted and unrestricted activity is counted in the proportional distribution of these indirect expenses. Cost sharing of research is the costs of the restricted research program of that department borne by the unrestricted budget under agreement with the sponsor. Indirect cost recovery is the indirect cost recoveries from all sponsored research activity in the department less that justified and accounted for departmental administration. The ICR are shown as negative unrestricted indirect costs to emphasize that their purpose is to cover the indirect costs associated with supporting the sponsored research activity.

Participation is a charge of 25 percent of direct unrestricted revenue. This charge helps fund the reallocation (subvention) pool. Subvention is a discretionary allocation to account for the different unit costs of different program activities historical, intrinsic, or desired. (In this after-the-fact presentation, the subvention is set to balance revenue to expenses.) If a particular department suffers rapid loss of student interest and income, for example, the central authority (general) can help phase the impact by increasing that department's subvention. In responsibility center budgeting, subvention is the primary means of institutional-level budgeting and control.

Table 46.2 presents an overview of the funds flow for the total institution in this decentralized financial model for 1991–92. The six columns identify academic operations (departments), other educational (summer school, continuing education, etc.), auxiliary operations (residences, dining, bookstore, etc.), general, administrative services, and total. Notice that at the institutional level, participation transfers revenues (25% of unrestricted) from the revenue centers to general (subvention pool). General collects revenues from participation, unrestricted gifts, and unrestricted endowment and transfers them to the revenue centers as subvention.

Indirect costs are generated as the net costs of the administrative services and distributed to the revenue centers by indirect cost type (academic support, general administrative, etc.,) using consistent algorithms based on use or potential use. The total column corresponds to the audited financial results, except indirect cost recoveries are shown as a reduction of indirect costs to emphasize that while the recoveries may be accounted as unrestricted revenues by FASB, they truly are not discretionary in purpose.

By normalizing the financial data, one can produce physical equivalents from which a number of interesting analyses can be made, both geographically (across schools or departments) and temporally. One could generate, for example, tuition equivalent student/salary equivalent faculty ratios by department or subvention ratios by department. The notion, of course, is not that these ratios should be identical across departments. Different teaching methodologies, lifestyles, lab-

TABLE 46.2
Total Resources Management, Revenue and Expense Area Summary, 1991–92 Fiscal Year

Description	Unrestricted						Restricted			
	Academic Oper.	Other Educ.	Auxiliary	General	Administrative	Institutional	Academic Oper.	Other Educ.	Administrative	Institutional
Direct revenue	41,993,658	2,737,229	6,349,005	5,983,153	342,218	57,405,263	14,688,841	611	330,664	15,020,116
Participation	(10,498,419)	(684,308)	(1,587,252)	12,769,979						
Subvention	14,871,969	986,208	2,930,849	(18,789,026)						
Total revenue	46,367,208	3,039,129	7,692,602	(35,894)	342,218	57,405,263	14,688,841	611	330,664	15,020,116
Direct expense	20,489,405	1,979,930	5,417,298	391	30,021,851	57,908,875	8,628,417	611	5,594,563	14,223,591
Dept. admin. ICR	(33,472)				(975)	(34,447)				
Indirect expense	18,112,601	1,059,199	2,275,304	(82,641)	(20,930,275)	434,188	(464,338)		(26,509)	(490,847)
Financial aid	8,721,517				(8,721,517)		5,265,231		(5,265,231)	
Indirect cost recovery	(922,843)			(1,299)	(26,866)	(951,008)	1,259,531		27,841	1,287,372
Total expenses	466,367,208	3,039,129	7,692,602	(83,549)	342,218	57,357,608	14,688,841	611	330,664	15,020,116
Variance				47,655		47,655				

oratory needs, and histories all contribute to very different measures. The important point is that these measures should be consistent with quality perceptions or expectations and priorities. If they are not, explicit actions should be taken to align these measures over time. Organizing data in a responsibility center budgeting format thus provides a lot of useful, financially consistent information even if departments are not managed according to strict RCB principles.

Budgeting Under Decentralized Management

To this point, most of the emphasis and all of the examples have been after-the-fact presentations of where revenues were earned and how they were spent. While this is an important educational tool, the real benefit of decentralized management is in prospective planning and budgeting. The general approach employed at both Pennsylvania and USC to budget the subsequent year is as follows:

1. Project the full institutional budget for next year(s) and make preliminary decisions for the (trade-offs of tuition rates, enrollments, salaries, benefits, new programs, and reallocation.

2. Decide on the general parameters for the administrative service centers and set their outline budgets.

3. Distribute the indirect costs for the next year based on the algorithms using data from the previous year.

4. Project tuition revenues for the next year based on the new rates and the expected enrollments.

5. Set subventions to reflect history, priority, and ability to change to achieve the goals of the strategic plan.

6. Ask the revenue centers to balance their budgets with particular care for enrollment assumptions.

Once this logic is in place, various refinements can be added to do planning and subvention settings over longer time periods. The institution also needs a mechanism, perhaps an intercenter bank, to hold centers responsible for deficits and to allow other centers to profit in future years from prior year surpluses.

Potential Benefits

Over the years, the following sorts of benefits have been realized at the University of Pennsylvania, USC, and elsewhere by measuring budget performance on the basis of revenues and expenses, indirect as well as direct, at the school and department level.

Accountability for both the full revenues and expenditures of a budget center has had several effects. Perhaps most important, the centers themselves now have incentives both to enhance revenues and control costs. Cost-benefit analysis is encouraged. On the revenue side, responsibility center budgeting focuses more attention on the importance of tuition revenue and on the professors or courses likely to attract that revenue. In addition, members of a budget center are encouraged to seek out gifts and grants from both philanthropic and governmental sources.

On the cost side, the members of a center become more aware of the total costs of the enterprise including benefits, financial aid, and overheads, since these are no longer charged to other units in the accounting. In fact, explicit charges for space related costs may cause a reappraisal for the need or value of space. Explicit charges for space and depreciation also emphasize the need to provide resources for maintaining the physical plant, making the cost of deferring those repairs more apparent. Finally, explicit portrayal of indirect costs helps reinforce the notion that indirect cost recovery is not discretionary income but rather income to cover real, and often frustratingly high, administrative costs.

Portrayal of revenues and expenses at the school or department level involves the faculty substantively, not just as consultants, in academic and financial policy issues where they can make a difference. Public presentation of all the data (except individual salaries) for all centers encourages peer pressure for appropriate behavior. The explicit, public identification of the sources and uses of indirect costs creates pressures to provide services more efficiently. At both Pennsylvania and USC, general administration and general institutional indirect costs were reduced dramatically relative to total expenditures in the years following the introduction of decentralized management. Moreover, at USC departmental administrative costs were reduced as well. Finally, allowing centers to carry forward surpluses and requiring them to be responsible for deficits at year-end provide incentives for prudent long-term operations.

Potential Pitfalls

Implementing responsibility center budgeting also gives rise to dangers that must be avoided. These systems facilitate management but do not automate it. Consequently, the chief academic officer, in particular, must be vigilant in emphasizing the incentives for good academic performance and in discouraging possible unfortunate side effects in the schools and departments. Among these possible side effects are centers restricting students from taking courses in other schools in order to retain their tuition, trying to attract students from other schools with gut courses, restricting interdisciplinary activity in order to retain tuition revenue or indirect cost recoveries, and finally restricting use of necessary administrative or academic support services in an attempt to minimize indirect cost allocations that are based on measured use.

In addition, subvention raises some problems of its own. Subvention provides a net measure of the relative unit costs of different programs both intrinsic and as a result of institutional history. Further, subvention can be used to express priority and to provide discretionary funding for new ventures. Unfortunately, this system can also lead to invidious comparison between peers over who is most favored. The chief academic officer must be prepared to defend the subvention distribution in terms of the relative academic benefits provided. Many deans and department heads will try to win this budget game by arguing with the rules rather than concentrating on performance. The correct response must be that subvention is based on a certain set of rules and any changes will be problem invariant.

A few other potential weaknesses remain. Department chairs elected by their faculty for short terms may have difficulty in providing the strong financial management needed with decentralized management. While the costs of central services should be tested against the marketplace and changes made where appropriate, care must be exercised to assure that these changes are not too precipitous and that institutional considerations are brought to bear when services are out-sourced.

Most important, as with all budgeting, the strategic plan must drive the tactical budget and not vice versa.

Guidelines

For those adventuresome enough to contemplate installing decentralized management at their institutions, here are some guidelines:

Keep it simple! Folks will argue both sides of any algorithm to distribute revenues or allocate costs.

Try to generate broadly based involvement and acceptance for the underlying concepts early on.

Maintain as much discretion as possible in the allocation of subvention.

Derive all reports directly from official information systems and make certain that reports reconcile. One simple mistake or inconsistency can destroy confidence for a long time.

Emphasize that while the numbers reconcile to the official information systems, the underlying decisions reflect academic priorities and judgment.

Display and budget restricted activity as well as unrestricted to emphasize the role of restricted funds in advancing the mission of that academic unit.

Avoid the temptation to deal solely with the direct revenues and expenses as this precludes the benefits of knowing the overheads, no matter how imprecisely they are allocated.

Never (ever!) compromise the principle that units must be responsible for their performance.

Embed the annual budgeting process in a multiyear strategic planning process.

Present all the data (except individual salaries) for all centers publicly, to encourage comparison and preclude suspicion.

The president and chief academic officer must believe! (i.e., walk it as well as talk it!)

Another Approach

While the examples given to this point are derived from a decentralized presentation of

WPI's financial performance on a departmental basis, WPI is not being managed on a decentralized basis. As at most colleges and universities, the WPI departments exercise significant authority over their expenditures and negotiate their annual expenditure budgets based on historical precedent and qualitative analyses of the academic benefits that will result. To date at least, the department heads have been skeptical of what benefits might accrue from taking responsibility for generating revenue and particularly for balancing expenses to revenues during an academic year. Moreover, they have been most reluctant to be held responsible for indirect expenses they don't control.

The attitudes encountered at WPI with respect to decentralized management are not peculiar; they were encountered at both Pennsylvania and USC. The enormous success of decentralized management at improving financial and service management, however, suggests potentially significant benefits for departmentally based decentralization in a small college environment similar to WPI if ways can be found to overcome these kinds of objections. Another approach based on responsibility center budgeting was undertaken at WPI with the full cooperation of the department heads.

Table 46.3 presents the reconfigured results for the department described in Table 46.1. Data from the registration systems from which student revenue can be computed are displayed as revenue statistics. The unrestricted direct expenses are the same for the individual categories as in Table 46.1. Indirect expenses are not presented, but specific employee counts from the human resource system are included.

This approach has some of the advantages of full decentralized management in that departments are alerted to the characteristic features of their direct revenue and expenditure patterns and can compare their behavior to others. This approach, however, neither establishes a logical tautology for setting expenditure levels relative to revenue nor facilitates peer-based control of indirect costs. This method does provide, however, the beginnings of an approach that may prove effective for departmentally based decentralized management, and is presented here as a possible intermediate step. The difficult times facing higher education now and for at least the next decade have stimulated general interest in better, more participatory financial management in public as well as private institutions. Decentralized management has provided demonstrated benefits, but a major challenge remains in bringing this system to individual academic departments.

THE USC EXPERIENCE

Currently Vice President for Business and Finance at the California Institute of Technology, John R. Curry was instrumental in implementing responsibility center management at the University of Southern California (USC) in the early 1980s. As executive director of the university budget, he first helped establish the School of Dentistry as a pilot program for decentralized budgeting, and then enlisted the help of Jon Strauss in 1980 when USC decided to implement responsibility center management on a university-wide basis. In the lively account that follows, he recalls the process of changing from a centralized budgeting system to a decentralize one and identifies five stages of implementation. His managerial perspective serves as a useful blueprint for understanding how principle translates into practice.–Ed.

In the first section, Jon Strauss discusses principles that underlie both academic governance and the management of complex organizations. His three academic principles of *openness*, *localness* and *merit* indicate why decentralization should be a natural state in universities. The eight companion organizational principles are normative: they state what ought to be the characteristics of a functional decentralized university; that is, they characterize the decentralization—the end product—not the *decentralizing*—the act or process of change. It is the *process* of change that I discuss here, beginning with the conditions at the University of Southern California in 1980–81 when decentralization became a salient issue. A backward looking cultural assessment runs the risk of self-serving revisionism, yet I believe the effort will prove worthwhile.

At the beginning of 1980, dissidents and dissonance were on the rise. Lore about who was financially supporting whom, or who was exploiting whom, was lurid. Most deans were saying, "The more money I find (in the form of enrollment or sponsored research), the more they (the ubiquitous despised *they*) take away."

TABLE 46.3
Decentralized Departmental Data for Budgeting Purposes

Revenue Statistics	Actual FY 1991	%	Actual FY 1992	%	Preliminary FY 1993	%
Undergraduate majors	209	7	186	7	211	8
Undergraduate advisees	200	7	185	7	206	7
Undergraduate courses	72	7	58	6	71	7
Undergraduate course credit	4,998	6	5,160	6	4,851	6
I Q P projects	35	4	61	8	48	7
I Q P credits	255	4	603	11	320	6
M Q P projects	87	7	100	9	65	6
M Q P credits	375	6	488	8	369	6
Other undergraduate projects	17	4	38	8	8	4
Other undergraduate project credit	44	1	131	4	23	1
Graduate majors	109	12	115	14	139	17
Graduate advisees	110	15	105	16	126	19
Graduate courses	24	11	26	13	16	14
Graduate course credits	1,104	14	1,449	18	832	21
Graduate projects (Thes/PhD/Dr/Isg)	44	10	36	9	20	11
Graduate project credits	250	10	188	9	84	9

Direct Expense Categories	Actual FY 1991	%	Actual FY 1992	%	Budget FY 1993	%
Tenure track faculty salaries	624,903	6	666,200	7	696,780	6
Non-tenure track faculty salaries	66,000	7	97,619	8	86,300	11
Staff salaries	94,818	6	99,215	6	103,040	6
Benefits	180,716	6	212,306	7	217,986	7
Reimbursed salaries					(10,000)	2
Teaching assistants	84,500	11	89,100	11	103,032	12
Student help	12,012	6	18,235	9	5,516	3
Total compensation	1,062,949	6	1,182,675	7	1,202,654	7
Graduate assistant tuition	85,536	11	90,620	11	107,232	12
Materials and supplies	77,962	8	59,895	6	51,550	6
Equipment, expensed	81,621	22	57,947	15	66,055	18
Travel	17,348	8	13,667	6	12,050	6
Telephone	6,566	5	6,088	5	5,400	5
Total other direct expenses	269,033	11	228,217	9	242,287	10
Total direct expenses	1,331,982	7	1,410,892	7	1,444,941	7

Employee Totals	Actual FY 1991	%	Actual FY 1992	%	Budget FY 1993	%
Tenure track faculty	12.50	6	12.00	6	12.00	6
Staff	4.00	7	4.00	7	4.00	7
Teaching assistants	11.00	11	11.00	11	12.00	12

The deans had specific and colorful examples. Central administrators, especially those in financial positions, held an equally flattering view of deans and faculty, saying, "If we didn't shut them down in the comptroller's office, they would spend the university into ruin." The administrators also had specific and colorful examples. Virtually every dean and faculty member believed that the athletic program was robbing the academic program blind.

Several deans, knowing that their revenues exceeded expenses (they could count enrollments and knew the research dollars their faculty had won), claimed bitterly and resentfully to be carrying everyone else around on their shoulders (thus suggesting that altruism is an unnatural act in the academy). Such claims were possible since neither fringe benefit costs nor indirect costs were included in their back-of-the-envelope calculations of net revenues, so no deans really knew the full costs associated with the revenues generated. Without that knowledge, everyone could proclaim the injustice of their forced role of benefactor. The word *disincentive* dripped from nearly everyone's lips.

On the other hand, numerous side deals licensed entrepreneurship and sometimes lunacy. The School of Medicine had a return-of-indirect cost recovery deal as an incentive to go after sponsored research. The School of Business had a tuition revenue deal as incentive to increase undergraduate enrollments. Some schools had Class II budgets that, if authorized, returned 80 percent of the marginal revenue to the finders for program support. Finally, having begun its transformation in 1977, the School of Dentistry had become a successful responsibility center pilot modeled after the system at the University of Pennsylvania. Lots of local entrepreneurship hovered around the edges.

The institution was learning a lot about entrepreneurship without accountability. Except for the School of Dentistry, there was not much local responsibility. For example, those entrepreneurs who had established Class II budgets, thus getting expenditure authority prior to realizing marginal revenues, were never sanctioned if they exceeded their expenditure authority, if they failed to deliver the revenue, or if the revenue they promised had already been promised elsewhere in the budget—a form of internal revenue piracy. Supposedly, budgets should have predicted financial outcomes with rewards for good fiscal behavior and sanctions for bad. Experience, however, too often proved otherwise. When entrepreneurial ventures failed financially, central administrators talked about deadbeat deans, but sanctions were not forthcoming. The sense of mismanagement was widespread and growing.

At the same time, senior management was putting the question of who was supporting whom to the test. In the smoke-filled rooms of central administration, the university had already begun to understand itself as a set of responsibility centers. For several years, at the fiscal close, the budget director had recreated the university in responsibility center guise, allocating all revenues and indirect expenses to the colleges, schools, and auxiliaries. Revenues minus all costs (direct plus indirect) had a name: net financial contribution (NFC). Some NFCs were positive, indicating exportation of a center's revenues; others were negative, denoting importation. The sum of all NFCs equaled the change in current fund balance in the university's year-end financial statements. Thus, revenue and cost allocation algorithms were in place, and some knowledge about the internal economy of USC was emerging,

A considerable barrier to campus-wide decentralized management, however, was the university's financial accounting system. Given that one could tell at a given time approximately where the university stood financially two months before, one wag suggested that a sophisticated model was needed just to forecast the past. And so the conversation went, "When you can't tell where you're going, how can you be held responsible for getting there?" Lewis Carroll would have written about this!

Many of these other conditions could have been ignored if it weren't for the university's financial condition. Dramatic enrollment growth in the late 1970s provided enough money to mollify the administration bashers. Grousing about disincentives, rip-offs, and what the infamous "they" were doing was background noise when the money was coming in faster than it could be spent. But when revenue growth attenuated and began shrinking in 1978, 1979, and 1980, and centrally imposed spring hiring freezes became as predictable as the swallows' return to Capistrano, the background noise came to the fore as a clear signal. An incredible number of things seemed in need of fixing.

Into the midst of this discontent came a new senior administration; a new president who had been charged by the board of trustees with rationalizing the organization; a new provost who immediately and intuitively grasped that neither he nor anyone else could micro-manage the complexity of a university comprising twenty-one colleges and schools and a farm club for the NFL; and an administrative vice president from the University of Pennsylvania who was a carrier of the decentralization virus. All three readily grasped the principle that decentralization should be proportional to size and complexity. All three understood that accountability measured by outcomes is preferable to accountability measured by controlling inputs. And the dean of the School of Dentistry was there to proclaim their perspicacity: the successful pilot of a system founded on these principles, he was an articulate and animated fan. He had begun affecting other deans.

In the process of decentralization at USC, the School of Dentistry was an important model for the rest of the university. During the 1970s, Zohrab Kaprielian, the executive vice president of USC, began to suspect that the School of Dentistry was losing money. Dental school tuitions at other schools were rising faster than undergraduate and other professional school tuitions while the dean at USC resisted all efforts to raise his school's tuitions. The dean had also resisted improving revenues in the school's clinical operations. Aware of the responsibility center system at the University of Pennsylvania, Kaprielian commissioned a full allocation of revenues and expenses to the schools and auxiliaries. Sure enough, revenues attributable to the School of Dentistry failed to cover expenses by more than a million dollars.

I was dispatched to the University of Pennsylvania to learn in depth about managing and living in their system. What were the incentives, the rewards, the sanctions? What were the disincentives, the pathologies? Having accounted for the USC schools and auxiliaries as responsibility centers, should we operate them that way? I returned an advocate and an enthusiast. We established dentistry as our first pilot in 1977, giving the school the goal of eliminating the annual revenue imbalance in three years. The pilot was a resounding success, although hiring a new "entrepreneur" dean was required.

All these various conditions contributed to *preparedness*: the cultural readiness for effecting change. By 1980, USC had reached the great conjunction: a high level of discontent, of lurid and unflattering lore about "this place," of accumulated anomalies; emerging awareness, if only centrally, of resource transfers among schools; a growing anxiety about financial well-being of the university, perhaps a sense of fiscal crisis; a confluence of interests in and zeal for decentralization among key new senior administrators who were still in their honeymoon period; and a successful pilot program, with other entrepreneurs wanting access to a predictable reward structure. Several of us knew that the times and timing were right, and we are certainly ready today to proclaim it with twenty-twenty hindsight: the great conjunction gave rise to a full tide.

Anyone wanting to alter an organization's direction needs to know the desired future state: the goal, the new paradigm, the "fortune." Knowing the goal and having an agenda, the change agent tries to determine when the right time has come in the affairs of the organization, when the organization is ready for change. Determining whither and when is never easy. The following guidelines can help establish a time of preparedness:

Be prepared for the end outcome—have a solution awaiting the definition of the problem.

Seed the culture with indications of what the organization would be like if the desired outcome were already in place.

Create from within or attract from without intellectual allies.

Take advantage of external influences when they create pressure internally for change (for example declines in college age populations or changes in government funding).

Stay attuned to the culture: seek the right tide and the right time.

In the foregoing discussion of preparedness, I reflected on seeding the culture as a prerequisite to, or necessary condition for, change. Among the techniques of seeding a culture are: conversion of colleagues into intellectual allies, recruiting allies into the organization, simulating a new system to show how current problems would be solved, forming ever-expanding workgroups or focus groups to diffuse the new concepts and to refine understanding of their application. For example, the dean of the College of Letters, Arts, and Sciences became an ardent supporter of RCM when he discovered that his school had been bringing in increasing tuition revenues without receiving any additional expenditure benefits. This second phase of adopting change, closely linked to preparedness, is *permeation:* the systematic but informal introduction of new management concepts into an organization

When the senior leadership at USC decided in 1981 that they wanted to implement RCM, and that the university's culture was ready for change, implementation had to move from the informal to the formal stage. In a university, that means: a committee! They were ready to begin the next stage—*prototyping.* President Zumberge appointed the Budget Incentives Task Force in the fall of 1981, comprising the "power deans" of the campus, proponents of RCM, representatives of the faculty senate, faculty members with expertise in management, and administrators whose service-unit budgets would be exposed under RCM as indirect costs. The task force was charged with defining a decentralized budget and financial management system with incentives for revenue generation and expenditure management and with sanctions for failure to comply with budget plans. One of the primary purposes of the task force was the facilitation of broad ownership of whatever system was defined.

President Zumberge appointed Robert Biller, then dean of public administration and a known master of process management, to chair the task force, and appointed me as staff to the chair. When Bob and I met to discuss the first meeting, he shocked me by saying, "Write the report; write it for the first meeting." This didn't sound quite like due process to me but Bob persisted: "You know a lot about RCM-like systems; you've helped create one here. So write a concept paper, but write it as if it were our report. That will really facilitate debate. Give task force members something hard to push against."

So I did. But being a mathematician, I liked to derive systems from "first principles." I set about to write down those organizational or

management principles from which our incarnation of RCM should flow.[1] They are:

P1. Responsibility should be commensurate with authority, and vice versa.

P2. Decentralization should be proportional to organizational size and complexity.

P3. Locally optimal decisions are not always globally optimal: central leverage is required to implement corporate (global) priorities.

P4. Outcome measures are preferable to process controls.

P5. Accountability is only as good as the tools that measure it.

P6. Quantitative measures of performance tend to drive out qualitative measures (a variant of Gresham's law).

P7. Outcomes should matter: plans that work should lead to rewards, plans that fail should lead to sanctions.

P8. Resource-expanding incentives are preferable to resource-dividing ones.

P9. People play better games when they own the rules.

Borrowing heavily from Penn's approach, I then specified a typical revenue and expense statement for a "center," proposed model revenue and indirect costs allocation rules, and described an internal banking system to account for year-end surpluses and deficits. I further specified how revenues would be shared between the centers and central administration. Finally, I showed how each aspect of the proposed system was consistent with the above set of principles.

At our first task force meeting, Bob Biller handed out my concept paper (which had been reviewed by the two senior vice presidents for whom I worked) saying something like, "Curry here has written a paper that—if you like it—will be our report. If you find any problems, however, we'll have to meet a few more times." We met a lot more times The report that emerged from the task force some four months later bore remarkable resemblance to the original concept paper, yet it represented a significant advance. For example, P6 above was not in my original paper. Reminding members of the task force that you get what you measure, management professor Steve Kerr urged us to introduce academic measures of performance along with the financial. Hence we connected the review of the performance of academic plans with the performance of annual budgets developed to implement them. Thus we added P6, a variant of Gresham's law, to the original principles in the final report.

By the time the task force fulfilled its charge, I was convinced of Bob Biller's wisdom: the power of a *prototype*, or straw report was undeniable. The more the prototype is based on principle, and the more internally consistent it is, the more likely its adoption in some consistently refined form. When individuals objected to some aspect of the prototype, typically over whose ox might be gored by changing to the new system, we could ask, "How would you change this aspect and still retain consistency with our principles?" or, "Are there some principles we should change?" As one colleague observed, the axiom-theorem-proof approach of the concept paper "elevated the debate from the plane of petty politics to the plateau of principle."

I distinguish this type of *conceptual prototyping* from *behavioral prototyping*. Both were indispensable to successful change implementation. The latter, creating the School of Dentistry as a pilot using a borrowed approach, created internal precedent, and allowed us—and most important, the dean and faculty of the school—to say, "it works!" In organizations characterized by multiple and conflicting goals, "organized anarchies" as Cohen and March characterize universities,[2] precedent from elsewhere and especially from within is powerful.

The conceptual prototype guided the broad deliberation required to move from one example to systemic implementation. Indeed, conceptual prototyping was contemporaneous with *participation*, yet another phase of implementation. Participation came in the judicious selection of task force members, and in their many debates leading ultimately to their ownership of the final report in December of 1981. The report defined USC's version of RCM: We called it Revenue Center Management to distinguish it from its forebears. The report was accepted by the president and adopted by the council of deans.

The length and quality of the decision process (really from 1975 to 1982) rendered implementation relatively swift. RCM went live at USC with the 1982–83 budget. There was much

to learn thereafter. From the time of the task force report, business managers from over sixty departments across the campus had to be trained; at the same time, they participated in specifying a new budgeting and financial accounting system required to enable them to take on their new authority and responsibility. As we lived with the system, we learned that some rules had unforeseen consequences and needed changing; that central administration cannot abrogate the system without consequence, that the rewards have to be honored, the sanctions enforced. We learned that some heads of revenue centers really didn't want responsibility. They preferred authority all by itself! And, above all, we learned that implementation never ends: rational systems, too, harbor disincentives, but when a system is explicit, anomalous behavior can be associated with specific rules, and the rules can be altered to improve outcomes. We kept the original task force in place for almost two years as an adaptation team. We should have kept it longer. Almost four years of living with the system passed before most of us agreed it had taken hold, that it was the way USC did business.

Persistence during that time paid off: preparation and implementation are more process than moment. The *persistence* phase of implementation is just as important as the permeation phase. The organizational propensity to recidivism, the regression to an old mean, is powerful indeed, and should not be underestimated.

The phases of implementation chart (Figure 46.1) summarizes most of the ideas discussed thus far, and allows us to extract additional insights into the management of change. First, although assessing the culture may be the earliest phase, it is continuous throughout the implementation process. The same is true of each successive phase. Indeed, they all should continue beyond the right-hand boundary of the chart! Second, the informal phases of implementation—assessing the culture, preparing the culture, and behavioral prototyping—occupy 86 percent (6/7) of the time to cut over, while the formal phases—conceptual prototyping, participation, and decision-occupy only 14 percent. Building the momentum for change is very time intensive, but if the time is well chosen, formal implementation occurs relatively rapidly. The chart also suggests an important behavioral consequence to this time asymmetry. As the talk (and gossip) about change

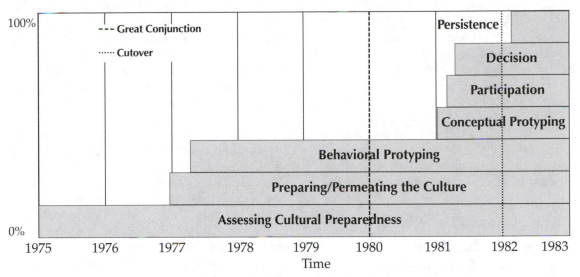

Figure 46.1 Phases of implementation

increases, and as more people become carriers of the change virus, frustration builds in the organization. People begin feeling as if something tangible should be happening, when nothing tangible is. If the informal phases are left adrift—that is, if leaders wait too long to introduce formal implementation measures—then momentum declines and the peak moment may be lost. More than one administration has drowned in a tidal wave of expectations.

THE CASE FOR ADOPTION BY PUBLIC INSTITUTIONS

Currently vice chancellor for administration and finance at the University of Houston, Edward L. Whalen has written extensively on implementing revenue responsibility budgeting systems at public institutions. His book, Responsibility Center Budgeting, *provides a detailed account of Indiana University's adoption of responsibility center budgeting in the late 1980s. Whalen served as assistant vice president and university director of budgeting during the transition on the eight-campus public system, and the book is filled with firsthand insights on the challenges of translating theory into practice. In the following piece, Whalen continues to address concerns specific to implementing revenue responsibility systems at public institutions.—Ed.*

In *Responsibility Center Budgeting,* we made the observation that, in the United States, there are about 2,000 four-year public and private institutions of higher education. Fewer than 600 of them are public; the rest—over 1,400—are private. That more private institutions than public ones have adopted responsibility center budgeting should not be surprising, since according to these aggregate numbers, more private institutions exist.

On the other hand, public institutions tend to be larger operations than private institutions, in terms of both enrollments and dollar volume. The number of public institutions with enrollments of more than 10,000 is four to five times larger than similarly sized private institutions. Responsibility center budgeting has greater applicability for larger and more complex institutions, since for a small college or university, managers of operating units (and for that matter, individual faculty and staff members) sense how their efforts contribute to the well-being of the whole enterprise. Their incentives tend to be consistent with those of the university. That sense of community tends to be lost in a big university with tens of thousands of students, hundreds of academic and support units, hundreds of millions of dollars of revenues and expenditures, and a wide variety of funding sources. In such an environment, implementing a decentralized budgeting and management system that motivates deans and heads of support units with incentives promoting the institution's objectives can offer real advantages. Nevertheless, in most cases, the budgeting and management structure of most large universities tends to resemble that of small liberal arts colleges more closely than that of the select institutions that have moved to responsibility center budgeting.

Why haven't public institutions taken the lead in moving toward responsibility center budgeting techniques in managing their affairs? Five possible areas of explanation occur to me:

Governing boards

Executive management

State funding arrangements

State administrative requirements

Coordinating boards or state legislature, executive branch

Other areas may exist as well. Although I shall explain the possible impediments to responsibility center budgeting linked with each area named above, I do not believe that any of these impediments to be insurmountable.

Governing Boards

Leadership is key. When moving to a new form of revenue and resource management and budgeting, a commitment at the top, the very top, is vital. And the very top of the university or college hierarchy is the board of trustees or board of regents. Although the university's president executes the move to responsibility center budgeting, the governing board must fully understand and enthusiastically endorse it. A president or provost or vice president who attempts to make such a change without the complete involvement of the board will find him or herself undone. Unless the board, a group of individuals, acts as one entity, the multitudes who resist change will corrode the vision, undermine the foundation, and compromise the structure.

The composition of governing boards of independent universities may be more receptive to the promise of alternative management techniques than that of public institutions. A business orientation may be more common in the former, while the latter must address a wide variety of societal and cultural concerns. Financial viability is seldom an item on the agenda of a public institution. In the case of the independent, however, survivability is not assured, so good business practice is more of a consideration.

Because responsibility center budgeting is a major change in the way institutions do business, governance must not only be strong but also continuous. Turnover in membership of public institutions' governing boards may sometimes be rather rapid. Because of changes in the political orientations of the governor's office and of the legislature, attitudes, philosophies, and backgrounds of new board members may differ markedly from their predecessors and incumbents. Thus windows of opportunity for the installation of responsibility center management or its counterparts may not last long.

The scope of responsibility that many governing boards of public institutions face may prevent the boards from focusing on the issue of expeditious internal management. In the public arena, a governing board often oversees a system or collection of universities. In certain cases, the governing board presides over a statewide system. Rarely are such systems composed of homogeneous units with common problems. With such broad and diffuse responsibilities, directing the attention necessary to reforming the internal management of a few of the largest and most complex units requires extraordinary resolve.

Despite the problems that governing boards of public institutions may pose, none, either alone or in combination, precludes a move to responsibility center budgeting. Especially during times like these, when states are confronted with serious financial exigencies and when taxpayers are resistant to revenue enhancing tax levies, publicly appointed board members may be more disposed to entertain promising structural and management changes. Turnover of board membership may actually serve to capture the moment. An active governing board of a public institution with a vision for innovative management need not be entirely passive in identifying prospective new appointees, even in situations where a change in political fortunes has occurred.

Executive Management

Leadership is key. The principal role of a governing board is not to implement responsibility center budgeting but to select and support a chief executive officer (president or chancellor) who will. That individual, in turn, must surround him or herself with those who will carry out its installation and inspire, convince, and cajole others about its merits. Both the governing board and the chief executive officer must share a common belief in responsibility center budgeting, but the chief executive officer and his colleagues must develop the vision for its installation.

No inherent character or personality differences appear to exist between the presidents of public institutions and those of private institutions. Indeed, some individuals manage in the course of their careers to serve as the chief executive officer of both types of institutions. So the scales should be fairly evenly balanced insofar as the predilection of public and private university presidents toward responsibility center budgeting is concerned.

While the predilection may be balanced between the two types of institutions, it's also liable to be uniformly low. Generally, chief executive officers are selected from among the academic ranks, and relatively few academic disciplines are concerned with management effectiveness and operating efficiencies. Rarely are management effectiveness and operating efficiency top priority selection criteria for faculty-dominated search and screening committees, so an institution's governing board may have to take the lead in identifying such a candidate. This difficulty, however, is common to both private and public universities.

Funding Arrangements

While the characteristics of chief executive officers do not differ significantly between public and private institutions, these institutions differ obviously and measurably in terms of their funding sources. Public institutions are public because of their access to public funds, which depend on political considerations rather than market forces. Does the nature of state support carry with it any conditions that impede the adoption of responsibility center budgeting?

At a time when fiscal difficulties have caused state appropriations to decrease in a number of examples, some argue that the inherent instability of public support precludes the adoption of responsibility center budget-

ing, I am not one of them, for the following two reasons.

First, fluctuating revenue creates a need for a responsibility center budgeting arrangement. At the University of Southern California, that incentive-based budgeting system is called revenue center management. Fluctuations in major revenue require an incentive-based approach that enlists the ingenuity and participation of deans and division heads in enhancing their own revenue opportunities and in adjusting their expenditures to what they perceive to be the resources available to them. Under traditional centralized approaches, dips in revenue are deemed to be central administration's problem until edicts are issued attempting to curtail expenditures of operating units. Responsibility center budgeting provides a mechanism for weathering a financial storm with minimum damage to the academic enterprise.

Second, fluctuations of state appropriation do not distinguish it from other revenue sources. Anyone who over an extended period of time has managed an investment portfolio or who has attempted to forecast student enrollments knows that endowment income, tuition, and student fees are also subject to substantial fluctuations, often in response to determinants that are very difficult to anticipate. Public institutions have no corner on the market of fickle sources of revenue.

Although the nature of state appropriation per se does not obstruct the implementation of responsibility center budgeting, the conditions under which that appropriation is made available to public institutions may. Under responsibility center budgeting, major operating units such as schools, colleges, support units—retain the income they earn, and at the end of a fiscal year any unspent balances (and deficits) are retained by them. Those two features, the ability to earn income and to retain year-end balances, are essential. An institution can hardly extend those features to its operating units if it does not possess them as well.

Conditions for implementing responsibility center budgeting in a public institution of higher education are propitious if it is recognized as a separate and independent financial entity able to supplement its state support with earned income and to retain unspent balances at the end of a fiscal year. On the other hand, if a public university's tuition, fees, and other revenues are swept into the state's general funds or if at the end of a fiscal year unspent balances revert, that institution's ability to implement responsibility center budgeting is seriously compromised. These ground rules, however, can be changed.

Once again, leadership is key. The university's president and the members of its governing board are not without influence and have access to the governor and members of the legislature. At a time when the public is concerned about efficiency in the public sector and is unwilling to accept additional tax burdens, public officials tend to be receptive to well-reasoned ideas for improving management. Decentralized budgeting techniques offer opportunities for developing pie-expanding incentives rather than pie-dividing incentives. Today's financial conditions make such techniques attractive to state legislators and other decision makers.

State Administrative Requirements

State appropriation sometimes arrives with various limitations on the ways in which it can be used. Sometimes expenses are classified by type of expenditure: so much for personnel, so much for supplies, so much for equipment, and so on. In other cases, functional categories are specified: so much for administration, so much for instruction, so much for academic support, and so on. Those conditions are awkward and tend to impede management discretion, but they are not as important for responsibility center budgeting as an institution's ability to earn income and retain its unspent balances. Certainly, such limitations on income are not unique to state appropriations. Administration of grants and contracts often labor under similar restrictions; private donors rarely dispense their philanthropy in the form of unrestricted gifts. Such impediments are common to both the private and public sectors of higher education.

Unlike private institutions of higher education that handle all their administrative functions, some of the administrative functions of certain public institutions are carried out by other state agencies. Examples of such functions include purchasing, personnel management, financial reporting, payroll, construction, and long-term debt financing. The existence of such service units operating outside the institution's management would require adaptation of responsibility center budgeting but does not prohibit it.

Coordinating Boards

A private university can adopt responsibility center budgeting, and since it is independent, the choice is unlikely to make anyone outside of the university uncomfortable. Not so with a public institution. Public institutions are like bananas: they are found in bunches. When one public institution distinguishes itself from the rest, other members of the bunch tend to become uncomfortable. Those who tend the bunch— higher education coordinating boards, other state reviewing agencies, legislative staff and committee—may be uncomfortable if these institutions are out of step with their counterparts in other states.

As a result, for the chief executive officer of a public institution and his colleagues, driven by a governing board keen on responsibility center budgeting, the process of communicating the nature of the new approach has to be extended to external constituencies. Public officials, the governor, key legislators, members of the coordinating board and other reviewing agencies, and legions of career state bureaucrats have to be informed of the approach.

If the Indiana University experience is any indication, receptivity to the idea will be high. One of the by-products of responsibility center budgeting is management information that addresses many of the key questions of interest to reviewing agencies and legislative committees, such as how much programs cost and how state funds are being used. The data are available automatically.

Full disclosure is a requirement of responsibility center budgeting. Such openness should not be restricted to those within the institution. A public university is accountable to the public who supports the institution: that public deserves to be informed as well.

Selling responsibility center budgeting, that is, generating a feeling of participation in state government, may not be such a problem. Constraining enthusiasm may be the greater hazard. Some will maintain that responsibility center budgeting should be adopted universally and immediately. Some will want to help by appropriating state support according to the internal allocation patterns among academic units—for example, directly on the basis of student enrollments without consideration of broader institutional needs. In any event, involvement and oversight of state government in a public institution's activities do not appear to present obstacles for responsibility center budgeting.

Conclusion

Can responsibility center budgeting work at a public institution of higher education? Of course, it can. What is required is leadership and the ability of an institution to earn income and retain unspent balances. And of the two, leadership is by far the most important.

NOTES

1. I listed a refined version of the original 1981 principles in my chapter, "Revenue Center Management at USC," in Edward Whalen's *Responsibility Center Budgeting: An Approach to Decentralized Management for Institutions of Higher Education* (Bloomington: Indiana University Press: 1991).
2. Michael D. Cohen and James G. March, *Leadership and Ambiguity: The American College President* (New York: McGraw-Hill, 1974).

SECTION VII

ETHICS AND HIGHER EDUCATION FINANCE

INTRODUCTION

Of all the areas within higher education institutions where ethics is a concern, perhaps the most prominent is the handling of finances. Here it is most obvious that conditions and occasions exist where moral abuses of authority and responsibility can lead to legal action. The following section presents articles about both theoretical and applied aspects of ethics in the area of finance. Constraints of space, as well as a dearth of peer-reviewed literature in this area, limit the selection to general rather than specific treatment of ethical issues.

As a branch of philosophy, ethics, like other disciplines, has its own technical language and concepts. Rather than plunging into this technical discourse, however, we have chosen from more widely accessible literature that carries some of the disciplinary language and concepts embedded within it. Thus Batson's article, "Why Act for the Public Good? Four Answers," while not directly treating aspects of higher education finance, sets the discourse stage for the subsequent readings. Batson outlines four motivations for acting for the public good: egoism (enlightened self-interest), collectivism (group self-interest), altruism (sacrifice for the sake of others), and principalism (goodness based on duty to a principle). In elucidating these concepts, Batson draws on classical philosophical writings, such as those by Aristotle, Mill, and Kant, as well as literature in social psychology. This article thus provides a simple matrix against which the terms and categories of the subsequent articles can be understood.

In their article, "Business Ethics and the Management of Non-profit Institutions," Bouckaert and Vandenhove contrast a social cost-benefit analysis of business ethics in the for-profit sector with social contract theory applicable to non-profit institutions, such as higher education. In a profit-making organization, management's primary responsibility is to shareholders, which may lead to tension with the goals of the larger society. By contrast, a non-profit institution is social at its core with a consequent responsibility (and the attendant tensions) to a multiplicity of stakeholders. Bouckaert and Vandenhove include a description and analysis of their research on these contrasting sets of constraints, and conclude with tables that explain the power of ethical values in determining perceptions of institutions as being socially responsible.

Tasker and Packham express concern about the growing number of alliances between universities and business interests as these alliances constrain the academic freedom and openness of research results that have long characterized higher education. Their view in "Freedom, Funding, and the Future of the Universities," draws on the experience of higher education institutions in the United Kingdom since the passage of the Education Reform Act of 1988. This act promotes closer cooperation with business whose competitive interests require a certain level of secrecy, as well as some managerial discretion in the staffing of research teams. Tasker and Packham warn that, although such cooperation can help increase university coffers, the ultimate price may be a loss of autonomy and the liberal spirit of free intellectual inquiry that Newman articulated in the 19th century.

The next two articles are book chapters. From *The Ethics of Asking: Dilemmas in Higher Education Fundraising*, Elliott and Gert's article outlines the moral foundations for fundraisers, while from his book, *Ethics for Fundraisers*, Anderson sets out the process of devising a code of ethics. In "The Moral Context of Fundraising," Elliott and Gert state that philanthropy is, in itself, a voluntary moral act that is not required of the donor. The fundraiser, therefore, must recognize this voluntary quality and act within highly ethical standards of behavior. This may mean, in some instances, refusing a donation that is inconsistent with the receiving institution's mission or interests, such as donor conditions that limit academic freedom. Moreover, the institution that accepts a gift is obliged to honor a donor's wishes for as long as the gift lasts, regardless of the institution's other competing needs. Elliott and Gert suggest devising a set of rules for fundraising that is made public and to which fundraisers and institutional officers can be held accountable.

In "A Practitioner's Code of Ethics," Anderson presents an argument for constructing a code of ethics by stating, "The code is a public witness that the organization recognizes and seeks to honor the value of trust in its rela-

tionships." Anderson distinguishes between "doing things right"—a matter of competence—and "doing the right thing"—a matter of ethics. He states that the process of developing a code of ethics can help an institution's stakeholders perceive and perhaps resolve areas of values conflict, but he warns that a code can be a "purely sentimental" item unless it is regularly used to guide conduct. Anderson recommends particular elements that ought to be present in any code of ethics and provides a guide for development and a sample code.

Counelis' article, "Toward Empirical Studies on University Ethics," concludes this section on ethics and higher education finance. Although not directly descriptive or prescriptive of conduct in the finance area, the article does present some of the highly salient ethical issues that confront college and university administrators. Further, Counelis provides a fairly comprehensive literature review on studies about ethics in higher education settings since the 1950s. He concludes that there is much work to be done in this area, and gives some recommendations for empirical research based on similar studies of corporations. It must be noted that this article overlooks an important compendium, Cahn (1990) *Morality, Responsibility, and the University: Studies in Academic Ethics* (Philadelphia: Temple University Press), and was in press when Wilcox and Ebbs (1992) published *The Leadership Compass: Values and Ethics in Higher Education* (Washington, D.C.: ASHE-ERIC Higher Education Report). Both of these latter texts concentrate on the academic side of the house, however, leaving the administrative area, especially finance, a rich and largely unexplored terrain for ethicists.

Members of the review panel for this section were:

Haithe Anderson, Bowling Green State University

John Boatwright, Loyola University Chicago

Kathleen Knight-Abowitz, Miami University of Ohio

Mark McKenzie, Illinois State University

Eugenie A. Potter, University of Michigan

CHAPTER 47

WHY ACT FOR THE PUBLIC GOOD?
FOUR ANSWERS

C. DANIEL BATSON

A conceptual analysis is offered that differentiates four motives for acting for the public good: egoism, collectivism, altruism, and principlism. Differentiation is based on identification of a unique ultimate goal for each motive. For egoism, the ultimate goal is self-benefit; for collectivism, it is to increase group welfare; for altruism, to increase one or more other individuals' welfare; for principlism, to uphold one or more moral principles. Advocates claim that these last three motives cannot be reduced to egoism. Evidence for this claim is limited, however, especially for collectivism and principlism. It is hoped that the conceptual distinctions proposed will permit broader, more precise empirical study of nonegoistic motives for acting for the public good.

Failure to act for the public good has created major social problems. As the population continues to explode, acting in ways that suit our own self-interests—or whims—without considering the consequences for others has led to crisis after crisis: trash-littered public parks, streets, and highways; polluted rivers and streams; dropping water tables and shrinking reservoirs; vanishing rain forests; the continuing slaughter of whales; reduced social services and underfunded schools; free riders who enjoy public TV but do not ante up.

Yet these crisises are only half the picture. There are times when we do act for the public good. We do, at times, pick up litter; we do recycle, carpool, and vote; we do contribute to public TV and the United Fund. We do help one another, and we do serve as volunteers in hospitals, nursing homes, AIDS hospices, fire departments, and rescue squads.

Acting for the public good, as I am using the phrase, means acting to increase the welfare of some person or persons other than oneself, thereby increasing the total welfare in society. In this sense, the public good includes not only economists' *public goods*, goods that can be used by more than one person (roads, parks, information, clean air, etc.), but also *private goods*, goods that can be used by only one person (food, clothing, shelter, rescue from danger, a comforting hug, etc.), if provided to others (Sen, 1977). Helping another individual is included within the present conception of the public good, or not, depending on whether, on balance, this help increases the total welfare in society, or not. One might argue that increasing one's own personal good increases the total welfare in society and therefore should also be considered acting for the public good. So it does; but the reason for speaking of public good is precisely to contrast it with exclusive regard for one's own personal good.

If not acting for the public good has created major problems for society, then acting for the public good has also created major problems—for behavioral and social scientists. The problems concern why people do it. It seems to violate an assumption about human motivation that has been foundational for virtually all major accounts of human action in psychology, sociology, economics, and political science. The assumption is that all human action is ultimately directed toward self-interest (Campbell, 1975; Mansbridge, 1990). Ecologist and social-policy analyst Garrett Hardin (1977) elevated this assumption to what he called the Cardinal Rule of Policy: "Never ask a person to act against his own self-interest" (p. 27).

WHY ACT FOR THE PUBLIC GOOD?

If self-interest motivates all human action, then why do people act for the public good? Over the last decade or so, this question has been asked with increasing frequency and acuity by a small number of behavioral and social scientists (see Mansbridge, 1990, for a useful sampling). In general, those asking this question all agree on two points: (a) Self-interest is an important motivator of human action, including action for the public good; (b) self-interest is not the only motive for acting for the public good. There is far less agreement, however, on what the motive or motives other than self-interest are.

One might think that social psychologists could clarify matters, that we could speak with authority on the nature and scope of motives for acting for the public good. Unfortunately, we have had relatively little to say. Unable as yet to speak with clarity, this essay is more at the stage of clearing one's throat.

FOUR ANSWERS

Reflection on the research and writings of others, as well as on some of my own research on empathy and altruism (Batson, 1991), leads me to suggest four answers to why we act for the public good. Each of these answers is based on a different motive. Following Lewin (1951), I am thinking of motives as goal-directed forces, and in this context it is important to distinguish among instrumental goals, ultimate goals, and unintended consequences. An *instrumental goal* is sought as a means to reach some other goal; an *ultimate goal* is sought as

an end in itself; an *unintended consequence* is a result of acting to reach a goal but is not itself sought as a goal. It is the ultimate goal that defines a motive; each different motive has a unique ultimate goal.

The four different motives for acting for the public good that I wish to consider are egoism, collectivism, altruism, and what—for lack of an existing term—I shall call principlism. I wish to suggest that each of these motives is possible, even plausible, and that each has its own unique ultimate goal, as well as its own distinct promise and problems as a source of action for the public good. I believe that an adequate answer to the question of why we act for the public good needs to consider all four. It needs to consider not only the existence of each but also their interplay.

Egoism: Serving the Public Good to Benefit Oneself

The most obvious and parsimonious answer to why we act for the public good, given the pervasive assumption that all human action is motivated by self-interest, is *egoism*. A motive is egoistic if the ultimate goal is to increase the actor's own welfare. Action that serves the public good can be egoistically motivated if this action serves either as an instrumental goal on the way to or as an unintended consequence of reaching the ultimate goal of self-benefit. A philanthropist may endow a hospital or university to gain recognition and a form of immortality; a capitalist, nudged by the Invisible Hand, may create jobs and enhance the standard of living by relentless pursuit of personal fortune. Both are egoistically motivated.

Self-benefits that can be the ultimate goal of acting for the public good
A number of self-benefits can be the ultimate goal of acting for the public good. Most obvious, perhaps, are material, social, and self-rewards (e.g., monetary reward, praise, esteem enhancement) and avoidance of material, social, and self-punishments (e.g., fines, censure, guilt, shame).

When one looks beyond the immediate situation to consider long-term consequences and intangible benefits of one's action, self-interest becomes *enlightened*. From an enlightened perspective, one may see that headlong pursuit of self-interest will lead to less long-term personal gain than will acting for the public good, and so one may decide to act for the public good as a means of reaching the ultimate goal of maximizing self-benefit. Appeals to enlightened self-interest are often used by politicians and social activists trying to encourage action for the public good: They warn us of the eventual consequences for ourselves and our children of pollution or of squandering natural resources; they remind us that if the plight of the poor becomes too severe, we may face revolution. The motive they seek to evoke is egoism, our enlightened self-interest.

Nontangible self-benefits of acting for the public good have sometimes been called *side payments*. Most side payments involve an appeal to social pressure or to conscience. As John Stuart Mill (1861/1987) put it in his defense of utilitarianism: "Why am I bound to promote the general happiness? If my own happiness lies in something else, why may I not give that the preference?" (p. 299). Mill's answer was that we will give our own happiness preference until, through education, we learn the sanctions for doing so. These include external sanctions stemming from social censure (including divine censure) and internal sanctions stemming from conscience. Freud (1930/1961) presented a very similar view, as have most social learning and norm theorists since.

Promise and problems of egoism as a source of action for the public good

Egoistic motives offer promise for promoting public good because they are easily aroused and potent. They also offer problems because they are fickle. If the egoistically motivated individual finds that self-interest can be served as well or better without enhancing the public good, then the public good be damned. If he or she can break free from Mill's external and internal sanctions, from the constraint of social and self-censure, from anticipated guilt and shame over norm violation, then narrow self-interest reigns supreme.

As noted, a number of behavioral and social scientists have begun to doubt that all action for the public good can be explained by egoism. Three alternatives have been suggested (though, as far as I know, never by one person—except perhaps Jenks, 1990). The first alternative is collectivism.

Collectivism: Serving the Public Good to Benefit a Group

Collectivism is motivation with the ultimate goal of increasing the welfare of a group or collective. The group may be large or small, from two to over 2 billion. It may be a marriage or a partnership; it may be a sports team, a university, a community, a nation; it may be all humanity. The group may be one's race, religion, sex, political party, or social class. One need not even be a member of the group. One may, for example, act to increase the welfare of a racial or ethnic minority, of the homeless, of gays and lesbians, without being a member of these groups.

Explanations of action for the public good in terms of collectivism have at times been linked to social identity theory, with its emphasis on acting for the group rather than for oneself (Tajfel, 1978; Tajfel & Turner, 1986). More recently, however, self-categorization theory (Turner, 1987) has recast group identity in terms of self-definition at the group level; one sees oneself as partner, team member, male, European, New Yorker, and so on. With self-definition recast in this way, acting for the group becomes another form of acting for the self. So, to the extent that group-level self-definition occurs, collectivism becomes a special case of egoism.

If, however, independent of group-level self-definition, one values a group's welfare and this welfare is threatened or can be enhanced in some way, then collectivist motivation may be aroused, promoting action to benefit the group. At times, we may act in a way that benefits the group as a whole; more often, we may benefit only some members, perhaps only a single person. Still, if enhancing the group's welfare is the ultimate goal, then the motive for benefiting this person is collectivism. From the Lewinian perspective adopted here, it is the ultimate goal, not the number of people benefited, that determines the nature of the motive.

To illustrate, the person who supports and comforts a spouse, not out of concern for the spouse per se or for the self-benefits imagined but "for the sake of the marriage," is displaying collectivist motivation. So is the person who contributes to the local United Way because it enriches the community. So is the senator who supports building shelters with the ultimate goal of easing the plight of the homeless. So is the rescuer of a Jewish family in Nazi Europe whose ultimate goal is to benefit humanity in whatever way possible. If the ultimate goal is to benefit some group, whether large or small, inclusive or exclusive, the motive is collectivism.

Problems

Collectivist motives are not problem free as a source of action for the public good. Typically, we care about collectives of which we are members, an *us*. Identifying with a group or collective in this way usually involves recognition of an out-group; an us implies a *them* who is not us. Indeed, a them-us comparison is often used to define a collective, as Henri Tajfel (1978) and John Turner (1987) have pointed out. When this occurs, harming *them* may be one way to enhance the comparative welfare of *us*. We rejoice at their difficulties and defeats, even if we do not directly benefit as a result (Tajfel & Turner, 1986). We scapegoat. Dawes, van de Kragt, and Orbell (1990) remind us that Rudolf Hoess, the commandant at Auschwitz, systematically murdered 2.9 million members of an out-group to benefit his National Socialist in-group.

Promise

In addition to this very real danger, collectivist motivation has some virtues that egoism does not. Egoism is directed toward our own self-interest. Yet many needs in the world are far removed from our self-interest, even our enlightened self-interest, and from worry about norm violation or the prick of conscience, each of which can be anesthetized with excuses and diffusion of responsibility.

Think, for example, of the plight of the homeless in the United States, of poverty and illiteracy in Central America, of pollution, global warming, overpopulation, energy conservation, endangered species—the list goes on and on. These problems are particularly difficult to address because they are *social dilemmas*. A social dilemma arises when (a) individuals in a group or collective have a choice about how to allocate personally held scarce resources (e.g., money, time, energy) and (b) allocation to the group provides more benefit for the group as a whole than does allocation to oneself, but allocation to oneself provides more self-benefit than does allocation to the group as a whole (Dawes, 1980). In such a situation, the action

that is best for me is to allocate resources to meet my needs, ignoring the needs of the group as a whole. But if everyone tries thus to maximize his or her own welfare, the attempt will backfire. Everyone, including me, is worse off. Unilateral pursuit of what is best for each individual creates a situation in which everyone suffers more.

If we rely on straightforward egoistic motivation to address the pressing social dilemmas we face, the prognosis looks bleak. Like lemmings heading for the sea, we will find ourselves racing pell-mell toward destruction. But the situation is not that grim. There is considerable evidence that when faced with a social dilemma, whether in a research laboratory or in real life, many people do not seek to maximize only their own welfare. Under certain conditions, people seek also to enhance the group welfare (Alfano & Marwell, 1980; Brewer & Kramer, 1986; Dawes, McTavish, & Shaklee, 1977; Kramer & Brewer, 1984; Orbell, van de Kragt, & Dawes, 1988; Yamagishi & Sato, 1986). The most common explanation for this attention to group welfare is in terms of collectivist motivation based on social or group identity (e.g., Brewer & Kramer, 1986; Dawes et al., 1990).

Does collectivism really exist?

Still, it is important to consider the possibility that what looks like collectivism is actually a subtle form of individual egoism. Perhaps attention to group welfare in a social dilemma is simply a result of enlightened self-interest or side payments.

The most direct evidence that collectivism is independent of egoism comes from research by Dawes and his colleagues (Dawes et al., 1990; Orbell et al., 1988). The research indicates that if individuals are placed in a social dilemma after discussing the dilemma with other members of the group, they give more to the group than if they had no prior discussion. Moreover, this effect is specific to the in-group with whom the discussion occurred; allocation to an out-group is not enhanced by discussion.

On the basis of this research, Dawes et al., (1990) claim evidence for collectivist motivation independent of egoism. They claim that participants acted to enhance the welfare of the group "in the absence of any expectation of future reciprocity, current reward or punishment, or even reputational consequences among other group members" (p. 99). They also claim that this action was independent of the dictates of conscience.

These are bold claims, perhaps too bold. Dawes et al., (1990) believe they eliminated all forms of enlightened self-interest and side payments from their experiments by having participants make a single, anonymous allocation decision. They believe they tested the effects of conscience by providing some participants with a choice between allocating to themselves and to the no-prior discussion out-group, whereas others chose between themselves and the prior-discussion in-group. Dawes et al., reasoned that a socially instilled norm to cooperate would dictate allocation to the out-group just as much as to the in-group. Yet this seems doubtful; the operative norm could easily be "Share with your buddies" rather than simply "Share."

Consistent with this suggestion, Dawes et al., (1990) found that, during the discussion period in their experiments, participants made lots of promises to cooperate. Promises were, of course, made only to members of the in-group with whom participants discussed, one's buddies, not to members of the out-group. Reneging on such a promise to gain a few dollars may be no small side cost for most people. Even if others will not know that you reneged, you will. Also consistent, in an earlier experiment, Dawes et al., (1977) found that prior discussion did not increase cooperative responses when subjects were not allowed to discuss the dilemma or possible strategies. This lack of increase seems hard to explain if the personalizing contact of discussion evoked group identity and collectivist motivation.

To discount these interpretative problems, Dawes et al., (1990) turned to research participants' self-reports of why they cooperated. When there was no prior discussion, most cooperators cited "doing the right thing" as their major motive; when there was discussion, most cited "group welfare." These self-reports are certainly of interest and are suggestive; yet are they enough to justify the conclusion that collectivist motivation is not reducible to egoism? Participants may not have known or, if they knew, may not have accurately reported their true reasons for acting. This seems especially likely given the multiplicity of potential motives and the value-laden decision.

The possibility that collectivism exists as a pro-social motive independent of egoism is certainly intriguing and worthy of pursuit. Before conclusions are drawn, however, more and better evidence is needed.

Altruism: Serving the Public Good to Benefit One or More Others

Altruism is motivation with the ultimate goal of increasing the welfare of one or more individuals other than oneself. If these individuals are members of a collective or if their welfare is linked to the welfare of the collective, then pursuit of this ultimate goal may increase the welfare of the collective. It increases the welfare of the collective not as an ultimate goal but as an instrumental goal or unintended consequence. Thus, although altruism is most often contrasted with egoism, it can be contrasted with collectivism as well.

Note that altruism is a form of possible motivation. As such, it should not be confused with *helping behavior*, which is one possible form of action for the public good. Helping may or may not be altruistically motivated. Nor should altruism be confused with self-sacrifice, which concerns cost to self, not benefit to the other (see Batson, 1991, for a discussion of conceptions and definitions of altruism).

The most commonly proposed source of altruistic motivation is empathic emotion. By *empathy* I mean other-oriented feelings congruent with the perceived welfare of another person. If the other is perceived to be in need, empathy includes feelings of sympathy, compassion, tenderness, and the like. Empathy is usually considered to be a product not only of perceiving the other as in need but also of adopting the perspective of the other, which means imagining how the other is affected by his or her situation (Scotland. 1969). It is for this reason that empathic feelings are called other oriented. Such feelings have been named as a source—if not *the* source—of altruism by Thomas Aquinas, David Hume, Adam Smith, Charles Darwin, Herbert Spencer, and William McDougall and, in contemporary psychology, by Martin Hoffman (1976), Dennis Krebs (1975), and myself (Batson, 1987, 1991). I have called the proposal that feeling empathy for a person in need evokes altruistic motivation the *empathy-altruism hypothesis*.

Does altruism really exist?

There is considerable evidence that feeling empathy for a person in need leads to increased helping of that person (see Eisenberg & Miller, 1987, for a review). Yet the motivation behind this relationship could be egoistic rather than altruistic. Obvious self-benefits result from helping a person for whom we feel empathy: We reduce our empathic arousal, which may be experienced as aversive; we avoid social and self-punishments for failing to help when we or others feel we should; and we gain social and self-rewards for doing what we or others feel is good and right. The empathy-altruism hypothesis does not deny that these self-benefits exist, but it claims that they are unintended consequences of the empathically aroused helper's reaching the ultimate goal of reducing the other's suffering. Egoistic explanations disagree; they claim that one or more of the self-benefits is the ultimate goal.

Over the past 15 years, other social psychologists and I have conducted more than 25 experiments designed to test the nature of the motivation to help evoked by empathy (see Batson, 1991, for a review). Results of these experiments have provided remarkably consistent support for the empathy-altruism hypothesis. None of the egoistic explanations proposed has received more than scattered support (see Cialdini et al., 1987; Schaller & Cialdini, 1988; Smith, Keating, & Stotland, 1989). This evidence has led me tentatively to accept the validity of the empathy-altruism hypothesis (Batson, 1991).

Problems

Even if empathy induced altruistic motivation exists, is it a plausible source of motivation to act for the public good? Altruism, especially empathy-induced altruism, appears to be directed toward the interest of specific other individuals. It may not be possible to feel empathy for an abstract social category like *women, humanity,* or *the homeless.* Further, the likelihood that needs of different individuals will evoke empathic feelings is not equal; these feelings are more likely to be felt for those (a) who are friends, kin, or similar to us, (b) to whom we are emotionally attached, (c) for whom we feel responsible, or (d) whose perspective we adopt (Batson, 1991; Krebs, 1975; Stotland, 1969).

These observations suggest that many of our most pressing social problems may evoke little empathy. The people in need are too remote or the problems too abstract. For this reason Hardin (1977) dismissed altruism as a potential solution to our environmental and population crises: "Is pure altruism possible? Yes, of course it is—on a small scale, over the short term, in certain circumstances, and within small, intimate groups. . . . But only the most naive hope to adhere to a noncalculating policy in a group that numbers in the thousands (or millions!), and in which many preexisting antagonisms are known and many more suspected" (p. 26). Hardin quickly returned to his cardinal rule of never asking a person to act against his own self-interest.

More generally, as a source of motivation for public good, altruism may be limited in much the same way as egoism. If benefiting the person or persons for whom empathy is felt leads to increased public good as an instrumental means or an unintended consequence, then altruism may enhance the public good. If benefiting the person or persons is in conflict with the larger public good, then altruism may diminish it. Consistent with this reasoning, colleagues and I recently found that inducing empathy for one of the other individuals in a social dilemma increased allocation of scarce resources to this individual to the detriment of the group as a whole, much as increased egoistic motivation might (Batson, Batson, & Todd, 1993).

Promise

Still, in certain circumstances the potential of empathy-evoked altruism to serve the public good may be quite powerful. A careful look at data collected by Oliner and Oliner (1988) and their colleagues on rescuers of Jews in Nazi Europe suggests that involvement in rescue activity frequently began with concern for a specific individual or individuals for whom compassion was felt—often an individual known previously. This initial involvement sometimes led to further contacts and rescue activity that extended well beyond the bounds of the initial empathic concern.

Attempting to induce empathy for an individual who is an exemplar of a larger group seems to be a key strategy of many fund-raising campaigns, whether for children with disabilities, starving refugees, or harp seals, spotted owls, and whales; it also seems effective (Shelton & Rogers, 1981). Isaacson (1992) suggested that empathy was a potent factor in the 1992 decision to send the Marines into Somalia, so potent that he raises the question of whether the world will ignore the Sudan but rescue Somalia mainly because photographic footage of the latter evokes more compassion.

Even the needs of the physical environment may not lie beyond the reach of empathy. Think of the tendency to personalize these needs by using metaphors such as Mother Earth, the rape of the landscape, or dying rivers. Could it be that these metaphors are used to evoke empathy—and so altruistic motivation—by personalizing the natural environment?

Principlism: Serving the Public Good to Uphold a Principle

Principlism is motivation with the ultimate goal of upholding some moral principle, such as justice or the utilitarian principle of the greatest good for the greatest number. Once again, this motive could easily increase the public good as an instrumental means or an unintended consequence.

It is not surprising that most moral philosophers have argued for the importance of a motive to act for the public good other than egoism. But most since Kant (1724–1804) have also argued for a motive other than collectivism or altruism. Moral philosophers reject appeals to collectivism because it is bounded by the limits of the collective; they reject appeals to altruism based on feelings of empathy, sympathy, and compassion because they find these emotions too fickle and circumscribed. Moral philosophers typically call for motivation with an ultimate goal of upholding some universal and impartial moral principle.

For example, Kant argued that the Judeo-Christian commandment to love one's neighbor as oneself should be understood as a moral principle to be upheld rather than as an expression of social identity or personal compassion (1785/1889, sec. 1, paragraph 13). Tolstoy echoed Kant's view, calling the law of love "the highest principle of life" and asserting that love should be "free from anything personal, from the smallest drop of personal bias towards its object. And such love can only be felt for one's

enemy, for those who hate and offend" (1908/1987, p. 230). Similarly, the utilitarian principle of the greatest good for the greatest number is universal and impartial; it affirms that one should give no more weight to what is good for oneself than to what is good for someone else (Mill, 1861/1987).

More recently, John Rawls (1971) has argued for a principle of justice based on the allocation of goods to the members of society from an initial position behind the veil of ignorance, where no one knows his or her place in society—prince or pauper, laborer or lawyer, male or female, Black or White. Why does Rawls require such a stance? Because it eliminates partiality and seduction by special interest. A universal, impartial principle of justice much like Rawls's is the basis for Lawrence Kohlberg's (1976) postconventional, or principled, moral reasoning, the highest level in his stage model of moral development.

Universalist, impartial views of morality have not gone unchallenged. Writers like Lawrence Blum (1980), Carol Gilligan (1982), Thomas Nagel (1991), Nel Noddings (1984), Joan Tronto (1987), and Bernard Williams (1981) call for recognition of forms of morality that allow for special interest in the welfare of certain others or certain relationships. In opposition to an ethic based on justice and fairness, these writers propose an ethic of care. Sometimes, it seems that these writers are proposing care as an alternative principle to justice, either as a substitute for justice or in dynamic tension with it; at other times, it seems that they are proposing care as an alternative to principled morality altogether. If care is an alternative principle, then it too might be an expression of principlism; one might act for the public good as a means of upholding the principle of care. If, however, care is a special feeling (a) for another individual, (b) for oneself, or (c) for a relationship that inclines one to act, then care would seem to be a form of altruism, egoism, or collectivism, respectively.

Does principlism really exist?

Is acting with an ultimate goal of upholding some moral principle really possible? When Kant briefly shifted his focus from an analysis of what ought to be to what is, he was ready to admit that even when the concern we show for others appears to be prompted by duty to principle, it may really be prompted by self-love (1785/1889, sec. 2, paragraph 2). The goal of upholding a moral principle may be only an instrumental goal, a means of reaching the ultimate goal of self-benefit. If so, the motivation is actually egoistic.

To date, I do not think anyone knows whether principlism is a distinct form of motivation or only a subtle and sophisticated form of egoism. We have empirical evidence, limited and weak, that espousal of at least some moral principles, such as Kohlberg's (1976) principle of universal justice, can lead to increased pro-social behavior (Eisenberg, 1991; Emler, Renwick, & Malone, 1983; Erkut, Jaquette, & Staub, 1981; Sparks & Durkin. 1987). To the best of my knowledge, however, there is no empirical evidence that upholding justice (or any other moral principle) can be an ultimate goal. Nor is there empirical evidence that rules this possibility out.

Problems and promise

The major problem with principlism as a source of motivation to act for the public good is knowing when and how a given principle applies. It may seem that moral principles, at least universal ones, always apply. But it is not that simple.

Most of us are adept at rationalization, at justifying to ourselves, if not to others, why a situation that benefits us or those we care about does not violate our moral principles— why, for example, the inequities in the public school systems of rich and poor communities in the United States are not really unjust (Kozol, 1991); why storing our nuclear waste in someone else's backyard is fair; why terrorist attacks by our side are regrettable but necessary evils, whereas terrorist attacks by the other side are atrocities; why we must obey orders even if it means killing innocents. The abstractness of most moral principles, and their multiplicity, makes rationalization all too easy. Skill in dodging the thrust of the moral principles we espouse may explain the weak empirical relation between principled morality and pro-social action. Perhaps moral principles serve more to censure or extol others' actions then to motivate our own.

However, if upholding moral principles can serve as an ultimate goal, defining a form of motivation independent of egoism, then perhaps these principles can provide a rational basis for acting for the public good that transcends reliance on self-interest or on vested interest in and feeling for the welfare of certain other individuals or groups. Quite an "if," but it seems well worth conducting research to find out.

INTERPLAY AND CONFLICT

What difference does it make why we act for the public good, as long as we do? Thinking about the different effects of the four proposed motives—egoism, collectivism, altruism, and principlism—suggests that it makes a lot of difference. Each motive has its own limiting conditions.

These different limiting conditions suggest that it is important to know which motives are operating in a given situation. It is also important to know what evokes each motive and how they interact. Sometimes, these motives may combine additively; at other times, they may be in conflict, one inhibiting or undermining another. The latter seems especially likely when self-benefits are made salient for behavior actually motivated by collectivism, altruism, or principlism. The self-benefits may lead to an interpretation of the motivation as egoistic, which may undermine the other motive, much as Lepper, Greene, and Nisbett (1973) found that extrinsic incentives can undermine the intrinsic motivation of children at play. In this way, the assumption that there is only one answer to the question of why we act for the public good— egoism—may become a self-fulfilling prophecy (Batson, Fultz, Schoenrade, & Paduano, 1987).

CONCLUSION

Obviously, there is much we do not know about the nature and function of motives for acting for the public good. The questions are subtle and difficult, and the stakes are high. But, building on the Lewinian tradition—both Lewin's rich conceptual framework for understanding motivation and his use of laboratory experimentation to isolate and identify complex social motives—social psychologists seem ideally situated to provide some answers. Perhaps we too can contribute to the public good.

REFERENCES

Alfano, G., & Marwell, G. (1980). Experiments on the provision of public goods by groups III: Non-divisibility and free riding in "real" groups. *Social psychology quarterly, 43*, 300–309.

Batson, C. D. (1987). Prosocial motivation: is it ever truly altruistic: In L. Berkowitz (Ed.), *Advances in experimental social psychology* (Vol. 20, pp. 65–122). New York: Academic Press.

Batson, C. D. (1991). *The altruism question: Toward a social-psychological answer.* Hillsdale, NJ: Lawrence Erlbaum.

Batson, C. D., Batson, J. G., & Todd, R M. (1993). *Empathy and the collective good: Caring for one of the others in a social dilemma.* Unpublished manuscript, University of Kansas.

Batson, C. D., Fultz, J., Schoenrade, P. A, & Paduano, A. (1987). Critical self-reflection and self-perceived altruism: When self-reward fails. *Journal of personality and social psychology, 53*, 594–602.

Blum, L. A (1980) . *Friendship, altruism, and morality.* London: Routledge.

Brewer, M. B., & Kramer, R M. (1986). Choice behavior in social dilemmas: Effects of social identity, group size, and decision framing. *Journal of personality and social psychology, 50*, 543–549.

Campbell, D. T. (1975). On the conflicts between biological and social evolution and between psychology and moral tradition. *American psychologist, 30*, 1103–1126.

Cialdini, R. B., Schaller, M., Houlihan, D., Arps, K., Fultz, J., & Beaman, A. L. (1987). Empathy-based helping: Is it selflessly or selfishly motivated? *Journal of personality and social psychology, 52*, 749–758.

Dawes, R. M. (1980). Social dilemmas. *Annual review of psychology, 31*, 169–193.

Dawes, R. M., McTavish, J., & Shaklee, H. (1977). Behavior, communication, and assumptions about other people's behavior in a commons dilemma situation. *Journal of personality and Social psychology, 35*,1–11.

Dawes, R., van de Kragt, A. J. C., & Orbell, J. M. (1990). Cooperation for the benefit of us—not me, or my conscience. In J. J. Mansbridge (Ed.), *Beyond self-interest* (pp. 97–110). Chicago: University of Chicago Press.

Eisenberg, N. (1991). Meta-analytic contributions to the literature on prosocial behavior. *Personality and social psychology bulletin, 17*, 273–282.

Eisenberg, N., & Miller, P. (1987). Empathy and prosocial behavior. *Psychological bulletin, 101*, 91–119.

Emler, N., Renwick, S., & Malone, B. (1983). The relationship between moral reasoning and political orientation. *Journal of personality and social psychology, 45*, 1073–1080.

Erkut, S., Jaquette, D. S., & Staub, E. (1981). Moral judgment-situation interaction as a basis for predicting pro-social behavior. *Journal of personality, 49*, 1–14.

Freud, S. (1961). *Civilisation and its discontents* (J. Strachey, Trans.). New York: W. W. Norton. (Original work published 1930).

Gilligan, C. (1982). *In a different voice: Psychological theory and women's development.* Cambridge, MA: Harvard University Press.

Hardin, G. (1977). *The limits of altruism: An ecologist's view of survival.* Bloomington: Indiana University Press.

Hoffman, M. L. (1976). Empathy, role-taking, guilt, and development of altruistic motives. In T. Lickona (Ed.), *Moral development and behavior. Theory, research, and social issues* (pp. 124–143). New York: Holt, Rinehart & Winston.

Isaacson, W. (1992, December 21). Sometimes, right makes might. *Time*, p. 82.

Jenks, C. (1990). Varieties of altruism. In J. J. Mansbridge (Ed.), *Beyond self-interest* (pp. 53–67). Chicago: University of Chicago Press.

Kant. I. (1889). *Kant's critique of practical reason and other works on the theory of ethics* (4th ed.) (T. K. Abbott, Trans.).New York: Longmans, Green. (Original work published 1785).

Kohlberg, L (1976). Moral stages and moralization: The cognitive-developmental approach. In T. Lickona (Ed.): *Moral development and behavior: Theory, research, and social issues* (pp. 31-53). New York: Holt, Rinehart & Winston.

Kozol, J. (1991). *Savage inequalities: Children in America's schools.* New York: Crown.

Kramer, R. M., & Brewer, M. B. (1984). Effects of group identity on resource use in a simulated commons dilemma. *Journal of personality and social psychology, 46*, 1044–1057.

Krebs. D. L (1975). Empathy and altruism. *Journal of personality and social psychology, 32*, 1134–1146.

Lepper, M. R., Greene, D., & Nisbett, R. E. (1973). Undermining children's intrinsic interest with extrinsic reward: A test of the "overjustification" hypothesis. *Journal of personality and social psychology, 28*, 129–137.

Lewin, K. (1951). *Field theory in social science* New York: Harper.

Mansbridge, J. J. (Ed.), (1990). *Beyond self-interest.* Chicago: University of Chicago Press.

Mill, J. S. (1987). Utilitarianism. In J. S. Mill & Jeremy Bentham (Eds.), *Utilitarianism and other essays* (pp. 272–338). London: Penguin. (Original work published 1861).

Nagel, T. (1991). *Equality and partiality.* New York. Oxford University Press.

Noddings, N. (1984). *Caring: A feminine approach to ethics and moral education.* Berkeley: University of California Press.

Oliner, S. P., & Oliner, P. M. (1988). *The altruistic personality: Rescuers of Jews in Nazi Europe.* New York: Free Press.

Orbell, J. M., van de Kragt, A J., & Dawes, R M. (1988). Explaining discussion-induced cooperation. *Journal of personality and social psychology*, 54, 811–819.

Rawls, J. (1971). *A theory of justice*. Cambridge, MA: Harvard University Press.

Schaller, M., & Cialdini, R. B. (1988). The economics of empathic helping: Support for a mood management motive. *Journal of experimental social psychology*, 24, 163–181.

Sen, A. K. (1977). Rational fools. *Philosophy and public affairs*, 6, 317–344.

Shelton, M. L., & Rogers, R. W. (1981). Fear-arousing and empathy-arousing appeals to help: The pathos of persuasion. *Journal of applied social psychology*, 11, 366–378.

Smith, K. D., Keating, J. P. & Stotland, E. (1989). Altruism reconsidered: The effect of denying feedback on a victim's status to empathic witnesses. *Journal of personality and social psychology*, 57, 641–650.

Sparks, P., & Durkin, K. (1987). Moral reasoning and political orientation: The context sensitivity of individual rights and democratic principles. *Journal of personality and social psychology*, 52, 931–936.

Stotland, E. (1969). Exploratory investigations of empathy. In L. Berkowitz (Ed.), *Advances in experimental social psychology* (Vol. 4, pp. 271–313). New York: Academic Press.

Tajfel, H. (1978). *Differentiation between social groups: Studies in the social psychology of intergroup relations*. London: Academic Press.

Tajfel, H., & Turner, J. C. (1986). The social identity theory of intergroup behavior. In S. Worchel & W. Austin (Eds.), *Psychology of intergroup relations* (pp. 7–24). Chicago: Nelson-Hall.

Tolstoy, L. (1987). The law of love and the law of violence. In *A confession and other religious writings* (J. Kentish, Trans.). London: Penguin. (Original work published 1908).

Tronto, J. (1987). Beyond gender differences to a theory of care. *Signs*, 12, 644–663.

Turner, J. C. (1987). *Rediscovering the social group: A self-categorization theory*. London: Basil Blackwell.

Williams, B. (1981). Persons, character, and morality. In B. Williams (Ed.), *Moral luck: Philosophical papers 1973–1980* (pp. 1–19). Cambridge: Cambridge University Press.

Yamagishi, T., & Sato, K. (1986). Motivational bases of the public goods problem. *Journal of personality and social psychology*, 50, 67–73.

CHAPTER 48

BUSINESS ETHICS AND THE MANAGEMENT OF NON-PROFIT INSTITUTIONS

LUK BOUCKAERT AND JAN VANDENHOVE

The core of business ethics literature is based upon the stakeholder theory of the firm. The normative function of this theory is to internalise the concept of social responsibility into the definition of the firm (the firm as a social contract) and into the managerial practice (participative management, social and ethical audit). But why should we introduce this business ethics approach into the field of the non-profit sector, which by its origin and mission has already a strong social dimension? Is there a genuine dilemma of social responsibility in non-profit institutions? The first part of the paper will give a more theoretical answer to this question. The second part will illustrate the relevance of the business ethics approach by presenting an empirical application of the stakeholder theory in the Belgian-Flemish non-profit sector.

I. The Managerial Responsibility Dilemma in the Non-profit Sector

(1) Consequential and Fiduciary Responsibility

We say that someone is socially responsible when he has due regard for the consequences of his acts. The minimum threshold of socially responsible behaviour is not to cause damage to others. Children who are not able to assess the consequences or potential damage of their actions are thus not considered to be responsible. If a person in one way or another creates damage or problems to third parties or society as a whole this will *subsequently* have to be put right, for example by paying compensation.

What applies to people also applies in a derived manner (with a number of restrictions) to companies and organisations. Social responsibility means the *liability* of an organisation for the *consequences* of its actions. The more concern there is for the harm that an organisation causes rather than the good that it does, the more likely the manager or institution will be called to account. This is done by using a *social cost-benefit analysis* which forms the basis of public opinion and government regulation. Since the 1960's, people have become more aware of the environmental effects of companies. This has led to a great deal of government regulation: environmental laws, town and country planning, environmental impact reports, anti-pollution taxes, etc. But at a time of substantial unemployment, the employment effect of companies is valued more highly and so the costs and benefits are weighed up against each other in a different way. In brief, social responsibility

Source: *Journal of Business Ethics*, Vol. 17: 1073–1081, 1998. © 1998 Kluwer Academic Publishers. Printed in the Netherlands.

refers to the social liability of persons and institutions. This approach is mainly external to the company, and is of a consequentialist and socio-political orientation.

There is another—more relational and internal corporate—approach to social responsibility. Being given responsibility means being given a *job* to do. Responsibility in this sense does not so much refer to the consequences, but rather to something that precedes the activity and which orients and directs the actions. The substance of assigned responsibility is much firmer than with the general social liability for the consequences of our actions. It also rests on a more direct relationship of trust between the person who delegates the responsibility and the person given the responsibility. We may call it a relationship of stewardship, or in the language of management theory: a principal-agent relationship. The person assigned with responsibility for making policy gets a specific mandate, authority and power upon being appointed. But he or she is in due course accountable to the principal for his or her own acts.

In a profit-making institution, the principal is the general meeting of shareholders and in a nonprofit-making institution it is the organisational authority. We can call such responsibility of the director or manager towards the principals, the internal or "fiduciary" responsibility. The message from agency theory is that the internal objectives of an organisation form the primary responsibility of the manager. The wider social liability in this respect is secondary and functional. When social liability is over-regulated by government, it is viewed as obstructive and irksome, an infringement of individual responsibility and self-regulation.

(2) Managing the Responsibility Dilemma

A manager or policy-maker is continually at the intersection of these two forms of responsibility. His prime responsibility is towards his principal, from whom he received the appointment and whose trust he enjoys. On the other hand, he is also the face of the company for the outside world and is responsible for the consequences of his policy towards what today are called the "stakeholders": all groups who in one way or another experience the effects of the activities of such an institution and who are therefore considered to be involved parties.

The area of tension between fiduciary responsibility towards shareholders and socio-consequential responsibility towards stakeholders is known in business ethics as the stakeholders' paradox (Goodpaster, 1991). The various solutions to this paradox are not simply the result of analytical arguments, but rather stem from different normative ideas that vary from radical libertarian (Friedman), through moderate liberal (Goodpaster), to social-democratic (Freeman).

Is there a similar tension between fiduciary and socio-consequential responsibility in the nonprofit-making sector? On first sight it would appear not, and with good reason. The object of non-profit institutions is social from start to finish. The content of fiduciary responsibility is not the private profit of shareholders but a social profit. There thus cannot be any question of a conflict between fiduciary and socio-consequential responsibility.

Yet this seems a rather superficial answer. It is of course true that a non-profit institution has a social and selfless purpose as its primary mission. But this social goal is of a very specific nature. It is, at least in the case of a private initiative, linked to a *particular* social perspective, the perspective of the founding group (the organisational authority) and is oriented towards a specific target group (for example, care of the disabled). This particular and *specific* goal is the direct and prime purpose of the organisation. However, the institution indirectly realises many other goals and expectations. These other social objectives include employment, income creation, development of new social technologies and therapies, social progress, social prestige, etc. This complex web of social interests and expectations can grow and may even be supported by government regulation to such an extent that a conflict arises between the original social objective and the derived social significance of the welfare institution.

The conflict can be explained in yet another way. The main purpose of the non-profit institution is to make a "social profit". But what does social profit mean? It means the cost-efficient use of the available capital such that the *social objective as defined by the organisational authority* is achieved to its best. But on the other hand, the added social value that the institution creates is also determined by the many socio-economic effects and benefits that the institution creates. That too, is an added social value or profit. Consequently, there can be a conflict between the added social value that the organisational authority pursues and the added social value that other social groups have in mind. In addition to the general objective of striving towards maximum social profit, there is also a *struggle surrounding the distribution of the social profit and the determination of its content*. Therefore, the stakeholders' theory may be a helpful tool to analyse and manage the responsibility dilemma.

The starting point of the stakeholders' theory of the firm is that an organisation (whether it is a profit or non-profit-making institution does not matter so much), must be considered as a social contract between several stakeholders or involved parties. This network of stakeholders must be quite widely interpreted. Applied to a nursing institution for example, it means that the institution can be considered (at least implicitly) as a social contract between different groups: the original founders who set up the institution on the basis of a certain inspiration, those in need of care who trust in the institution, those who provide the care who invest their work and talent in it, the government who regulates the sector by law, the taxpayers who co-finance it, the managers who make the policy, and the many intermediary bodies such as mutual societies, trade unions, professional associations, suppliers, banks, the neighbourhood, etc.

The purpose of the social contract is not only to create a social profit but also to fairly distribute it among the stakeholders. The questions that arise here are analogous to those in the profitmaking sector: by what actual project is social profit to be created? How are the expectations of the various stakeholders weighed up against each other? To what extent is it a case of real participation or stakeholder democracy?

The perspective of the social contract breaks down the rigid dualism between the principals—the shareholders or the organisational authority—and the other stakeholders. All stakeholders are co-principals. They co-determine the identity of the institution and are not just implementers, strategic objectives, or levels of performance for the organisation. In other words: the relationship with stakeholders changes from an instrumental relationship to a relationship of mutual responsibility or partnership.

(3) The Impact of Competition

Seen from a micro point of view, business ethics is a way to manage the responsibility dilemma. But from a macro perspective, the emergence of business ethics can be seen as a response to new forms of competition. Present-day competition is just as much, if not so more, quality competition as it is price competition. Quality competition compels companies to give due regard to ecological, social and ethical considerations. In this new type of socio-ethical competition, business ethics is of a strategic and market-oriented nature. It is an attempt to at least partially internalise external social responsibility into the objectives and mission of a company. This makes the company morally reliable. It creates trust, which against a background of insecurity is an essential condition for developing market activities. Transactions cannot come about without there being mutual trust. In addition, through moral self-regulation, a number of harmful social and ecological effects are prevented such that all too cumbersome government intervention is avoided.

What is the impact of these macro-developments on the non-profit-making sector? We see that political regulation is making way for increased market operations. The government is withdrawing somewhat and allowing more room for the independent policy of institutions. As a result of this, the importance of an internal and self-determined mission statement and the role of management as the implementer of this mission increases. Market elements such as quality competition, cost-efficiency, contract financing, customer-orientation, a flatter organisational structure, etc., all form part of the management of non-profit institutions. This undoubtedly creates many positive opportunities for quality improvement and internal delegation of responsibility. We may conclude that the macro-context is stimulating the business ethics approach in the social service sector.

Nevertheless, it would be naive to overestimate the ethics of business. The attention given to ethics in the profit sector is often very *selective and fragmentary*. Alongside the projects that are an expression of social and ecological responsibility, many types of *exclusion mechanisms* are developing, especially the exclusion of the low-skilled. Participation and delegating responsibility in companies sometimes go hand in hand with irresponsible behaviour *outside* the company pushing social costs onto the government and society. Political structures are for the time being unable to dismantle these exclusion mechanisms.

Exclusion mechanisms are also at work in the non-profit sector. Does the emphasis on quality improvement and autonomy not lead to a phenomenon of *social cocooning*, whereby every organisation is more strongly oriented towards its own specific tasks and general responsibility is left to a retreating and partly powerless central government? Does the increasing attention for the individual organisational ends not lead to a *selective* blindness towards the general interests of society? Our empirical research on the practice of social responsibility does not allow comparisons to be made over time. With regard to the current situation, we can however note that much less importance is attached to the wider expectations of society than to the core values of the institution (see Table 48.2).[1]

II. THE PRACTICE OF SOCIAL RESPONSIBILITY IN THE NON-PROFIT SECTOR

Those who place a strong emphasis on the practical role of business ethics tend to reduce business ethics to a *technology of ethical and social auditing*. Ranged against the pragmatists are the theoreticians who see business ethics more as a new social and political philosophy of institutions: a *micro-theory of social justice* based on the idea of genuine stakeholder democracy and participation. It is of course important for there to be some cross-fertilisation between theoretical and practical ethics. With this in mind, we will look at a practical model of social auditing that we applied to the Flemish-Belgian sector of social services.

(1) Aim of the Research

The current practices of ethical and social auditing have mainly been developed with respect to individual companies (e.g. Body Shop, SBN Bank Denmark, Trade Craft, etc.). Our research was aimed at the application of the social audit technique to an entire sector. In 1992 we interviewed 250 managers from the profit-making sector on the implementation of social responsibility in their institutions. Building further on this experience, and commissioned by the Flemish Ministry to do so, in 1994 we interviewed 450 managers of welfare institutions. The purpose was to examine the extent to which the idea of social responsibility had been implemented within the institution. Social responsibility was interpreted according to the stakeholder theory as the capability to effectively give due regard to the *expectations and interests* of the various stakeholders in determining and realising the *values and mission* of the company.

The methodology of our research was quite simple and consisted of two parts: an extensive *stakeholder analysis*, and to help explain our results, *an institutional analysis* describing the characteristics of the organisation concerned. By institutional analysis is meant elements such as the ethical structure, the company climate, the organisational structure, the relationship with society and a number of socio-biographical characteristics of the manager. Whereas the stakeholder analysis taught us how institutions deal with the expectations of the various stakeholders, and which institutions respond *strongly* or *weakly* to these expectations, the institutional analysis allowed us to see what significant factors could explain the difference between strong and weak social responsibility.

The stakeholder analysis was done in three steps:

(a) First step: identification of the stakeholders. For the welfare institutions we selected six stakeholders: those in need of care, the staff, management, board of directors, government, and the public at large.

(b) Second step: selection of the typical expectations and interests of each stakeholder. For each of our six stakeholders, we selected ten expectations from a long list that we drew up on the basis of a literature study. Thus we arrived at a series of sixty expectations or interests.

(c) Third step: the interview. The series of sixty items was presented, in random order, to the welfare managers of different institutions, together with two questions.

First: to what extent is attention actually given to these items in your institution (evaluated on a scale of 1 to 6). The second question: to what extent would the item be taken into account in a policy desired by yourself (also evaluated on a scale of 1 to 6). The responses to the two questions subsequently made it possible to see how large the difference is between the actual and the desired policies, or in other words, how great the requirement for change is in the institution concerned. The greater the distance between the desired and actual policy, the greater the frustration and desire to change.

(2) Some Conclusions

(a) A clear pattern emerged in the attention for stakeholder expectations. The expectations appear to be ordered according to a *hierarchy of three levels.* First of all there is a cluster of expectations and interests that score very highly and for which there is considerable consensus (small standard deviation), and which exhibit a statistically consistent internal pattern over and above the specific interest groups. We can speak of the core interests because they are apparently the most vital in determining the life and survival of the institution. In the second place there are the specific stakeholder interests and in the third place the items that relate to the wider community such as employment of the low-skilled, presence of women in management and executive functions, substantial contribution of voluntary workers, childcare, preference for environmentally-conscious suppliers, etc.

In Table 48.1 you can find the cluster of the *core interests* with their realised score. Attention is given to customer-orientation, innovation and expertise of staff:

(b) There is a clear distinction between *institutions with strong and weak social responsibility.* It is characteristic of those with strong responsibility that all expectations or interests were scored more highly. Social responsibility is, in other words, an integral attitude. Table 48.2 gives the scores for different levels of responsi-

TABLE 48.1
Core Values: The Ten Most Desired Values and Their Realised Scores (score on a 6 point-scale)

Value	Score	
	Desired	Realised
Person centered care	5.44	4.72
Concern for a long term vision	5.27	4.09
Maximal social integration of clients	5.21	4.51
Space for professional expertise	5.19	4.27
Critical reflection on working	5.17	4.29
Staff participation in on-going formation	5.14	4.53
Attention to new needs	5.13	4.32
Fidelity to original mission	5.08	4.36
Periodic and systematic staff evaluation	5.00	3.93
Individual counselling and guidance plans	4.98	4.30
Mean	*5.16*	*4.33*

Source: Bouckaert and Vandenhove, 1996, p. 56.

bility (strong, rather strong, rather weak and weak responsibility). The table illustrates also very well the pattern of hierachy between the core interests, the specific stakeholders interests and the attention for the community interests.

(c) Through regression analysis, we can try to work out which factors in our institutional analysis exert a significant influence on the difference in social responsibility. Table 48.3 gives an overview of the relevant explanatory variables for strong and weak social responsibility. The main explanatory factors are:

— *ethical structure:* organisations that build in institutional elements of ethical care such as codes of ethics, a complaints department, ethics committees or social-ethical training, for example, score better in the stakeholder analysis. However, in general, the formal ethical structure in welfare institutions is poorly developed. Only 15% of the organisations interviewed had a code of ethics, 6% an ethics committee, 35% a complaints department (mainly rest homes), and 18% provided participation in seminars or training sessions.

TABLE 48.2
Emphasis on Core Values and Stakeholders' Values by Level of Responsibility (score on a 6 point-scale)

Core values & Stakeholders' values	Responsibility			
	Strong	Rather strong	Rather Weak	Weak
Core values	5.24	4.55	3.85	2.77
Clients	4.76	4.11	3.35	2.53
Management	4.63	3.97	3.33	2.23
Personnel	4.54	3.93	3.35	2.53
Board of Directors	4.49	3.91	3.15	2.28
Government	4.46	3.75	3.05	2.45
Community	3.91	3.32	2.75	2.17
Number of organisations	*81*	*199*	*137*	*33*

Source: Bouckaert and Vandenhove, 1996, p. 73.

TABLE 48.3
Explanatory Factors for Different Levels of Responsibility (Results of regression analysis)

Variable	Description	Effect
Characteristics of the organisation		
Ethical Climate	Participatory	Positive
	Innovative	Positive
	Instrumental	Neutral
	Regulative	Negative
Ethical Structure	Presence of ethical code, ethical commission, complaint committee, ethical seminars	Positive
Type of Organisation	Professional	Positive
	Individualised	Neutral
	Familial	Neutral
	Bureaucratic	Neutral
Statute	Private Non Profit	Positive
	Public	Negative
Size	small (0–10)	neutral
	medium (11–50)	negative
	large (51 and more)	positive
Characteristics of the manager		
Tenure in sector	Slightly	Positive
Personal beliefs	Practising believer	Positive
	Non Practising believer	Negative
	Free thinker	Negative
	Neutral or Indifferent	Negative
Opinion on co-ordination	Consultation and negotiation	Positive

Source: Bouckaert and Vandenhove, 1996, pp. 76–77.

— *ethical climate:* Table 48.4a gives a typology of the four climates, characterised by a set of statements. Table 48.4b relates the scores of responsibility to the scores on ethical climate. The results are very clear. The more an institution is characterised by participation and a climate of innovation, the stronger its social

TABLE 48.4A
Types of Ethical Climate

Participatory

— team spirit is judged by our employees to be important in the organisation

— people in our organisation have a strong responsibility vis-à-vis the community

— our organisation is characterised by strong relations of trust among employees

Innovative

— innovative people are encouraged in our organisation

— openness for new social developments is considered to be essential

— our organisation is based on the personal creativity of all employees

Instrumental

— an important responsibility of our staff is monitoring costs

— the performances of our employees are judged according to their contribution to society

— much attention is paid to an efficient organisation of work

Regulatory

— people in our organisation clearly respect hierarchical relations

— in our organisation people follow strict legal stipulations and procedures

— powers in our organisation are clearly circumscribed

Source: Bouckaert and Vandenhove, 1996, pp. 148–149.

responsibility. The more the organisation has a regulatory climate, the weaker its responsibility score.

— *organisational structure:* an organisation with a highly structured hierarchy—a bureaucracy—is unfavourable for social responsibility. The professional organisation with characteristics such as a high degree of specialisation, little centralisation, small status differences, personal contact and high commitment is the most favourable for a policy of social responsibility. Table 48.5 illustrates this conclusion by relating the different organisational types and their characteristics to the core responsibility (core interests score).

In addition to organisational characteristics, the *characteristics and vision* of the *welfare manager* also play a significant role. The current literature on leadership quite strongly emphasises the personal role of the manager as the guardian of the institution's mission. Our research did not go into this deeply enough to form many conclusions in this respect. It certainly appears that one profile correlates better than others with a high score for the social responsibility of the organisation. Factors such as a certain seniority, a practising religious conviction, and a vision of society oriented towards open and direct democratic consultation, exhibit a significant positive effect on the social responsibility score.

TABLE 48.4B
Relation between ethical climate and level of social responsibility (mean and deviation from the mean)

Climate	Mean	Responsibility			
		Strong	*Rather strong*	*Rather weak*	*Weak*
Participatory	89	+5	+1	0	-12
Innovative	72	+2	+3	-4	-9
Instrumental	65	0	0	0	+2
Regulative	74	-6	-4	+4	+19

Source: Bouckaert and Vandenhove, 1996b.

TABLE 48.5
Organisational Structure and Core Interests (organisational characteristics on a 4 point-scale)

Organisational Characteristics	Type of Organisation			
	Professional	Familial	Individualised	Bureaucratic
Centralisation	2.88	2.66	2.50	3.70
Specialisation	3.21	1.72	1.82	2.02
Personal contact	3.67	3.65	1.95	2.73
Dedication	3.49	3.45	3.27	2.65
Differences in Status	1.86	1.73	1.95	2.67
Core interests	4.69	4.28	4.04	3.94

Source: Bouckaert and Vandenhove, 1997.

NOTES

1. We used also another technique to measure the gap between the organisational and the public interest. We presented six social objectives (economic growth, employment, income redistribution, restructuring of public finances, environmental protection) to the 450 managers participating in our research and asked them to rank them in order of importance, in two different ways. First of all with regard to their importance for their own organisation, and then their importance for society. The result of this exercise showed that the two lists were not ordered in the same way. Although the gap between organisational interests and social interests in the profit-making sector is much wider (almost twice as wide), there also appears to be a gap in the welfare sector (for the comparison between the profit-making and non-profit-making sectors, see Bouckaert and Vandenhove, 1996b).

REFERENCES

Bouckaert, L. & J. Vandenhove. (1994). *Méér dan strategie? Sociale verantwoordelijkheid als bedrijfsfilosofie.* Leuven: Acco.

Bouckaert, L. & J. Vandenhove. (1996). Het welzijn van de zorg. *Over sociale verantwoordelijkheid en management.* Leuven: Acco.

Bouckaert, L. & J. Vandenhove. (1996b) Sociaal verantwoord ondernemen, *Tijdschrift voor Economie en Management,* XLI, 449–472.

Goodpaster, E. (1991). Business Ethics and Stakeholder, Analysis. *Business Ethics Quarterly,* 1, 53–71.

Centrum voor Economie en Ethiek,
Catholic University of Leuven

CHAPTER 49

FREEDOM, FUNDING AND THE FUTURE OF THE UNIVERSITIES

M. E. TASKER AND D. E. PACKHAM

We argue that a university has an intellectual and a social purpose. The former involves the advancement of knowledge and the provision of a liberal education, purposes which are not inconsistent with vocational ends. The social purpose includes upholding standards of freedom and democracy in society and acting as an independent source of criticism within a university's area of competence. The scope of such criticism must reflect the scope of the university and so will often involve cultural and ethical, as well as scientific, technological and economic, dimensions. In order to achieve these purposes a university needs autonomy and freedom for its members in teaching and research. This concept of a university is being challenged in Britain partly by some within the universities who regard it as an impossible dream, and partly by a radical reforming Government. We discuss case studies of the erosion of university autonomy by means of the UGC and CVCP policies on academic standards, research selectivity and small departments. We suggest that the 'crisis' in universities is a philosophical rather than a financial one, and that it is being used to increase the control by government and industry. The dangers of large scale and uncritical acceptance of industrial funds are pointed out: as possibly leading to a value shift within universities with the result that technology generation would become a prime aim. In such a shift we suggest that there is a danger of compromising the proper role of the university in society. We point out that the problems facing Western industrialised society require primarily an ethical and cultural response. It is therefore of paramount importance for universities to address these problems from an ethical standpoint, and in this way play their part in the intellectual and moral development of society.

INTRODUCTION

The universities of Britain can be seen as the inheritors of an intellectual tradition going back for nearly a millenium to the *studia generalia* of medieval Europe. At a time of crisis it is natural for such institutions to examine their fundamental principles to try to determine what is central and what is peripheral to their essential purpose. In this paper we put forward one view of the nature of a university and discuss some of the pressures on universities in Britain today, and make some suggestions about the way forward.

THE PURPOSE OF A UNIVERSITY: ITS VALUES AND CONSTITUTION

In the first section of this paper we explore aspects of the 'liberal' concept of a university which are of particular contemporary relevance to its *intellectual* and *social* purposes, and emphasise some

---

Source: Studies in Higher Education, Vol. 15, No. 2, 1990.

important social contributions which a liberal university makes to a free society.

By 'liberal' we mean that idea of a university which, with obvious differences in emphasis, was expounded by Newman in 1852, by Jaspers in 1946, and which in the 1980s has been restated, *inter alios,* by scholars like Amy Gutmann and Anthony O'Hear arguing their cases from very different political and philosophical perspectives (Newman, 1852; Jaspers, 1946; Gutmann, 1987; O'Hear, 1988). The classic exposition of the liberal ideal is Newman's in *The Idea of a University.* Its aim is the cultivation of the intellect giving it a talent for speculation and original enquiry. This is achieved by study in an intellectually-balanced community where the mind is broadened by contact with those representing the 'whole circle' of knowledge.

In discharging its intellectual function, the university necessarily fulfils a social purpose. The values and ethos of the education system will influence, and be influenced by, those of society as a whole. For this reason the Robbins Committee, when considering the aims of higher education, argued for the fundamental importance of the transmission of a "common culture and common standards of citizenship", as well as for the "advancement of learning", and "instruction in skills" (Robbins, 1963, §25–28). A recent White Paper has endorsed these very words (Secretary of State for Education, 1987). On a European level, H. Carrier, formerly Rector of the Gregorian University, emphasised the importance of the universities' humanist mission and cultural role in enlivening social and economic development (Carrier, 1988).

The link between the nature of a state and its system of education was recognised by Aristotle who argued "the citizens of state should always be educated to suit the constitution of their state" (Aristotle). It follows, then, that in a free society a university has a moral purpose in the sense of upholding certain standards of truth, freedom and democracy. These may best be arrived at through rational debate and the practice of intellectual rigour in addressing questions which are of major significance to society. The university has the responsibility of extending these values to society at large and not confining them to an ivory tower. This duty of the university is even more pressing today, in late twentieth century Britain, where there is widespread moral confusion, little cultural

consensus and a marked decline in traditional cultural values, yet many of the most pressing problems facing society are ones which have to be addressed in moral and ethical terms. Questions such as pollution of the environment, genetic engineering and nuclear power have a serious moral element: they cannot adequately be resolved by technological and financial criteria alone.

It is almost a definition of a free society that the powers of the government should be circumscribed. Within the constitution there must be institutions, which, within their areas of competence, can act as a balance to government power, and challenge it when necessary. The independent judiciary and the free press are two such institutions, the autonomous university provides a third. For long it was beyond controversy that (except in the broadest outline) politicians should not have the power either to dictate the teaching curriculum or to control what research was or was not done. "Freedom of institutions as well as individual freedom is an essential constituent of a free society and the tradition of academic freedom in this country has deep roots in the whole history of our people" (Robbins, 1963, §703). This academic freedom carries with it a corresponding obligation on the part of the university to strive to conduct its teaching and research to the highest standards of integrity and impartiality.

The recognition which society gives to the universities' moral independence of both political and industrial power is shown by the frequent use of university teachers as unbiased arbiters in matters of controversy. Lord Frank's committee on the events leading to the Falklands War, Mary Warnock's report on embryo research and the CEGB's funding of university research into the causes of acid rain are three such examples of this kind of work. The intervention of academics into matters of public concern where their knowledge and expertise can be of practical benefit is also an acknowledgement of the obligation to society that academic freedom places on universities.

The need of medieval universities to combat external encroachments of a stifling nature, A. B. Cobban argues, helped them to formulate more sharply their views of corporate and individual academic freedom (Cobban, 1975, p. 75). Thus they fought with vigour to free themselves from both municipal and ecclesiastical control. From this has developed the concept of the university as 'a society of equal scholars who are able to govern their own affairs' which R. Eustace (1987) has described as an "ideal of university governance". This "ideal" he shows has become increasingly prominent in charters granted since the 1830s.

The broad concepts known by the terms 'autonomy' and 'academic freedom' emerge then as a requirement for a university to be able to fulfil its intellectual purpose—free and open enquiry in teaching and research—and its social purpose—a source of social criticism independent of political authority and economic power.

'Academic freedom' is a complex concept used by different authors in different ways. In a valuable chapter Robbins analysed some of its ramifications (Robbins, Chapter XVI). The present importance of the subject is shown by two recent publications, a collection of critical reviews published under the aegis of the Society for Research into Higher Education (Tight, 1988) and a declaration on 'Academic Freedom and Autonomy' issued by the general assembly of the World University Service (WUS, 1988). Both emphasise that freedom is not licence and that it places cognate responsibilities on academics to act "according to the canons of truth adopted by their academic disciplines" (Gutmann, 1987, p. 175) and to "respond to contemporary problems facing society" (WUS, 1988). In this paper we are concerned not to delineate the boundaries of the concept, but to consider its central territory—freedom of teaching, of research and of expression necessary for a university to achieve its purposes—and to determine whether the central territory has been, or is in serious danger of being, whittled away.

Neither academic freedom nor institutional autonomy can ever be absolute. Both are constrained by the law of the land and by the availability of funds. Both are ultimately dependent on the good will of the state. For a university to thrive, or even to exist, the state must have a sympathy with its basic purposes (cf. Aristotle *supra*). As Karl Jaspers says, "No state intolerant of any restriction on its power for fear of the consequences of a pure search for truth, will ever allow a genuine university to exist" (Jaspers, 1946). It is worth remembering that Jaspers wrote this in the light of his experience in Nazi Germany.

However, where this basic sympathy does exist, structures can be established whereby public money can be channelled to universities without compromising their integrity. A good example of such a structure was the University Grants Committee (UGC) in the United Kingdom. The UGC, originally set up at the end of the First World War, was designed to provide Government funds without prejudicing university autonomy. The grants originally came from the *Treasury*, not from the Board of Education, and the Committee which decided on how it should be allocated consisted of *academics* and only gave broad *advice*. As a contemporary commentator said "The creation of this intermediate body has, like the creation of a buffer state, preserved the complete autonomy of the university which has always been such a marked feature in English education" (Brereton, 1929). The Robbins Committee saw this arrangement as an essential safeguard for academic freedom: "There is no reason why the needs of the future should infringe the fundamental freedoms. Where co-ordination is necessary, there are means to achieve it that do not involve compulsion and that provide an effective insulation from inappropriate pressures" (Robbins, 1963, §732).

EROSION OF UNIVERSITY AUTONOMY IN CONTEMPORARY UNITED KINGDOM

(a) The Education Reform Act

The liberal concept of the university, with its emphasis on academic freedom and institutional autonomy, has occupied such an important place in the intellectual culture of the nation that it has an element of immunity from direct frontal attack. Nevertheless, a change in attitude on the part of the Government has been developing for more than a decade and has culminated in the Education Reform Act (1988). This Act replaced the UGC by the UFC as the body through which funds from *the Department of Education and Science* would come to universities. The members of the UFC, of whom the *majority* must be *non-academics*, are all appointed by the Secretary of State. They may attach to the payments "such *terms* and *conditions* as they think fit" (italics added).

Some indication of the consequences of this change can be predicted on the basis of experience as in recent years, particularly since 1981, the UGC operated in an increasingly 'UFC-like' mode. It had "been receiving much clearer indications from Ministers" (Jarratt, 1985, §3.9), grants "have been accompanied by more and, more specific, advice, and it was becoming harder for universities to ignore that advice" (ibid., §4.13). Here we see lip-service being paid to liberal ideas of autonomy by using words like 'indications' and 'advice' where the plain meaning is 'instructions'. It is significant that it was a report of a Committee of Vice-Chancellors and Principals (CVCP) committee which acknowledged that the UGC had come to be regarded by universities as "a tool of the DES" (Jarratt, 1985, §4.14). A logical consequence of "strengthening the relationship" between UGC and the CVCP, urged by the same Report (ibid., §4.15(c)), is that the latter too came to act as "a tool of the DES".

Thus fundamental values which, until now, have been safeguarded by university autonomy are under attack. Neither Government policies nor public opinion seem concerned with preserving such values. Indeed, Eustace (1987) quotes the misgivings of a number of senior academics about the ideal of a university of scholars governing their own affairs. Carrier, too, notes with concern that there are some within the university itself who see the traditional ideal as an impossible dream, and regard the institution not as a community, but as a service centre activated by the laws of supply and demand in providing specialised courses to satisfy the dictates of industry (Carrier, 1988, p. 24). Government pressure is being put on universities to implement the recommendations of the Jarratt Report (1985) which conceived the role of the UGC as 'managing' the university system (§4.18) and which advocated lay dominated university councils playing a much more active role in *academic* planning (§3.50(d)). The Education Reform Act (1988) gives the Government more formal power over the universities. A recent report by a committee consisting entirely of professors of physics on 'The Future of University Physics' considered that "the primary aims of universities coincide with the requirements of industry" (Edwards Report, 1988, 2.1).

In the light of these developments, it is worth asking whether these pressures repre-

sent a rational way ahead for the universities in the context of the present times, or whether they constitute a threat to the very nature of a university. In the rest of this paper we attempt to address these questions, first by analysing some recent examples of strong pressures by the UGC and the Committee of Vice-Chancellors and Principals and secondly, by considering in detail some of the implications of large-scale acceptance of industrial and commercial funding, a lifeline being urged on universities in their present crisis. We conclude by putting forward some guidelines for transcribing the liberal values and adapting them to the situation of the late twentieth century.

(b) The 'Action Plan'

As a consequence of the July, 1981 recurrent grant allocation by the UGC, many British universities were confronted by a financial crisis. "Reductions faced by individual universities varied from 44% to 6% with an average of 17% over the university system" (Jarratt, 1985, p. 10). A letter from the Chairman of the CVCP, published in Hansard in November, 1986, spoke of "the stark fact that the recurrent grant has fallen by one-fifth in real terms since 1980/81" (Baker, 1986). The effect in many universities was reduction of levels of academic staff and closure of courses.

The funding crisis has enabled the DES to exert stronger pressures on the universities through the UGC and CVCP. The extent to which both UGC and CVCP have fallen under the sway of the DES can be judged by the well-documented 'Action Plan' announced jointly by the Secretary of State and the Chairmen of the UGC and CVCP early in November, 1986. The Minister told Parliament ". . . additional funding for the universities [depends] crucially on evidence of real progress in the development of the policy of selectivity, the rationalisation of small departments . . . and improved standards of teaching. I have now agreed with the University Grants Committee and the Committee of Vice-Chancellors and Principals a major programme of work in these areas. . . . I shall expect individual universities to co-operate fully and positively in this programme. Progress will be closely monitored, and *future funding of the universities will depend significantly upon its implementation year by year*" (our italics) (Baker, 1986).

Complementary letters from the two Chairmen signified their acquiescence and threatened universities with annual reports to ministers on the implementation of the Plan, with submissions to Ministers of action the UGC intended to take where a university's response "appears to be unsatisfactory" (ibid.). It is interesting to contrast the style of these statements with the ideal of university autonomy "which has always been such a marked feature in English education"!

There is then an irresistible prima-facie case that the traditional autonomy of universities is being eroded by the attitude taken by the Government through the DES. On the other hand, autonomy, as such, is not compromised by the acceptance of advice. Does this 'Action Plan' represent a blatant attempt by the Government paymaster to dictate policy, if necessary overriding university autonomy, or does it represent a reasonable agreement between the two sides? An obvious objection to the latter view is that constitutionally the CVCP is not able to commit the individual universities to any course of action: the "major programme of work" to which the Minister referred was not agreed by the autonomous bodies expected to carry it out. The crucial test in these circumstances would seem to be the attitude of the adviser towards reasonable dissent on the part of the advised. If strong pressure is applied to overcome such dissent, particularly if this pressure is applied where no large sums of Government money are involved, the conclusions must be that university autonomy is not being respected.

In an attempt to elucidate this question, we examine pressures brought to bear on universities by the CVCP as part of its academic standards policy and the UGC policies of research selectivity and 'rationalisation' of small departments.

(c) Examiners of Research Degrees

As part of its work on academic standards the CVCP published the Reynolds Report in 1986, containing codes of practice for such things as examinations and appeals (CVCP, 1986a). In particular for research degrees it recommended (p. 26) that "the candidate's supervisor should be the internal examiner in exceptional circumstances only". This recommendation represented a departure from the practice most commonly found where the examining board consisted of the supervisor as internal examiner and an external examiner. Opinion in universities is divided on the wisdom of the change. An enquiry among academic staff at Bath, for example, found 57% of respondents to a questionnaire were against the CVCP recommendation (Meakin & Tasker, 1987). A similar lack of consensus in favour of change must have been widespread as many universities declined to accept the CVCP 'advice'.

It might have been expected that the matter would rest there: advice had been given, considered and, in some cases, rejected. However, in 1988 the CVCP, as it said "reiterates again [sic] its recommendation [about the supervisor]" (CVCP, 1988). It renewed its pressure on universities, expressing concern about non-compliance and promising "to discuss these matters further with relevant universities" (ibid.). In a report of an interview with the Chairman of the Committee, *The Times Higher Education Supplement (THES)* (8 July 1988) said that the CVCP would not hesitate to criticise individual universities which were thought to be dragging their heels and that recalcitrant universities were to be brought into line.

There is a basic contradiction between the attitude of the CVCP in 1988 and the Reynolds Report two years earlier which, in its introduction, lays emphasis on the importance of academic freedom and institutional autonomy. In particular, it said "Control of any of these matters by a body external to the university . . . could cause requirements to be formulated which in the best judgement of the properly-constituted university authorities were wrong. In that case the university would be unable to comply without breaking its charter" (CVCP, 1986a, p. 7). It might be that the Reynolds introduction was simply intended as verbal genuflection to a venerable, but outmoded, tradition. On the other hand the contradiction might reflect differing views within the CVCP or perhaps, what is most likely, a response to Government pressure to which the 'Action Plan' bears witness.

(d) Research Selectivity

In May, 1986, the UGC graded individual university 'cost centres' into three main categories: 'better than average', 'about average' and 'below average' (the 'average' referring to the United Kingdom). In addition, some cost centres were marked with an asterisk to designate their being 'outstanding' (*THES*, 30 May 1986). The assessment was made on the basis of data held by the UGC and supplied for the purpose by universities a year or so earlier (Swinnerton-Dyer, 1985). The grading exercise provoked an angry response throughout the universities, especially as would be expected, by those departments graded 'below average'. The uncertainty of the criteria used, the ambiguity of the UGC's initial request for information and the secrecy of the procedures used by the UGC subject sub-committees which were responsible for the gradings were all heavily criticised (*THES*, May-November 1986, *passim*; UGC, 1988). In one example where the Chairman of the UGC admitted an error, the financial penalty consequent upon it was not rescinded (*THES*, 1 August 1986). The rankings of politics departments were described by the Political Studies Association, representing the heads of 45 of the departments concerned, as commanding "no confidence within the profession" (*THES*, 18 July 1986, 5 September 1986).

It might be thought that in scientific disciplines obvious objective criteria of research quality were readily available. By examining the particular example of materials science and metallurgy, the problems associated with the selectivity exercise become apparent.

The assessment was formally made by the UGC technology sub-committee which consisted of 11 members, only one of whom belonged to the discipline concerned. Five departments, nearly a quarter of the total, were given 'below average' gradings. When the rank order is compared with available statistics on research activity, a strong suspicion emerges of heavy reliance on the *total* values of grants awarded by the *Materials Committee* of the SERC to each department. Such a criterion is unjust because it takes account neither of *department size*, nor of grants from *other SERC committees*. When these factors are examined, it becomes very difficult to understand many aspects of the ranking order. It might be argued that by taking into account more nebulous factors, such as the quality of the work and the perceived reputation of a department, the gradings by the sub-committee could be justified. Nevertheless, it is difficult to accept that

three of the departments coming in the top half of the per caput comparison of research income, should have been classified as 'below average'. It is clear that there was a marked arbitrary element in the assessment made.

The selectivity exercise had financial consequences: UGC recurrent grant allocations to *universities* were adjusted to take it into account. In addition, pressure has been put on universities to reflect these adjustments in their *internal* distribution of monies (Swinnerton-Dyer's letter in Baker, 1986; *THES*, 10 March 1989).

(e) Small Departments

An early statement of the UGC/DES policy talked of small departments not necessarily being weak, but expressed concern about departments which were both small and weak (UGC, 1984, §10.4). Since then the rhetoric, at least, has moved away from the reasonable position to one where small size as such is seen as objectionable. This can be seen in the reports of some of the subject review panels.

The panel on materials science and technology started with the statement that "industry needs more graduates of high quality than are currently available" and concluded, not with the recommendation that the subject area should be strengthened with more resources, but that four out of 18 undergraduate schools should be closed *without* transfer of resources to the survivors. The assertion was that this would cut off the 'tail' of undergraduates with low A-level scores. This accords badly with the emphasis currently being laid on widening access to university courses (UGC, 1984, §1.8; Secretary of State, 1985)!

The 'hispanics' panel report produced problems at Bath, where French and German were offered with a selection from Italian, Spanish and Russian as 'minor' languages. The UGC letter announcing the 1986/87 recurrent grant had expressed the hope that the university would "deploy some of the resources it had gained to strengthen provision in languages other than French and German". However, within a few months it became clear that the subject review panel would recommend closure of the Spanish course. The group responsible for the course was a small one (two lecturers, a lector and a tutor) and eventually it was closed, despite buoyant applications

(180–200 for 12–13 places), a high quality of intake (A-level point score 12 to 13), and despite the increased demand expected for graduates with a knowledge of Spanish following Spain's entry to the EEC.

These two examples show a number of common features. Each, in a different way, suggests inconsistency of policy within the UGC. In both cases the decision for closure appears arbitrary: cogent counter-arguments were readily suggested. Despite this, pressure was applied to the universities concerned to conform. As there was no net resources consequence for the UGC—the funds saved being transferred elsewhere within the same institution—the UGC was essentially making a purely academic judgement, and forcing it on the senates concerned.

(f) A Rational Way Forward?

Will these pressures from the CVCP and UGC lead to a rational way ahead for universities? There is much to be said for a systematic review of academic procedures such as the Reynolds Report provides. To support research strengths and to concentrate a university's attention on weak departments and research groups should in principle enable universities better to fulfil their academic and social purposes. However, in practice it has proved very difficult to establish rational criteria by which to judge the effectiveness of a department. Even where there are no misgivings about the soundness of the advice given, an autonomous institution should have the discretion to act upon it as it sees best.

Have the strong pressures on university autonomy from the UGC and CVCP impaired the ability of universities to fulfil their function? The early retirement or emigration of many of the most experienced academic staff may have reduced 'unit costs', but it is a manifestation of a widespread decline in morale. The pressures on university autonomy described in this paper have aggravated the demoralisation. They have also upset the intellectual coherence and balance of many institutions by forcing contractions and closures. There is now at least one technological university which has lost both physics and mathematic departments.

The continual chipping away at autonomy is generating a climate of opinion where universities are expected to engage in activities which are inimical to their primary function. For instance, it is worrying that the Government Training Agency (formerly Manpower Services Commission) sees "a substantial and productive role for employers . . . in the work of institutions particularly in curriculum *design,* delivery and *assessment*" (our italics) as the 'cornerstone' of the 'enterprise education' scheme which it is encouraging universities to adopt (Training Agency, 1989).

Again, both peers and MPs have been worried by a growing tendency on the part of the Government to retain a power of veto over the publication of university research it commissions, even in such fields as health, medicine and education (Hansard, 1988a-c).

Once a precedent is established of universities' giving way on significant academic issues against the better judgement of their 'properly-constituted authorities', or of responding to external judgements based on hidden or unintelligible criteria, the fundamental purpose of the university is under threat. A mechanism has then been established which an unscrupulous minister or official could use against a university or department which was deemed politically or ideologically embarrassing.

The 'action plan' shows how close are the links—almost a chain of command—between the DES, UGC, CVCP and individual universities. With the change from UGC to UFC this chain will become stronger. The question must be raised as to whether the Government in fact still has the sympathy which Jaspers implied was necessary for a university to flourish, or even to exist.

The nature of the pressure applied for securing acquiescence to inimical recommendations is quite clearly the threat, not necessarily explicit, of withdrawal of funds at a time of financial and economic crisis (Baker, 1986). It is difficult to resist the conclusions of M. Dummett (1987) that the apparent 'funding crisis' is being used as a justification for increasing governmental control over universities and that this form of control is to the universities' detriment. The economic crisis would appear to be a fact of life in all Western industrialised countries. But is the resulting 'funding crisis' more a crisis of priorities than of economics? In the United Kingdom there has been a radical re-evaluation of the function of universities in society by the current Government. Universities are to be seen in cost benefit terms and in what Hervé Carrier, writing in the Conference of European Rectors' publication 'Universities and Culture', calls *"la froide rationalité du pragmatisme, du profit; de la concurrence"* (Carrier, 1988). An important argument put forward in this paper is that there are other equally valid ways of perceiving the place of universities in society and that the 'crisis' that is before us is philosophical rather than financial.

INDUSTRIAL FUNDING AND UNIVERSITIES

At the University of Bath the reality of the 'financial crisis' and the strictures of Government have produced a swift response. The need for economic survival has always been high on the university's agenda, for Bath is a small (3500–4000 students) and minimally endowed institution. There is no financial 'fat' to fall back on. Economic resilience over the past few years has been maintained by several new and important ventures in the university/industry 'interface' which taken together amount to a significant shift in emphasis. By emphasising contract research and by markedly increasing its volume and value over the past few years, by instituting endowed chairs, by establishing a new structure of external relations with a strong marketing flavour and by pushing for a prestigious local science park, along the lines of the Research Triangle Park in the USA, Bath is 'signalling' its entry into the age of enterprise.

What is the rationale for such a policy shift? The Vice-Chancellor of Bath, opening the Second National PICKUP Conference at Lancaster University in 1988, stated that as a result of government pressures "universities are having to commercialise themselves much more than they use to" and that "this demands the emergence of a new type of academic" (Love, 1988). Certainly, since 1981, government pressures in the form of financial cuts have forced universities to look elsewhere for funding. They have turned increasingly to industry and have been encouraged to do so by the CVCP, for example (CVCP, 1986). In an official DTI publication dated January, 1988 the case is put for closer links with industry and commerce

and we read: "Such links have multiplied and strengthened over the past six or seven years, *though much remains to be done* [our italics]. University income from industry grew from £23 million in 1981/2 to £59 million in 1985/86" (DTI, 1988, p. 20). At the University of Leicester funding from industry rose by 162% in 1987 but at Bath the University Council is worried that the academics are not earning enough.

Industry's high profile and the extent of its penetration into the higher education domain is reflected in the publications of its national pressure group, CIHE (Council for Industry in Higher Education). In his speech to the CVCP in September 1988, Kenneth Baker referred twice to the CIHE, highlighting in particular its views on teaching. "A striking change is the corporate concern, now widespread and often passionate, in the process and output of teaching" (CIHE, 1988). It is, however, rather sinister to read in the CIHE document published in spring 1987 that "where research emphasis declines it should be matched by a much sharper focus on the business of teaching itself". The overall ends of the CIHE are unexceptionable: the opening up of higher education and the regeneration of national prosperity. But the means that are suggested are more open to question. The 1987 document urges that "the system [of higher education] be rationally organised for the type of expansion needed". But *whose* needs and who is to do the organising? It goes on "We must move progressively to a situation where the customers of Higher Education, both individuals and industry, contribute significantly to its cost, and exercise significant influence as customers" (CIHE, 1987). "Companies planning to invest in science will wish to know in the first place that their long run interests are, at least broadly, taken into account in the setting of national research priorities" (CIHE, 1987). Such close coincidence of Governmental and industrial interests and their mediation through the industrial 'arm' has worrying political overtones.

The CIHE agenda for 'reform' resonates strongly with some of the more radical provisions of the Education Reform Act. A majority industrial presence on the UFC, a core national secondary school curriculum and student loans had already been powerfully argued in the 1987 document *Towards a Partnership.* It is also worth noting an interconnection of right wing politics, and business interests. Thus, Kenneth Durham, Chairman of Unilever and founder member of CIHE, wrote about 'Refunding Higher Education to Increase Technological Application and Growth' in a 1984 publication entitled *Trespassing? Businessmen's Views on the Education System.* This was a publication of the Social Affairs Unit, (commonly described as a right wing 'think-tank') and took as its brief universities' "insulation from economic and technological reality" (Anderson, 1984). Kenneth Durham in his paper argues the case for 'responsiveness' by universities to industry's needs by claiming that "industry already largely provides the finance for education through the tax regime" (Durham, 1984).

In the United Kingdom university sector in the late 1980s, the industrial model would seem to be dominant and the evidence that universities have come to see industry as their most important lifeline is overwhelming. The argument that will be developed in the remainder of this paper is that we may clutch at this 'lifeline' at our peril. We argue that the development of intimate links between university and industry is a process fraught with dangers for traditional liberal values and that the rapidity with which we are proceeding down this path is blurring, even suppressing, the moral issues and value conflicts that should now be publicly debated.

The New Model University

It might be helpful to imagine the 'alternative' university that could emerge at the end of a process of university/industry interfacing. Intimations of such a future can be found in developments in higher education in the USA and in the Pacific Rim (specifically Australia and Japan). A 'new model' institution has been described by R. Stankiewicz in his book *Academics and Entrepreneurs* and the argument for an autonomous, privately funded university system put by Elie Kedourie in *Diamonds into Glass: the government and the universities.* In Stankiewicz's view the "ideal type" of university would "be designed to function as an integrating factor in the larger R&D system" and its prime aim would be "technology generation and transfer". In order to achieve this goal there would have to be major changes in academic organisation. In knowledge areas where the greatest commercial exploitation is likely, for

example, electronics, computer science and biotechnology, university interdisciplinary units, or centres, funded by industry, would provide the 'cutting edge' in research. Examples of such centres, known as Cooperative Research Centres, may be found in the USA where a policy of industry/university collaboration has been fostered by the National Science Foundation. The Centre funded by the Whitehead Institute (Edwin C. Whitehead is a multimillionaire entrepreneur, former owner of Technicon Inc. and now expanding into biotechnology) and the Biology Department of MIT, is well known for its outstanding 'curiosity driven' research record. The extent of private funding that this kind of university/industry collaboration entails would demand changes in the government of the university. Representatives from the Centres, who were not university appointments, would sit on the 'statutory committees' of the university. This 'crossing of boundaries' would be reflected in a changed policy towards staff appointments. Stankiewicz refers to the "emergence of new role-hybrids", people who could combine teaching in traditional university departments with research work in the cross-disciplinary centres and possibly with marketing the university's knowledge and service in the 'world outside'. Mobility and flexibility of personnel would be features of the 'new model'. In its relationship with the outside world the institution would pursue an active 'marketing strategy', tapping into as wide a constituency of 'users' and 'customers' as possible. Finally, for the 'new model' to be in the forefront of 'technology transfer', anticipating the fluctuations in the intellectual market, a high degree of institutional autonomy would be needed. Privatised or corporate universities would be in the best position to achieve this.

Such a future may have appeal to many university leaders as well as to industrialists. The idea of institutional autonomy, freedom from bureaucratic control and governmental intervention and the resulting 'managerial flexibility' may be particularly attractive to university vice-chancellors, or chief executives as they would presumably be called. To academics the prospect of working in exciting new areas like biotechnology in laboratories generously funded by industry must be tempting. And among the public at large, for so long indifferent or uncomprehending, there must be many who would give support to an entrepreneurial university released from its 'dependency mentality' and giving value for money at last.

There are, however, some objectionable features about the 'new model'. The idea of cross-disciplinary work is a welcome one towards which many universities are working in research and teaching. There is nevertheless a profound difference between a university academic trained in the critical demands of a subject discipline working with members of other departments within a community of scholars, and a 'role-hybrid' who is funded by industry and whose concern is with the commercial applications and profitability of the research topic. The task of the intellectual discipline is to advance knowledge and to do this an open and critical stance must be fostered. Industrially funded projects may, however, carry with them the demand for secrecy or delayed publication on the part of the sponsoring company, thus transgressing the academic principle of the free and unfettered dissemination of knowledge.

Attempts to foster collaborative research between private companies, or corporations, and university departments have met with problems of ownership and control. For example, the prestigious Whitehead Institute/MIT Biology Department ran into trouble over the appointment of academic staff, the selection of research topics and the nature of the relationship with commercial interests. The inclusion of corporate appointees on university committees and statutory bodies raises the issue of value of conflict: the norms and values of large industrial organisations and those of universities may be at different ends of an ideological continuum. A beginning has been made in the USA to discuss the ethical problems arising out of industry/university links and to create new ethical frameworks. The two 'Asilomar' conferences held in Pajaro Dunes in California in 1975 and 1981 were such an attempt. We are not aware of any such move taking place in the United Kingdom and no recommendation for ethical debate is made in either of the CIHE documents. Stankiewicz acknowledges this value chasm but his position is that it is the universities who will have to undergo cultural and organisational change in order to adapt to high-tech society. Finally, it needs to be stressed that most university/industry 'interfacing' is with big business. Thus in the USA it is

apparent that the Cooperative Research Centres, for example, are best adapted to serving the long term R&D needs of large companies (Dean, 1981). In Japan the coming together of big business, the higher education system and of government, all three arms of the state working together on the basis of cooperation and consensus, has, it is claimed, led to the economic miracle. Whether the 'Japan Incorporated' model of government, industry and universities, is transferable to the United Kingdom and if so, what consequences for academic freedom might follow, is a prospect worth debating.

Ten years ago the idea of a university as an 'integrating factor in a larger R&D system' would have sounded crassly reductionist. Nearly 20 years ago the publication of a book entitled *Warwick University Ltd* caused ripples of shock and even disdain (Thompson, 1971). Ten years ago liberal values prevailed, philosophy departments were still open, academic tenure was safe and the academic life was seen as a vocation. Today the language and values of entrepreneurialism and managerialism have become common currency in higher education: "*Le dur language de la productivité moderne ne s'accorde pas avec notre discours humaniste*" (Carrier, 1988).

The force of the new thinking can perhaps be judged by the extreme statement made by the newly formed Council for Academic Autonomy in its first publication *The State and Higher Education: restoring academic autonomy.* "Gone is the old idea of self-regulating communities of scholars and teachers, devoted to the common cause of the pursuit of knowledge. Instead we have a Government conception of academic institutions as 'cartels of knowledge', units of production with a managerial elite and a workforce of intellectual producers, whose labour will be increasingly casualised in the interests of 'managerial flexibility' and 'value for money'" (1988). This extraordinary value shift in higher education resonates with a profound cultural shift in society that has taken place over the last ten years. The devaluing of humanistic values, the primacy of 'making it' or 'loadsamoney' values, the elevation of entrepreneurial values into an ideology and the penetration of this ideology into areas of life, like education, that had previously been resistant; are trends which, if taken together, amount to a cultural revolution.

How have we arrived at this depressingly uncivilised state of affairs? The purpose of this section of the paper has not been to point the finger at businessmen and to place the responsibility for the collapse of liberal values on the shoulders of industry. Industrialists are only doing their job in demanding a supply of well qualified and competent young graduates to enter their ranks. It is the university's job to educate them and this must mean fostering in them a commitment to free scholarly enquiry—the disinterested pursuit of knowledge—as well as to the values pertaining to a democratic society.

Amy Gutmann (1987), writing about education in a democratic society, says "Universities are more likely to serve society well not by adopting the quantified values of the market but by preserving a realm where the non-quantifiable values of intellectual excellence and integrity and the supporting moral principles of non-repression and non-discrimination flourish. In serving society well by preserving such a realm, a university acts as an educator of office holders rather than simply a gatekeeper of office". Industry is an essential component of our democratic society and many industrialists share in its values. Thus, at a recent meeting of the Council of Bath University lay members, including several businessmen, voted in favour of the democratic principle in the governance of the university.

So, too, industry expects of universities a willingness to participate in scientific research which will advance productivity and profit. In responding to this quite justifiable expectation it behoves a university academic not to make a Faustian contract. Certain scholarly rules need to be followed: freedom to pursue lines of enquiry which may not be directly 'relevant' to the industrial sponsor and freedom to publish results. It is hypocritical for universities to persist in claiming academic freedom when at the same time researchers accept classified research which, by the demand for secrecy, negates the fundamental academic freedom— the right to publish. University academics should be aware of the dangers of accepting short term research with an immediate 'pay off.' Too much work of this kind would skew research in an unacceptable way, deflecting academics from research which in the long term might be of greater value to society, if of less immediate profit to the industrial sponsor

and to the university. It is important that university academics uphold the principle of social justice by serving not only those groups who can pay large sums for research, for example business corporations and governments, but also other less powerful and less established groups. In this way a university can carry out its social purpose of acting as a cutting edge in society, challenging established orthodoxies and forging new and possibly uncomfortable theories and value positions.

University academics, however, have failed to assert strongly and publicly their function of intellectual and moral leadership within society, and to assert it, moreover, in language proper to a university. The intellectual and linguistic vacuum that was the result has been filled by the values and terminology of the market place. Such is the bankruptcy of university leadership and the loss of faith and confidence amongst lecturers that we find resistance difficult and now, with some exceptions, we pay lip service to the primacy of the market. Resistance is nevertheless legitimate. We have an obligation to society to state publicly that governmental policy is destroying the proper environment for research and teaching in universities and that 'selling out' to industry is not in the interest of universities or of society.

The Council for Industry and Higher Education makes an urgent case for improving university teaching. The Government would for ideological reasons wish to see industry further involved in the work of universities and not only in a funding capacity. It would be of considerable benefit to society if industry and higher education could work together towards the common goal of regenerating the university, thus enabling it to carry out its proper role of moral leadership in society. But in any such partnership it is the university that must play the dominant part. Many of the most crucial questions facing society are, as Carrier points out, ethical and cultural. Thus, *"La premiere mission de l'Université est de servir l'élévation intellectuelle et morale des êtres humains"*. Universities, by virtue of their traditional freedoms, are equipped to fulfil this role but the debate that must take place needs to be carried forward not in the commercial language of profit and loss, of marketability and accountability, but in the ethical language of purposes and responsibilities.

CONCLUSIONS

The intention of this paper has not been to set up a defensive barrier against change by invoking traditional arguments for the liberal ideal of the university. We have tried to stress the value of an historical perspective which emphasises the principles on which university education rests. Much of the material we have presented stands as a depressing testimony to loss of a sense of purpose, failure of leadership, and an erosion of community. The case studies we have described should be seen as warnings, rather than self-fulfilling prophecies, for it is possible that the defensive and negative climate which oppresses university life in Britain today may lift. The effect of 1992 will be revivifying and will be challenging. In signing the Magna Charta of European universities on September 1988, the university rectors not only commemorated the 900 years of the university—*studium generale*—of Bologna, they also laid claim to the future. The 'new model' of the European university will be one in which programmes like COMETT (university-industry exchange) and ERASMUS (international mobility for staff and students) will be of increasing significance. The European university, while conscious of its historical past, will address itself even more urgently to the problems of the present and the future and will assume responsibility for reviving the economy and promoting employment. It will also see as its task the transforming of traditional values to meet the needs and values of the rising generation. To achieve these ends the European university will need to co-operate and interact with governments, with industry and with society as a whole, while affirming the basic need that, in the words of the Magna Charta, "a university's research and teaching must be morally and intellectually independent of all political authority and economic power" (Caputo, 1988).

REFERENCES

Anderson, D. (Ed.). (1984). *Trespassing? Businessmen's views on the education system.* London: Social Affairs Unit.

Aristotle. *The politics,* VIII, i, §2: E. Barker (Ed.), 1948 edn, p. 390, Oxford: Oxford University Press.

Baker, K. (1986). *House of commons official report,* 103, c. 489, 6 November.

Brereton, C. (1929). Education. *Encyclopedia britannica,* 14th edn, 7, p. 987.

Caputo, G. (1988). *For a magna charta of European universities.* CRE-action, No. 2, p. 81. The text of the charta is on pp. 85–86 and in French, pp. 79–80.

Carrier, H. (1988). *Les universitiés et le devenir de l'Europe.* CRE-action No. 2, *Université et Culture,* p. 19.

Committee of Vice-Chancellors and Principals. (1986a). *Academic standards in universities* (Reynolds Report). London: CVCP.

Committee of Vice-Chancellors and Principals. (1986b). *The future of the universities London, CVCP..*

Committee of Vice-Chancellors and Principals. (1988). *Academic standards in universities. Second Report.* London: CVCP.

Council for Academic Autonomy. (1988). *The state and higher education: Restoring academic autonomy.* London: CAA.

Council for Industry in Higher Education. (1987). *Towards a partnership. Higher education—government—industry.* London: CIHE.

Council For Industry in Higher Education. (1988). *Towards a partnership. The company response.* London: CIHE.

Cobban, A. B. (1975). *The medieval universities.* London: Methuen.

Dummett, M. (1987). Universities at risk. *The tablet,* 30 May, p. 578.

Dean, C. W. (1981). A study of university/small business interaction for technology transfer. *Technovation,* 1, p. 15.

Department of Trade and Industry. *Departmental Brochure,* Ch. 4. London: DTI.

Durham, K. (1984). In D. Anderson (Ed.) *Trespassing? Businessmen's views on the education system.* London: Social Affairs Unit.

Edward's Report. (1988). *The future of university physics.* London: UGC.

Eustace, R. (1987). The English ideal of university governance. *Studies in higher education,* 12, pp. 7–22.

Gutmann, A. (1987). *Democratic education.* Princeton, NJ: Princeton University Press.

Hansard. (1988a). Education reform bill, lords amendments further considered. *House of commons official report,* 137, c.1022–23, 19 July.

Hansard. (1988b). Health and medicines bill, report. *House of lords official report,* 500, c.942–960, 17 October.

Hansard. (1988c). Health and medicines bill, third reading. *House of lords official report,* 500, c.1489–97, 28 October.

Jarratt Report. (1985). *Report of the steering committee for efficiency studies in universities.* London: CVCP.

Jaspers, K. (1946). *The idea of the university.* (English trans. London, Peter Owen, 1960).

Love, J. (1988). 'Stop beating about the bush' says Quayle. *Pickup in progress.* Autumn, p. 20. London: DES.

Meakin, B. J. & Tasker, M. E. (1987). *Higher degree examination protocol.* (University of Bath) [available from the authors].

Newman, J. H. (1852). *The idea of a university* (frequently reprinted. Page references are to the Image Books Edition, New York, Doubleday, 1959).

O'Hear, A. (1988). Academic freedom and the university, in: M. Tight, *op. cit.,* p. 6.

Robbins, Report. (1963). *Committee on Higher Education.* London: HMSO.

Secretary of State for Education and Science *et al.* (1985). *The Development of Higher Education in the 1990s,* Green Paper §3.2. London: HMSO.

Secretary of State for Education and Science *et al.* (1987). *Higher education: Meeting the challenge.* London: HMSO.

Stankiewicz, R. (1986). *Academics and entrepreneurs developing university-industry relations.* London: Six Countries Programme.

Swinnerton-Dyer, P. (1985). *The times higher education supplement,* 15 November.

Thompson, E. P. (1971). *Warwick university ltd.* Harmondsworth: Penguin.

Tight, M. (1988). *Academic freedom and responsibility.* Milton Keynes, Open University & SRHE.

Training Agency. (1989). *Enterprise in higher education. Key features of the enterprise in higher education proposals, 1988–89.* Sheffield: Training Agency.

University Grants Committee. (1984). A strategy for higher education into the 1990s. London: HMSO.

University Grants Committee. (1988). *The next research selectivity exercise: Consultative. Circular Letter 15/88.* London: UGC.

Whitehead, A. N. (1932). *The aims of education and other essays,* p. 74 London: Benn.

WUS. (1988). *The Lima declaration on academic freedom and autonomy of institutions higher education.* Geneva: World University Service.

Chapter 50

The Moral Context of Fund Raising

Deni Elliott and Bernard Gert

The moral context of fund raising provides the foundation for establishing what fund raisers ought to do and what they ought not do.[1] That foundation is based on the universal agreement that it is wrong to cause other people to suffer harms, to deceive, or to break a promise unless one has sufficient reason. In addition, fund raisers have special responsibilities based on the nature of their job and on the nature of the institution that employs them. The moral foundation provides criteria for determining which actions are morally prohibited, which are morally required, which are morally permitted, and which are morally ideal for fund raisers in institutions of higher education.[2]

It is as important to be clear about the moral context of fund raising as it is to be clear about the social and legal contexts. Although moral and legal dictates often coincide, there are two relevant differences between them. The first is a difference in accountability. No matter how ill-conceived one might judge a federal or state law relating to the solicitation, acceptance, or recording of donations, the fear of accountability in terms of fines or other penalties keeps all but the most recalcitrant institution or fund raiser in line.

Accountability for moral infractions is of a different and more diffuse sort. The institution that treats prospects or donors in ways that are immoral but not illegal will suffer a loss of trust, credibility, and ultimately donations. But unless the immoral act is also illegal, no one will go to jail. The law proscribes a very narrow scope of activities that are almost always morally as well as legally prohibited. That is why it is almost always morally required that people obey the law. But the scope of moral prohibitions is far larger than the scope of law. It is generally wrong to act deceptively, but the law holds people accountable for only certain acts of deception, for example, deceiving the IRS.

Another important difference between law and ethics is the way they define compliance. Laws are straightforward. Institutions, fund raisers, and donors may sometimes search for loopholes in the law, but the laws are written, and precedents are established, in an attempt to make the minimal legal requirements increasingly more clear. The law holds in a very exacting way regardless of context.

Moral imperatives, while clear on the surface—"Don't cheat," "Don't deceive," "Keep your promises"—require interpretation and application for individual situations. Behavior that is morally permitted or even encouraged in a poker game, for example, is morally prohibited in most occupational relationships, including the relationship that exists between fund raisers and potential or actual donors. Even though the moral rules prohibiting deception, cheating, and breaking a promise are universal, whether a specific act counts as deception, cheating, or breaking a promise is determined by context. Moral problems in fund raising cannot be treated as isolated, as though their solutions will not have implications for all other moral problems. The moral imperatives of

Source: *The Ethics of Asking: Dilemmas in Higher Education Fundraising*, 1995, D. Elliott (ed.), Johns Hopkins University Press.

fund raising exist within a system of morality that extends to all other questions of applied and professional ethics.

Morality is a public system that applies to all moral agents. By *moral agents* we mean persons who are held morally responsible for their actions. Such persons must know at least some of the rules that everyone is morally prohibited from violating and be able to control their actions with respect to those rules; this includes almost all adults of near normal intelligence and above, as well as most children above the age of ten and even many below that age. They all know certain general facts, for example, that all people have only limited knowledge; that they do not want to suffer any harm or evil, namely, death, pain, disability, or loss of freedom or pleasure, unless they believe that someone, either they themselves or someone else, will avoid at least a comparable harm or gain some comparable benefits, namely, abilities, freedom, or pleasure. Further, such persons themselves want to avoid acting in a way that will cause them to suffer any harm unless they have such beliefs about someone benefiting. Acting in such a way is to act irrationally. Although all of us probably act irrationally at one time or another, for example, when we get very angry, most people would like this never to be the case.

All the persons to whom a public system applies—those whose behavior is to be guided and judged by it—understand it; that is, they know what behavior the system prohibits, requires, and encourages. And it is not irrational for any of them to accept being guided or judged by it. The clearest example of a public system is a game. The rules of the game are part of a system that is understood by all of the players, they all know what kinds of behavior are prohibited, required, and encouraged by the rules of the game, and it is not irrational for players to use the rules to guide their own behavior and to judge the behavior of other players by those rules. Morality is a public system that applies to all moral agents; people are subject to morality simply by virtue of being rational persons with sufficient knowledge to be held responsible for their actions. None of this is surprising. The high degree of consensus as to what counts as a moral question or an ethical violation goes unnoticed because we make so many moral judgments based on commonly understood and shared rules.

Is it morally acceptable for fund raisers to steer prospects to nonprofits rather than to the educational institution that employs them? Should fund raisers use sex or power to obtain gifts? Should educational institutions seek gifts under false pretenses? The answers to these questions are obvious, and obviously not what we are addressing in this book. There is not always a unique correct solution to every moral problem, but it does not follow that all solutions are morally acceptable. It may be that people cannot agree on a single correct solution but will agree that a number of solutions would be simply immoral.

Although most people use the same moral system when they think seriously about making a moral judgment or deciding how to act when confronting a moral problem, they probably are not conscious of doing so. Grammar provides a useful analogy. Most speakers cannot explicitly describe the grammatical system; they all know it in the sense that they use it when speaking themselves and in interpreting the speech of others. Although there are some variations in the grammatical system, no one should accept a description of the grammatical system that rules out speaking in a way that they regard as acceptable or permits speaking in a way that they regard as unacceptable to those who are competent speakers of the language.

Similarly, a moral system that promotes acting in a way that conflicts with one's considered moral judgments should not be accepted. However, recognition of the systematic character of morality may demonstrate some inconsistencies in one's moral judgments in much the same way that careful grammatical analysis can uncover a speaker's error in sentence construction. Making the moral system explicit, including making clear which facts are morally relevant and which are not, may reveal that some moral judgments are inconsistent with the vast majority of other moral judgments. Thus, one may come to see that what one accepted as a correct moral judgment is mistaken. . . .

Most of the moral judgments fund raisers make will be noncontroversial. Their understanding of what it means to act in morally permitted ways, combined with their special role-related responsibilities, provides the scope for determining they ought and ought not to do. Some of what appears as guidelines for ethical fund raising throughout this book should appear obvious to practitioners in the field.

We can think of the role of the university fund raiser in a nested way. The primary job responsibility for fund raisers is to raise money. The moral responsibility that surrounds them stems from their role as part of the institutional advancement team. Therefore, along with other advancement officers, they share the duty of promoting the university's interests. Still more broadly, fund raisers are administrators in their institutions of higher education. Thus, they also share the responsibility of actualizing the mission and operating philosophy of the institution.[3]

What counts as a role-related responsibility for fund raisers is important because fund raisers, like everyone else, are morally required to do their jobs. Specifically, fund raisers are morally required to bring in money in a way that reflects an understanding of the institutions mission and promotes the institution's interests. It is immoral to neglect one's duty, to fail to meet one's role-related responsibilities, but except in unusual cases it is also immoral to fulfill this duty through a process that involves causing harm, deception, cheating, or breaking one's promise. Fund raisers are morally required to raise money, but not at any cost. Their meritorious goal of bringing in money cannot justify deceiving prospective donors, violating a prospect's privacy to get information, or violating tax laws to help a donor.

REASONABLE EXPECTATIONS AND MORAL PERMISSIBILITY

An explanation of the relationship between the fund raiser and the donor can clarify some of what is morally permissible for fund raisers. The nature of the relationship between the fund raiser and potential or actual donor provides the basis for determining what the prospect or donor can reasonably expect from the fund raiser. Knowing what to expect from a business or professional relationship protects people from being too vulnerable. For example, it is reasonable to expect salespeople to withhold information about the positive qualities of competitors' products and the negative qualities of their own. This is a convention of the sales business that most of us have come to

expect. Consider what happens to customers who do not understand this convention and think that salespeople will give them all the pertinent information. Those customers perceive themselves to be less vulnerable than they really are. Because of their mistaken expectations, they are depending on the salesperson as their sole source of information.

It is more difficult to clarify the conventional expectations for fund raisers than it is to describe the conventional expectations for salespeople. Like sales personnel, fund raisers have a primary responsibility to their employer; however, unlike sales personnel, they are expected to develop trust relationships with actual and prospective donors. "Buyer beware" is the conventional standard for sales; there is no parallel "giver beware" in charitable solicitations.

It is important that fund raisers define and be able to describe the reasonable expectations that donors have of them. This sets the rules of the game. Then if fund raisers violate expected standards of behavior, they are acting in an unfair way; we may even regard it as cheating. What is it reasonable for actual or prospective donors to expect in their relationships with higher education fund raisers? The following understanding emerges from the literature and practice of conscientious fund raising:

> Philanthropy is a social relation between the donor and the recipient organization in which giving is a voluntary act. Fund raising is in service to that relationship and act.[4]

The relationship between a fund raiser and a prospective or actual donor differs in important ways from that between a salesperson and a customer. The fund-raising relationship begins with the assumption that the potential donor wants to provide a gift specifically to the recipient organization. A sales relationship begins with the assumption that the customer needs or wants to buy some product or service that can be found in various stores. Givers do not often approach a charitable organization with the view that they have a certain number of dollars to give away and that maybe they will give it to that charitable organization, and maybe they will not. The reasons that lead a donor to give to a specific charitable organization are far more complex than those that lead a buyer to purchase goods from a particular store.

Philanthropic giving is an expression of the donor's values and world-view. It is also an expression of ideal rather than required behavior. While one may want to encourage all people to give of themselves in some beneficent way, the giving of a particular gift to a particular institution is not a moral requirement for any donor. By bestowing gifts, donors act in a way that is morally ideal rather than morally required. It is morally permissible for donors to do any number of other things with their money or to give it to any number of worthy causes. The fund raisers exist to facilitate gift giving to the educational institutions that employ them.

Philanthropy scholar Robert Payton and colleagues state the facilitative role of the fund raiser succinctly: "We believe that fund raising for social purposes engages fund raisers in the lives of other people for their benefit or for some larger public benefit as well as for the benefit of the fund raisers themselves. Intervening in the lives of others for their benefit is a moral action."[5] These are laudable goals, but the fund raiser's intervention is a moral action only if the process of fund raising is as exemplary as its goal. Since giving is a voluntary act, any morally permissible methods of fund raising will be accompanied by the assumption of explicit or implicit consent on the part of the potential donor.

One can think of any number of beneficial actions that, if done without consent, would be immoral rather than moral actions. Rational adults are allowed to make incorrect decisions, to act in ways that are not necessarily in their benefit or in the public's benefit. No matter how strongly a fund raiser believes that alumni owe something to the college, taking their money in a way that circumvents their will is not permissible.

Except in rare, justifiable cases, it is immoral to deprive anyone of the opportunity to make choices. Being so deprived is a harm that any rational person normally wants to avoid. One might be justified in depriving an adult of the freedom to make choices through involuntary commitment when it is clear that the choices that person is making are likely to cause him serious harm; or one might be justified in imprisoning someone who has harmed others. But when we are speaking of an action such as giving money to one's alma mater,

there is no justification for depriving the donor, by deception or other immoral means, of the freedom to give or not to give. Donating one's extra money to a worthwhile cause is itself a morally exceptional act, rather than one that is morally required, and the freedom to decide whether and how to give is critical to the ethical nature of the relationship.

The relationship between the donor and fund raiser is based on trust, with the fund raiser working as a conduit between the donor and institution. The following reasonable expectations extend from that trust relationship:

1. Donors reasonably expect fund raisers to protect their gifts by understanding and safeguarding the donative intent.

2. Donors reasonably expect fund raisers to give them pertinent information to assist them in making decisions about whether and how to give.

3. Donors reasonably expect fund raisers not to deceive them as they make determinations relative to their donations.

Thus, it is reasonable for donors to expect their beliefs, concerns, and desires to be important features of their relationship with fund raisers. This is not to say that every belief, concern, or desire of every donor must be condoned. If the prospective donor's offer or conditions for the gift's use are inconsistent with the institutional mission or interest, the gift ought not to be accepted. The acceptance of a gift assumes that the donor's gift and conditions and the institution's acceptance reflect a shared understanding of institutional mission and interest. Consider how these reasonable donor expectations unfold.

PROTECTION OF THE GIFT

It is morally unjustifiable for an institution to fail to respect the donor's intent, just as it is morally unjustifiable for the fund raiser and the institution to fail to protect that intent. As time passes and the understanding of a donor's intent fades, preserving that intent may not be an easy task. It is unfair for fund raisers to fail to solicit, comprehend, and carry out the donor's wishes to the best of the institution's ability. The willingness of development staffs to regard such stewardship seriously long after the actual donation will be favorably noticed by other alumni who are concerned about the future of their gifts in perpetuity.

THE REQUIREMENT TO TELL

The disclosure requirement of fund raisers requires that they share all information that donors would consider relevant in the decision process. This clarifies the limits of deception in higher education fund raising: a lie is always morally unacceptable, that is, unless it is otherwise justified,[6] but omitting or withholding information is only sometimes morally unacceptable.

While it is not deceptive for fund raisers to fail to reveal details of their personal lives to prospective donors, there is some information that fund raisers have a moral obligation to reveal, namely, information that donors would reasonably consider relevant to their determination of whether to give. The fund raiser, as facilitator, has a good-faith obligation to find out what the prospective donor considers relevant and to provide that information even if the prospect might withhold the gift in light of the information. . . .

RESPECT FOR DONORS

Telling prospective donors information that they would consider relevant to the making of their gifts is one important way that fund raisers show respect for donors. Another way is through the collection and retention of information concerning the prospective donor. One of the standard tenets of the profession is that information that the prospective or actual donor might consider embarrassing or damaging should not be intentionally collected or retained by the institution.[7] . . .

MORALLY UNACCEPTABLE ACTIONS IN FUND RAISING

Causing pain, depriving freedom or opportunity, deceiving, cheating, or breaking the law are the kinds of action that require justification. The moral rules that prohibit such actions are not absolute, and all of them have justified exceptions. Most people would agree that even killing is justified in self-defense, for example. Further, one finds almost complete agreement on the features of justified exceptions. The first of these is *impartiality*. When all of the relevant features are the same, if a violation of a moral rule is justified for any person, it is justified for every person.

Simple slogans like the Golden Rule, "Do unto others as you would have them do unto you," and Kant's categorical imperative, "Act only on that maxim that you could will to be a universal law," serve as heuristic devices for people who are contemplating the violation of a moral rule: "Consider whether you would be prepared to impartially favor that kind of violation no matter who is doing the violating and to whom."

It is also generally agreed that there is some kind of publicity requirement, that is, that everyone know that this kind of violation is allowed. The publicity requirement guarantees genuine impartiality. It is not sufficient to justify allowing everyone to violate the rule in the same circumstances. One must also be willing to advocate the violation publicly. Consider a fund raiser who deceives a prospective donor in a situation in which failure to receive the donation would result in the loss of great benefits to the institution but the donor would suffer no harm other than being deceived and no one would become aware of the deception. This would be a justified violation of the rule "Do not deceive" only if everyone, including all fund raisers and all donors, knew that it was a justifiable exception. But logically, no one would favor everyone's knowing that this kind of deception was allowed. If everyone knew it, the kind of trust that is essential in the relationship between fund raiser and donor would be destroyed. And if no one favored publicly allowing this kind of deception, then practicing it would involve arrogance; that is, one would be making special exceptions for oneself, which is clearly immoral.

We do not claim that everyone agrees *which* violations satisfy these conditions, but no violation is justified unless it has satisfied these conditions. The proper attitude toward moral rules, therefore, is as follows: *Everyone is always to obey the rule unless an impartial rational person can advocate that violating it be publicly allowed.*

There are justifiable exceptions to the rules. For example, most people would consider it justifiable to cheat or deceive a hostage-taker if such behavior were likely to lead to the release of his hostages, especially if everyone, including potential hostage-takers, understood that that was how law enforcement officers were likely to react toward hostage-taking. If hostage-takers knew that they could not trust law enforcement officers to do what they said in a hostage-taking situation, the hostage-takers' power would be gone. Part of what makes this exception to the rule "Do not deceive" justifiable is that the law enforcement officers are deceiving those who have acted immorally by depriving innocent people of their freedom. It is far easier to justify deceiving those who are acting immorally than it is to justify those who are not. Many would favor deceiving hostage-takers even when everyone, including the hostage-takers, knew that such deception was allowed. Indeed, one point of having everyone know that deception is allowed in these cases is to establish future uncertainty on the part of would-be hostage-takers that law enforcement officers would meet their demands. But publicly allowing deception in fund raising would create an uncertainty that no one in the field of fund raising wants.

In order to avoid the kind of uncertainty that can arise if it is not clear what counts as deception, the rules of the fund-raising-game must be made public. . . . Institutions should adopt written rules for how to count various types of gifts. Publicly adopting such rules and sticking with the rules throughout the campaign allows all the players—donors as well as volunteers and development officers—to set reasonable expectations for the conduct of the campaign.

It is very difficult, if not impossible, for fund raisers to justify actions that are usually morally unacceptable, because the act that forms the basis of the relationship between fund raiser and prospect or donor is an act of philanthropy. Donors act on moral ideals when they give. Giving is not morally required. It is morally permissible for donors to refuse to give, to give elsewhere, or to give less. There is no basis from which to argue that it is ever morally acceptable for fund raisers to deceive, cheat, deprive prospects or donors of their free-

dom of choice, or otherwise cause them harm in the process of raising funds.

Two faulty justifications that are sometimes offered for morally unacceptable actions on the part of fund raisers are (1) that the donor is not acting out of meritorious donative intent and (2) that the institution has a desperate need for the money. Neither justification holds. It is very difficult to fully know the donor's intent. Motivations for giving vary from the psychological to the economic to the social.[8] The so-called charitable impulse is present as a theme in all the various conscious and unconscious motivations to give. Even if it were possible to determine with absolute certainty that a donor was providing the donation for some purely non-philanthropic reason, fund raisers would not be justified in treating that donor in a morally unacceptable way. Whatever the purpose, intent, or motivation, the donor's act is still a morally good one.

Fund raisers' guesses that a prospective donor's motivation is non-philanthropic are irrelevant unless the donor's motivation or gift conditions conflict with the institutional mission or interests. The sleazy donor is neither a problem for the fund raiser seeking to act in morally permissible ways nor a justification for morally prohibited behavior on the part of the fund raisers. If the donor's goals are inconsistent with the institution's mission or interests, then no gift ought to be accepted. On the other hand, if the donor's goals for the gift are consistent with the institution's mission, then fund raisers are morally required to do their job without engaging in actions that might cause the donor to suffer harm.

Nor is the desperation of the institution a justification for acting in morally unacceptable ways toward prospective or actual donors. Several years ago, at a seminar for Ivy League prospect research officers, a participant justified an unacceptable technique for obtaining information in the following words: "Don't you understand? This is about survival!" The school's multimillion-dollar endowment made the claim especially ironic, but this justification is morally lacking even in times when the institutional doors might really have to close.

The rule suggested in allowing the desperate situation of an institution to justify morally unacceptable behavior is that it is morally permissible to engage in actions that might cause individuals to suffer harm if those actions will bring about a good result for one's institution. This rule describes a world in which Robin Hood is the model fund raiser. The rule also would not stand up under the public scrutiny that is required for behavior that is generally morally unacceptable. That is, the fund raisers in this example would need to let everyone know that they are willing to deceive donors when the institution is in desperate need of funds. This obviously is not a practice that could be made known to donors, because then donors would never know whether or not to believe fund raisers. If fund raisers take Kant's categorical imperative—"Act only on the maxim that you could will to be a universal law"—as their guide, their proper moral behavior is to act only in those ways that they would be willing to be publicly allowed. This means never causing harm, deceiving, cheating, or breaking promises unless one would be willing for everyone to know that violating a moral rule in these kind of circumstances was allowed for everyone.

NOTES

Sections of this chapter appeared in Bernard Gert, "Morality, Moral Theory, and Applied and Professional Ethics," *Professional Ethics* 1, nos. 1 and 2 (1992): 5–24.

1. The terms *moral* and *ethical* are used synonymously here.
2. Much of what follows is based on the work of philosopher Bernard Gert. See his *Morality: A New Justification for the Moral Rules* (New York: Oxford Univ. Press, 1988).
3. The moral obligation of the fund raiser to support the institution rests, of course, on the assumption that the mission of the institution is itself moral.
4. Henry A. Rosso, "A Philosophy of Fund Raising," in Rosso et al., *Achieving Excellence in Fund Raising: A Comprehensive Guide to Principles, Strategies, and Methods* (San Francisco: Jossey-Bass, 1991), 3–7; S. Ostrander and P. Schervish, "Giving and Getting: Philanthropy

as a Social Relation," in *Critical Issues in American Philanthropy,* ed. Jon Van Til (San Francisco: Jossey-Bass, 1990); Robert L. Payton, *Major Challenges to Philanthropy: A Discussion Paper for Independent Sector* (New York: Independent Sector, 1984).
5. Robert L. Payton, Henry A. Rosso, and Eugene R. Tempel, "Toward a Philosophy of Fund Raising," in Dwight Burlingame and Lamont J. Hulse, *Taking Fund Raising Seriously: Advancing the Profession and Practice of Raising Money* (San Francisco: Jossey-Bass, 1991), 9.
6. Consent is one kind of justification for deception. I consent to be deceived when I go to a magic show; thus, deception in this case is not immoral. Other forms of justification include public acceptance (e.g., for unmarked police cars) and the prevention of greater evil, coupled with the requirement that all of the people being deceived have failed to meet a moral requirement. One would be hard-pressed to justify deceiving a prospective or actual donor, whose basic act is one that is morally encouraged rather than required. For more analysis of deception, see Deni Elliott, "On Deceiving One's Source," *International Journal of Applied Philosophy* 6, no. 1 (summer 1991): 1–8; Deni Elliott and Charles Culver, "Defining and Analyzing Journalistic Deception," *Journal of Mass Media Ethics* 7, no. 2 (spring 1992): 69–84; and Deni Elliott, "What Counts as Deception in Higher Education Development," in Burlingame and Hulse, *Taking Fund Raising Seriously,* 73-82.
7. Bobbie Strand, "Prospect Research Is Spelled R-e-s-p-e-c-t," in Bobbie Strand and Susan Hunt, eds., *Prospect Research: A How-To Guide* (Washington, D.C.: CASE, 1986).
8. On psychological motivations for giving, see, for example, Ernest Dichter, "Why People Give," in *Some Aspects of Educational Fund Raising,* ed. Jean D. Lineham (Washington, D.C.: American Alumni Council, 1962), 45–49; and Kathleen Teltsch, "The Ultimate Gift," *New York Times,* Educational suppl., Apr. 10, 1988, 22–24. On economic motivations, see, for example, Lynn Gatozzi, "Charitable Contributions as a Condition of Probation for Convicted Corporations: Using Philanthropy to Combat Corporate Crime." *Case Western Reserve Law Review* 37 (1987): 569. And on social motivations, see, for example, Letty Cottin Pogrebin, "Contributing to the Cause," *New York Times Magazine,* Apr. 22, 1990, 22–24.

CHAPTER 51

A PRACTITIONER'S CODE OF ETHICS

ALBERT ANDERSON

When Aristotle talks about responsibility he makes a distinction between our professional, social, or cultural role, and our moral obligation. It is quite possible to play the role of fundraiser, grant-maker, or nonprofit volunteer well, and yet fail to think and act in an ethically responsible way. The ultimate aim is to consistently fuse these responsibilities together.

The distinction is particularly important for understanding codes of ethics, where the two kinds of responsibility meet. No doubt Aristotle would affirm the need and usefulness of codes for business, government, and the professions as we know them today. With the almost daily allegations of influence-peddling, cover-ups, and deception of Congress under oath, not to mention white collar fraud, conflicts of interest, and intrusion into privacy, there is good reason to have effective codes of conduct in public, private, and nonprofit sectors of society.[1] Like a vast network of limited social contracts, these codes are both implicit and explicit. They are central to the pluralistic, patchwork fabric of personal and organizational commitments that uniquely hold contemporary American society together.

CODES AND CONFLICTS OF INTEREST

In a narrow sense, the process of developing a code characterizes ethics itself, seen by some as the locus for conflict of values. The provisions of a code are general resolutions of potential areas of tension and conflict that are part of the organization's environment.

For this reason, codes typically give special attention to actual and potential conflicts of interest, which can be very subtle. In fact, former President Bush once made the development of a new code governing the conduct of public servants a national priority, and declared that "apparent" conflict of interest, a concern basic to government service as well as corporate behavior, should be its guiding principle. That is, a government servant should avoid any action that has even the *appearance* of being at odds with public or corporate policy.

However, to define ethics solely in terms of conflict of interest is too simplistic. It makes some people content with the "smell test"—the presumption that we are all equipped with the capacity to sense when something is not right. We can just feel it.

Ironically, the concern for apparently conflicting interests can itself be abused, turning as it does upon intentions. To note that a particular relationship poses an apparent conflict can be a positive, well-intended request to erase suspicion, or it may be a mischievous charge intended solely to create suspicion. "Full disclosure" of the party's personal, business, or political interests is a common antidote. But at best, disclosure functions as a preventive measure in advance of possible

Source: *Ethics for Fundraising,* 1996, Indiana University Press.

conflict. It does little to resolve a conflict ethically in a framework for decision-making. Like the code itself, an apparent conflict of interest is basically an invitation to do ethics.

A related and intriguing test is offered by Harlan Cleveland in *The Future Executive*.[2] "If this action is held up to public scrutiny, will I still feel that it is what I should have done, and how I should have done it?" A colloquial version of this principle was offered recently by a major nonprofit director, who urged nonprofits to draft policy that considers how it will play "on a 20-second news bite or in a four-inch newspaper column."

Cleveland's principle assumes that our intentions will be found out. "Information leaks;" so we might as well reveal it in the best possible light. However, we may recall Plato's legend of the Ring of Gyges, described in his *Republic*.[3] Suppose, according to the legend—a test of moral intentions in its own right—one had a magic ring enabling a person to become invisible, allowing one to do anything one pleased with impunity. Would there be any reason to refrain from unqualified self-interest? Actually there is, argues Socrates (Plato's dramatic agent). Even if we had this ring—and occasionally we think we do—it would be self-destructive to use it, harmful to the "soul;" the seat of character, the basis for well-being.

Without careful qualification, Cleveland's test is a mixed blessing. Public scrutiny of policy affairs generally assures openness, a cornerstone of American democracy, but the weight of public opinion in no way assures rightness. As a test of consistency with implicit or explicit public policy, it may be fine. As a principle of *ethical adequacy*, it borders closely on the principle of expediency, or, as the cynical saying goes, whatever is "politically correct."

By themselves codes offer little improvement, but they do have two important public benefits. In the first place, they guide us to identify, objectify, and verbally safeguard important interests or values of the individual, the organization, and others including the public at large—every person who has a stake in our purposes.

A second benefit is a code's potential for eliciting trust. Neither the individual nor the public at large can have complete confidence in an organization whose norms run aground on the Scylla and Charybdis of inconsistency and hypocrisy. The code is a public witness that the organization recognizes and seeks to honor the value of trust in its relationships.

Thus, a code of ethics can be a powerful organizational instrument. Even so, if Aristotle is right about the importance of differentiating professional and moral responsibilities, there is a certain mischievous seduction about having a code.

THE PROBLEM WITH CODES

Codes have the look, but not the weight of moral principle. Unless they are supported by what it means to think and act in an ethically responsible manner . . ., codes tempt one to substitute their normative provisions for the ethical character and principles that justify them. As a set of commitments or values shared by a group with a common purpose, a code represents the normative role we as professionals or volunteers are willing to assume in our relationships with all who are perceived to have a stake in the organization. A code is specifically written to reflect the organization's mission, and its moral intentions. However, by its very nature a code has two major shortcomings: first, as a standard of ethical conduct, it is *not self-justifying;* and second, as a guide to practical action, it is *not self-clarifying*.

For example, we do not assume that because the Mafia has a code, its norms are ethically self-evident. Despite their moral ring, norms proposing "honor among thieves," or absolute loyalty to "the company," or "my country right or wrong" are not necessarily justified. That will not happen until they are derived from more fundamental, generally durable and widely acknowledged principles of conduct, such as truth-telling, promise-keeping, respect for persons, and the like.

A recent study of white-collar crime, principally fraud, reveals how the unethical mind works.[4] Ranging from employees who pad their expense accounts to those who steal money by altering an organization's records, the fraudulently disposed are represented at every level of responsibility. Typically tempted by the prospect of enriching themselves with impunity at the expense of the organization, then moved by greed, they seize the opportunity. If found out and questioned about their dishonesty, according to one convicted executive, most deny their culpability with "a million excuses, ranging from, 'I did it to keep the business afloat' to, 'Hey, I'm not some violent criminal. I didn't hurt anybody.'" In fact, some try to justify it as only right and fair considering that their real value to the organization goes unrecognized! However, the executive insists, "[white collar criminals are the worst in the world] because they use their intelligence, education, status and trust (that others have in them) for their own benefit." The study also finds that the most frequently cited step (79 percent) that companies may take to reduce the possibility of fraud—an increasingly substantial expense—is to establish a corporate code of conduct.

Nonetheless, content with a few normative provisions, we expect too much of a code. Without the ethical awareness and reasoning that clarify and justify its norms, a code has little power despite our best intentions to effect right action.

HABITS OF AN ETHICAL ORGANIZATION

Code provisions are only generalizations, static but open-ended guides for organizing the dynamic and often complex day-to-day experiences that demand specific, moral actions. A code's provisions are not self-clarifying, short of the concrete situations that make them meaningful.

National organizations such as the Council for the Advancement and Support of Education (CASE) have long had codes governing their members. In fundraising alone, the profession has become so complex and technical as to warrant specialized codes for areas such as planned giving, prospect research, telemarketing and direct mail, as well as volunteer and board development. The codes of national organizations make excellent models of the standards common to the professions. However, they are no substitute for codes specifically developed in each organization. Indeed, a footnote to the CASE code says it is "intended to stimulate ethical awareness and discussion."[5] A code that is skeined but never woven strategically into the fabric of day-to-day experience is purely sentimental, a cedar chest item. Printed and distributed merely to elicit good

will, it borders on moralistic promotionalism. Unless the organization regularly reviews its standards in the light of experience, developing a code can be a substantial waste of time and talent, and a potential object of cynicism for those who have a stake in it.

Ideally, a code is *programmatic*, begging to be examined in the course of carrying out the organization's multiple objectives. Its utility and meaningfulness are embodied by example, by the cases we encounter in the trenches. As Michael O'Neill, director of the Institute for Nonprofit Organization Management, has put it, ethics is the business of nonprofits. It should be examined broadly and regularly by practitioners, not only when the occasional crisis arises.[6]

Thus, regular occasion to discuss current strategies with reference to the code serves to heighten ethical issues, exemplify the code's norms, and test them—together with organizational plans—for adequacy. There is no substitute for developing a code that is tempered by local fires.

ETHICAL LEADERSHIP

A code is only as effective as the corporate will and leadership behind it. The topic of ethics and leadership has been covered amply by other authors,[7] though we noted at the outset that Aristotle's *Nichomachean Ethics* may well set the ideal example for the philanthropic community. Indeed, we could make the case that the essence of leadership, at least in philanthropy if not elsewhere, is to be ethical. Or perhaps better stated: leaders are not by definition morally virtuous, but they ought to be.

A study once sought to define the connection between character development and leadership by noting what leaders conspicuous by their efforts to address human needs have in common.[8] The researcher found that such leaders are all competent, are committed to a worthy and transcendent mission, have a positive impact on their organization and community, care about human beings, and have the integrity, perseverance, and courage to stand up for their convictions (at times to their own jeopardy). But they can also laugh at themselves.

For every practitioner of philanthropy, there is a profound lesson in this: we cannot all assume conspicuous leadership positions, but we can all be ethical leaders in the roles we do assume. We can be models of character, whenever integrity and courage to do the right thing are at stake. Achieving corporate responsibility will be difficult if not impossible without strong leadership at the top. Ethical leadership cannot effectively be delegated or left to consultants.

THE ELEMENTS OF A CODE

Every code is unique, tailored to the organization's aims and stakeholders. However, codes also tend to have elements in common.

Typically, they:

- begin with a statement of *purpose* that implies or affirms a service for the public good;
- identify major *stakeholders*, and the responsibilities that are as assumed in relation to each;
- affirm good *citizenship*, upholding both the letter and the spirit of state and federal laws;
- proclaim a commitment to *ethical principles* that exceed compliance with the law ("obedience to the unenforceable");
- promulgate a governing *ethical concept*, a dominant theme or relationship such as trust, that is central to the organization's nature;
- identify—where necessary—*private and public interests* consistent with the organization's accountability and the acknowledged democratic rights of all; and,
- give special attention to the principal *conflicts of interest* that can arise in pursuit of objectives.

ABOUT CORPORATE RESPONSIBILITY

There are three common views of corporate responsibility, from which every organization can learn. They tend to define the ethical culture.

First, there is the view, consistent with classical capitalism, that a corporation's primary duty is to generate profit, without which jobs, family security, and taxes cannot be sustained. Corporations that compete fairly and openly,

managed in the best interests of the *shareholder*, economically benefit society. For the nonprofit cause this means above all satisfying the donor's expectations that contributions are used efficiently and effectively to further the organization's mission.

The second view, the *stakeholder* concept, recognizes a broader accountability to society. In addition to serving their owners, corporations have responsibilities to everyone who has a stake in the business, including the community. Indeed, as firms aid in solving the community's social problems, they not only help society prosper but are likely to themselves be more profitable. Similarly, the nonprofit finds it in its own best interests to be attentive to a constituency larger than its donors and the targeted recipients of its funds; the whole community has a stake in the organization's efforts.

Third, there is the view that society is best served when corporations—and nonprofits—are *regulated*, by the government or some authoritative body, to conform to the highest possible standards of personal and community life. Left to its own self-interests, a corporation or organization may well make up its own rules as it goes along, to the detriment of the greater good. Thus, a state's charities agency may set a limit on how much of a nonprofit's funds raised, should be spent on raising them.

Most corporate bodies tend to favor the stakeholder view, and hold that self-regulation, wherever it is effective, is better than government intervention. However, a corporation's social responsibility, often reflected in its code, is a separate and major topic, worthy of its own forum and outside the limits of this book. For example, a strong case can be made for a corporation that, while actively committed to socially worthy causes, sees its first responsibility to the shareholder. That view has been demonstrated compellingly in recent cases where the well-promoted programs of corporations to serve a popular public good entailed short-sighted management strategies that resulted in significant layoffs and loss of benefits to long-time employees, substantial losses to shareholders (many of whom were employees), and a diminished corporate image.[9]

Among outstanding examples of corporate stakeholder codes of ethics are those of American Can Company, Johnson & Johnson, and Levi Strauss & Co.[10] For example, in its opening section, "Our Shared Responsibilities;" American Can makes the commitment to serve its stakeholders—customers, suppliers, shareholders, employees, and community—by noting (with Aristotle) that it is not enough to meet performance goals. Employment at American Can also requires a clear understanding and embodiment of the company's ethical standards. The basic rules are: to obey all laws applying to the business; to go beyond the letter of the law to its spirit, based on experience and conscience; and to let rules of fairness and honor govern one's conduct at all times. The code then develops the theme of accountability—in business relationships, to employees, to society, and to the law—with helpful examples of acceptable and unacceptable conduct. Moreover, the code is intended "to create a continuing dialogue producing thoughtful and positive action, characterized by mutual respect and understanding." It is an excellent statement of a corporation's responsibilities to its various stakeholders.

Of similar quality, and often held up as a model for corporate conduct, the succinct Johnson & Johnson code or "credo" stands out for placing its customers and the community before its shareholders. It begins: "WE believe our first responsibility is to the doctors, nurses and patients, to mothers and all others who use our products and services." A few brief provisions later: "WE are responsible to our employees, the men and women who work with us throughout the world. EVERYONE must be considered as an individual. WE must respect their dignity and recognize their merit." The final section begins, "OUR final responsibility is to our stockholders. BUSINESS must make a sound profit." The code is also noteworthy for undergoing intense review on a regular basis, to insure that it is a living document, embraced by all employees, including management. While these company-wide discussions have led some over the years to resist the credo's character, the company has continued to affirm the principles virtually without change since 1975. The firm's handling of the famous Tylenol tragedy, when it took millions of dollars worth of the product off the shelves to develop a tamper-proof container and stop any further attempts by culprits to lace it with cyanide, is legendary. It demonstrated the integrity of the company and the efficacy of its code. Among the results, though presumably not the governing motives, were heightened good will and profitability.

Like Johnson & Johnson, Levi Strauss & Co. has consistently demonstrated its commitment to a code of ethical principles, notable for the provision on integrity: "We will live up to LS&CO's ethical principles; even when confronted by personal, professional and social risks, as well as economic pressures." The code also provides its own governing principle, suggesting that "the best test whether something is ethically correct is whether you would be prepared to present it to our senior management and board of directors as being consistent with our ethical traditions. If you have any uneasiness about an action you are about to take or which you see, you should discuss the action with your supervisor or management."

The code of ethics developed by Stanford University's Office of Development is one of the oldest and finest examples for nonprofit fundraisers in education.[11] Again, more a "credo" than a comprehensive code of ethical principles, it effectively sets forth the office's "mission and values" in seven succinct paragraphs covering: a mission that recognizes dual accountability, to donors as well as to the institution; a responsibility for donor privacy and gift confidentiality; integrity; teamwork; quality; enthusiasm (to be effective, one must be positive!); and initiative. The paragraph on integrity, the dominant ethical theme, is an eloquent series of practitioner commitments:

> We live up to both the spirit and letter of promises to donors. As staff members, we avoid conflicts of interest between our Stanford jobs and outside activities, both paid and voluntary. We do not exploit relationships with donors or volunteers for personal benefit. We utilize University facilities and property only for official business. We travel with a sense of fiscal responsibility. When in doubt about the compatibility of an action or expenditure with these values, we have a responsibility to disclose and discuss the situation with relevant [Office of Development] managers.

A GUIDE TO CODE DEVELOPMENT

A guide, designed mainly for an organization's development operations, may be helpful. It may be viewed as a modest complement and follow-up to the principles, examples, and "key ethical questions" found in the Independent Sector (IS) study and follow-up workbook.[12] In the best traditions of American philanthropy, they provide a rationale, a set of values, and a self-study instrument to encourage ethical behavior in all nonprofit organizations. However, their purpose falls short of providing the practitioner with a comprehensive program—the aim of this book—for more fully understanding ethical awareness and decision-making. Code or no code, one's stated values, including a code's provisions, will be most effective when regularly clarified by experience and supported by principle.

Nonetheless, the essential values or behaviors the IS committee believes should be common to all independent sector organizations are eminently worthy of being reflected in a nonprofit's code, and consistent with what follows. For convenience they are repeated here:

- commitment beyond self
- commitment beyond the law
- commitment to the public good
- respect for the value and dignity of individuals
- tolerance, diversity and social justice
- accountability to the public
- openness and honesty
- prudent application of resources
- obedience to the laws

The IS companion workbook asks a number of key questions for self-evaluation by the nonprofit under each of these behavior categories. The workbook will serve the nonprofit well as a systematic means to "audit" its ethical dispositions both prior to the development of a code and afterwards on a regular basis to maintain the code's efficacy. Noteworthy among the workbook's key questions are these: "Are all persons associated with the organization educated in the meaning and importance of the code and ethical conduct?"; and, "Can I articulate the organization's mission and recognize my own role in achieving that mission?". What the workbook will not do (and was not intended to do) is to resolve the ethical tensions that the practitioner faces from day to day.

The model code offered below assumes that the nonprofit's basic mission and case statements have been reviewed. The headings and sample provisions are conceptual pieces only, intended for vigorous, ongoing discussion. They represent some basic elements that should be considered in a code, with room for others that may be needed to reflect the organization's unique culture.

The provisions reflect the three major ethical principles or dominant spheres of influence, and their supporting principles:

RESPECT
  Autonomy (self-determination)
  Privacy
  Protection (concern for others)

BENEFICENCE
  Serving the good
  Charitable intent

TRUST
  Truth-telling
  Promise-keeping
  Accountability (stewardship)
  Fairness
  Fidelity of purpose (consistency)

Of course, the principles are themselves subject to each nonprofit's own discussions and sound—quite possibly better—ethical judgment. Here are some provisions to consider in the development of a code for nonprofit practitioners of philanthropy:

Purpose

  As responsible persons organized to advance and support [the organization's mission], our primary objective is to aid [name of the organization] in accomplishing its purposes by rightly soliciting the contributions and enduring good will of our constituents.

Stakeholder Relationships

  In partnership with the philanthropic community, we will maintain our professional and ethical relationships with donors whose gifts are entrusted to us; with volunteers on whose aid we depend; with staff who are accountable for their actions; and with the public whose well-being we serve.

Responsible Citizenship

As responsible citizens of this community and nation, we uphold both the letter and the spirit of the law, and all rights and privileges afforded by the law to every citizen.

Ethical Principles beyond the Law

We also acknowledge the propriety and self-enforcement of ethical principles and human rights that may exceed compliance with existing laws.

[Here, the organization may wish to add its list of principles or ethical values, including the primary principles and related ones such as autonomy, privacy, protection, serving the good, charitable intent, truthfulness, promise-keeping, accountability, fairness, fidelity of purpose, or others suggested in the provisions to follow.]

The remaining provisions focus on the organization's concerns and values. For example, every nonprofit development operation has a responsibility to protect the organization's nonprofit autonomy and the donor's privacy even as the public good is served. The key to striking this balance lies in clarifying the relationship between two kinds of trust—private and public—and the "need to know:" The latter idea is, in principle, vague until the lines we draw specify and help to justify what we mean.

Based on the primary ethical principle of *trust*, and specifically on its derivative, *promise-keeping*, the donor/prospect must have confidence in the nonprofit to solicit, handle, and direct contributions properly and as advertised. By an ethical requirement that goes beyond law, these functions represent the organization's *fiduciary* duty, that is, what it holds in both public and private trust. Thus, a nonprofit might introduce this topic in the following way:

Public and Private Trust

In a pluralistic, democratic society the nonprofit organization exists in a variety of forms to serve the charitable, educational, and social good of all.

[For the typical development operation.] As an integral part of [the organization] and thus dedicated to support its purposes, we have a preeminent fiduciary responsibility to all who provide charitable gifts and services on our behalf.

[Or, the fundraising foundation:] Though the [name of the foundation] exists solely to support [the organization], it has a fiduciary responsibility to all who provide charitable gifts and services on its behalf.

The individual has the ethical and (in the case of public employees) legal right to personal *privacy*, grounded in the primary principle of *respect*. The organization accords the individual confidentiality, to safeguard this right against intrusiveness into gift records and intimately personal information, except when the individual consents to disclosure.

However, we are also committed to a *public* trust. Public disclosure of the organization's financial and other data safeguards the public and the organization against conflicts of interest and the abuse and misuse of policies and funds. Arm's-length audits of the sources and uses of funds avoid mischievous allegations that, for example, "slush funds" exist for surreptitious purposes. A policy for proper disclosure is also a preventive measure: its absence may encourage unnecessary intrusiveness of another kind, namely, governmental regulation.

Thus, the following provisions may serve to take these factors into account:

As an American institution, (the organization) values autonomy sufficient to safeguard a proper division of organizational, private, and public interests. Thus, we recognize a dual responsibility for the trust in which both public and private interests hold us; that is:

We disclose all financial statements, governing policies, and plans of action that add to public understanding, appreciation and confidence in our objectives. However, we are equally concerned to guard against unwarranted interference and intrusiveness into private matters, particularly confidential information, such as a donor's gift history or personal life.

These provisions lead directly into the next section of the code, covering the organization's position on fundraising, based on the primary principle of *beneficence*. For example:

Fundraising

As [the organization] seeks to raise funds, it joins with private individuals, firms, foundations, and the public at large to (statement of mission), which benefits the community and therefore is worthy of its support.

To that end, we are scrupulous in our efforts to accomplish our donors' purposes, to prudently manage all funds, and to direct discretionary gifts to objectives that are open to public scrutiny.

The last provisions focus on the responsibilities of fundraising staff and on volunteer commitment. Increasing sophistication in the gathering and management of donor/prospect information makes it more important than ever to be up front about the care one takes to assure donor confidentiality, consent to disclosure, and enduring trust.

Thus:

Information Management

Whether represented by volunteers or professional staff, (the organization) seeks to assure its own integrity and that of others in the use and management of information.

We are thorough and discreet in the process of learning to know and engage all donors and prospective supporters, to earn their enduring support.

We do this with sensitivity and respect for individual and corporate dignity; and we hold confidential, save with the person's or organization's consent to disclose it, private or corporate information such as gift transactions, personal identity, and anecdotal knowledge, whether on or off the record.

Next, the conflict of interest provisions of the code will underscore again the importance of trust as the fundraiser's *modus operandi*, and may even specify the unethical character of conflicting or competing interests. In addition, given the rightful, but also extremely vulnerable position of the "whistle-blower" in organizational activity, the section should offer a provision to anticipate such cases.

Conflict of Interest

As persons employed or enlisted for our willingness, competence, and effectiveness in philanthropy, we are committed to integrity in all our relationships, and place the long-term best interests of [the organization], its constituents, and the profession before our own.

To avoid even the appearance of conflicting or competing interests, we make no agreements that could result in favoritism,

unfair advantage, or monetarily significant reward for ourselves or [the organization].

Concerns about any transaction or relationship that could embarrass (the organization), breach confidentiality, or violate conscience will be discussed with those to whom we are accountable, fairly and without fear of recrimination.

The final provisions of the code are the most personal of all. They affirm the individual staff member's or volunteer's readiness—as the classical ethicists enjoin—to embody character that is worthy of philanthropy. As I have stressed throughout the book, individual as well as organizational character are the wellsprings of ethical thought and action, whatever the governing framework for their justification. Particularly in the nonprofit sector, character is the personal and corporate good will behind the respect, beneficence, and trust we seek to develop.

This provision of the code should include a practitioner's conduct in the profession at large as well as in his/her own organization. Disrespect for the work of others, misrepresenting personal expense accounts, careless use of the organization's property, negligent security, and indifference to the need for professional improvement all exemplify inappropriate behavior that we may wish to cite specifically. The provision serves as a personal credo for staff and board members and other volunteers who work for the organization.

Personal Character

As individuals we are ethically responsible to ourselves and our profession for embodying character that is worthy of the best traditions of philanthropy. To that end we will compromise neither our personal convictions nor those of the organization and its constituents.

As professionals we treat our colleagues here and elsewhere with respect and properly credit others for ideas not our own. We use budgeted funds prudently, and account for them honestly We are careful with facilities and equipment, and safeguard the integrity of records and systems to which we have access. And, we acknowledge the value of constructive criticism, to evaluate and improve our performance against the profession's highest standards.

As the examples of effectively ethical organizations suggest, a code may be shorter and more succinct, or more extensive and explicit, than the model above. What is important is that it be tailored to the organization's character and environment, and that it express the essential norms that define one's practice of philanthropy.

Above all, . . . practitioners must learn how to think and act in an ethically responsible way, how to make principled decisions, and how to consistently embody and regularly examine their own organizational code of ethics.

THE CASE FOR DOING THE RIGHT THING

No one said that being ethical would be easy, least of all Aristotle. To him, it means to take responsibility, be accountable for our actions. Why should we? Because, as reason and experience teach us, there are limits beyond which it is unwise for human beings to go. If so, we must learn how and where to draw the line. What is more, by doing so we begin to build admirable, virtuous character, realize our potential, and experience the kind of well-being in life we all seek.

To Aristotle, taking responsibility for one's actions means not only being self-conscious agents and skillful role-players who do things right. It also means doing the right thing, above all in matters of justice and beneficence, the realm of morality. However, as he observed, doing the right thing has never been as predictable as following the rules of geometry. Deciding where to draw the line—the Golden Mean—between action that goes too far or not far enough is an art one develops with experience. Indeed, beneficence demands two artful, right-seeking actions: gaining wealth and distributing it. And, since one's governing motive is to enhance the public good, charitable intent is fundamental to ethical philanthropy.

Aristotle's view of philanthropy is the classical ideal. Still, the long-standing tradition of sharing one's resources with those who are without them—the alternative idealized by Jesus—is clearly more popular today in both its religious and secular forms. For over a million nonprofits in this country, philanthropy—understood as volunteer action for the common good—is efficacious and vital.

Ethical responsibility—or accountability—is both an individual and a corporate matter. The intersection of agency, role-playing, and action is corporately expressed by its culture and ideally by its code of ethical values and behaviors. The responsible firm or nonprofit embodies its code, committing its members both to keep the law of the land and to exceed it by employing the organization's moral norms. However, a code is impotent unless its practitioners know how to think and act in an ethically responsible way; that is, how to focus, frame, and justify their actions.

Ethics is basically a matter of principle. Both Aristotle and Jesus offer broadly governing principles such as the Golden Mean and the Golden Rule. But neither is adequate without qualification. Aristotle's Mean is so general as to leave completely relative what is right for each person in each situation. And Jesus' Rule, secularly applied, is ambiguously self-interested unless one provides a carefully developed notion of self-respect.

The first challenge in doing the right thing is to avoid expediency and radical individualism—to find principles governing action that are if possible always right for most if not all people. Knowing right from wrong does not begin in a vacuum. We regularly make moral judgments and opinions based on personal experience and values. Some look to conscience developed from childhood, or to rules and traditions reinforced by laws. Others say common sense requires simple respect for others, and many seem to believe that one is free to do as one pleases, as long as it does no harm.

Indeed, we often give such judgments and opinions obligatory force, with an ought or a should. But no moral opinion is better or more obligatory than any other in the absence of criteria by which to judge them. Thinking ethically, not merely being opinionated or comfortable with what is culturally permissible, is about clarifying and resolving differences, conflicting attitudes, competing tensions between what we claim or judge to be right and wrong. But it is also about doing it, not merely saying it.

In short, we need an ethical framework that is adequate for relieving the tensions involved in doing the right thing. Ethical adequacy requires:

1. *Clarity of thinking.* We must know the facts, understand one another, be open and reasonable if we hope to get at the ethical issue we must address.

2. *Self-examination.* We must honestly confront the human condition and its capacity for good and evil, because the efficacy of moral action depends on what we as human beings can truly accomplish.

3. *Acknowledgment that ethical relationships are based on trust.* In matters of philanthropy, trust is the moral culture in which we operate.

4. Durable principles. We need these to consistently clarify moral ambiguities and ward off hypocrisy, which we find intolerable.

5. *Moral judgments that are justifiable.* These are achieved by conformity to principles we commonly respect and ultimately by a governing outlook that grounds and guides all our action.

From a secular standpoint, two classical frameworks exemplify these conditions: the utilitarian framework inspired by Mill, and the duty-based framework developed by Kant. For the utilitarian—or consequentialist—view, an act is ethically worthy when its consequences or effects are more beneficial than harmful for most people, most of the time. Truth-telling, for example, is ethically worthy for that reason. For the duty-based—or imperativist—view, an act is ethically worthy, independent of consequences, when done for the sake of duty, as determined by what is universally appropriate and consistent with reason. Truth-telling is such a duty.

Although as competing views they are popularly simplified as beneficial consequences versus good intentions, both the classic frameworks and the moral tensions they address are more complex. While these frameworks seem inadequate to resolve all of life's dilemmas, either is generally adequate to ground principled action for practitioners, and may be adopted.

Even with good moral instincts, one develops the art of detecting moral tensions mainly from experience with cases typical of the profession, that is: (1) those affecting donors or prospects, such as misusing donor funds and information, intruding on donor privacy, exploiting donors to one's advantage, etc.; and (2) those affecting the organization, like compromising its interests, misusing property, charging inappropriately for services, mistreating the whistle-blower, etc. To address these cases and issues we generally require two kinds of decision-making: (a) drawing lines, often related to potential abuse; and (b) choosing between competing or conflicting courses of action both of which seem right.

However, we cannot do the right thing without knowing which action is right and how to justify it. To that end we need at least two, and ideally three additional instruments:

1. *A set of ethical principles.* The principles of greatest influence in philanthropy are respect, beneficence, and trust. They, in turn, imply principles such as confidentiality, service, accountability, fairness, truth-telling, fidelity, etc.

2. *A decision-making procedure.* Certain questions should be asked as a matter of routine: What seems right or wrong about this situation? What course of action seems best? What principles (and governing framework) would justify the action?

The ideal framework for principled action would include 3. *A code of ethics.* We need a public set of shared values and behaviors regularly clarified and justified by the experience of those who have a stake in the organization. Tailored to the mission and environment of the nonprofit's philanthropic work, the code will include explicit ethical positions relating to purpose, stakeholders, citizenship, ethical principles, public trust, fundraising, information, conflict of interest, and personal character.

In matters of philanthropy and everywhere, being accountable to ourselves and others means taking ethically principled action: doing the right thing.

NOTES

1. Two articles in the May 25, 1987 issue of *Time* document the ethical improprieties of top government and business leaders during the mid-1980s: "Morality among the Supply-

Siders," by Richard Stengel, reported by David Beckwith, 18–20, notes cases alleging serious ethics violations representing over 100 Reagan era officials. Stengel concludes: "one of the sad commentaries . . . is that so many of those tainted . . . still seem unable to divine what was wrong with their concept of government service"; also, "Having It All, Then Throwing It All Away," by Stephen Koepp, reported by Harry Kelly and Rajl Samghabadl, 22–23, describes a rash of white-collar crimes among high-level executives, including insider trading, money laundering, and greenmail motivated by greed combined with technology, and the pressure to perform.

2. Harlan Cleveland, *The Future Executive* (New York: Harper & Row, 1972), 104. Chapters 8 and 9 are excellent essays on the topic of moral leadership for public executives.

3. Many versions; for example *The Republic of Plato* trans. Francis M. Cornford (Oxford: Oxford University Press, 1945), chapter 5, p. 44F.

4. "Stealing from the Hand That Feeds You," by Ann Merrill, staff writer for the *Minneapolis Star Tribune*, October 3, 1994.

5. The code for the Council for the Advancement and Support of Education is available from the council's offices, 11 Dupont Circle, Suite 400, Washington, DC, 20036. See also CASE CAMPAIGN STANDARDS, available from CASE Publications Order Department.

6. Quoted by Kristin A. Goss in "Internal Misconduct Leads Nonprofits to Look to Their Missions to Resolve Ethical Questions," *TCP,* July 2, 1991.

7. In addition to Cleveland's books, see Robert Terry, *Authentic Leadership: Courage in Action* (San Francisco: Jossey-Bass, 1993). For a pertinent and perceptive analysis of the corporate grantmaking milieu and of the "styles" of leadership one finds in it, see the essay by James E. Shannon, a distinguished veteran of corporate philanthropy, "Successful Corporate Grantmaking: Lessons to Build On" in *The Corporate Contributions Handbook,* ed. James E Shannon (San Francisco: Jossey-Bass, 1991), 343–46 and in Resource C of the same, 374.f, an excerpt from independent Sector's "Profiles of Effective Corporate Giving Programs." Styles include: the loyal soldier, the skillful tactician, the change agent, the broker-advocate, and the technocrat.

8. See "Ethical Leadership" by George Shapiro, a professor at the University of Minnesota, in *Focus,* a publication of the University of Minnesota Office of Educational Development Programs, vol. IV, no. 1, Fall 1988.

9. A discussion of current views of corporate responsibility is presented by Jeremy Iggers,

"How Should Companies Behave?," in the *Minneapolis Star Tribune* for April 18, 1994. As an ongoing forum for discussing these issues, see *Business Ethics,* a first-rate magazine that has as its mission "to promote ethical business practices, to serve that growing community of professionals striving to live and work in responsible ways, and to create a financially healthy company in the process." Kenneth E. Goodpaster has written a very helpful essay, "The Concept of Corporate Responsibility," in *Just Business: New Essays in Business Ethics,* ed. Tom Regan (New York: Random, 1984). An article by John J. Oslund of the *Minneapolis Star Tribune* for May 19, 1994, "Chinese Puzzle: Minnesotan Has Idea for Dealing with Trade Dilemma: A Code of Conduct" notes a proposal by Robert MacGregor, president of the Minnesota Center for Corporate Responsibility, urging corporations that do business in China to adopt a code of conduct similar to the Sullivan Principles adopted by major firms such as 3M to ameliorate apartheid in South Africa. The proposed China code would allow ongoing business while making various efforts to address human rights issues; in general, international business should be characterized by fairness, honesty, respect for human dignity, and respect for the environment, applied to all stakeholders.

10. The Johnson & Johnson code is succinctly written as "Our Credo"; American Can Company's code is a well-developed manual; the Levi Strauss & Co.'s position is brief and to the point: six "Ethical Principles" and a "Code of Ethics" based on four "values. Robert Dunn, Strauss's foundation executive, has coauthored with Judith Babbitts the essay "Being Ethical and Accountable in the Grantmaking Process," *The Corporate Contributions Handbook.* For an in-depth examination of the philosophies, policies, and procedures of ten major corporations, including Johnson & Johnson, see *Corporate Ethics: A Prime Business Asset* (New York: Business Roundtable, 1988).

11. "Mission And Values: Stanford University Office of Development," Henry E. Riggs, vice president for development.

12. The manual, *Everyday Ethics,* ed. Sandra Trice Gray (Washington, DC: Independent Sector, 1993), offers nonprofit organizations a list of "key ethical questions" by which to measure themselves against the recommendations of the Independent Sector study. The questions quoted are from page 4, under the heading "Commitment Beyond the Law."

CHAPTER 52

TOWARD EMPIRICAL STUDIES ON UNIVERSITY ETHICS

A New Role for Institutional Research

JAMES STEVE COUNELIS

August 28, 1991

> . . . the apologists for any means to achieve desired ends forget that the separation of "means" and "ends" is merely a verbal convenience. They forget that the means they employ are *included* in the ends.
>
> Anatole Rapoport,
> *Science and the Goals of Man*, 1950

PART 1: INTRODUCTION

On the Ethical Study of the University

The American university has a long history of concern for ethical matters.[1] Currently, the American Association of University Professors and the Association of Governing Boards of Universities and Colleges establish standards on the ethical governance of the university. Further, the regional and professional accrediting associations, together with the collective bargaining agreement, are other vehicles that affect the university's moral governance [39, 93, 94, 99, 101]. However, powerful and pervasive external influences affect university governance, especially economic and governmental power.

In the last thirty years or so, the ethos and argot of the business world have taken over the university. "Markets" are sought. "Contributions to margin" become goals. "Cost/benefit analysis" is used in deciding to drop a small-enrollment classical language department or in retaining a costly laboratory science curriculum. Students become customers. The faculty become employees excluded from the economic decisions relative to the curriculum. An economic engine, the university produces new and retrained employees, new arts, new sciences, and new technologies and provides packaged services for business, church, community, education, and government. Without doubt, the regional and professional accrediting associations act in the public interest protecting students and their parents as consumers [99, chap. 12 and p. 447]. Importantly, the accrediting associations serve as an important countervalent that sets governing standards for university boards of trustees, including the sheltering of their academic communities from attacks upon institutional autonomy and academic freedom [cf. 93, pp. 15–24; 99 pp. 442–48.].

Source: *Journal of Higher Education*, Vol. 64, No. 1 (January/February 1993). © 1993 by the Ohio State University Press.

The university's missions and goals no longer seem tied as imperatives to educational practice. With the exception of the university president, no one appears accountable for the cultivation and maintenance of institutional direction [67]. Like the American corporation, the university's broad dispersion of responsibility contributes to the university-wide practice of no one being specifically held accountable. If an institution's mission and goals become inapplicable, new general statements are drawn up, again without agential assignment of responsibility [cf. 26, 89].

One reads in *The Chronicle of Higher Education* and the daily press about administrative fraud, the scientific investigator who "fudges" data, faculty and student plagiarism, student cheating on tests, the "commercial production" of undergraduate term papers and their purchase by students, sexual harassment of students and staff, student athletes' use of drugs to enhance strength and stamina in athletic competition, and the "booster club's" corruption of student athletes. Of course, student activism is a perennial source of ethical controversy. What about recent revelations of dubious university accounting practices [cf. 67]? Such a continuing stream of disturbing reports sent me to seek empirical studies on the moral behavior of those who comprise the American university community.

No empirical studies on the university's moral deportment were found in reviewing bibliographies that concentrated on the professional higher education literature since the 1950s, though one bibliography on the university presidency began with literature since 1900 [28, 29, 30, 44, 63, 96]. Two encyclopedic works on higher education yielded no citations of empirical studies on ethical behavior in American higher education [49, 56]. At roughly ten-year intervals, Lunsford in 1963, Peterson in 1974, and Bess in 1984, provided status summaries of social science research on organizational behavior for American universities [10, 59, 76]. But these reviews yielded no moral behavioral studies on institutional and personnel matters in higher education. Further, the 1980 Jademus and Peterson institutional research volume, *Improving Academic Management*, did not mention the ethical dimensions of the university in administration, decision making, or planning [50], and

Muffo and McLaughlin, writing in 1987 for the Association for Institutional Research, did not refer to ethical studies on the university [68]. Taylor in the 1987 OECD publication, *Universities under Scrutiny*, also did not discuss moral behavior within the universities in OECD member states [88].

A computer search for empirical studies on the moral behaviors of university boards of trustees, their administrators, and faculty was without result. I found only personal testimonies and lamentations, a few surveys of administrator opinions, and philosophical disquisitions by former presidents and deans. This computer search did yield many social and psychological studies on college students, especially on academic deceit and sexual harassment. Generally, university faculties in education, psychology, and sociology have had ready access to "powerless" undergraduates, which accounts for the numerous student studies. One such study was Feldman and Newcomb's large scale 1967 study of undergraduates [cf. 1, 33].

I reviewed the Fall 1980-Summer 1991 issues of *Higher Education Abstracts* [46]. Under the index descriptor "ethics," there were fifty-two abstracts. Some forty-three abstracts (83 percent) were of non-empirical papers. The remaining nine abstracts (17 percent) were on studies having empirical data. Five studies were on the instruction of ethics; and four were about administrative matters. In an AIR conference paper from this set, R. G. Rodriguez and R. F. Agrella advocated a professional code of ethics for institutional research professionals [78].

The AAUP's cases of censured institutions (which do not appear to have been studied as a set) are well known.[2] One was the celebrated loyalty oath case at the University of California-Berkeley [37]. Since 1987, the well-publicized academic freedom case of the religious ethicist, the Reverend Charles E. Curran, S. J., at Catholic University of America is found. The Curran case was a continuation of some aspects of an earlier Catholic University case [47]. Both cases reflect the significant conjoined issues of liberty and order within a secular state and a religiously defined university community [3; 4, 25, part 3]. *The Chronicle of Higher Education, The New York Times, America,* and Fr. Curran extensively recorded his story [14; 15; 23; 24; 25, part 5; 35; 55; 70, 77].

Two higher education readers provided some empirical insights into the cognitive and moral development of undergraduates during collegiate matriculation. In 1962, Nevitt Sanford's *The American College* contained two studies of continuing interest, namely, George G. Stern's "Environments for Learning" and Christopher S. Jencks and David Riesman's "Patterns of Residential Education: A Case Study of Harvard"[51, 80, 85]. Christian Bay suggested studies be done on the undergraduates' educational processes that would include "the universalism of moral judgment" [7, pp. 993–94]. In 1973, Ellison and Simon [31] reviewed Chickering's 1967 "ideal" model of collegiate change. They noted the normative character of this model, which obviously did not account for various forms of academic cheating, the drug scene, the development of the counterculture movement, or increased religiosity, be it Eastern meditation or Christian fundamentalism. Under the topic of "persistence" of college students, Ellison and Simon noted that certain aspects of personal behavior had not been studied, such as, "Machiavellian skills," competitive skills in both acceptable and "cutthroat" forms, the capacity to exploit intellectual style and intellectual jargon to deceive or be deceived, and the skills of relating to persons from diverse backgrounds [26]. In the 1981 Chickering reader, *The Modern American College,* Bay's suggestion was partially reflected in the papers of Carol Gilligan and William G. Perry on the college students' stages of moral development [13, 41, 75]. Nucci and Pascarella reviewed the research literature on college influence on moral development. This 1983 review provided extensive evidence on the intellectual effects of collegiate education upon moral reasoning; however, no work had determined the behavioral results of that sophisticated reasoning [71]. However by 1987, Fritz K. Oser wrote in the third edition of the *Handbook of Research in Teaching* that, "there is no integrative and highly differentiated model of values and moral learning, despite a great interest in moral education" [72, p. 917].

For the American university, Parsons and Platt provide a detailed higher education extrapolation of Parson's social system concept in which there is a systemic place for morals in society's cultural institutions, in eluding the university [74]. Within this framework, one can place Burton R. Clark who has cross-nationally studied higher education systems. A holistic conceptualization of these studies led him to present an abstracted "normative theory," consisting of "basic values" (that is, justice, competence, liberty, and loyalty) and "institutional preferences" (that is, division of power, support of variety, legitimation of disorder, and the uniqueness of higher education). Clark reported on these normative habits and their relations to national societies [16, chaps. 7–8].

In addition, I have written two meta-ethical essays. The first is a 1977 general systems study, titled, "The Open Systems University," in which I outline the notion of organizational intelligence—an institutional epistemology—together with the internal valuational/ethical calculus used in the university—an operational axiology [19, pp. 153–69]. The second essay is a 1990 study, titled, "The Ethical Management of the University." In this second article, I present several meta-ethical aspects of university administration, a hierarchical set of generic sources for ethical principles, and university leadership as positive moral action [22, pp. 43–59]. A comprehensive anthological source can be found for many ethical aspects of American higher education in May's 1990 volume, *Ethics and Higher Education.* [61].

Studies on Ethics and Moral Behavior

Given this paucity of systematic and systemic empirical research on American university ethics, what is the general range of disciplinary studies on ethics and moral behavior? To date, there are four research approaches to the study of ethics and moral behavior. The first mode of inquiry is that of ethology or behaviorism when external observations are made of people. This inquiry approach is illustrated by Howard S. Becker and his colleagues in their participant observer study of student culture in a medical school. This study is their 1961 *Boys in White* [8]. The second approach is the systematic study and reflection upon moral behavior, as it is practiced by psychology and introspective commonsense, for example. Sigmund Freud's concept of the superego and Albert Bandura's cybernetic social learning theory come to mind [5; 36, chap. 3]. The third method of study is that of biology, sociology, and anthropology, wherein moral behavior is related to the environment—cultural, economic, natural, political, and social. At the macrosocietal level, Clifford Geertz's anthropological work on the relation of *Weltanschauungen*, religions and ideologies to culture represents this third class of study [38]. At the microsocial level of the person, Henry A. Murray's concept of the beta press—the psychological relationship of the proximate environment to the person—exhibits the same research approach [69]. These first three inquiry approaches to ethics are labeled *positive* scientific approaches. Their concerns are for the facts "about" moral behavior. However the fourth mode of inquiry is called *normative science* (or *meta-ethics*), that is, the formal and casuistic study on ethical reasoning, moral values, virtue and virtues, duties and obligations, prudential judgments and the moral quality of their consequences, along with the practical "oughts" of behaving [cf. 27, pp. 8–10; 40; 52; 53; 54; 83; 97].

As a result of this search, I have come to believe that universities ought to be studied as empirical ethical systems, describing their methods in ethical reasoning and consequent patterns of moral behavior. Case studies (in particular, ethnographic field descriptions and participant observer reports) are needed on the university community-in-action. Many case studies on the everyday moral acts of university boards of trustees, academic leaders, faculty, staff, and students are required to construct valid and reliable propositions. Such empirical propositions are necessary for developing policies on ethical behavior. Case studies, moreover, would provide grist for the task of meta-ethical discourse. Competent decision making and the right behavior of American institutions of higher education are dependent upon the quality and reasoned command of the meta-ethical underpinnings to behavior and decision making, whether undertaken by institution or person.

When a writer selectively presented and summarized empirical data on the ethical behavior of American business, I took special note to see what useful ethical lessons could be learned from corporate America. This small volume is Mathews' *Strategic Intervention in Organizations: Resolving Ethical Dilemmas* [60].

PART 2: THE EMPIRICAL STUDY OF AMERICAN CORPORATE ETHICS

Starting Point

In the preface of *Strategic Interventions in Organizations*, M. Cash Mathews wrote the following:

> The overall focus of the book is to provide guidelines and provoke discussion—discussion that is necessary to overcome the increasing tensions between the public and the business world. Only through such examination, debate, and action will we be able to avoid the spiraling effects that can result, not only in the imposition of harsh sanctions upon corporations and corporate executives, but may also ultimately threaten our economic system [60, p. 5].

The purposes of this book are thus pragmatic and therapeutic, the first purpose being appropriate and the second laudable. Chapters 1 and 2 contain brief descriptive discussions on ethics. The normative treatment of corporate ethics *per se* is apparently not a concern of the author. Mathews' chapters 2–8 reflect a mix of studies that use the first three methods of studying ethics. In chapter 9 and scattered elsewhere through the volume, Mathews' ethical concerns are with the pragmatics of alerting corporate leadership and altering unethical and illegal corporate behaviors [cf. 40, chap. 2; 52; 53; 92, pp. 115–18; 97, pp. 757–58].

Empirical Data

Mathews' chapters 3–8 contain descriptive social scientific facts on ethical behavior in America's corporate world. Generally, these empirical chapters are well written. She briefly outlines current social science research on such matters as criminality and corporate culture, social learning theory,[3] the contents and effects of ethical codes on corporate behavior, "whistle-blowing" within the corporation, the corporate response to victimization, together with corporate and managerial liability. For brevity, these empirical facts are summarized in the following seven propositions:

1. Corporate cultures that foster ethical and legal behavior use trust, concern for the individual, and positive reinforce-

ment of "prosocial" behavioral patterns [60, p. 39].

2. Criminal behavior patterns within corporations that have been learned can be unlearned, and new law-abiding behaviors can be learned and substituted by using differential reinforcement contingencies [60, p. 45].

3. The content analysis of the codes of conduct revealed that corporations are more concerned with acts against the firm or specific illegal activity—such as bribery—on behalf of the firm *than* with product safety and quality, environmental affairs, and other issues directly related to consumers [author's italics: 60, p. 61].

4. There is little relationship between corporate codes of conduct and corporate violations, contrary to the expectation that the codes serve as an effective form of self-regulation [60, p. 76].

5. Corporate self-protection against victimization increases the use of quasi-criminal justice apparatus within the corporation, through monitoring: (a) for conflict-of-interest behavior of employees; (b) for divulging of trade secrets and proprietary information; (c) for insider trading; (d) by lie detector testing; (e) by drug testing; (f) for alcoholism [60, chap. 6].

6. Whistle-blowing is defined as deviant behavior within the corporate organization; but it is defined as a conforming behavior by society. Corporate retaliation against whistle-blowers is counterproductive of trust and effective communication within the corporate organization [60, chap. 7].

7. The legal and social environment of business is continually changing and public discontent with the corporate world is clearly on the rise again. Unless corporate policy and decision-makers can convince consumers and the general public of the ability of corporations to police their own (e.g., self-regulation, law-abiding corporate cultures), the calls for increasing levels of deterrence will continue [60, p. 125].

Mathews clearly recognizes the practical complexity of moral issues in American corporate life. She also correctly asserts that society relies on two methods to insure compliance with legal and ethical standards, namely, sanctions and the internatization of norms. Mathews' interventions rely on scientific principles for modifying social behavior within organizations, hopefully, with newly internalized ethical standards.[4]

Interventions

Recognizing that business leaders must desire to foster a corporate culture in which illegal and unethical behavior is "unthinkable," Mathews suggests a long-term, two-prong intervention. The first prong is devising, instituting and maintaining certain structural changes. The second prong is the design, utilization and evaluation of contingency reinforcements that foster "prosocial" behavior.[5] There is no doubt that intervention effectiveness requires sustained effort. School effectiveness research has shown long ago that the most effective schools were a direct function of the sustained and consistent curricular leadership of the same school principal.

The recommended structural change would be the creation of an ethics committee with authority to inquire into all aspects of corporate operations. Additionally, the committee would establish ethical standards for behavior and provide for ethics workshops throughout the year. The committee's composition would include personnel from all significant levels of management. Other professionals within the organization—scientists, financial analysts, information specialists, legal experts, personnel specialists—would also be included. An outside professional ethicist is recommended, thereby supporting within the corporation the committee's credibility, efficacy, and impartiality.

Employees would be able to consult the committee about possible unethical or illegal activity or requests that appear questionable. Mathews believes that retaliatory measures against the employee would greatly diminish. Employees' concerns would be addressed, policies clarified, and investigations undertaken. Specific positive reinforcements would be designed to reward employees whose concerns over legal and moral actions supported the corporation's culture. In addition to resolving employee concerns, the committee would meet monthly to discuss general ethical strategy that would assist corporate planning [60, pp. 136–37]. And not the least, Mathews recommends a company newsletter and topical weekly handbills that would be posted on prominent bulletin boards [60, pp. 139–41].

Mathews emphasizes that a workable code of ethics should be written. The basic elements in her corporate code of ethics are to stress: (a) the concept of senior executives as role models; (b) the importance of the corporation's reputation; (c) legal and moral behavior as imperatives because it is unthinkable to behave otherwise; (d) social responsibility to clients, consumers, and the general public; (e) the significance of employer; employee trust in all aspects of the corporation's culture. The author makes specific suggestions on the writing of such ethics codes. An important general principle is the listing of ethical and unethical behaviors, both sets being clearly defined [60, pp. 138–39].

Without doubt, Mathews believes the success of her interventions depends upon sustained effort and vigorous support by corporate executives. However, Mathews' interventions, apparently, are untested. Hence, no practical experience for guidance is available. I believe, nonetheless, the university can learn much of ethical import from Mathews' brief volume.

PART 3: AN ETHICS TUTORIAL FOR THE UNIVERSITY

Lessons

Mathews' first lesson for the university is the need and utility for empirical research on the systemic moral behavior of university's community members: (a) the trustees: (b) the president and executive suite; (c) middle-level administrators and their staffs; (d) the ombudsperson; (e) faculty; (f) students and alumni. Intrainstitutional case studies (especially, ethnographic field descriptions and participant observer reports) and cross-institutional inquiries are necessary [cf. 2; 17; cf. 30; 34; cf. 42; cf. 44; cf. 45; cf. 79; 88; 87; 98]. The character and range of the moral behavior exhibited by community members of the university require description. Further, "categorical densities of

ethical and unethical behaviors" need to be estimated. The most troublesome areas of moral behavior can, thus, be mapped for institutional treatment. In response, ethical behavioral patterns become appropriate and robust niches for initiating institutional changes in organizational and individual behaviors.

Are any of Mathews' empirical findings applicable to the university? Yes! Several findings analogically appear to be true. Collectively, this second lesson consists of three such empirical findings.

One empirical finding is Mathews' first proposition, namely: Corporate cultures that foster ethical and legal behavior use trust, concern with the individual, and positive reinforcement of "prosocial" behavior patterns [60, p. 39]. The same is true for the university because human relations research since the 1930s has documented this proposition many times in different settings, including the university [48, 65, 94].

The second empirical finding is Mathews' seventh proposition, namely: Public discontent with business is noted to be on the rise, again, with increased pressure for public deterrence [60, chap. 8]. Higher education has already experienced this identical situation in a number of arenas. Review the following examples: (a) governmental scrutiny of university grants and contracts through financial audits with repayment entailments; (b) the protection of human subjects in scientific research; (c) post-degree guild/state certification of professional school graduates (that is, bar examinations, medical and dental licensing, CPA examinations); (d) state licensing of public school professionals—teachers, counselors, administrators: state-approved university programs and state defined professional standards; (e) anti-discrimination and affirmative action legislation; (f) the qualitative evaluation of higher education by the accreditation agencies. Indeed as of August 1991, some twenty states require public universities and colleges to set up programs to assess student learning in college [15]. Significantly, federal authorities are currently investigating two ethical problems in higher education: (a) conflicts-of-interest within the university; (b) tuition price-fixing and admissions practice among several elite undergraduate institutions. However, a question remains. What has American higher education collectively learned from the experiences of these examples? Obviously, these institutionalized practices are testimony about university morals that apparently require systematic surveillance if not episodic rule enforcement. New ethical patterns can be institutionally learned through positive reinforcement. Mathews' second proposition is the last of the three empirical findings. Derived from social learning theory, the shaping of organizational interventions for reinforcement of institutional and personal moral behavior is both possible and appropriate.[6] The university's will to learn this lesson itself requires buttressing by continual reinforcement!

Constructing University Interventions

I believe that a university's mission and goal statements ought to be written as standards with assigned agents being held accountable for their specific implementation. Continuing rather than episodic oversight would then be internally provided. Hence, Mathews' written code of ethics can be converted to the university's use.

An example is found in my 1986 University of Vienna paper on expert systems design for ethical organizational administration [21]. I presented several ethical behavioral standards for university trustees, administration, faculty, and students. Review the following:

1. The University has as its basic policy goal the building and continuance of a community life style, reflecting a selfless dedication to an education for personal growth and institutional development through university governance, teaching, research and service.

2. The University is motivated institutionally to conform the external actions of its board of trustees, administration and staff, faculty, students, and alumni in an informing harmony with their natural interior psychological dispositions for the humane and the right.

3. The University has a fundamental policy to pursue ethical ends only through moral means in all governance, administration, instruction, learning, and research, having special concern for the liberty, rights, dignity, and integrity of

all persons who comprise the university and its wider community.

4. The University has a fundamental policy of academic freedom for faculty, librarians, and students to pursue the true, the right, the moral, and the beautiful as the University's contribution to the society [21, pp. 162–63].

Explicit ethical behavioral standards can assist in raising the moral quality of institutional decision making and personal deportment within the university community. Such policy statements would become the expected and accountable (and hopefully internalized) behavior. Though constructed differently than Mathews' ethical code for corporate business, my example of university behavioral standards implicitly reflects several of Mathews' principles, namely, (a) institutional reputation; (b) the high expectation for ethical and legal behavior; (c) institutional responsibility to clients, consumers, and the public; (d) internalized trust [cf. 22].

Mathews' research documents that ethical codes do not guarantee moral behavior within businesses [60, chaps. 4–5]. Probably, this would be true for the university. Nonetheless, the traditional university ethos has certain reinforcing norms that set an ethical standard [4; 11; 12; 16, chaps. 3 and 7; 18, chap. 5; 19; cf. 25, part 3; 66, chaps. 5–6; 81]. These several norms are: (a) institutional autonomy; (b) the collegiality of faculty decision making; (c) *Lernfreiheit*; (d) *Lehrfreiheit*; (e) the moral imperative of truth; (f) the civility of discourse; (g) tolerance for differing opinion; (h) equity of access to higher education for current students and faculty; and (i) equity in evaluation of trustees, administrative and professional services, faculty competence for promotion in professional ranks and student learning. Indeed these pervasive academic norms are analogous to some elements in Mathews' first empirical proposition, namely: Corporate cultures that foster ethical and legal behavior use trust, concern for the individual, and positive reinforcement of "prosocial" behavioral patterns [cf. 4; 32; 73, pp. 104–12, 163–67 and chap. 8]. Egregious wrongs reach intra-institutional review boards, ombudspersons, union contract grievance procedures, arbitration processes or litigation. These are appropriate means to redress grievances and correct personal and institutional errors.

A second useful intervention from Mathews would be the university ethics committee. Separately, federal law requires a human subjects research committee to review and evaluate all research proposals that require human subject interventions. Perhaps the ombudsperson would head the all-university ethics committee, composed of trustees, administrators and staff from all levels, faculty and students. The jurisdiction of this committee would need to be broadly defined with authority to pursue any investigation within the university. The committee would report directly to the board of trustees through the committee's chairperson.

General systems theory asserts that studies on isomorphic epistemic structures—models, laws, and concepts—across disciplines provide both a unifying meta-theory and heuristic insights on a given set of cross-disciplinary ideas [86, pp. 20–34]. Therefore, it is reasonable to note that the American university and America's corporate business use analogous organizational information, employ a number of similar operating principles, and possess kindred concerns over right behavior. Mathews' book on American business ethics contains analogous insights for higher education leaders. With differing biographies and varying institutional circumstances, university and business leaders could find similar lessons in Mathews' brief volume.

A New Institutional Research Role

The absence of empirical data about a university's ethical behavior is a serious institutional deficit. Through creative institutional research, two new goals with ethical import for the university can be addressed vigorously. The first new goal for institutional research is to provide the solid science on the university's internal and external ethical behavior. Using such information, a university can fashion appropriate policies and design intra-institutional interventions to attain informed moral guidance. The second new institutional research goal would be to provide the casuistic (that is, case-based) grist for the university's internal meta-ethical discourse. This discourse would have the purpose to delineate those axiologically informed epistemic principles required for competent university decision making and provide appropriate ethical principles for guiding organizational and individual behavior [cf. 62].

Such institutional research and meta-ethical discourse would be conducted within the general purposes established in the Preamble of the federal *Constitution* [cf. 18]. University life is especially informed by the nation's general welfare clause, which entails America's historic academic ethos and traditions. Holistically, these constitute the American university's fundamental values, derived from its broader American *Weltanschauung*[7] [18, chap. 5; 20]. Matching these values with appropriate actions, the American university can reduce if not eliminate many of its moral tensions through solid science, the civility of ethically informed discourse, and through a willed integrity to pursue its nationally construed commonweal. The university's commonweal and a new institutional research role in the study of the university's moral behavior are, therefore, entwined.

NOTES

1. For this article, the word "university" is used as a collective term for undergraduate, graduate, and professional degree institutions of American higher education.

2. For two studies with empirical data on AAUP cases, see the 1978 Metzger doctoral dissertation [64] and Slaughter's 1981 essay [82]. Metzger's work is about the 1915–1956 cases: Slaughter's essay has gross data on 1970–1980 cases. Slaughter provides a set of reasons why there cannot be reasonable approximations on the number of academic freedom cases that have arisen since 1915 when the *General Report on Academic Freedom and Academic Tenure* was written by Arthur O. Lovejoy (Johns Hopkins University). E. R. A. Seligman, and John Dewey (Columbia University) together with others for the newly established American Association of University Professors.

3. For an encyclopedic summary and current research bibliographies on human development and education, see, R. Murray Thomas's 1990 volume, *The Encyclopedia of Human Development and Education: Theory, Research, and Studies* [81]. In this volume, see summary articles on social learning theory and prosocial behavior that inform Mathews' approaches for changing the moral character of American corporate behavior: (a) R. Murray Thomas, "Social Learning Theory" [83, pp. 75–78]; (b) D. Bar-Ial. "Prosocial Behavior"[6. pp. 427–31]. For the literature on moral development and moral education, see: K. Bergling. [83, pp. 423–27: (b) Leming [57, 58].

4. Ibid.
5. Ibid.
6. Ibid.
7. For the American world view, comprehensively but succinctly outlined, see: "Chart No. 1. American World View Principles and Data" [20. pp. 255–56].

REFERENCES

1. Altbach, P. G. & D. H. Kelly. (1973). *American students: A selected bibliography on student activism and related topics.* Lexington, Mass.: Lexington Books/D. C. Heath & Company, 1973.
2. Anderson, G. L. (Fall 1989). Critical ethnography in education: Origins, current status, and new directions. *Review of Educational Research*, 59, 249–70.
3. Andrews, J. L., et al. (Spring 1987). "Recent development: Church licensed professors—The Curran controversy." *Journal of college and university law*, 13, 375–95.
4. Annarelli, J. J. (1987). *Academic freedom and catholic higher education.* New York: Greenwood Press.
5. Bandura, A. (1977). *Social Learning Theory.* Englewood Cliffs, N. J.: Prentice-Hall.
6. Bar-Tel, D. (1990). Prosocial behavior." In R. M. Thomas (Ed.), *The encyclopedia of human development and education: Theory, research, studies*, pp. 427–31. Oxford, UK: Pergamon Press.
7. Bay, C. (1962). A social theory of intellectual development." In N. Sanford (Ed.), *The American college: A psychological and social interpretation of the higher learning*, chap. 28. New York: John Wiley & Sons, Inc.
8. Becker, H. S., et al. (1961). *Boys in white.* Chicago: The University of Chicago Press.
9. Bergling, K. (1990). "Moral development." In R. M. Thomas (Ed.), *The Encyclopedia of human development and education: Theory, research, and studies.* Oxford. UK: Pergamon Press.
10. Bess, James L. (Ed.). (1984). *College and university organization: Insights from the behavioral sciences.* New York: New York University Press.
11. Braxton, J. M. (1986). "The normative structure of science: Social control in the academic profession." In J. C. Smart (Ed.), *Higher Education: Handbook of Theory and Research*, vol. 2. New York: Agathon Press.
12. Brubacher, J. S. (1982). *On the philosophy of higher education.* San Francisco: Jossey-Bass, Inc.
13. Chickering, A. W., et al. (1981). *The modern American college.* San Francisco: Jossey-Bass, Inc.
14. *The Chronicle of higher education*, 8 March 1989, pp. 13A, 17A; 15 March 1989, pp. 13A, 18A.
15. *The Chronicle of higher education*, 28 August 1991, p. 10.
16. Clark, B. R. (1983). *The higher education system: Academic organization in cross-national perspec-*tive. Berkeley: The University of California Press.
17. Constans, M. A. (Summer 1992). "Qualitative analysis as a public event: The documentation of category development procedures." *American educational research journal*, 29, 253–66.
18. Counelis, J. S. (1961). "American government, higher education and the bar." Ph. D. dissertation, The University of Chicago, 1961.
19. _____. (1977). "The open systems university." In J. Rose & C. Bilciu (Eds.), *Modern Trends in Cybernetics and Systems*, vol. 1, pp. 153–69. Berlin: Springer-Verlag.
20. _____. (1980). "Cross-cultural education and an aristotelian model of *Weltanschauung.*" In R. V. Padilla (Ed.), *Ethnoperspectives in bilingual education research: Theory in bilingual education*, vol. 2, pp. 250–60. Ypsilanti, Mich.: Eastern University/Department of Foreign Languages and Bilingual Education.
21. _____. (1986). "On a generic process of modeling an expert system for ethical organizational administration." *Cybernetics and systems: An international journal*, 16, 151–67.
22. _____. 1990. "The ethical management of the university." In J. S. Counelis (Ed.), *Higher learning and orthodox christianity*, pp. 43–59, London/ Scranton: Associated University Presses/University of Scranton Press.
23. Curran, C. E. (1986). *Faithful dissert.* Kansas City, MO: Sheed & Ward.
24. _____. (25 April 1987). "A teaching moment continues." *America* 156, 336–40.
25. Curran. C. E. & R. A. McCormick, S. J. (Eds.). (1988). *Readings in moral theology, No. 6: Dissent in the church.* New York: Paulist Press.
26. Davies, G. K. (1986). "The importance of being general: Philosophy, politics, and institutional mission statements." In J. C. Smart (Ed.), *Higher Education: Handbook of theory and research*, vol. 1. New York: Agathon Press.
27. Edel, A. (1961). *Science and the structure of ethics.* In O. Neurath (Ed.), *International encyclopedia of unified science*, vol. 2, no. 3. Chicago: The University of Chicago Press.
28. Eells, W. C., & E. V. Hollis. (1960). *Administration of higher education: An annotated bibliography.* OE–53002/Bulletin No. 7; Washington, DC.: U. S. Department of Health, Education, and Welfare.
29. _____. (1961). *The college presidency, 1900–1960: An annotated bibliography.* OE-53008 Bulletin No. 9; Washington, D. C.: U. S. Department of Health, Education, and Welfare.
30. Ellis, J. M. (1989). *Against Deconstruction.* Princeton, N. J.: Princeton University Press.
31. Ellison, A., & B. Simon, (1973). "Does college make a person healthy and wise?" In L. C. Solmon & P. J. Taubman (Eds.), *Does College Matter?—Some evidence on the impacts of higher education*, pp. 35–63. New York: Academic Press.
32. Emmett, D. (1968). "Ethical systems and social structures. *International encyclopedia of the social sciences.*" 1968 ed. Vol. 5, pp. 157–60.

33. Feldman, K. A. & T. M. Newcomb. (1969). *The impact of college on students*, 2 vols. San Francisco: Jossey-Bass, Inc.

34. Fetterman, D. M. (Ed.). (1991). *Using qualitative methods for institutional research*, vol. 72 of *New directions for institutional research*, San Francisco: Jossey-Bass. Inc.

35. Fitch, D. (25 April 1987). "Curran and Dissent: The Case for the Holy See." *America*, 341–43, 349–50.

36. Freud, S. (1933). *New introductory lectures on psycho-analysis*. Translated by W. J. H. Sprott. New York: W. W. Norton & Company, Inc.

37. Gardner, D. P (1967). *The California oath controversy*. Berkeley: The University of California Press.

38. Geertz, C. (1973). *The interpretation of cultures: Selected essays*. New York: Basic Books. Inc.

39. Geis, J. C. [Ed.]. (1983). *The good steward: A guide to theological school trusteeship*. Washington. D. C.: Association of Governing Boards of Universities and Colleges.

40. Gewirth, A. (1978). *Reason and Morality*. Chicago: The University of Chicago Press.

41. Gilligan, C. (1981). "Moral development." In A. W. Chickering, et al. (Ed.), *The modern American college*, chap. 5. San Francisco: Jossey-Bass. Inc.

42. Glaser, B. C., & A. L. Strauss. (1967). *The discovery of grounded theory: Strategies for qualitative research*. Chicago: Aldine Publishing Company.

43. Good, C. V. (1955). "Personnel problems at the college level." *Review of educational research*, 25, 252–60.

44. Gordon, E. W., et al. (April 1990). "Coping with communicentric bias in knowledge production in the social sciences." *Educational Researcher*, 19, 14–19.

45. Habermas, J. (1988). *On the logic of the social sciences*, translated by S. W. Nicholsen & J. A. Stark. Cambridge, Mass.: MIT Press, 1988.

46. *Higher education abstracts*, 16, nos. 1–4 (1980–1981)—26, nos. 1–3 (1990–1991).

47. Hunt, J. F., & T. R. Connelly, et al. (1969). *The responsibility of dissent: The church and academic freedom*. New York: Sheed and Ward.

48. Immegart, G. L. (1988). "Leadership and leader behavior." In N. J. Boyan (Ed.). *Handbook of research on educational administration: A project of the American educational research association*, chap. 13. New York: Longman.

49. Knowles, A. S. (Ed.). (1986). *International encyclopedia of higher education*, 10 vols. San Francisco: Jossey-Bass, Inc.

50. Jedamus, P., M. W. Peterson, et al. (1980). *Improving academic management*. San Francisco: Jossey-Bass, Inc.

51. Jencks, C. S., & D. Riesman. (1962). "Patterns of residential education: A case study." In N. Sanford (Ed.), *The American college: A psychological and social interpretation of the higher learning*, chap. 22. New York: John Wiley & Sons, Inc.

52. Jonsen, A. R. (1986). "Casuistry." In J. F. Childress & J. Macquarrie (Eds.), *The Westminster dictionary of christian ethics*, pp. 78–80. Philadelphia: The Westminster Press.

53. Jonsen, A. R., & S. Toulmin. (1988). *The abuse of casuistry: A history of moral reasoning*. Berkeley, Calif.: The University of California Press, 1988.

54. Kallen, H. M. (1968). "Morals." *Encyclopedia of the social Sciences*, vol. 10, pp. 643–49.

55. Kirtland, R. (25 April 1987). "Authority and academic freedom." *America* 156, 348–49.

56. Knowles, A. S. (Ed.). (1970). *Handbook of college and university administration*, 2 vols. New York: McGraw-Hill Book Company.

57. Leming, J. S. (1983). *Contemporary approaches to moral education: An annotated bibliography and guide to research*. New York: Garland Publishing, Inc.

58. _____. (1983). *Foundations of moral education: An annotated bibliography*. Westport, Conn.: Greenwood Press.

59. Lunsford, T. F. (Ed.). (1963). *The study of academic administration*. Boulder. Colo.: Western Interstate Commission for Higher Education.

60. Mathews, M. C. (1988). *Strategic intervention in organizations: Resolving ethical dilemma*. Newbury Park, Calif.: Sage Publications.

61. May, W. W. (Ed.). (1990). *Ethics and higher education*. New York: American Council on Education/Macmillan Publishing Company.

62. Mead, G. H. (1938). "Essay XXIV: Moral behavior and reflective thinking." In C. W. Morris, et al. (1938). *The philosophy of the act*. Chicago: The University of Chicago Press.

63. Meeth, L. R. (Ed.). (1965). *Selected issues in higher education: An annotated bibliography*. New York: Institute of Higher Education/Teacher College Press.

64. Metzger, L. (1978). "Professors in trouble: A quantitative analysis of academic freedom and tenure." Ph.D. dissertation. Columbia University.

65. Miskel, C. & R. Ogawa. (1988). "Work motivation, job satisfaction, and climate." In N. J. Boyan (Ed.). *Handbook of research on educational administration: A project of the American educational research association*, chap. 14. New York: Longman.

66. Moberly, Sir W. (1949). *The crisis in the university*. London: SCM Press, Ltd.

67. Mortimer, K. P. (1972). "Accountability in higher education." Washington, D. C.: American Association for Higher Education.

68. Muffo, J. A., & G. W. McLaughlin (Eds.). (1987). *A primer on institutional research*. Tallahassee. Fla.: Association for Institutional Research, 1987.

69. Murray, H. A., et al. (1938). *Explorations in personality: A clinical and experimental study of fifty*

men of college age. New York: Oxford University Press.

70. *The New York times.* 8 April 1988, p. 16A; 13 April 1988, p. 17A; 18 May 1988, p. 21A: 18 December 1988, p. 30; 1 March 1989, p. 18A; 29 September 1989, p. 17A.

71. Nucci, L. & E. T. Pascarella. (1987). "The influence of college on moral development." In J. C. Smart (Ed.), *Higher education: Handbook of theory and research,* vol. 3. New York: Agathon Press. Inc.

72. Oser, F. K. (1986). "Moral education and values education: The discourse perspective." In M. C. Wittrock (Ed.), *Handbook of research on teaching,* 3d ed., chap. 32. New York: Macmillan Publishing Company.

73. Parsons. T. (1951). *The social system.* Glencoe, Ill.: The Free Press, 1951.

74. Parsons, T., & G. M. Platt. (1973). *The American university.* Cambridge, Mass.: Harvard University Press.

75. Perry, W. G. Jr. (1981). "Cognitive and ethical growth: The making of meaning." In A. W. Chickering, et al. (Ed.), *The modern American college,* chap. 3. San Francisco: Jossey-Bass. Inc.

76. Peterson, M. W. (1974). "Organization and administration in higher education." In F. M. Kerlinger & J. B. Carroll (Eds.), *Review of research in education,* vol. 2. Itasca, Ill.: AERA/E. F. Peacock Publishers, Inc.

77. Rausch, T. P. (25 April 1987). "Who speaks for the church? *America,*" 156, 344–46.

78. Rodriguez, R. G. & R. F. Argrella. (Winter 1990). "Ethical analysis in institutional research." Association for Institutional Research conference paper, Louisville, Ky. *Higher education abstracts,* 26, 236.

79. Rosenau, P. M. (1992). *Post-modernism and the social sciences: Insights, inroads, and intrusions.* Princeton, N.J.: Princeton University Press.

80. Sanford, N. (ed.). (1962). *The American college: A psychological and social interpretation of the higher learning.* New York: John Wiley & Sons, Inc.

81. Shils, E. (1983). *The academic ethic: The report of a study group of the international council on the future of the university.* Chicago: The University of Chicago Press.

82. Slaughter, S. (1981). "Political action, faculty autonomy and retrenchment: A decade of academic freedom." In P. G. Altbach & R. O. Berdahl (Eds.), *Higher education in American society,* chap. 5. Buffalo, N. Y.: Prometheus Books.

83. Smith, T. V. "Ethics." *Encyclopaedia of the social sciences,* 1931 ed., vol. 5, pp. 602–7.

84. Stenhouse, L. (1988). "Case study methods." In J. P. Keeves (Ed.), *Educational research, methodology, and measurement: An international handbook,* pp. 49–53. Oxford, UK: Pergamon Press.

85. Stern, G. G. (1962). "Environments of learning." In N. Sanford (Ed.), *The American college: A psychological and social interpretation of the higher learning,* chap. 21. New York: John Wiley & Sons, Inc.

86. Sutherland, J. W. (1973). *General systems philosophy for the social and behavioral sciences.* New York: George Braziller.

87. Taft, R. (1988). "Ethnographic research methods." In J. P. Keeves (Ed.), *Educational research, methodology, and management: An international handbook,* pp. 59–63. Oxford, UK: Pergamon Press.

88. [Taylor, W.] (1987). *Universities under scrutiny.* Paris: Organisation for Economic Cooperation and Development.

89. Thelin, J. R. (1986). "Postscript to 'The importance of being general,'" by Gordon K. Davies." In J. C. Smart (Ed.), *Higher education: Handbook of theory and research,* vol. 2. New York: Agathon Press.

90. Thomas, R. M. (Ed.) (1990). *The encyclopedia of human development and education: Theory, research, and studies.* Oxford, UK: Pergamon Press.

91. ———. (1990). "Social learning theory." In R. M. Thomas (Ed.). *The encyclopedia of human development and education: Theory, research, and studies,* pp. 75–78. Oxford, UK: Pergamon Press.

92. Weber, M. (1947). *The theory of social and economic organization,* translated by A. M. Henderson & T. Parsons, T. Parsons (Ed.). Glencoe, Ill.: The Free Press/The Falcon's Wing Press.

93. Western Association of Schools and Colleges/Accrediting Commission for Senior Colleges and Universities. (1988). *Handbook of accreditation.* Oakland, Calif.: Mills College.

94. Whetton, D. A., & K. Bettenhausen. (1987). "Diversity in university governance: Attitudes, structure, and satisfaction." In J. C. Smart (Ed.), *Higher Education: Handbook of theory and research,* vol. 3. New York: Agathon Press.

95. Williams, G. B., and P. A. Zirkel. (1988). "Academic penetration in faculty collective bargaining contracts in higher education." *Research in higher education,* 28, 76–95.

96. Willingham, W. W., et al. (1973). *The source book for higher education: A critical guide to literature and information on access to higher education.* New York: College Entrance Examination Board.

97. Wolf, A. "Ethics." *Encyclopaedia britannica.* 1955 ed. vol. 8, pp. 757–61.

98. Yin, R. K. (1984). *Case study research: Design and methods.* Beverly Hills, Calif.: Sage Publications.

99. Young, K. E., et al. (1983). *Understanding accreditation: Contemporary perspectives on issues in evaluating educational quality.* San Francisco: Jossey-Bass, Inc.

100. Zwingle, J. L. (1970). "Governing boards." In A. S. Knowles (Ed.), *Handbook of college and university administration,* vol. 1, section 2. New York: McGraw-Hill Book Company.

101. ———. (1982). *Effective trusteeship: Guidelines for board members.* Washington, D.C.: Association of Governing Boards of Universities and Colleges.

SECTION VIII

INTERNATIONAL
FINANCING OF
HIGHER EDUCATION

INTRODUCTION

This section of the *ASHE Reader on Finance in Higher Education* complements the *ASHE Reader on Comparative Education*. Acknowledging the rapid (and still accelerating) pace of economic and educational globalization, and the pressing need for American students and scholars of higher education to learn more about the development of higher education in other countries and regions of the world, this section features six articles which offer international and comparative analyses of critical issues, especially the powerful effects of market forces on higher education. In each article, readers will benefit from learning more about the experiences of other countries, and also from re-evaluating domestic circumstances from a comparative perspective.

The first article, by Mark Bray, is significant not only of its substance, but also its approach. In "Financing Higher Education in Asia: Patterns, Trends, and Options," Bray uses a world region—in this case, Asia—as his unit of analysis, and skillfully explores both the similarities and contrasts between thirty Asian nations related to higher education financing concerns, including government financing, unit costs, and privatization. Bray's analysis concludes with speculation regarding the future of higher education in Asia.

Privatization is the focus of the second article, "Privatization and Competition Policies for Australian Universities," by Jan Currie and Lesley Vidovich. Currie and Vidovich define privatization, discuss the promulgation of the privatization ideology by groups such as the World Bank and Organization for Economic Co-operation and Development, and the effects of privatization on higher education systems—particularly in Australia. The authors examine these effects, which they generally characterize as negative, and describe steps universities can take to prevent the loss of their public interest philosophy and identity. This is one of two articles in this section from a special issue of the *International Journal of Educational Development* (Vol. 20, No. 2, 2000) devoted to marketization and privatization of education.

Hans-Dieter Daniel, Stefanie Schwarz, and Ulrich Teichler turn the focus from Asia and Australia to Europe in their article, "Study Costs, Student Income, and Public Policy in Europe." Recognizing the pre-eminence of cost and funding schemes as issues of higher education policy in Europe, the authors provide a survey of higher education cost structures and funding systems in fifteen European countries, utilizing a cross-national comparative approach. This article is very useful, both as an introduction to the various cost and funding conditions in the member states of the European Union, and as a catalyst for a critical reassessment of American higher education policy and practices. Interested readers are referred to other related articles in this issue of the *European Journal of Education* (Vol. 34, No. 1, 1999) devoted to European higher education finance.

The fourth article, by Steve Michael and Edward Holdaway, discusses "Entrepreneurial Activities in Postsecondary Education" from a Canadian perspective. Arguing that higher education is currently in an "entrepreneurial phase," Michael and Holdaway describe the context and characteristics of this phase, and the implications of this entrepreneurial emphasis on institutions—specifically administrative competence, resource allocation, and student orientation. This article is an effective counterbalance to the Currie and Vidovich article by recasting privatization of higher education in a more positive, though not entirely uncritical, light.

Ka Ho Mok joins the discussion of privatization, or enterpreneurialism, with his article on "Marketizing Higher Education in Post-Mao China." Mok uses the term "marketization" to describe the influence of a socialist market system on Chinese educational development in the 1990s. Mok complements the articles by Currie and Vidovich, and Michael and Holdaway, by providing an illuminating history of the institutional origins of the marketization of Chinese education, and an enumeration of the effects of marketization, which in China have included the emergence of user fees, private education, internal competition, and increased consumer choice. Contrasting the Chinese experience with similar movements in other countries, this article offers readers an excellent opportunity to explore a global trend in a national context.

The final article, "Diversifying Finance of Higher Education Systems in the Third World: The Cases of Kenya and Mongolia," by John Weidman, examines the struggles of these countries to reduce the expenditures of scarce public resources on higher education. Weidman details numerous strategies for diversifying the sources of funding for higher education in developing countries, including direct cost recovery, income-generating activities, cultivating private contributions, and deferred cost recovery. As many nations around the world wrestle with how to pay for the relatively expensive enterprise of higher education, Weidman's article is both a how-to for these countries, and an accessible introduction for readers seeking to understand the challenges these countries face.

The following reviewers contributed to the selection of works included in this section:

Mark Bray, Hong Kong University

Steve O. Michael, Kent State University

José-Gines Mora, University of Valencia

Jamil Salmi, The World Bank

John C. Weidman, University of Pittsburgh

CHAPTER 53

FINANCING HIGHER EDUCATION

Patterns, Trends and Options

MARK BRAY

The value of the world region as a unit for analysis has been demonstrated in many comparative and other studies (e.g. Halls, 1990; Kazamias & Spillane, 1998; Arnove & Torres, 1999). Although most regions—and Asia is no exception—contain considerable internal diversity, many also have unifying features. Moreover, in the search for conceptual understanding, diversity can be as useful as uniformity because analysis of contrasts assists in the identification of features that might otherwise have been overlooked. Accordingly, this paper, which focuses on the financing of higher education, seeks to identify commonalties, grapple with the diversity, and highlight the lessons that can be learned. While much of the discussion focuses on Asia as a whole and on its components, parts of the discussion highlight similarities and differences between Asia and other parts of the world.

The paper begins with the context, identifying the geographical coverage and the nature of the societies encompassed. It then presents data on the nature of higher education, to indicate first what existing provision needs to be financed and then what gaps may need to be bridged, and thus paid for, in the future. This leads to commentary on the nature of public and private financing of higher education, and to patterns of fee-charging, grants and loans. Also noted are matters of institutional revenue generation and unit costs. The final section summarizes and concludes.

THE CONTEXT

A necessary starting point is the geographical boundaries of the region. Consensus on these boundaries is difficult to find, since the region may be defined in different ways for different purposes. As pointed out by Su (1999, p. 329), for example, classical definitions of Asia include five major sub-regions, namely Russian Asia, South-West Asia, South Asia, South-East Asia and East Asia. More modern definitions, however, tend to focus on the last three of these sub-regions and to exclude Russian Asia and South-West Asia. For some purposes Australia and the Pacific Islands are included, but for others they are excluded. This particular paper takes as its focus the region bounded by Afghanistan in the west, Mongolia in the north, Taiwan in the east and the Maldives in the south. The countries thus encompassed are listed in Table 53.1.

Table 53.1 also provides estimates of populations, per capita gross national product (GNP), real gross domestic product (GDP) adjusted for purchasing power parity (PPP), and the Human Development Index calculated by the United Nations Development Programme (UNDP). The table shows a huge range in populations, from just 300,000 in the Maldives to 1,230,400,000 in China. It

Source: *Prospects,* Vol. 3, September 2000, International Bureau of Education, UNESCO Publishing.

TABLE 53.1
Basic Statistics for Countries in Asia

	Population (millions)	GNP per Capita (US$)	Real GDP per Capita (PPP$)	Human Development Index
Afghanistan	17.7	...	...	...
Bangladesh	125.6	240	1,382	0.371
Bhutan	0.6	420	1,382	0.347
Brunei Darussalam	0.3	25,160	31,165	0.889
Cambodia	10.9	270	1,110	0.422
China, People's Republic of	1,230.4	620	2,935	0.650
Dem. People's Rep. of Korea	23.0	...	4,058	0.766
India	955.2	340	1,422	0.451
Indonesia	199.9	900	3,971	0.679
Japan	124.5	31,490	21,930	0.940
Kazakhstan	15.8	1,350	...	0.695
Kyrgyzstan	4.7	550	1,927	0.633
Lao People's Democratic Rep.	4.6	350	2,571	0.465
Malaysia	21.7	3,890	9,572	0.834
Maldives	0.3	990	3,540	0.683
Mongolia	2.4	310	3,916	0.669
Myanmar	46.4	...	1,130	0.481
Nepal	21.7	200	1,145	0.351
Pakistan	135.2	460	2,209	0.453
Philippines	73.5	1,050	2,762	0.672
Republic of Korea	46.0	9,700	11,594	0.894
Singapore	3.1	26,730	22,604	0.896
Sri Lanka	18.6	700	3,408	0.716
Tajikistan	5.8	470	943	0.575
Taiwan	21.6	13,310	...	...
Thailand	60.6	2,740	7,742	0.838
Uzbekistan	23.3	1,010	2,376	0.659
Viet Nam	76.7	240	1,236	0.560

... = not available.

Data refer to the most recent year available—in most cases the mid-1990s. *Sources:* Asian Development Bank, 1998; United Nations Development Programme, 1998; various national sources.

also shows a wide range in GNP per capita (from US$200 in Nepal to US$31,490 in Japan) and in real GDP per capita (from PPP$943 in Tajikistan to PPP$31,165 in Brunei Darussalam). These factors have a strong bearing on the size and shape of higher education, and also on modes of financing.

Other aspects of diversity among the countries under discussion should also be highlighted. Concerning political systems, for example, some countries have recently shifted from communism to capitalism (e.g. Cambo-dia, Kyrgyzstan, Mongolia); others have always had capitalist regimes (e.g. Republic of Korea, Pakistan, Philippines); and yet others (e.g. People's Republic of China, Lao People's Democratic Republic [Lao PDR], Viet Nam) retain socialist systems, albeit in most cases with a stronger element of market economy. Political ideology affects the official philosophy and orientation of higher education.

Several commonalties are also significant. For example, in common with other parts of the world, almost all Asian societies face issues concerning the role of the State in education. This includes questions about the size of the public and private sectors, and about cost-sharing in public institutions. Likewise, almost all societies face issues related to supply and demand of high-level manpower and to migration of educated personnel. Also, all societies both benefit from and have to grapple with the advances in technology that, among other effects, may change curricula and modes of delivery in higher education. All societies have to address tensions between well-established institutional structures and the new modes that may become necessary. One particularly striking feature of the last decade has been the advance of capitalist modes of operation in almost all parts of the region. This has been especially obvious in the States that formally abandoned socialism, but has also been evident in most of the States that officially maintained socialist regimes. Moreover, the advance of capitalist modes of operation has been apparent even in countries which have long operated basically capitalist economies but which have had government-protected education systems. The chief manifestation of the change has been the advance of privatization in such countries as different as Mongolia and India.

THE COVERAGE AND NATURE OF HIGHER EDUCATION

Just as the geographical boundaries of the Asia-Pacific region are open to debate, so are the definitional boundaries of higher education. This paper is primarily concerned with universities, though in some parts it takes a broader focus to include polytechnics, teachers' colleges, technical colleges and other institutions.

Table 53.2 presents information on the scale of higher education in some countries of the region. The table reports figures on the number of students in higher education (defined to include both university and other post-secondary studies) per 100,000 inhabitants. Compared with an enrollment rate, the advantage of the statistic is that it avoids stipulation of a specific age group for higher education. It also avoids reliance on precise data on the numbers of people within age groups.

The chief message from the table is again one of diversity. The reported range is from 119 students per 100,000 people in Cambodia to 4,955 students in the Republic of Korea. Other countries at the bottom of the scale include the Lao PDR, Viet Nam, Sri Lanka and China. Countries at the top of the scale include Japan, Uzbekistan and Kazakhstan. All three socialist States for which data are available (Lao PDR, China and Viet Nam) are at the bottom, but some former socialist States (e.g. Uzbekistan and Kazakhstan) are near the top. This was not just a function of capitalist enterprise in the latter States, because they had high enrollment rates even during the Soviet era. Other capitalist States are scattered throughout the spectrum. To some extent the figures reflect the ideologies of government planners, but they also

TABLE 53.2
Coverage of Higher Education in Selected Asia-Pacific Countries, 1995

Country	No. of Students per 100,000 Inhabitants	Country	No. of Students per 100,000 Inhabitants
Brunei Darussalam	514	Macau	1,874
Cambodia	119	Mongolia	1,569
China	478	Myanmar	564
India	601	Nepal	501
Indonesia	1,146	Philippines	2,701
Japan	3,139	Singapore	2,522
Kazakhstan	2,807	Sri Lanka	474
Korea, Republic of	4,955	Tajikistan	1,857
Kyrgyzstan	1,115	Thailand	2,096
Lao PDR	134	Uzbekistan	2,960
Malaysia	971	Viet Nam	404

Source: UNESCO, 1998, p. 149.

reflect the resources available to the States in question. Prosperous States could more easily afford large systems of higher education, and, by having stronger secondary school systems, supply larger numbers of potential recruits.

While the statistics on students per 100,000 inhabitants are useful, they do have limitations. One problem is that the age structure of populations may vary considerably—some are weighted towards people under the age of 15, and others are weighted towards people over the age of 40. For that reason, it remains instructive to examine enrollment rates for specifically designated higher-education age groups. Table 53.3 shows figures for enrollment rates by world region. It indicates that average enrollment rates among the less-developed countries of East Asia and Oceania and of South Asia were greater than those in sub-Saharan Africa, but considerably lower than in the Arab States and in Latin America and the Caribbean. They were also, of course, much lower than among the more developed countries of North America. However, enrollment rates in the more developed countries of Eastern Asia and Oceania were comparable with those of Europe. In all regions, enrollment rates increased between 1985 and 1995. The increase in the more developed countries of East Asia and Oceania was dramatic—from 28.1% to 45.3% in only a decade. This matched a comparable increase in Europe.

Institutions of higher education may be either public or private. The World Bank (1994, p. 35) has shown that in the late 1980s and early 1990s Asian countries generally had fairly high proportions of private enrollments in higher

education, particularly in comparison with Africa. However, considerable variation again existed within the region. Among the forty countries for which the World Bank presented data, the countries with the highest and lowest proportions were both Asian—the Philippines and Pakistan, respectively.

Since the period to which the World Bank figures referred, in some countries the balance has shifted markedly towards private systems. Pakistan was among them, to the extent that by 1996 ten private universities and institutes operated alongside twenty-five public sector universities, though the average size of the private institutions was much smaller than in the public sector (Sheikh, 1998; Kizilbash, 1998). In Indonesia, the number of private post-secondary institutions increased from 344 in 1980 to 1,035 in 1993; in Thailand the number of private universities and colleges rose from 11 in 1976 to 31 in 1994 (Woodhall, 1997, p. 2). Especially dramatic were changes in former socialist systems. In Mongolia, for example, within three years of relaxation of restrictions on private higher education in 1990, eighteen private institutions were established to operate in parallel with the fourteen public ones. The private bodies focused on specialist domains such as business, sports, law and languages (Bray et al., 1994, p. 37–38). Comparable patterns were evident in Kazakhstan and some other former Soviet States (Kitaev, 1996).

The scale of private higher education in Philippines deserves particular comment because it is at the extreme. In 1994/95, 794 out of 1,090 institutions (72.8%) were operated by private bodies. Of these, 247 institutions were run

TABLE 53.3
Gross Higher Education Enrollment Rates by World Region, 1985 and 1995 (%)

	1985	1995		1985	1995
Less-developed regions of which:	6.5	8.8	More-developed regions of which:	39.3	59.6
Sub-Saharan Africa	2.2	3.5	North America	61.2	84.0
Arab States	10.7	12.5	Asia/Oceania	28.1	45.3
Latin America/Caribbean	15.8	17.3	Europe	26.9	47.8
East Asia/Oceania	5.4	8.9			
South Asia	5.3	6.5	Countries in transition	36.5	34.2
Least developed countries	2.5	3.2			

Source: UNESCO, 1998, p. 108.

by sectarian organizations, particularly the Catholic Church. Some private universities were operated as companies, the shares of which were quoted on the stock exchange. Gonzales (1997, p. 264) described changing official attitudes to the private sector. Prior to 1969, the policy was one of *laissez faire* to the point that 85% of students attended private universities financed almost entirely from fees. This system led to a mismatch between the supply of graduates and the available jobs, and also to complaints about high fees. As a result, for over a decade starting in 1969 the Government regulated private institutions and attempted to make the sector conform to a central plan. However, the regulations threatened the viability of some institutions, and political change led to a reversal of policies in the 1980s. By 1992 deregulation was complete and the *laissez faire* approach had come full circle.

GOVERNMENT AND NON-GOVERNMENT FINANCING IN PUBLIC HIGHER EDUCATION

The public sector is, of course, not financed exclusively by governments. Individuals also contribute substantially, particularly through fees. Additionally, public institutions may have other sources of revenue. This section of the paper begins with some comments on public revenues and expenditures, before turning to matters of fees, grants and loans, and institutional incomes.

Public Revenues and Expenditures

The main way to finance public institutions is through income from taxation. Some countries have well-established systems of taxation, which include income and corporation taxes as well as sales and other indirect taxes. Countries in this group include Japan and Taiwan. Other countries have much weaker systems of taxation, either because of general underdevelopment or because of recent emergence from socialist regimes, which were financed on different principles. Countries in this group include Bhutan, China, Cambodia and Myanmar.

Information on the size of total government revenues, including taxation, may be discerned by comparing figures on the percentage of education in government budgets with figures on public expenditures on education as a percentage of GNP. Whereas Hong Kong's 2.8% of GNP consumed by public expenditures on education represented 17.0% of the budget, in Viet Nam the only slightly higher 2.9% of GNP represented only 7.4% of the budget (Table 53.4). Conversely, Kyrgyzstan's 23.1% of the budget represented 6.8% of GNP, while Singapore's 23.4% of the budget represented only 3.0% of GNP. The second column in Table 53.4 is also instructive in its own right as an indicator of government commitment to the education sector.

The next question concerns the priority for higher education within total education budgets. The right-hand column in Table 53.4 indicates a wide range—from 37.1% in Hong Kong to just 3.9% in the Lao PDR. However, higher education in the latter was set for rapid expansion (Weidman, 1997). Most analysts would consider allocations below 10% to be low, but ones above 25% to be rather high.

Fees in Public Institutions

The 1980s and 1990s brought a worldwide trend towards introduction and increase of fees in public higher education. This was in direct opposition to the view dominant in the 1950s and 1960s that public education, particularly at lower levels but also including higher education, should be free of charge. For example, Article 13 of the 1966 International Covenant on Economic, Social and Cultural Rights (United Nations, 1973, p. 5) stated that:

(a) primary education shall be compulsory and available free to all;

(b) secondary education in its different forms [. . .] shall be made generally available and accessible to all by every appropriate means, and in particular by the progressive introduction of free education; and

(c) higher education shall be made equally accessible to all, on the basis of capacity, by every appropriate means, and in particular by the progressive introduction of free education.

The chief justification was that education was a major route for social mobility, and the possi-

TABLE 53.4
Public Expenditures on Education in Selected Asian Countries, 1995

Country	Education as a % of GNP	Education as a % of Total Govt. Budget	Higher Education as a % of Total Public Education Expenditures
Bangladesh	2.3	8.7	7.9
China	2.3	...	16.5
India	3.5	12.1	13.6
Japan	3.8	10.8	13.5
Kazakhstan	4.5	17.6	12.5
Korea, Republic of	3.7	17.4	7.9
Kyrgyzstan	6.8	23.1	8.3
Lao PDR	2.4	...	3.9
Malaysia	5.3	15.5	16.8
Maldives	8.4	13.6	...
Mongolia	5.6	...	17.8
Myanmar	1.3	14.4	11.7
Nepal	2.9	13.2	28.1
Philippines	2.2	...	...
Singapore	3.0	23.4	34.8
Sri Lanka	3.1	8.1	12.2
Thailand	4.2	20.1	16.5
Uzbekistan	9.5	24.4	...
Viet Nam	2.7	7.4	9.7

.... = not available.

Source: UNESCO, 1998, p. 158–59.

bility of poor people being excluded from education by fees was considered inequitable.

By the 1990s, however, the third clause had been widely abandoned. This was not only because of financial stringency but also because of the realization that fee-free education at the tertiary level, far from being equitable, was likely to be *in*equitable. The reason is that young people from richer socio-economic groups are always more likely than their counterparts from poorer socio-economic groups to attend tertiary institutions, and subsidies for higher education are therefore more likely to benefit the rich than the poor. This observation was coupled with strong advocacy, particularly on the part of the World Bank, that investment in primary education gives better economic rates of return than secondary or tertiary education, and that in most contexts desirable policies should include reduced public investment in tertiary education in favour of increased public investment in primary education (World Bank, 1995, p. 56).

The Asian region has accompanied other parts of the world in the global shift in policy. The World Bank (1994, p. 42) presented data on the proportion of recurrent expenditures in public higher education institutions met from tuition fees in thirty-three countries in the late 1980s or early 1990s. In only twenty of these countries did tuition fees account for over 10% of recurrent expenditures. The scale of fees was not related to the incomes of countries, but there was variation across regions. Sub-Saharan Africa, North Africa, the Middle East and Eastern Europe had little or no tradition of cost recovery in public higher education. However, public-institution fees exceeded 10% of recurrent expenditures in one out of five Latin American countries and in half of the Asian countries in the sample.

TABLE 53.5
Sources of Recurrent Income of Selected Indian Universities, 1989/90–1991/92 (%)

Institution	Govt. Grants	Fees	Press	Farm	Loans	Endow-ments	Misc.
Central universities							
Aligarh Muslim	97.4	1.1	0.0	1.0	0.2	0.0	0.3
Banaras Hindu	89.4	0.8	0.6	7.2	0.0	0.4	1.6
Hyderabad	94.7	1.9	0.0	0.7	0.0	0.0	2.6
Jawaharlal Nehru	92.7	1.0	1.0	2.0	0.7	0.0	2.5
Pondicherry	86.7	8.3	0.5	0.3	0.0	0.0	4.1
Viswa Bharati	97.9	0.5	0.2	0.7	0.0	0.0	0.7
AVERAGE	93.2	1.2	0.4	3.7	0.1	0.1	1.3
State universities							
Bombay	11.5	39.0	28.3	2.2	4.1	0.0	15.1
Calcutta	91.2	7.5	0.0	0.1	0.0	0.3	0.8
Karnataka	53.5	5.5	1.8	0.1	12.7	15.1	11.3
Kerala	58.3	30.1	4.5	1.2	1.9	0.0	4.0
Madras	15.7	46.8	1.0	0.2	4.5	0.4	31.4
Mohanlal Sukhadia	91.3	8.1	0.0	0.3	0.0	0.0	0.2
Utkal	59.2	22.1	0.0	0.5	2.2	0.7	15.3
AVERAGE	54.3	21.2	5.3	0.6	4.3	5.3	9.0

Source: Tilak, 1997, p. 11.

For analysis of some countries, however, disaggregation of national averages is necessary. Table 53.5 shows fee incomes in selected universities in India. Fee incomes in the sample of central universities averaged below 2% of total income, but in state universities they averaged 21.2%. Among the state universities shown, the range was from 8.1% to as much as 46.7%.

As the 1990s progressed, in some parts of Asia fees increased further. In Hong Kong, for example, where the Government imposed uniform fees across all public institutions, the authorities decided in 1991 to raise fees from 12% of recurrent costs (which was already a substantial increase from the situation in the mid-1980s) to 18% in 1997 (Bray, 1993, p. 38). Moreover, as soon as the 18% target had nearly been achieved, the authorities considered raising the proportion to 20% or more (University Grants Committee of Hong Kong, 1996, p. 161, 174). The Government did not immediately implement this idea, but the fact that the notion was even considered was significant. Fees have also greatly increased in the People's Republic of China. Many institutions admitted self-sponsored students for high fees, and by 1997 the average fee in many institutions was between 25 and 30% of recurrent costs (Zhang, 1998, p. 246). In Singapore, differential fees were charged by academic discipline. In arts and social sciences, fees were increased from 10% of the recurrent cost in 1986/87 to 20% in 1992/93, and the Government declared its intent to raise fees further to 25% (Selvaratnam, 1994, p. 81–83).

Grants and Loans

People who oppose such increases in fees usually do so particularly on the grounds that fees are likely to exclude individuals from the poorest segments of society. Part of the response by policy-makers has been to provide an array of support schemes, including grants and loans. Grants may be linked not only to the incomes of applicants but also to academic performance and to efforts to attract students to particular types of training. Loan schemes usually contain a substantial proportion of hidden grants.

Among the international authorities on student loans are Woodhall (1987; 1991; 1997) and Ziderman and Albrecht (199S). These authors have highlighted a wide range of models, of which the two main types are mortgage loans and income-contingent loans. Mortgage loans are more common, and require students to repay sums over a specified period, usually with fixed monthly payments. Income-contingent loans provide faster avenues for repayment by high-income graduates, and safety nets for low-income graduates, by linking the size of repayment to graduates' incomes. Most loan schemes provide for living expenses as well as for tuition fees. Some loan schemes are administered by government agencies, while others are operated by commercial banks.

The hidden grant elements of loans take the form of subsidized interest rates, leniency for low-income students, and tolerance of default on repayment. Ziderman and Albrecht (1995, p. 70–71) compiled statistics of hidden subsidies and government losses in twenty countries. The hidden grant through subsidized interest rates ranged from 13% of the loans in Barbados to 93% in Venezuela; average loan recovery ratios ranged from just 2% in Brazil to 67% in Barbados. Asian countries were not well represented in Ziderman and Albrecht's sample, but data from Indonesia, Japan and Hong Kong contributed to the general conclusion that loan schemes may demand substantial administration, and that such schemes are much less efficient as a mechanism for recovery of costs than is widely assumed.

In the light of such statistics, much attention during the 1990s focused on ways to improve the efficiency of cost-recovery schemes. In Hong Kong, the Government was recommended in 1996 to simplify administration and raise interest charges. When the scheme was initiated in 1969, loans were interest-free. However, in 1987 a 2.5% charge was placed on loans, and a 1996 report recommended that this should be raised to between 5.8 and 8.5% (Ernst & Young, 1996, p. 122). Similarly, continued scrutiny of schemes in China is permitting the authorities to plug some of the leaks in the system set up in the early 1990s (World Bank, 1997; Zhang, 1997).

Institutional Revenue-Earning Schemes

Higher education institutions in Asia are increasingly being required to secure additional funds from other sources. Table 53.5 showed, somewhat unusually, an institution in India that reportedly raised 28.3% of its recurrent income from a press. It also referred to farms and to endowments. Several institutions in the region now solicit donations from alumni. Many are also encouraging teaching staff and others to undertake consultancy services; some are moving into direct business ventures (Harman & Selim, 1991).

The scale of revenue obtainable from such sources depends greatly on the general wealth of the societies in which the institutions operate, on the nature of specializations offered by the institutions, and on the frameworks set by governments. Prosperous societies are obviously better able to support such initiatives than impoverished ones, though the irony is that institutions in prosperous societies have in general faced less need to secure independent revenues because their governments have been more easily able to provide substantial budget allocations. In the marketing of skills, institutions and individuals specializing in applied science and commerce generally have more opportunities than their counterparts specializing in history or philosophy. Governments can facilitate moves by offering tax exemptions for donations to public institutions.

Viet Nam is among the countries in which higher education institutions have been forced by the escalating cost of living and the inadequacy of revenues from the Government to earn independent revenues. Pham and Sloper (1995, p. 174) indicate that in 1991, Viet Nam's College of Construction was able to add 28.3% to its budget by taking on external contracts. Comparable figures were 22.0% for the Foreign Languages University, 11.0% for the College of Mining and Geology, 10.5% for the Teachers Training College of Vinh, and 4.2% for the Technical Teachers College No. 1. Pham and Sloper comment that the scale of such income generation chiefly depends on:

- the product or service that can be provided (which does not always relate to the primary mission of the institution);
- the entrepreneurial capability and culture within the institution; and
- the state of institutional infrastructure—personnel, organizational and technical—which creates the basis for delivering a desired product or service.

Institutions in urban locations generally have greater opportunities than ones in rural locations. However, in Viet Nam rural institutions have been able to generate revenues by raising poultry, producing vegetables, managing restaurants and tailoring clothes. Critics observe that such activities deflect the staff from their primary mission as specialized providers of higher education. Advocates usually agree, but point out that the activities at least permit the institutions to survive in harsh economic climates.

An example of a very different sort may be taken from Singapore. Although the country has a buoyant economy and a government with continued budget surpluses, even in Singapore the 1990s brought a philosophy that higher education institutions should develop their own sources of revenue and reduce dependence on the government. In 1991, appeals were launched by Singapore's two universities for newly created Endowment Funds with a target of S$1 billion (Selvaratnam, 1994, p. 81). To boost the funds, the Government contributed S$500 million, and committed itself to match up to S$250 million during the following five years if the universities could secure that amount from non-government sources.

UNIT COSTS IN HIGHER EDUCATION

Official policies that fees should cover a given percentage of unit costs raise questions about the size and the determinants of those unit costs. In some systems, fees are determined in proportion to average unit costs for all disciplines. Hong Kong is in this category, with the result that in reality the fees of humanities students cover about 30% of recurrent costs, whereas those of medical students cover only about 6% (University Grants Committee of Hong Kong, 1996, p. 134). In other systems, differential fees are charged not only by discipline but also by year of study and by institution. This has been a practice in Mongolia, for example, though it has been considered an over-complex system (Bray et al., 1994).

In both types of arrangements, controversies may surround the components of unit costs (Tan & Mingat, 1992, p. 28–37). Asian universities are increasingly noted for their research output, which of course has to be paid for. Some students consider it reasonable to pay a proportion of direct instructional costs, but less reasonable to pay for research output. This issue has caused controversy in some systems, and is likely to be an increasingly prominent element of policy debate.

Unit costs are also partly determined by salaries, in which again the region has considerable diversity. Academics in Hong Kong are among the best paid in the world—a fact that is recognized by the academics themselves (Boyer, Altbach & Whitelaw, 1994, p. 50). In contrast, their counterparts in Viet Nam are among the worst paid. When in 1985 the minimum state salary level in Viet Nam was 220 dong per month, a higher education lecturer was paid 425 dong, equivalent to 87 kilograms of rice, plus subsidies of various sorts (Pham & Sloper, 1995, p. 169). Subsequent adjustments for inflation were inadequate, and by 1991 a lecturer's salary was equivalent to only thirty-six kilograms of rice plus subsidized housing and electricity. By 1993 the salary had again been raised to the equivalent of seventy-five kilograms of rice, but without the fringe benefits. Lecturers could only provide effectively for their families by securing additional sources of income.

Salaries have also been very low in China. As a result, personnel costs in 1994 did not exceed 50% of institutional budgets, and in some cases were only 11%, which in international terms was very low (World Bank, 1997, p. 49). However, between 1980 and 1993, real salaries and benefits of lecturers had increased at an average of 10.7% a year, compared with an 8.9% increase in average annual salaries for all types of employees. In 1994, average annual wages in higher education were 23% above those in secondary education, and 32% above the national average for all sectors. This remained a much smaller differential than in the majority of countries, although it reflected a policy increasing the wages of intellectuals in order to attract and retain capable individuals in higher education.

To justify and permit raising of salaries, some institutions in China endeavoured to raise student-staff ratios. In 1994, the average ratio of students for each full-time equivalent member of the teaching staff was just 7:1. In most North American and European universities the ratio was 15–20:1, in Taiwan 21:1 and in the Republic of Korea 33:1. From one perspective, Chinese institutions could afford low ratios because wages were low; but from another perspective it was desirable to raise both salaries and ratios—in the process keeping unit costs roughly constant.

A further determinant of unit costs is the size of institutions. Partly for nationalistic reasons, even the smallest States are anxious to have their own universities. Thus Samoa (population 163,000) and Brunei Darussalam (population 281,000) have their own national universities, though the Maldives (population 300,000) does not. Bhutan (population 600,000) has a college affiliated to the University of Delhi that aspires to gain autonomy as an independent institution. One way through which these institutions keep expenses under control is by avoiding high-cost science and other subjects. However, this is not always considered a satisfactory approach to national development.

However, small institutions are not a phenomenon only of small countries. Most countries with Soviet legacies have traditions of small specialist institutions that are not very appropriate to the new economic and social frameworks. In Viet Nam, some institutions were amalgamated during the early 1990s; but in 1994/95, sixty-six of the 100 remaining higher education institutions still had enrollments of below 2,000 students, forty-four had enrollments below 1,000, and eighteen had enrollments below 500 (World Bank, 1996, p. 81). Similar proportions were to be found in China (World Bank, 1997, p. 54). Amalgamation is not to be recommended for all institutions, but it would be a way to reduce unit costs in many cases.

Reduction of unit costs can also be achieved in other ways. Like their counterparts in other regions, many Asian institutions have made increasing use of distance learning as a supplement to, or a replacement of, face-to-face teaching. Since the early 1980s, distance education has expanded rapidly in Bangladesh, China, Hong Kong, India, Indonesia, Japan, Pakistan, the Philippines, the Republic of Korea, Sri Lanka, Thailand and Viet Nam (Asian Development Bank, 1987; 1990). It is noteworthy that eight of the eighteen autonomous distance education universities listed by Moore (1992)

were located in Asia. Three of them were highlighted as being among the largest in the world, namely the Indira Gandhi National Open University founded in India in 1985, the Sukhotai Thammathirat Open University founded in Thailand in 1978, and the Allama Iqbal Open University founded in Pakistan in 1974. In addition, China has a whole system of radio and television universities, numbering forty-six in 1994.

The World Bank (1994, p. 34) presented statistics on unit costs in distance education and conventional methods for four Asian institutions which showed that unit costs in distance education appeared dramatically lower. This type of finding is of considerable importance. Policy-makers need to exercise caution, however, because more research on this topic is needed (Perraton, 1994). Such research would include examination of the relative qualities of the two modes of delivery, and of the labour market outcomes of graduates from distance-education programmes. Dhand (1996) has highlighted serious deficiencies in the effectiveness of Bachelor of Education (B.Ed.) degrees offered by distance education in India, and it is likely that many of Dhand's remarks would be echoed in other contexts. Nevertheless, it seems certain that distance education will become an increasing feature of higher education in Asia as much as in other parts of the world. It will be facilitated by the expansion of the Internet and e-mail.

PRIVATIZATION IN HIGHER EDUCATION

Privatization in higher education, as previously noted, has been a growing feature in Asia, and the trend is likely to continue (Wongsothorn & Wang, 1997). Writing from the Indian perspective, for example, Deshpande (1994) sees it as 'inevitable'. The starting points for privatization vary according to the country, but growth of the private sector is evident throughout the region.

Some observers view this trend positively. For example, the World Bank (1994, p. S) has stated that:

> Private institutions are an important element of some of the strongest higher edu-

cation systems to be found today. [...] They can respond efficiently and effectively to changing demand, and they increase educational opportunities with little or no educational cost.

However, Yee & Lim (1995, p. 179) have pointed out that the private sector includes many 'opportunists and charlatans' as well as reputable providers. In addition to local entrepreneurs, the opportunists include some ventures that have bases in North America, Europe and Australia but which market their wares in Asia. The 1990s brought a rash of joint ventures and overseas operations in such countries as Malaysia and Japan, some of which were of questionable quality and which offered degrees that were not accredited in their home countries. *Laissez faire* policies towards the private sector may also exacerbate problems in the labour market. With reference to the Philippines, Gonzales (1997, p. 281) pointed out that permissiveness produced an overproduction of graduates in some fields and underproduction in others. He added that the 'magic hand' of the free market was not present at all times.

These comments imply that some government oversight is needed in this sector. As pointed out by the World Bank (1994, p. 9), for example, national policy-makers need to have 'a vision [...] for the sector as a whole and for the role of each type of institution within that whole, including private institutions'. The Bank recognizes that in most countries public institutions will continue to educate the majority of students, but recommends government planners to promote coherence in the sector as a whole by facilitating the flow of information on the costs and quality of different courses, and by establishing procedures for accrediting degrees from private institutions.

One dimension that will deserve continuing monitoring concerns the direct linkages between private and public institutions. In Indonesia, for example, three-quarters of the teachers in private institutions are employed on a part-time basis and simultaneously work full-time in public institutions (Yee & Lim, 1995, p. 191). Viewed positively, this can be described as symbiosis, but viewed negatively it might be considered parasitism.

CONCLUSIONS

This paper began by noting that regional analysis can be a useful tool within the domain of comparative analysis. Despite the internal diversity, examination of patterns and trends in the financing of higher education in Asia shows some commonalties across the region. For example, almost all governments are trying to identify the appropriate role of the State and the balance of public and private institutions, and all have competing priorities for resources within the education sector and between education and other sectors. Throughout the region, the 1980s and 1990s brought increased attention to forms of cost-sharing. Fees have generally been increased, in most cases supported by scholarships and loans of various kinds. Also, throughout the region there have been important experiments with distance education.

To a large extent, these features can also be found in other parts of the world (Wasser & Picken, 1998; Johnstone, 1998). However, Asia does have some distinctive emphases. One aspect, as noted above, was in the scale of cost-recovery through student fees. Another aspect, according to the World Bank (1994), is in the mix of institutions. The Bank identifies Asia (p. 30) as the 'continent where differentiation efforts have been the most extensive and most effective'. This remark chiefly referred to the mix of conventional and distance-learning universities, and to the balance of public and private operation. Some systems are also differentiating between the nature and role of specific institutions. Institutions in the United States have long been divided into ones that have a primary focus on teaching as opposed to others that have a strong research function. A similar form of differentiation is being developed in China and India, for example.

The question is then what can be expected during the coming decades. While prediction is always difficult and dangerous, several factors seem to be clear:

- *Expansion.* It seems probable that continued expansion will be a major feature. This will be particularly obvious in the socialist States that currently have low enrollment rates, including China, the Lao PDR and Viet Nam. Many capitalist

States will also make renewed thrusts to reach higher enrollment rates. The chief exceptions are likely to be Japan and the Republic of Korea. In many countries expansion will be financed through economic growth, but in some contexts restructuring and improved efficiency will be needed.

- *Research.* The pattern of increased emphasis on research in higher education is likely to be maintained. Countries that used to send students abroad for doctoral studies now have the capacity to train them at home. The emphasis on research is especially evident in countries with strong economies, including Japan, Singapore, the Republic of Korea and Taiwan.

- *The public-private* mix. Countries such as the Republic of Korea and the Philippines already have such high proportions of private higher education that it seems unlikely that the proportion will increase further. However, the private sector is likely to become increasingly evident in such countries as China, India, Kazakhstan, Uzbekistan and Viet Nam. Moreover, throughout the region the boundaries of the public and private sectors have become blurred as public institutions have charged increasing fees and generated larger proportions of income through entrepreneurial activity.

- *Fees and loans. No* sooner have populations become used to fees exceeding 10% of recurrent costs than authorities begin to talk of raising fees above 20%. It seems probable that present trends of cost-sharing will continue. They will be supported by loan schemes of various kinds, and renewed attention will be given to the efficiency of those schemes.

- *Cost-recovery through taxation.* Countries in the region with efficient taxation systems are likely to investigate in closer detail the possibility of using those systems for stronger cost-recovery. This may be linked to student loans, as in Australia (Creedy, 1995; OECD, 1998).

- *Distance education.* The 1980s and 1990s to some extent brought a revolution through which conventional forms of higher education were supplemented with new forms of distance education. These trends are likely to continue. The potential of the Internet in this domain is only beginning to become evident. At present, the Internet is dominated by the English language, but already it is being used for transmission in other languages, including those that are not based on alphabets, such as Chinese. Even libraries, conventionally conceived of as buildings full of books and journals, are changing. In the process, education is becoming more accessible to many (though not all) disadvantaged groups, and unit costs are likely to fall further.

Within this arena of changing patterns, policy-makers in individual countries will continue to have many options. Some policies can be free-standing, such as encouragement to institutions to generate independent revenues from alumni and consultancies. Other policies will need to be formed as packages, such as combinations of fee increases with expanded access to loans. The continued existence of a multitude of options, together with continuing diversity of social and economic characteristics, means that the overall mosaic in Asia is likely to remain full of variety and diversity. At the same time, both policy-makers and practitioners will continue to derive value from cross-national exchange of experiences and perspectives. They can learn from differences as well as from commonalties; they can learn from bold initiatives as well as from cautious ones.

REFERENCES

Arnove, R.F.; Torres, C.A., eds. 1999. *Comparative education: the dialectic of the global and the local.* Lanham, MD, Rowman & Littlefield.

Asian Development Bank. 1987. *Distance education in Asia and the Pacific,* Manila, Asian Development Bank.

_____. 1990. *Distance education in South Asia.* Manila, Asian Development Bank.

_____.1998. *Key indicators of developing Asian and Pacific countries 1998.* Manila, Asian Development Bank.

Boyer, E.; Altbach, P.G.; Whitelaw, M.J. 1994. *The academic profession: an international perspective.* Princeton, NJ, Carnegie Foundation for the Advancement of Teaching.

Bray, M. 1993. Financing higher education: a comparison of government strategies in Hong Kong and Macau. *In:* Bray, M., ed. *The economics and financing of education: Hong Kong and comparative perspectives,* p. 32–50. Hong Kong, Faculty of Education, University of Hong Kong. (Education paper, 20.)

Bray, M., et al. 1994. Transition from socialism and the financing of higher education: the case of Mongolia. *Higher education policy* (Oxford, UK), vol. 7, no. 4, p. 36–42.

Creedy, J. 1995. *The economics of higher education: an analysis of taxes versus fees.* Aldershot, UK, Edward Elgar.

Deshpande, V.S. 1994. Privatisation of higher education: inevitability, problems and remedies. *Journal of education and social change* (Pune, India), vol. 8, nos. 2/3, p. 1–11.

Dhand, H. 1996. How effective is teachers' training through distance education in India? *Perspectives in education* (Johannesburg, South Africa), vol. 12, no. 3, p. 127–42.

Ernst & Young Ltd. 1996. *Consultancy study on the local student finance scheme.* Hong Kong, Ernst & Young/Hong Kong Government Student Financial Assistance Agency.

Gonzales, A. 1997. Philippines. *In:* Postiglione, G.; Mak, G.C.L., eds. *Asian higher education: an international handbook and reference guide,* p. 265–84. Westport, CT, Greenwood Press.

Halls, W.D., ed. 1990. *Comparative education: contemporary issues and trends.* London, Jessica Kingsley.

Harman, G.; Selim, M.; eds. 1991. *Funding for higher education in Asia and the Pacific: strategies to increase cost efficiency and attract additional financial support.* Bangkok, UNESCO Principal Regional Office for Asia & the Pacific.

Johnstone, B.D. 1998. *The financing and management of higher education: a status report on worldwide reforms.* Washington, DC, World Bank. (Paper prepared as a contribution to the UNESCO World Conference on Higher Education, October 1998.)

Kazamias, A.M.; Spillane, M.G., eds. 1998. *Education and the structuring of European space: north-south, centre-periphery, identity-otherness.* Athens, Seirios Editions.

Kitaev, I., ed. 1996. *Educational finance in Central Asia and Mongolia.* Paris, International Institute for Educational Planning. (Educational Forum Series no. 7.)

Kizilbash, H.H. 1998. Higher education in Pakistan: the private sector. *In:* Talati, J., et al., eds. *Higher education: a pathway to development,* p. 45–50. Karachi, Oxford University Press.

Moore, M.G. 1992. Distance education at postsecondary level. *In:* Clark, B.R.; Neave, G., eds. *The encyclopedia of higher education,* vol. 2, p. 1097–106. Oxford, Pergamon Press.

OECD [Organisation for Economic Co-operation and Development]. 1998. Paying for tertiary education: the learner perspective. *In:* OECD. *Education policy analysis 1998,* p. 57–82. Paris, OECD.

Perraton, H. 1994. Comparative cost of distance teaching in higher education: scale and quality. In: Dhanarajan, G., et al., eds. *Economics of distance education: recent experience,* p. 19–30. Hong Kong, Open Learning Institute Press.

Pham, Q.S.; Sloper, D. 1995. Funding and financial issues. *In:* Sloper, D.; Le, T.C., eds. *Higher education in Vietnam: change and response,* p. 161–81. Singapore, Institute of Southeast Asian Studies.

Selvaratnam, V. 1994. *Innovations in higher education: Singapore at the competitive edge.* Washington, DC, World Bank. (Technical Paper no. 222.)

Sheikh, N.1998. Higher education in Pakistan: the public sector. *In:* Talati, J., et al., eds. *Higher education: a pathway to development,* p. 33–44. Karachi, Oxford University Press.

Su, Z. 1999. Asian education. *In:* Arnove, R.F.; Torres, C.A., eds. *Comparative education: the dialectic of the global and the local,* p. 329–44. Lanham, MD, Rowman & Littlefield.

Tan, J.-P.; Mingat, A. 1992. *Education in Asia: a comparative study of cost and financing.* Washington, DC, World Bank.

Tilak, J.B.G. 1997. The dilemma of reforms in financing higher education. *Higher education policy* (Oxford, UK), vol. 10, no. 1, p. 7–21.

UNESCO. 1998. *World education report 1998.* Paris, UNESCO.

United Nations. 1973. *Human rights: a compilation of international instruments of the United Nations.* New York, United Nations.

United Nations Development Programme. 1998. *Human development report 1998.* New York, United Nations Development Programme.

University Grants Committee of Hong Kong. 1996. *Higher education in Hong Kong.* Hong Kong, Government Printer.

Wasser, H.; Picken, R. 1998. Changing circumstances in funding public universities: a comparative view. *Higher education* (Amsterdam), vol. 11, no. 1, p. 29–35.

Weidman, J.C. 1997. Laos. *In:* Postiglione, G.; Mak, G.C.L., eds. *Asian higher education: an international handbook and reference guide,* p. 165–172. Westport, CT, Greenwood Press.

Wongsothorn, T.-I.; Wang, Y., eds. 1997. *Private higher education in Asia and the Pacific.* Bangkok, UNESCO Principal Regional Office for Asia & the Pacific (PROAP) and Southeast Asia Ministers of Education Organisation (SEAMEO) Regional Centre for Higher Education and Development (RIHED).

Woodhall, M. 1987. *Lending for learning: designing a student loan programme for developing countries.* London, Commonwealth Secretariat.

_____.1991. *Student loans in higher education: Asia.* Paris, International Institute for Educational Planning.

_____.1997. *The reform of higher education finance in developing countries: some implementation issues.* (Paper presented at the World Bank Human Development Week, University of Maryland, College Park, MD, 1997.)

World Bank. 1994. *Higher education: the lessons of experience.* Washington, DC, World Bank.

_____.1995. *Priorities and strategies for education: a World Bank review.* Washington, DC, World Bank.

_____.1996. *Vietnam education financing sector study.* Washington, DC, World Bank.

_____.1997. *China: higher education reform.* Washington, DC, World Bank.

Yee, A.H.; Lim, T.G. 1995. Educational supply and demand in East Asia: private higher education. *In:* Yee, A.H., ed. *East Asian higher education: traditions and transformations,* p. 179–92. Oxford, Pergamon Press.

Zhang, M. 1997. *Conceptions and choices: a comparative study on student financial support policies* [in Chinese]. Beijing, People's Education Press.

_____.1998. Changing conceptions of equity and student financial support policies. *In:* Agelasto, M.; Adamson, B., eds. *Higher education in post-Mao China,* p. 237–57. Hong Kong, Hong Kong University Press.

Ziderman, A.; Albrecht, D. 1995. *Financing universities in developing countries.* London, Falmer Press.

CHAPTER 54

PRIVATIZATION AND COMPETITION POLICIES FOR AUSTRALIAN UNIVERSITIES

JAN CURRIE AND LESLEY VIDOVICH

Jan Curry, School of Education, Murdoch University, Murdoch, Western Australia 6150, Australia

Lesley Vidovich, The Graduate School of Education, University of Western Australia, Nedlands, Western Australia 6009, Australia

"Privatization" encapsulates an ideological shift towards market principles such as competition, commercialization, deregulation, efficiency and changing forms of accountability. In higher education, the privatization trend includes the full gamut from the creation of fully private institutions which operate without government financial support, to reforms in largely government-funded institutions operating in more of a quasi-market mode. This article examines privatization policies and speculates on their origins and their ramifications for universities around the world. In particular, it describes the impact of corporate managerialism (the import of management practices from the private sector) in institutions still largely under the control of governments, and focuses on examples of the particular effects of this ideological shift in three Australian universities. It argues that some traditional academic values should be preserved as important attributes of universities that enable them to operate in the public interest and maintain their role as a critical voice in society.

1. INTRODUCTION

The ideological shift towards privatization includes both the increasing provision of education services for profit by private organizations and tendencies to marketization within institutions that continue to be publically funded and driven. It is the latter which is the main theme of this paper, given that changes in Australian universities are foregrounded, and the vast majority of these universities still receive a significant proportion of their funding from the federal government (only two of the 38 Australian universities are private institutions). Market principles, such as competition, deregulation, efficiency, changing forms of accountability, flexibility of staff and more enterprise-based industrial labor relations, have guided the restructuring of Australian universities during the last decade. Along with these market principles, there has been a shift in universities towards corporate managerialism, creating "leaner and meaner" decision making structures and processes in institutions and resulting in an intensification of academic work. In the decade from 1986 to 1996 Australian universities have seen a 33% increase in the student-staff ratio from 12:1 to 16:1 and a drop in government funding from 90% in 1981 to about 55% in 1996 with real grant funding per student declining about 7% since 1983 (Armitage, 1996). Since 1996 there have been further cuts of between 1–3% each year. This has resulted in a greater reliance on second and third stream funding as described by Clark in Entrepreneurial Universities (Clark, 1998). The second major source of funding is through competing for grants and contracts from the Australian Research Council and other public boards that distribute research funding. Third stream income sources are industrial firms, philanthropic foundations, campus services, student fees and alumni fundraising.

This article gives a description of privatization and how its ideology has influenced higher education in many countries around the world. It describes the way competition has entered the rhetoric of neo-liberal reforms and led to policies creating quasi-markets for universities. It focuses on the way privatization in Australian universities has led to increasing corporate managerialism, with associated changes in forms and mechanisms of accountability. Findings from case studies in three Australian universities give the perceptions of academics about changes in their universities, especially in relation to decision making structures and processes. The discussion argues that an ideology of privatization does not necessarily have to be accompanied by an erosion of collegiality. It suggests that universities need to preserve traditional academic values, especially their role as a critical voice within society. It also asserts that privatization can go too far and that public universities, well funded by tax-payers, are important to maintain for societies increasingly at risk due to the vicissitudes of global markets.

2. PRIVATIZATION

The World Bank and the Organization for Economic Co-operation and Development (OECD) have been crucial in encouraging governments to change public policy based on the social good to one based on economic goals. This has led to instituting greater deregulation and privatization policies. To carry out these market practices, governments have urged the corporatization of public sector organizations to make them function more like businesses. This has resulted in the reshaping of the administrative structure and also the culture of organiza-

tions to serve a 'competitive' state (Yeatman, 1993; Knight and Lingard, 1996).

The World Bank in its 1994 Report on Higher Education urged countries to shift from dependence on just one source of funding—the state, towards more money coming from student fees, consultancies and donations. It recommends, among a number of reforms, that governments link funding more closely to performance, develop private institutions and create greater differentiation among institutions (World Bank, 1994). "In short, higher education should resemble the United States model more closely" (Hodges, 1994, p. 24). There is little discussion of alternative models and their benefits; only the disadvantages of the policies of certain countries are given in defense of moving towards greater privatization of higher education.

In the OECD's (1998a) review of tertiary education in its member countries, the reviewers noted moves to transpose to educational institutions principles of private sector business management. They identified the Anglo-American countries as increasingly fitting the entrepreneurial model, having a more instrumental approach and being more responsive to "the market". Even though there was no explicit message that the entrepreneurial, instrumentalist, managerial approaches were better, there were indications that more of these practices would lead universities in the "correct" direction. They remarked that "the year-long use of space and the flexible use of personnel are marked features of the more dynamic institutions in the United States" (p. 25). In addition they noted that "the policy discourse in all countries is moving steadily in this direction" [entrepreneurial model] (p. 45). They recommended "the introduction of modern management and evaluation practices into those institutions not already familiar with them, not least in financial management, strategic planning, institutional profiling and quality assurance is needed in view of the scale and complexity of decision making" (p. 48).

One of the reasons given for the introduction of market forces in higher education is the need for States to become more competitive within a global economy. Universities are needed for wealth creation in this information age. However, it is increasingly difficult for nations to compete as capital itself has changed. It moves freely across boundaries in our increasingly borderless world, at least as far as markets are concerned (the borders are still there for unwanted immigrants). The global economy has enhanced the power of multinationals, bankers and the media in relation to the State. There has been a political mobilization of business that has developed into a worldwide network of a capitalist class.

Sklair (1995) has detailed how the transnational capitalist class develops political transnational practices to transform the world in terms of the global capitalist project. This class, in turn, has been influenced by particular think tanks which have helped shape public opinion. The main message of these 'free market' think tanks is that American corporate practices should be adopted, economies should be de-regulated and the power of trade unions limited (Wheelwright, 1995). Santamaria (1996) illustrates the power of the transnational capitalist class in an article. He claimed that international financiers have become "modern potentates with the power to dictate policy to states" (p. 24). He asserted that the Howard Government in Australia was moving on virtually all of the specifics nominated by a group of 100 top executives of the world's biggest banks which met in Sydney, 7 June 1996 and proclaimed that "more privatization, fewer subsidies and smaller public payrolls" were the order of the day (p. 24).

Not only has there been the influence of international financiers and supranational bodies like the World Bank and the OECD on each nation's policies but also that of regional trade organizations. Academics and labor activists from Canada, the United States and Mexico recently met in Monterrey, Mexico to safeguard higher education from the North American Free Trade Agreement's (NAFTAs) so called harmonization. A representative from Toronto remarked "Education is another institution our government has given away to the capital interests of North America" (Guerrero, 1996, p. 6). Buchbinder and Rajagopal (1996) writing about the impact of free trade and globalization on Canadian universities identify the specific chapters of NAFTA, particularly Cross Border Trade in Telecommunications and Investment, Services and Related Matters which affect education. They also believe that the last 20 years of changes have 'softened up' Canadian universities and left them "both vulnerable and to a great degree, acquiescent to the wide ranging influences of globalization" (pp. 289–290).

Fisher and Rubenson noted that in Canadian universities:

> Privatization continues to be the overwhelming trend. Institutions are changing their practices in order to accumulate power. Our universities are becoming more corporate, more technocratic, more utilitarian and far more concerned with selling products than with education. Jointly designing curriculum with private donors, the differentiation between teaching and research internally, and the reliance on non-tenure-track sessional or part-time labor are already established trends. Full cost recovery is a major theme (Fisher and Rubenson, 1998, p. 96).

There are constant reminders in Australia which suggest to politicians that there are still more market forces that can be applied to higher education. For example, in Australia, a report released in November 1995 by the Economic Planning Advisory Commission said "micro-economic reforms embracing 'market incentives' should be extended to the education and training sector" (Armitage, 1995, p. 8). Then the Hoare Committee in December 1995 found that work practices in Australian universities were "not keeping pace with the profound societal and economic changes affecting the sector and the Government needed to force universities to improve their management and governance policies" (Richardson, 1995, p. 1).

In Australia, the Chair of the Higher Education Review,[1] Roderick West, identified globalization as one of the very pressing issues facing higher education (Healy, 1997, p. 21). In his foreword to the final report (April 1998), West acknowledged that there is "anxiety in the academic community over globalization which involves supra-nationalism that straddles national boundaries, overriding the wishes of nations in respect of higher education". Nevertheless, he asserts that "Australia should prefer an unregulated international environment for the borderless delivery of higher education" (p. 7). Embedded within this last statement is the acceptance that neo-liberal economic policies that lead toward deregulation result in positive benefits for universities and that this conception of globalization should not alarm the higher education community.

Australian higher education has grown from an elite system enrolling 32,000 students in 1949 to 660,000 students (in 36 public and two private universities) in 1996. Nearly 40% of those who complete Year 12 enter higher education within two years of leaving school. Education is now Australia's fifth largest source of service export income, generating $3 billion in 1996. Relative to the size of its population, Australia is a highly successful exporter of higher education services, with more overseas students per capita than the USA, the UK or Canada (West Review of Higher Education Financing and Policy, 1997).

It is predicted that in the next few years government funding to universities will be reduced to less than 50% of their total budgets (Williams, 1997 in the West Report, 1997). Williams reports that government expenditure on tertiary education as a percentage of GDP is about at the OECD average although in nine OECD countries government expenditure relative to GDP is higher than in Australia. He concludes by stating that "the best international universities are much better funded than any Australian university" (p. 9). From 1989 to 1996 the required annual fees, known as the Higher Education Contribution Scheme (HECS), for a full-time student was approximately one-fifth of the average amount paid by the federal government to universities for a full-time student place. From 1997 the contribution was substantially increased and differentiated according to discipline ($3300 for Arts, Social Sciences, Humanities and Education; $4700 for Science, Engineering, Economics/Commerce and Architecture; and $5500 for Law, Medicine and Dentistry). The income threshold for repayments in 1997–98 was lowered to $20,700. DeBats and Ward, in a paper comparing American and Australian university policies, found that "the fee increase in Australia has been much greater than anything that has happened in the US" (Richardson, 1998, p. 38).

3. COMPETITION POLICY AND MARKETIZATION OF HIGHER EDUCATION

Competition among universities in most countries takes place in a quasi-market. Both public and (in some countries) private institutions are still supported by government subsidies so it is not a free market situation. Marginson described the OECD "ideal" form of higher education system, which was structured as a quasi-market guided by government:

> The OECD regarded American and Japanese higher education as model systems, because they combined high participation with user payments. The private share of costs was 50% in the USA and higher in Japan. At the bottom, these systems were cheap and accessible and there was a steep hierarchy of institutions in which capacity to pay and academic 'ability' were readily matched to cost and positional values of the institution, naturalizing the elite subsector at the top (Marginson, 1997, p. 222, taken from OECD, 1987, pp. 77–85).

The shift towards greater competition occurred in the United States in the early 1970s when the Nixon administration and other national policy groups introduced the idea of market forces in higher education. More of the costs of a university education shifted to students and universities became more entrepreneurial. This resulted in "a high tuition—high aid policy through which government gave aid to students rather than institutions, thus making students consumers in the tertiary education marketplace" (Slaughter and Leslie, 1997, p. 44). Slaughter and Leslie describe the process as one that forced colleges and universities to engage in 'academic capitalism'. The shift was largely in the area of Research and Development where political leaders developed a strong competitiveness coalition, concentrating on science and engineering and including the universities in profit making. Congress translated competitiveness policies into law which allowed "universities to participate in profit taking, permitted corporations exclusive access to government-funded research performed in universities and federal laboratories, and promoted joint ventures between universities and corporations" (p. 45).

Australia has not gone as far as the United States in 'academic capitalism'; however, a number of policies and reports may move the country along the same route traveled by American institutions. Marginson (1997) noted that Minister Dawkins (1987–91) had created a semi-market system in higher education and Minister Vanstone (1996) had made the competition more intense. Senator Vanstone underscored the kind of changes she wished Australian universities to make: "To survive and prosper in a rapidly changing world, universities must embrace the marketplace and become customer-focused business enterprises" (1996, p. A11). Competition has turned managers into entrepreneurs and their success is based on the institution's financial performance and by its competitive position in research performance and quality assurance. According to Marginson (1997), competitive bidding and profile negotiations between institutions and the federal government forged a culture of compliance. The market liberal reforms "enhanced the freedom and autonomy of universities in the entrepreneurial sense, and diminished them in the collegial sense" (p. 231). At the same time, "competition penalized horizontal diversity, pressing all institutions into a mould, so that universities competed on much the same set of activities" (p. 251).

In the United States, the influence of corporations seems to have had a greater impact on the independence of universities than in Australia. According to Soley:

> Corporate, foundation, and tycoon money has had a major, deleterious impact on universities. Financial considerations have altered academic priorities, reduced the importance of teaching, degraded the integrity of academic journals, and determined what research is conducted at universities. The social costs of this influence have been lower-quality education, a reduction in academic freedom, and a covert transfer of resources from the public to the private sector (Soley, 1995, p. 145).

In a critique of the commodification of higher education in the United States, Shumar made many of the same accusations: "One of the dangers in all of these changes is that universities are increasingly servants of the marketplace and in ways different from the past. The logic of the market is rapidly becoming the only logic on the university campus" (Shumar, 1997, p. 94). John Ralston Saul of Canada echoed this concern. He fears that universities—instead of easing the crisis of conforming to this market-oriented ideology and the corporate structures it has developed—are aligning themselves with specific market forces and no longer fulfil the role of active independent pub-

lic critics (Saul, 1995). In a more recent Business Magazine report (1998), Bill Graham, a philosophy professor and president of the University of Toronto's faculty association was reported as being dismayed at the interaction between academe and business: "The medieval scholar had to worry about the church. . . . We have to concern ourselves with the directing power of money. Its a seductive and driving influence" (Cole, 1998, p. 37).

Those policy-makers enforcing changes on Australian universities seem to have little concern for the potential damaging effects of business practices in universities. The following brief description of the competition policy shows how it is seen as a neutral policy instrument with only beneficial effects on universities. Hilmer[2] has written on how the current competition policy should affect Australian universities and the West Report endorsed his view. The West Report (West Review of Higher Education Financing, 1998) asserts that "the current higher education policy framework has a number of features which impede competition," namely that "restricting public funding to a certain set of 'public' institutions represents one of the greatest impediments to the development of a private higher education sector in Australia" (p. 95). The committee based its argument on the 'competitive neutrality principle' which has been enunciated by Hilmer. He said that choices should be made by "representatives of those who use and fund the services or goods provided and not by the providers" and that "no group in the community should be entitled to judge in its own cause" (Hilmer, unpublished paper prepared for the AVCC and provided to the West Committee). There is no doubt that the West Report endorses the benefits of competition in stating that "increased competition will produce a stronger Australian higher education sector while also benefiting Australian students and the community as a whole" (p. 101).

The West Report enunciated that "the principle of competitive neutrality requires the elimination of any net competitive advantages that publicly owned or funded organizations enjoy simply as a result of their public sector ownership or support. The prime goal of the policy is to promote competition as a way of effecting greater efficiency" (1998, p. 109). In essence any commercial activity undertaken by universities should not be tax-exempt and should be subject to appropriate pricing principles to achieve transparency. The requirements for "competitive neutrality" will also mean that existing public universities could be obliged to lease their facilities (libraries, computer centers, even student amenities) to private providers seeking to compete with them for government funds delivered indirectly through vouchers or directly by means of contracts obtained in competitive funding (Nicholls, 1997).

In reviewing the West Report, Marginson concluded that its arguments for technology and deregulation would result in a global free trade in higher education which would weaken even the strongest of Australian universities. He asserted that "few governments in the world would be so stupid as to sacrifice their university systems on the altar of an abstract economic model . . . the impression remains that deregulation is seen as an end in itself, regardless of the consequences" (1997, p. 43).

The threat to Australian universities has not come only through the West Report but another global accord, the Multilateral Agreement on Investment (MAI). MAI could have had the same consequences if it had been signed between Australia and other OECD countries. Under the proposed treaty obligations, local governments would have had to remove impediments to overseas investors to allow them to operate on the same basis as domestic public and private providers. Signatories to the agreement could not "enact laws to give local providers a market advantage" (Healy, 1998a, p. 37). Jane Nicholls warned public universities about MAI and argued that it is essential to have "international consensus which recognizes that nations have a right to determine their own direction in higher education policy". She warned that the information technology revolution and globalization of capital would subject university systems everywhere to destabilization and deregulation on a scale "that can be scarcely imagined" (Healy, 1998b, p. 47). Fortunately Australian policy makers among others heeded these warnings and decided not to sign the MAI Treaty. The Government decided that there were legitimate concerns about Australia's sovereignty under the treaty and did not see the OECD proceeding further with the treaty (Hudson, 1998, p. 17).

Apparently the French Government and the US Congress were also staunchly opposed to the MAI Treaty. This was despite its promotion by the OECD to all its Members as a means to secure further investment liberalization and to promote economic growth and efficiency. It also wanted to "reduce the risks of international business by providing predictability and security for international investors and their investments" (OECD, 1998b, p. 82). For those who opposed it, it was seen as an instrument of multinational corporations to have carte blanche entry into any country without maintaining the social values and safeguards necessary for the country's economy and national identity. An example of this kind of opposition is found in an email from Michael Sysiuk declaring that "San Francisco is a MAI Free zone!"

On Monday, 20 April 1998, the campaign against the MAI and corporate globalization scored a big victory when the San Francisco Board of Supervisors voted unanimously to approve a resolution to oppose the MAI and "similar international agreements that could restrict San Francisco's ability to regulate within its jurisdiction, decide how to spend its procurement funds and support local economic development". This proactive stance sends free-traders and the White House a much needed reality check: what's good for multinational corporations is not necessarily what's best for our communities, working people, the environment and human rights (Sysiuk, 1998).

4. GREATER ACCOUNTABILITY AND QUALITY CONTROL

The Australian higher education system was derived from the British universities and technical institutes but in the late 1980s and early 1990s it moved towards a more American style system, combining high participation, greater institutional differentiation, market competition and part private funding.

> The key moment in the "advanced liberal" modernization of the Australian system was the reforms implemented by the then Labor Government Minister for Employment, Education and Training, John Dawkins, in the 1987 to 1989 period. Dawkins restructured higher education in the form of a "Unified National System"

which was also a quasi-market in which each institution competed with every other for academic prestige, non-government funding and, in a growing number of areas, government support as well (Marginson, 1996, p. 81).

One key initiative of the Dawkins' White Paper (1988) was the enhanced accountability of universities to the federal government through the institutional profiles negotiations. These are an annual exercise where each institution is required to negotiate its teaching and research profile with bureaucrats from the federal government, within the framework of national priorities. In effect, with this mechanism, the federal government used funding levers to force compliance with its own agendas. The White Paper (Dawkins, 1998) also identified a preliminary range of performance indicators, including student satisfaction, completion rates, relative staffing levels, research publications and consultancy rates which could be used for accountability purposes. The subsequent and ongoing momentum of the Dawkins' reforms in relation to accountability was demonstrated by the rapid succession of groups reporting on the further development of performance indicators. The Performance Indicators Research Group chaired by Russell Linke reported in 1989 that the government could use performance indicators but stressed the need for caution with regard to their validity and reliability and the need to use multiple indicators to avoid promoting uniformity. Further, the report emphasized that quantitative indicators should only be an adjunct to qualitative judgements (Linke, 1991).

In the early 1990s, with a growing backlash to the proposed use of performance indicators from the sector, the federal Labor government introduced a new form of competition between universities through the quality audits and associated quality league tables which allocated differential financial rewards and (more importantly) status rewards. Following the ministerial quality policy statement in 1991, the Committee for Quality Assurance in Higher Education (CQAHE) was established to conduct a three year cycle of quality audits between 1993 and 1995. CQAHE members revealed that they had used some performance indicators in their assessments, but only to inform their more qualitative value judgements (Vidovich and Currie, 1998). However, these quality reviews significantly enhanced both accountability of institutions and competition between institutions (Vidovich, 1998). Further, as a result of the quality audits, universities began instituting their own quality management committees and developing internal performance indicators in preparation for each annual cycle in which the government budgeted approximately $76 million dollars to be distributed to universities based on their quality ranking. In addition to these quality audits, the government instituted the Research Index Fund based on a range of performance indicators, such as postgraduate completions, grants and publications. The total points scored on the research index determined a portion of each institution's budget. This was often distributed internally by the number of points scored by each Faculty/Department, leading to greater internal as well as external competition.

The current (1996–1999) Liberal-National Coalition Government has maintained the use of the Research Index Fund along with the institutional profiles process as two accountability mechanisms for universities. It has not continued the quality audits as a separate, high profile exercise but has "mainstreamed" quality assessments with the institutional profiles negotiations. However, in anticipation of more performance assessments, many universities have been implementing their own performance indicators in the areas of teaching and administration. In an open pool in The Australian Higher Education Supplement, in response to the question: have the demands on universities to provide data on quality gone too far?, two-thirds of respondents thought they had (The Australian Higher Education Supplement, 1997, p. 38). A few of their comments are worth quoting:

> Academics have among the highest standards of any professional group; fraud and slacking are not parts of the academic mindset. They can be trusted to do research and to teach well, provided they have the opportunity to do so (unidentified respondent).

> Universities are being forced to spend so much time collecting, analyzing and presenting data on how well they are doing that they do not actually have the resources to get around to doing 'good stuff (a Murdoch Staffer).

Universities provide data not on quality but on quantity and this has gone to 'ridiculous extremes'. Bureaucrats want mindless formulas, never a measured academic judgment (an Adelaide academic).

The rush for quality is having the opposite effect. "We're fluffing out the trimming but removing the content in a pretence designed simply to keep our rankings in the meaningless league tables that the bean counters continue to tabulate. Enough! Let's get back to education and scholarship, to what universities are supposed to be about and not the corporate jargon of clients and products" (a NSW academic whose university ranks within the first three universities on most of the league tables).

In a more recent article (Illing, 1998), the flaws of the current system were exposed by a well-respected, former Vice-Chancellor of the Australian National University. He said that the "naive use of arithmetic measures of performance" was one of several mechanisms imported from private business and public administration that were "arguably dysfunctional in a university setting". He felt that "many of the indicators failed to gauge performance in any meaningful way". Moreover, he said "they emphasized quantity and seldom took account of quality, greatly distorting conclusions drawn from them" (p. 35).

Through the use of both "quality" and performance indicators, the federal government is exerting control by "steering at a distance". Government sets the desired outcomes ("ends") but devolves decisions about the processes ("means") to institutions. This "steering at a distance" mechanism is also seen as a change in style of university governance, with devolution of budget responsibilities to lower levels within institutions at the same time that senior management gains greater central control over policy directions. This allows universities to respond to the market and enables middle-level managers to take more initiatives (Marceau, 1993; Marginson, 1996; Currie, 1998). Currie and Vidovich (1998) argue that this has resulted in greater managerialism within universities and a widening of the gap between academics and managers. This supports a similar case made by Bessant (1995) who studied the emergence of the senior executive as a separate and exclusive group and the adoption of corporate management practices in a number of Australian universities.

5. VIEWS OF THE CHANGES FROM AUSTRALIAN ACADEMICS

This section focuses on the views of Australian academics on the impact of the ideology of privatization, and its raft of market principles, within their universities. In this way, it offers micro level case studies of some of the general changes discussed in the previous sections, as perceived by academics working at three different types of institutional sites in Australian higher education. In particular, the focus here is on changing decision making structures and processes within institutions, but views on changing accountability are also briefly overviewed. The research project from which the interview data is drawn, The Changing Nature of Academic Work, follows Foucault's (1991) suggestion that power should be studied in an ascending way, starting from the bottom, investigating the micro-level of society to see how power circulates within it. The aim of Foucault's 'microphysics of power' is to discover the effective practices and techniques (often borrowed from business in this case) used by governments to control and shape our behavior (McHoul and Grace, 1993).

The interviews were conducted in the mid 1990s with 156 respondents at Sydney, Murdoch and Edith Cowan universities. These institutions were chosen to represent different contexts in Australian higher education, especially in terms of age, status and size. Sydney University is the oldest in Australia (established in the 1850s) with a current student population of approx. 30,000, and it has traditionally enjoyed a high status reputation. Murdoch University was established in the 1970s as an alternative university, and it has a current student enrollment of approx. 9000. Edith Cowan University was a college of advanced education (focusing almost exclusively on teaching rather than research) prior to the 1988 reforms by Minister Dawkins and it became a university in 1991, and has a current student enrollment of 17,000. The respondents represented a range of discipline areas across Education, Social Sciences/Arts, Business/Economics and the Sciences and a range of academic ranks from Professor to Associate Lecturer. About one-third of each sample was female academics, representing a similar range of ranks. The qualitative data was analysed using the NUD.IST software program. While the percentages of respondents in the different categories which emerged from the data provide a sense of the strength of the responses, these are supported with quotes which reveal the views of academics in greater depth.

When respondents were asked the question "Have you experienced any changes in accountability requirements over the last 5 years?", a large majority (85%) had experienced an increase in demands. No respondent at any of the three universities reported feeling less accountable over that time, and 15% reported no change. It seems, though, that the increased accountability was experienced by a larger percentage of the sample at the pre-Dawkins universities (92% at Sydney and 88% at Murdoch) than at Edith Cowan (75%). The finding possibly reflects the more bureaucratic structure Edith Cowan had historically inherited, where accountability to a superior was already a major feature, so that the effect of the changing accountability was less marked.

For most respondents, increased accountability meant growth in bureaucratic procedures, especially form filling. Such requirements appeared as extra tasks for academics in an already overloaded schedule, and hence they had contributed to further work intensification. Frustration was evident with the duplication of requests for the same information. The federal government was often identified as a major source of the push for greater accountability of academics, and the 1993–95 quality audits were clearly identified as exercises in raising accountability. Many respondents made the point that they were not opposed to accountability per se but to the form of the current requirements. They perceived bureaucratic mechanisms as time-consuming "busywork", which at best distracted from the "main game" and at worst distorted the academic enterprise to seriously impede attainment of academic "excellence".

The following quotes reflect some of the general themes raised by respondents:

> The need to be constantly responding to directives from Canberra (the federal bureaucracy) which intrude into everybody's lives. . . . Constant requests for

research information about both publications and research grants, requested in every conceivable format. So you no sooner seem to have finished one set of such information than they want pretty much the same thing but in a different format, which people find very frustrating (Murdoch).

> There's definitely more directives from DEET (federal bureaucracy), filling in forms. I'm actually rather resistant in that regard. Probably doesn't do me too much good. Just endless forms about your research activity, this, that, the other thing, and half the time I don't fill in the forms. They've clawed back the base grants—so in a sense what it will do is force individuals into some reporting mechanisms if they want to get the loading. If you resist you lose the money (Edith Cowan).

Focusing now on decision making structures and processes, when respondents were asked the question "How would you describe the style of decision making at your university?", they used a variety of labels such as bureaucratic, corporate managerial, democratic, and collegial. Responses were organized into the three categories of "non-participatory", "participatory" and a "combination" of both. The majority (59%) responded that decision making was non-participatory in their university. In their words, it was bureaucratic, corporate managerial, top-down, centralized and autocratic. Some (19%) identified that there was a combination of decision making styles operating in their universities, often identifying more democratic decision making procedures at the departmental or faculty level and more bureaucratic and corporate managerial procedures at the overall institutional level. About one-fifth (22%) responded that decision making was still participatory, and most of those respondents were at Murdoch and Edith Cowan universities. Only one respondent at Sydney found this to be the case.

The following quotes from each university represent the respondents who felt the university was becoming less democratic and more bureaucratic or more managerial:

> Its never been democratic. Its gone from oligarchic to bureaucratic. That's the reason that the university is running down—its never used the talents, interests and energies of the staff in its management. . . . It's

becoming more bureaucratic. Corporate managerialism dignifies it too much. . . . The oligarchic thing worked for a small institution but it was unable to adapt quickly enough to the requirements that were really corporate requirements. Melbourne was another old university and you might think just as incapable of change but they somehow had the leadership, or foresight or political nous (common sense) to see that the world was changing (Sydney).

Important decisions are passed down from the top, although there is quite a lot of flexibility about how people can allocate resources at the School and Departmental level. It's certainly a lot less dictatorial than in some universities. This university has made a decision about extending to another campus at Kwinana. I think that was probably one of the least democratic decisions but it had to be made quickly because we were in competition with other institutions. We were moved along very much by the instigators of the project because they said, "We are going to make a decision on the x of November and you will have to put up a case." So we were driven very much by outside forces (Murdoch).

Extraordinarily bureaucratic. It's amazing. I had felt that the Education Department (State Government) was unnecessarily bureaucratic but Edith Cowan beats it hands down. In this organization, there are many layers with forms to fill out for just about everything, approval is required to do the most trivial things and with very much a strong commitment among the administration to follow those rules (Edith Cowan).

There were also those who felt the university was still collegial (even to its own detriment is the tone often used) or even increasing its participatory style of decision making (from a fairly autocratic base). Since only one respondent at Sydney felt this, the following two quotes from Murdoch and Edith Cowan demonstrate this perception:

The University started off back in the 1970s by deciding that it should be democratic and based on a highly collegiate style and that is entirely appropriate to an institution that is very small. As an institution gets larger and as there are greater amounts of impositions from state and federal government, it becomes increasingly difficult to maintain that same democracy in which

everybody could be involved, even in the most trivial decisions, to what is now essentially the need for a managerial autocracy in which people are still involved in the decision making process but the whole thing is much more streamlined. We fall somewhere in the middle where we recognize the need to operate at a more managerial level, but we're still operating on a democratic level down here somewhere and what we're ending up with is poor decisions because very frequently it's not clear how policy decisions are made, on what basis, by whom. And when they are made, it is often the case that important ones are not being implemented (Murdoch).

With the new Vice-Chancellor, it is becoming more open. . . . Things are changing more towards the democratic approach, so it is quite noticeable that things are loosening up (Edith Cowan).

Finally there were some that felt that a combination of decision making was a more accurate description of the current state of play. Two quotes from Sydney and Murdoch demonstrate this viewpoint since only one person from Edith Cowan discussed decision making as a combination of different styles.

Badly; it's an unfortunate mix of all three; sometimes you need a corporate sense, then they say no, you have to consult and then the decision doesn't get made; another decision that was made corporately should have been made democratically. It's an inevitable conflict within universities working out the connections between these three, and I don't think they have been worked out successfully. At the corporate level there seems to be fragmentation (Sydney).

That is a hard one to answer. It is collegial in regard to academic decision making. It is bureaucratic in regard to financial and administrative decision making. There has been a definite shift over the last five years towards more centralized decision making; a managerial style organization—and I take that to be for the worse because it means that the academic collegiality of Murdoch is being set at a discount by the managerial style. Which is not to say that decisions made at the centre are necessarily wrong. I think that there have been some good decisions in recent years about university expansion and that sort of thing. But if it is setting a precedent of putting the academics to one side, and giving preference to a chancellorial hierarchy, then that is a cost that may not be one that we will be glad to bear in the future (Murdoch).

When respondents were asked the question "Have there been any changes in the decision making process over the last five years?", the majority response (between 64% and 80% across the three universities) was that there was increased non-participatory decision making over the previous five years. A few quotes, which demonstrate these changes towards top-down, corporate managerial style decision making, are given here:

It is more managerial. It is less democratic as a result. Any sense of a coherent university has been lost by the production of fiefdoms, where the different faculties are run by robber-barons who call themselves Pro-Vice-Chancellors and who get motor cars and so on. They are called senior management. It came with the previous Vice-Chancellor and the appointment of the Boston Consulting Group and the throwing of at least a million dollars at them to produce a bunch of flow charts. . . . It had almost no beneficial impact but it gave the green light to restructure or managerialize (Sydney).

It's changed because the sheer increasing size of the university has meant that more decisions are being made by smaller groups of people. For example, there was no Planning and Management Committee or anything that even looked like it four years ago (Murdoch).

I'm not sure what they're called, the Deans of the faculties come together with the Vice-Chancellor and the Deputy Vice-Chancellor and the representatives of the major service organizations, effectively that's where the power is and then their decisions are passed along to the Academic Council which effectively is a rubber stamper (Edith Cowan).

There were also some staff who said that the university is becoming more democratic. This was particularly the case at Edith Cowan. A typical quote follows:

A lot of decision making has devolved down to the schools. Much more than we ever had before. Much, much better (Edith Cowan).

At Murdoch a few respondents saw the benefit of devolution although they also identified the way in which it could harm morale because the tougher decisions are taken close at home:

Clearly the devolution to Schools of all financial matters and then in this particular School we devolved it down to Departments. So in terms of how we run ourselves in a resources sense, we have got that responsibility now. We don't have the comfort of falling back on an anonymous central body like RAAC (Resource Allocation Advisory Committee) to say "Well you make decisions for us." We have to make hard decisions. That's the significant change that the process of making choices is now firmly devolved onto the people who are affected by those choices. The problem is that it is harder in terms of the interpersonal relationships that are involved in actually making some of those hard decisions. Because there are gainers and losers out of those decisions. It was fine when we could blame RAAC but when we have to make a decision here then some people are going to gain in terms of whatever the issue may be, not necessarily in the monetary sense, some people may lose and that is hard. That is hard for the morale (Murdoch).

There were also some who did not see that major changes were occurring in the decision making process. Two quotes demonstrate this kind of response (the Murdoch one probably identifying that a collegial style remains, while the Edith Cowan one suggests the autocratic style is still there):

Clearly there have been changes in the structures of some of the major committees, things like Education Committee and RAAC but I don't think the basic decision making process has changed dramatically, no (Murdoch).

It seems that things are now getting less centralized. Decision making seems to be evolved through faculty or school but instead of having a dictator at the top, there is now this level of dictators lined up making decisions the same way as the central system used to be and in our group certainly there is no collegial or democratic process operating (Edith Cowan).

Overall this interview data revealed changes towards enhanced accountability and a predominance of non-participatory decision making at all three universities, with senior or middle managers (rather than academics) making key decisions, and grassroots academics feeling increasingly responsible for achieving the goals set by superordinates.

6. DISCUSSION

Despite their differing local contexts and the 'messiness' (Ball, 1994) of the policy process in any organization, the universities in this study appear to be moving towards a more common, corporate model with "leaner and meaner" decision making structures and processes (albeit at different rates of change). The need to respond rapidly to a changing external environment, especially economic constraints, is frequently cited as the rationale for the changes within universities. There is a connection between the ideological shift towards privatization of universities, the demands for greater accountability to government and increased managerialism within universities. This interconnectedness is captured in the following quote which identifies the push to run universities more like businesses and the impact this generates within institutions:

> Of course, much of the Dawkins' agenda was an argument about the lack of accountability of institutions. The inappropriateness of their governance structures demand that they be run much more like business corporations and the 'knock on' effect of that right down from reduced numbers in the Senate to the kind of line management universities are adopting (Professor, Murdoch).

This interconnectedness can also be seen in the latest Vision Statement of Murdoch University (Murdoch 21) which uses managerial terms throughout the document, demands speedy decision making on the part of the staff and wants to make staff more accountable to one person who would directly report to the Vice-Chancellor. Under a heading called: 'Make Productivity Gains and Manage Strategically', the Vice-Chancellor identified 23 actions to be voted on within 3 weeks that among other things would restructure the university into divisions and create a hierarchical management structure with appointed, Executive

Deans. In the rationale for changing academic structures, the main reasons given were to maximize the efficiency, quality and cost effectiveness of the administration and reduce academic committee workloads. Earlier in the year Murdoch's Vice-Chancellor eliminated 32 committees and in this document he advised Schools to eliminate more committees and leave decisions up to the Executive Deans. Despite some concern that there is little evidence that this type of line-management has led to greater productivity or efficiency (Treuren, 1996), the trend in this direction seems irreversible as one university after another moves towards a smaller number of divisions and the appointment of executive deans with more power over decision making. This trend is not only observed in Australia. In a comparative study of New Zealand with Australia and the United Kingdom, Kelsey identified the impact that these managerial reforms were having on academics as a group:

> Removed from the decision making process, academics become mere wage labourers selling their services for a price, subject to strict employment contracts, performance appraisals, and managerial oversight. Labour market deregulation reinforces this deprofessionalization, as national awards are replaced by enterprise or individual contracts with performance incentives and differential pay scales reflecting market demand (Kelsey, 1998, p. 61).

It appears that despite these attempts to restructure universities to gain more efficiencies, the overwhelming response from academics was about the inefficiencies of the new accountability regimes and the waste of their time in filling out forms. The duplication of requests for the same information on different forms emerged as a major frustration for academics. In addition, there was a growing concern that all of these forms were not making any difference to the quality of teaching or research. For example, one respondent spoke at length about the weaknesses in the current system of student evaluations, questioning the validity and reliability of the surveys, as well as the potential impact of always giving students what they wanted to avoid adverse evaluations. Perhaps the major impact of accountability that may lessen the quality of education for students and the quality of research for the community is the time it takes away from other important tasks academics perform. It adds to their already overloaded schedules and hence leads to further work intensification.

Of greater importance may be the responses that identified that accountability operated in such a way as to foster greater instrumentalism in both teaching and research, to the detriment of broader social goals. This has forced some researchers to steer away from pure, curiosity-driven research to tackle the areas of priority, chosen by the government, with more commercial application. Instrumentalism as applied to teaching means that subjects (philosophy, history, classics), once thought essential in a university, may be dropped in favor of those that are more popular with students and seen as having greater direct job applicability (commerce, computing, media).

The survival of universities in the present system means that there is greater compliance to accountability measures and to changing internal structures and procedures to match those the government advises are in the best interest of a particular university. For the individual academic, there is also a lot of pressure to comply with both internal regulations and those imposed by federal government agencies to procure funds for research. Although some academics continued to engage in a range of resistance techniques to accountability measures, the threat of funding withdrawal and job loss for other than tenured staff is often a sufficient sanction to force compliance.

7. CONCLUSION

Privatization and the market ideology have brought business practices into universities which have serious negative ramifications. The frightening aspect of privatization is the subtle way business practices infiltrate institutions so that the work culture of universities is changed. Unless there is greater organization of resistance to these practices, which link universities to markets, the result will be a shift from 'scholar' to 'entrepreneur' (from educator to trainer and from pure to applied researcher). A certain amount of entrepreneurialism and instrumentalism may be of benefit to universities. A certain degree of privatization of universities may be tolerated. However, the question

that each country must consider is at which point in the privatization process do market principles begin to destroy the "public interest" function of public universities.

With little concern for maintaining traditional academic values, Australian universities under threat from the neo-liberal reform agenda which is restructuring the higher education system. Kelsey describes the way global neo-liberalism is trying to silence universities, especially their ability to be a critical voice in society:

> Underpinning the privatization and internationalization agenda lies a deep ideological belief in the virtue and infallibility of global markets and a corresponding intolerance of alternative views. Universities provide a repository of historical knowledge, a source of critique, and a breeding ground for competing ideas which challenge the portrayal of neo-liberalism as immutable and indisputable orthodoxy. As such, they present an obvious target for radical market-oriented restructuring (Kelsey, 1998, p. 58).

The economic rationalists should listen to the arguments of Rodrik (1997) who wrote the book, Has Globalization Gone Too Far?. He quoted Katzenstein (1985, p. 5) who stated that "it is no accident that small, highly open European economies such as Sweden, Austria and the Netherlands have large governments. Governments in these economies have sought to provide a cushion against the risks of exposure to international economic forces and have done so by extending their powers" (p. 50). He summed up his argument by suggesting that those governments that risk the vicissitudes of global markets need to have more generous social programs. "Hence the conclusion that the social welfare state is the flip side of the open economy" (Rodrik, 1997, p. 53). The social welfare state gives more protection to higher education and believes in generating communities within institutions as well as in the wider society. Similarly, we argue that the privatization push needs to be curtailed and a higher level of public funding restored to universities.

Within their recently enhanced roles as Chief Executives of corporate universities, Vice-Chancellors might consider preserving and extending the fragments of collegial, participatory decision making identified in this study. Otherwise, universities and their 'clients' are likely to suffer in the longer term. It is salient to heed the advice of Burton Clark (1998) who feels that the heartland of universities is still found in the traditional academic departments where traditional values are most firmly rooted and these have to be blended with newer managerial practices. He asserts that it is through "collective entrepreneurial action" (p. 2) that universities can be transformed into entrepreneurial organizations and that academic values should guide this transformation.

To counter the movement towards corporate managerialism, there needs to be a lively debate generated within universities about decision making practices with the objective of ensuring that forms of democracy are maintained and critical voices are not silenced. Retaining tenure is an important plank in this resistance strategy because few contract academics would take the risk of speaking out against management and challenging them on what management sees as their managerial prerogative. Yet it is important to keep up the pressure and not lose ever more ground in the 'collegiality' stakes.

Slaughter urged American faculty who were concerned with restructuring to begin preparing for it through debate within their own universities and to open forums in which community and political groups can interact with professionals to form new coalitions built around concepts of the public interest (Slaughter, 1993, p. 249). However, Levine warns American institutions that the government is going to become more intrusive into their affairs because there is a perception that universities are dragging their feet and are selfish and unconcerned about the public good. He says that this criticism directed at higher education is likely to affect universities in a variety of ways.

> In the years ahead, the faculty role in governance is likely to diminish. Boards of trustees will become more active in the management of educational institutions. Government regulation of higher education will increase and encompass such matters as faculty workloads and tenure. . . . Demands for accountability from institutions and their faculties are also likely to increase and, if not heeded, to become mandates (Levine, 1997, p. 3).

A number of writers have commented on the dangers facing universities, but few have tried to develop programs of resistance or alternative policies that could counteract these global trends. Jones (1996) proposed the development of charters of collegial autonomy for Australian universities that would detail the democratic forms of self-governance that collegialism should entail. He identifies, in particular, the need to make middle managers accountable to their colleagues and specified collegial skills be made essential merit selection criteria for their appointments:

> Charters would thus register the dual accountability of academic 'middle managers': 'upward' to the university management primarily (and increasingly) via budgetary responsibilities and 'laterally' (not 'downward') to their colleagues, primarily as practitioner/advocate of the collegial norms and procedures articulated in the charters (Jones, 1996, p. 7).

There needs to be greater exchange of information among academics across the world to compare methods that work to preserve the quality of their institutions (remaining cognizant that methods may not translate across nations because of their different historical and material settings). If we, as academics, are not going to resist these global trends, then many of the most committed and dedicated of our colleagues will resign in despair. This feeling of despair is seen in a quote from a Murdoch University respondent:

> When your interest coincides with your work then you are not so much working for the money. So when I had time to think, to talk to people, to read the kind of stuff I wanted to, to do the kind of research that I wanted, the money was not such an issue. If I am going to be held to my desk, accounting to people all the time, filling in even more forms, I think "What the hell, I might just as well be a Stockbroker and earn lots of money" (Pears et al., 1996).

Embedded in this quote is the total sense of alienation from work that this academic is experiencing. He no longer sees his work as contributing to new knowledge because he is given no time to reflect and exchange ideas with other staff. This lack of time is invading universities as their work is intensified and the aims of the institution are to bring in ever more students, both locally and internationally and ever more money from industry and the private sector in general. If the frustration inherent in the above quote is not turned into political action, it will quickly lead to apathy and an atomization of staff. How can universities preserve the best of the past as they move into the 21st century when the pace of change will be ever greater and the external pressures to conform to these global practices ever more pressing?

NOTES

1. Roderick West was asked to chair a review of higher education financing and policy by the current Minister of Education, David Kemp. It was to set the agenda for higher education until the year 2010.
2. Frederick Hilmer is the Chair of the National Competition Council that has attempted to extend competition into the public sector.

ACKNOWLEDGEMENT

This research has been funded by the Australian Research Council and Murdoch University.

REFERENCES

Armitage, C. (1995). Competition may be bad for unis. *The Australian,* 30, November, 8.

Armitage, C. (1996). The threat to higher learning. *The weekend Australian,* 18–19 May, 1.

Ball, S.J. (1994). *Education reform: A critical and post-structural approach.* Open University Press, Milton Keynes.

Bessant, B. (1995). Corporate management and its penetration of university administration and government. *Australian universities' review,* 38 (1), 59–62.

Buchbinder, H., Rajagopal, P. (1996). Canadian universities: The impact of free trade and globalization. *Higher education,* 31, 283–299.

Cole, T. (1998). Ivy-league hustle: The University of Toronto fundraising team is raking in both cash and controversy as they put the touch on corporate Canada. *Business Magazine,* June, 35–44.

Clark, B. (1998). *Creating entrepreneurial universities: Organizational pathways of transformation.* Oxford: Pergamon Press. (International Association of Universities and Elsevier Science Ltd).

Currie, J., & Vidovich, L. (1998). Microeconomic reform through managerialism in Australian and American universities. In Currie, J., & Newson, J. (Eds.), *Universities and globalization: Critical perspective.* Thousand Oaks, CA: Sage, pp. 153–172.

Currie, J. (1998). Globalization practices and the professoriate in Anglo-Pacific and North American universities. *Comparative Education Review* 42 (1), 15–29.

Dawkins, J., (1998). *Higher education: A policy statement.* Canberra: Australian Government Publishing Service.

Fisher, D., & Rubenson, K. (1998). The changing political economy: the private and public lives of Canadian universities. In Currie, J., & Newson, J. (Eds.), *Universities and globalization: Critical perspective.* Thousand Oaks, CA: Sage, pp. 77–98.

Foucault, M. (1991). Governmentality. In Burchell, G., Gordon, C., & Miller, P. (Eds.), *The Foucault effect: Studies in governmentality.* London: Harvester Wheatsheaf, pp. 87–104.

Guerrero, J.C. (1996). The NAFTA threat: labor, academic, nonprofit activists discuss preserving public education. *Labor Notes,* August, 6.

Healy, G. (1997). West reveals 'pressing issues' in review plan. *The Australian Higher education supplement,* Wednesday, 21 January, 21.

Healy, G. (1998a). Foreign threat in global accord. *The Australian higher education supplement,* Wednesday, 4 February, 37.

Healy, G. (1998b). Union call to beware ideological reform bid. *The Australian higher education supplement ,*Wednesday, 4 February, 47.

Hodges, L. (1994). World bank pushes US tertiary model. *The Australian, Higher Education Supplement,* Wednesday, 27 July, 24.

Hudson, P. (1998). Australia drops MAI treaty. *The Age,* Tuesday, 3 November, 17.

Illing, D. (1998). Karmel warns of falling standards. *The Australian higher education supplement,* Wednesday, 3 June, 35.

Jones, P. (1996). *Time for charters of collegial autonomy.* Unpublished paper, Sydney: Department of Sociology and Social Anthropology, University of New South Wales.

Katzenstein, P.J. (1985). *Small states in world markets: Industrial policy in Europe.* Ithaca, NY: Cornell University Press.

Kelsey, J. (1998). Privatizing the universities. *Journal of law and society,* 25 (1), 51–70.

Knight, J., & Lingard, B. (1996). Australian higher education 1987–1995: some notes on a Labor policy regime and its dilemmas. In Warry, M., O'Brien, P., Knight, J., & Swendson, C. (Eds.), *Navigating in a sea of change.* Rockhampton, Queensland: Central Queensland University Press, pp. 4–15.

Levine, A. (1997). How the academic profession is changing. *Daedalus,* 126 (4), 1–20.

Linke, R. (1991). *Performance indicators in higher education.* Canberra: Australian Government Publishing Service.

Marceau, J. (1993). *Steering from a distance: International trends in the financing and governance of higher education*. Canberra: Australian Government Publishing Service.

Marginson, S. (1996). Power and modernisation in higher education: Australia after the reforms of 1987–1989. *Melbourne studies in education*, 37 (2), 77–101.

Marginson, S. (1997). Review needs broader focus. *The Australian higher education supplement*, Wednesday, 19 November, 43.

McHoul, A., & Grace, W. (1993). A Foucault primer: Discourse, power and the subject (Chapter on Power). Melbourne: Melbourne University Press.

Nicholls, J. (1997). Competition changing the public face of education. *The Australian higher education supplement*, Wednesday, 17 September, 44.

OECD. (1987). *Structural adjustment and economic performance*. Paris: OECD.

OECD. (1998a). *Redefining tertiary education*. Paris: OECD.

OECD. (1998b). *Open markets matter: The benefits of trade and investment liberalisation*. Paris: OECD.

Pears, H., Currie, J., & Vidovich, L. (1996). The importance of work in the lives of academics. *Trends report of project: the changing nature of academic work*. Case study of Murdoch University. School of Education, Murdoch University (August), Murdoch, Western Australia.

Richardson, J. (1995). Universities face radical reforms. *The Australian*, 13 December, 1.

Richardson, J. (1998). Why we're suffering shock from tertiary costs. *The Australian higher education supplement*, Wednesday, 18 March, 38.

Rodrik, A. (1997). *Has globalization gone too far?* Washington, DC: Institute for International Economics.

Santamaria, D. A. (1996). Bankers' hegemony creditworthy? *The weekend Australian*, 15–16 June, 24.

Saul. J.R. (1995). *The unconscious civilization*. New York: Free Press.

Shumar, W. (1997). *College for sale: A critique of the commodification of higher education*. London: Falmer Press.

Sklair, L. (1995). *Sociology of the global system*, 2nd ed. (1st ed., 1991). Baltimore, MD: Johns Hopkins University Press.

Slaughter, S. (1993). Introduction to special issue on retrenchment. *The journal of higher education*, 64 (3), 247–249.

Slaughter, S., & Leslie, L. L. (1997). Academic capitalism: Politics, policies and the entrepreneurial university. Baltimore, MD: Johns Hopkins University Press.

Foley, L. C. (1995). Leasing the ivory tower: The corporate takeover of academia. Boston: South End Press.

Sysiuk, M. (1998). *San Francisco is a MAI free zone*. Internet: email from sysiuk@hawaii.edu.

The Australian Higher Education Supplement (1997). Survey: Have the demands on universities to provide data on quality gone too far? Wednesday, 29 October, 38.

Treuren, G. (1996). The changing state-university relationship: State involvement in academic industrial relations since the Murray report. *Australian universities review*, 39 (1), 51–58.

Vanstone, Senator A. (1996). A vision of change. *The age*, Tuesday, 1 October, A 11.

Vidovich, L. (1998). "Quality" as accountability in Australian higher education of the 1990s: A policy trajectory. Ph.D. thesis, Murdoch University

Vidovich, L., & Currie, J. (1998). Changing accountability and autonomy at the "coalface" of academic work in Australia. In Currie, & J., Newson, J. (Eds.), *Universities and globalization: Critical perspective*. Thousand Oaks, CA: Sage, pp. 123–211.

West Review of Higher Education Financing and Policy. (1998). *Learning for life. Final Report*. Canberra: Australian Government Publishing Service.

West Review of Higher Education Financing and Policy. (1997). *Learning for life*. A policy discussion paper. Canberra: Australian Government Publishing Service.

Wheelwright, T. (1995). The complicity of think-tanks. In Rees, S., & Rodley, G. (Eds.), *The human costs of managerialism*. Leichardt, New South Wales: Pluto Press, pp. 29–37.

Williams, R. (1997). Funding higher education in Australia. A commissioned paper (Appendix 14) for *West review of higher education financing and policy* (November 1997) Learning for Life. A policy discussion paper. Canberra: Australian Government Publishing Service.

World Bank. (1994). Higher education: The lessons of experience. *The world bank*, Washington, DC.

Yeatman, A. (1993). Corporate managerialism and the shift from the welfare to the competition state. *Discourse*, 13 (2), 2–9.

CHAPTER 55

STUDY COSTS, STUDENT INCOME
AND PUBLIC POLICY IN EUROPE

HANS-DIETER DANIEL, STEFANIE SCHWARZ AND ULRICH TEICHLER

INTRODUCTION

Costs and funding of study have been amongst the major issues of higher education policy in industrialised societies for several decades (cf. Williams & Furth, 1990; Williams, 1992; Eicher, 1998). Attention is not only paid to financial issues in a narrow sense, i.e. the sums involved, their allocation, the payers, the beneficiaries, and abundance versus scarcity. The steering effects are also at stake: what balance between opportunity and meritocracy should be achieved? How are the cost and funding mechanisms of study, e.g. fees, stipends, tax regulations or services at reduced costs, embedded in the regulatory system of demand and supply for highly qualified labour? How is the role of the students defined through the conditions of the costs and funding of study? What impacts do the modes of costs and funding have on the behaviour of the students and their families and on the higher education institutions?

The debates gained momentum in the 1990s in Europe. Concern about the financial crisis of the Welfare State, deregulatory policies and the growing popularity of incentive steering of higher education in many European countries led to a greater popularity of positions advocating a heavier financial load for the students and their families, e.g. through the introduction and increase of fees (Eicher, 1998), through a reduction of grants or through the introduction of income-contingent loans or a graduate tax (Oosterbeek, 1998). Interest in comparing one's own traditions and modes with those of other countries tended to grow. And the substantial increase of student mobility within Europe challenged the countries to examine whether a growing integration of Europe called for a certain degree of 'harmonisation' of the existing modes of costs and funding of study.

The aim of the comparative study on which this article is based was not only to provide updated in-depth information on the various aspects of costs and funding of higher education, but also to establish the quantitative role public support continues to play in covering the overall costs of study. Moreover, we shall analyse the qualitative function of public support in shaping the students' role, i.e. as dependent children, investors or citizens.

THE APPROACH OF THE COMPARATIVE STUDY

Though students' costs and funding rank prominently in higher education policy, they are not well covered in major international statistical sources. The one that covers the largest number of countries,

Source: *European Journal of Education*, Vol. 34, No. 1 © 1999, European Institute of Education and Social Policy, Paris.

i.e. the UNESCO *Statistical Yearbook* (1997), does not inform on students' costs and funding at all. OECD and the European Commission try to cover this topic in their efforts to provide educational indicators which are partly based on data other than those delivered by the national statistical offices (OECD, 1995, 1997; European Commission, 1994, 1997) but they address only limited aspects. There are, however, various comparative studies on the major features of students and funding in Europe. Amongst the most recent is the one published in 1997 by Deutsches Studentenwerk.

This study aims to take stock of the most recent available information on the main elements of direct costs and funding of study in various European countries. Data were collected on the students' average or typical expenses, tuition and other fees and the conditions, modes and amounts of public support through the grant and loan systems of the respective countries. The results of the various studies (e.g. Dams, 1990; Eicher & Chevaillier, 1992; Dohmen, 1995, 1996) served as a source of reference. In addition, this study aims to show the quantitative role public support still plays. Model calculations are undertaken on how far public support covers the expenditures of students who are awarded the maximum support, the average expenditures of students who receive public grants and loans, and the average expenditures of all students. Finally, the principles and rationales which seem to underlie the composition of cost and funding components, and notably the amounts and modes of public support in the individual European countries, are discussed. Emphasis is placed on the social role of the students, which is obviously reinforced through the public funding scheme.

In the comparative study on which this article is based, information was also collected on additional components of funding of study which are often mentioned in national studies but seldom play a role in international comparisons: e.g. additional fellowship schemes and indirect support through family allowances, tax deductions, subsidies for food and housing, discounts on insurances, transport, learning material, etc. (see also Deutsches Studentenwerk, 1997). As many indirect means of support are available, one would ideally like to know the aggregate support for students from various social backgrounds. As the comparative study

elicited only information on the diversity of these modes of support, but not in sufficient detail to quantify their value for the various types of students, these findings are neither reported here nor taken into account in the model calculations of cost and funding of study.

The comparative study also aimed to summarise available information in the various countries on the steering impacts of the cost and funding pattern of higher education. Available research on the impact on study behaviour (Daniel, 1996; Leslie & Brinkman, 1998; Leszensky, 1993) sought to assess the plausibility of the claims made in public debates on the relationships between funding and study behaviour, the socially deterred effects of tuition fees or the pressures of fees on teachers' and students' efficiency. However, we realised that research on these issues was too scarce to draw any convincing conclusion. Therefore, it is not reported here.

The comparative study addressed all the countries of the European Union (except Luxembourg[1]), as well as Switzerland. Leading experts, either scholars or administrators involved in higher education policy in general or directly involved in matters of student costs and funding (see Table 55.1), were asked to compile available information on their country and write an extended country report both on the findings and the respective debates. The analysis of basic data on costs of study and student income as well as tuition fees and public support was based on the fiscal year of 1997 if information was already available, or otherwise on 1996. The reports of the country experts were written between autumn 1997 and spring 1998. However, the effects of the latest changes of student financing in some countries, e.g. the introduction of tuition fees in the UK in autumn 1998, can only be briefly referred to.

The study was commissioned in late 1996 by the German Ministry of Science and Research of the *Land* North Rhine-Westphalia, in the meantime renamed Ministry of Schools, Continuing Education, Science and Research. The Minister of the time, Anke Brunn, was one of the key advocates in the German higher education reform debates of preserving study opportunities without any tuition fees and introducing a mixed funding system for students similar to that in the Netherlands. She supported such an in-depth study both on established measures and financial conditions

TABLE 55.I
Country Experts in the European Union and Switzerland

Country	Country experts	Institution
Austria	Erich Schuster	Bundesministerium für Wissenschaft, Verkehr und Kunst, Wien
Belgium	Jan Fiers	Education Law Centre, Gent
Denmark	Esbjørn Molander, Susanne Anthony	SUstyrelsen, Copenhagen
Finland	Osmo Kivinen, Juha Hedman	RUSE, Research Unit for the Sociology of Education, University of Turku
France	Thierry Chevallier, Jean-Claude Eicher	IREDU Universite de Bourgogne, Dijon
Germany	Dieter Schäferbarthold	Deutsches Studentenwerk, Bonn
Greece	Vassiliki Georgiadou	University of Athens
Ireland	Patrick Clancy, Deirdre Kehoe	Department of Sociology, University College Dublin
Italy	Guiseppe Catalano, Paolo Silvestri	National University Evaluation Council, Ministry of University and Scientific and Technological Research, Rome
The Netherlands	Hans Vossensteyn	Centre of Higher Education Policy Studies, University of Twente
Portugal	Pedro Telhando Pereira, Tânia Couto d'Oliveira	Faculdade de Economia, Universidade Nova de Lisboa
Sweden	Peter Andersson	Ministry of Justice, Stockholm
Switzerland	Elke Staehelin-Witt, Patrick Parisi	B.S.S., Volkswirtschaftliche Beratung, Basel
Spain	José-Ginés Mora, Adela Garcia	Department of Applied Economics, University of Valencia
United Kingdom	Gareth Williams, Sharon Jones	Centre of Higher Education Studies, Institute of Education, London

as well as on major policies in order to enrich the debates through a sounder basis of comparative knowledge. As the study was initially undertaken to inform the public debate in the Federal Republic of Germany on costs and funding of higher education, these were calculated in DM (i.e. equivalent to 0.52 ECU).

STUDENTS' STUDY EXPENDITURES

Students' total monthly living expenditures vary greatly between the European countries addressed. According to the surveys or model calculations undertaken, they range from the equivalent of more than 1,500 DM to less than 700 DM. Even if allowance was made for different levels of pricing, great variety remained. It should be noted that these figures refer to costs incurred. Study costs borne by government or other sources and discounts and free provisions for students are not included if the students themselves do not pay them.

The average estimated expenditures of students in the countries included was less than 1,100 DM. As column IV of Table 55.2 shows:

- relatively high expenditures (i.e. about 1,400 DM and above) were reported for students in France, the Netherlands, Denmark and Switzerland;

- expenditures somewhat above or below the mean could be observed in Belgium, Sweden, Greece, Finland, Italy and Austria, Germany; and

- relatively low expenditures (i.e. below 900 DM) could be noted in Spain, the UK, Ireland and Portugal.

Living expenditures also vary greatly within countries. Support schemes often reflect three major factors:

TABLE 55.2
Maximum Support and Expenditure for First-Degree, Full-Time Students
Living Independently by Country (in DM/month)

	I Grant	II Loan	III Total Maximum Direct National Support per Student	IV Estimated Expenditure per Student	V Difference between Income and Expenditure	VI Percentage of Support (%)
Austria	1,033 (100%)	0	1,033	936	+ 97	110
Belgium	400 (100%)	0	400	**	**	**
Denmark	897 (66%)	466 (34%)	1,363	1,395	- 32	98
Finland	479 (54%)	410 (46%)	889	1,040	- 151	85
France	454 (100%)	0	454	1,540	- 1,086	30
Germany	505 (50%)	505 (50%)	1,010	1,170	- 160	86
Greece	173 (73%)	65 (27%)	238	1,144	- 971	15
Ireland	429 (100%)	0	429	813	- 384	53
Italy	279 (100%)	0	279	950	- 671	30
Netherlands	727 (69%)	320 (31%)	1,047	1,439	- 392	73
Portugal	527 (100%)	0	527	691	- 164	76
Switzerland	540 (51%)	531 (49%)	1,071	1,621	- 550	66
Sweden	428 (28%)	1,112 (72%)	1,540	1,174	+ 366	131
Spain	616 (100%)	0	616	847	- 231	73
UK	400 (58%)	291 (42%)	691	820	- 129	84

** = No data available.

- whether students live with their parents or independently;
- whether they have a family and are responsible for covering living expenses of children and possibly the partner;
- whether they have to pay tuition and other fees.

The variation according to the first two factors will be illustrated for a few countries. In addition, an overview will be provided on the tuition patterns in all the countries addressed.

Living with Parents or Independently

The differences in total students' living costs in different European countries result partly from the living arrangements that are predominant in the respective countries. Whereas the majority of students in Nordic countries do not live with their parents (Denmark 94%; Sweden 82%; Finland 93%), the majority of those in southern European countries do (Spain 80%). In mid-European countries the situation is different: in France 60%, Germany 77%, and the Netherlands 80% do not live with their parents. In Europe, the average amount students spend on accommodation per month ranges from 195 DM (Portugal) to 890 DM (Switzerland). Students in Northern and Mid-European countries spend on average (510 DM in Denmark, 479 DM in Sweden, and 569 DM in Germany) more than those in some Southern European countries (DM 312 in Greece).

Costs for Other Living Expenses

The average costs for living expenses other than accommodation—e.g. office supplies, food, travel and miscellaneous expenses—also vary. They range from 918 DM (the Netherlands) to 347 DM (Italy). Generally, countries that show above average costs for accommodation also show above average costs for other living expenses because a higher percentage of the student population does not live with their parents.

Nordic countries and the Netherlands show above average living expenses, as is seen in Table 55.3. In the Netherlands, students on

average spend 131 DM on office supplies, 219 DM on food, 125 DM on travel costs, and 443 DM on miscellaneous expenses. In Denmark, students on average spend 63 DM on office supplies, 497 DM on food, DM 25 on travel costs, and 300 DM on miscellaneous expenses. In the UK and Ireland, the costs of living are lower than in the Netherlands or Denmark, mainly because a higher percentage of students live with their parents. In Ireland, students on average spend 77 DM on office supplies, 207 DM on food, 77 DM on travel costs and 133 DM on miscellaneous expenses. Students in the UK spend more on office supplies, especially on books (112 DM) and on food (255 DM), than those in Ireland. The remaining costs of students in the UK are similar to those of Irish students. In the UK, they spend an average of 39 DM on travel costs and 140 DM on miscellaneous expenses. In Southern Europe, costs for living expenses are below the European average. In Spain and Portugal, stu-

TABLE 55.3
Monthly Living Expenditures of First Degree, Full-Time Students Living Independently (in DM)

	Books, Computers, Office Supplies	Accommodation	Food	Travel Costs	Other Living Expenses	Approx. Total
Austrian[1]	126	281	274	83	172	936
Belgium[2]	78	380	375	320	121	1,274
Denmark	63	510	497	25	300	1,395
Finland	No data available	301	229	94	416	1,040
France	95	246	171	242	768	1,522
Germany[3]	61	452	267	118	272	1,170
	53	320	219	119	202	913
Greece	104	312	286	130	312	1,144
Ireland	77	289	207	77	133	783
Italy[4]	54	493	203	22	68	840
Netherlands	131	346	219	125	443	1,264
Portugal	56	195	302	47	47	647
Switzerland	71	890	439	100	No data available	1,500
Sweden	80	479	320	87	208	1,174
Spain	89	446	223	89	No data available	847
UK	112	274	255	39	140	820

[1] Amounts based on students living in dormitories.

[2] 1991 data, partly estimated.

[3] Old Länder/new Länder; 'other living expenses' comprise expenses for medical insurance, telephone and postage, hobbies, sports etc.

[4] Data refer to a student living in Milan, attending the faculty of economics.

dents on average spend 89 DM and 56 DM for office supplies, 223 DM and 302 DM for food and 89 DM and 47 DM for travel costs.[2]

Tuition and Other Fees

Differences in total costs for tuition, registration fees, and administration fees in different European countries are less marked. The monthly costs range from 175 DM (the Netherlands) to no fees at all. Switzerland (116 DM) and Italy (110 DM) charge above average tuition fees. Spain (97 DM) and Portugal (44 DM) charge below average tuition fees. Eight European countries charge no tuition fees: Austria, Denmark, Finland, France, Greece, Ireland, Germany and Sweden.[3] Three countries which do not charge tuition fees charge a moderate registration fee. France charges registration fees of 18 DM per month and Ireland 30 DM per month. A few countries charge a modest student union fee of a maximum of 16 DM per month.

STUDENT SUPPORT SCHEMES

In all countries addressed, there are needs-based national support schemes. However, they vary substantially according to the rules for eligibility, social conditions for support and the students' specific needs (e.g. living independently, family responsibilities, etc.).

Model Support

A comparison of the ideal support for the needy student can be made if we compare the maximum support for a model student, i.e. a first-degree, full-time, student living independently without the responsibilities of a family of her or his own. This model support varies far more between the European countries than the living costs incurred. As the first three columns in Table 55.2 indicate:

- highest monthly support is provided in Switzerland (1,540 DM) and Denmark (1,363 DM);
- some 1,000 DM is the maximum monthly support for students in Sweden, the Netherlands, Austria, Germany and Finland;

- between 400 and 700 DM are provided in the UK, Spain, Portugal, France, Ireland and Belgium;
- the maximum support remains below 300 DM in Greece and Italy.

Grants and Loans

National need-based support systems aim to provide funds to cover the totality or part of the costs incurred by the students belonging to the target group of the scheme. Systems, however, differ enormously according to whether the funds made available are grants, which do not have to be reimbursed, or loans, i.e. support which, in principle, has to be reimbursed. We also note substantial differences in public support made available for a reduction of the rate of interest and the conditions under which the loans can be waived, reduced or the terms of reimbursement modified.

About half the countries provide need-based support partly on a loan basis. The model student defined above receives a monthly loan of:

- more than 1,000 DM in Sweden;
- some 400 to 500 DM in Denmark, Finland, Germany and Switzerland;
- some 300 DM in the Netherlands and the UK;
- less than 100 DM in Greece.

The support scheme is exclusively a grant system in Austria, Belgium, France, Ireland, Italy, Portugal and Spain. Obviously, countries which only support a small number of students tend to provide the direct financial support exclusively as grants.

The monthly grant provided to the model students is:

- highest, i.e. close to 1,000 DM, in Austria and Denmark;
- in the range of about 400 to 700 DM in most countries;
- lowest, i.e. less than 300 DM, in Italy and Greece.

Although the great diversity of the student aid schemes is a major feature, we can single out the following. Students defined as needy ought to be provided a grant which covers about half or slightly more of the monthly costs students in the country incur as a rule.

COVERAGE OF COSTS THROUGH STUDENT AID SCHEMES

A major aim of the study was to show how far national student systems cover the costs of study respectively and how far the students and their families assume these costs. We established three model calculations:

(a) the extent to which the maximum student aid covers the expenditures for students receiving maximum support;

(b) the extent to which the expenses of all beneficiaries of student aid are covered by the student aid;

(c) the extent to which the student aid system covers the expenditures of all students.

The calculations obviously have two major limitations. First, student loans are treated in the same way as student grants, i.e. as contributions aimed to cover current costs; the former, however, are expected to be paid back and thus constitute an additional burden for the students. Second, the costs to be covered by the students and their families might not be a financial load for them, since the calculation could not take into consideration other direct or indirect public subsidies, such as tax deductions for parents, public welfare eligibility for needy students, etc., because the information available was too limited to enable us to calculate the average values of the modes of support.

Maximum Coverage

The maximum support for the model student defined above is sufficient in some countries to cover the costs of study. If we consider the coverage of 90% of the average student expenditures as more or less full coverage of costs, we note that, as presented in Table 55.2:

- the student aid schemes in Austria (110%), Denmark (98%), and Sweden (131%) more or less cover the full costs;
- and those in Finland (85%), the UK (84%), Portugal (76%), Spain (73%), the

Netherlands (73%), Germany (66%) and Switzerland (66%) cover most of costs;

- the student aid system in Ireland (53%) covers roughly half the costs, whereas those in France (30%), Italy (30%) and Greece (15%) cover only a small share of the costs incurred even by the students defined as most needy.

It is obvious that student aid systems in some countries aim to cover the full costs for students defined as most needy. Some countries expect small contributions from these students. The student aid in the last four countries can be considered only as subsidising systems for the most needy students.

If we only consider the grant component of student aid, the Austrian and Swedish student aid systems are the only ones to aim to cover the full costs of the most needy students. In addition, only Spain, Portugal and Denmark aim to cover most of the costs of the most needy students. All other countries expect even the most needy students to assume, immediately or in the long run, about half or more of the costs they incur.

Proportion of Beneficiaries

Almost all European countries addressed in this study can be attributed to two groups as regards the target group of the student aid systems:

- The first aims to provide student aid for almost all students. Students are in principle eligible for support. They might not receive student aid, if obvious wealth makes this superfluous, if they are not eligible because they do not fit into the model of the regular student (e.g. part-time study, non-traditional age student, students who take a long time to obtain their degree, etc.) or if they forego the opportunity of being supported (e.g. because they do not accept loans so as to avoid future debts). At present, 70% or more students receive student aid in all the Nordic countries which were analysed, the Netherlands and the UK;
- The latter group of countries intends only to provide aid for a minority—between 40% and 20%—of socially needy stu-

dents. This holds true for Austria, Belgium, France and the Southern European countries included in the study.

Ireland does not fit into these groups. The Irish concept of student aid sets out to cover most students, but the actual number of students who do not receive aid is close to half. The student aid system in the Federal Republic of Germany concerned over 30% of the socially needy students, but the figure has gradually dropped to 19%. Hence, it can now be considered as belonging to the latter group of countries.

Coverage of Costs of Beneficiaries

Table 55.4 presents student aid *received on average by students who receive some support*. Again, we note great differences:

- in Austria and the Nordic countries, they receive between 650 DM and 900 DM on average (60% and more of the average student expenditures);
- the average support in the Netherlands, the UK and Germany is about half or just under the average student expenditures; the average amounts vary from less than 400 DM to more than 700 DM;

TABLE 55.4
Average National Support and Average Expenditure per Financial Aid Receiver by Country (in DM/month)

	I Financial Aid Receivers (in thousands)	II Grants/Loans Average Direct Financial Support per Student	III Estimated Expenditure per Student	IV II in % of III
Austria	28 (12%)	762	936	81
Belgium	31 (20 %)	495	**	**
Denmark	131 (77% grants) 99 (58% loans)	891	1,395	64
Finland	121 (59% grants) 99 (30% loans)	651	1,040	63
France	415 (20%)	341	1,540	22
Germany	337 (18,7%)	615	1,283	48
Greece	10 (3,6% grants) 12 (4% loans)	45	1,144	4
Ireland	68 (56%)	266	813	33
Italy	108 (6%)	280	950	29
Netherlands	42 3 (84%)	713	1,439	50
Portugal	45 (15%)	172	691	25
Switzerland	**	**	**	**
Sweden	194 (79%)	859	1,174	73
Spain	269 (17,6%)	197	847	23
UK	1,269 (70%)	361	820	44

**No data available.

- in several countries, the average support varies between one-fifth and one-third of the average student expenditures; the average amounts vary between more than 300 DM and less than 200 DM.

Greece is also an exception in this respect. Students who receive some type of aid are granted on average only about 4% of the mean student expenditures.

Funds for Student Aid

The total public expenditures for national student aid systems are bound to vary substantially between European countries, because the size of their population and the number of students differ considerably. At present, total public expenditure ranges from more than 5 billion DM in the UK to less than 100 million DM in Portugal and under 10 million DM in Greece.

Coverage of Costs of All Students

Student aid in the European countries analysed provides, on average, over 200 DM for all students per month. The highest amounts are provided in the Nordic countries and the Netherlands (see Table 55.5). In Denmark, a country with 170,000 students, an average of 686 DM is paid per student per month. Sweden, a country with a student population of 246,000, provides an average direct student support of 678 DM per student. The Finnish aid system supports the students on average with 384 DM per student. In the Netherlands, a country with an enrollment of 139,000 students receive on average 557 DM per month.

In other Mid- and Western European countries the amounts are lower. In Austria, a country with a student population of 234,000, the average per head amount of support is 91 DM. Students in the UK, a country with a student enrollment of 1.8 million, receive on average

TABLE 55.5
Average National Support and Average Expenditure per Student by Country (in DM)

	I Total National Expenditure per year (in million DM)	II Number of Students (in thousands)[1]	III Grants/Loans Average Direct Financial Support per Student/ per Month	IV Estimated Expenditure per Student/ per Month	V III in % of IV
Austria	256	234	91	936	10
Belgium	70	152	461	**	**
Denmark	1,400	170	686	1,395	49
Finland	945	205	384	1,040	37
France	**	**	**	**	**
Germany	1,780	1,838	82	1,283	7
Greece	6.5	290[2]	2	1,144	2
Ireland	217	122	148	813	18
Italy	363	1,792	17	950	2
The Netherlands	2,400	557	595	1,439	39
Portugal	93	301	26	691	4
Switzerland	**	**	**	**	**
Sweden	2,000	246	678	1,174	58
Spain	636	1,527	35	847	4
UK	5,500	1,813	253	820	31

[1] Eurydice, Report 1997: Key Data on Education in the European Union.

[2] 1994–95 data.

** No data available.

253 DM. The average direct national support for students in Ireland, a country with an enrollment of 122,000 students, is 148 DM. In Germany, a country with an enrollment of 1.8 million students, the average support is 82 DM per student.

Students in Southern Europe on average receive the lowest direct national student support. In Spain, a country with a student enrollment of 1.5 million, a student on average receives 35 DM. Italy, with a student population of 1.8 million, provides on average 17 DM per student and Portugal, a country with a student population of 301,000, provides 26 DM per student. In Greece, a country with a student enrollment of 290,000, direct financial aid amounts to only 2 DM on average per student.

Thus, the major financial aid system (including loans) covers more than half of all the students' expenditures in Sweden and about half in Denmark. It corresponds to about 40% of the students' expenses in the Netherlands and Finland, about 30% in the UK and almost 20% in Ireland. Finally, public support for students covers less than 10% of their direct costs in the remaining countries (in Greece less than 1%).

THE ASSUMED AND REINFORCED SOCIAL ROLE OF STUDENTS

The study has shown that public financial support for students varies substantially not only according to the amount provided, the quantitative distribution of funds and the modes of distribution, but also according to the rationales of support. We came to the conclusion that the major rationale of student support in European countries in the past has not so much been to steer study behaviour in a narrow sense, but rather to shape the social role of students:

- The *student as a learner and young citizen* is envisaged notably if substantial grants are provided regardless of parental financial resources;

- The *student as a child in a family social system* is taken as the prototype if hardly any public support is provided for covering direct student expenditures;

- The *student as a child in a family system with a strong welfare component* is reinforced, if student aid depends on parental resources, but financial aid is provided to a large number of all students;

- The *student as an investor in her/his future* is clearly borne in mind when establishing loan components in student aid systems.

It could be added that tuition and other fees seem to play the most ambiguous role in shaping and reinforcing the social role of students. In the current moves in the UK, fees are primarily viewed as part of an investment in the future. In the US, they are often seen primarily as reinforcing efficient behaviour of students and higher education institutions and additionally as reinforcing the student's role as an investor. In Japan, tuition fees are primarily viewed as underscoring the student as dependent on a family system.

In some countries, the system of costs and funding of studies in higher education seems to resemble one of these ideal-type rationales:

- the Danish system obviously has the young learner and citizen in mind;

- the Austrian and German systems seem clearly to reinforce the student as a child in a family society counterbalanced by the Welfare State;

- the Greek system clearly treats the student as a child in a family system;

- there is no country where the student as a young investor is the dominant approach.

Over the years, greater efforts have been made to establish mixed rationales. In Sweden, elements that lay emphasis on students as learners and young citizens are intertwined with those which consider them as young investors. In the UK, efforts are being made to reduce the elements of reinforcement of a young learner and citizen and to strengthen those of a child and a young investor. The Netherlands deliberately introduced the most mixed system in the 1980s. In-depth research would be needed to establish whether it succeeds in having a balanced effect of reinforcing concurrently the student as a citizen, an investor and a child in a Welfare State and in shaping him as an efficient actor, or whether its effect is simply diffused.

COMMON TRENDS, CONVERGENCES OR NEW VARIATIONS?

This study aimed to provide up-to-date information on costs and funding of study and describe recent rationales, policies and debates. The findings suggest that the systems of costs and funding of study vary greatly among European countries.

In asking whether we observe common trends, we have to take into consideration other sources as well. Our study, however, suggests that common trends or changes resulting in a convergence cannot have led very far.

Since the mid-1970s, policies have emerged in some Western European countries (and other countries followed in the 1980s) to reduce the public unit costs for study places and to increase the students' share with the introduction or increase of tuition and other fees (Eicher & Chevaillier, 1992; Kaiser *et al.*, 1993). In most European countries, public expenditures for higher education grew, but governments coped with the expansion of higher education by reducing the expenditures per student. This, however, did not result, as some neo-liberal advocates suggest, in any consistent policies of substituting past equal opportunity and welfare policies by policies which put the student as a young investor in the forefront or by steering mechanisms which reinforce the presumed 'efficient' behaviour of higher education students by seeking short periods of study.

In trying to explain the contrasting expectations of a trend, we have to point out that equal opportunity policies and social welfare approaches had even remained very weak in some European countries in the 1970s. The view of the social role of a student as a child in a family society had been hardly questioned.

Second, approaches towards underscoring the role of the student as an investor and using student costs and funding as a steering device for efficient study and institutional behaviour were often pursued at most very moderately. In this context, we must be aware of the weaknesses of the mechanism advocated for these purposes. The student fees obviously send divergent signals. The loan schemes are viewed as weak factors in reinforcing the role of the students as investors because public loans are created to reduce the investors' risks

and the difficulties of managing consistent and stable systems of loans and reimbursement dampen the enthusiasm of many of their potential advocates.

Third, the rationales of considering the student as a learner and young citizen, though under pressure because of the costs involved, cannot be disregarded because the potentials of steering study through professional rewards might loose further ground in the process of 'massification of higher education' (OECD, 1998) and the trend towards a 'knowledge society'. Also, the rationale of treating students as dependent on their family looses momentum if age of study continues to increase and further steps are taken in the direction of what could be called a 'lifelong learning society'.

Fourth, recent policy debates, informed by the international options, by awareness of the diversity of interests in a democratic society and by greater pessimism as regards the success of targeted societal action, tend to favour cautious changes and mixed models. Therefore, a growing variety of systems of costs and funding of study could be the most likely outcome.

NOTES

1. Student numbers are based on EUROSTAT (European Commission, 1997) which correspond to Unesco ISCED levels 5, 6 and 7 with full-time and part-time, university and non-university higher education being regarded as a whole. Therefore student numbers in column II exceed the number of first-degree full-time students. This is a methodological weakness of this model calculation. However, EUROSTAT provides the most complete database of student numbers in European countries.
2. For Spain and Portugal, data on miscellaneous expenses are not available.
3. In the UK, tuition fees of DM 2,600 were introduced in October 1998.

REFERENCES

Dams, T. (1990) Ausbildings-/Studienförderung im internationalen Vergleich—Empirische Befunde und denkbare Modelle für die zukünftige Bildungspolitik. In: Deutscher Bundestag (Ed.). *Anhangsband zum Schußbericht der Enquête-Kommisson "Zukünftige Bildungspolitik—Bildung 2000"*. Drucksache 11/7820 vom 5, 9.

Daniel, H. -D. (1996). Korrelate der Fachstudiendauer von Betriebswirten. In: H. Albach & K. Brockhoff. (Eds). *Betriebswirtschaftslehre and der Standort Deutschland, Zeitschrift für Betriebswirtschaft* (Ergänzungsheft 1/96), p. 114.

Deutsches Studentenwerk. (1992). *Die wirtschaftliche und Soziale Förderung der Studierenden in den Ländern der Europäischen Gemeinschaft.* Bonn, Deutsches: Studentenwerk.

Deutsches Studentenwerk. (1997). *Aktuelle Entwicklung der Systeme der Studienfinanzierung in Westeuropa in Zusammenhang mit dem Familienlastenausgleich.* Bonn, Deutsches: Studentenwerk.

Doumen, D. (1995). Studiengebüren and Studienfinanzierung im Internationalen Vergleich, *Recht der Jugend und des Bildungswesens,* 43, pp. 442–458.

Doumen, D. (1996). *Neuordnung der Studienfinanzierung—Eine Kritische Bestandsaufnahme des Heutigen Systems und der Vorliegenden Reform Vorschläge.* Frankfurt am Main: Peter Lang.

Dohmen, D. & Ullrich, R. (1996). *Ausbildungsförderung und studiengebühren in Westeuropa.* Köln: FIBS (FIBS—Forschungsbericht, 1).

Eicher, J.-C. (1998). The costs and funding of higher education in Europe. *European Journal of Education,* 33, pp. 31–39.

Eicher, J.-C. & Chevailler, T. (1992). Rethinking the financing of post-compulsory education. *Higher Education in Europe,* 17, pp. 6–32.

European Commission. (1994). *Higher Education in the European Union.* Luxembourg: Office for Official Publications of the European Communities.

European Commission. (1997). *Key Data on Education in the European Union.* Luxembourg: Office for Official Publications of the European Communities.

Freundlinger, A. & Wolfschläger, E. R. (1991). *Zur Sozialen Lage der Studierenden 1990: Internationaler Vergleich von Studienförderungssystemen* (Vol. 1) Wien: Bundesministerium für Wissenschaft und Forschung.

Kaiser, F., Koelman, J. B. J., Floraxi, R. J. G. M. & Van Vught, F. A. (1993*). Public Expenditure on Higher Education: A Comparative Study in the Member States of the European Community.* London: Jessica Kingsley Publishers.

Leslie, L. L. & Brinckman, P. T. (1988). *The Economic Value of Higher Education,* Chapter 8: *The Effects of Student Financial Aid.* New York: Macmillan.

Leszensky, M. (1993). *Der Trend zur Studentischen Selbstfinanzierung: Ursachen und Folgen.* Hannover: HIS GmbH (Hochschulplanung, Band 99).

Metais, J. Le. (1993). *Higher Education Fees, Grants and Loans in the European Community.* London: EURYDICE Unit for England, Wales and Northern Ireland.

Mora, J. G. (1998). Financing higher education: innovation and changes. *European Journal of Education,* 33, pp. 113–129.

OECD. (1995). *Education at a Glance.* Paris: OECD.

OECD. (1997). *Education at a Glance.* Paris: OECD.

OECD (1998) *Redefining Tertiary Education.* Paris: OECD.

Oijen, P. Van, Smid, E., & Broekmulen, R. (1990). *International Comparative Study of Financial Assistance to Students in Higher Education.* Zoetemeer: Ministry of Education and Science.

Oosterbeek, H. (1998). An economic analysis of student financial aid schemes. *European Journal of Education,* 33, pp. 21–29.

Vossensteyn, J. J. (1995). *Direct versus Indirect Student Support. An International Comparison.* Paper presented at the 17th Annual EAIR Forum, 27–30 August 1995, Zürich.

Williams, G. (1992). *Changing Patterns of Finance in Higher Education.* Buckingham: Open University Press.

Williams, G. & Furth, D. (1990). *Financing Higher Education: Current Patterns.* Paris: OECD.

Wolfschläger, E. R. (1991). *Zur sozialen lage der studierenden 1990: Internationaler Vergleich von Studienförderungssystemen* (Vol. 2). Wien: Bun-

Chapter 56

Entrepreneurial Activities in Postsecondary Education

ENTREPRENEURIAL ACTIVITIES IN POSTSECONDARY EDUCATION

STEVE O. MICHAEL AND
EDWARD A. HOLDAWAY

Steve O. Michael is Assistant Professor at the Bristol Bay Campus of the University of Alaska.

Edward A. Holdaway is Professor of Educational Administration at the University of Alberta.

Postsecondary education in western countries has experienced four major phases in this century. An elite phase persisted until about 1945 when a reconstructionist phase emerged, reflecting a more democratic approach. The third phase of reductions in funding and support characterized the 1980s. Inadequate revenues to meet rising costs, government measures, and institutional efforts to become more market-oriented can be viewed as complementary developments which were largely responsible for the current entrepreneurial phase.

Entrepreneurial aspects of postsecondary education include the extent to which users should pay, the balance between market-related and purely academic activities, the relative emphasis upon basic and applied research, fundraising, and greater involvement of institutions and individuals in obtaining patents, licenses, and cooperating with sizeable companies. A more entrepreneurial emphasis has implications for postsecondary administrators, especially in the matters of budget allocations, the need for more training of administrators, and increased attention to student needs. While a greater market orientation is warranted, care must be exercised to ensure that the academic mandate remains paramount.

ENTREPRENEURIAL ACTIVITIES IN POSTSECONDARY EDUCATION

Across Canada, and in many other countries, public postsecondary educational institutions are engaged in entrepreneurial activities to a greater extent than ever before. Both advocates and opponents of entrepreneurship exist, but the issues and implications have not been examined as critically as they deserve. The thesis of this paper is that postsecondary institutions are currently becoming more entrepreneurial as a result of three complementary developments involving underfunding, government influence, and institutional initiatives. Consequently, definitions and meanings of entrepreneurship and marketing in postsecondary education are addressed, some aspects of the history of institutions of higher education are reviewed, three complementary developments are described, and the issues and implications of entrepreneurialism for the administration of postsecondary education are examined.

Source: *The Canadian Journal of Higher Education*, Vol. XXII-2, 1992.

Definitions and Meanings

The word "entrepreneur" generally refers either to a planner or manager of an enterprise or to someone who assumes the risk of an enterprise. In economics, an entrepreneur is one of the four factors of production, the others being land, labour, and capital. An entrepreneur is the catalyst, the agent of change and economic progress, and the one who reaps the loss or profit of an enterprise. An "entrepreneurial activity" therefore refers to the act of planning, setting up, and/or managing a business enterprise. In postsecondary education, the terms have several different meanings. An "entrepreneurial initiative," for example, may be used to describe the coming together of a postsecondary institution and an industry for either research or cooperative education purposes. "Entrepreneurial higher education" may be used to describe a market-system of higher education, in which the administrators of a postsecondary institution think and act similarly to those of a business enterprise. Also, "entrepreneurial efforts" may be used to describe activities engaged in by a postsecondary institution to generate funds, for example, renting out an under-utilised facility, or buying and selling investments, or selling intellectual property. In this regard, Emery (1987) noted that:

> the most promising entrepreneurial avenues available to the tertiary educational sector appear to be: greater co-operation with commerce and industry; the development of private, fee-paying universities and colleges; and the provision of extension education services in the form of corporate consultancies and contracts, mainly as export commodities (p. 84).

In this paper, "entrepreneurial higher education" implies all the conditions previously described, but especially the structuring and administering of a postsecondary institution to reflect a market orientation and less dependence upon government funding.

Marketing activities have increased both quantitatively and qualitatively in postsecondary institutions as these institutions have become more entrepreneurial. Since the word "marketing" means different things to different people, it requires some elaboration. In this paper, marketing is viewed as both a process

and philosophy. As a process, marketing involves the sequential phases of identification of needs, development of appropriate programs, delivery of these programs, feedback about program effectiveness, and modification of existing programs. As a philosophy, marketing requires that institutional activities be planned, coordinated, and executed in a manner that optimally benefits the society, the clients, the relevant publics, and the institution. Marketing serves as an exchange-facilitating function between an entrepreneurial organization and its constituencies. The correct use of marketing, in the view of Kotler and Fox (1985), enables an organization to sense, serve, and satisfy targeted constituencies in a way that is beneficial to both the organization and its target constituencies.

Antecedents

In an attempt to map and analyze the historical development of postsecondary education in western countries, four major overlapping phases can be identified and given the following arbitrary names—"elitism," "reconstructionism," "reductionism," and "entrepreneurialism." The first phase, elitism, occurred when higher education was reserved for the privileged few. As observed in the Bulletin of the Canadian Society for the Study of Higher Education (1991), "the first universities, which began in 11th-century Europe, were like private clubs for privileged members" (p. 2). The second phase, reconstructionism, occurred when universal access to education was introduced as a result of perceived benefits of education to society. Education after the Second World War was essentially reconstructionist. The administration of educational systems and institutions reflected the need to rebuild nations. Governments were enthusiastic about funding education, which was perceived as an instrument to achieve development. Emphasis was placed on universal access and on central planning. Democratisation of education was based on many positive assumptions, including the following: (a) the number of graduates from higher educational institutions is positively correlated with the gross national product; (b) education possesses a capacity to develop a stronger moral sense; and (c) education ensures equal opportunity for all citizens (Tomlison,

1989; Burrup & Brimley, 1982). The second phase was characterized by hope and expectations; it was a period when education enjoyed generous financial support from governments.

The third phase, reductionism, occurred when resources and government financial support declined. Reductionism is used broadly to describe a situation where operating grants either decline or do not increase sufficiently to meet increased costs, and decreases occur in student enrollment (in some places), political support, and/or other resources. While some agreement is evident that benefit has resulted from reconstructionalist postsecondary educational activities, as hoped for after the Second World War, there is no agreement as to how much financial investment produces a particular level of education. Consequently, this important question remains unanswered: At what point will additional funding produce zero return in education? Ribich (1970) pointed out that "increased public spending on education is hardly the most direct way to attack the problem of poverty" (p. 207). He argued that the extra funding must result in additional learning, that the additional learning must lead to an increased capacity to produce, and that this capacity must lift the individual out of poverty. Within this period of reductionism, which is still present, several measures have been adopted by various governments in an attempt to achieve their goals. Some of these include measures to increase accountability, zero-based budgeting, system rationalization, and various measures to enhance efficiency. Apprehension among students and staff and lowering of morale have been common outcomes.

The fourth phase, entrepreneurialism, began when the entrepreneurial spirit was injected into educational systems. This phase incorporates many activities resulting from funding difficulties, government intervention, and the recognition that universities can undertake revenue-generating initiatives to a much greater extent than they have previously. These matters are addressed in the following sections.

Revenue and Costs

The need for fiscal restraint has forced the governments of many nations to make proportional reductions in their spending on traditional public services. Decore and Pannu (1989, p. 150) noted that, since the mid-1970s, Canada, the United States, the United Kingdom, Germany, Sweden, the USSR, and Japan experienced a continual decline in educational spending relative to their gross national products. For Canada, Gregor (1990) noted that the resources committed to postsecondary education as a percentage of GNP decreased from 2.5% in 1970 to 1.9% in 1987–88: in this latter year, 71% was provided by the provinces, 12% directly by the federal government, 9% from student fees, and 8% from other sources (p. 960). A provincial example is provided by Alberta Advanced Education (1989b) which has as one of its goals and priorities for the 1990–2000 AD decade the development of "a framework which will encourage and support a reduced reliance on provincial government revenues" (p. 2).

The European funding situation was assessed in the following three sections of Resolution 945 of the Parliamentary Assembly of the Council of Europe (1990):

> The Assembly . . .
>
> 3. Notes that the problems of financing universities and other institutions of higher education concern all member States, despite the considerable diversity in the situation and structure of higher education in Europe on the one hand and the heterogeneity of levels of economic development on the other;
>
> 4. Observes that, in most member States, the lack of sufficient financial means is mainly due to a rise in the number of students enrolled, to the major increase in the costs of education and research, and to stagnation in public funding;
>
> 5. Regrets the negative effects of this situation on the quality of higher education, on research (the results of which are rarely readily marketable), on the independence and autonomy of institutions of higher education and lastly on co-operation between them in Europe (as a result of the increasing disparity in their resources). (p. 13)

Further, the political support for a substantial increase in educational budgets, which would probably increase taxes, is presently at a low level in many nations. Education is forced to compete with other areas, such as health care, social programs, defense, and municipal services, for its share of government funds. The difficulty of identifying any clear cause-and-effect relationships in educational investments has not helped politicians who, more often than not, are interested in simple and direct answers and must provide tangible justifications for their presence in office. In many places, governments have instituted measures that have radical consequences for educational finance and for college and university administration.

Gregor (1990), however, noted that the perceived tendency of Canadian provincial governments to underfund the postsecondary system "does not reflect the public will" and that "opinion polls have indicated an overwhelming majority . . . in favour of increased postsecondary spending, and a substantial majority acknowledging the importance of postsecondary education to the community and the individual citizen" (p. 961). Gregor added that the raising of fees also was supported. A 1991 poll, conducted by the Angus Reid Group (Tausig, 1991), provided further evidence of positive public attitudes. This poll showed that 60 percent considered that "funding from the federal government should increase" and 69 percent agreed "that university education is 'very important' to Canada's economic competitiveness and social development" (p. 48).

While postsecondary institutions continue to be affected by inadequate government grants, the costs of running these institutions are increasing rapidly for the following three reasons: these institutions are not insulated from the general inflation in the environment; the number of students demanding higher education is rising; and centres of excellence are expensive to operate.

In summary, the level of government funding needed to support postsecondary institutions has declined in many countries. This is a concern to both governments and the institutions. While government grants continue to decline in relative terms and in some cases in absolute terms, student enrollment continues to grow. The costs of running modern libraries, installing modern laboratories, and hiring high-quality faculty have put extraordinary pressures on administrators of higher education. Consequently, increasing fees (which are usually under government control), engaging in more entrepreneurial activities, and shifting of costs through privatization of some func-

tions, are perceived to be popular measures to improve the financial picture.

GOVERNMENT INTERVENTION

In several countries, some realignment of postsecondary operations and offerings has occurred as a result of redirection of government funding. This is closely related to the extent to which postsecondary decision-making is decentralised. In a fully decentralised system, decisions about budgets, operations, administration, admissions, and curricula would be made locally. Such systems are rare, even in the private sector, as the high proportion of funding which comes from government and the need for coordination among institutions both require that governments or their agents exercise substantial influence. As Carter (1980) has stated, "society invests considerable resources in higher education, and evidently expects some benefit to follow" (p. 21).

For Canada, Axelrod (1986) provided this information:

> In the fall of 1981, Ottawa promised to reduce dramatically its support of higher education through the Established Programs Financing arrangement and to redirect its funds toward university programs and research designed to serve the country's economic needs. In every region, provincial governments took initial steps to control the growth of academic programs, to avoid "duplication" of facilities, and to encourage universities to "rationalize" their development in accordance with economic demand. (p. 56)

Throughout the late 1980s, Alberta Advanced Education (1989a) embarked upon rationalisation of the postsecondary education system; its *Guidelines for System Development* (1989) stated that "government has expressed its intention to rationalise the system, that is, to ensure that unnecessary duplication is minimised, that program gaps are addressed, [and] that the benefits of specialization are realized" (p. 1). These *Guidelines* emphasised the need for these institutions to strive for efficiency and effectiveness. A few months after the publication of this document, Alberta Advanced Education (1989b) released a statement which outlined its goals and priorities for postsecondary education and expressed its intentions to encourage institutions to reduce their reliance on provincial government revenues. While the purpose of rationalisation was to reduce cost, diversification of sources of funding was expected to supplement inadequate government funding.

Similar sentiments were expressed in the 1980s in the United Kingdom. A 1987 government White Paper entitled *Higher Education: Meeting the Challenge* (cited in Maclure, 1988), included these statements:

Higher education has a crucial role in helping the nation to meet the economic and social challenges of the final decade of this century and beyond. . . . Higher education should:

- serve the country more effectively
- pursue basic scientific research and scholarship in the arts and humanities
- have closer links with industry and commerce and promote enterprise.

But above all there is an urgent need, in the interests of the nation as a whole, and therefore of universities, polytechnics and colleges themselves, for higher education to take increasing account of the economic requirements of the country.

Meeting the needs of the economy is not the sole purpose of higher education nor can higher education alone achieve what is needed. But this aim, with its implications for the scale and quality of higher education, must be vigorously pursued. . . .

The Government and its central funding agencies will do all they can to encourage and reward approaches by higher education institutions which bring them close to the world of business. . . . (pp. 83–84)

The same principles were to be applied to research. Research councils were directed to give greater priority to targeted efforts that could yield better results with respect to commercial exploitation. Maclure (1988, pp. 87–88), in commenting on the British government's decision to replace the University Grants Committee by a University Funding Council (UFC) on which academics lost the majority that they had previously held, noted that the UFC would receive directions from the Secretary of State about terms and conditions under which payments were to be made to universities. As a result, more policies would be made centrally, more attention would be directed to performance indicators, and the role of civil servants would be enhanced.

A final assessment by Maclure (1988) warrants special emphasis:

It is difficult to exaggerate the magnitude of the change in the management of British higher education implicit in these sections of the Act. One set of long-standing conventions has been swept away. The foundations have shifted. The idea of universities as independent centres of learning and research, capable of standing out against government and society, and offering critical judgments of varying objectivity, informed by learning and protected by the autonomy of historic institutions, is discarded. Instead, universities are made the servants of the State and its priorities. In the context of the late twentieth century they, like the rest of the education system, are to be used in the attempt to create a nation of enterprise and to discredit the 'dependency culture' associated with the forty years after World War Two. (p. 88)

Recent developments in Australia parallel those in Canada, the United Kingdom, and elsewhere. The following statements from the Australian federal government's document entitled *Higher Education: A Policy Statement* (Dawkins, 1988) clearly identify its desires:

The Government intends to shift a proportion of general infrastructure research funding to competitive research schemes, in line with its goal of maximizing the research potential of the higher education system and achieving a closer alignment with broader national objectives. (p. 83)

The Government supports the development of a funding system that responds to institutional performance and the achievement of mutually agreed goals. It intends to develop funding arrangements that take into account a range of output, quality and performance measures, and will initiate moves in this direction during the 1989–91 triennium. (p. 85)

The Government . . . expects that Commonwealth funding for research should be focused more effectively on those institutions and staff with a demonstrated capacity and record of research performance. (p. 92).

In England and Wales, Australia, New Zealand, and some American states, governments also have recently introduced measures to alter organizational arrangements substantially and to provide a greater market orientation in the school sector. This information is included in order to point out that, although the K-12 and postsecondary situations are not analogous, the reorganizational and market aspects are not restricted to the postsecondary sector. Of course, English independent schools have for many years provided prime examples of entrepreneurial activity in the K-12 sector. In Great Britain, the movement toward devolution of authority in order to achieve what is called "school-site management" has been one of the attempts to foster competition among educational institutions. Tomlison (1989) concluded that "in 1988 the state [Britain] is ceding its responsibilities to the market place and it is legitimate to conclude that the long-term effect must be to widen the differences in opportunities" (p. 279). In support of the Bill that would ensure a market-led educational system and to explain the crucial nature of this system to the "health and wealth" of Great Britain, the Secretary of State was reported by Tomlison (1989) to have said that the new system is:

> about enhancing the life chances of young people, about competition, choice and freedom, and about quality and standards. Additionally, it is about the devolution of authority and responsibility, and about harnessing the energies and commitment of teachers, parents and business people. (p. 276)

Further, Sexton (1987) suggested that:

> the more that those customers, parents of children, have a direct relationship, preferably direct financial relationship, with the schools, the more that they can exert their "market" demands, and the more that free market will raise the quality of education— far more so than any dozens of government departments or any hundreds of local education authorities. (p. 9)

In New South Wales, Australia, similar opinions were expressed by the Management Review (1989) which conducted a comprehensive examination of the state education department. It concluded that the centralised and state-controlled educational system seriously impaired the ability of schools to respond to their local needs, that is, to "the market."

The loose and elusive input-output relationship in education, the mounting criticism over government inefficiency, the global economic recession, and a projected decline in enrollments appear to have provided some governments with the momentum to institute several radical changes. The challenges of the 1990s, which are summed up in the terms "globalization of business" and "internationalization of education," have further justified the need to restructure educational systems (see, for example Naisbitt, 1990, and Tye, 1991). Also, the worldwide developments in technology add to these challenges. A shrinking world implies that "territorial walls" are crumbling; therefore, competition will be found where there was none before and intensified where it exists. (For example, Gonzaga University, located in Spokane, Washington, is offering graduate programs which extend to the northern part of Alberta, Canada.) Governments are increasingly concerned about the ability of their countries to compete in the global market. The Second Report of the House of Commons Standing Committee on Industry, Science, and Technology (Sparrow, 1990) stated that "education is central in meeting this challenge [of providing the education and training needed in jobs related to Canada's competitiveness]. From kindergarten through university, to job training and retraining, every aspect of our educational system must work to prepare Canadians for the future" (p. 2). While governments recognize the importance of education to achieve these objectives, there seems to be little or no faith in the present system to accomplish the task. The injection of competition into educational systems therefore is seen by many governments as a preparation for the 1990s and beyond.

Where politically feasible, governments have introduced varying degrees of privatization, that is, the transfer of assets and services in part or whole from the public to the private sector. This is seen by some governments to be a better alternative to public funding of public services. Fixler (1986) stated that "increasing reports of privatization in other nations indicate that it is a worldwide phenomenon. Developed and underdeveloped nations, and even some communist countries, are privatizing services and activities to one degree or another" (p. 1). With the mounting criticism of the quality and relevance of some aspects of education on the one hand, and the inefficiency of protected industries on the other hand, a logical reaction for many governments is to withdraw their responsibility for full funding of education. Policies that would enhance private participation in education whereby the public would have more say, institutions would be more accountable, and governments would have less financial burden, are becoming increasingly popular in many nations.

The initiatives described clearly demonstrate that the governments of several countries wish to restructure some aspects of the organization of educational institutions (both postsecondary and K-12) and the means by which they are funded in an attempt to ensure that they are more involved in helping to achieve national and provincial economic objectives. The directed nature of research grants and the desired restriction of research funding to institutions and individuals with demonstrated records of research effectiveness provide two of the most radical examples of direct intervention. The implications for greater emphasis on marketing and entrepreneurial activities are very clear.

INSTITUTIONAL INITIATIVES

The notion of "public education in the marketplace" has gained in popularity among politicians, administrators, and even educators. Shatlock, Booth, Wagner, and Williams (1989) acknowledged that "it is impossible to deny the world-wide ideological currents which mean that most political leaders now consider fragmented individual choices by consumers to be preferable to centralized decisions by planners and producers" (p. 96). The public also wants greater transferability of academic credit for students who move among educational systems.

Belief in private competition as the most viable way to achieve creativity, innovations, quality, and cost-efficiency in education is not new. Adam Smith (cited in Friedman, 1975) argued over 200 years ago, that "those parts of education, it is observed, for the teaching of which there are no public institutions, are generally the best taught" (p. 272), and John Stuart Mill (cited in Garforth, 1980) stated about a century ago that

a general State education is a mere contrivance for moulding people to be exactly like one another: and the mould in which it casts them is that which pleases the predominant power in the government, whether this be a monarch, a priesthood, an aristocracy or the majority of the existing generation, in proportion as it is efficient and successful, it establishes a despotism over the mind, leading by natural tendency to one over the body. (p. 123)

Praise for the achievement of the market system in various sectors is growing. Friedman (1975) argued that "music or dance, secretarial skills, automobile driving, airplane piloting, technical skills—all are taught best when they are taught privately. Try talking French with someone who studied it in public schools, then with a Berlitz graduate" (p. 284). Some private higher educational institutions in the United States have become centres of excellence with international reputations.

In a shrinking world, competition is unavoidable, especially as corporate industries are increasingly offering educational services, perhaps more efficiently, and effectively. Those who favour competition, therefore, argue that the injection of competition in educational systems is aimed at preparing higher educational institutions for the challenges of a shrinking world. Although an indisputable need exists for liberal education, any society that generally favours competition is more likely to move toward a market-led educational system. Bélanger (1989) made this relevant assessment:

All universities nowadays, of whatever size, find themselves in a competitive struggle, the consequences of which are beneficial for some and costly for others, depending on the mission they have selected for themselves and the leaders they have installed to pursue their particular paths of excellence. (p. 14)

This struggle also involves the search for corporate donations. Many universities envy Harvard's total endowment, identified by Footlick (1990) as "a stupefying $5 billion" (p. 52), and few universities have any chance of approaching it. However, in 1988–90, the University of Toronto raised $125 million, described as "the largest private fundraising effort in Canadian history," and the University of British Columbia raised $66 million in 1989–90 ("Over the top," 1991). Some academics consider that chasing donations compromises their freedom, but Douglas Wright, President of the University of Waterloo, in an interview in the *Bulletin* of the Canadian Society for the Study of Higher Education (1990b), expressed the view that "universities would enhance their independence, rather than endanger losing it, by accepting more contributions from business and corporations. 'Independence comes out of pluralism. You lose independence if you have only one paymaster'" (p. 1). Raising money to assist with operating budgets can lead to an increase in financial autonomy. One implication of this for the internal management of postsecondary institutions, the Council of Europe (1990, p. 15) noted, is a concomitant growth in the direction of professionalism and market-orientation.

Another important initiative involves the matching by governments of funds raised from private sources. In 1991, Alberta and British Columbia were the only two provinces with post-secondary matching funds programs. Brief descriptions of Alberta's three matching initiatives in the 1980s, which are prime examples of this thrust, are provided below:

1. *1980s Endowment Fund:* $80 million government contribution; the original timetable was 1980–90, but funds were expended by 1985.

2. *Endowment and Incentive Fund 1:* $80 million government contribution for 1986–1994; overwhelming private sector support changed the parameters to $128 million for 1986–1988.

3. *Endowment and Incentive Fund 2:* $80 million government contribution for 1989–1999; more restrictions have been placed upon this fund, as identified in Note 1.

As of March 1992, these three programs had injected approximately $428 million in new government and private funds into public postsecondary institutions in Alberta.

Probably the greatest manifestation of university entrepreneurial initiatives lies in the marketing of staff expertise, inventions, and discoveries. The move to foster the university/industry relationship, recommended by the Council of Europe (1990, p. 13), is geared toward "research for dollars"; hence, this type of research is, in many cases, applied and industry-specific. Academics often criticize this arrangement on the ground that it would cripple basic or curiosity-driven research, which is equally important to the society. Because the results of industry-specific research cannot always be published freely, a cooperative approach may achieve one of the goals of a university, that is, to disseminate information. Fairweather (1988) observed that

> The growth of alliances between business and higher education reflects the perception by government, industry, and academe that a significant overlap of interests exists. Academic institutions, for example, require additional resources. Industry is willing to provide resources in exchange for access to students, faculty, and resources. Only at the most general level (e.g., desire for an improved economy), however, can academe and industry be said to have identical interests; in most cases, institutions of higher education participate in alliances for reasons different from those of their industrial counterparts. (p. 23)

Gregor (1990) has provided the following assessments about this university-industry relationship:

> Efforts to foster research excellence at the provincial level appear increasingly to emphasize technological development.
>
> At both levels of government there is also an increasing inclination to have appropriate ministries more active in entering into research partnerships with universities or other agencies.
>
> Related university initiatives are to be seen in the increased number of institutional offices set up to facilitate co-operative ventures with business and industry; and in the establishment of research or technological parks in juxtaposition with university campuses . . . and thus foster more effective collaboration.
>
> The message has been conveyed that the postsecondary curriculum must take better cognizance of the country's place and future in a world community. (p. 962)

The importance being placed on this relationship is further demonstrated by the holding of a Business and Education Conference sponsored by The Conference Board of Canada

(Toronto, 24–26 April 1991). Also, Weston (1991) reported that 14 university-related research parks are either currently planned or established in Canada, with the world total now being 175.

In order to provide a concrete example of university entrepreneurial activities, information is included here about the Intellectual Property and Contracts Office IPCO) at the University of Alberta (1991). In a document which describes its operations, IPCO lists these benefits of technology transfer: "increased competitiveness in the international market place, economic diversification, creation of jobs, industries and companies, and increased funding opportunities through collaborative industrial research" (p. 1). The first Canadian technology-transfer office was established at the University of Toronto in 1981, while the majority were formed in 1985–86; most rely on both government and university funding (p. 1). In 1990, the University of Alberta's Office of Research Services was split into IPCO and the Research Grants Office in recognition of the growing importance of intellectual property transfer. IPCO has these three objectives:

1. To enhance and expand the research horizons of the University

2. To facilitate intellectual property transfer out of the University

3. To achieve financial recovery on intellectual property transfer (p. 3)

The Faculty Agreement between the University of Alberta (1988) and its Academic Staff Association includes this statement:

> The University Patent Policy has the purpose of encouraging the staff to patent inventions and to provide a mechanism for the commercial application and utilization of the inventions while at the same time rewarding the inventor and protecting the rights of the University where the inventions were made using University facilities. (p. 72)

Inventors can either seek patent protection and commercial partners on their own initiative or offer the technology to the University which can then patent and commercialize the invention. The inventors and the University share the royalties in either case.

IPCO noted that "financial returns from University technologies most often come from licensing," but, because the University is in the early phase of writing such licences, royalty revenue has been minimal (p. 5). Individual faculty members also have been encouraged to start companies based on technologies that they have developed; examples are Chembiomed Ltd., Biomira Inc., and Synthetic Peptides Inc. The University benefits directly from equity interests in these companies and from royalties. Further, IPCO staff maintain close relationships with several government departments and crown corporations involved in technology transfer, e.g., the National Research Council, the Alberta Research Council, Science and Technology Canada, and Alberta Technology, Research and Telecommunications. The recent Report of the House of Commons (Sparrow, 1990) included this relevant statement: "The Committee recommends that the federal government facilitate technology transfer throughout the country by such means as a National Technology Information Network: enhanced technological personnel exchange among government, industry and the universities; government-industry sponsored technology centres; etc." (p. 11).

To recapitulate, universities themselves can act in entrepreneurial ways which are not necessarily triggered by government underfunding or restructuring. Of special significance in North American universities are many activities related to cooperative linkages with business, patents, inventions, and discoveries. Individual institutional initiatives also involve attracting students and funds, greater privatization, new programs, and greater coordination and cooperation.

DISCUSSION

The thesis presented at the beginning of this paper, namely, that postsecondary institutions are becoming more entrepreneurial as a result of three complementary developments, is supported by the evidence provided. In many countries, one or more of the following, i.e. declining real revenue and rising costs, an increase in government influence upon restructuring, and an increase in institutional interest in entrepreneurialism, have been associated

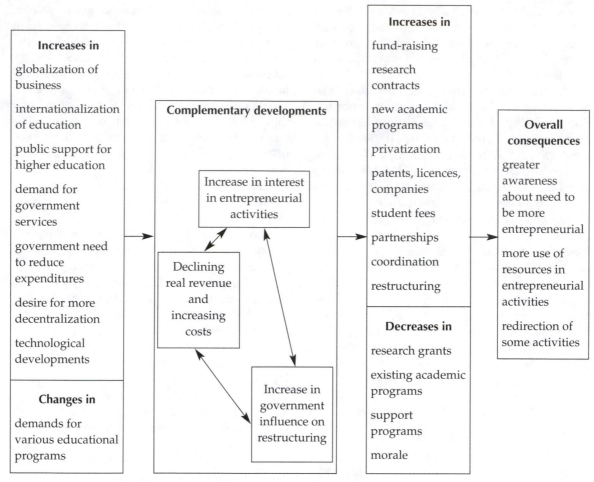

Figure 56.1 Stimuli for and effects of increasing entrepreneurialism

with an overall increase in entrepreneurial activities in postsecondary institutions. The stimuli for this increase and their relationships with the other variables discussed in this article are presented in Figure 56.1.

Some educational administrators have urged higher educational institutions to seize this opportunity to restructure rather than resist the changes of the 1980s and the 1990s. For example, Shapiro (cited in O'Brien and Siyahi, 1989) remarked that

> if American higher education is to retain its vitality as a cultural institution, it will have to continue to adapt and change in a manner that both serves the society that supports it and remains constant to the sustaining traditions and values of higher education itself. To imagine that higher education institutions have reached their final and most perfect form would be a special intellectual arrogance indeed. (pp.1–2)

Burgess (1982) has succinctly described the two major autonomous and service traditions of higher education. The autonomous tradition is "aloof, academic, conservative and exclusive"; education is seen as "an activity with its own values and purposes, affecting the rest of society obliquely and as a kind of bonus." The service tradition "explicitly expects education to serve individuals and society and defends it in these terms" (p. 70).

In its deliberations about the financing of higher education and research, the Council of Europe (1990) associated its activities with those of the Organization for Economic Co-operation and Development (OECD) which had drawn the following conclusions based on 12 in-depth national case studies:

> The main finding of this report is the growing diversity of higher education and its funding mechanisms in most OECD countries. The university has too many missions

for the means available and, by decreasing their contributions, governments are hoping that diversification of financial sources will become the solution to the problems they themselves have allowed to develop. (p. 14)

Further, Massy (1990) identified these six ways by which "the gap between long-run growth rates of revenue and expense" can be closed: (a) increasing investment return; (b) enhancing revenue from mainline academic activities; (c) improving the productivity of administrative and support activities; (d) obtaining revenue from non-traditional sources; (e) improving the productivity of academic functions; and (f) terminating selected academic programs. (p. 25)

These changes have major implications for many aspects of the operation of postsecondary institutions. Those implications that deal with administrative competence, allocation of resources, student orientation, and related matters are addressed below.

Administrative Competence

A market-led Canadian educational system would be a radical departure from the traditional system of education and would have far-reaching implications for everybody involved with higher educational institutions. For example, it would move some of the responsibility for determining the quality of education from institutions to students, employers, and the general public. These groups would have to know what constitutes quality and how to identify the difference among various higher educational institutions.

Also, a shift would be necessary from the traditional approach of appointing academics, who typically have little or no administrative training, to positions which have substantial administrative responsibility. Emery (1987) acknowledged that

> academics have been trained to teach and research rather than to administer and invest. Yet, over recent years, the promotional path for an academic has meant less teaching and research and more administration, management and institutional planning. This is not the ideal recipe for the creation of a senior management expert in fund-raising, sales promotion, investment portfolios and the export of educational

services. Nevertheless, institutional viability is now largely dependent upon selling additional services. (p. 84)

More training in personnel administration, finance/budgeting, organizational analysis, office management, and public relations would probably be necessary. In a competitive environment, educational leaders would be expected to be entrepreneurs and "intrapreneurs—individuals who possess the skills necessary to ensure institutional survival and growth and who understand the business of education. In this regard, McWilliam (1990) observed that "the bureaucratic structure and functioning of colleges as a sub-set of a bureaucratic government prohibited refinement of organizational purposes. . . . Poorly executed communication and collaboration linkages ensured that innovative efforts went unlinked with opportunities for meaningful exploitation of them" (p. 93). This author further stated that "individuals bemoaned limited strategic planning, absence of a clear college mission, role, and mandate, lack of educational leadership, centralised decision-making and control, a 'pigeonholing structure,' lack of linkages between committees, polarised and competing factions, and incongruence between stated and enacted philosophy" (p. 95).

In a market-led educational system where leaders would be expected to act decisively and promptly, the planning and monitoring of changes within each institution would have to be much more centralized and more focused than they currently are.

Allocation of Resources

Traditionally, the allocation of resources within higher educational institutions has been based on program need. In many instances, program development and delivery reflect the interests of academics. Consequently, a program-based budgetary allocation may not necessarily reflect the demand or utility of such a program, at least from the point of view of the general public. Once programs are developed they become parts of a faculty's territory and must be protected, and the review of academic programs may have little relevance to societal need. Even where program reviews are carried out, the process and outcome often represent the views of the academics rather than the views of students, employers, and the general public. A greater customer orientation in conducting program reviews is probably warranted. In an article which both criticized many university practices and offered suggestions for effective strategies for the 1990s, Chaffee (1990) considered that service to "customers"—students, employers of graduates, research funding agencies, etc.—should be the guide for action even though many people in higher education are uncomfortable with the term "customers" (p. 61).

Under a market-led educational system, the allocation of resources would depend more on the needs of identifiable targeted groups and would be reflected through their demand for programs. When a particular program suffers low enrollment, the department concerned would be required to examine the reason. When low enrollment is related to lack of knowledge of the existence or importance of the program, a concerted effort to educate the public and popularise the program could be carried out. When the problem is obsolescence, a review to update or phase-out the program would be conducted. A general liberal education need not suffer under a market-led educational system if the benefits of such education are appropriately communicated to the relevant publics. To be able to respond to changes in the environment, a market-led system of higher education would require resources that would be more redeployable. In many places, a budgetary system has already been adopted to enable institutions to redeploy their resources to meet local needs.

Student Orientation

A greater emphasis on students would mean that attracting students, keeping them at the institution, and producing larger numbers of graduates, without sacrificing quality, would be central concerns of administrators. A different administrative approach towards students can become necessary, because of changes that are occurring in the composition of the student body in postsecondary institutions. Some of these changes include declining percentages of the 18–24-year-old cohort, increasing participation of matriculated and non-matriculated adult students, and increasing percentages of part-time students and students with special needs, such as single parents and minority students (West, 1988). To meet the needs of such

students, higher educational institutions should examine different aspects of administration, such as greater use of credit cards, increased library hours, reduced residency requirements, and more day-care facilities.

Contrary to the common notion that market-led educational systems would concentrate institutional efforts on enrollments at the expense of academic standards, the long-term attraction possessed by an institution under this system would be its perceived quality of education. Different kinds of institutions for different kinds of people may result. Of course, special provisions for various disadvantaged groups would still be necessary.

Other Issues

Greater emphasis on university initiatives with respect to attracting students, donations and funds from non-traditional sources, privatization, research grants and contracts, patents and licences, coordination, and new programs raise several important issues which should be identified before particular initiatives are discussed:

- what should be the relative contributions of governments, "users," and alumni to the cost of postsecondary education?

- to what extent is education a "public good" or a "private good"?

- where should university activities focus on development of students and the development of the economy?

- where should university research activities be located on the basic-applied continuum?

- to what extent does the "search for dollars" interfere with teaching, research, and service?

University initiatives with respect to raising instructional fees need to be examined to ascertain whether they restrict access. Free education does not necessarily result in equal participation among the various social and economic classes within a society. Granting that there is some correlation between educational cost and accessibility, the purpose of a social welfare program in a capitalist state is to assist the less advantaged people to gain access to equitable participation, health, food, and education. Governments can therefore be more relevant to society by assisting the less advantaged to gain access to these services. Some advocates of the voucher system, such as Friedman (1975), argued that, contrary to the common notion, a voucher system of education would indeed increase the participation rate of the less advantaged and minority groups. A market-led educational system is possible without the government abdicating its educational responsibility—which is to ensure that every person has access to educational services. Perhaps the most common criticism is the effect of a market-led educational system on accessibility. Some fear that higher educational institutions would charge exorbitant fees and thus exclude the less advantaged but equally competent students. With respect to fees and accessibility, the *Bulletin* of the Canadian Society for the Study of Higher Education (1990a) reported that "research, however, has shown little or no correlation between low fees and student enrollment" (p. 1). The Society also noted that various countries that have experimented with zero fees have met with limited success; for example, "Swedish universities charge no tuition fees, and have found that students from less affluent homes still enroll in shorter programs than students from wealthier backgrounds" (p. 1).

CONCLUSIONS

Many current moves are characterized by increasing emphasis on competition, self-reliance, and responsiveness. Several advantages of a market-led educational system are laudable, but equally convincing are some of the arguments against the system. The possibility of increasing inequality in society is paramount among the arguments against a market-led education system. Some researchers have responded to this by indicating that there is little or no correlation between the level of student fees and the extent to which eligible citizens enroll.

The major implication or conclusion to be drawn from this debate appears to be the need for balance between conflicting forces and demands. Katz (1986) reminded us that "the conflict between the forces of the marketplace and of the community in higher education echoes an old struggle" (p. 6). Also, Massy (1990) cautioned that "common sense and sensitivity to the world around us are as important to

achieving our objectives as intellectual prowess" (p. 27). Postsecondary institutions need to be more responsive (i.e., more entrepreneurial, more market-oriented) to a variety of societal needs, while still maintaining academic standards, values, and relevant traditions.

Finally, we must recognize that adoption of more entrepreneurial activities in higher educational institutions will have consequences for their administration. Special attention will need to be directed towards institutional missions, communication channels, coordination of activities, criteria used in personnel decisions, and informing the public about the importance and contributions to society of postsecondary institutions. Although the balance between the marketplace and academic concerns must always be preserved, perhaps the time has now come to recognize that the fulcrum has moved, and may continue to move, somewhat towards the marketplace. Greater emphasis on entrepreneurialism in higher education may well prove to have more advantages than disadvantages.

NOTES

1. Alberta Advanced Education provided the following additional information about its Endowment and Incentive Fund 2:

   The major difference between this program and its two predecessors is the establishment of maximum institutional allocations to ensure the full life of the program. The institutions are responsible for establishing their priorities within their annual allocations and making the appropriate matching grant applications. Cash gifts for endowments, operating expenses and capital purposes can be matched on a 1:1 basis and gifts of books and equipment for teaching or research purposes can be matched up to an amount that does not exceed the value of the books or equipment, as determined by the Minister of Advanced Education.

   Also, private donations to universities were not eligible for matching grants after 1 April 1992, except those provided for capital projects of an exceptional nature.

2. The assistance provided in the preparation of this article by Michael Andrews, Marc Arnal, Ronald Boivin, Joe Fris, Bing Mah, David Norwood, Janice Park, and Eva Radford is gratefully acknowledged. The authors also wish to recognize the valuable comments pro-

vided by reviewers of an earlier draft of the article.

REFERENCES

Alberta Advanced Education. (1989). *Goals and priorities: Post-secondary education 1989 to the year 2000.* Edmonton, AB: Author.

Alberta Advanced Education. (1989). *Guidelines for system development.* Edmonton, AB: Author.

Association for Supervision and Curriculum Development. (1990). *ASCD issues analysis: Public schools of choice.* Alexandria, VA: Author.

Axelrod, P. (1986). Service or captivity? Business-university relations in the twentieth century. In W. A. W. Neilson, R C. Gaffield (Eds.), *Universities in crisis: A mediaeval institution in the twenty-first century* (pp. 45-68). Montréal, Que.: The Institute for Research on Public Policy.

Bélanger, C. H. (1989). University entrepreneurship and competition: The case of the small universities. *The Canadian journal of higher education, 19* (2), 13–22.

Burgess, T. (1982). Autonomous and service traditions. In L. Wagner (Ed.), *Agenda for institutional change in higher education* (pp. 70–79). Guilford, Surrey, U.K.: The Society for Research into Higher Education.

Burrup, P. E., & Brimley, V. (1982). *Financing education in a climate of change* (3rd ed.). Boston, MA: Allyn & Bacon.

Canadian Society for the Study of Higher Education. (1991). Commission boss fears universities changing too slowly. *Bulletin,* (Winter), 2.

Canadian Society for the Study of Higher Education. (1990a). Universities struggle with cost of tuition for higher education. *Bulletin,* (Winter), 1–2.

Canadian Society for the Study of Higher Education. (1990b). University of Waterloo head to set panel on education. *Bulletin,* (Spring), 1.

Carter, C. (1980). *Higher education for the future.* Oxford, UK: Basil Blackwell.

Chaffee, E. E. (1990). Strategies for the 1990s. *New directions for higher Education,* No. 70 (Summer). San Francisco, CA: Jossey-Bass.

Cooper, B. S. (1988). School reform in the 1980s: The new right's legacy. *Educational administration quarterly, 24* (3), 282–298.

Council of Europe. (1990). Financing higher education and research—Resolution 945 of the Parliamentary Assembly, adopted 11 May 1990. *Educational newsletter, 4/90.* Strasbourg, France: Author.

Dawkins, J. S. (1988). *Higher education: A police statement.* Canberra, Australia: Australian Government Printing Service.

Decore, A. M., & Pannu, R. S. (1989). Alberta political economy in crisis: Whither education? *Canadian journal of education, 14* (2), 150–169.

Dennison, W. F. (1990). Performance indicators and consumer choice. *International journal of educational management, 4* (1), 8–11.

Emery, J. S. (1987). Education and enterprise. *UNICORN: Bulletin of the Australian college of education, 13* (2), 83–88.

Fairweather, J. S. (1988). *Entrepreneurship and higher education: Lessons for colleges, universities, and industry.* Washington, D.C.: ERIC Clearinghouse on Higher Education.

Fixler, P. E. (1986). Privatization 1986. *Annual report on privatization of government services.* Santa Monica, CA: Reason Foundation.

Footlick, J. K. (1990, June 11). Giving Harvard notice. *Newsweek,* pp. 52, 54.

Friedman, M. (1975). *An economist's protest.* Glen Ridge, NJ: Thomas Hoctor.

Garforth, F. W. (1980). *Educative democracy: John Stuart Mill on education in society.* Oxford: Oxford University Press.

Gregor, A. D. (1990). *The universities of Canada commonwealth universities Yearbook 1990* (pp. 955–968). London: The Association of Commonwealth Universities.

Hogbin, G. (1987). Privatizing the consumption of education. In P. Abelson (Ed.), *Privatization: An Australian perspective* (pp. 227–248). Sydney, Australia: Australian Professional Publications.

Katz. M. B. (1986). The moral crisis of the university, or, the tension between marketplace and community in higher learning. In W. A. W. Neilson, & C. Gaffield (Eds.), *Universities in crisis: A medieval institution in the twenty-first century* (pp. 3–27). Montréal, QC: The Institute for Research on Public Policy.

Kogan, M. (1988). Normative models of accountability. In R. Glatter, M. Preedy, C. Riches, & M. Masterton (Eds.), *Understanding school management* (pp. 139–153). Philadelphia, PA: Open University.

Kotler, P. & Fox, K. F. A. (1985). *Strategic marketing for noneducational institutions,* (3rd ed.). Englewood Cliffs, NJ: Prentice-Hall.

Maclure, S. (1988). *Education reformed.* Sevenoaks, Kent, UK: Hodder & Stoughton.

Management Review. (1989). *Schools renewal: A strategy to revitalise schools in the New South Wales state education system.* Milsons Point: NSW, Australia: NSW Education Portfolio.

Massy, W. F. (1990). A paradigm for research on higher education. In J. C. Smart (Ed.), *Higher education: Handbook of theory and research: Vol. 6* (pp. 1–34). New York: Agathon.

Maynard, A. (1982). Privatization and market mechanisms. In A. Morris & J. C. Sizer (Eds.). *Resources and higher education* (pp. 58–80). Guildford, Surrey, UK: Society for Research into Higher Education.

McWilliam, C. L. (1990). Innovation and entrepreneurship in colleges: An interpretive study of the piloting of innovation centres. *The Canadian journal of higher education*, 20 (3), 85–102.

Naisbitt, J. (1990). Global education. *Inside Guide*, 4 (3). 8–9.

O'Brien, P., & Siyahi, C. (1989, November). *Challenging old standards: Strategy and planning for a new metropolitan model.* Paper presented at the American Marketing Association National Symposium for the Marketing of Higher Education, Cincinnati, OH.

Over the top. (1991, February). *University affairs*, 32 (2), 19.

Perot, H. R. (1989). *Educating our children for the next century.* Educom Review. 24 (1), 14–17.

Ribich, T. I. (1970). The effect of educational spending on poverty reduction. In R. L. Johns, (Ed.), *Economic factors affecting the financing of education* (pp. 207-234). Gainsville, FL: National Educational Finance Project.

Sexton, S. (1987). Our schools. In S. Sexton (Ed.), *The funding and management of education* (pp. 5–12). Warlingham, Surrey, UK: Institute of Economic Affairs, Education Unit.

Shapiro, H. T. (1986, May). *American higher education: A special tradition faces a special challenge.* Occasional Paper (16). Paper presented at the Annual Dinner of the Academy for Educational Development, New York.

Shatlock, M., Booth, C., Wagner, L., & Williams, G. (1989). Editorial. *Higher educational quarterly.* 43 (2), 95–188.

Sparrow, B. J. (1990). *Canada must compete. Second report of the standing committee on industry, science and technology, regional and northern development.* Presented to the House of Commons, Ottawa, ON: Queen's Printer.

Tausig, C. (1991). Recent poll reveals majority support increased university funding. *University affairs*, 32 (3), 48.

Tomlison, J. (1989). The education reform bill—44 years of progress? *Education Policy*, 4 (3), 275–279.

Tye, K. A. (Ed.) (1991). *Global education: Front thought to action.* Alexandria, VA: Association for Supervision and Curriculum Development.

University of Alberta. (1991). *University technology transfer.* Unpublished paper. Edmonton, AB: Intellectual Property and Contracts Office.

Weston, J. (1991, January). *University affairs*, 32 (1), 10.

West, E. G. (1988). *Higher education in Canada.* Vancouver, BC: The Fraser Institute.

CHAPTER 57

MARKETIZING HIGHER EDUCATION IN POST-MAO CHINA

KA HO MOK

Dr. Ka Ho Mok is Convenor, Comparative Education Policy Research Unit of the Department of Public and Social Administration at the City University of Hong Kong. His major research interests include social and political development issues in contemporary China and East Asia, comparative education policy, and intellectuals and politics. He is the author of Intellectuals and the State in Post-Mao China *(London: Macmillan, 1998) and* Social and Political Development in Post-Reform China *(London: Macmillan and New York: St. Martin Press, forthcoming 1999) and the Editor of a book on* Socio-Structural Change and Educational Development in the Asia Pacific Region *(with Anthony Welch) (London: Macmillan and New York: St. Martin Press, forthcoming). His recent work published in* Comparative Education Review, Comparative Education, International Education Review, International Journal of Educational Development. Higher Education, *etc.*

In the post-Mao era, reformers in the People's Republic of China have taken significant steps to privatize social welfare services. After the adoption of a socialist market system in the 1990s, educational development has been affected by strong market forces. It is argued that the emergence of private educational institutions, the shift of state responsibility in educational provision to families and individuals, the prominence of fee-charging, as well as the introduction of internal competition among educational institutions, clearly suggest that China's education has been going through a process of marketization. The principal goal of this paper is to examine institutional origins of the policy change in education, with particular reference to the process and implications of such changes. The paper will also appraise the Chinese experience in the light of global practices on marketization of social welfare services.

1. INTRODUCTION

In the post-Mao era, the reformers have taken significant steps to privatize social welfare services. After the adoption of a socialist market system in the 1990s, strong market forces have affected educational development. Despite the post-Mao leaders' discomfort about the term "privatization", signs of state withdrawal from the provision of social welfare are clear. The present paper argues that the emergence of private educational institutions, the shift of state responsibility in educational provision to families and individuals, the prominence of fee-charging, as well as the introduction of internal competition among educational institutions, have clearly suggested that China's education has been going through a process of marketization. Though the Chinese experience of marketization may be different from the West, there is no doubt that education is increasingly "marketized". Despite the fact that the Chinese Communist Party has never actively pro-

Source: Department of Public and Social Administration, City University of Hong Kong, Kowloon, Hong Kong, People's Republic of China.

moted the establishment of an independent "internal education market", its passive facilitation of internal education markets has inevitably "marketized" China's education. The principal goal of this paper is to examine institutional origins of the policy change in education, with particular reference to the process and implications of such changes. The paper will also appraise the Chinese experience in the light of global practices on marketization of social policy.

2. THE RESTRUCTURING OF THE STATE AND PUBLIC POLICY DEVELOPMENT

Recent decades have brought considerable questioning the state's ability to continue monopolizing the provision of public services. Realizing the importance of productivity, performance and control, governments have begun to engage themselves in transforming the way that services are managed (Flynn, 1997). Undoubtedly, the role of the state in relation to the formulation of public policies and the delivery of public services has significantly been affected by various forces—the impact of globalization, crises of the state, the search for a post-Keynesian settlement, fragmentary impulses in society and the contradictions of identity politics—which have created immense pressures for the restructuring of the state. Corporate managerialism, devolution, the role of markets, and the popularity of "economic rationality" are some of the key elements of the restructuring of the state in the public domain (Taylor et al., 1997; Welch, 1998).

Being one of the major public responsibilities, education is unquestionably affected by the strong tide of managerialism. Central to "corporate managerialism" is a "rational, output-oriented, plan-based and management-led view of organizational reform" (Sinclair, 1989, p. 389). Under the rubric of "managerialism", some new slogans such as "focusing on outcomes and results" (effectiveness), "doing more with less" (efficiency), and "managing change better" are becoming very popular in the public sector (Yeatman, 1987, p. 341). With a paradigm shift to public management, the running of public services (including education, of course) has focused on "results and

efficiency and effectiveness, decentralized management environments, flexibility to explore alternatives to public provision of services, establishment of productivity targets and a competitive environment between public sector organizations, along with the strengthening of strategic capacities at the centre of organization" (Taylor et al., 1997, p. 82). In short, the impact of managerialism suggests a less state directed approach is adopted while market ideologies and practices are becoming more popular in the running of the public sector.

3. CORPORATE MANAGEMENT AND EDUCATIONAL RESTRUCTURING: A GLOBAL TREND

The fundamental change in the philosophy and practices of governance has caused similar process of transformation in the educational sector. In its recent reviews, the World Bank has shown its support to a "managerial approach" in reforming education. The dominant rationale for education within the *Priorities and Strategies for Education and Higher Education: The Lessons of Experience* is economic (World Bank 1994, 1995). "It is largely concerned with finance, economic returns, human resource development, efficiency, effectiveness, costings, private funding and the like" (Watson, 1996, p. 49). Despite the fact that the Bank's rethink of the substantial import of the state's role in education in its most recent annual reports of 1997/98 and 1998/99 (World Bank 1997, 1998), the impetus for change initiated by the Bank a few years ago has undoubtedly shaped the educational restructuring along the line of a managerial approach.

The economic rhetoric of individual rights and ideologies of "efficiency" are gaining momentum not only in industrialized countries like the UK, the USA and Australia (see, for example, Bridges and McLaughlin, 1994; Brown, 1995; Currie and Newson, 1998) but also in less developed ones (Bray, 1996). Other scholars have also noted that different countries (regardless of their levels of development) have a mixture of public and private services (James, 1992; Tilak, 1991; Bray, 1997). Many empirical studies reveal that the private sector is playing a more important role in education (e.g. Mok, 1999a; Yee and Lim, 1995; World Bank, 1996). Bray's (1996) work on the financing of education in East Asia also points out that in some setting parents and local communities have played a more important role than the government in the financing of education, while the state has gradually withdrawn from the frontier of educational provision. Similar experience has been reported in Vietnam, the Philippines and Malaysia, leading to a new definition of the public/private boundaries (Cheng, 1995b; Bray, 1996). Increasing critical attention is now being paid to the application of this ideology and processes to schools, and more recently to the academic profession (Hartley, 1995; Mok, 1999a; Lo, 1997). In short, unlike the traditional notion of education, which was dominated by the public sector, the emergence of "internal markets" and the prominence of "economic rationalism" in the educational sphere seems to be a feature of the globalization agenda.

4. MARKETS IN EDUCATION: RATIONALES, ASSUMPTIONS AND FEATURES

As Whitty and Power argue in this issue that recent reforms taking place in the educational sphere have sought to dismantle centralized bureaucracies, devolving systems of schooling with more emphasis given to parental choice and competition between different modes of school. Such development suggests that education has been going through processes of "marketization" and "privatization". Despite the fact that the terms "marketization" and "privatization" are meant differently to different people. Nonetheless, central to the notion of "marketization" is the evolution of "quasi-markets" whereby internal competition is introduced with intention to enhance "consumer choice". Basically, there are three major aspects when we talk about "marketization" of public service. First, it is believed that the private sector approach is comparatively superior to traditional approaches adopted in the public sector. Second, principles and practices of the private sector are adopted by the public sector as operating principles. Third, private decision-making is encouraged to replace bureaucratic fiat (Le Grand and Robinson, 1984).

The underlying assumption of adopting a market-oriented approach to restructure education is that "the empowerment of parents and students through resources-related choices in education has the potential to produce greater responsiveness and academic effectiveness" (Chubb and Moe, 1992, quoted in Grace, 1995, p. 206). It is also assumed that private providers should be free to establish schools and to compete with each other and thus people are given more choices in schooling. Another rationale for employing market mechanisms is that customers are themselves the rightful and best judges about what they really want to buy in the education market.

In the process, several major features can be found: the clear private-public distinction between state activities and those of the market have become blurred; traditionally private sector practices are becoming more popular in the public sector; residualization of the universal provision of many state services; changing practices of decentralization and devolution and the emphasis on market individualism. In mainland China, similar features of "marketization" can easily be found, we now find it difficult to draw a very clear public-private distinction in China's educational sector, especially when public schools are becoming more "private" as ideas/principles and practices which are popular in the market/private sector are also employed by publicly-run schools. In his studies of educational reforms in the UK and elsewhere, Ball identified five major elements in the education market place, namely, *choice, competition, diversity, funding* and *organization* (Ball, 1990, p. 61).

By "choice", we mean parents should be provided with a choice of different types of schooling in terms of curriculum, language of instruction, education provision, and school ethos. Advocates for market education believe "competition" between schools would best serve not only the consumers (parents and students), but also the nation, by ensuring an orientation to "continuous adaptation". When school funding is directly linked with the performance of individual schools, it is argued that the introduction of "internal competition" can ensure quality education. Another principle of the education market is closely related to "diversity" of "products" to make choice a real one for parents (consumers). More importantly, "a real market is driven by rewards and by failure" (Ball, 1990, p. 63). Following this logic, the choices made by the consumers should have a direct impact on "funding", thereby rewarding those performing well but penalizing those less competitive ones by allocating fewer resources. The last aspect of the education market is to improve school management and initiate reforms/re-engineering in "organization". Figure 57.1 shows these five major elements in Marketizing education.

In this paper, when talking about "marketization of education", we refer to "a process whereby education becomes a commodity provided by competitive suppliers, educational services are priced and access to them depends on consumer calculations and ability to pay" (Yin and White, 1994, p. 217). According to Buchbinder and Newson (1990), marketization takes two distinct forms, the first involves attempts to market their academic wares in the commercial world by educational institutions; while the other form is to restructure educational institutions in terms of business principles and practices. These two forms of marketization are also known as "inside-out" and "outside-in" practices to make the delivery of educational services more efficient and cost-effective. In short, the adoption of a market-oriented approach in running education would have the following consequences:

- adoption of the fee-paying principle in education

- reduction in state provision, subsidy and regulation

- popularity of revenue generation activities

- market-driven courses and curricula

- emphasis on parental choice

- managerial approach in educational administration/management.

Having discussed some major conceptual issues related to education and the market place, the following sections will examine whether China's education has similar experience of marketization or not. If so, the implications of the marketization of China's education will be examined. Much of the material reported in the paper is based on my field visits and intensive interviews conducted in the mainland in the past few years.

5. INSTITUTIONAL ORIGINS OF MARKETIZING EDUCATION IN CHINA

Under the reign of Mao Zedong (1949–1976), the CCP regarded education as a means to indoctrinate people with socialist ideas, and the state exerted a tight control over educational provision. After the CCP had consolidated its political power, a nationalization policy, which included education, was implemented. After 1956, all private schools were converted into public schools under the leadership of the Ministry of Education of the State Council (China National Institute of Educational Research, 1995). The adoption of a centralization policy in the educational sphere gave the central government a relatively tight control over financing, provision and management of education. Living in this policy context, Chinese citizens were accustomed to free education provided by the state sector (Yao, 1984).

With the introduction of economic reform in 1978, China entered a new stage of development. Economic modernization has not only fostered the growth of a market economy but has also caused a structural change in education. Under the slogan of "socialist construction", the CCP has tried to reduce its involvement in direct provision of educational services. In the immediate post-Mao era (i.e. 1978-present), the CCP initiated a decentralization policy in the educational realm to allow local governments, local communities, individuals and even other non-state actors to create more educational opportunities. Reshuffling the monopolistic role of the state in educational provision, reform in the educational structure started in the mid-1980s and has manifested a mix of private and public consumption (Mok, 1996; Cheng, 1995a; Hayhoe, 1996). A policy paper entitled "The Decision of Reform of the Educational System" issued in 1985 by the Central Committee of the CCP indicated that the state attempted to diversify educational services by encouraging all democratic parties, people bodies, social organizations, retired cadres and intellectuals, collective economic organizations and individuals subject to the Party and governmental policies, actively and voluntarily to contribute to developing education by various forms and methods (Wei and Zhang, 1995, p. 5).

In 1987, the "Provisional Regulations on the Establishment of Schools by Societal Forces" gave further detail and more concrete legal guidelines on the establishment and management of non-state schools (Zhu, 1996). Coinciding with "multiple channels" in financing, the state describes the use of a mixed economy of welfare as a "multiple-channel" *(duoqudao)* and "multi-method" *(duofangfa)* approach to the provision of educational services during the "primary state of socialism" *(shehui zhuyi chuji jieduan),* indicating a diffusion of responsibility from the state to society (Mok, 1996; Cheng, 1990).

Economic development in the first half of the 1990s was dominated by the impact of the

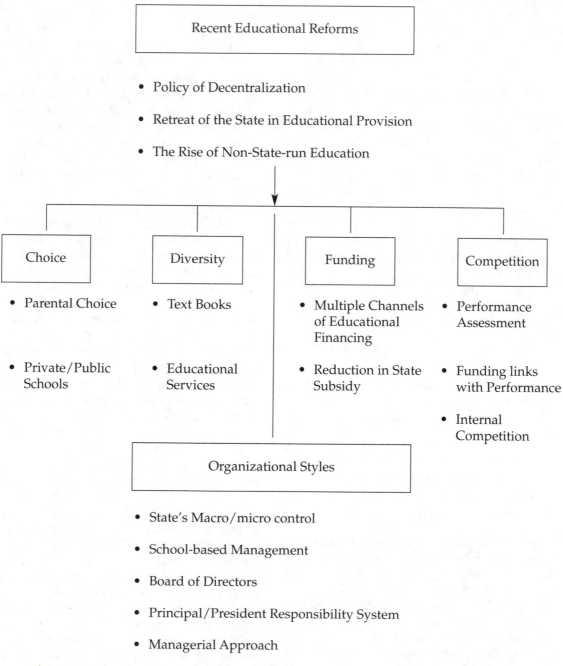

Figure 57.1 The education market place: recent educational restructuring in mainland China

Source: Modified from Ball (1990, p. 60).

tour of southern China, which Deng Xiaoping undertook at the beginning of 1992. In the wake of economic retrenchment for more than two years, coupled with severe inflation in 1988–89, Deng was keen to make use of his "southern inspection tour" to advocate renewed economic reform and accelerated growth. After Deng's tour to Southern China, the CCP openly endorsed the adoption of a socialist market economy in its 14th Party Congress. Hence, the role of the "market" has received a proper recognition not only in the Chinese economy (Ash and Kueh, 1996) but also in the welfare sector (Wong, 1994). It is in such a policy context that fee charges, diversification of non-state services, market-driven curricula, internal competition, and cost recovery activities are becoming more and more popular in China's education (Mok, 1999c).

Openly recognizing the fact that the state alone can never meet people's pressing educational needs, the CCP has deliberately devolved responsibilities to other non-state sectors to engage in educational development. In late 1993, "The Program for reform and the development of China's Education" stipulated that the national policy was actively to encourage and fully support social institutions and citizens to establish schools according to laws and to provide right guidelines and strengthen administration (CCPCC, 1993). Article 25 of the *Education Law* promulgated in 1995 reconfirmed once again the state would give full support to enterprises, social institutions, local communities and individuals to establish schools under the legal framework of the People's Republic of China (PRC) (State Education Commission, 1995). In short, the state's attitude towards the development of non-state-run education can be summarized by the phrase "active encouragement, strong support, proper guidelines, and sound management" (*jiji guli, dali zhichi, zhengque yindao, jiaqiang guanli*). Under such a legal framework, coupled with the "decentralization" policy context, China's education has been significantly affected by strong market forces, and I would argue such changes could clearly demonstrate China's education is going through a process of "marketization". Let us now examine the major features of "marketized" education in mainland China.

6. FEATURES OF "MARKETIZED" EDUCATION

6.1. The changing structure of financing in public schools: towards user charges

In line with the 1985 programmatic document "Decision of the Central Committee of the Communist Party of China on the Reform of the Educational Structure" and "The Outline of Education Reform and Development in China" promulgated by the Central Committee of the Communist Party of China and the State Council, local governments and educational practitioners have searched for "multiple channels" for the financing of education (Cheng, 1990). Instead of relying upon the state's financial support, educational funding has been diversified by seeking other resources such as overseas donations, financial support levied from local government taxes and subsidies, and tuition fees (Mok, 1996).

Realizing that the state was financially unable to meet people's pressing need for educational services, the CCP adopted a policy of "walking on two legs", whereby a shared responsibility between the state and the people was developed in financing primary education (Cheng, 1995a). In order to mobilize local communities, enterprises, individuals and even the market to engage themselves in educational endeavor, the state promoted a scheme of sponsorship at three levels, i.e. village, township and county. Under this scheme, the state would not bear more than one-third of the expenditure involved in the construction of school buildings and purchasing of school furniture. What the state was responsible for was to pay teachers' salaries. However, not all of the teachers in mainland China are employed by the state. For those teachers working for *minban* (people-run) schools, their salaries are paid by their school authorities, who mainly derive funds from educational surcharges, local communities, tuition fees, as well as collection of taxes for educational use from local government. For most schools at village, township and county level, educational funding is generated mainly from the local community, tuition fees and overseas donations (Cheng, 1995b).

In the 1990s, the CCP has shifted the responsibility from the state further to individuals and families by the introduction of a "fee-paying" principle.[2] Early in the 1980s, the plan for fee-charging students was regarded as "ultra-plan", implying that the intake of these "self-supporting" students was beyond the state plan (Cheng, 1996). But after the endorsement of a socialist market economy in the CCP's 14th Congress, the State Education Commission officially approved institutions of higher education admitting up to 25% students in the "commissioned training" or "fee-paying" categories in 1992. In 1993, 30 higher learning institutions were selected for a pilot study for a scheme known as "merging the rails", whereby students were admitted either because of public examination scores or because they were willing and able to pay a fee though their scores were lower than what was required. In 1994, more institutions entered the scheme and the fee-charging principle was thus legitimatized (Cheng, 1996).

The structural change in the financing of education in China is more obvious in higher education. Before the 1990s, the number of fee-paying students was only a very tiny group but it has been increasing after the adoption of the "user charge" principle. The percentage of fee-paying students of higher educational institutions in Shanghai increased from 7.5% in 1988 to 32.1% in 1994, showing a jump of "self-financing" students (Yuan and Wakabayashi, 1996). Table 57.1 shows that the number of self-supporting students has expanded throughout the country since 1988. Despite the fact that the number of self-support students dropped from 25,800 in 1989 to 11,300 in 1992 because of political reasons,[3] the number of self-support stu-

dents has grown again since the formal endorsement of the socialist market economy in 1992 when the role of the non-state sector (including the market) received a due recognition. From 1997 onwards, all students who want to enroll in higher education have to pay tuition fees. For those students who are from poor family can apply for scholarship or subsidy from their universities/institutions.

During my field visits to Guangdong, a laboratory for the economic reforms and the most prosperous province, I learned that all students (from primary to tertiary level) should pay for their tuition fees. In the higher education sector, Zhongshan University, for instance, has started to "merge the tracks" from 1995, implying there are no longer any differences between "publicly-funded students", "self-paying students" and "commissioned students". Professor Cai He, Head of the Department of Sociology, and Professor Zhang Minqiang, Director of the Institute of Higher Education of Zhongshan University, told me that students had begun to accept the fee-paying principle. In the present academic year, the range of tuition fees is varied among courses; students have to pay from 2500 to 3500 yuan (while the average per capita monthly salary in Guangzhoou was around 1000 yuan in 1997). Mr. Wu Yechun, Deputy Director of the Office of Administration, South China University of Technology, told me that in his view students had far more incentives to study hard after the adoption of a "fee-charging" principle in the university sector. He said:

> In the past, university education was entirely supported by the state and students seemed to take higher education for granted and thus their motivation was low once they were admitted. But the situation has changed since the adoption of "self-paying" principle in the university sector. Students are strongly motivated to study because they have to pay for the courses and they are eager to learn a wider range of subjects to broaden their knowledge base. Despite the fact that some students particularly for those who are from poor families may have difficulties to pay for tuition fees, many of them are able to secure financial support to obtain higher education. . . . More fundamentally, people are generally supportive of the "fee-paying" principle in higher education because they believe that

TABLE 57.1
Enrollment Change in Higher Educational Institutions in Mainland China[a]

Year	Total No. of Students	No. of Self-Support Students	Percentage
1988	669,700	42,200	6.3
1989	579,100	25,800	4.5
1990	608,600	17,300	2.8
1991	616,000	11,800	1.9
1992	628,400	11,300	1.8
1993	924,000	336,000	39.0
1994	899,800	364,000	40.5

a. *Source:* Yuan and Wakabayashi (1996, p. 195).

higher education is an investment. With higher qualifications university graduates would find it easier to get jobs in the open labour market, "value" is thus added to the students after university training (Field Interview, Guangzhou, March 1998).[4]

6.2. The Emergence of Private Education in China

The 14th Congress of the CCP, held in 1992, endorsed the principle of introducing the socialist market economy, thereafter creating a favourable environment for the emergence of private education (Mok, 1996). To foster further economic development in China, the State Education Commission issued the document "Points Regarding How to Expedite Reforms and Vigorously Develop Ordinary Higher Education", giving key guidelines for Chinese higher education to adapt it to the socialist market economy (Yin and White, 1994). The development of private education was supported by "Provisional Regulations for the Establishment of People-Run Schools of Higher Education" promulgated in 1993 by the State Education Commission. In late 1993, "The Program for Reform and the Development of China's Education" stipulated that the national policy was actively to encourage and fully support social institutions and citizens to establish schools according to laws and to provide right guidelines and strengthen administration (CCPCC, 1993).

Under such a legal framework, different types of school systems have been flourishing, and privately-run educational institutions have become popular in China's big cities (Mok and Chan, 1996). Realizing the importance of education, Chinese citizens believe that achieving a higher educational level may enable them to earn more money. Many surveys report that people are of the view that education is vital to their career development. A survey in Shanghai found that more than 60% of the parents hope that their children can receive higher education (Zhang, 1996). Another survey carried out by the Central Education Science Institute in Guangzhou in 1993 showed that 73% of 500 respondents favoured the establishment of non-governmental schools at the basic education level (Zhang, 1996). Under this favourable policy environment, non-state run educational institutions are developing rapidly in China, ranging from kindergartens to higher learning institutions.

By 1994, there were more than 800 non-state higher educational institutions across the nation, of which 18 were fully recognized by the State Education Commission and with authority to grant their own diplomas (China National Institute of Educational Research, 1995, p. 11). A 1996 report suggested that the number of private/*minban* institutions included around 20,780 kindergartens, 3159 primary/secondary schools, 672 secondary vocational schools and 1230 higher educational institutions (Cheng, 1997).

In the past few years, I have been studying the resurgence and development of private higher education institutions in Guangdong (see Mok and Chan, 1996; Mok, 1997a,b, 1998a). In 1998, there were three non-governmental higher education institutions in the Guangdong area and they have adopted different strategies to run their colleges. Hualian Private College, the first privately owned higher education institution in Guangdong, primarily relies upon students' tuition fees to run the institution; while Non-governmental [*Minban*] Nanhua Industrial and Business is financed partially by students' tuition fees and partly supported by the Trade Union of Guangdong Province. Another newly established private college, Pei Zheng Business College, adopts a *Minban Gongzhu* model (i.e. people-run and publicly assisted) to run the college. The college is financially supported by the local government (Hua Du City) in terms of a subsidised land price for college building and paying teachers' salaries. In addition to local government's support, Pei Zheng Alumni also raises funds to run the college (Mok, 1997a; Wu, 1996).

Realizing the pressing demand for higher education, these non-governmental institutions take advantage of this relatively liberal sociopolitical environment to develop courses and programmes catering for market needs. For instance, Nanhua Industrial and Business College offers programmes falling into four major areas: law, catering and tourism, business management, and administrative management. In order to be competitive in the "education market", the College adopts a "Five Gears Strategy". First, courses are geared to the market. Second, courses are geared to availability. Third, English courses are geared to international needs. Fourth, Education is geared to students' needs. And finally, The College is geared to becoming a famous school to attract more students (Niu, 1997). Professor Niu Xian-min, President of the College, told us that students were the "lifeblood of the College and the market had actually guided the development of non-governmental colleges" (Field Interview, July 1995; Mok, 1997a).

Knowing that non-governmental higher education institutions would face immense difficulties to compete with their formal counterparts, these private colleges have a clear vision to differentiate themselves from state-funded higher education institutions by specializing in courses which are geared to newly emerging market needs. In addition, they are committed to serve the local communities in which they are located. For example, Pei Zheng Business College has a mission to produce educated people for Hua Du City and has established a very close link with local enterprises to create more opportunities for its students to enrich their internship and placement experiences (Wu, 1996). Following a similar path, other non-governmental colleges are in the process of formation, Private Chaoshan College and Private Nanling College, have already secured financial support from local governments and they are ready to launch in the Guangdong area in near future (Wu, 1996).

More interesting, private/*minban* education is also popular in Shanghai where a *"Minban Gongzhu"* (People-run and Publicly-assisted) Model is adopted to create more educational opportunities. I visited several colleges of this kind in 1997 and 1998. Shanghai Guang Qi College, one of these *minban gongzhu* colleges in Shanghai, was established in 1996 by Professor Chen Quanfu, Dean of Adult Education of Shanghai Jiao Tong University. When asked about the nature of *minban gongzhu*, Professor Chen told me that:

> *Minban Gongzhu* means that the college is not entirely funded by the non-state sector but partially supported by the government in terms of financial support of school building. Guang Qi College is one of these *minban gongzhu* colleges. The Xuhui Qu, a local government in Shanghai, is committed to establish a local higher educational institution to train educated people to assist in modernization and match the needs of the local community created by rapid economic development. Therefore, the local government has given financial

support to found the Guang Qi College in the hope of creating more people with knowledge and skills to serve in the local community. (Field Interview, April 1998).

With the support from local government in providing school building and financial support, Guang Qi College was founded in October 1996 as *a minban gongzhu* college. Professor Chen shared with me the fact that the College is very conscious about its mission to train people for the local needs.

Seeing a gap between demand and supply in formal higher education, a group of old and experienced professors from Shanghai Jiaotong University and Fudan University therefore secured local government support and they are very committed to run a *minban* college to create additional quality educational opportunities. Professor Chen proudly told me that Guang Qi College was a "community-based" higher educational institution. In order to make the college more known to the local community, Guang Qi has identified several selected areas for teaching, offering programmes which give emphasis on practical knowledge, computing skills, foreign languages and advanced technology. Sharing the facilities and libraries of Shanghai Jiao Tong University, coupled with a stable teaching team from retired but experienced professors from Fudan and Jiaoda, Quang Qi College has proved itself a success in its students' public examination. Its good record has attracted 9000 applicants for only 250 places in the 1997/98 academic year.

The formation of Hua Xia College, another *minban gongzhu* college in Shanghai, was initiated by the East China Normal University to create more learning opportunities for Shanghai citizens. Like Guang Qi College, Hua Xia College is another community-based college. Despite the fact that Hua Xia has not got formal recognition from the central government, the Shanghai municipal government has approved it and its foundation has received support from the local community and East China Normal University. With financial sources generated from tuition fees, overseas donations and the local community, Hua Xia was founded in August 1996. Having a strong affiliation with East China Normal University, Hua Xia students can share the library and laboratory facilities of the University. In my interview with Professor Zian Hong, President of Hua Xia College, I was told that Hua Xia had a degree of autonomy, which her formal counterparts had not enjoyed.

Realizing that the state alone can never meet the pressing demand for higher education in the mainland, Professor Zian strongly believes that *minban* colleges have a role to play, particularly to fill the gap between the existing supply and demand left over by the formal university sector. Professor Zian feels the central government should allow more autonomy to local educationalists and intellectuals to run *minban* colleges. Moreover, he also urges the state to formally recognize the qualifications and the standard of these *minban* colleges. He told me:

> There is no harm at all to have *minban* colleges in China. First, we can create additional learning opportunities for students. Second, we can make use of the expertise, knowledge and experience of retired professors and they are very keen to serve and teach in the higher educational sector. Third, it is a better utilization of existing facilities and space from formal public universities. Calculating all these advantages together, I think the state must support and recognize the development of *minban* colleges. (Field Interview, May 1997).

Despite the fact that the state has not formally granted *minban* colleges university status, the state has gradually accepted the existence of *minban* as a reality, which it cannot deny. In the Education law promulgated in 1995 and the most recent Higher Education Law issued in 1998, the role of *minban* education has been formally recognized and proper systems and mechanisms would be worked out to monitor the qualifications awarded by and academic standards of these colleges. No matter how the state perceives the role of *minban* higher educational institutions, there is no doubt that *minban* education has developed as a part of the educational system in the mainland. The discussion above has only focused on two major models of private/*minban* education, it is worthy mentioned that there are other approaches and models of non-state-run schools throughout the country.[5] All these developments have suggested that educational services have become diversified, different

types of schools have emerged other than the state-run educational institutions and that they have emerged in response to market generated demands.

6.3. The Introduction of Internal Competition Among Educational Institutions

Drawing comparative insights from leading universities in other countries, the CCP has begun to realize the importance of bringing about substantial improvements in its university education. In order to enhance quality education at the tertiary level, the CCP introduced "Project 211" a few years ago to select 100 institutions of higher education to promote development in selected disciplines. The state is going to attach a new financial and strategic importance to about 100 universities and some subject areas in order to try to ensure that these identified 100 universities become world class universities in the early 21st century. Central to the scheme is a plan to introduce "competition" among universities, rewarding the top 100 higher educational institutions. Universities are assessed by quantifiable, objective criteria on staffing, buildings, libraries, laboratories, research, funds, etc. to determine whether they are "qualified" to be included as top institutions. Most important of all, the selected universities will attract more funding from the central government. In order to be chosen as top universities, many universities have tried to merge with other universities to improve their research and academic profile (Christiansen, 1996; Rosen, 1997). For instance, old Shanghai University announced a plan to merge with other local colleges to become a more comprehensive university. After the "merger" the new Shanghai University has proved itself a more competitive university and has successfully been selected as one of the top "211" universities in the mainland. More significantly, the 211 programme means that "internal competition" has been introduced among universities. Seemingly an "internal market" is evolving in the Chinese university sector.

After the introduction of "competition" in the Chinese university sector, the resources and funds of individual universities are determined by their research output and the proportion of graduates getting employment. According to Hayhoe (1996), university authorities have a general expectation that faculty in research institutions should spend two-thirds of their time on research and one-third on teaching; while the reverse expectation is commonly held in teaching institutions. Inevitably, when "competition" is introduced among higher educational institutions rewarding winners and showing up losers, faculty members have experienced intensified work pressure to improve their research profile.

In 1997, the State Education Committee (SEC) (now Education Bureau) issued a new direction for higher education in the mainland, universities are encouraged to share resources and facilities; to merge universities to enhance research and teaching quality; to consolidate and strengthen existing good work, and to establish new universities in collaboration with local governments (Wu, 1997). Under such a policy direction, I learned that different local universities in Guangzhou (the provincial capital of Guangdong) have attempted to merge with others to strengthen their common strengths, hoping the undertaking may enable them to be selected into the "top 100". In order to upgrade the Guangzhou city-run higher education institutions, Guangzhou Normal University, Guangzhou Institute of Education and Guangzhou Teacher College will merge and form a new Guangzhou Normal University. At the same time, Guangzhou Medical College, South China Construction College and Guangzhou University are committed to improve their research and teaching, establishing closer links with local industries and businesses to make their courses more attractive and competitive in the market (Wu, 1997).

Another growth area will be the establishment of a "University City" in Guangzhou. Realizing the limitations faced by the Guangzhou city-run higher education institutions (particularly in terms of the small size of the student population, limited space for school buildings, and inadequate resources and faculty members, it is proposed that a University City could be developed, comprising various local institutions of higher learning such as Jiaotong College, Vocational College, Industrial and Business College, College of Arts and Law, and College of Finance. The proposed "merge" will draw resources and strengths together. Coupled with the existing 100 college-run research centres and enter-

prises, students would very much benefit from sharing more resources, better facilities, well-qualified faculty members and enhanced research and teaching in the future University City (Wu, 1997). Most recently, the Ministry of Education, a newly established administrative body replacing the SEC, has announced that the central government has decided to allocate additional funding to develop Beijing University and Qinghua University, while other universities have to search for alternatives to generate educational funds.

6.4. Stressing Consumers' Choice in Education

Considering students' choice as a very prominent factor affecting course design, educational institutions in China have adopted a "customer-oriented" approach to running their educational services. For instance, the Department of Teaching, People's University of China (Rends), conducted a survey on teaching matters among faculty members and concluded that new teaching materials must be introduced to cater for newly emerging market needs. Thereafter, a "Textbook Revolution" was initiated by using and publicizing 100 kinds of new textbooks throughout the university in 1993. New teaching materials were written and compiled and a special "Teaching Material Working Committee"[6] was set up to coordinate a comprehensive reform in teaching (Wei, 1996). In addition to "teaching material reform", another major action which Renda has taken is to reshuffle the disciplines and specializations to cater for newly emerging needs from the market. Not unexpectedly, programmes like international commerce, international enterprise management, marketing, taxation, national economic management, real estate business and management, etc. are introduced and have successfully attracted far more students.

One striking example, which I learned from my field visits, is that the Department of History of Zhongshan University, has been confronted with a reduction of students under the market economy. In order to attract more students, the department has started to repackage courses to make them more "marketable". Courses such as "culture and history" and "tourism and history" are therefore introduced, with similar practices also adopted by other departments of pure academic studies. "Applied" value is emphasized such as applied mathematics, applied physics and applied chemistry to attract students. Similar cases can easily be observed elsewhere in China's schools especially when computer literacy, spoken English, diversified subjects and practical value are stressed in course design and curriculum development.

In order to "please" the consumers, "quality control" systems and measures are introduced. For instance, Hading Chemical Industry Institute proposed a reform measure called "teachers hanging up their shingles and students choosing their own courses". This means that, for the same course, classes of different specializations, requiring different amount of study time, providing different amount of credits, and using a diversity of teaching methods are employed. These are taught by teachers with varied teaching styles, each of whom "hangs out" his or her "shingle", while students may choose whichever teacher they like best. As a result, students face fierce competition if they desire the opportunity to be personally taught by the best teachers. Teachers "hanging out their shingles" is something new in Shanghai as well as throughout China (Wei, 1996).

Since the implementation of the system of teaching by "shingle-hanging", teachers have acquired control over students' examinations and grading, and students are in control of teachers' standards and the amount of wages and bonuses they receive. More importantly, the scheme is seen as a means to raise teachers' sense of responsibility toward teaching. As well, this reform is used to inspire excellence and to encourage everyone to put all their energies into teaching and research. This institute also introduces "competition" among its colleagues, rewarding those working hard with monetary prizes to induce faculty members to engage actively in research activities (Wei, 1996, pp. 84–88). Educational services are priced, and access to them depends on consumer calculations and the ability to pay. All in all, re-focusing curricula to meet emerging market needs and emphasizing the importance of vocational training and responsiveness to student and market demand are highly suggestive that China's education has been going through a marketization process (Yin and White, 1994; Mok, 1997a).

6.5. A New Educational Mandate: Revenue Generation Activities

Unlike the Mao era when educational development was entirely directed by the central government, there has been a strong tide of diversification and decentralization of education in post-reform China. Starting from the mid-eighties onwards, senior leaders of the CCP have begun to encourage administrators, principals and presidents of schools and universities to search for additional funding to run educational services (Mok and Wat, 1998). Zhao Ziyang, the former Party Secretary, openly admitted that the state did not have sufficient funds to meet the pressing demands for education. He therefore encouraged educational institutions to join in the nationwide proliferation of commercial activities in 1985. Similarly, Li Peng, the former commissioner of education in 1987, also urged local governments to multiply financial sources to support educational development. It is in such a policy context that *chuan shou* (income-generating activity) was initiated and officially endorsed (Kwong, 1996).

In order to generate more income to support educational development, school principals and university administrators have ventured into the business and commercial fields to get additional funds. Through the opening of business firms and enterprises *(xiaoban qiye)*, running commissioned courses, offering adult education and evening courses to attract more students, or charging consultant fees are becoming more popular. With the increasing pressure to find alternative resources, school principals and university administrators have tried different ways to generate additional incomes. For instance, renting out their premises, running cafeterias, "salons", "bars" or even turning their assembly halls into discos or other places for entertainment (Kwong, 1996; Mok, 1997a, 1998a).

Many of the renowned universities in the mainland have run business firms to create additional educational funds. Beida is one of these higher educational institutions doing business and commerce to generate extra funds to support teaching and research activities. New mode of education—"integrate the school and business units, support the schools with factories"—have gained momentum among other schools and colleges in China to diversify sources of financial support. Ren Yanshen, Vice-Secretary of the Party Committee of Beijing University believes that universities' ventures into the commercial and business activities could support universities' scholastic and research activities. He openly said that the "financial income obtained [from doing business] will be used to improve teaching conditions, provide teachers and staff with opportunities to exercise their professional skills, and relieve them of any anxieties about their livelihood" (Ren, cited in Wei, 1996, pp. 72–73). Qinghua University, another key-point university, has run factories and business firms for years. In addition, many faculty staff have established a close link with the industrial sector, playing either the role of consultant or a managerial role in some enterprises (Mok, 1998a; Pepper, 1995; Zhou, 1995).

According to another report, among 50 higher educational institutions, there are 238 companies, 144 factories, 43 three-tier enterprises *(sanzi qiyi)*, diverting about 40% of the profit from these enterprises to support scholastic activities (Zhou et al., 1996). Other activities such as "holding international conferences and charging registration fees to foreign participants, conducting training courses for local industry workers, organizing tours to Chinese archaeological sites, assisting in computerization activities [for] businesses, offering preparatory courses for individuals who may wish to pursue advanced degrees and the like" are organized (Julius, 1997, p. 148). With additional income gained after ventures in the "commercial sea", educational institutions can allocate more money to raise the salaries of teachers and improve teaching and research facilities (China News Analysis, 1993; Cheng, 1996).

7. DISCUSSION AND CONCLUSION: CHINESE EXPERIENCE OF MARKETIZATION

In the light of the conceptual framework which I set out at the beginning of the paper, the adoption of a fee-charging principle, the diversification of educational services offered by the non-state sector, the creation of market-driven courses and curricula, the introduction of "internal competition" in the educational sec-

tor, and revenue generation activities have suggested that China's education has been going through a process of marketization. Even though the state has not deliberately set out to promote private education, the state's persistent call for decentralization and diversification of educational services has created ample room for the growth of private education as well as creating a much more mixed economy within the public sector. Despite the fact that the state has never called for the development of an education market in the mainland, it is beyond doubt that the recent educational restructuring in China shows major elements of a movement towards an education market. Going through a process of marketization, diversity of services and consumers' choice have received due attention, internal competition is introduced to ensure "value for money". The growth of private higher educational institutions, coupled with the adoption of market principles and strategies in recovering educational costs, suggest that the mainland is moving in a similar though identical trajectory to the global process of privatization/marketization in education (Mok, 1997a). Putting all the observations discussed above together, we can argue that the recent transformation of China's educational realm has taken two forms of marketization as Buchbinder and Newson suggested (1990). Both "inside-out" and "outside-in" approaches have been adopted in an attempt to make the delivery of educational services more efficient and responsive to market needs.

Despite the process of marketization, internal markets in Chinese education have not yet evolved. The split of purchaser and provider is not clear in China's educational realm (Mok, 1997a). The strategies adopted by the CCP in creating more educational opportunities in response to emerging market needs are highly instrumental. The aim is to improve administrative efficiency and effectiveness as well as resolve the financial difficulty of the state to provide its citizens with free education rather than to make a fundamental shift of value orientation. This is because the CCP has never committed itself theoretically and ideologically to public choice theory or "economic rationalism", the philosophical basis of marketization and privatization. Even though the move to user pays and the rise of non-state provision in China suggests a withdrawal of the state in provision and subsidy, such practices are compatible with the development of a more effective state role in the socialist market economy context.

Unlike "marketization" experiences in the West, the Chinese "marketization of education" has not yet entirely oriented toward a "managerial approach" thereby reforms in managing educational institutions and the introduction of control mechanisms in the university sector are believed to be effective ways to improve the performance, efficiency and effectiveness of service delivery (Henry et al., 1997; Welch, 1998). What really characterizes Chinese experience of "marketization" is closely related to the "institutional transition" taken place in the mainland. By "institutional transition", we mean a transition from a highly-centralized economic planning system to the market economy (Li, 1997). In the midst of the transition, the CCP has gradually retreated from the public domain, trying to mobilize non-state sectors or governments at the local level to engage in public service/policy provision. As such, market forces are being adopted to generate additional resources to run education. Clearly commercial aspects, user pays and a limited role for private provision in the PRC does suggest the reduced state role in educational provision and financing, but this process does not constitute a total withdrawal from state control/shaping (Mok, 1999b). Similar to the privatization experience of the Czech Republic suggested by Svecova in this issue, the "marketization" project in China is to encourage the non-state sector and even the market/private sector to create more educational opportunities while the state alone is proved to be unable to meet people's pressing demand for education (Yin and White, 1994). Therefore, market principles and mechanisms are adopted in education under a new paradigm of social welfare, i.e. the concept of the market economy plays a key role in shaping public and social policy development (Wong and Flynn, unpublished manuscript).

It is worth noting that even though China's education has been going through a process of "marketization", the CCP still fears that the emergence of private education in the mainland would greatly challenge the conventional order. In spite of the fact that the traditional social/public policy paradigm practiced in the Mao era has proved to be ineffective in the socialist market context (Wong, 1998), the state still has a problem to openly acknowledge the ideological conflict between socialism and the principles of market economy. This point is clearly revealed by the condemnation of the "private element" in the educational sector by not allowing "profit-making" arrangements (Mok and Chan, 1996). Trying to uphold the socialist ideal in order that the legitimacy of the CCP would be maintained, the CCP has tried very hard to protect this last "battle-field" of socialism—public education.

But the CCP's efforts to protect the last "bastion" of a command economy (as popular in the Mao era) may prove to be ineffective especially when the public and state run schools are starting to look private. Our above discussion has already demonstrated how schools and universities in the public sector have begun by choice and necessity to adopt market principles and strategies in refashioning their courses. A fee-charging system is not only operating in non-state run schools but state run and even key-point schools are using similar strategies in financing education. Public schools are very active in business activities to generate revenue to finance education (Zhou et al., 1996). Our foregoing discussion has also highlighted that there is a strong trend in China's educational realm towards diversity and plurality because the state has deliberately demonopolized its role as service provider. Local initiatives, individual efforts and the private sector have tried to create more educational opportunities, resulting in a division of labour between the state, local government, the community, and the school. As a result, diversity and variety can now be found not only in the structure of education but also in the versions of textbooks (Cheng, 1995a; Mok, 1997b). Particularly striking is that publicly-run educational institutions are becoming more "marketized".

The Chinese experience of "marketization of education" has suggested that the private and public boundary is merging. In this regard, the most crucial question in the debate over the "public and private" distinction is not "public or private". In order to reduce the burden of the state in educational provision, economic factors are considered by public administrators the most important ones, and it is economic considerations that drive individuals and shape social and public policy. The university sector is not the only sector affected by strong market forces: other fields like welfare, health, and housing are going through a similar trend of marketization (Wong and Flynn, unpublished manuscript). Reductions in state subsidy, provision and regulation, and a transfer of state responsibility to other non-state sectors, are good indicators of the breakdown of public/private borders. The growing impact of market forces on the educational realm has inevitably led to a border-crossing process, whereby both public and private schools in the mainland have to make themselves more competitive in a market environment. In this regard, a discussion of the marketization of education in China would seem to include not only schools that call themselves private but also public schools that in many ways appear increasingly to be private, thus making the distinction between private and public more problematic.

In addition, the retreat of the state has also led to a process of re-negotiation between the state and society of their division of social responsibilities, and eventually to a new definition of state/society relationship in general and public/private boundaries in particular (Mok, 1997b,c). Thus, the "public/private" debate is essentially related to the question of "*how* [people] choose between public and private provision and *how* [they] establish the proper balance between them" (Wilding, 1990, p. 27, italic original). What is clear, then, is that the future of educational provision in China is a much more overtly mixed economy.

NOTES

1. The author wants to thank the City University of Hong Kong to offer him conference grants to present the present paper to the 14th World Congress of Sociology, which was held in Montreal, Canada in August 1998. The paper was selected in the Congress for publication. Thanks must be expressed to two referees for their very useful and constructive suggestions to improve the paper. Of course, the author is solely responsible for any errors and mistakes in the paper.

2. By "fee-paying" principle, I mean that students have to pay for their higher education. Before the reform took place in the higher education sector in the early 1990s, Chinese citizens were entitled to have free higher education so long as they could perform well in open university entrance examination. Nonetheless, the CCP has adopted a "user-charge" principle to recover costs of higher education since the mid-1990s and thereafter students have to pay for their tuition fees.

3. In the 1989 June Fourth Incident, university students complained about inadequate state financial support to higher education and the reduction of state subsidies had increased the financial burden of students in university education. For this reason, the CCP intentionally controlled the number of self-support students.

4. The inequality of access to higher education with increasing tuition fees has called for social concern and governments at both the central and local levels have adopted different strategies to help students from poor socio-economic backgrounds to continue their learning in higher education (see, for example, Agelasto and Adamson, 1998).

5. By other approaches and models, I refer to different types of non-state-run schools in the mainland and they adopt different ways to finance and manage their schools (for details, see, Mok, 1998b).

6. In the Mao era, the CCP had a very tight control over course design and curricula of university. Hence, the establishment of a special "Teaching Material Working Committee" in recent years has a very significant implication that universities in the mainland nowadays enjoy far more autonomy and flexibility in the design of programmes and courses.

REFERENCES

Agelasto, M., & Adamson, B. (Eds.). (1998). *Higher Education in Post-Mao China*. Hong Kong: Hong Kong University Press.

Ash, R., & Kueh, Y. Y. (Eds.), 1996. *The Chinese economy under Deng Xiaoping*. Oxford: Clarendon.

Ball, S. J. (1990). *Politics and policy making in education*. London: Routledge.

Bray, M. (1996). *Counting the full cost: Parental and community financing of education in East Asia*. Washington, DC: World Bank in collaboration with the United Nations Children's Fund.

Bray, M. (1997). *Financing higher education in Asia and the Pacific: Patterns, trends and options*. Paper presented to the World Congress on Higher Education and Human Resource Development in Asia and the Pacific for the 21st Century, Manila.

Buchbinder, H., & Newson, J. (1990). Corporate-university linkages in Canada: Transforming a public institution. *Higher education*, 20 (4), 355–379.

Bridges, D., & McLaughlin, T.H. (Eds.). (1994). *Education and the market place*. London: The Falmer Press.

Brown. F. (1995). Privatization of public education: theories and concepts. *Education and urban society,* 27 (2), 114–126.

CCPCC. (1993). The program for educational reform and development in China. *Zhonghun Renmin Gongheguo Guowuyuan Gongbao,* 2, 58–66.

Cheng, K. M. (1990). Financing education in mainland China: What are the real problems? *Issues and studies,* 3 (March), 54–75.

Cheng, K. M. (1995a). Education—decentralization and the market. In Wong, L. & MacPherson, S. (Eds.), *Social change and social policy in contemporary China.* Aldershot: Avebury.

Cheng, K. M. (1995b). Zhongguo jiaoyu (China's education). In Lee, X. M. (Ed.), *Zhongguo Shehui Fenxi (China's social development).* Hong Kong: Hong Kong Educational.

Cheng, K. M. (1996). Markets in a socialist system: Reform of higher education. In Watson, K., Modgil, S., & Modgil, C. (Eds.), *Educational dilemmas: Debate and diversity,* vol. 2, Higher Education. London: Cassell.

Cheng, K. M. (1997). *What have been reformed? Review of two decades' reform in China's education.* Paper presented at the Conference on Education and Development: Education and Geo-political Change, New College, Oxford.

China National Institute of Educational Research. (1995). *A study of NGO-sponsored and private higher education in China.* Sponsored by UNESCO, Beijing.

China News Analysis, 15 October 1993.

Christiansen, F. (1996). Devolution in Chinese higher education policy in the 1990s: Common establishment and the "211" program. *Leeds East Asia papers,* No. 36.

Currie, J., & Newson, J. (1998). *Universities and globalization: Critical perspectives.* Newbury, CA: Sage.

Flynn, N. (1997). *Public sector management,* 3rd ed. Hempstead: Harvester Wheatsheaf.

Grace, G. (1995). *School leadership: Beyond educational management.* London: The Falmer Press.

Hartley, D. (1995). The "MacDonaldization" of higher education: Food for thought? *Oxford review of education,* 21 (4), 409–423.

Hayhoe, R. (1996). *China's universities 1985–1995: A century of cultural conflict.* New York: Garland.

Henry, M. et al. (1997). Globalization, the state and education policy making. In Taylor, S. et al. (Eds.), *Educational policy and the politics of change.* London: Routledge.

James, E. (1992). Why do different countries choose a different public-private mix of educational services. *The journal of human resources,* June, 571–592.

Julius, D. (1997). Will Chinese universities survive in emerging market economy? *Higher education management,* 9 (1), 141–156.

Kwong, J. (1996). The new educational mandate in China: Running schools running businesses. *International journal of educational development,* 16 (2), 185–194.

Le Grand, J., & Robinson, R. (Eds.). (1984). *Privatization and the welfare state.* London: Allen & Unwin.

Li, P. (1997). Institutional innovation and interest allocation under China's reform. In Lu, X. Y., & Li, P. L. (Eds.), *Zhongguo Xinsiqi Shehui Fazhang Baogao (Report of the social development in New China).* Shenyang: Liaoning Renmin Chubanshe.

Lo, A. (1997). *Towards a market-oriented school system in Hong Kong: Impacts and anticipated consequences.* Paper presented to the 14th Annual Conference of HKERA.

Mok, K. H. (1996). Marketization and decentralization: Development of education and paradigm shift in social policy. *Hong Kong public administration,* 5 (1), 35–56.

Mok, K. H. (1997a). Marketization and quasi-marketization: Educational development in post-Mao China. *International review of education,* 43 (5–6), 1–21.

Mok, K. H. (1997b). Professional autonomy and private education in Guangdong province. *Leeds East Asia papers,* 41, 1–40.

Mok, K.H., 1997c. Private challenges to public dominance: the resurgence of private education in the Pearl River Delta. *Comparative education,* 31 (1), 43–60.

Mok, K. H., 1998a. *Intellectuals and the state in post-Mao China.* Houndmills: Macmillan.

Mok, K. H. (1998b). The resurgence of private education in post-Mao China. In Mok, K. H., & Yu, K. M. (Eds.), *Social and political transformation in post-Mao China.* Hong Kong: Hong Kong Humanities Press.

Mok, K. H. (1999a). The cost of manageralism: the implications for the "McDonaldisation" of higher education in Hong Kong. *Journal of higher education policy and management,* 21 (1), 117–127.

Mok, K. H. (1999b). Education and the market place in mainland China and Hong Kong. *Higher education,* 37, 133–158.

Mok, K. H(1999c). *Social and political development in post-reform China.* Houndmills: Macmillan. In press.

Mok, K. H., & Chan, D. (1996). The emergence of private education in the Pearl River Delta: Implications for social development. In MacPherson, S., & Cheng, J. (Eds.), *Social and economic development in south China.* London: Elgar.

Mok, K. H., & Wat, K. Y. (1998). Merging of the public and private boundary: Education and the market place in China. *International journal of educational development,* 18 (3), 255–267.

Niu, X. (1997). The practical experience of the nongovernmental Nanhua industurial and business college. *Chinese education and society,* 30 (1), 84–89.

Pepper, S. (1995). Regaining the initiative for education reform and development. In Lo, C. K. et al. (Eds.) *China review, 1995.* Hong Kong: The Chinese University Press.

Rosen, S. (1997). *The impact of economic reform on Chinese education: Markets and the growth of differentiation.* Paper presented to the Conference on Social Consequences of Chinese Economic Reform, John K. Fairbank Center, Harvard University.

Sinclair, C. (1989). Public sector culture: management or multiculturalism? *Australian journal of public administration,* 48 (4), 382–397.

State Education Commission (SEC). (1995). *Education law.* State Education Commission, Beijing.

Taylor, S. et al. (1997). *Educational policy and the politics of change.* London: Routledge.

Tilak, J. (1991). The privatization of higher education. *Prospects,* 21 (2), 227–239.

Watson, K. (1996). Banking on key reforms for educational development: A critique of the World Bank review. *Mediterranean journal of educational studies,* 1 (1), 43–61.

Wei, F. 1996. The great tremors in China's intellectuals circles: An overview of intellectuals floundering in the sea of commercialism. *Chinese education and society,* 29 (6), 7–104.

Wei, Y., & Zhang, G. (1995). *A historical perspective on non-governmental higher education in China.* Paper presented to the International Conference of Private Higher Education in Asia and the Pacific Region, November, The University of Xiamen, Xiamen.

Welch, A. (1998). The cult of efficiency in education: comparative reflections on the reality and the rhetoric. *Comparative education,* 34 (2), 157–175.

Wilding, P. (1990). Privatization: An introduction and a critique. In Parry, R. (Ed.), *Privatazation.* London: Kingsley.

World Bank. (1994). *Priorities and strategies for education.* Washington, DC: The World Bank.

World Bank. (1995). *Higher education: The lessons of experience.* Washington. DC: The World Bank.

World Bank. (1996). *Vietnam: Education financing sector study.* Washington, DC: The World Bank.

World Bank. (1997). *Annual report 1997.* Washington, DC: The World Bank.

World Bank. (1998). *Annual report 1998.* Washington, DC: The World Bank.

Wong, L. (1994). Privatization of social welfare in post-Mao China. *Asian survey,* 34 (4), 307–325.

Wong, L. (1998). *Marginalization and social welfare in China.* London: Routledge.

Wong, L., & Flynn, N. (Eds.). (1999). *Social policy in post-reform China: Marketization and societalization.* Unpublished manuscript.

Wu, N. (1996). Guangdong silidaixue fazhan chuyi (A proposal for private university development in Guangdong). *Gaojiao Tansuo,* February, 40–44.

Wu, Z. (1997). Guangzhou si jiaoyu fazhan zhanlue yinjiu di huigu jiqi rensi (Review and study of the strategies of the education development in Guangzhou). In Wu, Z. (Ed.), *Zhanshe Xindaihua Jiaoyu Jiangsi Guangzhousi Jiaoyu Fazhan Zhanlue Yinjiu (Building a strong educational province— Strategies of the education development in Guangdong).* Guangdong: Guangdong Higher Education Press.

Yao, R. (1984). *Zhongguo Jiaoyu 1949–1982 (China's education 1949–1982).* Hong Kong: Wah Fong Bookshop Press.

Yeatman, A. (1987). The concept of public management and the Australian state in the 1980s. *Australian journal of public administration,* 46 (4), 339–353.

Yee, A. H., & Lim, T. G. (1995). Education supply and demand in east Asia: Private higher education. In Yee, A. H. (Ed.), *East Asian higher education: Traditions and transformations.* Oxford: Pergamon Press.

Yin, Q., & White, G. (1994). The marketization of Chinese higher education: A critical assessment. *Comparative education,* 30 (3), 217–237.

Yuan, Z., & Wakabayashi, M. (1996). Chinese higher education reform from the "state model" to the "social model": Based on a Sino-Japan comparative perspective. *Forum of international development studies,* 6, 173–200.

Zhang, Z. (1996). Summary of a symposium on non-governmental basic education. *Chinese education and society,* 29 (5), 73–81.

Zhou, N. (1995). Strengthening the connection between education and economic development: major issues in China's educational reform and suggested solutions. In Postilglione, G., & Lee, W. O. (Eds.), *Social change and educational development, mainland China, Taiwan, and Hong Kong.* Hong Kong: Centre of Asian Studies, The University of Hong Kong.

Zhou, N. et al. (1996). *Private higher education in China in the1990s: Background, current status, and research findings.* Beijing: China National Institute of Educational Research.

Zhu, Y. (1996). *Perspectives on Minban schools in China.* Paper presented to the Shanghai International House for Education, Shanghai.

CHAPTER 58

DIVERSIFYING FINANCE OF HIGHER EDUCATION SYSTEMS IN THE THIRD WORLD

The Cases of Kenya and Mongolia

JOHN C. WEIDMAN

John C. Weidman is at the Maseno University College, Kenya, University of Pittsburgh, Professor of Education and Sociology School of Education, Department of Administrative and Policy Studies.

In countries throughout the world, there are increasing pressures to reduce the government share of costs for goods and services with high payoffs to individuals so that the limited available public funds can be used for other needs. This paper suggests several strategies for reducing government expenditures on higher education, including direct cost recovery, grants from and contracts with external agencies, income-producing enterprises, private contributions, and expansion of the private sector. Policy implications and examples (e.g., student access and financial aid, tax status of revenues from enterprises, deferred cost recovery) are presented for both developing and developed countries.

As developing countries struggle to meet the financial demands for full participation in the world economy, there is strong pressure to change patterns of government expenditures in order to meet changing budgetary needs (e.g., funding neglected infrastructure improvements, especially transportation and communication). International donor agencies and development banks support fiscal policies that reduce what are considered to be patterns of inordinately high expenditures on education and human resources in order to facilitate necessary reallocation of scarce government resources. This is an example of what are commonly known as "structural adjustment policies" (SAPS).

To implement SAPS, governments are encouraged to identify those sectors of their economies in which there are possibilities for "cost sharing," namely, shifting greater portions of the burden of payment to the individuals who are the recipients or users of the services provided. Hence, it is understandable that a frequent target for cost sharing is higher education, a service that is both very expensive to provide and from which recipients can expect to receive significant financial benefits. Recent research suggests that even in the Philippines, an "educationally advanced developing country" (40% baccalaureate-level enrollment ratio and more than half of the institutions in the private sector), higher education has demonstrable individual as well as national development payoffs (Hossain & Psacharopoulos, 1994).

Several options for "widening and diversifying sources of finance" of higher education (Woodhall, 1993) are explored in this paper, including (a) direct cost recovery, (b) grants from and contracts with external agencies, (c) income-producing enterprises, (d) voluntary contributions, and (d) expansion of the private sector. Comparisons are made between the strategies and approaches used to implement various options in Kenya and Mongolia, two Third World countries under strong pressure to implement SAPs. While both countries have well-developed higher

Source: Education Policy Analysis Archives, Vol. 3 Num. 5, February 24, 1995, ISSN (1068-2341). Editor: Gene V. Glass, Glass © ASU.EDU. College of Education, Arizona State University, Tempe AZ 85287-2411. © 1995, the EDUCATION POLICY ANALYSIS.

education systems, the prospects for maintaining vitality and reaching an internationally competitive standard have become increasingly remote because neither government can afford to pay world market prices to supply each of their institutions with state-of-the-art educational, scientific, and technological materials and equipment. Hence, both countries are involved in efforts to reform higher education through more efficient use of existing resources, strategic planning for new resource acquisition, and organizational changes that reduce the role of central government and provide greater institutional autonomy.

The paper begins with (a) some general background information on the national development contexts and higher education systems in Kenya and Mongolia, and (b) a general framework for understanding the notion of "revenue diversification" (Albrecht & Ziderman, 1992) in higher education which illustrates the relationships among various public and private funding sources. It includes discussion of policy issues related to specific types of financial diversification, presenting examples and implications for higher education in both developed and developing countries.

DEVELOPMENT CONTEXTS AND HIGHER EDUCATION SYSTEMS IN KENYA AND MONGOLIA

Kenya gained its independence from Great Britain in 1963. It had a one-party political system until the end of the 1980's when opposition parties were legalized, though none is a viable threat to the ruling party. According to the World Bank (1994, Table 58.1), Kenya is among the poorest countries in the world, ranking 19th from the bottom of its list of 132 economies. Per capita Gross National Product (GNP) was $310 in 1992. Education constituted 20% of central

government expenditures which represented 6% of GNP (World Bank, 1994, Table 10).

The contemporary history of university-level education in Kenya dates only from 1963 when there were just 571 students enrolled in what was to become the University of Nairobi (Weidman, 1995, Table 2). Education in the newly independent Kenya was modeled on the British 7–4–2 system, with 7 years of primary schooling followed by 4 years of secondary school and an additional 2 years of advanced secondary education (signified by successful completion of the A-level exams) to qualify for entrance to 3-year university bachelor's degree programs. In the 1980's, there was a shift to an American-style 8–4–4 system with 8 years of primary education followed by 4 years of secondary school and a 4-year bachelor's degree curriculum (Mwiria & Nyukuri, 1994, pp. 10–12). Under both systems, students seeking admission to universities were required to take a competitive national examination.

Mongolia gained its independence from China in 1921, and following 3 years of a constitutional monarchy headed by Buddhist leaders, established the Mongolian People's Democratic Republic in 1924. Mongolia maintained its independence for the next 65 years but had a strong alliance with the Soviet Union that included very close economic ties. In the 1986–89 period, inflows of resources from the Soviet Union averaged about 32% of Gross Domestic Product (GDP)! These resources, which included books and scientific equipment for the universities, stopped by the end of 1990 following the break-up of the Soviet Union (World Bank, 1992, pp. 2, 8). The Asian Development Bank (1993, p. 1) estimated the 1992 per capita GNP of Mongolia to be $ 299. According to the World Bank

TABLE 58.1
Enrollment in Baccalaureate-Level Institutions of Higher Education by Country and Sector

	1992* Population (millions)	*BA-level** Enrollment (thousands)*		*Enrollment per 100,000 People*	
		Public	*Private*	*Public*	*Private*
Kenya	25.7	40.7	2.0	158	8
Mongolia	2.4	17.5	3.9	762	169

*   *Source:* World Bank, 1994, Table 1.

**   *Source:* For Kenya—public universities (1991–92), Republic of Kenya, 1994, Table 1.13; private institutions (1990–91), Saint, 1992, p. 42. For Mongolia (1993–94)—Bray, et al., Tables 1 and 2.

(1992, p. 82), expenditures on education at the end of 1990 were 25% of the government's total budget which constituted a sizable 14% of GDP.

The oldest contemporary university-level institution of higher education, now named the Mongolia National University, was founded in 1942. Mongolia has a 6–2–2–4 educational system, with primary education lasting 6 years, followed by either a vocationally-oriented 2-year secondary program or a 4-year, university-oriented secondary program. Higher education in Mongolia was originally modeled on the Soviet system in which curricula were highly specialized and student places were determined on the basis of projected manpower needs. Universities were primarily teaching institutions, with responsibility for research and the awarding of the highest scientific degrees vested in independent institutes under the Academy of Science.

A shift is now underway to a less specialized American-style system in which students will earn bachelor's degrees at the end of four years and places are determined, at least in part, by student demand. Efforts are underway to integrate the research institutes of the Academy of Science into the universities. Each higher education institution administers its own competitive admissions examinations.

Data on higher education enrollments for both countries are shown in Table 58.1. Mongolia has a much smaller population but its overall higher education enrollment rate is 5.6 times greater than Kenya's. Mongolia also has a much larger private higher education sector. To put these enrollment rates in perspective, both countries are above the Sub-Saharan average of 89, but well below both the Latin American average of 1468 and the OECD (Organization for Economic Cooperation and Development) average of 2392 (Zymelman, 1990, p. 22).

The historical funding patterns of higher education in Kenya and Mongolia are similar to many developing countries in Africa and the emerging formerly socialist countries of Eastern Europe and Central Asia. Higher education was not only free of charge, but students received additional allowances from the government for their living expenses and study materials. Sanyal and Martin (1991) describe "the relatively high cost of African higher education" as follows:

> . . . cost of a graduate of Sub-Saharan Africa, according to one estimate is eight times GNP per capita whereas it is only 3.7 times the GNP per capita for all the developing countries combined (Mingat and Psacharopoulos, 1985). The ratio between unit costs in higher and in primary education varies between 30:1 and 50:1 in African countries as against 10:1 in Asia or Latin America (Hinchliffe, 1987).

In Kenya, 1992/93 national "recurrent" expenditures per student in public universities were 46 times higher than those for each primary school student, even though actual total "recurrent" expenditures for primary education were almost three times larger than those for public universities (Weidman, 1995, Table 58.3; Republic of Kenya, 1993, p. 184). Just a small fraction of the eligible age cohort is enrolled in Kenyan universities. While virtually all children in Kenya enter primary school, only half of the original entering students are still enrolled at the end of primary school. Because just half of the primary school leavers gain admission to secondary school, there is an effective secondary school enrollment ratio of 24% of the nation's young people of secondary school age (Opondo & Noormohamed, 1989, p. 88). In 1990, there were enough available university places for just 7.5% of the secondary school leavers (Mwiria & Nyukuri, 1994, pp. 10–11), so the effective university enrollment ratio was less than 2% of university-age Kenyans. Only 37% of the students enrolled in government universities are women (Weidman, 1995, Table 58.2).

In Mongolia, virtually all children also enter primary school, but 89% complete the eighth grade, and 50% complete secondary school (i.e., tenth grade). Among Mongolians under the age of 34, only 2% did not complete secondary school. In the total workforce, 16% have completed at least some higher education (World Bank, 1992, pp. 82–83). Women constitute 64% of the students in baccalaureate-level government institutions of higher education. In private baccalaureate-level programs, 76% of the students are women (Bray, et al., 1994, Tables 58.1 and 58.2).

TABLE 58.2
Funding Sources for Higher Education Systems by Sector*

	Public Sector	Private Sector
Government	X	
Grants Commission	X	
Research Councils	X	X
Loan Agency	X	X
Students	X	X
Alumni		X
Industry		X

*   Adapted from Albrecht & Ziderman, 1992, Chart 1.3, p. 14.

A "REVENUE DIVERSIFICATION MODEL" OF HIGHER EDUCATION FINANCE

Table 58.2 illustrates the combination of public and private sector sources from which funding for higher education systems is generated that has been called the "revenue diversification model" (Albrecht & Ziderman, 1992) of higher education finance. Even though the model was developed with specific reference to the type of funding structure that exists in Great Britain, the basic components appear in a variety of national higher education systems.

Table 58.2 also suggests the interaction between the public and private sectors in university finance. The public sector is shown to fund universities in five different ways, four of which do not provide resources directly to the institutions but rather through intermediary agencies or through students. In this example, funds are provided by the government to students in two ways: (1) through direct grants which can be used to pay university costs, but are not subject to repayment; and (2) through partial funding to an agency which offers loans to students. The "private sector" component of the "loan agency" is self-perpetuating, namely, through loan payments made by former students.

Many developed countries have been placing increasing emphasis on loans rather than direct grants to students, thereby reducing the government share of higher education costs. In the USA, for instance, student aid provided by the federal government shifted from 20% loans

and 76% grants in 1975–76 to 64% loans and 33% grants in 1992–93 (Gladieux et al., 1994, p. 134).

The British government also finances a "grants commission" (for capital projects) and "research councils" (for research projects) which provide funds to universities on a competitive basis. In this model, industry "may contribute to university finances directly or indirectly through research councils and sponsored students" (Albrecht & Ziderman, 1992, p.13). Alumni of higher education institutions also contribute funds privately to universities. Not shown in Table 58.2, but certainly worth noting, is the contribution made by industry and alumni to the pool of available government funds through the proportion of their income taxes that is allocated to higher education. It is important, however, to keep the following cautionary note in mind when considering this type of model:

> . . . Since revenue diversification implies also diversifying the outputs and activities of the university system, this process may lead to a change in the role of universities away from traditional teaching for degrees and research. If revenue diversification is pressed too far, on too broad a front, serious issues concerning the role of the university may arise (Albrecht & Ziderman, 1992, p. 13).

TABLE 58.3
Revenues of Colleges and Universities in the USA by Sector, 1990–91*

	Public	Private
Tuition and fees	16%	40%
Federal government	10%	15%
State governments	40%	2%
Local governments	4%	1%
Private gifts, grants, contracts	4%	9%
Endowment income	1%	5%
Sales and services		
Educational activities	3%	3%
Auxilliary enterprises	10%	11%
Hospitals	10%	10%
Other	3%	4%

* *Source:* The Almanac of Higher Education, 1994, p. 76.

An example of the scope of revenue diversification in a highly developed country is contained in Table 58.3 which shows the average proportions of different revenue streams for public and private colleges and universities in the USA. The fundamental differences in revenue streams between the two sectors lie in the greater reliance of private higher education institutions on tuition, private gifts, and endowments. At least in the USA, both public and private institutions generate equal amounts through sales and services. It should also be noted that even the public higher education institutions generate, on average, almost half of their revenues from non-government sources. In the next section of this paper, actual strategies for diversifying revenues are described.

DIVERSIFYING THE SOURCES OF FINANCE FOR HIGHER EDUCATION

The following are several strategies for diversifying the funding base of higher education systems suggested in a recent paper by Woodhall (1993, pp. 8–10) that are also designed to reduce the government's share of costs. Where relevant, specific reference is made to the current status of efforts to employ the strategies in Kenya and Mongolia.

1. Direct Cost Recovery

a. Charge fees to students for tuition. The largest potential source of funds results from requiring students to pay fees for tuition (basic instruction) and related instructional services (e.g., registration, examinations, computer, access to library, etc.). There is considerable variability, both among institutions and among countries, in the proportion of costs recovered via tuition and student fees.

Some Mongolian students were assessed fees for the 1992–93 academic year and all students enrolled in public higher education in 1993–94 were being charged. At least as initially determined, it appeared that tuition fees for the public higher education institutions in Mongolia were being set at levels that provided for full recovery of all costs. Particularly during this period of transition into a market economy and entry into the world economic system, it is important that there not be radical shifts in funding patterns that would materially harm Mongolia's well-established higher education system. Further, even as students are required to share costs at increasingly greater levels, it is essential that there be some government funds available for much-needed maintenance and improvement of buildings (Harsh winters take their toll.), for instructional facilities such as libraries and laboratories, for support of students from poor families, and for faculty and program development. Requiring total cost recovery provides virtually no allowance for such investments in the future.

With respect to the notion of "cost recovery," it is instructive to note the following observation in a World Bank discussion paper:

> . . . There are no university systems which are characterized by cost recovery in a pure form (though there are particular universities that are financed in this way); in practice, cost recovery operates in tandem with, and complements, state subsidy of higher education. Characterizing a system as one of cost recovery in practice relates to the breadth of student coverage of fees and their size in relation to costs (Albrecht & Ziderman, 1992, p. 11).

In Kenya, public university students are required to pay fees, but the amount continues to be quite low, currently 300 Kenya pounds (6000 Kenya shillings, or about 150 US$) per year. This amount was equal to just over 10% of the total estimated government recurrent expenditures per university student in 1992/93 of 2889 Kenya pounds (Republic of Kenya, 1993). Any increase in fees should, however, also incorporate some scheme for providing scholarships to poor students with high academic potential.

b. Eliminate student stipends. Requiring students to pay charges for board and lodging from their own funds would allow the government to eliminate the costs of providing student stipends for personal expenses, though it may still be desirable to provide small stipends for books and instructional materials. Government stipends for Mongolian students were virtually eliminated in 1993–94. In Kenya, stipends for personal expenses are covered under the student loan scheme.

2. Contracts and Agreements with Private and Public Sector Agencies

a. Sponsorship of students. Institutions of higher education can seek to establish agreements with private sector employers willing to sponsor promising students by paying their tuition and other fees, or by providing scholarships.

b. Contracts for consulting services. Funds can be obtained by contracting with external agencies (e.g., commerce, industry, government, etc.) for the provision of expert services by professors and other skilled staff. This could include contracts for consulting, for applied research, or for other expertise represented within the higher education community. Efforts along these particular lines are now occurring in Mongolia, especially in the Technical University.

c. Paid internships. Arrangements can be made for students to receive salaries and/or tuition support from employers for internships related to their fields of study. Such internships could be done either during a vacation period or during a semester away from campus.

3. Income Producing Enterprises

This method of generating funds is currently used by all of the public higher education institutions in Mongolia. The most common of these is maintaining a herd of livestock (cattle, sheep, goats, etc.), but there are others (renting space for a shop, providing copying services, running bookstores, etc.). The public universities in Mongolia which have such enterprises generate income, on the average, equal to roughly 10% of their total operating budgets. Most of the government universities in Kenya as well as several private ones also maintain farms to generate revenue.

4. Private Contributions and Endowments

In many parts of the world, there are annual campaigns to solicit gifts from alumni and staff as well as private donors. When higher education institutions get sufficiently large contributions (either alone or when several gifts are combined), endowments can be established by making investments from which all or part of the income can be used, usually for specific purposes. Governments often encourage private contributions by providing income tax deductions for gifts made to eligible, non-profit higher education institutions. Neither Kenya nor Mongolia generate any significant revenues for higher education in this way.

Higher education institutions should have sufficient autonomy to be able to keep any additional revenue generated from contracts, enterprises, and contributions, and not have either to return it to the government or to have subsequent budget allocations reduced by the amount of the income (Woodhall, 1993, p. 12). Institutions should be allowed to control and monitor their own expenditures, preferably using standard reporting procedures supported by an automated financial accounting system. It is also essential that those government funds which are appropriated to higher education institutions be received in a regular and timely way.

5. Student Employment and National Service Scholarships

a. Work-study. This is wage earning employment, not necessarily limited to campus jobs but administered through higher education institutions. There are usually some financial need criteria which must be satisfied before a student can get a work-study job.

b. Scholarships for national service. These programs provide participants with the opportunity to accumulate funds, on the basis of established formulae, that can be applied to higher education expenses. Often the government matches the participants' contributions at some pre-determined rate. Both of these approaches involve government expenditures, but the funds are disbursed in exchange for specified productive activity rather than as outright subsidies. Examples of such programs that have existed in the USA are the Civilian Conservation Corps of the 1930's, the Peace Corps, VISTA, and the National Health Service Corps (Gladieux et al., 1994, p. 138).

6. Deferred Cost Recovery

a. Tax on future earnings of graduates. While likely to be politically unpopular, this approach requires payment of a tax based on salaries earned by graduates of publicly supported higher education institutions. It could be a payroll tax paid by employers or be assessed on the graduates, themselves.

b. Tax on private sector employers. This would be a tax based on either the proportion of graduates from higher education employed or on a percentage of total earnings by the company, again depending on the proportion of graduates among all employees.

c. Student loans. This is the most widely used mode of deferred cost recovery. The students who borrow money generally either do not have the financial resources necessary to pay for higher education during the period of their enrollment or wish to pay back the tuition costs in inflated currency some years later. If well-structured and efficiently operated, loan programs can be virtually self-perpetuating. There are five basic issues that need to be considered in the design of any higher education student loan program:

. . . First, a deferred payment program requires the participation of a credible collection institution with incentives to collect, which in most instances required the direct participation of commercial banks, a taxation department or a social security agency.

. . . Second, with loans, there must be a willingness to charge interest rates equal to or above inflation in order to minimize subsidies.

. . . Third, the relationship between necessary repayments and the likely income of students must be examined to ensure that repayment burdens never pose an excessive burden on graduates.

. . . Fourth, developing a means of targeting support to needier and more academically deserving students will be crucial to a program's efficiency.

. . . Fifth, loan losses can be justified if there are potential social gains that would not be reflected in a graduate's income (Albrecht & Ziderman, 1992, p. 100).

Loan programs may include such incentives as deferred interest payments while a student is enrolled in higher education, loan forgiveness for graduates working in areas of national need, subsidized interest rates, and

government guarantees to private lenders offering student loans. In all of these cases, the loan programs are not self-funding and require government support, though certainly at a much lower level than direct scholarship grants. Further, if the government is the primary source of loans, its financial outlay will not be reduced until a significant amount of money is being returned through loan repayment. For a more detailed discussion of specific loan schemes in African and Asian countries, see Woodhall (1991 a and b).

The government's inability (or unwillingness) to finance the student loan scheme that was to have been fully implemented for the 1993–94 academic year seems to be a fundamental problem in Mongolia. The national government has apparently tried to shift the burden of financial responsibility for guaranteeing loans to the local government (aimag) level in Mongolia, but local authorities are understandably reluctant to make commitments on the basis of an uncertain future. Until recently, there has been no effective agency in Kenya for collection of outstanding student loans, with 75–80% never being repaid (Woodhall, 1991a, p. 55). In 1994, the government increased its effort to collect loans from public employees by instituting a more aggressive program of withholding monthly payments from their paychecks.

7. Expanding the Private Sector

One additional way for national governments to reduce their share of the total costs of providing higher education is to encourage the establishment and growth of private institutions. Asian countries with large private higher education sectors are Indonesia (58% of national enrollment), South Korea (66% of enrollment), Japan (76% of enrollment), and the Philippines (85% of enrollment). The private higher education institutions in Indonesia and Japan receive 20–30% of their expenses from the government; those in South Korea and the Philippines receive less than 10% of their funding from the government (James, 1991, p. 6). As is shown in Table 58.1, only 5% of the BA-level students in Kenya are enrolled in private higher education institutions. In Mongolia, the corresponding private enrollment is 18%.

The growth of private higher education institutions in Mongolia appears to be driven by "excess demand:"

> Excess demand for education often exists when the capacity of the public school system is less than full enrollment; that is, the option of attending a free or low-price public school is not available to everyone. If the private benefits from education are high (e.g., because of labour market rewards), many people who are left out of the public schools will seek places in private schools, as a "second best" solution (James, 1991, p. 3).

In areas such as foreign languages and market-oriented economics, the public higher education sector in Mongolia is not able to accommodate the numbers of qualified students who seek admission. This is partly due to a vestigial pattern of the old "command economy" in which government, through its National Planning Board, continues to determine the number of places available for each course of study on the basis of projected manpower needs, independent of student demand. It is also partly due to the lack of sufficient numbers of qualified teachers in these areas within the public higher education institutions.

Largely because of the Mongolian government's failure to fund adequately the national loan scheme in 1993–94, public higher education institutions admitted a significant number of self-paying students beyond the centrally established quotas into high demand fields. This was a way of generating revenue to meet operating expenses during the beginning of the academic year while the government tried to get commitments from local authorities to guarantee students' loans. Funds are not being released to higher education institutions by the government until the loans are guaranteed.

In Kenya, the private sector has only recently been allowed to expand as the government has been more willing to authorize the establishment of private higher education institutions. The secondary level in Kenya can, however, be also characterized as being driven by "excess demand," with just over half of all students attending private secondary schools (James, 1991, p. 5).

A fundamental concern for government authorities in any country is making certain that private higher education institutions meet reasonable standards of academic quality and operational procedures. Four areas in which governments regulate private educational institutions are (1) physical facilities—health and safety standards, space and furniture, target enrollments related to physical facilities; (2) academic regulations—curriculum, degree requirements, national examinations, language of instruction; (3) organizational and reporting requirements—periodic financial reports, minimum investment, tax status; and (4) teachers and students—teacher qualifications, procedures for hiring and firing teachers, allowable student fees, student selection criteria, government representatives on institutional governing bodies (James, 1991, p. 25).

Governments vary, of course, in the emphasis placed on any specific area of regulation. With respect to allowable profits, for instance, the governments of Korea and the Philippines regulate both the amount of tuition that can be charged in private higher education institutions and the numbers of students, thereby limiting income. There is also the issue of tax status of revenues generated by auxiliary enterprises in both public and private higher education institutions as well as fairness of price competition with private enterprise providers of similar products and services. Such concerns are common in both developed and developing countries.

Ultimately, however, it is the responsibility of governments to establish policy with respect to the diversity of funding sources for higher education; the levels of student fees, the types of loan or subsidy programs that will be made available to assist needy students in the payment of fees in order to ensure broad access to higher education; the mix of public and private sector institutions; standards for the accreditation and operational authorization of both public and private sector higher education institutions; and the degree of autonomy higher education institutions will have in the control and management of their finances. This paper has provided some specific examples, but any application of the various strategies for revenue diversification mentioned will have to be adapted to fit the particular social, political, cultural, and economic environment of the host country.

NOTE

This is the revised version of a paper that was originally presented at a conference on "Reform of Higher Education in Mongolia" sponsored by the German Foundation for International Development (DSE) in Ulaanbaatar, Mongolia, 18 November 1993. It was subsequently revised and the material on Kenya added for presentation in a seminar held on 8 June 1994 at the Institute of Research and Postgraduate Studies, Maseno University College, Maseno, Kenya. Grateful acknowledgement is accorded to participants in both the DSE conference and the Maseno seminar as well as three anonymous reviewers for their helpful comments.

REFERENCES

Albrecht, Douglas & Adrian Ziderman. (1992, August). *Financing universities in developing countries.* Washington, DC: Education and Employment Division, Population and Human Resources Department, The World Bank (Document No. PHREE/92/61).

The almanac of higher education. (1994). Prepared by the Editors of The Chronicle of Higher Education. Chicago: University of Chicago Press.

Asian Development Bank. (1993). *Mongolia: Country performance indicators.* Manila: Asian Development Bank.

Bray, Mark, Surengiin Davaa, Seth Spaulding, & John C. Weidman. (1994). "Transition from socialism and the financing of higher education: The case of Mongolia." *Higher education policy,* Vol. 7 (No. 4), 36–42.

Gladieux, Lawrence E., Arthur M. Hauptman, & Laura Greene Knapp. (1994). "The federal government and higher education." Pp. 12–154. In Philip G. Altbach, Robert O. Berdahl, & Patricia J. Gumport (Eds.), *Higher education in American society.* Third Edition. Amherst, NY: Prometheus Books.

James, Estelle. (1991). Private Finance and Management of Education in Developing Countries: Major Policy and Research Issues. *Issues and methodologies in education development: An IIEP series for orientation and training,* 5. Paris: International Institute for Educational Planning (UNESCO).

Hinchliffe, K. (1987). *Higher education in sub-Saharan Africa.* London: Croom Helm.

Hossain, Shaikh I. & George Psacharopoulos. (1994). "The profitability of school investments in an educationally advanced developing country". *International journal of educational development,* Vol. 14 (No. 1), pp. 35–42.

Mingat, Alain & George Psacharopoulos. (1985). "Financing education in sub-Saharan Africa: Issues of equity and efficiency of investment—Some policy alternatives. *Finance and development,* Vol. 22 (March), pp. 35–38.

Mwiria, Kilemi & Mulati S. Nyukuri. (1994). The management of double intakes: A case study of Kenyatta University. *IIEP research and studies programme: Improving the managerial effectiveness of higher education institutions.* Paris: International Institute for Educational Planning (UNESCO).

Opondo, Fred & Sodik Osman Noormohamed. (1989). "Cost-sharing in Education." Annex 4 (pp. 87–107). In J. E. O. Odada & L. O. Odhiambo (Eds.), *Report of the proceeding of the workshop on cost-sharing in Kenya: Naivasha,* 29 March–2 April 1989. Nairobi: UNICEF, Kenya Country Office, Ministry of Planning and National Development, and Kenyan Economic Association.

Republic of Kenya. (1994). *Development plan, 1994–96.* Nairobi: Government Printing Office.

Republic of Kenya. (1993). *Economic survey 1993.* Central Bureau of Statistics, Office of the Vice President, and Ministry of Planning and National Development. Nairobi: Government Printer.

Saint, William S. (1992). Universities in Africa: Strategies for stabilization and revitalization. *World Bank technical paper number 194,* Africa Technical Department Series. Washington, DC: World Bank.

Sanyal, Bikas C. in association with Michaela Martin. (1991). *"Staff management in African universities."* Document prepared within the framework of the IIEP research programme on "Improving the effectiveness of higher education institutions: Studies of the management of change." Paris: International Institute for Educational Planning (UNESCO). Document IIEP/Prg.BS/91.160.

Weidman, John C. (1995). "Prospects for the development of higher education in Kenya." *Journal of the third world spectrum,* Spring.

Woodhall, Maureen. (1993, September). *Financial diversification in higher education: A review of international experience.* Unpublished paper.

Woodhall, Maureen. (1991a). *Student loans in higher education: 3. English-speaking Africa.* Educational Forum Series No. 3. Paris: International Institute for Educational Planning (UNESCO).